B. M. Thompson
Washington. D. C.
1864.

ENGRAVED BY A. B. WALTER

Revd. Sydney Smith

THE
WORKS
OF
THE REV. SYDNEY SMITH.

THREE VOLUMES,

COMPLETE IN ONE.

NEW-YORK:
D. APPLETON AND COMPANY,
346 & 348 BROADWAY.
M.DCCC.LX.

PREFACE.

When first I went into the Church, I had a curacy in the middle of lisbury Plain. The Squire of the parish took a fancy to me, and requested me to go with his son to reside at the University of Weimar; before we could get there, Germany became the seat of war, and in stress of politics we put into Edinburgh, where I remained five years. The principles of the French Revolution were then fully afloat, and it is impossible to conceive a more violent and agitated state of society. Among the first persons with whom I became acquainted were, Lord Jeffrey, Lord Murray (late Lord Advocate for Scotland), and Lord Brougham; all of them maintaining opinions upon political subjects a little too liberal for the dynasty of Dundas, then exercising supreme power over the northern division of the island.

One day we happened to meet in the eighth or ninth story or flat in Buccleugh-place, the elevated residence of the then Mr. Jeffrey. I proposed that we should set up a Review; this was acceded to with acclamation. I was appointed Editor, and remained long enough in Edinburgh to edit the first number of the Edinburgh Review. The motto I proposed for the Review was,

"*Tenui musam meditamur avena.*"
"We cultivate literature upon a little oatmeal."

But this was too near the truth to be admitted, and so we took our present grave motto from *Publius Syrus*, of whom none of us had, I am sure, ever read a single line; and so began what has since turned out to be a very important and able journal. When I left Edinburgh, it fell into the stronger hands of Lord Jeffrey and Lord Brougham, and reached the highest point of popularity and success. I contributed from England many articles, which I have been foolish enough to collect and publish with some other tracts written by me.

To appreciate the value of the Edinburgh Review, the state of England at the period when that journal began should be had in remembrance. The Catholics were not emancipated—the Corporation and Test Acts were unrepealed—the Game Laws were horribly oppressive—Steel Traps and Spring

Guns were set all over the country—Prisoners tried for their Lives cou have no Counsel—Lord Eldon and the Court of Chancery pressed heavi upon mankind—Libel was punished by the most cruel and vindictive ir prisonments—the principles of Political Economy were little understood- the Law of Debt and of Conspiracy were upon the worst possible footing- the enormous wickedness of the Slave Trade was tolerated—a thousand evi were in existence, which the talents of good and able men have sin lessened or removed; and these effects have been not a little assisted l the honest boldness of the Edinburgh Review.

I see very little in my Reviews to alter or repent of: I always ende voured to fight against evil; and what I thought evil then, I think ev now. I am heartily glad that all our disqualifying laws for religious opinio are abolished, and I see nothing in such measures but unmixed good ar real increase of strength to our Establishment.

The idea of danger from the extension of the Catholic religion in En land I utterly deride. The Catholic faith is a misfortune to the worl but those whose faith it conscientiously is, are quite right in professing boldly, and in promoting it by all means which the law allows. A ph sician does not say "You will be well *as soon as* the bile is got rid of; but he says, "You will not be well *until after* the bile is got rid of. He knows after the cause of the malady is removed, that morbid habi are to be changed, weakness to be supported, organs to be called bac to their proper exercise, subordinate maladies to be watched, secondary an vicarious symptoms to be studied. The physician is a wise man—but th anserous politician insists, after 200 years of persecution, and ten of emanc pation, that Catholic Ireland should be as quiet as Edmonton, or Tooting

Not only are just laws wanted for Catholic Ireland, but the just adminis tration of just laws; such as they have in general experienced under th Whig government; and this system steadily preserved in will, after a laps of time and O'Connell, quiet, conciliate, and civilize that long injured an irritable people.

I have printed in this Collection the Letters of Peter Plymley. Th Government of that day took great pains to find out the author; all tha they *could* find was, that they were brought to Mr. Budd, the publishe by the Earl of Lauderdale. Somehow or another, it came to be conjec tured that I was that author: I have always denied it; but finding tha I deny it in vain, I have thought it might be as well to include the Let ters in this Collection; they had an immense circulation at the time, an I think above 20,000 copies were sold.

From the beginning of the century (about which time the Review began to the death of Lord Liverpool, was an awful period for those who had the misfortune to entertain liberal opinions, and who were too honest to sell them for the ermine of the judge, or the lawn of the prelate:—a long and hopeless career in your profession, the chuckling grin of noodles, the sarcastic leer of the genuine political rogue—prebendaries, deans, and bishops made over your head—reverend renegadoes advanced to the highest dignities of the Church, for helping to rivet the fetters of Catholic and Protestant Dissenters, and no more chance of a Whig administration than of a thaw in Zembla—these were the penalties exacted for liberality of opinion at that period; and not only was there no pay, but there were many stripes. It is always considered as a piece of impertinence in England, if a man of less than two or three thousand a year has any opinions at all upon important subjects; and in addition he was sure at that time to be assailed with all the Billingsgate of the French Revolution—Jacobin, Leveller, Atheist, Deist, Socinian, Incendiary, Regicide, were the gentlest appellations used; and the man who breathed a syllable against the senseless bigotry of the two Georges, or hinted at the abominable tyranny and persecution exercised upon Catholic Ireland, was shunned as unfit for the relations of social life. Not a murmur against any abuse was permitted; to say a word against the suitorcide delays of the Court of Chancery, or the cruel punishments of the Game Laws, or against any abuse which a rich man inflicted, or a poor man suffered, was treason against the *Plousiocracy*, and was bitterly and steadily resented. Lord Grey had not then taken off the bearing-rein from the English people, as Sir Francis Head has now done from horses.

To set on foot such a Journal in such times, to contribute towards it for many years, to bear patiently the reproach and poverty which it caused, and to look back and see that I have nothing to retract, and no intemperance and violence to reproach myself with, is a career of life which I must think to be extremely fortunate. Strange and ludicrous are the changes in human affairs. The Tories are now on the treadmill, and the well-paid Whigs are riding in chariots: with many faces, however, looking out of the windows, (including that of our Prime Minister,) which I never remember to have seen in the days of the poverty and depression of Whiggism. Liberality is now a lucrative business. Whoever has any institution to destroy, may consider himself as a commissioner, and his fortune as made; and to my utter and never ending astonishment, I, an old Edinburgh Reviewer, find myself fighting, in the year 1839, against the Archbishop of Canterbury and the Bishop of London, for the existence of the National Church.

SYDNEY SMITH.

CONTENTS.

WORKS

OF THE

REV. SYDNEY SMITH.

DR. PARR.*

[Edinburgh Review, 1802.]

Whoever has had the good fortune to see Dr. Parr's wig, must have observed, that while it trespasses a little on the orthodox magnitude of perukes in the anterior parts, it scorns even Episcopal limits behind, and swells out into boundless convexity of frizz, the μεγα θαυμα of barbers, and the terror of the literary world. After the manner of his wig, the Doctor† has constructed his sermon, giving us a discourse of no common length, and subjoining an immeasurable mass of notes, which appear to concern every learned thing, every learned man, and almost every unlearned man since the beginning of the world.

For his text, Dr. Parr has chosen *Gal.* vi. 10. *As we have therefore opportunity, let us do good to all men, especially to those who are of the household of faith.* After a short preliminary comparison between the dangers of the selfish system, and the modern one of universal benevolence, he divides his sermon into two parts: in the first, examining how far, by the constitution of human nature, and the circumstances of human life, the principles of particular and universal benevolence are compatible: in the last, commenting on the nature of the charitable institution for which he is preaching.

The former part is levelled against the doctrines of Mr. Godwin; and, here, Dr. Parr exposes, very strongly and happily, the folly of making universal benevolence the *immediate motive* of our actions. As we consider this, though of no very difficult execution, to be by far the best part of the sermon, we shall very willingly make some extracts from it.

"To me it appears, that the modern advocates for universal philanthropy have fallen into the error charged upon those who are fascinated by a violent and extraordinary fondness for what a celebrated author calls 'some moral species.' Some men, it has been remarked, are hurried into romantic adventures, by their excessive admiration of fortitude. Others are actuated by a headstrong zeal for disseminating the true religion. Hence, while the only properties, for which fortitude or zeal can be esteemed, are scarcely discernible, from the enormous bulkiness to which they are swollen, the ends to which alone they can be directed usefully are overlooked or defeated; the public good is impaired, rather than increased; and the claims that other virtues equally obligatory have to our notice are totally disregarded. Thus, too, when any dazzling phantoms of universal philanthropy have seized our attention, the objects that formerly engaged it shrink and fade. All considerations of kindred, friends, and countrymen, drop from the mind, during the struggles it makes to grasp the collective interests of the species; and when the association that attached us to them has been dissolved, the notions we have formed of their comparative insignificance will prevent them from recovering, I do not say any hold whatsoever, but that *strong* and *lasting* hold they once had upon our conviction and our feelings. Universal benevolence, should it, from any strange combination of circumstances, ever become passionate, will, like every other passion, justify itself; and the importunity of its demands to obtain a hearing will be proportionate to the weakness of its cause. But what are the consequences? A perpetual wrestling for victory between the refinements of sophistry, and the remonstrances of indignant nature—the agitations of secret distrust in opinions which gain few or no proselytes, and feelings which excite little or no sympathy—the neglect of all the usual duties, by which social life is preserved or adorned; and in the pursuit of other duties which are unusual, and indeed imaginary, a succession of airy projects eager hopes, tumultuous efforts, and galling disappointments, such, in truth, as every wise man foresaw, and a good man would rarely commiserate."

In a subsequent part of his sermon, Dr. Parr handles the same topic with equal success.

---

* *Spital Sermon*, preached at Christ Church upon Easter-Tuesday, April 15, 1800. To which are added, Notes by Samuel Parr, LL.D. Printed for J. Mawman in the Poultry. 1801.

† A great scholar, as rude and violent as most Greek scholars are, unless they happen to be Bishops. He has left nothing behind him worth leaving: he was rather fitted for the law than the church, and would have been a more considerable man, if he had been more knocked about among his equals. He lived with country gentlemen and clergymen, who flattered and feared him.

"The stoics, it has been said, were more successful in weakening the tender affections, than in animating men to the stronger virtues of fortitude and self-command; and possible it is, that the influence of our modern reformers may be greater, in furnishing their disciples with pleas for the neglect of their ordinary duties, than in stimulating their endeavours for the performance of those which are extraordinary, and perhaps ideal. If, indeed, the representations we have lately heard of universal philanthropy served only to amuse the fancy of those who approve of them, and to communicate that pleasure which arises from contemplating the magnitude and grandeur of a favourite subject, we might be tempted to smile at them as groundless and harmless. But they tend to debase the dignity, and to weaken the efficacy of those particular affections, for which we have daily and hourly occasion in the events of real life. They tempt us to substitute the ease of speculation, and the pride of dogmatism, for the toil of practice. To a class of artificial and ostentatious sentiments, they give the most dangerous triumph over the genuine and salutary dictates of nature. They delude and inflame our minds with pharisaical notions of superior wisdom and superior virtue; and, what is the worst of all, they may be used as 'a cloke to us' for insensibility, where other men feel; and for negligence, where other men act with *visible* and *useful*, though *limited*, effect."

In attempting to show the connection between particular and universal benevolence, Dr. Parr does not appear to us to have taken a clear and satisfactory view of the subject. Nature impels us both to good and bad actions; and, even in the former, gives us no measure by which we may prevent them from degenerating into excess. Rapine and revenge are not less natural than parental and filial affection; which latter class of feelings may themselves be a source of crimes, if they overpower (as they frequently do) the sense of justice. It is not, therefore, a sufficient justification of our actions, that they are natural. We must seek, from our reason, some principle which will enable us to determine what impulses of nature we are to obey, and what we are to resist: such is that of general utility, or, what is the same thing, of universal good; a principle which sanctifies and limits the more particular affections. The duty of a son to a parent, or a parent to a son, is not an ultimate principle of morals, but depends on the principle of universal good, and is only praiseworthy because it is found to promote it. At the same time, our spheres of action and intelligence are so confined, that it is better, in a great majority of instances, to suffer our conduct to be guided by those affections which have been long sanctioned by the approbation of mankind, than to enter into a process of reasoning, and investigate the relation which every trifling event might bear to the general interests of the world. In his principle of universal benevolence, Mr. Godwin is unquestionably right. That it is the grand principle on which all morals rest—that it is the corrective for the excess of all particular affections, we believe to be undeniable: and he is only erroneous in excluding the particular affections, because, in so doing, he deprives us of our most powerful means of promoting his own principle of universal good; for it is as much as to say, that all the crew ought to have the *general* welfare of the ship so much at heart that no sailor should ever pull any *particular* rope, or hand any *individual* sail. By universal benevolence, we mean, and understand Dr. Parr to mean, not a barren affection for the species, but a desire to promote their real happiness; and of this principle, he thus speaks:

"I admit, and I approve of it, as an *emotion* of which general happiness is the cause, but not as a passion, of which, according to the usual order of human affairs, it could often be the object. I approve of it as a disposition to wish, and, as opportunity may occur, to desire and do good, rather than harm, to those with whom we are quite unconnected."

It would appear, from this kind of language, that a desire of promoting the universal good were a pardonable weakness, rather than a fundamental principle of ethics; that the particular affections were incapable of excess; and that they never wanted the corrective of a more generous and exalted feeling. In a subsequent part of his sermon, Dr. Parr atones a little for this over-zealous depreciation of the principle of universal benevolence; but he nowhere states the particular affections to derive their value and their limits from their subservience to a more extensive philanthropy. He does not show us that they exist only as virtues, from their instrumentality in promoting the general good; and that, to preserve their true character, they should be frequently referred to that principle as their proper criterion.

In the latter part of his sermon, Dr. Parr combats the general objections of Mr. Turgot to all charitable institutions, with considerable vigour and success. To say that an institution is necessarily bad, because it will not always be administered with the same zeal, proves a little too much; for it is an objection to political and religious, as well as to charitable institutions; and, from a lively apprehension of the fluctuating characters of those who govern, would leave the world without any government at all. It is better there should be an asylum for the mad, and a hospital for the wounded, if they were to squander away 50 *per cent.* of their income, than that we should be disgusted with sore limbs, and shocked by straw-crowned monarchs in the streets. All institutions of this kind must suffer the risk of being governed by more or less of probity and talents. The good which one active character effects, and the wise order which he establishes, may outlive him for a long period and we all hate each other's crimes, by which we gain nothing, so much, that in proportion as public opinion acquires ascendency in any particular country, every public institution becomes more and more guarantied from abuse.

Upon the whole, this sermon is rather the production of what is called a sensible, than of a very acute man; of a man certainly more remarkable for his learning than his originality. It refutes the very refutable positions of Mr. Godwin, without placing the doctrine of benevolence in a clear light; and it almost leaves us to suppose, that the particular affections are themselves ultimate principles of action, instead of convenient instruments of a more general principle.

The style is such as to give a general impression of heaviness to the whole sermon. The Doctor is never simple and natural for a single instant. Every thing smells of the rhetorician. He never appears to forget himself, or to be hurried by his subject into obvious language. Every expression seems to be the result of artifice and intention; and as to the worthy dedicatees, the Lord Mayor and Aldermen, unless the sermon be *done into English by a person of honour*, they may perhaps be flattered by the Doctor's politeness, but they can never be much edified by his meaning. Dr. Parr seems to think, that eloquence consists not in exuberance of beautiful images—not in simple and sublime conceptions—not in the feelings of the passions; but in a studious arrangement of *sonorous, exotic, and sesquipedal* words: a very ancient error, which corrupts the style of young, and wearies the patience of sensible men. In some of his combinations of words the Doctor is singularly unhappy. We have the *din of superficial cavillers, the prancings of giddy ostentation, flattering vanity, hissing scorn, dank clod*, &c. &c. &c. The following intrusion of a technical word into a pathetic description renders the whole passage almost ludicrous.

"Within a few days, mute was the tongue that uttered these celestial sounds, and the hand which signed your indenture lay cold and motionless in the dark and dreary chambers of death."

In page 16, Dr. Parr, in speaking of the indentures of the hospital, a subject (as we should have thought) little calculated for rhetorical panegyric, says of them—

"If the writer of whom I am speaking had perused, as I have, your indentures, and your rules, he would have found in them seriousness without austerity, earnestness without extravagance, good sense without the trickeries of art, good language without the trappings of rhetoric, and the firmness of conscious worth, rather than the prancings of giddy ostentation."

The latter member of this eloge would not be wholly unintelligible, if applied to a spirited coach horse; but we have never yet witnessed the phenomenon of a *prancing indenture*.

It is not our intention to follow Dr. Parr through the copious and varied learning of his notes; in the perusal of which we have been as much delighted with the richness of his acquisitions, the vigour of his understanding, and the genuine goodness of his heart, as we have been amused with his ludicrous self-importance, and the miraculous simplicity of his character. We would rather recommend it to the Doctor to publish an annual list of worthies, as a kind of stimulus to literary men; to be included in which, will unquestionably be considered as great an honour, as for a commoner to be elevated to the peerage. A line of Greek, a line of Latin, or no line at all, subsequent to each name, will distinguish, with sufficient accuracy, the shades of merit, and the degree of immortality conferred.

Why should Dr. Parr confine this *eulogomania* to the literary characters of this island alone? In the university of Benares, in the lettered kingdom of Ava, among the Mandarins at Pekin, there must, doubtless, be many men who have the eloquence of* Βαρρουος, the feeling of Ταιλωρος, and the judgment of Ωκηρος, of whom Dr. Parr might be happy to say, that they have profundity without obscurity—perspicuity without prolixity—ornament without glare—terseness without barrenness—penetration without subtlety—comprehensiveness without digression—and a great number of other things without a great number of other things.

In spite of 32 pages of very close printing, in defence of the University of Oxford, is it, or is it not true, that very many of its Professors enjoy ample salaries, without reading any lectures at all? The character of particular colleges will certainly vary with the character of their governors; but the University of Oxford so far differs from Dr. Parr in the commendation he has bestowed upon its state of *public* education, that they have, since the publication of his book, we believe, and forty years after Mr. Gibbon's residence, completely abolished their very ludicrous and disgraceful exercises for degrees, and have substituted in their place a system of exertion, and a scale of academical honours, calculated (we are willing to hope) to produce the happiest effects.

We were very sorry, in reading Dr. Parr's note on the Universities, to meet with the following passage:—

"Ill would it become me tamely and silently to acquiesce in the strictures of this formidable accuser upon a seminary to which I owe many obligations, though I left it, as must not be dissembled, before the usual time, and, in truth, had been almost compelled to leave it, *not* by the want of proper education, for I had arrived at the first place in the first form of Harrow School, when I was not quite fourteen—not by the want of useful tutors, for mine were eminently able, and to me had been uniformly kind—not by the want of ambition, for I had begun to look up ardently and anxiously to academical distinctions—not by the want of attachment to the place, for I regarded it then, as I continue to regard it now, with the fondest and most unfeigned affection—but by another want, which it were unnecessary to name, and for the supply of which, after some hesitation, I determined to provide by patient toil and resolute self-denial, when I had not completed my twentieth year. I ceased, therefore, to reside, with an aching heart: I looked back with mingled feelings of regret and humiliation to advantages of which I could no longer partake, and honours to which I could no longer aspire."

To those who know the truly honourable

* *Πάντες μὲν σοφοί· ἐλῶ δε Ὤκηρον μὲν σέβω, θαυμάζω δὲ Βάῤῥουον καὶ φιλῶ Ταίλωρον.* See Lucian in Vita Dæmonact. vol. ii. p. 394.—(Dr. Parr's note.)

and respectable character of Dr. Parr, the vast extent of his learning, and the unadulterated benevolence of his nature, such an account cannot but be very affecting, in spite of the bad taste in which it is communicated. How painful to reflect, that a truly devout and attentive minister, a strenuous defender of the church establishment, and by far the most learned man of his day, should be permitted to languish on a little paltry curacy in Warwickshire!

—— Dii meliora, &c. &c.*

DR. RENNEL.†

[Edinburgh Review, 1802.]

We have no modern sermons in the English language that can be considered as very eloquent. The merits of Blair (by far the most popular writer of sermons within the last century) are plain good sense, a happy application of scriptural quotation, and a clear harmonious style, richly tinged with scriptural language. He generally leaves his readers pleased with his judgment, and his just observations on human conduct, without ever rising so high as to touch the great passions, or kindle any enthusiasm in favour of virtue. For eloquence, we must ascend as high as the days of Barrow and Jeremy Taylor: and even there, while we are delighted with their energy, their copiousness, and their fancy, we are in danger of being suffocated by a redundance which abhors all discrimination; which compares till it perplexes, and illustrates till it confounds.

To the *Oases* of Tillotson, Sherlock, and Atterbury, we must wade through many a barren page, in which the weary Christian can descry nothing all around him but a dreary expanse of trite sentiments and languid words.

The great object of modern sermons is to hazard nothing: their characteristic is, decent debility; which alike guards their authors from ludicrous errors, and precludes them from striking beauties. Every man of sense, in taking up an English sermon, expects to find it a tedious essay, full of commonplace morality; and if the fulfilment of such expectations be meritorious, the clergy have certainly the merit of not disappointing their readers. Yet it is curious to consider, how a body of men so well educated, and so magnificently endowed as the English clergy, should distinguish themselves so little in a species of composition to which it is their peculiar duty, as well as their ordinary habit, to attend. To solve this difficulty, it should be remembered, that the eloquence ot the Bar and of the Senate force themselves into notice, power, and wealth—that the penalty which an individual client pays for choosing a bad advocate, is the loss of his cause—that a prime minister must infallibly suffer in the estimation of the public, who neglects to conciliate the eloquent men, and trusts the defence of his measures to those who have not adequate talents for that purpose: whereas the only evil which accrues from the promotion of a clergyman to the pulpit, which he has no ability to fill as he ought, is the fatigue of the audience, and the discredit of that species of public instruction; an evil so general, that no individual patron would dream of sacrificing to it his particular interest. The clergy are generally appointed to their situations by those who have no interest that they should please the audience before whom they speak; while the very reverse is the case in the eloquence of the Bar, and of Parliament. We by no means would be understood to say, that the clergy should owe their promotion principally to their eloquence, or that eloquence ever could, consistently with the constitution of the English Church, be made out a common cause of preferment. In pointing out the total want of connection between the privilege of preaching, and the power of preaching well, we are giving no opinion as to whether it might, or might not be remedied; but merely stating a fact. Pulpit discourses have insensibly dwindled from speaking to reading; a practice, of itself, sufficient to stifle every germ of eloquence. It is only by the fresh feelings of the heart, that mankind can be very powerfully affected. What can be more ludicrous, than an orator delivering stale indignation, and fervour of a week old; turning over whole pages of violent passions, written out in German text; reading the tropes and apostrophes into which he is hurried by the ardour of his mind; and so affected at a preconcerted line, and page, that he is unable to proceed any farther!

The prejudices of the English nation have proceeded a good deal from their hatred to the French; and because that country is the native soil of elegance, animation, and grace, a certain patriotic solidity, and loyal awkwardness, have become the characteristics of this; so that an adventurous preacher is afraid of violating the ancient tranquillity of the pulpit; and the audience are commonly apt to consider the man who tires them less than usual, as a trifler, or a charlatan.

Of British education, the study of eloquence makes little or no part. The exterior graces of a speaker are despised; and debating societies (admirable institutions, under proper regulations) would hardly be tolerated either at Oxford or Cambridge. It is commonly answered to any animadversions upon the eloquence of

* The courtly phrase was, that Dr. Parr was not a *producible* man. The same phrase was used for the neglect of Paley.

† *Discourses on Various Subjects.* By Thomas Rennel, D.D. Master of the Temple. Rivington, London.

the English pulpit, that a clergyman is to recommend himself, not by his eloquence, but by the purity of his life, and the soundness of his doctrine; an objection good enough, if any connection could be pointed out between eloquence, heresy, and dissipation; but if it is possible for a man to live well, preach well, and teach well, at the same time, such objections, resting only upon a supposed incompatibility of these good qualities, are duller than the dulness they defend.

The clergy are apt to shelter themselves under the plea, that subjects so exhausted are utterly incapable of novelty; and, in the very strictest sense of the word *novelty*, meaning that which was never said before, at any time, or in any place, this may be true enough, of the first principles of morals; but the modes of expanding, illustrating, and enforcing a particular theme are capable of infinite variety; and, if they were not, this might be a very good reason for preaching commonplace sermons, but is a very bad one for publishing them.

We had great hopes, that Dr. Rennel's Sermons would have proved an exception to the character we have given of sermons in general; and we have read through his present volume with a conviction rather that he has misapplied, than that he wants, talents for pulpit eloquence. The subjects of his sermons, fourteen in number, are, 1. The consequences of the vice of gaming: 2. On old age: 3. Benevolence exclusively an evangelical virtue: 4. The services rendered to the English nation by the Church of England, a motive for liberality to the orphan children of indigent ministers: 5. On the grounds and regulation of national joy: 6. On the connection of the duties of loving the brotherhood, fearing God, and honouring the King: 7. On the guilt of blood-thirstiness: 8. On atonement: 9. A visitation sermon: 10. Great Britain's naval strength, and insular situation, a cause of gratitude to Almighty God: 11. Ignorance productive of atheism, anarchy, and superstition: 12, 13, 14. On the sting of death, the strength of sin, and the victory over them both by Jesus Christ.

Dr. Rennel's first sermon, upon the consequences of gaming, is admirable for its strength of language, its sound good sense, and the vigour with which it combats that detestable vice. From this sermon, we shall, with great pleasure, make an extract of some length.

"Farther to this sordid habit the gamester joins a disposition to FRAUD, and that of the *meanest* cast. To those who soberly and fairly appreciate the real nature of human actions, nothing appears more inconsistent than that societies of men, who have incorporated themselves for the express purpose of gaming, should disclaim fraud or indirection, or affect to drive from their assemblies those among their associates whose crimes would reflect disgrace on them. Surely this, to a considerate mind, is as solemn and refined a banter as can well be exhibited: for when we take into view the vast latitude allowed by the most upright gamesters, when we reflect that, according to their precious casuistry, every advantage may be legitimately taken of the young, the unwary, and the inebriated, which superior coolness, skill, address, and activity can supply, we must look upon pretences to honesty as a most shameless aggravation of their crimes. Even if it were possible that, in his own practices, a man might be a FAIR GAMESTER, yet, for the result of the extended frauds committed by his fellows, he stands deeply accountable to God, his country, and his conscience. To a system necessarily implicated with fraud; to associations of men, a large majority of whom subsist by fraud; to habits calculated to poison the source and principle of all integrity, he gives efficacy, countenance, and concurrence. Even his *virtues* he suffers to be subsidiary to the cause of vice. He sees with calmness, depredation committed daily and hourly in his company, perhaps under his very roof. Yet men of this description declaim (so desperately deceitful is the heart of man) against the very knaves they cherish and protect, and whom, perhaps, with some poor sophistical refuge for a worn-out conscience, they even imitate. To such, let the Scripture speak with emphatical decision —*When thou sawest a thief, then thou consentedst with him.*"

The reader will easily observe, in this quotation, a command of language, and a power of style, very superior to what is met with in the great mass of sermons. We shall make one more extract.

"But in addition to fraud, and all its train of crimes, propensities and habits of a very different complexion enter into the composition of a gamester: a most ungovernable FEROCITY OF DISPOSITION, however for a time disguised and latent, is invariably the result of his system of conduct. Jealousy, rage, and revenge, exist among gamesters in their worst and most frantic excesses, and end frequently in consequences of the most atrocious violence and outrage. By perpetual agitation the malignant passions spurn and overwhelm every boundary which discretion and conscience can oppose. From what source are we to trace a very large number of those murders, sanctioned or palliated indeed by custom, but which stand at the tribunal of God precisely upon the same grounds with every other species of murder?—From the gaming-table, from the nocturnal receptacles of distraction and frenzy, the duellist rushes with his hand lifted up against his brother's life!—Those who are as yet on the threshold of these habits should be warned, that however calm their *natural* temperament, however meek and placable their disposition, yet that, by the events which every moment arise, they stand exposed to the ungovernable fury of themselves and others. In the midst of fraud, protected by menace on the one hand, and on the other, of despair; irritated by a recollection of the meanness of the artifices and the baseness of the hands by which utter and remediless ruin has been inflicted; in the midst of these feelings of horror and distraction it is, that the voice of brethren's blood '*crieth unto God from the ground*'—'*and now art thou cursed from the earth, which hath opened her mouth to receive thy brother's blood from thy hand.*' Not only THOU who actually sheddest that blood, but THOU who art the artificer of death—thou who administerest incentives to these habits—who dissemi natest the practice of them—improvest the skill in them—sharpenest the propensity to them—at THY hands will it be required, surely, at the tribunal of God in the next world, and perhaps, in most instances, in his distributive and awful dispensations towards thee and thine here on earth."

Having paid this tribute of praise to Dr. Rennel's first sermon, we are sorry so soon to change our eulogium into censure, and to blame him for having selected for publication so many sermons touching directly and indirectly upon the French Revolution. We confess ourselves long since wearied with this kind of discourses, bespattered with blood and brains, and ringing eternal changes upon atheism, cannibalism, and apostasy. Upon the enormities of the French Revolution there can be but one opinion; but the subject is not fit for the pulpit. The public are disgusted with it to satiety; and we can never help remembering, that this politico-orthodox rage in the mouth of a preacher may be profitable as well as sincere. Upon such subjects as the murder of the Queen of France, and the great events of these days, it is not possible to endure the draggling and the daubing of such a ponderous limner as Dr. Rennel, after the ethereal touches of Mr. Burke. In events so truly horrid in themselves, the field is so easy for a declaimer, that we set little value upon the declamation; and the mind, on such occasions, so easily outruns ordinary description, that we are apt to feel more, before a mediocre oration begins, than it even aims at inspiring.

We are surprised that Dr. Rennel, from among the great number of subjects which he must have discussed in the pulpit (the interest in which must be permanent and universal), should have published such an empty and frivolous sermon as that upon the victory of Lord Nelson; a sermon good enough for the garrulity of joy, when the phrases, and the exultation of the Porcupine, or the True Briton, may pass for eloquence or sense; but utterly unworthy of the works of a man who aims at a place among the great teachers of morality and religion.

Dr. Rennel is apt to put on the appearance of a holy bully, an evangelical swaggerer, as if he could carry his point against infidelity by big words and strong abuse, and kick and cuff men into Christians. It is a very easy thing to talk about the shallow impostures, and the silly ignorant sophisms of Voltaire, Rousseau, Condorcet, D'Alembert, and Volney, and to say that Hume is not worth answering. This affectation of contempt will not do. While these pernicious writers have power to allure from the church great numbers of proselytes, it is better to study them diligently, and to reply to them satisfactorily, than to veil insolence, want of power, or want of industry, by a pretended contempt; which may leave infidels and wavering Christians to suppose that such writers are abused, because they are feared; and not answered, because they are unanswerable. While every body was abusing and despising Mr. Godwin, and while Mr. Godwin was, among a certain description of understandings, increasing every day in popularity, Mr. Malthus* took the trouble of refuting him and we hear no more of Mr. Godwin. We recommend this example to the consideration of Dr. Rennel, who seems to think it more useful, and more pleasant, to rail than to fight.

After the world has returned to its sober senses upon the merits of the ancient philosophy, it is amusing enough to see a few *bad heads* bawling for the restoration of exploded errors and past infatuation. We have some dozen of plethoric phrases about Aristotle, who is, in the estimation of the Doctor, *et rex et sutor bonus*, and every thing else; and to the neglect of whose works he seems to attribute every moral and physical evil under which the world has groaned for the last century. Dr. Rennel's admiration of the ancients is so great, that he considers the works of Homer to be the region and depository of natural law, and natural religion.† Now, if, by natural religion, is meant the will of God collected from his works, and the necessity man is under of obeying it; it is rather extraordinary that Homer should be so good a natural theologian, when the divinities he has painted are certainly a more drunken, quarrelsome, adulterous, intriguing, lascivious set of beings, than are to be met with in the most profligate court in Europe. There is, every now and then, some plain coarse morality in Homer; but the most bloody revenge, and the most savage cruelty in warfare, the ravishing of women, and the sale of men, &c. &c. &c. are circumstances which the old bard seems to relate as the ordinary events of his times, without ever dreaming that there could be much harm in them; and if it be urged that Homer took his ideas of right and wrong from a barbarous age, that is just saying, in other words, that Homer had very imperfect ideas of natural law.

Having exhausted all his powers of eulogium upon the times that are gone, Dr. Rennel indemnifies himself by the very novel practice of declaiming against the present age. It is an *evil age*—an *adulterous age*—an *ignorant age*—an *apostate age*—and a *foppish age*. Of the propriety of the last epithet, our readers may perhaps be more convinced, by calling to mind a class of fops not usually designated by that epithet—men clothed in profound black, with large canes, and strange amorphous hats—of big speech, and imperative presence—talkers about Plato—great affecters of senility—despisers of women, and all the graces of life—fierce foes to common sense—abusive of the living, and approving no one who has not been dead for at least a century. Such fops, as vain and as shallow as their fraternity in Bond street, differ from these only as Gorgonius differed from Rufillus.

In the ninth Discourse (p. 226), we read of St. Paul, that he had "an heroic zeal, directed, rather than bounded, by the nicest discretion—a conscious and commanding dignity, softened by the meekest and most profound humility."

* I cannot read the name of Malthus without adding my tribute of affection for the memory of one of the best men that ever lived. He loved philosophical truth more than any man I ever knew,—was full of practical wisdom,—and never indulged in contemptuous feelings against his inferiors in understanding.

† Page 318

This is intended for a fine piece of writing; but it is without meaning: for, if words have any limits, it is a *contradiction in terms* to say of the *same* person, at the *same* time, that he is nicely discreet, and heroically zealous; or that he is profoundly humble, and imperatively dignified: and if Dr. Rennel means, that St. Paul displayed these qualities at different times, then could not any one of them direct or soften the other.

Sermons are so seldom examined with any considerable degree of critical vigilance, that we are apt to discover in them sometimes a great laxity of assertion: such as the following:—

"Labour to be undergone, afflictions to be borne, contradictions to be endured, danger to be braved, interest to be despised in the best and most flourishing ages of the church, are the perpetual badges of far the greater part of those who take up their cross and follow Christ."

This passage, at first, struck us to be untrue; and we could not immediately recollect the afflictions Dr. Rennel alluded to, till it occurred to us, that he must undoubtedly mean the eight hundred and fifty actions which, in the course of eighteen months, have been brought against the clergy for non-residence.

Upon the danger to be apprehended from Roman Catholics in this country, Dr. Rennel is laughable. We should as soon dream that the wars of York and Lancaster would break out afresh, as that the Protestant religion in England has any thing to apprehend from the machinations of Catholics. To such a scheme as that of Catholic emancipation, which has for its object to restore their natural rights to three or four millions of men, and to allay the fury of religious hatred, Dr. Rennel is, as might be expected, a very strenuous antagonist. Time, which lifts up the veil of political mystery, will inform us if the Doctor has taken that side of the question which may be as lucrative to himself as it is inimical to human happiness, and repugnant to enlightened policy.

Of Dr. Rennel's talents as a reasoner, we certainly have formed no very high opinion. Unless dogmatical assertion, and the practice (but too common among theological writers) of taking the thing to be proved, for part of the proof, can be considered as evidence of a logical understanding, the specimens of argument Dr. Rennel has afforded us are very insignificant. For putting obvious truths into vehement language; for expanding and adorning moral instruction; this gentleman certainly possesses considerable talents: and if he will moderate his insolence, steer clear of theological metaphysics, and consider rather those great laws of Christian practice, which must interest mankind through all ages, than the petty questions which are important to the Chancellor of the Exchequer for the time being, he may live beyond his own days, and become a star of the third or fourth magnitude in the English Church.

JOHN BOWLES.*

[Edinburgh Review, 1802.]

If this piece be, as Mr. Bowles asserts,† the death-warrant of the liberty and power of Great Britain, we will venture to assert, that it is also the death-warrant of Mr. Bowles's literary reputation; and that the people of this island, if they verify his predictions, and cease to read his books, whatever they may lose in political greatness, will evince no small improvement in critical acumen. There is a political, as well as a bodily hypochondriasis; and there are empirics always on the watch to make their prey, either of the one or of the other. Dr. Solomon, Dr. Brodum, and Mr. Bowles, have all commanded their share of the public attention: but the two former gentlemen continue to flourish with undiminished splendour; while the patients of the latter are fast dwindling away, and his drugs falling into disuse and contempt.

The truth is, if Mr. Bowles had begun his literary career at a period when superior discrimination, and profound thought, not vulgar violence, and the eternal repetition of rabble-rousing words, were necessary to literary reputation, he would never have emerged from that obscurity to which he will soon turn. The intemperate passions of the public, not his own talents, have given him some temporary reputation; and now, when men hope and fear with less eagerness than they have been lately accustomed to do, Mr. Bowles will be compelled to descend from that moderate eminence, where no man of real genius would ever have condescended to remain.

The pamphlet is written in the genuine spirit of the Windham and Burke School; though Mr. Bowles cannot be called a servile copyist of either of these gentlemen, as he has rejected the logic of the one, and the eloquence of the other, and imitated them only in their head strong violence, and exaggerated abuse. There are some men who continue to astonish and please the world, even in the support of a bad cause. They are mighty in their fallacies, and beautiful in their errors. Mr. Bowles sees only one half of the precedent; and thinks, in

---

* *Reflections at the Conclusion of the War:* Being a Sequel to Reflections on the Political and Moral State of Society at the Close of the Eighteenth Century. The Third Edition, with Additions. By John Bowles, Esq.

† It is impossible to conceive the mischievous power of the corrupt alarmists of those days, and the despotic manner in which they exercised their authority. They were fair objects for the Edinburgh Review.

order to be famous, that he has nothing to do but to be in the wrong.

War, eternal war, till the wrongs of Europe are avenged, and the Bourbons restored, is the master-principle of Mr. Bowles's political opinions, and the object for which he declaims through the whole of the present pamphlet.

The first apprehensions which Mr. Bowles seems to entertain, are of the boundless ambition and perfidious character of the First Consul, and of that military despotism he has established, which is not only impelled by the love of conquest, but interested, for its own preservation, to desire the overthrow of other states. Yet the author informs us, immediately after, that the life of Buonaparte is exposed to more dangers than that of any other individual in Europe who is not actually in the last stage of an incurable disease; and that his death, whenever it happens, must involve the dissolution of that machine of government, of which he must be considered not only as the sole director, but the main spring. Confusion of thought, we are told, is one of the truest indications of terror; and the panic of this alarmist is so very great, that he cannot listen to the consolation which he himself affords: for it appears, upon summing up these perils, that we are in the utmost danger of being destroyed by a despot, whose system of government, as dreadful as himself, cannot survive him, and who, in all human probability, will be shot or hanged before he can execute any one of his projects against us.

We have a good deal of flourishing in the beginning of the pamphlet, about the effect of the moral sense upon the stability of governments; that is, as Mr. Bowles explains it, the power which all old governments derive from the opinion entertained by the people of the justice of their rights. If this sense of ancient right be (as is here confidently asserted) strong enough ultimately to restore the Bourbons, why are we to fight for that which will be done without any fighting at all? And if it be strong enough to restore, why was it weak enough to render restoration necessary?

To notice every singular train of reasoning into which Mr. Bowles falls, is not possible; and, in the copious choice of evils, we shall, from feelings of mercy, take the least.

It must not be forgotten, he observes, that "those rights of government, which, because they are ancient, are recognised by the moral sense as lawful, are the only ones which are compatible with civil liberty." So that all questions of right and wrong, between the governors and the governed, are determinable by chronology alone. Every political institution is favourable to liberty, not according to its spirit, but in proportion to the antiquity of its date; and the slaves of Great Britain are groaning under the trial by jury, while the free men of Asia exult in the bold privilege transmitted to them by their fathers, of being trampled to death by elephants.

In the 8th page, Mr. Bowles thinks that France, if she remains without a king, will conquer all Europe; and, in the 19th page, that she will be an object of Divine vengeance till she takes one. In the same page, all the miseries of France are stated to be a judgment of Heaven for their cruelty to the king; and, in the 33d page, they are discovered to proceed from the perfidy of the same king to this country in the American contest. So that certain misfortunes proceed from the maltreatment of a person, who had himself occasioned these identical misfortunes before he was maltreated; and while Providence is compelling the French, by every species of affliction, to resume the monarchical government, they are to acquire such extraordinary vigour, from not acting as Providence would wish, that they are to trample on every nation which co-operates with the Divine intention.

In the 60th page, Mr. Bowles explains what is meant by Jacobinism; and, as a concluding proof of the justice with which the character is drawn, triumphantly quotes the case of a certain R. Mountain, who was tried for damning all kings and all governments upon earth; for, adds R. Mountain, "I am a Jacobin." Nobody can more thoroughly detest and despise that restless spirit of political innovation, which, we suppose, is meant by the name of Jacobinism, than we ourselves do; but we were highly amused with this proof, *ab ebriis sutoribus*, of the prostration of Europe, the last hour of human felicity, the perdition of man, discovered in the crapulous eructations of a drunken cobler.

This species of evidence might certainly have escaped a common observer: But this is not all; there are other proofs of treason and sedition, equally remote, sagacious, and profound. Many good subjects are not very much pleased with the idea of the Whig Club dining together; but Mr. Bowles has the merit of first calling the public attention to the alarming practice of singing after dinner at these political meetings. He speaks with a proper horror of tavern dinners,

> "—where conviviality is made a stimulus to disaffection—where wine serves only to inflame disloyalty—where toasts are converted into a vehicle of sedition—and where the powers of harmony are called forth in the cause of Discord by those hireling singers, who are equally ready to invoke the Divine favour on the head of their King, or to strain their venal throats in chanting the triumphs of his bitterest enemies."

All complaint is futile, which is not followed up by appropriate remedies. If Parliament, or Catarrh, do not save us, Dignum and Sedgwick will quaver away the King, shake down the House of Lords, and warble us into all the horrors of republican government. When, in addition to these dangers, we reflect also upon those with which our national happiness is menaced, by the present thinness of ladies' petticoats (p. 78), temerity may hope our salvation, but how can reason promise it?

One solitary gleam of comfort, indeed, beams upon us in reading the solemn devotion of this modern Curtius to the cause of his King and country—

"My attachment to the British monarchy, and to the reigning family, is rooted in my 'heart's core.'—My anxiety for the British throne, pending the dangers to which, in common with every other throne, it has lately been exposed, has imbittered my choicest comforts. And I must solemnly vow, before Almighty God, to devote myself, to the end of my days, to the maintenance of that throne."

Whether this patriotism be original, or whether it be copied from the Upholsterer in Foote's Farces, who sits up whole nights watching over the British constitution, we shall not stop to inquire; because, when the practical effect of sentiments is good, we would not diminish their merits by investigating their origin. We seriously commend in Mr. Bowles this future dedication of his life to the service of his King and country; and consider it as a virtual promise that he will write no more in their defence. No wise or good man has ever thought of either, but with admiration and respect. That they should be exposed to that ridicule, by the forward imbecility of friendship, from which they appear to be protected by intrinsic worth, is so painful a consideration, that the very thought of it, we are persuaded, will induce Mr. Bowles to desist from writing on political subjects.

DR. LANGFORD.*

[EDINBURGH REVIEW, 1802.]

AN accident which happened to the gentleman engaged in reviewing this Sermon proves, in the most striking manner, the importance of this charity for restoring to life persons in whom the vital power is suspended. He was discovered, with Dr. Langford's† discourse lying open before him, in a state of the most profound sleep; from which he could not, by any means, be awakened for a great length of time. By attending, however, to the rules prescribed by the Humane Society, flinging in the smoke of tobacco, applying hot flannels, and carefully removing the discourse itself to a great distance, the critic was restored to his disconsolate brothers.

The only account he could give of himself was, that he remembers reading on, regularly, till he came to the following pathetic description of a drowned tradesman; beyond which he recollects nothing.

"But to the individual himself, as a man, let us add the interruption to all the temporal business in which his interest was engaged. To him indeed, now apparently lost, the world is as nothing: but it seldom happens, that man can live for himself alone: society parcels out its concerns in various connections; and from one head issue waters which run down in many channels.—The spring being suddenly cut off, what confusion must follow in the streams which have flowed from its source? It may be, that all the expectations reasonably raised of approaching prosperity, to those who have embarked in the same occupation, may at once disappear; and the important interchange of commercial faith be broken off before it could be brought to any advantageous conclusion."

This extract will suffice for the style of the sermon. The charity itself is above all praise.

ARCHDEACON NARES.‡

[EDINBURGH REVIEW, 1802.]

FOR the swarm of ephemeral sermons which issue from the press, we are principally indebted to the vanity of popular preachers, who are puffed up by female praises into a belief, that what may be delivered, with great propriety, in a chapel full of visitors and friends, is fit for the deliberate attention of the public, who cannot be influenced by the decency of a clergyman's private life, flattered by the sedulous politeness of his manners, or misled by the fallacious circumstances of voice and action. A clergyman cannot be always considered as reprehensible for preaching an indifferent sermon; because, to the active piety, and correct life, which the profession requires, many an excellent man may not unite talents for that species of composition; but every man who prints, imagines he gives to the world something which they had not before, either in matter or style; that he has brought forth new truths, or adorned old ones; and when, in lieu of novelty and ornament, we can discover nothing but trite imbecility, the law must take its course, and the delinquent suffer

* *Anniversary Sermon of the Royal Humane Society.* By W. LANGFORD, D. D. Printed for F. and C. Rivington.

† To this exceedingly foolish man, the first years of Etonian Education were intrusted. How is it possible to inflict a greater misfortune on a country, than to fill up such an office with such an officer?

‡ *A Thanksgiving for Plenty, and Warning against Avarice.* A Sermon. By the Reverend ROBERT NARES, Archdeacon of Stafford, and Canon Residentiary of Litchfield. London: Printed for the author, and sold by Rivingtons, St. Paul's Churchyard.

This was another gentleman of the alarmist tribe.

that mortification from which vanity can rarely be expected to escape, when it chooses dulness for the minister of its gratifications.

The learned author, after observing that a large army praying would be a much finer spectacle than a large army fighting, and after entertaining us with the old anecdote of Xerxes, and the flood of tears, proceeds to express his sentiments on the late scarcity, and the present abundance; then, stating the manner in which the Jews were governed by the immediate interference of God, and informing us, that other people expect not, nor are taught to look for, miraculous interference, to punish or reward them, he proceeds to talk of the visitation of Providence, for the purposes of trial, warning, and correction, as if it were a truth of which he had never doubted.

Still, however, he contends, though the Deity does interfere, it would be presumptuous and impious to pronounce the purposes for which he interferes; and then adds, that it has pleased God, within these few years, to give us a most awful lesson of the vanity of agriculture and importation without piety, and that he has proved this to the conviction of every thinking mind.

"Though he interpose not (says Mr. Nares) by positive miracle, he influences by means unknown to all but himself, and directs the winds, the rain, and the glorious beams of heaven to execute his judgment, or fulfil his merciful designs."—Now, either the wind, the rain, and the beams, are here represented to act as they do in the ordinary course of nature, or they are not. If they are, how can their operations be considered as a judgment on sins? and if they are not, what are their extraordinary operations, but positive miracles? So that the archdeacon, after denying that any body knows *when*, *how*, and *why*, the Creator works a miracle, proceeds to specify the *time*, *instrument*, and *object* of a miraculous scarcity; and then, assuring us that the elements were employed to execute the judgments of Providence, denies that this is any proof of a positive miracle.

Having given us this specimen of his talents for theological metaphysics, Mr. Nares commences his attack upon the farmers; accuses them of cruelty and avarice; raises the old cry of monopoly; and expresses some doubts, in a note, whether the better way would not be, to subject their granaries to the control of an exciseman; and to levy heavy penalties upon those, in whose possession corn, beyond a certain quantity to be fixed by law, should be found.—This style of reasoning is pardonable enough in those who argue from the belly rather than the brains; but in a well-fed, and well-educated clergyman, who has never been disturbed by hunger from the free exercise of cultivated talents, it merits the severest reprehension. The farmer has it not in his power to raise the price of corn; he never has fixed and never can fix it. He is unquestionably justified in receiving any price he can obtain: for it happens very beautifully, that the effect of his efforts to better his fortune is as beneficial to the public as if their motive had not been selfish. The poor are not to be supported, in time of famine, by abatement of price on the part of the farmer, but by the subscription of residentiary canons, archdeacons, and all men rich in public or private property; and to these subscriptions the farmer should contribute according to the amount of his fortune. To insist that he should take a less price when he can obtain a greater, is to insist upon laying on that order of men the whole burden of supporting the poor; a convenient system enough in the eyes of a rich ecclesiastic; and objectionable only, because it is impracticable, pernicious, and unjust.*

The question of the corn trade has divided society into two parts—those who have any talents for reasoning, and those who have not. We owe an apology to our readers for taking any notice of errors that have been so frequently and so unanswerably exposed; but when they are echoed from the bench and the pulpit, the dignity of the teacher may perhaps communicate some degree of importance to the silliest and most extravagant doctrines.

No reasoning can be more radically erroneous than that upon which the whole of Mr. Nares's sermon is founded. The most benevolent, the most Christian, and the most profitable conduct the farmer can pursue, is, to sell his commodities for the highest price he can possibly obtain. This advice, we think, is not in any great danger of being rejected: we wish we were equally sure of success in counselling the Reverend Mr. Nares to attend, in future, to practical rather than theoretical questions about provisions. He may be a very hospitable archdeacon; but nothing short of a *positive miracle* can make him an acute reasoner.

* If it is pleasant to notice the intellectual growth of an individual, it is still more pleasant to see the public growing wiser. This absurdity of attributing the high price of corn to the combinations of farmers, was the common nonsense talked in the days of my youth. I remember when ten judges out of twelve laid down this doctrine in their charges to the various grand juries on the circuits. The lowest attorney's clerk is now better instructed.

MATTHEW LEWIS.*

[Edinburgh Review, 1803.]

Alfonso, king of Castile had, many years previous to the supposed epoch of the play, left his minister and general, Orsino, to perish in prison, from a false accusation of treason. Cæsario, son to Orsino, (who by accident had liberated Amelrosa, daughter of Alfonso, from the Moors, and who is married to her, unknown to the father,) becomes a great favourite with the king, and avails himself of the command of the armies, with which he is intrusted, to gratify his revenge for his father's misfortunes, to forward his own ambitious views, and to lay a plot by which he may deprive Alfonso of his throne and his life. Marquis Guzman, poisoned by his wife Ottilia, in love with Cæsario, confesses to the king that the papers upon which the suspicion of Orsino's guilt was founded were forged by him: and the king, learning from his daughter Amelrosa that Orsino is still alive, repairs to his retreat in the forest, is received with the most implacable hauteur and resentment, and in vain implores forgiveness of his injured minister. To the same forest Cæsario, informed of the existence of his father, repairs and reveals his intended plot against the king. Orsino, convinced of Alfonso's goodness to his subjects, though incapable of forgiving him for his unintentional injuries to himself, in vain dissuades his son from the conspiracy; and at last, ignorant of their marriage, acquaints Amelrosa with the plot formed by her husband against her father. Amelrosa, already poisoned by Ottilia, in vain attempts to prevent Cæsario from blowing up a mine laid under the royal palace; information of which she had received from Ottilia, stabbed by Cæsario to avoid her importunity. In the mean time, the king had been removed from the palace by Orsino to his ancient retreat in the forest: the people rise against the usurper Cæsario; a battle takes place: Orsino stabs his own son at the moment the king is in his son's power; falls down from the wounds he has received in battle; and dies in the usual dramatic style, repeating twenty-two hexameter verses. Mr. Lewis says in his preface,

"To the assertion, that my play is *stupid*, I have nothing to object; if it be found so, even let it be so said; but if (as was most *falsely* asserted of Adelmorn) any anonymous writer should advance that this Tragedy is *immoral*, I expect him to prove his assertion by quoting the objectionable passages. This I demand as an act of *justice*."

We confess ourselves to have been highly delighted with these symptoms of returning, or perhaps nascent purity in the mind of Mr. Lewis; a delight somewhat impaired, to be sure, at the opening of the play, by the following explanation which Ottilia gives of her early rising.

"ACT I. Scene I.—*The palace-garden.—Day-break.*
Ottilia *enters in a night-dress: her hair flows dishevelled.*

"Ottil. Dews of the morn descend! Breathe summer gales:
My flushed cheeks woo ye! Play, sweet wantons, play
'Mid my loose tresses, fan my panting breast,
Quench my blood's burning fever!—Vain, vain prayer!
Not Winter throned 'midst Alpine snows, whose will
Can with one breath, one touch, congeal whole realms,
And blanch whole seas: not that fiend's self could ease
This heart, this gulf of flames, this purple kingdom,
Where passion rules and rages!"

Ottilia at last becomes quite furious, from the conviction that Cæsario has been sleeping with a second lady, called Estella; whereas he has really been sleeping with a third lady, called Amelrosa. Passing across the stage, this gallant gentleman takes an opportunity of mentioning to the audience, that he has been passing his time very agreeably, meets Ottilia, quarrels, makes it up; and so end the first two or three scenes.

Mr. Lewis will excuse us for the liberty we take in commenting on a few passages in his play which appear to us rather exceptionable. The only information which Cæsario, imagining his father to have been dead for many years, receives of his existence, is in the following short speech of Melchior.

"Melch. The Count San Lucar, long thought dead but saved,
It seems, by Amelrosa's care.—Time presses—
I must away: farewell."

To this laconic, but important information, Cæsario makes no reply; but merely desires Melchior to meet him at one o'clock, under the Royal Tower, and for some other purposes.

In the few cases which have fallen under our observation, of fathers restored to life after a supposed death of twenty years, the parties concerned have, on the first intimation, appeared a little surprised, and generally ask a few questions; though we do not go the length of saying it is natural so to do. This same Cæsario (whose love of his father is a principal cause of his conspiracy against the king) begins criticising the old warrior, upon his first seeing him again, much as a virtuoso would criticise an ancient statue that wanted an arm or a leg.

"Orsino *enters from the cave.*
"Cæsario. Now by my life
A noble ruin!"

Amelrosa, who imagines her father to have banished her from his presence for *ever*, in the first transports of joy for pardon, obtained by earnest intercessions, thus exclaims:—

"Lend thy doves, dear Venus,
That I may send them where Cæsario strays:
And while he smooths their silver wings, and gives them
For drink the honey of his lips, I'll bid them
Coo in his ear, his Amelrosa's happy!"

What judge of human feelings does not re

* *Alfonso, King of Castile.* A Tragedy, in five Acts. By M. G. Lewis. Price 2*s.* 6*d.*

cognise in these images of silver wings, doves and honey, the genuine language of the passions?

If Mr. Lewis is really in earnest in pointing out the coincidence between his own dramatic sentiments,and the Gospel of St. Matthew, such a reference (wide as we know this assertion to be) evinces a want of judgment, of which we did not think him capable. If it proceeded from irreligious levity, we pity the man who has bad taste enough not to prefer honest dulness to such paltry celebrity.

We beg leave to submit to Mr. Lewis, if Alfonso, considering the great interest he has in the decision, might not interfere a little in the long argument carried on between Cæsario and Orsino, upon the propriety of putting him to death. To have expressed any decisive opinion upon the subject, might perhaps have been incorrect; but a few gentle hints as to that side of the question to which he leaned, might be fairly allowed to be no very unnatural incident.

This tragedy delights in explosions. Alfonso's empire is destroyed by a blast of gunpowder, and restored by a clap of thunder. After the death of Cæsario, and a short exhortation to that purpose by Orsino, all the conspirators fall down in a thunder-clap, ask pardon of the king, and are forgiven. This mixture of physical and moral power is beautiful! How interesting a water-spout would appear among Mr. Lewis's kings and queens! We anxiously look forward, in his next tragedy, to a fall of snow three or four feet deep; or expect that a plot shall gradually unfold itself by means of a general thaw.

All is not so bad in this play. There is some strong painting, which shows, every now and then, the hand of a master. The agitation which Cæsario exhibits upon his first joining the conspirators in the cave, previous to the blowing up of the mine, and immediately after stabbing Ottilia, is very fine.

"CÆSARIO. Ay, shout, shout,
And kneeling greet your blood-anointed king,
This steel his sceptre! Tremble, dwarfs in guilt,
And own your master! Thou art proof, Henriquez,
'Gainst pity; I once saw thee stab in battle
A page who clasped thy knees: And Melchior there
Made quick work with a brother whom he hated.
But what did I this night? Hear, hear, and reverence!
There was a breast, on which my head had rested
A thousand times; a breast which loved me fondly
As heaven loves martyred saints; and yet this breast
I stabbed, knave—stabbed it to the heart—Wine! wine there?
For my soul's joyous!"—p. 86.

The resistance which Amelrosa opposes to the firing of the mine, is well wrought out; and there is some good poetry scattered up and down the play, of which we should very willingly make extracts, if our limits would permit. The ill success which it has justly experienced, is owing, we have no doubt, to the want of nature in the characters, and of probability and good arrangement in the incidents; objections of some force.

AUSTRALIA.*

[EDINBURGH REVIEW, 1803.]

To introduce an European population, and consequently, the arts and civilization of Europe, into such an untrodden country as New Holland, is to confer a lasting and important benefit upon the world. If man be destined for perpetual activity, and if the proper objects of that activity be the subjugation of physical difficulties, and of his own dangerous passions, how absurd are those systems which proscribe the acquisitions of science and the restraints of law, and would arrest the progress of man in the rudest and earliest stages of his existence! Indeed, opinions so very extravagant in their nature must be attributed rather to the wantonness of paradox, than to sober reflection and extended inquiry.

To suppose the savage state permanent, we must suppose the numbers of those who compose it to be stationary, and the various passions by which men have actually emerged from it to be extinct; and this is to suppose man a very different being from what he really is. To prove such a permanence beneficial, (if it were possible,) we must have recourse to matter of fact, and judge of the rude state of society, not from the praises of tranquil *literati*, but from the narratives of those who have seen it, through a nearer and better medium than that of imagination. There is an argument, however, for the continuation of evil, drawn from the ignorance of good; by which it is contended, that to teach men their situation *can* be better, is to teach them that it *is* bad, and to destroy that happiness which always results from an ignorance that any greater happiness is within our reach. All pains and pleasures are clearly by comparison; but the most deplorable savage enjoys a sufficient contrast of good, to know that the grosser evils from which civilization rescues him *are* evils. A New Hollander seldom passes a year without suffering from famine; the small-pox falls upon him like a plague; he dreads those calamities, though he does not know how to avert them; but, doubtless, would find his happiness increased, if they *were* averted. To deny this, is to suppose that men are reconciled to evils, because they are inevitable; and yet hurricanes, earthquakes, bodily decay, and death, stand highest in the catalogue of human calamities.

* *Account of the English Colony of New South Wales.* By Lieutenant-Colonel COLLINS of the Royal Marines. Vol. ii. 4to. Cadell and Davies, London.

Where civilization gives new birth to new comparisons unfavourable to savage life, with the information that a greater good is possible, it generally connects the means of attaining it. The savage no sooner becomes ashamed of his nakedness, than the loom is ready to clothe him; the forge prepares for him more perfect tools, when he is disgusted with the awkwardness of his own: his weakness is strengthened, and his wants supplied as soon as they are discovered; and the use of the discovery is, that it enables him to derive from comparison the best proof of present happiness. A man born blind is ignorant of the pleasures of which he is deprived. After the restoration of his sight, his happiness will be increased from two causes;—from the delight he experiences at the novel accession of power, and from the contrast he will always be enabled to make between his two situations, long after the pleasure of novelty has ceased. For these reasons it is humane to restore him to sight.

But, however beneficial to the general interests of mankind the civilization of barbarous countries may be considered to be, in this particular instance of it, the interest of Great Britain would seem to have been very little consulted. With fanciful schemes of universal good we have no business to meddle. Why we are to erect penitentiary houses and prisons at the distance of half the diameter of the globe, and to incur the enormous expense of feeding and transporting their inhabitants to and at such a distance, it is extremely difficult to discover. It certainly is not from any deficiency of barren islands near our own coast, nor of uncultivated wastes in the interior; and if we were sufficiently fortunate to be wanting in such species of accommodation, we might discover in Canada, or the West Indies, or on the coast of Africa, a climate malignant enough, or a soil sufficiently sterile, to revenge all the injuries which have been inflicted on society by pickpockets, larcenists, and petty felons. Upon the foundation of a new colony, and especially one peopled by criminals, there is a disposition in Government (where any circumstance in the commission of the crime affords the least pretence for the commutation) to convert capital punishments into transportation; and by these means to hold forth a very dangerous, though certainly a very unintentional, encouragement to offences. And when the history of the colony has been attentively perused in the parish of St. Giles, the ancient avocation of picking pockets will certainly not become more discreditable from the knowledge, that it may eventually lead to the possession of a farm of a thousand acres on the river Hawkesbury. Since the benevolent Howard attacked our prisons, incarceration has become not only healthy but elegant; and a county jail is precisely the place to which any pauper might wish to retire to gratify his taste for magnificence as well as for comfort. Upon the same principle, there is some risk that transportation will be considered as one of the surest roads to honour and to wealth; and that no felon will hear a verdict of "*not guilty*" without considering himself as cut off in the fairest career of prosperity. It is foolishly believed, that the colony of Botany Bay unites our moral and commercial interests, and that we shall receive hereafter an ample equivalent, in bales of goods, for all the vices we export. Unfortunately, the expenses we have incurred in founding the colony, will not retard the natural progress of its emancipation, or prevent the attacks of other nations, who will be as desirous of reaping the fruit, as if they had sown the seed. It is a colony, besides, begun under every possible disadvantage; it is too distant to be long governed, or well defended; it is undertaken, not by the voluntary association of individuals, but by Government, and by means of compulsory labour. A nation must, indeed, be redundant in capital, that will expend it where the hopes of a just return are so very small.

It may be a very curious consideration, to reflect what we are to do with this colony when it comes to years of discretion. Are we to spend another hundred millions of money in discovering its strength, and to humble ourselves again before a fresh set of Washingtons and Franklins? The moment after we have suffered such serious mischief from the escape of the old tiger, we are breeding up a young cub, whom we cannot render less ferocious, or more secure. If we are gradually to manumit the colony, as it is more and more capable of protecting itself, the degrees of emancipation, and the periods at which they are to take place, will be judged of very differently by the two nations. But we confess ourselves not to be so sanguine as to suppose, that a spirited and commercial people would, in spite of the example of America, ever consent to abandon their sovereignty over an important colony, without a struggle. Endless blood and treasure will be exhausted to support a tax on kangaroos' skins; faithful Commons will go on voting fresh supplies to support a *just and necessary* war; and Newgate, then become a quarter of the world, will evince a heroism, not unworthy of the great characters by whom she was originally peopled.

The experiment, however, is not less interesting in a moral, because it is objectionable in a commercial point of view. It is an object of the highest curiosity, thus to have the growth of a nation subjected to our examination; to trace it by such faithful records, from the first day of its existence; and to gather that knowledge of the progress of human affairs, from actual experience, which is considered to be only accessible to the conjectural reflections of enlightened minds.

Human nature, under very old governments, is so trimmed, and pruned, and ornamented, and led into such a variety of factitious shapes, that we are almost ignorant of the appearance it would assume, if it were left more to itself. From such an experiment as that now before us, we shall be better able to appreciate what circumstances of our situation are owing to those permanent laws by which all men are influenced, and what to the accidental positions in which we have been placed. New circumstances will throw new light upon the effects of our religious, political, and economical institutions, if we cause them to be adopted as models in our rising empire; and if we do not, we shall estimate the effects of their presence, by observing those which are produced by their non-existence.

The history of the colony is at present, however, in its least interesting state, on account of the great preponderance of depraved inhabitants, whose crimes and irregularities give a monotony to the narrative, which it cannot lose, till the respectable part of the community come to bear a greater proportion to the criminal.

These Memoirs of Colonel Collins resume the history of the colony from the period at which he concluded it in his former volume, September 1796, and continue it down to August 1801. They are written in the style of a journal, which, though not the most agreeable mode of conveying information, is certainly the most authentic, and contrives to banish the suspicion (and most probably the reality) of the interference of a book-maker—a species of gentlemen who are now almost become necessary to deliver naval and military authors in their literary labours, though they do not always atone, by orthography and grammar, for the sacrifice of truth and simplicity. Mr. Collins's book is written with great plainness and candour: he appears to be a man always meaning well; of good, plain common sense; and composed of those well-wearing materials, which adapt a person for situations where genius and refinement would only prove a source of misery and of error.

We shall proceed to lay before our readers an analysis of the most important matter contained in this volume.

The natives in the vicinity of Port Jackson stand extremely low, in point of civilization, when compared with many other savages, with whom the discoveries of Captain Cook have made us acquainted. Their notions of religion exceed even that degree of absurdity which we are led to expect in the creed of a barbarous people. In politics, they appear to have scarcely advanced beyond family-government. Huts they have none; and, in all their economical inventions, there is a rudeness and deficiency of ingenuity, unpleasant, when contrasted with the instances of dexterity with which the descriptions and importations of our navigators have rendered us so familiar. Their numbers appear to us to be very small: a fact, at once, indicative either of the ferocity of manners in any people, or, more probably, of the sterility of their country; but which, in the present instance, proceeds from both these causes.

"Gaining every day (says Mr. Collins) some further knowledge of the inhuman habits and customs of these people, their being so thinly scattered through the country ceased to be a matter of surprise. It was almost daily seen, that from some trifling cause or other, they were continually living in a state of warfare: to this must be added their brutal treatment of their women, who are themselves equally destructive to the measure of population, by the horrid and cruel customs of endeavouring to cause a miscarriage, which their female acquaintances effect by pressing the body in such a way, as to destroy the infant in the womb which violence not unfrequently occasions the death of the unnatural mother also To this they have recourse to avoid the trouble of carrying the infant about when born, which, when it is very young, or at the breast, is the duty of the woman. The operation for this destructive purpose is termed Mee-bră. The burying an infant (when at the breast) with the mother, if she should die, is another shocking cause of the thinness of population among them. The fact that such an operation as the Mee-bră was practised by these wretched people, was communicated by one of the natives to the principal surgeon of the settlement."—(p. 124, 125.)

It is remarkable, that the same paucity of numbers has been observed in every part of New Holland which has hitherto been explored; and yet there is not the smallest reason to conjecture that the population of it has been very recent; nor do the people bear any marks of descent from the inhabitants of the numerous islands by which this great continent is surrounded. The force of population can only be resisted by some great physical evils; and many of the causes of this scarcity of human beings, which Mr. Collins refers to the ferocity of the natives, are ultimately referable to the difficulty of support. We have always considered this phenomenon as a symptom extremely unfavourable to the future destinies of this country. It is easy to launch out into eulogiums of the fertility of nature in particular spots; but the most probable reason why a country that has been long inhabited, is not well inhabited, is, that it is not calculated to support many inhabitants without great labour. It is difficult to suppose any other causes powerful enough to resist the impetuous tendency of man, to obey that mandate for increase and multiplication, which has certainly been better observed than any other declaration of the Divine will ever revealed to us.

There appears to be some tendency to civilization, and some tolerable notions of justice, in a practice very similar to our custom of duelling; for duelling, though barbarous in civilized, is a highly civilized institution among barbarous people: and when compared to assassination, is a prodigious victory gained over human passions. Whoever kills another in the neighbourhood of Botany Bay, is compelled to appear at an appointed day before the friends of the deceased, and to sustain the attacks of their missile weapons. If he is killed, he is deemed to have met with a deserved death; if not, he is considered to have expiated the crime for the commission of which he was exposed to the danger. There is in this institution a command over present impulses, a prevention of secrecy in the gratification of revenge, and a wholesome correction of that passion by the effect of public observation, which evince such a superiority to the mere animal passions of ordinary savages, and form such a contrast to the rest of the history of this people, that it may be considered as altogether an anomalous and inexplicable fact. The natives differ very much in the progress they have made in the arts of economy. Those to the north of Port Jackson evince a considerable degree of ingenuity and contrivance in the structure of their houses, which are rendered quite impervious to the weather, while the inhabitants at Port Jackson have no houses at all. At Port Dalrymple, in Van Diemen's Land, there was every reason to believe the natives were unacquainted with the use of canoes; a fact extremely embarrassing to those who indulge themselves in speculating on the genealogy of nations; because it reduces them to the necessity of supposing that the progenitors of this insular people swam over from the main land, or that they were aboriginal; a species of dilemma, which effectually bars all conjecture upon the intermixture of nations. It is painful to learn, that the natives have begun to plunder and rob in so very alarming a manner, that it has been repeatedly found necessary to fire upon them; and many have, in consequence, fallen victims to their rashness.

The soil is found to produce coal in vast abundance, salt, lime, very fine iron ore, timber fit for all purposes, excellent flax, and a tree, the bark of which is admirably adapted for cordage. The discovery of coal (which, by the by, we do not believe was ever before discovered so near the line) is probably rather a disadvantage than an advantage; because, as it lies extremely favourable for sea carriage, it may prove to be a cheaper fuel than wood, and thus operate as a discouragement to the clearing of lands. The soil upon the sea-coast has not been found to be very productive, though it improves in partial spots in the interior. The climate is healthy, in spite of the prodigious heat of the summer months, at which period the thermometer has been observed to stand in the shade at 107, and the leaves of garden-vegetables to fall into dust, as if they had been consumed with fire. But one of the most insuperable defects in New Holland, considered as the future country of a great people, is, the want of large rivers penetrating very far into the interior, and navigable for small crafts. The Hawkesbury, the largest river yet discovered, is not accessible to boats for more than twenty miles. This same river occasionally rises above its natural level, to the astonishing height of fifty feet; and has swept away, more than once, the labours and the hopes of the new people exiled to its banks.

The laborious acquisition of any good we have long enjoyed is apt to be forgotten. We walk and talk, and run and read, without remembering the long and severe labour dedicated to the cultivation of these powers, the formidable obstacles opposed to our progress, or the infinite satisfaction with which we overcame them. He who lives among a civilized people, may estimate the labour by which society has been brought into such a state, by reading these annals of Botany Bay, the account of a whole nation exerting itself to new floor the government-house, repair the hospital, or build a wooden receptacle for stores. Yet the time may come, when some Botany Bay Tacitus shall record the crimes of an emperor lineally descended from a London pick-pocket, or paint the valour with which he has led his New Hollanders into the heart of China. At that period, when the Grand Lahma is sending to supplicate alliance; when the spice islands are purchasing peace with nutmegs; when enormous tributes of green tea and nankeen are wafted into Port Jackson, and landed on the quays of Sydney, who will ever remember that the sawing of a few planks, and the knocking together a few nails, were such a serious trial of the energies and resources of the nation?

The Government of the colony, after enjoying some little respite from this kind of labour, has begun to turn its attention to the coarsest and most necessary species of manufactures, for which their wool appears to be well adapted. The state of stock in the whole settlement, in June 1801, was about 7,000 sheep, 1,300 head of cattle, 250 horses, and 5,000 hogs. There were under cultivation at the same time, between 9 and 10,000 acres of corn. Three years and a-half before this, in December 1797, the numbers were as follows:—Sheep, 2,500; cattle 350; horses, 100; hogs, 4,300; acres of land in cultivation, 4,000. The temptation to salt pork, and sell it for Government store, is probably the reason why the breed of hogs has been so much kept under. The increase of cultivated lands between the two periods is prodigious. It appears (p. 319) that the whole number of convicts imported between January 1788 and June 1801 (a period of thirteen years and a half) has been about 5,000, of whom 1,157 were females. The total amount of the population on the continent, as well as at Norfolk Island, amounted, June 1801, to 6,500 persons; of these 766 were children born at Port Jackson. In the returns from Norfolk Island, children are not discriminated from adults. Let us add to the imported population of 5,000 convicts, 500 free people, which (if we consider that a regiment of soldiers has been kept up there) is certainly a very small allowance; then, in thirteen years and a half, the imported population has increased only by two-thirteenths. If we suppose that something more than a fifth of the free people were women, this will make the total of women 1,270; of whom we may fairly presume that 800 were capable of child-bearing; and if we suppose the children of Norfolk Island to bear the same proportion to the adults as at Port Jackson, their total number at both settlements will be 913;—a state of infantine population which certainly does not justify the very high eulogiums which have been made on the fertility of the female sex in the climate of New Holland.

The Governor, who appears on all occasions to be an extremely well-disposed man, is not quite so conversant in the best writings on political economy as we could wish: and indeed (though such knowledge would be extremely serviceable to the interests which this Romulus of the Southern Pole is superintending), it is rather unfair to exact from a superintendent of pick-pockets, that he should be a philosopher. In the 18th page we have the following information respecting the price of labour:—

"Some representations having been made to the Governor from the settlers in different parts of the colony, purporting that the wages demanded by the free labouring people, whom they had occasion to hire, were so exorbitant as to run away with the greatest part of the profit of their farms, it was recommended to them to appoint quarterly meetings among themselves, to be held in each district, for the purpose of settling the rate of wages to labourers in every different kind of work; that, to this end, a written agreement should be entered into, and subscribed by each settler, a breach of which should be punished by a penalty, to be fixed by the general opinion, and made recoverable in a court of civil judicature. It was recommended to them to apply this forfeiture to the common benefit; and they were to transmit to the head-quarters a copy of their agreement, with the rate of wages which they should from time to time establish, for the Governor's information, holding their first meeting as early as possible."

And again, at p. 24, the following arrangements on that head are enacted:—

"In pursuance of the order which was issued in January last recommending the settlers to appoint meetings, at which they should fix the rate of wages that it might be proper to pay for the different kinds of labour which their farms should require, the settlers had submitted to the Governor the several resolutions that they had entered into, by which he was enabled to fix a rate that he conceived to be fair and equitable between the farmer and the labourer.

"The following prices of labour were now established, viz.

	£	s.	d.
Felling forest timber, per acre, - -	0	9	0
Ditto in brushwood, ditto - -	1	10	6
Burning off open ground, ditto - -	1	5	0
Ditto brush ground, ditto - -	1	10	0
Breaking up new ground, ditto - -	1	4	0
Chipping fresh ground, ditto - -	1	12	3
Chipping in wheat, ditto - -	0	7	0
Breaking up stubble or corn ground, 1¼d. per rod, or ditto - -	0	16	8
Planting Indian corn, ditto - -	0	7	0
Hilling ditto ditto - -	0	7	0
Reaping wheat, ditto - -	0	10	0
Thrashing ditto, pr. bush., ditto - -	0	0	9
Pulling and husking Indian corn, per bushel	0	0	6
Splitting paling of seven feet long, per hundred	0	3	0
Ditto of five feet long, ditto - - -	0	1	6
Sawing plank, ditto - - -	0	7	0
Ditching per rod, three feet wide, and 3 ft. deep	0	0	10
Carriage of wheat, per bushel, per mile -	0	0	2
Ditto Indian corn, neat - - -	0	0	3
Yearly wages for labour, with board -	10	0	0
Wages per week, with provisions, consisting of 4 lb. of salt pork, or 6 lb. of fresh, and 21 lb. of wheat with vegetables - -	0	6	0
A day's wages with board - - -	0	1	0
Ditto without board - - - -	0	2	6
A government-man allowed to officers or settlers in their own time - - -	0	0	10
Price of an axe - - - - -	0	2	0
New steeling ditto - - - -	0	0	6
A new hoe - - - - - -	0	1	9
A sickle - - - - - -	0	1	6
Hire of a boat to carry grain, per day -	0	5	0

"The settlers were reminded, that, in order to prevent any kind of dispute between the master and servant, when they should have occasion to hire a man for any length of time, they would find it most convenient to engage him for a quarter, half-year, or year, and to make their agreement in writing; on which, should any dispute arise, an appeal to the magistrates would settle it."

This is all very bad; and if the Governor had cherished the intention of destroying the colony, he could have done nothing more detrimental to its interests. The high price of labour is the very corner-stone on which the prosperity of a new colony depends. It enables the poor man to live with ease; and is the strongest incitement to population, by rendering children rather a source of riches than of poverty. If the same difficulty of subsistence existed in new countries as in old, it is plain that the progress of population would be equally slow in each. The very circumstances which cause the difference are, that, in the latter, there is a competition among the labourers to be employed; and, in the former, a competition among the occupiers of land to obtain labourers. In the one, land is scarce and men plenty; in the other, men are scarce, and land is plenty. To disturb this natural order of things (a practice injurious at all times) must be particularly so where the predominant disposition of the colonist is an aversion to labour, produced by a long course of dissolute habits. In such cases the high prices of labour, which the Governor was so desirous of abating, bid fair not only to increase the agricultural prosperity, but to effect the moral reformation of the colony. We observe the same unfortunate ignorance of the elementary principles of commerce in the attempts of the Governor to reduce the prices of the European commodities, by bulletins and authoritative interference, as if there were any other mode of lowering the price of an article (while the demand continues the same) but by increasing its quantity. The avaricious love of gain, which is so feelingly deplored, appears to us a principle which, in able hands, might be guided to the most salutary purposes. The object is to encourage the love of labour, which is best encouraged by the love of money. We have very great doubts on the policy of reserving the best timber on the estates as government timber. Such a reservation would probably operate as a check upon the clearing of lands without attaining the object desired; for the timber, instead of being immediately cleared, would be slowly destroyed, by the neglect or malice of the settlers whose lands it encumbered. Timber is such a drug in new countries, that it is at any time to be purchased for little more than the labour of cutting. To secure a supply of it by vexatious and invidious laws, is surely a work of supererogation and danger. The greatest evil which the government has yet to contend with is, the inordinate use of spirituous liquors; a passion which puts the interests of agriculture at variance with those of morals: for a dram-drinker will consume as much corn, in the form of alcohol, in one day, as would supply him with bread for three; and thus, by his vices, opens an admirable market to the industry of a new settlement. The only mode, we believe, of encountering this evil, is by deriving from it such a revenue as will not admit of smuggling. Beyond this it is almost invincible by authority; and is probably to be cured only by the progressive refinement of manners.

To evince the increasing commerce of the

settlement, a *list is subjoined of* 140 ships, which have arrived there since its first foundation, forty only of which were from England. The colony at Norfolk Island is represented to be in a very deplorable situation, and will most probably be abandoned for one about to be formed on Van Diemen's Land,* though the capital defect of the former settlement has been partly obviated, by a discovery of the harbour for small craft.

The most important and curious information contained in this volume, is the discovery of straits which separate Van Diemen's Land (hitherto considered as its southern extremity) from New Holland. For this discovery we are indebted to Mr. Bass, a surgeon, after whom the straits have been named, and who was led to a suspicion of their existence by a prodigious swell which he observed to set in from the westward, at the mouth of the opening which he had reached on a voyage of discovery, prosecuted in a common whale-boat. To verify this suspicion, he proceeded afterwards in a vessel of 25 tons, accompanied by Mr. Flanders, a naval gentleman; and, entering the straits between the latitudes of 39° and 40° south, actually circumnavigated Van Diemen's Land. Mr. Bass's ideas of the importance of this discovery, we shall give from his narrative, as reported by Mr. Collins.

"The most prominent advantage which seemed likely to accrue to the settlement from this discovery was, the expediting of the passage from the Cape of Good Hope to Port Jackson: for, although a line drawn from the Cape to 44° of south latitude, and to the longitude of the South Cape of Van Diemen's Land, would not sensibly differ from one drawn to the latitude of 40° to the same longitude; yet it must be allowed, that a ship will be four degrees nearer to Port Jackson in the latter situation than it would be in the former. But there is, perhaps, a greater advantage to be gained by making a passage through the strait, than the mere saving of four degrees of latitude along the coast. The major part of the ships that have arrived at Port Jackson have met with N. E. winds, on opening the sea round the South Cape and Cape Pillar; and have been so much retarded by them, that a fourteen days' passage to the port is reckoned to be a fair one, although the difference of latitude is but ten degrees, and the most prevailing winds at the latter place are from S. E. to S. in summer, and from W. S. W. to S. in winter. If, by going through Bass Strait, these N. E. winds can be avoided, which in many cases would probably be the case, there is no doubt but a week or more would be gained by it; and the expense, with the wear and tear of a ship for one week, are objects to most owners, more especially when freighted with convicts by the run.

* It is singular that Governments are not more desirous of pushing their settlements rather to the north than the south of Port Jackson. The soil and climate would probably improve, in the latitude nearer the equator; and settlements in that position would be more contiguous to our Indian colonies.

"This strait likewise presents another advantage. From the prevalence of the N. E. and easterly winds of the South Cape, many suppose that a passage may be made from thence to the westward, either to the Cape of Good Hope, or to India; but the fear of the great unknown bight between the South Cape and the S. W. Cape of Lewen's Land, lying in about 35° south and 113° east, has hitherto prevented the trial being made. Now, the strait removes a part of this danger, by presenting a certain place of retreat, should a gale oppose itself to the ship in the first part of the essay: and should the wind come at S. W. she need not fear making a good stretch to the W. N. W., which course, if made good, is within a few degrees of going clear of all. There is, besides, King George the Third's Sound, discovered by Captain Vancouver, situate in the latitude of 35° 30′ south, and longitude 118° 12′ east; and it is to be hoped, that a few years will disclose many others upon the coast, as well as the confirmation or futility of the conjecture that a still larger than Bass Strait dismembers New Holland."—(p. 192, 193.)

We learn from a note subjoined to this passage, that, in order to verify or refute this conjecture, of the existence of other important inlets on the west coast of New Holland, Captain Flinders has sailed with two ships under his command, and is said to be accompanied by several professional men of considerable ability.

Such are the most important contents of Mr Collins's book, the style of which we very much approve, because it appears to be written by himself; and we must repeat again, that nothing can be more injurious to the opinion the public will form of the authenticity of a book of this kind, than the suspicion that it has been tricked out and embellished by other hands. Such men, to be sure, have existed as Julius Cæsar; but, in general, a correct and elegant style is hardly attainable by those who have passed their lives in action: and no one has such a pedantic love of good writing, as to prefer mendacious finery to rough and ungrammatical truth. The events which Mr. Collins's book records, we have read with great interest. There is a charm in thus seeing villages, and churches, and farms, rising from a wilderness, where civilized man has never set his foot since the creation of the world. The contrast between fertility and barrenness, population and solitude, activity and indolence, fills the mind with the pleasing images of happiness and increase. Man seems to move in his proper sphere, while he is thus dedicating the powers of his mind and body to reap those rewards which the bountiful Author of all things has assigned to his industry. Neither is it any common enjoyment, to turn for a while from the memory of those distractions which have so recently agitated the Old World, and to reflect that its very horrors and crimes may have thus prepared a long era of opulence and peace for a people yet involved in the womb of time.

J. FIEVEE.*

[EDINBURGH REVIEW, 1809.]

OF all the species of travels, that which has moral observation for its object is the most liable to error, and has the greatest difficulties to overcome, before it can arrive at excellence. Stones, and roots, and leaves, are subjects which may exercise the understanding without rousing the passions. A mineralogical traveller will hardly fall fouler upon the granite and the feldspar of other countries than his own; a botanist will not conceal its non-descripts; and an agricultural tourist will faithfully detail the average crop per acre; but the traveller who observes on the manners, habits, and institutions of other countries, must have emancipated his mind from the extensive and powerful dominion of association, must have extinguished the agreeable and deceitful feelings of national vanity, and cultivated that patient humility which builds general inferences only upon the repetition of individual facts. Every thing he sees shocks some passion or flatters it; and he is perpetually seduced to distort facts, so as to render them agreeable to his system and his feelings! Books of travels are now published in such vast abundance, that it may not be useless, perhaps, to state a few of the reasons why their value so commonly happens to be in the inverse ratio of their number.

1st, Travels are bad, from a want of opportunity for observation in those who write them. If the sides of a building are to be measured, and the number of its windows to be counted, a very short space of time may suffice for these operations; but to gain such a knowledge of their prevalent opinions and propensities, as will enable a stranger to comprehend (what is commonly called) the *genius* of people, requires a long residence among them, a familiar acquaintance with their language, and an easy circulation among their various societies. The society into which a transient stranger gains the most easy access in any country, is not often that which ought to stamp the national character; and no criterion can be more fallible, in a people so reserved and inaccessible as the British, who (even when they open their doors to letters of introduction) cannot for years overcome the awkward timidity of their nature. The same expressions are of so different a value in different countries, the same actions proceed from such different causes, and produce such different effects, that a judgment of foreign nations, founded on rapid observation, is almost certainly a mere tissue of ludicrous and disgraceful mistakes; and yet a residence of a month or two seems to entitle a traveller to present the world with a picture of manners in London, Paris, or Vienna, and even to dogmatize upon the political, religious, and legal institutions, as if it were one and the same thing to speak of *abstract* effects of such institutions, and of their effects combined with all the peculiar circumstances in which any nation may be placed.

2dly, An affectation of quickness in observation, an intuitive glance that requires only a *moment*, and a *part*, to judge of a *perpetuity*, and a *whole*. The late Mr. Petion, who was sent over into this country to acquire a knowledge of our criminal law, is said to have declared himself thoroughly informed upon the subject after remaining precisely *two and thirty minutes* in the Old Bailey.

3dly, The tendency to found observation on a system, rather than a system upon observation. The fact is, there are very few original eyes and ears. The great mass see and hear as they are directed by others, and bring back from a residence in foreign countries nothing but the vague and customary notions concerning it, which are carried and brought back for half a century, without verification or change. The most ordinary shape in which this tendency to prejudge makes its appearance among travellers, is by a disposition to exalt, or, a still more absurd disposition to depreciate their native country. They are incapable of considering a foreign people but under one single point of view—the relation in which they stand to their own; and the whole narrative is frequently nothing more than a mere triumph of national vanity, or the ostentation of superiority to so common a failing.

But we are wasting our time in giving a theory of the faults of travellers, when we have such ample means of exemplifying them all from the publication now before us, in which Mr. Jacob Fievée, with the most surprising talents for doing wrong, has contrived to condense and agglomerate every species of absurdity that has hitherto been made known, and even to launch out occasionally into new regions of nonsense, with a boldness which well entitles him to the merit of originality in folly, and discovery in impertinence. We consider Mr. Fievée's book as extremely valuable in one point of view. It affords a sort of limit or mind-mark, beyond which we conceive it to be impossible in future that pertness and petulance should pass. It is well to be acquainted with the boundaries of our nature on both sides; and to Mr. Fievée we are indebted for this valuable approach to *pessimism*. The height of knowledge no man has yet scanned; but we have now pretty well fathomed the gulf of ignorance.

We must, however, do justice to Mr. Fievée when he deserves it. He evinces, in his preface, a lurking uneasiness at the apprehension of exciting war between the two countries, from the anger to which his letters will

* *Lettres sur l'Angleterre.* Par J. FIEVEE. 1802.

give birth in England. He pretends to deny that they will occasion a war; but it is very easy to see he is not convinced by his own arguments; and we confess ourselves extremely pleased by this amiable solicitude at the probable effusion of human blood. We hope Mr. Fievée is deceived by his philanthropy, and that no such unhappy consequences will ensue, as he really believes, though he affects to deny them. We dare to say the dignity of this country will be satisfied if the publication in question is disowned by the French government, or, at most, if the author is given up. At all events, we have no scruple to say, that to sacrifice 20,000 lives, and a hundred millions of money to resent Mr. Fievée's book, would be an unjustifiable waste of blood and treasure; and that to take him off privately by assassination would be an undertaking hardly compatible with the dignity of a great empire.

To show, however, the magnitude of the provocation, we shall specify a few of the charges which he makes against the English. That they do not understand fireworks as well as the French; that they charge a shilling for admission to the exhibition; that they have the misfortune of being incommoded by a certain disgraceful privilege, called the liberty of the press; that the opera band plays out of tune; that the English are so fond of drinking that they get drunk with a certain air called the gas of Paradise; that the privilege of electing members of Parliament is so burthensome that cities sometimes petition to be exempted from it; that the great obstacle to a Parliamentary reform is the mob; that women sometimes have titles distinct from those of their husbands, although, in England, any body can sell his wife at market, with a rope about her neck. To these complaints he adds—that the English are so far from enjoying that equality of which their partisans boast, that none but the servants of the higher nobility can carry canes behind a carriage; that the power which the French kings had of pardoning before trial is much the same thing as the English mode of pardoning after trial; that he should conceive it to be a good reason for rejecting any measure in France that it was imitated from the English, who have no family affections, and who love money so much that their first question, in an inquiry concerning the character of any man, is, as to his degree of fortune. Lastly, Mr. Fievée alleges against the English, that they have great pleasure in contemplating the spectacle of men deprived of their reason. And, indeed, we must have the candour to allow that the hospitality which Mr. Fievée experienced seems to afford some pretext for this assertion.

One of the principal objects of Mr. Fievée's book is to combat the Anglomania which has raged so long among his countrymen, and which prevailed at Paris to such an excess that even M. Neckar, a foreigner (incredible as it may seem), *after having been twice minister of France*, retained a considerable share of admiration for the English government. This is quite inexplicable. But this is nothing to the treason of the *Encyclopedists*, who, instead of attributing the merit of the experimental philosophy and the reasoning by induction to a Frenchman, have shown themselves so lost to all sense of duty which they owed their country, that they have attributed it to an Englishman* *of the name of Bacon*, and this for no better reason than that he really was the author of it. The whole of this passage is written so entirely in the genius of Mr Fievée, and so completely exemplifies that very caricature species of Frenchmen from which our gross and popular notions of the whole people are taken, that we shall give the whole passage at full length, cautiously abstaining from the sin of translating it.

"Quand je reproche aux philosophes d'avoir vanté l'Angleterre, par haine pour les institutions qui soutenoient la France, je ne hasarde rien, et je fournirai une nouvelle preuve de cette assertion, en citant les encyclopédistes, chefs avoués de la philosophie moderne.

"Comment nous ont-ils présenté l'Encyclopédie? Comme un monument immortel, comme le dépôt précieux de toutes les connoissances humaines. Sous quel patronage l'ont-ils élevé ce monument immortel? Est ce sous l'égide des écrivains dont la France s'honoroit? Non, ils ont choisi pour maître et pour idole un Anglais, Bâcon; ils lui on fait dire tout ce qu'ils ont voulu, parce que cet auteur, extraordinairement volumineux, n'étoit pas connu en France, et ne l'est guère en Angleterre que de quelques hommes studieux; mais les philosophes sentoient que leur succès, pour introduire des nouveautés, tenoit à faire croire qu'elles n'étoient pas *neuves* pour les grands esprits; et comme les grands esprits Français, trop connus, ne ce prêtoient pas à un pareil dessein, les philosophes ont eu recours à l'Angleterre. Ainsi, un ouvrage fait en France, et offert à l'admiration de l'Europe comme l'ouvrage par excellence, fut mis par des Français sous la protection du génie Anglais. O honte! Et les philosophes se sont dit patriotes, et la France, pour prix de sa dégradation, leur a élevé des statues! La siècle qui commence, plus juste, parce qu'il a le sentiment de la véritable grandeur, laissera ces statues et l'Encyclopédie s'ensevelir sous la même poussière."

When to this are added the commendations that have been bestowed on Newton, the magnitude and the originality of the discoveries which have been attributed to him, the admiration which the words of Locke have excited, and the homage that has been paid to Milton and Shakspeare, the treason which lurks at the bottom of it all will not escape the penetrating glance of Mr. Fievée; and he will discern that same cause from which every good Frenchman knows the defeat of Aboukir and of the first of June to have proceeded—*the monster Pitt, and his English guineas.*

---

* "Gaul was conquered by a person of the name of Julius Cæsar," is the first phrase in one of Mr. Newberry's little books.

EDGEWORTH ON BULLS.*

[EDINBURGH REVIEW, 1803.]

WE hardly know what to say about this rambling, scrambling book; but that we are quite sure the author, when he began any sentence in it, had not the smallest suspicion of what it was about to contain. We say the author; because, in spite of the mixture of sexes in the title-page, we are strongly inclined to suspect that the male contributions exceed the female in a very great degree. The Essay on Bulls is written much with the same mind, and in the same manner, as a schoolboy takes a walk: he moves on for ten yards on the straight road, with surprising perseverance; then sets out after a butterfly, looks for a bird's nest, or jumps backwards and forwards over a ditch. In the same manner, this nimble and digressive gentleman is away after every object which crosses his mind. If you leave him at the end of a comma, in a steady pursuit of his subject, you are sure to find him, before the next full stop, a hundred yards to the right or left, frisking, capering, and grinning in a high paroxysm of merriment and agility. Mr. Edgeworth seems to possess the sentiments of an accomplished gentleman, the information of a scholar, and the vivacity of a first-rate harlequin. He is fuddled with animal spirits, giddy with constitutional joy; in such a state he must have written on, or burst. A discharge of ink was an evacuation absolutely necessary, to avoid fatal and plethoric congestion.

The object of the book is to prove, that the practice of making bulls is not more imputable to the Irish than to any other people; and the manner in which he sets about it, is to quote examples of bulls produced in other countries. But this is surely a singular way of reasoning the question: for there are goîtres out of Valais, extortioners who do not worship Moses, oat cakes out of the Tweed, and balm beyond the precincts of Gilead. If nothing can be said to exist pre-eminently and emphatically in one country, which exists at all in another, then Frenchmen are not gay, nor Spaniards grave, nor are gentlemen of the Milesian race remarkable for their disinterested contempt of wealth in their connubial relations. It is probable there is some foundation for a character so generally diffused; though it is also probable that such foundation is extremely enlarged by fame. If there were no foundation for the common opinion, we must suppose national characters formed by chance; and that the Irish might, by accident, have been laughed at as bashful and sheepish; which is impossible. The author puzzles himself a good deal about the nature of bulls, without coming to any decision about the matter. Though the question is not a very easy one, we shall venture to say, that a bull is an apparent congruity, and real incongruity, of ideas, suddenly discovered. And if this account of bulls be just, they are (as might have been supposed) the very reverse of wit; for as wit discovers real relations, that are not apparent, bulls admit apparent relations that are not real. The pleasure arising from wit proceeds from our surprise at suddenly discovering two things to be similar, in which we suspected no similarity. The pleasure arising from bulls proceeds from our discovering two things to be dissimilar, in which a resemblance might have been suspected. The same doctrine will apply to wit, and to bulls in action. Practical wit discovers connection or relation between actions, in which duller understandings discover none; and practical bulls originate from an *apparent* relation between two actions, which more correct understandings immediately perceive to have no relation at all.

Louis XIV. being extremely harassed by the repeated solicitations of a veteran officer for promotion, said one day, loud enough to be heard, "That gentleman is the most troublesome officer I have in my service." "That is precisely the charge (said the old man) which your majesty's enemies bring against me."

"An English gentleman," (says Mr. Edgeworth, in a story cited from Joe Millar,) "was writing a letter in a coffee-house; and perceiving that an Irishman stationed behind him was taking that liberty which Parmenio used with his friend Alexander, instead of putting his seal upon the lips of the *curious impertinent*, the English gentleman thought proper to reprove the Hibernian, if not with delicacy, at least with poetical justice. He concluded writing his letter in these words: 'I would say more, but a damned tall Irishman is reading over my shoulder every word I write.'

"'You lie, you scoundrel,' said the self-convicted Hibernian.'"—(p. 29.)

The pleasure derived from the first of these stories, proceeds from the discovery of the relation that subsists between the object he had in view, and the assent of the officer to an observation so unfriendly to that end. In the first rapid glance which the mind throws upon his words, he appears, by his acquiescence, to be pleading against himself. There seems to be no relation between what he says and what he wishes to effect by speaking.

In the second story, the pleasure is directly the reverse. The lie given was *apparently* the readiest means of proving his innocence, and *really* the most effectual way of establishing his guilt. There seems for a moment to be a strong relation between the means and the ob-

* *Essay on Irish Bulls.* By RICHARD LOVELL EDGEWORTH, and MARIA EDGEWORTH. London, 1802.

ject; while, in fact, no irrelation can be so complete.

What connection is there between pelting stones at monkeys, and gathering cocoa-nuts from lofty trees? Apparently none. But monkeys sit upon cocoa-nut trees; monkeys are imitative animals; and if you pelt a monkey with a stone, he pelts you with a cocoa-nut in return. This scheme of gathering cocoa-nuts is very witty, and would be more so, if it did not appear useful: for the idea of utility is always inimical to the idea of wit.* There appears, on the contrary, to be some relation between the revenge of the Irish rebels against a banker, and the means which they took to gratify it, by burning all his notes wherever they found them; whereas they could not have rendered him a more essential service. In both these cases of bulls, the one verbal, the other practical, there is an apparent congruity, and real incongruity of ideas. In both the cases of wit, there is an apparent incongruity and a real relation.

It is clear that a bull cannot depend upon mere incongruity alone; for if a man were to say that he would ride to London upon a cocked hat, or that he would cut his throat with a pound of pickled salmon, this, though completely incongruous, would not be to make bulls, but to talk nonsense. The stronger the apparent connection, and the more complete the real disconnection of the ideas, the greater the surprise, and the better the bull. The less apparent, and the more complete the relations established by wit, the higher gratification does it afford. A great deal of the pleasure experienced from bulls, proceeds from the sense of superiority in ourselves. Bulls which we invented, or knew to be invented, might please, but in a less degree, for want of this additional zest.

As there must be apparent connection, and real incongruity, it is seldom that a man of sense and education finds any form of words by which he is conscious that he might have been deceived into a bull. To conceive how the person has been deceived, he must suppose a degree of information very different from, and a species of character very heterogeneous to, his own; a process which diminishes surprise, and consequently pleasure In the above-mentioned story of the Irishman overlooking the man writing, no person of ordinary sagacity can suppose himself betrayed into such a mistake; but he can easily represent to himself a kind of character that might have been so betrayed. There are some bulls so extremely fallacious, that any man may imagine himself to have been betrayed into them; but these are rare: and, in general, it is a poor, contemptible species of amusement; a delight in which evinces a very bad taste in wit.

Whether the Irish make more bulls than their neighbours, is, as we have before remarked, not a point of much importance; but it is of considerable importance, that the character of a nation should not be degraded; and Mr. Edgeworth has great merit in his very benevolent intention of doing justice to the excellent qualities of the Irish. It is not possible to read his book, without feeling a strong and a new disposition in their favour. Whether the imitation of the Irish manner be accurate in his little stories we cannot determine; but we feel the same confidence in the accuracy of the imitation, that is often felt in the resemblance of a portrait, of which we have never seen the original. It is no very high compliment to Mr. Edgeworth's creative powers, to say, he could not have formed any thing, which was not real, so like reality; but such a remark only robs Peter to pay Paul; and gives every thing to his powers of observation, which it takes from those of his imagination. In truth, nothing can be better than his imitation of the Irish manner: It is first-rate painting.

Edgeworth and Co. have another faculty in great perfection. They are eminently masters of the *pathos*. The Firm drew tears from us in the stories of little Dominick, and of the Irish beggar, who killed his sweetheart: Never was any grief more natural or simple. The first, however, ends in a very foolish way;

——— *formosa superne*
Desinit in piscem.

We are extremely glad that our avocations did not call us from Bath to London on the day that the Bath coach conversation took place. We except from this wish the story with which the conversation terminates; for as soon as Mr. Edgeworth enters upon a story he excels.

We must confess we have been much more pleased with Mr. Edgeworth in his laughing and in his pathetic, than in his grave and reasoning moods. He meant, perhaps, that we should; and it certainly is not very necessary that a writer should be profound on the subject of bulls. Whatever be the deficiencies of the book, they are, in our estimation, amply atoned for by its merits; by none more than that lively feeling of compassion which pervades it for the distresses of the wild, kind hearted, blundering poor of Ireland.

* It must be observed, that all the great passions, and many other feelings, extinguish the relish for wit. Thus *lympha pudica Deum vidit et erebuit*, would be witty, were it not bordering on the sublime. The resemblance between the sandal tree imparting (while it falls) its aromatic flavour to the edge of the axe, and the benevolent man rewarding evil with good, would be witty, did it not excite virtuous emotions. There are many mechanical contrivances which excite sensations very similar to wit; but the attention is absorbed by their utility. Some of Merlin's machines, which have no utility at all, are quite similar to wit. A small model of a steam-engine, or mere squirt, is wit to a child. A man speculates on the causes of the first, or in its consequences, and so loses the feelings of wit; with the latter, he is too familiar to be surprised. In short, the essence of every species of wit is surprise; which *vi termini*, must be sudden; and the sensations which wit has a tendency to excite, are impaired or destroyed as often as they are mingled with much thought or passion.

TRIMMER AND LANCASTER.*

[Edinburgh Review, 1806.]

This is a book written by a lady who has gained considerable reputation at the corner of St. Paul's churchyard; who flames in the van of Mr. Newberry's shop; and is, upon the whole, dearer to mothers and aunts than any other author who pours the milk of science into the mouths of babes and sucklings. Tired at last of scribbling for children, and getting ripe in ambition, she has now written a book for grown-up people, and selected for her antagonist as stiff a controversialist as the whole field of dispute could well have supplied. Her opponent is Mr. Lancaster,† a Quaker, who has lately given to the world new and striking lights upon the subject of Education, and come forward to the notice of his country by spreading order, knowledge, and innocence among the lowest of mankind.

Mr. Lancaster, she says, wants method in his book; and therefore her answer to him is without any arrangement. The same excuse must suffice for the desultory observations we shall make upon this lady's publication.

The first sensation of disgust we experienced at Mrs. Trimmer's book, was from the patronizing and protecting air with which she speaks of some small part of Mr. Lancaster's plan. She seems to suppose, because she has dedicated her mind to the subject, that her opinion must necessarily be valuable upon it; forgetting it to be barely possible, that her application may have made her more wrong, instead of more right If she can make out her case, that Mr. Lancaster is doing mischief in so important a point as that of national education, she has a right, in common with every one else, to lay her complaint before the public; but a right to publish praises must be earned by something more difficult than the writing sixpenny books for children. This may be very good; though we never remember to have seen any one of them; but if they be no more remarkable for judgment and discretion than parts of the work before us, there are many thriving children quite capable of repaying the obligations they owe to their amiable instructress, and of teaching, with grateful retaliation, "the *old* idea how to shoot."

In remarking upon the work before us, we shall exactly follow the plan of the authoress, and prefix, as she does, the titles of those subjects on which her observations are made· doing her the justice to presume, that her quotations are fairly taken from Mr. Lancaster's book.

1. *Mr. Lancaster's Preface.*—Mrs. Trimmer here contends, in opposition to Mr. Lancaster, that ever since the establishment of the Protestant Church, the education of the poor has been a national concern in this country; and the only argument she produces in support of this extravagant assertion, is an appeal to the act of uniformity. If there are millions of Englishmen who cannot spell their own names, or read a sign-post which bids them turn to the right or left, is it any answer to this deplorable ignorance to say, there is an act of Parliament for public instruction?—to show the very line and chapter where the King, Lords, and Commons, in Parliament assembled, ordained the universality of reading and writing, when, centuries afterwards, the ploughman is no more capable of the one or the other than the beast which he drives? In point of fact, there is no Protestant country in the world where the education of the poor has been so grossly and infamously neglected as in England. Mr. Lancaster has the very high merit of calling the public attention to this evil, and of calling it in the best way, by new and active remedies; and this uncandid and feeble lady, instead of using the influence she has obtained over the anility of these realms, to join that useful remonstrance which Mr. Lancaster has begun, pretends to deny that the evil exists; and when you ask where are the schools, rods, pedagogues, primers, histories of Jack the Giant-killer, and all the usual apparatus for education, the only thing she can produce is *the act of uniformity and common prayer.*

2. *The Principles on which Mr. Lancaster's Institution is conducted.*—"Happily for mankind," says Mr. Lancaster, "it is possible to combine precept and practice together in the education of youth: that public spirit, or general opinion, which gives such strength to vice, may be rendered serviceable to the cause of virtue; and in thus directing it, the whole secret, the beauty, and simplicity of national education consists. Suppose, for instance, it be required to train a youth to strict veracity. He has learnt to read at school: he there reads the declaration of the Divine will respecting liars: he is there informed of the pernicious effects that practice produces on society at large; and he is enjoined, for the fear of God, for the approbation of his friends, and for the good of his school-fellows, never to tell an untruth. This is a most excellent precept; but let it be taught, and yet, if the contrary practice be treated with indifference by parents,

---

* *A Comparative View of the New Plan of Education promulgated by Mr. Joseph Lancaster, in his Tracts concerning the Instruction of the Children of the Labouring Part of the Community; and of the System of Christian Education founded by our pious Forefathers for the Initiation of the Young Members of the Established Church in the Principles of the Reformed Religion.* By Mrs. Trimmer. 1805.

† Lancaster invented the new method of education. The Church was sorely vexed at his success, endeavoured to set up Dr. Bell as the discoverer, and to run down poor Lancaster. George the Third was irritated by this shabby conduct, and always protected Lancaster. He was delighted with this Review, and made Sir Herbert Taylor read it a second time to him.

teachers, or associates, it will either weaken or destroy all the good that can be derived from it: But if the parents or teachers tenderly nip the rising shoots of vice; if the associates of youth pour contempt on the liar; he will soon hide his head with shame, and most *likely leave off the practice."—(p. 24, 25.)*

The objection which Mrs. Trimmer makes to this passage, is, that it is *exalting the fear of man above the fear of God.* This observation is as mischievous as it is unfounded. Undoubtedly the fear of God ought to be the paramount principle from the very beginning of life, if it were possible to make it so; but it is a feeling which can only be built up by degrees. The awe and respect which a child entertains for its parent and instructor, is the first scaffolding upon which the sacred edifice of religion is reared. A child *begins* to pray, to act, and to abstain, not to please God, but to please the parent, who tells him that such is the will of God. The religious principle gains ground from the power of association and the improvement of reason; but without the fear of man,—the desire of pleasing, and the dread of offending those with whom he lives,—it would be extremely difficult, if not impossible, to cherish it at all in the minds of the children. If you tell (says Mr. Lancaster) a child not to swear, because it is forbidden by God, and he finds everybody whom he lives with addicted to that vice, the mere precept will soon be obliterated; which would acquire its just influence if aided by the effect of example. Mr. Lancaster does not say that the fear of man ever *ought* to be a stronger motive than the fear of God, or that, in a thoroughly formed character, it ever *is:* he merely says, that the fear of man may be made the most powerful mean to raise up the fear of God; and nothing, in our opinion, can be more plain, more sensible, or better expressed, than his opinions upon these subjects. In corroboration of this sentiment, Mr. Lancaster tells the following story:—

"A benevolent friend of mine," says he, "who resides at a village near London, where he has a school of the class called *Sunday Schools,* recommended several lads to me for education. He is a pious man, and these children had the advantage of *good precepts* under his instruction in an *eminent degree,* but had reduced them to very little practice. As they came to my school from some distance, they were permitted to bring their dinners; and, in the interval between morning and afternoon school hours, spent their time with a number of lads under similar circumstances in a play-ground adjoining the school-room. In this play-ground the boys usually enjoy an hour's recreation; tops, balls, races, or what best suits their inclination or the season of the year; but with this charge, 'Let all be kept in innocence.' These lads thought themselves very happy at play with their new associates; but on a sudden they were seized and overcome by numbers, were brought into school just as people in the street would seize a pickpocket, and bring him to the police office. Happening at that time to be within, I inquired, Well, boys, what is all this bustle about?'—'Why, sir,' was the general reply, 'these lads have been swearing." This was announced with as much emphasis and solemnity as a judge would use in passing sentence upon a criminal. The culprits were, as may be supposed, in much terror. After the examination of witnesses and proof of the facts, they received admonition as to the offence; and, on promise of better behaviour, were dismissed. No more was ever heard of their swearing; yet it was observable, that they were better acquainted with *the theory of Christianity,* and could give a more rational answer to *questions from the scripture,* than several of the boys who had thus treated them, on comparison *as constables would do a thief.* I call this," adds Mr. Lancaster, "*practical religious instruction,* and could, if needful, give many such anecdotes." —(p. 26, 27.)

All that Mrs. Trimmer has to observe against this very striking illustration of Mr. Lancaster's doctrine, is, that the monitors behaved to the swearers in a very rude and unchristian-like manner. She begins with being cruel, and ends with being silly. Her first observation is calculated to raise the *posse comitatus* against Mr. Lancaster, to get him stoned for impiety; and then, when he produces the most forcible example of the effect of opinion to encourage religious precept, she says such a method of preventing swearing is too rude for the gospel. True, modest, unobtrusive religion—charitable, forgiving, indulgent Christianity, is the greatest ornament and the greatest blessing that can dwell in the mind of man. But if there is one character more base, more infamous, and more shocking than another, it is him who, for the sake of some paltry distinction in the world, is ever ready to accuse conspicuous persons of irreligion—to turn common informer for the church—and to convert the most beautiful feelings of the human heart to the destruction of the good and great, by fixing upon talents the indelible stigma of irreligion. It matters not how trifling and how insignificant the accuser; cry out that the *church is in danger,* and your object is accomplished; lurk in the walk of hypocrisy, to accuse your enemy of the crime of Atheism, and his ruin is quite certain; acquitted or condemned, is the same thing; it is only sufficient that he be accused, in order that his destruction be accomplished. If we could satisfy ourselves that such were the real views of Mrs. Trimmer, and that she were capable of such baseness, we would have drawn blood from her at every line, and left her in a state of martyrdom more piteous than that of St. Uba. Let her attribute the milk and mildness she meets with in this review of her book, to the conviction we entertain, that she knew no better—that she really did understand Mr. Lancaster as she pretends to understand him—and that if she had been aware of the extent of the mischief she was doing, she would have tossed the manuscript spelling-book in which she was engaged into the fire, rather than have done it. As a proof that we are in earnest in speaking of Mrs. Trimmer's simplicity, we must state the objection she makes to one of Mr. Lancaster's punishments. "When I meet,' says Mr. Lancaster, "with a slovenly boy, I put a label upon his breast, I walk him round the school with a tin or a paper crown upon his head." "Surely," says Mrs. Trimmer (in reply to this), "surely it should be remembered, that *the Saviour of the world was crowned with thorns, in derision, and that this is the reason why crowning is an improper punishment for a slovenly boy*"!!!

Rewards and Punishments.—Mrs. Trimmer objects to the fear of ridicule being made an instrument of education, because it may be hereafter employed to shame a boy out of his religion. She might, for the same reason, object to the cultivation of the reasoning faculty, because a boy may hereafter be reasoned out of his religion: she surely does not mean to say that she would make boys insensible to ridicule, the fear of which is one curb upon the follies and eccentricities of human nature. Such an object it would be impossible to effect, even if it were useful: Put a hundred boys together, and the fear of being laughed at will always be a strong influencing motive with every individual among them. If a master can turn this principle to his own use, and get boys to laugh at vice, instead of the old plan of laughing at virtue, is he not doing a very new, a very difficult, and a very laudable thing?

When Mr. Lancaster finds a little boy with a very dirty face, he sends for a little girl, and makes her wash off the dirt before the whole school: and she is directed to accompany her ablutions with a gentle box of the ear. To us, this punishment appears well adapted to the offence; and in this, and in most other instances of Mr. Lancaster's interference in scholastic discipline, we are struck with his good sense, and delighted that arrangements apparently so trivial, really so important, should have fallen under the attention of so ingenious and so original a man. Mrs. Trimmer objects to this practice, that it destroys female modesty, and inculcates, in that sex, *a habit of giving boxes on the ear.*

"When a boy gets into a singing tone in reading," says Mr. Lancaster, "the best mode of cure that I have hitherto found effectual is by the *force* of ridicule.—Decorate the offender with matches, ballads, (dying speeches if needful;) and in this garb send him round the school, with some boys before him crying matches, &c., exactly imitating the dismal tones with which such things are hawked about London streets, as will readily recur to the reader's memory. I believe many boys behave rudely to Jews more on account of the manner in which they cry 'old clothes,' than because they are Jews. I have always found excellent effects from treating boys, who sing or tone in their reading, in the manner described. It is sure to turn the laugh of the whole school upon the delinquent; it provokes risibility, in spite of every endeavour to check it, in all but *the offender.* I have seldom known a boy thus punished once, for whom it was needful a second time. It is also very seldom that a boy deserves both a log and a shackle at the same time. Most boys are wise enough, *when under* one punishment, not to transgress immediately, lest it should be doubled."—(p 47, 48.)

This punishment is objected to on the part of Mrs. Trimmer, because it inculcates a dislike to Jews, and an indifference about dying speeches! Toys, she says, given as rewards, are worldly things; children are to be taught that there are eternal rewards in store for them. It is very dangerous to give prints as rewards, because prints may hereafter be the vehicle of indecent ideas. It is, above all things, perilous to create an order of merit in the borough school, because it gives the boys an idea of the origin of nobility, "*especially in times* (we use Mrs. Trimmer's own words) *which furnish instances of the extinction of a race of ancient nobility, in a neighbouring nation, and the elevation of some of the lowest people to the highest stations. Boys accustomed to consider themselves the nobles of the school, may, in their future lives, form a conceit of their own merits* (*unless they have very sound principles*), *aspire to be nobles of the land, and to take place of the hereditary nobility.*"

We think these extracts will sufficiently satisfy every reader of common sense, of the merits of this publication. For our part, when we saw these ragged and interesting little nobles, shining in their tin stars, we only thought it probable that the spirit of emulation would make them better ushers, tradesmen, and mechanics. We did, in truth, imagine we had observed, in some of their faces, a bold project for procuring better breeches for keeping out the blast of heaven, which howled through those garments in every direction, and of aspiring hereafter to greater strength of seam, and more perfect continuity of cloth. But for the safety of the titled orders we had no fear; nor did we once dream that the black rod which whipt these dirty little dukes, would one day be borne before them as the emblem of legislative dignity, and the sign of noble blood.

Order.—The order of Mr. Lancaster has displayed in the school is quite astonishing. Every boy seems to be the cog of a wheel—the whole school a perfect machine. This is so far from being a burden or constraint to the boys, that Mr. Lancaster has made it quite pleasant and interesting to them, by giving to it the air of military arrangement; not foreseeing, as Mrs. Trimmer foresees, that, in times of public dangers, this plan furnishes the disaffected with the immediate means of raising an army; for what have they to do but to send for all the children educated by Mr. Lancaster, from the different corners of the kingdom into which they are dispersed,—to beg it as a particular favour of them to fall into the same order as they adopted in the spelling class twenty-five years ago; and the rest is all matter of course—

Jamque faces, et Saxa volant.

The main object, however, for which this book is written, is to prove that the church establishment is in danger, from the increase of Mr. Lancaster's institutions. Mr. Lancaster is, as we have before observed, a Quaker. As a Quaker, he says, I cannot teach your creeds:

but I pledge myself not to teach my own. I pledge myself (and if I deceive you, desert me, and give me up) to confine myself to those points of Christianity in which all Christians agree. To which Mrs. Trimmer replies, that, in the first place, he cannot do this; and, in the next place, if he did do it, it would not be enough. But why, we would ask, cannot Mr. Lancaster effect his first object? The practical and the feeling parts of religion are much more likely to attract the attention and provoke the questions of children than its speculative doctrines. A child is not very likely to put any questions at all to a catechising master, and still less likely to lead him into subtle and profound disquisition. It appears to us not only practicable, but very easy, to confine the religious instruction of the poor, in the first years of life, to those general feelings and principles which are suitable to the established church, and to every sect; afterwards, the discriminating tenets of each subdivision of Christians may be fixed upon this general basis. To say this is not enough, that a child should be made an Antisocinian, or an Antipelagian, in his tenderest years, may be very just; but what prevents you from making him so? Mr. Lancaster, purposely and intentionally, to allay all jealousy, leaves him in a state as well adapted for one creed as another. Begin; make your pupil a firm advocate for the peculiar doctrines of the English church; dig round about him, on every side, a trench that shall guard him from every species of heresy. In spite of all this clamour you do nothing; you do not stir a single step; you educate alike the swineherd and his hog; and then, when a man of real genius and enterprise rises up, and says, Let me dedicate my life to this neglected object; I will do every thing but that which must necessarily devolve upon you alone; you refuse to do your little, and compel him, by the cry of infidel and Atheist, to leave you to your ancient repose, and not to drive you, by insidious comparisons, to any system of active utility. We deny, again and again, that Mr. Lancaster's instruction is any kind of impediment to the propagation of the doctrines of the church; and if Mr. Lancaster was to perish with his system to-morrow, these boys would positively be taught nothing; the doctrines which Mrs. Trimmer considers prohibited would not rush in, but there would be an absolute vacuum. We will, however, say this in favour of Mrs. Trimmer, that if every one who has joined in her clamour, had laboured one-hundredth part as much as she has done in the cause of national education, the clamour would be much more rational, and much more consistent, than it now is. By living with a few people as active as herself, she is perhaps somehow or another persuaded that there is a national education going on in this country. But our principal argument is, that Mr. Lancaster's plan is at least better than the *nothing* which preceded it. The authoress herself seems to be a lady of respectable opinions, and very ordinary talents; defending what is right without judgment, and believing what is holy without charity.

PARNELL AND IRELAND.*

[Edinburgh Review, 1807.]

If ever a nation exhibited symptoms of downright madness, or utter stupidity, we conceive these symptoms may be easily recognized in the conduct of this country upon the Catholic question.† A man has a wound in his great toe, and a violent and perilous fever at the same time; and he refuses to take the medicines for the fever, because it will disconcert his toe! The mournful and folly-stricken blockhead forgets that his toe cannot survive him;—that if he dies, there can be no digital life apart from him; yet he lingers and fondles over this last part of his body, soothing it madly with little plasters, and anile fomentations, while the neglected fever rages in his entrails, and burns away his whole life. If the comparatively little questions of Establishment are all that this country is capable of discussing or regarding, for God's sake let us remember, that the foreign conquest which destroys all, destroys this beloved *toe* also. Pass over freedom, industry, and science—and look upon this great empire, by which we are about to be swallowed up, only as it affects the manner of collecting tithes, and of reading the liturgy—still, if all goes, these must go too; and even, for their interests, it is worth while to conciliate Ireland, to avert the hostility, and to employ the strength of the Catholic population. We plead the question as the sincerest friends to the Establishment;—as wishing to it all the prosperity and duration its warmest advocates can desire,—but remembering always, what these advocates seem to forget, that the Establishment cannot be threatened by any danger so great as the perdition of the kingdom in which it is established.

We are truly glad to agree so entirely with Mr. Parnell upon this great question; we admire his way of thinking; and most cordially

* *Historical Apology for the Irish Catholics.* By William Parnell, Esq. Fitzpatrick, Dublin, 1807.

† I do not retract one syllable (or *one iota*) of what I have said or written upon the Catholic question. What was wanted for Ireland was emancipation, time and justice, abolition of present wrongs; time for forgetting past wrongs, and that continued and even justice which would make such oblivion wise. It is now only difficult to tranquillize Ireland, before emancipation it was impossible. As to the danger from Catholic doctrines, I must leave such apprehensions to the respectable anility of these realms. I will not meddle with it.

recommend his work to the attention of the public. The general conclusion which he attempts to prove is this; that religious sentiment, however perverted to bigotry or fanaticism, has always a *tendency* to moderation; that it seldom assumes any great portion of activity or enthusiasm, except from novelty of opinion, or from opposition, contumely and persecution, when novelty ceases; that a government has little to fear from any religious sect, except while that sect is new. Give a government only time, and, provided it has the good sense to treat folly with forbearance, it must ultimately prevail. When, therefore, a sect is found, after a lapse of years, to be ill disposed to the government, we may be certain that government has widened its separation by marked distinctions, roused its resentment by contumely, or supported its enthusiasm by persecution.

The *particular* conclusion Mr. Parnell attempts to prove is, that the Catholic religion in Ireland had sunk into torpor and inactivity, till government roused it with the lash: that even then, from the respect and attachment, which men are always inclined to show towards government, there still remained a large body of loyal Catholics; that these only decreased in number from the rapid increase of persecution; and that, after all, the effects which the resentment of the Roman Catholics had in creating rebellions had been very much exaggerated.

In support of these two conclusions, Mr. Parnell takes a survey of the history of Ireland from the conquest under Henry, to the rebellion under Charles the First, passing very rapidly over the period which preceded the Reformation, and dwelling principally upon the various rebellions which broke out in Ireland between the Reformation and the grand rebellion in the reign of Charles the First. The celebrated conquest of Ireland by Henry the Second, extended only to a very few counties in Leinster; nine-tenths of the whole kingdom were left, as he found them, under the dominion of their native princes. The influence of example was as strong in this, as in most other instances; and great numbers of the English settlers who came over under various adventurers, resigned their pretensions to superior civilization, cast off their lower garments, and lapsed into the nudity and barbarism of the Irish. The limit which divided the possessions of the English settler from those of the native Irish, was called the pale; and the expression of inhabitants *within pale*, and *without the pale*, were the terms by which the two nations were distinguished. It is almost superfluous to state, that the most bloody and pernicious warfare was carried on upon the borders—sometimes for something—sometimes for nothing—most commonly for cows. The Irish, over whom the sovereigns of England affected a sort of nominal dominion, were entirely governed by their own laws; and so very little connection had they with the justice of the invading country, that it was as lawful to kill an Irishman, as it was to kill a badger or a fox. The instances are innumerable, where the defendant has pleaded that the deceased was an Irishman, and that therefore defendant had a right to kill him;—and upon the proof of Hibernicism, acquittal followed of course.

When the English army mustered in any great strength, the Irish chieftains would do exterior homage to the English Crown; and they very frequently, by this artifice, averted from their country the miseries of invasion: but they remained completely unsubdued, till the rebellion which took place in the reign of Queen Elizabeth, of which that politic woman availed herself to the complete subjugation of Ireland. In speaking of the Irish about the reign of Elizabeth, or James the First, we must not draw our comparisons from England, but from New Zealand; they were not civilized men, but savages; and if we reason about their conduct, we must reason of them as savages.

"After reading every account of Irish history," (says Mr. Parnell,) "one great perplexity appears to remain: How does it happen, that, from the first invasion of the English, till the reign of James I., Ireland seems not to have made the smallest progress in civilization or wealth?

"That it was divided into a number of small principalities, which waged constant war on each other; or that the appointment of the chieftains was elective; do not appear sufficient reasons, although these are the only ones assigned by those who have been at the trouble of considering the subject: neither are the confiscations of property quite sufficient to account for the effect. There have been great confiscations in other countries, and still they have flourished: the petty states of Greece were quite analogous to the chiefries (as they were called) in Ireland; and yet they seemed to flourish almost in proportion to their dissensions. Poland felt the bad effects of an elective monarchy more than any other country; and yet, in point of civilization, it maintained a very respectable rank among the nations of Europe; but Ireland never, for an instant, made any progress in improvement till the reign of James I.

"It is scarcely credible, that in a climate like that of Ireland, and at a period so far advanced in civilization as the end of Elizabeth's reign, the greater part of the natives should go naked. Yet this is rendered certain by the testimony of an eye-witness, Fynes Moryson. 'In the remote parts,' he says, 'where the English laws and manners are unknown, the very chief of the Irish, as well men as women, go naked in the winter time, only having their privy parts covered with a rag of linen, and their bodies with a loose mantle. This I speak of my own experience; yet remembering that a Bohemian Baron coming out of Scotland to us by the north parts of the wild Irish, told me in great earnestness, that he, coming to the house of O'Kane, a great lord amongst them, was met at the door by sixteen women all naked, excepting their loose mantles, whereof eight or ten were very fair; with which strange sight his eyes being dazzled, they led him into the house, and then sitting down by the fire with crossed legs, like tailors, and so low as could not but offend chaste eyes, desired him *to sit down* with them. Soon after, O'Kane, the lord of the country, came in all naked, except a loose mantle and shoes, which he put off as soon as he came in; and, entertaining the Baron after his best manner in the Latin tongue, desired him to put off his apparel, which he thought to be a burden to him, and to sit naked.

"'To conclude, men and women at night, going to sleep, lye thus naked in a round circle about the fire, with their feet towards it. They fold their heads and their upper parts in woollen mantles, first steeped in water to keep them warm; for they say, that woollen cloth, wetted, preserves heat, (as linen, wetted, preserves cold,) when the smoke of their bodies has warmed the woollen cloth.'

"The cause of this extreme poverty, and of its long continuance, we must conclude, arose from the peculiar laws of property, which were in force under the Irish dynasties. These laws have been described by most writers as similar to the Kentish custom of gavelkind; and indeed so little attention was paid to the subject, that were it not for the researches of Sir J. Davis, the knowledge of this singular usage would have been entirely lost.

"The Brehon law of property, he tells us, was similar to the custom (as the English lawyers term it) of hodge-podge. When any one of the sept died, his lands did not descend to his sons, but were divided among the whole sept: and, for this purpose, the chief of the sept made a new division of the whole lands belonging to the sept, and gave every one his part according to seniority. So that no man had a property which could descend to his children; and even during his own life, his possession of any particular spot was quite uncertain, being liable to be constantly shuffled and changed by new partitions. The consequence of this was that there was not a house of brick or stone, among the Irish, down to the reign of Henry VII.; not even a garden or orchard, or well fenced or improved field, neither village or town, or in any respect the least provision for posterity. This monstrous custom, so opposite to the natural feelings of mankind, was probably perpetuated by the policy of the chiefs. In the first place, the power of partitioning being lodged in their hands, made them the most absolute of tyrants, being the dispensers of the property as well as of the liberty of their subjects. In the second place, it had the appearance of adding to the number of their savage armies; for, where there was no improvement or tillage, war was pursued as an occupation.

"In the early history of Ireland, we find several instances of chieftains discountenancing tillage; and so late as Elizabeth's reign, Moryson says, that 'Sir Neal Garve restrained his people from ploughing, that they might assist him to do any mischief.'"—(p. 98—102.)

These quotations and observations will enable us to state a few plain facts for the recollection of our English readers. 1*st.* Ireland was never subdued till the rebellion in the reign of Queen Elizabeth. 2*d.* For four hundred years before that period, the two nations had been almost constantly at war; and in consequence of this, a deep and irreconcileable hatred existed between the people within and without the pale. 3*d.* The Irish, at the accession of Queen Elizabeth, were unquestionably the most barbarous people in Europe. So much for what had happened previous to the reign of Queen Elizabeth: and let any man, who has the most superficial knowledge of human affairs, determine, whether national hatred, proceeding from such powerful causes, could possibly have been kept under by the defeat of one single rebellion; whether it would not have been easy to have foreseen, at that period, that a proud, brave, half-savage people, would cherish the memory of their wrongs for centuries to come, and break forth into arms at every period when they were particularly exasperated by oppression, or invited by opportunity. If the Protestant religion had spread in Ireland as it did in England, and if there never had been any difference of faith between the two countries,—can it be believed that the Irish, ill-treated, and infamously governed as they have been, would never have made any efforts to shake off the yoke of England? Surely there are causes enough to account for their impatience of that yoke, without endeavouring to inflame the zeal of ignorant people against the Catholic religion, and to make that mode of faith responsible for all the butchery which the Irish and English, for these last two centuries, have exercised upon each other. Every body, of course, must admit, that if to the causes of hatred already specified, there be added the additional cause of religious distinction, this last will give greater force (and what is of more consequence to observe, give *a name*) to the whole aggregate motive. But what Mr. Parnell contends for, and clearly and decisively proves, is, that many of those sanguinary scenes attributed to the Catholic religion, are to be partly imputed to causes totally disconnected from religion; that the unjust invasion, and the tyrannical, infamous policy of the English, are to take their full share of blame with the sophisms and plots of Catholic priests. In the reign of Henry the Eighth, Mr. Parnell shows, that feudal submission was readily paid to him by all the Irish chiefs; that the Reformation was received without the slightest opposition; and that the troubles which took place at that period in Ireland, are to be entirely attributed to the ambition and injustice of Henry. In the reign of Queen Mary, there was no recrimination upon the Protestants;—a striking proof, that the bigotry of the Catholic religion had not, at that period, risen to any great height in Ireland. The insurrections of the various Irish princes were as numerous, during this reign, as they had been in the two preceding reigns,—a circumstance rather difficult of explanation, if, as is commonly believed, the Catholic religion was at that period the main spring of men's actions.

In the reign of Elizabeth, the Catholic in the pale regularly fought against the Catholic out of the pale. O'Sullivan, a bigoted Papist, reproaches them with doing so. Speaking of the reign of James the First, he says, "And now the eyes even of the English Irish" (the Catholics of the pale) "were opened; and they cursed their former folly for helping the heretic." The English government were so sensible of the loyalty of the Irish English Catholics, that they entrusted them with the most confidential services. The Earl of Kildare was the principal instrument in waging war against the chieftains of Leix and Offal. William O'Bourge, another Catholic, was created Lord Castle Connel for his eminent services; and MacGully Patrick, a priest, was the state spy. We presume that this wise and *manly* conduct of Queen Elizabeth was utterly unknown both to the Pastrycook and the Secretary of State, who have published upon the dangers of employing Catholics even against foreign enemies; and in those publications have said a great deal about the wisdom of our ancestors—the usual topic whenever the folly of their descendants is to be defended. To whatever other of our ancestors they may allude, they may spare all compliments to this illustrious Princess, who would certainly have kept the worthy confectioner to the composition of tarts, and most probably furnished him with the productions of the Right Honourable Secretary, as the means of conveying those juicy delicacies to an hungry and discerning public.

In the next two reigns, Mr. Parnell shows by what injudicious measures of the English government the spirit of Catholic opposition was gradually formed; for that it did produce powerful effects at a subsequent period, he does not deny; but contends only (as we have before stated), that these effects have been much overrated, and ascribed *solely* to the Catholic religion, when other causes have at least had an equal agency in bringing them about. He concludes with some general remarks on the dreadful state of Ireland, and the contemptible folly and bigotry of the English;*—remarks full of truth, of good sense, and of political courage. How melancholy to reflect, that there would be still some chance of saving England from the general wreck of empires, but that it may not be saved, because one politician will lose two thousand a year by it, and another three thousand—a third a place in reversion, and a fourth a pension for his aunt!—Alas! these are the powerful causes which have always settled the destiny of great kingdoms, and which may level Old England, with all its boasted freedom, and boasted wisdom, to the dust. Nor is it the least singular among the political phenomena of the present day, that the sole consideration which seems to influence the unbigoted part of the English people, in this great question of Ireland, is a regard for the personal feelings of the Monarch. Nothing is said or thought of the enormous risk to which Ireland is exposed,—nothing of the gross injustice with which the Catholics are treated,—nothing of the lucrative apostasy of those from whom they experience this treatment: but the only concern by which we all seem to be agitated is, that the King must not be vexed in his old age. We have a great respect for the King; and wish him all the happiness compatible with the happiness of his people. But these are not times to pay foolish compliments to Kings, or the sons of Kings, or to any body else: this journal has always preserved its character for courage and honesty; and it shall do so to the last. If the people of this country are solely occupied in considering what is personally agreeable to the King, without considering what is for his permanent good, and for the safety of his dominions; if all public men, quitting the common vulgar scramble for emolument, do not concur in conciliating the people of Ireland; if the unfounded alarms, and the comparatively trifling interests of the clergy, are to supersede the great question of freedom or slavery, it does appear to us quite impossible that so mean and so foolish a people can escape that destruction which is ready to burst upon them;—a destruction so imminent, that it can only be averted by arming all in our defence who would evidently be sharers in our ruin,—and by such a change of system as may save us from the hazard of being ruined by the ignorance and cowardice of any general, by the bigotry or the ambition of any minister, or by the well-meaning scruples of any human being, let his dignity be what it may. These minor and domestic dangers we must endeavour firmly and temperately to avert as we best can; but, at all hazards, we must keep out the destroyer from among us, or perish like wise and brave men in the attempt.

* It would be as well, in future, to say no more of the revocation of the edict of Nantz.

METHODISM.*

[Edinburgh Review, 1808.]

This is the production of an honest man, possessed of a fair share of understanding. He cries out lustily (and not before it is time), upon the increase of Methodism; proposes various remedies for the diminution of this evil; and speaks his opinions with a freedom which does him great credit, and convinces us that he is a respectable man. The clergy are accused of not exerting themselves. What temporal motive, Mr. Ingram asks, have they for exertion? Would a curate, who had served thirty years upon a living in the most exemplary manner, secure to himself, by such a conduct, the slightest right or title to promotion in the church? What can you expect of a whole profession, in which there is no more connection between merit and reward, than between merit and beauty, or merit and strength? This is the substance of what Mr. Ingram says upon this subject; and he speaks the truth. We regret, however, that this gentleman has thought fit to use against the dissenters, the exploded clamour of Jacobinism; or that he deems it necessary to call into the aid of the Church, the power of intolerant laws, in spite of the odious and impolitic tests to which the dissenters are still subjected. We believe them to be very good subjects; and we have no doubt but that any further attempt upon their religious liberties, without reconciling them to the Church, would have a direct tendency to render them disaffected to to the State.

Mr. Ingram (whose book, by the by, is very dull and tedious) has fallen into the common mistake of supposing his readers to be as well acquainted with his subject as he is himself; and has talked a great deal about dissenters, without giving us any distinct notions of the spirit which pervades these people—the objects they have in view—or the degree of talent which is to be found among them. To remedy this very capital defect, we shall endeavour to set before the eyes of the reader a complete section of the tabernacle; and to present him with a near view of those sectaries, who are at present at work upon the destruction of the orthodox churches, and are destined hereafter, perhaps, to act as conspicuous a part in public affairs, as the children of Sion did in the time of Cromwell.

The sources from which we shall derive our extracts, are the Evangelical and Methodistical Magazines for the year 1807;—works which are said to be circulated to the amount of 18,000 or 20,000 each, every month; and which contain the sentiments of Arminian and Calvinistic Methodists, and of the *evangelical* clergymen of the Church of England. We shall use the general term of Methodism, to designate these three classes of fanatics, not troubling ourselves to point out the finer shades, and nicer discriminations of lunacy, but treating them all as in one general conspiracy against common sense, and rational orthodox Christianity.

In reading these very curious productions, we seemed to be in a new world, and to have got among a set of beings, of whose existence we had hardly before entertained the slightest conception. It has been our good fortune to be acquainted with many truly religious persons, both in the Presbyterian and Episcopalian churches; and from their manly, rational, and serious characters, our conceptions of true practical piety have been formed. To these confined habits, and to our want of proper introductions among the children of light and grace, any degree of surprise is to be attributed, which may be excited by the publications before us; which, under opposite circumstances, would (we doubt not) have proved as great a source of instruction and delight to the Edinburgh reviewers, as they are to the most melodious votaries of the tabernacle.

It is not wantonly, or with the most distant intention of trifling upon serious subjects, that we call the attention of the public to these sort of publications. Their circulation is so enormous, and so increasing,—they contain the opinions, and display the habits of so many human beings,—that they cannot but be objects of curiosity and importance. The common and the middling classes of the people are the purchasers; and the subject is religion,—though not that religion certainly which is established by law, and encouraged by national provision. This may lead to unpleasant consequences, or it may not; but it carries with it a sort of aspect, which ought to insure to it serious attention and reflection.

It is impossible to arrive at any knowledge of a religious sect, by merely detailing the settled articles of their belief: it may be the fashion of such a sect to insist upon some articles very slightly; to bring forward others prominently; and to consider some portion of their formal creed as obsolete. As the knowledge of the jurisprudence of any country can never be obtained by the perusal of volumes which contain some statutes that are daily enforced, and others that have been silently antiquated: in the same manner, the practice, the preaching, and the writing of sects, are comments absolutely necessary to render the perusal of their creed of any degree of utility.

It is the practice, we believe, with the orthodox, both in the Scotch and English churches, to insist very rarely, and very discreetly, upon the particular instances of the interference of Divine Providence. They do not contend that the world is governed only by general laws,—

* *Causes of the Increase of Methodism and Dissension.* By Robert Acklem Ingram, B. D. Hatchard.

that a Superintending Mind never interferes for particular purposes; but such purposes are represented to be of a nature very awful and sublime,—when a guilty people are to be destroyed, when an oppressed nation is to be lifted up, and some remarkable change introduced into the order and arrangement of the world. With this kind of theology we can have no quarrel; we bow to its truth; we are satisfied with the moderation which it exhibits; and we have no doubt of the salutary effect which it produces upon the human heart. Let us now come to those special cases of the interference of Providence as they are exhibited in the publications before us.

An interference with respect to the Rev. James Moody.

"Mr. James Moody was descended from pious ancestors, who resided at Paisley;—his heart was devoted to music, dancing, and theatrical amusements; of the latter he was so fond, that he used to meet with some men of a similar cast to rehearse plays, and used to entertain a hope that he should make a figure upon the stage. To improve himself in music, he would rise very early, even in severely cold weather, and practise on the German flute: by his skill in music and singing, with his general powers of entertaining, he became a desirable companion: he would sometimes venture to profane the day of God, by turning it into a season of carnal pleasure: and would join in excursions on the water, to various parts of the vicinity of London. But the time was approaching, *when the Lord, who had designs of mercy for him, and for many others by his means, was about to stop him in his vain career of sin and folly.* There were two professing servants in the house where he lived; one of these was a porter, who, in brushing his clothes, would say, 'Master James, this will never do—you must be otherwise employed—you must be a minister of the gospel.' This worthy man, earnestly wishing his conversion, put into his hands that excellent book which God hath so much owned, *Alleine's Alarm to the Unconverted.*

"About this time, it pleased God to visit him with a disorder in his eyes, occasioned, as it was thought, by his sitting up in the night to improve himself in drawing. The apprehension of losing his sight occasioned many serious reflections; his mind was impressed with the importance and necessity of seeking the salvation of his soul, and he was induced to attend the preaching of the gospel. The first sermon that he heard with a desire to profit, was at Spa-fields Chapel; a place where he had formerly frequented, when it was a temple of vanity and dissipation. Strong convictions of sin fixed on his mind; and he continued to attend the preached word, particularly at Tottenham-court Chapel. Every sermon increased his sorrow and grief that he had not earlier sought the Lord. It was a considerable time before he found comfort from the gospel. He has stood in the free part of the chapel, hearing with such emotion, that the tears have flowed from his eyes in torrents; and, when he has returned home, he has continued a great part of the night on his knees, praying over what he had heard.

"The change effected by the power of the Holy Spirit on his heart now became visible to all. Nor did he halt between two opinions, as some persons do; he became at once a decided character, and gave up for ever all his vain pursuits and amusements; devoting himself with as much resolution and diligence to the service of God, as he had formerly done to folly." *Ev. Mag.* p. 194.

An interference respecting Cards.

"A clergyman not far distant from the spot on which these lines were written, was spending an evening—not in his closet wrestling with his Divine Master for the communication of that grace which is so peculiarly necessary for the faithful discharge of the ministerial function,—not in his study searching the sacred oracles of divine truth for materials wherewith to prepare for his public exercises and feed the flock under his care,—not in pastoral visits to that flock, to inquire into the state of their souls, and endeavour, by his pious and affectionate conversation, to conciliate their esteem, and promote their edification,—but at the *card table.*" —After stating that when it was his turn to deal, he dropped down dead, "It is worthy of remark (says the writer), that within a very few years this was the third character in the neighbourhood which had been summoned from the card table to the bar of God."—*Ev. Mag.* p. 262.

Interference respecting Swearing—a Bee the instrument.

"A young man is stung by a bee, upon which he buffets the bees with his hat, uttering at the same time the most dreadful oaths and imprecations. In the midst of his fury, one of these little combatants stung him upon the tip of that unruly member (his tongue), which was then employed in blaspheming his Maker. Thus can the Lord engage one of the meanest of his creatures in reproving the bold transgressor who dares to take his name in vain."—*Ev. Mag.* p. 363.

Interference with respect to David White, who was cured of Atheism and Scrofula by one Sermon of Mr. Coles.

This case is too long to quote in the language and with the evidences of the writers. The substance of it is what our title implies.—David Wright was a man with scrofulous legs and atheistical principles;—being with difficulty persuaded to hear one sermon from Mr. Coles, he limped to the church in extreme pain, and arrived there after great exertion;—during church time he was entirely converted, walked home with the greatest ease, and never after experienced the slightest return of scrofula or infidelity.—*Ev. Mag.* p. 444.

The displeasure of Providence is expressed at Captain Scott's going to preach in Mr. Romaine's Chapel.

The sign of this displeasure is a violent storm of thunder and lightning just as he came into town.—*Ev. Mag.* p. 537.

Interference with respect to an Innkeeper, who was destroyed for having appointed a cock-fight at the very time that the service was beginning at the Methodist Chapel.

"'Never mind,' says the innkeeper, 'I'll get a greater congregation than the Methodist parson;—we'll have a cock-fight.' But what is man! how insignificant his designs, how impotent his strength, how ill-fated his plans, when opposed to that Being who is infinite in wisdom, boundless in power, terrible in judgment, and who frequently reverses, and suddenly renders abortive, the projects of the wicked! A few days after the avowal of his intention, the innkeeper sickened," &c. &c. And then the narrator goes on to state, that his corpse was carried by the meeting-house, "*on the day, and exactly at the time*, the deceased had fixed for the cock-fight."—*Meth. Mag.* p. 126.

In page 167, *Meth. Mag.*, a father, mother, three sons, and a sister, are destroyed by particular interposition.

In page 222, *Meth. Mag.*, a dancing-master is destroyed for irreligion,—another person for swearing at a cock-fight,—and a third for pretending to be deaf and dumb. These are called *recent and authentic accounts* of God's avenging providence.

So much for the miraculous interposition of Providence in cases where the Methodists are concerned: we shall now proceed to a few specimens of the energy of their religious feelings.

Mr. Roberts's feelings in the month of May, 1793.

"But, all this time, my soul was stayed upon God; my desires increased, and my mind was kept in a sweet praying frame, a going out of myself, as it were, and taking shelter in Him. Every breath I drew, ended in a prayer. I felt myself helpless as an infant, dependent upon God for all things. I was in a constant daily expectation of receiving all I wanted; and, on Friday, May 31st, under Mr. Rutherford's sermon, though entirely independent of it, (for I could not give any account of what he had been preaching about,) I was given to feel that God was waiting to be very gracious to me; the spirit of prayer and supplication was given me, and such an assurance that I was accepted in the Beloved, as I cannot describe, but which I shall never forget."—*Meth. Mag.* p. 35.

Mrs. Elizabeth Price and her attendants hear sacred music on a sudden.

"A few nights before her death, while some neighbours and her husband were sitting up with her, a sudden and joyful sound of music was heard by all present, *although some of them were carnal people:* at which time she thought she saw her crucified Saviour before her, speaking these words with power to her soul, 'Thy sins are forgiven thee, and I love thee freely.' After this she never doubted of her acceptance with God; and on Christmas day following was taken to celebrate the Redeemer's birth in the Paradise of God. MICHAEL COUSIN."—*Meth. Mag.* p. 137.

T. L., a Sailor on board of the Stag frigate has a special revelation from our Saviour.

"October 26th, being the Lord's day, he had a remarkable manifestation of God's love to his soul. That blessed morning, he was much grieved by hearing the wicked use profane language, when Jesus revealed himself to him, and impressed on his mind those words, 'Follow Me.' This was a precious day to him." *Meth. Mag.* p. 140.

The manner in which Mr. Thomas Cook was accustomed to accost S. B.

"Whenever he met me in the street, his salutation used to be, 'Have you free and lively intercourse with God to-day? Are you giving your whole heart to God?' I have known him on such occasions speak in so pertinent a manner, that I have been astonished at his knowledge of my state. Meeting me one morning, he said, 'I have been praying for you; you have had a sore conflict, though all is well now.' At another time he asked, 'Have you been much exercised these few days, for I have been led to pray that you might especially have suffering grace.'"—*Meth. Mag.* p. 247.

Mr. John Kestin on his death-bed.

"'Oh, my dear, I am now going to glory, happy, happy, happy. I am going to sing praises to God and the Lamb; I am going to Abraham, Isaac, and Jacob. I think I can see my Jesus without a glass between. I can, I feel I can, discern 'my title clear to mansions in the skies.' Come, Lord Jesus, come! why are thy chariot-wheels so long delaying?'" *Ev. Mag.* p. 124.

The Reverend Mr. Mead's sorrow for his sins.

"This wrought him up to temporary desperation; his inexpressible grief poured itself forth in groans: 'Oh, that I had never sinned against God! I have a hell here upon earth, and there is a hell for me in eternity!' One Lord's day, very early in the morning, he was awoke by a tempest of thunder and lightning; and imagining it to be the end of the world, his agony was great, supposing the great day of divine wrath was come, and he unprepared: but happy to find it not so."—*Ev. Mag.* p. 147.

Similar case of Mr. John Robinson.

"About two hours before he died, he was in great agony of body and mind: it appeared that the enemy was permitted to struggle with him; and being greatly agitated, he cried out, 'Ye powers of darkness begone!' This, however, did not last long: 'the prey was taken from the mighty, and the lawful captive delivered,' although he was not permitted to tell of his deliverance, but lay quite still and composed."—*Ev. Mag.* p. 177.

The Reverend William Tennant in an heavenly trance.

"'While I was conversing with my brother,' said he, 'on the state of my soul, and the fears I had entertained for my future welfare, I found myself in an instant, in another state of existence, under the direction of a superior being, who ordered me to follow him. I was wafted along, I know not how, till I beheld at a distance an ineffable glory, the impression of which on my mind it is impossible to communicate to mortal man. I immediately reflected on my happy change; and thought, Well, blessed be God! I am safe at last, notwithstanding all my fears. I saw an innumerable host of happy beings surrounding the inexpressible glory, in acts of adoration and joyous worship; but I did not see any bodily shape or representation in the glorious appearance. I heard things unutterable. I heard their songs and hallelujahs of thanksgiving and praise, with unspeakable rapture. I felt joy unutterable and full of glory. I then applied to my conductor, and requested leave to join the happy throng.' "—*Ev. Mag.* p. 251.

The following we consider to be one of the most shocking histories we ever read. God only knows how many such scenes take place in the gloomy annals of Methodism.

"A young man, of the name of S—— C——, grandson to a late eminent Dissenting minister, and brought up by him, came to reside at K——g, about the year 1803. He attended at the Baptist place of worship, not only on the Lord's day, but frequently at the week-day lectures and prayer-meetings. He was supposed by some to be seriously inclined; but his opinion of himself was, that he had never experienced that divine change, without which no man can be saved.

"However that might be, there is reason to believe he had been for some years under powerful convictions of his miserable condition as a sinner. In June, 1806, these convictions were observed to increase, and that in a more than common degree. From that time he went into no company; but, when he was not at work, kept in his chamber, where he was employed in singing plaintive hymns, and bewailing his lost and perishing state.

"He had about him several religious people; but could not be induced to open his mind to them, or to impart to any one the cause of his distress. Whether this contributed to increase it or not, it did increase, till his health was greatly affected by it, and he was scarcely able to work at his business.

"While he was at meeting on Lord's day, September 14th, he was observed to labour under very great emotion of mind, especially when he heard the following words: 'Sinner, if you die without an interest in Christ, you will sink into the regions of eternal death.'

"On the Saturday evening following, he intimated to the mistress of the house where he lodged, that some awful judgment was about to come upon him; and as he should not be able to be at meeting next day, requested that an attendant might be procured to stay with him. She replied, that she would herself stay at home, and wait upon him; which she did.

"On the Lord's day he was in great agony of mind. His mother was sent for, and some religious friends visited him; but all was of no avail. That night was a night dreadful beyond conception. The horror which he endured brought on all the symptoms of raging madness. He desired the attendants not to come near him, lest they should be burnt. He said that 'the bed-curtains were in flames,—that he smelt the brimstone,—that devils were come to fetch him,—that there was no hope for him, for that he had sinned against light and conviction, and that he should certainly go to hell.' It was with difficulty he could be kept in bed.

"An apothecary being sent for, as soon as he entered the house, and heard his dreadful howlings, he inquired if he had not been bitten by a mad dog. His appearance, likewise, seemed to justify such a suspicion, his countenance resembling that of a wild beast more than of a man.

"Though he had no feverish heat, yet his pulse beat above 150 in a minute. To abate the *mania*, a quantity of blood was taken from him, a blister was applied, his head was shaved, cold water was copiously poured over him, and fox-glove was administered. By these means his fury was abated; but his mental agony continued, and all the symptoms of madness which his bodily strength, thus reduced, would allow, till the following Thursday. On that day he seemed to have recovered his reason, and to be calm in his mind. In the evening he sent for the apothecary; and wished to speak with him by himself. The latter, on his coming, desired every one to leave the room, and thus addressed him: 'C——, have you not something on your mind?' 'Ay,' answered he, '*that is it!*' He then acknowledged that, early in the month of June, he had gone to a fair in the neighbourhood, in company with a number of wicked young men: that they drank at a public-house together till he was in a measure intoxicated; and that from thence they went into other company, where he was criminally connected with a harlot. 'I have been a miserable creature,' continued he, 'ever since; but during the last three days and three nights, I have been in a state of desperation.' He intimated to the apothecary, that he could not bear to tell this story to his minister: 'But,' said he, 'do you inform him that I shall not die in despair; for light has broken in upon me; I have been led to the great Sacrifice for sin, and I now hope in him for salvation.'

"From this time his mental distress ceased, his countenance became placid, and his conversation, instead of being taken up as before with fearful exclamations concerning devils and the wrath to come, was now confined to the dying love of Jesus! The apothecary was of opinion, that if his strength had not been so much exhausted, he would now have been in a state of religious transport. His nervous system, however, had received such a shock, that his recovery was doubtful; and it seemed certain, that if he did recover, he would sink into a state of idiocy. He survived this interview but a few days."—*Ev. Mag.* p. 412, 413.

A religious observer stands at a turnpike gate on a Sunday, to witness the profane crowd passing by; he sees a man driving very clumsily in a gig; the inexperience of the driver provokes the following pious observations.

"'What (said I to myself) if a single untoward circumstance should happen! Should the horse take fright, or the wheel on either side get entangled, or the gig upset,—in either case what can preserve them? And should a morning so fair and promising bring on evil before night,—should death on his pale horse appear,—what follows? My mind shuddered at the images I had raised.' "—*Ev. Mag.* p. 558, 559.

Miss Louisa Cooke's rapturous state.

"From this period she lived chiefly in retirement, either in reading the sacred volume on her knees, or in pouring out her soul in prayer to God. While thus employed, she was not unfrequently indulged with visits from her gracious Lord; and sometimes she felt herself to be surrounded, as it were, by his glorious presence. After her return to Bristol, her frame of mind became so heavenly, that she seemed often to be dissolved in the love of God her Saviour."—*Ev. Mag.* p. 576, 577.

Objection to Almanacks.

"Let those who have been partial to such vain productions, only read Isaiah xlvii. 13, and Daniel ii. 27; and they will here see what they are to be accounted of, and in what company they are to be found; and let them learn to despise their equivocal and artful insinuations, which are too frequently blended with profanity; for is it not profanity in them to attempt to palm their frauds upon mankind by Scripture quotations, which they seldom fail to do, especially Judges v. 20, and Job xxxviii. 31? neither of which teaches nor warrants any such practice. Had Baruch or Deborah consulted the stars? No such thing."—*Ev. Mag.* p. 600.

This energy of feeling will be found occasionally to meddle with, and disturb the ordinary occupations and amusements of life, and to raise up little qualms of conscience, which, instead of exciting respect, border, we fear, somewhat too closely upon the ludicrous.

A Methodist Footman.

"A gentleman's servant, who has left a good place because he was ordered to deny his master when actually at home, wishes something on this subject may be introduced into this work, that persons who are in the habit of denying themselves in the above manner may be convinced of its evil."—*Ev. Mag.* p. 72.

Doubts if it is right to take any interest for money.

"*Usury.*—Sir, I beg the favour of you to insert the following case of conscience. I frequently find in Scripture, that *Usury* is particularly condemned; and it is represented as the character of a good man, that 'he hath not given forth upon usury, neither hath taken any increase,' Ezek. xviii. 8, &c. I wish, therefore, to know how such passages are to be understood; and whether the taking of interest for money, as it is universally practised among us, can be reconciled with the word and will of God? Q."—*Ev. Mag.* p. 74.

Dancing ill suited to a creature on trial for eternity

"If dancing be a waste of time; if the precious hours devoted to it may be better employed; if it be a species of trifling ill suited to a creature on trial for eternity, and hastening towards it on the swift wings of time; if it be incompatible with genuine repentance, true faith in Christ, supreme love to God, and a state of genuine devotedness to him,—then is dancing a practice utterly opposed to the whole spirit and temper of Christianity, and subversive of the best interests of the rising generation."—*Meth. Mag.* p. 127, 128.

The Methodists consider themselves as constituting a chosen and separate people, living in a land of atheists and voluptuaries. The expressions by which they designate their own sects, are the *dear people—the elect—the people of God.* The rest of mankind are *carnal people, the people of this world,* &c. &c. The children of Israel were not more separated, through the favour of God, from the Egyptians, than the Methodists are, in their own estimation, from the rest of mankind. We had hitherto supposed that the disciples of the Established churches in England and Scotland had been Christians; and that, after baptism, duly performed by the appointed minister, and participation in the customary worship of these two churches, Christianity was the religion of which they were to be considered as members. We see, however, in these publications, men of twenty or thirty years of age first called to a knowledge of Christ *under a sermon* by the Rev. Mr. Venn,—or first admitted into the church of Christ *under a sermon* by the Rev. Mr. Romaine. The apparent admission turns out to have been a mere mockery; and the pseudo-christian to have had no religion at all, till the business was really and effectually done under these sermons by Mr. Venn and Mr. Romaine.

An awful and general departure from the Christian Faith in the Church of England.

"A second volume of Mr. Cooper's sermons is before us, stamped with the same broad seal of truth and excellence as the former. Amidst the awful and general departure from the faith, as once delivered to the saints, in the Church of England, and sealed by the blood of our Reformers, it is pleasing to observe that there is a remnant, according to the election of grace, who continue rising up to testify the gospel of the grace of God, and to call back their fellows to the consideration of the great and leading doctrines on which the Reformation was built, and the Church of England by law established. The author of these sermons, avoiding all matters of more doubtful disputation, avowedly attaches himself to the great fundamental truths; and on the two substantial pillars, the Jachin and Boaz of the living temple, erects his superstructure. 1. Justification by faith, without works, free and full, by grace alone, through the redemption which is in Jesus Christ, stands at the commencement of the first volume; and on its side rises in the beauty of holiness," &c.—*Ev. Mag.* p. 79.

Mr. Robinson called to the knowledge of Christ under Mr. Venn's Sermon.

"Mr. Robinson was called in early life to the knowledge of Christ, under a sermon at St. Dunstan's, by the late Rev. Mr. Venn, from Ezek. xxxvi. 25, 26; the remembrance of which greatly refreshed his soul upon his death bed."—*Ev. Mag* p. 176.

Christianity introduced into the Parish of Launton, near Bicester, in the year 1807.

"A very general spirit of inquiry having appeared for some time in the village of Launton, near Bicester, some serious persons were excited to communicate to them the word of life." *Ev. Mag.* p. 380.

We learn in page 128, *Meth. Mag.*, that twelve months had elapsed from the time of Mrs. Cocker's joining *the people of God*, before she obtained a clear sense of forgiveness.

A religious Hoy sets off every week for Margate.

"*Religious Passengers accommodated.—To the Editor.*—Sir, it afforded me considerable pleasure to see upon the cover of your Magazine for the present month, an advertisement, announcing the establishment of a packet, to sail weekly between London and Margate, during the season; which appears to have been set on foot for the accommodation of religious characters; and in which 'no profane conversation is to be allowed.'

"To those among the followers of a crucified Redeemer, who are in the habit of visiting the Isle of Thanet in the summer, and who, for the sea air, or from other circumstances, prefer travelling by water, such a conveyance must certainly be a *desideratum*, especially if they have experienced a mortification similar to that of the writer, in the course of the last summer, when shut up in a cabin with a mixed multitude, who spake almost all languages but that of Canaan. Totally unconnected with the concern, and personally a stranger to the worthy owner, I take the liberty of recommending this vessel to the notice of my fellow-Christians; persuaded that they will think themselves bound to patronise and encourage an undertaking that has the honour of the dear Redeemer for its professed object. It ought ever to be remembered, that every talent we possess, whether large or small, is given us in trust to be laid out for God;—and I have often thought that Christians act inconsistently with their high profession, when they omit, even in their most common and trivial expenditures, to give a decided preference to the friends of their Lord. I do not, however, anticipate any such ground of complaint in this instance; but rather believe that the religious world in general will cheerfully unite with me, while I most cordially wish success to the Princess of Wales Yacht, and pray that she may ever sail under the divine protection and blessing;—that the humble followers of Him who spoke the storm into a calm, when crossing the lake of Gennesareth, may often feel their hearts glowing with sacred ardour, while in her cabins they enjoy sweet communion with their Lord and with each other;—and that strangers, who may be providentially brought among them, may see so much of the beauty and excellency of the religion of Jesus exemplified in their conduct and conversation, that they may be constrained to say, 'We will go with you, for we perceive that God is with you.—Your God shall be our God, and his people shall henceforth be our chosen companions and associates.' I am, Mr. Editor, your obliged friend and sister in the gospel, E T."—*Ev. Mag.* p. 268.

A religious newspaper is announced in the Ev. M. for September.—It is said of common newspapers, "That *they are absorbed in temporal concerns, while the consideration of those which are eternal is postponed;* the business of this life has superseded the claims of immortality; and the monarchs of the world have engrossed an attention which would have been more properly devoted to the Saviour of the universe." It is then stated, "that the columns of this paper (*The Instructor, price 6d.*) will be supplied by pious reflections; suitable comments to improve the dispensations of Providence will be introduced; and the whole conducted with an eye to our spiritual, as well as temporal, welfare. The work will contain the latest news up to four o'clock on the day of publication, together with the most recent religious occurrences. The prices of stock, and correct market-tables, will also be accurately detailed." *Ev. Mag. September Advertisement.* The Eclectic Review is also understood to be carried on upon Methodistical principles.

Nothing can evince more strongly the influence which Methodism now exercises upon common life, and the fast hold it has got of the people, than the advertisements which are circulated every month in these very singular publications. On the cover of a single number, for example, we have the following:—

"Wanted, by Mr. Turner, shoemaker, a steady apprentice; he will have the privilege of attending the ministry of the gospel;—a premium expected, p. 3.—Wanted, a serious young woman, as servant of all work, 3.—Wanted, a man of serious character, who can shave, 3.—Wanted, a serious woman to assist in a shop, 3.—A young person in the millinery line wishes to be in a serious family, 4.—Wants a place, a young man who has brewed in a serious family, 4.—Ditto, a young woman of evangelical principles, 4.—Wanted, an active serious shopman, 5.—To be sold, an eligible residence, with sixty acres of land; gospel preached in three places within half a mile, 5.—A single gentleman may be accommodated with lodging in a small serious family, 5.—To let, a genteel first floor in an airy situation near the Tabernacle, 6.—Wanted, a governess, of evangelical principles and corresponding character, 10."

The religious vessel we have before spoken of, is thus advertised:—

"The Princess of Wales Yacht, J. Chapman, W. Bourn, master, by divine permission, will leave Ralph's Quay every Friday, 11," &c. &c. —*July Ev. Mag.*

After the specimens we have given of these people, any thing which is said of their activity can very easily be credited. The army and navy appear to be particular objects of their attention.

"*British Navy.*—It is with peculiar pleasure we insert the following extract of a letter from the pious chaplain of a man-of-war, to a gentleman at Gosport, intimating the power and grace of God manifested towards our brave seamen. "*Off Cadiz, Nov.* 26, 1806.—My dear friend—A fleet for England found us in the night, and is just going away. I have only to tell you that the work of God seems to prosper. Many are under convictions;—some, I trust, are converted. I preach every night, and am obliged to have a private meeting afterwards with those who wish to speak about their souls. But my own health is suffering much, nor shall I probably be able long to bear it. The ship is like a tabernacle; and really there is much external reformation. Capt. ——— raises no objection. I have near a hundred hearers every night at six o'clock. How unworthy am I!—Pray for us.' "—*Ev. Mag.* 84.

The Testimony of a profane Officer to the worth of Pious Sailors.

"Mr. Editor—In the mouth of two or three witnesses a truth shall be established. I recently met with a pleasing confirmation of a narrative, stated sometime since in your Magazine. I was surprised by a visit from an old acquaintance of mine the other day, who is now an officer of rank in his Majesty's navy. In the course of conversation, I was shocked at the profane oaths that perpetually interrupted his sentences; and took an opportunity to express my regret that such language should be so common among so valuable a body of men. 'Sir,' said he, still interspersing many solemn imprecations, 'an officer cannot live at sea without swearing;—not one of my men would mind a word without an oath; it is common sea-language. If we were not to swear, the rascals would take us for lubbers, stare in our faces, and leave us to do our commands ourselves. I never knew but one exception; and that was extraordinary. I declare, believe me 'tis true (suspecting that I might not credit it), there was a set of fellows called *Methodists*, on board the Victory, Lord Nelson's ship (to be sure he was rather a religious man himself!), and those men never wanted swearing at. The dogs were the best seamen on board. Every man *knew* his duty, and every man *did* his duty. They used to meet together and sing hymns; and nobody dared molest them. The commander would not have suffered it, had they attempted it. They were allowed a mess by themselves; and never mixed with the other men. I have often heard them singing away myself; and 'tis true, I assure you, but not one of them was either killed or wounded at the battle of Trafalgar, though they did their duty as well as any men. No, not one of the psalm-singing gentry was even hurt; and there the fellows are swimming away in the Bay of Biscay at this very time, singing like the d——. They are now under a new commander; but still are allowed the same privileges, and mess by themselves. These were the only fellows that ever I knew do their duty without swearing; and I will do them the justice to say they do it.' J. C."—*Ev. Mag.* p. 119, 120.

These people are spread over the face of the whole earth in the shape of missionaries.—Upon the subject of missions we shall say very little or nothing at present, because we reserve it for another article in a subsequent Number. But we cannot help remarking the magnitude of the collections made in favour of the missionaries at the Methodistical chapels, when compared with the collections for any common object of charity in the orthodox churches and chapels.

"*Religious Tract Society*.—A most satisfactory report was presented by the committee; from which it appeared that, since the commencement of the institution in the year 1799, upwards of *four millions* of religious tracts have been issued under the auspices of the society; and that considerably more than one-fourth of that number have been sold during the last year."—*Ev. Mag.* p. 284.

These tracts are dropped in villages by the Methodists, and thus every chance for conversion afforded to the common people. There is a proposal in one of the numbers of the volumes before us, that travellers, for every pound they spend on the road, should fling one shilling's worth of these tracts out of the chaise window;—thus taxing his pleasures at 5 *per cent.* for the purposes of doing good.

"Every Christian who expects the protection and blessing of God ought to take with him as many *shillings' worth*, at least, of cheap tracts to throw on the road, and leave at inns, as he takes out *pounds* to expend on himself and family. This is really but a trifling sacrifice. It is a highly reasonable one; and one which God will accept."—*Ev. Mag.* p. 405.

It is part of their policy to have a great change of Ministers.

"Same day, the Rev. W. Haward, from Hoxton Academy, was ordained over the Independent church at Rendham, Suffolk. Mr. Pickles, of Walpole, began with prayer and reading; Mr. Price, of Woodbridge, delivered the introductory discourse, and asked the questions; Mr. Dennant, of Halesworth, offered the ordination prayer; *Mr. Shufflebottom, of Bungay, gave the charge* from Acts xx. 28; Mr. Vincent, of Deal, the general prayer; and Mr. Walford, of Yarmouth, preached to the people from 2 Phil. ii. 16."—*Ev. Mag.* p. 429.

Chapels opened.—"Hambledon, Bucks, Sept. 22.—Eighteen months ago this parish was destitute of the gospel; the people have now one of the Rev. G. Collison's students, the Rev. Mr. Eastmead, settled among them. Mr. English, of Wooburn, and Mr. Frey, preached on the occasion; and Mr. Jones, of London, Mr. Churchill, of Henley, Mr. Redford, of Windsor, and Mr. Barratt, now of Petersfield, prayed."—*Ev. Mag.* p. 533.

Methodism in his Majesty's ship Tonnant—A Letter from the Sail-maker.

"It is with great satisfaction that I can now inform you God has deigned, in a yet greater degree, to own the weak efforts of his servant to turn many from Satan to himself. Many are called here, as is plain to be seen by their pensive looks and deep sighs. And if they would be obedient to the heavenly call, instead of grieving the Spirit of grace, I dare say we should soon have near half the ship's company brought to God. I doubt not, however, but, as I have cast my bread upon the waters, it will be found after many days. Our 13 are now increased to upwards of 30. Surely the Lord delighteth not in the death of him that dieth."—*Meth. Mag*. p. 188.

It appears, also, from p. 193, *Meth. Mag*., that the same principles prevail on board his Majesty's ship Sea-horse, 44 guns. And in one part of *Evan. Mag*. great hopes are entertained of the 25th regiment. We believe this is the number; but we quote this fact from memory.

We must remember, in addition to these trifling specimens of their active disposition, that the Methodists have found a powerful party in the House of Commons, who, by the neutrality which they affect, and partly adhere to, are courted both by ministers and opposition; that they have gained complete possession of the India-House; and under the pretence, or perhaps with the serious intention of educating young people for India, will take care to introduce (as much as they dare without provoking attention) their own particular tenets. In fact, one thing must always be taken for granted respecting these people,—that wherever they gain a footing, or whatever be the institutions to which they give birth, *proselytism will be their main object;* every thing else is a mere instrument—this is their principal aim. When every proselyte is not only an addition to their temporal power, but when the act of conversion which gains a vote, saves (as they suppose) a soul from destruction,—it is quite needless to state, that every faculty of their minds will be dedicated to this most important of all temporal and eternal concerns.

Their attack upon the Church is not merely confined to publications; it is generally understood that they have a very considerable fund for the purchase of livings, to which, of course, ministers of their own profession are always presented.

Upon the foregoing facts, and upon the spirit evinced by these extracts, we shall make a few comments.

1. It is obvious that this description of Christians entertain very erroneous and dangerous notions of the present judgments of God. A belief that Providence interferes in all the little actions of our lives, refers all merit and demerit to bad and good fortune; and causes the successful man to be always considered as a good man, and the unhappy man as the object of divine vengeance. It furnishes ignorant and designing men with a power which is sure to be abused:—the cry of a *judgment*, a *judgment*, it is always easy to make, but not easy to resist. It encourages the grossest superstitions; for if the Deity rewards and punishes on every slight occasion, it is quite impossible, but that such an helpless being as man will set himself at work to discover the will of Heaven in the appearances of outward nature, to apply all the phenomena of thunder, lightning, wind, and every striking appearance to the regulation of his conduct; as the poor Methodist, when he rode into Piccadilly in a thunder storm, and imagined that all the uproar of the elements was a mere hint to him not to preach at Mr. Romaine's chapel. Hence a great deal of error, and a great deal of secret misery. This doctrine of a theocracy must necessarily place an excessive power in the hands of the clergy: it applies so instantly and so tremendously to men's hopes and fears, that it must make the priest omnipotent over the people, as it always has done where it has been established. It has a great tendency to check human exertions, and to prevent the employment of those secondary means of effecting an object which Providence has placed in our power. The doctrine of the immediate and perpetual interference of Divine providence is not true. If two men travel the same road, the one to rob, the other to relieve a fellow-creature who is starving; will any but the most fanatic contend that they do not both run the same chance of falling over a stone and breaking their legs? and is it not matter of fact, that the robber often returns safe, and the just man sustains the injury? Have not the soundest divines, of both churches, always urged this unequal distribution of good and evil, in the present state, as one of the strongest natural arguments for a future state of retribution? Have not they contended, and well, and admirably contended, that the supposition of such a state is absolutely necessary to our notion of the justice of God,—absolutely necessary to restore order to that moral confusion which we all observe and deplore in the present world? The man who places religion upon a false basis is the greatest enemy to religion. If victory is always to the just and good,—how is the fortune of impious conquerors to be accounted for? Why do they erect dynasties and found families which last for centuries? The reflecting mind whom you have instructed in this manner, and for present effect only, naturally comes upon you hereafter with difficulties of this sort; he finds he has been deceived; and you will soon discover that, in breeding up a fanatic, you have unwittingly laid the foundation of an atheist. The honest and the orthodox method is to prepare young people for the world as it actually exists; to tell them that they will often find vice perfectly successful, virtue exposed to a long train of afflictions; that they must bear this patiently, and look to another world for its rectification.

2. The second doctrine which it is necessary to notice among the Methodists, is the doctrine of inward impulse and emotions, which, it is quite plain, must lead, if universally insisted upon, and preached among the common people, to every species of folly and enormity. When an human being believes that his internal feelings are the monitions of God, and that these monitions must govern his conduct; and when a great stress is purposely laid upon these inward feelings in all the discourses from the pulpit; it is impossible to say to what a pitch of extravagance mankind may not be carried, under the influence of such dangerous doctrines.

3. The Methodists hate pleasure and amusements; no theatre, no cards, no dancing, no punchinello, no dancing dogs, no blind fiddlers;—all the amusements of the rich and of the poor must disappear wherever these

gloomy people get a footing. It is not the abuse of pleasure which they attack, but the interspersion of pleasure, however much it is guarded by good sense and moderation;—it is not only wicked to hear the licentious plays of Congreve, but wicked to hear Henry the Vth, or the School for Scandal:—it is not only dissipated to run about to all the parties in London and Edinburgh,—*but dancing is not fit for a being who is preparing himself for Eternity. Ennui,* wretchedness, melancholy, groans and sighs, are the offerings which these unhappy men make to a Deity who has covered the earth with gay colours, and scented it with rich perfumes; and shown us, by the plan and order of his works, that he has given to man something better than a bare existence, and scattered over his creation a thousand superfluous joys, which are totally unnecessary to the mere support of life.

4. The Methodists lay very little stress upon practical righteousness. They do not say to their people, do not be deceitful; do not be idle; get rid of your bad passions; or at least (if they do say these things) they say them very seldom. Not that they preach faith without works; for if they told the people that they might rob and murder with impunity, the civil magistrate must be compelled to interfere with such doctrine:—but they say a great deal about faith, and very little about works. What are commonly called the mysterious parts of our religion, are brought into the foreground much more than the doctrines which lead to practice;—and this among the lowest of the community.

The Methodists have hitherto been accused of dissenting from the Church of England. This, as far as it relates to mere subscription to articles, is not true; but they differ in their choice of the articles upon which they dilate and expand, and to which they appear to give a preference, from the stress which they place upon them. There is nothing heretical in saying, that God *sometimes* intervenes with his special providence; but these people differ from the Established Church, in the degree in which they insist upon this doctrine. In the hands of a man of sense and education, it is a safe doctrine;—in the management of the Methodists, we have seen how ridiculous and degrading it becomes. In the same manner, a clergyman of the Church of England would not do his duty, if he did not insist upon the necessity of faith, as well as of good works; but as he believes that it is much more easy to give credit to doctrines than to live well, he labours most in those points where human nature is the *most* liable to prove defective. Because he does so, he is accused of giving up the articles of his faith, by men who have their partialities also in doctrine; but parties, not founded upon the same sound discretion, and knowledge of human nature.

5. The Methodists are always desirous of making men more religious than it is possible, from the constitution of human nature, to make them. If they could succeed as much as they wish to succeed, there would be at once an end of delving and spinning, and of every exertion of human industry. Men must eat, and drink, and work; and if you wish to fix upon them high and elevated notions, as the *ordinary* furniture of their minds, you do these two things: you drive men of warm temperaments mad,—and you introduce in the rest of the world, a low and shocking familiarity with words and images, which every real friend to religion would wish to keep sacred. *The friends of the dear Redeemer, who are in the habit of visiting the Isle of Thanet*—(as in the extract we have quoted)—Is it possible that this mixture of the most awful with the most familiar images, so common among Methodists now, and with the enthusiasts in the time of Cromwell, must not, in the end, divest religion of all the deep and solemn impressions which it is calculated to produce? In a man of common imagination (as we have before observed), the terror, and the feeling which it first excited, must necessarily be soon separated: but, where the fervour of impression is long preserved, piety ends in Bedlam. Accordingly, there is not a mad-house in England, where a considerable part of the patients have not been driven to insanity by the extravagance of these people. We cannot enter such places without seeing a number of honest artisans, covered with blankets, and calling themselves angels and apostles, who, if they had remained contented with the instruction of men of learning and education, would have been sound masters of their own trade, sober Christians, and useful members of society.

6. It is impossible not to observe how directly all the doctrine of the Methodists is calculated to gain power among the poor and ignorant. To say, that the Deity governs this world by general rules, and that we must wait for another and a final scene of existence, before vice meets with its merited punishment, and virtue with its merited reward; to preach this up daily, would not add a single votary to the Tabernacle, nor sell a Number of the Methodistical Magazine:—but to publish an account of a man who was cured of scrofula by a single sermon—of Providence destroying the innkeeper at Garstang for appointing a cock-fight near the Tabernacle;—this promptness of judgment and immediate execution is so much like human justice, and so much better adapted to vulgar capacities, that the system is at once admitted as soon as any one can be found who is impudent or ignorant enough to teach it; and being once admitted, it produces too strong an effect upon the passions to be easily relinquished. The case is the same with the doctrine of inward impulse, or, as they term it, experience. If you preach up to ploughmen and artisans, that every singular feeling which comes across them is a visitation of the Divine Spirit—can there be any difficulty, *under* the influence of this nonsense, in converting these simple creatures into active and mysterious fools, and making them your slaves for life? It is not possible to raise up any dangerous enthusiasm, by telling men to be just, and good, and charitable; but keep this part of Christianity out of sight—and talk long and enthusiastically before ignorant people, of the mysteries of our religion, and you will not fail to attract a crowd of fol

lowers:—verily the Tabernacle loveth not that which is simple, intelligible, and leadeth to good sound practice.

Having endeavoured to point out the spirit which pervades these people, we shall say a few words upon the causes, the effects, and the cure of this calamity.—The fanaticism so prevalent in the present day, is one of those evils from which society is never wholly exempt; but which bursts out at different periods, with peculiar violence, and sometimes overwhelms every thing in its course. The last eruption took place about a century and a half ago, and destroyed both Church and Throne with its tremendous force. Though irresistible, it was short; enthusiasm spent its force—the usual reaction took place; and England was deluged with ribaldry and indecency, because it had been worried with fanatical restrictions. By degrees, however, it was found out that orthodoxy and loyalty might be secured by other methods than licentious conduct and immodest conversation. The public morals improved; and there appeared as much good sense and moderation upon the subject of religion as ever can be expected from mankind in large masses. Still, however, the mischief which the Puritans had done was not forgotten; a general suspicion prevailed of the dangers of religious enthusiasm; and the fanatical preacher wanted his accustomed power among a people recently recovered from a religious war, and guarded by songs, proverbs, popular stories, and the general tide of humour and opinion, against all excesses of that nature. About the middle of the last century, however, the character of the genuine fanatic was a good deal forgotten, and the memory of the civil wars worn away; the field was clear for extravagance in piety; and causes, which must always produce an immense influence upon the mind of man, were left to their own unimpeded operations. Religion is so noble and powerful a consideration—it is so buoyant and so insubmergible—that it may be made, by fanatics, to carry with it any degree of error and of perilous absurdity. In this instance Messrs. Whitefield and Wesley happened to begin. They were men of considerable talents; they observed the common decorums of life; they did not run naked into the streets, or pretend to the prophetical character;—and therefore they were not committed to Newgate. They preached with great energy to weak people; who first stared—then listened—then believed—then felt the inward feeling of grace, and became as foolish as their teachers could possibly wish them to be;—in short, folly ran its ancient course,—and human nature evinced itself to be what it always has been under similar circumstances. The great and permanent cause, therefore, of the increase of Methodism, is the cause which has given birth to fanaticism in all ages,—*the facility of mingling human errors with the fundamental truths of religion.* The formerly imperfect residence of the clergy may, perhaps, in some trifling degree, have aided this source of Methodism. But unless a man of education, and a gentleman, could stoop to such disingenuous arts as the Methodist preachers, unless he hears heavenly music all of a sudden, and enjoys *sweet experiences,*—it is quite impossible that he can contend against such artists as these. More active than they are at present the clergy might perhaps be: but the calmness and moderation of an Establishment can never possibly be a match for sectarian activity.—If the common people are *ennui'd* with the fine acting of Mrs. Siddons, they go to Sadler's Wells. The subject is too serious for ludicrous comparisons:—but the Tabernacle really is to the Church, what Sadler's Wells is to the Drama. There popularity is gained by vaulting and tumbling,—by low arts, which the regular clergy are not too idle to have recourse to, but too dignified: their institutions are chaste and severe,—they endeavour to do that which, *upon the whole, and for a great number of years,* will be found to be the most admirable and the most useful: it is no part of their plan to descend to small artifices for the sake of present popularity and effect. The religion of the common people under the government of the Church may remain as it is for ever;—enthusiasm must be progressive, or it will expire.

It is probable that the dreadful scenes which have lately been acted in the world, and the dangers to which we are exposed, have increased the numbers of the Methodists. To what degree will Methodism extend in this country?—This question is not easy to answer. That it has rapidly increased within these few years, we have no manner of doubt; and we confess we cannot see what is likely to impede its progress. The party which it has formed in the legislature; and the artful neutrality with which they give respectability to their small number, the talents of some of this party, and the unimpeached excellence of their characters, all make it probable that fanaticism will increase rather than diminish. The Methodists have made an alarming inroad into the Church, and they are attacking the army and navy. The principality of Wales, and the East India Company, they have already acquired. All mines and subterraneous places belong to them; they creep into hospitals and small schools, and so work their way upwards. It is the custom of the religious neutrals to beg all the little livings, particularly in the north of England, from the minister for the time being; and from these fixed points they make incursions upon the happiness and common sense of the vicinage. We most sincerely deprecate such an event; but it will excite in us no manner of surprise, if a period arrives when the churches of the sober and orthodox part of the English clergy are completely deserted by the middling and lower classes of the community. We do not prophesy any such event; but we contend that it is not impossible,—hardly improbable. If such, in future, should be the situation of this country, it is impossible to say what political animosities may not be ingrafted upon this marked and dangerous division of mankind into the *godly* and the *ungodly.* At all events, we are quite sure that happiness will be destroyed, reason degraded, sound religion banished from the world; and that when fanaticism becomes too foolish and too prurient to be endured, (as is at last sure to be the case,) it will be succeeded by a long period of the grossest immorality, atheism, and debauchery.

We are not sure that this evil admits of any cure,—or of any considerable palliation. We most sincerely hope that the government of this country will never be guilty of such indiscretion as to tamper with the Toleration Act, or to attempt to put down these follies by the intervention of the law. If experience has taught us any thing, it is the absurdity of controlling men's notions of eternity by acts of Parliament. Something may perhaps be done, in the way of ridicule, towards turning the popular opinion. It may be as well to extend the privileges of the dissenters to the members of the Church of England; for, as the law now stands, any man who dissents from the established church may open a place of worship where he pleases. No orthodox clergyman can do so, without the consent of the parson of the parish,—who always refuses, because he does not choose to have his monopoly disturbed; and refuses in parishes where there are not accommodations for one half of the persons who wish to frequent the Church of England, and in instances where he knows that the chapels from which he excludes the established worship will be immediately occupied by sectaries. It may be as well to encourage in the early education of the clergy, as Mr. Ingram recommends, a better and more animated method of preaching; and it may be necessary, hereafter, if the evil gets to a great height, to relax the articles of the English Church, and to admit a greater variety of Christians within the pale. The greatest and best of all remedies is perhaps the education of the poor;—we are astonished, that the Established Church of England is not awake to this mean of arresting the progress of Methodism. Of course, none of these things will be done; nor is it *clear*, if they were done, they would do *much* good. Whatever happens, we are for common sense and orthodoxy. Insolence, servile politics, and the spirit of persecution, we condemn and attack, whenever we observe them;—but to the learning, the moderation, and the rational piety of the Establishment, we most earnestly wish a decided victory over the nonsense, the melancholy, and the madness of the Tabernacle.*

God send that our wishes be not in vain.

* There is one circumstance to which we have neglected to advert in the proper place,—the dreadful pillage of the earnings of the poor which is made by the Methodists. A case is mentioned in one of the Numbers of these two magazines for 1807, of a poor man with a family, earning only twenty-eight shillings a week, who has made *two donations of ten guineas each to the missionary fund!*

INDIAN MISSIONS.*

(EDINBURGH REVIEW, 1808.)

AT two o'clock in the morning, July the 10th, 1806, the European barracks, at Vellore, containing then four complete companies of the 69th regiment, were surrounded by two battalions of Sepoys in the Company's service, who poured in an heavy fire of musketry, at every door and window, upon the soldiers: at the same time the European sentries, the soldiers at the main-guard, and the sick in the hospital, were put to death; the officers' houses were ransacked, and every body found in them murdered. Upon the arrival of the 19th Light Dragoons under Colonel Gillespie, the Sepoys were immediately attacked; 600 cut down upon the spot; and 200 taken from their hiding places, and shot. There perished, of the four European companies, about 164, besides officers; and many British officers of the native troops were murdered by the insurgents.

Subsequent to this explosion, there was a mutiny at Nundydroog; and, in one day, 450 Mahomedan Sepoys were disarmed, and turned out of the fort, on the ground of an intended massacre. It appeared, also, from the information of the commanding officer at Tritchinopoly, that, at that period, a spirit of disaffection had manifested itself at Bangalore, and other places; and seemed to gain ground in every direction. On the 3d of December, 1806, the government of Madras issued the following proclamation:—

"A PROCLAMATION.—The Right Hon. the Governor in Council, having observed that, in some late instances, an extraordinary degree of agitation has prevailed among several corps of the native army of this coast, it has been his Lordship's particular endeavour to ascertain the motives which may have led to conduct so different from that which formerly distinguished the native army. From this inquiry, it has appeared that many persons of evil intention have endeavoured, for malicious purposes, to impress upon the native troops a belief that it is the wish of the British government to convert them by forcible means to Christianity; and his Lordship in Council has observed with concern, that such malicious reports have been believed by many of the native troops.

"The Right Hon. the Governor in Council, therefore, deems it proper, in this public manner, to repeat to the native troops his assurance, that the same respect which has been invariably shown by the British government for their religion and for their customs, will be always continued; and that no interruption will be given to any native, whether Hindoo or Mussulman, in the practice of his religious ceremonies.

"His Lordship in Council desires that the native troops will not give belief to the idle rumours which are circulated by enemies of their happiness, who endeavour, with the basest designs, to weaken the confidence of the troops in the British government. His Lordship in Council desires that the native troops will remember the constant attention and humanity which have been shown by the British government, in providing for their comfort, by augmenting the pay of the native officers and Sepoys; by allowing liberal pensions to those who have done their duty faithfully; by making ample provisions for the families of those who may have died in battle; and by receiving their children into the service of the Honourable Company, to be treated with the same care and bounty as their fathers had experienced.

"The Right Hon. the Governor in Council trusts, that the native troops, remembering these circumstances, will be sensible of the happiness of their situation, which is greater than what the troops of any other part of the world enjoy; and that they will continue to observe the same good conduct for which they were distinguished in the days of Gen. Lawrence, of Sir Eyre Coote, and of other renowned heroes.

"The native troops must at the same time be sensible, that if they should fail in the duties of their allegiance, and should show themselves disobedient to their officers, their conduct will not fail to receive merited punishment, as the British government is not less prepared to punish the guilty, than to protect and distinguish those who are deserving of its favour.

"It is directed that this paper be translated with care into the Tamul, Telinga, and Hindoostany languages; and that copies of it be circulated to each native battalion, of which the European officers are enjoined and ordered to be careful in making it known to every native officer and Sepoy under his command.

"It is also directed, that copies of the paper be circulated to all the magistrates and collectors under this government, for the purpose of

---

* *Considerations on the Policy of communicating the Knowledge of Christianity to the Natives in India.* By a late Resident in Bengal. London. Hatchard, 1807.

An Address to the Chairman of the East India Company occasioned by Mr. Twining's Letter to that Gentleman. By the Rev. John Owen. London. Hatchard.

A Letter to the Chairman of the East India Company, on the Danger of interfering in the religious Opinions of the Natives of India. By Thomas Twining. London. Ridgeway.

Vindication of the Hindoos. By a Bengal Officer. London. Rodwell.

Letter to John Scott Waring. London. Hatchard.

Cunningham's Christianity in India. London. Hatchard.

Answer to Major Scott Waring. Extracted from the Christian Observer.

Observations on the Present State of the East India Company. By Major Scott Waring. Ridgeway. London.

being fully understood in all parts of the country.

"Published by order of the Right Hon. the Governor in Council.

"G. Buchan, Chief Secretary to Government.
"*Dated in Fort St. George, 3d Dec.* 1806."

Scott Waring's Preface, iii.—v.

So late as March 1807, three months after the date of this proclamation, so universal was the dread of a general revolt among the native troops, that the British officers attached to the native troops constantly slept with loaded pistols under their pillows.

It appears that an attempt had been made by the military men at Madras, to change the shape of the Sepoy turban into something resembling the helmet of the light infantry of Europe, and to prevent the native troops from wearing, on their foreheads, the marks characteristic of their various castes. The sons of the late Tippoo, with many noble Mussulmen deprived of office at that time, resided in the fortress of Vellore, and in all probability contributed very materially to excite, or to inflame those suspicions of design against their religion, which are mentioned in the proclamation of the Madras government, and generally known to have been a principal cause of the insurrection at Vellore. It was this insurrection which first gave birth to the question upon missions to India; and before we deliver any opinion upon the subject itself, it will be necessary to state what had been done in former periods towards disseminating the truths of the gospel in India, and what new exertions had been made about the period at which this event took place.

More than a century has elapsed since the first Protestant missionaries appeared in India. Two young divines, selected by the University of Halle, were sent out in this capacity by the king of Denmark, and arrived at the Danish settlement of Tranquebar in 1706. The mission thus begun, has been ever since continued, and has been assisted by the Society for the Promotion of Christian Knowledge established in this country. The same Society has, for many years, employed German missionaries, of the Lutheran persuasion, for propagating the doctrines of Christianity among the natives of India. In 1799, their number was six; it is now reduced to five.

The Scriptures translated into the Tamulic language, which is vernacular in the southern parts of the peninsula, have, for more than half a century, been printed at the Tranquebar press, for the use of Danish missionaries and their converts. A printing press, indeed, was established at that place by the two first Danish missionaries; and, in 1714, the Gospel of St. Matthew, translated into the dialect of Malabar, was printed there. Not a line of the Scriptures, in any of the languages current on the coast, had issued from the Bengal press on September 13, 1806.

It does appear, however, about the period of the mutiny at Vellore, and a few years previous to it, that the number of the missionaries on the coast had been increased. In 1804, the *Missionary Society*, a recent institution, sent a new mission to the coast of Coromandel; from whose papers, we think right to lay before our readers the following extracts.*

"*March* 31*st*, 1805.—Waited on A. B. He says, *Government seems to be very willing to forward our views.* We may stay at Madras as long as we please; and when we intend to go into the country, on our application to the governor by letter, he would issue orders for granting us passports, which would supersede the necessity of a public petition.—Lord's Day."—*Trans. of Miss. Society*, II. p. 365.

In a letter from Brother Ringletaube to Brother Cran, he thus expresses himself;—

"The passports Government has promised you are so valuable, that I should not think a journey too troublesome to obtain one for myself, if I could not get it through your interference In hopes that your application will suffice to obtain one for me, I enclose you my Gravesend passport, that will give you the particulars concerning my person."—*Trans. of Miss. Society*, II. p. 369.

They obtain their passports from Government; and the plan and objects of their mission are printed, free of expense, at the Government press.

"1805, *June* 27, Dr. ——— sent for one of us to consult with him on particular business. He accordingly went. The Doctor told him, that he had read the publications which the brethren lately brought from England, and was so much delighted with the report of the Directors, that he wished 200 or more copies of it were printed, together with an introduction, giving an account of the rise and progress of the Missionary Society, in order to be distributed in the different settlements in India. He offered *to print them at the Government press free of expense*. On his return, we consulted with our two brethren on the subject, and resolved to accept the Doctor's favour. We have begun to prepare it for the press."—*Trans. of Miss. Society*, II. p. 394.

In page 89th of the 18th Number, Vol. III., the Missionaries write thus to the Society in London, about a fortnight before the massacre at Vellore.

"Every encouragement is offered us by the established government of the country. Hitherto they have granted us every request, whether solicited by ourselves or others. Their permission to come to this place; their allowing us an acknowledgment for preaching in the fort, which sanctions us in our work; together with the grant which they have lately given us to hold a large spot of ground every way suited for missionary labours, are objects of the last importance, and remove every impediment which might be apprehended from this source. We trust not to an arm of flesh; but when we reflect on these things, we cannot but behold the loving kindness of the Lord."

* There are six societies in England for converting Heathens to the Christian religion. 1. Society for *Missions to Africa and the East*; of which Messrs. Wilberforce, Grant, Parry, and Thorntons, are the principal encouragers. 2. Methodist Society for Missions. 3. Anabaptist Society for Missions. 4. Missionary Society. 5. Society for Promoting Christian Knowledge. 6. Moravian Missions. They all publish their proceedings.

In a letter of the same date, we learn, from Brother Ringletaube, the following fact:—

"The Dewan of Travancore sent me word, that if I despatched one of our Christians to him, he would give me leave to build a church at Magilandy. Accordingly, I shall send in a short time. For this important service, our society is indebted alone to Colonel ——, without *whose determined and fearless interposition, none of their missionaries would have been able to set a foot in that country.*"

In page 381, Vol. II., Dr. Kerr, one of the chaplains on the Madras establishment, baptizes a Mussulman who had applied to him for that purpose; upon the first application, it appears that Dr. Kerr hesitated; but upon the Mussulman threatening to rise against him on the day of judgment, Dr. Kerr complies.

It appears that in the Tinevelly district, about a year before the massacre of Vellore, not only riots, but very serious persecutions of the converted natives had taken place, from the jealousy evinced by the Hindoos and Mussulmen at the progress of the gospel.

"'Rev. Sir,—I thought you sufficiently acquainted with the late vexations of the Christians in those parts, arising from the blind zeal of the Heathens and Mahometans; the latter viewing with a jealous eye the progress of the gospel, and trying to destroy, or at least to clog it, by all the crafty means in their power. I therefore did not choose to trouble you; but as no stop has been put to these grievances, things go on from bad to worse, as you will see from what has happened at Hickadoe. The Catechist has providentially escaped from that outrageous attempt, by the assistance of ten or twelve of our Christians, and has made good his flight to Palamcotta; whilst the exasperated mob, coming from Padeckepalloe, hovered round the village, plundering the houses of the Christians, and ill-treating their families, by kicking, flogging, and other bad usage; these monsters not even forbearing to attack, strip, rob, and miserably beat the Catechist Jesuadian, who, partly from illness and partly through fear, had shut himself up in his house. I have heard various accounts of this sad event; but yesterday the Catechist himself called on me, and told me the truth of it. From what he says, it is plain that the Manikar of Wayrom (a Black peace-officer of that place) has contrived the whole affair, with a view to vex the Christians. I doubt not that these facts have been reported to the Rev. Mr. K. by the country-priest; and if I mention them to you, it is with a view to show in what a forlorn state the poor Christians hereabout are, and how desirable a thing it would be, if the Rev. Mr. Ringletaube were to come hither as soon as possible; then tranquillity would be restored, and future molestations prevented. I request you to communicate this letter to him with my compliments. I am, sir, &c. *Manapaar, June* 8, 1805.'

"This letter left a deep impression on my mind, especially when I received a fuller account of the troubles of the Christians. By the Black underlings of the Collectors, they are frequently driven from their homes, put in the stocks, and exposed for a fortnight together to the heat of the raging sun, and the chilling dews of the night, all because there is no European Missionary to bring their complaints to the ear of Government, who, I am happy to add, have never been deficient in their duty of procuring redress, where the Christians have had to complain of real injuries. One of the most trying cases, mentioned in a postscript of the above letter, is that of Christians being flogged till they consent to hold the torches to the Heathen idols. The letter says 'the Catechist of Collesigrapatuam has informed me, that the above Manikar has forced a Christian, of the Villally caste, who attends at our church, to sweep the temple of the idol. A severe flogging was given on this occasion.'—From such facts, the postscript continues, 'You may guess at the deplorable situation of our fellow-believers, as long as every Manikar thinks he has a right to do them what violence he pleases.'

"It must be observed, to the glory of the Saviour who is strong in weakness, that many of the Neophytes in that district have withstood all these fiery trials with firmness. Many also, it is to be lamented, have fallen off in the evil day, and at least so far yielded to the importunity of their persecutors, as again to daub their faces with paint and ashes, after the manner of the Heathen. How great this falling off has been I am not yet able to judge. But I am happy to add, that the Board of Revenue has issued the strictest orders against all unprovoked persecution."—*Trans. of Miss. Society*, II. 431, 433.

The following quotations evince how far from indifferent the natives are to the progress of the Christian religion in the East.

"1805. *Oct.* 10.—A respectable Brahmin in the Company's employ called on us. We endeavoured to point out to him the important object of our coming to India, and mentioned some of the great and glorious truths of the gospel, which we wished to impart in the native language. He seemed much hurt, and told us the Gentoo religion was of a divine origin as well as the Christian;—that heaven was like a palace which had many doors, at which people may enter;—that variety is pleasing to God, &c.—and a number of other arguments which we hear every day. On taking leave, he said, 'the Company has got the country, (for the English are very clever,) and, perhaps, they may succeed in depriving the Brahmins of their power, and let you have it.'"

"*November* 16*th*. Received a letter from the Rev. Dr. Taylor; we are happy to find he is safely arrived at Calcutta, and that our Baptist brethren are labouring with increasing success. The natives around us are astonished to hear this news. It is bad news to the Brahmins, who seem unable to account for it; they say the world is going to ruin."—*Trans. of Miss. Society*, II. 422 & 426.

"While living in the town, our house was watched by the natives from morning to night, to see if any person came to converse about religion. This prevented many from coming who have been very desirous of hearing of *the good way.*"—*Trans. of Miss. Society*, No. 16, p. 87.

"If Heathen, of great influence and connections, or Brahmins, were inclined to join the Christian church, it would probably cause commotions and even rebellions, either to prevent them from it, or to endanger their life. In former years, we had some instances of this kind at Tranquebar; where they were protected by the assistance of government. If such instances should happen now in our present times, we don't know what the consequence would be."—*Trans. of Miss. Society*, II. 185.

This last extract is contained in a letter from Danish Missionaries at Tranquebar, to the Directors of the Missionary Society at London.

It is hardly fair to contend, after these extracts, that no symptoms of jealousy upon the subject of religion had been evinced on the coast, except in the case of the insurrection at Vellore; or that no greater activity than common had prevailed among the missionaries. We are very far, however, from attributing that insurrection exclusively, or even principally, to any apprehensions from the zeal of the missionaries. The rumor of that zeal might probably have more readily disposed the minds of the troops for the corrupt influence exercised upon them; but we have no doubt that the massacre was principally owing to the adroit use made by the sons of Tippoo, and the high Mussulmen living in the fortress, of the abominable military foppery of our people.

After this short sketch of what has been lately passing on the coast, we shall attempt to give a similar account of the missionary proceedings in Bengal; and it appears to us, it will be more satisfactory to do so as much as possible in the words of the missionaries themselves. In our extracts from their publications, we shall endeavour to show the character and style of the men employed in these missions, the extent of their success, or rather of their failure, and the general impression made upon the people by their efforts for the dissemination of the gospel.

It will be necessary to premise, that the missions in Bengal, of which the public have heard so much of late years, are the missions of Anabaptist dissenters, whose peculiar and distinguishing tenet it is, to baptize the members of their church by plunging them into the water when they are grown up, instead of sprinkling them with water when they are young. Among the subscribers to this society, we perceive the respectable name of the Deputy Chairman of the East India Company, who, in the common routine of office, will succeed to the chair of that Company at the ensuing election. The Chairman and Deputy Chairman of the East India Company, are also both of them trustees to another religious society for *missions to Africa and the East.*

The first number of the *Anabaptist Missions* informs us that the origin of the society will be found in *the workings of Brother Carey's mind, whose heart appears to have been set upon the conversion of the Heathen in* 1786, *before he came to reside at Moulton.* (No. I. p. 1.) These workings produced a sermon at Northampton, and the sermon a subscription to convert 420 millions of Pagans. Of the subscription we have the following account: "Information has come from Brother Carey that a gentleman from Northumberland had promised to send him 30*l.* for the Society, and to subscribe four guineas annually."

"At this meeting at Northampton two other friends subscribed, and paid two guineas apiece, two more one guinea each, and another half a guinea, making six guineas and a half in all. And such members as were present of the first subscribers, paid their subscriptions into the hands of the treasurer; who proposed to put the sum now received into the hands of a banker, who will pay interest for the same." —*Bapt. Mis. Soc.* No. I. p. 5.

In their first proceedings they are a good deal guided by Brother Thomas, who has been in Bengal before, and who lays before the Society an history of his life and adventures, from which we make the following extract:—

"On my arrival in Calcutta, I sought for religious people, but found none. At last, how was I rejoiced to hear that a very religious man was coming to dine with me at a house in Calcutta; a man who would not omit his closet hours, of a morning or evening, at sea or on land, for all the world. I concealed my impatience as well as I could, till the joyful moment came: and a moment it was, for I soon heard him take the Lord's name in vain, and it was like a cold dagger, with which I received repeated stabs in the course of half an hour's conversation; and he was ready to kick me when I spoke of some things commonly believed by other hypocrites, concerning our Lord Jesus Christ; and with fury put an end to our conversation, by saying I was a mad enthusiast, to suppose that Jesus Christ had any thing to do in the creation of the world, who was born only seventeen hundred years ago. When I returned, he went home in the same ship, and I found him a strict observer of devotional hours, but an enemy to all religion, and horribly loose, vain, and intemperate in his life and conversation.

"After this *I advertised for a Christian;* and that I may not be misunderstood, I shall subjoin a copy of the advertisement, from the Indian Gazette of November 1, 1783, which now lies before me."—*Bapt. Mis. Soc.* No. I. p. 14, 15.

Brother Thomas relates the Conversion of an Hindoo on the Malabar Coast to the Society.

"A certain man, on the Malabar coast, had inquired of various devotees and priests, how he might make atonement for his sins; and at last he was directed to drive iron spikes, sufficiently blunted, through his sandals, and on these spikes he was to place his naked feet, and walk (if I mistake not) 250 coss, that is about 480 miles. If, through loss of blood, or weakness of body, he was obliged to halt, he might wait for healing and strength. He undertook the journey; and while he halted under a large shady tree where the gospel was sometimes preached, one of the missionaries came, and preached in his hearing from these words, *The blood of Jesus Christ cleanseth from all sin.* While he was preaching, the man rose up, threw off his torturing sandals, and cried out aloud, '*This is what I want!*'"—*Bapt. Mis. Soc.* No. I. p. 29.

On June 13, 1793, the missionaries set sail, carrying with them letters to three supposed converts of Brother Thomas, Parbotee, Ram Ram Boshoo, and Mohun Chund. Upon their arrival in India, they found, to their inexpressible mortification, that Ram Ram had relapsed into paganism: and we shall present our readers with a picture of the present and worldly misery to which an Hindoo is subjected, who becomes a convert to the Christian religion. Every body knows that the population of Hindostan is divided into castes, or classes of persons; and that when a man loses his caste, he is shunned by his wife, children, friends, and relations; that it is considered as an abomination to lodge or eat with him; and that he is a wanderer and an outcast upon the earth. Caste can be lost by a variety of means, and the Protestant missionaries have always made the loss of it a previous requisite to admission into the Christian church.

"On our arrival at Calcutta, we found poor Ram Boshoo waiting for us: but, to our great grief, he has been bowing down to idols again. When Mr. T. left India, he went from place to place; but, forsaken by the Hindoos, and neglected by the Europeans, he was seized with a flux and fever. In this state, he says, 'I had nothing to support me or my family; a relation offered to save me from perishing for want of necessaries, on condition of my bowing to the idol; I knew that the Roman Catholic Christians worshipped idols; I thought they might be commanded to honour images in some part of the Bible which I had not seen; I hesitated, and complied; but I love Christianity still.'" —*Bapt. Mis. Soc.* Vol. I. p. 64, 65.

"*Jan.* 8, 1794. We thought to write to you long before this, but our hearts have been burthened with cares and sorrows. It was very afflicting to hear of Ram Boshoo's great persecution and fall. Deserted by Englishmen, and persecuted by his own countrymen, he was nigh unto death. The natives gathered in bodies, and threw dust in the air as he passed along the streets in Calcutta. At last one of his relations offered him an asylum on condition of his bowing down to their idols."—*Bapt. Mis. Soc.* Vol. I. p. 78.

Brother Carey's Piety at Sea.

"Brother Carey, while very sea-sick, and leaning over the ship to relieve his stomach from that very oppressive complaint, said his mind was even then filled with consolation in contemplating the wonderful goodness of God." —*Ibid.* p. 76.

Extracts from Brother Carey's and Brother Thomas's Journals, at sea and by land.

"1793. *June* 16. *Lord's Day.* A little recovered from my sickness; met for prayer and exhortation in my cabin; had a dispute with a French deist."—*Ibid.* p. 158.

"—— 30. *Lord's Day.* A pleasant and profitable day: our congregation composed of ten persons."—*Ibid.* p. 159.

"*July* 7. Another pleasant and profitable Lord's day; our congregation increased with one. Had much sweet enjoyment with God."—*Ibid.*

"1794. *Jan.* 26. *Lord's Day.* Found much pleasure in reading Edwards' *Sermon on the Justice of God in the damnation of Sinners.*"—*Ib.* p. 165.

"*April* 6. Had some sweetness to-day, especially in reading Edwards' Sermon."—*Ibid.* p. 171.

"*June* 8. This evening reached Bowlea, where we lay to for the Sabbath. Felt thankful that God had preserved us, and wondered at his regard for so mean a creature. I was unable to wrestle with God in prayer for many of my dear friends in England."—*Ibid.* p. 179.

"—— 16. This day I preached twice at Malda, where Mr. Thomas met me. Had much enjoyment; and though our congregation did not exceed *sixteen*, yet the pleasure I felt in having my tongue once more set at liberty, I can hardly describe. Was enabled to be faithful, and felt a sweet affection for immortal souls."—*Ibid.* p. 180.

"1796. *Feb.* 6. I am now in my study; and oh, it is a sweet place, because of the presence of God with the vilest of men. It is at the top of the house; I have but one window in it."—*Ibid.* p. 295.

"The work to which God has set his hand will infallibly prosper. Christ has begun to bombard this strong and ancient fortress, and will assuredly carry it."—*Bapt. Miss.* Vol. I. p 328.

"More missionaries I think *absolutely necessary* to the support of the interest. Should any natives join us, they would become outcast immediately, and must be consequently supported by us. The missionaries on the coast are to this day obliged to provide for those who join them, as I learn from a letter sent to brother Thomas by a son of one of the missionaries." —*Ibid.* p. 334.

In the last extract our readers will perceive a new difficulty attendant upon the progress of Christianity in the East. The convert must not only be subjected to degradation, but his degradation is so complete, and his means of providing for himself so entirely destroyed, that he must be fed by his instructor. The slightest success in Hindostan would eat up the revenues of the East India Company.

Three years after their arrival these zealous and most active missionaries give the following account of their success.

"I bless God, our prospect is considerably brightened up, and our hopes are more enlarged than at any period since the commencement of the mission, owing to very pleasing appearances of the gospel having been made effectual to FOUR poor labouring Mussulmen, who have been setting their faces towards Zion ever since the month of August last. I hope their baptism will not be much longer deferred; and that might encourage Mohun Chund, Parbottee, and Cassi Naut (who last year appeared to set out in the ways of God), to declare for the Lord Jesus Christ, by an open profession of their faith in him. *Seven* of the natives, *we hope*, are indeed converted."—*Bapt. Miss.* Vol. I. p. 345, 346.

Effects of Preaching to an Hindoo Congregation.

"I then told them, that if they could not tell *me*, I would tell *them;* and that God, who had permitted the Hindoos to sink into a sea of darkness, had at length commiserated them; and sent me and my colleagues to preach life to them. I then told them of Christ, his death, his person, his love, his being the surety of sinners, his power to save, &c., and exhorted them earnestly and affectionately to come to him. Effects were various; one man came before I had well done, and wanted to sell stockings to me."—*Bapt. Miss.* Vol. I. p. 357.

Extracts from Journals.

"After worship, I received notice that the printing-press was just arrived at the Ghàt from Calcutta. Retired, and thanked God for furnishing us with a press."—*Ibid.* p. 469.

Success in the Sixth Year.

"We lament that several who did run well are now hindered. We have faint hopes of a few, and pretty strong *hopes* of *one* or *two;* but if I say more, it must either be a dull recital of our journeying to one place or another to preach the gospel, or something else relating to ourselves, of which I ought to be the last to speak."—*Ibid.* p. 488.

Extracts from Mr. Ward's Journal, a new Anabaptist Missionary sent out in 1799.

Mr. Ward admires the Captain.

"Several of our friends who have been sick begin to look up. This evening we had a most precious hour at prayer. Captain Wickes read from the 12th verse of the 33d of Exodus, and then joined in prayer. Our hearts were all warmed. We shook hands with our dear captain, and, in design, clasped him to our bosoms."—*Ibid.* Vol. II. p. 2.

Mr. Ward is frightened by a Privateer.

"*June* 11. Held our conference this evening. A vessel is still pursuing us, which the Captain believes to be a Frenchman. I feel some alarm: considerable alarm. Oh Lord, be thou our defender! the vessel seems to gain upon us. (Quarter past eleven at night.) There is no doubt of the vessel being a French privateer: when we changed our tack, she changed hers. We have, since dark, changed into our old course, so that possibly we shall lose her. Brethren G. and B. have engaged in prayer: we have read Luther's psalm, and our minds are pretty well composed. Our guns are all loaded, and the captain seems very low. All hands are at the guns, and the matches are lighted. I go to the end of the ship. I can just see the vessel, though it is very foggy. A ball whizzes over my head, and makes me tremble. I go down, and go to prayer with our friends."—*Bapt. Miss.* Vol. II. p. 3, 4.

Mr. Ward feels a regard for the Sailors.

"*July* 12. I never felt so much for any men as for our sailors; a tenderness which could weep over them. Oh, Jesus! let thy blood cover some of them! A sweet prayer meeting. Verily God is here."—*Ibid.* p. 7.

Mr. Ward sees an American Vessel, and longs to preach to the Sailors.

"*Sept.* 27. An American vessel is along-side, and the captain is speaking to their captain through his trumpet. How pleasant to talk to a friend! I have been looking at them through the glass; the sailors sit in a group, and are making their observations upon us. I long to go and preach to them."—*Ibid.* p. 11.

Feelings of the Natives upon hearing their Religion attacked.

"1800. *Feb.* 25. Brother C. had some conversation with one of the Mussulmen, who asked, upon his denying the divine mission of Mahommed, what was to become of Mussulmen and Hindoos! Brother C. expressed his fears that they would all be lost. The man seemed as if he would have torn him to pieces."—*Ibid.* p. 51.

"*Mar.* 30. The people seem quite anxious to get the hymns which we give away. The Brahmins are rather uneasy. *The Governor* advised his Brahmins to send their children to learn English. They replied, that we seemed to take pains to make the natives Christians; and they were afraid that, their children being of tender age, would make them a more easy conquest."—*Ibid.* p. 158.

"*April* 27. *Lord's Day.* One Brahmin said, he had no occasion for a hymn, for they were all over the country. He could go into any house and read one."—*Ibid.* p. 61.

"*May* 9. Brother Fountain was this evening at Buddabarry. At the close, the Brahmins having collected a number of boys, they set up a great shout, and followed the brethren out of the village with noise and shoutings."—*Ibid.*

"*May* 16. Brother Carey and I were at Buddabarry this evening. No sooner had we begun, than a Brahmin went round to all the rest that were present, and endeavoured to pull them away."—*Bapt. Miss.* Vol. II. p. 62.

"—— 30. This evening at Buddabarry, the man mentioned in my journal of March 14th insulted Brother Carey. He asked why we came; and said, if we could employ the natives as carpenters, blacksmiths, &c. it would be very well; but that they did not *want our holiness.* In exact conformity with this sentiment, our Brahmin told Brother Thomas when here, that he did not want the favour of God."—*Ibid.* p. 63.

"*June* 22. *Lord's Day.* A Brahmin has been several times to disturb the children, and to curse Jesus Christ! Another Brahmin complained to Brother Carey that, by our school and printing, we were now teaching the gospel to their children from their infancy."—*Ibid.* p. 65.

"*June* 29. *Lord's Day.* This evening a Brahmin went round amongst the people who were collected to hear Brother Carey, to persuade them not to accept of our papers. Thus 'darkness struggles with the light.'"—*Ibid.* p. 66.

"It was deemed advisable to print 2000 copies of the New Testament, and also 500 additional copies of Matthew, for immediate distribution; to which are annexed some of the most remarkable prophecies in the Old Testament respecting Christ. These are now distributing, together with copies of several evangelical hymns, and a very earnest and pertinent address to the natives, respecting the gospel. It was written by Ram Boshoo, and contains a hundred lines in Bengalee verse. We hear that these papers are read with much attention, and that apprehensions are rising in the minds of some of the Brahmins whereunto these things may grow."—*Ibid.* p. 69.

"We have printed several small pieces in Bengalee, which have had a large circulation." —*Ibid.* p. 77.

Mr. Fountain's gratitude to Hervey.

"When I was about eighteen or nineteen years of age, *Hervey's Meditations* fell into my hands. Till then I had read nothing but my Bible and the prayer book. This ushered me as it were into a new world! It expanded my mind, and excited a thirst after knowledge: and this was not all; I derived spiritual as well as intellectual advantages from it. I shall bless God for this book while I live upon earth, *and when I get to heaven, I will thank dear Hervey himself.*"—*Bapt. Miss.* Vol. II. p. 90.

Hatred of the Natives to the Gospel.

"*Jan.* 27. The inveterate hatred that the Brahmins every where show to the gospel, and the very name of Jesus, in which they are joined by many lewd fellows of the baser sort, requires no common degree of self-possession, caution, and prudence. The seeming failure of some we hoped well of is a source of considerable anxiety and grief."—*Ibid.* p. 110.

"*Aug.* 31. *Lord's Day.* We have the honour of printing the first book that was ever printed in Bengalee; and this is the first piece in which Brahmins have been opposed, perhaps for thousands of years. All their books are filled with accounts to establish Brahminism, and raise Brahmins to the seat of God. Hence they are believed to be inferior gods. All the waters of salvation in the country are supposed to meet in the foot of a Brahmin. It is reckoned they have the keys of heaven and hell, and have power over sickness and health, life and death. O pray that Brahminism may come down!"—*Ibid.* p. 111.

"*Oct.* 3. Brother Marshman having directed the children in the Bengalee school to write out a piece written by Brother Fountain (a kind of catechism), the schoolmaster reported yesterday that all the boys would leave the school rather than write it; that it was designed to make them lose caste, and make them *Feringas;* that is, persons who have descended from those who were formerly converted by the papists, and who are to this day held in the greatest contempt by the Hindoos. From this you may gather how much contempt a converted native would meet with."—*Ibid.* p. 113, 114.

"*Oct.* 26. *Lord's Day. Bharratt* told Brother Carey to-day what the people talked among themselves—'Formerly,' say they, 'here were no white people amongst us. Now the English have taken the country, and it is getting full of whites. Now also the white man's shaster is publishing. Is it not going to be fulfilled which is written in our shasters, that *all shall be of one caste;* and will not this caste be the gospel?'"—*Ibid* p. 115.

"*Nov.* 7. He also attempted repeatedly to introduce Christ and him crucified; but they would immediately manifest the utmost dislike of the very name of him. Nay, in their turn they commended Creeshnoo, and invited Brother C. to believe in him."—*Ibid.* p. 118.

"*Dec.* 23. This forenoon Gokool came to tell us that Kristno and his whole family were in confinement! Astonishing news! It seems the whole neighbourhood, as soon as it was noised abroad that these people had lost caste, was in an uproar. It is said that two thousand people were assembled pouring their anathemas on these new converts."—*Bapt. Miss.* Vol. II. p. 125.

"*Jan.* 12. The Brahmins and the young people show every degree of contempt; and the name of Christ is become a by-word, like the name *methodist* in England formerly."—*Ibid.* p. 130.

"*Sept.* 25. I then took occasion to tell them that the Brahmins only wanted their money, and cared nothing about their salvation. To this they readily assented."—*Ibid.* p. 134.

"*Nov.* 23. *Lord's Day.* Went with Brother Carey to the new pagoda, at the upper end of the town. About ten Brahmins attended. They behaved in the most scoffing and blasphemous manner, treating the name of Christ with the greatest scorn; nor did they discontinue their ridicule while Brother Carey prayed with them. No name amongst men seems so offensive to them as that of our adorable Redeemer!"—*Ibid.* p. 138.

"*Dec.* 24. The Governor had the goodness to call on us in the course of the day, and desired us to secure the girl, at least within our walls, for a few days, as he was persuaded the people round the country were so exasperated at Kristno's embracing the gospel, that he could not answer for their safety. A number of the mob might come from twenty miles distant in the night, *and murder them all,* without the perpetrators being discovered. He believed, that had they obtained the girl, they would have murdered her before the morning, and thought they had been doing God service!"—*Ibid.* p. 143, 144.

"*Jan.* 30. After speaking about ten minutes, a rude fellow began to be very abusive, and, with the help of a few boys, raised such a clamour that nothing could be heard. At length, seeing no hope of their becoming quiet, I retired to the other part of the town. They followed, hallooing, and crying, 'Hurree boll!' (an exclamation in honour of Veeshno). They at last began to pelt me with stones and dirt. One of the men, who knew the house to which Brother Carey was gone, advised me to accompany him thither, saying, that these people would not hear our words. Going with him, I met Brother C. We were not a little pleased that the devil had begun to bestir himself, inferring from hence that he suspected danger." —*Ibid.* p. 148, 149.

Feelings of an Hindoo Boy upon the eve of Conversion.

"*Nov.* 18. One of the boys of the school, called Benjamin, is under considerable concern· indeed there is a general stir amongst are children, which affords us great encouragement. The following are some of the expressions used in prayer by poor *Benjamin*:—

"'Oh Lord, the day of judgment is coming: the sun, and moon, and stars will all fall down. Oh, what shall I do in the day of judgment! Thou wilt break me to pieces. [literal.] The Lord Jesus Christ was so good as to die for us poor souls: Lord, keep us all this day! Oh hell! gnashing, and beating, and beating! One hour weeping, another gnashing! We shall stay there for ever! I am going to hell I am going to hell! O Lord, give me a new heart; give me a new heart; and wash away all my sins! Give me a new heart, that I may praise Him, that I may obey Him, that I may speak the truth, that I may never do evil things! Oh, I have many times sinned against thee, many times broken thy commandments, oh, many times; and what shall I do in the day of judgment!'"—*Bapt. Miss.* Vol. II. p. 162, 163.

Alarm of the Natives at the preaching of the Gospel.

"From several parts of Calcutta he hears of people's attention being excited by reading the papers which we have scattered among them. Many begin to wonder that they never heard these things before, since the English have been so long in the country."—*Ibid.* p. 223.

"Many of the natives have expressed their astonishment at seeing the converted Hindoos sit and eat with Europeans. It is what they thought would never come to pass. The priests are much alarmed for their tottering fabric, and rack their inventions to prop it up. They do not like the institution of the college in Calcutta, and that their sacred shasters should be explored by the unhallowed eyes of Europeans."—*Ibid.* p. 233.

"Indeed, by the distribution of many copies of the Scriptures, and of some thousands of small tracts, a spirit of inquiry has been excited to a degree unknown at any former period."—*Ibid.* p. 236.

"As he and Kristno walked through the street, the natives cried out, 'What will this joiner do? (meaning Kristno.) Will he destroy the caste of us all? Is this Brahmin going to be a Feringa?'"—*Ibid.* p. 245.

Account of success in 1802.—*Tenth year of the Mission.*

"Wherever we have gone we have uniformly found, that *so long as people did not understand the report of our message, they appeared to listen; but the moment they understood something of it, they either became indifferent, or began to ridicule. This in general has been our reception.*"—*Bapt. Miss.* Vol. I. p. 273.

Hatred of the Natives.

"*Sept.* 27. This forenoon three of the people arrived from Ponchetalokpool, who seemed very happy to see us. They inform us that the Brahmins had raised a great persecution against them; and when they set out on their journey hither, the mob assembled to hiss them away. After Brother Marshman had left that part of the country, they hung him in effigy, and some of the printed papers which he had distributed amongst them."—*Ibid.* p. 314.

Difficulty which the Mission experiences from not being able to get Converts shaved.

"Several persons there seemed willing to be baptized; but if they should, the village barber, forsooth, will not shave them! When a native loses his caste, or becomes unclean, his barber and his priest will not come near him; and as they are accustomed to shave the head nearly all over, and cannot well perform this business themselves, it becomes a serious inconvenience."—*Ibid.* p. 372.

Hatred of the Natives.

"*Apr.* 24. *Lord's Day.* Brother Chamberlain preached at home, and Ward at Calcutta; Brother Carey was amongst the brethren, and preached at night. Kristno Prisaud, Ram Roteen and others, were at Buddabatty, where they met with violent opposition. They were set upon as Feringas, as destroyers of the caste, as having eaten fowls, eggs, &c. As they attempted to return, the mob began to beat them, putting their hands on the back of their necks, and pushing them forward; and one man, even a civil officer, grazed the point of a spear against the body of Kristno Prisaud. When they saw that they could not make our friends angry by such treatment, they said, You *salla;* you will not be angry, will you? They then insulted them again, threw cow-dung mixed in gonga water at them; talked of making them a necklace of old shoes; beat Neeloo with Ram Roteen's shoe, &c.; and declared that if they ever came again, they would make an end of them."—*Bapt. Miss.* Vol. II. p. 378.

A plan for procuring an order from Government to shave the Converts.

"After concluding with prayer, Bhorud Ghose, Sookur, and Torribot Bichess, took me into the field, and told me that their minds were quite decided; there was no necessity for exhorting them. There was only one thing that kept them from being baptized in the name of Jesus Christ. Losing caste in a large town like Serampore, was a very different thing from losing caste in their village. If they declared themselves Christians, the barber of their village would no longer shave them; and, without shaving their heads and their beards, they could not live. If an order could be obtained from the magistrate of the district for the barber to shave Christians as well as others, they would be immediately baptized."—*Ibid.* p. 397.

We meet in these proceedings with the account of two Hindoos who had set up as gods, *Dulol* and *Ram Dass.* The missionaries, conceiving this schism from the religion of the Hindoos to be a very favourable opening for them, wait upon the two deities. With Dulol, who seems to have been a very shrewd fellow, they are utterly unsuccessful; and the following is an extract from the account of their conference with Ram Dass:—

"After much altercation, I told him he might put the matter out of all doubt as to himself; he had only to come as a poor, repenting, suppliant sinner, and he would be saved, whatever became of *others.* To this he gave no other answer than a smile of contempt. I then asked him in what way the sins of these his fol lowers would be removed; urging it as a matter of the last importance, as he knew that they were all sinners, and must stand before the righteous bar of God? After much evasion, he replied that he had fire in his belly, which would destroy the sins of all his followers."—*Bapt. Miss.* Vol. II. p. 401.

A Brahmin Converted.

"*Dec.* 11. *Lord's day.* A Brahmin came from Nuddea. After talking with him about the gospel, which he said he was very willing to embrace, we sent him to Kristno's. He ate with them without hesitation, but discovered such a thirst for Bengalee rum, as gave them a disgust."

"*Dec.* 13. This morning *the Brahmin decamped suddenly*."—*Bapt. Miss.* Vol. II. p. 424.

Extent of Printing.

"*Sept.* 12. We are building an addition to our printing office, where we employ seventeen printers and five book-binders. The Brahmin from near Bootan gives some hope that he has received the truth in love."—*Ibid.* p. 483

"The news of Jesus Christ, and of the church at Serampore, seems to have gone much further than I expected; it appears to be known to a few in most villages."—*Ibid.* p. 487.

Hatred to the Gospel.

"The caste (says Mr. W.) is the great millstone round the necks of these people. Roteen wants shaving; but the barber here will not do it. He is run away lest he should be compelled. He says he will not shave Yesoo Kreest's people!"—*Ibid.* p. 493.

Success greater by importunity in prayer.

"With respect to their *success*, there are several particulars attending it worthy of notice. One is, *that it was preceded by a spirit of importunate prayer*. The brethren had all along committed their cause to God; but in the autumn of 1800, they had a special weekly prayer-meeting for a blessing on the work of the mission. At these assemblies, Mr. Thomas, who was then present on a visit, seems to have been more than usually strengthened to wrestle for a blessing; and writing to a friend in America, he speaks of 'the holy unction appearing on *all the missionaries*, especially of late; and of times of refreshing from the presence of the Lord, being solemn, frequent and lasting.' In connecting these things, we cannot but remember that previous to the outpouring of the Spirit in the days of Pentecost, the disciples 'continued with one accord in prayer and supplication.'"—*Bapt. Miss. Pref.* Vol. III. p. vii.

What this success is, we shall see by the following extract:

"The whole number baptized in Bengal since the year 1795, is *forty-eight*. Over many of these we rejoice with great joy; for others we tremble; and over some we are compelled to weep."—*Bapt. Miss.* Vol. III. p. 21, 22.

Hatred to the Gospel.

"*April* 2. This morning, several of our chief printing servants presented a petition, desiring they might have some relief, as they were compelled, in our Bengalee worship, to hear so many blasphemies against their gods! Brother Carey and I had a strong contention with them in the printing-office, and invited them to argue the point with Petumber, as his sermon had given them offence; but they declined it though we told them that they were ten, and he was only one; that they were Brahmins, and he was only a sooder!"—*Ibid.* p. 36.

"The enmity against the gospel and its professors is universal. One of our baptized Hindoos wanted to rent a house: after going out two or three days, and wandering all the town over, he at last persuaded a woman to let him have a house: but though she was herself a Feringa, yet when she heard that he was a Brahmin who had become a Christian, she insulted him, and drove him away: so that we are indeed made the offscouring of all things."—*Ibid.* p. 38.

"I was sitting among our native brethren, at the Bengalee school, hearing them read and explain a portion of the word in turn, when an aged, gray-headed Brahmin, well-dressed, came in; and standing before me, said, with joined hands, and a supplicating tone of voice, 'Sahib! I am come to ask an alms." Beginning to weep, he repeated these words hastily; 'I am come to ask ... an alms.' He continued standing, with his hands in a supplicating posture, weeping. I desired him to say what alms; and told him, that by his looks, it did not seem as if he wanted any relief. At length, being pressed, he asked me to give him his son, pointing with his hand into the midst of our native brethren. I asked him which was his son? He pointed to a young Brahmin, named Soroop; and setting up a plaintive cry, said, that was his son. We tried to comfort him, and at last prevailed upon him to come and sit down upon the veranda. Here he began to weep again; and said that the young man's mother was dying with grief."—*Bapt. Miss.* Vol. III. p. 43.

"This evening Buxoo, a brother, who is servant with us, and Soroop, went to a market in the neighbourhood, where they were discovered to be *Yesoo Khreestare Loke* (Jesus Christ's people). The whole market was in a hubbub: they clapped their hands, and threw dust at them. Buxoo was changing a rupee for cowries, when the disturbance began; and in the scuffle, the man ran away with the rupee without giving the cowries."—*Ibid.* p. 55.

"*Nov.* 24. This day Hawnye and Ram Khunt returned from their village. They relate that our brother Fotick, who lives in the same village, was lately seized by the chief Bengalee man there; dragged from his house; his face, eyes and ears clogged with cow-dung—his hands tied—and in this state confined several hours. They also tore to pieces all the papers, and the copy of the Testament, which they found in Fotick's house. A relation of these persecutors being dead, they did not molest Hawnye and Ram Khunt; but the townsfolk would not hear about the gospel: they only insulted them for becoming Christians."—*Ibid.* p. 57.

"*Cutwa on the Ganges, Sept.* 3, 1804. This place is about seventy miles from Serampore, by the Hoogley river. Here I procured a spot of ground, perhaps about two acres, pleasantly situated by two tanks, and a fine grove of man-go trees, at a small distance from the town. It was with difficulty I procured a spot. I was forced to leave one, after I had made a beginning, through the violent opposition of the people. Coming to this, opposition ceased; and therefore I called it Rehoboth; for Jehovah hath made room for us. Here I have raised a spacious bungalo."—*Ibid.* p. 59.

It would perhaps be more prudent to leave the question of sending missions to India to the effect of these extracts, which appear to us to be quite decisive, both as to the danger of insurrection from the prosecution of the scheme, the utter unfitness of the persons employed in it, and the complete hopelessness of the attempt while pursued under such circumstances as now exist. But, as the Evangelical party who have got possession of our eastern empire have brought forward a great deal of argument upon the question, it may be necessary to make it some sort of reply.

We admit it to be the general duty of Christian people to disseminate their religion among the pagan nations who are subjected to their empire. It is true they have not the aid of miracles; but it is their duty to attempt such conversion by the earnest and abundant employment of the best human means in their power. We believe that we are in possession of a revealed religion; that we are exclusively in possession of a revealed religion; and that the possession of that religion can alone confer immortality, and best confer present happiness. This religion, too, teaches us the duty of general benevolence: and how, under such a system, the conversion of heathens can be a matter of indifference, we profess not to be able to understand.

So much for the general rule:—now for the exceptions.

No man (not an Anabaptist) will, we presume, contend that it is our duty to preach the natives into an insurrection, or to lay before them, so fully and emphatically, the scheme of the gospel, as to make them rise up in the dead of the night and shoot their instructors through the head. If conversion be the greatest of all objects, the possession of the country to be converted is the only mean, in this instance, by which that conversion can be accomplished; for we have no right to look for a miraculous conversion of the Hindoos; and it would be little short of a miracle, if General *Oudinot* was to display the same spirit as the *serious* part of the Directors of the East India Company. Even for missionary purposes, therefore, the utmost discretion is necessary; and if we wish to teach the natives a better religion, we must take care to do it in a manner which will not inspire them with a passion for political change, or we shall inevitably lose our disciples altogether. To us it appears quite clear, from the extracts before us, that neither Hindoo nor Mahomedan is at all indifferent to the attacks made upon his religion; the arrogance and the irritability of the Mahomedan are universally acknowledged; and we put it to our readers, whether the Brahmins seem in these extracts to show the smallest disposition to behold the encroachments upon their religion with passiveness and unconcern. A missionary who converted only a few of the refuse of society, might live for ever in peace in India, and receive his salary from his fanatical masters for pompous predictions of universal conversion, transmitted by the ships of the season; but, if he had any marked success among the natives, it could not fail to excite much more dangerous specimens of jealousy and discontent than those which we have extracted from the Anabaptist Journal. How is it in human nature that a Brahmin should be indifferent to encroachments upon his religion? His reputation, his dignity, and in great measure his wealth, depend upon the preservation of the present superstitions; and why is it to be supposed that motives which are so powerful with all other human beings, are inoperative with him alone? If the Brahmins, however, are disposed to excite a rebellion in support of their own influence, no man, who knows any thing of India, can doubt that they have it in their power to effect it.

It is in vain to say, that these attempts to diffuse Christianity do not originate from the government in India. The omnipotence of government in the East is well known to the natives. If government does not prohibit, it tolerates; if it tolerates the conversion of the natives, the suspicion may be easily formed that it encourages that conversion. If the Brahmins do not believe this themselves, they may easily persuade the common people that such is the fact; nor are there wanting, besides the activity of these new missionaries, many other circumstances to corroborate such a rumor. Under the auspices of the College at Fort William, the Scriptures are in a course of translation into the languages of almost the whole continent of Oriental India, and we perceive, that in aid of this object the Bible Society has voted a very magnificent subscription. The three principal chaplains of our Indian settlements are (as might be expected) of principles exactly corresponding with the enthusiasm of their employers at home; and their zeal upon the subject of religion has shone and burnt with the most exemplary fury. These circumstances, if they do not really impose upon the minds of the leading natives, may give them a very powerful handle for misrepresenting the intentions of government to the lower orders.

We see from the massacre of Vellore, what a powerful engine attachment to religion may be rendered in Hindostan. The rumors might all have been false; but that event shows they were tremendously powerful when excited. The object, therefore, is not only not to do any thing violent and unjust upon subjects of religion, but not to give any stronger colour to jealous and disaffected natives for misrepresenting your intentions.

All these observations have tenfold force when applied to an empire which rests so entirely upon opinion. If physical force could be called in to stop the progress of error, we could afford to be misrepresented for a season; but 30,000 white men living in the midst of 70 million sable subjects, must be always in the right, or at least never represented as grossly in the wrong. Attention to the prejudices of the subject is wise in all governments, but quite indispensable in a government constituted as our empire in India is constituted; where an uninterrupted series of dexterous conduct is not only necessary to our prosperity, but to our existence.

These reasonings are entitled to a little more consideration, at a period when the French threaten our existence in India by open force, and by every species of intrigue with the native powers. In all governments, every thing takes its tone from the head; fanaticism has got into the government at home; fanaticism will lead to promotion abroad. The civil servant in India will not only not dare to exercise his own judgment, in checking the indiscretions of ignorant missionaries; but he will strive to recommend himself to his holy masters in Leadenhall Street, by imitating Brother Cran and Brother Ringletaube, and by every species of fanatical excess. Methodism at home is no unprofitable game to play. In the East it will soon be the infallible road to promotion. This is the great evil; if the management was in the hands of men who were as discreet and wise in their devotion as they are in matters of temporal welfare, the desire of putting an end to missions might be premature and indecorous. But the misfortune is, the men who wield the instrument, ought not, in common sense and propriety, to be trusted with it for a single instant. Upon this subject, they are quite insane and ungovernable; they would deliberately, piously, and conscientiously expose our whole Eastern empire to destruction, for the sake of converting half a dozen Brahmins, who, after stuffing themselves with rum and rice, and borrowing money from the missionaries, would run away and cover the gospel and its possessors with every species of impious ridicule and abuse.

Upon the whole, it appears to us hardly possible to push the business of proselytism in India to any length without incurring the utmost risk of losing our empire. The danger is more tremendous, because it may be so sudden; religious fears are very probable causes of disaffection in the troops; if the troops are generally disaffected, our Indian empire may be lost to us as suddenly as a frigate or a fort; and that empire is governed by men who, we are very much afraid, would feel proud to lose it in such a cause.

"But I think it my duty to make a solemn appeal to all who still retain the fear of God, and who admit that religion and the course of conduct which it prescribes are not to be banished from the affairs of nations—now when the political sky, so long overcast, has become more lowering and black than ever—whether this is a period for augmenting the weight of our national sins and provocations, by an *exclusive* TOLERATION *of idolatry;* a crime which, unless the Bible be a forgery, has actually drawn forth the heaviest denunciations of vengeance, and the most fearful inflictions of Divine displeasure."—*Considerations, &c.* p. 98.

Can it be credited that this is an extract from a pamphlet generally supposed to be written by a noble Lord at the Board of Control, from whose official interference the public might have expected a corrective to the pious temerity of others?

The other leaders of the party, indeed, make at present great professions of toleration, and express the strongest abhorence of using violence to the natives. This does very well for a beginning; but we have little confidence in such declarations. We believe their fingers itch to be at the stone and clay gods of the Hindoos; and that, in common with the noble Controller, they attribute a great part of our national calamities to these ugly images of deities on the one side of the world. We again repeat, that upon such subjects, the best and ablest men, if once tinged by fanaticism, are *not to be trusted for a single moment.*

2dly, Another reason for giving up the task of conversion, is the want of success. In India, religion extends its empire over the minutest actions of life. It is not merely a law for moral conduct, and for occasional worship; but it dictates to a man his trade, his dress, his food, and his whole behaviour. His religion also punishes a violation of its exactions, not by eternal and future punishments, but by present infamy. If an Hindoo is irreligious, or, in other words, if he loses his caste, he is deserted by father, mother, wife, child, and kindred, and becomes instantly a solitary wanderer upon the earth; to touch him, to receive him, to eat with him, is a pollution producing a similar loss of caste; and the state of such a degraded man is worse than death itself. To these evils an Hindoo must expose himself before he becomes a Christian; and this difficulty must a missionary overcome, before he can expect the smallest success; a difficulty which, it is quite clear, they themselves, after a short residence in India, consider to be insuperable.

As a proof of the tenacious manner, in which the Hindoos cling to their religious prejudices, we shall state two or three very short anecdotes, to which any person who has resided in India might easily produce many parallels.

"In the year 1766, the late Lord Clive and Mr. Verelst employed the whole influence of Government to restore a Hindoo to his caste, who had forfeited it, not by any neglect of his own, but by having been compelled, by a most unpardonable act of violence, to swallow a drop of cow broth. The Brahmins, from the peculiar circumstances of the case, were very anxious to comply with the wishes of Government; the principal men among them met once at Kishnagur, and once at Calcutta; but after consultations, and an examination of their most ancient records, they declared to Lord Clive, that as there was no precedent to justify the act, they found it *impossible* to restore the unfortunate man to his caste, and he died soon after of a broken heart."—*Scott Waring's Preface*, p. lvi.

It is the custom of the Hindoos to expose dying people upon the banks of the Ganges. There is something peculiarly holy in that river; and it soothes the agonies of death to look upon its waters in the last moments. A party of English were coming down in a boat, and perceived upon the bank a pious Hindoo, in a state of the last imbecility—about to be drowned by the rising of the tide, after the most approved and orthodox manner of their religion. They had the curiosity to land; and as they perceived some more signs of life than were at first apparent, a young Englishman poured down his throat the greatest part of a bottle of lavender water, which he happened to have in his pocket. The effects of such a stimulus, applied to a stomach accustomed to nothing stronger than water, were instantaneous and powerful. The Hindoo revived sufficiently to admit of his being conveyed to the boat, was carried to Calcutta, and perfectly recovered. He had drunk, however, in the company of Europeans;—no matter whether voluntary or involuntary,—the offence was committed: he lost caste, was turned away from his home, and avoided, of course, by every relation and friend. The poor man came before the police, making the bitterest complaints upon being restored to life; and for three years the burden of supporting him fell upon the mistaken Samaritan who had rescued him from death. During that period, scarcely a day elapsed in which the degraded resurgent did not appear before the European, and curse him with the bitterest curses—as the cause of all his misery and desolation. At the end of that period he fell ill, and of course was not again thwarted in his passion for dying. The writer of this article vouches for the truth of this anecdote; and many persons who were at Calcutta at the time must have a distinct recollection of the fact, which excited a great deal of conversation and amusement, mingled with compassion.

It is this institution of castes which has preserved India in the same state in which it existed in the days of Alexander; and which would leave it without the slightest change in habits and manners, if we were to abandon the country to-morrow. We are astonished to observe the *late resident* in Bengal speaking of the fifteen millions of Mahomedans in India as converts from the Hindoos; an opinion, in support of which he does not offer the shadow of an argument, except by asking, whether the Mahomedans have the Tartar face? and if not, how they can be the descendants of the first conquerors of India? Probably not altogether. But does this writer imagine, that the Mahomedan empire could exist in Hindostan for 700 years without the intrusion of Persians, Arabians, and every species of Mussulmen adventurers from every part of the East, which had embraced the religion of Mahomed? And let them come from what quarter they would, could they ally themselves to Hindoo women without producing in their descendants an approximation to the Hindoo features? Dr. Robertson, who has investigated this subject with the greatest care, and looked into all the authorities, is expressly of an opposite opinion; and considers the Mussulman inhabitants of Hindostan to be merely the descendants of Mahomedan adventurers, and not converts from the Hindoo faith.

"The armies" (says Orme) "which made the first conquests for the heads of the respective dynasties, or for other invaders, left behind them numbers of Mahomedans, who, seduced by a finer climate, and a richer country, forgot their own.

"The Mahomedan princes of India naturally gave a preference to the service of men of their own religion, who, from whatever country they came, were of a more vigorous constitution than the stoutest of the subjected nation. This preference has continually encouraged adventurers from Tartary, Persia, and Arabia, to seek their fortunes under a government from which they were sure of receiving greater encouragement than they could expect at home. From these origins, time has formed in India a mighty nation of near ten millions of Mahomedans."—*Orme's Indostan*, I. p. 24.

Precisely similar to this is the opinion of Dr. Robertson, Note xl.—*Indian Disquisition.*

As to the religion of the Ceylonese, from which the Bengal *resident* would infer the facility of making converts of the Hindoos, it is to be observed, that the religion of Boudhou, in ancient times, extended from the north of Tartary to Ceylon, from the Indus to Siam, and (if Foe and Boudhou are the same persons) over China. That of the two religions of Boudhou and Bramá, the one was the parent of the other, there can be very little doubt; but the comparative antiquity of the two is so very disputed a point, that it is quite unfair to state the case of the Ceylonese as an instance of conversion from the Hindoo religion to any other: and even if the religion of Bramá is the most ancient of the two, it is still to be proved, that the Ceylonese professed that religion before they changed it for their present faith. In point of fact, however, the boasted Christianity of the Ceylonese is proved by the testimony of the missionaries themselves, to be little better than nominal. The following extract from one of their own communications, dated Columbo, 1805, will set this matter in its true light:—

"The elders, deacons, and some of the members of the Dutch congregation, came to see us, and we paid them a visit in return, and made a little inquiry concerning the state of the church on this island, which is, in one word, *miserable!* One hundred thousand of those who are called Christians (because they are baptized) need not go back to heathenism, for *they never have been any thing else but heathens*, worshippers of Budda: they have been induced, for worldly reasons, to be baptized. O Lord have mercy on the poor inhabitants of this populous island!" —*Trans. Miss. Soc.* II. 265.

What success the Syrian Christians had in making converts; in what degree they have gained their numbers by victories over the native superstition, or lost their original numbers by the idolatrous examples to which for so many centuries they have been exposed; are points wrapt up in so much obscurity, that no kind of inference, as to the facility of converting the natives, can be drawn from them. Their present number is supposed to be about 150,000.

It would be of no use to quote the example of Japan and China, even if the progress of the faith in these empires had been much greater than it is. We do not say it is difficult to convert the Japanese, or the Chinese; but the

Hindoos. We are not saying it is difficult to convert human creatures; but difficult to convert human creatures with such institutions. To mention the example of other nations who have them not, is to pass over the material objection, and to answer others which are merely imaginary, and have never been made.

3dly, The duty of conversion is less plain, and less imperious, when conversion exposes the convert to great present misery. An African or an Otaheite proselyte might not perhaps be less honoured by his countrymen if he became a Christian; an Hindoo is instantly subjected to the most perfect degradation. A change of faith might increase the immediate happiness of any other individual; it annihilates for ever all the *human* comforts which an Hindoo enjoys. The eternal happiness which you proffer him, is therefore less attractive to him than to any other heathen, from the life of misery by which he purchases it.

Nothing is more precarious than our empire in India. Suppose we were to be driven out of it to-morrow, and to leave behind us twenty thousand converted Hindoos, it is most probable they would relapse into heathenism; but their original station in society could not be regained. The duty of making converts, therefore, among such a people, as it arises from the general duty of benevolence, is less strong than it would be in many other cases; because, situated as we are, it is quite certain we shall expose them to a great deal of misery, and not quite certain we shall do them any future good.

4thly, Conversion is no duty at all, if it merely destroys the old religion, without really and effectually teaching the new one. Brother Ringletaube may write home that he makes a Christian, when, in reality, he ought only to state that he has destroyed an Hindoo. Foolish and imperfect as the religion of an *Hindoo* is, it is at least some restraint upon the intemperance of human passions. It is better a Brahmin should be respected, than that nobody should be respected. An Hindoo had better believe that a deity with an hundred legs and arms, will reward and punish him hereafter, than that he is not to be punished at all. Now, when you have destroyed the faith of an Hindoo, are you quite sure that you will graft upon his mind fresh principles of action, and make him any more than a nominal Christian?

You have 30,000 Europeans in India, and 60 millions of other subjects. If proselytism were to go on as rapidly as the most visionary Anabaptist could dream or desire, in what manner are these people to be taught the genuine truths and practices of Christianity? Where are the clergy to come from? Who is to defray the expense of the establishment? and who can foresee the immense and perilous difficulties of bending the laws, manners, and institutions of a country to the dictates of a new religion? If it were easy to persuade the Hindoos that their own religion was folly, it would be indefinitely difficult effectually to teach them any other. They would tumble their own idols into the river, and you would build them no churches: you would destroy all their present motives for doing right and avoiding wrong, without being able to fix upon their minds the more sublime motives by which you profess to be actuated. What a missionary will do hereafter with the heart of a convert, is a matter of doubt and speculation. He is quite certain, however, that he must accustom the man to see himself considered infamous; and good principles can hardly be exposed to a ruder shock. Whoever has seen much of Hindoo Christians must have perceived, that the man who bears that name is very commonly nothing more than a drunken reprobate, who conceives himself at liberty to eat and drink anything he pleases, and annexes hardly any other meaning to the name of Christianity. Such sort of converts may swell the list of names, and gratify the puerile pride of a missionary; but what real, discreet Christian can wish to see such Christianity prevail? But it will be urged, if the present converts should become worse Hindoos, and very indifferent Christians, still the next generation will do better; and by degrees, and at the expiration of half a century, or a century, true Christianity may prevail. We may apply to such sort of Jacobin converters what Mr. Burke said of the Jacobin politicians in his time,—"To such men a whole generation of human beings are of no more consequence than a frog in an air-pump." For the distant prospect of doing what most probably after all, they will never be able to effect, there is no degree of present misery and horror to which they will not expose the subjects of their experiment.

As the duty of making proselytes springs from the duty of benevolence, there is a priority of choice in conversion. The greatest zeal should plainly be directed to the most desperate misery and ignorance. Now, in comparison to many other nations who are equally ignorant of the truths of Christianity, the Hindoos are a civilized and a moral people. That they have remained in the same state for so many centuries, is at once a proof that the institutions which established that state could not be highly unfavourable to human happiness. After all that has been said of the vices of the Hindoos, we believe that an Hindoo is more mild and sober than most Europeans, and as honest and chaste. In astronomy the Hindoos have certainly made very high advances;—some, and not an unimportant progress in many sciences. As manufacturers, they are extremely ingenious—and as agriculturists, industrious. Christianity would improve them; (whom would it not improve?) but if Christianity cannot be extended to all, there are many other nations who want it more.*

The Hindoos have some very savage customs, which it would be desirable to abolish. Some swing on hooks, some run knives through their hands, and widows burn themselves to death: but these follies (even the last) are quite voluntary on the part of the sufferers. We dislike all misery, voluntary or involuntary; but the difference between the torments which a man chooses, and those which he endures from

* We are here, of course, arguing the question only in a worldly point of view. This is one point of view in which it must be placed, though certainly the lowest and least important.

the choice of others, is very great. It is a considerable wretchedness that men and women should be shut up in religious houses; but it is only an object of legislative interference, when such incarceration is compulsory. Monasteries and nunneries with us would be harmless institutions; because the moment a devotee found he had acted like a fool, he might avail himself of the discovery and run away; and so may an Hindoo, if he repents of his resolution of running hooks into his flesh.

The duties of conversion appear to be of less importance, when it is impossible to procure proper persons to undertake them, and when such religious embassies, in consequence, devolve upon the lowest of the people. Who wishes to see scrofula and atheism cured by a single sermon in Bengal? who wishes to see the religious hoy riding at anchor in the Hoogly river? or shoals of jumpers exhibiting their nimble piety before the learned Brahmins of Benares? This madness is disgusting and dangerous enough at home:—Why are we to send out little detachments of maniacs to spread over the fine regions of the world the most unjust and contemptible opinion of the gospel? The wise and rational part of the Christian ministry find they have enough to do at home to combat with passions unfavourable to human happiness, and to make men act up to their professions. But if a tinker is a devout man, he infallibly sets off for the East. Let any man read the Anabaptist missions:—can he do so without deeming such men pernicious and extravagant in their own country,—and without feeling that they are benefiting us much more by their absence, than the Hindoos by their advice?

It is somewhat strange, in a duty which is stated by one party to be so clear and so indispensable, that no man of moderation and good sense can be found to perform it. And if no other instruments remain but visionary enthusiasts, some doubt may be honestly raised whether it is not better to drop the scheme entirely.

Shortly stated, then, our argument is this:—We see not the slightest prospect of success;—we see much danger in making the attempt;—and we doubt if the conversion of the Hindoos would ever be more than nominal. If it is a duty of general benevolence to convert the Heathen, it is less a duty to convert the Hindoos than any other people, because they are already highly civilized, and because you must infallibly subject them to infamy and present degradation. The instruments employed for these purposes are calculated to bring ridicule and disgrace upon the gospel; and in the discretion of those at home, whom we consider as their patrons, we have not the smallest reliance; but, on the contrary, we are convinced they would behold the loss of our Indian empire, not with the humility of men convinced of erroneous views and projects, but with the pride, the exultation, and the alacrity of martyrs.

Of the books which have handled this subject on either side, we have little to say. Major Scott Waring's book is the best against the Missions; but he wants arrangement and prudence. The late resident writes well; but is miserably fanatical towards the conclusion. Mr. Cunningham has been diligent in looking into books upon the subject: and though an *evangelical* gentleman, is not uncharitable to those who differ from him in opinion. There is a passage in the publication of his reverend brother, Mr. Owen, which, had we been less accustomed than we have been of late to this kind of writing, would appear to be quite incredible.

"I have not pointed out the comparative indifference, upon Mr. Twining's principles, between one religion and another, to the welfare of a people; nor the impossibility, on those principles, of India being Christianized by any human means, so long as it shall remain under the dominion of the Company; nor *the alternative to which Providence is by consequence reduced, of either giving up that country to everlasting superstition, or of working some miracle in order to accomplish its conversion.*"—*Owen's Address*, p. 28.

This is really beyond any thing we ever remember to have read. The hoy, the cock-fight, and the religious newspaper, are pure reason when compared to it. The idea of *reducing Providence to an alternative!!* and, by a motion at the India House, carried by ballot! We would not insinuate, in the most distant manner, that Mr. Owen is not a gentleman of the most sincere piety; but the misfortune is, all extra superfine persons accustom themselves to a familiar phraseology upon the most sacred subjects, which is quite shocking to the common and inferior orders of Christians. *Providence reduced to an alternative!!!!!* Let it be remembered, this phrase comes from a member of a religious party, who are loud in their complaints of being confounded with enthusiasts and fanatics.

We cannot conclude without the most pointed reprobation of the low mischief of the Christian Observer; a publication which appears to have no other method of discussing a question fairly open to discussion, than that of accusing their antagonists of infidelity. No art can be more unmanly, or, if its consequences are foreseen, more wicked. If this publication had been the work of a single individual, we might have passed it over in silent disgust; but as it is looked upon as the organ of a great political religious party in this country, we think it right to notice the very unworthy manner in which they are attempting to extend their influence. For ourselves, if there were a fair prospect of carrying the gospel into regions where it was before unknown,—if such a project did not expose the best possessions of the country to extreme danger, and if it was in the hands of men who were discreet, as well as devout, we should consider it to be a scheme of true piety, benevolence, and wisdom: but the baseness and malignity of fanaticism shall never prevent us from attacking its arrogance, its ignorance, and its activity. For what vice can be more tremendous than that which, while it wears the outward appearance of religion, destroys the happiness of man, and dishonours the name of God?

CATHOLICS.*

[Edinburgh Review, 1808.]

The various publications which have issued from the press in favour of religious liberty, have now nearly silenced the arguments of their opponents; and, teaching sense to some, and inspiring others with shame, have left those only on the field who can neither learn nor blush.

But, though *the argument* is given up, and the justice of the Catholic cause admitted, it seems to be generally conceived, that their case, at present, is utterly hopeless; and that, to advocate it any longer, will only irritate the oppressed, without producing any change of opinion in those by whose influence and authority that oppression is continued. To this opinion, unfortunately too prevalent, we have many reasons for not subscribing.

We do not understand what is meant in this country by the notion, that a measure, of consummate wisdom and imperious necessity, is to be deferred for any time, or to depend upon any contingency. Whenever it can be made clear to the understanding of the great mass of enlightened people, that any system of political conduct is necessary to the public welfare, every obstacle (as it ought) will be swept away before it; and as we conceive it to be by no means improbable, that the country may, ere long, be placed in a situation where its safety or ruin will depend upon its conduct towards the Catholics, we sincerely believe we are doing our duty in throwing every possible light on this momentous question. Neither do we understand where this passive submission to ignorance and error is to end. Is it confined to religion? or does it extend to war and peace, as well as religion? Would it be tolerated, if any man were to say, "Abstain from all arguments in favour of peace; the court have resolved upon eternal war; and, as you cannot have peace, to what purpose urge the necessity of it?" We answer,—that courts must be presumed to be open to the influence of reason; or, if they were not, to the influence of prudence and discretion, when they perceive the public opinion to be loudly and clearly against them. To lie by in timid and indolent silence,—to *suppose* an inflexibility, in which no court ever could, under pressing circumstances, persevere—and to neglect a regular and vigorous appeal to public opinion, is to give up all chance of doing good, and to abandon the only instrument by which the few are ever prevented from ruining the many.

It is folly to talk of any other *ultimatum* in government than perfect justice to the fair claims of the subject. The concessions to the Irish Catholics in 1792 were to be the *ne plus ultra*. Every engine was set on foot to induce the grand juries in Ireland to petition against further concessions; and, in six months afterwards, government were compelled to introduce, themselves, those further relaxations of the penal code, of which they had just before assured the Catholics they must abandon all hope. Such is the absurdity of supposing that a few interested and ignorant individuals can postpone, at their pleasure and caprice, the happiness of millions.

As to the feeling of irritation with which such continued discussion may inspire the Irish Catholics, we are convinced that no opinion could be so prejudicial to the cordial union which we hope may always subsist between the two countries, as that all the efforts of the Irish were unavailing,—that argument was hopeless,—that their case was prejudged with a sullen inflexibility which circumstances could not influence, pity soften, or reason subdue.

We are by no means convinced, that the decorous silence recommended upon the Catholic question would be rewarded by those future concessions, of which many persons appear to be so certain. We have a strange incredulity where persecution is to be abolished, and any class of men restored to their indisputable rights. When we see it done, we will believe it. Till it is done, we shall always consider it to be highly improbable—much too improbable—to justify the smallest relaxation in the Catholics themselves, or in those who are well-wishers to their cause. When the fanciful period at present assigned for the emancipation arrives, new scruples may arise—fresh forbearance be called for—and the operations of common sense be deferred for another generation. Toleration never had a present tense, nor taxation a future one. The answer which Paul received from Felix, he owed to the subject on which he spoke. When justice and righteousness were his theme, Felix told him to go away, and he would hear him some other time. All men who have spoken to courts upon such disagreeable topics, have received the same answer. Felix, however, trembled when he gave it; but his fear was ill-directed. He trembled at the subject—he ought to have trembled at the delay.

Little or nothing is to be expected from the shame of deferring what it is so wicked and perilous to defer. Profligacy in taking office is so extreme, that we have no doubt public men may be found, who, for half a century, would postpone all remedies for a *pestilence*, if the preservation of their places depended upon the propagation of the virus. To us, such kind of conduct conveys no other action than that of sordid avaricious impudence:—it puts to sale the best interests of the country for some improvement in the wines and meats and carriages which a

* *History of the Penal Laws against the Irish Catholics, from the Treaty of Limerick to the Union.* By Henry Parnell Esq. M.P.

man uses,—and encourages a new political morality which may always postpone any other great measure—and every other great measure as well as the emancipation of the Catholics.

We terminate this apologetical preamble with expressing the most earnest hope that the Catholics will not, from any notion that their cause is effectually carried, relax in any one constitutional effort necessary to their purpose. Their cause is the cause of common sense and justice;—the safety of England and of the world may depend upon it. It rests upon the soundest principles; leads to the most important consequences; and therefore cannot be too frequently brought before the notice of the public.

The book before us is written by Mr. Henry Parnell, the brother of Mr. William Parnell, author of the Historical Apology, reviewed in one of our late numbers; and it contains a very well written history of the penal laws enacted against the Irish Catholics, from the peace of Limerick, in the reign of King William, to the late Union. Of these we shall present a very short, and, we hope even to loungers, a readable abstract.

The war carried on in Ireland against King William cannot deserve the name of a rebellion: it was a struggle for their lawful Prince, whom they had sworn to maintain; and whose zeal for the Catholic religion, whatever effect it might have produced in England, could not by them be considered as a crime. This war was terminated by the surrender of Limerick, upon conditions by which the Catholics hoped, and very rationally hoped, to secure to themselves the free enjoyment of their religion in future, and an exemption from all those civil penalties and incapacities which the reigning creed is so fond of heaping upon its subjugated rivals.

By the various articles of this treaty, they are to enjoy such privileges in the exercise of their religion, as they did enjoy in the time of Charles II.: and the King promises upon the meeting of Parliament, "to endeavor to procure for them such *further security* in that particular, as may preserve them *from any disturbance* on account of their said religion." They are to be restored to their estates, privileges, and immunities, as they enjoyed them in the time of Charless II. The gentlemen are to be allowed to carry arms; and no other oath is to be tendered to the Catholics who submit to King William than the oath of allegiance. These and other articles, *King William ratifies for himself, his heirs and successors, as far as in him lies; and confirms the same, and every other clause and matter therein contained.*

These articles were signed by the English general on the 3d of October, 1691; and diffused comfort, confidence, and tranquillity among the Catholics. On the 22d of October, the English Parliament excluded Catholics from the Irish Houses of Lords and Commons, by compelling them to take the oaths of supremacy before admission.

In 1695, the Catholics were deprived of all means of educating their children, at home or abroad, and of the privilege of being guardians to their own or to other persons' children. Then all the Catholics were disarmed,—and then all the priests banished. *After this* (probably by way of joke), an act was passed to *confirm* the treaty of Limerick,—the great and glorious King William totally forgetting the contract he had entered into of recommending the religious liberties of the Catholics to the attention of Parliament.

On the 4th of March, 1704, it was enacted, that any son of a Catholic who would turn Protestant, should succeed to the family estate, which from that moment could no longer be sold, or charged with debt and legacy. On the same day, Popish fathers were debarred, by a penalty of 500*l*., from being guardians to their own children. If the child, however young, declared himself a Protestant, he was to be delivered immediately to the custody of some Protestant relation. No Protestant to marry a Papist. No Papist to purchase land, or take a lease of land for more than thirty-one years. If the profits of the lands so leased by the Catholics amounted to above a certain rate settled by the act,—*farm to belong to the first Protestant who made the discovery*. No Papist to be in a line of entail; but the estate to pass on to the next Protestant heir, as if the Papist were dead. If a Papist dies intestate, and no Protestant heir can be found, property to be equally divided among all the sons; or, if he has none, among all the daughters. By the 16th clause of this bill, no Papist to hold any office civil or military. Not to dwell in Limerick or Galway, except on certain conditions. Not to vote at elections. Not to hold advowsons.

In 1709, Papists were prevented from holding an annuity for life. If any son of a Papist chose to turn Protestant, and enrol the certificate of his conversion in the Court of Chancery, that court is empowered to compel his father to state the value of his property upon oath, and to make out of that property a competent allowance to the son, at their own discretion, not only for his present maintenance, but for his future portion after the death of his father. An increase of jointure to be enjoyed by Papist wives upon their conversion. Papists keeping schools to be prosecuted as convicts. Popish priests who are converted, to receive 30*l*. *per annum*.

Rewards are given by the same act for the discovery of the Popish clergy;—50*l*. for discovering a Popish bishop; 20*l*. for a common Popish clergyman; 10*l*. for a Popish usher. Two justices of the peace can compel any Papist above eighteen years of age to disclose every particular which has come to his knowledge respecting Popish priests, celebration of mass, or Papist schools. Imprisonment for a year if he refuses to answer. Nobody can hold property in trust for a Catholic. Juries, in all trials growing out of these statutes, to be Protestants. No Papist to take more than two apprentices, except in the linen trade. All the Catholic clergy to give in their names and places of abode at the quarter-sessions, and to keep no curates. Catholics not to serve on grand juries. In any trial upon statutes for strengthening the Protestant interest, a Papist juror may be peremptorily challenged.

In the next reign, Popish horses were at

tached, and allowed to be seized for the militia. Papists cannot be either high or petty constables. No Papists to vote at elections. Papists in towns to provide Protestant watchmen;—and not to vote at vestries.

In the reign of George II., Papists were prohibited from being barristers. Barristers and solicitors marrying Papists, considered to be Papists, and subjected to all penalties as such. Persons robbed by privateers, during a war with a Popish prince, to be indemnified by grand jury presentments, and the money to be levied on the *Catholics* only. No Papist to marry a Protestant;—any priest celebrating such a marriage *to be hanged.*

During all this time there was not the slightest rebellion in Ireland.

In 1715 and 1745, while Scotland and the north of England were up in arms, not a man stirred in Ireland; yet the spirit of persecution against the Catholics continued till the 18th of his present Majesty, and then gradually gave way to the increase of knowledge, the humanity of our Sovereign, the abilities of Mr. Grattan, the weakness of England struggling in America, and the dread inspired by the French revolution.

Such is the rapid outline of a code of laws which reflects indelible disgrace upon the English character, and explains but too clearly the cause of that hatred in which the English name has been so long held in Ireland. It would require centuries to efface such an impression; and yet, when we find it fresh, and operating at the end of a few years, we explain the fact by every cause which can degrade the Irish, and by none which can remind us of our own scandalous policy. With the folly and the horror of such a code before our eyes,—with the conviction of recent and domestic history, that mankind are not to be lashed and chained out of their faith,—we are striving to teaze and worry them into a better theology. Heavy oppression is removed; light insults and provocations are retained; the scourge does not fall upon their shoulders, but it sounds in their ears. And this is the conduct we are pursuing, when it is still a great doubt whether this country alone may not be opposed to the united efforts of the whole of Europe. It is really difficult to ascertain which is the most utterly destitute of common sense,—the capricious and arbitrary stop we have made in our concessions to the Catholics, or the precise period we have chosen for this grand effort of obstinate folly.

In whatsoever manner the contest now in agitation on the Continent may terminate, its relation to the emancipation of the Catholics will be very striking. If the Spaniards succeed in establishing their own liberties, and in rescuing Europe from the tyranny under which it at present labours, it will still be contended, within the walls of our own Parliament, that the Catholics cannot fulfil the duties of social life. Venal politicians will still argue that the time is not yet come. Sacred and lay sycophants will still lavish upon the Catholic faith their well-paid abuse, and England still passively submit to such a disgraceful spectacle of ingratitude and injustice. If, on the contrary (as may probably be the case), the Spaniards fall before the numbers and military skill of the French, then are we left alone in the world, without another ray of hope; and compelled to employ against internal disaffection that force which, exalted to its utmost energy, would in all probability prove but barely equal to the external danger by which we should be surrounded. Whence comes it that these things are universally admitted to be true, but looked upon in servile silence by a country hitherto accustomed to make great efforts for its prosperity, safety and independence?

METHODISM.*

[Edinburgh Review, 1809.]

In routing out a nest of consecrated cobblers, and in bringing to light such a perilous heap of trash as we were obliged to work through, in our articles upon the Methodists and Missionaries, we are generally conceived to have rendered an useful service to the cause of rational religion. Every one, however, at all acquainted with the true character of Methodism, must have known the extent of the abuse and misrepresentation to which we exposed ourselves in such a service. All this obloquy, however, we were very willing to encounter, from our conviction of the necessity of exposing and correcting the growing evil of fanaticism. In spite of all misrepresentation, we have ever been, and ever shall be, the sincere friends of sober and rational Christianity. We are quite ready, if any fair opportunity occur, to defend it, to the best of our ability, from the tiger-spring of infidelity; and we are quite determined, if we can prevent such an evil, that it shall not be eaten up by the nasty and numerous vermin of Methodism. For this purpose, we shall proceed to make a few short remarks upon the sacred and silly gentleman before us,—not, certainly, because we feel any sort of anxiety as to the effect of his strictures on our own credit or reputation, but because his direct and articulate defence of the principles and practices which we have condemned, affords us the fairest opportunity of exposing, still more clearly, both the extravagance and the danger of these popular sectaries.

These very impudent people have one ruling canon, which pervades every thing they say and do. *Whoever is unfriendly to Methodism, is an infidel and an atheist.* This reasonable and amiable maxim, repeated, in every form of dulness, and varied in every attitude of malignity, is the sum and substance of Mr. Styles's pamphlet. Whoever wishes to rescue religion from the hands of didactic artisans,—whoever prefers a respectable clergyman for his teacher to a delirious mechanic,—whoever wishes to keep the intervals between churches and lunatic asylums as wide as possible,—all such men, in the estimation of Mr. Styles, are nothing better than open or concealed enemies of Christianity. His catechism is very simple. In what hoy do you navigate? By what shoemaker or carpenter are you instructed? What miracles have you to relate? Do you think it sinful *to reduce Providence to an alternative*, &c. &c. &c. Now, if we were to content ourselves with using to Mr. Styles, while he is dealing about his imputations of infidelity, the uncourtly language which is sometimes applied to those who are little curious about truth or falsehood, what Methodist would think the worse of him for such an attack? Who is there among them that would not glory to lie for the tabernacle? who that would not believe he was pleasing his Maker, by sacrificing truth, justice and common sense, to the interests of his own little chapel, and his own deranged instructor? Something more than contradiction or confutation, therefore, is necessary to discredit those charitable dogmatists, and to diminish their pernicious influence;—and the first accusation against us is, that we have endeavoured to add ridicule to reasoning.

We are a good deal amused, indeed, with the extreme disrelish which Mr. John Styles exhibits to the humour and pleasantry with which he admits the Methodists to have been attacked; but Mr. John Styles should remember, that it is not the practice with destroyers of vermin to allow the little victims a *veto* upon the weapons used against them. If this were otherwise, we should have one set of vermin banishing small-tooth combs; another protesting against mouse-traps; a third prohibiting the finger and thumb; a fourth exclaiming against the intolerable infamy of using soap and water. It is impossible, however, to listen to such pleas. They must all be caught, killed and cracked, in the manner, and by the instruments which are found most efficacious to their destruction; and the more they cry out, the greater plainly is the skill used against them. We are convinced a little laughter will do them more harm than all the arguments in the world. Such men as the author before us cannot understand when they are out-argued; but he has given us a specimen, from his irritability, that he fully comprehends when he has become the object of universal contempt and derision. We agree with him, that ridicule is not exactly the weapon to be used in matters of religion; but the use of it is excusable, when there is no other which can make fools tremble. Besides, he should remember the particular sort of ridicule we have used, which is nothing more than accurate quotation from the Methodists themselves. It is true, that this is the most severe and cutting ridicule to which we could have had recourse; but, whose fault is that?

Nothing can be more disingenuous than tne attacks Mr. Styles has made upon us for our use of Scripture language. *Light and grace* are certainly terms of Scripture. It is not to the words themselves that any ridicule can ever attach. It is from the preposterous application of those words, in the mouths of the most arrogant and ignorant of human beings;—it is from their use in the most trivial, low and familiar scenes of life;—it is from the illiterate and ungrammatical prelacy of Mr. John Styles, that any tinge of ridicule ever is

* *Strictures on two Critiques in the Edinburgh Review, on the Subject of Methodism and Missions; with Remarks on the Influence of Reviews, in general, on Morals and Happiness.* By John Styles. 8vo. London, 1809.

or ever can be imparted to the sacred language of Scripture.

We admit also, with this gentleman, that it would certainly evince the most vulgar and contracted heart, to ridicule any religious opinions, methodistical or otherwise, because they were the opinions of the poor, and were conveyed in the language of the poor. But are we to respect the poor, when they wish to step out of their province, and become the teachers of the land?—when men, whose proper "talk is of bullocks, pretend to have wisdom and understanding," is it not lawful to tell them they have none? An ironmonger is a very respectable man, so long as he is merely an ironmonger,—an admirable man if he is a religious ironmonger; but a great blockhead if he sets up for a bishop or a dean, and lectures upon theology. It is not the poor we have attacked,—but the writing poor, the publishing poor,—the limited arrogance which mistakes its own trumpery sect for the world: nor have we attacked them for want of talent, but for want of modesty, want of sense, and want of true rational religion,—for every fault which Mr. John Styles defends and exemplifies.

It is scarcely possible to reduce the drunken declamations of Methodism to a point, to grasp the wriggling lubricity of these cunning animals, and to fix them in one position. We have said, in our review of the Methodists, that it is extremely wrong to suppose that Providence interferes with special and extraordinary judgments on every trifling occasion of life: that to represent an innkeeper killed for preventing a Methodist meeting, or loud claps of thunder rattling along the heavens, merely to hint to Mr. Scott that he was not to preach at a particular tabernacle in Oxford-road, appeared to us to be blasphemous and mischievous nonsense. With great events, which change the destiny of mankind, we might suppose such interference, the discovery of which, upon every trifling occasion, we considered to be pregnant with very mischievous consequences. To all which Mr. Styles replies, that, with Providence, nothing is great, or nothing little,—nothing difficult, or nothing easy; that a worm and a whale are equal in the estimation of a Supreme Being. But did any human being but a Methodist, and a third or fourth rate Methodist, ever make such a reply to such an argument? We are not talking of what is great or important to Providence, but to us. The creation of a worm or a whale, a Newton or a Styles, are tasks equally easy to Omnipotence. But are they, in their results, equally important to us? The lightning may as easily strike the head of the French emperor, as of an innocent cottager; but we are surely neither impious nor obscure, when we say, that one would be an important interference of Providence, and the other comparatively not so. But it is a loss of time to reply to such trash; it presents no stimulus of difficulty to us, nor would it offer any of novelty to our readers.

To our attack upon the melancholy tendency of Methodism, Mr. Styles replies, "that a man must have studied in the *schools of Hume, Voltaire, and Kotzebue*, who can plead in behalf of the theatre; that, at fashionable ball-rooms and assemblies, seduction is drawn out to a system; that dancing excites the fever of the passions, and raises a delirium too often fatal to innocence and peace; and that, for the poor, instead of the common rough amusements to which they are now addicted, there remain the simple beauties of nature, the gay colours, and scented perfumes of the earth." These are the blessings which the common people have to expect from their Methodistical instructors. They are pilfered of all their money,—shut out from all their dances and country wakes,—and are then sent pennyless into the fields, to gaze on the clouds, and to smell dandelions!

Against the orthodox clergy of all descriptions, our sour devotee proclaims, as was to have been expected, the most implacable war,—declaring that, "*in one century, they would have obliterated all the remaining practical religion in the church, had it not been for this new sect, everywhere spoken against.*" Undoubtedly, the distinction of mankind into godly and ungodly—if by godly is really meant those who apply religion to the extinction of bad passions—would be highly desirable. But when, by that word, is only intended a sect more desirous of possessing the appellation than of deserving it,—when, under that term, are comprehended thousands of canting hypocrites and raving enthusiasts—men despicable from their ignorance, and formidable from their madness,—the distinction may hereafter prove to be truly terrific; and a dynasty of fools may again sweep away both church and state in one hideous ruin. There may be, at present, some very respectable men at the head of these maniacs, who would insanify them with some degree of prudence, and keep them only half mad, if they could. But this won't do; Bedlam will break loose, and overpower its keepers. If the preacher sees visions, and has visitations, the clerk will come next, and then the congregation; every man will be his own prophet, and dream dreams for himself: the competition in extravagance will be hot and lively, and the whole island a receptacle for incurables. There is, at this moment, a man in London who prays for what garments he wants, and finds them next morning in his room, tight and fitting. This man, as might be expected, gains between two and three thousand a year from the common people, by preaching. Anna, the prophetess, encamps in the woods of America, with thirteen or fourteen thousand followers, and has visits every night from the prophet *Elijah*. *Joanna Southcote* raises the dead, &c. &c. Mr. Styles will call us atheists, and disciples of the French school, for what we are about to say; but it is our decided opinion, that there is some fraud in the prophetic visit; and it is but too probable, that the clothes are merely human, and the man measured for them in the common way. When such blasphemous deceptions are practised upon mankind, how can remonstrance be misplaced, or exposure mischievous? If the choice rested with us, we should say,—give us back our wolves again,—restore our Danish invaders,—curse us with any evil but the evil of a canting, deluded, and Methodistical populace. Wherever Methodism extends its baneful influence, the character of the English people is constantly changed by it. Boldness and rough honesty are broken down into meanness, prevarication, and fraud.

While Mr. Styles is so severe upon the indolence of the Church, he should recollect that his Methodists are the ex-party; that it is not in human nature, that any persons who quietly possess power can be as active as those who are pursuing it. The fair way to state the merit of the two parties is, to estimate what the exertions of the lachrymal and suspirious clergy would be, if they stepped into the endowments of their competitors. The moment they ceased to be paid by the groan,—the instant that Easter offerings no longer depended upon jumping and convulsions,—Mr. Styles may assure himself, that the character of his darling preachers would be totally changed; their bodies would become quiet, and their minds reasonable.

It is not true, as this bad writer is perpetually saying, that the world hates piety. That modest and unobtrusive piety which fills the heart with all human charities, and makes a man gentle to others, and severe to himself, is an object of universal love and veneration. But mankind hate the lust of power when it is veiled under the garb of piety;—they hate canting and hypocrisy;—they hate advertisers and quacks and piety;—they do not choose to be insulted;—they love to tear folly and imprudence from that altar which should only be a sanctuary for the wretched and the good.

Having concluded his defence of Methodism, this fanatical writer opens upon us his Missionary battery, firing away with the most incessant fury, and calling names, all the time, as loud as lungs accustomed to the eloquence of the tub usually vociferate. In speaking of the cruelties which their religion entails upon the Hindoos, Mr. Styles is peculiarly severe upon us for not being more shocked at their piercing their limbs with *kimes*. This is rather an unfair mode of alarming his readers with the idea of some unknown instrument. He represents himself as having paid considerable attention to the manners and customs of the Hindoos; and, therefore, the peculiar stress he lays upon this instrument is naturally calculated to produce, in the minds of the humane, a great degree of mysterious terror. A drawing of the *kime* was imperiously called for; and the want of it is a subtle evasion, for which Mr. Styles is fairly accountable. As he has been silent on this subject, it is for us to explain the plan and nature of this terrible and unknown piece of mechanism. A *kime*, then, is neither more nor less than a false print in the Edinburgh Review for a *knife;* and from this blunder of the printer has Mr. Styles manufactured this Dædalean instrument of torture, called a *kime!* We were at first nearly persuaded by his arguments against *kimes;*—we grew frightened;—we stated to ourselves the horror of not sending missionaries to a nation which used *kimes;*—we were struck with the nice and accurate information of the Tabernacle upon this important subject:—but we looked in the errata, and found Mr. Styles to be always Mr. Styles,—always cut off from every hope of mercy, and remaining for ever himself.

Mr. Styles is right in saying we have abolished many practices of the Hindoos since the establishment of our empire; but then we have always consulted the Brahmins, whether or not such practices were conformable to their religion; and it is upon the authority of their condemnation that we have proceeded to abolition.

To the whole of Mr. Styles's observations upon the introduction of Christianity into India, we have one short answer:—it is not Christianity which is introduced there, but the debased mummery and nonsense of Methodists, which has little more to do with the Christian religion than it has to do with the religion of China. We would as soon consent that *Brodum* and *Solomon* should carry the medical art of Europe into India, as that Mr. Styles and his Anabaptists should give to the Eastern World their notions of our religion. We send men of the highest character for the administration of justice and the regulation of trade,—nay, we take great pains to impress upon the minds of the natives the highest ideas of our arts and manufactures, by laying before them the finest specimens of our skill and ingenuity,—why, then, are common sense and decency to be forgotten in religion alone? and so foolish a set of men allowed to engage themselves in this occupation, that the natives almost instinctively duck and pelt them? But the missionaries, we are told, have mastered the languages of the East. They may also, for aught we know, in the same time, have learnt perspective, astronomy, or any thing else. What is all this to us? Our charge is, that they want sense, conduct, and sound religion; and that, if they are not watched, the throat of every European in India will be cut:—the answer to which is, that their progress in languages is truly astonishing! If they expose us to eminent peril, what matters it if they have every virtue under heaven? We are not writing dissertations upon the intellect of Brother Carey, but stating his character so far as it concerns us and caring for it no further. But these pious gentlemen care nothing about the loss of the country. The plan, it seems, is this:—We are to educate India in Christianity, as a parent does his child; and, when it is perfect in its catechism, then to pack up, quit it entirely, and leave it to its own management. This is the evangelical project for separating a colony from the parent country. They see nothing of the bloodshed, and massacres, and devastations, nor of the speeches in parliament, squandered millions, fruitless expeditions, jobs and pensions, with which the loss of our Indian possessions would necessarily be accompanied; nor will they see that these consequences could arise from the *attempt*, and not from the completion, of their scheme of conversion. We should be swept from the peninsula by Pagan zealots; and should lose, among other things, all chance of ever really converting them.

What is the use, too, of telling us what these men endure? Suffering is not a merit, but only useful suffering. Prove to us that they are fit men, doing a fit thing, and we are ready to praise the missionaries; but it gives us no pleasure to hear that a man has walked a thousand miles with peas in his shoes, unless we know why, and wherefore, and to what good purpose he has done it.

But these men, it is urged, foolish and extravagant as they are, may be very useful precursors of the established clergy. This is much as if a regular physician should send a quack doctor before him, and say, do you go and look after this disease for a day or two, and ply the patient well with your nostrums, and then I will step in and complete the cure; a more notable expedient we have seldom heard of. Its patrons forget that these self-ordained ministers, with Mr. John Styles at their head, abominate the established clergy ten thousand times more than they do Pagans, who cut themselves with cruel *kimes*. The efforts of these precursors would be directed with infinitely more zeal to make the Hindoos disbelieve in bishops, than to make them believe in Christ. The darling passion in the soul of every missionary is, not to teach the great leading truths of the Christian faith, but to enforce the little paltry modification and distinction which he first taught from his own tub. And then what a way of teaching Christianity is this! There are five sects, if not six, now employed as missionaries, every one instructing the Hindoos in their own particular method of interpreting the Scriptures; and, when these have completely succeeded, the Church of England is to step in, and convert them all over again to its own doctrines. There is, indeed, a very fine varnish of probability over this ingenious and plausible scheme. Mr. John Styles, however, would much rather see a *kime* in the flesh of an Hindoo than the hand of a bishop on his head.

The missionaries complain of intolerance. A weasel might as well complain of intolerance when he is throttled for sucking eggs. Toleration for their own opinions,—toleration for their domestic worship, for their private groans and convulsions, they possess in the fullest extent; but who ever heard of toleration for intolerance? Who ever before heard men cry out that they were persecuted, because they might not insult the religion, shock the feelings, irritate the passions of their fellow-creatures, and throw a whole colony into bloodshed and confusion? We did not say that a man was not an object of pity who tormented himself from a sense of duty, but that he was not so great an object of pity as one equally tormented by the tyranny of another, and without any sense of duty to support him. Let Mr. Styles first inflict forty lashes upon himself, then let him allow an Edinburgh Reviewer to give him forty more,—he will find no comparison between the two flagellations.

These men talk of the loss of our possessions in India, as if it made the argument against them only more or less strong; whereas, in our estimation, it makes the argument against them conclusive, and shuts up the case. Two men possess a cow, and they quarrel violently how they shall manage this cow. They will surely both of them (if they have a particle of common sense) agree, that there is an absolute necessity for preventing the cow from running away. It is not only the loss of India that is in question,—but how will it be lost? By the massacre of ten or twenty thousand English, by the blood of our sons and brothers, who have been toiling so many years to return to their native country. But what is all this to a ferocious Methodist? What care brothers *Barrel* and *Ringletub* for us and our colonies?

If it were possible to invent a method by which a few men sent from a distant country could hold such masses of people as the Hindoos in subjection, that method would be the institution of *castes*. There is no institution which can so effectually curb the ambition of genius, reconcile the individual more completely to his station, and reduce the varieties of human character to such a state of insipid and monotonous tameness; and yet the religion which destroys castes is said to render our empire in India more certain! It may be our duty to make the Hindoos Christians,—that is another argument: but, that we shall by so doing strengthen our empire, we utterly deny. What signifies identity of religion to a question of this kind? Diversity of bodily colour and of language would soon overpower this consideration. Make the Hindoos enterprising, active, and reasonable as yourselves,—destroy the eternal track in which they have moved for ages—and, in a moment, they would sweep you off the face of the earth. Let us ask, too, if the Bible is universally diffused in Hindostan, what must be the astonishment of the natives to find that we are forbidden to rob, murder, and steal;—we who, in fifty years, have extended our empire from a few acres about Madras over the whole peninsula, and sixty millions of people, and exemplified in our public conduct every crime of which human nature is capable. What matchless impudence to follow up such practice with such precepts! If we have common prudence, let us keep the gospel at home, and tell them that Machiavel is our prophet, and the god of the Manicheans our god.

There is nothing which disgusts us more than the familiarity which these impious coxcombs affect with the ways and designs of Providence. Every man, now-a-days, is an *Amos* or a *Malachi*. One rushes out of his chambers, and tells us we are beaten by the French, because we do not abolish the slave trade. Another assures us, that we have no chance of victory till India is evangelized. The new Christians are now come to speak of the ways of their Creator with as much confidence as they would of the plans of an earthly ruler. We remember when the ways of God to man were gazed upon with trembling humility,—when they were called inscrutable,—when piety looked to another scene of existence for the true explanation of this ambiguous and distressing world. We were taught in our childhood that this was true religion; but it turns out now to be nothing but atheism and infidelity. If any thing could surprise us from the pen of a Methodist, we should be truly surprised at the very irreligious and presumptuous answer which Mr. Styles makes to some of our arguments. Our title to one of the anecdotes from the Methodist Magazine is as follows:—"*A sinner punished—a Bee the instrument;*" to which Mr. Styles replies, that we might as well ridicule the Scriptures, by relating their contents in the same ludicrous manner. *An interference with respect to a travelling Jew; blindness the consequence. Acts, the ninth chapter, and first nine verses. The account of Paul's conversion, &c. &c. &c. page* 38. But does Mr. Styles forget that the one is a shameless falsehood, introduced to sell a twopenny book, and the other a miracle recorded by inspired writers? In the same manner, when we express our surprise that sixty millions of Hindoos should be converted by four men and sixteen guineas, he asks, what would have become of Christianity if the twelve Apostles had argued in the same way? It is impossible to make this infatuated gentleman understand that the lies of the Evangelical Magazine are not the miracles of Scripture; and that the Baptist Missionaries are not the Apostles. He seriously expects that we should speak of Brother Carey as we would speak of St. Paul; and treat with an equal respect the miracles of the Magazine and the Gospel.

Mr. Styles knows very well that we have never said, because a nation has present happiness, that it can therefore dispense with immortal happiness; but we have said that, where of two nations both cannot be made Christians, it is more the duty of a missionary to convert the one, which is exposed to every evil of barbarism, than the other possessing every blessing of civilization. Our argument is merely comparative: Mr. Styles must have known it to be so:—but who does not love the Tabernacle better than truth? When the tenacity of the Hindoos on the subject of their religion is adduced as a reason against the success of the missions, the friends of this understanding are always fond of reminding us how patiently the Hindoos submitted to the religious persecutions and butchery of Tippoo. The inference from such citations is truly alarming. It is the imperious duty of Government to watch some of these men most narrowly.—There is nothing of which they are not capable. And what, after all, did Tippoo effect in the way of conversion? How many Mahomedans did he make? There was all the carnage of Medea's Kettle, and none of the transformation. He deprived multitudes of Hindoos of their caste, indeed; and cut them off from all the benefits of their religion. That he did, and we may do, by violence; but, did he make Mahomedans?—or shall we make Christians? This, however, it seems, is a matter of pleasantry. To make a poor Hindoo hateful to himself and his kindred, and to fix a curse upon him to the end of his days!—we have no doubt but that this is very entertaining; and particularly to the friends of toleration. But our ideas of comedy have been formed in another school. We are dull enough to think, too, that it is more innocent to exile pigs than to offend conscience, and destroy human happiness. The scheme of baptizing with beef broth is about as brutal and preposterous as the assertion that you may vilify the gods and priests of the Hindoos with safety, provided you do not meddle with their turbans and toupees, (which are cherished solely on a principle of religion,) is silly and contemptible. After all, if the Mahomedan did persecute the Hindoo with impunity, is that any precedent of safety to a government that offends every feeling *both* of Mahomedan and Hindoo at the same time? You have a tiger and a buffalo in the same enclosure; and the tiger drives the buffalo before him;—is it therefore prudent in *you* to do that which will irritate them both, and bring their united strength upon you?

In answer to the low malignity of this author, we have only to reply, that we are, as we always have been, sincere friends to the conversion of the Hindoos. We admit the Hindoo religion to be full of follies, and full of enormities;—we think conversion a great duty; and should think, if it could be effected, a great blessing; but our opinion of the missionaries and of their employer is such, that we most firmly believe, in less than twenty years, for the conversion of a few degraded wretches, who would be neither Methodists nor Hindoos, they would infallibly produce the massacre of every European in India;* the loss of our settlements; and, consequently, of the chance of that slow, solid, and temperate introduction of Christianity, which the superiority of the European character may ultimately effect in the Eastern world. The Board of Control (all Atheists, and disciples of Voltaire, of course) are so entirely of our way of thinking, that the most peremptory orders have been issued to send all the missionaries home upon the slightest appearance of disturbance. Those who have sons and brothers in India may now sleep in peace. Upon the transmission of this order, Mr. Styles is said to have destroyed himself with a *kime*.

*Every opponent says of Major Scott's book, "What a dangerous book! the arrival of it at Calcutta may throw the whole Indian empire into confusion;" and yet these are the people whose religious prejudices may be insulted with impunity.

HANNAH MORE.*

[Edinburgh Review, 1809.]

This book is written, or supposed to be written, (for we would speak timidly of the mysteries of superior beings,) by the celebrated Mrs. Hannah More! We shall probably give great offence by such indiscretion; but still we must be excused for treating it as a book merely human,—an uninspired production,—the result of mortality left to itself, and depending on its own limited resources. In taking up the subject in this point of view, we solemnly disclaim the slightest intention of indulging in any indecorous levity, or of wounding the religious feelings of a large class of very respectable persons. It is the only method in which we can possibly make this work a proper object of criticism. We have the strongest possible doubts of the attributes usually ascribed to this authoress; and we think it more simple and manly to say so at once, than to admit nominally superlunary claims, which, in the progress of our remarks, we should virtually deny.

Cœlebs wants a wife: and, after the death of his father, quits his estate in Northumberland to see the world, and to seek for one of its best productions, a woman, who may add materially to the happiness of his future life. His first journey is to London, where, in the midst of the gay society of the metropolis, of course, he does not find a wife; and his next journey is to the family of Mr. Stanley, the head of the Methodists, a serious people, where, of course, he does find a wife. The exaltation, therefore, of what the authoress deems to be the religious, and the depreciation of what she considers to be the worldly character, and the influence of both upon matrimonial happiness, form the subject of this novel,—rather of this *dramatic sermon.*

The machinery upon which the discourse is suspended is of the slightest and most inartificial texture, bearing every mark of haste, and possessing not the slightest claim to merit. Events there are none; and scarcely a character of any interest. The book is intended to convey religious advice; and no more labour appears to have been bestowed upon the story, than was merely sufficient to throw it out of the dry, didactic form. Lucilla is totally uninteresting; so is Mr. Stanley; Dr. Barlow still worse; and Cœlebs a mere clod or dolt. Sir John and Lady Belfield are rather more interesting—and for a very obvious reason: they have some faults; they put us in mind of men and women; they seem to belong to one common nature with ourselves. As we read, we seem to think we might act as such people act, and therefore we attend; whereas imitation is hopeless in the more perfect characters which Mrs. More has set before us; and therefore they inspire us with very little interest.

There are books, however, of all kinds; and those may not be unwisely planned which set before us very pure models. They are less probable, and therefore less amusing, than ordinary stories; but they are more amusing than plain, unfabled precept. Sir Charles Grandison is less agreeable than Tom Jones; but it is more agreeable than Sherlock and Tillotson; and teaches religion and morality to many who would not seek it in the productions of these professional writers.

But, making every allowance for the difficulty of the task which Mrs. More has prescribed to herself, the book abounds with marks of negligence and want of skill; with representations of life and manners which are either false or trite.

Temples to friendship and virtue must be totally laid aside, for many years to come, in novels. Mr. Lane, of the Minerva Press, has given them up long since; and we were quite surprised to find such a writer as Mrs. More busied in moral brick and mortar. Such an idea, at first, was merely juvenile; the second time, a little nauseous; but the ten thousandth time it is quite intolerable. Cœlebs, upon his first arrival in London, dines out,—meets with a bad dinner,—supposes the cause of that bad dinner to be the erudition of the ladies of the house,—talks to them upon learned subjects, and finds them as dull and ignorant as if they had piqued themselves upon all the mysteries of housewifery. We humbly submit to Mrs. More, that this is not humorous, but strained and unnatural. Philippics against frugivorous children after dinner are too common. Lady Melbury has been introduced into every novel for these four years last past. Peace to her ashes!

The characters in this novel which evince the greatest skill are unquestionably those of Mrs. Ranby and her daughters. There are some scenes in this part of the book extremely well painted, and which evince that Mrs. More could amuse, in no common degree, if amusement was her object.

"At tea I found the young ladies took no more interest in the conversation than they had done at dinner, but sat whispering and laughing, and netting white silk gloves, till they were summoned to the harpsichord. Despairing of getting on with them in company, I proposed a walk in the garden. I now found them as willing to talk as destitute of any thing to say. Their conversation was vapid and frivolous. They laid great stress on small things. They seemed to have no shades in their understanding, but used the

* *Cœlebs in Search of a Wife; comprehending Observations on Domestic Habits and Manners, Religion and Morals.* 2 vols. London, 1809.

strongest terms for the commonest occasions; and admiration was excited by things hardly worthy to command attention. They were extremely glad and extremely sorry on subjects not calculated to excite affections of any kind. They were animated about trifles, and indifferent on things of importance. They were, I must confess, frank and good-natured; but it was evident that, as they were too open to have any thing to conceal, so they were too uninformed to have any thing to produce; and I was resolved not to risk my happiness with a woman who could not contribute her full share towards spending a wet winter cheerfully in the country."—(I. 54, 55.)

This trait of character appears to us to be very good. The following passage is still better.

"In the evening, Mrs. Ranby was lamenting in general, in rather customary terms, her own exceeding sinfulness. Mr. Ranby said, 'You accuse yourself rather too heavily, my dear; you have sins to be sure.' 'And pray what sins have I, Mr. Ranby?' said she, turning upon him with so much quickness that the poor man started. 'Nay,' said he, meekly, 'I did not mean to offend you; so far from it, that, hearing you condemn yourself so grievously, I intended to comfort you, and to say that, except a few faults———' 'And pray what faults?' interrupted she, continuing to speak, however, lest he should catch an interval to tell them. 'I defy you, Mr. Ranby, to produce one.' 'My dear,' replied he, 'as you charged yourself with all, I thought it would be letting you off cheaply, by naming only two or three, such as———' Here, fearing matters would go too far, I interposed; and, softening things as much as I could for the lady, said, 'I conceived that Mr. Ranby meant, that though she partook of the general corruption———' Here Ranby, interrupting me with more spirit than I thought he possessed, said, 'General corruption, sir, must be the source of particular corruption. I did not mean that my wife was worse than other women.'—'Worse, Mr. Ranby, worse?' cried she. Ranby, for the first time in his life, not minding her, went on, 'As she is always insisting that the whole species is corrupt, she cannot help allowing that she herself has not quite escaped the infection. Now, to be a sinner in the gross, and a saint in the detail—that is, to have all sins, and no faults—is a thing I do not quite comprehend.'

"After he had left the room, which he did as the shortest way of allaying the storm, she, apologizing for him, said, 'he was a well-meaning man, and acted up to the little light he had;' but added, 'that he was unacquainted with religious feelings, and knew little of the nature of conversion.'

"Mrs. Ranby, I found, seems to consider Christianity as a kind of free-masonry; and therefore thinks it superfluous to speak on serious subjects to any but the initiated. If they do not *return the sign*, she gives them up as blind and dead. She thinks she can only make herself intelligible to those to whom certain peculiar phrases are familiar: and though her friends may be correct, devout, and both doctrinally and practically pious; yet, if they cannot catch a certain mystic meaning,—if there is not a sympathy of intelligence between her and them,—if they do not fully conceive of impressions, and cannot respond to mysterious communications, she holds them unworthy of intercourse with her. She does not so much insist on high moral excellence as the criterion of their worth, as on their own account of their internal feelings."—(I. 60—63.)

The great object kept in view, throughout the whole of this introduction, is the enforcement of religious principle, and the condemnation of a life lavished in dissipation and fashionable amusement. In the pursuit of this object, it appears to us that Mrs. More is much too severe upon the ordinary amusements of mankind, many of which she does not object to in this or that degree, but altogether. Cœlebs and Lucilla, her *optimus* and *optima*, never dance, and never go to the play. They not only stay away from the comedies of Congreve and Farquhar, for which they may easily enough be forgiven; but they never go to see Mrs. Siddons in the Gamester, or in Jane Shore. The finest exhibition of talent, and the most beautiful moral lessons, are interdicted at the theatre. There is something in the word *Playhouse* which seems so closely connected, in the minds of these people, with sin and Satan,—that it stands in their vocabulary for every species of abomination. And yet why? Where is every feeling more roused in favour of virtue than at a good play? Where is goodness so feelingly, so enthusiastically learnt? What so solemn as to see the excellent passions of the human heart called forth by a great actor, animated by a great poet? To hear Siddons repeat what Shakspeare wrote? To behold the child and his mother—the noble and the poor artisan—the monarch and his subjects—all ages and all ranks convulsed with one common passion—wrung with one common anguish, and, with loud sobs and cries, doing involuntary homage to the God that made their hearts! What wretched infatuation to interdict such amusements as these! What a blessing that mankind can be allured from sensual gratification, and find relaxation and pleasure in such pursuits! But the excellent Mr. Stanley is uniformly paltry and narrow,—always trembling at the idea of being entertained, and thinking no Christian safe who is not dull. As to the spectacles of impropriety which are sometimes witnessed in parts of the theatre, such reasons apply, in a much stronger degree, to not driving along the Strand, or any of the great public streets of London, after dark; and, if the virtue of well-educated young persons is made of such very frail materials, their best resource is a nunnery at once. It is a very bad rule, however, never to quit the house for fear of catching cold.

Mrs. More practically extends the same doctrine to cards and assemblies. No cards—because cards are employed in gaming; no assemblies—because many dissipated persons pass their lives in assemblies. Carry this but a little further, and we must say, no wine—because of drunkenness; no meat—because of gluttony; no use, that there may be no abuse! The fact is, that Mr. Stanley wants, not only to be religious, but to be at the head of the religious. These little abstinences are the cockades by which the party are known,—the rallying points for the evangelical faction. So natural is the love of power, that it sometimes becomes the influencing motive with the sincere advocates of that blessed religion whose very characteristic excellence is the humility which it inculcates.

We observe that Mrs. More, in one part of her work, falls into the common error about dress. She first blames ladies for exposing their persons in the present style of dress, and then says, if they knew their own interest,—if they were aware how much more alluring they were to men when their charms are less displayed, they would make the desired alteration from motives merely selfish.

"Oh! if women in general knew what was their real interest, if they could guess with what a charm even the *appearance* of modesty invests its possessor, they would dress decorously from mere self-love, if not from principle. The designing would assume modesty as an artifice; the coquette would adopt it as an allurement; the pure as her appropriate attraction; and the voluptuous as the most infallible art of seduction."—(I. 189.)

If there is any truth in this passage, nudity becomes a virtue; and no decent woman, for the future, can be seen in garments.

We have a few more of Mrs. More's opinions to notice.—It is not fair to attack the religion of the times, because, in large and indiscriminate parties, religion does not become the subject of conversation. Conversation must and ought to grow out of materials on which men can agree, not upon subjects which try the passions. But this good lady wants to see men chatting together upon the Pelagian heresy—to hear, in the afternoon, the theological rumours of the day—and to glean polemical tittle-tattle at a tea-table rout. All the disciples of this school uniformly fall into the same mistake. They are perpetually calling upon their votaries for religious thoughts and religious conversation in every thing; inviting them to ride, walk, row, wrestle, and dine out religiously;—forgetting that the being to whom this impossible purity is recommended, is a being compelled to scramble for his existence and support for ten hours out of the sixteen he is awake;—forgetting that he must dig, beg, read, think, move, pay, receive, praise, scold, command, and obey;—forgetting, also, that if men conversed as often upon religious subjects as they do upon the ordinary occurrences of the world, they would converse upon them with the same familiarity and want of respect,—that religion would then produce feelings not more solemn or exalted than any other topics which constitute at present the common furniture of human understandings.

We are glad to find in this work some strong compliments to the efficacy of works,—some distinct admissions that it is necessary to be honest and just, before we can be considered as religious. Such sort of concessions are very gratifying to us; but how will they be received by the children of the Tabernacle? It is quite clear, indeed, throughout the whole of the work, that an apologetical explanation of certain religious opinions is intended; and there is a considerable abatement of that tone of insolence with which the improved Christians are apt to treat the bungling specimens of piety to be met with in the more ancient churches.

So much for the extravagances of this lady.—With equal sincerity, and with greater pleasure, we bear testimony to her talents, her good sense, and her real piety. There occur every now and then, in her productions, very original and very profound observations. Her advice is very often characterized by the most amiable good sense, and conveyed in the most brilliant and inviting style. If, instead of belonging to a trumpery faction, she had only watched over those great points of religion in which the hearts of every sect of Christians are interested, she would have been one of the most useful and valuable writers of her day. As it is, every man would wish his wife and his children to read *Cœlebs*;—watching himself its effects—separating the piety from the puerility;—and showing that it is very possible to be a good Christian, without degrading the human understanding to the trash and folly of Methodism.

PROFESSIONAL EDUCATION.*

[EDINBURGH REVIEW, 1809.]

THERE are two questions to be asked respecting every new publication. Is it worth buying? Is it worth borrowing? and we would advise our readers to weigh diligently the importance of these interrogations, before they take any decided step as to this work of Mr. Edgeworth; the more especially as the name carries with it considerable authority, and seems, in the estimation of the unwary, almost to include the idea of purchase. For our own part, we would rather decline giving a direct answer to these questions; and shall content ourselves for the present with making a few such slight observations as may enable the sagacious to conjecture what our direct answer would be were we compelled to be more explicit.

One great and signal praise we think to be the eminent due of Mr. Edgeworth: in a canting age, he does not cant;—at a period when hypocrisy and fanaticism will almost certainly insure the success of any publication, he has constantly disdained to have recourse to any such arts;—without ever having been accused of disloyalty or irreligion, he is not always harping upon Church and King, in order to catch at a little popularity, and sell his books;—he is manly, independent, liberal—and maintains enlightened opinions with discretion and honesty. There is also in this work of Mr. Edgeworth an agreeable diffusion of anecdote and example, such as a man acquires who reads with a view to talking or writing. With these merits, we cannot say that Mr. Edgeworth is either very new, very profound, or very apt to be right in his opinion. He is active, enterprising, and unprejudiced; but we have not been very much instructed by what he has written, or always satisfied that he has got to the bottom of his subject.

On one subject, however, we cordially agree with this gentleman; and return him our thanks for the courage with which he has combated the excessive abuse of classical learning in England. It is a subject upon which we have long wished for an opportunity of saying something; and one which we consider to be of the very highest importance.

"The principal defect," says Mr. Edgeworth, "in the present system of our great schools is, that they devote too large a portion of time to Latin and Greek. It is true, that the attainment of classical literature is highly desirable; but it should not, or rather it need not, be the exclusive object of boys during eight or nine years.

"Much less time, judiciously managed, would give them an acquaintance with the classics sufficient for all useful purposes, and would make them as good scholars as gentlemen or professional men need to be. It is not requisite that every man should make Latin or Greek verses; therefore, a knowledge of prosody beyond the structure of hexameter and pentameter verses, is as worthless an acquisition as any which folly or fashion has introduced amongst the higher classes of mankind. It must indeed be acknowledged that there are some rare exceptions; but even party prejudice would allow, that the persons alluded to must have risen to eminence though they had never written sapphics or iambics. Though preceptors, parents, and the public in general, may be convinced of the absurdity of making boys spend so much of life in learning what can be of no use to them; such are the difficulties of making any change in the ancient rules of great establishments, that masters themselves, however reasonable, dare not, and cannot make sudden alterations.

"The only remedies that can be suggested might be, perhaps, to take those boys, who are not intended for professions in which deep scholarship is necessary, away from school before they reach the highest classes, where prosody and Greek and Latin verses are required.

"In the college of Dublin, where an admirable course of instruction has been long established, where this course is superintended by men of acknowledged learning and abilities, and pursued by students of uncommon industry, such is the force of example, and such the fear of appearing inferior in trifles to English universities, that much pains have been lately taken to introduce the practice of writing Greek and Latin verses, and much solicitude has been shown about the prosody of the learned languages, without any attention being paid to the prosody of our own.

"Boarding-houses for the scholars at Eton and Westminster, which are at present mere lodging houses, might be kept by private tutors, who might, during the hours when the boys were not in their public classes, assist them in acquiring general literature, or such knowledge as might be advantageous for their respective professions.

"New schools, that are not restricted to any established routine, should give a fair trial to experiments in education, which afford a rational prospect of success. If nothing can be altered in the old schools, leave them as they are. Destroy nothing—injure none—but let the public try whether they cannot have something better. If the experiment do not succeed, the public will be convinced that they ought to acquiesce in the established methods of instruction, and parents will send their children to the ancient seminaries with increased confidence."—(p. 47—49.)

We are well aware that nothing very new

* *Essays on Professional Education.* By R. L. EDGEWORTH, Esq., F. R. S., &c. London. 1809.

can remain to be said upon a topic so often debated. The complaints we have to make are at least as old as the time of Locke and Dr. Samuel Clarke; and the evil which is the subject of these complaints has certainly rather increased than diminished since the period of those two great men. An hundred years, to be sure, is a very little time for the duration of a national error; and it is so far from being reasonable to look for its decay at so short a date, that it can hardly be expected, within such limits, to have displayed the full bloom of its imbecility.

There are several feelings to which attention must be paid, before the question of classical learning can be fairly and temperately discussed.

We are apt, in the first place, to remember the immense benefits which the study of the classics once conferred on mankind; and to feel for those models on which the taste of Europe has been formed, something like sentiments of gratitude and obligation. This is all well enough, so long as it continues to be a mere feeling; but, as soon as it interferes with action, it nourishes dangerous prejudices about education. Nothing will do in the pursuit of knowledge but the blackest ingratitude; the moment we have got up the ladder we must kick it down;—as soon as we have passed over the bridge, we must let it rot;—when we have got upon the shoulders of the ancients, we must look over their heads. The man who forgets the friends of his childhood in real life, is base: but he who clings to the props of his childhood in literature, must be content to remain as ignorant as he was when a child. His business is to forget, disown, and deny—to think himself above every thing which has been of use to him in time past—and to cultivate that exclusively from which he expects future advantage: in short, to do every thing for the advancement of his knowledge which it would be infamous to do for the advancement of his fortune. If mankind still derive advantage from classical literature proportionate to the labour they bestow upon it, let their labour and their study proceed; but the moment we cease to read Latin and Greek for the solid utility we derive from them, it would be a very romantic application of human talents to do so from any feeling of gratitude, and recollection of past service.

To almost every Englishman up to the age of three or four and twenty, classical learning has been the great object of existence; and no man is very apt to suspect, or very much pleased to hear, that what he has done for so long a time was not worth doing. His classical literature, too, reminds every man of the scenes of his childhood, and brings to his fancy several of the most pleasing associations which we are capable of forming. A certain sort of vanity, also, very naturally grows among men occupied in a common pursuit. Classical quotations are the watchwords of scholars, by which they distinguish each other from the ignorant and illiterate; and Greek and Latin are insensibly become almost the only test of a cultivated mind.

Some men through indolence, others through ignorance, and most through necessity, submit to the established education of the times; and seek for their children that species of distinction which happens, at the period in which they live, to be stamped with the approbation of mankind. This mere question of convenience every parent must determine for himself. A poor man, who has his fortune to gain, must be a quibbling theologian, or a classical pedant, as fashion dictates; and he must vary his error with the error of the times. But it would be much more fortunate for mankind, if the public opinion, which regulates the pursuits of individuals, were more wise and enlightened than it at present is.

All these considerations make it extremely difficult to procure a candid hearing on this question; and to refer this branch of education to the only proper criterion of every branch of education—its utility in future life.

There are two questions which grow out of this subject: 1st, How far is any sort of classical education useful? 2d, How far is that particular classical education adopted in this country useful?

Latin and Greek are, in the first place, useful, as they inure children to intellectual difficulties, and make the life of a young student what it ought to be, a life of considerable labour. We do not, of course, mean to confine this praise exclusively to the study of Latin and Greek; or to suppose that other difficulties might not be found which it would be useful to overcome: but though Latin and Greek have this merit in common with many arts and sciences, still they have it; and, if they do nothing else, they at least secure a solid and vigorous application at a period of life which materially influences all other periods.

To go through the grammar of one language thoroughly is of great use for the mastery of every other grammar; because there obtains, through all languages, a certain analogy to each other in their grammatical construction. Latin and Greek have now mixed themselves etymologically with all the languages of modern Europe—and with none more than our own; so that it is necessary to read these two tongues for other objects than themselves.

The two ancient languages are, as mere inventions—as pieces of mechanism—incomparably more beautiful than any of the modern languages of Europe: their mode of signifying time and case by terminations, instead of auxiliary verbs and participles, would of itself stamp their superiority. Add to this, the copiousness of the Greek language, with the fancy, majesty, and harmony of its compounds; and there are quite sufficient reasons why the classics should be studied for the beauties of language. Compared to them, merely as vehicles of thought and passion, all modern languages are dull, ill-contrived, and barbarous.

That a great part of the Scriptures has come down to us in the Greek language, is of itself a reason, if all others were wanting, why education should be planned so as to produce a supply of Greek scholars.

The cultivation of style is very justly made

a part of education. Every thing which is written is meant either to please or to instruct. The second object it is difficult to effect, without attending to the first; and the cultivation of style is the acquisition of those rules and literary habits which sagacity anticipates, or experience shows to be the most effectual means of pleasing. Those works are the best which have longest stood the test of time, and pleased the greatest numbers of exercised minds. Whatever, therefore, our conjectures may be, we cannot be so sure that the best modern writers can afford us as good models as the ancients;—we cannot be certain that they will live through the revolutions of the world, and continue to please in every climate—under every species of government—through every stage of civilization. The moderns have been well taught by their masters; but the time is hardly yet come when the necessity for such instruction no longer exists. We may still borrow descriptive power from Tacitus; dignified perspicuity from Livy; simplicity from Cæsar; and from Homer some portion of that light and heat which, dispersed into ten thousand channels, has filled the world with bright images and illustrious thoughts. Let the cultivator of modern literature addict himself to the purest models of taste which France, Italy, and England could supply, he might still learn from Virgil to be majestic, and from Tibullus to be tender; he might not yet look upon the face of nature as Theocritus saw it; nor might he reach those springs of pathos with which Euripides softened the hearts of his audience. In short, it appears to us, that there are so many excellent reasons why a certain number of scholars should be kept up in this and in every civilized country, that we should consider every system of education from which classical education was excluded, as radically erroneous and completely absurd.

That vast advantages, then, may be derived from classical learning, there can be no doubt. The advantages which are derived from classical learning by the English manner of teaching, involve another and a very different question; and we will venture to say, that there never was a more complete instance in any country of such extravagant and overacted attachment to any branch of knowledge as that which obtains in this country with regard to classical knowledge. A young Englishman goes to school at six or seven years old; and he remains in a course of education till twenty-three or twenty-four years of age. In all that time, his sole and exclusive occupation is learning Latin and Greek:* he has scarcely a notion that there is any other kind of excellence; and the great system of facts with which he is the most perfectly acquainted, are the intrigues of the heathen gods: with whom Pan slept?—with whom Jupiter?—whom Apollo ravished? These facts the English youth get by heart the moment they quit the nursery; and are most sedulously and industriously instructed in them till the best and most active part of life is passed away. Now, this long career of classical learning, we may, if we please, denominate a foundation; but it is a foundation so far above ground, that there is absolutely no room to put any thing upon it. If you occupy a man with one thing till he is twenty-four years of age, you have exhausted all his leisure time: he is called into the world, and compelled to act; or is surrounded with pleasures, and thinks and reads no more. If you have neglected to put other things in him, they will never get in afterwards;—if you have fed him only with words, he will remain a narrow and limited being to the end of his existence.

The bias given to men's minds is so strong, that it is no uncommon thing to meet with Englishmen, whom, but for their gray hairs and wrinkles, we might easily mistake for schoolboys. Their talk is of Latin verses; and it is quite clear, if men's ages are to be dated from the state of their mental progress, that such men are eighteen years of age, and not a day older. Their minds have been so completely possessed by exaggerated notions of classical learning, that they have not been able, in the great school of the world, to form any other notion of real greatness. Attend, too, to the public feelings—look to all the terms of applause. A learned man!—a scholar!—a man of erudition! Upon whom are these epithets of approbation bestowed? Are they given to men acquainted with the science of government? thoroughly masters of the geographical and commercial relations of Europe? to men who know the properties of bodies, and their action upon each other? No: this is not learning: it is chemistry, or political economy—not learning. The distinguishing abstract term, the epithet of Scholar, is reserved for him who writes on the Œolic reduplication, and is familiar with the Sylburgian method of arranging defectives in ω and μι. The picture which a young Englishman, addicted to the pursuit of knowledge, draws—his *beau idéal* of human nature—his top and consummation of man's powers—is a knowledge of the Greek language. His object is not to reason, to imagine, or to invent; but to conjugate, decline, and derive. The situations of imaginary glory which he draws for himself, are the detection of an anapæst in the wrong place, or the restoration of a dative case which Cranzius had passed over, and the never-dying Ernesti failed to observe. If a young classic of this kind were to meet the greatest chemist or the greatest mechanician, or the most profound political economist of his time, in company with the greatest Greek scholar, would the slightest comparison between them ever come across his mind?—would he ever dream that such men as Adam Smith and Lavoisier were equal in dignity of understanding to, or of the same utility as, Bentley and Heyné? We are inclined to think, that the feeling excited would be a good deal like that which was expressed by Dr. George about the praises of the great King of Prussia, who entertained considerable doubts whether the king, with all his victories, knew how to conjugate a Greek verb in μι.

Another misfortune of classical learning, as taught in England, is, that scholars have come

* Unless he goes to the University of Cambridge; and then classics occupy him entirely for about ten years; and divide him with mathematics for four or five more.

in process of time, and from the effects of association, to love the instrument better than the end;—not the luxury which the difficulty encloses, but the difficulty;—not the filbert, but the shell;—not what may be read in Greek, but Greek itself. It is not so much the man who has mastered the wisdom of the ancients, that is valued, as he who displays his knowledge of the vehicle in which that wisdom is conveyed. The glory is to show I am a scholar. The good sense and ingenuity I may gain by my acquaintance with ancient authors is matter of opinion; but if I bestow an immensity of pains upon a point of accent or quantity, this is something positive; I establish my pretensions to the name of scholar, and gain the credit of learning, while I sacrifice all its utility.

Another evil in the present system of classical education is the extraordinary perfection which is aimed at in teaching those languages; a needless perfection; an accuracy which is sought for in nothing else. There are few boys who remain to the age of eighteen or nineteen at a public school, without making above ten thousand Latin verses;—a greater number than is contained in the *Æneid:* and after he has made this quantity of verses in a dead language, unless the poet should happen to be a very weak man indeed, he never makes another as long as he lives. It may be urged, and it is urged, that this is of use in teaching the delicacies of the language. No doubt it is of use for this purpose, if we put out of view the immense time and trouble sacrificed in gaining these little delicacies. It would be of use that we should go on till fifty years of age making Latin verses, if the price of a whole life were not too much to pay for it. We effect our object; but we do it at the price of something greater than our object. And whence comes it, that the expenditure of life and labour is totally put out of the calculation, when Latin and Greek are to be attained? In every other occupation, the question is fairly stated between the attainment, and the time employed in the pursuit;—but, in classical learning, it seems to be sufficient if the least possible good is gained by the greatest possible exertion; if the end is any thing, and the means every thing. It is of some importance to speak and write French; and innumerable delicacies would be gained by writing ten thousand French verses: but it makes no part of our education to write French poetry. It is of some importance that there should be good botanists; but no botanist can repeat, by heart, the names of all the plants in the known world; nor is any astronomer acquainted with the appellation and magnitude of every star in the map of the heavens. The only department of human knowledge in which there can be no excess, no arithmetic, no balance of profit and loss, is classical learning.

The prodigious honour in which Latin verses are held at public schools, is surely the most absurd of all absurd distinctions. You rest all reputation upon doing that which is a natural gift, and which no labour can attain. If a lad won't learn the words of a language, his degradation in the school is a very natural punishment for his disobedience, or his indolence but it would be as reasonable to expect that all boys should be witty, or beautiful, as that they should be poets. In either case, it would be to make an accidental, unattainable, and not a very important gift of nature, the only, or the principal, test of merit. This is the reason why boys, who make a very considerable figure at school, so very often make no figure in the world;—and why other lads, who are passed over without notice, turn out to be valuable, important men. The test established in the world is widely different from that established in a place which is presumed to be a preparation for the world; and the head of a public school, who is a perfect miracle to his contemporaries, finds himself shrink into absolute insignificance, because he has nothing else to command respect or regard, but a talent for fugitive poetry in a dead language.

The present state of classical education cultivates the imagination a great deal too much, and other habits of mind a great deal too little: and trains up many young men in a style of elegant imbecility, utterly unworthy of the talents with which nature has endowed them. It may be said, there are profound investigations, and subjects quite powerful enough for any understanding, to be met with in classical literature. So there are; but no man likes to add the difficulties of a language to the difficulties of a subject; and to study metaphysics, morals, and politics in Greek, when the Greek alone is study enough without them. In all foreign languages, the most popular works are works of imagination. Even in the French language, which we know so well, for one serious work which has any currency in this country, we have twenty which are mere works of imagination. This is still more true in classical literature; because what their poets and orators have left us, is of infinitely greater value than the remains of their philosophy; for, as society advances, men think more accurately and deeply, and imagine more tamely; works of reasoning advance, and works of fancy decay. So that the matter of fact is, that a classical scholar of twenty-three or twenty-four years of age, is a man principally conversant with the works of imagination. His feelings are quick, his fancy lively, and his taste good. Talents for speculation and original inquiry he has none; nor has he formed the invaluable habit of pushing things up to their first principles, or of collecting dry and unamusing facts as the materials of reasoning. All the solid and masculine parts of his understanding are left wholly without cultivation; he hates the pain of thinking, and suspects every man whose boldness and originality call upon him to defend his opinions and prove his assertions.

A very curious argument is sometimes employed in justification of the learned minutiæ to which all young men are doomed, whatever be their propensities in future life. What are you to do with a young man up to the age of seventeen? Just as if there was such a want of difficulties to overcome, and of important tastes to inspire, that from the mere necessity of doing something, and the impossibility of doing any thing else, you were driven to the expedient of metre and poetry;—as if a young man within that period might not acquire the modern languages, modern history, experimental philosophy, geography, chronology, and a considerable share of mathematics;—as if the memory of things was not more agreeable and more profitable than the memory of words.

The great objection is, that we are not making the most of human life, when we constitute such an extensive, and such minute classical erudition, an indispensable article in education. Up to a certain point we would educate every young man in Latin and Greek; but to a point far short of that to which this species of education is now carried. Afterwards, we would grant to classical erudition as high honours as to every other department of knowledge, but not higher. We would place it upon a footing with many other objects of study; but allow it no superiority. Good scholars would be as certainly produced by these means as good chemists, astronomers, and mathematicians are now produced, without any direct provision whatsoever for their production. Why are we to trust to the diversity of human tastes, and the varieties of human ambition in every thing else, and distrust it in classics alone? The passion for language is just as strong as any other literary passion. There are very good Persian and Arabic scholars in this country. Large heaps of trash have been dug up from Sanscrit ruins. We have seen, in our own times, a clergyman of the University of Oxford complimenting their majesties in Coptic and Syrophœnician verses; and yet we doubt whether there will be a sufficient avidity in literary men to get at the beauties of the finest writers which the world has yet seen; and though the *Bagvat Gheeta* has (as can be proved) met with human beings to translate, and other human beings to read it, we think that, in order to secure an attention to Homer and Virgil, we must catch up every man—whether he is to be a clergyman or a duke,—begin with him at six years of age, and never quit him till he is twenty; making him conjugate and decline for life and death; and so teaching him to estimate his progress in real wisdom as he can scan the verses of the Greek tragedians.

The English clergy, in whose hands education entirely rests, bring up the first young men of the country as if they were all to keep grammar schools in little country towns; and a nobleman, upon whose knowledge and liberality the honour and welfare of his country may depend, is diligently worried, for half his life, with the small pedantry of longs and shorts. There is a timid and absurd apprehension, on the part of ecclesiastical tutors, of letting out the minds of youth upon difficult and important subjects. They fancy that mental exertion must end in religious scepticism; and, to preserve the principles of their pupils, they confine them to the safe and elegant imbecility of classical learning. A genuine Oxford tutor would shudder to hear his young men disputing upon moral and political truth, forming and pulling down theories, and indulging in all the boldness of youthful discussion. He would augur nothing from it but impiety to God and treason to kings. And yet, who vilifies both more than the holy poltroon who carefully averts from them the searching eye of reason, and who knows no better method of teaching the highest duties, than by extirpating the finest qualities and habits of the mind? If our religion is a fable, the sooner it is exploded the better. If our government is bad, it should be amended. But we have no doubt of the truth of the one, or of the excellence of the other; and are convinced that both will be placed on a firmer basis in proportion as the minds of men are more trained to the investigation of truth. At present, we act with the minds of our young men as the Dutch did with their exuberant spices. An infinite quantity of talent is annually destroyed in the universities of England by the miserable jealousy and littleness of ecclesiastical instructors. It is in vain to say we have produced great men under this system. We have produced great men under all systems. Every Englishman must pass half his life in learning Latin and Greek; and classical learning is supposed to have produced the talents which it has not been able to extinguish. It is scarcely possible to prevent great men from rising up under any system of education, however bad. Teach men demonology or astrology, and you will still have a certain portion of original genius, in spite of these or any other branches of ignorance and folly.

There is a delusive sort of splendour in a vast body of men pursuing one object, and thoroughly obtaining it; and yet, though it is very splendid, it is far from being useful. Classical literature is the great object at Oxford. Many minds so employed have produced many works and much fame in that department; but if all liberal arts and sciences useful to human life had been taught there,—if some have dedicated themselves to chemistry, some to mathematics, some to experimental philosophy,—and if every attainment had been honoured in the mixed ratio of its difficulty and utility,—the system of such an University would have been much more valuable, but the splendour of its name something less.

When an University has been doing useless things for a long time, it appears at first degrading to them to be useful. A set of lectures upon political economy would be discouraged in Oxford,* probably despised, probably not permitted. To discuss the inclosure of commons, and to dwell upon imports and exports, —to come so near to common life, would seem to be undignified and contemptible. In the same manner, the Parr, or the Bentley of his day, would be scandalized in an University to be put on a level with the discoverer of a neutral salt; and yet, what other measure is there of dignity in intellectual labour, but usefulness and difficulty? And what ought the term University to mean, but a place where every science is taught which is liberal, and at the same time useful to mankind? Nothing would so much tend to bring classical literature within proper bounds, as a steady and invariable appeal to these tests in our appre-

* They have since been established.

ciation of all human knowledge. The puffed up pedant would collapse into his proper size, and the maker of verses, and the rememberer of words, would soon assume that station which is the lot of those who go up unbidden to the upper places of the feast.

We should be sorry if what we have said should appear too contemptuous towards classical learning, which we most sincerely hope will always be held in great honour in this country, though we certainly do not wish to it that exclusive honour which it at present enjoys. A great classical scholar is an ornament, and an important acquisition to nis country; but, in a place of education, we would give to all knowledge an equal chance for distinction; and would trust to the varieties of human disposition that every science worth cultivation would be cultivated. Looking always to real utility as our guide, we should see, with equal pleasure, a studious and inquisitive mind arranging the productions of nature, investigating the qualities of bodies, or mastering the difficulties of the learned languages. We should not care whether he were chemist, naturalist, or scholar; because we know it to be as necessary that matter should be studied, and subdued to the use of man, as that taste should be gratified, and imagination inflamed.

In those who were destined for the church, we would undoubtedly encourage classical learning more than in any other body of men; but if we had to do with a young man going out into public life, we would exhort him to contemn, or at least not to affect, the reputation of a great scholar, but to educate himself for the offices of civil life. He should learn what the constitution of his country really was, —how it had grown into its present state,—the perils that had threatened it,—the malignity that had attacked it,—the courage that had fought for it, and the wisdom that had made it great. We would bring strongly before his mind the characters of those Englishmen who have been the steady friends of the public happiness; and by their examples, would breathe into him a pure public taste which should keep him untainted in all the vicissitudes of political fortune. We would teach him to burs through the well paid, and the pernicious can of indiscriminate loyalty; and to know his sovereign only as he discharged those duties, and displayed those qualities, for which the blood and the treasure of his people are confided to his hands. We should deem it of the utmost importance that his attention was directed to the true principles of legislation,—what effect laws can produce upon opinions, and opinions upon laws,—what subjects are fit for legislative interference, and when men may be left to the management of their own interests. The mischief occasioned by bad laws, and the perplexity which arises from numerous laws,—the causes of national wealth, —the relations of foreign trade,—the encouragement of manufactures and agriculture,—the fictitious wealth occasioned by paper credit,—the laws of population,—the management of poverty and mendicity,—the use and abuse of monopoly,—the theory of taxation,—the consequences of the public debt. These are some of the subjects, and some of the branches of civil education to which we would turn the minds of future judges, future senators, and future noblemen. After the first period of life had been given up to the cultivation of the classics, and the reasoning powers were now beginning to evolve themselves, these are some of the propensities in study which we would endeavour to inspire. Great knowledge, at such a period of life, we could not convey; but we might fix a decided taste for its acquisition, and a strong disposition to respect it in others. The formation of some great scholars we should certainly prevent, and hinder many from learning what, in a few years, they would necessarily forget; but this loss would be well repaid,—if we could show the future rulers of the country that thought and labour which it requires to make a nation happy,—or if we could inspire them with that love of public virtue, which, after religion, we most solemnly believe to be the brightest ornament of the mind of man.

FEMALE EDUCATION.*

EDINBURGH REVIEW, 1810.

MR. BROADHURST is a very good sort of a man, who has not written a very bad book upon a very important subject. His object (a very laudable one) is to recommend a better system of female education than at present prevails in this country—to turn the attention of women from the trifling pursuits to which they are now condemned—and to cultivate faculties which, under the actual system of management, might almost as well not exist. To the examination of his ideas upon these points, we shall very cheerfully give up a portion of our time and attention.

A great deal has been said of the original difference of capacity between men and women; as if women were more quick, and men more judicious—as if women were more remarkable for delicacy of association, and men for stronger powers of attention. All this, we confess, appears to us very fanciful. That there is a difference in the understandings of the men and the women we every day meet with, every body, we suppose, must perceive; but there is none surely which may not be accounted for by the difference of circumstances in which they have been placed, without referring to any conjectural difference of original conformation of mind. As long as boys and girls run about in the dirt, and trundle hoops together, they are both precisely alike. If you catch up one half of these creatures, and train them to a particular set of actions and opinions, and the other half to a perfectly opposite set, of course their understandings will differ, as one or the other sort of occupations has called this or that talent into action. There is surely no occasion to go into any deeper or more abstruse reasoning, in order to explain so very simple a phenomenon. Taking it, then, for granted, that nature has been as bountiful of understanding to one sex as the other, it is incumbent on us to consider what are the principal objections commonly made against the communication of a greater share of knowledge to women than commonly falls to their lot at present: for though it may be doubted whether women should learn all that men learn, the immense disparity which now exists between their knowledge we should hardly think could admit of any rational defence. It is not easy to imagine that there can be any just cause why a woman of forty should be more ignorant than a boy of twelve years of age. If there be any good at all in female ignorance, this (to use a very colloquial phrase) is surely too much of a good thing.

Something in this question must depend, no doubt, upon the leisure which either sex enjoys for the cultivation of their understandings:—and we cannot help thinking, that women have fully as much, if not more, idle time upon their hands than men. Women are excluded from all the serious business of the world; men are lawyers, physicians, clergymen, apothecaries, and justices of the peace—sources of exertion which consume a great deal more time than producing and suckling children; so that, if the thing is a thing that ought to be done—if the attainments of literature are objects really worthy the attention of females, they cannot plead the want of leisure as an excuse for indolence and neglect. The lawyer who passes his day in exasperating the bickerings of Roe and Doe, is certainly as much engaged as his lady who has the whole of the morning before her to correct the children and pay the bills. The apothecary, who rushes from an act of phlebotomy in the western parts of the town to insinuate a bolus in the east, is surely as completely absorbed as that fortunate female who is darning the garment, or preparing the repast of her Æsculapius at home; and, in every degree and situation of life, it seems that men must necessarily be exposed to more serious demands upon their time and attention than can possibly be the case with respect to the other sex. We are speaking always of the fair demands which ought to be made upon the time and attention of women; for, as the matter now stands, the time of women is considered as worth nothing at all. Daughters are kept to occupations in sewing, patching, mantua-making, and mending, by which it is impossible they can earn tenpence a day. The intellectual improvement of women is considered to be of such subordinate importance, that twenty pounds paid for needlework would give to a whole family leisure to acquire a fund of real knowledge. They are kept with nimble fingers and vacant understandings till the season for improvement is utterly passed way, and all chance of forming more important habits completely lost. We do not therefore say that women have more leisure than men, if it be necessary that they should lead the life of artisans; but we make this assertion only upon the supposition, that it is of some importance women should be instructed; and that many ordinary occupations, for which a little money will find a better substitute, should be sacrificed to this consideration.

We bar, in this discussion, any objection which proceeds from the mere novelty of teaching women more than they are already taught. It may be useless that their education should be improved, or it may be pernicious; and these are the fair grounds on which the question may be argued. But those who cannot bring their minds to consider such an unusual extension of knowledge, without connecting with it some sensation of the ludicrous, should remember that, in the progress from absolute ignorance, there is a period when cultivation of mind is new to every rank and description of persons. A century ago, who would have believed that country gentlemen could be brought to read and spell with the ease and accuracy which we now so frequently remark,—or supposed that they could be carried up even to the

* Advice to Young Ladies on the Improvement of the Mind. By THOMAS BROADHURST. 8vo. London, 1808.

elements of ancient and modern history? Nothing is more common, or more stupid, than to take the actual for the possible—to believe that all which is, is all which can be; first to laugh at every proposed deviation from practice as impossible—then, when it is carried into effect, to be astonished that it did not take place before.

It is said, that the effect of knowledge is to make women pedantic and affected; and that nothing can be more offensive than to see a woman stepping out of the natural modesty of her sex to make an ostentatious display of her literary attainments. This may be true enough; but the answer is so trite and obvious, that we are almost ashamed to make it. All affectation and display proceed from the supposition of possessing something better than the rest of the world possesses. Nobody is vain of possessing two legs and two arms;—because that is the precise quantity of either sort of limb which every body possesses. Who ever heard a lady boast that she understood French?—for no other reason, that we know of, but because every body in these days does understand French; and though there may be some disgrace in being ignorant of that language, there is little or no merit in its acquisition. Diffuse knowledge generally among women, and you will at once cure the conceit which knowledge occasions while it is rare. Vanity and conceit we shall of course witness in men and women as long as the world endures: but by multiplying the attainments upon which these feelings are founded, you increase the difficulty of indulging them, and render them much more tolerable, by making them the proofs of a much higher merit. When learning ceases to be uncommon among women, learned women will cease to be affected.

A great many of the lesser and more obscure duties of life necessarily devolve upon the female sex. The arrangement of all household matters, and the care of children in their early infancy, must of course depend upon them. Now, there is a very general notion, that the moment you put the education of women upon a better footing than it is at present, at that moment there will be an end of all domestic economy; and that, if you once suffer women to eat of the tree of knowledge, the rest of the family will very soon be reduced to the same kind of aerial and unsatisfactory diet. These, and all such opinions, are referable to one great and common cause of error; that man does every thing, and that nature does nothing; and that every thing we see is referable to positive institution rather than to original feeling. Can any thing, for example, be more perfectly absurd than to suppose that the care and perpetual solicitude which a mother feels for her children, depends upon her ignorance of Greek and mathematics; and that she would desert an infant for a quadratic equation? We seem to imagine that we can break in pieces the solemn institution of nature, by the little laws of a boarding-school; and that the existence of the human race depends upon teaching women a little more or a little less;—that Cimmerian ignorance can aid paternal affection, or the circle of arts and sciences produce its destruction. In the same manner, we forget the principles upon which the love of order, arrangement, and all the arts of economy depend. They depend not upon ignorance nor idleness; but upon the poverty, confusion, and ruin which would ensue for neglecting them. Add to these principles, the love of what is beautiful and magnificent, and the vanity of display;—and there can surely be no reasonable doubt but that the order and economy of private life is amply secured from the perilous inroads of knowledge.

We would fain know, too, if knowledge is to produce such baneful effects upon the material and the household virtues, why this influence has not already been felt? Women are much better educated now than they were a century ago; but they are by no means less remarkable for attention to the arrangements of their household, or less inclined to discharge the offices of parental affection. It would be very easy to show, that the same objection has been made at all times to every improvement in the education of both sexes, and all ranks—and been as uniformly and completely refuted by experience. A great part of the objections made to the education of women, are rather objections made to human nature than to the female sex: for it is surely true, that knowledge, where it produces any bad effects at all, does as much mischief to one sex as to the other,—and gives birth to fully as much arrogance, inattention to common affairs, and eccentricity among men, as it does among women. But it by no means follows, that you get rid of vanity and self-conceit because you get rid of learning. Self-complacency can never want an excuse; and the best way to make it more tolerable, and more useful, is to give to it as high and as dignified an object as possible. But at all events it is unfair to bring forward against a part of the world an objection which is equally powerful against the whole. When foolish women think they have any distinction, they are apt to be proud of it; so are foolish men. But we appeal to any one who has lived with cultivated persons of either sex, whether he has not witnessed as much pedantry, as much wrong-headedness, as much arrogance, and certainly a great deal more rudeness, produced by learning in men, than in women; therefore, we should make the accusation general—or dismiss it altogether; though, with respect to pedantry, the learned are certainly a little unfortunate, that so very emphatic a word, which is occasionally applicable to all men embarked eagerly in any pursuit, should be reserved exclusively for them: for, as pedantry is an ostentatious obtrusion of knowledge, in which those who hear us cannot sympathize, it is a fault of which soldiers, sailors, sportsmen, gamesters, cultivators, and all men engaged in a particular occupation, are quite as guilty as scholars; but thay have the good fortune to have the vice only of pedantry,—while scholars have both the vice and the name for it too.

Some persons are apt to contrast the acquisition of important knowledge with what they call simple pleasures; and deem it more becoming that a woman should educate flowers, make friendships with birds, and pick up plants, than enter into more difficult and fatiguing studies. If a woman has no taste and genius for higher occupation, let her engage in these to be sure rather than remain destitute of any pursuit. But why are we necessarily to doom a girl, whatever be her taste or her capacity, to one unvaried line of petty and frivolous occupation? If she is full of strong sense and elevated curiosity, can there be any reason why she should be diluted and enfeebled down to a mere culler of simples, and fancier of birds?—why books of history and reasoning are to be torn out of her hand, and why she is to be sent, like a butterfly, to hover over the idle flowers of the field? Such amusements are innocent to those whom they can occupy; but they are not innocent to those who have too powerful understandings to be occupied by them. Light broths and fruits are innocent food only to weak or to infant stomachs; but they are poison to that organ in its perfect and mature state. But the great charm appears to be in the word *simplicity*—simple pleasure! If by a simple pleasure is meant an innocent pleasure, the observation is best answered by showing, that the pleasure which results from the acquisition of important knowledge is quite as innocent as any pleasure whatever: but if by a simple pleasure is meant one, the cause of which can be easily analyzed, or which does not last long, or which in itself is very faint, then simple pleasures seem to be very nearly synonymous with small pleasures; and if the simplicity were to be a little increased, the pleasure would vanish altogether.

As it is impossible that every man should have industry or activity sufficiently to avail himself of the advantages of education, it is natural that men who are ignorant themselves, should view, with some degree of jealousy and alarm, any proposal for improving the education of women. But such men may depend upon it, however the system of female education may be exalted, that there will never be wanting a due proportion of failures; and that after parents, guardians, and preceptors have done all in their power to make every body wise, there will still be a plentiful supply of women who have taken special care to remain otherwise; and they may rest assured, if the utter extinction of ignorance and folly is the evil they dread, that their interests will always be effectually protected, in spite of every exertion to the contrary.

We must in candour allow that those women who begin will have something more to overcome than may probably hereafter be the case. We cannot deny the jealousy which exists among pompous and foolish men respecting the education of women. There is a class of pedants who would be cut short in the estimation of the world a whole cubit if it were generally known that a young lady of eighteen could be taught to decline the tenses of the middle voice, or acquaint herself with the Æolic varieties of that celebrated language. Then women have, of course, all ignorant men for enemies to their instruction, who being bound (as they think,) in point of sex, to know more, are not well pleased, in point of fact, to know less. But, among men of sense and liberal politeness, a woman who has successfully cultivated her mind, without diminishing the gentleness and propriety of her manners, is always sure to meet with a respect and attention bordering upon enthusiasm.

There is in either sex a strong and permanent disposition to appear agreeable to the other: and this is the fair answer to those who are fond of supposing, that an higher degree of knowledge would make women rather the rivals than the companions of men. Presupposing such a desire to please, it seems much more probable, that a common pursuit should be a fresh source of interest than a cause of contention. Indeed, to suppose that any mode of education can create a general jealousy and rivalry between the sexes, is so very ridiculous, that it requires only to be stated in order to be refuted. The same desire of pleasing secures all that delicacy and reserve which are of such inestimable value to women. We are quite astonished, in hearing men converse on such subjects, to find them attributing such beautiful effects to ignorance. It would appear, from the tenour of such objections, that ignorance had been the great civilizer of the world. Women are delicate and refined only because they are ignorant;—they manage their household, only because they are ignorant;—they attend to their children, only because they know no better. Now, we must really confess, we have all our lives been so ignorant as not to know the value of ignorance. We have always attributed the modesty and the refined manners of women, to their being well taught in moral and religious duty,—to the hazardous situation in which they are placed,—to that perpetual vigilance which it is their duty to exercise over thought, word, and action,—and to that cultivation of the mild virtues, which those who cultivate the stern and magnanimous virtues expect at their hands. After all, let it be remembered, we are not saying there are no objections to the diffusion of knowledge among the female sex. We would not hazard such a proposition respecting any thing; but we are saying, that, upon the whole, it is the best method of employing time; and that there are fewer objections to it than to any other method. There are, perhaps, 50,000 females in Great Britain who are exempted by circumstances from all necessary labour: but every human being must do something with their existence; and the pursuit of knowledge is, upon the whole, the most innocent, the most dignified, and the most useful method of filling up that idleness, of which there is always so large a portion in nations far advanced in civilization. Let any man reflect, too, upon the solitary situation in which women are placed,—the ill treatment to which they are sometimes exposed, and which they must endure in silence, and without the power of complaining,—and he must feel convinced that the happiness of a woman will be materially increased in proportion as education has given to her the habit and the means of drawing her resources from herself.

There are a few common phrases in circulation, respecting the duties of women, to which we wish to pay some degree of attention, because they are rather inimical to those opinions which we have advanced on this subject. Indeed, independently of this, there is nothing which requires more vigilance than the current phrases of the day, of which there are always some resorted to in every dispute, and from the sovereign authority of which it is often vain to make any appeal. "The true theatre for a woman is the sick-chamber;"—"Nothing so honourable to a woman as not to be spoken of at all." These two phrases, the delight of *Noodledom*, are grown into common-places upon the subject; and are not unfrequently employed to extinguish that love of knowledge in women, which, in our humble opinion, it is of so much importance to cherish. Nothing, certainly, is so ornamental and delightful in women as the benevolent affections; but time cannot be filled up, and life employed, with high and impassioned virtues. Some of these feelings are of rare occurrence—all of short duration—or nature would sink under them. A scene of distress and anguish is an occasion where the finest qualities of the female mind may be displayed; but it is a monstrous exaggeration to tell women that they are born only for scenes of distress and anguish. Nurse father, mother, sister, and brother, if they want it;—it would be a violation of the plainest duties to neglect them. But, when we are talking of the common occupations of life, do not let us mistake the accidents for the occupations;—when we are arguing how the twenty-three hours of the day are to be filled up, it is idle to tell us of those feelings and agitations above the level of common existence, which may employ the remaining hour. Compassion, and every other virtue, are the great objects we all ought to have in view; but no man (and no woman) can fill up the twenty-four hours by acts of virtue. But one is a lawyer, and the other a ploughman, and the third a merchant; and then, acts of goodness, and intervals of compassion and fine feeling, are scattered up and down the common occupations of life. We know women are to be compassionate; but they cannot be compassionate from eight o'clock in the morning till twelve at night:—and what are they to do in the interval? This is the only question we have been putting all along, and is all that can be meant by literary education.

Then, again, as to the notoriety which is incurred by literature.—The cultivation of knowledge is a very distinct thing from its publication; nor does it follow that a woman is to become an author merely because she has talent enough for it. We do not wish a lady to write books,—to defend and reply,—to squabble about the tomb of Achilles, or the plain of Troy,—any more than we wish her to dance at the opera, to play at a public concert, or to put pictures in the exhibition, because she has learned music, dancing and drawing. The great use of her knowledge will be that it contributes to her private happiness. She may make it public: but it is not the principal object which the friends of female education have in view. Among men, the few who write bear no comparison to the many who read. We hear most of the former, indeed, because they are, in general, the most ostentatious part of literary men; but there are innumerable persons who, without ever laying themselves before the public, have made use of literature to add to the strength of their understandings, and to improve the happiness of their lives. After all, it may be an evil for ladies to be talked of: but we really think those ladies who are talked of only as Mrs. Marcet, Mrs. Somerville, and Miss Martineau are talked of, may bear their misfortunes with a very great degree of Christian patience.

Their exemption from all the necessary business of life is one of the most powerful motives for the improvement of education in women. Lawyers and physicians have in their professions a constant motive to exertion; if you neglect their education, they must in a certain degree educate themselves by their commerce with the world: they must learn caution, accuracy, and judgment, because they must incur responsibility. But if you neglect to educate the mind of a woman, by the speculative difficulties which occur in literature, it can never be educated at all: if you do not effectually rouse it by education, it must remain for ever languid. Uneducated men may escape intellectual degradation; uneducated women cannot. They have nothing to do; and if they come untaught from the schools of education, they will never be instructed in the school of events.

Women have not their livelihood to gain by knowledge; and that is one motive for relaxing all those efforts which are made in the education of men. They certainly have not; but they have happiness to gain, to which knowledge leads as probably as it does to profit; and that is a reason against mistaken indulgence. Besides, we conceive the labour and fatigue of accomplishments to be quite equal to the labour and fatigue of knowledge; and that it takes quite as many years to be charming as it does to be learned.

Another difference of the sexes is, that women are attended to, and men attend. All acts of courtesy and politeness originate from the one sex, and are received by the other. We can see no sort of reason, in this diversity of condition, for giving to women a trifling and insignificant education; but we see in it a very powerful reason for strengthening their judgment, and inspiring them with the habit of employing time usefully. We admit many striking differences in the situation of the two sexes, and many striking differences of understanding, proceeding from the different circumstances in which they are placed: but there is not a single difference of this kind which does not afford a new argument for making the education of women better than it is. They have nothing serious to do;—is that a reason why they should be brought up to do nothing but what is trifling? They are exposed to greater dangers;—is that a reason why their faculties are to be purposely and industriously weakened? They are to form the characters of future men;—is that a cause why their own characters are to be broken and frittered down as they now are? In short, there is not a single trait in that diversity of circumstances, in which the two sexes are placed, that does not decidedly prove the magnitude of the error we commit in neglecting (as we do neglect) the education of women.

If the objections against the better education of women could be overruled, one of the great advantages that would ensue would be the extinction of innumerable follies. A decided and prevailing taste for one or another mode of education there must be. A century past, it was for housewifery—now it is for accomplishments. The object now is, to make women artists,—to give them an excellence in drawing, music, painting and dancing,—of which, persons who make these pursuits the occupation of their lives, and derive from them their subsistence, need not be ashamed. Now, one great evil of this is, that it does not last. If the whole of life were an Olympic game,—if we could go on feasting and dancing to the end,—this might do; but it is in truth merely a provision for the little interval between coming into life, and settling in it; while it leaves a long and dreary expanse behind, devoid both of dignity and cheerfulness. No mother, no woman who has passed over the few first years of life, sings, or dances, or draws, or plays upon musical instruments. These are merely means for displaying the grace and vivacity of youth, which every woman gives up, as she gives up the dress and manners of eighteen: she has no wish to retain them, or, if she has, she is driven out of them by diameter and derision. The system of female education, as it now stands, aims only at embellishing a few years of life, which are in themselves so full of grace and happiness, that they hardly want it; and then leaves the rest of existence a miserable prey to idle insignificance. No woman of understanding and reflection can possibly conceive she is doing justice to her children by such kind of education. The object is, to give to children resources that will endure as long as life endures,—habits that time will ameliorate, not destroy,—occupations that will render sickness tolerable, solitude pleasant, age venerable, life more dignified and useful, and therefore death less terrible: and the compensation which is offered for the omission of all this, is a short-lived blaze,—a little temporary effect, which has no other consequence than to deprive the remainder of life of all taste and relish. There may be women who have a taste for the fine arts, and who evince a decided talent for drawing, or for music. In that case, there can be no objection to the cultivation of these arts; but the error is, to make such things the grand and universal object,—to insist upon it that every woman is to sing, and draw, and dance—with nature, or against nature,—to bind her apprentice to some accomplishment, and if she cannot succeed in oil or water-colours, to prefer gilding, varnishing, burnishing, box-making, to real solid improvement in taste, knowledge, and understanding.

A great deal is said in favour of the social nature of the fine arts. Music gives pleasure to others. Drawing is an art, the amusement of which does not centre in him who exercises it, but it is diffused among the rest of the world. This is true; but there is nothing, after all, so social as a cultivated mind. We do not mean to speak slightingly of the fine arts, or to depreciate the good humour with which they are sometimes exhibited; but we appeal to any man, whether a little spirited and sensible conversation—displaying, modestly, useful acquirements—and evincing rational curiosity, is not well worth the highest exertions of musical or graphical skill. A woman of accomplishments may entertain those who have the pleasure of knowing her for half an hour with great brilliancy; but a mind full of ideas, and with that elastic spring which the love of knowledge only can convey, is a perpetual source of exhilaration and amusement to all that come within its reach;—not collecting its force into single and insulated achievements, like the effort made in the fine arts—but diffusing, equally over the whole of existence, a calm pleasure—better loved as it is longer felt—and suitable to every variety and every period of life. Therefore, instead of hanging the understanding of a woman upon walls, or hearing it vibrate upon strings,—instead of seeing it in clouds, or hearing it in the wind, we would make it the first spring and ornament of society, by enriching it with attainments upon which alone such power depends.

If the education of women were improved, the education of men would be improved also. Let any one consider (in order to bring the matter more home by an individual instance) of what immense importance to society it is, whether a nobleman of first-rate fortune and distinction is well or ill brought up;—what a taste and fashion he may inspire for private and for political vice!—and what misery and mischief he may produce to the thousand human beings who are dependent on him! A country contains no such curse within its bosom. Youth, wealth, high rank, and vice, form a combination which baffles all remonstrance and beats down all opposition. A man of high rank who combines these qualifications for corruption, is almost the master of the manners of the age, and has the public happiness within his grasp. But the most beautiful possession which a country can have is a noble and rich man, who loves virtue and knowledge;—who without being feeble or fanatical is pious—and who without being factious is firm and independent;—who, in his political life, is an equitable mediator between king and people; and in his civil life, a firm promoter of all which can shed a lustre upon his country, or promote the peace and order of the world. But if these objects are of the importance which we attribute to them, the education of women must be important, as the formation of character for the first seven or eight years of life seems to depend almost entirely upon them. It is certainly in the power of a sensible and well-educated mother to inspire, within that period, such tastes and propensities as shall nearly decide the destiny of the future man; and this is done, not only by the intentional exertions of the mother, but by the gradual and insensible imitation of the child; for there is something extremely contagious in greatness and rectitude of thinking, even at that age; and the character of the mother with whom he passes his early infancy, is always an event of the utmost importance to the child. A merely accomplished woman cannot infuse her tastes into the minds of her sons; and, if she could, nothing could be more unfortunate than her success. Besides, when her accomplishments are given up, she has nothing left for it but to amuse herself in the best way she can; and, becoming entirely frivolous, either declines altogether the fatigue of attending to her children, or, attending to them, has neither talents nor knowledge to succeed; and, therefore, here is a plain and fair answer to those who ask so triumphantly, why should a woman dedicate herself to this branch of knowledge? or why should she be attached to such science?—Because, by having gained information on these points, she may inspire her son with valuable tastes, which may abide by him through life, and carry him up to all the sublimities of knowledge; because she cannot lay the foundation of a great character, if she is absorbed in frivolous amusements, nor inspire her child with noble desires, when a long course of trifling has destroyed the little talents which were left by a bad education.

It is of great importance to a country, that there should be as many understandings as possible actively employed within it. Mankind are much happier for the discovery of barometers, thermometers, steam-engines, and all the innumerable inventions in the arts and sciences. We are every day and every hour reaping the benefit of such talent and ingenuity. The same observation is true of such works as those of Dryden, Pope, Milton and Shakspeare. Mankind are much happier that such individuals have lived and written; they add every day to the stock of public enjoyment—and perpetually gladden and embellish life. Now, the number of those who exercise their understandings to any good purpose, is exactly in proportion to those who exercise it at all; but, as the matter stands at present, half the talent in the universe runs to waste, and is totally unprofitable. It would have been almost as well for the world, hitherto, that women, instead of possessing the capacities they do at present, should have been born wholly destitute of wit, genius, and every other attribute of mind, of which men make so eminent a use: and the ideas of use and possession are so united together, that, because it has been the custom in almost all countries to give to women a different and a worse education than to men, the notion has obtained that they do not possess faculties which they do not cultivate. Just as, in breaking up a common, it is sometimes very difficult to make the poor believe it will carry corn, merely because they have been hitherto accustomed to see it produce nothing but weeds and grass—they very naturally mistake present condition for general nature. So completely have the talents of women been kept down, that there is scarcely a single work, either of reason or imagination, written by a woman, which is in general circulation either in the English, French, or Italian literature;—scarcely one that has crept even into the ranks of our minor poets.

If the possession of excellent talents is not a conclusive reason why they should be improved, it at least amounts to a very strong presumption; and, if it can be shown that women may be trained to reason and imagine as well as men, the strongest reasons are certainly necessary to show us why we should not avail ourselves of such rich gifts of nature; and we have a right to call for a clear statement of those perils which make it necessary that such talents should be totally extinguished, or, at most, very partially drawn out. The burthen of proof does not lie with those who say, increase the quanity of talent in any country as much as possible—for such a proposition is in conformity with every man's feelings: but it lies with those who say, take care to keep that understanding weak and trifling, which nature has made capable of becoming strong and powerful. The paradox is with them, not with us. In all human reasoning, knowledge must be taken for a good, till it can be shown to be an evil. But now, nature makes to us rich and magnificent presents; and we say to her—You are too luxuriant and munificent—we must keep you under, and prune you;—we have talents enough in the other half of the creation;—and, if you will not stupefy and enfeeble the mind of women to our hands, we ourselves must expose them to a narcotic process, and educate away that fatal redundance with which the world is afflicted, and the order of sublunary things deranged.

One of the greatest pleasures of life is conversation;—and the pleasures of conversation are of course enhanced by every increase of knowledge: not that we should meet together to talk of alkalies and angles, or to add to our stock of history and philology—though a little of these things is no bad ingredient in conversation; but let the subject be what it may, there is always a prodigious difference between the conversation of those who have been well educated and of those who have not enjoyed this advantage. Education gives fecundity of thought, copiousness of illustration, quickness, vigour, fancy, words, images and illustrations;—it decorates every common thing, and gives the power of trifling without being undignified and absurb. The subjects themselves may not be wanted, upon which the talents of an educated man have been exercised; but there is always a demand for those talents which his education has rendered strong and quick. Now, really, nothing can be further from our intention than to say any thing rude and unpleasant; but we must be excused for observing, that it is not now a very common thing to be interested by the variety and extent of female knowledge, but it is a very common thing to lament, that the finest faculties in the world have been confined to trifles utterly unworthy of their richness and their strength.

The pursuit of knowledge is the most innocent and interesting occupation which can be given to the female sex; nor can there be a better method of checking a spirit of dissipation than by diffusing a taste for literature. The true way to attack vice, is by setting up something else against it. Give to women, in early youth, something to acquire, of sufficient interest and importance to command the application of their mature faculties, and to excite their perseverance in future life;—teach them that happiness is to be derived from the acquisition of knowledge, as well as the gratification of vanity; and you will raise up a much more formidable barrier against dissipation than a host of invectives and exhortations can supply.

It sometimes happens that an unfortunate man gets drunk with very bad wine,—not to gratify his palate, but to forget his cares: he does not set any value on what he receives, but on account of what it excludes;—it keeps out something worse than itself. Now, though it were denied that the acquisition of serious knowledge is of itself important to a woman, still it prevents a taste for silly and pernicious works of imagination; it keeps away the horrid trash of novels; and, in lieu of that eagerness for emotion and adventure which books of that sort inspire, promotes a calm and steady temperament of mind.

A man who deserves such a piece of good fortune, may generally find an excellent companion for all the vicissitudes of his life; but it is not so easy to find a companion for his understanding, who has similar pursuits with himself, or who can comprehend the pleasure he derives from them. We really can see no reason why it should not be otherwise; nor comprehend how the pleasures of domestic life can be promoted by diminishing the number of subjects in which persons who are to spend their lives together take a common interest.

One of the most agreeable consequences of knowledge is the respect and importance which it communicates to old age. Men rise in character often as they increase in years;—they are venerable from what they have acquired, and pleasing from what they can impart. If they outlive their faculties, the mere frame itself is respected for what it once contained; but women (such is their unfortunate style of education) hazard every thing upon one cast of the die;—when youth is gone, all is gone. No human creature gives his admiration for nothing either the eye must be charmed, or the understanding gratified. A woman must talk wisely or look well. Every human being must put up with the coldest civility, who has neither the charms of youth nor the wisdom of age. Neither is there the slightest commiseration for decayed accomplishments;—no man mourns over the fragments of a dancer, or drops a tear on the relics of musical skill. They are flowers destined to perish; but the decay of great talents is always the subject of solemn pity; and, even when their last memorial is over, their ruins and vestiges are regarded with pious affection.

There is no connexion between the ignorance in which women are kept, and the preservation of moral and religious principle; and yet certainly there is, in the minds of some timid and respectable persons, a vague, indefinite dread of knowledge, as if it were capable of producing these effects. It might also be supposed, from the dread which the propagation of knowledge has excited, that there was some great secret which was to be kept in impenetrable obscurity,—that all moral rules were a species of delusion and imposture, the detection of which, by the improvement of the understanding, would be attended with the most fatal consequences to all, and particularly to women. If we could possibly understand what these great secrets were, we might perhaps be disposed to concur in their preservation; but believing that all the salutary rules which are imposed on women are the result of true wisdom, and productive of the greatest happiness, we cannot understand how they are to become less sensible of this truth in proportion as their power of discovering truth in general is increased, and the habit of viewing questions with accuracy and comprehension established by education. There are men, indeed, who are always exclaiming against every species of power, because it is connected with danger: their dread of abuses is so much stronger than their admiration of uses, that they would cheerfully give up the use of fire, gunpowder, and printing, to be freed from robbers, incendiaries, and libels. It is true, that every increase of knowledge may possibly render depravity more depraved, as well as it may increase the strength of virtue. It is in itself only power; and its value depends on its applicalion. But, trust to the natural love of good where there is no temptation to be bad—it operates no where more forcibly than in education. No man, whether he be tutor, guardian, or friend, ever contents himself with infusing the mere ability to acquire; but giving the power, he gives with it a taste for the wise and rational exercise of that power; so that an educated person is not only one with stronger and better faculties than others, but with a more useful propensity—a disposition better cultivated—and associations of a higher and more important class.

In short, and to recapitulate the main points upon which we have insisted:—Why the disproportion in knowledge between the two sexes should be so great, when the inequality in natural talents is so small; or why the understanding of women should be lavished upon trifles, when nature has made it capable of higher and better things, we profess ourselves not able to understand. The affectation charged upon female knowledge is best cured by making that knowledge more general: and the economy devolved upon women is best secured by the ruin, disgrace, and inconvenience which proceeds from neglecting it. For the care of children, nature has made a direct and powerful provision; and the gentleness and elegance of women is the natural consequence of that desire to please, which is productive of the greatest part of civilization and refinement, and which rests upon a foundation too deep to be shaken by any such modifications in education as we have proposed. If you educate women to attend to dignified and important subjects, you are multiplying beyond measure the chances of human improvement, by preparing and *medicating* those early impressions, which always come from the mother; and which, in a great majority of instances, are quite decisive of character and genius. Nor is it only in the business of education that women would influence the destiny of men. If women knew more, men must learn more—for ignorance would then be shameful—and it would become the fashion to be instructed. The instruction of women improves the stock of national talents, and employs more minds for the instruction and amusement of the world;—it increases the pleasures of society, by multiplying the topics upon which the two sexes take a common interest; and makes marriage an intercourse of understanding as well as of affection, by giving dignity and importance to the female character. The education of women favours public morals; it provides for every season of life, as well as for the brightest and the best: and leaves a woman when she is stricken by the hand of time, not as she now is, destitute of every thing, and neglected by all; but with the full power and the splendid attractions of knowledge,—diffusing the elegant pleasures of polite literature, and receiving the just homage of learned and accomplished men.

PUBLIC SCHOOLS.*

(Edinburgh Review, 1810.)

There is a set of well-dressed, prosperous gentlemen, who assemble daily at Mr. Hatchard's shop;—clean, civil personages, well in with people in power,—delighted with every existing institution—and almost with every existing circumstance: and, every now and then, one of these personages writes a little book;—and the rest praise that little book—expecting to be praised, in their turn, for their own little books:—and of these little books, thus written by these clean, civil personages, so expecting to be praised, the pamphlet before us appears to be one.

The subject of it is the advantage of public schools; and the author, very creditably to himself, ridicules the absurd clamour, first set on foot by Dr. Rennel, of the irreligious tendency of public schools: he then proceeds to an investigation of the effects which public schools may produce upon the moral character; and here the subject becomes more difficult, and the pamphlet worse.

In arguing any large or general question, it is of infinite importance to attend to the first feelings which the mention of the topic has a tendency to excite; and the name of a public school brings with it immediately the idea of brilliant classical attainments: but, upon the importance of these studies, we are not now offering any opinion. The only points for consideration are, whether boys are put in the way of becoming good and wise men by these schools; and whether they actually gather there those attainments which it pleases mankind, for the time being, to consider as valuable, and to decorate by the name of learning.

By a public school, we mean any endowed place of education, of old standing, to which the sons of gentlemen resort in considerable numbers, and where they continue to reside, from eight or nine, to eighteen years of age. We do not give this as a definition which would have satisfied Porphyry or Duns-Scotus, but as one sufficiently accurate for our purpose. The characteristic features of these schools are, their antiquity, the numbers, and the ages of the young people who are educated at them. We beg leave, however, to premise, that we have not the slightest intention of insinuating any thing to the disparagement of the present discipline or present rulers of these schools, as compared with other times and other men: we have no reason whatever to doubt that they are as ably governed at this as they have been at any preceding period. Whatever objections we may have to these institutions, they are to faults, not depending on present administration, but upon original construction.†

At a public school (for such is the system established by immemorial custom), every boy is alternately tyrant and slave. The power which the elder part of these communities exercises over the younger is exceedingly great—very difficult to be controlled—and accompanied, not unfrequently, with cruelty and caprice. It is the common law of the place, that the young should be implicitly obedient to the elder boys; and this obedience resembles more the submission of a slave to his master, or of a sailor to his captain, than the common and natural deference which would always be shown by one boy to another a few years older than himself. Now, this system we cannot help considering as an evil,—because it inflicts upon boys, for two or three years of their lives, many painful hardships, and much unpleasant servitude. These sufferings might perhaps be of some use in military schools; but, to give a boy the habit of enduring privations to which he will never again be called upon to submit—to inure him to pains which he will never again feel—and to subject him to the privation of comforts with which he will always in future abound—is surely not a very useful and valuable severity in education. It is not the life in miniature which he is to lead hereafter—nor does it bear any relation to it:—he will never again be subjected to so much insolence and caprice; nor ever, in all human probability, be called upon to make so many sacrifices. The servile obedience which it teaches might be useful to a menial domestic; or the habits of enterprise which it encourages prove of importance to a military partisan; but we cannot see what bearing it has upon the calm, regular, civil life, which the sons of gentlemen, destined to opulent idleness, or to any of the three learned professions, are destined to lead. Such a system makes many boys very miserable; and produces those bad effects upon the temper and disposition, which unjust suffering always does produce;—but what good it does we are much at a loss to conceive. Reasonable obedience is extremely useful in forming the disposition. Submission to tyranny lays the foundation of hatred, suspicion, cunning, and a variety of odious passions. We are convinced that those young people will turn out to be the best men, who have been guarded most effectually in their childhood, from every species of useless vexation; and experienced, in the greatest degree, the blessings of a wise and rational indulgence. But even if these effects upon future character are not produced, still four or five years in childhood make a very considerable period of human existence; and it is by no means a trifling consideration whether they are passed happily or unhappily. The wretchedness of school tyranny is trifling enough to a man who only contemplates it in

* Remarks on the System of Education in Public Schools. 8vo. Hatchard. London, 1809.

† A public school is thought to be the best cure for the insolence of youthful aristocracy. This insolence, however, is not a little increased by the homage of masters, and would soon meet with its natural check in the world. There can be no occasion to bring five hundred boys together to teach to a young noblemen that proper demeanour which he would learn so much better from the first English gentleman whom he might think proper to insult.

ease of body and tranquillity of mind, through the medium of twenty intervening years; but it is quite as real, and quite as acute, while it lasts, as any of the sufferings of mature life: and the utility of these sufferings, or the price paid in compensation for them, should be clearly made out to a conscientious parent before he consents to expose his children to them.

This system also gives to the elder boys an absurd and pernicious opinion of their own importance, which is often with difficulty effaced by a considerable commerce with the world. The *head* of a public school is generally a very conceited young man, utterly ignorant of his own dimensions, and losing all that habit of conciliation towards others, and that anxiety for self-improvement, which result from the natural modesty of youth. Nor is this conceit very easily and speedily gotten rid of;—we have seen (if we mistake not) public school importance lasting through the half of after life, strutting in lawn, swelling in ermine, and displaying itself, both ridiculously and offensively, in the haunts and business of bearded men.

There is a manliness in the athletic exercises of public schools which is as seductive to the imagination as it is utterly unimportant in itself. Of what importance is it in after life whether a boy can play well or ill at cricket; or row a boat with the skill and precision of a waterman? If our young lords and esquires were hereafter to wrestle together in public, or the gentlemen of the Bar to exhibit Olympic games in Hilary Term, the glory attached to these exercises at public schools would be rational and important. But of what use is the body of an athlete, when we have good laws over our heads,—or when a pistol, a postchaise, or a porter, can be hired for a few shillings? A gentleman does nothing but ride or walk; and yet such a ridiculous stress is laid upon the manliness of the exercises customary at public schools—exercises in which the greatest blockheads commonly excel the most—which often render habits of idleness inveterate—and often lead to foolish expense and dissipation at a more advanced period of life.

One of the supposed advantages of a public school is the greater knowledge of the world which a boy is considered to derive from those situations; but if, by a knowledge of the world, is meant a knowledge of the forms and manners which are found to be the most pleasing and useful in the world, a boy from a public school is almost always extremely deficient in these particulars; and his sister, who has remained at home at the apron-strings of her mother, is very much his superior in the science of manners. It is probably true, that a boy at a public school has made more observation on human character, because he has had more opportunities of observing than have been enjoyed by young persons educated either at home or at private schools: but this little advance gained at a public school is so soon overtaken at college or in the world, that, to have made it, is of the least possible consequence, and utterly underserving of any risk incurred in the acquisition. Is it any injury to a man of thirty or thirty-five years of age—to a learned serjeant or venerable dean—that at eighteen they did not know so much of the world as some other boys of the same standing? They have probably escaped the arrogant character so often attendant upon this trifling superiority; nor is there much chance that they have ever fallen into the common and youthful error of mistaking a premature initiation into vice for a knowledge of the ways of mankind; and, in addition to these salutary exemptions, a winter in London brings it all to a level; and offers to every novice the advantages which are supposed to be derived from this precocity of confidence and polish.

According to the general prejudice in favour of public schools, it would be thought quite as absurd and superfluous to enumerate the illustrious characters who have been bred at our three great seminaries of this description, as it would be to descant upon the illustrious characters who have passed in and out of London over our three great bridges. Almost every conspicuous person is supposed to have been educated at public schools; and there are scarcely any means (as it is imagined) of making an actual comparison; and yet, great as the rage is, and long has been, for public schools, it is very remarkable, that the most eminent men in every art and science have not been educated in public schools; and this is true, even if we include, in the term of public schools, not only Eton, Winchester, and Westminster, but the Charter-House, St. Paul's School, Merchant Tailors', Rugby, and every school in England, at all conducted upon the plan of the three first. The great schools of Scotland we do not call public schools; because, in these, the mixture of domestic life gives to them a widely different character. Spenser, Pope, Shakspeare, Butler, Rochester, Spratt, Parnell, Garth, Congreve, Gay, Swift, Thomson, Shenstone, Akenside, Goldsmith, Samuel Johnson, Beaumont and Fletcher, Ben Jonson, Sir Philip Sydney, Savage, Arbuthnot, and Burns, among the poets, were not educated in the system of English schools. Sir Isaac Newton, Maclaurin, Wallis, Hamstead, Saunderson, Simpson, and Napier, among men of science, were not educated in public schools.

The three best historians that the English language has produced, Clarendon, Hume, and Robertson, were not educated at public schools. Public schools have done little in England for the fine arts—as in the examples of Inigo Jones, Vanbrugh, Reynolds, Gainsborough, Garrick, &c. The great medical writers and discoverers in Great Britain, Harvey, Cheselden, Hunter, Jenner, Meade, Brown, and Cullen, were not educated at public schools. Of the great writers on morals and metaphysics, it was not the system of public schools which produced Bacon, Shaftesbury, Hobbes, Berkeley, Butler, Hume, Hartley, or Dugald Stewart. The greatest discoverers in chemistry have not been brought up at public schools;—we mean Dr. Priestley, Dr. Black, and Mr. Davy. The only Englishmen who have evinced a remarkable genius, in modern times, for the art of war,—the Duke of Marlborough, Lord Peterborough, General Wolfe, and Lord Clive, were all trained in private schools. So were Lord Coke, Sir Matthew Hale, and Lord Chancellor Hardwicke, and Chief Justice Holt, among the lawyers. So also, among statesmen, were Lord Burleigh, Walsingham, the Earl of Strafford, Thurloe, Cromwell, Hampden, Lord Clarendon, Sir Walter Raleigh, Sydney, Russel, Sir W. Temple, Lord Somers, Burke, Sheridan, Pitt. In addition to this list, we must not forget the names of such eminent scholars and men of letters, as

Cudworth, Chillingworth, Tillotson, Archbishop King, Selden, Conyers, Middleton, Bentley, Sir Thomas More, Cardinal Wolsey, Bishops Sherlock and Wilkins, Jeremy Taylor, Isaac Hooker, Bishops Usher, Stillingfleet, and Spelman, Dr. Samuel Clarke, Bishop Hoadley, and Dr. Lardner. Nor must it be forgotten, in this examination, that none of the conspicuous writers upon political economy which this country has as yet produced, have been brought up in public schools. If it be urged that public schools have only assumed their present character within this last century, or half century, and that what are now called public schools partook, before this period, of the nature of private schools, there must then be added to our lists the names of Milton, Dryden, Addison, &c., &c.: and it will follow, that the English have done almost all that they have done in the arts and sciences, without the aid of that system of education to which they are now so much attached. Ample as this catalogue of celebrated names already is, it would be easy to double it; yet, as it stands, it is obviously sufficient to show that great eminence may be attained in any line of fame without the aid of public schools. Some more striking inferences might perhaps be drawn from it; but we content ourselves with the simple fact.

The most important peculiarity in the constitution of a public school is its numbers, which are so great, that a close inspection of the master into the studies and conduct of each individual is quite impossible. We must be allowed to doubt, whether such an arrangement is favourable either to literature or morals.

Upon this system, a boy is left almost entirely to himself, to impress upon his own mind, as well as he can, the distant advantages of knowledge, and to withstand, from his own innate resolution, the examples and the seductions of idleness. A firm character survives this brave neglect; and very exalted talents may sometimes remedy it by subsequent diligence: but schools are not made for a few youths of preeminent talents, and strong characters; such prizes can, of course, be drawn but by a very few parents. The best school is that which is best accommodated to the greatest variety of characters, and which embraces the greatest number of cases. It cannot be the main object of education to render the splendid more splendid, and to lavish care upon those who would almost thrive without any care at all. A public school does this effectually; but it commonly leaves the idle almost as idle, and the dull almost as dull as it found them. It disdains the tedious cultivation of those middling talents of which only the great mass of human beings are possessed. When a strong desire of improvement exists, it is encouraged, but no pains are taken to inspire it. A boy is cast in among five or six hundred other boys, and is left to form his own character;—if his love of knowledge survives this severe trial, it, in general, carries him very far: and, upon the same principle, a savage, who grows up to manhood, is, in general, well made, and free from all bodily defects; not because the severities of such a state are favourable to animal life, but because they are so much the reverse, that none but the strongest can survive them. A few boys are incorrigibly idle, and a few incorrigibly eager for knowledge; but the great mass are in a state of doubt and fluctuation; and they come to school for the express purpose, not of being left to themselves—for that could be done any where—but that their wavering tastes and propensities should be decided by the intervention of a master. In a forest, or public school for oaks and elms, the trees are left to themselves; the strong plants live, and the weak ones die: the towering oak that remains is admired; the saplings that perish around it are cast into the flames and forgotten. But it is not surely to the vegetable struggle of a forest, or the hasty glance of a forester, that a botanist would commit a favourite plant; he would naturally seek for it a situation of less hazard, and a cultivator whose limited occupations would enable him to give to it a reasonable share of his time and attention. The very meaning of education seems to us to be, that the old should teach the young, and the wise direct the weak; that a man who professes to instruct, should get among his pupils, study their characters, gain their affections, and form their inclinations and aversions. In a public school, the numbers render this impossible; it is impossible that sufficient time should be found for this useful and affectionate interference. Boys, therefore, are left to their own crude conceptions and ill-formed propensities; and this neglect is called a spirited and manly education.

In by far the greatest number of cases, we cannot think public schools favourable to the cultivation of knowledge; and we have equally strong doubts if they be so to the cultivation of morals,—though we admit, that, upon this point, the most striking arguments have been produced in their favour.

It is contended by the friends to public schools, that every person, before he comes to man's estate, must run through a certain career of dissipation; and that if that career is, by the means of a private education, deferred to a more advanced period of life, it will only be begun with greater eagerness, and pursued into more blameable excess. The time must, of course, come when every man must be his own master; when his conduct can be no longer regulated by the watchful superintendence of another, but must be guided by his own discretion. Emancipation must come at last; and we admit, that the object to be aimed at is, that such emancipation should be gradual, and not premature. Upon this very invidious point of the discussion, we rather wish to avoid offering any opinion. The manners of great schools vary considerably from time to time; and what may have been true many years ago, is very possibly not true at the present period. In this instance, every parent must be governed by his own observations and means of information. If the license which prevails at public schools is only a fair increase of liberty, proportionate to advancing age, and calculated to prevent the bad effects of a sudden transition from tutelary thraldom to perfect self-government, it is certainly a good rather than an evil. If, on the contrary, there exists in these places of education a system of premature debauchery, and if they only prevent men from being corrupted by the world, by corrupting them before their entry into the world, they can then only be looked upon as evils of the greatest magnitude, however they may be sanctioned by opinion, or rendered familiar to us by habit.

The vital and essential part of a school is the master; but, at a public school, no boy, or, at the best, only a very few, can see enough of him to derive any considerable benefit from his character, manners, and information. It is certainly of eminent use, particularly to a young man of rank, that he should have lived among boys; but it is only so when they are all moderately watched by some superior understanding. The morality of boys is generally very imperfect; their notions of honour extremely mistaken; and their objects of ambition frequently very absurd. The probability then is, that the kind of discipline they exercise over each other will produce (when left to itself) a great deal of mischief; and yet this is the discipline to which every child at a public school is not only necessarily exposed, but principally confined. Our objection (we again repeat) is not to the interference of boys in the formation of the character of boys; their character, we are persuaded, will be very imperfectly formed without their assistance; but our objection is to that almost exclusive agency which they exercise in public schools.

After having said so much in opposition to the general prejudice in favour of public schools, we may be expected to state what species of school we think preferable to them; for if public schools, with all their disadvantages, are the best that can actually be found, or easily attained, the objections to them are certainly made to very little purpose.

We have no hesitation, however, in saying, that that education seems to us to be the best which mingles a domestic with a school life; and which gives to a youth the advantage which is to be derived from the learning of a master, and the emulation which results from the society of other boys, together with the affectionate vigilance which he must experience in the house of his parents. But where this species of education, from peculiarity of circumstances or situation, is not attainable, we are disposed to think a society of twenty or thirty boys, under the guidance of a learned man, and, above all, of a man of good sense, to be a seminary the best adapted for the education of youth. The numbers are sufficient to excite a considerable degree of emulation, to give to a boy some insight into the diversities of the human character, and to subject him to the observation and control of his superiors. It by no means follows, that a judicious man should always interfere with his authority and advice because he has always the means; he may connive at many things which he cannot approve, and suffer some little failures to proceed to a certain extent, which, if indulged in wider limits, would be attended with irretrievable mischief: he will be aware, that his object is to fit his pupil for the world; that constant control is a very bad preparation for complete emancipation from all control; that it is not bad policy to expose a young man, under the eye of superior wisdom, to some of those dangers which will assail him hereafter in greater number, and in greater strength—when he has only his own resources to depend upon. A private education, conducted upon these principles, is not calculated to gratify quickly the vanity of a parent who is blest with a child of strong character and pre-eminent abilities: to be the first scholar of an obscure master, at an obscure place, is no very splendid distinction; nor does it afford that opportunity, of which so many parents are desirous, of forming great connexions for their children: but if the object be, to induce the young to love knowledge and virtue, we are inclined to suspect, that, for the average of human talents and characters, these are the situations in which such tastes will be the most effectually formed.

TOLERATION.*

[Edinburgh Review, 1811.]

If a prudent man sees a child playing with a porcelain cup of great value, he takes the vessel out of his hand, pats him on the head, tells him his mamma will be sorry if it is broken, and gently cheats him into the use of some less precious substitute. Why will Lord Sidmouth meddle with the Toleration Act, when there are so many other subjects in which his abilities might be so eminently useful—when enclosure bills are drawn up with such scandalous negligence—turnpike roads so shamefully neglected—and public conveyances illegitimately loaded in the face of day, and in defiance of the wisest legislative provisions? We confess our trepidation at seeing the Toleration Act in the hands of Lord Sidmouth; and should be very glad if it were fairly back in the statute book, and the sedulity of this well-meaning nobleman diverted into another channel.

The alarm and suspicion of the Dissenters upon these measures are wise and rational. They are right to consider the Toleration Act as their palladium; and they may be certain that in this country there is always a strong party ready, not only to prevent the further extension of tolerant principles, but to abridge (if they dared) their present operation within the narrowest limits. Whoever makes this attempt, will be sure to make it under professions of the most earnest regard for mildness and toleration, and with the strongest declarations of respect for King William, the Revolution, and the principles which seated the House of Brunswick on the throne of these realms;—and then will follow the clauses for whipping Dissenters, imprisoning preachers, and subjecting them to rigid qualifications, &c. &c. &c. The infringement on the militia acts is a mere pretence. The real object is to diminish the number of Dissenters from the Church of England, by abridging the liberties and privileges they now possess. This is the project which we shall examine, for we sincerely believe it to be the project in agitation. The mode in which it is proposed to attack the Dissenters is, first, by exacting greater qualifications in their teachers: next, by preventing the interchange or itinerancy of preachers, and fixing them to one spot.

It can never, we presume, be intended to subject dissenting ministers to any kind of *theological* examination. A teacher examined in doctrinal opinions, by another teacher who differs from him, is so very absurd a project, that we entirely acquit Lord Sidmouth of any intention of this sort. We rather presume his lordship to mean, that a man who professes to teach his fellow creatures, should at least have made some progress in human learning;—that he should not be wholly without education;—that he should be able at least to read and write. If the test is of this very ordinary nature, it can scarcely exclude many teachers of religion; and it was hardly worth while, for the very insignificant diminution of numbers which this must occasion to the dissenting clergy, to have raised all the alarm which this attack upon the Toleration Act has occasioned.

But, without any reference to the magnitude of the effects, is the principle right? or, What is the meaning of religious toleration? That a man should hold, without pain or penalty, any religious opinions,—and choose for his instruction, in the business of salvation, any guide whom he pleases;—care being taken that the teacher and the doctrine injure neither the policy nor the morals of the country. We maintain that perfect religious toleration applies as much to the teacher as the thing taught; and that it is quite as intolerant to make a man hear Thomas, who wants to hear John, as it would be to make a man profess Arminian, who wished to profess Calvinistical principles. What right has any government to dictate to any man who shall guide him to heaven, any more than it has to persecute the religious tenets by which he hopes to arrive there? You believe that the heretic professes doctrines utterly incompatible with the true spirit of the gospel;—first you burnt him for this,—then you whipt him, then you fined him,—then you put him in prison. All this did no good;—and, for these hundred years last past, you have let him alone. The heresy is now firmly protected by law;—and you know it must be preached: What matters it then, who preaches it? If the evil must be communicated, the organ and instrument through which it is communicated cannot be of much consequence. It is true, this kind of persecution against persons, has not been quite so much tried as the other against doctrines; but the folly and inexpediency of it rest precisely upon the same grounds.

Would it not be a singular thing if the friends of the Church of England were to make the most strenuous efforts to render their enemies eloquent and learned?—and to found places of education for Dissenters? But, if their learning would not be a good, why is their ignorance an evil?—unless it be necessarily supposed, that all increase of learning must bring men over to the Church of England; in which supposition, the Scottish and Catholic universities, and the college at Hackney, would hardly acquiesce. Ignorance surely matures and quickens the progress, by insuring the dissolution of absurdity. Rational and learned Dissenters remain:—religious mobs, under some ignorant

* *Hints on Toleration, in Five Essays, &c. suggested for the consideration of Lord Viscount Sidmouth, and the Dissenters.* By Philagatharches. London. 1810.

fanatic of the day, become foolish overmuch,—dissolve, and return to the Church. The Unitarian, who reads and writes gets some sort of discipline, and returns no more.

What connection is there (as Lord Sidmouth's plan assumes) between the zeal and piety required for religious instruction and the common attainments of literature? But, if knowledge and education are required for religious instruction, why be content with the common elements of learning? why not require higher attainments in dissenting candidates for orders; and examine them in the languages in which the books of their religion are conveyed?

A dissenting minister of vulgar aspect and homely appearance, declares that he entered into that holy office because he felt a call;—and a clergyman of the Establishment smiles at him for the declaration. But it should be remembered, that no minister of the Establishment is admitted into orders, before he has been expressly interrogated by the bishop whether he feels himself called to that sacred office. The doctrine of calling, or inward feeling, is quite orthodox in the English Church;—and, in arguing this subject in Parliament, it will hardly be contended, that the Episcopalian only is the judge when that call is genuine, and when it is only imaginary.

The attempt at making the dissenting clergy stationary, and persecuting their circulation, appears to us quite as unjust and inexpedient as the other measure of qualifications. It appears a gross inconsistency to say—"I admit that what you are doing is legal,—but you must not do it thoroughly and effectually. I allow you to propagate your heresy,—but I object to all means of propagating it which appear to be useful and effective." If there are any other grounds upon which the circulation of the dissenting clergy is objected to, let these grounds be stated and examined; but to object to their circulation merely because it is the best method of effecting the object which you allow them to effect, does appear to be rather unnatural and inconsistent.

It is persumed, in this argument, that the only reason urged for the prevention of itinerant preachers is the increase of heresy; for, if heresy is not increased by it, it must be immaterial to the feelings of Lord Sidmouth, and of the imperial Parliament, whether Mr. Shufflebottom preaches at Bungay, and Mr. Ringletub at Ipswich· or whether an artful vicissitude is adopted, and the order of insane predication reversed.

But, supposing all this new interference to be just, what good will it do? You find a dissenting preacher, whom you have prohibited, still continuing to preach,—or preaching at Ealing when he ought to preach at Acton;—his number is taken, and the next morning he is summoned. Is it believed that this description of persons can be put down by fine and imprisonment? His fine is paid for him; and he returns from imprisonment ten times as much sought after and as popular as he was before. This is a receipt for making a stupid preacher popular, and a popular preacher more popular, but can have no possible tendency to prevent the mischief against which it is leveled. It is precisely the old history of persecution against opinions turned into a persecution against persons. The prisons will be filled,—the enemies of the Church made enemies of the state also,—and the Methodists rendered ten times more actively mad than they are at present. This is the direct and obvious tendency of Lord Sidmouth's plan.

Nothing dies so hard and rallies so often as intolerance. The fires are put out, and no living nostril has scented the nidor of a human creature roasted for faith;—then, after this, the prison doors were got open, and the chains knocked off; and now Lord Sidmouth only begs that men who disagree with him in religious opinions may be deprived of all civil offices and not be allowed to hear the preachers they like best. Chains and whips he would not hear of; but these mild gratifications of his bill every orthodox mind is surely entitled to. The hardship would indeed be great if a churchman were deprived of the amusement of putting a dissenting parson in prison. We are convinced Lord Sidmouth is a very amiable and well-intentioned man: his error is not the error of his heart, but of his time, above which few men ever rise. It is the error of some four or five hundred thousand English gentlemen of decent education and worthy characters, who conscientiously believe that they are punishing, and continuing incapacities, for the good of the state; while they are, in fact (though without knowing it), only gratifying that insolence, hatred, and revenge, which all human beings are unfortunately so ready to feel against those who will not conform to their own sentiments.

But, instead of making the dissenting churches less popular, why not make the English church more popular, and raise the English clergy to the privileges of the Dissenters? In any parish of England, any layman, or clergyman, by paying sixpence, can open a place of worship,—provided it be not the worship of the Church of England. If he wishes to attack the doctrines of the bishop or the incumbent, he is not compelled to ask the consent of any person; but if, by any evil chance, he should be persuaded of the truth of those doctrines, and build a chapel or mount a pulpit to support them, he is instantly put in the spiritual court; for the regular incumbent, who has a legal monopoly of this doctrine, does not choose to suffer any interloper; and without his consent, it is illegal to preach the doctrines of the church within his precincts.* Now this appears to us a great

* It might be supposed that the general interests of the Church would outweigh the particular interests of the rector; and that any clergyman would be glad to see places of worship opened within his parish for the doctrines of the Established Church. The fact, however, is directly the reverse. It is scarcely possible to obtain permission from the established clergyman of the parish to open a chapel there; and, when it is granted, it is granted upon very hard and interested conditions. The parishes of St. George—of St. James—of Mary-le bone—and of St. Anne's, in London—may, in the parish churches, chapels of ease, and mercenary chapels, contain, perhaps, one-hundredth part of their Episcopalian inhabitants. Let the rectors, lay and clerical, meet together, and give notice that any clergyman of the Church of England, approved by the bishop, may preach there; and we will venture to say, that places of wor-

and manifest absurdity, and a disadvantage against the Established Church which very few establishments could bear. The persons who preach and who build chapels, or for whom chapels are built, among the Dissenters, are active clever persons, with considerable talents for that kind of employment. These talents have, with them, their free and unbounded scope; while in the English Church they are wholly extinguished and destroyed. Till this evil is corrected, the Church contends with fearful odds against its opponents. On the one side, any man who can command the attention of a congregation—to whom nature has given the animal and intellectual qualifications of a preacher—such a man is the member of every corporation;—all impediments are removed;—there is not a single position in Great Britain which he may not take, provided he is hostile to the Established Church. In the other case, if the English Church were to breed up a Massillon or a Bourdaloue, he finds every place occupied, and every where a regular and respectable clergyman ready to put him in the spiritual court, if he attracts, within his precincts, any attention to the doctrines and worship of the Established Church.

The necessity of having the bishop's consent would prevent any improper person from preaching. That consent should be withheld, not capriciously, but for good and lawful cause to be assigned.

The profits of an incumbent proceed from fixed or voluntary contributions. The fixed could not be affected; and the voluntary ought to vary according to the exertions of the incumbent and the good will of the parishioners; but, if this is wrong, pecuniary compensation might be made (at the discretion of the ordinary) from the supernumerary to the regular clergyman.*

Such a plan, it is true, would make the Church of England more popular in its nature; and it ought to be made more popular, or it will not endure for another half century. There are two methods; the Church must be made more popular or the Dissenters less so. To effect the latter object by force and restriction is unjust and impossible. The only remedy seems to be, to grant to the Church the same privileges which are enjoyed by the Dissenters, and to excite, in one party, that competition of talent which is of such palpable advantage to the other.

A remedy suggested by some well-wishers to the Church, is the appointment of men to benefices who have talents for advancing the interests of religion; but, till each particular patron can be persuaded to care more for the general good of the Church than for the particular good of the person whom he patronizes, little expectation of improvement can be derived from this quarter.

The competition between the Established clergy, to which this method would give birth, would throw the incumbent in the back-ground only when he was unfit to stand forward,—immoral, negligent, or stupid. His income would still remain; and, if his influence were superseded by a man of better qualities and attainments, the general good of the Establishment would be consulted by the change. The beneficed clergyman would always come to the contest with great advantages; and his deficiencies must be very great indeed, if he lost the esteem of his parishioners. But the contest would rarely or never take place, where the friends of the Establishment were not numerous enough for all. At present, the selfish incumbent, who cannot accommodate the fiftieth part of his parishioners, is determined that no one else shall do it for him. It is in such situations that the benefit to the Establishment would be greatest, and the injury to the appointed minister none at all.

We beg of men of sense to reflect, that the question is not whether they wish the English Church to stand as it now is, but whether the English Church can stand as it now is; and whether the moderate activity here recommended is not the minimum of exertion necessary for its preservation. At the same time, we hope nobody will rate our sagacity so very low as to imagine we have much hope that any measure of the kind will ever be adopted. *All establishments die of dignity.* They are too proud to think themselves ill, and to take a little physic.

To show that we have not misstated the obstinacy or the conscience of sectaries, and the spirit with which they will meet the regulations of Lord Sidmouth, we will lay before our readers the sentiments of Philagatharches—a stern subacid Dissenter.

"I shall not here enter into a comprehensive discussion of the nature of a call to the ministerial office; but deduce my proposition from a sentiment admitted equally by conformists and nonconformists. It is essential to the nature of a call to preach 'that a man be moved by the Holy Ghost to enter upon the work of the ministry:' and, if the Spirit of God operate powerfully upon his heart to contrain him to appear as a public teacher of religion, who shall command him to desist? We have seen that the sanction of the magistrate can give no authority to preach the gospel; and if he were to forbid our exertions, we must persist in the work; we dare not relinquish a task that God has required us to perform; we cannot keep our consciences in peace, if our lips are closed in silence, while the Holy Ghost is moving our hearts to proclaim the tidings of salvation:—'Yea, woe is unto me,' saith St. Paul, 'if I preach not the gospel.' Thus, when the Jewish priests had taken Peter and John into custody and after examining them concerning their doc

ship capable of containing 20,000 persons would be built within ten years. But, in these cases, the interest of the rector and of the Establishment is not the same. A chapel belonging to the Swedenborgians, or Methodists of the New Jerusalem, was offered, two or three years since, in London, to a clergyman of the Establishment. The proprietor was tired of his irrational tenants, and wished for better doctrine. The rector (since a dignitary), with every possible compliment to the fitness of the person in question, positively refused the application; and the church remains in the hands of Methodists. No particular blame is intended, by this anecdote, against the individual rector. He acted as many have done before and since; but the incumbent clergyman ought to possess no such power. It is his interest, but not the interest of the Establishment.

* All this has been since placed on a better footing.

trine, 'commanded them not to speak at all, nor to teach in the name of Jesus,' these apostolical champions of the cross undauntedly replied, 'Whether it be right in the sight of God to hearken unto you more than unto God, judge ye: for we cannot but speak the things which we have seen and heard.' Thus, also, in our day, when the Holy Ghost excites a man to preach the gospel to his fellow sinners, his message is sanctioned by an authority which is 'far above all principality and power;' and, consequently, neither needs the approbation of subordinate rulers, nor admits of revocation by their countermanding edicts.

"3dly. He who receives a license should not expect to derive from it a testimony of qualification to preach.

"It would be grossly absurd to seek a testimony of this description from any single individual, even though he were an experienced veteran in the service of Christ; for all are fallible; and, under some unfavourable prepossession, even the wisest or the best of men might give an erroneous decision upon the case. But this observation will gain additional force when we suppose the power of judging transferred to the person of the magistrate.—We cannot presume that a civil ruler understands as much of theology as a minister of the gospel. His necessary duties prevent him from critically investigating questions upon divinity; and confine his attention to that particular department which society has deputed him to occupy; and hence to expect at his hands a testimony of qualification to preach would be almost as ludicrous as to require an obscure country curate to fill the office of Lord Chancellor.

"But again—admitting that a magistrate who is nominated by the sovereign to issue forth licenses to dissenting ministers, is competent to the task of judging of their natural and acquired abilities, it must still remain a doubtful question whether they are moved to preach by the influences of the Holy Ghost; for it is the prerogative of God alone to 'search the heart and try the reins' of the children of men. Consequently, after every effort of the ruling powers to assume to themselves the right of judging whether a man be or be not qualified to preach, the most essential property of the call must remain to be determined by the conscience of the individual.

"It is further worthy of observation that the talents of a preacher may be acceptable to many persons, if not to him who issues the license. The taste of a person thus high in office may be too refined to derive gratification from any but the most learned, intelligent, and accomplished preachers. Yet, as the gospel is sent to the poor as well as to the rich, perhaps hundreds of preachers may be highly acceptable, much esteemed, and eminently useful in their respective circles, who would be despised as men of mean attainments by one whose mind is well stored with literature, and cultivated by science. From these remarks, I infer, that a man's own judgment must be the criterion, in determining what line of conduct to pursue before he begins to preach; and the opinion of the people to whom he ministers must determine whether it be desirable that he should continue to fill their pulpit."—(168—173.)

The sentiments of Philagatharches are expressed still more strongly in a subsequent passage.

"Here a question may arise—what line of conduct conscientious ministers ought to pursue, if laws were to be enacted, forbidding either all dissenting ministers to preach, or only lay preachers; or forbidding to preach in an unlicensed place; and, at the same time, refusing to license persons and places, except under such security as the property of the parties would not meet, or under limitations to which their consciences could not accede. What has been advanced ought to outweigh every consideration of temporal interest; and if the evil genius of persecution were to appear again, I pray God that we might all be faithful to Him who hath called us to preach the gospel. Under such circumstances, let us continue to preach: if fined, let us pay the penalty, and persevere in preaching; and, when unable to pay the fine, or deeming it impolitic so to do, let us submit to go quietly to prison, but with the resolution still to preach upon the first opportunity, and, if possible, to collect a church even within the precincts of the gaol. He who, by these zealous exertions, becomes the honoured instrument of converting one sinner unto God, will find that single seal to his ministerial labours an ample compensation for all his sufferings. In this manner the venerable apostle of the Gentiles both avowed and proved his sincere attachment to the cause in which he had embarked:—'The Holy Ghost witnesseth, in every city, that bonds and afflictions abide me. But none of these things move me, neither count I my life dear unto myself, so that I might finish my course with joy, and the ministry which I have received of the Lord Jesus, to testify the gospel of the grace of God.'

"In the early ages of Christianity martyrdom was considered an eminent honour; and many of the primitive Christians thrust themselves upon the notice of their heathen persecutors, that they might be brought to suffer in the cause of that Redeemer whom they ardently loved. In the present day Christians in general incline to estimate such rash ardour as a species of enthusiasm, and feel no disposition to court the horrors of persecution; yet, if such dark and tremendous days were to return in this age of the world, ministers should retain their stations; they should be true to their charge; they should continue their ministrations, each man in his sphere, shining with all the lustre of genuine godliness, to dispel the gloom in which the nation would then be enveloped. If this line of conduct were to be adopted, and acted upon with decision, the cause of piety, of nonconformity, and of itinerant preaching, must eventually triumph. All the gaols in the country would speedily be filled: those houses of correction which were erected for the chastisement of the vicious in the community, would be replenished with thousands of the most pious, active, and useful men in the kingdom, whose characters are held in general esteem. But the ultimate result of such despotic proceedings is beyond the ken of human prescience:—probably, appeals to the public and the legislature would teem from the press, and, under such circumstances, might diffuse a revolutionary spirit throughout the country."—(239—243.)

We quote these opinions at length, not because they are the opinions of Philagatharches, but because we are confident that they are the opinions of ten thousand hot-headed fanatics, and that they would firmly and conscientiously be acted upon.

Philagatharches is an instance (not uncommon, we are sorry to say, even among the most rational of the Protestant Dissenters) of a love of toleration combined with a love of persecution. He is a Dissenter, and earnestly demands religious liberty for that body of men; but as for the Catholics, he would not only continue their present disabilities, but load them with every new one that could be conceived. He expressly says that an Atheist or a Deist may be allowed to propagate their doctrines, but not a Catholic; and then proceeds with all the customary trash against that sect which nine schoolboys out of ten now know how to refute. So it is with Philagatharches;—so it is with weak men in every sect. It has ever been our object, and (in spite of misrepresentation and abuse) ever shall be our object, to put down this spirit—to protect the true interests, and to diffuse the true spirit, of toleration. To a well-supported national Establishment, effectually discharging its duties, we are very sincere friends. If any man, after he has paid his contribution to this great security for the existence of religion in any shape, chooses to adopt a religion of his own, that man should be permitted to do so without let, molestation, or disqualification for any of the offices of life. We apologize to men of sense for sentiments so trite; and patiently endure the anger which they will excite among those with whom they will pass for original.

CHARLES FOX.*

[EDINBURGH REVIEW, 1811.]

THOUGH Mr. Fox's history was, of course, as much open to animadversion and rebuke as any other book, the task, we think, would have become any other person better than Mr. Rose. The whole of Mr. Fox's life was spent in opposing the profligacy and exposing the ignorance of his own court. In the first half of his political career, while Lord North was losing America, and in the latter half, while Mr. Pitt was ruining Europe, the creatures of the government were eternally exposed to the attacks of this discerning, dauntless, and most powerful speaker. Folly and corruption never had a more terrible enemy in the English House of Commons—one whom it was so impossible to bribe, so hopeless to elude, and so difficult to answer. Now it so happened that, during the whole of this period, the historical critic of Mr. Fox was employed in subordinate offices of government;—that the detail of taxes passed through his hands;—that he amassed a large fortune by those occupations;—and that, both in the measures which he supported, and in the friends from whose patronage he received his emoluments, he was completely and perpetually opposed to Mr. Fox.

Again, it must be remembered, that very great people have very long memories for the injuries which they receive, or which they think they receive. No speculation was so good, therefore, as to vilify the memory of Mr. Fox,—nothing so delicious as to lower him in the public estimation,—no service so likely to be well rewarded—so eminently grateful to those of whose favour Mr. Rose had so often tasted the sweets, and of the value of whose patronage he must, from long experience, have been so thoroughly aware.

We are almost inclined to think that we might at one time have worked ourselves up to suspect Mr. Rose of being actuated by some of these motives:—not because we have any reason to think worse of that gentleman than of most of his political associates, but merely because it seemed to us so very probable that he should have been so influenced. Our suspicions, however, were entirely removed by the frequency and violence of his own protestations. He vows so solemnly that he has no bad motive in writing his critique, that we find it impossible to withhold our belief in his purity. But Mr. Rose does not trust to his protestations alone. He is not satisfied with assurances that he did not write this book from any bad motive, but he informs us that his motive was excellent,—and is even obliging enough to tell us what that motive was. The Earl of Marchmont, it seems, was Mr. Rose's friend. To Mr. Rose he left his manuscripts; and among these manuscripts was a narrative written by Sir Patrick Hume, an ancestor of the Earl of Marchmont, and one of the leaders in Argyle's rebellion. Of Sir Patrick Hume Mr. Rose conceives (a little erroneously to be sure, but he assures us he does conceive) Mr. Fox to have spoken disrespectfully; and the case comes out, therefore, as clearly as possible, as follows.

Sir Patrick was the progenitor, and Mr. Rose was the friend and sole executor, of the Earl of Marchmont; and therefore, says Mr. Rose, I consider it as a *sacred* duty to vindicate the character of Sir Patrick, and, for that purpose, to publish a long and elaborate critique upon all the doctrines and statements contained in Mr. Fox's history! This appears to us about as satisfactory an explanation of Mr. Rose's authorship as the exclamation of the traveller was of the name of Stony Stratford.

Before Mr. Rose gave way to this intense value for Sir Patrick, and resolved to write a book, he should have inquired what accurate men there were about in society; and if he had once received the slightest notice of the existence of Mr. Samuel Heywood, serjeant-at-law, we are convinced he would have transfused into his own will and testament the feelings he derived from that of Lord Marchmont, and devolved upon another executor the sacred and dangerous duty of vindicating Sir Patrick Hume.

The life of Mr. Rose has been principally employed in the painful, yet perhaps necessary, duty of increasing the burdens of his fellow-creatures. It has been a life of detail, onerous to the subject—onerous and lucrative to himself. It would be unfair to expect from one thus occupied any great depth of thought, or any remarkable graces of composition; but we have a fair right to look for habits of patient research and scrupulous accuracy. We might naturally expect industry in collecting facts, and fidelity in quoting them; and hope, in the absence of commanding genius, to receive a compensation from the more humble and ordinary qualities of the mind. How far this is the case, our subsequent remarks will enable the reader to judge. We shall not extend them to any great length, as we have before treated on the same subject in our review of Mr. Rose's work. Our great object at present is to abridge the observations of Serjeant Heywood. For Serjeant Heywood, though a most respectable, honest, and enlightened man, really does require an abridger. He has not the talent of saying what he has to say quickly; nor is he aware that brevity is in writing what charity is to all other virtues. Righteousness is worth nothing without the one, nor authorship without the other. But whoever will forgive this little defect will find in all his productions great learning, immaculate honesty, and the most scrupulous accu

* *A Vindication of Mr. Fox's History of the Early Part of the Reign of James the Second.* By SAMUEL HEYWOOD, Serjeant-at-Law. London. Johnson & Co. 1811.

racy. Whatever detections of Mr. Rose's inaccuracies are made in this Review are to be entirely given to him; and we confess ourselves quite astonished at their number and extent.

"Among the modes of destroying persons (says Mr. Fox, p. 14,) in such a situation (*i. e.* monarchs deposed), there can be little doubt but that adopted by Cromwell and his adherents *is the least dishonourable.* Edward II., Richard II., Henry VI., Edward V., had none of them long survived their deposal; but this was the first instance, in our history at least, when of such an act it could be truly said it was not done in a corner."

What Mr. Rose can find in this sentiment to quarrel with, we are utterly at a loss to conceive. If a human being is to be put to death unjustly, is it no mitigation of such a lot that the death should be public? Is any thing better calculated to prevent secret torture and cruelty? And would Mr. Rose, in mercy to Charles, have preferred that red-hot iron should have been secretly thrust into his entrails?—or that he should have disappeared as Pichegru and Toussaint have disappeared in our times? The periods of the Edwards and Henrys were, it is true, barbarous periods: but this is the very argument Mr. Fox uses. All these murders, he contends, were immoral and bad; but that where the *manner* was the least objectionable, was the murder of Charles the First,—because it was public. And can any human being doubt, in the first place, that these crimes would be marked by less intense cruelty if they were public; and, secondly, that they would become less frequent, where the perpetrators incurred responsibility, than if they were committed by an uncertain hand in secrecy and concealment? There never was, in short, not only a more innocent, but a more obvious sentiment; and to object to it in the manner which Mr. Rose has done, is surely to love Sir Patrick Hume too much,—if there can be any excess in so very commendable a passion in the breast of a sole executor.

Mr. Fox proceeds to observe, that "he who has discussed this subject with foreigners, must have observed, that the act of the execution of Charles, even in the minds of those who condemn it, excites more admiration than disgust." If the sentiment is bad, let those who feel it answer for it. Mr. Fox only asserts the fact, and explains, without justifying it. The only question (as concerns Mr. Fox) is, whether such is, or is not, the feeling of foreigners; and whether that feeling (if it exists) is rightly explained? We have no doubt either of the fact or of the explanation. The conduct of Cromwell and his associates was not to be excused in the main act; but, in the manner, it *was* magnanimous. And among the servile nations of the Continent, it must naturally excite a feeling of joy and wonder, that the power of the people had for once been felt, and so memorable a lesson read to those whom *they* must naturally consider as the great oppressors of mankind.

The most unjustifiable point of Mr. Rose's accusation, however, is still to come. "If such high praise," says that gentleman, "was, in the judgment of Mr. Fox, due to Cromwell for the publicity of the proceedings against the king, how would he have found language sufficiently commendatory to express his admiration of the magnanimity of those who brought Lewis the Sixteenth to an open trial?" Mr. Rose accuses Mr. Fox, then, of approving the execution of Lewis the Sixteenth: but, on the 20th of December, 1792, Mr. Fox said, in the House of Commons, *in the presence of Mr. Rose,*

"The proceedings with respect to the royal family of France are so far from being magnanimity, justice, or mercy, that they are directly the reverse; they are injustice, cruelty, and pusillanimity." And afterwards declared his wish for an address to his majesty, to which he would add an expression "of our abhorrence of the proceedings against the royal family of France, in which, I have no doubt, we shall be supported by the whole country. If there can be any means suggested that will be better adapted to produce the unanimous concurrence of this House, and of all the country, with respect to the measure now under consideration in Paris, I should be obliged to any person for his better suggestion upon the subject." Then, after stating that such address, especially if the Lords joined in it, must have a decisive influence in France, he added, "I have said thus much in order to contradict one of the most cruel misrepresentations of what I had before said in our late debates; and that my language may not be interpreted from the manner in which other gentlemen have chosen to answer it. I have spoken the genuine sentiments of my heart, and I anxiously wish the House to come to some resolution upon the subject." And on the following day, when a copy of instruction sent to Earl Gower, signifying that he should leave Paris, was laid before the House of Commons, Mr. Fox said, "he had heard it said, that the proceedings against the King of France are unnecessary. He would go a great deal farther, and say, he believed them to be highly unjust; and not only repugnant to all the common feelings of mankind, but also contrary to all the fundamental principles of law."—(p. 20, 21.)

On Monday the 28th January, he said,—

"With regard to that part of the communication from his majesty, which related to the late detestable scene exhibited in a neighbouring country, he could not suppose there were two opinions in that House; he knew they were all ready to declare their abhorrence of that abominable proceeding."—(p. 21.)

Two days afterwards, in the debate on the message, Mr. Fox pronounced the condemnation and execution of the king to be

—"an act as disgraceful as any that history recorded: and whatever opinions he might at any time have expressed in private conversation, he had expressed none certainly in that House on the justice of bringing kings to trial: revenge being unjustifiable, and punishment useless, where it could not operate either by way of prevention or example; he did not view with less detestation the injustice and inhumanity that had been committed towards that unhappy monarch. Not only were the rules of criminal justice—rules that more than any other ought to be strictly observed—violated with respect to him: not only was he tried and condemned without existing law, to which he was personally amenable, and even contrary to laws that did actually exist, but the degrading circumstances of his imprisonment, the unnecessary and insulting asperity with which he had been treated, *the total want of republican magnanimity in the whole transaction*, (for even in that House it could be no offence to say, that there might be such a thing as magnanimity in a republic,) added every aggravation to the inhumanity and injustice."

That Mr. Fox had held this language in the House of Commons, Mr. Rose knew perfectly well, when he accused that gentleman of approving the murder of the King of France. Whatever be the faults imputed to Mr. Fox, duplicity and hypocrisy were never among the number; and no human being ever doubted but that Mr. Fox, in this instance, spoke his real sentiments: but the love of Sir Patrick Hume is an overwhelming passion; and no man who gives way to it, can ever say into what excesses he may be hurried.

Non simul cuiquam conceditur, amare et sapere.

The next point upon which Sergeant Heywood attacks Mr. Rose, is that of General Monk. Mr. Fox says of Monk, "that he acquiesced in the insult so meanly put upon the illustrious corpse of Blake, under whose auspices and command he had performed the most creditable services of his life." This story, Mr. Rose says, rests upon the authority of Neale, in his History of the Puritans. This is the first of many blunders made by Mr. Rose upon this particular topic: for Anthony Wood, in his Fasti Oxonienses, enumerating Blake among the bachelors, says, "His body was taken up, and, with others, *buried in a pit in St. Margaret's church-yard* adjoining, near to the back door of one of the prebendaries of Westminster, *in which place it now remaineth*, enjoying no other monument but what it reared by its valour, which time itself can hardly efface." But the difficulty is to find how the denial of Mr. Rose affects Mr. Fox's assertion. Mr. Rose admits that Blake's body was dug up by an order of the king; and does not deny that it was done with the acquiescence of Monk. But if this be the case, Mr. Fox's position that Blake was insulted, and that Monk acquiesced in the insult, is clearly made out. Nor has Mr. Rose the shadow of an authority for saying that the corpse of Blake was reinterred *with great decorum*. Kennet is silent upon the subject. We have already given Serjeant Heywood's quotation from Anthony Wood; and this statement, for the present, rests entirely upon the assertion of Mr. Rose; and upon that basis will remain to all eternity.

Mr. Rose, who, we must say, on all occasions through the whole of this book, makes the greatest parade of his accuracy, states that the bodies of Cromwell, Ireton, and Blake, were taken up at the same time; whereas the fact is, that those of Cromwell and Ireton were taken up on the 26th of January, and that of Blake on the 10th of September, nearly nine months afterwards. It may appear frivolous to notice such errors as these; but they lead to very strong suspicions in a critic of history and of historians. They show that those habits of punctuality, on the faith of which he demands implicit confidence from his readers, really do not exist; they prove that such a writer will be exact only when he thinks the occasion of importance, and as he himself is the only judge of that importance, it is necessary to examine his proofs in every instance, and impossible to trust him anywhere.

Mr. Rose remarks that, in the weekly paper entitled Mercurius Rusticus, No. 4, where an account is given of the disinterment of Cromwell and Ireton, not a syllable is said respecting the corpse of Blake. This is very true; but the reason (which does not seem to have occurred to Mr. Rose) is, that Blake's corpse was *not touched till six months afterwards*. This is really a little too much. That Mr. Rose should quit his usual pursuits, erect himself into an historical critic, perch upon the body of the dead lion, impugn the accuracy of one of the greatest, as well as most accurate men of his time,—and himself be guilty of such gross and unpardonable negligence, looks so very much like an insensibility to shame, that we should be loth to characterize his conduct by the severe epithets which it appears to merit, and which, we are quite certain, Sir Patrick, the defendee, would have been the first to bestow upon it.

The next passage in Mr. Fox's work objected to is that which charges Monk, at the trial of Argyle, "with having produced letters of friendship and confidence to take away the life of a nobleman, the zeal and cordiality of whose co-operation with him, proved by such documents, was the chief ground of his execution." This accusation, says Mr. Rose, rests upon the sole authority of Bishop Burnet; and yet no sooner has he said this, than he tells us, Mr. *Laing* considers the bishop's authority to be confirmed by Cunningham and Baillie, both contemporary writers. Into Cunningham or Baillie Mr. Rose never looks to see whether or not they do really confirm the authority of the bishop; and so gross is his negligence, that the very misprint from Mr. Laing's work is copied, and page 431 of Baillie is cited instead of 451. If Mr. Rose had really taken the trouble of referring to these books, all doubt of the meanness and guilt of Monk must have been instantly removed. "Monk was moved," says Baillie, "*to send down four or five of Argyle's letters to himself and others, promising his full compliance with them, that the king should not reprieve him*."—*Baillie's Letters*, p. 451. "He endeavoured to make his defence," says Cunningham; "*but chiefly by the discoveries of Monk* was condemned of high treason, and lost his head."—*Cunningham's History*, i. p. 13.

Would it have been more than common decency required, if Mr. Rose, who had been apprised of the existence of these authorities, had

had recourse to them, before he impugned the accuracy of Mr. Fox? Or is it possible to read, without some portion of contempt, this slovenly and indolent corrector of supposed inaccuracies in a man, not only so much greater than himself in his general nature, but a man who, as it turns out, excels Mr. Rose in his own little arts of looking, searching, and comparing; and is as much his superior in the retail qualities which small people arrogate to themselves, as he was in every commanding faculty to the rest of his fellow creatures?

Mr. Rose searches Thurloe's State Papers; but Serjeant Heywood searches them after Mr. Rose: and, by a series of the plainest references, proves the probability there is that Argyle did receive letters which might materially have affected his life.

To Monk's duplicity of conduct may be principally attributed the destruction of his friends, who were prevented, by their confidence in him, from taking measures to secure themselves. He selected those among them whom he thought fit for trial—sat as a commissioner upon their trial—and interfered not to save the lives even of those with whom he had lived in habits of the greatest kindness.

"I cannot," says a witness of the most unquestion ble authority, "I cannot forget *one passage that I saw.* Monk and his wife, before they were moved to the Tower, while they were yet prisoners at Lambeth House, came one evening to the garden, and caused them to be brought down, only to stare at them; which was such a barbarism, for that man who had betrayed so many poor men to death and misery, that never hurt him, but had honoured him, and trusted their lives and interests with him, to glut his bloody eyes with beholding them in their bondage, as no story can parallel the inhumanity of."—(p. 83.) *Hutchinson's Memoirs*, 378.

This, however, is the man whom Mr. Fox, at the distance of a century and a half, may not mark with infamy, without incurring, from the candour of Mr. Rose, the imputation of republican principles;—as if attachment to monarchy could have justified, in Monk, the coldness, cruelty, and treachery of his character,—as if the historian became the advocate, or the enemy of any form of government, by praising the good, or blaming the bad men which it might produce Serjeant Heywood sums up the whole article as follows:

"Having examined and commented upon the evidence produced by Mr. Rose, than which 'it is hardly possible,' he says, 'to conceive that stronger could be formed in any case to establish a negative,' we now safely assert that Mr. Fox had fully informed himself upon the subject before he wrote, and was amply justified in the condemnation of Monk, and the consequent severe censures upon him. It has been already demonstrated that the character of Monk had been truly given, when of him he said, 'the army had fallen into the hands of one, than whom a baser could not be found in its lowest ranks.' The transactions between him and Argyle for a certain period of time were such as must naturally, if not necessarily, have led them into an epistolary correspondence; and it was in exact conformity with Monk's character and conduct to the regicides, that he should betray the letters written to him, in order to destroy a man whom he had, in the latter part of his command in Scotland, both feared and hated. If the fact of the production of these letters had stood merely on the testimony of Bishop Burnet, we have seen that nothing has been produced by Mr. Rose and Dr. Campbell to impeach it; on the contrary, an inquiry into the authorities and documents they have cited, strongly confirm it. But, as before observed, it is a surprising instance of Mr. Rose's indolence, that he should state the question to depend now, as it did in Dr. Campbell's time, on the bishop's authority solely. But that authority is, in itself, no light one Burnet was almost eighteen years of age at the time of Argyle's trial; he was never an unobserving spectator of public events; he was probably at Edinburgh, and, for some years afterwards, remained in Scotland, with ample means of information respecting events which had taken place so recently. Baillie seems also to have been upon the spot, and expressly confirms the testimony of Burnet. To these must be added Cunningham, who, writing as a person perfectly acquainted with the circumstances of the transaction, says it was owing to the interference of Monk, who had been his great friend in Oliver's time, that he was sent back to Scotland, and brought to trial; and that he was condemned chiefly by his discoveries. We may now ask where is the improbability of this story, when related of such a man? and what ground there is for not giving credit to a fact attested by three witnesses of veracity, each writing at a distance, and separate from each other? In this instance Bishop Burnet is so confirmed, that no reasonable being, who will attend to the subject, can doubt of the fact he relates being true; and we shall hereafter prove that the general imputation against his accuracy, made by Mr. Rose, is totally without foundation. If facts so proved are not to be credited, historians may lay aside their pens, and every man must content himself with the scanty pittance of knowledge he may be able to collect for himself in the very limited sphere of his own immediate observation."—(p. 86—88.)

This, we think, is conclusive enough: but we are happy to be enabled, out of our own store, to set this part of the question finally to rest, by an authority which Mr. Rose himself will probably admit to be decisive. Sir George Mackenzie, the great tory lawyer of Scotland in that day, and Lord Advocate to Charles II. through the greater part of his reign, was the leading counsel for Argyle on the trial alluded to. In 1678, this learned person, who was then Lord Advocate to Charles, published an elaborate treatise on the criminal law of Scotland; in which, when treating of probation, or evidence, he observes, that missive letters, not written, but only signed by the party, should not be received in evidence; and immediately adds, "And yet *the Marquis of Argyle was convict of treason* UPON LETTERS WRITTEN BY HIM TO GENERAL MONK; these letters being only subscribed by him, and not holograph, and the subscription being proved *per comparationem literarum;* which were very hard in other cases," &c.—*Mackenzie's Criminals,* first edit. p. 524, Part II. tit. 25, § 3. Now this, we conceive, is neither more nor less than a solemn professional report of the case,—and leaves just as little room for doubt as to the fact, as if the original record of the trial had been recovered.

Mr. Rose next objects to Mr. Fox's assertion, that "the king kept from his cabal ministry the real state of his connection with France—and from some of them the secret of what he was pleased to call his religion;" and Mr. Fox doubts whether to attribute this conduct to the habitual treachery of Charles, or to an apprehension that his ministers might demand for themselves some share of the French money; which he was unwilling to give them. In answer to this conjecture, Mr. Rose quotes Barillon's Letters to Lewis XIV., to show that Charles's ministers were fully apprised of his money transactions with France. The letters so quoted were, however, written *seven years after the cabal ministry were in power*—for Barillon did not come to England as ambassador till 1677—and these letters were not written till after that period. Poor Sir Patrick—It was for thee and thy defence this book was written!!!!

Mr. Fox has said, that from some of the ministers of the cabal the secret of Charles's religion was concealed. It was known to Arlington, admitted by Mr. Rose to be a concealed Catholic; it was known to Clifford, an avowed Catholic: Mr. Rose admits it not to have been known to Buckingham, though he explains the reserve, with respect to him, in a different way. He has not, however, attempted to prove that Lauderdale or Ashley were consulted;—on the contrary, in Colbert's letter of the 25th August, 1670, cited by Mr. Rose, it is stated that Charles had proposed the *traité simulé,* which should be a repetition of the former one in all things, except the article relative to the king's declaring himself a Catholic, and that the *Protestant ministers,* Buckingham, Ashley, Cooper, and Lauderdale, should be brought to be parties to it:—Can there be a stronger proof (asks Serjeant Heywood), that they were ignorant of the same treaty made the year before, and remaining then in force? Historical research is certainly not the peculiar talent of Mr. Rose; and as for the official accuracy of which he is so apt to boast, we would have Mr. Rose to remember, that the term *official accuracy* has of late days become one of very ambiguous import. Mr. Rose, we can see, would imply by it the highest possible accuracy—as we see *office pens* advertised in the window of a shop, by way of excellence. The public reports of those, however, who have been appointed to look into the manner in which public offices are conducted, by no means justify this usage of the term;—and we are not without apprehensions, that Dutch politeness, Carthaginian faith, Bœotian genius, and official accuracy, may be terms equally current in the world; and that Mr. Rose may, without intending it, have contributed to make this valuable addition to the mass of our ironical phraseology.

Speaking of the early part of James's reign, Mr. Fox says, it is by no means certain that he had yet thoughts of obtaining for his religion any thing more than a complete toleration; and if Mr. Rose had understood the meaning of the French word *établissement,* one of his many incorrect corrections of Mr. Fox might have been spared. A system of religion is said to be established when it is enacted and endowed by Parliament; but a toleration (as Serjeant Heywood observes) is established, when it is recognised and protected by the supreme power. And in the letters of *Barillon,* to which Mr. Rose refers for the justification of his attack upon Mr. Fox, it is quite manifest that it is in this latter sense that the word *établissement* is used· and that the object in view was, not the substitution of the Catholic religion for the Established Church, but merely its toleration. In the first letter cited by Mr. Rose, James says, that "he knew well he should never be in safety unless *liberty of conscience* for them should be fully established in England." The letter of the 24th of April is quoted by Mr. Rose, as if the French king had written, the *establishment of the Catholic religion;* whereas the real words are, the *establishment of the free exercise of the Catholic religion.* The world are so inveterately resolved to believe, that a man who has no brilliant talents must be accurate, that Mr. Rose, in referring to authorities, has a great and decided advantage. He is, however, in point of fact, as lax and incorrect as a poet; and it is absolutely necessary, in spite of every parade of line, and page, and number, to follow him in the most minute particular. The Serjeant, like a bloodhound of the old breed, is always upon his track; and always looks if there are any such passages in the page quoted, and if the passages are accurately quoted or accurately translated. Nor will he by any means be content with *official accuracy,* nor submit to be treated, in historical questions, as if he were hearing financial statements in the House of Commons.

Barillon writes, in another letter to Lewis XIV.—"What your majesty has most besides at heart, that is to say, for the establishment of a free exercise of the Catholic religion." On the 9th of May, *Lewis* writes to *Barillon,* that he is persuaded Charles will employ all his authority to establish the *free exercise* of the Catholic religion: he mentions also, in the same letter, the Parliament consenting to the *free exercise of our religion.* On the 15th of June, he writes to Barillon—"There now remains only *to obtain the repeal of the penal laws in favour of the Catholics, and the free exercise of our religion in all his states.*" Immediately after Monmouth's execution, when his views of success must have been as lofty as they ever could have been, Lewis writes—"It will be easy to the King of England, and as useful for the security of his reign as for the repose of his conscience, to re-establish *the exercise* of the Catholic religion." In a letter of Barillon, July 16th, Sunderland is made to say, that the king would always be exposed to the indiscreet zeal of those who would inflame the people against the Catholic religion, so *long as it should not be more fully established.* The French expression is *tant qu'elle ne sera pas plus pleinement établie;* and this Mr. Rose has had the modesty to translate, *till it shall be com-*

pletely established, and to mark the passage with italics, as of the greatest importance to his argument. These false quotations and translations being detected, and those passages of early writers, from which Mr. Fox had made up his opinion, brought to light, it is not possible to doubt, but that the object of James, before Monmouth's defeat, was not the destruction of the Protestant, but the toleration of the Catholic religion; and after the execution of Monmouth, Mr. Fox admits, that he became more bold and sanguine upon the subject of religion.

We do not consider those observations of Serjeant Heywood to be the most fortunate in his book, where he attempts to show the republican tendency of Mr. Rose's principles. Of any disposition to principles of this nature, we most heartily acquit that right honourable gentleman. He has too much knowledge of mankind to believe their happiness can be promoted in the stormy and tempestuous regions of republicanism; and, besides this, that system of slender pay, and deficient perquisites, to which the subordinate agents of government are confined in republics, is much too painful to be thought of for a single instant.

We are afraid of becoming tedious by the enumeration of blunders into which Mr. Rose has fallen, and which Serjeant Heywood has detected. But the burthen of this sole executor's song is accuracy—his own official accuracy—and the little dependence which is to be placed on the accuracy of Mr. Fox. We will venture to assert, that, in the whole of his work, he has not detected Mr. Fox in *one single error*. Whether Serjeant Heywood has been more fortunate with respect to Mr. Rose, might be determined, perhaps with sufficient certainty, by our previous extracts from his remarks. But for some indulgent readers, these may not seem enough: and we must proceed in the task, till we have settled Mr. Rose's pretensions to accuracy on a still firmer foundation. And if we be thought minutely severe, let it be remembered that Mr. Rose is himself an accuser; and if there is justice upon earth, every man has a right to pull stolen goods out of the pocket of him who cries, "*Stop thief!*"

In the story which Mr. Rose states of the seat in Parliament sold for five pounds (Journal of the Commons, vol. v.), he is wrong, both in the sum and the volume. The sum is four pounds; and it is told, not in the fifth volume, but the first. Mr. Rose states, that a perpetual excise was granted to the crown, in lieu of the profits of the court of wards; and adds, that the question in favour of the crown was carried by a majority of two. The real fact is, that the half only of an excise upon certain articles was granted to government in lieu of these profits; and this grant was *carried without a division.* An attempt was made to grant the other half, and this *was negatived by a majority of two.* The Journals are open;—Mr. Rose reads them;—he is officially accurate. What can the meaning be of these most extraordinary mistakes?

Mr. Rose says that, in 1679, the writ *de hæretico comburendo* had been a dead letter for more than a century. It would have been extremely agreeable to Mr. Bartholomew Legate, if this had been the case; for, in 1612, he was burnt at Smithfield for being an Arian. Mr. Wightman would probably have participated in the satisfaction of Mr. Legate; as he was burnt also, the same year, at Lichfield, for the same offence. With the same correctness, this scourge of historians makes the Duke of Lauderdale, who died in 1682, a confidential adviser of James II. after his accession in 1689. In page 13, he quotes, as written by Mr. Fox, that which was written by Lord Holland. This, however, is a familiar practice with him. Ten pages afterward, in Mr. Fox's History, he makes the same mistake. "Mr. *Fox* added"—whereas it was *Lord Holland* that added. The same mistake again, in p. 147 of his own book; and after this, he makes Mr. Fox the person who selected the appendix of Barillon's papers; whereas it is particularly stated in the preface to the History, that this appendix was selected by Laing.

Mr. Rose affirms, that compassing to levy war against the king was made high treason by the statute of 25 Edward the Third; and, in support of this affirmation, he cites Coke and Blackstone. His stern antagonist, a professional man, is convinced he has read neither. The former says, "*a compassing to levy war is no treason,*" (Inst. 3, p. 9;) and Blackstone, "a bare conspiracy to levy war does not amount to this species of treason." (Com. iv. p. 82.) This really does not look as if the Serjeant had made out his assertion.

Of the bill introduced in 1685, for the preservation of the person of James II., Mr. Rose observes—"Mr. Fox has not told us for which of our modern statutes this bill was used as a model; and it will be difficult for any one to show such an instance." It might have been thought, that no prudent man would have made such a challenge, without a tolerable certainty of the ground upon which it was made. Serjeant Heywood answers the challenge by citing the 36 Geo. III. c. 7, which is a mere copy of the act of James.

In the fifth section of Mr. Rose's work is contained his grand attack upon Mr. Fox for his abuse of Sir Patrick Hume; and his observations upon this point admit of a fourfold answer. 1st, Mr. Fox does not use the words quoted by Mr. Rose; 2dly, He makes no mention whatever of Sir Patrick Hume in the passage cited by Mr. Rose; 3dly, Sir Patrick Hume is attacked by nobody in that history; 4thly, If he had been so attacked he would have deserved it. The passage from Mr. Fox is this:—

"In recounting the failure of his expedition, it is impossible for him not to touch upon what *he deemed* the misconduct of his friends; and this is the subject upon which, of all others, his temper must have been most irritable. A certain description of friends (the words describing them are omitted) were all of them, without exception, his greatest enemies, both to betray and destroy him: —— and —— and (the names again omitted) were the greatest cause of his rout, and his being taken, though not designedly, he acknowledges, but by ignorance, cowardice, and faction. This sentence had scarce escaped him, when, notwithstanding the qualifying words with which his candour has acquitted *the last mentioned persons of intentional treachery,* it appeared too harsh to his gentle nature; and, declaring himself displeased with the hard epithets he had used, he desires that they may be put out of any account that is to be given of these transactions."—*Heywood,* p. 365, 366.

Argyle names neither the description of friends who were his greatest enemies, nor the two individuals who were the principal cause of the failure of his scheme. Mr. Fox leaves the blanks as he finds them. *But* two notes are added by the editor, which Mr. Rose might have observed are marked with an *E.* In the latter of them we are told, that Mr. Fox observes, in *a private letter,* "Cochrane and Hume certainly filled up the two principal blanks." But is this communication of a private letter any part of Mr. Fox's history? And would it not have been equally fair in Mr. Rose to have commented upon any private conversation of Mr. Fox, and then to have called it his history? Or, if Mr. Fox had filled up the blanks in the body of his history, does it follow that he adopts Argyle's censure because he shows against whom it is levelled? Mr. Rose has described the charge against Sir Patrick Hume to be, of faction, cowardice, and *treachery.* Mr. Rose has more than once altered the terms of a proposition before he has proceeded to answer it; and, in this instance, the charge of treachery against Sir Patrick Hume is not made either in Argyle's letter, Mr. Fox's text, or the editor's note, or any where but in the imagination of Mr. Rose. The sum of it all is, that Mr. Rose first supposes the relation of Argyle's opinion to be the expression of the relator's opinion, that Mr. Fox adopts Argyle's insinuations because he explains them;—then he looks upon a quotation from a private letter, made by the editor, to be the same as if included in a work intended for publication by the author;—then he remembers that he is the sole executor of Sir Patrick's grandson, whose blank is so filled up;—and goes on blundering and blubbering,—grateful and inaccurate,—teeming with false quotations and friendly recollections to the conclusion of his book. *Multa gemens ignominiam.*

Mr. Rose came into possession of the Earl of Marchmont's papers, containing, among other things, the narrative of Sir Patrick Hume. He is very severe upon Mr. Fox for not having been more diligent in searching for original papers; and observes, that if any application had been made to him (Mr. Rose), this narrative should have been at Mr. Fox's service. We should be glad to know, if Mr. Rose saw a person tumbled into a ditch, whether he would wait for a regular application till he pulled him out? Or, if he happened to espy the lost piece of silver for which the good woman was diligently sweeping the house, would he wait for formal interrogation before he imparted his discovery, and suffer the lady to sweep on till the question had been put to him in the most solemn forms of politeness? The established practice, we admit, is to apply, and to apply vigorously and incessantly, for sinecure places and pensions—or they cannot be had. This is true enough. But did any human being ever think of carrying this practice into literature, and compelling another to make interest for papers essential to the good conduct of his undertaking? We are perfectly astonished at Mr. Rose's conduct in this particular; and should have thought that the ordinary exercise of his good nature would have led him to a very different way of acting.

"*On the whole, and upon the most attentive consideration of every thing which has been written upon the subject,* there does not appear to have been any intention of applying torture in the case of the Earl of Argyle." (*Rose,* p. 182.) If this *every thing* had included the following extract from *Barillon,* the above cited, and very disgraceful inaccuracy of Mr. Rose would have been spared. "The Earl of Argyle has been executed at Edinburgh, and has left a full confession in writing, in which he discovers all those who have assisted him with money, and have aided his designs. *This has saved him from the torture.*" And Argyle, in his letter to Mrs. Smith, confesses he has made discoveries. In his very inaccurate history of torture in the southern part of this island, Mr. Rose says, that except in the case of Felton,—in the attempt to introduce the civil law in Henry VI.'s reign,—and in some cases of treason in Mary's reign, torture was never attempted in this country. The fact, however, is, that in the reign of Henry VIII., Anne Askew was tortured by the chancellor himself. Simson was tortured in 1558; Francis Throgmorton in 1571; Charles Baillie, and Banastie, the Duke of Norfolk's servant, were tortured in 1581; Campier, the Jesuit, was put upon the rack; and Dr. Astlow is supposed to have been racked in 1558. So much for Mr. Rose as the historian of punishments. We have seen him, a few pages before, at the stake,—where he makes quite as bad a figure as he does now upon the rack. Precipitation and error are his foibles. If he were to write the history of sieges, he would forget the siege of Troy;—if he were making a list of poets, he would leave out Virgil:—Cæsar would not appear in his catalogue of generals;—and Newton would be overlooked in his collection of eminent mathematicians.

In some cases, Mr. Rose is to be met only with flat denial. Mr. Fox *does not* call the soldiers who were defending James against Argyle *authorized assassins;* but he uses that expression against the soldiers who were murdering the peasants, and committing every sort of licentious cruelty in the twelve counties given up to military execution; and this Mr. Rose must have known, by using the most ordinary diligence in the perusal of the text,—and would have known it in any other history than that of Mr. Fox.

"Mr. Rose, in his concluding paragraph, boasts of his speaking 'impersonally,' and he hopes it will be allowed justly, when he makes a general observation respecting the proper province of history. But the last sentence evidently shows that, though he might be speaking justly, he was not speaking *impersonally,* if by that word is meant, without refe rence to any person. His words are, 'But history cannot connect itself with party, without forfeiting its name; without departing from the truth, the dignity, and the usefulness of its functions.' After the remarks he has made in some of his preceding pages, and the apology he has offered for Mr. Fox, in his last preceding paragraph, for having been mistaken in his view of some leading points, there can be no difficulty in concluding, that this general observation is meant to be applied to the historical work. The charge intended to be insinuated must be, that, in Mr. Fox's hands, history has forfeited the name by being connected with party; and has departed from the truth, the dignity, and the usefulness of its functions. It were to be wished that Mr. Rose had explained himself more fully; for, after assuming that the application of this observation is too obvious to be mistaken, there still remains some difficulty with respect to its meaning. If it is confined to such publications as are written under the title of histories, but are intended to serve the purposes of a party; and truth is sacrificed, and facts perverted, to defend and give currency to their tenets, we do not dispute its propriety; but, if that is the character which Mr. Rose would give to Mr. Fox's labours, he has not treated him with candour, or even common justice. Mr. Rose has never, in any one instance, intimated that Mr. Fox has wilfully departed from truth, or strayed from the proper province of history, for the purpose of indulging his private or party feelings. But, if Mr. Rose intends that the observation should be applied to all histories, the authors of which have felt strongly the influence of political connections and principles, what must become of most of the histories of England? Is the title of historian to be denied to Mr. Hume? and in what class are to be placed Echard, Kennet, Rapin, Dalrymple, or Macpherson? In this point of view the principle laid down is too broad. A person, though connected with party, may write an impartial history of events which occurred a century before; and, till this last sentence, Mr. Rose has not ventured to intimate that Mr. Fox has not done so. On the contrary, he has declared his approbation of a great portion of the work; and his attempts to discover material errors in the remainder have uniformly failed in every particular. If it might be assumed that there existed in the book no faults, besides those which the scrutinizing eye of Mr. Rose has discovered, it might be justly deemed the most perfect work that ever came from the press; for not a single deviation from the strictest duty of an historian has been pointed out; while instances of candour and impartiality present themselves in almost every page; and Mr. Rose himself has acknowledged and applauded many of them."—(pp. 422—424.)

These extracts from both books are sufficient to show the nature of Serjeant Heywood's examination of Mr. Rose,—the boldness of this latter gentleman's assertions,—and the extreme inaccuracy of the researches upon which these assertions are founded. If any credit could be gained from such a book as Mr. Rose has published, it could be gained from accuracy alone. Whatever the execution of his book had been, the world would have remembered the infinite disparity of the two authors, and the long political opposition in which they lived—if that, indeed, can be called opposition, where the thunderbolt strikes, and the clay yields. They would have remembered also that Hector was dead; and that every cowardly Grecian could now thrust his spear into the hero's body. But still, if Mr. Rose had really succeeded in exposing the inaccuracy of Mr. Fox,—if he could have fairly shown that authorities were overlooked, or slightly examined, or wilfully perverted,—the incipient feelings to which such a controversy had given birth must have yielded to the evidence of facts; and Mr. Fox, however qualified in other particulars, must have appeared totally defective in that laborious industry and scrupulous good faith so indispensable to every historian. But he absolutely comes out of the contest not worse even in a single tooth or nail—unvilified even by a wrong date—without one misnomer proved upon him—immaculate in his years and days of the month—blameless to the most musty and limited pedant that ever yellowed himself amidst rolls and records.

But how fares it with his critic? He rests his credit with the world as a man of labour,—and he turns out to be a careless inspector of proofs, and an historical sloven. The species of talent which he pretends to is humble,—and he possesses it not. He has not done that which all men may do, and which every man ought to do, who rebukes his superiors for not doing it. His claims, too, it should be remembered, to these every-day qualities, are by no means enforced with gentleness and humility. He is a braggadocio of minuteness—a swaggering chronologer;—a man bristling up with small facts—prurient with dates—wantoning in obsolete evidence—loftily dull, and haughty in his drudgery;—and yet all this is pretence. Drawing is no very unusual power in animals; but he cannot draw; he is not even the ox which he is so fond of being. In attempting to vilify Mr. Fox, he has only shown us that there was no labour from which that great man shrunk, and that no object connected with his history was too minute for his investigation. He has thoroughly convinced us that Mr. Fox was as industrious, and as accurate, as if these were the only qualities upon which he had ever rested his hope of fortune or of fame. Such, indeed, are the customary results when little people sit down to debase the characters of great men, and to exalt themselves upon the ruins of what they have pulled down. They only provoke a spirit of inquiry, which places every thing in its true light and magnitude,—shows those who appear little to be still less, and displays new and unexpected excellence in others who were before known to excel. These are the usual consequences of such attacks. The fame of Mr. Fox has stood this, and will stand much ruder shocks.

Non hiemes illam, non flabra neque imbres
Convellunt; immota manet, multosque per annos
Multa virûm volvens durando sæcula vincit.

MAD QUAKERS.*

[Edinburgh Review, 1814.]

The Quakers always seem to succeed in any institution which they undertake. The gaol at Philadelphia will remain a lasting monument of their skill and patience; and, in the plan and conduct of this retreat for the insane, they have evinced the same wisdom and perseverance.

The present account is given us by Mr. Tuke, a respectable tea-dealer, living in York, —and given in a manner which we are quite sure the most opulent and important of his customers could not excel. The long account of the subscription, at the beginning of the book, is evidently made tedious for the Quaker market; and Mr. Tuke is a little too much addicted to quoting. But, with these trifling exceptions, his book does him very great credit;—it is full of good sense and humanity, right feelings and rational views. The retreat for insane Quakers is situated about a mile from the city of York, upon an eminence commanding the adjacent country, and in the midst of a garden and fields belonging to the institution. The great principle on which it appears to be conducted is that of kindness to the patients. It does not appear to them, because a man is mad upon one particular subject, that he is to be considered in a state of complete mental degradation, or insensible to the feelings of kindness and gratitude. When a madman does not do what he is bid to do, the shortest method, to be sure, is to knock him down; and straps and chains are the species of prohibition which are the least frequently disregarded. But the Society of Friends seem rather to consult the interest of the patient than the ease of his keeper; and to aim at the government of the insane, by creating in them the kindest disposition towards those who have the command over them. Nor can any thing be more wise, humane, or interesting, than the strict attention to the feelings of their patients which seems to prevail in their institutions. The following specimens of their disposition upon this point we have great pleasure in laying before our readers:—

"The smallness of the court," says Mr. Tuke, "would be a serious defect, if it was not generally compensated by taking such patients as are suitable into the garden; and by frequent excursions into the city, or the surrounding country, and into the fields of the institution. One of these is surrounded by a walk interspersed with trees and shrubs.

"The superintendent has also endeavoured to furnish a source of amusement to those patients whose walks are necessarily more circumscribed, by supplying each of the courts with a number of animals, such as rabbits, sea gulls, hawks, and poultry. These creatures are generally very familiar with the patients; and it is believed they are not only the means of innocent pleasure, but that the intercourse with them sometimes tends to awaken the social and benevolent feelings."—(p. 95, 96.)

Chains are never permitted at the Retreat; nor is it left to the option of the lower attendants when they are to impose an additional degree of restraint upon the patients; and this compels them to pay attention to the feelings of the patients, and to attempt to gain an influence over them by kindness. Patients who are not disposed to injure themselves are merely confined by the strait waistcoat, and left to walk about the room, or lie down on the bed, at pleasure; and even in those cases where there is a strong tendency to self-destruction, as much attention is paid to the feelings and ease of the patient as is consistent with his safety.

"Except in cases of violent mania, which is far from being a frequent recurrence at the Retreat, coercion, when requisite, is considered as a necessary evil; that is, it is thought abstractedly to have a tendency to retard the cure, by opposing the influence of the moral remedies employed. It is therefore used very sparingly; and the superintendent has often assured me, that he would rather run some risk than have recourse to restraint where it was not absolutely necessary, except in those cases where it was likely to have a salutary moral tendency.

"I feel no small satisfaction in stating, upon the authority of the superintendents, that during the last year, in which the number of patients has generally been sixty-four, there has not been occasion to seclude, on an average, two patients at one time. I am also able to state, that although it is occasionally necessary to restrain, by the waistcoat, straps, or other means, several patients at one time, yet that the average number so restrained does not exceed four, including those who are secluded.

"The safety of those who attend upon the insane is certainly an object of great importance; but it is worthy of inquiry whether it may not be attained without materially interfering with another object,—the recovery of the patient. It may also deserve inquiry, whether the extensive practice of coercion, which obtains in some institutions, does not arise from erroneous views of the character of insane persons; from indifference to their comfort or from having rendered coercion necessary by previous unkind treatment.

* *Description of the Retreat, an Institution near York, for Insane Persons of the Society of Friends. Containing an account of its Origin and Progress, the Modes of Treatment, and a Statement of Cases.* By Samuel Tuke. York, 1813.

"The power of judicious kindness over this unhappy class of society is much greater than is generally imagined. It is, perhaps, not too much to apply to kind treatment the words of our great poet,—

> 'She can unlock
> The clasping charm, and thaw the numbing spell.'
> MILTON.

"In no instances has this power been more strikingly displayed, or exerted with more beneficial effects, than in those deplorable cases in which the patient refuses to take food. The kind persuasions and ingenious arts of the superintendents have been singularly successful in overcoming this distressing symptom; and very few instances now occur in which it is necessary to employ violent means for supplying the patient with food.

"Some patients, who refuse to partake of the family meals, are induced to eat by being taken into the larder, and there allowed to help themselves. Some are found willing to eat when food is left with them in their rooms, or when they can obtain it unobserved by their attendants. Others, whose determination is stronger, are frequently induced, by repeated persuasion, to take a small quantity of nutritious liquid; and it is equally true in these, as in general cases, that every breach of resolution weakens the power and disposition to resistance.

"Sometimes, however, persuasion seems to strengthen the unhappy determination. In one of these cases the attendants were completely wearied with their endeavours; and, on removing the food, one of them took a piece of meat which had been repeatedly offered to the patient, and threw it under the fire-grate, at the same time exclaiming that she should not have it. The poor creature, who seemed governed by the rule of contraries, immediately rushed from her seat, seized the meat from the ashes, and devoured it. For a short time she was induced to eat, by the attendants availing themselves of this contrary disposition; but it was soon rendered unnecessary by the removal of this unhappy feature of the disorder."—(p. 166, 167, 168, 169.)

When it is deemed necessary to apply any mode of coercion, such an overpowering force is employed as precludes all possibility of successful resistance; and most commonly, therefore, extinguishes every idea of making any at all. An attendant upon a madhouse exposes himself to some risk—and to some he ought to expose himself, or he is totally unfit for his situation. If the security of the attendants were the only object, the situation of the patients would soon become truly desperate. The business is, not to risk nothing, but not to risk too much. The generosity of the Quakers, and their courage in managing mad people, are placed, by this institution, in a very striking point of view. This cannot be better illustrated than by the two following cases:—

"The superintendent was one day walking in a field adjacent to the house, in company with a patient who was apt to be vindictive on very slight occasions. An exciting circumstance occurred. The maniac retired a few paces, and seized a large stone, which he immediately held up, as in the act of throwing at his companion. The superintendent, in no degree ruffled, fixed his eye upon the patient, and in a resolute tone of voice, at the same time advancing, commanded him to lay down the stone. As he approached, the hand of the lunatic gradually sunk from its threatening position, and permitted the stone to drop to the ground. He then submitted to be quietly led to his apartment."

"Some years ago, a man, about thirty-four years of age, of almost herculean size and figure, was brought to the house. He had been afflicted several times before; and so constantly, during the present attack, had he been kept chained, that his clothes were contrived to be taken off and put on by means of strings, without removing his manacles. They were, however, taken off when he entered the Retreat, and he was ushered into the apartment where the superintendents were supping. He was calm: his attention appeared to be arrested by his new situation. He was desired to join in the repast, during which he behaved with tolerable propriety. After it was concluded the superintendent conducted him to his apartment, and told him the circumstances on which his treatment would depend; that it was his anxious wish to make every inhabitant in the house as comfortable as possible; and that he sincerely hoped the patient's conduct would render it unnecessary for him to have recourse to coercion. The maniac was sensible of the kindness of his treatment. He promised to restrain himself; and he so completely succeeded, that, during his stay, no coercive means were ever employed towards him. This case affords a striking example of the efficacy of mild treatment. The patient was frequently very vociferous, and threatened his attendants, who, in their defence, were very desirous of restraining him by the jacket. The superintendent on these occasions went to his apartment: and though the first sight of him seemed rather to increase the patient's irritation, yet, after sitting some time quietly beside him, the violent excitement subsided, and he would listen with attention to the persuasions and arguments of his friendly visitor. After such conversations the patient was generally better for some days or a week; and in about four months he was discharged perfectly recovered.

"Can it be doubted that, in this case, the disease had been greatly exasperated by the mode of management? or that the subsequent kind treatment had a great tendency to promote his recovery?"—(p. 172, 173, 146, 147.)

And yet, in spite of this apparent contempt of danger, for eighteen years not a single accident has happened to the keepers.

In the day room the sashes are made of cast-iron, and give to the building the security of bars, without their unpleasant appearance. With the same laudable attention to the feelings of these poor people, the straps of their strait waistcoats are made of some showy colour, and are not unfrequently considered by them as ornaments. No advantage whatever has been found to arise from reasoning with patients on their particular delusions: it is found rather to exasperate than convince them. Indeed, that state of mind would hardly deserve the name of insanity where argument was sufficient for the refutation of error.

The classification of patients according to their degree of convalescence is very properly attended to at the Retreat, and every assistance given to returning reason by the force of example. We were particularly pleased with the following specimens of Quaker sense and humanity:—

"The female superintendent, who possesses an uncommon share of benevolent activity, and who has the chief management of the female patients, as well as of the domestic department, occasionally gives a general invitation to the patients to a tea-party. All who attend dress in their best clothes, and vie with each other in politeness and propriety. The best fare is provided, and the visitors are treated with all the attention of strangers. The evening generally passes in the greatest harmony and enjoyment. It rarely happens that any unpleasant circumstance occurs. The patients control, in a wonderful degree, their different propensities; and the scene is at once curious and affectingly gratifying.

"Some of the patients occasionally pay visits to their friends in the city; and female visitors are appointed every month by the committee to pay visits to those of their own sex, to converse with them, and to propose to the superintendents, or the committee, any improvements which may occur to them. The visitors sometimes take tea with the patients, who are much gratified with the attention of their friends, and mostly behave with propriety.

"It will be necessary here to mention that the visits of former intimate friends have frequently been attended with disadvantage to the patients, except when convalescence had so far advanced as to afford a prospect of a speedy return to the bosom of society. It is, however, very certain that, as soon as reason begins to return, the conversation of judicious indifferent persons greatly increases the comfort, and is considered almost essential to the recovery of many patients. On this account the convalescents of every class are frequently introduced into the society of the rational parts of the family. They are also permitted to sit up till the usual time for the family to retire to rest, and are allowed as much liberty as their state of mind will admit."—(p. 178, 179.)

To the effects of kindness in the Retreat are superadded those of constant employment. The female patients are employed as much as possible in sewing, knitting, and domestic affairs; and several of the convalescents assist the attendants. For the men are selected those species of bodily employments most agreeable to the patient, and most opposite to the illusions of his disease. Though the effect of fear is not excluded from the institution, yet the love of esteem is considered as a still more powerful principle.

"That fear is not the only motive which operates in producing *self-restraint* in the minds of maniacs, is evident from its being often exercised in the presence of strangers who are merely passing through the house; and which, I presume, can only be accounted for from that desire of esteem which has been stated to be a powerful motive to conduct.

"It is, probably, from encouraging the action of this principle, that so much advantage has been found, in this institution, from treating the patient as much in the manner of a rational being as the state of his mind will possibly allow. The superintendent is particularly attentive to this point in his conversation with the patients. He introduces such topics as he knows will most interest them; and which, at the same time, allows them to display their knowledge to the greatest advantage. If the patient is an agriculturist, he asks him questions relative to his art; and frequently consults him upon any occasion in which his knowledge may be useful. I have heard one of the worst patients in the house, who, previously to his indisposition, had been a considerable grazier, give very sensible directions for the treatment of a diseased cow.

"These considerations are undoubtedly very material as they regard the comfort of insane persons; but they are of far greater importance as they relate to the cure of the disorder. The patient, feeling himself of some consequence, is induced to support it by the exertion of his reason, and by restraining those dispositions which, if indulged, would lessen the respectful treatment he receives, or lower his character in the eyes of his companions and attendants.

"They who are unacquainted with the character of insane persons are very apt to converse with them in a childish, or, which is worse, in a domineering manner; and hence it has been frequently remarked, by the patients at the Retreat, that a stranger who has visited them seemed to imagine they were children.

"The natural tendency of such treatment is to degrade the mind of the patient, and to make him indifferent to those moral feelings which, under judicious direction and encouragement, are found capable, in no small degree, to strengthen the power of self-restraint, and which render the resort to coercion in many cases unnecessary. Even when it is absolutely requisite to employ coercion, if the patient promises to control himself on its removal, great confidence is generally placed upon his word. I have known patients, such is their sense of honour and moral obligation under this kind of engagement, hold, for a long time, a successful struggle with the violent propensities of their disorder; and such attempts ought to be sedulously encouraged by the attendant.

"Hitherto we have chiefly considered those modes of inducing the patient to control his disordered propensities which arise from an application to the general powers of the mind; but considerable advantage may certainly be derived, in this part of moral management, from an acquaintance with the previous habits, manners, and prejudices of the individual. Nor must we forget to call to our aid, in endeavouring to promote self-restraint, the mild but powerful influence of the precepts of our holy religion. Where these have been strongly imbued in early life, they become little less than principles of our nature: and their restraining power is frequently felt, even under the delirious excitement of insanity. To encourage the influence of religious principles over the mind of the insane is considered of great consequence as a means of cure. For this purpose, as well as for others still more important, it is certainly right to promote in the patient an attention to his accustomed modes of paying homage to his Maker.

"Many patients attend the religious meetings of the society held in the city; and most of them are assembled, on a first day afternoon, at which time the superintendent reads to them several chapters in the Bible. A profound silence generally ensues; during which, as well as at the time of reading, it is very gratifying to observe their orderly conduct, and the degree in which those who are much disposed to action restrain their different propensities."—(p. 158—161.)

Very little dependence is to be placed on medicine alone for the cure of insanity. The experience, at least, of this well-governed institution is very unfavourable to its efficacy. Where an insane person happens to be diseased in body as well as in mind, medicine is not only of as great importance to him as to any other person, but much greater; for the diseases of the body are commonly found to aggravate those of the mind; but against mere insanity, unaccompanied by bodily derangement, it appears to be almost powerless.

There is one remedy, however, which is very frequently employed at the Retreat, and which appears to have been attended with the happiest effect, and that is the warm bath,—the least recommended, and the most important, of all remedies in melancholy madness. Under this mode of treatment, the number of recoveries, in cases of *melancholia*, has been very unusual; though no advantage has been found from it in the case of mania.

At the end of the work is given a table of all the cases which have occurred in the institution from its first commencement. It appears that, from its opening in the year 1796 to the end of 1811, 149 patients have been admitted. Of this number 61 have been recent cases: 31 of these patients have been maniacal; of whom 2 have died, 6 remain, 21 have been discharged perfectly recovered, 2 so much improved as not to require further confinement. The remainder, 30 recent cases, have been those of melancholy madness; of whom 5 have died, 4 remain, 19 have been discharged cured, and 2 so much improved as not to require further confinement. The old cases, or, as they are commonly termed, incurable cases, are divided into 61 cases of mania, 21 of melancholia, and 6 of dementia; affording the following tables:—

"*Mania.*

"11 died.
31 remain in the house.
5 have been removed by their friends improved.
10 have been discharged perfectly recovered.
4 so much improved as not to require further confinement."

"*Melancholia.*

"6 died.
6 remain.
1 removed somewhat improved.
6 perfectly cured.
2 so much improved as not to require further confinement."

"*Dementia.*

"2 died.
2 remain.
2 discharged as unsuitable objects."

The following statement shows the ages of patients at present in the house:—

"15 to 20 inclusive		2
20 to 30	—	8
30 to 40	—	12
40 to 50	—	7
60 to 70	—	11
70 to 80	—	4
80 to 90	—	2"

Of 79 patients it appears that

"12 went mad from disappointed affections.
2 from epilepsy.
49 from constitutional causes.
8 from failure in business.
4 from hereditary disposition to madness.
2 from injury of the skull.
1 from mercury.
1 from parturition."

The following case is extremely curious: and we wish it had been authenticated by name, place, and signature.

"A young woman, who was employed as a domestic servant by the father of the relator when he was a boy, became insane, and at length sunk into a state of perfect idiocy. In this condition she remained for many years, when she was attacked by a typhus fever; and my friend, having then practised some time, attended her. He was surprised to observe, as the fever advanced, a development of the mental powers. During that period of the fever, when others were delirious, this patient was entirely rational. She recognised in the face of her medical attendant the son of her old master, whom she had known so many years before; and she related many circumstances respecting his family, and others which had happened to herself in her earlier days. But, alas! it was only the gleam of reason. As the fever abated, clouds again enveloped the mind: she sunk into her former deplorable state, and remained in it until her death, which happened a few years afterwards. I leave to the metaphysical reader further speculation on this, certainly, very curious case." —(p. 137.)

Upon the whole, we have little doubt that this is the best managed asylum for the insane that has ever yet been established; and a part of the explanation no doubt is, that the Quakers take more pains than other people with their madmen. A mad Quaker belongs to a small and rich sect; and is, therefore, of greater importance than any other mad person of the same degree in life. After every allowance, however, which can be made for the feelings of sectaries, exercised towards their own disciples, the Quakers, it must be allowed, are a very charitable and humane people. They are always ready with their money, and, what is of far more importance, with their time and attention, for every variety of human misfortune.

They seem to set themselves down systematically before the difficulty, with the wise conviction that it is to be lessened or subdued only by great labour and thought; and that it is always increased by indolence and neglect. In this instance, they have set an example of courage, patience, and kindness, which cannot be too highly commended, or too widely diffused; and which, we are convinced, will gradually bring into repute a milder and better method of treating the insane. For the aversion to inspect places of this sort is so great, and the temptation to neglect and oppress the insane so strong, both from the love of power, and the improbability of detection, that we have no doubt of the existence of great abuses in the interior of many madhouses. A great deal has been done for prisons; but the order of benevolence has been broken through by this preference; for the voice of misery may sooner come up from a dungeon, than the oppression of a madman be healed by the hand of justice.†

† The Society of Friends have been extremely fortunate in the choice of their male and female superintendents at the asylum, Mr. and Mrs. Jephson. It is not easy to find a greater combination of good sense and good feeling than these two persons possess:—but then the merit of selecting them rests with their employers

AMERICA.*

[EDINBURGH REVIEW, 1818.]

THESE four books are all very well worth reading, to any person who feels, as we do, the importance and interest of the subject of which they treat. They contain a great deal of information and amusement; and will probably decide the fate, and direct the footsteps, of many human beings, seeking a better lot than the Old World can afford them. Mr. Hall is a clever, lively man, very much above the common race of writers; with very liberal and reasonable opinions, which he expresses with great boldness,—and an inexhaustible fund of good humour. He has the elements of wit in him; but sometimes is trite and flat when he means to be amusing. He writes verses, too, and is occasionally long and metaphysical: but, upon the whole, we think highly of Mr. Hall; and deem him, if he is not more than twenty-five years of age, an extraordinary young man. He is not the less extraordinary for being a lieutenant of Light Dragoons—as it is certainly somewhat rare to meet with an original thinker, an indulgent judge of manners, and a man tolerant of neglect and familiarity, in a youth covered with tags, feathers, and martial foolery.

Mr. Palmer is a plain man, of good sense and slow judgment. Mr. Bradbury is a botanist, who lived a good deal among the savages, but worth attending to. Mr. Fearon is a much abler writer than either of the two last, but no lover of America,—and a little given to exaggeration in his views of vices and prejudices.

Among other faults with which our government is chargeable, the vice of *impertinence* has lately crept into our cabinet; and the Americans have been treated with ridicule and contempt. But they are becoming a little too powerful, we take it, for this cavalier sort of management; and are increasing with a rapidity which is really no matter of jocularity to us, or the other powers of the Old World. In 1791, Baltimore contained 13,000 inhabitants; in 1810, 46,000; in 1817, 60,000. In 1790, it possessed 13,000 tons of shipping; in 1798, 59,000, in 1805, 72,000; in 1810, 103,444. The progress of Philadelphia is as follows:—

	Houses.	Inhabitants.
"In 1683 there were in the city	80 and	600
1700 - - - - - -	700	5,000
1749 - - - - - -	2,076	15,000
1760 - - - - - -	2,969	20,000
1769 - - - - - -	4,474	30,000
1776 - - - - - -	5,460	40,000
1783 - - - - - -	6,000	42,000
1806 - - - - - -	13,000	90,000
1810 - - - - - -	22,769	100,000

"Now it is computed there are at least 120,000 inhabitants in the city and suburbs, of which 10,000 are free coloured people."—*Palmer*, p. 254, 255.

The population of New York (*the city*), in 1805, was 60,000; it is now 120,000. Their shipping, at present, amounts to 300,000 tons. The population of *the state* of New York was, at the accession of his present majesty, 87,000, and is now nearly 1,000,000. Kentucky, first settled in 1773, had, in 1792, a population of 100,000; and in 1810, 406,000. Morse reckons the whole population of the western territory, in 1790, at 6,000; in 1810 it was near half a million; and will probably exceed a million in 1820. These, and a thousand other equally

* 1. *Travels in Canada and the United States, in 1816 and 1817. By* LIEUTENANT FRANCIS HALL, 14th Light Dragoons, H. P. London. Longman & Co. 1818.
2. *Journal of Travels in the United States of North America, and in Lower Canada, performed in the year* 1817, *&c.* By JOHN PALMER. London. Sherwood, Neely & Jones. 1818.
3. *A Narrative of a Journey of Five Thousand Miles through the Eastern and Western States of America; contained in Eight Reports, addressed to the Thirty-nine English Families by whom the Author was deputed, in June,* 1817, *to ascertain whether any and what Part of the United States would be suitable for their Residence. With Remarks on Mr. Birkbeck's "Notes" and "Letters."* By HENRY BRADSHAW FEARON. London. Longman & Co. 1818.
4. *Travels in the Interior of America, in the years* 1809, 1810, *and* 1811, *&c.* By JOHN BRADBURY, F. L. S. Lond. 8vo. London. Sherwood, Neely & Jones. 1817.

strong proofs of their increasing strength, tend to extinguish pleasantry, and provoke thought.

We were surprised and pleased to find from these accounts that the Americans on the Red River and the Arkansas River have begun to make sugar and wine. Their importation of wool into this country is becoming also an object of some consequence; and they have inexhaustible supplies of salt and coal. But one of the great sources of wealth in America is and will be an astonishing command of inland navigation. The Mississippi, flowing from the north to the Gulf of Mexico, through seventeen degrees of latitude; the Ohio and the Alleghany almost connecting it with the Northern Lakes; the Wabash, the Illinois, the Missouri, the Arkansas, the Red River, flowing from the confines of New Mexico;—these rivers, all navigable, and most of them already frequented by steamboats, constitute a facility of internal communication not, we believe, to be paralleled in the whole world.

One of the great advantages of the American government is its cheapness. The American king has about 5000*l.* per annum, the vice-king 1000*l.* They hire their Lord Liverpool at about a thousand per annum, and their Lord Sidmouth (a good bargain) at the same sum. Their Mr. Crokers are inexpressibly reasonable,—somewhere about the price of an English doorkeeper, or bearer of a mace. Life, however, seems to go on very well, in spite of these low salaries; and the purposes of government to be very fairly answered. Whatever may be the evils of universal suffrage in other countries, they have not yet been felt in America; and one thing at least is established by her experience, that this institution is not necessarily followed by those tumults, the dread of which excites so much apprehension in this country. In the most democratic states, where the payment of direct taxes is the only qualification of a voter, the elections are carried on with the utmost tranquillity; and the whole business, by taking votes in each parish or section, concluded all over the state in a single day. A great deal is said by Fearon about *Caucus*, the cant word of the Americans for the committees and party meetings in which the business of the elections is prepared —the influence of which he seems to consider as prejudicial. To us, however, it appears to be nothing more than the natural, fair, and unavoidable influence which talent, popularity and activity always must have upon such occasions. What other influence can the leading characters of the democratic party in Congress possibly possess? Bribery is entirely out of the question—equally so is the influence of family and fortune. What then can they do, with their caucus or without it, but recommend? And what charge is it against the American government to say that those members of whom the people have the highest opinion meet together to consult whom they shall recommend for president, and that their recommendation is successful in their different states? Could any friend to good order wish other means to be employed, or other results to follow? No statesman can wish to exclude influence, but only bad influence;—not the influence of sense and character, bu the influence of money and punch.

A very disgusting feature in the character of the present English government is its extreme timidity, and the cruelty and violence to which its timidity gives birth. Some hot-headed young person, in defending the principles of liberty, and attacking those abuses to which all governments are liable, passes the bounds of reason and moderation, or is thought to have passed them by those whose interest it is to think so. What matters it whether he has or has not? You are strong enough to let him alone. With such institutions as ours he can do no mischief; perhaps he may owe his celebrity to your opposition; or, if he must be opposed, write against him, —set Candidus, Scrutator, Vindex, or any of the conductitious penmen of government to write him down;—any thing but the savage spectacle of a poor wretch, perhaps a very honest man, contending in vain against the weight of an immense government, pursued by a jealous attorney, and sentenced, by some candidate, perhaps, for the favour of the crown, to the long miseries of the dungeon.* A still more flagrant instance may be found in our late suspensions of the habeas corpus act. Nothing was trusted to the voluntary activity of a brave people, thoroughly attached to their government—nothing to the good sense and prudence of the gentlemen and yeomen of the country—nothing to a little forbearance, patience, and watchfulness. There was no other security but despotism; nothing but the alienation of that right which no king nor minister can love, and which no human beings but the English have had the valour to win, and the prudence to keep. The contrast between our government and that of the Americans, upon the subject of suspending the habeas corpus, is drawn in so very able a manner by Mr. Hall, that we must give the passage at large.

"It has ever been the policy of the federalists to 'strengthen the hands of government.' No measure can be imagined more effectual for this purpose, than a law which gifts the ruling powers with infallibility; but no sooner was it enacted, than it revealed its hostility to the principles of the American system, by

* A great deal is said about the independence and integrity of English judges. In causes between individuals they are strictly independent and upright; but they have strong temptations to be otherwise, in cases where the crown prosecutes for libel. Such cases often involve questions of party, and are viewed with great passion and agitation by the minister and his friends. Judges have often favours to ask for their friends and families, and dignities to aspire to for themselves. It is human nature, that such powerful motives should create a great bias against the prisoner. Suppose the chief justice of any court to be in an infirm state of health, and a government libel-cause to be tried by one of the puisne judges,—of what immense importance is it to that man to be called a strong friend to government—how injurious to his natural and fair hopes to be called lukewarm, or addicted to popular notions—and how easily the runners of the government would attach such a character to him! The useful inference from these observations is, that, in all government cases, the jury, instead of being influenced by the cant phrases about the integrity of English judges, should suspect the operation of such motives—watch the judge with the most acute jealousy —and compel him to be honest, by throwing themselves into the opposite scale whenever he is inclined to be otherwise.

generating oppression under the cloak of defending social order.

"If there ever was a period when circumstances seemed to justify what are called energetic measures, it was during the administrations of Mr. Jefferson and his successor. A disastrous war began to rage, not only on the frontiers, but in the very penetralia of the republic. To oppose veteran troops, the ablest generals, and the largest fleets in the world, the American government had raw recruits, officers who had never seen an enemy, half a dozen frigates, and a population unaccustomed to sacrifices, and impatient of taxation. To crown these disadvantages, a most important section of the Union, the New England states, openly set up the standard of separation and rebellion. A convention sat for the express purpose of thwarting the measures of government; while the press and pulpit thundered every species of denunciation against whoever should assist their own country in the hour of danger.* And this was the work, not of jacobins and democrats, but of the stanch friends of religion and social order, who had been so zealously attached to the government, while it was administered by their own party, that they suffered not the popular breath 'to visit the president's breech too roughly.'

"The course pursued, both by Mr. Jefferson and Mr. Madison throughout this season of difficulty, merits the gratitude of their country, and the imitation of all governments pretending to be free.

"So far were they from demanding any extraordinary powers from Congress, that they did not even enforce, to their full extent, those with which they were by the constitution invested. The process of reasoning, on which they probably acted, may be thus stated. The majority of the nation is with us, because the war is national. The interests of a minority suffer; and self-interest is clamorous when injured. It carries its opposition to an extreme inconsistent with its political duty. Shall we leave it in an undisturbed career of faction, or seek to put it down with libel and sedition laws? In the first case it will grow bold from impunity; its proceedings will be more and more outrageous: but every step it takes to thwart us will be a step in favour of the enemy, and, consequently, so much ground lost in public opinion. But, as public opinion is the only instrument by which a minority can convert a majority to its views, impunity, by revealing its motives, affords the surest chance of defeating its intent. In the latter case, we quit the ground of reason to take that of force; we give the factious the advantage of seeming persecuted; by repressing intemperate discussion, we confess ourselves liable to be injured by it. If we seek to shield our reputation by a libel-law, we acknowledge, either that our conduct will not bear investigation, or that the people are incapable of distinguishing betwixt truth and falsehood: but for a popular government to impeach the sanctity of the nation's judgment is to overthrow the pillars of its own elevation.

"The event triumphantly proved the correctness of this reasoning. The federalists awoke from the delirium of factious intoxication, and found themselves covered with contempt and shame. Their country had been in danger, and they gloried in her distress. She had exposed herself to privations from which they had extracted profit. In her triumphs they had no part, except that of having mourned over and depreciated them. Since the war federalism has been scarcely heard of."—*Hall*, 508—511.

The Americans, we believe, are the first persons who have discarded the tailor in the administration of justice, and his auxiliary the barber—two persons of endless importance in codes and pandects of Europe. A judge administers justice, without a calorific wig and particoloured gown, in a coat and pantaloons. He is obeyed, however; and life and property are not badly protected in the United States. We shall be denounced by the laureate as atheists and jacobins; but we must say, that we have doubts whether one atom of useful influence is added to men in important situations by any colour, quantity, or configuration of cloth and hair. The true progress of refinement, we conceive, is to discard all the mountebank drapery of barbarous ages. One row of gold and fur falls off after another from the robe of power, and is picked up and worn by the parish beadle and the exhibitor of wild beasts. Meantime, the afflicted wiseacre mourns over equality of garment; and wotteth not of two men, whose doublets have cost alike, how one shall command and the other obey.

The dress of lawyers, however, is, at all events, of less importance than their charges. Law is cheap in America: in England, it is better, in a mere pecuniary point of view, to give up forty pounds than to contend for it in a court of common law. It costs that sum in England to win a cause; and, in the court of equity, it is better to abandon five hundred or a thousand pounds than to contend for it. We mean to say nothing disrespectful of the chancellor—who is an upright judge, a very great lawyer, and zealous to do all he can; but we believe the Court of Chancery to be in a state which imperiously requires legislative correction. We do not accuse it of any malversation, but of a complication, formality, entanglement, and delay, which the life, the wealth, and the patience of man cannot endure. How such a subject comes not to have been taken up in the House of Commons, we are wholly at a loss to conceive. We feel for climbing boys as much as anybody can do; but what is a climbing boy in a chimney to a full-grown suitor in the Master's office. And whence comes it, in the midst of ten thousand com

* "In Boston, associations were entered into for the purpose of preventing the filling up of government loans. Individuals disposed to subscribe were obliged to do it in secret, and conceal their names, as if the action had been dishonest."—*Vide* 'Olive Branch,' p. 307. At the same time, immense runs were made by the Boston banks on those of the Central and Southern states; while the specie thus drained was transmitted to Canada, in payment for smuggled goods and British government bills, which were drawn in Quebec, and disposed of in great numbers, on advantageous terms, to moneyed men in the states. Mr. Henry's mission is the best proof of the result anticipated by our government from these proceedings in New England.

passions and charities, that no Wilberforce, or Sister Fry, has started up for the suitors in Chancery?* and why, in the name of these afflicted and attorney-worn people, are there united in their judge three or four offices, any one of which is sufficient to occupy the whole time of a very able and active man?

There are no very prominent men at present in America; at least none whose fame is strong enough for exportation. Monroe is a man of plain, unaffected good sense. Jefferson, we believe, is still alive; and has always been more remarkable, perhaps, for the early share he took in the formation of the republic, than from any very predominant superiority of understanding. Mr. Hall made him a visit:—

"I slept a night at Monticello, and left it in the morning with such a feeling as the traveller quits the mouldering remains of a Grecian temple, or the pilgrim a fountain in the desert. It would indeed argue great torpor both of understanding and heart, to have looked without veneration and interest on the man who drew up the declaration of American independence; who shared in the councils by which her freedom was established; whom the unbought voice of his fellow-citizens called to the exercise of a dignity from which his own moderation impelled him, when such example was most salutary, to withdraw; and who, while he dedicates the evening of his glorious days to the pursuits of science and literature, shuns none of the humbler duties of private life; but, having filled a seat higher than that of kings, succeeds with graceful dignity to that of the good neighbour, and becomes the friendly adviser, lawyer, physician, and even gardener of his vicinity. This is the 'still small voice' of philosophy, deeper and holier than the lightnings and earthquakes which have preceded it. What monarch would venture thus to exhibit himself in the nakedness of his humanity? On what royal brow would the laurel replace the diadem?"—*Hall*, 384, 385.

Mr. Fearon dined with another of the Ex-Kings, Mr. Adams.

"The ex-president is a handsome old gentleman of eighty-four;—his lady is seventy-six;—she has the reputation of superior talents, and great literary acquirements. I was not perfectly a stranger here; as, a few days previous to this, I had received the honour of an hospitable reception at their mansion. Upon the present occasion the minister (the day being Sunday) was of the dinner party. As the table of a '*late King*' may amuse some of you, take the following particulars:—first course, a pudding made of Indian corn, molasses, and butter;—second, veal, bacon, neck of mutton, potatoes, cabbages, carrots, and Indian beans; Madeira wine, of which each drank two glasses. We sat down to dinner at one o'clock; at two, nearly all went a second time to church. For tea, we had pound-cake, sweet bread and butter, and bread made of Indian corn and rye (similar to our brown home-made). Tea was brought from the kitchen, and handed round by a neat, white servant-girl. The topics of conversation were various—England, America, religion, politics, literature, science, Dr. Priestley, Miss Edgeworth, Mrs. Siddons, Mr. Kean, France, Shakspeare, Moore, Lord Byron, Cobbett, American Revolution, the traitor General Arnold.

"The establishment of this political patriarch consists of a house two stories high, containing, I believe, eight rooms; of two men and three maid-servants; three horses, and a plain carriage. How great is the contrast between this individual—a man of knowledge and information—without pomp, parade, or vicious and expensive establishments, as compared with the costly trappings, the depraved characters, and the profligate expenditure of —— house, and ——! What a lesson *in this* does America teach! There are now in this land no less than three Cincinnati!"—*Fearon*, 111—113.

The travellers agree, we think, in complaining of the insubordination of American children—and do not much like American ladies. In their criticisms upon American gasconade, they forget that vulgar people of all countries are full of gasconade. The Americans love titles. The following extract from the Boston Sentinel of last August (1817), is quoted by Mr Fearon.

"'*Dinner to Mr. Adams.*—Yesterday a public dinner was given to the *Hon.* John Q. Adams, in the Exchange Coffee-House, by his fellow-citizens of Boston. The *Hon.* Wm. Gray presided, assisted by the *Hon.* Harrison Gray Otis, George Blake, Esq., and the *Hon.* Jonathan Mason, vice-presidents. Of the guests were, the *Hon.* Mr. Adams, late president of the United States, his *Excellency* Governor Brooks, his *Honour* Lt. Gov. Phillips, Chief Justice Parker, Judge Story, President Kirkland, Gen. Dearborn, Com. Hull, Gen. Miller, several of the reverend clergy, and many public officers, and strangers of eminence.'"

They all, in common with Mr. Birkbeck, seem to be struck with the indolence of the American character. Mr. Fearon makes the charge; and gives us below the right explanation of its cause.

"The life of boarders at an American tavern presents the most senseless and comfortless mode of killing time which I have ever seen. Every house of this description that I have been in, is thronged to excess; and there is not a man who appears to have a single earthly object in view, except spitting, and smoking segars. I have not seen a book in the hands of any person since I left Philadelphia. Objectionable as these habits are, they afford decided evidence of the prosperity of that country, which can admit so large a body of its

* This is still one of the great uncorrected evils of the country. Nothing can be so utterly absurd as to leave the head of the Court of Chancery a political officer, and to subject forty millions of litigated property to all the delays and interruptions which are occasioned by his present multiplicity of offices. (1839.)—The Chancellor is Speaker of the House of Lords; he might as well be made Archbishop of Canterbury;—it is one of the greatest of existing follies.

citizens to waste in indolence three-fourths of their lives, and would also appear to hold out encouragement to Englishmen with *English habits*, who could retain their industry amid a nation of indolence, and have sufficient firmness to live in America, and yet bid defiance to the deadly example of its natives." — *Fearon*, p. 252, 253.

Yet this charge can hardly apply to the north-eastern parts of the Union.

The following sample of American vulgarity is not unentertaining

"On arriving at the tavern door the landlord makes his appearance.—*Landlord.* Your servant, gentlemen, this is a fine day. — *Answer.* Very fine.—*Land.* You've got two *nice creatures; they are right elegant* matches. *Ans.* Yes, we bought them for matches.—*Land.* They cost a *heap* of dollars, (a pause, and knowing look); 200 I *calculate*. *Ans.* Yes, they cost a good sum. *Land. Possible!* (a pause); going westward to Ohio, gentlemen? *Ans.* We are going to Philadelphia. — *Land.* Philadelphia, ah! that's a *dreadful* large place, three or four times as *big* as Lexington. *Ans.* Ten times as large.—*Land.* Is it, by George! what a *mighty heap* of houses, (a pause); but I *reckon* you was not *reared* in Philadelphia. *Ans.* Philadelphia is not our native place. — *Land.* Perhaps *away up* in Canada. *Ans.* No; we are from England.—*Land. Is it possible!* well, I *calculated* you were from abroad, (pause); how long have you been from the *old country?* *Ans.* We left England last March.—*Land.* And in August here you are in *Kentuck*. Well, I should have *guessed* you had been in the state some years; you speak almost as good English as we do!

"This dialogue is not a literal copy; but it embraces most of the frequent and improper applications of words used in the back country, with a few New England phrases. By the log-house farmer and tavern keeper, they are used as often, and as erroneously, as they occur in the above discourse."—*Palmer*, p. 129, 130.

This is of course intended as a representation of the manners of the low, or, at best, the middling class of people in America.

The four travellers, of whose works we are giving an account, made extensive tours in every part of America, as well in the old as in the new settlements; and, generally speaking, we should say their testimony is in favour of American manners. We must except, perhaps, Mr. Fearon; — and yet he seems to have very little to say against them. Mr. Palmer tells us that he found his companions, officers and farmers, unobtrusive, civil and obliging; — that what the servants do for you, they do with alacrity;—that at their *tables d'hôte* ladies are treated with great politeness. We have real pleasure in making the following extract from Mr. Bradbury's tour.

"In regard to the manners of the people west of the Alleghanies, it would be absurd to expect that a general character could be now formed, or that it will be, for many years yet to come. The population is at present compounded of a great number of nations, not yet amalgamated, consisting of emigrants from every state in the Union, mixed with English, Irish, Scotch, Dutch, Swiss, Germans, French and almost from every country in Europe. In some traits they partake in common with the inhabitants of the Atlantic states, which results from the nature of their government. That species of hauteur which one class of society in some countries shows in their intercourse with the other, is here utterly unknown. By their constitution, the existence of a privileged order, vested by birth with hereditary privileges, honours or emoluments, is for ever interdicted. If, therefore, we should here expect to find that contemptuous feeling in man for man, we should naturally examine amongst those clothed with judicial or military authority; but we should search in vain. The justice on the bench, or the officer in the field, is respected and obeyed whilst discharging the functions of his office, as the representative or agent of the law, enacted for the *good of all;* but should he be tempted to treat even the least wealthy of his neighbours or fellow-citizens with contumely, he would soon find that he could not do it with impunity. Travellers from Europe, in passing through the western country, or indeed any part of the United States, ought to be previously acquainted with this part of the American character, and more particularly if they have been in the habit of treating with contempt, or irritating with abuse, those whom accidental circumstances may have placed in a situation to administer to their wants. Let no one here indulge himself in abusing the waiter or ostler at an inn; that waiter or ostler is probably a citizen, and does not, nor cannot conceive, that a situation in which he discharges a duty to society, not in itself dishonourable, should subject him to insult: but this feeling, so far as I have experienced, is entirely defensive. I have travelled near 10,000 miles in the United States, and never met with the least incivility or affront.

"The Americans, in general, are accused by travellers of being inquisitive. If this be a crime, the western people are guilty; but, for my part, I may say that it is a practice that I never was disposed to complain of, because I always found them as ready to answer a question as to ask one, and therefore I always came off a gainer by this kind of barter; and if any traveller does not, it is his own fault. As this leads me to notice their general conduct to strangers, I feel myself bound, by gratitude and regard to truth, to speak of their hospitality. In my travels through the inhabited parts of the United States, not less than 2000 miles was through parts where there were no taverns, and where a traveller is under the necessity of appealing to the hospitality of the inhabitants. In no one instance has my appeal been fruitless; although, in many cases, the furnishing of a bed has been evidently attended with inconvenience, and in a great many instances no remuneration would be received. Other European travellers have experienced this liberal spirit of hospitality, and some have repaid it by calumny."—*Bradbury*, p. 304—306.

We think it of so much importance to do justice to other nations, and to lessen that hatred and contempt which race feels for race, that we subjoin two short passages from Mr. Hall to the same effect.

"I had bills on Philadelphia, and applied to a respectable storekeeper, that is, tradesman, of the village, to cash me one; the amount, however, was beyond any remittance he had occasion to make, but he immediately offered me whatever sum I might require for my journey, with no better security than my word for its repayment at Philadelphia: he even insisted on my taking more than I mentioned as sufficient. I do not believe this trait of liberality would surprise an American; for no one in the states, to whom I mentioned it, seemed to consider it as more than any stranger of respectable appearance might have looked for, in similar circumstances: but it might well surprise an English traveller, who had been told, as I had, that the Americans never failed to cheat and insult every Englishman who travelled through their country, especially if they knew him to be an officer. This latter particular they never failed to inform themselves of, for they are by no means bashful in inquiries: but if the discovery operated in any way upon their behaviour, it was rather to my advantage; nor did I meet with a single instance of incivility betwixt Canada and Charleston, except at the Shenandoah Point, from a drunken English deserter. My testimony in this particular, will certainly not invalidate the complaints of many other travellers, who, I doubt not, have frequently encountered rude treatment, and quite as frequently deserved it; but it will at least prove the possibility of traversing the United States without insult or interruption, and even of being occasionally surprised by liberality and kindness."—*Hall*, p. 255, 256.

"I fell into very pleasant society at Washington. Strangers who intend staying some days in a town, usually take lodgings at a boarding-house, in preference to a tavern: in this way they obtain the best society the place affords; for there are always gentlemen and frequently ladies, either visitors or temporary residents, who live in this manner to avoid the trouble of housekeeping. At Washington, during the sittings of Congress, the boarding-houses are divided into messes, according to the political principles of the inmates, nor is a stranger admitted without some introduction, and the consent of the whole company. I chanced to join a democratic mess, and name a few of its members with gratitude, for the pleasure their society gave me—Commodore Decatur and his lady, the Abbè Correa, the great botanist and plenipotentiary of Portugal, the Secretary of the Navy, the Secretary of the Navy Board, known as the author of a humorous publication entitled 'John Bull and Brother Jonathan,' with eight or ten members of Congress, principally from the western states, which are generally considered as most decidedly hostile to England, but whom I did not on this account find less good-humoured and courteous. It is from thus living in daily intercourse with the leading characters of the country, that one is enabled to judge with some degree of certainty of the practices of its government; for to know the paper theory is nothing, unless it be compared with the instruments employed to carry it into effect. A political constitution may be nothing but a cabalistic form, to extort money and power from the people; but then the jugglers must be in the dark, and "no admittance behind the curtain." This way of living affords, too, the best insight into the best part of society: for if in a free nation the depositaries of the public confidence be ignorant or vulgar, it is a very fruitless search to look for the opposite qualities in those they represent; whereas, if these be well-informed in mind and manners, it proves at the least an inclination towards knowledge and refinement in the general mass of citizens by whom they are selected. My own experience obliges me to a favourable verdict in this particular. I found the little circle into which I had happily fallen full of good sense and good humour, and never quitted it without feeling myself a gainer, on the score either of useful information or of social enjoyment."—*Hall*, p. 329—331.

In page 252 Mr. Hall pays some very handsome compliments to the gallantry, high feeling and humanity of the American troops. Such passages reflect the highest honour upon Mr. Hall. They are full of courage as well as kindness, and will never be forgiven at home.

Literature the Americans have none—no native literature, we mean. It is all imported. They had a Franklin, indeed; and may afford to live for half a century on his fame. There is, or was a Mr. Dwight, who wrote some poems; and his baptismal name was Timothy. There is also a small account of Virginia by Jefferson, and an epic by Joel Barlow; and some pieces of pleasantry by Mr. Irving. But why should the Americans write books, when a six weeks' passage brings them, in their own tongue, our sense, science and genius, in bales and hogsheads? Prairies, steam-boats, grist-mills, are their natural objects for centuries to come. Then, when they have got to the Pacific Ocean—epic poems, plays, pleasures of memory and all the elegant gratifications of an ancient people who have tamed the wild earth, and set down to amuse themselves.—This is the natural march of human affairs.

The Americans, at least in the old states, are a very religious people: but there is no sect there which enjoys the satisfaction of excluding others from civil offices; nor does any denomination of Christians take for their support a tenth of produce. Their clergy, however, are respectable, respected, and possess no small share of influence. The places of worship in Philadelphia in 1810, were as follows:—Presbyterian, 8; Episcopalian, 4; Methodists, 5; Catholic, 4; Baptist, 5; Quakers, 4; Fighting Quakers, 1; Lutheran, 3; Calvinist, 3; Jews, 2; Universalists, 1; Swedish Lutheran, 1; Moravian, 1; Congregationalists, 1; Unitarians, 1; Covenanters, 1; Black Baptists, 1; Black Episcopalians, 1; Black Methodists, 2. The Methodists, Mr. Palmer tells us, are becoming the most numerous sect in the United States.

Mr. Fearon gives us this account of the state of religion at New York.

"Upon this interesting topic I would repeat, what, indeed, you are already acquainted with, that *legally* there is the most unlimited liberty. There is no state religion, and no government prosecution of individuals for conscience sake

Whether those halcyon days, which I think would attend a similar state of things in England, are in existence here, must be left for future observation. There are five Dutch Reformed churches; six Presbyterian; three Associated Reformed ditto, one Associated Presbyterian; one Reformed ditto; five Methodist; two ditto *for blacks;* one German Reformed; one Evangelical Lutheran; one Moravian; four Trinitarian Baptist; one Universalist; two Catholic; three Quaker; eight Episcopalian; one Jews' Synagogue; and to this I would add a small meeting which is but little known, at which the priest is dispensed with, every member following what they call the apostolic plan of instructing each other, and 'building one another up in their most holy faith.' The Presbyterian and Episcopalian, or Church of England sects, take the precedence in numbers and in respectability. Their ministers receive from two to eight thousand dollars per annum. All the churches are well filled: they are the fashionable places for *display;* and the sermons and talents of the minister offer never-ending subjects of interest when social converse has been exhausted upon the bad conduct and inferior nature of *niggars* (negroes); the price of flour at Liverpool; the capture of the *Guerrière;* and the battle of New Orleans. The perfect equality of all sects seems to have deadened party feeling: controversy is but little known."—*Fearon*, p. 45, 46.

The absence of controversy, Mr. Fearon seems to imagine, has produced indifference; and he heaves a sigh to the memory of departed oppression. "Can it be possible (he asks) that the non-existence of religious oppression has lessened religious knowledge, and made men superstitiously dependent upon outward form, instead of internal purity?" To which question (a singular one from an enlightened man like Mr. Fearon), we answer, that the absence of religious oppression has not lessened religious knowledge, but theological animosity; and made men more dependent upon pious actions, and less upon useless and unintelligible wrangling.*

The great curse of America is the institution of slavery—of itself far more than the foulest blot upon their national character, and an evil which counterbalances all the excisemen, licensers, and tax-gatherers of England. No virtuous man ought to trust his own character, or the character of his children, to the demoralizing effects produced by commanding slaves. Justice, gentleness, pity and humility soon give way before them. Conscience suspends its functions. The love of command—the impatience of restraint, get the better of every other feeling; and cruelty has no other limit than fear.

"'There must doubtless,' says Mr. Jefferson, 'be an unhappy influence on the manners of the people produced by the existence of slavery among us. The whole commerce between master and slave is a perpetual exercise of the most boisterous passions; the most unremitting despotism on the one part, and degrading submissions on the other. Our children see this, and learn to imitate it; for man is an imitative animal. The parent storms, the child looks on, catches the lineaments of wrath, puts on the same airs in the circle of smaller slaves, gives loose to the worst of passions; and thus nursed, educated, and daily exercised in tyranny, cannot but be stamped by it with odious peculiarities. The man must be a prodigy who can retain his morals and manners undepraved by such circumstances.'—Notes, p. 241."—*Hall*, p. 459.

The following picture of a slave song is quoted by Mr. Hall from the "Letters on Virginia."

"'I took the boat this morning, and crossed the ferry over to Portsmouth, the small town which I told you is opposite to this place. It was court-day, and a large crowd of people was gathered about the door of the court-house. I had hardly got upon the steps to look in, when my ears were assailed by the voice of singing; and turning round to discover from what quarter it came, I saw a group of about thirty negroes, of different sizes and ages, following a rough-looking white man, who sat carelessly lolling in his sulky. They had just turned round the corner, and were coming up the main street to pass by the spot where I stood, on their way out of town. As they came nearer, I saw some of them loaded with chains to prevent their escape; while others had hold of each other's hands, strongly grasped, as if to support themselves in their affliction. I particularly noticed a poor mother, with an infant suckling at her breast as she walked along, while two small children had hold of her apron on either side, almost running to keep up with the rest. They came along singing a little wild hymn, of sweet and mournful melody, flying, by a divine instinct of the heart, to the consolation of religion, the last refuge of the unhappy, to support them in their distress. The sulky now stopped before the tavern, at a little distance beyond the court-house, and the driver got out. 'My dear sir,' said I to a person who stood near me, 'can you tell me what these poor people have been doing? What is their crime? and what is to be their punishment?' 'O,' said he, 'it's nothing at all but a parcel of negroes sold to Carolina; and that man is their driver, who has bought them' 'But what have they done, that they should be sold into banishment?' 'Done,' said he, 'nothing at all, that I know of; their masters wanted money, I suppose, and these drivers give good prices.' Here the driver having supplied himself with brandy, and his horse with water, (the poor negroes, of course, wanted nothing,) stepped into his chair again, cracked his whip, and drove on, while the miserable exiles followed in funeral procession behind him.'"—*Hall*, 358—360.

The law by which slaves are governed in the Carolinas, is a provincial law as old as 1740. but made perpetual in 1783. By this law it is enacted, that every negro shall be presumed a slave, unless the contrary appear. The 9th clause allows two justices of the peace, and

* Mr. Fearon mentions a religious lottery for building a Presbyterian church. What will Mr. Littleton say to this? he is hardly prepared, we suspect, for this union of Calvin and the Little Go. Every advantage will be made of it by the wit and eloquence of his fiscal opponent;—nor will it pass unheeded by Mr. Bish.

three freeholders, power to put them to any manner of death; the evidence against them may be without oath.—No slave is to traffic on his own account.—Any person murdering a slave is to pay 100*l*.—or 14*l*. if he cuts out the tongue of a slave.—Any white man meeting seven slaves together on an high road, may give them twenty lashes each.—No man must teach a slave to write, under penalty of 100*l*. currency. We have Mr. Hall's authority for the existence and enforcement of this law at the present day. Mr. Fearon has recorded some facts still more instructive.

"Observing a great many coloured people, particularly females, in these boats, I concluded that they were emigrants, who had proceeded thus far on their route towards a settlement. The fact proved to be, that fourteen of the flats were freighted with human beings for sale. They had been collected in the several states by slave dealers, and shipped from Kentucky for a market. They were dressed up to the best advantage, on the same principle that jockeys do horses upon sale. The following is a specimen of advertisements on this subject.

'TWENTY DOLLARS REWARD

"'Will be paid for apprehending and lodging in jail, or delivering to the subscriber, the following slaves, belonging to JOSEPH IRVIN, of *Iberville*.—TOM, a very light mulatto, blue eyes, 5 feet 10 inches high, appears to be about 35 years of age; an artful fellow—can read and write, and *preaches* occasionally.—CHARLOTTE, a black wench, round and full faced, tall, straight and likely—about 25 years of age, and wife of the above-named Tom.—These slaves decamped from their owner's plantation on the night of the 14th September inst.' "—*Fearon*, p. 270.

"The three 'African churches,' as they are called, are for all those native Americans who are black, or have any shade of colour darker than white. These persons, though many of them are possessed of the rights of citizenship, are not admitted into the churches which are visited by whites. There exists a penal law, deeply written in the *mind* of the whole white population, which subjects their coloured fellow-citizens to unconditional contumely and never-ceasing insult. No respectability, however unquestionable, —no property, however large,—no character, however unblemished, will gain a man, whose body is (in American estimation) *cursed* with even a twentieth portion of the blood of his African ancestry, admission into society!!! They are considered as mere Pariahs—as outcasts and vagrants upon the face of the earth! I make no reflection upon these things, but leave the facts for your consideration."—*Ibid.*, p. 168, 169.

That such feelings and such practices should exist among men who know the value of liberty, and profess to understand its principles, is the consummation of wickedness. Every American who loves his country, should dedicate his whole life, and every faculty of his soul, to efface this foul stain from its character. If nations rank according to their wisdom and their virtue, what right has the American, a scourger and murderer of slaves, to compare himself with the least and lowest of the European nations?—much more with this great and humane country, where the greatest lord dare not lay a finger upon the meanest peasant? What is freedom, where all are not free? where the greatest of God's blessings is limited, with impious caprice, to the colour of the body? And these are the men who taunt the English with their corrupt Parliament, with their buying and selling votes. Let the world judge which is the most liable to censure—we who, in the midst of our rottenness, have torn off the manacles of slaves all over the world;—or they who, with their idle purity and useless perfection, have remained mute and careless, while groans echoed and whips clanked round the very walls of their spotless Congress. We wish well to America—we rejoice in her prosperity—and are delighted to resist the absurd impertinence with which the character of her people is often treated in this country: but the existence of slavery in America is an atrocious crime, with which no measures can be kept—for which her situation affords no sort of apology —which makes liberty itself distrusted, and the boast of it disgusting.

As for emigration, every man, of course, must determine for himself. A carpenter under thirty years of age, who finds himself at Cincinnati with an axe over his shoulder, and ten pounds in his pocket, will get rich in America, if the change of climate does not kill him. So will a farmer who emigrates early with some capital. But any person with tolerable prosperity here had better remain where he is. There are considerable evils, no doubt, in England: but it would be madness not to admit that it is, upon the whole, a very happy country,—and we are much mistaken if the next twenty years will not bring with it a great deal of internal improvement. The country has long been groaning under the evils of the greatest foreign war we were ever engaged in; and we are just beginning to look again into our home affairs. Political economy has made an astonishing progress since they were last investigated; and every session of Parliament brushes off some of the cobwebs and dust of our ancestors.* The Apprentice Laws have been swept away; the absurd nonsense of the Usury Laws will probably soon follow; Public Education and Saving Banks have been the invention of these last ten years; and the strong fortress of bigotry has been rudely assailed. Then, with all its defects, we have a Parliament of inestimable value. If there be a place in any country where 500 well-educated men can meet together and talk with impunity of public affairs, and if what they say is published, that country must improve. It is not pleasant to emigrate into a country of changes and revolution, the size and integrity of whose empire no man can predict.

* In a scarcity which occurred little more than twenty years ago, every judge, (except the lord chancellor, then Justice of the Common Pleas, and Serjeant Remington,) when they charged the grand jury, attributed the scarcity to the combinations of the farmers; and complained of it as a very serious evil. Such doctrines would not now be tolerated in the mouth of a schoolboy.

The Americans are a very sensible, reflecting people, and have conducted their affairs extremely well; but it is scarcely possible to conceive that such an empire should very long remain undivided, or that the dwellers on the Columbia should have common interest with the navigators of the Hudson and the Delaware.

England is, to be sure, a very expensive country; but a million of millions has been expended in making it habitable and comfortable; and this is a constant source of revenue, or, what is the same thing, a constant diminution of expense to every man living in it. The price an Englishman pays for a turnpike road is not equal to the tenth part of what the delay would cost him without a turnpike. The New River Company brings water to every inhabitant of London at an infinitely less price than he could dip for it out of the Thames. No country, in fact, is so expensive as one which human beings are just beginning to inhabit;—where there are no roads, no bridges, no skill, no help, no combination of powers, and no force of capital.

How, too, can any man take upon himself to say that he is so indifferent to his country that he will not begin to love it intensely, when he is 5000 or 6000 miles from it? And what a dreadful disease Nostalgia must be on the banks of the Missouri! Severe and painful poverty will drive us all anywhere: but a wise man should be quite sure that he has so irresistible a plea, before he ventures on the Great or the Little Wabash. He should be quite sure that he does not go there from ill temper—or to be pitied—or to be regretted—or from ignorance of what is to happen to him—or because he is a poet—but because he has not enough to eat here, and is sure of abundance where he is going.

GAME LAWS.*

[EDINBURGH REVIEW, 1819.]

THE evil of the Game Laws, in their present state, has long been felt, and of late years has certainly rather increased than diminished. We believe that they cannot long remain in their present state; and we are anxious to express our opinion of those changes which they ought to experience.

We thoroughly acquiesce in the importance of encouraging those field sports which are so congenial to the habits of Englishmen, and which, in the present state of society, afford the only effectual counterbalance to the allurements of great towns. We cannot conceive a more pernicious condition for a great nation, than that its aristocracy should be shut up from one year's end to another in a metropolis, while the mass of its rural inhabitants are left to the management of factors and agents. A great man returning from London to spend his summer in the country, diffuses his intelligence, improves manners, communicates pleasure, restrains the extreme violence of subordinate politicians, and makes the middling and lower classes better acquainted with, and more attached to their natural leaders. At the same time, a residence in the country gives to the makers of laws an opportunity of studying those interests which they may afterwards be called upon to protect and arrange. Nor is it unimportant to the character of the higher orders themselves, that they should pass a considerable part of the year in the midst of these their larger families; that they should occasionally be thrown among simple, laborious, frugal people, and be stimulated to resist the prodigality of courts, by viewing with their own eyes the merits and the wretchedness of the poor.

Laws for the preservation of game are not only of importance, as they increase the amusements of the country, but they may be so constructed as to be perfectly just. The game which my land feeds is certainly mine; or, in other words, the game which all the land feeds certainly belongs to all the owners of the land; and the only practical way of dividing it is, to give to each proprietor what he can take on his own ground. Those who contribute nothing to the support of the animal, can have no possible right to a share in the distribution. To say of animals, that they are *feræ Naturâ*, means only, that the precise place of their birth and nurture is not known. How they shall be divided, is a matter of arrangement among those whose collected property certainly has produced and fed them; but the case is completely made out against those who have no land at all, and who cannot, therefore, have been in the slightest degree instrumental to their production. If a large pond were divided by certain marks into four parts, and allotted to that number of proprietors, the fish contained in that pond would be, in the same sense, *feræ Naturâ*. Nobody could tell in which particular division each carp had been born and bred. The owners would arrange their respective rights and pretensions in the best way they could; but the clearest of all possible propositions would be, that the four proprietors, among them, made a complete title to all the fish; and that nobody but them had the smallest title to the smallest share. This we say in answer to those who contend that there is no foundation for any system of game laws; that animals born wild are the property of the public; and that their appropriation is nothing but tyranny and usurpation.

In addition to these arguments, it is perhaps scarcely necessary to add, that nothing which is worth having, which is accessible, and supplied only in limited quantities, could exist at all, if it was not considered as the property of some individual. If every body might take game wherever they found it, there would soon be an end of every species of game. The advantage would not be extended to fresh classes, but be annihilated for all classes. Besides all this, the privilege of killing game could not be granted without the privilege of trespassing on landed property;—an intolerable evil, which would entirely destroy the comfort and privacy of a country life.

But though a system of game laws is of great use in promoting country amusements, and may, in itself, be placed on a footing of justice, its effects, we are sorry to say, are by no means favourable to the morals of the poor.

It is impossible to make an uneducated man understand in what manner a bird hatched nobody knows where,—to-day living in my field, to-morrow in yours,—should be as strictly property as the goose whose whole history can be traced, in the most authentic and satisfactory manner, from the egg to the spit. The arguments upon which this depends are so contrary to the notions of the poor,—so repugnant to their passions,—and, perhaps, so much above their comprehension, that they are totally unavailing. The same man who would respect an orchard, a garden or an hen-roost, scarcely thinks he is committing any fault at all in invading the game-covers of his richer neighbour; and as soon as he becomes wearied of honest industry, his first resource is in plundering the rich magazine of hares, pheasants and partridges—the top and bottom dishes, which on every side of his village are running and flying before his eyes. As these things cannot be done with safety in the day, they must be done in the night;—and in this manner a lawless marauder is often formed, who proceeds from

* *Three Letters on the Game Laws.* Rest Fenner, Black & Co.' London, 1818.

one infringement of law and property to another, till he becomes a thoroughly bad and corrupted member of society.

These few preliminary observations lead naturally to the two principal considerations which are to be kept in view, in reforming the game laws;—to preserve, as far as is consistent with justice, the amusements of the rich and to diminish, as much as possible, the temptations of the poor. And these ends, it seems to us, will be best answered,

1. By abolishing qualifications. 2. By giving to every man a property in the game upon his land. 3. By allowing game to be bought by any body, and sold by its lawful possessors.*

Nothing can be more grossly absurd than the present state of the game laws, as far as they concern the qualification for shooting. In England, no man can possibly have a legal right to kill game, who has not 100*l.* a year in land rent. With us in Scotland, the rule is not quite so inflexible, though in principle not very different. But we shall speak to the case which concerns by far the greatest number: and certainly it is scarcely possible to imagine a more absurd and capricious limitation. For what possible reason is a man, who has only 90*l.* per annum in land, not to kill the game which his own land nourishes? If the legislature really conceives, as we have heard surmised by certain learned squires, that a person of such a degree of fortune should be confined to profitable pursuits, and debarred from that pernicious idleness into which he would be betrayed by field sports, it would then be expedient to make a qualification for bowls or skittles—to prevent small landowners from going to races or following a pack of hounds—and to prohibit to men of a certain income, every other species of amusement as well as this. The only instance, however, in which this paternal care is exercised, is that in which the amusement of the smaller landowner is supposed to interfere with those of his richer neighbour. He may do what he pleases, and elect any other species of ruinous idleness but that in which the upper classes of society are his rivals.

Nay, the law is so excessively ridiculous in the case of small landed proprietors, that on a property of less than 100*l.* per annum, *no human being* has the right of shooting. It is not confined but annihilated. The lord of the manor may be warned off by the proprietor; and the proprietor may be informed against by any body who sees him sporting. The case is still stronger in the instance of large farms. In Northumberland, and on the borders of Scotland, there are large capitalists who farm to the amount of two or three thousand per annum, who have the permission of their distant non-resident landlords to do what they please with the game, and yet who dare not fire off a gun upon their own land. Can any thing be more utterly absurd and preposterous, than that the landlord and the wealthy tenant *together* cannot make up a title to the hare which is fattened upon the choicest produce of their land? That the landlord, who can let to farm the fertility of the land for growing wheat, cannot let to farm its power of growing partridges? That he may reap by deputy, but cannot on that manor shoot by deputy? Is it possible that any respectable magistrate could fine a farmer for killing a hare upon his own grounds with his landlord's consent, without feeling that he was violating every feeling of common sense and justice?

Since the enactment of the game laws, there has sprung up an entirely new species of property, which of course is completely overlooked by their provisions. An Englishman may possess a million of money in funds or merchandize—may be the *Baring* or the *Hope* of Europe—provide to government the sudden means of equipping fleets and armies, and yet be without the power of smiting a single partridge, though invited by the owner of the game to participate in his amusement. It is idle to say that the difficulty may be got over by purchasing land: the question is, upon what principle of justice can the existence of the difficulty be defended? If the right of keeping men-servants was confined to persons who had more than 100*l.* a year in the funds, the difficulty might be got over by every man who would change his landed property to that extent. But what could justify so capricious a partiality to one species of property? There might be some apology for such laws at the time they were made; but there can be none for their not being now accommodated to the changes which time has introduced. If you choose to exclude poverty from this species of amusement, and to open it to wealth, why is it not opened to every species of wealth? What amusement can there be morally lawful to an holder of turnip land, and criminal in a possessor of exchequer bills? What delights ought to be tolerated to long annuities, from which wheat and beans should be excluded? What matters whether it is scrip or short-horned cattle? If the *locus quo* is conceded—if the trespass is waived—and if the qualification for any amusement is wealth, let it be any probable wealth—

Dives agris, dives positis in fœnore nummis.

It will be very easy for any country gentleman who wishes to monopolize to himself the pleasures of shooting, to let to his tenant every other right attached to the land, except the right of killing game; and it will be equally easy, in the formation of a new game act, to give to the landlord a summary process against his tenant, if such tenant fraudulently exercises the privileges he has agreed to surrender.

The case which seems most to alarm country gentlemen, is that of a person possessing a few acres in the heart of a manor, who might, by planting food of which they are fond, allure the game into his own little domain, and thus reap an harvest prepared at the expense of the neighbour who surrounded him. But, under the present game laws, if the smaller possession belongs to a qualified person, the danger of intrusion is equally great as it would be under the proposed alteration; and the danger from the poacher would be the same in both cases. But if it is of such great consequence to keep clear from all interference, may not such a piece of land be rented or bought? Or, may not the food which tempts the game be sown in the same abundance in the surrounding as in the enclosed

* All this has since been established.

After all, it is only common justice, that he whose property is surrounded on every side by a preserver of game, whose corn and turnips are demolished by animals preserved for the amusement of his neighbour, should himself be entitled to that share of game which plunders upon his land. The complaint which the landed grandee makes is this. "Here is a man who has only a twenty-fourth part of the land, and he expects a twenty-fourth part of the game. He is so captious and litigious, that he will not be contented to supply his share of the food without requiring his share of what the food produces. I want a neighbour who has talents only for suffering, not one who evinces such a fatal disposition for enjoying." Upon such principles as these, many of the game laws have been constructed, and are preserved. The interference of a very small property with a very large one; the critical position of one or two fields, is a very serious source of vexation on many other occasions besides those of game. He who possesses a field in the middle of my premises, may build so as to obstruct my view; and may present to me the hinder parts of a barn, instead of one of the finest landscapes in nature. Nay, he may turn his fields into tea-gardens, and destroy my privacy by the introduction of every species of vulgar company. The legislature, in all these instances, has provided no remedy for the inconveniences which a small property, by such intermixture, may inflict upon a large one, but has secured the same rights to unequal proportions. It is very difficult to conceive why these equitable principles are to be violated in the case of game alone.

Our securities against that rabble of sportsmen which the abolition of qualifications might be supposed to produce, are, the consent of the owner of the soil as an indispensable preliminary, guarded by heavy penalties—and the price of a certificate, rendered, perhaps, greater than it is at present. It is impossible to conceive why the owner of the soil, if the right of game is secured to him, has not a right to sell, or grant the right of killing it to whom he pleases—just as much as he has the power of appointing whom he pleases to kill his ducks, pigeons and chickens. The danger of making the poor idle is a mere pretence. It is monopoly calling in the aid of hypocrisy, and tyranny veiling itself in the garb of philosophical humanity. A poor man goes to wakes, fairs and horse-races, without pain and penalty; a little shopkeeper, when his work is over, may go to a bullbait, or to the cock-pit; but the idea of his pursuing an hare, even with the consent of the landowner, fills the Bucolic senator with the most lively apprehensions of relaxed industry and ruinous dissipation. The truth is, if a poor man does not offend against morals or religion, and supports himself and his family without assistance, the law has nothing to do with his amusements. The real barriers against increase of sportsmen (if the proposed alteration were admitted), are, as we have before said, the prohibition of the landowner; the tax to the state for a certificate; the necessity of labouring for support.—Whoever violates none of these rights, and neglects none of these duties in his sporting, sports without crime;—and to punish him would be gross and scandalous tyranny

The next alteration which we would propose is that game should be made property; that is, that every man should have a right to the game found upon his land—and that the violation of it should be punished as poaching now is, by pecuniary penalties, and summary conviction before magistrates. This change in the game laws would be an additional defence of game: for the landed proprietor has now no other remedy against the qualified intruder upon his game, than an action at law for a trespass on the land; and if the trespasser has received no notice, this can hardly be called any remedy at all. It is now no uncommon practice for persons who have the exterior, and perhaps the fortunes of gentlemen, as they are travelling from place to place, to shoot over manors where they have no property, and from which, as strangers, they cannot have been warned. In such case (which, we repeat again, is by no means one of rare occurrence), it would, under the reformed system, be no more difficult for the lord of the soil to protect his game, than it would be to protect his geese and ducks. But though game should be considered as property it should still be considered as the lowest species of property—because it is in its nature more vague and mutable than any other species of property, and because depredations upon it are carried on at a distance from the dwelling, and without personal alarm to the proprietors. It would be very easy to increase the penalties, in proportion to the number of offences committed by the same individual.

The punishments which country gentlemen expect by making game property, are the punishments affixed to offences of a much higher order: but country gentlemen must not be allowed to legislate exclusively on this, more than on any other subject. The very mention of hares and partridges in the country, too often puts an end to common humanity and common sense. Game must be protected; but protected without violating those principles of justice, and that adaptation of punishment to crime, which (incredible as it may appear), are of infinitely greater importance than the amusements of country gentlemen.

We come now to the sale of game.—The foundation on which the propriety of allowing this partly rests, is the impossibility of preventing it. There exists, and has sprung up since the game laws, an enormous mass of wealth, which has nothing to do with land. Do the country gentlemen imagine that it is in the power of human laws to deprive the three per cents of pheasants? That there is upon earth, air, or sea, a single flavour (cost what crime it may to procure it), that mercantile opulence will not procure? Increase the difficulty, and you enlist vanity on the side of luxury; and make that be sought for as a display of wealth, which was before valued only for the gratification of appetite. The law may multiply penalties by reams. Squires may fret and justices commit, and gamekeepers and poachers continue their nocturnal wars. There must be game on Lord Mayor's day, do what you will. You may multiply the crimes by which it is procured; but nothing can arrest its inevitable progress, from the wood of the esquire to the spit of the citizen. The late law for preventing the sale of game produced some little temporary difficulty in London at the beginning of the season. The poulterers were alarmed, and came to some resolutions. But the alarm soon began to subside and the difficulties to vanish. In another season, the law will be entirely nugatory and forgotten. The experiment was tried of increased severity, and a law passed to punish poachers with transportation who were caught poaching in the night time with arms. What has the consequence been?—Not a cessation of poaching, but a succession of village guerillas;—an internecive war between the gamekeepers and marauders of game:—the whole country flung into brawls and convulsions, for the unjust and exorbitant pleasures of country gentlemen. The poacher hardly believes he is doing any wrong in taking partridges and pheasants. He would admit the justice of being transported for stealing sheep; and his courage in such a transaction would be impaired by a consciousness he was doing wrong: but he has no such feeling in taking game; and the preposterous punishment of transportation makes him desperate, and not timid. Single poachers are gathered into large companies, for their mutual protection; and go out, not only with the intention of taking game, but of defending what they take with their lives. Such feelings soon produce a rivalry of personal courage, and a thirst of revenge between the villagers and the agents of power. We extract the following passages on this subject from the Three Letters on the Game Laws.

"The first and most palpable effect has naturally been, an exaltation of all the savage and desperate features in the poacher's character. The war between him and the gamekeeper has necessarily become a '*bellum internecivum.*' A marauder may hesitate perhaps at killing his fellow man, when the alternative is only six months' imprisonment in the county jail; but when the alternative is to overcome the keeper, or to be torn from his family and connections, and sent to hard labour at the antipodes, we cannot be much surprised that murders and midnight combats have considerably increased this season; or that information, such as the following, has frequently enriched the columns of the country newspapers."

"'Poaching.—Richard Barnett was on Tuesday convicted before T. Clutterbuck, Esq., of keeping and using engines or wires for the destruction of game in the parish of Dunkerton, and fined 5*l.* He was taken into custody by C. Coates, keeper to Sir Charles Bamfylde, Bart., who found upon him seventeen wire-snares. The new act that has just passed against these illegal practices, seems only to have irritated the offenders, and made them more daring and desperate. The following is a copy of an anonymous circular letter, which has been received by several magistrates, and other eminent characters in this neighbourhood.

"'Take notice.—We have lately heard and seen that there is an act passed, and whatever poacher is caught destroying the game, is to be transported for seven years.—*This is English liberty!*

"'Now, we do swear to each other, that the first of our company that this law is inflicted on, that there shall not one gentleman's seat in our country escape the rage of fire. We are nine in number, and we will burn every gentleman's house of note. The first that impeaches shall be shot. We have sworn not to impeach. You may think it a threat, but they will find it reality. The game-laws were too severe before. The Lord of all men sent these animals for the peasants as well as for the prince. God will not let his people be oppressed. He will assist us in our undertaking, and we will execute it with caution.'"—*Bath Paper.*

"'Death of a Poacher.—On the evening of Saturday se'ennight, about eight or nine o'clock, a body of poachers, seven in number, assembled by mutual agreement on the estate of the Hon. John Dutton at Sherborne, Gloucestershire, for the purpose of taking hares and other game. With the assistance of two dogs, and some nets and snares which they brought with them, they had succeeded in catching nine hares, and were carrying them away, when they were discovered by the gamekeeper and seven others who were engaged with him in patroling the different covers, in order to protect the game from nightly depredators. Immediately on perceiving the poachers, the keeper summoned them in a civil and peaceable manner to give up their names, the dogs, implements, &c. they had with them, and the game they had taken; at the same time assuring them, that his party had firearms (which were produced for the purpose of convincing and alarming them), and representing to them the folly of resistance, as, in the event of an affray, they must inevitably be overpowered by superior numbers, even without firearms, which they were determined not to resort to unless compelled in self-defence. Notwithstanding this remonstrance of the keeper, the men unanimously refused to give up on any terms, declaring, that if they were followed, they would give them "a brush," and would repel force by force. The poachers then directly took off their great coats, threw them down with the game, &c. behind them, and approached the keepers in an attitude of attack. A smart contest instantly ensued, both parties using only the sticks or bludgeons they carried: and such was the confusion during the battle, that some of the keepers were occasionally struck by their own comrades in mistake for their opponents. After they had fought in this manner about eight or ten minutes, one of the poachers named Robert Simmons, received a violent blow upon his left temple, which felled him to the ground, where he lay, crying out murder, and asking for mercy. The keepers very humanely desired that all violence might cease on both sides: upon which three of the poachers took to flight and escaped, and the remaining three, together with Simmons, were secured by the keepers. Simmons, by the assistance of the other men, walked to the keeper's house, where he was placed in a chair: but he soon after died. His death was no doubt caused by the pressure of blood upon the brain, occasioned by the rupture of a vessel from the blow he had received. The three poachers who had been taken were committed to Northleach prison. The inquest upon the body of Simmons was taken on Monday, before W. Trigge, Gent., Coroner; and the above account is extracted from the evidence given upon that occasion. The poachers were all armed with bludgeons, except the deceased, who had provided himself with the thick part of a flail, made of firm knotted crabtree, and pointed at the extremity, in order to thrust with, if occasion required. The deceased was an athletic muscular man, very active, and about twenty-eight years of age. He resided at Bowle, in Oxfordshire, and has left a wife but no child. The three prisoners were heard in evidence; and all concurred in stating that the keepers were in no way blameable, and attributed their disaster to their own indiscretion and imprudence. Several of the keepers' party were so much beat as to be now confined to their beds. The two parties are said to be total strangers to each other, consequently no malice prepense could have existed between them; and as it appeared to the jury, after a most minute and deliberate investigation, that the confusion during the affray was so great, that the deceased was as likely to be struck by one of his own party as by the keepers', they returned a verdict of—*Manslaughter* against some person or persons unknown.'

"Wretched as the first of these productions is, I think it can scarcely be denied, that both its spirit and its probable consequences are wholly to be ascribed to the exasperation naturally consequent upon the severe enactment just alluded to. And the last case is at least a strong proof that severity of enactment is quite inadequate to correct the evil."—(P. 356–359.)

Poaching will exist in some degree, let the laws be what they may; but the most certain method of checking the poacher seems to be by underselling him. If game can be lawfully sold, the quantity sent to market will be increased, the price lowered, and, with that, the profits and temptations of the poacher. Not only would the prices of the poacher be lowered, but we much doubt if he would find any sale at all. Licenses to sell game might be confined to real poulterers, and real occupiers of a certain portion of land. It might be rendered penal to purchase it from any but licensed persons; and in this way the facility of the lawful, and the danger of the unlawful trade, would either annihilate the poacher's trade, or reduce his prices so much, that it would be hardly worth his while to carry it on. What poulterer in London, or in any of the large towns, would deal with poachers, and expose himself to indictment for receiving stolen goods, when he might supply his customers at fair prices by dealing with the lawful proprietor of game? Opinion is of more power than law. Such conduct would soon become infamous; and every respectable tradesman would be shamed out of it. The consumer himself would rather buy his game of a poulterer at an increase of price, than pick it up clandestinely, and at a great risk, though a somewhat smaller price, from porters and boothkeepers. Give them a chance of getting it fairly, and they will not get it unfairly. At present, no one has the slightest shame at violating a law which every body feels to be absurd and unjust.

Poultry-houses are sometimes robbed;—but stolen poultry is rarely offered to sale;—at least, nobody pretends that the shops of poulterers and the tables of moneyed gentlemen are supplied by these means. Out of one hundred geese that are consumed at Michaelmas, ninety-nine come into the jaws of the consumer by honest means;—and yet, if it had pleased the country gentlemen to have goose laws as well as game laws;—if goose-keepers had been appointed, and the sale and purchase of this savoury bird prohibited, the same enjoyments would have been procured by the crimes and convictions of the poor; and the periodical gluttony of Michaelmas have been rendered as guilty and criminal, as it is indigestible and unwholesome. Upon this subject we shall quote a passage from the very sensible and spirited letters before us.

"In favourable situations, game would be reared and preserved for the express purpose of regularly supplying the market in fair and open competition; which would so reduce its price, that I see no reason why a partridge should be dearer than a rabbit, or a hare and pheasant than a duck or goose. This is about the proportion of price which the animals bear to each other in France, where game can be legally sold, and is regularly brought to market; and where, by the way, game is as plentiful as in any cultivated country in Europe. The price so reduced would never be enough to compensate the risk and penalties of the unlawful poacher, who must therefore be driven out of the market. Doubtless, the great poulterers of London and the commercial towns, who are the *principal instigators of poaching*, would cease to have any temptation to continue so, as they could fairly and lawfully procure game for their customers at a cheaper rate from the regular breeders. They would, as they now do for rabbits and wild-fowl, contract with persons to rear and preserve them for the regular supply of their shops, which would be a much more commodious and satisfactory, and less hazardous way for them, than the irregular and dishonest and corrupting methods now pursued. It is not saying very much in favour of human nature to assert, that men in respectable stations of society had rather procure the *same ends* by honest than dishonest means. Thus would all the temptations to offend against the game laws, arising from the change of society, together with the long chain of moral and political mischiefs, at once disappear.

"But then, in order to secure a sufficient breed of game for the supply of the market, in fair and open competition, it will be necessary to authorize a certain number of persons, likely to breed game for sale, to take and dispose of it when reared at their expense. For this purpose, I would suggest the propriety of permitting by law occupiers of land to take and kill game, for sale or otherwise, on their *own occupations only*, unless, (if tenants,) they are specifically prohibited by agreement with their landlord; reserving the game and the power of taking it to himself, (as is now frequently done in leases.) This permission should not, of course, operate during the current leases, unless by agreement. With this precaution, nothing could be fairer than such an enactment; for it is certainly at the expense of the *occupier* that the game is raised and maintained: and unless he receive an equivalent for it, either by abatement of rent upon agreement, or by permission to take and dispose of it, he is certainly an injured man. Whereas it is perfectly just that the owner of the land should have the option either to increase his rent by leaving the disposal of his game to his tenant, or *vice versâ*. Game would be held to be (as in fact it is) an *outgoing* from the land, like tithe and other burdens, and therefore to be considered in a bargain; and land would either be let *game-free*, or a special reservation of it made by agreement.

"Moreover, since the breed of game must always depend upon the occupier of the land, who may, and frequently does, destroy every head of it, or prevent its coming to maturity, unless it is considered in his rent; the license for which I am now contending, by affording an inducement to preserve the breed in particular spots, would evidently have a considerable effect in increasing the stock of game in other parts, and in the country at large. There would be introduced a general system of protection depending upon individual interest, instead of a general system of destruction. I have, therefore, very little doubt that the provision here recommended would, upon the whole, add facilities to the amusements of the sportsman, rather than subtract from them. A sportsman without land might also hire from the occupier of a large tract of land the privilege of shooting over it, which would answer to the latter as well as sending his game to the market. In short, he might in various ways get a fair return, to which he is well entitled for the expense and trouble incurred in rearing and preserving that particular species of stock upon his land."—(P. 337—339.)

There are sometimes 400 or 500 head of game killed in great manors on a single day. We think it highly probable the greater part of this harvest (if the game laws were altered) would go to the poulterer, to purchase poultry or fish for the ensuing London season. Nobody is so poor and so distressed as men of very large fortunes, who are fond of making an unwise display to the world; and if they had recourse to these means of supplying game, it is impossible to suppose that the occupation of the poacher could be continued.—The smuggler can compete with the spirit merchant on account of the great duty imposed by the revenue; but where there is no duty to be saved, the mere thief—the man who brings the article to market with a halter around his neck—the man of whom it is disreputable and penal to buy—who hazards life, liberty and property, to procure the articles which he sells; such an adventurer can never be long the rival of him who honestly and fairly produces the articles in which he deals.—Fines, imprisonments, concealment, loss of character, are great deductions from the profits of any trade to which they attach, and great discouragement to its pursuit.

It is not the custom at present for gentlemen to sell their game; but the custom would soon begin, and public opinion soon change. It is not unusual for men of fortune to contract with their gardeners to supply their own table and to send the residue to market, or to sell their venison; and the same thing might be done with the manor. If game could be bought, it would not be sent in presents:—barn-door fowls are never so sent, precisely for this reason.

The price of game would, under the system of laws of which we are speaking, be further lowered by the introduction of foreign game, the sale of which, at present prohibited, would tend very much to the preservation of English game by underselling the poacher. It would not be just, if it were possible, to confine any of the valuable productions of nature to the use of one class of men, and to prevent them from becoming the subject of barter, when the proprietor wished so to exchange them. It would be just as reasonable that the consumption of salmon should be confined to the proprietors of that sort of fishery—that the use of charr should be limited to the inhabitants of the lakes—that maritime Englishmen should alone eat oysters and lobsters as that every other class of the community than landowners should be prohibited from the acquisition of game.

It will be necessary, whenever the game laws are revised, that some of the worst punishments now inflicted for an infringement of these laws should be repealed. To transport a man for seven years, on account of partridges, and to harass a poor wretched peasant in the Crown Office, are very preposterous punishments for such offences; humanity revolts against them—they are grossly tyrannical—and it is disgraceful that they should be suffered to remain on our statute books. But the most singular of all abuses, is the new class of punishments which the squirarchy have themselves enacted against depredations on game. The law says, that an unqualified man who kills a pheasant, shall pay five pounds; but the squire says he shall be shot;—and accordingly he places a spring-gun in the path of the poacher, and does all he can to take away his life. The more humane and mitigated squire mangles him with traps; and the suprafine country gentleman only detains him in machines, which prevent his escape, but do not lacerate their captive. Of the gross illegality of such proceedings, there can be no reasonable doubt. Their immorality and cruelty are equally clear. If they are not put down by some declaratory law, it will be absolutely necessary that the judges, in their invaluable circuits of Oyer and Terminer, should leave two or three of his majesty's squires to a fate too vulgar and indelicate to be alluded to in this journal.

Men have certainly a clear right to defend their property; but then it must be by such means as the law allows:—their houses by pistols, their fields by actions for trespass, their game by information. There is an end of law, if every man is to measure out his punishment for his own wrong. Nor are we able to distinguish between the guilt of two persons,—the one of whom deliberately shoots a man whom he sees in his fields—the other of whom purposely places such instruments as he knows will shoot trespassers upon his fields. Better that it should be lawful to kill a trespasser face to face than to place engines which will kill him. The trespasser may be a child—a women—a son or friend. The spring-gun cannot accommodate itself to circumstances,—the squire or the game keeper may.

These, then, are our opinions respecting the alterations in the game laws, which, as they now stand, are perhaps the only system which could possibly render the possession of game so very insecure as it now is. We would give to every man an absolute property in the game upon his land, with full power to kill—to permit others to kill—and to sell;—we would punish any violation of that property by summary conviction, and pecuniary penalties—rising in value according to the number of offences. This would of course abolish all qualifications; and we sincerely believe it would lessen the profits of selling game illegally, so as very materially to lessen the number of poachers. It would make game as an article of food, accessible to all classes, without infringing the laws. It would limit the amusement of country gentlemen within the boundaries of justice—and would enable the magistrate cheerfully and conscientiously to execute laws, of the moderation and justice of which he must be thoroughly convinced. To this conclusion, too, w have no doubt we shall come at the last. Afte many years of scutigeral folly—loaded prisons* —nightly battles—poachers tempted—and families ruined, these principles will finally prevail, and make law once more coincident with reason and justice.

* In the course of the last year, no fewer than *twelve hundred* persons were committed for offences against the game; besides those who ran away from their families for the fear of commitment. This is no slight quantity of misery

---

BOTANY BAY.*

[Edinburgh Review, 1819.]

This land of convicts and kangaroos is beginning to rise into a very fine and flourishing settlement:—And great indeed must be the natural resources, and splendid the endowments of that land that has been able to survive the system of neglect† and oppression experienced from the mother country, and the series of ignorant and absurd governors that have been selected for the administration of its affairs. But mankind live and flourish not only in spite of storms and tempests, but (which could not have been anticipated previous to experience) in spite of colonial secretaries expressly paid to watch over their interests. The supineness and profligacy of public officers cannot always overcome the amazing energy with which human beings pursue their happiness, nor the sagacity with which they determine on the means by which that end is to be promoted. Be it our care, however, to record for the future inhabitants of Australasia, the political sufferings of their larcenous forefathers; and let them appreciate, as they ought, that energy which founded a mighty empire in spite of the afflicting blunders and marvellous cacœconomy of their government.

Botany Bay is situated in a fine climate, rather Asiatic than European,—with a great variety of temperature,—but favourable on the whole to health and life. It, conjointly with Van Diemen's Land, produces coal in great abundance, fossil salt, slate, lime, plumbago, potter's clay; iron; white, yellow and brilliant topazes; alum and copper. These are all the important fossil productions which have been hitherto discovered; but the epidermis of the country has hardly as yet been scratched; and it is most probable that the immense mountains which divide the eastern and western settlements, Bathurst and Sydney, must abound with every species of mineral wealth. The harbours are admirable; and the whole world, perhaps, cannot produce two such as those of Port Jackson and Derwent. The former of these is land-locked for fourteen miles in length, and of the most irregular form; its soundings are more than sufficient for the largest ships; and all the navies of the world might ride in safety within it. In the harbour of Derwent there is a road-stead forty-eight miles in length, completely land-locked;—varying in breadth from eight to two miles,—in depth from thirty to four fathoms,—and affording the best anchorage the whole way

The mean heat, during the three summer months, December, January, and February, is about 80° at noon. The heat which such a degree of the thermometer would seem to indicate, is considerably tempered by the sea-breeze, which blows with considerable force from nine in the morning till seven in the evening. The three autumn months are March, April and May, in which the thermometer varies from 55° at night to 75° at noon. The three winter months are June, July, and August. During this inter-

*1. *A Statistical, Historical and Political Description of the Colony of New South Wales, and its dependent Settlements in Van Diemen's Land; with a particular Enumeration of the Advantages which these colonies offer for Emigration, and their Superiority in many respects over those possessed by the United States of America.* By W. C. Wentworth, Esq., a Native of the Colony. Whittaker. London, 1819.

2. *Letter to Viscount Sidmouth, Secretary of State for the Home Department, on the Transportation Laws, the State of the Hulks, and of the Colonies in New South Wales.* By the Hon. Henry Grey Bennet, M. P. Ridgway. London, 1819.

3. O'Hara's *History of New South Wales.* Hatchard. London, 1818.

† One and no small excuse for the misconduct of colonial secretaries is, the enormous quantity of business by which they are distracted. There should be two or three colonial secretaries instead of one: the office is dreadfully overweighed. The government of the colonies is commonly a series of blunders.

val, the mornings and evenings are very chilly, and the nights excessively cold; hoar-frosts are frequent; ice, half an inch thick, is found twenty miles from the coast; the mean temperature, at daylight, is from 40° to 45,° and at noon, from 55° to 60°. In the three months of spring, the thermometer varies from 60° to 70°. The climate to the westward of the mountains is colder. Heavy falls of snow take place during the winter; the frosts are more severe, and the winters of longer duration. All the seasons are much more distinctly marked, and resemble much more those of this country.

Such is the climate of Botany Bay; and, in this remote part of the earth, Nature (having made horses, oxen, ducks, geese, oaks, elms, and all regular and useful productions for the rest of the world), seems determined to have a bit of play, and to amuse herself as she pleases. Accordingly, she makes cherries with the stone on the outside; and a monstrous animal, as tall as a grenadier, with the head of a rabbit, a tail as big as a bed-post, hopping along at the rate of five hops to a mile, with three or four young kangaroos looking out of its false uterus to see what is passing. Then comes a quadruped as big as a large cat, with the eyes, colour and skin of a mole, and the bill and web-feet of a duck—puzzling Dr. Shaw, and rendering the latter half of his life miserable, from his utter inability to determine whether it was a bird or a beast. Add to this a parrot, with the legs of a sea-gull; a skate with the head of a shark; and a bird of such monstrous dimensions, that a side bone of it will dine three real carniverous Englishmen;—together with many other productions that agitate Sir Joseph, and fill him with mingled emotions of distress and delight.

The colony has made the following progress:—

Stock in 1788.		Stock in 1817.	
Horned Cattle	5	Do.	44,753
Horses	7	Do.	3,072
Sheep	29	Do.	170,920
Hogs	74	Do.	17,842
Land in cultivation	0 acres.	Do.	47,564
Inhabitants	1000	Do.	20,379

The colony has a bank, with a capital of 20,000*l.*; a newspaper; and a capital (the town of Sydney) containing about 7000 persons. There is also a Van Diemen's Land Gazette. The perusal of these newspapers, which are regularly transmitted to England, and may be purchased in London, has afforded us considerable amusement. Nothing can paint in a more lively manner the state of the settlement, its disadvantages and prosperities, and the opinions and manners which prevail there.

"On Friday, Mr. James Squires, settler and brewer, waited on his excellency at Government House, with two vines of hops taken from his own grounds, &c.—As a public recompense for the unremitted attention shown by the grower in bringing this valuable plant to such a high degree of perfection, his excellency has directed a cow to be given to Mr. Squires from the government herd."—*O'Hara*, p. 255.

"*To Parents and Guardians.*

"A person who flatters herself her character will bear the strictest scrutiny, being desirous of receiving into her charge a proposed number of children of her own sex, as boarders, respectfully acquaints parents and guardians that she is about to situate herself either in Sydney or Paramatta, of which notice will be shortly given. She doubts not, at the same time, that her assiduity in the inculcation of moral principles in the youthful mind, joined to an unremitting attention and polite diction, will insure to her the much-desired confidence of those who may think proper to favour her with such a charge.—Inquiries on the above subject will be answered by G. Howe, at Sydney, who will make known the name of the advertiser."—(p. 270.)

"*Lost,*

"(supposed to be on the governor's wharf,) two small keys, a tortoise shell comb, and a packet of papers. Whoever may have found them, will, on delivering them to the printer, receive a reward of half a gallon of spirits."—(p. 272.)

"*To the Public.*

"As we have no certainty of an immediate supply of paper, we cannot promise a publication next week."—(p. 290.)

"*Fashionable Intelligence, Sept. 7th.*

"On Tuesday his excellency the late governor, and Mrs. King, arrived in town from Paramatta; and yesterday Mrs. King returned thither, accompanied by Mrs. Putland."—(*Ibid.*)

"*To be sold by private Contract, by Mr. Bevan,*

"An elegant four-wheeled chariot, with plated mounted harness for four horses complete; and handsome lady's side-saddle and bridle. May be viewed, on application to Mr. Bevan."—(p. 347.)

"*From the Derwent Star.*

"Lieutenant Lord, of the Royal Marines, who, after the death of Lieutenant-Governor Collins, succeeded to the command of the settlement at Hobart Town, arrived at Port Jackson in the Hunter, and favours us with the perusal of the ninth number published of the *Derwent Star and Van Diemen's Land Intelligencer;* from which we copy the following extracts."—(p. 353.)

"*A Card.*

"The subscribers to the Sydney Race Course are informed that the Stewards have made arrangements for two balls during the race week, viz., on Tuesday and Thursday.—Tickets, at 7*s.* 6*d.* each, to be had at Mr. E. Wills's, George Street.—An ordinary for the subscribers and their friends each day of the races, at Mr. Wills's. Dinner on table at five o'clock."—(p. 356.)

"*The Ladies' Cup.*

"The ladies' cup, which was of very superior workmanship, won by Chase, was presented to Captain Richie by Mrs. M'Quarie; who, accompanied by his excellency, honoured each day's race with her presence, and who, with her usual affability, was pleased to preface the donation with the following short address.—'In the name of the Ladies of New South Wales, I have the pleasure to present you with this cup Give me leave to congratulate you on being the successful candidate for it; and to hope that it is a prelude to future success and lasting prosperity.'"—(p. 357.)

"*Butchers.*

"Now killing, at Matthew Pimpton's, Cumberland street, Rocks, beef, mutton, pork, and lamb. By retail, 1*s.* 4*d.* per lib. Mutton by the carcass, 1*s.* per lib. sterling, or 14*d.* currency; warranted to weigh from 10 lib. to 12 lib. per quarter. Lamb per ditto.—Captains of ships supplied at the wholesale price, and with punctuality.—*N.B.* Beef, pork, mutton, and lamb, at E Lamb's, Hunter street, at the above prices."—(p. 376.)

"*Salt Pork and Flair from Otaheite.*

"On sale, at the warehouse of Mrs. S. Willis, 96 George street, a large quantity of the above articles, well cured, being the Mercury's last importation from Otaheite. The terms per cask are 10*d.* per lib. sterling, or 1*s.* currency.—*N.B.* For the accommodation of families, it will be sold in quantities not less than 112 lib."—(p. 377.)

"*Painting.—A Card.*

"Mr. J. W. Lewin begs leave to inform his friends and the public in general, that he intends opening an academy for painting on the days of Monday, Wednesday, and Friday, from the hours of 10 to 12 in the forenoon.—Terms 5*s.* a lesson: Entrance 20*s.*—*N.B.* The evening academy for drawing continued as usual."—(p. 384.)

"*Sale of Rams.*

"Ten rams of the Merino breed, lately sold by auction from the flocks of John M'Arthur, Esq., produced upwards of 200 guineas."—(p. 388.)

"*Mrs. Jones's Vacation Ball, December 12th.*

"Mrs. Jones, with great respect, informs the parents and guardians of the young ladies entrusted to her tuition, that the vacation ball is fixed for Tuesday the 22d instant, at the seminary, No. 45 Castlereagh street, Sydney. Tickets 7*s.* 6*d.* each."—(p. 388.)

"*Sporting Intelligence.*

"A fine hunt took place the 8th instant at the Nepean, of which the following is the account given by a gentleman present. 'Having cast off by the government hut on the Nepean, and drawn the cover in that neighbourhood for a native Dog unsuccessfully, we tried the forest ground for a Kangaroo, which we soon found. It went off in excellent style along the sands by the river side, and crossed to the Cow-pasture Plains, running a circle of about two miles; then recrossed, taking a direction for Mr. Campbell's stock-yard, and from thence at the back of Badge Allen Hill, to the head of Boorroobaham Creek, where he was headed; from thence he took the main range of hills between the Badge Allen and Badge Allenabinjee, in a straight direction for Mr. Throsbey's farm, where the hounds ran into him; and he was killed, after a good run of about two hours.'—The weight of the animal was upwards of 120 lib."—(p. 380.)

Of the town of Sydney, Mr. Wentworth observes, that there are in it many public buildings, as well as houses of individuals, that would not disgrace the best parts of London; but this description we must take the liberty to consider as more patriotic than true. We rather suspect it was penned before Mr. Wentworth was in London; for he is (be it said to his honour) a native of Botany Bay. The value of lands (in the same spirit he adds) is half as great in Sydney as in the best situations in London; and is daily increasing: The proof of this which Mr. Wentworth gives is, that "it is not a commodious house which can be rented for 100*l.* per annum unfurnished." The town of Sydney contains two good public schools, for the education of 224 children of both sexes. There are establishments, also, for the diffusion of education in every populous district throughout the colony; the masters of these schools are allowed stipulated salaries from the Orphans' fund. Mr. Wentworth states that one-eighth part of the whole revenue of the colony is appropriated to the purposes of education; this eighth he computes at 2500*l.* Independent of these institutions, there is an Auxiliary Bible Society, a Sunday School, and several good private schools. This is all as it should be: the education of the poor, important everywhere, is indispensable at Botany Bay. Nothing but the earliest attention to the habits of children can restrain the erratic finger from the contiguous scrip, or prevent the hereditary tendency to larcenous abstraction. The American arrangements respecting the education of the lower orders is excellent. Their unsold lands are surveyed, and divided into districts. In the centre of every district, an ample and well-selected lot is provided for the support of future schools. We wish this had been imitated in New Holland; for we are of opinion that the elevated nobleman, Lord Sidmouth, should imitate what is good and wise, even if the Americans are his teachers. Mr. Wentworth talks of 15,000 acres set apart for the support of the Female Orphan Schools; which certainly does sound a little extravagant: but then 50 or 100 acres of this reserve are given as a portion to each female orphan; so that all this pious tract of ground will be soon married away. This dotation of women, in a place where they are scarce, is amiable and foolish enough. There is a school also for the education and civilization of the natives, we hope not to the exclusion of the children of convicts, who have clearly a prior claim upon public charity.

Great exertions have been made in public roads and bridges. The present governor has wisely established toll-gates in all the principal roads. No tax can be more equitable, and no money more beneficially employed. The herds of wild cattle have either perished through the long droughts, or been destroyed by the remote settlers. They have nearly disappeared; and their extension is a good rather than an evil. A very good horse for cart or plough may now be bought for 5*l.* to 10*l.*; working oxen for the same price; fine young breeding ewes from 1*l.* to 3*l.*, according to the quality of the fleece. So lately as 1808, a cow and calf were sold by public auction for 105*l.*; and the price of middling cattle was from 80*l.* to 100*l.* A breeding mare was, at the same period, worth from 150 to 200 guineas; and ewes from 10*l.* to 20*l.* The inhabitants of New South Wales have now 2000 years before them of cheap beef and mutton. The price of land is of course regulated by its situation and quality. Four years past, an hundred and fifty acres of very indifferent ground, about three quarters of a mile from Sydney, were sold, by virtue of an execution, in lots of 12 acres each, and averaged 14*l.* per acre. This is the highest price given for land not situated in a town. The general average of unimproved land is 5*l.* per acre. In years when the crops have not suffered from flood or drought, wheat sells for 9*s.* per bushel; maize for 3*s.* 6*d.*; barley for 5*s.*; oats for 4*s.* 6*d.*; potatoes for 6*s.* per cwt. By the last accounts received from the colony, mutton and beef were 6*d.* per lib.; veal 8*d.*; pork 9*d.* Wheat 8*s.* 8*d.* per bushel; oats 4*s.*, and barley 5*s.* per ditto. Fowls 4*s.* 6*d.* per couple; ducks 6*s.* per ditto; geese 5*s.* each; turkeys 7*s.* 6*d.* each; eggs 2*s* 6*d.* per dozen; butter 2*s.* 6*d.* per lib. There are manufacturers of coarse woollen cloths, hats, earthenware, pipes, salt, candles, soap. There are extensive breweries and tanneries; and all sorts of mechanics and artificers necessary for an infant colony. Carpenters, stone masons, bricklayers, wheel and plough wrights, and all the most useful description of artificers, can earn from 8*s.* to 10*s.* per day. Great attention has been paid to the improvement of wool; and it is becoming a very considerable article of export to this country.

The most interesting circumstance in the accounts lately received from Botany Bay, is the discovery of the magnificent river on the western side of the Blue Mountains. The public are aware that a fine road has been made from Sydney to Bathurst, and a new town founded at the foot of a western side of these mountains, a distance of 140 miles. The country in the neighbourhood of Bathurst has been described as beautiful, fertile, open, and eminently fit for all the purposes of a settlement. The object was to find a river; and such an one has been found, the description of which it is impossible to read without the most lively interest. The intelligence is contained in a dispatch from Mr. Oxley, surveyor-general of the settlement, to the governor, dated 30th August, 1817.

"'On the 19th, we were gratified by falling in with a river running through a most beautiful country, and which I would have been well contented to have believed the river we were in search of. Accident led us down this stream about a mile, when we were surprised by its junction with a river coming from the south, of such width and magnitude, as to dispel all doubts as to this last being the river we had so long anxiously looked for. Short as our resources were, we could not resist the temptation this beautiful country offered us to remain two days on the junction of the river, for the purpose of examining the vicinity to as great an extent as possible.

"'Our examination increased the satisfaction we had previously felt. As far as the eye could reach in every direction, a rich and picturesque country extended, abounding in limestone, slate, good timber and every other requisite that could render an *uncultivated* country desirable. The soil cannot be excelled; whilst a noble river of *the first magnitude* affords the means of conveying its productions from one part to the other. Where I quitted it, its course was northerly; and we were then north of the parallel of Port Stevens, being in latitude 32° 45′ south, and 148° 58′ east longitude.

"'It appeared to me that the Macquarrie had taken a north-north-west course from Bathurst, and that it must have received immense accessions of water in its course from that place. We viewed it at a period best calculated to form an accurate judgment of its importance, when it was neither swelled by floods beyond its natural and usual height, nor contracted within limits by summer droughts. Of its magnitude when it should have received the streams we had crossed, independent of any it may receive from the east, which, from the boldness and height of the country, I presume must be at least as many, some idea may be formed, when at this point it exceeded in breadth and apparent depth, the Hawkesbury at Windsor. Many of the branches were of grander and more extended proportion than the admired one on the Nepean river from the Warragambia to Emu plains.

"'Resolving to keep as near the river as possible during the remainder of our course to Bathurst, and endeavour to ascertain, at least on the west side, what waters fell into it, on the 22d we proceeded up the river; and between the point quitted and Bathurst, crossed the sources of numberless streams, all running into the Macquarrie. Two of them were nearly as large as that river itself at Bathurst. The country whence all these streams derive their source was mountainous and irregular, and appeared equally so on the east side of the Macquarrie. This description of country extended to the immediate vicinity of Bathurst; but to the west of those lofty ranges the country was broken into low, grassy hills and fine valleys, watered by rivulets rising on the west side of the mountains, which, on their eastern side, pour their waters directly into the Macquarrie.

"'These westerly streams appeared to me to join that which I had at first sight taken for the Macquarrie; and when united, fall into it at the point at which it was first discovered on the 19th inst.

"'We reached this place last evening, without a single accident having occurred during the whole progress of the expedition, which from this point has encircled, with the parallels of 34° 0′ south and 32° south, and between the meridians of 149° 43′ and 143° 40′ east, a space of nearly one thousand miles.'"—*Wentworth*, pp. 72—75.

The nearest distance from the point at which Mr. Oxley left off, to any part of the western coast, is very little short of 2000 miles. The Hawkesbury, at Windsor, (to which he compares his new river in magnitude,) is 250 yards in breadth, and of sufficient depth to float a 74 gun ship. At this point it has 2000 miles in a straight line to reach the ocean; and if it winds as rivers commonly do wind, it has a space to flow over of between 5000 and 6000 miles. The course and direction of the river have since become the object of two expeditions, one by land under Mr. Oxley, the other by sea under Lieu tenant King, to the results of which we look forward with great interest. Enough of the country on the western side of the Blue Mountains has been discovered, to show that the settlement has been made on the wrong side. The space between the Mountains and the Eastern Sea is not above 40 miles in breadth, and the five or six miles nearest the coast are of very barren land. The country, on the other side, is boundless, fertile, well watered, and of very great beauty. The importance of such a river as the Macquarrie is incalculable. We cannot help remarking here, the courtly appellations in which Geography delights;—the river *Hawkesbury;* the town of *Windsor* on its banks; *Bathurst* Plains; *Nepean* River. Shall we never hear of the Gulf of *Tierney; Brougham* Point; or the Straits of *Mackintosh* on the river *Grey?*

The mistakes which have been made in settling this fine colony are of considerable importance, and such as must very seriously retard its progress to power and opulence. The first we shall mention is the settlement on the Hawkesbury. Every work of nature has its characteristic defects. Marshes should be suspected of engendering disease—a volcanic country of eruptions—rivers of overflowing. A very little portion of this kind of reflection would have induced the disposers of land in New South Wales to have become a little better acquainted with the Hawkesbury before they granted land on its banks, and gave that direction to the tide of settlement and cultivation. It turns out that the Hawkesbury is the embouchure through which all the rain that falls on the eastern side of the Blue Mountain makes its way to the sea; and accordingly, without any warning, or any fall of rain on the settled part of the river, the stream has often risen from 70 to 90 feet above its common level.

"These inundations often rise seventy or eighty feet above low water mark; and the instance of what is still emphatically termed 'the great flood,' attained an elevation of ninety-three feet. The chaos of confusion and distress that presents itself on these occasions cannot be easily conceived by any one who has not been a witness of its horrors. An immense expanse of water, of which the eye cannot in many directions discover the limits, everywhere interspersed with growing timber, and crowded with poultry, pigs, horses, cattle, stacks and houses, having frequently men, women and children, clinging to them for protection and shrieking out in an agony of despair for assistance:—such are the principal objects by which these scenes of death and devastation are characterized.

"These inundations are not periodical, but they most generally happen in the month of March. Within the last two years there have been no fewer than four of them, one of which was nearly as high as the great flood. In the six years preceding, there had not been one. Since the establishment of the colony, they have happened, upon an average, about once in three years.

"The principal cause of them is the contiguity of this river to the Blue Mountains. The Grose and Warragambia rivers, from which two sources it derives its principal supply, issue direct from these mountains; and the Nepean river, the other principal branch of it, runs along the base of them for fifty or sixty miles; and receives, in its progress, from the innumerable mountain torrents connected with it, the whole of the rain which these mountains collect in that great extent. That this is the principal cause of these calamitous inundations has been fully proved; for shortly after the plantation of this colony, the Hawkesbury overflowed its banks (which are in general about thirty feet in height,) in the midst of harvest, when not a single drop of rain had fallen on the Port Jackson side of the mountains. Another great cause of the inundations which take place in this and the other rivers in the colony, is the small fall that is in them and the consequent slowness of their currents. The current in the Hawkesbury, even when the tide is in full ebb, does not exceed two miles an hour. The water, therefore, which during the rains rushes in torrents from the mountains, cannot escape with sufficient rapidity; and from its immense accumulation soon overtops the banks of the river and covers the whole of the low country."—*Wentworth,* pp. 24–26.

It appears to have been a great oversight not to have built the town of Sydney upon a regular plan. Ground was granted, in the first instance, without the least attention to this circumstance; and a chaos of pigstyes and houses was produced, which subsequent governors have found it extremely difficult to reduce to a state of order and regularity.

Regularity is of consequence in planning a metropolis; but fine buildings are absurd in the infant state of any country. The various governors have unfortunately displayed rather too strong a taste for architecture—forgetting that the real Palladio for Botany Bay, in its present circumstances, is he who keeps out the sun, wind and rain with the smallest quantity of bricks and mortar.

The appointment of Governor Bligh appears to have been a very serious misfortune to the colony—at such an immense distance from the mother-country, with such an uncertainty of communication, and with a population so peculiarly circumstanced. In these extraordinary circumstances, the usual jobbing of the treasury should really be laid aside, and some little attention paid to the selection of a proper person. It is common, we know, to send a person who is somebody's cousin; but, when a new empire is to be founded, the treasury should send out into some other part of the town, for a man of sense and character.

Another very great absurdity which has been committed at Botany Bay, is the diminution of their strength and resources by the foundation of so many subordinate settlements. No sooner had the settlers unpacked their boxes at Port Jackson, than a fresh colony was settled in Norfolk Island under Lieutenant King, which was afterwards abandoned, after considerable labour and expense, from the want of a harbour: besides four or five settlements on the main land, two or three thousand persons, under a lieutenant-governor, and regular officers, are settled in Van Diemen's Land. The difficulties of a new colony are such, that the exertions of all the arms and legs are wanted merely to cover their bodies and fill their bellies: the passage from one settlement to another, necessary for common intercourse, is a great waste of strength; ten thousand men, within a given compass, will do much more for the improvement of a country than the same number spread over three times the space—will make more miles of roads, clear more acres of wood, and build more bridges. The judge, the windmill, and the school, are more accessible; and one judge, one windmill, and one school, may do instead of two;—there is less waste of labour. We do not, of course, object to the natural expansion of a colony over uncultivated lands—the more rapidly that takes place the greater is the prosperity of the settlement; but we reprobate the practice of breaking the first population of a colony, by the interposition of government, into small detached portions, placed at great intervals. It is a bad economy of their resources; and as such, is very properly objected to by the committee of the House of Commons.

This colony appears to have suffered a good deal from the tyranny as well as the ignorance of its governors. On the 7th of December, 1816, Governor Macquarrie issued the following order:—

"His excellency is also pleased further to declare, order and direct, that in consideration of the premises, the under-mentioned sums, amounts and charges, and no more, with regard to and upon the various denominations of work, labour and services, described and set forth, shall be allowed, claimed or demandable within this territory and its dependencies in respect thereof."—*Wentworth*, pp. 105, 106.

And then follows a schedule of every species of labour, to each of which a maximum is affixed. We have only to observe, that a good stout inundation of the Hawkesbury would be far less pernicious to the industry of the colony than such gross ignorance and absurdity as this order evinces. Young surgeons are examined in Surgeon's Hall on the methods of cutting off legs and arms before they are allowed to practise surgery. An examination on the principles of Adam Smith, and a license from Mr. Ricardo, seem to be almost a necessary preliminary for the appointment of governors. We must give another specimen of Governor Macquarrie's acquaintance with the principles of political economy.

"*General Orders.*

"His excellency has observed, with much concern, that, at the present time of scarcity, most of the garden ground attached to the allotments, whereon different descriptions of persons have been allowed to build huts, are totally neglected, and no vegetable growing thereon: —as such neglect in the occupiers, points them out as unfit to profit by such indulgence, those who do not put the garden ground attached to the allotments they occupy in cultivation, on or before the 10th day of July next, will be dispossessed (except in cases wherein ground is held by lease), and more industrious persons put in possession of them; as the present necessities of the settlement require every exertion being used to supply the wants of families, by the ground attached to their dwellings being made as productive as possible.—By command of his excellency. G. Blaxwell, Sec. *Government House, Sydney, June 21st*, 1806."—*O'Hara*, p. 275.

This compulsion to enjoy, this despotic benevolence, is something quite new in the science of government.

The sale of spirits was, first of all, monopolized by the government, and then let out to individuals for the purpose of building an hospital. Upon this subject Mr. Bennet observes,—

"Heretofore all ardent spirits brought to the colony were purchased by the government, and served out at fixed prices to the officers, civil and military, according to their ranks; hence arose a discreditable and gainful trade on the part of these officers, their wives and mistresses. The price of spirits at times was so high, that one and two guineas have been given for a single bottle. The thirst after ardent spirits became a mania among the settlers: all the writers on the state of the colony, and all who have resided there, and have given testimony concerning it, describe this rage and passion for drunkenness as prevailing in all classes, and as being the principal foundation of all the crimes committed there. This extravagant propensity to drunkenness was taken advantage of by the governor, to aid him in the building of the hospital. Mr. Wentworth, *the surgeon*, Messrs. Riley and Blaxwell, obtained permission to enter a certain quantity of spirits;—they were to pay a duty of five or seven shillings a gallon on the quantity they introduced, which duty was to be set apart for the erection of the hospital. To prevent any other spirits from being landed, a monopoly was given to these contractors. As soon as the agreement was signed, these gentlemen sent off to Rio Janeiro, the Mauritius and the East Indies, for a large quantity of rum and arrack, which they could purchase at about the rate of 2*s.* or 2*s.* 6*d.* per gallon, and disembarked it at Sydney. From there being but few houses that were before permitted to sell this poison, they abounded in every street; and such was the enormous consumption of spirits, that money was soon raised to build the hospital, which was finished in 1814. Mr. Marsden informs us, that in the small town of Paramatta, thirteen houses were licensed to deal in spirits, though he should think five at the utmost would be amply sufficient for the accommodation of the public."—*Bennet*, pp. 77–79.

The whole coast of Botany Bay and Van Diemen's Land abounds with whales; and, accordingly, the duty levied upon train oil procured by the subjects in New South Wales, or imported there, is twenty times greater than that paid by the inhabitants of this country; the duty on spermaceti oil, imported, is *sixty times greater*. The duty levied on train oil, spermaceti and head matter, procured by the inhabitants of Newfoundland, is only three times the amount of that which is levied on the same substance procured by British subjects residing in the United Kingdom. The duty levied on oil procured by British subjects residing in the Bahama or Bermuda islands, or on the plantations of North America, is only eight times the amount on train oil, and twelve times the amount on spermaceti, of that which is levied on the same substances taken by British subjects within the United Kingdom. The duty, therefore, which is payable on train oil in vessels belonging to this colony is nearly seven times greater than that which is payable on the same description of oil taken in vessels belonging to the island of Newfoundland, and considerably more than double of that which is payable on the same commodity taken in vessels belonging to the Bahama or Bermuda islands, or to the plantations in North America; while the duty which is levied on spermaceti oil, procured in vessels belonging to this colony, is five times the amount of that which is levied on vessels belonging to the abovementioned places, and twenty times the amount of that which is levied on vessels belonging to Newfoundland. The injustice of this seems to us to be quite enormous. The statements are taken from Mr. Wentworth's book.

The inhabitants of New South Wales have no trial by jury; the governor has not even a council to restrain him. There is imposed in this country a very heavy duty on timber and coals exported; but for which, says Mr. Wentworth, some hundred tons of these valuable productions would have been sent annually to the Cape of Good Hope and India, since the vessels which have been in the habit of trading between those countries and the colony have always returned in ballast. The owners and consignees would gladly have shipped cargoes of timber and coals, if they could have derived the most minute profit from the freight of them.

The Australasians grow corn; and it is necessarily their staple. The Cape is their rival in the corn trade. The food of the inhabitants of the East Indies is rice; the voyage to Europe is too distant for so bulky an article as corn. The supply to the government stores furnished the cultivators of New South Wales with a market in the first instance, which is now become too insignificant for the great excess of the supply above the consumption. Population goes on with immense rapidity; but while so much new and fertile land is before them, the supply continues in the same proportion greater than the demand. The most obvious method of affording a market for this redundant corn is by encouraging distilleries within the colony; a measure repeatedly pressed upon the government at home, but hitherto as constantly refused. It is a measure of still greater importance to the colony, because its agriculture is subjected to the effects both of severe drought and extensive inundations, and the corn raised for the distillers would be a magazine in times of famine. A recommendation to this effect was long since made by a committee of the House of Commons; but, as it was merely a measure for the increase of human comforts, was stuffed into the improvement baskets and forgotten. There has been in all governments a great deal of absurd canting about the consumption of spirits. We believe the best plan is to let people drink what they like, and wear what they like; to make no sumptuary laws either for the belly or the back. In the first place laws against rum and rum water are made by men who can change a wet coat for a dry one whenever they choose, and who do not often work up to their knees in mud and water; and, in the next place, if this stimulus did all the mischief it is thought to do by the wise men of claret, its cheapness and plenty would rather lessen than increase the avidity with which it is at present sought for.

The governors of Botany Bay have taken the liberty of imposing what taxes they deemed proper, without any other authority than their own; and it seemed very frivolous and vexatious not to allow this small effusion of despotism in so remote a corner of the globe; but it was noticed by the opposition in the House of Commons, and reluctantly confessed and given up by the administration. This great portion of the earth begins civil life with noble principles of freedom:—may God grant to its inhabitants that wisdom and courage which are necessary for the preservation of so great a good!

Mr. Wentworth enumerates, among the evils to which the colony is subjected, that clause in the last settlement of the East India Company's charter, which prevents vessels of less than 300 tons burden from navigating the Indian seas; a restriction from which the Cape of Good Hope has been lately liberated, and which ought, in the same manner, to be removed from New South Wales, where there cannot be for many years to come sufficient capital to build vessels of so large a burden.

"The disability," says Mr. Wentworth, "might be removed by a simple order in council. Whenever his majesty's government shall have freed the colonists from this useless and cruel prohibition, the following branches of commerce would then be opened to them. First, they would be enabled to transport, in their own vessels, their coals, timbers, spars, flour, meat, &c to the Cape of Good Hope, the Isle of France, Calcutta, and many other places in the Indian seas; in all of which, markets more or less extensive exist for those various other productions which the colony might furnish. Secondly, they would be enabled to carry directly to Canton the sandal wood, bêche la mer, dried seal skins, and, in fact, all the numerous productions which the surrounding seas and islands afford for the China market, and return freighted with cargoes of tea, silks, nankeens, &c.; all of which commodities are in great demand in the colony, and are at present altogether furnished by East India or American merchants, to the great detriment and dissatisfaction of the colonial. And, lastly, they would be enabled, in a short time, from the great increase of capital which these important privileges would of themselves occasion, as well as attract from other countries, to open the fur-trade with the northwest coast of America, and dispose of the cargoes procured in China,—a trade which has hitherto been exclusively carried on by the Americans and Russians, although the colonists possess a local superiority for the prosecution of this valuable branch of commerce, which would insure them at least a successful competition with the subjects of those two nations."—*Wentworth*, pp. 317, 318.

The means which Mr. Wentworth proposes

for improving the condition of Botany Bay, are —trial by jury—colonial assemblies, with whom the right of taxation should rest—the establishment of distilleries, and the exclusion of foreign spirits—alteration of duties, so as to place New South Wales upon the same footing as other colonies—removal of the restriction to navigate the Indian seas in vessels of a small burden—improvements in the courts of justice—encouragement for the growth of hemp, flax, tobacco and wine; and, if a colonial assembly cannot be granted, that there should be no taxation without the authority of Parliament.

In general, we agree with Mr. Wentworth in his statement of evils, and in the remedies he has proposed for them. Many of the restrictions upon the commerce of New South Wales are so absurd that they require only to be stated in Parliament to be corrected. The fertility of the colony so far exceeds its increase of population, and the difficulty of finding a market for corn is so great—or rather the impossibility so clear—that the measure of encouraging domestic distilleries ought to be had recourse to. The colony, with a soil fit for every thing, must, as Mr. Wentworth proposes, grow other things besides corn, and excite that market in the interior which it does not enjoy from without. The want of demand, indeed, for the excess of corn, will soon effect this without the intervention of government. Government, we believe, have already given up the right of taxation without the sanction of Parliament; and there is an end, probably, by this time, to that grievance. A council and a colonial secretary they have also expressed their willingness to concede. Of trial by jury and a colonial assembly, we confess that we have great doubts. At some future time they must come, and ought to come. The only question is, is the colony fit for such institutions at present? Are there a sufficient number of respectable persons to serve that office in the various settlements? If the English law is to be followed exactly, to compose a jury of twelve persons, a panel of forty-eight must be summoned. Could forty-eight intelligent convicted men, be found in every settlement of New South Wales? or must they not be fetched from great distances, at an enormous expense and inconvenience? Is such an institution calculated for so very young a colony? A good government is an excellent thing; but it is not the first in the order of human wants. The first want is to subsist; the next to subsist in freedom and comfort; first to live at all, then to live well. A parliament is still a greater demand upon the wisdom and intelligence and opulence of a colony than trial by jury. Among the twenty thousand inhabitants of New South Wales, are there ten persons out of the employ of government whose wisdom and prudence could reasonably be expected to advance the interests of the colony without embroiling it with the mother-country? Who has leisure, in such a state of affairs, to attend such a parliament? Where wisdom and conduct are so rare, every man of character, we will venture to say, has, like strolling players in a barn, six or seven important parts to perform. Mr. M'Arthur, who, from his character and understanding, would probably be among the first persons elected to the colonial legislature, besides being a very spirited agriculturist, is, we have no doubt, justice of the peace, curator and rector of a thousand plans, charities and associations, to which his presence is essentially necessary. If he could be cut into as many pieces as a tree is into planks, all his subdivisions would be eminently useful. When a member of Parliament, and what is called a really respectable country gentleman, sets off to attend his duty in our Parliament, such diminution of intelligence as is produced by his absence, is, God knows, easily supplied; but in a colony of 20,000 persons, it is impossible this should be the case. Some time hence, the institution of a colonial assembly will be a very wise and proper measure, and so clearly called for, that the most profligate members of administration will neither be able to ridicule nor refuse it. At present we are afraid that a Botany Bay parliament would give rise to jokes; and jokes at present have a great agency in human affairs.

Mr. Bennet concerns himself with the settlement of New Holland, as it is a school for criminals; and, upon this subject, has written a very humane, enlightened and vigorous pamphlet. The objections made to this settlement by Mr. Bennet are, in the first place, its enormous expense. The colony of New South Wales, from 1788 to 1815 inclusive, has cost this country the enormous sum of 3,465,983*l.* In the evidence before the transportation committee, the annual expense of each convict, from 1791 to 1797, is calculated at 33*l.* 9*s.* 5¾*d.* per annum, and the profits of his labour are stated to be 20*l.* The price paid for the transport of convicts has been, on an average, 37*l.* exclusive of food and clothing. It appears, however, says Mr. Bennet, by an account laid before Parliament, that in the year 1814, 109,746*l.* were paid for the transport, food and clothing of 1016 convicts, which will make the cost amount to about 108*l.* per man. In 1812, the expenses of the colony were 176,000*l.*; in 1813, 235,000*l.*; in 1814, 231,362*l.*; but in 1815 they had fallen to 150,000*l.*

The cruelty and neglect in the transportation of convicts have been very great—and in this way a punishment inflicted which it never was in the contemplation of law to enact. During the first eight years, according to Mr. Bennet's statements, one-tenth of the convicts died on the passage; on the arrival of three of the ships, 200 sick were landed, 281 persons having died on board. These instances, however, of criminal inattention to the health of the convicts no longer take place; and it is mentioned rather as an history of what is past than a censure upon any existing evil.

In addition to the expense of Botany Bay, Mr. Bennet contends that it wants the very essence of punishment, terror; that the common people do not dread it; that instead of preventing crimes, it rather excites the people to their commission, by the hopes it affords of bettering their condition in a new country.

"All those who have had an opportunity of witnessing the effect of this system of transportation agree in opinion, that it is no longer an object of dread—it has, in fact, generally ceased to be a punishment: true it is, to a father of a family, to the mother who leaves her children, this perpetual separation from those whom they love and whom they support, is a cruel blow, and when I consider the merciless character of the law which inflicts it, a severe penalty: but by far the greater number of persons who suffer this punishment, regard it in quite a different light. Mr. Cotton, the ordinary of Newgate, informed the police committee last year, 'that the generality of those who are transported consider it as a party of pleasure—as going out to see the world; they evince no penitence, no contrition, but seem to rejoice in the thing,—many of them to court it. I have heard them, when the sentence of transportation has been passed by the recorder, return thanks for it, and seem overjoyed at their sentence: the very last party that went off, when they were put into the caravan, shouted and huzzaed, and were very joyous: several of them called out to the keepers who were there in the yard, the first fine Sunday we will have a glorious kangaroo hunt at the Bay,—seeming to anticipate a great deal of pleasure.' He was asked if those persons were married or single, and his answer was, 'by far the greater number of them were unmarried. Some of them are anxious that their wives and children should follow them; others care nothing about either wives or children, and are glad to get rid of them.'"—*Bennet*, pp. 60, 61

It is a scandalous injustice in this colony, that persons transported for seven years, have no power of returning when that period is expired. A strong active man may sometimes work his passage home; but what is an old man or an aged female to do? Suppose a convict were to be confined in prison for seven years, and then told he might get out if he could climb over the walls, or break open the locks, what in general would be his chance of liberation? But no lock nor doors can be so secure a means of detention as the distance of Botany Bay. This is a downright trick and fraud in the administration of criminal justice. A poor wretch who is banished from his country for seven years, should be furnished with the means of returning to his country when these seven years are expired.—If it is intended he should never return, his sentence should have been banishment for life.

The most serious charge against the colony, as a place for transportation, and an experiment in criminal justice, is the extreme profligacy of manners which prevails there, and the total want of reformation among the convicts. Upon this subject, except in the regular letters officially varnished and filled with fraudulent beatitudes for the public eye, there is, and there can be, but one opinion. New South Wales is a sink of wickedness, in which the great majority of convicts of both sexes become infinitely more depraved than at the period of their arrival. How, as Mr. Bennet very justly observes, can it be otherwise? The felon, transported to the American plantations, became an insulated rogue among honest men. He lived for years in the family of some industrious planter, without seeing a picklock, or indulging in pleasant dialogues on the delicious burglaries of his youth. He imperceptibly glided into honest habits, and lost not only the tact for pockets, but the wish to investigate their contents. But in Botany Bay, the felon, as soon as he gets out of the ship, meets with his ancient trull, with the footpad of his heart, the convict of his affections,—the man whose hand he has often met in the same gentleman's pocket—the being whom he would choose from the whole world to take to the road, or to disentangle the locks of Bramah. It is impossible that vice should not become more intense in such society.

Upon the horrid state of morals now prevalent in Botany Bay, we would counsel our readers to cast their eyes upon the account given by Mr. Marsden, in a letter, dated July, 1815, to Governor Macquarrie. It is given at length in the appendix to Mr. Bennet's book. A more horrid picture of the state of any settlement was never penned. It carries with it an air of truth and sincerity, and is free from all enthusiastic cant.

"I now appeal to your excellency," (he says, at the conclusion of his letter,) "whether, under such circumstances any man of common feeling, possessed of the least spark of humanity or religion, who stood in the same official relation that I do to these people, as their spiritual pastor and magistrate, could enjoy one happy moment from the beginning to the end of the week!

"I humbly conceive that it is incompatible with the character and wish of the British nation, that her own exiles should be exposed to such privations and dangerous temptations, when she is daily feeding the hungry and clothing the naked, and receiving into her friendly, and I may add pious bosom, the stranger, whether savage or civilized, of every nation under heaven. There are, in the whole, under the two principal superintendents, Messrs. Rouse and Oakes, one hundred and eight men, and one hundred and fifty women, and several children; and nearly the whole of them have to find lodgings for themselves when they have performed their government tasks.

"I trust that your excellency will be fully persuaded, that it is totally impossible for the magistrate to support his necessary authority, and to establish a regular police, under such a weight of accumulated and accumulating evils. I am as sensible as any one can be, that the difficulty of removing these evils will be very great; at the same time, their number and influence may be greatly lessened, if the abandoned male and female convicts are lodged in barracks, and placed under the eye of the police, and the number of licensed houses is reduced. Till something of this kind is done, all attempts of the magistrate, and the public administration of religion, will be attended with little benefit to the general good. I have the honour to be, your excellency's most obedient, humble servant, SAMUEL MARSDEN."—*Bennet*, p. 134.

Thus much for Botany Bay. As a mere colony, it is too distant and too expensive; and, in future, will of course involve us in many of those just and necessary wars, which deprive Englishmen so rapidly of their comforts, and make England scarcely worth living in. If considered as a place of reform for criminals, its distance, expense, and the society to which it dooms the objects of the experiment, are insuperable objections to it. It is in vain to say, that the honest people in New South Wales will soon bear a greater proportion to the rogues, and the contamination of bad society will be less fatal. This only proves that it may be a good place for reform hereafter, not that it is a good one now. One of the principal reasons for peopling Botany Bay at all, was, that it would be an admirable receptacle, and a school of reform, for our convicts. It turns out, that for the first half century, it will make them worse than they were before, and that, after that period, they may probably begin to improve. A marsh, to be sure, may be drained and cultivated; but no man who has his choice, would select it in the mean time for his dwelling-place.

The three books are all books of merit. Mr. O'Hara's is a bookseller's compilation, done in a useful and pleasing manner. Mr. Wentworth is full of information on the present state of Botany Bay. The humanity, the exertions and the genuine benevolence of Mr. Bennet, are too well known to need our commendation

All persons who have a few guineas in their pocket, are now running away from Mr. Nicholas Vansittart to settle in every quarter of the globe. Upon the subject of emigration to Botany Bay, Mr. Wentworth observes, 1st, that any respectable person emigrating to that colony, receives as much land gratis as would cost him 400*l.* in the United States; 2dly, he is allowed as many servants as he may require, at one-third of the wages paid for labour in America; 3dly, himself and family are victualled at the expense of government for six months. He calculates that a man, wife and two children, with an allowance of five tons for themselves and baggage, could emigrate to Botany Bay for 100*l.* including every expense, provided a whole ship could be freighted; and that a single man could be taken out thither for 30*l.* These points are worthy of serious attention to those who are shedding their country.

CHIMNEY SWEEPERS.*

[Edinburgh Review, 1819.]

An excellent and well-arranged dinner is a most pleasing occurrence, and a great triumph of civilized life. It is not only the descending morsel and the enveloping sauce—but the rank, wealth, wit and beauty which surround the meats—the learned management of light and heat—the silent and rapid services of the attendants—the smiling and sedulous host, proffering gusts and relishes—the exotic bottles—the embossed plate—the pleasant remarks—the handsome dresses—the cunning artifices in fruit and farina! The hour of dinner, in short, includes every thing of sensual and intellectual gratification which a great nation glories in producing.

In the midst of all this, who knows that the kitchen chimney caught fire half an hour before dinner!—and that a poor little wretch, of six or seven years old, was sent up in the midst of the flames to put it out? We could not, previous to reading this evidence, have formed a conception of the miseries of these poor wretches, or that there should exist, in a civilized country, a class of human beings destined to such extreme and varied distress. We will give a short epitome of what is developed in the evidence before the two Houses of Parliament.

Boys are made chimney sweepers at the early age of five or six.

Little boys for small flues, is a common phrase in the cards left at the door by itinerant chimney sweepers. Flues made to ovens and coppers are often less than nine inches square; and it may be easily conceived how slender the frame of that human body must be, which can force itself through such an aperture.

"What is the age of the youngest boys who have been employed in this trade, to your knowledge? About five years of age: I know one now between five or six years old; it is the man's own son in the Strand: now there is another at Somer's Town, I think, said he was between four and five, or about five; Jack Hall, a little lad, takes him about.—Did you ever know any female children employed? Yes, I know one now. About two years ago there was a woman told me she had climbed scores of times, and there is one at Paddington now whose father taught her to climb: but I have often heard talk of them when I was an apprentice, in different places.—What is the smallest sized flue you have ever met with in the course of your experience? About eight inches by nine; these they are always obliged to climb in this posture (*describing it*), keeping the arms up straight; if they slip their arms down, they get jammed in; unless they get their arms close over their head they cannot climb."—*Lord's Minutes*, No. 1. p. 8.

The following is a specimen of the manner in which they are taught this art of climbing chimneys.

"Do you remember being taught to climb chimneys? Yes.—What did you feel upon the first attempt to climb a chimney? The first chimney I went up, they told me there was some plum-pudding and money up at the top of it, and that is the way they enticed me up; and when I

**Account of the Proceedings of the Society for superseding the Necessity of Climbing Boys.* Baldwin, &c. London, 1816.

got up, I would not let the other boy get from under me to get at it; I thought he would get it; I could not get up, and shoved the pot and half the chimney down into the yard.—Did you experience any inconvenience to your knees, or your elbows? Yes, the skin was off my knees and elbows too, in climbing up the new chimneys they forced me up.—How did they force you up? When I got up, I cried out about my sore knees. —Were you beat or compelled to go up by any violent means? Yes, when I went to a narrow chimney, if I could not do it, I durst not go home; when I used to come down, my master would well beat me with the brush; and not only my master, but when he used to go with the journeymen, if we could not do it, they used to hit us three or four times with the brush."—*Lords' Minutes*, No. 1. p. 5.

In practising the art of climbing they are often crippled.

"You talked of the pargetting to chimneys; are many chimneys pargetted? There used to be more than are now; we used to have to go and sit all a-twist to parge them, according to the floors, to keep the smoke from coming out; then I could not straighten my legs; and that is the reason that many are cripples,—from parging and stopping the holes."—*Lords' Minutes*, No. 1. p. 17.

They are often stuck fast in a chimney, and, after remaining there many hours, are cut out.

"Have you known, in the course of your practice, boys stick in chimneys at all? Yes, frequently.—Did you ever know an instance of a boy being suffocated to death? No; I do not recollect any one at present, but I have assisted in taking boys out when they have been nearly exhausted.—Did you ever know an instance of its being necessary to break open a chimney to take the boy out? O yes.—*Frequently? Monthly I might say;* it is done with a cloak, if possible, that it should not be discovered; a master in general wishes it not to be known, and therefore speaks to the people belonging to the house not to mention it, for it was merely the boy's neglect; they often say it was the boy's neglect.—Why do they say that? The boy's climbing shirt is often very bad; the boy coming down, if the chimney be very narrow, and numbers of them are only nine inches, gets his shirt rumpled underneath him, and he has no power after he is fixed in that way (*with his hand up.*) Does a boy frequently stick in the chimney? Yes, I have known more instances of that the last twelvemonth than before.—Do you ever have to break open in the inside of a room? Yes, I have helped to break through into a kitchen chimney in a dining room."—*Lords' Minutes*, p. 34.

To the same effect is the evidence of John Daniels, (*Minutes*, p. 100,) and of James Ludford, (*Lords' Minutes*, p. 147.)

"You have swept the Penitentiary? I have. —Did you ever know a boy stick in any of the chimneys there? Yes, I have.—Was it one of your boys? It was.—Was there one or two that stuck? Two of them.—How long did they stick there? Two hours.—How were they got out? They were cut out.—Was there any danger while they were in that situation? It was the core from the pargetting of the chimney, and the rubbish that the labourers had thrown down, that stopped them, and when they got it aside them, they could not pass.—They both stuck together? Yes."—*Lords' Minutes*, p. 147.

One more instance we shall give from the evidence before the Commons.

"Have you heard of any accidents that have recently happened to climbing boys in the small flues? Yes; I have *often* met with accidents myself when I was a boy; there was lately one in Mary-le-bone, where the boy *lost his life* in a flue, a boy of the name of Tinsey (his father was of the same trade); that boy I think was about eleven or twelve years old.—Was there a coroner's inquest sat on the body of that boy you mentioned? Yes, there was; he was an apprentice of a man of the name of Gay.—How many accidents do you recollect which were attended with loss of life to the climbing boys? I have heard talk of many more than I know of; I never knew of more than three since I have been at the trade, but I have heard talk of many more.—Of twenty or thirty? I cannot say; I have been near losing my own life several times."—*Commons' Report*, p. 53.

We come now to burning little chimney sweepers. A large party are invited to dinner —a great display is to be made;—and about an hour before dinner, there is an alarm that the kitchen chimney is on fire! It is impossible to put off the distinguished personages who are expected. It gets very late for the soup and fish —the cook is frantic—all eyes are turned upon the sable consolation of the master chimney sweeper—and up into the midst of the burning chimney is sent one of the miserable little infants of the brush! There is a positive prohibition of this practice, and an enactment of penalties in one of the acts of Parliament which respects chimney sweepers. But what matter acts of Parliament, when the pleasures of genteel people are concerned? Or what is a toasted child, compared to the agonies of the mistress of the house with a deranged dinner?

"Did you ever know a boy get burnt up a chimney? Yes.—Is that usual? Yes, I have been burnt myself, and have got the scars on my legs; a year ago I was up a chimney in Liquor Pond Street; I have been up *more than forty chimneys where I have been burnt.*—Did your master or the journeymen ever direct you to go up a chimney that was on fire? Yes, it is a general case.—Do they compel you to go up a chimney that is on fire? Oh yes, it was the general practice for two of us to stop at home on Sunday to be ready in case of a chimney being a-fire.—You say it is general to compel the boys to go up chimneys on fire? Yes, boys get very ill-treated if they do not go up."—*Lords' Minutes*, p. 34.

"Were you ever forced up a chimney on fire? Yes, I was forced up one once, and, because I could not do it, I was taken home and well hided with a brush by the journeyman.—Have you frequently been burnt in ascending chimneys on fire? Three times.—Are such hardships as you have described common in the trade with other boys? Yes, they are."—*Ibid.*, p. 100.

"What is the price for sending a boy up a chimney badly on fire? The price allowed is five shillings, but most of them charge half a guinea.—Is any part of that given to the boy? No, but very often the boy gets half a crown, and then the journeyman has half, and his mistress takes the other part to take care of against Sunday.—Have you never seen water thrown down from the top of a chimney when it is on fire? Yes.—Is not that generally done? Yes; I have seen that done twenty times, and the boy in the chimney; at the time when the boy has hallooed out, 'It is so hot I cannot go any further;' and then the expression is, with an oath, 'Stop, and I will heave a pail of water down.' " —*Ibid.*, p. 39.

Chimney sweepers are subject to a peculiar sort of cancer, which often brings them to a premature death.

"He appeared perfectly willing to try the machines everywhere? I must say the man appeared perfectly willing; he had a fear that he and his family would be ruined by them; but I must say of him that he is very different from other sweeps I have seen; he attends very much to his own business; he was as black as any boy he had got, and unfortunately in the course of conversation he told me he had got a cancer; he was a fine healthy strong looking man; he told me he dreaded having an operation performed, but his father died of the same complaint, and his father was sweeper to King George the Second."—*Lords' Minutes*, p. 84.

"What is the nature of the particular diseases? The diseases that we particularly noticed, to which they were subject, were of a cancerous description. In what part? The scrotum in particular, &c.—Did you ever hear of cases of that description that were fatal? No, I do not think them as being altogether fatal, unless they will not submit to the operation; they have such a dread of the operation that they will not submit to it, and if they do not let it be perfectly removed they will be liable to the return of it. To what cause do you attribute that disease? I think it begins from a want of care: the scrotum being in so many folds or crevices, the soot lodges in them and creates an itching, and I conceive, that by scratching it and tearing it, the soot gets in and creates the irritability; which disease we know by the name of the chimney sweeper's cancer, and is always lectured upon separately as a distinct disease. —Then the committee understands that the physicians who are entrusted with the care and management of those hospitals think that disease of such common occurrence, that it is necessary to make it a part of surgical education? Most assuredly; I remember Mr. Cline and Mr. Cooper were particular on that subject. —Without an operation there is no cure? I conceive not; I conceive without the operation it is death; for cancers are of that nature that unless you extirpate them entirely they will never be cured."—*Commons' Rep.* pp. 60, 61.

In addition to the life they lead as chimney sweepers, is superadded the occupation of nightmen.

"(*By a Lord.*) Is it generally the custom that many masters are likewise nightmen? Yes: I forgot that circumstance, which is very grievous; I have been tied round the middle and let down several privies, for the purpose of fetching watches and such things; it is generally made the practice to take the smallest boy, to let him through the hole without taking up the seat, and to paddle about there until he finds it; they do not take a big boy, because it disturbs the seat." —*Lords' Minutes*, p. 38.

The bed of these poor little wretches is often the soot they have swept in the day.

"How are the boys generally lodged; where do they sleep at night? Some masters may be better than others, but I know I have slept on the soot that was gathered in the day myself.—Where do boys generally sleep? Never on a bed; I never slept on a bed myself while I was apprentice—Do they sleep in cellars? Yes, very often: I have slept in the cellar myself on the sacks I took out.—What had you to cover you? The same.—Had you any pillow? No further than my breeches and jacket under my head. How were you clothed? When I was apprentice we had a pair of leather breeches and a small flannel jacket. Any shoes and stockings? Oh dear, no; no stockings.—Had you any other clothes for Sunday? Sometimes we had an old bit of a jacket, that we might wash out ourselves, and a shirt."—*Lords' Minutes*, p. 40.

Girls are occasionally employed as chimney sweepers.

"Another circumstance, which has not been mentioned to the committee, is, that there are several little girls employed; there are two of the name of Morgan at Windsor, daughters of the chimney sweeper, who is employed to sweep the chimneys of the castle; another instance at Uxbridge, and at Brighton, and at Whitechapel (which was some years ago), and at Hadley near Barnet, and Witham in Essex, and elsewhere."—*Commons' Report*, p. 71.

Another peculiar danger to which chimney sweepers are exposed, is the rottenness of the pots at the top of chimneys;—for they must ascend to the very summit, and show their brushes above them, or there is no proof that the work is properly completed. These chimney-pots from their exposed situation, are very subject to decay; and when the poor little wretch has worked his way up to the top, pot and boy give way together, and are both shivered to atoms. There are many instances of this in the evidence before both Houses. When they outgrow the power of going up a chimney, they are fit for nothing else. The miseries they have suffered lead to nothing. They are not only enormous, but unprofitable: having suffered, in what is called the happiest part of life, every misery which an human being can suffer, they are then cast out to rob and steal, and given up to the law.

Not the least of their miseries, while their trial endures, is their exposure to cold. It will easily be believed that much money is not expended on the clothes of a poor boy stolen from his parents, or sold by them for a few shillings, and constantly occupied in dirty work. Yet the nature of their occupations renders chimney sweepers peculiarly susceptible of cold. And as chimneys must be swept very early, at four or five o'clock of a winter morning, the poor boys are shivering at the door, and attempting by repeated ringings to rouse the profligate footman; but the more they ring the more the footman does not come.

"Do they go out in the winter time without stockings? Oh yes.—Always? I never saw one go out *with* stockings; I have known masters make their boys pull off their leggins, and cut off the feet, to keep their feet warm when they have chilblains.—Are chimney sweepers' boys peculiarly subject to chilblains? Yes; I believe it is owing to the weather: they often go out at two or three in the morning, and their shoes are generally very bad. Do they go out at that hour at Christmas? Yes; a man will have twenty jobs at four, and twenty more at five or six.—Are chimneys generally swept much about Christmas time? Yes; they are in general; it is left to the Christmas week.—Do you suppose it is frequent that, in the Christmas week, boys are out from three o'clock in the morning to nine or ten? Yes, further than that; I have known that a boy has been only in and out again directly all day till five o'clock in the evening.—Do you consider the journeymen and masters treat those boys generally with greater cruelty than other apprentices in other trades are treated? They do, most horrid and shocking."—*Lords' Minutes*, p. 33.

The following is the reluctant evidence of a master.

"At what hour in the morning did your boys go out upon their employment? According to orders.—At any time? To be sure; suppose a nobleman wished to have his chimney done before four or five o'clock in the morning, it was done, or how were the servants to get their things done?—Supposing you had an order to attend at four o'clock in the morning in the month of December, you sent your boy? I was generally with him, or had a careful follower with him. Do you think those early hours beneficial for him? I do; and I have heard that 'early to bed and early to rise, is the way to be healthy, wealthy and wise.'—Did they always get in as soon as they knocked? No; it would be pleasant to the profession if they could.—How long did they wait? *Till the servants please to rise.*—How long might that be? According how heavy they were to sleep.—How long was that? It is impossible to say; ten minutes at one house, and twenty at another.—Perhaps half an hour? *We cannot see in the dark how the minutes go.*—Do you think it healthy to let them stand there twenty minutes at four o'clock in the morning in the winter time? He has a cloth to wrap himself in like a mantle, and keep himself warm."—*Lords' Minutes*, pp. 138, 139.

We must not forget sore eyes. Soot lodges on their eyelids, produces irritability, which requires friction; and the friction of dirty hands of course increases the disease. The greater proportion of chimney sweepers are in consequence blear-eyed. The boys are very small, but they are compelled to carry heavy loads of soot.

"Are you at all lame yourself? No: but I am 'knapped-kneed' with carrying heavy loads when I was an apprentice. That was the occasion of it? It was. In general, are persons employed in your trade either stunted or knock-kneed by carrying heavy loads during their childhood? It is owing to their masters a great deal; and when they climb a great deal it makes them weak."—*Commons' Report*, p. 58.

In climbing a chimney, the great hold is by the knees and elbows. A young child of 6 or 7 years old, working with knees and elbows against hard bricks soon rubs off the skin from these bony projections, and is forced to climb high chimneys with raw and bloody knees and elbows.

"Are the boys' knees and elbows rendered sore when they first begin to learn to climb? Yes, they are, and pieces out of them.—Is that almost generally the case? It is; *there is not one out of twenty who is not;* and they are sure to take the scars to their grave: I have some now.—Are they usually compelled to continue climbing while those sores are open? *Yes;* the way they use to make them hard is that way.—Might not this severity be obviated by the use of pads in learning to climb? Yes; but they consider in the business, learning a boy, that he is never thoroughly learned until the boy's knees are hard after being sore; then they consider it necessary to put a pad on, from seeing the boys have bad knees; the children generally walk stiff-kneed.—Is it usual among the chimney sweepers to teach their boys to learn by means of pads? No; they learn them with nearly naked knees.—Is it done in one instance in twenty? No, nor one in fifty."—*Lords' Minutes*, p. 32.

According to the humanity of the master, the soot remains upon the bodies of the children, unwashed off, for any time from a week to a year.

"Are the boys generally washed regularly? No, unless they wash themselves.—Did not your master take care you were washed? No.—Not once in three months? No, *not once a year.*—Did not he find you soap? No; I can take my oath on the Bible that he never found me one piece of soap during the time I was apprentice."—*Lords' Minutes*, p. 41.

The life of these poor little wretches is so miserable, that they often lie sulking in the flues unwilling to come out.

"Did you ever see severity used to boys that were not obstinate and perverse? Yes.—Very often? Yes, very often. The boys are rather obstinate; some of them are; some of them will get half-way up the chimney, and will not go any further, and then the journeyman will swear at them to come down, or go on; but the boys are too frightened to come down; they halloo out, we cannot get up, and they are afraid to come down; sometimes they will send for another boy, and drag them down; sometimes get up to the top of the chimney, and throw down water, and drive them down; then, when they get them down, they will begin to drag, or beat, or kick them about the house; then, when they get home, the master will beat them all round the kitchen afterwards, and give them no breakfast, perhaps."—*Lords' Minutes*, pp. 9, 10.

When a chimney boy has done sufficient work for the master he must work for the man; and he thus becomes for several hours after his morning's work a perquisite to the journeyman.

"It is frequently the perquisite of the journeyman, when the first labour of the day on account of the master is finished, to 'call the streets,' in search of employment on their own account, with the apprentices, whose labour is thus unreasonably extended, and whose limbs are weakened and distorted by the weights which they have to carry, and by the distance which they have to walk. John Lawless says, 'I have known a boy to climb from twenty to thirty chimneys for his master in the morning; he has then been sent out instantly with the journeyman, who has kept him out till three or four o'clock, till he has accumulated from six to eight bushels of soot.' "—*Lords' Report*, p. 24.

The sight of a little chimney sweeper often excites pity: and they have small presents made to them at the houses where they sweep. These benevolent alms are disposed of in the following manner:—

"Do the boys receive little presents of money from people often in your trade? Yes, it is in general the custom.—Are they allowed to keep that for their own use? Not the whole of it,—the journeymen take what they think proper. The journeymen *are entitled to half* by the master's orders; and whatever a boy may get, if two boys and one journeyman are sent to a large house to sweep a number of chimneys, and after they have done, there should be a shilling or eighteen pence given to the boys, the journeyman has his full half, and the two boys in general have the other. Is it usual or customary for the journeymen to play at chuck farthing or other games with the boys? Frequently.—Do they win the money from the boys? Frequently: the children give their money to the journeymen to screen for them.—What do you mean by screening? Such a thing as sifting the soot.—The child is tired, and he says, 'Jem, I will give you two-pence if you will sift my share of the soot;' there is sometimes twenty or thirty bushels to sift. Do you think the boys retain one quarter of that given them for their own use? No." —*Lords' Minutes*, p. 35.

To this most horrible list of calamities is to be added the dreadful deaths by which chimney sweepers are often destroyed. Of these we once thought of giving two examples; one from London, the other from our own town of Edinburgh: but we confine ourselves to the latter.

"James Thomson, chimney-sweeper.—One day, in the beginning of June, witness and panel (that is, the master, the party accused) had been sweeping vents together. About *four* o'clock in the afternoon, the panel proposed to go to Albany street, where the panel's brother was cleaning a vent, with the assistance of Frazer, whom he had borrowed from the panel for the occasion. When witness and panel got to the house in Albany street, they found Frazer, who had gone up the vent *between eleven and twelve* o'clock, not yet come down. On entering the house they found a mason making a hole in the wall. Panel said, what was he doing? I suppose he has taken a lazy fit. The panel called to the boy, 'What are you doing? what's keeping you?' The boy answered that he could not come. The panel worked a long while, sometimes persuading him, sometimes threatening and swearing at the boy to get him down. Panel then said, 'I will go to a hardware shop and get a barrel of gunpowder, and blow you and the vent to the devil, if you do not come down.'—Panel then began to slap at the wall—witness then went up a ladder, and spoke to the boy through a small hole in the wall previously made by the mason—but the boy did not answer Panel's brother told witness to come down, as the boy's master knew best how to manage him. Witness then threw off his jacket, and put a handkerchief about his head, and said to the panel, let me go up the chimney to see what's keeping him. The panel made no answer, but pushed witness away from the chimney, and continued bullying the boy. At this time the panel was standing on the grate, so that witness could not go up the chimney; witness then said to panel's brother, there is no use for me here, meaning that panel would not permit him to use his services. He prevented the mason making the hole larger, saying, Stop, and I'll bring him down in five minutes' time. Witness then put on his jacket, and continued an hour in the room, *during all which time the panel continued bullying the boy.* Panel then desired witness to go to Reid's house to get the loan of his boy Alison. Witness went to Reid's house, and asked Reid to come and speak to panel's brother. Reid asked if panel was there? Witness answered he was; Reid said he would send his boy to the panel, but not to the panel's brother. Witness and Reid went to Albany street; and when they got into the room, panel took his head out of the chimney and asked Reid if he would lend him his boy; Reid agreed; witness then returned to Reid's house for his boy, and Reid called after him, 'Fetch down a set of ropes with you.' By this time witness had been ten minutes in the room, during which time panel was swearing, and asking what's keeping you, you scoundrel? When witness returned with the boy and ropes, Reid took hold of the rope, and having loosed it, gave Alison one end, and directed him to go up the chimney, saying, do not go farther than his feet, and when you get there fasten it to his foot. Panel said nothing all this time. Alison went up, and having fastened the rope, Reid desired him to come down; Reid took the rope and pulled, but did not bring down the boy; the rope broke! Alison was sent up again with the other end of the rope, which was fastened to the boy's foot. When Reid was pulling the rope, panel said, 'You have not the strength of a cat;' he took the rope into his own hands, *pulling as strong as he could.* Having pulled *about a quarter of an hour*, panel and Reid fastened the rope round a crow bar, which they applied to the wall as a lever, and both *pulled with all their strength for about a quarter of an hour longer*, when it broke.—During this time witness heard the boy cry, and say, 'My God Almighty!' Panel said, 'If I had you here, I would God Almighty you.' Witness thought the cries were in agony. The master of the house brought a new piece of rope, and the panel's brother spliced an eye on it. Reid expressed a wish to have it fastened on both thighs, to have greater purchase. Alison was sent up for this purpose, but came down, and said he could not get it fastened. Panel then began to slap at the wall. After striking a long while at the wall, he got out a large stone; he then put in his head and called to Frazer, 'Do you hear, you sir?' but got no answer: he then put in his hands, and threw down deceased's breeches. He then came down from the ladder

At this time the panel was in a state of perspiration: he sat down on a stool, and the master of the house gave him a dram. Witness did not hear panel make any remarks as to the situation of the boy Frazer. Witness thinks that, from panel's appearance, he knew that the boy was dead." — *Commons' Report*, pp. 136—138.

We have been thus particular in stating the case of the chimney sweepers, and in founding it upon the basis of facts, that we may make an answer to those profligate persons who are always ready to fling an air of ridicule upon the labours of humanity, because they are desirous that what they have not virtue to do themselves, should appear to be foolish and romantic when done by others. A still higher degree of depravity than this, is to want every sort of compassion for human misery, when it is accompanied by filth, poverty and ignorance,—to regulate humanity by the income tax, and to deem the bodily wretchedness and the dirty tears of the poor, a fit subject for pleasantry and contempt. We should have been loath to believe that such deep-seated and disgusting immorality existed in these days; but the notice of it is forced upon us. Nor must we pass over a set of marvellously weak gentlemen who discover democracy and revolution in every effort to improve the condition of the lower orders, and to take off a little of the load of misery from those points where it presses the hardest. Such are the men into whose heart Mrs. Fry has struck the deepest terror,—who abhor Mr. Bentham and his penitentiary; Mr. Bennet and his hulks; Sir James Mackintosh and his bloodless assizes; Mr. Tuke and his sweeping machines,—and every human being who is great and good enough to sacrifice his quiet to his love for his fellow-creatures. Certainly we admit that humanity is sometimes the veil of ambition or of faction; but we have no doubt that there are a great many excellent persons to whom it is misery to see misery, and pleasure to lessen it; and who, by calling the public attention to the worst cases, and by giving birth to judicious legislative enactments for their improvement, have made, and are making, the world somewhat happier than they found it. Upon these principles we join hands with the friends of the chimney sweepers, and most heartily wish for the diminution of their numbers, and the limitation of their trade.

We are thoroughly convinced, there are many respectable master chimney sweepers; though we suspect their numbers have been increased by the alarm which their former tyranny excited, and by the severe laws made for their coercion: but even with good masters the trade is miserable,—with bad ones it is not to be endured; and the evidence already quoted shows us how many of that character are to be met with in the occupation of sweeping chimneys.

After all, we must own that it was quite right to throw out the bill for prohibiting the sweeping of chimneys by boys—because humanity is a modern invention; and there are many chimneys in old houses which cannot possibly be swept in any other manner. But the construction of chimneys should be attended to in some new building act; and the treatment of boys be watched over with the most severe jealousy of the law. Above all, those who have chimneys accessible to machinery, should encourage the use of machines,* and not think it beneath their dignity to take a little trouble, in order to do a great deal of good. We should have been very glad to have seconded the views of the Climbing Society, and to have pleaded for the complete abolition of climbing boys, if we could conscientiously have done so. But such a measure, we are convinced from the evidence, could not be carried into execution without great injury to property, and great increased risk of fire. The lords have investigated the matter with the greatest patience, humanity and good sense; and they do not venture, in their report, to recommend to the House the abolition of climbing boys.

* The price of a machine is fifteen shillings.

AMERICA.*

[Edinburgh Review, 1820.]

This is a book of character and authority; but it is a very large book; and therefore we think we shall do an acceptable service to our readers, by presenting them with a short epitome of its contents, observing the same order which has been chosen by the author. The whole, we conceive, will form a pretty complete picture of America, and teach us how to appreciate that country, either as a powerful enemy or a profitable friend. The first subject with which Mr. Seybert begins, is the population of the United States.

Population.—As representatives and direct taxes are apportioned among the different states in proportion to their numbers, it is provided for in the American constitution, that there shall be an actual enumeration of the people every ten years. It is the duty of the marshals in each state to number the inhabitants of their respective districts: and a correct copy of the lists, containing the names of the persons returned, must be set up in a public place within each district, before they are transmitted to the secretary of state:—they are then laid before Congress by the president. Under this act three census, or enumerations of the people, have been already laid before Congress—for the years 1790, 1800 and 1810. In the year 1790, the population of America was 3,921,326 persons, of whom 697,697 were slaves. In 1800, the numbers were 5,319,762, of which 896,849 were slaves. In 1810, the numbers were 7,239,903, of whom 1,191,364 were slaves; so that at a rate at which free population has proceeded between 1790 and 1810, it doubles itself, in the United States, in a very little more than 22 years. The slave population, according to its rate of proceeding in the same time, would be doubled in about 26 years. The increase of the slave population in this statement is owing to the importation of negroes between 1800 and 1808, especially in 1806 and 1807, from the expected prohibition against importation. The number of slaves was also increased by the acquisitions of territory in Louisiana, where they constituted nearly half the population. From 1801 to 1811, the inhabitants of Great Britain acquired an augmentation of 14 per cent.; the Americans, within the same period, were augmented 36 per cent.

Emigration seems to be of very little importance to the United States. In the year 1817, by far the most considerable year of emigration, there arrived in ten of the principal ports of America, from the old world, 22,000 persons as passengers. The number of emigrants, from 1790 to 1810, is not supposed to have exceeded 6000 per annum. None of the separate states have been retrograde during these three enumerations, though some have been nearly stationary. The most remarkable increase is that of New York, which has risen from 340,120 in the year 1790, to 959,049 in the year 1810. The emigration from the eastern to the western states is calculated at 60,000 persons per annum. In all the American enumerations, the males uniformly predominate in the proportion of about 100 to 92. We are better off in Great Britain and Ireland,—where the women were to the men, by the census of 1811, as 110 to 100. The density of population in the United States is less than 4 persons to a square mile; that of Holland, in 1803, was 275 to the square mile; that of England and Wales, 169. So that the fifteen provinces which formed the union in 1810, would contain, if they were as thickly peopled as Holland, 135 million souls.

The next head is that of *Trade* and *Commerce.*—In 1790, the exports of the United States were above 19 millions of dollars; in 1791, above 20 millions; in 1792, 26 millions; in 1793, 33 millions of dollars. Prior to 1795, there was no discrimination, in the American treasury accounts, between the exportation of domestic, and the re-exportation of foreign articles. In 1795, the aggregate value of the merchandize exported was 67 millions of dollars, of which the foreign produce re-exported was 26 millions. In 1800, the total value of exports was 94 millions; in 1805, 101 millions; and in 1808, when they arrived at their maximum, 108 million dollars. In the year 1809, from the effects of the French and English orders in council, the exports fell to 52 millions of dollars; in 1810 to 66 millions; in 1811, to 61 millions; In the first year of the war with England, to 38 millions; in the second to 27; in the year 1814, when peace was made, to 6 millions. So that the exports of the republic, in six years, had tumbled down from 108 to 6 millions of dollars: after the peace, in the years 1815-16-17, the exports rose to 52, 81, 87 million dollars.

In 1817, the exportation of cotton was 85 million pounds. In 1815, the sugar made on the banks of the Mississippi was 10 million pounds. In 1792, when the wheat trade was at the maximum, a million and a half of bushels were exported. The proportions of the exports to Great Britain, Spain, France, Holland and Portugal, on an average of ten years ending 1812, are as 27, 16, 13, 12 and 7; the actual value of exports to the dominions of Great Britain, in the three years ending 1804, were consecutively, in millions of dollars, 16, 17, 13.

Imports.—In 1791, the imports of the United States were 19 millions; on an average of three consecutive years, ending 1804 inclusive, they

---

* *Statistical Annals of the United States of America.* By Adam Seybert, 4to. Philadelphia, 1818.

were 68 millions; in 1806-7, they were 138 millions; and in 1815, 133 millions of dollars. The annual value of the imports, on an average of three years ending 1804, was 75,000,000, of which the dominions of Great Britain furnished nearly one half. On an average of three years ending in 1804, America imported from Great Britain to the amount of about 36 millions, and returned goods to the amount of about 23 millions. Certainly these are countries that have some better employment for their time and energy than cutting each other's throats, and may meet for more profitable purposes.—The American imports from the dominions of Great Britain, before the great American war, amounted to about 3 millions sterling; soon after the war, to the same. From 1805 to 1811, both inclusive, the average annual exportation of Great Britain to all parts of the world, in real value, was about 43 millions sterling, of which one-fifth, or nearly 9 millions, was sent to America.

Tonnage and *Navigation.*—Before the revolutionary war, the American tonnage, whether owned by British or American subjects, was about 127,000 tons; immediately after that war, 108,000. In 1789, it had amounted to 437,733 tons, of which 279,000 was American property. In 1790, the total was 605,825, of which 354,000 was American. In 1816, the tonnage, all American, was 1,300,000. On an average of three years, from 1810 to 1812, both inclusive, the registered tonnage of the British empire was 2,459,000; or little more than double the American.

Lands.—All public lands are surveyed before they are offered for sale, and divided into townships of six miles square, which are subdivided into thirty-six sections of one mile square, containing each 640 acres. The following lands are excepted from the sales. One thirty-sixth part of the lands, or a section of 640 acres in each township, is uniformly reserved for the support of schools; seven entire townships, containing each 23,000 acres, have been reserved in perpetuity for the support of learning: all salt springs and lead mines are also reserved. The Mississippi, the Ohio, and all the navigable rivers and waters leading into either, or into the river St. Lawrence, remain common highways, and forever free to all the citizens of the United States, without payment of any tax. All the other public lands, not thus excepted, are offered for public sale in quarter sections of 160 acres, at a price not less than two dollars per acre, and as much more as they will fetch by public auction. It was formerly the duty of the secretary of the treasury to superintend the sales of lands. In 1812, an office, denominated the General Land-Office, was instituted. The public lands sold prior to the opening of the land-offices, amounted to one million and a half of acres. The aggregate of the sales since the opening of the land-offices, N. W. of the river Ohio, to the end of September, 1817, amounted to 8,469,644 acres; and the purchase-money to 18,000,000 dollars. The lands sold since the opening of the land-offices in the Mississippi territory, amount to 1,600,000 acres. The stock of unsold land on hand is calculated at 400,000,000 acres. In the year 1817 there were sold above two millions of acres.

Post-Office.—In 1789, the number of post-offices in the United States was 75; the amount of postage 38,000 dollars; the miles of post-road 1800. In 1817, the number of post-offices was 3,459; the amount of postage 961,000 dollars; and the extent of post-roads 51,600 miles.

Revenue.—The revenues of the United States are derived from the customs; from duties on distilled spirits, carriages, snuff, refined sugar, auctions, stamped paper, goods, wares and merchandise manufactured within the United States, household furniture, gold and silver watches and postage of letters; from money arising from the sale of public lands and from fees on letters-patent. The following are the duties paid at the custom-house for some of the principal articles of importation:—7½ per cent. on dyeing drugs, jewellery and watch-work; 15 per cent. on hempen cloth and on all articles manufactured from iron, tin, brass and lead—on buttons, buckles, china, earthenware and glass, except window glass; 25 per cent. on cotton and woollen goods and cotton twist; 30 per cent. on carriages, leather and leather manufactures, &c.

The average annual produce of the customs, between 1801 and 1810, both inclusive, was about twelve millions of dollars. In the year 1814, the customs amounted *only to four millions;* and, in the year 1815, the first year after the war, rose to thirty-seven millions. From 1789 to 1814, the customs have constituted 65 per cent. of the American revenues; loans 26 per cent.; and all other branches 8 to 9 per cent. They collect their customs at about 4 per cent.;—the English expense of collection is 6*l.* 2*s.* 6*d.* per cent.

The duty upon spirits is extremely trifling to the consumer—not a penny per gallon. The number of distilleries is about 15,000. The licenses produce a very inconsiderable sum. The tax laid upon carriages in 1814, varied from fifty dollars to one dollar, according to the value of the machine. In the year 1801, there were more than fifteen thousand carriages of different descriptions paying duty. The furniture-tax seems to have been a very singular species of tax, laid on during the last war. It was an *ad valorem* duty upon all the furniture in any man's possession, the value of which exceeded 600 dollars. Furniture cannot be estimated without domiciliary visits, nor domiciliary visits allowed without tyranny and vexation. An information laid against a new arm-chair, or a clandestine sideboard—a search-warrant, and a conviction consequent upon it—have much more the appearance of English than American liberty. The license for a watch, too, is purely English. A truly free Englishman walks out covered with licenses. It is impossible to convict him. He has paid a guinea for his powdered head—a guinea for the coat of arms upon his seals—a three guinea license for the gun he carries upon his shoulder to shoot game: and is so fortified with permits and official sanctions, that the most eagle-eyed informer cannot obtain the most trifling advantage over him.

America has borrowed, between 1791 and 1815, one hundred and seven millions of dollars, of which forty-nine millions were borrowed in 1813 and 1814. The internal revenue in the year 1815 amounted to eight million dollars; the gross revenue of the same year, including the loan, to fifty-one million dollars.

Army.—During the late war with Great Britain, Congress authorized the raising of 62,000 men for the armies of the United States,—though the actual number raised never amounted to half that force. In February, 1815, the army of the United States did not amount to more than 32,000 men; in January, 1814, to 23,000.* The recruiting service, as may be easily conceived, where the wages of labour are so high, goes on very slowly in America. The military peace establishment was fixed in 1815 at 10,000 men. The Americans are fortunately exempt from the insanity of garrisoning little rocks and islands all over the world; nor would they lavish millions upon the ignoble end of the Spanish Peninsula—the most useless and extravagant possession with which any European power was ever afflicted. In 1812, any recruit honourably discharged from the service, was allowed three months' pay, and 160 acres of land. In 1814, every non-commissioned officer, musician and private, who enlisted and was afterwards honourably discharged, was allowed, upon such discharge, 320 acres. The enlistment was for five years, or during the war. The widow, child or parent of any person enlisted, who was killed, or died in the service of the United States, was entitled to receive the same bounty in land.

Every free white male between eighteen and forty-five, is liable to be called out in the militia, which is stated, in official papers, to amount to 748,000 persons.

Navy.—On the 8th of June, 1781, the Americans had only one vessel of war, the *Alliance;* and that was thought to be too expensive; it was sold! The attacks of the Barbary powers first roused them to form a navy; which, in 1797, amounted to three frigates. In 1814, besides a great increase of frigates, four seventy-fours were ordered to be built. In 1816, in consequence of some brilliant actions of their frigates, the naval service had become very popular throughout the United States. One million of dollars was appropriated annually, for eight years to the gradual increase of the navy; nine seventy-fours,† and twelve forty-four gun-ships were ordered to be built. Vacant and unappropriated lands belonging to the United States, fit to produce oak and cedar, were to be selected for the use of the navy. The peace establishment of the marine corps was increased, and six navy yards were established. We were surprised to find Dr. Seybert complaining of a want of ship timber in America. "Many persons (he says) believe that our stock of live oak is very considerable; but upon good authority we have been told, in 1801, that supplies of live oak from Georgia will be obtained with great difficulty, and that the larger pieces are very scarce." In treating of naval affairs, Dr. Seybert, with a very different purpose in view, pays the following involuntary tribute to the activity and effect of our late naval warfare against the Americans.

"For a long time the majority of the people of the United States was opposed to an extensive and permanent naval establishment; and the force authorized by the legislature, until very lately, was intended for temporary purposes. A navy was considered to be beyond the financial means of our country; and it was supposed the people would not submit to be taxed for its support. Our brilliant success in the late war has changed the public sentiment on this subject: many persons who formerly opposed the navy, now consider it as an essential means for our defence. The late transactions on the borders of the Chesapeake Bay, cannot be forgotten; the extent of that immense estuary enabled the enemy to sail triumphant into the interior of the United States. For hundreds of miles along the shores of that great bay, our people were insulted; our towns were ravaged and destroyed; a considerable population was teased and irritated; depredations were hourly committed by an enemy who could penetrate into the bosom of the country, without our being able to molest him whilst he kept on the water. By the time a sufficient force was collected to check his operations in one situation, his ships had already transported him to another, which was feeble, and offered a booty to him. An army could make no resistance to this mode of warfare; the people were annoyed; and they suffered in the field only to be satisfied of their inability to check those who had the dominion upon our waters. The inhabitants who were in the immediate vicinity, were not alone affected by the enemy; his operations extended their influence to our great towns on the Atlantic coast; domestic intercourse and internal commerce were interrupted, whilst that with foreign nations was, in some instances, entirely suspended. The treasury documents for 1814, exhibit the phenomenon of the State of Pennsylvania not being returned in the list of the exporting states. We were not only deprived of revenue, but our expenditures were very much augmented. It is probable the amount of the expenditures incurred on the borders of the Chesapeake would have been adequate to provide naval means for the defence of those waters: the people might then have remained at home, secure from depredation in the pursuit of their tranquil occupations. The expenses of the government, as well as of individuals, were very much augmented for every species of transportation. Every thing had to be conveyed by land carriage. Our communication with the ocean was cut off. One thousand dollars were paid for the transportation of each of the thirty-two pounder cannon from Washington city to Lake Ontario for the public service. Our roads became almost impassable from the heavy loads which were carried over them. These facts should induce us, in times of tranquillity, to provide for the national defence, and execute such internal improvements as cannot be effected during the agitations of war."—(p. 679.)

Expenditure.—The President of the United States receives about 6000*l.* a year; the Vice-President about 600*l.*; the deputies to Congress

* Peace with Great Britain was signed in December, 1814, at Ghent.

† The American seventy-four gun ships are as big as our first-rates, and their frigates nearly as big as ships of the line.

have 8 dollars per day, and 8 dollars for every 20 miles of journey. The first clerk of the House of Representatives receives about 750*l.* per annum; the Secretary of State, 1200*l.*; the Postmaster-General, 750*l.*; the Chief Justice of the United States, 1000*l.*; a Minister Plenipotentiary, 2200*l.* per annum. There are, doubtless, reasons why there should be two noblemen appointed in this country as postmasters-general, with enormous salaries, neither of whom know a twopenny post letter from a general one, and where further retrenchments are stated to be impossible. This is clearly a case to which that impossibility extends. But these are matters where a prostration of understanding is called for; and good subjects are not to reason, but to pay. If, however, we were ever to indulge in the Saxon practice of looking into our own affairs, some important documents might be derived from these American salaries. Jonathan, for instance, sees no reason why the first clerk of his House of Commons should derive emoluments from his situation to the amount of 6000*l.* or 7000*l.* per annum; but Jonathan is vulgar and arithmetical. The total expenditure of the United States varied, between 1799 and 1811, both inclusive, from 11 to 17 millions of dollars. From 1812 to 1814, both inclusive, and all these years of war with this country, the expenditure was consecutively, 22, 29, and 38 millions of dollars. The total expenditure of the United States, for 14 years from 1791 to 1814, was 333 millions of dollars; of which, in the three last years of war with this country, from 1812 to 1814, there were expended 100 millions of dollars, of which only 35 were supplied by revenue, the rest by loans and government paper. The sum total received by the American treasury from the 3d of March, 1789, to the 31st of March, 1816, is 354 millions of dollars; of which 107 millions have been raised by loan, and 222 millions by the customs and tonnage: so that, exclusive of the revenue derived from loans, 222 parts out of 247 of the American revenue have been derived from foreign commerce. In the mind of any sensible American, this consideration ought to prevail over the few splendid actions of their half dozen frigates, which must, in a continued war, have been, with all their bravery and activity, swept from the face of the ocean by the superior force and equal bravery of the English. It would be the height of madness in America to run into another naval war with this country, if it could be averted by any other means than a sacrifice of proper dignity and character. They have, comparatively, no land revenue; and, in spite of the *Franklin* and *Guerrière*, though lined with cedar and mounted with brass cannon, they must soon be reduced to the same state which has been described by Dr. Seybert, and from which they were so opportunely extricated by the treaty of Ghent. David Porter and Stephen Decatur are very brave men; but they will prove an unspeakable misfortune to their country, if they inflame Jonathan into a love of naval glory, and inspire him with any other love of war than that which is founded upon a determination not to submit to serious insult and injury.

We can inform Jonathan what are the inevitable consequences of being too fond of glory;—Taxes *upon every article which enters into the mouth, or covers the back, or is placed under the foot—taxes upon every thing which it is pleasant to see, hear, feel, smell, or taste—taxes upon warmth, light and locomotion—taxes on every thing on earth, and the waters under the earth—on every thing that comes from abroad, or is grown at home—taxes on the raw material—taxes on every fresh value that is added to it by the industry of man—taxes on the sauce which pampers man's appetite, and the drug that restores him to health—on the ermine which decorates the judge, and the rope which hangs the criminal—on the poor man's salt, and the rich man's spice—on the brass nails of the coffin, and the ribbons of the bride—at bed or board, couchant or levant, we must pay.—The school-boy whips his taxed top—the beardless youth manages his taxed horse, with a taxed bridle, on a taxed road:—and the dying Englishman, pouring his medicine, which has paid 7 per cent., into a spoon that has paid 15 per cent.,—flings himself back upon his chintz bed, which has paid 22 per cent.,—and expires in the arms of an apothecary, who has paid a license of a hundred pounds for the privilege of putting him to death. His whole property is then immediately taxed from 2 to 10 per cent. Besides the probate, large fees are demanded for burying him in the chancel; his virtues are handed down to posterity on taxed marble; and he is then gathered to his fathers,—to be taxed no more.* In addition to all this, the habit of dealing with large sums will make the government avaricious and profuse; and the system itself will infallibly generate the base vermin of spies and informers, and a still more pestilent race of political tools and retainers of the meanest and most odious description;—while the prodigious patronage which the collecting of this splendid revenue will throw into the hands of government, will invest it with so vast an influence, and hold out such means and temptations to corruption, as all the virtue and public spirit, even of republicans, will be unable to resist.

Every wise Jonathan should remember this, when he sees the rabble huzzaing at the heels of the truly respectable Decatur, or inflaming the vanity of that still more popular leader, whose justification has lowered the character of his government with all the civilized nations of the world.

Debt.—America owed 42 million dollars after the Revolutionary war; in 1790, 79 millions; in 1803, 70 millions; and in the beginning of January, 1812, the public debt was diminished to 45 million dollars. After the last war with England, it had risen to 123 millions; and so it stood on the 1st of January, 1816. The total amount carried to the credit of the commissioners of the sinking fund, on the 31st of December, 1816, was about 34 millions of dollars.

Such is the land of Jonathan—and thus has it been governed. In his honest endeavours to better his situation, and in his manly purpose of resisting injury and insult we most cordially sympathize. We hope he will always continue to watch and suspect his government as he now does—remembering that it is the constant tendency of those entrusted with power, to conceive that they enjoy it by their own merits, and for their own use, and not by delegation, and for the benefit of others. Thus far we are the friends and admirers of Jonathan. But he must not grow vain and ambitious; or allow himself to be dazzled by that galaxy of epithets by which his orators and newspaper scribblers endeavour to persuade their supporters that they are the greatest, the most refined, the most enlightened and most moral people upon earth. The effect of this is unspeakably ludicrous on this side of the Atlantic—and, even on the other, we shall imagine, must be rather humiliating to the reasonable part of the population. The Americans are a brave, industrious and acute people; but they have, hitherto, given no indications of genius, and made no approaches to the heroic, either in their morality or character. They are but a recent offset, indeed, from England; and should make it their chief boast, for many generations to come, that they are sprung from the same race with Bacon and Shakspeare and Newton. Considering their numbers, indeed, and the favourable circumstances in which they have been placed, they have yet done marvellously little to assert the honour of such a descent, or to show that their English blood has been exalted or refined by their republican training and institutions.—Their Franklins and Washingtons, and all the other sages and heroes of their Revolution, were born and bred subjects of the King of England,—and not among the freest or most valued of his subjects. And since the period of their separation, a far greater proportion of their statesmen and artists and political writers have been foreigners than ever occurred before in the history of any civilized and educated people. During the thirty or forty years of their independence, they have done absolutely nothing for the Sciences, for the Arts, for Literature or even for the statesman-like studies of Politics or Political Economy. Confining ourselves to our own country, and to the period that has elapsed since *they* had an independent existence, we would ask, where are their Foxes, their Burkes, their Sheridans, their Windhams, their Horners, their Wilberforces?—where their Arkwrights, their Watts, their Davys?—their Robertsons, Blairs, Smiths, Stewarts, Paleys, and Malthuses?—their Porsons, Parrs, Burneys, or Bloomfields?—their Scotts, Rogers's, Campbells, Byrons, Moores, or Crabbes?—their Siddons's, Kembles, Keans, or O'Neils?—their Wilkies, Lawrences, Chantrys?—or their parallels to the hundred other names that have spread themselves over the world from our little island in the course of the last thirty years, and blest or delighted mankind by their works, inventions or examples? In so far as we know, there is no such parallel to be produced from the whole annals of this self-adulating race. In the four quarters of the globe, who reads an American book? or goes to an American play? or looks at an American picture or statue? What does the world yet owe to American physicians or surgeons? What new substances have their chemists discovered? or what old ones have they analyzed? What new constellations have been discovered by the telescopes of Americans? What have they done in the mathematics? Who drinks out of American glasses? or eats from American plates? or wears American coats or gowns? or sleeps in American blankets? Finally, under which of the old tyrannical governments of Europe is every sixth man a slave, whom his fellow-creatures may buy and sell and torture?

When these questions are fairly and favourably answered, their laudatory epithets may be allowed: but till that can be done, we would seriously advise them to keep clear of superlatives.

IRELAND.*

[Edinburgh Review, 1820.]

These are all the late publications that treat of Irish interests in general,—and none of them are of first-rate importance. Mr. Gamble's Travels in Ireland are of a very ordinary description—low scenes and low humour making up the principal part of the narrative. There are readers, however, whom it will amuse; and the reading market becomes more and more extensive, and embraces a greater variety of persons every day. Mr. Whitelaw's History of Dublin is a book of great accuracy and research, highly creditable to the industry, good sense and benevolence of its author. Of the Travels of Mr. Christian Curwen, we hardly know what to say. He is bold and honest in his politics—a great enemy to abuses—vapid in his levity and pleasantry, and infinitely too much inclined to declaim upon common-place topics of morality and benevolence. But, with these drawbacks, the book is not ill written; and may be advantageously read by those who are desirous of information upon the present state of Ireland.

So great and so long has been the misgovernment of that country, that we verily believe the empire would be much stronger if every thing was open sea between England and the Atlantic, and if *skates and codfish* swam over the fair land of Ulster. Such jobbing, such profligacy—so much direct tyranny and oppression—such an abuse of God's gifts—such a profanation of God's name for the purposes of bigotry and party spirit, cannot be exceeded in the history of civilized Europe, and will long remain a monument of infamy and shame to England. But it will be more useful to suppress the indignation which the very name of Ireland inspires, and to consider impartially those causes which have marred this fair portion of the creation, and kept it wild and savage in the midst of improving Europe.

The great misfortune of Ireland is, that the mass of the people have been given up for a century to a handful of Protestants, by whom they have been treated as *Helots*, and subjected to every species of persecution and disgrace. The sufferings of the Catholics have been so loudly chaunted in the very streets, that it is almost needless to remind our readers that, during the reigns of George I. and George II., the Irish Roman Catholics were disabled from holding any civil or military office, from voting at elections, from admission into corporations, from practising law or physic. A younger brother, by turning Protestant, might deprive his elder brother of his birthright; by the same process he might force his father, under the name of a liberal provision, to yield up to him a part of his landed property: and, if an eldest son, he might, in the same way, reduce his father's fee-simple to a life estate. A papist was disabled from purchasing freehold lands—and even from holding long leases—and any person might take his Catholic neighbour's house by paying 5*l.* for it. If the child of a Catholic father turned Protestant, he was taken away from his father and put into the hands of a Protestant relation. No papist could purchase a freehold, or lease for more than thirty years—or inherit from an intestate Protestant—nor from an intestate Catholic—nor dwell in Limerick or Galway—nor hold an advowson, nor buy an annuity for life. 50*l.* was given for discovering a popish archbishop—30*l.* for a popish clergyman—and 10*s.* for a schoolmaster. No one was allowed to be trustee for Catholics; no Catholic was allowed to take more than two apprentices; no papist to be solicitor, sheriff, or to serve on grand juries. Horses of papists might be seized for the militia; for which militia papists were to pay double, and to find Protestant substitutes. Papists were prohibited from being present at vestries, or from being high or petty constables; and, when resident in towns, they were compelled to find Protestant watchmen. Barristers and solicitors marrying Catholics, were exposed to the penalties of Catholics. Persons plundered by privateers during a war with any popish prince, were reimbursed by a levy on the Catholic inhabitants where they lived. All popish priests celebrating marriages contrary to 12 Geo. I. cap. 3, were to be hanged.

The greater part of these incapacities are removed, though many of a very serious and oppressive nature still remain. But the grand misfortune is, that the spirit which these oppressive laws engendered remains. The Protestant still looks upon the Catholic as a degraded being. The Catholic does not yet consider himself upon an equality with his former tyrant and taskmaster. That religious hatred which required all the prohibiting vigilance of the law for its restraint, has found in the law its strongest support; and the spirit which the law first exasperated and embittered, continues to act long after the original *stimulus* is withdrawn. The law which prevented Catholics from serving on grand juries is repealed; but Catholics are not called upon grand juries in the proportion in which they are entitled, by their rank and fortune. The Duke of Bedford did all he could to give them the benefit of those laws which are already passed in their favour. But power is seldom entrusted in this country to one of the Duke of Bedford's liberality; and

* 1. *Whitelaw's History of the City of Dublin.* 4to. Cadell and Davies.

2. *Observations on the State of Ireland, principally directed to its Agriculture and Rural Population; in a series of Letters written on a Tour through that Country.* In 2 vols. By J. C. Curwen, Esq., M. P. London, 1818.

3. *Gamble's Views of Society in Ireland.*

every thing has fallen back in the hands of his successors into the ancient division of the privileged and degraded castes. We do not mean to cast any reflection upon the present secretary for Ireland, whom we believe to be upon this subject a very liberal politician, and on all subjects an honourable and excellent man. The government under which he serves allows him to indulge in a little harmless liberality; but it is perfectly understood that nothing is intended to be done for the Catholics; that no loaves and fishes will be lost by indulgence in Protestant insolence and tyranny; and, therefore, among the generality of Irish Protestants, insolence, tyranny and exclusion continue to operate. However eligible the Catholic may be, he is not elected; whatever barriers may be thrown down, he does not advance a step. He was first kept out by law; he is now kept out by opinion and habit. They have been so long in chains, that nobody believes they are capable of using their hands and feet.

It is not, however, the only or the worst misfortune of the Catholics, that the relaxations of the law are hitherto of little benefit to them; the law is not yet sufficiently relaxed. A Catholic, as every body knows, cannot be made sheriff; cannot be in Parliament; cannot be a director of the Irish Bank; cannot fill the great departments of the law, the army and the navy; is cut off from all the high objects of human ambition, and treated as a marked and degraded person.

The common admission now is, that the Catholics are to the Protestants in Ireland as about 4 to 1—of which Protestants, not more than *one half* belong to the Church of Ireland. This, then, is one of the most striking features in the state of Ireland. That the great mass of the population is completely subjugated and overawed by a handful of comparatively recent settlers,—in whom all the power and patronage of the country are vested,—who have been reluctantly compelled to desist from still greater abuses of authority,—and who look with trembling apprehension to the increasing liberality of the Parliament and the country towards these unfortunate persons whom they have always looked upon as their property and their prey.

Whatever evils may result from these proportions between the oppressor and the oppressed—to whatever dangers a country so situated may be considered to be exposed—these evils and dangers are rapidly increasing in Ireland. The proportion of Catholics to Protestants is infinitely greater now than it was thirty years ago, and is becoming more and more favourable to the former. By a return made to the Irish House of Lords in 1732, the proportion of Catholics to Protestants was not 2 to 1. It is now (as we have already observed) 4 to 1; and the causes which have thus altered the proportion in favour of the Catholics are sufficiently obvious to any one acquainted with the state of Ireland. The Roman Catholic priest resides; his income entirely depends upon the number of his flock; and he must exert himself, or he starves. There is some chance of success, therefore, in *his* efforts to convert; but the Protestant clergyman, if he were equally eager, has little or no probability of persuading so much larger a proportion of the population to come over to his church. The Catholic clergyman belongs to a religion that has always been more desirous of gaining proselytes than the Protestant church; and he is animated by a sense of injury and a desire of revenge. Another reason for the disproportionate increase of Catholics is, that the Catholics will marry upon means which the Protestant considers as insufficient for marriage. A few potatoes and a shed of turf are all that Luther has left for the Romanist; and, when the latter gets these, he instantly begins upon the great Irish manufacture of children. But a Protestant belongs to the sect that eats the fine flour, and leaves the bran to others; he must have comforts, and he does not marry till he gets them. He would be ashamed, if he were seen living as a Catholic lives. This is the principal reason why the Protestants who remain attached to their church do not increase so fast as the Catholics. But in common minds, daily scenes, the example of the majority, the power of imitation, decide their habits, religious as well as civil. A Protestant labourer who works among Catholics, soon learns to think and act and talk as they do—he is not proof against the eternal panegyric which he hears of Father O'Leary. His Protestantism is rubbed away; and he goes at last, after some little resistance, to the chapel, where he sees every body else going.

These eight Catholics not only hate the ninth man, the Protestant of the Establishment, for the unjust privileges he enjoys—not only remember that the lands of their fathers were given to his father—but they find themselves forced to pay for the support of his religion. In the wretched state of poverty in which the lower orders of Irish are plunged, it is not without considerable effort that they can pay the few shillings necessary for the support of their Catholic priest; and when this is effected, a tenth of the potatoes in the garden is to be set out for the support of a persuasion, the introduction of which into Ireland they consider as the great cause of their political inferiority, and all their manifold wretchedness. In England, a labourer can procure constant employment—or he can, at the worst, obtain relief from his parish. Whether tithe operates as a tax upon him, is known only to the political economist: if he does pay it, he does not know that he pays it; and the burthen of supporting the clergy is at least kept out of his view. But, in Ireland, the only method in which a poor man lives, is by taking a small portion of land, in which he can grow potatoes: seven or eight months out of twelve, in many parts of Ireland, there is no constant employment of the poor: and the potato farm is all that shelters them from absolute famine. If the pope were to come in person, and seize upon every tenth potato, the poor peasant would scarcely endure it. With what patience then, can he see it tossed into the cart of the heretic rector who has a church without a congregation, and a revenue without duties?

We do not say whether these things are right or wrong—whether they want a remedy at all—or what remedy they want; but we paint them in those colours in which they appear to the eye of poverty and ignorance, without saying whether those colours are false or true. Nor is the case at all comparable to that of Dissenters paying tithe in England; which case is precisely the reverse of what happens in Ireland, for it is the contribution of a very small minority to the religion of a very large majority; and the numbers on either side make all the difference in the argument. To exasperate the poor Catholic still more, the rich grazier of the parish—or the squire in his parish—pay no tithe at all for their grass land. Agistment tithe is abolished in Ireland; and the burthen of supporting two churches seems to devolve upon the poorer Catholics, struggling with plough and spade in small scraps of dearly-rented land. Tithes seem to be collected in a more harsh manner than they are collected in England. The minute subdivisions of land in Ireland—the little connection which the Protestant clergyman commonly has with the Catholic population of his parish, have made the introduction of tithe proctors very general—sometimes as the agent of the clergyman—sometimes as the lessee or middleman between the clergyman and the cultivator of the land; but, in either case, practised, dexterous estimators of tithe. The English clergymen in general, are far from exacting the whole of what is due to them, but sacrifice a little to the love of popularity or to the dread of odium. A system of tithe-proctors established all over England (as it is in Ireland,) would produce general disgust and alienation from the Established Church.

"During the administration of Lord Halifax," says Mr. Hardy, in quoting the opinion of Lord Charlemont upon tithes paid by Catholics, "Ireland was dangerously disturbed in its southern and northern regions. In the south principally, in the counties of Kilkenny, Limerick, Cork and Tipperary, the White Boys now made their first appearance; those White Boys, who have ever since occasionally disturbed the public tranquillity, without any rational method having been as yet pursued to eradicate this disgraceful evil. When we consider that the very same district has been for the long space of seven-and-twenty years liable to frequent returns of the same disorder into which it has continually relapsed, in spite of all the violent remedies from time to time administered by our political quacks, we cannot doubt but that some real, peculiar and topical cause must exist; and yet, neither the removal nor even the investigation of this cause has ever once been seriously attempted. Laws of the most sanguinary and unconstitutional nature have been enacted; the country has been disgraced and exasperated by frequent and bloody executions; and the gibbet, that perpetual resource of weak and cruel legislators, has groaned under the multitude of starving criminals: yet, while the cause is suffered to exist, the effects will ever follow. The amputation of limbs will never eradicate a prurient humour, which must be sought in its source, and there remedied."

"I wish," continues Mr. Wakefield, "for the sake of humanity, and for the honour of the Irish character, that the gentlemen of that country would take this matter into their serious consideration. Let them only for a moment place themselves in the situation of the half-famished cotter, surrounded by a wretched family, clamorous for food; and judge what his feelings must be, when he sees the tenth part of the produce of his potato garden exposed at harvest time to public *cant;* or, if he have given a promissory note for the payment of a certain sum of money, to compensate for such tithe when it becomes due, to hear the heart-rending cries of his offspring clinging round him, and lamenting for the milk of which they are deprived, by the cows being driven to the pound, to be sold to discharge the debt. Such accounts are not the creation of fancy; the facts do exist, and are but too common in Ireland. Were one of them transferred to canvas by the hand of genius, and exhibited to English humanity, that heart must be callous, indeed, that could refuse its sympathy. I have seen the cow, the favourite cow, driven away, accompanied by the sighs, the tears and the imprecations of a whole family, who were paddling after, through wet and dirt, to take their last affectionate farewell of this their only friend and benefactor, at the pound gate. I have heard with emotions which I can scarcely describe, deep curses repeated from village to village as the cavalcade proceeded. I have witnessed the group pass the domain walls of the opulent grazier, whose numerous herds were cropping the most luxuriant pastures, while he was secure from any demand for the tithe of their food, looking on with the most unfeeling indifference."—*Wakefield*, p. 486.

In Munster, where tithe of potatoes is exacted, risings against the system have constantly occurred during the last forty years. In Ulster, where no such tithe is required, these insurrections are unknown. The double church which Ireland supports, and that painful visible contribution towards it which the poor Irishman is compelled to make from his miserable pittance, is one great cause of those never-ending insurrections, burnings, murders and robberies, which have laid waste that ill-fated country for so many years. The unfortunate consequence of the civil disabilities, and the church payments under which the Catholics labour, is a rooted antipathy to this country. They hate the English government from historical recollection, actual sufferings and disappointed hope; and till they are better treated, they will continue to hate it. At this moment, in a period of the most profound peace, there are twenty-five thousand of the best disciplined and best appointed troops in the world in Ireland, with bayonets fixed, presented arms, and in the attitude of present war: nor is there a man too much—nor would Ireland be tenable without them. When it was necessary last year (or thought necessary) to put down the children of reform, we were forced to make a new levy of troops in this country—not a man could be spared from Ireland. The moment they had embarked, Peep-of-day Boys, Heart-of-Oak Boys, Twelve-o'clock Boys, Heart-of-Flint Boys, and all the bloody boyhood of the Bog of Allen, would have proceeded to the ancient work of riot, rapine and disaffection. Ireland, in short, till her wrongs are redressed, and a more liberal policy is adopted towards her, will always be a cause of anxiety and suspicion to this country; and, in some moment of our weakness and depression, will forcibly extort what she would now receive with gratitude and exultation.

Ireland is situated close to another island of greater size, speaking the same language, very superior in civilization, and the seat of government. The consequence of this is the emigration of the richest and most powerful part of the community—a vast drain of wealth—and the absence of all that wholesome influence which the representatives of ancient families residing upon their estates, produce upon their tenantry and dependents. Can any man imagine that the scenes which have been acted in Ireland within these last twenty years, would have taken place, if such vast proprietors as the Duke of Devonshire, the Marquis of Hertford, the Marquis of Lansdowne, Earl Fitzwilliam, and many other men of equal wealth, had been in the constant habit of residing upon their Irish, as they are upon their English estates? Is it of no consequence to the order and the civilization of a large district, whether the great mansion is inhabited by an insignificant, perhaps a mischievous, attorney, in the shape of agent, or whether the first and greatest men of the United Kingdoms, after the business of Parliament is over, come with their friends and families, to exercise hospitality, to spend large revenues, to diffuse information and to improve manners? This evil is a very serious one to Ireland; and, as far as we see, incurable. For if the present large estates were, by the dilapidation of families, to be broken to pieces and sold, others equally great would, in the free circulation of property, speedily accumulate; and the moment any possessor arrived at a certain pitch of fortune, he would probably choose to reside in the better country,—near the Parliament or the court.

This absence of great proprietors in Ireland necessarily brings with it, or if not necessarily, has actually brought with it, the employment of middlemen, which forms one other standing and regular Irish grievance. We are well aware of all that can be said in defence of middlemen; that they stand between the little farmer and the great proprietor, as the shop-keeper does between the manufacturer and consumer; and, in fact, by their intervention, save time, and therefore expense. This may be true enough in the abstract; but the particular nature of land must be attended to. The object of the man who makes cloth is to sell his cloth at the present market, for as high a price as he can obtain. If that price is too high, it soon falls; but no injury is done to his machinery by the superior price he has enjoyed for a season—he is just as able to produce cloth with it, as if the profits he enjoyed had always been equally moderate; he has no fear, therefore, of the middlemen, or of any species of moral machinery which may help to obtain for him the greatest present prices. The same would be the feeling of any one who let out a steam-engine, or any other machine, for the purposes of manufacture; he would naturally take the highest price he could get: for he might either let his machine for a price proportionate to the work it did, or the repairs, estimable with the greatest precision, might be thrown upon the tenant; in short, he could hardly ask any rent too high for his machine which a responsible person would give; dilapidation would be so visible, and so calculable in such instances, that any secondary lease, or subletting, would be rather an increase of security than a source of alarm. Any evil from such a practice would be improbable, measurable and remediable. In land, on the contrary, the object is not to get the highest prices absolutely, but to get the highest prices which will not injure the machine. One tenant may offer and pay double the rent of another, and in a few years leave the land in a state which will effectually bar all future offers of tenancy. It is of no use to fill a lease full of clauses and covenants; a tenant who pays more than he ought to pay, or who pays even to the last farthing which he ought to pay, will rob the land, and injure the machine, in spite of all the attorneys in England. He will rob it even if he means to remain upon it—driven on by present distress, and anxious to put off the day of defalcation and arrear. The damage is often difficult of detection--not easily calculated, not easily to be proved; such for which juries (themselves, perhaps, farmers) would not willingly give sufficient compensation. And if this is true in England, it is much more strikingly true in Ireland, where it is extremely difficult to obtain verdicts for breaches of covenant in leases.

The only method then of guarding the machine from real injury is, by giving to the actual occupier such advantage in his contract, that he is unwilling to give it up--that he has a real interest in retaining it, and is not driven by the distresses of the present moment to destroy the future productiveness of the soil. Any rent which the landlord accepts more than this, or any system by which more rent than this is obtained, is to borrow money upon the most usurious and profligate interest--to increase the revenue of the present day by the absolute ruin of the property. Such is the effect produced by a middleman: he gives high prices that he may obtain higher from the occupier; more is paid by the actual occupier than is consistent with the safety and preservation of the machine; the land is run out, and in the end, that maximum of rent we have described is not obtained: and not only is the property injured by such a system, but in Ireland the most shocking consequences ensue from it. There is little manufacture in Ireland; the price of labour is low, the demand for labour irregular. If a poor man is driven, by distress of rent, from his potato garden, he has no other resource--all is lost: he will do the impossible (as the French say) to retain it: and subscribe any bond, and promise any rent. The middleman has no character to lose; and he knew, when he took up the occupation, that it was one with which pity had nothing to do. On he drives; and backward the poor peasant recedes, losing something at every step, till he comes to the very brink of despair; and then he recoils and murders his oppressor, and is a *White boy* or a *Right boy*:--the soldier shoots him, and the judge hangs him.

In the debate which took place in the Irish House of Commons, upon the bill for preventing tumultuous risings and assemblies, on the 31st of January, 1787, the attorney-general submitted to the House the following narrative of facts.

"The commencement," said he, "was in one or two parishes in the county of Kerry; and they proceeded thus. The people assembled in a Catholic chapel, and there took an oath to obey the laws of Captain Right, and to starve the clergy. They then proceeded to the next parishes, on the following Sunday, and there swore the people in the same manner; with this addition, that they (the people last sworn) should, on the ensuing Sunday, proceed to the chapels of their next neighbouring parishes, and swear the inhabitants of those parishes in like manner. Proceeding in this manner they very soon went through the province of Munster. The first object was the *reformation of tithes.* They swore not to give more than a certain price per acre; not to assist, or allow them to be assisted, in drawing the tithe, and to permit *no proctor.* They next took upon them to prevent the collection of parish cesses; next to nominate parish clerks, and in some cases curates: to say what church should or should not be repaired; and in one case to threaten that they would burn a *new* church, if the *old* one were not given for a mass-house. At last, they proceeded to regulate the price of lands; to raise the price of labour; and to oppose the collection of the hearth money, and other taxes. Bodies of 5000 of them have been seen to march through the country unarmed, and if met by any magistrate, *they never offered the smallest rudeness or offence;* on the contrary, they had allowed persons charged with crimes to be taken from amongst them by the magistrate *alone*, unaided by any force."

"The attorney-general said he was well acquainted with the province of Munster, and that it was impossible for human wretchedness to *exceed that of the peasantry of that province.* The unhappy tenantry were *ground to powder* by relentless landlords; that, far from being able to give the clergy their just dues, they had not food nor raiment for themselves—the landlord grasped the whole; and sorry was he to add, that, not satisfied with the present extortion, some landlords had been so base as to instigate the insurgents to rob the clergy of their tithes, not in order to alleviate the distresses of the tenantry, but that they might add the clergy's share to the cruel rack-rents they already paid. The poor people of Munster lived in a *more abject state of poverty than human nature could be supposed equal to bear.*"—*Grattan's Speeches*, vol. i. 292.

We are not, of course, in such a discussion, to be governed by names. A middleman might be tied up by the strongest legal restriction, as to the price he was to exact from the undertenants, and then he would be no more pernicious to the estate than a steward. A steward might be protected in exactions as severe as the most rapacious middleman; and then, of course, it would be the same thing under another name. The practice to which we object is, the too common method in Ireland of extorting the last farthing which the tenant is willing to give for land, rather than quit it: and the machinery by which such practice is carried into effect, is that of the middleman. It is not only that it ruins the land; it ruins the people also. They are made so poor—brought so near the ground that they can sink no lower; and burst out at last into all the acts of desperation and revenge for which Ireland is so notorious. Men who have money in their pockets, and find that they are improving in their circumstances, don't do these things. Opulence, or the hope of opulence or comfort, is the parent of decency, order and submission to the laws. A landlord in Ireland understands the luxury of carriages and horses; but has no relish for the greater luxury of surrounding himself with a moral and grateful tenantry. The absent proprietor looks only to revenue, and cares nothing for the disorder and degradation of a country which he never means to visit. There are very honourable exceptions to this charge: but there are too many living instances that it is just. The rapacity of the Irish landlord induces him to allow of the extreme division of his lands. When the daughter marries, a little portion of the little farm is broken off—another corner for Patrick, and another for Dermot—till the land is broken into sections, upon one of which an English cow could not stand. Twenty mansions of misery are thus reared instead of one. A louder cry of oppression is lifted up to Heaven; and fresh enemies to the English name and power are multiplied on the earth. The Irish gentlemen, too, extremely desirous of political influence, multiply freeholds and split votes; and this propensity tends of course to increase the miserable redundance of living beings, under which Ireland is groaning. Among the manifold wretchedness to which the poor Irish tenant is liable, we must not pass over the practice of driving for rent. A lets land to B, who lets it to C, who lets it again to D. D pays C his rent, and C pays B. But if B fails to pay A, the cattle of B, C, D are all driven to the pound, and after the interval of a few days, sold by auction. A general driving of this kind very frequently leads to a bloody insurrection. It may be ranked among the classical grievances of Ireland.

Potatoes enter for a great deal into the present condition of Ireland. They are much cheaper than wheat; and it is so easy to rear a family upon them, that there is no check to population from the difficulty of procuring food. The population, therefore, goes on with a rapidity approaching almost to that of new countries, and in a much greater ratio than the improving agriculture and manufactures of the country can find employment for it. All degrees of all nations begin with living in pig-styes. The king or the priest first gets out of them; then the noble, then the pauper, in proportion as each class becomes more and more opulent. Better tastes arise from better circumstances; and the luxury of one period is the wretchedness and poverty of another. English peasants, in the time of Henry the Seventh, were lodged as badly as Irish peasants now are; but the population was limited by the difficulty of procuring a corn subsistence. The improvements of this kingdom were more rapid; the price of labour rose; and, with it, the luxury and comfort of the peasant, who is now decently lodged and clothed, and who would think himself in the last stage of wretchedness, if he had nothing but an iron pot in a turf house, and plenty of potatoes in it. The use of the potato was introduced into Ireland when the wretched accommodation of her own peasantry bore some proportion to the state of those accommodations all over Europe. But they have increased their population so fast, and, in conjunction with the oppressive government of Ireland retarding improvement, have kept the price of labour so low, that the Irish poor have never been able to emerge from their mud cabins, or to acquire any taste for cleanliness and decency of appearance. Mr. Curwen has the following description of Irish cottages.

"These mansions of miserable existence, for so they may truly be described, conformably to our general estimation of those indispensable comforts requisite to constitute the happiness of rational beings, are most commonly composed of two rooms on the ground floor, a most appropriate term, for they are literary on the earth; the surface of which is not unfrequently reduced a foot or more, to save the expense of so much outward walling. The one is a refectory, the other the dormitory. The furniture of the former, if the owner ranks in the upper part of the scale of scantiness, will consist of a kitchen dresser, well provided and highly decorated with crockery—not less apparently the pride of the husband than the result of female vanity in the wife: which, with a table, a chest, a few stools and an iron pot, complete the catologue of conveniences generally found as belonging to the cabin; while a spinning-wheel, furnished by the Linen Board, and a loom, ornament vacant spaces, that otherwise would remain unfurnished. In fitting up the latter, which cannot, on any occasion, or by any display, add a feather to the weight or importance expected to be excited by the appearance of the former, the inventory is limited to one, and sometimes two beds, serving for the repose of the whole family! However downy these may be to limbs impatient for rest, their coverings appeared to be very slight; and the whole of the apartment created reflections of a very painful nature. Under such privations, with a wet mud floor, and a roof in tatters, how idle the search for comforts!"—*Curwen*, I. 112, 113.

To this extract we shall add one more on the same subject.

"The gigantic figure, bare-headed before me, had a beard that would not have disgraced an ancient Israelite—he was without shoes or stockings—and almost a sans-culotte—with a coat or rather a jacket, that appeared as if the first blast of wind would tear it to tatters. Though his garb was thus tattered he had a manly commanding countenance. I asked permission to see the inside of his cabin, to which I received his most courteous assent. On stooping to enter at the door I was stopped and found that permission from another was necessary before I could be admitted. A pig, which was fastened to a stake driven into the floor, with length of rope sufficient to permit him the enjoyment of sun and air, demanded some courtesy, which I showed him, and was suffered to enter. The wife was engaged in boiling thread; and by her side, near the fire, a lovely infant was sleeping, without any covering, on a bare board. Whether the fire gave additional glow to the countenance of the babe, or that Nature impressed on its unconscious cheek a blush that the lot of man should be exposed to such privations, I will not decide; but if the cause be referable to the latter, it was in perfect unison with my own feelings. Two or three other children crowded round the mother: on their rosy countenances health seemed established in spite of filth and ragged garments. The dress of the poor woman was barely sufficient to satisfy decency. Her countenance bore the impression of a set melancholy, tinctured with an appearance of ill health. The hovel, which did not exceed twelve or fifteen feet in length and ten in breadth, was half obscured by smoke—chimney or window I saw none; the door served the various purposes of an inlet to light, and the outlet to smoke. The furniture consisted of two stools, an iron pot and a spinning-wheel—while a sack stuffed with straw, and a single blanket laid on planks, served as a bed for the repose of the whole family. Need I attempt to describe my sensations? The statement alone cannot fail of conveying, to a mind like yours, an adequate idea of them—I could not long remain a witness to this acmé of human misery. As I left the deplorable habitation, the mistress followed me to repeat her thanks for the trifle I had bestowed. This gave me an opportunity of observing her person more particularly. She was a tall figure, her countenance composed of interesting features, and with every appearance of having once been handsome.

"Unwilling to quit the village without first satisfying myself whether what I had seen was a solitary instance, or a sample of its general state; or whether the extremity of poverty I had just beheld had arisen from peculiar improvidence and want of management in one wretched family; I went into an adjoining habitation, where I found a poor old woman of eighty, whose miserable existence was painfully continued by the maintenance of her granddaughter. Their condition, if possible, was more deplorable."—*Curwen*, I. 181. 183.

This wretchedness, of which all strangers who visit Ireland are so sensible, proceeds certainly, in great measure, from their accidental use of a food so cheap, that it encourages population to an extraordinary degree, lowers the price of labour, and leaves the multitudes which it calls into existence almost destitute of every thing but food. Many more live in consequence of the introduction of potatoes; but all live in greater wretchedness. In the progress of population, the potato must, of course, become at last as difficult to be procured as any other food; and then let the political economist calculate what the immensity and wretchedness of a people must be where the farther progress of population is checked by the difficulty of procuring potatoes.

The consequence of the long mismanagement and oppression of Ireland, and of the singular circumstances in which it is placed, is, that it is a semi-barbarous country:—more shame to those who have thus ill treated a fine country, and a fine people; but it is part of the present case of Ireland. The barbarism of Ireland is evinced by the frequency and ferocity of duels,—the hereditary clannish feuds of the common people, —and the fights to which they give birth,—the atrocious cruelties practised in the insurrections of the common people—and their proneness to insurrection. The lower Irish live in a state of greater wretchedness than any other people in Europe, inhabiting so fine a soil and climate. It is difficult, often impossible, to execute the processes of law. In cases where gentlemen are concerned, it is often not even attempted. The conduct of under-sheriffs is often very corrupt.* We are afraid the magistracy of Ireland is very inferior to that of this country; the spirit of jobbing and bribery is very widely diffused, and upon occasions when the utmost purity prevails in the sister kingdom. Military force is necessary all over the country, and often for the most common and just operations of government. The behaviour of the higher to the lower orders is much less gentle and decent than in England. Blows from superiors to inferiors are more frequent, and the punishment for such aggression more doubtful. The word *gentleman* seems, in Ireland, to put an end to most processes of law. Arrest a gentleman!!!!—take out a warrant against a gentleman—are modes of operation not very common in the administration of Irish justice. If a man strikes the meanest peasant in England, he is either knocked down in his turn, or immediately taken before a magistrate. It is impossible to live in Ireland without perceiving the various points in which it is inferior in civilization. Want of unity in feeling and interest among the people,—irritability, violence and revenge,—want of comfort and cleanliness in the lower orders,—habitual disobedience to the law,—want of confidence in magistrates,—corruption, venality, the perpetual necessity of recurring to military force,—all carry back the observer to that remote and early condition of mankind, which an Englishman can learn only in the pages of the antiquary or the historian. We do not draw this picture for censure but for truth. We admire the Irish,—feel the most sincere pity for the state of Ireland, and think the conduct of the English to that country to have been a system of atrocious cruelty and contemptible meanness. With such a climate, such a soil and such a people, the inferiority of Ireland to the rest of Europe is directly chargeable to the long wickedness of the English government.

A direct consequence of the present uncivilized state of Ireland, is that very little English capital travels there. The man who deals in steam-engines and warps and woofs, is naturally alarmed by Peep-of-Day Boys, and nocturnal Carders; his object is to buy and sell as quicklly and quietly as he can; and he will naturally bear high taxes and rivalry in England, or emigrate to any part of the Continent, or to America, rather than plunge into the tumult of Irish politics and passions. There is nothing which Ireland wants more than large manufacturing towns to take off its superfluous population. But internal peace must come first, and then the arts of peace will follow. The foreign manufacturer will hardly think of embarking his capital where he cannot be sure that his existence is safe. Another check to the manufacturing greatness of Ireland, is the scarcity—not of coal—but of good coal, cheaply raised; an article in which (in spite of papers in the Irish Transactions) they are lamentably inferior to the English.

Another consequence from some of the causes we have stated, is the extreme idleness of the Irish labourer. There is nothing of the value of which the Irish seem to have so little notion as that of time. They scratch, pick, daudle, stare, gape, and do any thing but strive and wrestle with the task before them. The most ludicrous of all human objects is an Irishman ploughing.—A gigantic figure—a seven foot machine for turning potatoes into human nature, wrapt up in an immense great coat, and urging on two starved ponies, with dreadful imprecations, and uplifted shillala. The Irish crow discerns a coming perquisite, and is not inattentive to the proceedings of the steeds. The furrow which is to be the depository of the future crop, is not unlike, either in depth or regularity, to those domestic furrows which the nails of the meek and much-injured wife plough, in some family quarrel, upon the cheeks of the deservedly punished husband. The weeds seem to fall contentedly, knowing that they have fulfilled their destiny, and left behind them, for the resurrection of the ensuing spring, an abundant and healthy progeny. The whole is a scene of idleness, laziness and poverty, of which it is impossible, in this active and enterprising country, to form the most distant conception; but strongly indicative of habits, whether secondary or original, which will long present a powerful impediment to the improvement of Ireland.

The Irish character contributes something to retard the improvements of that country. The Irishman has many good qualities: he is brave witty, generous, eloquent, hospitable and open hearted; but he is vain, ostentatious, extravagant, and fond of display—light in counsel—deficient in perseverance—without skill in private or public economy—an enjoyer, not an acquirer—one who despises the slow and patient virtues—who wants the superstructure without the foundation—the result without the previous operation—the oak without the acorn and the three hundred years of expectation. The Irish are irascible, prone to debt and to fight, and very impatient of the restraints of law. Such a people are not likely to keep their eyes steadily upon the main chance, like the Scotch or the Dutch. England strove very hard, at one period, to compel the Scotch to pay a double church;—but Sawney took his pen and ink; and finding what a sum it amounted to, became furious, and drew his sword. God forbid the Irishman should do the same! the remedy, now, would be worse than the disease; but if the oppressions of England had been more steadily resisted a century ago, Ireland would not have been the scene of poverty, misery and distress which it now is.

The Catholic religion, among other causes, contributes to the backwardness and barbarism of Ireland. Its debasing superstition, childish ceremonies, and the profound submission to the priesthood which it teaches, all tend to darken men's minds, to impede the progress of knowledge and inquiry, and to prevent Ireland from becoming as free, as powerful, and as rich as

* The difficulty often is to catch the sheriff.

the sister kingdom. Though sincere friends to Catholic emancipation, we are no advocates for the Catholic religion. We should be very glad to see a general conversion to Protestantism among the Irish; but we do not think that violence, privations and incapacities are the proper methods of making proselytes.

Such, then, is Ireland, at this period,—a land more barbarous than the rest of Europe, because it has been worse treated and more cruelly oppressed. Many of the incapacities and privations to which the Catholics were exposed, have been removed by law; but, in such instances, they are still incapacitated and deprived by custom. Many cruel and oppressive laws are still enforced against them. A ninth part of the population engrosses all the honours of the country; the other nine pay a tenth of the product of the earth for the support of a religion in which they do not believe. There is little capital in the country. The great and rich men are called by business, or allured by pleasure, into England; their estates are given up to factors, and the utmost farthing of rent extorted from the poor, who, if they give up the land, cannot get employment in manufactures, or regular employment in husbandry. The common people use a sort of food so very cheap, that they can rear families, who cannot procure employment, and who have little more of the comforts of life than food. The Irish are light-minded—want of employment has made them idle—they are irritable and brave—have a keen remembrance of the past wrongs they have suffered, and the present wrongs they are suffering from England. The consequence of all this is, eternal riot and insurrection, a whole army of soldiers in time of profound peace, and general rebellion whenever England is busy with other enemies, or off her guard! And thus it will be while the same causes continue to operate, for ages to come,—and worse and worse as the rapidly increasing population of the Catholics becomes more and more numerous.

The remedies are, time and justice; and that justice consists in repealing all laws which make any distinction between the two religions; in placing over the government of Ireland, not the stupid, amiable, and insignificant noblemen who have too often been sent there, but men who feel deeply the wrongs of Ireland, and who have an ardent wish to heal them; who will take care that Catholics, when eligible, shall be elected;* who will share the patronage of Ireland proportionally among the two parties, and give to just and liberal laws the same vigour of execution which has hitherto been reserved only for decrees of tyranny, and the enactments of oppression. The injustice and hardship of supporting two churches must be put out of sight, if it cannot or ought not to be cured. The political economist, the moralist and the satirist, must combine to teach moderation and superintendence to the great Irish proprietors. Public talk and clamour may do something for the poor Irish, as it did for the slaves in the West Indies. Ireland will become more quiet under such treatment, and then more rich, more comfortable, and more civilized; and the horrid spectacle of folly and tyranny which it at present exhibits, may in time be removed from the eyes of Europe.

There are two eminent Irishmen now in the House of Commons, Lord Castlereagh and Mr. Canning, who will subscribe to the justness of every syllable we have said upon this subject; and who have it in their power, by making it the condition of their remaining in office, to liberate their native country and raise it to its just rank among the nations of the earth. Yet the court buys them over, year after year, by the pomp and perquisites of office, and year after year they come into the House of Commons, feeling deeply and describing powerfully, the injuries of five millions of their countrymen, —and continue members of a government that inflicts those evils, under the pitiful delusion that it is not a cabinet question,—as if the scratchings and quarrellings of kings and queens could alone cement politicians together in indissoluble unity, while the fate and fortune of one-third of the empire might be complimented away from one minister to another, without the smallest breach in their cabinet alliance. Politicians, at least honest politicians, should be very flexible and accommodating in little things, very rigid and inflexible in great things. And is this not a great thing? Who has painted it in finer and more commanding eloquence than Mr. Canning? Who has taken a more sensible and statesmanlike view of our miserable and cruel policy than Lord Castlereagh? You would think, to hear them, that the same planet could not contain them and the oppressors of their country,—perhaps not the same solar system. Yet for money, claret and patronage, they lend their countenance, assistance and friendship, to the ministers who are the stern and inflexible enemies to the emancipation of Ireland!

Thank God that all is not profligacy and corruption in the history of that devoted people—and that the name of Irishman does not always carry with it the idea of the oppressor or the oppressed—the plunderer or the plundered—the tyrant or the slave. Great men hallow a whole people and lift up all who live in their time. What Irishman does not feel proud that he has lived in the days of GRATTAN? who has not turned to him for comfort, from the false friends and open enemies of Ireland? who did not remember him in the days of its burnings and wastings and murders? No government ever dismayed him—the world could not bribe him—he thought only of Ireland—lived for no other object—dedicated to her his beautiful fancy, his elegant wit, his manly courage and all the splendour of his astonishing eloquence. He was so born and so gifted, that poetry, forensic skill, elegant literature and all the highest attainments of human genius, were within his reach; but he thought the noblest occupation of a man was to make other men happy and free; and in that straight line he went on for fifty years, without one side-look, without one yielding thought, without one motive in his heart which he might not have laid open to the view of God and man. He is gone!—but there is not a single day of his honest life of which every good

* Great merit is due to the Whigs for the patronage bestowed on Catholics.

Irishman would not be more proud, than of the whole political existence of his countrymen—the annual deserters and betrayers of their native land.

SPRING-GUNS.*

[Edinburgh Review, 1821.]

When Lord Dacre (then Mr. Brand) brought into the House of Commons his bill for the amendment of the game laws, a system of greater mercy and humanity was in vain recommended to that popular branch of the legislature. The interests of humanity, and the interests of the lord of the manor, were not, however, opposed to each other; nor any attempt made to deny the superior importance of the last. No such bold or alarming topics were agitated; but it was contended that, if laws were less ferocious, there would be more partridges—if the lower orders of mankind were not torn from their families and banished to Botany Bay, hares and pheasants would be increased in number, or, at least, not diminished. It is not, however, till after long experience that mankind ever think of recurring to humane expedients for effecting their objects. The rulers who ride the people never think of coaxing and petting till they have worn out the lashes of their whips, and broken the rowels of their spurs. The legislators of the trigger replied, that two laws had lately passed which would answer their purpose of preserving game: the one, an act for transporting men found with arms in their hands for the purposes of killing game in the night; the other, an act for rendering the buyers of the game equally guilty with the seller, and for involving both in the same penalty. Three seasons have elapsed since the last of these laws was passed; and we appeal to the experience of all the great towns in England, whether the difficulty of procuring game is in the slightest degree increased?—whether hares, partridges and pheasants are not purchased with as much facility as before the passing this act?—whether the price of such unlawful commodities is even in the slightest degree increased? Let the Assize and Sessions' calendars bear witness, whether the law for transporting poachers has not had the most direct tendency to encourage brutal assaults and ferocious murders. There is hardly now a jail-delivery in which some gamekeeper has not murdered a poacher—or some poacher a gamekeeper. If the question concerned the payment of five pounds, a poacher would hardly risk his life rather than be taken; but when he is to go to Botany Bay for seven years, he summons together his brother poachers—they get brave from rum, numbers and despair—and a bloody battle ensues.

Another method by which it is attempted to defeat the depredations of the poacher, is by setting spring-guns to murder any person who comes within their reach; and it is to this last new feature in the *supposed* game laws, to which, on the present occasion, we intend principally to confine our notice.

We utterly disclaim all hostility to the game laws in general. Game ought to belong to those who feed it. All the landowners in England are fairly entitled to all the game in England. These laws are constructed upon a basis of substantial justice; but there is a great deal of absurdity and tyranny mingled with them, and a perpetual and vehement desire on the part of the country gentlemen to push the provisions of these laws up to the highest point of tyrannical severity.

"Is it lawful to put to death by a spring-gun, or any other machine, an unqualified person trespassing upon your woods or fields in pursuit of game, and who has received due notice of your intention, and of the risk to which he is exposed?" This, we think, is stating the question as fairly as can be stated. We purposely exclude gardens, orchards and all contiguity to the dwelling-house. We exclude, also, all felonious intention on the part of the deceased. The object of his expedition shall be proved to be game; and the notice he received of his danger shall be allowed to be as complete as possible. It must also be part of the case, that the spring-gun was placed there for the express purpose of defending the game, by killing or wounding the poacher, or spreading terror, or doing any thing that a reasonable man ought to know would happen from such a proceeding.

Suppose any gentleman were to give notice that all other persons must abstain from his manors; that he himself and his servants paraded the woods and fields with loaded pistols and blunderbusses, and would shoot any body who fired at a partridge; and suppose he were to keep his word, and shoot through the head some rash trespasser who defied this bravado, and was determined to have his sport:—Is there any doubt that he would be guilty of murder? We suppose no resistance on the part of the trespasser; but that, the moment he passes the line of demarcation with his dogs and gun, he is shot dead by the proprietor of the land from behind a tree. If this is not murder, what is murder? We will make the case a little better for the homicide squire. It shall be night; the poacher, an unqualified person, steps over the line of demarcation with his nets and snares, and is instantly shot through the head by the

* *The Shooter's Guide.* By J. B. Johnson. 12mo. Edwards and Knibb, 1819.

pistol of the proprietor. We have no doubt that this would be murder—that it ought to be considered as murder, and punished as murder. We think this so clear that it would be a waste of time to argue it. There is no kind of resistance on the part of the deceased; no attempt to run away; he is not even challenged: but instantly shot dead by the proprietor of the wood, for no other crime than *the intention* of killing game unlawfully. We do not suppose that any man, possessed of the elements of law and common sense, would deny this to be a case of murder, let the previous notice to the deceased have been as perfect as it could be. It is true, a trespasser in a park may be killed; but then it is when he will not render himself to the keepers, upon a hue and cry to stand to the king's peace. But deer are property, game is not; and this power of slaying deer-stealers is by the 21st Edward I., *de Malefactoribus in Parcis*, and by 3d and 4th William & Mary, c. 10. So rioters may be killed, house-burners, ravishers, felons refusing to be arrested, felons escaping, felons breaking jail, men resisting a civil process—may all be put to death. All these cases of justifiable homicide are laid down and admitted in our books. But who ever heard that to pistol a poacher was justifiable homicide? It has long been decided that it is unlawful to kill a dog who is pursuing game in a manor. "To decide the contrary," says Lord Ellenborough, "would outrage reason and sense." (Vere *v.* Lord Cawdor and King, 11 *East*, 368.) Pointers have always been treated by the legislature with great delicacy and consideration. To "*wish to be a dog and to bay the moon*," is not quite so mad a wish as the poet thought it.

If these things are so, what is the difference between the act of firing yourself, and placing an engine which does the same thing? In the one case your hand pulls the trigger; in the other, it places the wire which communicates with the trigger, and causes the death of the trespasser. There is the same intention of slaying in both cases—there is precisely the same human agency in both cases; only the steps are rather more numerous in the latter case. As to the bad effects of allowing proprietors of game to put trespassers to death at once, or to set guns that will do it, we can have no hesitation in saying, that the first method, of giving the power of life and death to esquires, would be by far the most humane. For, as we have observed in a previous Essay on the Game Laws, a live armigeral spring-gun would distinguish an accidental trespasser from a real poacher—a woman or a boy from a man—perhaps might spare a friend or an acquaintance—or a father of a family with ten children—or a small freeholder who voted for administration. But this new rural artillery must destroy, without mercy and selection, every one who approaches it.

In the case of Ilot *versus* Wilks, Esq., the four judges, Abbot, Bailey, Holroyd and Best, gave their opinions *seriatim* on points connected with this question. In this case, as reported in Chetwynd's edition of Burn's Justice, 1820, vol. ii. p. 500, Abbot, C. J. observes as follows:—

"I cannot say that repeated and increasing acts of aggression may not reasonably call for increased means of defence and protection. I believe that many of the persons who cause engines of this description to be placed in their grounds, do not do so with an intention to injure any person, but really believe that the publication of notices will prevent any person from sustaining an injury; and that no person having the notice given him, will be weak and foolish enough to expose himself to the perilous consequences of his trespass. Many persons who place such engines in their grounds, do so for the purpose of preventing, by means of terror, injury to their property, rather than from any motive of doing malicious injury."

"Increased means of defence and protection," but increased (his lordship should remember) from the payment of five pounds to instant death—and instant death inflicted, not by the arm of law, but by the arm of the proprietor;—could the Lord Chief Justice of the King's Bench intend to say, that the impossibility of putting an end to poaching by other means would justify the infliction of death upon the offender? Is he so ignorant of the philosophy of punishing, as to imagine he has nothing to do but to give ten stripes instead of two, an hundred instead of ten, and a thousand, if an hundred will not do? to substitute the prison for pecuniary fines, and the gallows instead of the jail? It is impossible so enlightened a judge can forget, that the sympathies of mankind must be consulted; that it would be wrong to break a person upon the wheel for stealing a penny loaf, and that gradations in punishments must be carefully accommodated to gradations in crime; that if poaching is punished more than mankind in general think it ought to be punished, the fault will either escape with impunity, or the delinquent be driven to desperation; that if poaching and murder are punished equally, every poacher will be an assassin. Besides, too, if the principle is right in the unlimited and unqualified manner in which the chief justice puts it—if defence goes on increasing with aggression, the legislature at least must determine upon their equal pace. If an act of Parliament made it a capital offence to poach upon a manor, as it is to commit a burglary in a dwelling-house, it might then be as lawful to shoot a person for trespassing upon your manor as it is to kill a thief for breaking into your house. But the real question is—and so in sound reasoning his lordship should have put it—"If the law at this moment determines the aggression to be in such a state that it merits only a pecuniary fine after summons and proof, has any sporadic squire the right to say, that it shall be punished with death, before any summons and without any proof?"

It appears to us, too, very singular to say that many persons who cause engines of this description to be placed in their ground, do not do so with an intention of injuring any person, but really believe that the publication of notices will prevent any person from sustaining an injury, and that no person, having the notice given him, will be weak and foolish enough to expose himself to the perilous consequences of his trespass. But if this is the real belief of the engineer—if he thinks the mere notice will keep people away—then he must think it a mere inutility that the guns should be placed at all; if he thinks that many will be deterred, and a few come, then he must mean to shoot those few. He who believes his gun will never be called upon to do its duty, need set no gun, and trust to rumour of their being set, or being loaded for his protection. Against the gun and the powder we have no complaint; they are perfectly fair and admissible: our quarrel is with the bullets. He who sets a *loaded* gun, means that it should go off if it is touched. But what signifies the mere empty wish that there may be no mischief, when I perform an action which my common sense tells me may produce the worst mischief? If I hear a great noise in the street, and fire a bullet to keep people quiet, I may not, perhaps, have intended to kill; I may have wished to have produced quiet by mere terror, and I may have expressed a strong hope that my object has been effected without the destruction of human life. Still I have done that which every man of sound intellect knows is likely to kill; and if any one falls from my act, I am guilty of murder.—"Further," (says Lord Coke,) "if there be an evil intent, though that intent extendeth not to death, it is murder. Thus, if a man, knowing that many people are in the street, throw a stone over the wall, intending only to frighten them, or to give them a little hurt, and thereupon one is killed—this is murder—for he had an ill intent; though that intent extended not to death, and though he knew not the party slain." (3 *Inst.* 57.) If a man is not mad, he must be presumed to foresee common consequences if he puts a bullet into a spring gun—he may be supposed to foresee that it will kill any poacher who touches the wire—and to that consequence he must stand. We do not suppose all preservers of game to be so bloodily inclined that they would prefer the death of a poacher to his staying away. Their object is to preserve game; they have no objection to preserve the lives of their fellow-creatures, also, if both can exist at the same time; if not, the least worthy of God's creatures must fall—the rustic without a soul—not the Christian partridge—not the immortal pheasant—not the rational woodcock, or the accountable hare.

The chief justice quotes the instance of glass and spikes fixed upon walls. He cannot mean to infer from this, because the law connives at the infliction of such small punishments for the protection of property, that it does allow, or ought to allow, proprietors to proceed to the punishment of death. Small means of annoying trespassers may be consistently admitted by the law, though more severe ones are forbidden, and ought to be forbidden; unless it follows, that what is good in any degree, is good in the highest degree. You may correct a servant boy with a switch; but if you bruise him sorely, you are to be indicted—if you kill him, you are hanged. A blacksmith corrected his servant with a bar of iron; the boy died, and the blacksmith was executed. (Grey's Case, *Kel.* 64, 65.) A woman kicked and stamped on the belly of her child—she was found guilty of murder. (1 *East, P. C.* 261.) *Si immoderate suo jure utatur, tunc reus homicidii sit.* There is, besides, this additional difference in the two cases put by the chief justice, that no publication of notices can be so plain, in the case of the guns, as the sight of the glass or the spikes; for a trespasser may not believe in the notice which he receives, or he may think he shall see a gun, and so avoid it, or that he may have the good luck to avoid it, if he does not see it; whereas, of the presence of the glass or the spikes he can have no doubt; and he has no hope of placing his hand in any spot where they are not. In the one case, he cuts his fingers upon full and perfect notice, the notice of his own senses; in the other case, he loses his life after a notice which he may disbelieve, and by an engine which he may hope to escape.

Mr. Justice Bailey observes, in the same case, that it is not an indictable offence to set spring-guns: perhaps not. It is not an indictable offence to go about with a loaded pistol, intending to shoot any body who grins at you; but if you do it, you are hanged; many inchoate acts are innocent, the consummation of which is a capital offence.

This is not a case where the motto applies of *Volenti non fit injuria.* The man does not will to be hurt, but he wills to get the game; and, with that rash confidence natural to many characters, believes he shall avoid the evil and gain the good. On the contrary, it is a case which exactly arranges itself under the maxim, *Quando aliquid prohibetur ex directo, prohibetur et per obliquum.* Give what notice he may, the proprietor cannot lawfully shoot a trespasser (who neither runs nor resists) with a loaded pistol;—he cannot do it *ex directo;*—how then can he do it *per obliquum*, by arranging on the ground the pistol which commits the murder?

Mr. Justice Best delivers the following opinion. His lordship concluded as follows:—

"This case has been discussed at the bar, as if these engines were exclusively resorted to for the protection of game; but I consider them as lawfully applicable to the protection of every species of property against unlawful trespassers. But if even they might not lawfully be used for the protection of game, I, for one, should be extremely glad to adopt such means, if they were found sufficient for that purpose; because I think it a great object that gentlemen should have a temptation to reside in the country, amongst their neighbours and tenantry, whose interests must be materially advanced by such a circumstance. The links of society are thereby better preserved, and the mutual advantage and dependence of the higher and lower classes of society, existing between each other, more beneficially maintained. We have seen, in a neighbouring country, the baneful consequences of the non-residence of the landed gentry; and in an ingenious work, lately published by a foreigner, we learn the fatal effects of a like system on the Continent. By preserving game, gentlemen are tempted to reside in the country; and, considering that the diversion of the field is the only one of which they can partake on the estates, I am of opinion that, for the purpose I have stated, it is of essential importance that this species of property should be inviolably protected."

If this speech of Mr. Justice Best is correctly reported, it follows, that a man may put his fellow-creatures to death for any infringement of his property—for picking the sloes and black berries off his hedges—for breaking a few dead sticks out of them by night or by day—with resistance or without resistance—with warning or without warning;—a strange method this of keeping up the links of society, and maintaining the dependence of the lower upon the higher classes. It certainly is of importance that gentlemen should reside on their estates in the country; but not that gentlemen with such opinions as these should reside. The more they are absent from the country, the less strain will there be upon those links to which the learned judge alludes—the more firm that dependence upon which he places so just a value. In the case of Dean *versus* Clayton, Bart., the Court of Common Pleas were equally divided upon the lawfulness of killing a dog coursing an hare by means of a concealed dog-spear. We confess that we cannot see the least difference between transfixing with a spear, or placing a spear so that it will transfix; and, therefore, if Vere *versus* Lord Cawdor and King is good law, the action could have been maintained in Dean *versus* Clayton; but the solemn consideration concerning the life of the pointer is highly creditable to all the judges. They none of them say that it is lawful to put a trespassing pointer to death under any circumstances, or that they themselves would be glad to do it; they all seem duly impressed with the recollection that they are deciding the fate of an animal faithfully ministerial to the pleasures of the upper classes of society; there is an awful desire to do their duty, and a dread of any rash and intemperate decision. Seriously speaking, we can hardly believe this report of Mr. Justice Best's speech to be correct; yet we take it from a book which guides the practice of nine-tenths of all the magistrates in England. Does a judge,—a cool, calm man, in whose hands are the issues of life and death—from whom so many miserable, trembling human beings await their destiny—does he tell us, and tell us in a court of justice, that he places such little value on the life of man, that he himself would plot the destruction of his fellow-creatures for the preservation of a few hares and partridges? "Nothing which falls from me" (says Mr. Justice Bailey) "shall have a tendency to encourage the practice."—"I consider them" (says Mr. Justice Best) "as lawfully applicable to the protection of every species of property; but even if they might not lawfully be used for the protection of game, *I for one should be extremely glad to adopt them*, if they were found sufficient for that purpose." Can any man doubt to which of these two magistrates he would rather entrust a decision on his life, his liberty and his possessions? We should be very sorry to misrepresent Mr. Justice Best, and will give to his disavowal of such sentiments, if he does disavow them, all the publicity in our power; but we have cited his very words conscientiously and correctly, as they are given in the Law Report. We have no doubt he meant to do his duty; we blame not his motives, but his feelings and his reasoning.

Let it be observed that, in the whole of this case, we have put every circumstance in favour of the murder. We have supposed it to be in the night time; but a man may be shot in the day* by a spring-gun. We have supposed the deceased to be a poacher; but he may be a very innocent man, who has missed his way—an unfortunate botanist, or a lover. We have supposed notice; but it is a very possible event that the dead man may have been utterly ignorant of the notice. This instrument, so highly approved of by Mr. Justice Best—this knitter together of the different orders of society—is levelled promiscuously against the guilty or the innocent, the ignorant and the informed. No man who sets such an infernal machine, believes that it can reason or discriminate; it is made to murder all alike, and it does murder all alike.

Blackstone says, that the law of England, like that of every other well-regulated community, is tender of the public peace, and careful of the lives of the subjects; "that it will not suffer with impunity any crime to be prevented by death, *unless the same, if committed, would also be punished by death.*" (*Commentaries*, vol. iv. 182.) "The law sets so high a value upon the life of a man, that it always intends some misbehaviour in the person who takes it away, unless by the command, or express permission of the law."—"And as to the necessity which excuses a man who kills another *se defendendo*, Lord Bacon calls even that *necessitas culpabilis*." (*Commentaries*, vol. iv. p. 187.) So far this luminary of the law.—But the very amusements of the rich are, in the estimation of Mr. Justice Best, of so great importance, that the poor are to be exposed to sudden death who interfere with them. There are other persons of the same opinion with this magistrate respecting the pleasures of the rich. In the last session of Parliament a bill was passed, entitled "An act for the summary punishment, in certain cases, of persons wilfully or maliciously damaging, or committing trespasses on public or private property." *Anno primo*—(a bad specimen of what is to happen)—*Georgii IV. Regis*, cap. 56. In this act it is provided, that "if any person shall wilfully, *or* maliciously, commit any damage, injury, or spoil, upon any building, fence, hedge, gate, stile, guide-post, milestone, tree, wood, underwood, orchard, garden, nursery-ground, crops, vegetables, plants, land, or other matter or thing growing or being therein, or to or upon real or personal property of any nature or kind soever, he may be immediately seized by any body, without a warrant, taken before a magistrate, and fined (according to the mischief he has done) to the extent of 5*l.*; or, in default of payment, may be committed to the jail for three months." And at the end comes a clause, exempting from the operation of this act *all mischief done in hunting, and by shooters who are qualified.* This is surely the most impudent piece of legislation that ever crept into the statute-book; and, coupled with Mr. Justice Best's declaration, constitutes the following affectionate relation between the different orders of society. Says the higher link to the lower, "If you meddle with my game, I will immediately murder you;—if you commit the slightest injury upon my real or personal property, I will take you before a magistrate, and fine you five pounds. I am in

* Large damages have been given for wounds inflicted by spring-guns set in a garden in the day-time, where the party wounded had no notice

Parliament, and you are not; and I have just brought in an act of Parliament for that purpose. But so important is it to you that my pleasures should not be interrupted, that I have exempted myself and friends from the operation of this act; and we claim the right (without allowing you any such summary remedy) of riding over your fences, hedges, gates, stiles, guide-posts, milestones, woods, underwoods, orchards, gardens, nursery-grounds, crops, vegetables, plants, lands or other matters or things growing or being thereupon—including your children and yourselves, if you do not get out of the way." Is there, upon earth, such a mockery of justice as an act of Parliament, pretending to protect property, sending a poor hedge-breaker to jail, and specially exempting from its operation the accusing and the judging squire, who, at the tail of the hounds, have that morning, perhaps, ruined as much wheat and seeds as would purchase fuel a whole year for a whole village?

It cannot be urged, in extenuation of such a murder as we have described, that the artificer of death had no particular malice against the deceased; that his object was general, and his indignation leveled against offenders in the aggregate. Every body knows that there is a malice by implication of law.

"In general, any formal design of doing mischief may be called malice; and therefore, not such killing only as proceeds from premeditated hatred and revenge against the person killed, but also, in many other cases, such as is accompanied with those circumstances that show the heart to be perversely wicked, is adjudged to be of malice prepense."—2 *Haw.* c. 31.

"For where the law makes use of the term, malice aforethought, as descriptive of the crime of murder, it is not to be understood in that narrow restrained sense in which the modern use of the word *malice* is apt to lead one, a principle of malevolence to particulars; for the law, by the term malice, *malitia*, in this instance, meaneth, that the fact hath been attended with such circumstances as are the ordinary symptoms of a wicked heart, regardless of social duty, and fatally bent upon mischief."—*Fost.* 256, 257.

Ferocity is the natural weapon of the common people. If gentlemen of education and property contend with them at this sort of warfare, they will probably be defeated in the end. If spring-guns are generally set—if the common people are murdered by them, and the legislature does not interfere, the posts of gamekeeper and lord of the manor will soon be posts of honour and danger. The greatest curse under heaven (witness Ireland) is a peasantry demoralized by the barbarity and injustice of their rulers.

It is expected by some persons, that the severe operation of these engines will put an end to the trade of a poacher. This has always been predicated of every fresh operation of severity, that it was to put an end to poaching. But if this argument is good for one thing, it is good for another. Let the first pickpocket who is taken be hung alive by the ribs, and let him be a fortnight in wasting to death. Let us seize a little grammar boy, who is robbing orchards, tie his arms and legs, throw over him a delicate puff paste, and bake him in a bun-pan in an oven. If poaching can be extirpated by intensity of punishment, why not all other crimes? If racks and gibbets and tenter-hooks are the best method of bringing back the golden age, why do we refrain from so easy a receipt for abolishing every species of wickedness? The best way of answering a bad argument is not to stop it, but to let it go on in its course till it leaps over the boundaries of common sense. There is a little book called *Beccaria on Crimes and Punishments*, which we strongly recommend to the attention of Mr. Justice Best. He who has not read it, is neither fit to make laws, nor to administer them when made.

As to the idea of abolishing poaching altogether, we will believe that poaching is abolished when it is found impossible to buy game; or when they have risen so greatly in price, that none but people of fortune can buy them. But we are convinced this never can, and never will happen. All the traps and guns in the world will never prevent the wealth of the merchant and manufacturer from commanding the game of the landed gentleman. You may, in the pursuit of this visionary purpose, render the common people savage, ferocious and vindictive; you may disgrace your laws by enormous punishments, and the national character by these new secret assassinations; but you will never separate the wealthy glutton from his pheasant. The best way is, to take what you want, and sell the rest fairly and openly. This is the real spring-gun and steel trap which will annihilate, not the unlawful trader, but the unlawful trade.

There is a sort of horror in thinking of a whole land filled with lurking engines of death—machinations against human life under every green tree—traps and guns in every dusky dell and bosky bourn—the *feræ naturâ*, the lords of manors eyeing their peasantry as so many butts and marks, and panting to hear the click of the trap, and to see the flash of the gun. How any human being, educated in liberal knowledge and Christian feeling, can doom to certain destruction a poor wretch tempted by the sight of animals that naturally appear to him to belong to one person as well as another, we are at a loss to conceive. We cannot imagine how he could live in the same village, and see the widow and orphans of the man whose blood he had shed for such a trifle. We consider a person who could do this, to be deficient in the very elements of morals—to want that sacred regard to human life which is one of the corner stones of civil society. If he sacrifices the life of man for his mere pleasures, he would do so, if he dared, for the lowest and least of his passions. He may be defended, perhaps, by the abominable injustice of the game laws—though we think and hope he is not. But there rests upon his head, and there is marked in his account, the deep and indelible sin of *blood-guiltiness.*

PRISONS.*

[Edinburgh Review, 1821.]

There are, in every county in England, large public schools, maintained at the expense of the county, for the encouragement of profligacy and vice, and for providing a proper succession of house-breakers, profligates and thieves. They are schools, too, conducted without the smallest degree of partiality or favour; there being no man (however mean his birth, or obscure his situation,) who may not easily procure admission to them. The moment any young person evinces the slightest propensity for these pursuits, he is provided with food, clothing and lodging, and put to his studies under the most accomplished thieves and cut-throats the county can supply. There is not, to be sure, a formal arrangement of lectures, after the manner of our universities; but the petty larcenous stripling, being left destitute of every species of employment and locked up with accomplished villains as idle as himself, listens to their pleasant narrative of successful crimes, and pants for the hour of freedom, that he may begin the same bold and interesting career.

This is a perfectly true picture of the prison establishments of many counties in England, and was so, till very lately, of almost all; and the effects so completely answered the design, that, in the year 1818, there were committed to the jails of the United Kingdom more than one hundred and seven thousand persons!† a number supposed to be greater than that of all the commitments in the other kingdoms of Europe put together.

The bodily treatment of prisoners has been greatly improved since the time of Howard. There is still, however, much to do; and the attention of good and humane people has been lately called to their state of moral discipline.

It is inconceivable to what a spirit of party this has given birth;—all the fat and sleek people,—the enjoyers,—the mumpsimus, and "well as we are" people, are perfectly outrageous at being compelled to do their duty, and to sacrifice time and money to the lower orders of mankind. Their first resource was, to deny all the facts which were brought forward for the purposes of amendment; and the alderman's sarcasm of the Turkey carpet in jails was bandied from one hard-hearted and fat-witted gentleman to another: but the advocates of prison improvement are men in earnest—not playing at religion, but of deep feeling, and of indefatigable industry in charitable pursuits. Mr. Buxton went in company with men of the most irreproachable veracity; and found, in the heart of the metropolis, and in a prison of which the very Turkey carpet alderman was an official visitor, scenes of horror, filth and cruelty, which would have disgraced even the interior of a slave-ship.

This dislike of innovation proceeds sometimes from the disgust excited by false humanity, canting hypocrisy, and silly enthusiasm. It proceeds, also, from a stupid and indiscriminate horror of change, whether of evil for good, or good for evil. There is also much party spirit in these matters. A good deal of these humane projects and institutions originates from Dissenters. The plunderers of the public, the jobbers, and those who sell themselves to some great man, who sells himself to a greater, all scent from afar the danger of political change—are sensible that the correction of one abuse may lead to that of another—feel uneasy at any visible operation of public spirit and justice—hate and tremble at a man who exposes and rectifies abuses from a sense of duty—and think, if such things are suffered to be, that their candle-ends and cheese-parings are no longer safe: and these sagacious persons, it must be said for them, are not very wrong in this feeling. Providence, which has denied to them all that is great and good, has given them a fine tact for the preservation of their plunder: their real enemy is the spirit of inquiry—the dislike of wrong—the love of right—and the courage and diligence which are the concomitants of these virtues. When once this spirit is up, it may be as well directed to one abuse as another. To say you must not torture a prisoner with bad air and bad food, and to say you must not tax me without my consent or that of my representative, are both emanations of the same principle, occurring to the same sort of understanding, congenial to the same disposition, published, protected and enforced by the same qualities. This it is that really excites the horror against Mrs. Fry, Mr. Gurney, Mr. Bennet, and Mr. Buxton. Alarmists such as we have described have no particular wish that prisons should be dirty, jailers cruel, or prisoners wretched; they care little about such matters either way; but all their malice and meanness are called up into action when they see secrets brought to light, and abuses giving way before the diffusion of intelligence, and the aroused feelings of justice and compassion. As for us, we have neither love of change, nor fear of it; but a love of what is just and wise, as far as we are able to find it out. In this spirit we shall offer a few observa-

---

*1. *Thoughts on the Criminal Prisons of this Country, occasioned by the Bill now in the House of Commons, for Consolidating and amending the Laws relating to Prisons; with some Remarks on the Practice of looking to the Task-Master of the Prison rather than to the Chaplain for the Reformation of Offenders; and of purchasing the Work of those whom the Law has condemned to Hard Labour as a Punishment, by allowing them to spend a Portion of their Earnings during their Imprisonment.* By George Holford, Esq. M. P. Rivington. 1821.

2. *Gurney on Prisons.* Constable and Co. 1819.

3. *Report of Society for bettering the Condition of Prisons.* Bensley. 1820.

† Report of Prison Society, xiv.

tions upon prisons, and upon the publications before us.

The new law should keep up the distinction between jails and houses of correction. One of each should exist in every country, either at a distance from each other, or in such a state of juxtaposition that they might be under the same governor. To the jail should be committed all persons accused of capital offences, whose trials would come on at the assizes; to the house of correction, all offenders whose cases would be cognizable at the Quarter Sessions. Sentence of imprisonment in the house of correction, after trial, should carry with it hard labour; sentence of imprisonment in the jail, after trial, should imply an exemption from compulsory labour. There should be no compulsory labour in jails—only in houses of correction. In using the terms *Jail* and House of Correction, we shall always attend to these distinctions. Prisoners for trial should not only not be compelled to labour, but they should have every indulgence shown to them compatible with safety. No chains—much better diet than they commonly have — all possible access to their friends and relations—and means of earning money if they choose it. The broad and obvious distinction between prisoners before and after trial should constantly be attended to; to violate it is gross tyranny and cruelty.

The jails for men and women should be so far separated, that nothing could be seen or heard from one to the other. The men should be divided into two classes: 1*st*, those who are not yet tried; 2*d*, those who are tried and convicted. The first class should be divided into those who are accused as misdemeanants and as felons; and each of these into first misdemeanants and second misdemeanants, men of better and worse character; and the same with felons. The second class should be divided into, 1*st*, persons condemned to death; 2*dly*, persons condemned for transportation; 3*dly*, first class of confined, or men of the best character under sentence of confinement; 4*thly*, second *confined*, or men of worse character under sentence of confinement. To these are to be added separate places for king's evidence, boys, lunatics, and places for the first reception of prisoners, before they can be examined and classed:—a chapel, hospital, yards and workshops for such as are willing to work.

The classifications in jails will then be as follows:—

Men before Trial.	*Men after Trial.*
1*st* Misdemeanants.	Sentenced to death.
2*d* Ditto.	Ditto transportation.
1*st* Felons.	1*st* Confined.
2*d* Ditto.	2*d* Confined.

Other Divisions in a Jail.

King's Evidence.
Criminal Lunatics.
Boys.
Prisoners on their first reception.
And the same divisions for Women.

But there is a division still more important than any of these; and that is, a division into much smaller numbers than are gathered together in prisons:—40, 50 and even 70 and 80 felons are often placed together in one yard and live together for months previous to their trial. Any classification of offences, while there is such a multitude living together of one class, is perfectly nugatory and ridiculous; no character can escape from corruption and extreme vice in such a school. The law ought to be peremptory against the confinement of more than fifteen persons together of the same class. Unless some measure of this kind is resorted to, all reformation in prisons is impossible.*

A very great, and a very neglected object in prisons, is diet. There should be, in every jail and house of correction, four sorts of diet;—1*st*, Bread and water; 2*dly*, Common prison diet, to be settled by the magistrates; 3*dly*, Best prison diet, to be settled by ditto; 4*thly*, Free diet, from which spirituous liquors altogether and fermented liquors in excess, are excluded. All prisoners, before trial, should be allowed best prison diet and be upon free diet if they could afford it. Every sentence for imprisonment should expressly mention to which diet the prisoner is confined; and no other diet should be, on any account, allowed to such prisoner after his sentence. Nothing can be so preposterous and criminally careless as the way in which persons confined upon sentence are suffered to live in prison. Misdemeanants, who have money in their pockets, may be seen in many of our prisons with fish, buttered veal, rump steaks and every other kind of luxury; and as the practice prevails of allowing them to purchase a pint of ale each, the rich prisoner purchases many pints of ale in the name of his poorer brethren and drinks them himself. A jail should be a place of punishment, from which men recoil with horror—a place of real suffering, painful to the memory, terrible to the imagination; but if men can live idly, and live luxuriously, in a clean, well-aired, well-warmed, spacious habitation, is it any wonder that they set the law at defiance, and brave that magistrate who restores them to their former luxury and ease? There are a set of men well known to jailers, called *Familymen*, who are constantly returning to jail, and who may be said to spend the greater part of their life there,—up to the time when they are hanged.

Minutes of Evidence taken before Select Committee on Gaols

"Mr. WILLIAM BEEBY, *Keeper of the New Clerkenwell Prison.*—Have you many prisoners that return to you on re-commitment? A vast number; some of them are frequently discharged in the morning and I have them back again in the evening; or they have been discharged in the evening, and I have had them back in the morning."—*Evidence before the Committee of the House of Commons in* 1819, p. 278.

"FRANCIS CONST, Esq., *Chairman of the Middlesex Quarter-sessions.*—Has that opinion been confirmed by any conduct you have observed in prisoners that have come before you for trial? I only judge from the opposite thing, that, going into a place where they can be idle, and well protected from any inconveniences of the weather and other things that poverty is open

* We should much prefer solitary imprisonment; but are at present speaking of the regulations in jails where that system is excluded.

to, they are not amended at all; they laugh at it frequently, and desire to go to the house of correction. Once or twice, in the early part of the winter, upon sending a prisoner for two months, he has asked whether he could not stay longer, or words to that effect. It is an insulting way of saying they like it."—*Evidence before the Committee of the House of Commons in* 1819, p. 285.

The fact is, that a thief is a very dainty gentleman. *Male parta cito dilabuntur.* He does not rob to lead a life of mortification and self-denial. The difficulty of controlling his appetites, in all probability, first led him to expenses, which made him a thief to support them. Having lost character and become desperate, he orders crab and lobster and veal cutlets at a public house, while a poor labourer is refreshing himself with bread and cheese. The most vulnerable part of a thief is his belly; and there is nothing he feels more bitterly in confinement than a long course of water-gruel and flour-puddings. It is a mere mockery of punishment to say, that such a man shall spend his money in luxurious viands, and sit down to dinner with fetters on his feet, and fried pork in his stomach.

Restriction to diet in prisons is still more necessary, when it is remembered that it is impossible to avoid making a prison, in some respects, more eligible than the home of a culprit. It is almost always more spacious, cleaner, better ventilated, better warmed. All these advantages are inevitable on the side of the prison. The means, therefore, that remain of making a prison a disagreeable place, are not to be neglected; and of these, none are more powerful than the regulation of diet. If this is neglected, the meaning of sentencing a man to prison will be this—and it had better be put in these words—

"Prisoner at the bar, you are fairly convicted, by a jury of your country, of having feloniously stolen two pigs, the property of Stephen Muck, farmer. The court having taken into consideration the frequency and enormity of this offence, and the necessity of restraining it with the utmost severity of punishment, do order and adjudge that you be confined for six months in a house larger, better aired, and warmer than your own, in company with 20 or 30 young persons in as good health and spirits as yourself. You need do no work, and you may have any thing for breakfast, dinner and supper, you can buy. In passing this sentence, the court hope that your example will be a warning to others; and that evil-disposed persons will perceive, from your suffering, that the laws of their country are not to be broken with impunity."

As the diet, according to our plan, is always to be a part of the sentence, a judge will, of course, consider the nature of the offence for which the prisoner is committed, as well as the quality of the prisoner: and we have before stated, that all prisoners, before trial, should be upon the best prison diet, and unrestricted as to what they could purchase, always avoiding intemperance.

These gradations of diet being fixed in all prisons, and these definitions of Jail and House of Correction being adhered to, the punishment of imprisonment may be apportioned with the greatest nicety, either by the statute, or at the discretion of the judge, if the law chooses to give him that discretion. There will be—

Imprisonment for different degrees of time.

Imprisonment solitary, or in company, or in darkness.

In jails without labour.

In houses of correction with labour.

Imprisonment with diet on bread and water.

Imprisonment with common prison diet.

Imprisonment with best prison diet.

Imprisonment with free diet.

Every sentence of the judge should state diet, as well as light or darkness, time, place, solitude, society, labour or ease; and we are strongly of opinion, that the punishment in prisons should be sharp and short. We would, in most cases, give as much of solitary confinement as would not injure men's minds, and as much of bread and water diet as would not injure their bodies. A return to prison should be contemplated with horror—horror, not excited by the ancient filth, disease and extortion of jails; but by calm, well-regulated, well-watched austerity—by the gloom and sadness wisely and intentionally thrown over such an abode. Six weeks of such sort of imprisonment would be much more efficacious than as many months of jolly company and veal cutlets.

It appears, by the Times newspaper of the 24th of June, 1821, that two persons, a man and his wife, were committed at the Surrey Sessions for three years. If this county jail is bad, to three years of idleness and good living—if it is a manufacturing jail, to three years of regular labour, moderate living and accumulated gains. They are committed *principally* for a warning to others, partly for their own good. Would not these ends have been much more effectually answered, if they had been committed for nine months, to solitary cells upon bread and water; the first and last month in dark cells? If this is too severe, then lessen the duration still more, and give them more light days and fewer dark ones; but we are convinced the whole good sought may be better obtained in much shorter periods than are now resorted to.

For the purpose of making jails disagreeable, the prisoners should remain perfectly alone all night, if it is not thought proper to render their confinement entirely solitary during the whole period of their imprisonment. Prisoners dislike this—and *therefore* it should be done; it would make their residence in jails more disagreeable, and render them unwilling to return there. At present, eight or ten women sleep in a room with a good fire, pass the night in sound sleep or pleasant conversation; and this is called confinement in a prison. A prison is a place where men, after trial and sentence, should be made unhappy by public lawful enactments, not so severe as to injure the soundness of mind or body. If this is not done, prisons are a mere invitation to the lower classes to wade through felony and larceny to better accommodations than they can procure at home And here, as it appears to us, is the mistake of the many excellent men who busy themselves (and wisely and humanely busy themselves) about prisons. Their first object seems to be the reformation of the prisoners, not the reformation of the public; whereas the first object should be, the discomfort and discontent of their prisoners; that they should become a warning, feel unhappy, and resolve never to act so again as to put themselves in the same predicament; and then as much reformation as is compatible with this the better. If a man says to himself, this prison is a comfortable place, while he says to the chaplain or the visitor that he will come there no more, we confess we have no great confidence in his public declaration; but if he says "this is a place of misery and sorrow, you shall not catch me here again," there is much reason to believe he will be as good as his word; and he then becomes (which is of much more consequence than his own reformation) a warning to others. Hence it is we object to that spectacle of order and decorum—carpenters in one shop, tailors in another, weavers in a third, sitting down to a meal by ring of bell, and receiving a regular portion of their earnings. We are afraid it is better than real life on the other side of the wall, or so very little worse that nobody will have any fear to encounter it. In Bury jail, which is considered as a pattern jail, the prisoners under a sentence of confinement are allowed to spend their weekly earnings (two, three, and four shillings per week) in fish, tobacco and vegetables; so states the jailer in his examination before the House of Commons —and we have no doubt it is well meant; but is it punishment? We were most struck, in reading the evidence of the jail committee before the House of Commons, with the opinions of the jailer of the Devizes jail, and with the practice of the magistrates who superintend it.*

"Mr. T. Brutton, *Governor of the Gaol at Devizes.*—Does this confinement in solitude make prisoners more averse to return to prison? I think it does.—Does it make a strong impression upon them? I have no doubt of it. —Does it make them more obedient and orderly while in gaol? I have no doubt it does.—Do you consider it the most effectual punishment you can make use of? I do.—Do you think it has a greater effect upon the minds of prisoners than any apprehensions of personal punishment? I have no doubt of it.—Have you any dark cells for the punishment of refractory prisoners? I have. —Do you find it necessary occasionally to use them? Very seldom.—Have you, in any instance, been obliged to use the dark cell, in the case of the same prisoner twice? Only on one occasion, I think.—What length of time is it necessary to confine a refractory prisoner to bring him to his senses? Less than one day.—Do you think it essential, for the purpose of keeping up the discipline of the prison, that you should have it in your power to have recourse to the punishment of dark cells? I do; I consider punishment in a dark cell for one day, has a greater effect upon a prisoner than to keep him on bread and water for a month."—*Evidence before the Committee of the House of Commons in* 1819, p. 359.

The evidence of the governor of Gloucester jail is to the same effect.

"Mr. Thomas Cunningham, *Keeper of Gloucester Gaol.*—Do you attribute the want of those certificates entirely to the neglect of enforcing the means of solitary confinement? I do most certainly. Sometimes, where a certificate has not been granted, and a prisoner has brought a certificate of good behaviour for one year, Sir George and the committee ordered one pound or a guinea from the charity.—Does that arise from your apprehension that the prisoners have not been equally reformed, or only from the want of the means of ascertaining such reformation? It is for want of not knowing; and we cannot ascertain it, from their working in numbers.—They may be reformed? Yes, but we have not the means of ascertaining it. There is one thing I do which is not provided for by the rules, and which is the only thing in which I deviate from the rules. When a man is committed for a month, I never give him any work; he sits in solitude, and walks in the yard by himself for air; he has no other food but his bread and water, except twice a week a pint of peas soup. I never knew an instance of a man coming in a second time who had been committed for a month. I have done that for these seventeen or eighteen years.—What has been the result? They dread so much coming in again. If a man is committed for six weeks we give him work. Do you apprehend that solitary confinement for a month, without employment, is the most beneficial means of working reform? I conceive it is.—Can it operate as the means of reform, any more than it operates as a system of punishment? It is only for small offences they commit for a month.—Would not the same effect be produced by corporeal punishment? Corporeal punishment may be absolutely necessary sometimes; but I do not think corporeal punishment would reform them so much as solitary confinement.—Would not severe corporeal punishment have the same effect? No, it would harden them more than any thing else.—Do you think benefit is derived from the opportunity of reflection afforded by solitary confinement? Yes.— And very low diet also? Yes."—*Evidence before the Committee of the House of Commons in* 1819, p. 391.

We must quote, also, the evidence of the governor of Horsley jail.

"Mr. William Stokes, *Governor of the House of Correction at Horsley.*—Do you observe any difference in the conduct of prisoners who are employed, and those who have no employment? Yes, a good deal; I look upon it, from what judgment I can form, and I have been a long while in it, that to take a prisoner and discipline him according to the rules as the law allows, and if he have no work, that that man goes through more punishment in one month than a man who is employed and receives a portion of his labour three months; but still I should like to have employment, because a great number of times I took men away, who have been in the habit of earning sixpence a week to buy a loaf, and put them in solitary confinement; and the punishment is a great deal more without work.—Which of the prisoners, those that have been employed, or those unemployed, do you think would go out of the prison the better men? I think, that let me have a prisoner, and I never treat any one with severity, any further than that they should be obedient, and to let them see that I will do

* The Winchester and Devizes jails seem to us to be conducted upon better principles than any other, though even these are by no means what jails should be

my duty, I have reason to believe, that, if a prisoner is committed under my care, or any other man's care, to a house of correction, and he has to go under the discipline of the law, if he is in for the value of a month or six weeks, that man is in a great deal better state than though he stays for six months; he gets hardened by being in so long, from one month to another.—You are speaking now of solitude without labour; do you think he would go out better, if he had been employed during the month you speak of? No, nor half; because I never task those people, in order that they should not say I force them to do more than they are able, that they should not slight it; for if they perform any thing in the bounds of reason, I never find fault with them. The prisoner who is employed, his time passes smooth and comfortable, and he has a proportion of his earnings, and he can buy additional diet; but if he has no labour, and kept under the discipline of the prison, it is a tight piece of punishment to go through.—Which of the two should you think most likely to return immediately to habits of labour on their own account? The dispositions of all men are not alike; but my opinion is this, if they are kept and disciplined according to the rules of the prison, and have no labour, that one month will do more than six; I am certain, that a man who is kept there without labour once, will not be very ready to come there again."—*Evidence before the Committee of the House of Commons*, pp. 398, 399.

Mr. Gurney and Mr. Buxton both lay a great stress upon the quiet and content of prisoners, upon their subordination and the absence of all plans of escape; but, where the happiness of prisoners is so much consulted, we should be much more apprehensive of a conspiracy to break into, than to break out of, prison. The mob outside may, indeed, envy the wicked ones within; but the felon who has left, perhaps, a scolding wife, a battered cottage, and six starving children, has no disposition to escape from regularity, sufficient food, employment which saves him money, warmth, ventilation, cleanliness and civil treatment. These symptoms, upon which these respectable and excellent men lay so much stress, are by no means proofs to us that prisons are placed upon the best possible footing.

The governor of Bury jail, as well as Mr. Gurney, insist much upon the few prisoners who return to the jail a second time, the manufacturing skill which they acquire there, and the complete reformation of manners for which the prisoner has afterwards thanked him the governor. But this is not the real criterion of the excellence of a jail, nor the principal reason why jails were instituted. The great point is, not the average recurrence of the same prisoners, but the paucity or frequency of commitments, upon the whole. You may make a jail such an admirable place of education, that it may cease to be infamous to go there. Mr. Holford tells us (and a very curious anecdote it is,) that parents actually accuse their children falsely of crimes, in order to get them into the Philanthropic Charity! and that it is consequently a rule with the governors of that charity never to receive a child upon the accusation of the parents alone. But it is quite obvious what the next step will be, if the parents cannot get their children in by fibbing. They will take good care that the child is *really* qualified for the Philanthropic, by impelling him to those crimes which are the passport to so good an education.

"If, on the contrary, the offender is to be punished simply by being placed in a prison, where he is to be well lodged, well clothed, and well fed, to be instructed in reading and writing, to receive a moral and religious education, and to be brought up to a trade; and if this prison is to be within the reach of the parents, so that they may occasionally visit their child, and have the satisfaction of knowing, from time to time, that all these advantages are conferred upon him, and that he is exposed to no hardships, although the confinement and the discipline of the prison may be irksome to the boy; yet the parents may be apt to congratulate themselves on having got him off their hands into such a good berth, and may be considered by other parents as having drawn a prize in the lottery of human life by their son's conviction. This reasoning is not theoretical, but is founded in some degree upon experience. Those who have been in the habit of attending the committee of the Philanthropic Society know, that parents have often accused their children of crimes falsely, or have exaggerated their real offences, for the sake of inducing that society to take them; and so frequent has been this practice, that it is a rule with those who manage that institution, never to receive an object upon the representation of its parents, unless supported by other strong testimony."—*Holford*, pp. 44, 45.

It is quite obvious that, if men were to appear again, six months after they were hanged, handsomer, richer, and more plump than before execution, the gallows would cease to be an object of terror. But here are men who come out of jail, and say, 'Look at us,—we can read and write, we can make baskets and shoes, and we went in ignorant of every thing: and we have learnt to do without strong liquors, and have no longer any objection to work; and we did work in the jail, and have saved money, and here it is." What is there of terror and detriment in all this? and how are crimes to be lessened if they are thus rewarded? Of schools there cannot be too many. Penitentiaries, in the hands of wise men, may be rendered excellent institutions; but a prison must be a prison—a place of sorrow and wailing; which should be entered with horror, and quitted with earnest resolution never to return to such misery; with that deep impression, in short, of the evil which breaks out into perpetual warning and exhortation to others. This great point effected, all other reformation must do the greatest good.

There are some very sensible observations upon this point in Mr. Holford's book, who upon the whole has, we think, best treated the subject of prisons, and best understands them.

"In former times, men were deterred from pursuing the road that led to a prison, by the apprehension of encountering there disease and hunger, of being loaded with heavy irons, and of remaining without clothes to cover them, or a bed to lie on; we have done no more than what justice required in relieving the inmates of a prison from these hardships; but there is no reason that they should be freed from the fear of all other sufferings and privations. And I hope that those whose duty it is to take up the consideration of these subjects, will see, that in penitentiaries, offenders should be subjected to separate confinement, accompanied by such work as may be found consistent with that system of imprisonment; that in jails or houses of correction, they should perform that kind of labour which the law has enjoined; and that in prisons of both descriptions, instead of being allowed to cater for themselves, they should be sustained by such food as the rules and regulations of the establishment should have provided for them; in short, that prisons should be considered as places of punishment, and not as scenes of cheerful industry, where a compromise must be made with the prisoner's appetite to make him do the common work of a journeyman or manufacturer, and the labours of the spinning-wheel and the loom must be alleviated by indulgence."*

This is good sound sense; and it is a pity that it is preceded by the usual nonsense about "*the tide of blasphemy and sedition.*" If Mr. Holford is an observer of tides and currents, whence comes it that he observes only those which set one way? Whence comes it that he says nothing of the tides of canting and hypocrisy which are flowing with such rapidity?—of abject political baseness and sycophancy—of the disposition so prevalent among Englishmen, to sell their conscience and their country to the Marquis of Londonderry for a living for the second son—or a silk gown for the nephew—or for a frigate for my brother the captain? How comes our loyal carcerist to forget all these sorts of tides?

There is a great confusion, as the law now stands, in the government of jails. The justices are empowered, by several statutes, to make subordinate regulations for the government of the jails; and the sheriff supersedes those regulations. Their respective jurisdictions and powers should be clearly arranged.

The female prisoners should be under the care of a matron, with proper assistants. Where this is not the case, the female part of the prison is often a mere brothel for the turnkeys. Can any thing be so repugnant to all ideas of reformation, as a male turnkey visiting a solitary female prisoner? Surely, women can take care of women as effectually as men can take care of men; or, at least, women can do so properly assisted by men. This want of a matron is a very scandalous and immoral neglect in any prison system.

The presence of female visitors, and instructors for the women, is so obviously advantageous and proper, that the offer of forming such an institution must be gladly and thankfully received by any body of magistrates. That they should feel any jealousy of such interference is too absurd a supposition to be made or agreed upon. Such interference may not effect all that zealous people suppose it will effect; but, if it does any good, it had better be.

Irons should never be put upon prisoners before trial; after trial, we cannot object to the humiliation and disgrace which irons and a parti-coloured prison dress occasion. Let them be a part of solitary confinement, and let the words "Solitary Confinement," in the sentence, imply permission to use them. The judge then knows what he inflicts.

We object to the office of prison inspector, for reasons so very obvious, that it is scarcely necessary to enumerate them. The prison inspector would, of course, have a good salary; that, in England, is never omitted. It is equally matter of course that he would be taken from among treasury retainers; and that he never would look at a prison. Every sort of attention should be paid to the religious instruction of these unhappy people; but the poor chaplain should be paid a little better;—every possible duty is expected from him—and he has one hundred per annum.

Whatever money is given to prisoners, should be lodged with the governor for their benefit, to be applied as the visiting magistrates point out—no other donations should be allowed or accepted.

If voluntary work before trial, or compulsory work after trial, is the system of a prison, there should be a task-master; and it should be remembered, that the principal object is not profit.

Wardsmen, selected in each yard among the best of the prisoners, are very serviceable. If prisoners work, they should work in silence. At all times, the restrictions upon seeing friends should be very severe; and no food should be sent from friends.

Our general system then is—that a prison should be a place of real punishment; but of known, enacted, measurable and measure

* "That I am guilty of no exaggeration in thus describing a prison conducted upon the principles now coming into fashion, will be evident to any person who will turn to the latter part of the article, 'Penitentiary, Millbank,' in Mr. Buxton's Book on Prisons. He there states what passed in conversation between himself and the governor of Bury jail, (which jail, by the bye, he praises as one of the three best prisons he has ever seen, and strongly recommends to our imitation at Millbank.) Having observed that the governor of Bury jail had mentioned his having counted 34 spinning-wheels in full activity when he left that jail at 5 o'clock in the morning on the preceding day, Mr. Buxton proceeds as follows:—'After he had seen the Millbank Penitentiary, I asked him what would be the consequence, if the regulations there used were adopted by him?' 'The consequence would be,' he replied, 'that every wheel would be stopped.' Mr. Buxton then adds, 'I would not be considered as supposing that the prisoners will altogether refuse to work at Millbank—they will work during the stated hours; but the present incentive being wanting, the labour will, I apprehend, be languid and desultory.' I shall not, on my part, undertake to say that they will do as much work as will be done in those prisons in which work is the primary object; but, besides the encouragement of the portion of earnings laid up for them, they know that diligence is among the qualities that will recommend them to the mercy of the crown, and that the want of it is, by the rules and regulations of the prison, an offence to be punished. The governor of Bury jail, who is a very intelligent man, must have spoken hastily, in his eagerness to support his own system, and did not, I conceive, give himself credit for as much power and authority in his prison as he really possesses. It is not to be wondered at, that the keepers of prisons should like the new system: there is less trouble in the care of a manufactory than in that of a jail: but I am surprised to find that so much reliance is placed in argument on the declaration of some of these officers, that the prisoners are quieter where their work is encouraged, by allowing them to spend a portion of their earnings. It may naturally be expected, that offenders will be least discontented, and consequently least turbulent, where their punishment is lightest, or where, to use Mr. Buxton's own words, 'by making labour productive of comfort or convenience, you do much towards rendering it agreeable;' but I must be permitted to doubt, whether these are the prisons of which men will live in most dread."—*Holford*, pp. 78—80.

punishment. A prisoner (not for assault, or refusing to pay parish dues, but a bad felonious prisoner), should pass a part of his three months in complete darkness; the rest in complete solitude, perhaps in complete idleness, (for solitary idleness leads to repentance, idleness in company to vice.) He should be exempted from cold, be kept perfectly clean, have sufficient food to prevent hunger or illness, wear the prison dress and moderate irons, have no communication with any body but the officers of the prison and the magistrates, and remain otherwise in the most perfect solitude. We strongly suspect this is the way in which a bad man is to be made afraid of prisons; nor do we think that he would be less inclined to receive moral and religious instruction than any one of seven or eight carpenters in jail, working at a common bench, receiving a part of their earnings, and allowed to purchase with them the delicacies of the season. If this system is not resorted to, the next best system is severe work, ordinary diet, no indulgences, and as much seclusion and solitude as are compatible with work; — always remarking, that perfect sanity of mind and body are to be preserved.

To this system of severity in jails there is but one objection. The present duration of punishments was calculated for prisons conducted upon very different principles;—and if the discipline of prisons was rendered more strict, we are not sure that the duration of imprisonment would be practically shortened; and the punishments would then be quite atrocious and disproportioned. There is a very great disposition, both in judges and magistrates, to increase the duration of imprisonment; and, if that is done, it will be dreadful cruelty to increase the bitterness as well as the time. We should think, for instance, six months' solitary imprisonment to be a punishment of dreadful severity; but we find, from the House of Commons' report, that prisoners are sometimes committed by county magistrates for two years* of solitary confinement. And so it may be doubted, whether it is not better to wrap up the rod in flannel, and make it a plaything, as it really now is, than to show how it may be wielded with effectual severity. For the pupil, instead of giving one or two stripes, will whip his patient to death.— But if this abuse were guarded against, the real way to improve would be, now we have made prisons healthy and airy, to make them odious and austere — engines of punishment and objects of terror.

In this age of charity and of prison improvement, there is one aid to prisoners which appears to be wholly overlooked; and that is, the means of regulating their defence, and providing them witnesses for their trial. A man is tried for murder, or for house-breaking or robbery without a single shilling in his pocket. The nonsensical and capricious institutions of the English law prevent him from engaging counsel to speak in his defence, if he had the wealth of Crœsus; but he has no money to employ even an attorney, or to procure a single witness, or to take out a subpœna. The judge, we are told, is his counsel;—this is sufficiently absurd; but it is not pretended that the judge is his witness. He solemnly declares that he has three or four witnesses who could give a completely different colour to the transaction;—but they are sixty or seventy miles distant, working for their daily bread, and have no money for such a journey, nor for the expense of a residence of some days in an assize town. They do not know even the time of the assize, nor the modes of tendering their evidence if they could come. When every thing is so well marshaled against him on the opposite side, it would be singular if an innocent man, with such an absence of all means of defending himself, should not occasionally be hanged or transported: and accordingly we believe that such things have happened.* Let any man, immediately previous to the assizes, visit the prisoners for trial, and see the many wretches who are to answer to the most serious accusations, without one penny to defend themselves. If it appeared probable, upon inquiry that these poor creatures had important evidence which they could not bring into court for want of money, would it not be a wise application of compassionate funds, to give them this fair chance of establishing their innocence? — It seems to us no bad *finale* of the pious labours of those who guard the poor from ill-treatment during their imprisonment, to take care that they are not unjustly hanged at the expiration of the term.

* House of Commons' Report, 355.

* From the Clonmell Advertiser it appears, that John Brien, *alias* Captain Wheeler, was found guilty of murder at the late assizes for the county of Waterford. Previous to his execution he made the following confession:—

"I now again most solemnly aver, in the presence of that God by whom I will soon be judged, and who sees the secrets of my heart, that only three, viz, Morgan Brien, Patrick Brien and my unfortunate self, committed the horrible crimes of murder and burning at Ballygarron, and that the four unfortunate men who have before suffered for them, were not in the smallest degree accessary to them. I have been the cause for which they have innocently suffered death. I have contracted a death of justice with them—and the only and least restitution I can make them, is thus publicly, solemnly, and with death before my eyes, to acquit their memory of any guilt in the crimes for which I shall deservedly suffer!!" —*Philanthropist*, No. 6. 208.

Pereunt et imputantur.

PRISONS.*

[EDINBURGH REVIEW, 1822.]

THERE never was a society calculated, upon the whole, to do more good than the Society for the Improvement of Prison Discipline; and, hitherto, it has been conducted with equal energy and prudence. If now, or hereafter, therefore, we make any criticisms on their proceedings, these must not be ascribed to any deficiency of good will or respect. We may differ from the society in the means—our ends, we are proud to say, are the same.

In the improvement of prisons, they consider the small number of *recommitments* as the great test of amelioration. Upon this subject we have ventured to differ from them in a late number; and we see no reason to alter our opinion. It is a mistake, and a very serious and fundamental mistake, to suppose that the principal object in jails is the reformation of the offender. The principal object undoubtedly is, to prevent the repetition of the offence by the punishment of the offender; and, therefore, it is quite possible to conceive that the offender himself may be so kindly, gently and agreeably led to reformation, by the efforts of good and amiable persons, that the effect of the punishment may be destroyed, at the same time that the punished may be improved. A prison may lose its terror and discredit, though the prisoner may return from it a better scholar, a better artificer, and a better man. The real and only test, in short, of a good prison system is, the diminution of offences by the terror of the punishment. If it can be shown, that in proportion as attention and expense have been employed upon the improvement of prisons, the number of commitments has been diminished, this indeed would be a convincing proof that such care and attention were well employed. But the very reverse is the case; the number of commitments within these last ten years having nearly doubled all over England.

The following are stated to be the committals in Norfolk county jail. From 1796 to 1815, the number averaged about 80.

In 1816	it was	134
1817	-	142
1818	-	159
1819	-	161
1820	-	223.—*Report*, p. 57.

In Staffordshire, the commitments have gradually increased from 195 to 1815, to 443 in 1820—though the jail has been built since Howard's time, at an expense of 30,000*l*.—(*Report*, p. 67.) In Wiltshire, in a prison which has cost the county 40,000*l*., the commitments have increased from 207 in 1817 to 504 in 1821. Within this perriod, to the eternal scandal and disgrace of our laws, 378 persons have been committed for game offences—constituting a sixth part of all the persons committed;—so much for what our old friend, Mr. Justice Best, would term the unspeakable advantages of country gentlemen residing upon their own property!

When the committee was appointed in the county of Essex, in the year 1818, to take into consideration the state of the jail and houses of correction, they found that the number of prisoners annually committed had increased, within the ten preceding years, from 559 to 1993; and there is little doubt (adds Mr. Western) of this proportion being a tolerable specimen of the whole kingdom. We are far from attributing this increase solely to the imperfection of prison discipline. Increase of population, new statutes, the extension of the breed of pheasants, landed and mercantile distress, are very operative causes. But the increase of commitments is a stronger proof against the present state of prison discipline, than the decrease of recommitments is in its favour.—We may, possibly, have made some progress in the art of teaching him who has done wrong to do so no more; but there is no proof that we have learnt the more important art of deterring those from doing wrong who are doubting whether they shall do it or not, and who, of course, will be principally guided in their decision by the sufferings of those who have previously yielded to temptation.

There are some assertions in the report of the society, to which we can hardly give credit,—not that we have the slightest suspicion of any intentional misrepresentation, but that we believe there must be some unintentional error.

"The Ladies' Committees visiting Newgate and the Borough Compter, have continued to devote themselves to the improvement of the female prisoners, in a spirit worthy of their enlightened zeal and Christian charity. The beneficial effects of their exertions have been evinced by the progressive decrease in the number of female prisoners recommitted, which has diminished, since the visits of the ladies to Newgate, no less than 40 per cent."

That is, that Mrs. Fry and her friends have reclaimed forty women out of every hundred, who, but for them, would have reappeared in jails. Nobody admires and respects Mrs. Fry more than we do; but this fact is scarcely credible; and, if accurate, ought, in justice to the reputation of the society and its real interests, to have been thoroughly substantiated by names and documents. The ladies certainly lay claim

* 1. *The Third Report of the Committee of the Society for the Improvement of Prison Discipline, and for the Reformation of Juvenile Offenders.* London, 1821.

2. *Remarks upon Prison Discipline, &c. &c., in a Letter addressed to the Lord-Lieutenant and Magistrates of the County of Essex.* By C. C. Western, Esq. M. P. London, 1821.

to no such extraordinary success in their own report quoted in the Appendix: but speak with becoming modesty and moderation of the result of their labours. The enemies of all these reforms accuse the reformers of enthusiasm and exaggeration. It is of the greatest possible consequence, therefore, that their statements should be correct, and their views practical; and that all strong assertions should be supported by strong documents. The English are a calm, reflecting people; they will give time and money when they are convinced; but they love dates, names and certificates. In the midst of the most heart-rending narratives, Bull requires the day of the month, the year of our Lord, the name of the parish and the countersign of three or four respectable householders. After these affecting circumstances, he can no longer hold out; but gives way to the kindness of his nature—puffs, blubbers and subscribes!

A case is stated in the Hertford house of correction, which so much more resembles the sudden conversions of the Methodist Magazine, than the slow and uncertain process by which repentance is produced in real life, that we are a little surprised the society should have inserted it.

"Two notorious poachers, as well as bad men, were committed for three months, for not paying the penalty after conviction, but who, in consequence of extreme contrition and good conduct, were, at the intercession of the clergymen of their parish, released before the expiration of their term of punishment. Upon leaving the house of correction, they declared that they had been completely brought to their senses—spoke with gratitude of the benefit they had derived from the advice of the chaplain, and promised, upon their return to their parish, that they would go to their minister, express their thanks for his interceding for them; and moreover that they would, for the future, attend their duty regularly at church. It is pleasing to add, that these promises have been faithfully fulfilled."—*App. to Third Report*, pp. 29, 30.

Such statements prove nothing, but that the clergyman who makes them is an amiable man, and probably a college tutor. Their introduction however, in the report of a society depending upon public opinion for success, is very detrimental.

It is not fair to state the recommitments of one prison, and compare them with those of another, perhaps very differently circumstanced, —the recommitments, for instance, of a county jail, where offences are generally of serious magnitude, with those of a borough, where the most trifling faults are punished. The important thing would be, to give a table of recommitments, in the same prison, for a series of years,—the average of recommitments, for example, every five years in each prison for twenty years past. If the society can obtain this, it will be a document of some importance, (though of less, perhaps, than they would consider it to be.) At present they tell us, that the average of recommitments in certain prisons is 3 per cent.: in certain other prisons 5 per cent.: but what were they twenty years ago in the same prison?—what were they five years ago? If recommitments are to be the test, we must know whether these are becoming, *in any given prison*, more or less frequent, before we can determine whether that prison is better or worse governed than formerly. Recommitments will of course be more numerous where prisoners are received from large towns, and from the resorts of soldiers and sailors; because it is in these situations that we may expect the most hardened offenders. The different nature of the two soils which grow the crimes, must be considered before the produce gathered into prisons can be justly compared.

The quadruple column of the state of prisons for each year, is a very useful and important document; and we hope, in time, the society will give us a general and particular table of commitments and recommitments carried back for twenty or thirty years; so that the table may contain (of Gloucester jail, for instance,) 1st, the greatest number it can contain; 2dly, the greatest number it did contain at any one period in each year; 3dly, its classification; 4thly, the greatest number committed in any given year; 5thly, four averages of five years each, taken from the twenty years preceding, and stating the greatest number of commitments; 6thly, the greatest number of recommitments in the year under view; and four averages of recommitments, made in the same manner as the average of the commitments; and then totals at the bottom of the columns. Tables so constructed would throw great light upon the nature and efficacy of imprisonment.

We wish the society would pay a little more attention to the question of solitary imprisonment, both in darkness and in light; and to the extent to which it may be carried. Mr. Western has upon this subject some ingenious ideas.

"It appears to me, that if relieved from these impediments, and likewise from any idea of the necessity of making the labour of prisoners profitable, the detail of corrective prison discipline would not be difficult for any body to chalk out. I would first premise, that the only punishment for refractory conduct, or any misbehaviour in the gaol, should, in my opinion, be solitary confinement; and that, instead of being in a dark hole, it should be in some part of the house where they could fully see the light of the day; and I am not sure that it might not be desirable, in some cases, if possible, that they should see the surrounding country and moving objects at a distance, and every thing that man delights in, removed, at the same time, from any intercourse or word or look with any human being, and quite out of the reach of being themselves seen. I consider such confinement would be a punishment very severe, and calculated to produce a far better effect than darkness. All the feelings that are good in men would be much more likely to be kept alive; the loss of liberty, and all the blessings of life which honesty will insure, more deeply to be felt. There would not be so much danger of any delinquent sinking into that state of sullen, insensible condition, of incorrigible obstinacy, which sometimes occurs. If he does, under those circumstances, we have a right to keep him out of the way of mischief, and let him there remain. But I believe such solitary confinement as I have described, with scanty fare, would very rarely fail of its effect."—*Western's Remarks*, pp. 59, 60.

There is a good deal in this; it is well worth the trial; and we hope the society will notice it in their next report.

It is very difficult to hit upon degrees; but we cannot help thinking the society lean too much to a system of indulgence and education in jails. We shall be very glad to see them more stern and Spartan in their discipline. They recommend work, and even hard work; but they do not insist upon it, that the only work done in jails by felons should be hard, dull and uninteresting; they do not protest against the conversion of jails into schools and manufactories. Look, for example, to "Preston House of Correction."

"Preston House of Correction is justly distinguished by the industry which prevails. Here an idle hand is rarely to be found. There were lately 150 looms in full employ, from each of which the average weekly earnings are 5*s*. About 150 pieces of cotton goods are worked off per week. A considerable proportion of the looms are of the prisoners' own manufacture. In one month, an inexperienced workman will be able to earn the cost of his gaol allowance of food. Weaving has these advantages over other prison labour: the noise of the shuttle prevents conversation, and the progress of the work constantly requires the eye. The accounts of this prison contained in the Appendix, deserve particular attention, as there appears to be a balance of clear profit to the county, from the labour of the prisoners, in the year, of 1398*l*. 9*s*. 1*d*. This sum was earned by weaving and cleaning cotton only; the prisoners being besides employed in tailoring, white-washing, flagging, slating, painting, carpentering and labourers' work, the earnings of which are not included in the above account."—*Third Report*, pp. 21, 22.

"At Worcester county gaol, the system of employment is admirable. Every article of dress worn by the prisoners is made from the raw material; sacking and bags are the only articles made for sale."—*Ib*. p. 23.

"In many prisons, the instruction of the prisoners in reading and writing has been attended with excellent effects. Schools have been formed at Bedford, Durham, Chelmsford, Winchester, Hereford, Maidstone, Leicester house of correction, Shrewsbury, Warwick, Worcester, &c. Much valuable assistance has been derived in this department from the labours of respectable individuals, especially females, acting under the sanction of the magistrates, and direction of the chaplain."—*Ib*. pp. 30, 31.

We again enter our decided protest against these modes of occupation in prisons; they are certainly better than mere idleness spent in society; but they are not the kind of occupations which render prisons terrible. We would banish all the looms of Preston jail, and substitute nothing but the tread-wheel, or the capstan, or some species of labour where the labourer could not see the results of his toil,—where it was as monotonous, irksome and dull as possible,—pulling and pushing, instead of reading and writing,—no share of the profits—not a single shilling. There should be no tea and sugar —no assemblage of female felons round the washing-tub,—Nothing but beating hemp, and pulling oakum, and pounding bricks,—no work but what was tedious, unusual and unfeminine. Man, woman, boy and girl, should all leave the jail, unimpaired, indeed, in health, but heartily wearied of their residence; and taught, by sad experience, to consider it as the greatest misfortune of their lives to return to it. We have the strongest belief that the present lenity of jails, the education carried on there—the cheerful assemblage of workmen—the indulgence in diet—the shares of earnings enjoyed by prisoners, are one great cause of the astonishingly rapid increase of commitments.

Mr. Western, who entirely agrees with us upon these points, has the following judicious observations upon the severe system:—

"It may be imagined by some persons, that the rules here prescribed are too severe; but such treatment is, in my opinion, the tenderest mercy, compared with that indulgence which is so much in practice, and which directly tends to ruin, instead of saving, its unfortunate victim. This severity it is which in truth forms the sole effective means which imprisonment gives; only one mitigation, therefore, if such it may be termed, can be admissible, and that is, simply to shorten the duration of the imprisonment. The sooner the prisoner comes out the better, if fully impressed with dread of what he has suffered, and communicates information to his friends what they may expect if they get there. It appears to me, indeed, that one great and primary object we ought to have in view is, generally, to shorten the duration of imprisonment, at the same time that we make it such a punishment as is likely to deter, correct and reform; shorten the duration of imprisonment before trial, which we are called upon, by every principle of moral and political justice, to do; shorten also the duration of imprisonment after trial, by the means here described; and I am satisfied our prisons would soon lose, or rather would never see, half the number of their present inhabitants. The long duration of imprisonment, where the discipline is less severe, renders it perfectly familiar, and, in consequence, not only destitute of any useful influence, but obviously productive of the worst effects; yet this is the present practice; and I think, indeed, criminals are now sentenced to a longer period of confinement than formerly.

"The deprivation of liberty certainly is a punishment under any circumstances; but the system generally pursued in our gaols might rather be considered as a palliative of that punishment, than to make it effectual to any good purpose. An idle life, society unrestrained, with associates of similar character and habits, better fare and lodgings in many cases, and in few, if any, worse than falls to the lot of the hard-working and industrious peasant; and very often much better than the prisoners were in the enjoyment of before they were apprehended.

"I do not know what could be devised more agreeable to all the different classes of offenders than this sort of treatment: the old hardened sinner, the juvenile offender, or the idle vagabond, who runs away and leaves a sick wife and family to be provided for by his parish, alike have little or no apprehension, at present, of any imprisonment to which they may be sentenced; and thus are the most effective means we possess to correct and reform rendered totally unavailable, and even perverted, to the more certain ruin of those who might be restored to society good and valuable members of it.

"There are, it is true, various occupations now introduced into many prisons, but which, I confess, I think of very little use; drawing and preparing straws, platting, knitting, heading pins, &c., weaving and working at a trade even, as it is generally carried on—prisoners coaxed to the performance of it, the task easy, the reward immediate—afford rather the means of passing away the time agreeably. These occupations are, indeed, better than absolute idleness, notwithstanding that imprisonment may be rendered less irksome thereby. I am far from denying the advantage, still less would I be supposed to derogate from the merits of those who, with every feeling of humanity, and with indefatigable pains, in many instances, have established such means of employment; and some of them for women, with washing, &c., amount to hard labour; but I contend that, for men, they are applicable only to a house of industry and by no means suited to the corrective discipline which should be found in a prison. Individuals are sent here to be punished and for that sole purpose; in many cases for crimes which have induced the forfeiture of life: they are not sent to be educated, or apprenticed to a trade. The horrors of dungeon imprisonment, to the credit of the age, no longer exist. But, if no cause of dread is substituted, by what indication of common sense is it that we send criminals there at all? If prisons are to be made into places in which persons of both sexes and all ages may be well fed, clothed, lodged, educated and taught a trade, where they may find pleasant society, and are required not to take heed for the morrow, the present inhabitants should be turned out, and the most deserving and industrious of our poorest fellow-subjects should be invited to take their place, which I have no doubt they would be eager to do."—*Western*, pp. 13–17.

In these sentiments we most cordially agree. They are well worth the most serious attention of the society.

The following is a sketch from Mr. Western's book of what a prison life should be. It is impossible to write with more good sense, and a more thorough knowledge of the subject.

"The operations of the day should begin with the greatest punctuality at a given hour; and as soon as the prisoners have risen from their beds, they should be, according to their several classes, marched to the workhouses, where they should be kept to hard labour two hours at least; from thence they should be taken back to wash, shave, comb and clean themselves; thence to the chapel to hear a short prayer, or the governor or deputy should read to them in their respective day-rooms; and then their breakfast, which may, altogether, occupy an hour and a half or more. I have stated, in a former part of my letter, that the hours of meals and leisure should be in solitude, in the sleeping cells of the prison; but I presume, for the moment, this may not always be practicable. I will, therefore, consider the case as if the classes assembled at meal-times in the different day-rooms. After breakfast they should return to hard labour for three or four hours, and then take another hour for dinner; labour after dinner two or three hours, and their supper given them to eat in solitude in their sleeping cells.

"This marching backwards and forwards to chapel and mill-house, &c., may appear objectionable, but it has not been so represented to me in the prisons where it actually now takes place; and it is, to my apprehension, materially useful in many respects. The object is to keep the prisoners in a state of constant motion, so that there shall be no lounging time or loitering, which is always favourable to mischief or cabal. For the same reason it is I propose two hours' labour the moment they are up, and before washing, &c., that there may be no time lost, and that they may begin the day by a portion of labour, which will tend to keep them quiet and obedient the remainder of it. Each interval for meal, thus occurring between labour hours, has also a tendency to render the mischief of intercourse less probable, and at the same time the evening association, which is most to be apprehended in this respect, is entirely cut off. The frequent moving of the prisoners from place to place keeps the governor and sub-officers of the prison in a similar state of activity and attention, which is likewise of advantage, though their numbers should be such as to prevent their duty becoming too arduous or irksome. Their situation is not pleasant and their responsibility is great. An able and attentive governor, who executes all his arduous duties with unremitting zeal and fidelity, is a most valuable public servant and entitled to the greatest respect. He must be a man of no ordinary capacity, with a liberal and comprehensive mind, possessing a control over his own passions, firm and undaunted, a character that commands from those under him, instinctively, as it were, respect and regard. In vain are our buildings, and rules, and regulations, if the choice of a governor is not made an object of primary and most solicitous attention and consideration.

"It does not appear to me necessary for the prisoners to have more than three hours' leisure, inclusive of meal-times; and I am convinced the close of the day must be in solitude. Eight or ten hours will have passed in company with their fellow-prisoners of the same class (for I am presuming that a separate compartment of the workhouse will be allotted to each) where, though they cannot associate to enjoy society as they would wish, no gloom of solitude can oppress them: there is more danger even then of too close an intercourse and conversation, though a ready cure is in that case to be found by a wheel put in motion, the noise of which speedily overcomes the voice. Some time after Saturday night should be allowed to them, more particularly to cleanse themselves and their clothes, and they should have a bath, cold or warm, if necessary; and on the Sunday they should be dressed in their best clothes, and the day should be spent wholly in the chapel, the cell, and the airing-ground; the latter in presence of a day-watchman, as I have described to be in practice at Warwick. I say nothing about teaching to read, write, work, &c. &c.; any proportion of time necessary for any useful purpose may be spared from the hours of labour or of rest, according to circumstances; but I do not place any reliance upon improvement in any branch of education: they would not, indeed, be there long enough. All I want them to learn is, that there exists the means of punishment for crime, and be fully impressed with dread of repetition of what they have undergone; and a short time will suffice for that purpose. Now, if each successive day was spent in this manner, can it be doubted that the frequent commission of crime would be checked, and more done to deter, correct and reform than could be accomplished by any other punishment? A period of such discipline, longer or shorter, according to the nature of the offence, would surely be sufficient for any violation of the law short of murder, or that description of outrage which is likely to lead on to the perpetration of it. This sort of treatment is not to be overcome: it cannot be braved, or laughed at, or disregarded, by any force of animal spirits, however strong or vigorous of mind or body the individual may be. The dull, unvarying course of hard labour, with hard fare and seclusion, must in time become so painfully irksome, and so wear and distress him, that he will inevitably, in the end, be subdued."—*Western*, pp. 64–69.

There is nothing in the Report of the Prison Society so good as this.

The society very properly observe upon the badness of town jails, and the necessity for their suppression. Most towns cannot spare the funds necessary for building a good jail. Shopkeepers cannot spare the time for its superintendence; and hence it happens that town jails are almost always in a disgraceful state. The society frequently allude to the diffusion of tracts. If education is to be continued in jails, and tracts are to be dispersed, we cannot help lamenting that the tracts, though full of good principles, are so intolerably stupid—and all apparently constructed upon the supposition, that a thief or a peccant ploughman is inferior in common sense to a boy of five years old. The story generally is, that a labourer with six children has nothing to live upon but mouldy bread and dirty water; yet nothing can exceed his cheerfulness and content—no murmurs—no discontent: of mutton he has scarcely heard—of bacon he never dreams: furfurous bread and the water of the pool constitute his food, establish his felicity, and excite his warmest gratitude. The squire or parson of the parish always happens to be walking by and overhears him praying for the king and the members for the county, and for all in authority; and it generally ends with their offering him a shilling, which this excellent man declares he does not want, and will not accept! These are the pamphlets which Goodies and Noodles are dispersing with unwearied diligence. It would be a great blessing if some genius would arise who had a talent of writing for the poor. He would be of more value than many poets living upon the banks of lakes—or even (though we think highly of ourselves) of greater value than many reviewing men living in the garrets of the north.

The society offer some comments upon the prison bill now pending, and which unfortunately* for the cause of prison improvement, has been so long pending in the legislature. In the copy of this bill, as it stands at present, nothing is said of the limitation of numbers in any particular class. We have seen forty felons of one class in one yard before trial. If this is to continue, all prison improvement is a mere mockery. Separate sleeping cells should be enacted positively, and not in words, which leave this improvement optional. If any visiting justice dissents from the majority,† it should be lawful for him to give a separate report upon the state of the prison and prisoners to the judge or the quarter sessions. All such reports of any visiting magistrate or magistrates, not exceeding a certain length, should be published in the county papers. The chairman's report to the secretary of state should be published in the same manner. The great panacea is publicity; it is this which secures compliance with wise and just laws, more than all the penalties they contain for their own preservation.

We object to the reading and writing clause. A poor man, who is lucky enough to have his son committed for a felony, educates him, under such a system, for nothing; while the virtuous simpleton on the other side of the wall is paying by the quarter for these attainments. He sees clergymen and ladies busy with the larcenous pupil; while the poor lad, who respects the eighth commandment, is consigned, in some dark alley, to the frowns and blows of a ragged pedagogue. It would be the safest way, where a prisoner is kept upon bread and water alone, to enact that the allowance of bread should not be less than a pound and a half for men, and a pound for women and boys. We strongly recommend, as mentioned in a previous number, that four sorts of diet should be enacted for every prison; 1st, Bread and water; 2d, Better prison diet; 3d, Best prison diet; 4th, Free diet—the second and third to be defined by the visiting magistrates. All sentences of imprisonment should state to which of these diets the prisoner is to be confined; and all deviation from it on the part of the prison officers should be punished with very severe penalties. The regulation of prison diet in a prison is a point of the very highest importance; and to ask of visiting magistrates that they should doom to bread and water a prisoner whom the law has left at liberty to purchase whatever he has the money to procure, is a degree of severity which it is hardly fair to expect from country gentlemen, and, if expected, those expectations will not be fulfilled. The whole system of diet, one of the main-springs of all prison discipline, will get out of order, if its arrangement is left to the interference of magistrates and not to the sentence of the judge. Free diet and bread diet need no interpretation: and the jailer will take care to furnish the judge with the definitions of

* The county of York, with a prison under presentment, has been waiting nearly three years for this bill, in order to proceed upon the improvement of their county jail.

† It would be an entertaining change in human affairs to determine every thing by *minorities*. They are almost always in the right.

better prison diet and best prison diet. A knowledge of the diet prescribed in a jail is absolutely necessary for the justice of the case. Diet differs so much in different prisons, that six weeks in one prison is as severe a punishment as three months in another. If any country gentleman, engaged in legislation for prisons, is inclined to undervalue the importance of these regulations, let him appeal to his own experience, and remember, in the vacuity of the country, how often he thinks of his dinner, and of what there will be for dinner; and how much his amenity and courtesy for the evening depend upon the successful execution of this meal. But there is nobody so gluttonous and sensual as a thief; and he will feel much more bitterly fetters on his mouth than his heels. It sometimes happens that a gentleman is sentenced to imprisonment for manslaughter in a duel, or for a libel. Are visiting justices to doom such a prisoner to bread and water, or are *they* to make an invidious distinction between him and the other prisoners? The diet should be ordered by the judge, or it never will be well ordered—or ordered at all:

The most extraordinary clause in the bill is the following—

"And be it further enacted, that in case any criminal prisoner shall be guilty of any repeated offence against the rules of the prison, or shall be guilty of *any greater offence* which the jailer or keeper is not by this act empowered to punish, the said jailer or keeper shall report the same to the visiting justices, or one of them, for the time being; and such justices, or one of them, shall have power to inquire upon oath, and determine concerning any such offence so reported to him or them, and shall order the offender to be punished, either by moderate whipping, repeated whippings, or by close confinement, for any term not exceeding .'—*Act*, p. 21.

Upon this clause, any one justice may order repeated whippings for any offence greater than that which the jailer may punish. Our respect for the committee will only allow us to say, that we hope this clause will be reconsidered. We beg leave to add, that there should be a return to the principal secretary of state of recommitments as well as commitments.

It is no mean pleasure to see this attention to jail-discipline travelling from England to the detestable and despotic governments of the continent,—to see the health and life of captives admitted to be of any importance,—to perceive that human creatures in dungeons are of more consequence than rats and black beetles. All this is new—is some little gained upon tyranny; and for it we are indebted to the labours of the Prison Society. Still the state of prisons, on many parts of the continent, is shocking beyond all description.

It is a most inconceivable piece of cruelty and absurdity in the English law, that the prisoner's counsel, when he is tried for any capital felony, is not allowed to speak for him; and this we hope the new prison bill will correct. Nothing can be more ridiculous in point of reasoning, or more atrociously cruel and unjust in point of fact. Any number of counsel may be employed to take away the poor man's life. They are at full liberty to talk as long as they like; but not a syllable is to be uttered in his defence—not a sentence to show why the prisoner is not to be hung. This practice is so utterly ridiculous to any body but lawyers (to whom nothing that is customary is ridiculous), that men not versant with courts of justice will not believe it. It is, indeed, so utterly inconsistent with the common cant of the humanity of the English law, that it is often considered to be the mistake of the narrator, rather than the imperfection of the system. We must take this opportunity, therefore, of making a few observations on this very strange and anomalous practice.

The common argument used in its defence is that the judge is counsel for the prisoner. But the defenders of this piece of cruel and barbarous nonsense must first make their election, whether they consider the prisoner to be, by this arrangement, in a better, a worse or an equally good situation as if his counsel were allowed to plead for him. If he is in a *worse* situation, *why* is he so placed? Why is a man, in a solemn issue of life or death, deprived of any fair advantage which any suitor in any court of justice possesses? This is a plea of guilty to the charge we make against the practice; and its advocates, by such concession, are put out of court. But, if it is an advantage, or no disadvantage, whence comes it that the choice of this advantage, in the greatest of all human concerns, is not left to the party or to his friends? If the question concerns a footpath—or a fat ox—every man may tell his own story, or employ a barrister to tell it for him. The law leaves the litigant to decide on the method most conducive to his own interest. But, when the question is whether he is to live or die, it is at once decided for him that his counsel are to be dumb! And yet, so ignorant are men of their own interests, that there is not a single man tried who would not think it a great privilege if counsel were allowed to speak in his favour, and who would not be supremely happy to lay aside the fancied advantage of their silence. And this is true not merely of ignorant men; but there is not an Old Bailey barrister who would not rather employ another Old Bailey barrister to speak for him, than enjoy the advantage (as the phrase is) of having the judge for his counsel. But in what sense, after all, is the judge counsel for the prisoner? He states, in his summing up, facts as they have been delivered in evidence; and he tells the jury upon what points they are to decide: he mentions what facts are in favour of the prisoner, and what bear against him; and he leaves the decision to the jury. Does he do more than this in favour of the prisoner? Does he misstate? does he mislead? does he bring forward arguments on one side of the question, and omit equally important arguments on the other? If so, he is indeed counsel for the prisoner; but then who is judge? who takes care of the interests of the public? But the truth is, he does no such thing; he does merely what we have stated him to do; and would he do less, *could* he do less, if the prisoner's counsel spoke for him? If an argument was just, or an inference legitimate, he would not omit the one, or refute the other, because they had been put or drawn in the speech of the prisoner's counsel. He would be no more prejudiced against the defendant in a criminal than in a civil suit. He would select from the speeches of both counsel all that could be *fairly* urged for or against the defendant, and he would reply to their fallacious reasonings. The pure administration of justice requires of him, in either case, the same conduct. Whether the whole bar spoke for the prisoner, or whether he was left to defend himself, what can the judge do, or what ought he to do, but to state to the jury the facts as they are given in evidence, and the impression these facts have made upon his own mind? In the mean time, while the prisoner's counsel have been compelled to be silent, the accuser's, the opposite party, have enjoyed an immense advantage. In considering what bears against the prisoner, the judge has heard, not only the suggestions of his own understanding, but he has been exposed to the able and artful reasoning of a practised advocate, who has been previously instructed in the case of which the judge never heard a syllable before he came into court. Suppose it to be a case depending upon circumstantial evidence; in how many new points of view may a man of genius have placed those circumstances, which would not have occurred to the judge himself! How many inferences may he have drawn, which would have been unnoticed but for the efforts of a man whose bread and fame depend upon his exertions, and who has purposely, and on contract, flung the whole force of his understanding into one scale! In the mean time, the prisoner can say nothing, for he has not the gift of learned speech; his counsel can say nothing, though he has communicated with the prisoner, and could place the whole circumstances, perhaps, in the fairest and clearest point of view for the accused party. By the courtesy of England this is called *justice*—we in the north cannot admit of the correctness of the appellation.

It seems utterly to be forgotten, in estimating this practice, that two understandings are better than one. The judge must inevitably receive many new views against the prisoner by the speech of one counsel, and lose many views in favour of the prisoner by the silence of the other. We are not to suppose (like ladies going into court in an assize town) that the judge would have thought of every thing which the counsel against the prisoner has said, and which the counsel for the prisoner would have said. The judge, wigged and robed as he is, is often very inferior in acuteness to either of the persons who are pleading under him—a cold, slow, parchment and precedent man, without passions or præcordia,—perhaps a sturdy brawler for church and king,—or a quiet man of ordinary abilities, steadily, though perhaps conscientiously, following those in power through thick and thin—through right and wrong. Whence comes it that the method of getting at truth, which is so excellent on all common occasions, should be considered as so improper on the greatest of all occasions, where the life of a man is concerned? If an acre of land is to be lost or won, one man says all that can be said on one side of the question—another on the other; and the jury, aided by the impartiality of the judge, decide. The wit of man can devise no better method of disentangling difficulty, exposing falsehood, and detecting truth. "*Tell me why I am hurried away to a premature death, and no man suffered to speak in my defence, when at this very moment, and in my hearing, all the eloquence of the bar, on the other side of your justice hall, is employed in defending a path or a hedge? Is a foot of land dearer to any man than my life is to me? The civil plaintiff has not trusted the smallest part of his fate or fortune to his own efforts; and will you grant me no assistance of superior wisdom, who have suffered a long famine to purchase it—who am broken by prison—broken by chains—and so shamed by this dress of guilt, and abashed by the presence of my superiors, that I have no words which you could hear without derision—that I could not give way for a moment to the fulness and agitation of my rude heart without moving your contempt?*" So spoke a wretched creature to a judge in our hearing! and what answer could be given but "Jailer, take him away?"

We are well aware that a great decency of language is observed by the counsel employed against the prisoner, in consequence of the silence imposed upon the opposite counsel; but then, though there is a decency as far as concerns impassioned declamation, yet there is no restraint, and there can be no restraint, upon the reasoning powers of a counsellor. He may put together the circumstances of an imputed crime in the most able, artful and ingenious manner, without the slightest vehemence or passion. We have no objection to this, if any counter statement were permitted. We want only fair play. Speech for both sides, or speech for none. The first would be the wiser system; but the second would be clear from the intolerable cruelty of the present. We see no harm that would ensue, if both advocates were to follow their own plan without restraint. But, if the feelings are to be excluded in all causes of this nature (which seems very absurd), then let the same restraint be exacted from both sides. It might very soon be established, as the etiquette of the bar, that the pleadings on both sides were expected to be calm, and to consist of reasoning upon the facts. In high treason, where the partiality of the judge and power of the court are suspected, this absurd incapacity of being heard by counsel is removed. No body pretends to say, in such cases, that the judge would be counsel for the prisoner; and yet, how many thousand cases are there in a free country which have nothing to do with high treason, and where the spirit of party, unknown to himself, may get possession of a judge? Suppose any trial for murder to have taken place in the Manchester riots,—will any man say that the conduct of many judges on such a question ought not to have been watched with the most jealous circumspection? Would any prisoner—would any fair mediator between the prisoner and the public—be satisfied at such a period with the axiom that the judge is counsel for the prisoner? We are not saying that there is no judge who might not be so trusted, but that all judges are not, at all times, to be so intrusted. We are not saying that any judge would wilfully do wrong; but that many might be led to do wrong by passions and prejudices of which they were unconscious; and that the real safeguard to the prisoner, the best, the only safeguard, is full liberty of speech for the counsel he has employed.

What would be the discipline of that hospital where medical assistance was allowed in all trifling complaints, and withheld in every case of real danger? where Bailey and Halford were lavished upon stomach-aches and refused in typhus fever? where the dying patient beheld the greatest skill employed upon trifling evils of others, and was told, because his was a case of life and death, that the cook or the nurse was to be his physician?

Suppose so intolerable an abuse (as the attorney and solicitor-general would term it) had been established, and that a law for its correction was now first proposed, entitled an *Act to prevent the Counsel for Prisoners from being heard in their Defence!!!*

What evil would result from allowing counsel to be heard in defence of prisoners? Would too many people be hung from losing that valuable counsellor, the judge? or would too few people be hung? or would things remain much as they are at present? We never could get the admirers of this practice to inform us what the results would be of deviating from it; and we are the more particularly curious upon this point, because *our* practice is decidedly the reverse, and we find no other results from it than a fair administration of criminal justice. In all criminal cases that require the intervention of a jury in Scotland, a prisoner must have, 1st, a copy of the indictment, which must contain a minute specification of the offence charged; 2dly, a list of witnesses; 3dly, a list of the assize; and, 4thly, in every question that occurs, and in all addresses to the jury, the prisoner's counsel has the last word. Where is the boasted mercy of the English law after this?

The truth is, it proceeds from the error which, in all dark ages, pervades all codes of laws, of confounding the accused with the guilty. In the early part of our state trials, the prisoners were not allowed to bring evidence against the witnesses of the crown. For a long period after this, the witnesses of the prisoner were not suffered to be examined upon oath. One piece of cruelty and folly has given way after another. Each has been defended by the attorney and solicitor-general for the time, as absolutely necessary to the existence of the state, and the most perfect performance of our illustrious ancestors. The last grand hope of every foolish person is the silence of the prisoner's counsel. In the defence of this, it will be seen what stupidity driven to despair can achieve. We beg pardon for this digression; but flesh and blood cannot endure the nonsense of lawyers upon this subject.

The society have some very proper remarks upon the religious instructions of the chaplain—an appointment of vast importance and utility; unfortunately very ill paid, and devolving entirely upon the lower clergy. It is said that the present Bishop of Gloucester, Dr. Ryder, goes into jails and busies himself with the temporal wretchedness and the eternal welfare of the prisoners. If this is so, it does him great honour, and is a noble example to all ranks of clergy who are subject to him. Above all, do not let us omit the following beautiful anecdote, while we are talking of good and pious men.

"The committee cannot refrain from extracting from the report of the Paris Society, the interesting anecdote of the excellent Père Joussony, who being sent, by the Consul at Algiers, to minister to the slaves, fixed his residence in their prison; and, during a period of thirty years, never quitted his post. Being compelled to repair to France, for a short period, he returned again to the prison, and at length resigned his breath in the midst of those for whose interests he had laboured, and who were dearer to him than life."—*Report*, p. 30.

It seems to be a very necessary part of the prison system, that any poor person, when acquitted, should be passed to his parish; and that all who are acquitted should be *immediately* liberated. At present, a prisoner, after acquittal, is not liberated till the grand jury are dismissed,* in case (as it is said) any more bills should be preferred against him. This is really a considerable hardship; and we do not see, upon the same principle, why the prisoner may not be detained for another assize. To justify such a practice, notice should, at all events, be given to the jailer of intention to prefer other charges against him. To detain a man who is acquitted of all of which he has been accused, and who is accused of nothing more, merely because he *may be accused of something more*, seems to be a great perversion of justice. The greatest of all prison improvements, however, would be the delivery of jails four times in the year. It would save expense; render justice more terrible, by rendering it more prompt; facilitate classification, by lessening numbers; keep constantly alive, in the minds of wicked men, the dread of the law; and diminish the unjust sufferings of those who, after long imprisonment, are found innocent.

"From documents," says Mr. Western, "upon the table of the House of Commons in 1819, I drew out an account, which I have already adverted to in part, but which I shall restate here, as it places, in a strong point of view, the extent of injustice, and inconsistency, too, arising out of the present system. It appeared that, at the Maidstone Lent Assizes of that year there were one hundred and seventy-seven prisoners for trial; of these, seventeen were in prison before the 1st of October, eighty-three before the 1st of January, the shortest period of confinement before trial being six months of the former, three months of the latter. Nothing can show us more plainly the injustice of such confinement than the known fact of six months' imprisonment being considered a sufficient punishment for half the felonies that are committed: but the case is stronger, when we consider the number acquitted; seventeen of the twenty-seven first mentioned were acquitted, nine of the seventeen were discharged, not being prosecuted, or having no bill found against them. On the other side it appeared, that twenty-five convicted felons were sentenced to six months' imprisonment, or under, the longest period of whose confinement did not, therefore, exceed

* This has since been done away with.

the shortest of the seventeen acquitted, or that of the nine, against whom no charge was adduced; there were three, who, after being about seven months in prison, were then discharged, whilst various convicted felons suffered six-sevenths only of the punishment, including the time before trial as well as after condemnation. By the returns from the Lent Assizes at Chelmsford, the same year, the cases were not less striking than those of Maidstone: the total number was one hundred and sixty-six; of these, twenty-five were in prison before the 1st of October, of whom eleven were acquitted, and of these eleven, six were discharged without any indictment preferred; two were in prison eight months; three, seven months and fifteen days. three, six months and fifteen days. On the other hand, sixteen convicted of felony, were considered to be sufficiently punished by imprisonment under six months. Upon the whole, it appeared that four hundred and five persons had been in gaol before the 1st of October, whilst eight hundred convicted felons were sentenced to a lighter punishment, to a shorter duration of imprisonment, than these four hundred and five had actually undergone.

"It is a curious fact, that, upon an average, more than one-third of the total number committed for trial are acquitted. In the seven years ending 1819, seventy-two thousand two hundred and sixteen persons were committed; of these, fourteen thousand two hundred and ninety-one were acquitted on trial, eleven thousand two hundred and seventy-four were discharged, there being no prosecutions, or no bills found against them. This large proportion of acquittals aggravates the evil and injustice of long confinement before trial; but were it otherwise, what possible right can we have to detain a man in custody six months, upon any charge exhibited against him, before he is brought to trial? What excuse or palliation can be found for so barbarous a violation of all the principles of justice and humanity? How contemptible it is, by way of defence, to talk of the inexpediency of increasing the number of the judges, the expense, inconvenience, trouble, &c.! It is wrong to contend with such arguments against the unanswerable claims of justice, as it is only to admit they are entitled to weight. The fact is, we are so completely under the influence of habitual respect for established practice, that we do not stop to question the possibility of the existence of any serious defects in the administration of the law that can be capable of remedy. The public attention has never been earnestly and steadily fixed and devoted to the attainment of a better system."—*Western*, pp. 80—83.

The public cannot be too grateful to Mr. Western for his labours on this subject. We strongly recommend his tract for general circulation. It is full of stout good sense, without one particle of nonsense or fanaticism:—good English stuff, of the most improved and best sort. Lord Londonderry has assented to the measure; and his assent does him and the government very great credit. It is a measure of first-rate importance. The multiplicity of imprisonments is truly awful.

Within the distance of ten miles round London, thirty-one fairs are annually held, which continue eighty days within the space of seven months. The effect of these fairs, in filling the prisons of the metropolis, it is easy to imagine; and the topic is very wisely and properly brought forward by the society.

Nothing can be so absurd as the reasoning used about *flash houses.* They are suffered to exist, it seems, because it is easy to the officers of justice to find, in such places, the prisoners of whom they are in search! But the very place where the thief is found is most probably the place which made him a thief. If it facilitates the search, it creates the necessity for searching, and multiplies guilt while it promotes detection. Wherever thieves are known to haunt, that place should be instantly purged of thieves.

We have pushed this article to a length which will prevent us from dwelling upon that part of the plan of the Prison Society which embraces the reformation of juvenile delinquents, of whom it is calculated there are not less than 8000 in London who gain their livelihood by thieving. To this subject we may, perhaps, refer in some future number. We must content ourselves at present with a glimpse at the youthful criminals of the metropolis.

"Upon a late occasion (in company with Mr. Samuel Hoare, the chairman of the Society for the Reform of Juvenile Delinquents), I visited, about midnight, many of those receptacles of thieves which abound in this metropolis. We selected the night of that day in which an execution had taken place; and our object was, to ascertain whether that terrible demonstration of rigour could operate even a short suspension of iniquity, and keep for a single night the votaries of crime from their accustomed orgies. In one room, I recollect, we found a large number of children of both sexes, the oldest under eighteen years of age, and in the centre of these a man who had been described to me by the police as one of the largest sellers of forged bank-notes. At another part, we were shown a number of buildings, into which only children were allowed to enter, and in which, if you could obtain admission, which you cannot, you would see scenes of the most flagrant, the most public, and the most shocking debauchery. Have I not, then, a right to say, that you are growing crimes at a terrible rate, and producing those miscreants who are to disturb the public peace, plunder the public property, and to become the scourge and the disgrace of the country?"—*Buxton*, pp. 66, 67.

Houses dedicated to the debauchery of children, where it is impossible to enter!!! Whence comes this impossibility?

To show that their labours are not needlessly continued, the society make the following statement of the present state of prisons:—

"But although these considerations are highly encouraging, there is yet much to accomplish in this work of national improvement. So extensive are the defects of classification, that in thirty gaols, constructed for the confinement of 2985 persons, there were, at one time in the last year, no fewer than 5837 prisoners; and the whole number imprisoned in those gaols, during that period, amounted to 26,703 There are yet prisons where idleness and its attendant evils reign unrestrained—where the sexes are not separated—where all distinctions of crime are confounded—where few can enter, if uncorrupted, without pollution; and, if guilty, without incurring deeper stains of criminality.—There are yet prisons which receive not the pious visits of a Christian minister—which the light of knowledge never enters—and where the truths and consolations of the Gospel are never heard.—There are yet prisons where, for the security of the prisoners, measures are resorted to as revolting to British feeling as they are repugnant to the spirit and letter of English law."—*Report*, pp. 63, 64.

With this statement we take our leave of the subject of prisons, thoroughly convinced that, since the days of their cleanliness and salubrity, they have been so managed as to become the great school for crimes and wretchedness; and that the public, though beginning to awake, are not yet sufficiently aware of this fact, and sufficiently alarmed at it. Mrs. Fry is an amiable, excellent woman, and ten thousand times better than the infamous neglect that preceded her; but hers is not the method to stop crimes. In prisons, which are really meant to keep the multitude in order, and to be a terror to evil doers, there must be no sharing of profits—no visiting of friends—no education but religious education—no freedom of diet—no weavers' looms or carpenters' benches. There must be a great deal of solitude; coarse food; a dress of shame; hard, incessant, irksome, eternal labour; a planned and regulated and unrelenting exclusion of happiness and comfort.

PERSECUTING BISHOPS.*

[EDINBURGH REVIEW, 1822.]

It is a great point in any question to clear away encumbrances, and to make a naked circle about the object in dispute, so that there may be a clear view of it on every side. In pursuance of this disencumbering process, we shall first acquit the bishop of all wrong intentions. He has a very bad opinion of the practical effects of high Calvinistic doctrines upon the common people; and he thinks it his duty to exclude those clergymen who profess them from his diocese. There is no moral wrong in this. He has accordingly devised no fewer than *eighty-seven* interrogatories, by which he thinks he can detect the smallest taint of Calvinism that may lurk in the creed of the candidate; and in this also, whatever we may think of his reasoning, we suppose his purpose to be blameless. He believes, finally, that he has legally the power so to interrogate and exclude; and in this perhaps he is not mistaken. His intentions, then, are good, and his conduct, perhaps, not amenable to the law. All this we admit in his favour: but against him we must maintain, that his conduct upon the points in dispute has been singularly injudicious, extremely harsh, and, in its effects (though not in its intentions), very oppressive and vexatious to the clergy.

We have no sort of intention to avail ourselves of an anonymous publication to say unkind, uncivil, or disrespectful things to a man of rank, learning, and character—we hope to be guilty of no such impropriety; but we cannot believe we are doing wrong in ranging ourselves on the weaker side, in the cause of propriety and justice. The mitre protects its wearer from indignity; but it does not secure impunity.

It is a strong presumption that a man is wrong, when all his friends, whose habits naturally lead them to coincide with him, think him wrong. If a man were to indulge in taking medicine till the apothecary, the druggist, and the physician, all called upon him to abandon his philo-cathartic propensities—if he were to gratify his convivial habits till the landlord demurred and the waiter shook his head—we should naturally imagine that advice so wholly disinterested was not given before it was wanted, and that it merited some little attention and respect. Now, though the Bench of Bishops certainly love power, and love the church, as well as the Bishop of Peterborough, yet not one defended him—not one rose to say, "I have done, or I would do the same thing." It was impossible to be present at the last debate on this question, without perceiving that his lordship stood alone—and this in a very gregarious profession, that habitually combines and butts against an opponent with a very extended front. If a lawyer is wounded, the rest of the profession pursue him, and put him to death. If a churchman is hurt, the others gather round for his protection, stamp with their feet, push with their horns, and demolish the dissenter who did the mischief.

The bishop has at least done a very unusual thing in his Eighty-seven Questions. The two archbishops, and we believe every other bishop, and all the Irish hierarchy, admit curates into their dioceses without any such precautions. The necessity of such severe and scrupulous inquisition, in short, has been apparent to nobody but the Bishop of Peterborough; and the authorities by which he seeks to justify it are any thing but satisfactory. His lordship states, that forty years ago, he was himself examined by written interrogatories, and that he is not the only bishop who has done it; but he mentions no names; and it was hardly worth while to state such extremely slight precedents for so strong a deviation from the common practice of the church.

The bishop who rejects a curate upon the Eighty-seven Questions is necessarily and inevitably opposed to the bishop who ordained him. The Bishop of Gloucester ordains a young man of twenty-three years of age, not thinking it necessary to put to him these interrogatories, or putting them perhaps, and approving of answers diametrically opposite to those that are required by the Bishop of Peterborough. The young clergyman then comes to the last-mentioned bishop, and the bishop, after *putting him to the question*, says, "You are unfit for a clergyman,"—though, ten days before, the Bishop of Gloucester has made him one! It is bad enough for ladies to pull caps, but still worse for bishops to pull mitres. Nothing can be more mischievous or indecent

* 1. *An Appeal to the Legislature and Public; or, the Legality of the Eighty-seven Questions proposed by Dr. Herbert Marsh, the Bishop of Peterborough, to Candidates for Holy Orders, and for Licenses, within that Diocese, considered.* 2d Edition. London, Seely, 1821.

2. *A Speech, delivered in the House of Lords, on Friday, June 7, 1822, by Herbert, Lord Bishop of Peterborough, on the Presentation of a Petition against his Examination Questions: with Explanatory Notes, a Supplement, and a Copy of the Questions.* London, Rivington. 1822.

3. *The Wrongs of the Clergy of the Diocese of Peterborough stated and illustrated.* By the Rev. T. S. GRIMSHAWE, M. A., Rector of Burton, Northamptonshire; and Vicar of Biddenham, Bedfordshire. London, Seely, 1822.

4. *Episcopal Innovation: or, the Test of Modern Orthodoxy, in Eighty-seven Questions, imposed, as Articles of Faith, upon Candidates for Licenses and for Holy Orders, in the Diocese of Peterborough; with a distinct Answer to each Question, and General Reflections Relative to their Illegal Structure and Pernicious Tendency.* London, Seely, 1820.

5. *Official Correspondence between the Right Rev. Herbert, Lord Bishop of Peterborough, and the Rev. John Green, respecting his Nomination to the Curacy of Blatherwycke, in the Diocese of Peterborough, and County of Northampton: Also, between His Grace Charles, Lord Archbishop of Canterbury, and the Rev. Henry William Nevile, M. A., Rector of Blatherwycke, and of Cottesmore in the County of Rutland.* 1821

than such scenes; and no man of common prudence, or knowledge of the world, but must see that they ought immediately to be put a stop to. If a man is a captain in the army in one part of England, he is a captain in all. The general who commands north of the Tweed does not say, You shall never appear in my district, or exercise the functions of an officer, if you do not answer eighty-seven questions on the art of war, according to my notions. The same officer who commands a ship of the line in the Mediterranean, is considered as equal to the same office in the North Seas. The sixth commandment is suspended, by one medical diploma, from the north of England to the south. But, by this new system of interrogation, a man may be admitted into orders at Barnet, rejected at Stevenage, re-admitted at Brogden, kicked out as a Calvinist at Witham Common, and hailed as an ardent Arminian on his arrival at York.

It matters nothing to say that sacred things must not be compared with profane. In their importance, we allow, they cannot; but in their order and discipline they may be so far compared as to say, that the discrepancy and contention which would be disgraceful and pernicious in worldly affairs, should, in common prudence, be avoided in the affairs of religion. Mr. Greenough has made a map of England, according to its geological varieties;—blue for the chalk, green for the clay, red for the sand, and so forth. Under this system of Bishop Marsh, we must petition for the assistance of the geologist in the fabrication of an ecclesiastical map. All the Arminian districts must be purple. Green for one theological extremity—sky-blue for another—as many colours as there are bishops—as many shades of these colours as there are archdeacons—a tailor's pattern card—the picture of vanity, fashion, and caprice!

The bishop seems surprised at the resistance he meets with; and yet, to what purpose has he read ecclesiastical history, if he expects to meet with any thing but the most determined opposition? Does he think that every sturdy supralapsarian bullock whom he tries to sacrifice to the genius of orthodoxy, will not kick, and push, and toss; that he will not, if he *can*, shake the axe from his neck, and hurl his mitred butcher into the air? His lordship has undertaken a task of which he little knows the labour or the end. We know these men fully as well as the bishop; he has not a chance of success against them. If one motion in Parliament will not do, they will have twenty. They will ravage, roar, and rush, till the very chaplains, and the masters and Misses Peterborough request his lordship to desist. He is raising up a storm in the English church, of which he has not the slightest conception; and which will end, as it ought to end, in his lordship's disgrace and defeat.

The longer we live, the more we are convinced of the justice of the old saying, that an *ounce of mother wit is worth a pound of clergy;* that discretion, gentle manners, common sense, and good nature, are, in men of high ecclesiastical station, of far greater importance than the greatest skill in discriminating between sublapsarian and supralapsarian doctrines. Bishop Marsh should remember, that all men wearing the mitre work by character, as well as doctrine; that a tender regard to men's rights and feelings, a desire to avoid sacred squabbles, a fondness for quiet, and an ardent wish to make everybody happy, would be of far more value to the Church of England than all his learning and vigilance of inquisition. The Irish tithes will probably fall next session of Parliament; the common people are regularly receding from the Church of England—baptizing, burying, and confirming for themselves. Under such circumstances, what would the worst enemy of the English church require?—a bitter, bustling, theological bishop, accused by his clergy of tyranny and oppression—the cause of daily petitions and daily debates in the House of Commons—the idoneous vehicle of abuse against the Establishment—a stalking-horse to bad men for the introduction of revolutionary opinions, mischievous ridicule, and irreligious feelings. Such will be the advantages which Bishop Marsh will secure for the English Establishment in the ensuing session. It is inconceivable how such a prelate shakes all the upper works of the church, and ripens it for dissolution and decay. Six such bishops, multiplied by eighty-seven, and working with five hundred and twenty-two questions, would fetch every thing to the ground in less than six months. But what if it pleased Divine Providence to afflict every prelate with the spirit of putting eighty-seven queries, and the two archbishops with the spirit of putting twice as many, and the Bishop of Sodor and Man with the spirit of putting only forty-three queries?—there would then be a grand total of two thousand three hundred and thirty-five interrogations flying about the English church; and sorely vexed would the land be with Question and Answer.

We will suppose this learned prelate, without meanness or undue regard to his worldly interests, to feel that fair desire of rising in his profession, which any man, in any profession, may feel without disgrace. Does he forget that his character in the ministerial circles will soon become that of a violent, impracticable man—whom it is impossible to place in the highest situations—who has been trusted with too much already, and must be trusted with no more? Ministers have something else to do with their time, and with the time of Parliament, than to waste them in debating squabbles between bishops and their clergy. They naturally wish, and, on the whole, reasonably expect, that every thing should go on silently and quietly in the church. They have no objection to a learned bishop; but they deprecate one atom more of learning than is compatible with moderation, good sense, and the soundest discretion. It must be the grossest ignorance of the world to suppose, that the cabinet has any pleasure in watching Calvinists.

The bishop not only puts the question, but he actually assigns the limits within which they are to be answered. Spaces are left in the paper of interrogations, to which limits the answer is to be confined;—two inches to original sin; an inch and a half to justification; three quarters to predestination; and to free will only a quarter of an inch. But if his lordship gives them an inch they will take an ell. His lordship is himself a theological writer, and by no means remarkable for his conciseness. To deny space to his brother theologians, who are writing on the most difficult subjects, not from choice, but necessity; not for fame, but for bread; and to award rejection as the penalty of prolixity, does appear to us no slight deviation from Christian gentleness. The tyranny of calling for such short answers is very strikingly pointed out in a letter from Mr. Thurtell to the Bishop of Peterborough; the style of which pleads, we think, very powerfully in favour of the writer.

"*Beccles, Suffolk, August 28th,* 1821.

"My Lord—I ought, in the first place, to apologise for delaying so long to answer your lordship's letter: but the difficulty in which I was involved, by receiving another copy of your lordship's Questions, with positive directions to give short answers, may be sufficient to account for that delay.

"It is my sincere desire to meet your lordship's wishes, and to obey your lordship's directions in every particular; and I would therefore immediately have returned answers, without any 'restrictions or modifications,' to the Questions which your lordship has thought fit to send me, if, in so doing, I could have discharged the obligations of my conscience, by showing what my opinions really are. But it appears to me, that the Questions proposed to me by your lordship are so constructed as to elicit only two sets of opinions; and that by answering them in so concise a manner, I should be representing myself to your lordship as one who believes in either of two particular creeds, to neither of which I do *really* subscribe. For instance, to answer Question I. chap. ii., in the manner your lordship desires, I am reduced to the alternative of declaring, either that 'mankind are a mass of *mere* corruption,' which expresses more than I intend, or of leaving room for the inference, that they are only *partially* corrupt, which is opposed to the plainest declarations of the Homilies; such as these, 'Man is *altogether* spotted and defiled' (Hom. on Nat.), 'without a *spark* of goodness in him' (Serm. on Mis. of Man, &c.).

"Again, by answering the Questions comprised in the chapter on 'Free Will,' according to your lordship's directions, I am compelled to acknowledge either that man has such a share in the work of his own salvation as to exclude the *sole* agency of God, or that he has no share whatever; when the Homilies for Rogation Week and Whitsunday positively declare, that God is the 'only Worker,' or, in other words, *sole* Agent; and at the same time assign to man a certain share in the work of his own salvation. In short, I could, with your lordship's permission, point out twenty Questions, involving doctrines of the utmost importance, which I am unable to answer, so as to convey my real sentiments, without more room for explanation than the printed sheet affords.

"In this view of the subject, therefore, and in the most deliberate exercise of my judgment, I deem it indispensable to my acting with that candour and truth with which it is my wish and duty to act, and with which I cannot but believe your lordship desires I should act, to state my opinions in that language which expresses them most fully, plainly, and unreservedly. This I have endeavoured to do in the answers now in the possession of your lordship. If any further explanation be required, I am most willing to give it, even to a minuteness of opinion beyond what the Articles require. At the same time, I would humbly and respectfully appeal to your lordship's candour, *whether it is not hard to demand my decided opinion upon points which have been the themes of volumes; upon which the most pious and learned men of the church have conscientiously differed; and upon which the Articles in the judgment of Bishop Burnet have pronounced no definite sentence.* To those Articles, my lord, I have already subscribed; and I am willing again to subscribe to every one of them, 'in its literal and grammatical sense,' according to his majesty's declaration prefixed to them.

"I hope, therefore, in consideration of the above statement, that your lordship will not compel me, by the conciseness of my answers to assent to the doctrines which I do not believe, or to expose myself to inferences which do not fairly and legitimately follow from my opinions. "I am, my Lord, &c. &c."

We are not much acquainted with the practices of courts of justice; but, if we remember right, when a man is going to be hanged, the judge lets him make his defence in his own way, without complaining of its length. We should think a Christian bishop might be equally indulgent to a man who is going to be ruined. The answers are required to be clear, concise, and correct—short, plain, and positive. In other words, a poor curate, extremely agitated at the idea of losing his livelihood, is required to write with brevity and perspicuity on the following subjects;—Redemption by Jesus Christ—Original Sin—Free Will—Justification—Justification in reference to its causes—Justification in reference to the time when it takes place—Everlasting Salvation—Predestination—Regeneration on the New Birth—Renovation, and the Holy Trinity. As a specimen of these questions, the answer to which is required to be so brief and clear, we shall insert the following quotation:—

"*Section II.—Of Justification in reference to its cause.*

"1. Does not the eleventh Article declare, that we are 'justified by Faith *only?*'

"2. Does not the expression 'Faith only' derive additional strength from the negative expression in the same Article 'and *not* for our own works?'

"3. Does not therefore the eleventh Article *exclude* good works from all share in the office of Justifying? Or can we so construe the term 'Faith' in that Article, as to make it *include* good works?

"4. Do not the twelfth and thirteenth Articles *further* exclude them, the one by asserting that good works *follow after* Justification, the other by maintaining that they *cannot precede* it?

"5. Can that, which never precedes an effect, be reckoned among *the causes* of that effect?

"6. Can we then, consistently with our Articles, reckon the performance of good works among the *causes* of Justification, whatever qualifying epithet be used with the term *cause?*"

We entirely deny that the Calvinistical clergy are bad members of their profession. We maintain that as many instances of good, serious, and pious men—of persons zealously interesting themselves in the temporal and spiritual welfare of their parishioners are to be found among them, as among the clergy who put an opposite interpretation on the Articles. The Articles of Religion are older than Arminianism, *eo nomine*. The early reformers leant to Calvinism; and would, to a man, have answered the bishop's questions in a way which would have induced him to refuse them ordination and curacies; and those who drew up the Thirty-nine Articles, if they had not prudently avoided all precise interpretation of their creed on free-will, necessity, absolute decrees, original sin, reprobation, and election, would have, in all probability, given an interpretation of them like that which the bishop considers as a disqualification for holy orders. Laud's Lambeth Articles were illegal, mischievous, and are generally condemned. The Irish clergy in 1641 drew up one hundred and four articles as the creed of their church; and these are Calvinistic, and not Arminian. They were approved and signed by Usher, and never abjured by him; though dropped as a test or qualification. Usher was promoted (even in the days of Arminianism) to bishoprics and archbishoprics—so little did a Calvinistic interpretation of the Articles in a man's own breast, or even an avowal of Calvinism, beyond what was required by the Articles, operate even then as a disqualification for the cure of souls, or of any other office in the church. Throughout Charles II. and William III.'s time, the best men and greatest names of the church not only allowed latitude in interpreting the Articles, but thought it would be wise to diminish their number, and render them more lax than they are; and be it observed, that these latitudinarians leant to Arminianism rather than to high Calvinism; and thought, consequently, that the Articles, if objectionable at all, were exposed to the censure of being "too Calvinistic," rather than too Arminian. How preposterous, therefore, to twist them, and the subscription to them required by law, by the machinery of a long string of explanatory questions, into a barrier against Calvinists, and to give the Arminians a monopoly in the church!

Archbishop Wake, in 1716, after consulting all the bishops then attending Parliament, thought it incumbent on him "*to employ the authority which the ecclesiastical laws then in force, and the custom and laws of the realm, vested in him*," and taking care that "*no unworthy person might hereafter be admitted into the sacred ministry of the church;*" and he drew up twelve recommendations to the bishops of England, in which he earnestly exhorts them not to ordain persons of bad conduct or character, or incompetent learning; but he does not require from the candidates for holy orders or preferment, any explanation whatever of the Articles which they had signed.

The correspondence of the same eminent prelate with Professor Turretin in 1718, and with Mr. Le Clerc and the pastors and professors of Geneva in 1719, printed in London, 1782, recommends union among Protestants, and the omission of controverted points in confessions of faith, as a means of obtaining that union; and a constant reference to the practice of the Church of England is made in elucidation of the charity and wisdom of such policy. Speaking of men who act upon a contrary principle he says, *O quantum potuit insana* φιλαυτια!

These passages, we think, are conclusive evidence of the practice of the church till 1719. For Wake was not only at the time Archbishop of Canterbury, but both in his circular recommendations to the bishops of England, and in his correspondence with foreign churches, was acting in the capacity of metropolitan of the Anglican church. He, a man of prudence and learning, publicly boasts to Protestant Europe, that his church does *not* exact, and that he *de facto* has never avowed, and never will, his opinions on those very points upon which Bishop Marsh obliges every poor curate to be explicit, upon pain of expulsion from the church.

It is clear, then, the practice was, to extract subscription and nothing else, as the test of orthodoxy—to that Wake is an evidence. As far as he is authority on a point of opinion, it is his conviction that his practice was wholesome, wise, and intended to preserve peace in the church; that it would be wrong at least, if not illegal, to do otherwise; and that the observance of this forbearance is the only method of preventing schism. The Bishop of Peterborough, however, is of a different opinion; he is so thoroughly convinced of the pernicious effects of Calvinistic doctrines, that he does what no other bishop does, or ever did do, for their exclusion. This may be either wise or injudicious, but it is at least zealous and bold; it is to encounter rebuke, and opposition, from a sense of duty. It is impossible to deny this merit to his lordship. And we have no doubt, that, in pursuance of the same theological gallantry, he is preparing a set of interrogatories for those clergymen who are presented to benefices in his diocese. The patron will have his action of *Quare impedit*, it is true; and the judge and jury will decide whether the bishop has the right of interrogation at all; and whether Calvinistical answers to his interrogatories disqualify any man from holding preferment in the Church of England. If either of these points are given against the Bishop of Peterborough, he is in honour and conscience bound to give up his examination of curates. If Calvinistic ministers are, in the estimation of the bishops, so dangerous as curates, they are of course much more dangerous as rectors and vicars. He has as much right to examine one as the other. Why then does he pass over the greater danger, and guard against the less? Why does he not show his zeal when he would run some risk, and where the excluded person (if excluded unjustly) could appeal to the laws of his country? If his conduct is just and right, has he any thing to fear from that appeal? What should we say of a police officer who acted in all cases of petty larceny, where no opposition was made, and let off all persons guilty of felony who threatened to knock him down? If the bishop values his own character, he is bound to do less,—or to do more. God send his choice may be right! The law, as it stands at present, certainly affords very unequal protection to rector and to curate; but if the bishop will not act so as to improve the law, the law must be so changed as to improve the bishop; an action of *Quare impedit* must be given to the curate also—and then the fury of interrogation will be calmed.

We are aware that the Bishop of Peterborough, in his speech, disclaims the object of excluding the Calvinists by this system of interrogation. We shall take no other notice of his disavowal, than expressing our sincere regret that he ever made it; but the question is not at all altered by the intention of the interrogator. Whether he aims at the Calvinists only, or includes them with other heterodox respondents—the fact is, they *are* included in the proscription, and excluded from the church. The practical effect of the practice being, that men are driven out of the church, who have as much right to exercise the duties of clergymen as the bishop himself. If heterodox opinions are the great objects of the bishop's apprehensions, he has his ecclesiastical courts, where regular process may bring the offender to punishment, and from whence there is no appeal to higher courts. This would be the fair thing to do. The curate and the bishop would be brought into the light of day, and subjected to the wholesome restraint of public opinion.

His lordship boasts that he has excluded only two curates. So the Emperor of Hayti boasted that he had only cut off two persons' heads for disagreeable behaviour at his table. In spite of the paucity of the visitors executed, the example operated as a considerable impediment to conversation; and the intensity of the punishment was found to be a full compensation for its rarity. How many persons have been deprived of curacies which they might have enjoyed, but for the tenour of these interrogatories? How many respectable clergymen have been deprived of the assistance of curates connected with them by blood, friendship, or doctrine, and compelled to choose persons, for no other qualification than that they could pass through the eye of the bishop's needle? Violent measures are not to be judged of merely by the number of times they have been resorted to, but by the terror, misery, and restraint which the severity is likely to have produced.

We never met with any style so entirely clear of all redundant and vicious ornament, as that which the ecclesiastical Lord of Peterborough has adopted towards his clergy. It, in fact, may be all reduced to these few words—"Reverend Sir, I shall do what I please. Peterborough."—Even in the House of Lords, he speaks what we must call very plain language. Among other things, he says, that the allegations of the petitions are *false*. Now, as every bishop is, besides his other qualities, a gentleman; and as the word *false* is used only by laymen, who mean to hazard their lives by the expression; and as it cannot be supposed that foul language is ever used because it can be used with personal impunity, his lordship must, therefore, be intended to mean not *false*, but *mistaken*—not a wilful deviation from truth, but an accidental and unintended departure from it.

His lordship talks of the drudgery of wading through ten pages of answers to his eighty-seven questions. Who has occasioned this drudgery, but the person who means to be so much more active, useful, and important, than all other bishops, by proposing questions which nobody has thought to be necessary but himself? But to be intolerably strict and harsh to a poor curate, who is trying to earn a morsel of hard bread, and then to complain of the drudgery of reading his answers, is much like knocking a man down with a bludgeon, and then abusing him for splashing you with his blood, and pestering you with his groans. It is quite monstrous, that a man who inflicts eighty-seven new questions in theology upon his fellow-creatures, should talk of the drudgery of reading their answers.

A curate—there is something which excites compassion in the very name of a curate!!! How any man of purple, palaces, and preferment, can let himself loose against this poor workman of God, we are at a loss to conceive, —a learned man in a hovel, with sermons and saucepans, lexicons and bacon, Hebrew books and ragged children—good and patient—a comforter and a preacher—the first and purest pauper in the hamlet, and yet showing, that, in the midst of his worldly misery, he has the heart of a gentleman, and the spirit of a Christian, and the kindness of a pastor; and this man, though he has exercised the duties of a clergyman for twenty years—though he has most ample testimonies of conduct from clergymen as respectable as any bishop—though an archbishop add his name to the list of witnesses, is not good enough for Bishop Marsh; but is pushed out in the street, with his wife and children, and his little furniture, to surrender his honour, his faith, his conscience, and his learning—or to starve?

An obvious objection to these innovations is, that there can be no end to them. If eighty-seven questions are assumed to be necessary by one bishop, eight hundred may be considered as the minimum of interrogation by another. When once the ancient faith-marks of the church are lost sight of and despised, any misled theologian may launch out on the boundless sea of polemical vexation.

The Bishop of Peterborough is positive, that the Arminian interpretation of the articles is the right interpretation, and that Calvinists should be excluded from it; but the country gentlemen who are to hear these matters debated in the Lower House, are to remember, that other bishops have written upon these points before the Bishop of Peterborough, and have arrived at conclusions diametrically opposite. When curates are excluded because their answers are Calvinistical, a careless layman might imagine that this interpretation of the Articles had never been heard of before in the church—that it was a gross and palpable perversion of their sense, which had been scouted by all writers on church matters, from the day the Articles were promulgated, to this hour—that such an unheard-of monster as a Calvinistical curate had never leapt over the pale before, and been detected browsing in the sacred pastures.

The following is the testimony of Bishop Sherlock:—

"'The church has left a latitude of sense to prevent schisms and breaches upon every different opinion. It is evident the Church of England has so done in some articles, which are most liable to the hottest disputes; which yet are penned with that temper as to be willingly subscribed by men of different apprehensions in those matters.'—SHERLOCK's *Defence of Stillingfleet's Unreasonableness of Separation.*"

Bishop Cleaver, describing the difficulties attending so great an undertaking as the formation of a national creed, observes:—

"'These difficulties, however, do not seem to have discouraged the great leaders in this work from forming a design as wise as it was liberal, that of framing a confession, which, in the enumeration and method of its several articles, should meet the approbation, and engage the consent, of the whole reformed world.

"'If, upon trial, it was found that a comprehension so extensive could not be reduced to practice, still as large a comprehension as could be contrived, within the narrower limits of the kingdom, became, for the same reasons which first suggested the idea, at once an object of prudence and duty, in the formation and government of the English church.'

"After dwelling on the means necessary to accomplish this object, the bishop proceeds to remark:—'Such evidently appears to have been the origin, and such the actual complexion of the confession comprised in the Articles of our church; *the true scope and design of which will not, I conceive, be correctly apprehended in any other view than that of one drawn up and adjusted with an intention to comprehend the assent of all, rather than to exclude that of any who concurred in the necessity of a reformation.*

"'The means of comprehension intended were, not any general ambiguity or equivocation of terms, *but a prudent forbearance in all parties not to insist on the full extent of their opinions in matters not essential or fundamental; and in all cases to wave, as much as possible, tenets which might divide, where they wish to unite.*'—Remarks on the Design and Formation of the Articles of the Church of England, by WILLIAM, Lord Bishop of Bangor, 1802."—pp. 23—25.

We will finish with Bishop Horsley.

"It has been the fashion of late to talk about Arminianism as the system of the Church of England, and of Calvinism as something opposite to it, to which the church is hostile. That I may not be misunderstood in what I have stated, or may have occasion further to say upon this subject, I must here declare, that I use the words Arminianism and Calvinism in that restricted sense in which they are now generally taken, to denote the doctrinal part of each system, as unconnected with the principles either of Arminians or Calvinists upon church discipline and church government. This being premised, I assert, what I often have before asserted, and by God's grace I will persist in the assertion to my dying day, that so far is it from the truth that the Church of England is decidedly Arminian, and hostile to Calvinism, that the truth is this, *that upon the principal points in dispute between the Arminians and the Calvinists upon all the points of doctrine characteristic of the two sects, the Church of England maintains an absolute neutrality; her articles explicitly assert nothing but what is believed both by Arminians and by Calvinists.* The Calvinists indeed hold some opinions relative to the same points, which the Church of England has not gone the length of asserting in her Articles; but neither has she gone the length of explicitly contradicting those opinions; insomuch that *there is nothing to hinder the Arminian and the highest supralapsarian Calvinists from walking together in the Church of England and Ireland as friends and brothers, if they both approve the discipline of the church, and both are willing to submit to it.* Her discipline has been approved; it has been submitted to; it has been in former times most ably and zealously defended by the highest supralapsarian Calvinists. Such was the great Usher; such was Whitgift; such were many more, burning and shining lights of our church in her early days (when first she shook off the Papal tyranny), long since gone to the resting place of the spirits of the just.—*Bishop* HORSLEY's *Charges*, p. 216."—pp. 25, 26.

So that these unhappy curates are turned out of their bread for an exposition of the Articles which such men as Sherlock, Cleaver, and Horsley think may be fairly given of their meaning. We do not quote their authority to show that the right interpretation is decided, but that it is doubtful—that there is a balance of authorities—that the opinion which Bishop Marsh has punished with poverty and degradation, has been considered to be legitimate, by men at least as wise and learned as himself. In fact, it is to us perfectly clear, that the Articles were originally framed to prevent the very practices which Bishop Marsh has used for their protection—they were purposely so worded, that Arminians and Calvinists could sign them without blame. They were intended to combine both these descriptions of Protestants, and were meant principally for a bulwark against Catholics.

"Thus," says Bishop Burnet, "was the doctrine of the church cast into a short and plain form; in which they took care both to establish the positive articles of religion, and to cut off the errors formerly introduced in the time of popery, or of late broached by the Anabaptists and enthusiasts of Germany;

avoiding the niceties of schoolmen, or the peremptoriness of the writers of controversy; leaving, in matters that are more justly controvertible, a liberty to divines to follow their private opinions, without thereby disturbing the peace of the church."—History of the Reformation, Book I. part ii. p. 168, folio edition.

The next authority is that of Fuller.

"In the convocation now sitting, wherein Alexander Nowel, Dean of St. Paul's, was prolocutor, the nine-and-thirty Articles were composed. For the main they agree with those set forth in the reign of King Edward the Sixth, though in some particulars allowing more liberty to dissenting judgments. For instance, in this King's Articles it is said, that it is to be believed that Christ went down to hell (to preach to the spirits there); which last clause is left out in these Articles, and men left to a latitude concerning the cause, time, and manner of his descent.

"Hence some have unjustly taxed the composers for too much favour extended in their large expressions, clean through the contexture of these Articles, which should have tied men's consciences up closer, in more strict and particularizing propositions, *which indeed proceeded from their commendable moderation.* Children's clothes ought to be made of the biggest, because afterwards their bodies will grow up to their garments. Thus the Articles of this English Protestant Church, in the infancy thereof, they thought good to draw up in general terms, foreseeing that posterity would grow up to fill the same: I mean these holy men did prudently prediscover, that differences in judgments would unavoidably happen in the church, *and were loath to unchurch any, and drive them off from an ecclesiastical communion, for such petty differences, which made them pen the Articles in comprehensive words, to take in all who, differing in the branches, meet in the root of the same religion.*

"Indeed most of them had formerly been sufferers themselves, and cannot be said, in compiling these Articles, (an acceptable service, no doubt,) to offer to God what cost them nothing, some having paid imprisonment, others exile, all losses in their estates, for this their experimental knowledge in religion, *which made them the more merciful and tender in stating those points*, seeing such who themselves have been most patient in bearing, will be most pitiful in burdening the consciences of others."—See FULLER's *Church History*, book ix. p. 72, folio edit.

But this generous and pacific spirit gives no room for the display of zeal and theological learning. The gate of admission has been left too widely open. I may as well be without power at all, if I cannot force my opinions upon other people. What was purposely left indefinite, I must make definite and exclusive. Questions of contention and difference must be laid before the servants of the church, and nothing like neutrality in theological metaphysics allowed to the ministers of the Gospel. *I come not to bring peace*, &c.

The bishop, however, seems to be quite satisfied with himself, when he states, that he has a *right to do* what he has done—just as if a man's character with his fellow-creatures depended upon legal rights alone, and not upon a discreet exercise of those rights. A man may persevere in doing what he has a right to do, till the chancellor shuts him up in Bedlam, or till the mob pelt him as he passes. It must be presumed, that all men whom the law has invested with rights, nature has invested with common sense, to use those rights. For these reasons, children have no rights till they have gained common sense, and old men have no rights after they lose their common sense. All men are at all times accountable to their fellow-creatures for the discreet exercise of every right they possess.

Prelates are fond of talking of *my* see, *my* clergy, *my* diocese, as if these things belonged to them, as their pigs and dogs belonged to them. They forget that the clergy, the diocese, and the bishops themselves, all exist only for the public good; that the public are a third, and principal party in the whole concern. It is not simply the tormenting Bishop *versus* the tormented Curate, but the public against the system of tormenting; as tending to bring scandal upon religion and religious men. By the late alteration in the laws, the labourers in the vineyard are given up to the power of the inspectors of the vineyard. If he has the meanness and malice to do so, an inspector may worry and plague to death any labourer against whom he may have conceived an antipathy. As often as such cases are detected, we believe they will meet, in either House of Parliament, with the severest reprehension. The noblemen and gentlemen of England will never allow their parish clergy to be treated with cruelty, injustice, and caprice, by men who were parish clergymen themselves yesterday, and who were trusted with power for very different purposes.

The Bishop of Peterborough complains of the insolence of the answers made to him. This is certainly not true of Mr. Grimshawe, Mr. Neville, or of the author of the Appeal. They have answered his lordship with great force, great manliness, but with perfect respect. Does the bishop expect that humble men, as learned as himself, are to be driven from their houses and homes by his new theology, and then to send him letters of thanks for the kicks and cuffs he has bestowed upon them? Men of very small incomes, be it known unto his lordship, have very often very acute feelings; and a curate trod on feels a pang as great as when a bishop is refuted.

We shall now give a specimen of some answers, which, we believe, would exclude a curate from the diocese of Peterborough, and contrast these answers with the articles of the church to which they refer. The 9th Article of the Church of England is upon Original Sin. Upon this point his lordship puts the following question:—

"Did the Fall of Adam produce such an effect on his posterity, that mankind became thereby a mass of mere corruption, or of absolute and entire depravity? Or is the effect only such, that we are very *far gone* from original righteousness, and of our own nature *inclined* to evil?"

Excluding Answer.	*The Ninth Article.*
"The fall of Adam produced such an effect on his posterity, that mankind became thereby a mass of mere corruption, or of absolute and entire depravity."	"Original Sin standeth not in the following of Adam (as the Pelagians do vainly talk); but it is the fault or corruption of the nature of every man, that naturally is engendered of the offspring of Adam, whereby man is very far gone from original righteousness, and is of his own nature inclined to evil, so that the flesh lusteth always contrary to the spirit; and therefore, in every person born into the world, it deserveth God's wrath and damnation."

The 9th Question, Cap. 3d, on Free Will, is as follows:—Is it not contrary to Scripture to say, that man has no share in the work of his salvation?

Excluding Answer.	*Tenth Article.*
"It is quite agreeable to Scripture to say, that man has no share in the work of his own salvation."	"The condition of man after the fall of Adam is such, that he cannot turn and prepare himself, by his own natural strength and good works, to faith, and calling upon God. Wherefore, we have no power to do good works pleasant and acceptable to God, without the grace of God by Christ preventing us, that we may have a good will, and working with us when we have that good will."

On Redemption, his lordship has the following question, Cap. 1st, Question 1st:—Did Christ die for all men, or did he die only for a chosen few?

Excluding Answer.	*Part of Article Seventeenth.*
"Christ did not die for all men, but only for a chosen few."	"Predestination to life is the everlasting purpose of God, whereby (before the foundations of the world were laid) he hath constantly decreed by his counsel, secret to us, to deliver from curse and damnation those whom he hath chosen in Christ out of mankind, and to bring them by Christ unto everlasting salvation, as vessels made to honour."

Now, whether these answers are right or wrong, we do not presume to decide; but we cannot help saying, there appears to be some little colour in the language of the Articles for the errors of the respondent. It does not appear at first sight to be such a deviation from the plain, literal, and grammatical sense of the Articles, as to merit rapid and ignominious ejectment from the bosom of the church.

Now we have done with the Bishop. We give him all he asks as to his legal right; and only contend, that he is acting a very indiscreet and injudicious part—fatal to his quiet—fatal to his reputation as a man of sense—blamed by ministers—blamed by all the Bench of Bishops—vexatious to the clergy, and highly injurious to the church. We mean no personal disrespect to the Bishop; we are as ignorant of him as of his victims. We should have been heartily glad if the debate in Parliament had put an end to these blameable excesses; and our only object, in meddling with the question, is to restrain the arm of power within the limits of moderation and justice—one of the great objects which first led to the establishment of this Journal, and which, we hope, will always continue to characterize its efforts.

BOTANY BAY.*

[Edinburgh Review, 1823.]

Mr. Bigge's Report is somewhat long, and a little clumsy; but it is altogether the production of an honest, sensible, and respectable man, who has done his duty to the public, and justified the expense of his mission to the fifth or pickpocket quarter of the globe.

What manner of man is Governor Macquarrie?—Is all that Mr. Bennet says of him in the House of Commons true? These are the questions which Lord Bathurst sent Mr. Bigge, and very properly sent him, 28,000 miles to answer. The answer is, that Governor Macquarrie is not a dishonest man, nor a jobber; but arbitrary, in many things scandalously negligent, very often wrong-headed, and, upon the whole, very deficient in that good sense, and vigorous understanding, which his new and arduous situation so manifestly requires.

Ornamental architecture in Botany Bay! how it could enter into the head of any human being to adorn public buildings at the Bay, or to aim at any other architectural purpose but the exclusion of wind and rain, we are utterly at a loss to conceive. Such an expense is not only lamentable for the waste of property it makes in the particular instance, but because it destroys that guarantee of sound sense which the government at home must require in those who preside over distant colonies. A man who thinks of pillars and pilasters, when half the colony are wet through for want of any covering at all, cannot be a wise or prudent person. He seems to be ignorant, that the prevention of rheumatism in all young colonies is a much more important object than the gratification of taste, or the display of skill.

"I suggested to Governor Macquarrie the expediency of stopping all work then in progress that was merely of an ornamental nature, and of postponing its execution till other more im-

* 1. *Letter to Earl Bathurst,* By the Honourable H. Grey Bennet, M. P.
2. *Report of the Commissioner of Inquiry into the state of the Colony of New South Wales. Ordered by the House of Commons to be printed, 19th June, 1822.*

portant buildings were finished. With this view it was, that I recommended to the governor to stop the progress of a large church, the foundation of which had been laid previous to my arrival, and which, by the estimate of Mr. Greenway the architect, would have required six years to complete. By a change that I recommended, and which the governor adopted, in the destination of the new court-house at Sydney, the accommodation of a new church is probably by this time secured. As I conceived that considerable advantage had been gained by inducing Governor Macquarrie to suspend the progress of the larger church, I did not deem it necessary to make any pointed objection to the addition of these ornamental parts of the smaller one; though I regretted to observe in this instance, as well as in those of the new stables at Sydney, the turnpike-gate house and the new fountain there, as well as in the repairs of an old church at Paramatta, how much more the embellishment of these places had been considered by the governor than the real and pressing wants of the colony. The buildings that I had recommended to his early attention in Sydney were, a new gaol, a school-house, and a market-house. The defects of the first of these buildings will be more particularly pointed out when I come to describe the buildings that have been erected in New South Wales. It is sufficient for me now to observe, that they were striking, and of a nature not to be remedied by additions or repairs. The other two were in a state of absolute ruin; they were also of undeniable importance and necessity. Having left Sydney in the month of November, 1820, with these impressions, and with a belief that the suggestions I had made to Governor Macquarrie respecting them had been partly acted upon, and would continue to be so during my absence in Van Diemen's Land, it was not without much surprise and regret that I learnt, during my residence in that settlement, the resumption of the work at the large church in Sydney, and the steady continuation of the others that I had objected to, especially the governor's stables at Sydney. I felt the greater surprise in receiving the information respecting this last-mentioned structure, during my absence in Van Diemen's Land, as the governor himself had, upon many occasions, expressed to me his own regret at having ever sanctioned it, and his consciousness of its extravagant dimensions and ostentatious character."—*Report*, pp. 51, 52.

One of the great difficulties in Botany Bay is to find proper employment for the great mass of convicts who are sent out. Governor Macquarrie selects all the best artisans, of every description, for the use of government; and puts the poets, attorneys, and politicians, up to auction. The evil consequences of this are manifold. In the first place, from possessing so many of the best artificers, the governor is necessarily turned into a builder; and immense drafts are drawn upon the treasury at home, for buildings better adapted for Regent street than the Bay. In the next place, the poor settler, finding that the convict attorney is very awkward at cutting timber, or catching kangaroos, soon returns him upon the hands of government, in a much worse plight than that in which he was received. Not only are governors thus debauched into useless and expensive builders, but the colonists, who are scheming and planning with all the activity of new settlers, cannot find workmen to execute their designs.

What two ideas are more inseparable than beer and Britannia?—what event more awfully important to an English colony than the erection of its first brewhouse?—and yet it required, in Van Diemen's land, the greatest solicitation to the government, and all the influence of Mr. Bigge, to get it effected. The government, having obtained possession of the best workmen, keep them; their manumission is much more infrequent than that of the useless and unprofitable convicts; in other words, one man is punished for his skill, and another rewarded for his inutility. Guilty of being a locksmith—guilty of stone-masonry, or brick-making;—these are the second verdicts brought in, in New South Wales; and upon them is regulated the duration or mitigation of punishment awarded in the mother country. At the very period when the governor assured Lord Bathurst, in his despatches, that he kept and employed so numerous a gang of workmen, only because the inhabitants could not employ them, Mr. Bigge informs us, that their services would have been most acceptable to the colonists. Most of the settlers, at the time of Mr. Bigge's arrival, from repeated refusals and disappointments, had been so convinced of the impossibility of obtaining workmen, that they had ceased to make application to the governor. Is it to be believed that a governor, placed over a land of convicts, and capable of guarding his limbs from any sudden collision with odometrous stones, or vertical posts of direction, should make no distinction between the simple convict and the double and treble convict—the man of three juries, who has three times appeared at the Bailey, trilarcenous—three times driven over the seas?

"I think it necessary to notice the want of attention that has prevailed, until a very late period, at Sydney, to the circumstances of those convicts who have been transported a second and a third time. Although the knowledge of these facts is transmitted to the hulk lists, or acquired without difficulty during the passage, it never has occurred to Governor Macquarrie or to the superintendent of convicts, to make any difference in the condition of these men, not even to disappoint the views that they may be supposed to have indulged by the success of a criminal enterprise in England, and by transferring the fruits of it to New South Wales.

"To accomplish this very simple but important object, nothing more is necessary than to consign these men to any situation rather than that which their friends had selected for them, and distinctly to declare in the presence of their comrades at the first muster on their arrival, that no consideration or favour would be shown to those who had violated the law a second time, and that the mitigation of their sentences must be indefinitely postponed."—*Report*, p. 19.

We were not a little amused at Governor Macquarrie's laureate—a regular Mr. Southey—who, upon the king's birth-day, sings the praises of Governor Macquarrie.* The case of this votary of Apollo and Mercury was a case for life; the offence a menacing epistle, or, as low people call it, a *threatening letter*. He has been pardoned, however—bursting his shackles, like Orpheus of old, with song and metre, and is well spoken of by Mr. Bigge, but no specimen of his poetry given. One of the best and most enlightened men in the settlement appears to be Mr. Marsden, a clergyman at Paramatta. Mr. Bennet represents him as a gentleman of great feeling, whose life is embittered by the scenes of horror and vice it is his lot to witness at Paramatta. Indeed, he says of himself, that, in consequence of these things, "he does not enjoy one happy moment from the beginning to the end of the week!" This letter, at the time, produced a very considerable sensation in this country. The idea of a man of refinement and feeling wearing away his life in the midst of scenes of crime and debauchery to which he can apply no corrective, is certainly a very melancholy and affecting picture; but there is no story, however elegant and eloquent, which does not require, for the purposes of justice, to be turned to the other side, and viewed in reverse. The Rev. Mr. Marsden (says Mr. Bigge), *being himself accustomed to traffic in spirits*, must necessarily feel displeased at having so many public houses licensed in the neighbourhood.—(p. 14.)

"As to Mr. Marsden's troubles of mind (says the governor), and pathetic display of sensibility and humanity, they must be so deeply seated, and so far removed from the surface, as to escape all possible observation. His habits are those of a man for ever engaged in some active, animated pursuit. No man travels more from town to town, or from house to house. His deportment is at all times that of a person the most gay and happy. When I was honoured with his society, he was by far the most cheerful person I met in the colony. Where his hours of sorrow were spent, it is hard to divine; for the variety of his pursuits, both in his own concerns, and in those of others, is so extensive, in farming, grazing, manufactories, transactions, that, with his clerical duties, he seems, to use a common phrase, to have his hands full of work. And the particular subject to which he imputes this extreme depression of mind, is, besides, one for which few people here will give him much credit."—*Macquarrie's Letter to Lord Sidmouth*, p. 18.

There is certainly a wide difference between a man of so much feeling that he has not a moment's happiness from the beginning to the end of the week, and a little, merry, bustling clergyman, largely concerned in the sale of rum, and brisk at a bargain for barley. Mr. Bigge's evidence, however, is very much in favour of Mr. Marsden. He seems to think him a man of highly respectable character and superior understanding, and that he has been dismissed from the magistracy by Governor Macquarrie, in a very rash, unjustifiable, and even tyrannical manner; and in these opinions, we must say, the facts seem to bear out the report of the commissioner.

Colonel Macquarrie not only dismisses honest and irreproachable men in a country where their existence is scarce, and their services inestimable, but he advances convicts to the situation and dignity of magistrates. Mr. Bennet lays great stress upon this, and makes it one of his strongest charges against the governor; and the commissioner also takes part against it. But we confess we have great doubts on the subject; and are by no means satisfied that the system of the governor was not, upon the whole, the wisest and best adapted to the situation of the colony. Men are governed by words; and by the infamous word *convict* are comprehended crimes of the most different degrees and species of guilt. One man is transported for stealing three hams and a pot of sausages; and in the next berth to him on board the transport is a young surgeon, who has been engaged in the mutiny at the Nore; the third man is for extorting money; the fourth was in a respectable situation of life at the time of the Irish rebellion, and was so ill read in history as to imagine that Ireland had been ill-treated by England, and so bad a reasoner as to suppose that nine Catholics ought not to pay tithes to one Protestant. Then comes a man who set his house on fire, to cheat the Phœnix office; and, lastly, the most glaring of all human villains, a poacher, driven from Europe, wife and child, by thirty lords of manors, at the Quarter Sessions, for killing a partridge. Now, all these are crimes no doubt—particularly the last; but they are surely crimes of very different degrees of intensity, to which different degrees of contempt and horror are attached—and from which those who have committed them may, by subsequent morality, emancipate themselves, with different degrees of difficulty, and with more or less of success. A warrant granted by a reformed bacon stealer would be absurd; but there is hardly any reason why a foolish, hot-brained young blockhead, who chose to favour the mutineers at the Nore, when he was sixteen years of age, may not make a very loyal subject, and a very respectable and respected magistrate when he is forty years of age, and has cast his Jacobin teeth, and fallen into the practical jobbing and loyal baseness which so commonly developes itself about that period of life. Therefore, to say that a man must be placed in no situation of trust or elevation, as a magistrate, merely because he is a convict, is to govern mankind with a dictionary, and to surrender sense and usefulness to sound. Take the following case, for instance, from Mr. Bigge:—

"The next person, from the same class, that was so distinguished by Governor Macquarrie, was the Rev. Mr. Fulton. He was transported by the sentence of a court martial in Ireland, during the Rebellion; and on his arrival in

* *Vide* Report, p. 146.

New South Wales in the year 1800, was sent to Norfolk Island to officiate as chaplain. He returned to New South Wales in the year 1804, and performed the duties of chaplain at Sydney and Paramatta.

"In the divisions that prevailed in the colony previous to the arrest of Governor Bligh, Mr. Fulton took no part; but, happening to form one of his family when the person of the governor was menaced with violence, he courageously opposed himself to the military party that entered the house, and gave an example of courage and devotion to the authority of Governor Bligh, which, if partaken either by the officer or his few adherents, would have spared him the humiliation of a personal arrest, and rescued his authority from the disgrace of open and violent suspension."—*Report*, pp. 83, 84.

The particular nature of the place, too, must be remembered. It is seldom, we suspect, that absolute dunces go to the Bay, but commonly men of active minds, and considerable talents in their various lines—who have not learnt, indeed, the art of self-discipline and control, but who are sent to learn it in the bitter school of adversity. And when this medicine produces its proper effect—when sufficient time has been given to show a thorough change in character and disposition—a young colony really cannot afford to dispense with the services of any person of superior talents. Activity, resolution, and acuteness, are of such immense importance in the hard circumstances of a new state, that they must be eagerly caught at, and employed as soon as they are discovered. Though all may not be quite so unobjectionable as could be wished—

"Res dura, et regni novitas me talia cogunt
Moliri"—

as Colonel Macquarrie probably quoted to Mr. Commissioner Bigge. As for the conduct of those extra-moralists, who come to settle in a land of crime, and refuse to associate with a convict legally pardoned, however light his original offence, however perfect his subsequent conduct—we have no toleration for such folly and foppery. To sit down to dinner with men who have not been tried for their lives is a luxury which cannot be enjoyed in such a country. It is entirely out of the question; and persons so dainty, and so truly admirable, had better settle at Clapham Common than at Botany Bay. Our trade in Australasia is to turn scoundrels into honest men. If you come among us, and bring with you a good character, and will lend us your society, as a stimulus and reward to men recovering from degradation, you will confer the greatest possible benefit upon the colony; but if you turn up your nose at repentance, insult those unhappy people with your character, and fiercely stand up as a moral bully, and a virtuous braggadocio, it would have been far better for us if Providence had directed you to any other part of the globe than to Botany Bay—which was colonized, not to gratify the insolence of Pharisees, but to heal the contrite spirit of repentant sinners. Mr. Marsden, who has no happiness from six o'clock Monday morning, till the same hour the week following, will not meet pardoned convicts in society. We have no doubt Mr. Marsden is a very respectable clergyman; but is there not something very different from this in the Gospel? The most resolute and inflexible persons in the rejection of pardoned convicts were some of the marching regiments stationed at Botany Bay—men, of course, who had uniformly shunned, in the Old World, the society of gamesters, prostitutes, drunkards, and blasphemers—who had ruined no tailors, corrupted no wives, and had entitled themselves, by a long course of solemnity and decorum, to indulge in all the insolence of purity and virtue.

In this point, then, of restoring convicts to society, we side, as far as the principle goes, with the governor; but we are far from undertaking to say that his application of the principle has been on all occasions prudent and judicious. Upon the absurdity of his conduct in attempting to *force* the society of the pardoned convicts upon the undetected part of the colony, there can be no doubt. These are points upon which every body must be allowed to judge for themselves. The greatest monarchs of Europe cannot control opinion upon those points—sovereigns far exceeding Colonel Lachlan Macquarrie, in the antiquity of their dynasty, and the extent, wealth, and importance of their empire.

"It was in vain to assemble them" (the pardoned convicts), "even on public occasions, at Government House, or to point them out to the especial notice and favour of strangers, or to favour them with particular marks of his own attention upon these occasions, if they still continued to be shunned, or disregarded by the rest of the company.

"With the exception of the Reverend Mr. Fulton, and, on some occasions, of Mr. Redfern, I never observed that the other persons of this class participated in the general attentions of the company; and the evidence of Mr. Judge-Advocate Wylde and Major Bell both prove the embarrassment in which they were left on occasions that came within their notice.

"Nor has the distinction that has been conferred upon them by Governor Macquarrie produced any effect in subduing the prejudices or objections of the class of free inhabitants to associate with them. One instance only has occurred, in which the wife of a respectable individual, and a magistrate, has been visited by the wives of the officers of the garrison, and by a few of the married ladies of the colony. It is an instance that reflects equal credit upon the individual herself, as upon the feelings and motives of those by whom she has been so noticed; but the circumstances of her case were very peculiar, and those that led to her introduction to society were very much of a personal kind. It has generally been thought, that such instances would have been more numerous if Governor Macquarrie had allowed every person to have followed the dictates of their own judgment upon a subject, on which, of all others, men are least disposed to be dictated to, and most disposed to judge for themselves.

"Although the emancipated convicts, whom he has selected from their class, are persons who generally bear a good character in New South Wales, yet that opinion of them is by no means universal. Those, however, who entertained a good opinion of them would have proved it by their notice, as Mr. M'Arthur has been in the habit of doing, by the kind and marked notice that he took of Mr. Fitzgerald; and those who entertained a different opinion, would not have contracted an aversion to the principle of their introduction, from being obliged to witness what they considered to be an indiscreet and erroneous application of it."—*Report*, p. 150.

We do not think Mr. Bigge exactly seizes the sense of Colonel Macquarrie's phrase, when the colonel speaks of restoring men to the rank of society they have lost. Men may either be classed by wealth and education, or by character. All honest men, whether counts or cobblers, are of the same rank, if classed by moral distinctions. It is a common phrase to say that such a man can no longer be ranked among honest men; that he has been degraded from the class of respectable persons; and, therefore, by restoring a convict to the rank he has lost, the governor may very fairly be supposed to mean the moral rank. In discussing the question of granting offices of trust to convicts, the importance of the *Scelerati* must not be overlooked. Their numbers are very considerable. They have one-eighth of all the granted land in the colony; and there are among them individuals of very large fortune. Mr. Redfern has 2600 acres, Mr. Lord 4365 acres, and Mr. Samuel Terry 19,000 acres. As this man's history is a specimen of the mud and dirt out of which great families often arise, let the *Terry Filii*, the future warriors, legislators, and nobility of the Bay, learn from what, and whom, they sprang.

"The first of these individuals, Samuel Terry, was transported to the colony when young. He was placed in a gang of stone-masons at Paramatta, and assisted in the building of the gaol. Mr. Marsden states, that during this period he was brought before him for neglect of duty, and punished; but, by his industry in other ways, he was enabled to set up a small retail shop, in which he continued till the expiration of his term of service. He then repaired to Sydney, where he extended his business, and, by marriage, increased his capital. He for many years kept a public house and retail shop, to which the smaller settlers resorted from the country, and where, after intoxicating themselves with spirits, they signed obligations and powers of attorney to confess judgment, which were always kept ready for execution. By these means, and by an active use of the common arts of over-reaching ignorant and worthless men, Samuel Terry has been able to accumulate a considerable capital, and a quantity of land in New South Wales, inferior only to that which is held by Mr. D'Arcy Wentworth. He ceased, at the late regulations introduced by the magistrates at Sydney, in February, 1820, to sell spirituous liquors, and he is now become one of the principal speculators in the purchase of investments at Sydney, and lately established a water-mill in the swampy plains between that town and Botany Bay, which did not succeed. Out of the 19,000 acres of land held by Samuel Terry, 140 only are said to be cleared; but he possesses 1450 head of horned cattle, and 3800 sheep."—*Report*, p. 141.

Upon the subject of the New South Wales Bank, Mr. Bigge observes,—

"Upon the first of these occasions, it became an object both with Governor Macquarrie and Mr. Judge-Advocate Wyld, who took an active part in the establishment of the bank, to unite in its favour the support and contributions of the individuals of all classes of the colony. Governor Macquarrie felt assured that, without such co-operation, the bank could not be established; for he was convinced that the emancipated convicts were the most opulent members of the community. A committee was formed for the purpose of drawing up the rules and regulations of the establishment, in which are to be found the names of George Howe, the printer of the Sydney Gazette, who was also a retail dealer; Mr. Simon Lord, and Mr. Edward Eager, all emancipated convicts, and the last only conditionally.

"Governor Macquarrie had always understood, and strongly wished, that in asking for the co-operation of all classes of the community in the formation of the bank, a share in its direction and management should also be communicated to them."—*Report*, p. 150.

In the discussion of this question, we became acquainted with a piece of military etiquette, of which we were previously ignorant. An officer, invited to dinner by the governor, cannot refuse, unless in case of sickness. This is the most complete tyranny we ever heard of. If the officer comes out to his duty at the proper minute, with his proper number of buttons and epaulettes, what matters it to the governor or any body else, where he dines? He may as well be ordered what to eat, as where to dine—be confined to the upper or under side of the meat—be denied gravy, or refused melted butter. But there is no end to the small tyranny and puerile vexations of a military life.

The mode of employing convicts upon their arrival appears to us very objectionable. If a man is skilful as a mechanic, he is added to the government gangs; and in proportion to his skill and diligence, his chance of manumission, or of remission of labour, is lessened. If he is not skilful, or not skilful in any trade wanted by government, he is applied for by some settler, to whom he pays from 5*s.* to 10*s.* a week; and is then left at liberty to go where, and work for whomsoever, he pleases. In the same manner, a convict who is rich is applied for, and obtains his weekly liberty and idleness by the purchased permission of the person to whom he is consigned.

The greatest possible inattention or ignorance appears to have prevailed in manumitting convicts for labour—and for *such* labour! not for cleansing Augean stables, or draining

Pontine marshes, or damming out a vast length of the Adriatic, but for working five weeks with a single horse and cart in making the road to Bathurst Plains. Was such labour worth five pounds? And is it to be understood, that liberty is to be restored to any man who will do five pounds' worth of work in Australasia? Is this comment upon transportation to be circulated in the cells of Newgate, or in the haunts of those persons who are doomed to inhabit them?

"Another principle by which Governor Macquarrie has been guided in bestowing pardons and indulgences, is that of considering them as rewards for any particular labour or enterprise. It was upon this principle, that the men who were employed in working upon the Bathurst road, in the year 1815, and those who contributed to that operation by the loan of their own carts and horses, or of those that they procured, obtained pardons, emancipations, and tickets of leave. To 39 men who were employed as labourers in this work, three free pardons were given, one ticket of leave, and 35 emancipations; and two of them only had held tickets of leave before they commenced their labour. Seven convicts received emancipations for supplying horses and carts for the carriage of provisions and stores as the party was proceeding; six out of this number having previously held tickets of leave.

"Eight other convicts (four of whom held tickets of leave) received emancipations for assisting with carts, and one horse to each, in the transport of provisions and baggage for the use of Governor Macquarrie and his suite, on their journey from the river Nepean to Bathurst, in the year 1816; a service that did not extend beyond the period of five weeks, and was attended with no risk, and very little exertion.

"Between the months of January, 1816, and June, 1818, nine convicts, of whom six held tickets of leave, obtained emancipations for sending carts and horses to convey provisions and baggage from Paramatta to Bathurst, for the use of Mr. Oxley, the surveyor-general, in his two expeditions into the interior of the country. And in the same period, 23 convict labourers and mechanics obtained emancipations for labour and service performed at Bathurst.

"The nature of the services performed by these convicts, and the manner in which some of them were recommended, excited much surprise in the colony, as well as great suspicion of the purity of the channels through which the recommendations passed."—*Report*, pp. 122, 123.

If we are to judge from the number of jobs detected by Mr. Bigge, Botany Bay seems very likely to do justice to the mother-country from whence it sprang. Mr. Redfern, surgeon, seems to use the public rhubarb for his private practice. Mr. Hutchinson, superintendent, makes a very comfortable thing of the assignment of convicts. Major Druit was found selling their own cabbages to government in a very profitable manner; and many comfortable little practices of this nature are noticed by Mr. Bigge.

Among other sources of profit, the superintendent of convicts was the banker; two occupations which seem to be eminently compatible with each other, inasmuch as they afford to the superintendent the opportunity of evincing his impartiality and loading with equal labour every convict, without reference to their banking accounts, to the profit they afford, or the trouble they create. It appears, however (very strangely), from the report, that the money of convicts was not always recovered with the same readiness it was received.

Mr. Richard Fitzgerald, in September, 1819, was comptroller of provisions in Emu Plains, storekeeper at Windsor, and superintendent of government works at the same place. He was also a proprietor of land and stock in the neighbourhood, and kept a public house in Windsor, of which an emancipated Jew was the ostensible manager, upon whom Fitzgerald gave orders for goods and spirits in payment for labour on the public works. These two places are fifteen miles distant from each other, and convicts are to be watched and managed at both. It cannot be imagined that the convicts are slow in observing or following these laudable examples; and their conduct will add another instance of the vigilance of Macquarrie's government.

"The stores and materials used in the different buildings at Sydney are kept in a magazine in the lumber yard, and are distributed according to the written requisitions of the different overseers that are made during the day, and that are addressed to the storekeeper in the lumber yard. They are conveyed from thence to the buildings by the convict mechanics; and no account of the expenditure or employment of the stores is kept by the overseers, or rendered to the storekeeper. It was only in the early part of the year 1820 that an account was opened by him of the different materials used in each work or building; and in February, 1821, this account was considerably in arrear. The temptation, therefore, that is afforded to the convict mechanics who work in the lumber yard, in secreting tools, stores, and implements, and to those who work at the different buildings, is very great, and the loss to government is considerable. The tools, moreover, have not latterly been mustered as they used to be once a month, except where one of the convicts is removed from Sydney to another station."—*Report*, pp. 36, 37.

If it was right to build fine houses in a new colony, common sense seems to point out a control upon the expenditure, with such a description of workmen. What must become of that country where the buildings are useless, the governor not wise, the public the paymaster, the accounts not in existence, and all the artisans thieves?

An horrid practice prevailed, of the convicts accepting a sum of money from the captain, in their voyage out, in lieu of their regular ration of provisions. This ought to be restrained by the severest penalties.

What is it that can be urged for Governor Macquarrie, after the following picture of the hospital at Paramatta? It not only justifies his recall, but seems to require (if there are means of reaching such neglect) his severe punishment.

"The women, who had become most profligate and hardened by habit, were associated in their daily tasks with those who had very lately arrived, to whom the customs and practices of the colony were yet unknown, and who might have escaped the consequences of such pernicious lessons, if a little care, and a small portion of expense, had been spared in providing them with a separate apartment during the hours of labour. As a place of employment, the factory of Paramatta was not only very defective, but very prejudicial. The insufficient accommodation that it afforded to those females who might be well disposed presented an early incitement, if not an excuse, for their resorting to indiscriminate prostitution; and on the evening of their arrival at Paramatta, those who were not deploring their state of abandonment and distress, were traversing the streets in search of the guilty means of future support. The state in which the place itself was kept, and the state of disgusting filth in which I found it, both on an early visit after my arrival, and on one preceding my departure; the disordered, unruly, and licentious appearance of the women, manifested the little degree of control in which the female convicts were kept, and the little attention that was paid to any thing beyond the mere performance of a certain portion of labour."—*Report*, p. 70.

It might naturally be supposed, that any man sent across the globe with a good salary, for the express purpose of governing, and, if possible, of reforming convicts, would have preferred the morals of his convicts to the accommodation of his horses. Let Mr. Bigge, a very discreet and moderate man, be heard upon these points.

"Having observed, in Governor Macquarrie's answer to Mr. Marsden, that he justified the delay that occurred, and was still to take place, in the construction of a proper place of reception for the female convicts, by the want of any specific instructions from your lordship to undertake such a building, and which he states that he solicited at an early period of his government, and considered indispensable, I felt it to be my duty to call to the recollection of Governor Macquarrie, that he had undertaken several buildings of much less urgent necessity than the factory at Paramatta, without waiting for any such indispensable authority: and I now find that the construction of it was announced by him to your lordship in the year 1817, as then in his contemplation, without making any specific allusion to the evils which the want of it had so long occasioned; that the contract for building it was announced to the public on the 21st May, 1818, and that your lordship's approval of it was not signified until the 24th August, 1818, and could not have reached Governor Macquarrie's hands until nearly a year after the work had been undertaken. It appears, therefore, that if want of authority had been the sole cause of the delay in building the factory at Paramatta, that cause would not only have operated in the month of March, 1818, but it would have continued to operate until the want of authority had been formally supplied. Governor Macquarrie, however, must be conscious, that after he had stated to Mr. Marsden in the year 1815, and with an appearance of regret, that the want of authority prevented him from undertaking the construction of a building of such undeniable necessity and importance as the factory at Paramatta, he had undertaken several buildings, which, though useful in themselves, were of less comparative importance; *and had commenced, in the month of August,* 1817, *the laborious and expensive construction of his own stables at Sydney, to which I have already alluded,* without any previous communication to your lordship, and in direct opposition to an instruction that must have then reached him, and that forcibly warned him of the consequences."—*Report*, p. 71.

It is the fashion very much among the tories of the House of Commons, and all those who love the effects of public liberty, without knowing or caring how it is preserved, to attack every person who complains of abuses, and to accuse him of gross exaggeration. No sooner is the name of any public thief, or of any tormentor, or oppressor, mentioned in that honourable house, than out bursts the spirit of jobbing eulogium, and there is not a virtue under heaven which is not ascribed to the delinquent in question, and vouched for by the most irrefragable testimony. If Mr. Bennet or Sir Francis Burdett had attacked them, and they had now been living, how many honourable members would have vouched for the honesty of Dudley and Empson, the gentleness of Jeffries, or the genius of Blackmore? What human virtue did not Aris and the governor of Ilchester gaol possess? Who was not ready to come forward to vouch for the attentive humanity of Governor Macquarrie? What scorn and wit would it have produced from the treasury bench, if Mr. Bennet had stated the superior advantages of the horses over the convicts?—and all the horrors and immoralities, the filth and wretchedness, of the female prison of Paramatta? Such a case, proved as this now is beyond the power of contradiction, ought to convince the most hardy and profligate scoffers, that there is really a great deal of occasional neglect and oppression in the conduct of public servants; and that in spite of all the official praise, which is ever ready for the perpetrators of crime, there is a great deal of real malversation which should be dragged to the light of day, by the exertions of bold and virtuous men. If we had found, from the report of Mr. Bigge, that the charges of Mr. Bennet were without any, or without adequate foundation, it would have given us great pleasure to have vindicated the governor; but Mr. Bennet has proved his indictment. It is impossible to read the foregoing quotation, and not to perceive that the conduct and proceedings of Governor Macquarrie imperiously required the exposure they have received; and that it would have been much to the credit of government if he had been removed long ago from a situation which, but for the exertions of Mr. Bennet, we believe he would have held to this day.

The sick, from Mr. Bigge's report, appear to have fared as badly as the sinful. Good water was scarce, proper persons to wait upon the patients could not be obtained; and so numerous were the complaints from this quarter, that the governor makes an order for the exclusion of all hospital grievances and complaints, *except on one day in the month*—dropsy swelling, however, fever burning, and ague shaking, in the mean time, without waiting for the arrangements of Governor Macquarrie, or consulting the *Mollia tempora fandi.*

In permitting individuals to distil their own grain, the government of Botany Bay appears to us to be quite right. It is impossible, in such a colony, to prevent unlawful distillation to a considerable extent; and it is as well to raise upon spirits (as something must be taxed) that slight duty which renders the contraband trade not worth following. Distillation, too, always insures a magazine against famine, by which New South Wales has more than once been severely visited. It opens a market for grain where markets are very distant, and where redundance and famine seem very often to succeed each other. The cheapness of spirits, to such working people as know how to use them with moderation, is a great blessing; and we doubt whether that moderation, after the first burst of ebriety, is not just as likely to be learnt in plenty as in scarcity.

We were a little surprised at the scanty limits allowed to convicts for sleeping on board the transports. Mr. Bigge (of whose sense and humanity we really have not the slightest doubt) states eighteen inches to be quite sufficient—twice the length of a small sheet of letter-paper. The printer's devil, who carries our works to the press, informs us, that the allowance to the demons of the type is double foolscap length, or twenty-four inches. The great city upholsterers generally consider six feet as barely sufficient for a person just rising in business, and assisting occasionally at offficial banquets.

Mrs. Fry's* system is well spoken of by Mr. Bigge; and its useful effect in promoting order and decency among floating convicts fully admitted.

In a voyage to Botany Bay by Mr. Read, he states that, while the convict vessel lay at anchor, about to sail, a boat from shore reached the ship, and from it stepped a clerk of the Bank of England. The convicts felicitated themselves upon the acquisition of so gentleman-like a companion; but it soon turned out that the visitant had no intention of making so long a voyage. Finding that they were not to have the pleasure of his company, the convicts very naturally thought of picking his pockets; the necessity of which professional measure was prevented by a speedy distribution of their contents. Forth from his bill-case, this votary of Plutus drew his nitid Newlands; all the forgers and utterers were mustered on deck; and to each of them was well and truly paid into his hand a five pound note; less acceptable, perhaps, than if privately removed from the person, but still joyfully received. This was well intended on the part of the directors: but the consequences it is scarcely necessary to enumerate; a large stock of rum was immediately laid in from the circumambient slop boats; and the materials of constant intoxication secured for the rest of the voyage.

The following account of pastoral convicts is striking and picturesque:—

"I observed that a great many of the convicts in Van Diemen's Land wore jackets and trowsers of the kangaroo skin, and sometimes caps of the same material, which they obtain from the stock-keepers who are employed in the interior of the country. The labour of several of them differs, in this respect, from that of the convicts in New South Wales, and is rather pastoral than agricultural. Permission having been given, for the last five years, to the settlers to avail themselves of the ranges of open plains and valleys that lie on either side of the road leading from Austin's Ferry to Launceston, a distance of 120 miles, their flocks and herds have been committed to the care of convict shepherds and stock-keepers, who are sent to these cattle ranges, distant sometimes thirty or forty miles from their masters' estates.

"The boundaries of these tracts are described in the tickets of occupation by which they are held, and which are made renewable every year, on payment of a fee to the lieutenant governor's clerk. One or more convicts are stationed on them, to attend to the flocks and cattle, and are supplied with wheat, tea, and sugar, at the monthly visits of the owner. They are allowed the use of a musket and a few cartridges to defend themselves against the natives; and they have also dogs, with which they hunt the kangaroos, whose flesh they eat, and dispose of their skins to persons passing from Hobart Town to Launceston, in exchange for tea and sugar. They thus obtain a plentiful supply of food, and sometimes succeed in cultivating a few vegetables. Their habitations are made of turf and thatched, as the bark of the dwarf eucalyptus, or gum-trees of the plains; and the interior, in Van Diemen's Land, is not of sufficient expanse to form covering or shelter."—*Report*, pp. 107, 108.

A London thief, clothed in kangaroo's skins,

* We are sorry it should have been imagined, from some of our late observations on prison discipline, that we meant to disparage the exertions of Mrs. Fry. For prisoners before trial, it is perfect; but where imprisonment is intended for punishment, and not for detention, it requires, as we have endeavoured to show, a very different system. The Prison Society (an excellent, honourable, and most useful institution of some of the best men in England) have certainly, in their first numbers, fallen into the common mistake of supposing that the reformation of the culprit, and not the prevention of the crime, was the main object of imprisonment; and have, in consequence, taken some false views of the method of treating prisoners—the exposition of which, after the usual manner of flesh and blood, makes them a little angry. But, in objects of so high a nature, what matters *who* is right—the only question is, *what* is right?

lodged under the bark of the dwarf eucalyptus, and keeping sheep, fourteen thousand miles from Piccadilly, with a crook bent into the shape of a picklock, is not an uninteresting picture; and an engraving of it might have a very salutary effect—provided no engraving were made of his convict master, to whom the sheep belong.

The Maroon Indians were hunted by dogs—the fugitive convicts are recovered by the natives.

"The native blacks that inhabit the neighbourhood of Port Hunter and Port Stephens have become very active in retaking the fugitive convicts. They accompany the soldiers who are sent in pursuit, and, by the extraordinary strength of sight they possess, improved by their daily exercise of it in pursuit of kangaroos and opossums, they can trace to a great distance, and with wonderful accuracy, the impressions of the human foot. Nor are they afraid of meeting the fugitive convicts in the woods, when sent in their pursuit, without the soldiers; by their skill in throwing their long and pointed wooden darts, they wound and disable them, strip them of their clothes, and bring them back as prisoners, by unknown roads and paths, to the Coal river.

"They are rewarded for these enterprizes by presents of maize and blankets; and, notwithstanding the apprehensions of revenge from the convicts whom they bring back, they continue to live in Newcastle and its neighbourhood; but are observed to prefer the society of the soldiers to that of the convicts." —*Report*, p. 117.

Of the convicts in New South Wales, Mr. Bigge found about eight or nine in an hundred to be persons of respectable character and conduct, though the evidence respecting them is not quite satisfactory. But the most striking and consolatory passage in the whole report is the following:—

"The marriages of the native-born youths with female convicts are very rare; a circumstance that is attributable to the general disinclination to early marriage that is observable amongst them, and partly to the abandoned and dissolute habits of the female convicts; but chiefly to a sense of pride in the native-born youths, approaching to contempt for the vices and depravity of the convicts, even when manifested in the persons of their own parents."—*Report*, p. 105.

Every thing is to be expected from these feelings. They convey to the mother-country the first proof that the foundations of a mighty empire are laid.

We were somewhat surprised to find Governor Macquarrie contending with Mr. Bigge, that it was no part of his, the governor's duty, to select and separate the useless from the useful convicts, or to determine, except in particular cases, to whom they are to be assigned. In other words, he wishes to effect the customary separation of salary and duty—the grand principle which appears to pervade all human institutions, and to be the most invincible of all human abuses. Not only are church, king, and state, allured by this principle of vicarious labour, but the pot-boy has a lower pot-boy, who, for a small portion of the small gains of his principal, arranges, with inexhaustible sedulity, the subdivided portions of drink, and, intensely perspiring, disperses, in bright pewter, the frothy elements of joy.

There is a very awkward story of a severe flogging inflicted upon three freemen by Governor Macquarrie, without complaint to, or intervention of, any magistrate; a fact not denied by the governor, and for which no adequate apology, nor any thing approaching to an adequate apology, is offered. These Asiatic and Satrapical proceedings, however, we have reason to think, are exceedingly disrelished by London juries. The profits of having been unjustly flogged at Botany Bay (Scarlett for the plaintiff) is good property, and would fetch a very considerable sum at the auction mart. The governor, in many instances, appears to have confounded diversity of opinion upon particular measures, with systematic opposition to his government, and to have treated as disaffected persons those whom, in favourite measures, he could not persuade by his arguments, nor influence by his example, and on points where every man has a right to judge for himself, and where authority has no legitimate right to interfere, much less to dictate.

To the charges confirmed by the statement of Mr. Bigge, Mr. Bennet adds, from the evidence collected by the gaol committee, that the fees in the governor's court, collected by the authority of the governor, are most exorbitant and oppressive; and that illegal taxes are collected under the sole authority of the governor. It has been made, by colonial regulations, a capital offence to steal the wild cattle; and, in 1816, three persons were convicted of stealing a wild bull, *the property of our sovereign lord the king*. Now our sovereign lord the king (whatever be his other merits or demerits) is certainly a very good-natured man, and would be the first to lament that an unhappy convict was sentenced to death for killing one of his wild bulls on the other side of the world. The cases of Mr. Moore and of William Stewart, as quoted by Mr. Bennet, are very strong. If they are answerable, they should be answered. The concluding letter to Mr. Stewart is, to us, the most decisive proof of the unfitness of Colonel Macquarrie for the situation in which he was placed. The ministry at home, after the authenticity of the letter was proved, should have seized upon the first decent pretext of recalling the governor, of thanking him, in the name of his sovereign, for his valuable services (not omitting his care of the wild bulls), and of dismissing him to half pay—and insignificance.

As to the trial by jury, we cannot agree with Mr. Bennet, that it would be right to introduce it at present, for reasons we have given in a previous article, and which we see no reason for altering. The time of course will come when it would be in the highest degree unjust and absurd to refuse to that settlement the benefit of popular institutions. But they are too young, too few, and too deficient for such civilized machinery at present. "I cannot come to serve upon the jury—the waters of the Hawksbury are out, and I have a mile to swim—the kangaroos will break into my corn—the convicts have robbed me—my little boy has been bitten by an ornithorynchus paradoxus—I have sent a man fifty miles with a sack of flour to buy a pair of breeches for the assizes, and he is not returned." These are the excuses which, in new colonies, always prevent trial by jury; and make it desirable for the first half century of their existence, that they should live under the simplicity and convenience of despotism—such modified despotism (we mean) as a British House of Commons (always containing men as bold and honest as the member for Shrewsbury) will permit, in the governors of their distant colonies.

Such are the opinions formed of the conduct of Governor Macquarrie by Mr. Bigge. Not the slightest insinuation is made against the integrity of his character. Though almost every body else has a job, we do not perceive that any is imputed to this gentleman; but he is negligent, expensive, arbitrary, ignorant, and clearly deficient in abilities for the task committed to his charge. It is our decided opinion, therefore, that Mr. Bennet has rendered a valuable service to the public, in attacking and exposing his conduct. As a gentleman and an honest man, there is not the smallest charge against the governor; but a gentleman, and a very honest man, may very easily ruin a very fine colony. The colony itself, disencumbered of Colonel Lachlan Macquarrie, will probably become a very fine empire; but we can scarcely believe it is of any present utility as a place of punishment. The history of emancipated convicts, who have made a great deal of money by their industry and their speculations, necessarily reaches this country, and prevents men who are goaded by want, and hovering between vice and virtue, from looking upon it as a place of suffering—perhaps leads them to consider it as the land of hope and refuge, to them unattainable, except by the commission of crime. And so they lift up their heads at the bar, hoping to be transported,—

> "Stabant orantes primi transmittere cursum
> Tendebantque manus, ripæ ulterioris amore."

It is not possible, in the present state of the law, that these enticing histories of convict prosperity should be prevented, by one uniform system of severity exercised in New South Wales, upon all transported persons. Such different degrees of guilt are included under the term of convict, that it would violate every feeling of humanity, and every principle of justice, to deal out one measure of punishment to all. We strongly suspect that this is the root of the evil. We want new gradations of guilt to be established by law—new names for those gradations—and a different measure of good and evil treatment attached to those denominations. In this manner, the mere *convict*, the *rogue and convict*, and the *incorrigible convict*, would expect, upon their landing, to be treated with very different degrees of severity. The first might be merely detained in New South Wales without labour or coercion; the second compelled, at all events, to work out two-thirds of his time, without the possibility of remission; and the third be destined at once for the Coal River.* If these consequences steadily followed these gradations of conviction, they would soon be understood by the felonious world at home. At present, the prosperity of the best convicts is considered to be attainable by all; and transportation to another hemisphere is looked upon as the renovation of fallen fortunes, and the passport to wealth and power.

Another circumstance, which destroys all idea of punishment in transportation to New South Wales, is the enormous expense which that settlement would occasion, if it really was made a place of punishment. A little wicked tailor arrives, of no use to the architectural projects of the governor. He is turned over to a settler, who leases this sartorial Borgia his liberty for five shillings per week, and allows him to steal and snip, what, when, and where he can. The excuse for all this mockery of law and justice is, that the expense of his maintenance is saved to the government at home. But the expense is not saved to the country at large. The nefarious needleman writes home, that he is as comfortable as a finger in a thimble! that though a fraction only of humanity, he has several wives, and is filled every day with rum and kangaroo. This, of course, is not lost upon the shop-board; and, for the saving of fifteen pence per day, the foundation of many criminal tailors is laid. What is true of tailors, is true of tinkers and all other trades. The chances of escape from labour, and of manumission in the Bay, we may depend upon it, are accurately reported, and perfectly understood in the flash-houses of St. Giles; and, while Earl Bathurst is full of jokes and joy, public morals are thus sapped to their foundation.

* This practice is now resorted to.

GAME LAWS.*

[Edinburgh Review, 1823.]

About the time of the publication of this little pamphlet of Mr. Herbert, a committee of the House of Commons published a Report on the Game Laws, containing a great deal of very curious information respecting the sale of game, an epitome of which we shall now lay before our readers. The country higglers who collect poultry, gather up the game from the depots of the poachers, and transmit it in the same manner as poultry, and in the same packages, to the London poulterers, by whom it is distributed to the public; and this traffic is carried on (as far as game is concerned) even from the distance of Scotland. The same business is carried on by the porters of stage coaches; and a great deal of game is sold clandestinely by lords of manors, or by gamekeepers, without the knowledge of lords of manors; and principally, as the evidence states, from Norfolk and Suffolk, the great schools of steel traps and spring guns. The supply of game, too, is proved to be quite as regular as the supply of poultry; the number of hares and partridges supplied rather exceeds that of pheasants; but any description of game may be had to any amount. Here is a part of the evidence.

"Can you at any time procure any quantity of game? I have no doubt of it.—If you were to receive almost an unlimited order, could you execute it? Yes, I would supply the whole city of London, any fixed day once a week, all the year through, so that every individual inhabitant should have game for his table.—Do you think you could procure a thousand pheasants? Yes; I would be bound to produce *ten thousand* a week.—You would be bound to provide every family in London with a dish of game? Yes; a partridge, or a pheasant, or a hare, or a grouse, or something or other.—How would you set about doing it? I should, of course, request the persons with whom I am in the habit of dealing, to use their influence to bring me what they could by a certain day; I should speak to the dealers and the mail-guards, and coachmen, to produce a quantity; and I should send to my own connections in one or two manors where I have the privilege of selling for those gentlemen: and should send to Scotland to say, that every week the largest quantity they could produce was to be sent.—Being but a petty salesman, I sell a very small quantity; but I have had about 4000 head direct from one man.—Can you state the quantity of game which has been sent to you during the year? No; I may say, perhaps, 10,000 head; mine is a limited trade; I speak comparatively to that of others; I only supply private families."—*Report*, p. 20.

Poachers who go out at night cannot, of course, like regular tradesmen, proportion the supply to the demand, but having once made a contract, they kill all they can; and hence it happens that the game market is sometimes very much overstocked, and great quantities of game either thrown away, or disposed of by Irish hawkers to the common people at very inferior prices.

"Does it ever happen to you to be obliged to dispose of poultry at the same low prices you are obliged to dispose of game? It depends upon the weather; often, when there is a considerable quantity on hand, and owing to the weather, it will not keep till the following day, I am obliged to take any price that is offered; but we can always turn either poultry or game into some price or other; and if it was not for the Irish hawkers, hundreds and hundreds of heads of game would be spoiled and thrown away. It is out of the power of any person to conceive for one moment the quantity of game that is hawked in the streets. I have had opportunity more than other persons of knowing this; for I have sold, I may say, more game than any other person in the city; and we serve hawkers indiscriminately, persons who come and purchase probably six fowls or turkeys and geese, and they will buy heads of game with them."—*Report*, p. 22.

Live birds are sent up as well as dead; eggs as well as birds. The price of pheasants' eggs last year was 8*s*. per dozen; of partridges' eggs, 2*s*. The price of hares was from 3*s*. to 5*s*. 6*d*.; of partridges, from 1*s*. 6*d*. to 2*s*. 6*d*.; of pheasants, from 5*s*. to 5*s*. 6*d*. each, and sometimes as low as 1*s*. 6*d*.

"What have you given for game this year? It is very low indeed; I am sick of it; I do not think I shall ever deal again. We have got game this season as low as half-a-crown a brace (birds), and pheasants as low as 7*s*. a brace. It is so plentiful there has been no end to spoiling it this season. It is so plentiful, it is of no use. In war time it was worth having; then they fetched 7*s*. and 8*s*. a brace."—*Report*, p. 33.

All the poulterers, too, even the most respectable, state that it is absolutely necessary they should carry on this illegal traffic in the present state of the game laws; because their regular customers for poultry would infallibly leave any poulterer's shop from whence they could not be supplied with game.

"I have no doubt that it is the general wish at present of the trade not to deal in the article; but they are all, of course, compelled from their connections. If they cannot get game from one person, they can from another.

"Do you believe that poulterers are not to be found who would take out licenses, and

* *A Letter to the Chairman of the Committee of the House of Commons, on the Game Laws*. By the Hon. and Rev. William Herbert. Ridgway, 1823.

would deal with those very persons, for the purposes of obtaining a greater profit than they would have dealing as you would do? I think the poulterers in general are a respectable set of men, and would not countenance such a thing; they feel now that they are driven into a corner; that there may be men who would countenance irregular proceedings, I have no doubt.—Would it be their interest to do so, considering the penalty? No, I think not. The poulterers are perfectly well aware that they are committing a breach of the law at present.—Do you suppose that those persons, respectable as they are, who are now committing a breach of the law, would not equally commit that breach if the law were altered? No, certainly not; at present it is so connected with their business that they cannot help it.—You said just now, that they were driven into a corner; what did you mean by that? We are obliged to aid and abet those men who commit those depredations, because of the constant demand for game, from different customers whom we supply with poultry.—Could you carry on your business as a poulterer, if you refused to supply game? By no means; because some of the first people in the land require it of me."—*Report*, p. 15.

When that worthy errorist, Mr. Bankes, brought in his bill of additional severities against poachers, there was no man of sense and reflection who did not anticipate the following consequences of the measure.

"Do you find that less game has been sold in consequence of the bill rendering it penal to sell game? Upon my word, it did not make the slightest difference in the world.—Not immediately after it was made? No; I do not think it made the slightest difference.—It did not make the slightest sensation? No, I never sold a bird less.—Was not there a resolution of the poulterers not to sell game? I was secretary to that committee.—What was the consequence of that resolution? A great deal of ill blood in the trade. One gentleman who just left the room did not come into my ideas. I never had a head of game in my house; all my neighbours sold it; and as we had people on the watch, who were ready to watch it into the houses, it came to this, we were prepared to bring our actions against certain individuals, after sitting, perhaps from three to four months, every week, which we did at the Crown and Anchor in the Strand, but we did not proceed with our actions, to prevent ill blood in the trade. We regularly met, and, as we conceived at the time, formed a committee of the most respectable of the trade. I was secretary of that committee. The game was sold in the city, in the vicinity of the Royal Exchange, cheaper than ever was known, because the people at our end of the town were afraid. I, as a point of honour, never had it in my house. I never had a head of game in my house that season.—What was the consequence?—I lost my trade, and gave offence to gentlemen; a nobleman's steward, or butler, or cook, treated it as contumely; 'Good God, what is the use of your running your head against the wall?'—You were obliged to begin the trade again? Yes, and sold more than ever."—*Report*, p. 18.

These consequences are confirmed by the evidence of every person before the committee.

All the evidence is very strong as to the fact, that dealing in game is not discreditable; that there are a great number of respectable persons, and, among the rest, the first poulterers in London, who buy game knowing it to have been illegally procured, but who would never dream of purchasing any other article procured by dishonesty.

"Are there not, to your knowledge, a great many people in this town who deal in game, by buying or selling it, that would not on any account buy or sell stolen property? Certainly; there are many capital tradesmen, poulterers, who deal in game, that would have nothing to do with stolen property; and yet I do not think there is a poulterer's shop in London where they could not get game, if they wanted it.—Do you think any discredit attaches to any man in this town for buying or selling game? I think none at all: and I do not think that the men to whom I have just referred would have any thing to do with stolen goods. Would it not, in the opinion of the inhabitants of London, be considered a very different thing dealing in stolen game, or stolen poultry? Certainly.—The one would be considered disgraceful, and the other not? Certainly; they think nothing of dealing in game; and the farmers in the country will not give information; they will have a hare or two of the very men who work for them, and they are afraid to give us information."—*Report*, p. 31.

The evidence of Daniel Bishop, one of the Bow Street officers, who has been a good deal employed in the apprehension of poachers, is curious and important, as it shows the enormous extent of the evil, and the ferocious spirit which the game laws engender in the common people. "The poachers," he says, "came 16 miles. The whole of the village from which they were taken were poachers; the constable of the village, and the shoemaker, and other inhabitants of the village. I fetched one man 22 miles. There was the son of a respectable gardener; one of these was a sawyer, and another a baker, who kept a good shop there. If the village had been alarmed, we should have had some mischief; but we were all prepared with fire-arms. If poachers have a spite with the gamekeeper, that would induce them to go out in numbers to resist him. This party I speak of had something in their hats to distinguish them. They take a delight in setting to with the gamekeepers; and talk it over afterwards how they served so and so. They fought with the butt-ends of their guns at Lord Howe's; they beat the gamekeepers shockingly."—"Does it occur to you (Bishop is asked) to have had more applications, and to have detected more persons this season than in any former one? Yes; I think within four months there have been twenty-one transported that I have been at the taking of, and through one man turning evidence in each case, and without that they could not have been identified; the gamekeepers could not, or would not, identify them. The poachers go to the public house and spend their money; if they have a good night's work, they will go and get drunk with the money. The gangs are connected together at different public houses, just like a club at a public house; they are all sworn together. If the keeper took one of them, they would go and attack him for so doing."

Mr. Stafford, chief clerk of Bow Street, says, "All the offences against the game laws which are of an atrocious description I think are generally reported to the public office in Bow Street, more especially in cases where the keepers have either been killed, or dangerously wounded, and the assistance of an officer from Bow Street is required. The applications have been much more numerous of late years* than they were formerly. Some of them have been cases of murder; but I do not think many have amounted to murder. There are many instances in which keepers have been very ill treated—they have been wounded, skulls have been fractured, and bones broken; and they have been shot at. A man takes an hare, or a pheasant, with a very different feeling from that with which he would take a pigeon or a fowl out of a farm-yard. The number of persons that assemble together is more for the purpose of protecting themselves against those that may apprehend them, than from any idea that they are actually committing depredation upon the property of another person; they do not consider it as property. I think there is a sense of morality and a distinction of crime existing in the men's minds, although they are mistaken about it. Men feel that if they go in a great body together, to break into a house, or to rob a person, or to steal his poultry, or his sheep, they are committing a crime against that man's property; but I think with respect to the game, they do not feel that they are doing any thing which is wrong; but think they have committed no crime when they have done the thing, and their only anxiety is to escape detection." In addition, Mr. Stafford states that he remembers not *one single conviction under Mr. Bankes's Act against buying game;* and not one conviction for buying or selling game within the last year has been made at Bow Street.

The inferences from these facts are exactly as we predicted, and as every man of common sense must have predicted—that to prevent the sale of game is absolutely impossible. If game is plentiful, and cannot be obtained at any lawful market, an illicit trade will be established, which it is utterty impossible to prevent by any increased severity of the laws. There never was a more striking illustration of the necessity of attending to public opinion in all penal enactments. Mr. Bankes (a perfect representative of all the ordinary notions about forcing mankind by pains and penalties) took the floor. To buy a partridge (though still considered as inferior to murder) was visited with the very heaviest infliction of the law; and yet, though game is sold as openly in London as apples and oranges, though three years have elapsed since this legislative mistake, the officers of the police can hardly recollect a single instance where the information has been laid, or the penalty levied: and why? because every man's feelings and every man's understanding tell him, that it is a most absurd and ridiculous tyranny to prevent one man, who has more game than he wants, from exchanging it with another man, who has more money than he wants—because magistrates will not (if they can avoid it) inflict such absurd penalties—because even common informers know enough of the honest indignation of mankind, and are too well aware of the coldness of pump and pond to act under the bill of the Lycurgus of Corfe Castle.

The plan now proposed is, to undersell the poacher, which may be successful or unsuccessful; but the threat is, if you attempt this plan there will be no game—and if there is no game there will be no country gentlemen. We deny every part of this enthymeme—the last proposition as well as the first. We really cannot believe that all our rural mansions would be deserted, although no game was to be found in their neighbourhood. Some come into the country for health, some for quiet, for agriculture, for economy, from attachment to family estates, from love of retirement, from the necessity of keeping up provincial interests, and from a vast variety of causes. Partridges and pheasants, though they form nine-tenths of human motives, still leave a small residue, which may be classed under some other head. Neither is a great proportion of those whom the love of shooting brings into the country c the smallest value or importance to the country. A colonel of the Guards, the second son just entered at Oxford, three diners out from Piccadilly—Major Rock, Lord John, Lord Charles, the colonel of the regiment quartered at the neighbouring town, two Irish peers, and a German baron;—if all this honourable company proceed with fustian jackets, dog-whistles, and chemical inventions, to a solemn destruction of pheasants, how is the country benefited by their presence? or how would earth, air, or sea, be injured by their annihilation? There are certainly many valuable men brought into the country by a love of shooting, who, coming there for that purpose, are useful for many better purposes; but a vast multitude of shooters are of no more service to the country than the ramrod which condenses the charge, or the barrel which contains it. We do not deny that the annihilation of the game laws would thin the aristocratical population of the country; but it would not thin that population so much as is contended; and the loss of many of the persons so banished would be a good rather than a misfortune. At all events, we cannot at all comprehend the policy of alluring the better classes of society into the country, by the temptation of petty tyranny and injustice, or of monopoly in sports. How absurd it would be to offer to the higher orders the exclusive use of peaches, nectarines, and apricots, as the premium of rustication—to put vast quantities of men into prison as apricot eaters, apricot buyers, and apricot sellers—to appoint a regular day for beginning to eat, and another for leav-

* It is only of late years that men have been transported for shooting at night. There are instances of men who have been transported at the Sessions for night poaching, who made no resistance at all when taken; but then their characters as old poachers weighed against them—characters estimated probably by the very lords of manors who had lost their game. This disgraceful law is the occasion of all the murders committed for game.

ing off—to have a lord of the manor for green gages—and to rage with a penalty of five pounds against the unqualified eater of the gage! And yet the privilege of shooting a set of wild poultry is stated to be the bonus for the residence of country gentlemen. As far as this immense advantage can be obtained without the sacrifice of justice and reason, well and good—but we would not oppress any order of society, or violate right and wrong, to obtain any population of squires, however dense. It is the grossest of all absurdities to say the present state of the law is absurd and unjust; but it must not be altered, because the alteration would drive gentlemen out of the country! If gentlemen cannot breathe fresh air without injustice, let them putrefy in Cranborne Alley. Make just laws, and let squires live and die where they please.

The evidence collected in the House of Commons respecting the game laws is so striking and so decisive against the gentlemen of the trigger, that their only resource is to represent it as not worthy of belief. But why not worthy of belief? It is not stated what part of it is incredible. Is it the plenty of game in London for sale? the unfrequency of convictions? the occasional but frequent excess of supply above demand in an article supplied by stealing? or its destruction when the sale is not without risk, and the price extremely low? or the readiness of grandees to turn the excess of their game into fish or poultry? All these circumstances appear to us so natural and so likely, that we should, without any evidence, have but little doubt of their existence. There are a few absurdities in the evidence of one of the poulterers; but, with this exception, we see no reason whatever for impugning the credibility and exactness of the mass of testimony prepared by the committee.

It is utterly impossible to teach the common people to respect property in animals bred the possessor knows not where—which he cannot recognize by any mark, which may leave him the next moment, which are kept, not for his profit, but for his amusement. Opinion never will be in favour of such property; if the *animus furandi* exists, the propensity will be gratified by poaching. It is in vain to increase the severity of the protecting laws. They make the case weaker, instead of stronger; and are more resisted and worse executed, exactly in proportion as they are contrary to public opinion:—the case of the game laws is a memorable lesson upon the philosophy of legislation. If a certain degree of punishment does not cure the offence, it is supposed, by the Bankes School, that there is nothing to be done but to multiply this punishment by two, and then again and again, till the object is accomplished. The efficient maximum of punishment, however, is not what the legislature chooses to enact, *but what the great mass of mankind think the maximum ought to be.* The moment the punishment passes this Rubicon, it becomes less and less, instead of greater and greater. Juries and magistrates will not commit—informers* are afraid of public indignation—poachers will not submit to be sent to Botany Bay without a battle—blood is shed for pheasants—the public attention is called to this preposterous state of the law—and even ministers—(whom nothing pesters so much as the interests of humanity) are at least compelled to come forward and do what is right. Apply this to the game laws. It was before penal to sell game: within these few years it has been made penal to buy it. From the scandalous cruelty of the law, night poachers are transported for seven years. And yet, never was so much game sold, or such a spirit of ferocious resistance excited to the laws. One-fourth of all the commitments in Great Britain are for offences against the game laws. There is a general feeling that some alteration must take place—a feeling not only among Reviewers, who never see nor eat game, but among the double-barreled, shot-belted members of the House of Commons, who are either alarmed or disgusted by the vice and misery which their cruel laws and childish passion for amusement are spreading among the lower orders of mankind.

It is said, "In spite of all the game sold, there is game enough left; let the laws therefore remain as they are;" and so it was said formerly, "There is sugar enough; let the slave trade remain as it is." But at what expense of human happiness is this quantity of game or of sugar, and this state of poacher law and slave law, to remain! The first object of a good government is, not that rich men should have their pleasures in perfection, but that all orders of men should be good and happy; and if crowded covies and chuckling cock-pheasants are only to be procured by encouraging the common people in vice, and leading them into cruel and disproportionate punishment, it is the duty of the government to restrain the cruelties which the country members, in reward for their assiduous loyalty, have been allowed to introduce into the game laws.

The plan of the new bill (long since anticipated, in all its provisions, by the acute author of the pamphlet before us,) is, that the public at large should be supplied by persons licensed by magistrates, and that all qualified persons should be permitted to sell their game to these licensed distributors; and there seems a fair chance that such a plan would succeed. The questions are, Would sufficient game come into the hands of the licensed salesman? Would the licensed salesman confine himself to the purchase of game from qualified persons?—Would buyers of game purchase elsewhere than from the licensed salesman? Would the poacher be under-sold by the honest dealer?—Would game remain in the same plenty as before? It is understood that the game laws are to remain as they are; with this only differ-

* There is a remarkable instance of this in the new Turnpike Act. The penalty for taking more than the legal number of outside passengers is ten pounds per head, if the coachman is in part or wholly the owner. This will rarely be levied; because it is too much. A penalty of 100*l.* would produce perfect impunity. The maximum of practical severity would have been about five pounds. Any magistrate would cheerfully levy this sum; while doubling it will produce reluctance in the judge, resistance in the culprit, and unwillingness in the informer.

ence, that the qualified man can sell to the licensed man, and the licentiate to the public.

It seems probable to us, that vast quantities of game would, after a little time, find their way into the hands of licensed poulterers. Great people are very often half eaten up by their establisments. The quantity of game killed in a large shooting party is very great; to eat it is impossible, and to dispose of it in presents very troublesome. The preservation of game is very expensive; and, when it could be bought, it would be no more a compliment to send it as a present than it would be to send geese and fowls. If game were sold, very large shooting establishments might be made to pay their own expenses. The shame is made by the law; there is a disgrace in being detected and fined. If that barrier were removed, superfluous partridges would go to the poulterers as readily as superfluous venison does to the venison butcher—or as a gentleman sells the corn and mutton off his farm which he cannot consume. For these reasons, we do not doubt that the shops of licensed poulterers would be full of game in the season; and this part of the argument, we think, the arch-enemy, Sir John Shelley, himself would concede to us.

The next question is, From whence they would procure it? A license for selling game, granted by country magistrates, would, from their jealousy upon these subjects, be granted only to persons of some respectability and property. The purchase of game from unqualified persons would, of course, be guarded against by very heavy penalties, both personal and pecuniary; and these penalties would be inflicted, because opinion would go with them. "Here is a respectable tradesman," it would be said, "who might have bought as much game as he pleased in a lawful manner, but who, in order to increase his profits by buying it a little cheaper, has encouraged a poacher to steal it." Public opinion, therefore, would certainly be in favour of a very strong punishment; and a licensed vender of game, who exposed himself to these risks, would expose himself to the loss of liberty, property, character, and license.—The persons interested to put a stop to such a practice, would not be the paid agents of government, as in cases of smuggling; but all the gentlemen of the country, the customers of the tradesman for fish, poultry, or whatever else he dealt in, would have an interest in putting down the practice. In all probability, the practice would become disreputable, like the purchase of stolen poultry; and this would be a stronger barrier than the strongest laws. There would, of course, be some exceptions to this statement. A few shabby people would, for the chance of gaining sixpence, incur the risk of ruin and disgrace; but it is probable that the general practice would be otherwise.

For the same reasons, the consumers of game would rather give a little more for it to a licensed poulterer, than expose themselves to severe penalties by purchasing from poachers. The great mass of London consumers are supplied now, not from shabby people, in whom they can have no confidence—not from hawkers and porters, but from respectable tradesmen, in whose probity they have the most perfect confidence. Men will brave the law for pheasants, but not for sixpence or a shilling; and the law itself is much more difficult to be braved, when it allows pheasants to be bought at some price, than when it endeavours to render them utterly inaccessible to wealth. All the licensed salesmen, too, would have a direct interest in stopping the contraband trade of game. They would lose no character in doing so; their informations would be reasonable and respectable.

If all this is true, the poacher would have to compete with a great mass of game fairly and honestly poured into the market. He would be selling with a rope about his neck, to a person who bought with a rope about his neck; his description of customers would be much the same as the customers for stolen poultry, and his profits would be very materially abridged. At present, the poacher is in the same situation as the smuggler would be, if rum and brandy could not be purchased of any fair trader. The great check to the profits of the smuggler are, that if you want his commodities, and will pay an higher price, you may have them elsewhere without risk or disgrace. But forbid the purchase of these luxuries at any price. Shut up the shop of the brandy merchant, and you render the trade of the smuggler of incalculable value. The object of the intended bill is, to raise up precisely the same competition to the trade of the poacher, by giving the public an opportunity of buying lawfully and honestly the tempting articles in which he now deals exclusively. Such an improvement would not, perhaps, altogether annihilate his trade; but it would, in all probability, act as a very material check upon it.

The predominant argument against all this is, that the existing prohibition against buying game, though partially violated, does deter many persons from coming into the market; that if this prohibition were removed, the demand for game would be increased, the legal supply would be insufficient, and the residue would, and must be, supplied by the poacher, whose trade would, for these reasons, be as lucrative and flourishing as before. But it is only a few years since the purchase of game has been made illegal: and the market does not appear to have been at all narrowed by the prohibition; not one head of game the less has been sold by the poulterers; and scarcely one single conviction has taken place under that law. How, then, would the removal of the prohibition, and the alteration of the law, extend the market and increase the demand, when the enactment of the prohibition has had no effect in narrowing it? But if the demand increases, why not the legal supply also? Game is increased upon an estate by feeding them in winter, by making some abatement to the tenants for guarding against depradations, by a large apparatus of gamekeepers and spies—in short by expense. But if this pleasure of shooting, so natural to country gentlemen, is made to pay its own expenses, by sending superfluous game to market, more men, it is reasonable to suppose, will thus preserve and augment their game. The love of pleasure and amusement will produce in the owners of game that desire to multiply game, which the love of gain does in the farmer to multiply poultry. Many gentlemen of small fortune will remember, that they cannot enjoy to any extent this pleasure without this resource; that the legal sale of poultry will discountenance poaching; and they will open an account with the poulterer, not to get richer, but to enjoy a great pleasure without an expense, in which, upon other terms, they could not honourably and conscientiously indulge. If country gentlemen of moderate fortune will do this (and we think after a little time they will do it), game may be multiplied and legally supplied to any extent. Another keeper, and another bean-stack, will produce their proportional supply of pheasants. The only reason why the great lord has more game per acre than the little squire is, that he spends more money per acre to preserve it.

For these reasons, we think the experiment of legalizing the sale of game ought to be tried. The game laws have been carried to a pitch of oppression which is a disgrace to the country. The prisons are half filled with peasants, shut up for the irregular slaughter of rabbits and birds—a sufficient reason for killing a weasel, but not for imprisoning a man. Something should be done; it is disgraceful to a government to stand by, and see such enormous evils without interference. It is true, they are not connected with the struggles of party; but still, the happiness of the common people, whatever gentlemen may say, ought every now and then to be considered.

CRUEL TREATMENT OF UNTRIED PRISONERS.*

[EDINBURGH REVIEW, 1824.]

IT has been the practice, all over England, for these last fifty years,† not to *compel* prisoners to work before guilt was proved. Within these last three or four years, however, the magistrates of the North Riding of Yorkshire, considering it improper to support any idle person at the county expense, have resolved, that prisoners committed to the house of correction for trial, and requiring county support, should work for their livelihood; and no sooner was the treadmill brought into fashion, than that machine was adopted in the North Riding as the species of labour by which such prisoners were to earn their maintenance. If these magistrates did not consider themselves empowered to burden the county rates for the support of prisoners before trial, who would not contribute to support themselves, it does not appear, from the publication of the reverend chairman of the sessions, that any opinions of counsel were taken as to the legality of so putting prisoners to work, or of refusing them maintenance if they choose to be idle; but the magistrates themselves decided that such was the law of the land. Thirty miles off, however, the law of the land was differently interpreted; and in the Castle of York large sums were annually expended in the maintenance of idle prisoners before trial, and paid by the different Ridings, without remonstrance or resistance.‡

Such was the state of affairs in the county of York before the enactment of the recent prison bill. After that period, enlargements and alterations were necessary in the county jail; and it was necessary also for these arrangements, that the magistrates should know whether or not they were authorized to maintain such prisoners at the expense of the county, as, being accounted able and unwilling to work, still claimed the county allowance. To questions proposed upon these points to three barristers, the following answers were returned:—

"2dly, I am of opinion, that the magistrates are empowered, and are compelled to maintain, at the expense of the county, such prisoners *before* trial as are able to work, unable to maintain themselves, and not willing to work; and that they have not the power of compelling such prisoners to work, either at the treadmill, or any other species of labour.

"J. GURNEY.

"*Lincoln's Inn Fields, 2d September*, 1823."

"I think the magistrates are empowered, under the tenth section (explained by the 37th and 38th), to maintain prisoners before trial, who are able to work, unable to maintain themselves by their own means, or by employment which they themselves can procure, and not willing to work; and I think also, that the words "shall be lawful," in that section, do not leave them a discretion on the subject, but are compulsory. *Such* prisoners can only be employed in prison labour with *their own consent;* and it cannot be intended that the justices may force such consent, by withholding from them the necessaries of life, if they do not give it. Even those who are convicted cannot be employed at the treadmill, which I consider as a species of *severe* labour.

"*September 4th*, 1823." "J. PARKE.

"2dly, As to the point of compelling prisoners confined on criminal charges, and receiving relief from the magistrates, to reasonable labour; to that of the treadmill for instance, in which, when properly conducted, there is nothing severe or unreasonable; had the question arisen prior to the late act, I should with confidence have said, I thought the magistrates had a compulsory power in this respect. Those who cannot live without relief in a jail, cannot live without labour out of it. Labour then is their avocation. Nothing is so injurious to the morals and habits of the prisoner as the indolence prevalent in prisons; nothing so injurious to good order in the prison. The analogy between this and other cases of public support is exceedingly strong; one may almost consider it a general principle, that those who live at the charge of the community shall, as far as they are able, give the community a compensation through their labour. But the question does not depend on mere abstract reasoning. The stat. 19 Ch. 2, c. 4, sec. 1, entitled, 'An Act for Relief of poor Prisoners, and setting them on work,' speaks of persons committed for felony and other misdemeanours to the common jail, who many times *perish before trial;* and then proceeds as to setting poor prisoners on work. Then stat. 31 G. 3, c. 46, sec. 13, orders money to be raised for such prisoners of every description, as, being confined within the said jails, or other places of confinement, *are not able to work.* A late stat. (52 G. 3, c. 160) orders parish relief to such debtors on mesne process in jails, not county jails, as are not able to support themselves; but says nothing of finding or compelling work. Could it be doubted, that if the justices were to provide work, and the prisoner refused it, such debtors might, like any other

---

* 1. *A Letter to the Right Honourable Robert Peel, one of His Majesty's Principal Secretaries of State, &c. &c. &c. on Prison Labour.* By JOHN HEADLAM, M. A., Chairman of the Quarter Sessions for the North Riding of the County of York. London. Hatchard and Son, 1823.

2. *Information and Observations, respecting the proposed Improvements at York Castle.* Printed by Order of the Committee of Magistrates. September, 1823.

† Headlam, p. 6.

‡ We mention the case of the North Riding, to convince our readers that the practice of condemning prisoners to work before trial has existed in some parts of England; for in questions like this we have always found it more difficult to prove the existence of the facts, than to prove that they were mischievous and unjust.

parish paupers, be refused the relief mentioned by the statute? In all the above cases, the authority to insist on the prisoner's labour, as the condition and consideration of relief granted him, is, I think, either expressed, or necessarily implied; and thus viewing the subject, I think it was in the power of magistrates, prior to the late statute, to compel prisoners, subsisting in all or in part on public relief, to work at the treadmill. The objection commonly made is, that prisoners, prior to trial, are to be accounted innocent, and to be detained, merely that they may be secured for trial; to this the answer is obvious, that the labour is neither meant as a punishment or a disgrace, but simply as a compensation for the relief, at their own request, afforded them. Under the present statute, I, however, have no doubt, that poor prisoners are entitled to public support, and that there can be no compulsory labour prior to trial. The two statutes adverted to (19 Ch. 2, c. 4, and 31 G. 3) are, as far as this subject is concerned, expressly repealed. The legislature then had in contemplation the existing power of magistrates to order labour before trial, and having it in contemplation, repeals it; substituting (sec. 38) a power of setting to labour *only sentenced persons.* The 13th rule, too (p. 177), speaks of labour as connected with convicted prisoners, and sec. 37 speaks in general terms of persons committed for trial, as labouring with their own consent. In opposition to these clauses, I think it impossible to speak of implied power, or power founded on general reasoning or analogy. So strong, however, are the arguments in favour of a more extended authority in justices of the peace, that it is scarcely to be doubted, that Parliament, on a calm revision of the subject, would be willing to restore, in a more distinct manner than it has hitherto been enacted, a general discretion on the subject. Were this done, there is one observation I will venture to make, which is, that should some unfortunate association of ideas render the treadmill a matter of ignominy to common feelings, an enlightened magistracy would scarcely compel an untried prisoner to a species of labour which would disgrace him in his own mind, and in that of the public.

"S. W. Nicoll.

"*York, August 27th,* 1823."

In consequence, we believe, of these opinions, the North Riding magistrates, on the 13th of October (the new bill commencing on the 1st of September), passed the following resolution:—"That persons committed for trial, who are able to work, and have the means of employment offered them by the visiting magistrates, by which they may earn their support, but who obstinately refuse to work, shall be allowed bread and water only."

By this resolution they admit, of course, that the counsel are right in their interpretation of the present law; and that magistrates are forced to maintain prisoners before trial who do not choose to work. The magistrates say, however, by their resolution, that the food shall be of the plainest and humblest kind, bread and water; meaning, of course, that such prisoners should have a sufficient quantity of bread and water, or otherwise the evasion of the law would be in the highest degree mean and reprehensible. But it is impossible to suppose any such thing to be intended by gentlemen so highly respectable. Their intention is not that idle persons before trial shall starve, but that they shall have barely enough of the plainest food for the support of life and health.

Mr. Headlam has written a pamphlet to show that the old law was very reasonable and proper; that it is quite right that prisoners before trial, who are able to support themselves, but unwilling to work, should be compelled to work, and at the treadmill, or that all support should be refused them. We are entirely of an opposite opinion; and maintain that it is neither legal nor expedient to *compel* prisoners before trial to work at the treadmill, or at any species of labour, and that those who refuse to work should be supported upon a plain, healthy diet. We impute no sort of blame to the magistrates of the North Riding, or to Mr. Headlam, their chairman. We have no doubt but that they thought their measures the wisest and the best for correcting evil, and that they adopted them in pursuance of what they thought to be their duty. Nor do we enter into any discussion with Mr. Headlam, as chairman of a Quarter Sessions, but as the writer of a pamphlet. It is only in his capacity of author that we have any thing to do with him. In answering the arguments of Mr. Headlam, we shall notice, at the same time, a few other observations commonly resorted to in defence of a system which we believe to be extremely pernicious, and pregnant with the worst consequences; and so thinking, we contend against it, and in support of the law as it now stands.

We will not dispute with Mr. Headlam, whether his exposition of the old law is right or wrong: because time cannot be more unprofitably employed than in hearing gentlemen who are not lawyers discuss points of law. We dare to say Mr. Headlam knows as much of the laws of his country as magistrates in general do; but he will pardon us for believing, that for the moderate sum of three guineas a much better opinion of what the law is now, or was then, can be purchased, than it is in the power of Mr. Headlam, or any other county magistrate, to give for nothing—*Cuilibet in arte sua credendum est.* It is concerning the expediency of such laws, and upon that point alone, that we are at issue with Mr. Headlam; and do not let this gentleman suppose it to be any answer to our remarks to state what is done in the prison in which he is concerned, now the law is altered. The question is, whether he is right or wrong in his reasoning upon what the law *ought* to be; we wish to hold out such reasoning to public notice, and think it important it should be refuted—doubly important, when it comes from an author, the leader of the quorum, who may say with the pious Æneas,—

——Quæque ipse miserrima vidi,
Et *quorum* pars magna fui.

If, in this discussion, we are forced to insist upon the plainest and most elementary truths, the fault is not with us, but with those who forget them; and who refuse to be any longer restrained by those principles which have hitherto been held to be as clear as they are important to human happiness.

To begin, then, with the nominative case and the verb—we must remind those advocates for the treadmill, *a parte ante* (for which the millers *a parte post* we have no quarrel), that it is one of the oldest maxims of common sense, common humanity, and common law, to consider every man as innocent till he is proved to be guilty; and not only to consider him to be innocent, but to treat him as if he was so; to exercise upon his case not merely a barren speculation, but one which produces practical effects, and which secures to a prisoner the treatment of an honest, unpunished man. Now, to compel prisoners before trial to work at the treadmill, as the condition of their support, must, in a great number of instances, operate as a very severe punishment. A prisoner may be a tailor, a watchmaker, a bookbinder, a printer, totally unaccustomed to any such species of labour. Such a man may be cast into jail at the end of August,* and not tried till the March following; is it no punishment to such a man to walk up hill like a turnspit dog, in an infamous machine, for six months? and yet there are gentlemen who suppose that the common people do not consider this as punishment!—that the gayest and most joyous of human beings is a treader, untried by a jury of his countrymen, in the fifth month of lifting up the leg, and striving against the law of gravity, supported by the glorious information which he receives from the turnkey, that he has all the time been grinding flour on the other side of the wall! If this sort of exercise, necessarily painful to sedentary persons, is agreeable to persons accustomed to labour, then make it voluntary—give the prisoners their choice—give more money and more diet to those who can and will labour at the treadmill, if the treadmill (now so dear to magistrates) is a proper punishment for untried prisoners. The position we are contending against is, that all poor prisoners who are able to work should be put to work upon the treadmill, the inevitable consequence of which practice is, a repetition of gross injustice by the infliction of undeserved punishment; for punishment, and severe punishment, to such persons as we have enumerated, we must consider it to be.

But punishments are not merely to be estimated by pain to the limbs, but by the feelings of the mind. Gentlemen punishers are sometimes apt to forget that the common people have any mental feelings at all, and think, if body and belly are attended to, that persons under a certain income have no right to likes and dislikes. The labour of the treadmill is irksome, dull, monotonous, and disgusting to the last degree. A man does not see his work, does not know what he is doing, what progress he is making; there is no room for art, contrivance, ingenuity, and superior skill—all which are the cheering circumstances of human labour. The husbandman sees the field gradually subdued by the plough; the smith beats the rude mass of iron by degrees into its meditated shape, and gives it a meditated utility; the tailor accommodates his parallelogram of cloth to the lumps and bumps of the human body, and, holding it up, exclaims, "This will contain the lower moiety of an human being." But the treader does nothing but tread; he sees no change of objects, admires no new relation of parts, imparts no new qualities to matter, and gives to it no new arrangements and positions; or, if he does, he sees and knows it not, but is turned at once from a rational being, by a justice of peace, into a *primum mobile*, and put upon a level with a rush of water or a puff of steam. It is impossible to get gentlemen to attend to the distinction between raw and roasted prisoners, without which all discussion on prisoners is perfectly ridiculous. Nothing can be more excellent than this kind of labour for persons to whom you mean to make labour as irksome as possible; but for this very reason, it is the labour to which an untried prisoner ought not to be put.

It is extremely uncandid to say that a man is obstinately and incorrigibly idle, because he will not submit to such tiresome and detestable labour as that of the treadmill. It is an old feeling among Englishmen that there is a difference between tried and untried persons, between accused and convicted persons. These old opinions were in fashion before this new magistrate's plaything was invented; and we are convinced that many industrious persons, feeling that they have not had their trial, and disgusted with the nature of the labour, would refuse to work at the treadmill, who would not be averse to join in any common and fair occupation. Mr. Headlam says, that labour may be a privilege as well as a punishment. So may taking physic be a privilege, in cases where it is asked for as a charitable relief, but not if it is stuffed down a man's throat whether he say yea or nay. Certainly labour is not necessarily a punishment: nobody has said it is so; but Mr. Headlam's labour is a punishment, because it is irksome, infamous, unasked for, and undeserved. This gentleman, however, observes, that committed persons *have offended the laws;* and the sentiment expressed in these words is the true key to his pamphlet and his system—a perpetual tendency to confound the convicted and the accused.

"With respect to those sentenced to labour as a punishment, I apprehend there is no difference of opinion. All are agreed that it is a great defect in any prison where such convicts are unemployed. But as to all *other* prisoners, whether debtors, *persons committed for trial,* or convicts not sentenced to hard labour, if they have no means of subsisting themselves, and must, if discharged, either labour for their livelihood or apply for parochial relief, it seems unfair to society at large, and

*Mr. Headlam, as we understand him, would extend this labour to all poor prisoners before trial in jails which are delivered twice a year at the assizes, as well as to houses of correction delivered four times a year at the Sessions; *i. e.* not to extend the labour, but to refuse all support to those who refuse the labour—a distinction, but not a difference.

especially to those who maintain themselves by honest industry, that those who, *by offending the laws, have subjected themselves to imprisonment,* should be lodged, and clothed, and fed, without being called upon for the same exertions, which others have to use to obtain such advantages."—*Headlam*, pp. 23, 24.

Now nothing can be more unfair than to say that such men have offended the laws. That is the very question to be tried, whether they have offended the laws or not? It is merely because this little circumstance is taken for granted, that we have any quarrel at all with Mr. Headlam and his school.

"I can make," says Mr. Headlam, "every delicate consideration for the rare case of a person perfectly innocent being committed to jail on suspicion of crime. Such person is deservedly an object of compassion, for having fallen under circumstances which subject him to be charged with crime, and, consequently, to be deprived of his liberty: but if he has been in the habit of labouring for his bread before his commitment, there does not appear to be any addition to his misfortune in being called upon to work for his subsistence in prison."—*Headlam*, p. 24.

And yet Mr. Headlam describes this very punishment, which does not add to the misfortunes of an innocent man, to be *generally disagreeable, to be dull, irksome, to excite a strong dislike, to be a dull, monotonous labour, to be a contrivance which connects the idea of discomfort with a jail.* (p. 36.) So that Mr. Headlam looks upon it to be no increase of an innocent man's misfortunes, to be constantly employed upon a dull, irksome, monotonous labour, which excites a strong dislike, and connects the idea of discomfort with a jail. We cannot stop, or stoop to consider, whether beating hemp is more or less dignified than working in a mill. The simple rule is this,—whatever felons do, men not yet proved to be felons should not be compelled to do. It is of no use to look into laws become obsolete by alteration of manners. For these fifty years past, and before the invention of treadmills, untried men were not put upon felons' work; but with the mill came in the mischief. Mr. Headlam asks, How can men be employed upon the ancient trades in a prison?—certainly they cannot; but are human occupations so few, and is the ingenuity of magistrates and jailers so limited, that no occupations can be found for innocent men, but those which are shameful and odious? Does Mr. Headlam really believe, that grown up and baptized persons are to be satisfied with such arguments, or repelled by such difficulties?

It is some compensation to an acquitted person, that the labour he has gone through unjustly in jail has taught him some trade, given him an insight into some species of labour in which he may hereafter improve himself; but Mr. Headlam's prisoner, after a verdict of acquittal, has learnt no other art than of walking up hill; he has nothing to remember or recompense him but three months of undeserved and unprofitable torment. The verdict of the jury has pronounced him steady in his morals; the conduct of the justices has made him stiff in his joints.

But it is next contended by some persons, that the poor prisoner is not compelled to work, because he has the alternative of starving, if he refuses to work. You take up a poor man upon suspicion, deprive him of all his usual methods of getting his livelihood, and then giving him the first view of the treadmill, he of the quorum thus addresses him:—"My amiable friend, we use no compulsion with untried prisoners. You are free as air till you are found guilty; only it is my duty to inform you, as you have no money of your own, that the disposition to eat and drink which you have allowed you sometimes feel, and upon which I do not mean to cast any degree of censure, cannot possibly be gratified but by constant grinding in this machine. It has its inconveniences, I admit; but balance them against the total want of meat and drink, and decide for yourself. You are perfectly at liberty to make your choice, and I by no means wish to influence your judgment." But Mr. Nicoll has a curious remedy for all this miserable tyranny; he says it is not meant as a punishment. But if I am conscious that I never have committed the offence, certain that I have never been found guilty of it, and find myself tossed into the middle of an infernal machine, by the folly of those who do not know how to use the power entrusted to them, is it any consolation to me to be told, that it is not *intended* as a punishment, that it is a lucubration of justices, a new theory of prison discipline, a valuable county experiment going on at the expense of my arms, legs, back, feelings, character, and rights? We must tie those prægustant punishers down by one question. Do you mean to inflict any degree of punishment upon persons merely for being suspected?—or at least any other degree of punishment than that without which criminal justice cannot exist, detention? If you do why let any one out upon bail? For the question between us is not, how suspected persons are to be treated, and whether or not they are to be punished; but how suspected *poor* persons are to be treated, who want county support in prison. If to be suspected is deserving of punishment, then no man ought to be let out upon bail, but *every one* should be kept grinding from accusation to trial; and so ought *all* prisoners to be treated for offences not bailable, and who do not want the county allowance. And yet no grinding philosopher contends, that all suspected persons should be put in the mill—but only those who are too poor to find bail, or buy provisions.

If there are, according to the doctrines of the millers, to be two punishments, the first for being suspected of committing the offence, and the second for committing it, there should be two trials as well as two punishments. Is the man really suspected, or do his accusers only pretend to suspect him? Are the suspecting of better character than the suspected? Is it a light suspicion which may be atoned for by grinding a peck a day? Is it a bushel case? or is it one deeply criminal, which requires the flour to be ground fine enough for

French rolls? But we must put an end to such absurdities.

It is very untruly stated, that a prisoner, before trial, not compelled to work, and kept upon a plain diet, merely sufficient to maintain him in health, is better off than he was previous to his accusation; and it is asked, with a triumphant leer, whether the situation of any man ought to be improved, merely because he has become an object of suspicion to his fellow-creatures? This happy and fortunate man, however, is separated from his wife and family; his liberty is taken away; he is confined within four walls; he has the reflection that his family are existing upon a precarious parish support, that his little trade and property are wasting, that his character has become infamous, that he has incurred ruin by the malice of others, or by his own crimes, that in a few weeks he is to forfeit his life, or be banished from every thing he loves upon earth. This is the improved situation, and the redundant happiness which requires the penal circumvolutions of the justice's mill to cut off so unjust a balance of gratification, and bring him a little nearer to what he was before imprisonment and accusation. It would be just as reasonable to say, that an idle man in a fever is better off than a healthy man who is well and earns his bread. He may be better off if you look to the idleness alone, though that is doubtful; but is he better off if all the aches, agonies, disturbances, deliriums, and the nearness to death, are added to the lot?

Mr. Headlam's panacea for all prisoners before trial is the treadmill: we beg his pardon—for all *poor* prisoners; but a man who is about to be tried for his life, often wants all his leisure time to reflect upon his defence. The exertions of every man within the walls of a prison are necessarily crippled and impaired. What can a prisoner answer who is taken hot and reeking from the treadmill, and asked what he has to say in his defence; his answer naturally is—"I have been grinding corn instead of thinking of my defence, and have never been allowed the proper leisure to think of protecting my character and my life." This is a very strong feature of cruelty and tyranny in the mill. We ought to be sure that every man has had the fullest leisure to prepare for his defence, that his mind and body have not been harassed by vexations and compulsory employment. The public purchase, at a great price, legal accuracy, and legal talent, to accuse a man who has not, perhaps, one shilling to spend upon his defence. It is atrocious cruelty not to leave him full leisure to write his scarcely legible letters to his witnesses, and to use all the melancholy and feeble means which suspected poverty can employ for its defence against the long and heavy arm of power.

A prisoner, upon the system recommended by Mr. Headlam, is committed, perhaps at the end of August, and brought to trial the March following; and, after all, the bill is either thrown out by the grand jury, or the prisoner is fully acquitted; and it has been found, we believe, by actual returns, that, of committed prisoners, about a half are actually acquitted, or their accusations dismissed by the grand jury. This may be very true, say the advocates of this system, but we know that many men who are acquitted are guilty. They escape through some mistaken lenity of the law, or some corruption of evidence; and as they have not had their deserved punishment after trial, we are not sorry they had it before. The English law says, better many guilty escape, than that one innocent man perish; but the humane notions of the mill are bottomed upon the principle, that all had better be punished lest any escape. They evince a total mistrust in the jurisprudence of the country, and say the results of trial are so uncertain, that it is better to punish all the prisoners before they come into court. Mr. Headlam forgets that general rules are not beneficial in each individual instance, but beneficial upon the whole; that they are preserved because they do much more good than harm, though in some particular instances they do more harm than good; yet no respectable man violates them on that account, but holds them sacred for the great balance of advantage they confer upon mankind. It is one of the greatest crimes, for instance, to take away the life of a man; yet there are many men whose death would be a good to society, rather than an evil. Every good man respects the property of others; yet to take from a worthless miser, and to give it to a virtuous man in distress, would be an advantage. Sensible men are never staggered when they see the exception. They know the importance of the rule, and protect it most eagerly at the very moment when it is doing more harm than good. The plain rule of justice is, that no man should be punished till he is found guilty; but because Mr. Headlam occasionally sees a bad man acquitted under this rule, and sent out unpunished upon the world, he forgets all the general good and safety of the principle are debauched by the exception, and applauds and advocates a system of prison discipline which renders injustice certain, in order to prevent it from being occasional.

The meaning of all preliminary imprisonment is, that the accused person should be forthcoming at the time of trial. It was never intended as a punishment. Bail is a far better invention than imprisonment, in cases where the heavy punishment of the offence would not induce the accused person to run away from any bail. Now, let us see the enormous difference this new style of punishment makes between two men, whose only difference is, that one is poor and the other rich. A and B are accused of some bailable offence. A has no bail to offer, and no money to support himself in prison, and takes, therefore, his four or five months in the treadmill. B gives bail, appears at his trial, and both are sentenced to two months' imprisonment. In this case, the one suffers three times as much as the other for the same offence: but suppose A is acquitted and B found guilty,—the innocent man has then laboured in the treadmill five months because he was poor, and the guilty man labours two months because he was rich. We are aware that there must be, even without the treadmill, a great and an inevitable difference between men (*in pari delicto*), some of whom can give bail, and some not; but that difference becomes infinitely more bitter and objectionable, in proportion as detention before trial assumes the character of severe and degrading punishment.

If motion in the treadmill was otherwise as fascinating as millers describe it to be, still the mere degradation of the punishment is enough to revolt every feeling of an untried person. It is a punishment consecrated to convicted felons—and it has every character that such punishment ought to have. An untried person feels at once, in getting into the mill, that he is put to the labour of the guilty; that a mode of employment has been selected for him, which renders him infamous before a single fact or argument has been advanced to establish his guilt. If men are put into the treadmill before trial, it is literally of no sort of consequence whether they are acquitted or not. Acquittal does not shelter them from punishment, for they have already been punished. It does not screen them from infamy, for they have already been treated as if they were infamous; and the association of the treadmill and crimes is not to be got over. This machine flings all the power of juries into the hands of the magistrates, and makes every simple commitment more terrible than a conviction; for, in a conviction, the magistrate considers whether the offence has been committed or not; and does not send the prisoner to jail unless he thinks him guilty; but in a simple commitment, a man is not sent to jail because the magistrate is convinced of his guilt, but because he thinks a fair question may be made to a jury whether the accused person is guilty or not. Still, however, the convicted and the suspected both go to the same mill; and he who is there upon the doubt, grinds as much flour as the other whose guilt is established by a full examination of conflicting evidence.

Where is the necessity for such a violation of common sense and common justice? Nobody asks for the idle prisoner before trial more than a very plain and moderate diet. Offer him, if you please, some labour which is less irksome, and less infamous than the treadmill,—bribe him by improved diet, and a share of the earnings; there will not be three men out of an hundred who would refuse such an invitation, and spurn at such an improvement of their condition. A little humane attention and persuasion, among men who ought, upon every principle of justice, to be considered as innocent, we should have thought much more consonant to English justice, and to the feelings of English magistrates, than the rack and wheel of Cubitt.*

Prison discipline is an object of considerable importance; but the common rights of mankind, and the common principles of justice, and humanity, and liberty, are of greater consequence even than prison discipline. Right and wrong, innocence and guilt, must not be confounded, that a prison-fancying justice may bring his friend into the prison and say, "Look what a spectacle of order, silence, and decorum we have established here! no idleness, all grinding!—we produce a penny roll every second—our prison is supposed to be the best regulated prison in England,—Cubitt is making us a new wheel of forty felon power,—look how white the flour is, all done by untried prisoners—as innocent as lambs!" If prison discipline is to supersede every other consideration, why are pennyless prisoners alone to be put into the mill before trial? If idleness in jails is so pernicious, why not put all prisoners in the treadmill, the rich as well as those who are unable to support themselves? Why are the debtors left out? If fixed principles are to be given up, and prisons turned into a plaything for magistrates, nothing can be more unpicturesque than to see one-half of the prisoners looking on, talking, gaping, and idling, while their poorer brethren are grinding for dinners and suppers.

It is a very weak argument to talk of the prisoners earning their support, and the expense to a county of maintaining prisoners before trial,—as if any rational man could ever expect to gain a farthing by an expensive mill, where felons are the moving power, and justices the superintendents, or as if such a trade must not necessarily be carried on at a great loss. If it were just and proper that prisoners, before trial, should be condemned to the mill, it would be of no consequence whether the county gained or lost by the trade. But the injustice of the practice can never be defended by its economy; and the fact is, that it increases expenditure, while it violates principle. We are aware, that by leaving out repairs, alterations, and first costs, and a number of little particulars, a very neat account, signed by a jailer, may be made up, which shall make the mill a miraculous combination of mercantile speculation and moral improvement; but we are too old for all this. We accuse nobody of intentional misrepresentation. This is quite out of the question with persons so highly respectable; but men are constantly misled by the spirit of system, and egregiously deceive themselves—even very good and sensible men.

Mr. Headlam compares the case of a prisoner before trial, claiming support, to that of a pauper claiming relief from his parish. But it seems to us that no two cases can be more dissimilar. The prisoner was no pauper before you took him up, and deprived him of his customers, tools, and market. It is by your act and deed that he is fallen into a state of pauperism; and nothing can be more preposterous, than first to make a man a pauper, and then to punish him for being so. It is true, that the apprehension and detention of the prisoner were necessary for the purposes of criminal justice; but the consequences arising from this necessary act cannot be imputed to the prisoner. He has brought it upon himself, it will be urged; but that remains to be seen, and will not be known till he is tried; and till it is known you have no right to take it for granted, and to punish him as if it were proved.

There seems to be in the minds of some

* It is singular enough, that we use these observations in reviewing the pamphlet and system of a gentleman remarkable for the urbanity of his manners, and the mildness and humanity of his disposition.

gentlemen a notion, that when once a person is in prison, it is of little consequence how he is treated afterwards. The tyranny which prevailed, of putting a person in a particular dress before trial, now abolished by act of Parliament, was justified by this train of reasoning:—The man has been rendered infamous by imprisonment. He cannot be rendered more so, dress him as you will. His character is not rendered worse by the treadmill, than it is by being sent to the place where the treadmill is at work. The substance of this way of thinking is, that when a fellow-creature is in the frying-pan, there is no harm in pushing him into the fire; that a little more misery—a little more infamy—a few more links, are of no sort of consequence in a prison-life. If this monstrous style of reasoning extended to hospitals as well as prisons, there would be no harm in breaking the small bone of a man's leg, because the large one was fractured, or in peppering with small shot a person who was wounded with a cannon-ball. The principle is, because a man is very wretched, there is no harm in making him a little more so. The steady answer to all this is, that a man is imprisoned before trial, *solely* for the purpose of securing his appearance at his trial; and that no punishment nor privation, not clearly and candidly necessary for that purpose, should be inflicted upon him. I keep you in prison, because criminal justice would be defeated by your flight, if I did not: but criminal justice can go on very well without degrading you to hard and infamous labour, or denying you any reasonable gratification. For these reasons, the first of those acts is just, the rest are mere tyranny.

Mr. Nicoll, in his opinion, tells us, that he has no doubt Parliament would amend the bill, if the omission was stated to them. We, on the contrary, have no mannor of doubt that Parliament would treat such a petition with the contempt it deserved. Mr. Peel is too much enlightened and sensible to give any countenance to such a great and glaring error. In this case,—and we wish it were a more frequent one—the wisdom comes from within, and the error from without the walls of Parliament.

A prisoner before trial who can support himself, ought to be allowed every fair and rational enjoyment which he can purchase, not incompatible with prison discipline. He should be allowed to buy ale or wine in moderation,—to use tobacco, or any thing else he can pay for within the above-mentioned limits. If he cannot support himself, and declines work, then he should be supported upon a very plain, but still a plentiful diet (something better, we think, than bread and water); and all prisoners before trial should be *allowed* to work. By a liberal share of earnings (or rather by rewards, for there would be no earnings), and also by an improved diet, and in the hands of humane magistrates,* there would soon appear to be no necessity for appealing to the treadmill till trial was over.

This treadmill, after trial, is certainly a very excellent method of punishment, as far as we are yet acquainted with its effects. We think, at present, however, it is a little abused; and hereafter it is our intention to express our opinion upon the limits to which it ought to be confined. Upon this point, however, we do not much differ from Mr. Headlam; although, in his remarks on the treatment of prisoners before trial, we think he has made a very serious mistake, and has attempted (without knowing what he was doing, and meaning, we are persuaded, nothing but what was honest and just) to pluck up one of the ancient landmarks of human justice.†

* All magistrates should remember, that nothing is more easy to a person entrusted with power than to convince himself it is his duty to treat his fellow-creatures with severity and rigour,—and then to persuade himself that he is doing it very reluctantly, and contrary to his real feeling.

† We hope this article will conciliate our old friend Mr. Roscoe; who is very angry with us for some of our former lucubrations on prison discipline,—and, above all, because we are not grave enough for him. The difference is thus stated:—Six ducks are stolen. Mr. Roscoe would commit the man to prison for six weeks, perhaps, —reason with him, argue with him, give him tracts, send clergymen to him, work him gently at some useful trade, and try to turn him from the habit of stealing poultry. *We* would keep him hard at work twelve hours every day at the treadmill, feed him only so as not to impair his health, and then give him as much of Mr. Roscoe's system as was compatible with our own; and we think our method would diminish the number of duck-stealers more effectually than that of the historian of Leo X. The primary duck-stealer would, we think, be as effectually deterred from repeating the offence by the terror of our imprisonment, as by the excellence of Mr. Roscoe's education—and, what is of infinitely greater consequence, innumerable duck-stealers would be prevented. Because punishment does not annihilate crime, it is folly to say it does not lessen it. It did not stop the murder of Mrs. Donatty; but how many Mrs. Donattys has it kept alive! When we recommend severity, we recommend, of course, that degree of severity which will not excite compassion for the sufferer, and lessen the horror of the crime. This is why we do not recommend torture and amputation of limbs. When a man has been proved to have committed a crime, it is expedient that society should make use of that man for the diminution of crime: he belongs to them for that purpose. Our primary duty, in such a case, is so to treat the culprit that many other persons may be rendered better, or prevented from being worse by dread of the same treatment; and, making this the principal object, to combine with it as much as possible the improvement of the individual. The ruffian who killed Mr. Mumford was hung within forty-eight hours. Upon Mr. Roscoe's principles, this was wrong; for it certainly was not the way to reclaim the man:—We say, on the contrary, the object was to do any thing with the man which would render murders less frequent, and that the conversion of the man was a mere trifle compared to this. His death probably prevented the necessity of reclaiming a dozen murderers. That death will not, indeed, prevent all murders in that county; but many who have seen it, and many who have heard of it, will swallow their revenge from the dread of being hanged. Mr. Roscoe is very severe upon our style, but poor dear Mr. Roscoe should remember that men have different tastes, and different methods of going to work. We feel these matters as deeply as he does. But why so cross upon this or any other subject?

AMERICA.*

[Edinburgh Review, 1824.]

There is a set of miserable persons in England, who are dreadfully afraid of America and every thing American—whose great delight is to see that country ridiculed and vilified—and who appear to imagine that all the abuses which exist in this country acquire additional vigour and chance of duration from every book of travels which pours forth its venom and falsehood on the United States. We shall from time to time call the attention of the public to this subject, not from any party spirit, but because we love truth, and praise excellence wherever we find it; and because we think the example of America will in many instances tend to open the eyes of Englishmen to their true interests.

The *economy* of America is a great and important object for our imitation. The salary of Mr. Bagot, our late ambassador, was, we believe, rather higher than that of the President of the United States. The vice-president receives rather less than the second clerk of the House of Commons; and all salaries, civil and military, are upon the same scale; and yet no country is better served than America! Mr. Hume has at last persuaded the English people to look a little into their accounts, and to see how sadly they are plundered. But we ought to suspend our contempt for America, and consider whether we have not a very momentous lesson to learn from this wise and cautious people on the subject of economy.

A lesson upon the importance of religious toleration, we are determined, it would seem, *not* to learn,—either from America, or from any other quarter of the globe. The High Sheriff of New York, last year, was a Jew. It was with the utmost difficulty that a bill was carried this year to allow the first Duke of England to carry a gold stick before the king —because he was a Catholic!—and yet we think ourselves entitled to indulge in impertinent sneers at America,—as if civilization did not depend more upon making wise laws for the promotion of human happiness, than in having good inns, and post-horses, and civil waiters. The circumstances of the Dissenters' marriage bill are such as would excite the contempt of a Choctaw or Cherokee, if he could be brought to understand them. A certain class of Dissenters beg they may not be compelled to say that they marry in the name of the Trinity, because they do not believe in the Trinity. Never mind, say the corruptionists, you must go on saying you marry in the name of the Trinity, whether you believe in it or not. We know that such a protestation from you will be false: but, unless you make it, your wives shall be concubines, and your children illegitimate. Is it possible to conceive a greater or more useless tyranny than this?

"In the religious freedom which America enjoys, I see a more unquestioned superiority. In Britain we enjoy toleration, but here they enjoy liberty. If government has a right to grant toleration to any particular set of religious opinions, it has also a right to take it away; and such a right with regard to opinions exclusively religious I would deny in all cases, because totally inconsistent with the nature of religion, in the proper meaning of the word, and equally irreconcilable with civil liberty, rightly so called. God has given to each of us his inspired word, and a rational mind to which that word is addressed. He has also made known to us, that each for himself must answer at his tribunal for his principles and conduct. What man, then, or body of men, has a right to tell me, 'You do not think aright on religious subjects, but we will tolerate your error?' The answer is a most obvious one, 'Who gave you authority to dictate?—or what exclusive claim have you to infallibility?' If my sentiments do not lead me into conduct inconsistent with the welfare of my fellow-creatures, the question as to their accuracy or fallacy is one between God and my own conscience; and, though a fair subject for argument, is none for compulsion.

"The Inquisition undertook to regulate astronomical science, and kings and parliaments have with equal propriety presumed to legislate upon questions of theology. The world has outgrown the former, and it will one day be ashamed that it has been so long of outgrowing the latter. The founders of the American republic saw the absurdity of employing the attorney-general to refute deism and infidelity, or of attempting to influence opinion on abstract subjects by penal enactment; they saw also the injustice of taxing the whole to support the religious opinions of the few, and have set an example which older governments will one day or other be compelled to follow.

"In America the question is not, What is his creed?—but, what is his conduct? Jews have all the privileges of Christians; Episcopalians, Presbyterians, and Independents, meet on common ground. No religious test is required to qualify for public office, except in some cases a mere verbal assent to the truth of the Christian religion; and in every court throughout the country, it is optional whether

---

* 1. *Travels through Part of the United States and Canada, in* 1818 *and* 1819. By John M. Duncan, A. B. Glasgow, 1823.

2. *Letters from North America, written during a Tour in the United States and Canada.* By Adam Hodgson. London, 1824.

3. *An Excursion through the United States and Canada, during the years* 1822-3. By an English Gentleman. London, 1824.

you give your affirmation or your oath."—*Duncan's Travels*, II. 328—330.

In fact, it is hardly possible for any nation to show a greater superiority over another than the Americans, in this particular, have done over this country. They have fairly and completely, and probably for ever, extinguished that spirit of religious persecution which has been the employment and the curse of mankind for four or five centuries; not only that persecution which imprisons and scourges for religious opinions, but the tyranny of incapacitation, which, by disqualifying from civil offices, and cutting a man off from the lawful objects of ambition, endeavours to strangle religious freedom in silence, and to enjoy all the advantages, without the blood, and noise, and fire of persecution. What passes in the mind of one mean blockhead is the general history of all persecution. "This man pretends to know better than me—I cannot subdue him by argument; but I will take care he shall never be mayor or alderman of the town in which he lives; I will never consent to the repeal of the test act or to Catholic emancipation; I will teach the fellow to differ from me in religious opinions!" So says the Episcopalian to the Catholic—and so the Catholic says to the Protestant. But the wisdom of America keeps them all down—secures to them all their just rights—gives to each of them their separate pews, and bells, and steeples—makes them all aldermen in their turns—and quietly extinguishes the fagots which each is preparing for the combustion of the other. Nor is this indifference to religious subjects in the American people, but pure civilization—a thorough comprehension of what is best calculated to secure the public happiness and peace—and a determination that this happiness and peace shall not be violated by the insolence of any human being, in the garb, and under the sanction, of religion. In this particular, the Americans are at the head of all the nations of the world: and at the same time they are, especially in the Eastern and Midland States, so far from being indifferent on subjects of religion, that they may be most justly characterized as a very religious people: but they are devout without being unjust (the great problem in religion); an higher proof of civilization than painted tea-cups, water-proof leather, or broadcloth at two guineas a yard.

America is exempted, by its very newness as a nation, from many of the evils of the old governments of Europe. It has no mischievous remains of feudal institutions, and no violations of political economy sanctioned by time, and older than the age of reason. If a man finds a partridge upon his ground eating his corn, in any part of Kentucky or Indiana, he may kill it, even if his father is not a doctor of divinity. The Americans do not exclude their own citizens from any branch of commerce which they leave open to all the rest of the world.

"One of them said, that he was well acquainted with a British subject, residing at Newark, Upper Canada, who annually smuggl d from 500 to 1000 chests of tea into that province from the United States. He mentioned the name of this man, who he said was growing very rich in consequence; and he stated the manner in which the fraud was managed. Now, as all the tea ought to be brought from England, it is of course very expensive; and therefore the Canadian tea dealers, after buying one or two chests at Montreal or elsewhere, which have the custom-house mark upon them, fill them up ever afterwards with tea brought from the United States. It is calculated that near 10,000 chests are annually consumed in the Canadas, of which not more than 2000 or 3000 come from Europe. Indeed, when I had myself entered Canada, I was told that of every fifteen pounds of tea sold there thirteen were smuggled. The profit upon smuggling this article is from 50 to 100 per cent., and with an extensive and wild frontier like Canada, cannot be prevented. Indeed it every year increases, and is brought to a more perfect system. But I suppose that the English government, which is the perfection of wisdom, will never allow the Canadian merchants to trade direct to China, in order that (from pure charity) the whole profit of the tea trade may be given up to the United States."—*Excursion*, pp. 394, 395.

"You will readily conceive, that it is with no small mortification that I hear these American merchants talk of sending their ships to London and Liverpool, to take in goods or specie, with which to purchase tea for the supply of European ports, almost within sight of our own shores. They often taunt me, asking me what our government can possibly mean by prohibiting us from engaging in a profitable trade, which is open to them and to all the world? or where can be our boasted liberties, while we tamely submit to the infraction of our natural rights, to supply a monopoly as absurd as it is unjust, and to humour the caprice of a company who exclude their fellow-subjects from a branch of commerce which they do not pursue themselves, but leave to the enterprise of foreigners, or commercial rivals? On such occasions I can only reply, that both our governments and people are growing wiser; and that if the charter of the East India Company be renewed, when it next expires, I will allow them to infer, that the people of England have little influence in the administration of their own affairs."—*Hodgson's Letters*, II. 128, 129.

Though America is a confederation of republics, they are in many cases much more amalgamated than the various parts of Great Britain. If a citizen of the United States can make a shoe, he is at liberty to make a shoe any where between Lake Ontario and New Orleans,—he may sole on the Mississippi—heel on the Missouri—measure Mr. Birkbeck on the little Wabash, or take (which our best politicians do not find an easy matter) the length of Munroe's foot on the banks of the Potomac. But wo to the cobbler, who, having made Hessian boots for the aldermen of Newcastle, should venture to invest with these coriaceous integuments the leg of a liege subject at York. A yellow ant in a nest of red ants a butcher's dog in a fox-kennel—a mouse in a bee-hive,—all feel the effects of untimely intrusion;—but far preferable their fate to that of the misguided artisan, who, misled by sixpenny histories of England, and conceiving his country to have been united at the Heptarchy, goes forth from his native town to stitch freely within the sea-girt limits of Albion. Him the mayor, him the alderman, him the recorder, him the quarter sessions would worry. Him the justices before trial would long to get into the treadmill;* and would much lament that, by a recent act, they could not do so, even with the intruding tradesman's consent; but the moment he was tried, they would push him in with redoubled energy, and leave him to tread himself into a conviction of the barbarous institutions of his corporation-divided country.

Too much praise cannot be given to the Americans for their great attention to the subject of education. All the public lands are surveyed according to the direction of Congress. They are divided into townships of six miles square, by lines running with the cardinal points, and consequently crossing each other at right angles. Every township is divided into 36 sections, each a mile square, and containing 640 acres. One section in each township is reserved, and given in perpetuity for the benefit of common schools. In addition to this, the states of Tennessee and Ohio have received grants for the support of colleges and academies. The appropriation generally in the new states for seminaries of the higher orders, amounts to one-fifth of those for common schools. It appears from Seybert's Statistical Annals, that the land in the states and territories on the east side of the Mississippi, in which appropriations have been made, amounts to 237,300 acres; and according to the ratio above mentioned, the aggregate on the east side of the Mississippi is 7,900,000. The same system of appropriation applied to the west, will make, for schools and colleges, 6,600,000; and the total appropriation for literary purposes, in the new states and territories, 14,500,000 acres, which, at two dollars per acre, would be 29,000,000 dollars. These facts are very properly quoted by Mr. Hodgson; and it is impossible to speak too highly of their value and importance. They quite put into the back ground every thing which has been done in the Old World for the improvement of the lower orders, and confer deservedly upon the Americans the character of a wise, a reflecting, and a virtuous people.

It is rather surprising that such a people, spreading rapidly over so vast a portion of the earth, and cultivating all the liberal and useful arts so successfully, should be so extremely sensitive and touchy as the Americans are said to be. We really thought at one time they would have fitted out an armament against the Edinburgh and Quarterly Reviews, and burnt down Mr. Murray's and Mr. Constable's shops, as we did the American Capitol. We, however, remember no other anti-American crime of which we were guilty, than a preference of Shakspeare and Milton over Joel Barlow and Timothy Dwight. That opinion we must still take the liberty of retaining. There is nothing in Dwight comparable to the finest passages of Paradise Lost, nor is Mr. Barlow ever humorous or pathetic, as the great bard of the English stage is humorous and pathetic. We have always been strenuous* advocates for, and admirers of, America—not taking our ideas from the overweening vanity of the weaker part of the Americans themselves, but from what we have observed of their real energy and wisdom. It is very natural that we Scotch, who live in a little, shabby, scraggy corner of a remote island, with a climate which cannot ripen an apple, should be jealous of the aggressive pleasantry of more favoured people; but that Americans, who have done so much for themselves, and received so much from nature, should be flung into such convulsions by English reviews and magazines, is really a sad specimen of Columbian juvenility. We hardly dare to quote the following account of an American route, for fear of having our motives misrepresented,—and strongly suspect that there are but few Americans who could be brought to admit that a Philadelphia or Boston concern of this nature is not quite equal to the most brilliant assemblies of London or Paris.

"A tea party is a serious thing in this country; and some of those at which I have been present, in New York and elsewhere, have been on a very large scale. In the modern houses the two principal apartments are on the first floor, and communicated by large folding doors, which on gala days throw wide their ample portals, converting the two apartments into one. At the largest party which I have

* This puts us in mind of our friend Mr. Headlam, who, we hear, has written an answer to our Observations on the Treadmill, before Trial. It would have been a very easy thing for us to have hung Mr. Headlam up as a spectacle to the United Kingdoms of England, Scotland, and Ireland, the principality of Wales, and the town of Berwick-on-Tweed; but we have no wish to make a worthy and respectable man ridiculous. For these reasons we have not even looked at his pamphlet, and we decline entering into a controversy upon a point, where, among men of sense and humanity (who have not heated themselves in the dispute), there cannot possibly be any difference of opinion. All members of both houses of Parliament were unanimous in their condemnation of the odious and nonsensical practice of working prisoners in the treadmill before trial. It had not one single advocate. Mr. Headlam and the magistrates of the North Riding, in their eagerness to save a relic of their prison system, forgot themselves so far as to petition to be entrusted with the power of putting prisoners to work before trial, *with their own consent*—the legislature was, "We will not trust you,"—the severest practical rebuke ever received by any public body. We will leave it to others to determine whether it was deserved. We have no doubt the great body of magistrates meant well. They *must* have meant well—but they have been sadly misled, and have thrown odium on the subordinate administration of justice, which it is far from deserving on other occasions, in their hands. This strange piece of nonsense is, however, now well ended.—*Requiescat in pace!*

* Ancient women, whether in or out of breeches, will of course imagine that we are the enemies of the institutions of our country, because we are the admirers of the institutions of America: but circumstances differ. American institutions are too new, English institutions are ready made to our hands. If we were to build the house afresh, we might perhaps avail ourselves of the improvements of a new plan; but we have no sort of wish to pull down an excellent house, strong, warm, and comfortable, because, upon second trial, we might be able to alter and amend it,—a principle which would perpetuate demolition and construction. Our plan, where circumstances are tolerable, is to sit down and enjoy ourselves.

seen, there were about thirty young ladies present, and more than as many gentlemen. Every sofa, chair, and footstool, were occupied by the ladies, and little enough room some of them appeared to have after all. The gentlemen were obliged to be content with walking up and down, talking now with one lady, now with another. Tea was brought in by a couple of blacks, carrying large trays, one covered with cups, the other with cake. Slowly making the round, and retiring at intervals for additional supplies, the ladies were gradually gone over; and after much patience the gentlemen began to enjoy the beverage 'which cheers but not inebriates;' still walking about, or leaning against the wall, with the cup and saucer in their hand.

"As soon as the first course was over, the hospitable trays again entered, bearing a chaos of preserves—peaches, pineapples, ginger, oranges, citrons, pears, &c. in tempting display. A few of the young gentlemen now accompanied the revolution of the trays, and sedulously attended to the pleasure of the ladies. The party was so numerous that the period between the commencement and the termination of the round was sufficient to justify a new solicitation: and so the ceremony continued, with very little intermission, during the whole evening. Wine succeeded the preserves, and dried fruit followed the wine; which, in its turn, was supported by sandwiches in name of supper, and a forlorn hope of confectionary and frost work. I pitied the poor blacks, who, like Tantalus, had such a profusion of dainties the whole evening at their finger ends, without the possibility of partaking of them. A little music and dancing gave variety to the scene; which to some of us was a source of considerable satisfaction; for when a number of ladies were on the floor, those who cared not for the dance had the pleasure of getting a seat. About eleven o'clock I did myself the honour of escorting a lady home, and was well pleased to have an excuse for escaping."—*Duncan's Travels*, II. 279, 280.

The coaches must be given up; so must the roads, and so must the inns. They are of course what these accommodations are in all new countries; and much like what English great-grandfathers talk about as existing in this country at the first period of their recollection. The great inconvenience of American inns, however, in the eyes of an Englishman, is one which more sociable travellers must feel less acutely—we mean the impossibility of being alone, of having a room separate from the rest of the company. There is nothing which an Englishman enjoys more than the pleasure of sulkiness,—of not being forced to hear a word from any body which may occasion to him the necessity of replying. It is not so much that Mr. Bull disdains to talk, as that Mr. Bull has nothing to say. His forefathers have been out of spirits for six or seven hundred years, and, seeing nothing but fog and vapour, he is out of spirits too; and when there is no selling or buying, or no business to settle, he prefers being alone and looking at the fire. If any gentleman was in distress, he would willingly lend an helping hand; but he thinks it no part of neighbourhood to talk to a person because he happens to be near him. In short, with many excellent qualities, it must be acknowledged that the English are the most disagreeable of all the nations of Europe,—more surly and morose, with less disposition to please, to exert themselves for the good of society, to make small sacrifices, and to put themselves out of their way. They are content with Magna Charta and trial by jury: and think they are not bound to excel the rest of the world in small behaviour, if they are superior to them in great institutions.

We are terribly afraid that some Americans spit upon the floor, even when that floor is covered by good carpets. Now, all claims to civilization are suspended till this secretion is otherwise disposed of. No English gentleman has spit upon the floor since the Heptarchy.

The curiosity for which the Americans are so much laughed at, is not only venial, but laudable. Where men live in woods and forests, as is the case, of course, in remote American settlements, it is the duty of every man to gratify the inhabitants by telling them his name, place, age, office, virtues, crimes, children, fortune, and remarks: and with fellow-travellers, it seems to be almost a matter of necessity to do so. When men ride together for 300 or 400 miles through the woods and prairies, it is of the greatest importance that they should be able to guess at subjects most agreeable to each other, and to multiply their common topics. Without knowing who your companion is, it is difficult to know both what to say and what to avoid. You may talk of honour and virtue to an attorney, or contend with a Virginia planter that men of a fair colour have no right to buy and sell men of a dusky colour. The following is a lively description of the rights of interrogation, as understood and practised in America.

"As for the *inquisitiveness* of the Americans, I do not think it has been at all exaggerated.—They certainly are, as they profess to be, a very inquiring people; and if we may sometimes be disposed to dispute the claims of their *love of knowing* to the character of a liberal curiosity, we must at least admit that they make a most liberal use of every means in their power to gratify it. I have seldom, however, had any difficulty in repressing their home questions, if I wished it, and without offending them; but I more frequently amused myself by putting them on the rack; civilly, and apparently unconsciously, eluded their inquiries for a time, and then awakening their gratitude by such a discovery of myself as I might choose to make. Sometimes a man would place himself at my side in the wilderness, and ride for a mile or two without the smallest communication between us, except a slight nod of the head. He would then, perhaps, make some grave remark on the weather, and if I assented, in a monosyllable, he would stick to my side for another mile or two, when he would commence his attack. 'I reckon, stranger, you do not belong to these parts?'—'No, sir; I am not of Alabama.'—'I guess you are from the north?'—'No, sir,

I am not from the north.'—'I guess you found the roads mighty muddy, and the creeks swimming. You are come a long way, I guess?'—'No, not so very far; we have travelled a few hundred miles since we turned our faces westward.'—'I guess you have seen Mr. ——, or General ——?' (mentioning the names of some well-known individuals in the middle and southern states, who were to serve as guide-posts to detect our route); but, 'I have not the pleasure of knowing any of them,' or, 'I have the pleasure of knowing all,' equally defeated his purpose, but not his hopes. 'I reckon, stranger, you have had a good crop of cotton this year?'—'I am told, sir, the crops have been unusually abundant in Carolina and Georgia.'—'You grow tobacco, then, I guess?' (to track me to Virginia). 'No; I do not grow tobacco.' Here a modest inquirer would give up in despair, and trust to the chapter of accidents to develope my name and history; but I generally rewarded his modesty, and excited his gratitude, by telling him I would torment him no longer.

"The courage of a thorough-bred Yankee* would rise with his difficulties; and after a decent interval, he would resume: 'I hope no offence, sir; but you know we Yankees lose nothing for want of asking. I guess, stranger, you are from the old country?'—'Well, my friend, you have guessed right at last, and I am sure you deserve something for your perseverance; and now I suppose it will save us both trouble if I proceed to the second part of the story, and tell you where I am going. I am going to New Orleans.' This is really no exaggerated picture: dialogues, not indeed in these very words, but *to this effect*, occurred continually; and some of them more minute and extended than I can venture upon in a letter. I ought, however, to say, that many questions lose much of their familiarity when travelling in the wilderness. 'Where are you from?' and 'whither are you bound?' do not appear impertinent interrogations at sea; and often in the western wilds I found myself making inquiries which I should have thought very free and easy at home."—*Hodgson's Letters*, II. 32—35.

In all new and distant settlements the forms of law must, of course, be very limited. No justice's warrant is current in the Dismal Swamp; constables are exceedingly puzzled in the neighbourhood of the Mississippi; and there is no treadmill, either before or after trial, on the Little Wabash. The consequence of this is, that the settlers take the law into their own hands, and give notice to a justice-proof delinquent to quit the territory,—if this notice is disobeyed, they assemble and whip the culprit, and this failing, on the second visit they cut off his ears. In short, Captain Rock has his descendants in America. Mankind cannot live together without some approximation to justice; and if the actual government will not govern well, or cannot govern well, is too wicked or too weak to do so—then men prefer Rock to anarchy. The following is the best account we have seen of this system of irregular justice.

"After leaving Carlyle, I took the Shawneetown road, that branches off to the S. E., and passed the Walnut Hills, and Moore's Prairie. These two places had a year or two before been infested by a notorious gang of robbers and forgers, who had fixed themselves in these wild parts in order to avoid justice. As the country became more settled, these desperadoes became more and more troublesome. The inhabitants, therefore, took that method of getting rid of them that had been adopted not many years ago in Hopkinson and Henderson counties, Kentucky, and which is absolutely necessary in new and thinly settled districts, where it is almost impossible to punish a criminal according to legal forms.

"On such occasions, therefore, all the quiet and industrious men of a district form themselves into companies, under the name of 'Regulators.' They appoint officers, put themselves under their orders, and bind themselves to assist and stand by each other. The first step they then take is to send notice to any notorious vagabonds, desiring them to quit the state in a certain number of days, under the penalty of receiving a domiciliary visit. Should the person who receives the notice refuse to comply, they suddenly assemble, and, when unexpected, go in the night-time to the rogue's house, take him out, tie him to a tree, and give him a severe whipping, every one of the party striking him a certain number of times.

"This discipline is generally sufficient to drive off the culprit; but should he continue obstinate, and refuse to avail himself of another warning, the Regulators pay him a second visit, inflict a still severer whipping, with the addition probably of cutting off both his ears. No culprit has ever been known to remain after a second visit. For instance, an old man, the father of a family, all of whom he educated as robbers, fixed himself at Moore's Prairie, and committed numerous thefts, &c. &c. He was hard enough to remain after the first visit, when both he and his sons received a whipping. At the second visit the Regulators punished him very severely, and cut off his ears. This drove him off, together with his whole gang, and travellers can now pass in perfect safety where it was once dangerous to travel alone.

"There is also a company of Regulators near Vincennes, who have broken up a notorious gang of coiners and thieves who had fixed themselves near that place. These rascals, before they were driven off, had parties settled at different distances in the woods, and thus held communication and passed horses and stolen goods from one to another, from the Ohio to Lake Erie, and from thence into Canada or the New England States. Thus it was next to impossible to detect the robbers, or to recover the stolen property.

"This practice of *Regulating* seems very strange to an European. I have talked with some of the chief men of the Regulators, who all lamented the necessity of such a system. They very sensibly remarked, that when the country became more thickly settled, there

* "In America, the term Yankee is applied to the natives of New England only, and is generally used with an air of pleasantry.

would no longer be any necessity for such proceedings, and that they should all be delighted at being able to obtain justice in a more formal manner. I forgot to mention, that the rascals punished have sometimes prosecuted the Regulators for an assault. The juries, however, knowing the bad character of the prosecutors, would give but trifling damages, which, divided among so many, amounted to next to nothing for each individual."—*Excursion*, pp. 233—236.

This same traveller mentions his having met at table three or four American ex-kings—presidents who had served their time, and had retired into private life; he observes also upon the effect of a democratical government in preventing mobs. Mobs are created by opposition to the wishes of the people:—but when the wishes of the people are consulted so completely as they are consulted in America—all motives for the agency of mobs are done away.

"It is, indeed, entirely a government of opinion. Whatever the people wish is done. If they want any alteration of laws, tariffs, &c., they inform their representatives, and if there be a majority that wish it, the alteration is made at once. In most European countries there is a portion of the population denominated the *mob*, who, not being acquainted with real liberty, give themselves up to occasional fits of licentiousness. But in the United States there is no *mob*, for every man feels himself free. At the time of Burr's conspiracy, Mr. Jefferson said, that there was little to be apprehended from it, as every man felt himself a part of the general sovereignty. The event proved the truth of this assertion; and Burr, who in any other country would have been hanged, drawn, and quartered, is at present leading an obscure life in the city of New York, despised by every one."—*Excursion*, p. 70.

It is a real blessing for America to be exempted from that vast burthen of taxes, the consequences of a long series of foolish, just and necessary wars, carried on to please kings and queens, or the waiting maids and waiting lords and gentlemen, who have always governed kings and queens in the old world. The Americans owe this good to the newness of their government; and though there are few classical associations, or historical recollections in the United States, this barrenness is well purchased by the absence of all the feudal nonsense, inveterate abuses, and profligate debts of an old country.

"The good effects of a free government are visible throughout the whole country. There are no tithes, no poor-rates, no excise, no heavy internal taxes, no commercial monopolies. An American can make candles if he have tallow, can distil brandy if he have grapes or peaches, and can make beer if he have malt and hops, without asking leave of any one, and much less with any fear of incurring punishment. How would a farmer's wife there be astonished, if told that it was contrary to law for her to make soap out of the potass obtained on the farm, and of the grease she herself had saved! When an American has made these articles, he may build his little vessel, and take them without hinderance to any part of the world; for there is no rich company of merchants that can say to him, 'You shall not trade to India; and you shall not buy a pound of tea of the Chinese; as, by so doing, you would infringe upon our privileges.' In consequence of this freedom, all the seas are covered with their vessels, and the people at home are active and independent. I never saw a beggar in any part of the United States; nor was I ever asked for charity but once—and that was by an Irishman."—*Excursion*, pp. 70, 71.

America is so differently situated from the old governments of Europe, that the United States afford no political precedents that are exactly applicable to our old governments. There is no idle and discontented population. When they have peopled themselves up to the Mississippi, they cross to the Missouri, and will go on until they are stopped by the Western Ocean; and then, when there are a number of persons who have nothing to do, and nothing to gain, no hope for lawful industry and great interest in promoting changes, we may consider their situation as somewhat similar to our own, and their example as touching us more nearly. The changes in the constitution of the particular states seem to be very frequent, very radical, and to us very alarming;—they seem, however, to be thought very little of in that country, and to be very little heard of in Europe. Mr. Duncan, in the following passage, speaks of them with European feelings.

"The other great obstacle to the prosperity of the American nation, universal suffrage,* will not exhibit the full extent of its evil tendency for a long time to come; and it is possible that ere that time some antidote may be discovered, to prevent or alleviate the mischief which we might naturally expect from it. It does, however, seem ominous of evil, that so little ceremony is at present used with the constitutions of the various states. The people of Connecticut, not contented with having prospered abundantly under their old system, have lately assembled a convention, composed of delegates from all parts of the country, in which the former order of things has been condemned entirely, and a completely new constitution manufactured; which, among other things, provides for the same process being again gone through, as soon as the *profanum vulgus* takes it into his head to desire it.† A sorry legacy the British Constitution would be to us, if it were at the mercy of a meeting of delegates, to be summoned whenever a majority of the people took a fancy for a new one; and I am afraid, that if the Americans continue to cherish a fondness for such repairs, the Highlandman's pistol, with its new stock,

* In the greater number of the States, every white person, 21 years of age, who has paid taxes for one year, is a voter; in others, some additional qualifications are required, but they are not such as materially to limit the privilege.

† The people of the State of New York have subsequently taken a similar fancy to *clout the cauldron*. (1822.)

lock, and barrel, will bear a close resemblance to what is ultimately produced."—*Duncan's Travels*, II. 335, 336.

In the Excursion there is a list of the American navy, which, in conjunction with the navy of France, will one day or another, we fear, settle the Catholic question in a way not quite agreeable to the Earl of Liverpool for the time being, nor very creditable to the wisdom of those ancestors of whom we hear, and from whom we suffer so much. The regulations of the American navy seem to be admirable. The states are making great exertions to increase this navy; and since the capture of so many English ships, it has become the favourite science of the people at large. Their flotillas on the lakes completely defeated ours during the last war.

Fanaticism of every description seems to rage and flourish in America, which has no establishment, in about the same degree which it does here under the nose of an established church;—they have their prophets and prophetesses, their preaching encampments, female preachers, and every variety of noise, folly, and nonsense, like ourselves. Among the most singular of these fanatics, are the Harmonites. Rapp, their founder, was a dissenter from the Lutheran church, and therefore, of course, the Lutheran clergy of Stutgard (near to which he lived) began to put Mr. Rapp in white sheets, to prove him guilty of theft, parricide, treason, and all the usual crimes of which men dissenting from established churches are so often guilty,—and delicate hints were given respecting fagots! Stutgard abounds with underwood and clergy; and—away went Mr. Rapp to the United States, and, with a great multitude of followers, settled about twenty-four miles from our countryman, Mr. Birkbeck. His people have here built a large town, and planted a vineyard, where they make very agreeable wine. They carry on also a very extensive system of husbandry, and are the masters of many flocks and herds. They have a distillery, brewery, tannery, make hats, shoes, cotton and woollen cloth, and every thing necessary to the comfort of life. Every one belongs to some particular trade. But in bad weather, when there is danger of losing their crops, Rapp blows a horn, and calls them all together. Over every trade there is a head man, who receives the money and gives a receipt, signed by Rapp, to whom all the money collected is transmitted. When any of these workmen wants a hat or a coat, Rapp signs him an order for the garment, for which he goes to the store, and is fitted. They have one large store where these manufactures are deposited. This store is much resorted to by the neighbourhood, on account of the goodness and cheapness of the articles. They have built an excellent house for their founder, Rapp,—as it might have been predicted they would have done. The Harmonites profess equality, community of goods, and celibacy; for the men and women (let Mr. Malthus hear this) live separately, and are not allowed the slightest intercourse. In order to keep up their numbers, they have once or twice sent over for a supply of Germans, as they admit no Americans, of any intercourse with whom they are very jealous. Harmonites dress and live plainly. It is a part of their creed that they should do so. Rapp, however, and the head men have no such particular creed for themselves, and indulge in wine, beer, grocery, and other irreligious diet. Rapp is both governor and priest,—preaches to them in church, and directs all their proceedings in their working hours. In short, Rapp seems to have made use of the religious propensities of mankind, to persuade one or two thousand fools to dedicate their lives to his service; and if they do not get tired, and fling their prophet into a horse-pond, they will in all probability disperse as soon as he dies.

Unitarians are increasing very fast in the United States, not being kept down by charges from bishops and archdeacons, their natural enemies.

The author of the Excursion remarks upon the total absence of all games in America. No cricket, foot-ball, nor leap-frog—all seems solid and profitable.

"One thing that I could not help remarking with regard to the Americans in general, is the total want of all those games and sports that obtained for our country the appellation of 'Merry England.' Although children usually transmit stories and sports from one generation to another, and although many of our nursery games and tales are supposed to have been imported into England in the vessels of Hengist and Horsa, yet our brethren in the United States seem entirely to have forgotten the childish amusements of our common ancestors. In America I never saw even the schoolboys playing at any game whatsoever. Cricket, foot-ball, quoits, &c., appear to be utterly unknown; and I believe that if an American were to see grown-up men playing at cricket, he would express as much astonishment as the Italians did when some Englishmen played at this finest of all games, in the Cascina at Florence. Indeed, that joyous spirit which, in our country, animates not only childhood, but also maturer age, can rarely or never be seen among the inhabitants of the United States."—*Excursion*, pp. 502, 503.

These are a few of the leading and prominent circumstances respecting America, mentioned in the various works before us: of which works we can recommend the Letters of Mr. Hudson, and the Excursion into Canada, as sensible, agreeable books, written in a very fair spirit.

America seems, on the whole, to be a country possessing vast advantages, and little inconveniences; they have a cheap government, and bad roads; they pay no tithes, and have stage-coaches without springs. They have no poor laws and no monopolies—but their inns are inconvenient, and travellers are teased with questions. They have no collections in the fine arts; but they have no lord-chancellor, and they can go to law without absolute ruin. They cannot make Latin verses, but they expend immense sums in the education of the poor. In all this the balance is prodigiously in their favour: but then comes the great disgrace and danger of America—the existence of slavery, which, if not timously corrected, will one day entail (and ought to entail) a bloody servile war upon the Americans—which will separate America into slave states and states disclaiming slavery, and which remains at present as the foulest blot in the moral character of that people. An high-spirited nation, who cannot endure the slightest act of foreign aggression, and who revolt at the very shadow of domestic tyranny—beat with cart-whips, and bind with chains, and murder for the merest trifles, wretched human beings who are of a more dusky colour than themselves; and have recently admitted into their Union a new state, with the express permission of ingrafting this atrocious wickedness into their constitution! No one can admire the simple wisdom and manly firmness of the Americans more than we do, or more despise the pitiful propensity which exists among government runners to vent their small spite at their character; but on the subject of slavery, the conduct of America is, and has been, most reprehensible. It is impossible to speak of it with too much indignation and contempt; but for it, we should look forward with unqualified pleasure to such a land of freedom, and such a magnificent spectacle of human happiness.

BENTHAM ON FALLACIES.*

[Edinburgh Review, 1825.]

There are a vast number of absurd and mischievous fallacies, which pass readily in the world for sense and virtue, while in truth they tend only to fortify error and encourage crime. Mr. Bentham has enumerated the most conspicuous of these in the book before us.

Whether it is necessary there should be a middleman between the cultivator and possessor, learned economists have doubted; but neither gods, men, nor booksellers can doubt the necessity of a middleman between Mr. Bentham and the public. Mr. Bentham is long; Mr. Bentham is occasionally involved and obscure; Mr. Bentham invents new and alarming expressions; Mr. Bentham loves division and subdivision—and he loves method itself, more than its consequences. Those only, therefore, who know his originality, his knowledge, his vigour, and his boldness, will recur to the works themselves. The great mass of readers will not purchase improvement at so dear a rate; but will choose rather to become acquainted with Mr. Bentham through the medium of reviews—after that eminent philosopher has been washed, trimmed, shaved, and forced into clean linen. One great use of a review, indeed, is to make men wise in ten pages, who have no appetite for an hundred pages; to condense nourishment, to work with pulp and essence, and to guard the stomach from idle burden and unmeaning bulk. For half a page, sometimes for a whole page, Mr. Bentham writes with a power which few can equal; and by selecting and omitting, an admirable style may be formed from the text. Using this liberty, we shall endeavour to give an account of Mr. Bentham's doctrines, for the most part in his own words. Wherever any expression is particularly happy, let it be considered to be Mr. Bentham's:—the dulness we take to ourselves.

Our Wise Ancestors—the Wisdom of our Ancestors—the Wisdom of Ages—Venerable Antiquity—Wisdom of Old Times.—This mischievous and absurd fallacy springs from the grossest perversion of the meaning of words. Experience is certainly the mother of wisdom, and the old have, of course, a greater experience than the young; but the question is, who are the old? and who are the young? Of *individuals* living at the same period, the oldest has, of course, the greatest experience; but among *generations* of men the reverse of this is true. Those who come first (our ancestors), are the young people, and have the least experience. We have added to their experience the experience of many centuries; and, therefore, as far as experience goes, are wiser, and more capable of forming an opinion than they were. The real feeling should be, *not* can we be so presumptuous as to put our opinions in opposition to those of our ancestors? but can such young, ignorant, inexperienced persons as our ancestors necessarily were, be expected to have understood a subject as well as those who have seen so much more, lived so much longer, and enjoyed the experience of so many centuries? All this cant, then, about our ancestors is merely an abuse of words, by transferring phrases true of contemporary men to succeeding ages. Whereas (as we have before observed) of living men the oldest has, *cæteris paribus*, the most experience; of generations, the oldest has, *cæteris paribus*, the least experience. Our ancestors, up to the Conquest, were children in arms; chubby boys in the time of Edward the First; striplings under Elizabeth; men in the reign of Queen Anne; and *we* only are the white-bearded, silver-headed ancients, who have treasured up, and are prepared to profit by, all the experience which human life can supply. We are not disputing with our ancestors the palm of talent, in which they may or may not be our superiors, but the palm of experience, in which it is utterly impossible they can be our superiors. And yet, whenever the chancellor comes forward to protect some abuse, or to oppose some plan which has the increase of human happiness for its

* *The Book of Fallacies: from Unfinished Papers of Jeremy Bentham.* By a Friend. London, J. and H. L. Hunt. 1824.

object, his first appeal is always to the wisdom of our ancestors; and he himself, and many noble lords who vote with him, are, to this hour, persuaded that all alterations and amendments on their devices are an unblushing controversy between youthful temerity and mature experience!—and so, in truth, they are—only that much-loved magistrate mistakes the young for the old, and the old for the young—and is guilty of that very sin against experience which he attributes to the lovers of innovation.

We cannot of course be supposed to maintain that our ancestors wanted wisdom, or that they were necessarily mistaken in their institutions, because their means of information were more limited than ours. But we do confidently maintain that when we find it expedient to change any thing which our ancestors have enacted, we are the experienced persons, and not they. The quantity of talent is always varying in any great nation. To say that we are more or less able than our ancestors, is an assertion that requires to be explained. All the able men of all ages, who have ever lived in England, probably possessed, if taken altogether, more intellect than all the able men now in England can boast of. But if authority must be resorted to rather than reason, the question is, What was the wisdom of that single age which enacted the law, compared with the wisdom of the age which proposes to alter it? What are the eminent men of one and the other period? If you say that our ancestors were wiser than us, mention your date and year. If the splendour of names is equal, are the circumstances the same? If the circumstances are the same, we have a superiority of experience, of which the difference between the two periods is the measure. It is necessary to insist upon this; for upon sacks of wool, and on benches forensic, sit grave men, and agricolous persons in the Commons, crying out "Ancestors, Ancestors! *hodie non!* Saxons, Danes, save us! Fiddlefrig, help us! Howel, Ethelwolf, protect us."—Any cover for nonsense—any veil for trash—any pretext for repelling the innovations of conscience and of duty!

"So long as they keep to vague generalities—so long as the two objects of comparison are each of them taken in the lump—wise ancestors in one lump, ignorant and foolish mob of modern times in the other—the weakness of the fallacy may escape detection. But let them assign for the period of superior wisdom any determinate period whatsoever, not only will the groundlessness of the notion be apparent (class being compared with class in that period and the present one), but, unless the antecedent period be, comparatively speaking, a very modern one, so wide will be the disparity, and to such an amount in favour of modern times, that, in comparison of the lowest class of the people in modern times (always supposing them proficients in the art of reading, and their proficiency employed in the reading of newspapers), the very highest and best informed class of these wise ancestors will turn out to be grossly ignorant.

"Take, for example, any year in the reign of Henry the Eighth, from 1509 to 1546. At that time the House of Lords would probably have been in possession of by far the larger proportion of what little instruction the age afforded: in the House of Lords, among the laity it might even then be a question whether, without exception, their lordships were all of them able so much as to read. But even supposing them all in the fullest possession of that useful and political science being the science in question, what instruction on the subject could they meet with at that time of day?

"On no one branch of legislation was any book extant from which, with regard to the circumstances of the then present times, any useful instruction could be derived: distributive law, penal law, international law, political economy, so far from existing as sciences, had scarcely obtained a name: in all those departments, under the head of *quid faciendum*, a mere blank: the whole literature of the age consisted of a meager chronicle or two, containing short memorandums of the usual occurrences of war and peace, battles, sieges, executions, revels, deaths, births, processions, ceremonies, and other external events; but with scarce a speech or an incident that could enter into the composition of any such work as a history of the human mind—with scarce an attempt at investigation into causes, characters, or the state of the people at large. Even when at last, little by little, a scrap or two of political instruction came to be obtainable, the proportion of error and mischievous doctrine mixed up with it was so great, that whether a blank unfilled might not have been less prejudicial than a blank thus filled, may reasonably be matter of doubt.

"If we come down to the reign of James the First, we shall find that Solomon of his time eminently eloquent as well as learned, not only among crowned but among uncrowned heads, marking out for prohibition and punishment the practices of devils and witches, and without any the slightest objection on the part of the great characters of that day in their high situations, consigning men to death and torment for the misfortune of not being so well acquainted as he was with the composition of the Godhead.

"Under the name of exorcism, the Catholic liturgy contains a form of procedure for driving out devils;—even with the help of this instrument, the operation cannot be performed with the desired success, but by an operator qualified by holy orders for the working of this as well as so many other wonders. In our days and in our country the same object is attained, and beyond comparison more effectually, by so cheap an instrument as a common newspaper: before this talisman, not only devils but ghosts, vampires, witches, and all their kindred tribes, are driven out of the land, never to return again! The touch of the holy water is not so intolerable to them as the bare smell of printers' ink."—(pp. 74—77.)

Fallacy of irrevocable Laws.—A law, says Mr. Bentham, (no matter to what effect,) is proposed to a legislative assembly, who are called upon to reject it, upon the single ground, that by those who in some former period exercised the same power, a regulation was made, having for its object to preclude for ever, or to the end of an unexpired period, all succeed ing legislators from enacting a law to any such effect as that now proposed.

Now it appears quite evident that, at every period of time, every legislature must be endowed with all those powers which the exigency of the times may require: and any attempt to infringe on this power is inadmissible and absurd. The sovereign power, at any one period, can only form a blind guess at the measures which may be necessary for any future period: but by this principle of immutable laws, the government is transferred from those who are necessarily the best judges of what they want, to others who can know little or nothing about the matter. The thirteenth century decides for the fourteenth. The fourteenth makes laws for the fifteenth. The fifteenth hermetically seals up the sixteenth, which tyrannizes over the seventeenth, which again tells the eighteenth how it is to act, under circumstances which cannot be foreseen, and how it is to conduct itself in exigencies which no human wit can anticipate.

"Men who have a century more of experience to ground their judgments on, surrender their intellect to men who had a century less experience, and who, unless that deficiency constitutes a claim, have no claim to preference. If the prior gentlemen were, in respect of intellectual qualification, ever so much superior to the subsequent generation—if it understood so much better than the subsequent generation itself the interest of that subsequent generation—could it have been in an equal degree anxious to promote that interest, and consequently equally attentive to those facts with which, though in order to form a judgment it ought to have been, it is impossible that it should have been acquainted? In a word, will its love for that subsequent generation be quite so great as that same generation's love for itself?

"Not even here, after a moment's deliberate reflection, will the assertion be in the affirmative. And yet it is their prodigious anxiety for the welfare of their posterity that produces the propensity of these sages to tie up the hands of this same posterity for evermore—to act as guardians to its perpetual and incurable weakness, and take its conduct for ever out of its own hands.

"If it be right that the conduct of the 19th century should be determined not by its own judgment, but by that of the 18th, it will be equally right that the conduct of the 20th century should be determined, not by its own judgment, but by that of the 19th. And if the same principle were still pursued, what at length would be the consequence?—that in process of time the practice of legislation would be at an end. The conduct and fate of all men would be determined by those who neither knew nor cared any thing about the matter; and the aggregate body of the living would remain for ever in subjection to an inexorable tyranny, exercised as it were by the aggregate body of the dead."—(pp. 84—86.)

The despotism, as Mr. Bentham well observes, of Nero or Caligula, would be more tolerable than an *irrevocable law*. The despot, through fear or favour, or in a lucid interval, might relent; but how are the Parliament, who made the Scotch Union, for example, to be awakened from that dust in which they repose—the jobber and the patriot, the speaker and the doorkeeper, the silent voters and the men of rich allusions—Cannings and cultivators, Barings and Beggars—making irrevocable laws for men who toss their remains about with spades, and use the relics of these legislators to give breadth to brocoli, and to aid the vernal eruption of asparagus?

If the law is good, it will support itself; if bad, it should not be supported by the *irrevocable theory*, which is never resorted to but as the veil of abuses. All living men must possess the supreme power over their own happiness at every particular period. To suppose that there is any thing which a whole nation cannot do, which they deem to be essential to their happiness, and that they cannot do it, because *another* generation, long ago dead and gone, said it must not be done, is mere nonsense. While you are captain of the vessel, do what you please; but the moment you quit the ship, I become as omnipotent as you. You may leave me as much *advice* as you please, but you cannot leave me *commands;* though, in fact, this is the only meaning which can be applied to what are called irrevocable laws. It appeared to the legislature for the time being to be of immense importance to make such and such a law. Great good was gained, or great evil avoided by enacting it. Pause before you alter an institution which has been deemed to be of so much importance. This is prudence and common sense; the rest is the exaggeration of fools, or the artifice of knaves, who eat up fools. What endless nonsense has been talked of our navigation laws! What wealth has been sacrificed to either before they were repealed! How impossible it appeared to Noodledom to repeal them! They were considered of the irrevocable class—a kind of law over which the dead only were omnipotent, and the living had no power. Frost, it is true, cannot be put off by act of Parliament, nor can spring be accelerated by any majority of both houses. It is, however, quite a mistake to suppose that any alteration of any of the articles of union is as much out of the jurisdiction of Parliament as these meteorological changes. In every year, and every day of that year, living men have a right to make their own laws, and manage their own affairs; to break through the tyranny of the ante-spirants—the people who breathed before them,—and to do what they please for themselves. Such supreme power cannot, indeed, be well exercised by the people at large; it must be exercised therefore by the delegates, or Parliament whom the people choose; and such Parliament, disregarding the superstitious reverence for *irrevocable laws,* can have no other criterion of wrong and right than that of public utility.

When a law is considered as immutable, and the immutable law happens at the same time to be too foolish and mischievous to be endured, instead of being repealed, it is clandestinely evaded, or openly violated; and thus the authority of all law is weakened.

Where a nation has been ancestorially bound by foolish and improvident treaties, ample notice must be given of their termination. Where the state has made ill-advised grants, or rash bargains with individuals, it is necessary to grant proper compensation. The most difficult case, certainly, is that of the union of nations, where a smaller number of the weaker nation is admitted into the larger senate of the greater nation, and will be overpowered if the question comes to a vote; but the lesser nation must run this risk: it is not probable that any violation of articles will take place, till they are absolutely called for by extreme necessity. But let the danger be what it may, no danger is so great, no supposition so foolish, as to consider any human law as irrevocable. The shifting attitude of human affairs would often render such a condition an intolerable evil to all parties. The absurd jealousy of our countrymen at the union secured heritable jurisdiction to the owners; nine-and-thirty years afterwards they were abolished, in the very teeth of the act of union, and to the evident promotion of the public good.

Continuity of a Law by Oath.—The sovereign of England at his coronation takes an oath to maintain the laws of God, the true profession of the gospel, and the Protestant religion as established by law, and to preserve to the bishops and clergy of this realm the rights and privileges which by law appertain to them, and to preserve inviolate the doctrine, discipline, worship, and government of the church. It has been suggested that by this oath the king stands precluded from granting those indulgences to the Irish Catholics, which are included in the bill for their emancipation. The true meaning of these provisions is of course to be decided, if doubtful, by the same legislative authority which enacted them. But a different notion, it seems, is now afloat. The king for the time being (we are putting an imaginary case) thinks, as an individual, that he is not maintaining the doctrine, discipline, and rights of the Church of England, if he grants any extension of civil rights to those who are not members of that church; that he is violating his oath by so doing. This oath, then, according to this reasoning, is the great palladium of the church. As long as it remains inviolate the church is safe. How, then, can any monarch who has taken it ever consent to repeal it? How can he, consistently with his oath for the preservation of the privileges of the church, contribute his part to throw down so strong a bulwark as he deems this oath to be? The oath, then, cannot be altered. It must remain under all circumstances of society the same. The king, who has taken it, is bound to continue it, and to refuse his sanction to any bill for its future alteration; because it prevents him, and, he must needs think, will prevent others from granting dangerous immunities to the enemies of the church.

Here, then, is an irrevocable law—a piece of absurd tyranny exercised by the rulers of Queen Anne's time upon the government of 1825—a certain art of potting and preserving a kingdom, in one shape, attitude and flavour—and in this way it is that an institution appears like old Ladies' Sweetmeats and made Wines—Apricot Jam 1822—Currant Wine 1819—Court of Chancery 1427—Penal Laws against Catholics 1676. The difference is, that the ancient woman is a better judge of mouldy commodities than the illiberal part of his majesty's ministers. The potting lady goes sniffing about and admitting light and air to prevent the progress of decay; while to him of the woolsack, all seems doubly dear in proportion as it is antiquated, worthless, and unusable. It ought not to be in the power of the sovereign to tie up his own hands, much less the hands of his successors. If the sovereign is to oppose his own opinion to that of the two other branches of the legislature, and himself to decide what he considers to be for the benefit of the Protestant church, and what not, a king who has spent his whole life in the frivolous occupation of a court, may, by perversion of understanding, conceive measures most salutary to the church to be most pernicious; and persevering obstinately in his own error, may frustrate the wisdom of his Parliament, and perpetuate the most inconceivable folly! If Henry VIII. had argued in this manner, we should have had no reformation. If George III. had always argued in this manner, the Catholic code would never have been relaxed. And thus, a king, however incapable of forming an opinion upon serious subjects, has nothing to do but to pronounce the word *conscience*, and the whole power of the country is at his feet.

Can there be greater absurdity than to say that a man is acting contrary to his conscience who surrenders his opinion, upon any subject, to those who must understand the subject better than himself? I think my ward has a claim to the estate; but the best lawyers tell me he has none. I think my son capable of undergoing the fatigues of a military life; but the best physicians say he is much too weak. My Parliament say this measure will do the church no harm; but I think it very pernicious to the church. Am I acting contrary to my conscience because I apply much higher intellectual powers than my own to the investigation and protection of these high interests?

"According to the form in which it is conceived, any such engagement is in effect either a check or a license:—a license under the appearance of a check, and for that very reason but the more efficiently operative.

"Chains to the man in power? Yes:—but only such as he figures with on the stage: to the spectators as imposing, to himself as light as possible. Modelled by the wearer to suit his own purposes, they serve to rattle, but not to restrain.

"Suppose a king of Great Britain and Ireland to have expressed his fixed determination, in the event of any proposed law being tendered to him for his assent, to refuse such assent, and this not on the persuasion that the law would not be 'for the utility of the subjects,' but that by his coronation oath he stands precluded from so doing:—the course proper to be taken by Parliament, the course pointed out by principle and precedent, would be, a vote of abdication:—a vote declaring the king to have abdicated his royal authority, and that, as in case of death or incurable mental derangement, now is the time for the person next in succession to take his place.

"In the celebrated case in which a vote to this effect was actually passed, the declaration of abdication was in lawyers' language a fiction—in plain truth a falsehood—and that falsehood a mockery; not a particle of his power was it the wish of James to abdicate, to part with; but to increase it to a maximum was the manifest object of all his efforts. But in the case here supposed, with respect to a part, and that a principal part of the royal authority, the will and purpose to abdicate are actually declared: and this, being such a part, without which the remainder cannot, 'to the utility of the subjects,' be exercised, the remainder must of necessity be, on their part, and for their sake, added."—(pp. 110, 111.)

Self-trumpeter's fallacy.—Mr. Bentham explains the self-trumpeter's fallacy as follows.

"There are certain men in office who, in discharge of their functions, arrogate to themselves a degree of probity, which is to exclude all imputations and all inquiry. Their assertions are to be deemed equivalent to proof; their virtues are guarantees for the faithful discharge of their duties; and the most implicit confidence is to be reposed in them on all occasions. If you expose any abuse, propose any reform, call for securities, inquiry, or measures to promote publicity, they set up a cry of surprise, amounting almost to indignation, as if their integrity were questioned, or their honour wounded. With all this, they dexterously mix up intimations, that the most exalted patriotism, honour, and perhaps religion, are the only sources of all their actions."—(p. 120.)

Of course every man will try what he can effect by these means; but (as Mr. Bentham observes) if there be any one maxim in politics more certain than another, it is that no possible degree of virtue in the governor can render it expedient for the governed to dispense with good laws and good institutions. Madame de Stael (to her disgrace) said to the Emperor of Russia, "Sire, your character is a constitution for your country, and your conscience its guarantee." His reply was, "Quand cela serait, je ne serais jamais qu'un accident heureux;" and this we think one of the truest and most brilliant replies ever made by monarch.

Laudatory Personalities.—"The object of laudatory personalities is to effect the rejection of a measure on account of the alleged good character of those who oppose it; and the argument advanced is, 'The measure is rendered unnecessary by the virtue of those who are in power—their opposition is sufficient authority for the rejection of the measure. The measure proposed implies a distrust of the members of his majesty's government; but so great is their integrity, so complete their disinterestedness, so uniformly do they prefer the public advantage to their own, that such a measure is altogether unnecessary. Their disapproval is sufficient to warrant an opposition; precautions can only be requisite where danger is apprehended; here, the high character of the individuals in question is a sufficient guarantee against any ground of alarm.'"—(pp. 123, 124.)

The panegyric goes on increasing with the dignity of the lauded person. All are honourable and delightful men. The person who opens the door of the office is a person of approved fidelity; the junior clerk is a model of assiduity; all the clerks are models—seven years' models, eight years' models, nine years' models and upwards. The first clerk is a paragon—and ministers the very perfection of probity and intelligence; and as for the highest magistrate of the state, no adulation is equal to describe the extent of his various merits! It is too condescending, perhaps, to refute such folly as this. But we would just observe that if the propriety of the measure in question be established by direct arguments, these must be at least as conclusive against the character of those who oppose it as their character can be against the measure.

The effect of such an argument is, to give men of good or reputed good character the power of putting a negative on any question—not agreeable to their inclinations.

"In every public trust, the legislator should, for the purpose of prevention, suppose the trustee disposed to break the trust in every imaginable way in which it would be possible for him to reap, from the breach of it, any personal advantage. This is the principle on which public institutions ought to be formed; and when it is applied to all men indiscriminately, it is injurious to none. The practical inference is, to oppose to such possible (and what will always be probable) breaches of trust every bar that can be opposed, consistently with the power requisite for the efficient and due discharge of the trust. Indeed, these arguments, drawn from the supposed virtues of men in power, are opposed to the first principles on which all laws proceed.

"Such allegations of individual virtue are never supported by specific proof, are scarce ever susceptible of specific disproof; and specific disproof, if offered, could not be admitted in either house of Parliament. If attempted elsewhere, the punishment would fall, not on the unworthy trustee, but on him by whom the unworthiness had been proved."—(pp. 125, 126.)

Fallacies of pretended Danger.—Imputation of bad design—of bad character—of bad motives—of inconsistency—of suspicious connections.

The object of this class of fallacies is to draw aside attention from the measure to the man, and this in such a manner, that, for some real or supposed defect in the author of the measure, a corresponding defect shall be imputed to the measure itself. Thus "the author of the measure entertains a bad design: therefore the measure is bad. His character is bad.

therefore the measure is bad; his motive is bad, I will vote against the measure. On former occasions, this same person who proposed the measure was its enemy, therefore the measure is bad. He is on a footing of intimacy with this or that dangerous man, or has been seen in his company, or is suspected of entertaining some of his opinions, therefore the measure is bad. He bears a name that at a former period was borne by a set of men now no more, by whom bad principles were entertained—therefore the measure is bad!"

Now, if the measure be really inexpedient, why not at once show it to be so? If the measure is good, is it bad because a bad man is its author? If bad, is it good because a good man has produced it? What are these arguments, but to say to the assembly who are to be the judges of any measure, that their imbecility is too great to allow them to judge of the measure by its own merits, and that they must have recourse to distant and feebler probabilities for that purpose?

"In proportion to the degree of efficiency with which a man suffers these instruments of deception to operate upon his mind, he enables bad men to exercise over him a sort of power, the thought of which ought to cover him with shame. Allow this argument the effect of a conclusive one, you put it into the power of any man to draw you at pleasure from the support of every measure, which in your own eyes is good, to force you to give your support to any and every measure which in your own eyes is bad. Is it good?—the bad man embraces it, and, by the supposition, you reject it. Is it bad?—he vituperates it, and that suffices for driving you into its embrace. You split upon the rocks, because he has avoided them; you miss the harbour, because he has steered into it? Give yourself up to any such blind antipathy, you are no less in the power of your adversaries, than if, by a correspondently irrational sympathy and obsequiousness, you put yourself into the power of your friends."—(pp. 132, 133.)

"Besides, nothing but laborious application, and a clear and comprehensive intellect, can enable a man, on any given subject, to employ successfully relevant arguments drawn from the subject itself. To employ personalities, neither labour nor intellect is required. In this sort of contest, the most idle and the most ignorant are quite on a par with, if not superior to, the most industrious and the most highly gifted individuals. Nothing can be more convenient for those who would speak without the trouble of thinking. The same ideas are brought forward over and over again, and all that is required is to vary the turn of expression. Close and relevant arguments have very little hold on the passions, and serve rather to quell than to inflame them; while in personalities there is always something stimulant, whether on the part of him who praises or him who blames. Praise forms a kind of connection between the party praising and the party praised, and vituperation gives an air of courage and independence to the party who blames.

"Ignorance and indolence, friendship and enmity, concurring and conflicting interest, servility and independence, all conspire to give personalities the ascendency they so unhappily maintain. The more we lie under the influence of our own passions, the more we rely on others being affected in a similar degree. A man who can repel these injuries with dignity, may often convert them into triumph: 'Strike me, but hear,' says he, and the fury of his antagonist redounds to his own discomfiture."—(pp. 141, 142.)

No Innovation!—To say that all new things are bad, is to say that all old things were bad in their commencement: for of all the old things ever seen or heard of, there is not one that was not once new. Whatever is now establishment was once innovation. The first inventor of pews and parish clerks was no doubt considered as a Jacobin in his day. Judges, juries, criers of the court, are all the inventions of ardent spirits, who filled the world with alarm, and were considered as the great precursors of ruin and dissolution. No inoculation, no turnpikes, no reading, no writing, no popery! The fool sayeth in his heart, and crieth with his mouth, "I will have nothing new!"

Fallacy of Distrust.—"What's at the Bottom?"—This fallacy begins with a virtual admission of the propriety of the measure considered in itself, and thus demonstrates its own futility, and cuts up from under itself the ground which it endeavours to make. A measure is to be rejected for something that, by bare possibility, may be found amiss in some other measure! This is vicarious reprobation; upon this principle Herod instituted his massacre. It is the argument of a driveller to other drivellers, who says, We are not able to decide upon the evil when it arises—our only safe way is to act upon the general apprehension of evil.

Official Malefactor's Screen.—"Attack us—you attack Government."

If this notion is acceded to, every one who derives at present any advantage from misrule has it in fee-simple; and all abuses, present and future, are without remedy. So long as there is any thing amiss in conducting the business of government, so long as it can be made better, there can be no other mode of bringing it nearer to perfection, than the indication of such imperfections as at the time being exist.

"But so far is it from being true that a man's aversion or contempt for the hands by which the powers of government, or even for the system under which they are exercised, is a proof of his aversion or contempt towards government itself, that, even in proportion to the strength of that aversion or contempt, it is a proof of the opposite affection. What, in consequence of such contempt or aversion, he wishes for, is, not that there be no hands at all to exercise these powers, but that the hands may be better regulated;—not that those powers should not be exercised at all, but that they should be better exercised;—not that, in the exercise of them, no rules at all should be pursued, but that the rules by which they are exercised should be a better set of rules.

"All government is a trust; every branch of government is a trust; and immemorially acknowledged so to be: it is only by the magnitude of the scale that public differ from private trusts. I complain of the conduct of a person in the character of guardian, as domestic guardian, having the care of a minor or insane person. In so doing, do I say that guardianship is a bad institution? Does it enter into the head of any one to suspect me of so doing? I complain of an individual in the character of a commercial agent, or assignee of the effects of an insolvent. In so doing, do I say that commercial agency is a bad thing? that the practice of vesting in the hands of trustees or assignees the effects of an insolvent, for the purpose of their being divided among his creditors, is a bad practice? Does any such conceit ever enter into the head of man, as that of suspecting me of so doing?"—(pp. 162, 163.)

There are no complaints against government in Turkey—no motions in Parliament, no Morning Chronicles, and no Edinburgh Reviews: yet, of all countries in the world, it is that in which revolts and revolutions are the most frequent.

It is so far from true, that no good government can exist consistently with such disclosure, that no good government can exist without it. It is quite obvious, to all who are capable of reflection, that by no other means than by lowering the governors in the estimation of the people, can there be hope or chance of beneficial change. To infer from this wise endeavour to lessen the existing rulers in the estimation of the people, a wish of dissolving the government, is either artifice or error. The physician who intentionally weakens the patient by bleeding him has no intention he should perish.

The greater the quantity of respect a man receives, independently of good conduct, the less good is his behaviour likely to be. It is the interest, therefore, of the public, in the case of each, to see that the respect paid to him should, as completely as possible, depend upon the goodness of his behaviour in the execution of his trust. But it is, on the contrary, the interest of the trustee, that the respect, the money, or any other advantage he receives in virtue of his office, should be as great, as secure, and as independent of conduct as possible. Soldiers expect to be shot at; public men must expect to be attacked, and sometimes unjustly. It keeps up the habit of considering their conduct as exposed to scrutiny; on the part of the people at large, it keeps alive the expectation of witnessing such attacks, and the habit of looking out for them. The friends and supporters of government have always greater facility in keeping and raising it up, than its adversaries have for lowering it.

Accusation-scarer's Device.—"*Infamy must attach somewhere.*"

This fallacy consists in representing the character of a calumniator as necessarily and justly attaching upon him who, having made a charge of misconduct against any persons possessed of political power or influence, fails of producing evidence sufficient for their conviction.

"If taken as a general proposition, applying to all public accusations, nothing can be more mischievous as well as fallacious. Supposing the charge unfounded, the delivery of it may have been accompanied with *mala fides* (consciousness of its injustice), with *temerity* only, or it may have been perfectly blameless. It is in the first case alone that infamy can with propriety attach upon him who brings it forward. A charge really groundless may have been honestly *believed* to be well founded, *i. e.* believed with a sort of provisional credence, sufficient for the purpose of engaging a man to do his part towards the bringing about an investigation, but without sufficient reasons. But a charge may be perfectly groundless without attaching the smallest particle of blame upon him who brings it forward. Suppose him to have heard from one or more, presenting themselves to him in the character of percipient witnesses, a story which, either *in toto*, or perhaps only in *circumstances*, though in circumstances of the most material importance, should prove false and mendacious—how is the person who hears this, and acts accordingly, to blame? What sagacity can enable a man previously to legal investigation, a man who has no power that can enable him to insure correctness or completeness on the part of this extrajudicial testimony, to guard against deception in such a case?"—(pp. 185, 186.)

Fallacy of false Consolation.—"*What is the matter with you?—What would you have? Look at the people there, and there; think how much better off you are than they are. Your prosperity and liberty are objects of their envy; your institutions models of their imitation.*"

It is not the desire to look to the bright side that is blamed: but when a particular suffering, produced by an assigned cause, has been pointed out, the object of many apologists is to turn the eyes of inquirers and judges into any other quarter in preference. If a man's tenants were to come with a general encomium on the prosperity of the country, instead of a specified sum, would it be accepted? In a court of justice, in an action for damages, did ever any such device occur as that of pleading assets in the hands of a third person? There is, in fact, no country so poor and so wretched in every element of prosperity, in which matter for this argument might not be found. Were the prosperity of the country tenfold as great as at present, the absurdity of the argument would not in the least degree be lessened. Why should the smallest evil be endured, which can be cured; because others suffer patiently under greater evils? Should the smallest improvement attainable be neglected, because others remain contented in a state of still greater inferiority?

"Seriously and pointedly in the character of a bar to any measure of relief, no, nor to the most trivial improvement, can it ever be employed. Suppose a bill brought in for con verting an impassable road any where into a passable one, would any man stand up to oppose it, who could find nothing better to urge against it than the multitude and goodness of the roads we have already? No: when in the character of a serious bar to the measure in hand, be that measure what it may, an argument so palpably inapplicable is employed, it can only be for the purpose of creating a diversion;—of turning aside the minds of men from the subject really in hand, to a picture, which, by its beauty, it is hoped, may engross the attention of the assembly, and make them forget for the moment for what purpose they came there."—(pp. 196, 197.)

The Quietist, or no Complaint.—"A new law or measure being proposed in the character of a remedy for some incontestable abuse or evil, an objection is frequently started to the following effect:—'The measure is unnecessary. Nobody complains of disorder in that shape, in which it is the aim of your measure to propose a remedy to it. But even when *no* cause of complaint has been found to exist, especially under governments which admit of complaints, men have in general not been slow to complain; much less where any just cause of complaint has existed.' The argument amounts to this:—Nobody complains, therefore nobody suffers. It amounts to a *veto* on all measures of precaution or prevention, and goes to establish a maxim in legislation directly opposed to the most ordinary prudence of common life;—it enjoins us to build no parapets to a bridge till the number of accidents has raised an universal clamour."—(pp. 190, 191.)

Procrastinator's Argument.—"*Wait a little, this is not the time.*"

This is the common argument of men, who, being in reality hostile to a measure, are ashamed or afraid of appearing to be so. *To-day* is the plea—*eternal exclusion* commonly the object. It is the same sort of quirk as a plea of abatement in law—which is never employed but on the side of a dishonest defendant, whose hope it is to obtain an ultimate triumph, by overwhelming his adversary with despair, impoverishment, and lassitude. Which is the properest day to do good? which is the properest day to remove a nuisance? we answer, the very first day a man can be found to propose the removal of it; and whoever opposes the removal of it on that day will (if he dare) oppose it on every other. There is in the minds of many feeble friends to virtue and improvement, an imaginary period for the removal of evils, which it would certainly be worth while to wait for, if there was the smallest chance of its ever arriving—a period of unexampled peace and prosperity, when a patriotic king and an enlightened mob united their ardent efforts for the amelioration of human affairs; when the oppressor is as delighted to give up the oppression, as the oppressed is to be liberated from it; when the difficulty and unpopularity would be to continue the evil, not to abolish it! These are the periods when fair-weather philosophers are willing to venture out, and hazard a little for the general good. But the history of human nature is so contrary to all this, that almost all improvements are made after the bitterest resistance, and in the midst of tumults and civil violence—the worst period at which they can be made, compared to which any period is eligible, and should be seized hold of by the friends of salutary reform.

Snail's Pace argument.—"*One thing at a time! Not too fast! Slow and sure!*—Importance of the business—extreme difficulty of the business—danger of innovation—need of caution and circumspection—impossibility of foreseeing all consequences—danger of precipitation—every thing should be gradual—one thing at a time—this is not the time—great occupation at present—wait for more leisure—people well satisfied—no petitions presented—no complaints heard—no such mischief has yet taken place—stay till it has taken place!—Such is the prattle which the magpie in office, who, understanding nothing, yet understands that he must have something to say on every subject, shouts out among his auditors as a succedaneum to thought."—(pp. 203, 204.)

Vague Generalities.—Vague generalities comprehend a numerous class of fallacies resorted to by those who, in preference to the determinate expressions which they might use, adopt others more vague and indeterminate.

Take, for instance, the terms, government, laws, morals, religion. Every body will admit that there are in the world bad governments, bad laws, bad morals, and bad religions. The bare circumstance, therefore, of being engaged in exposing the defects of government, law, morals, and religion, does not of itself afford the slightest presumption that a writer is engaged in any thing blamable. If his attack is only directed against that which is bad in each, his efforts may be productive of good to any extent. This essential distinction, however, the defender of abuses uniformly takes care to keep out of sight; and boldly imputes to his antagonists an intention to subvert all *government, law, morals, and religion.* Propose any thing with a view to the improvement of the existing practice, in relation to law, government, and religion, he will treat you with an oration upon the necessity and utility of law, government, and religion. Among the several cloudy appellatives which have been commonly employed as cloaks for misgovernment, there is none more conspicuous in this atmosphere of illusion than the word order. As often as any measure is brought forward which has for its object to lessen the sacrifice made by the many to the few, *social order* is the phrase commonly opposed to its progress.

"By a defalcation made from any part of the mass of factitious delay, vexation, and expense, out of which, and in proportion to which, lawyers' profit is made to flow—by any defalcation made from the mass of needless and worse than useless emolument to office, with or without service or pretence of service—by any addition endeavoured to be made to the quantity, or improvement in the quality of service rendered, or time bestowed in service rendered in return for such emolument—by every endeavour that has for its object the persuading the people to place their fate at the disposal of any other agents than those in whose hands breach of trust is certain, due fulfilment of it morally and physically impossible—*social order* is said to be endangered, and threatened to be destroyed."—(p. 234.)

In the same way *establishment* is a word in use to protect the bad parts of establishments, by charging those who wish to remove or alter them with a wish to subvert all good establishments.

Mischievous fallacies also circulate from the convertible use of what Mr. B. is pleased to call dyslogistic and eulogistic terms. Thus a vast concern is expressed for the *liberty of the press*, and the utmost abhorrence for its *licentiousness:* but then, by the licentiousness of the press is meant every disclosure by which any abuse is brought to light and exposed to shame—by the *liberty of the press* is meant only publications from which no such inconvenience is to be apprehended; and the fallacy consists in employing the sham approbation of liberty as a mask for the real opposition to all free discussion. To write a pamphlet so ill that nobody will read it; to animadvert in terms so weak and insipid upon great evils, that no disgust is excited at the vice, and no apprehension in the evil-doer, is a fair use of the liberty of the press, and is not only pardoned by the friends of government, but draws from them the most fervent eulogium. The licentiousness of the press consists in doing the thing boldly and well, in striking terror into the guilty, and in rousing the attention of the public to the defence of their highest interests. This is the licentiousness of the press held in the greatest horror by timid and corrupt men, and punished by semianimous, semicadaverous judges, with a captivity of many years. In the same manner the dyslogistic and eulogistic fallacies are used in the case of reform.

"Between all abuses whatsoever, there exists that connection;—between all persons who see each of them any one abuse in which an advantage results to himself, there exists, in point of interest, that close and sufficiently understood connection, of which intimation has been given already. To no one abuse can correction be administered without endangering the existence of every other.

"If, then, with this inward determination not to suffer, so far as depends upon himself, the adoption of any reform which he is able to prevent, it should seem to him necessary or advisable to put on, for a cover, the profession or appearance of a desire to contribute to such reform—in pursuance of the device or fallacy here in question, he will represent that which goes by the name of reform as distinguishable into two species; one of them a fit subject for approbation, the other for disapprobation. That which he thus professes to have marked for approbation, he will accordingly, for the expression of such approbation, characterize by some adjunct of the *eulogistic* cast, such as moderate, for example, or temperate, or practical, or practicable.

"To the other of these nominally distinct species, he will, at the same time, attach some adjunct of the *dyslogistic* cast, such as violent, intemperate, extravagant, outrageous, theoretical, speculative, and so forth.

"Thus, then, in profession and to appearance, there are in his conception of the matter two distinct and opposite species of reform, to one of which his approbation, to the other his disapprobation is attached. But the species to which his approbation is attached is an *empty* species—a species in which no individual is, or is intended to be, contained.

"The species to which his disapprobation is attached is, on the contrary, a crowded species, a receptacle in which the whole contents of the *genus*—of the genus *Reform* are intended to be included."—(pp. 277, 278.)

Anti-rational Fallacies.—When reason is in opposition to a man's interests, his study will naturally be to render the faculty itself, and whatever issues from it, an object of hatred and contempt. The sarcasm and other figures of speech employed on the occasion are directed not merely against reason but against thought, as if there were something in the faculty of thought that rendered the exercise of it incompatible with useful and successful practice. Sometimes a plan, which would not suit the official person's interest, is without more ado pronounced a *speculative* one; and, by this observation, all need of rational and deliberate discussion is considered to be superseded. The first effort of the corruptionist is to fix the epithet *speculative* upon any scheme which he thinks may cherish the spirit of reform. The expression is hailed with the greatest delight by bad and feeble men, and repeated with the most unwearied energy; and, to the word speculative, by way of reinforcement, are added, *theoretical, visionary, chimerical, romantic, Utopian.*

"Sometimes a distinction is taken, and thereupon a concession made. The plan is *good in theory*, but it would be *bad in practice*, i. e. its being good in theory does not hinder its being bad in practice.

"Sometimes, as if in consequence of a farther progress made in the art of irrationality, the plan is pronounced to be *too good to be practicable;* and its being so good as it is, is thus represented as the very cause of its being bad in practice.

"In short, such is the perfection at which this art is at length arrived, that the very circumstance of a plan's being susceptible of the appellation of a *plan*, has been gravely stated as a circumstance sufficient to warrant its being rejected, if not with hatred, at any rate with a sort of accompaniment, which, to the million, is commonly felt still more galling—with contempt."—(p. 296.)

There is a propensity to push theory too far; but what is the just inference? not that theoretical propositions (*i. e.* all propositions of any considerable comprehension or extent) should, from such their extent, be considered to be false *in toto*, but only that, in the particular case, inquiry should be made whether, supposing the proposition to be in the character of a rule generally true, an exception ought to be taken out of it. It might almost be imagined that there was something wicked or unwise in the exercise of thought; for everybody feels a necessity for disclaiming it. "I am not given to speculation; I am no friend to theories." Can a man disclaim theory, can he disclaim speculation, without disclaiming thought?

The description of persons by whom this fallacy is chiefly employed are those who, regarding a plan as adverse to their interests, and not finding it on the ground of general utility exposed to any predominant objection, have recourse to this objection in the character of an instrument of contempt, in the view of preventing those from looking into it who might have been otherwise disposed. It is by the fear of seeing it practised that they are drawn to speak of it as impracticable. "Upon the face of it (exclaims some feeble or pensioned gentleman), it carries that air of plausibility, that, if you were not upon your guard, might engage you to bestow more or less of attention upon it; but were you to take the trouble, you would find that (as it is with all these plans which promise so much) practicability would at last be wanting to it. To save yourself from this trouble, the wisest course you can take is to put the plan aside, and to think no more about the matter." This is always accompanied with a peculiar grin of triumph.

The whole of these fallacies may be gathered together in a little oration, which we will denominate the

Noodle's Oration.

"What would our ancestors say to this, sir? How does this measure tally with their institutions? How does it agree with their experience? Are we to put the wisdom of yesterday in competition with the wisdom of centuries? (*Hear, hear!*) Is beardless youth to show no respect for the decisions of mature age? (*Loud cries of hear! hear!*) If this measure is right, would it have escaped the wisdom of those Saxon progenitors to whom we are indebted for so many of our best political institutions? Would the Dane have passed it over? Would the Norman have rejected it? Would such a notable discovery have been reserved for these modern and degenerate times? Besides, sir, if the measure itself is good, I ask the honourable gentleman if this is the time for carrying it into execution—whether, in fact, a more unfortunate period could have been selected than that which he has chosen? If this were an ordinary measure, I should not oppose it with so much vehemence; but, sir, it calls in question the wisdom of an irrevocable law—of a law passed at the memorable period of the Revolution. What right have we, sir, to break down this firm column, on which the great men of that day stamped a character of eternity? Are not all authorities against this measure, Pitt, Fox, Cicero, and the Attorney and Solicitor-General? The proposition is new, sir; it is the first time it was ever heard in this house. I am not prepared, sir—this house is not prepared, to receive it. The measure implies a distrust of his majesty's government; their disapproval is sufficient to warrant opposition. Precaution only is requisite where danger is apprehended. Here the high character of the individuals in question is a sufficient guarantee against any ground of alarm. Give not, then, your sanction to this measure; for, whatever be its character, if you do give your sanction to it, the same man by whom this is proposed, will propose to you others to which it will be impossible to give your consent. I care very little, sir, for the ostensible measure; but what is there behind? What are the honourable gentleman's future schemes? If we pass this bill, what fresh concessions may he not require? What farther degradation is he planning for his country? Talk of evil and inconvenience, sir! look to other countries—study other aggregations and societies of men, and then see whether the laws of this country demand a remedy, or deserve a panegyric. Was the honourable gentleman (let me ask him) always of this way of thinking? Do I not remember when he was the advocate in this house of very opposite opinions? I not only quarrel with his present sentiments, sir, but I declare very frankly I do not like the party with which he acts. If his own motives were as pure as possible, they cannot but suffer contamination from those with whom he is politically associated. This measure may be a boon to the constitution, but I will accept no favour to the constitution from such hands. (*Loud cries of hear! hear!*) I profess myself, sir, an honest and upright member of the British Parliament, and I am not afraid to profess myself an enemy to all change, and all innovation. I am satisfied with things as they are; and it will be my pride and pleasure to hand down this country to my children as I received it from those who preceded me. The honourable gentleman pretends to justify the severity with which he has attacked the noble lord who presides in the Court of Chancery. But I say such attacks are pregnant with mischief to government itself. Oppose ministers, you oppose government: disgrace ministers, you disgrace government: bring ministers into contempt, you bring government into contempt; and anarchy and civil war are the consequences. Besides, sir, the measure is unnecessary. Nobody complains of disorder in that shape in which it is the aim of your measure to propose a remedy to it. The business is one of the greatest importance; there is need of the greatest caution and circumspection. Do not let us be precipitate, sir; it is impossible to foresee all consequences. Every thing should be gradual; the example of a neighbouring nation should fill us with alarm! The honourable gentleman has taxed me with illiberality, sir. I deny the charge. I hate innovation, but I love improvement. I am an enemy to the corruption of government, but I defend its influence. I dread reform, but I dread it only when it is intemperate. I consider the liberty of the press as the great palladium of the constitution; but, at the same time, I hold the licentiousness of the press in the greatest abhorrence. Nobody is more conscious than I am of the splendid abilities of the honourable mover, but I tell him at once, his scheme is too good to be practicable. It savours of Utopia. It looks well in theory, but it won't do in practice. It will not do, I repeat, sir, in practice; and so the advocates of the measure will find, if, unfortunately, it should find its way through Parliament. (*Cheers.*) The source of that corruption to which the honourable member alludes, is in the minds of the people; so rank and extensive is that corruption, that no political reform can have any effect in removing it. Instead of reforming others—instead of reforming the state, the constitution, and every thing that is most excellent, let each man reform himself! let him look at home, he will find there enough to do, without looking abroad, and aiming at what is out of his power. (*Loud cheers.*) And now, sir, as it is frequently the custom in this house to end with a quotation, and as the gentleman who preceded me in the debate has anticipated me in my favourite quotation of the 'Strong pull and the long pull,' I shall end with the memorable words of the assembled Barons—*Nolumus leges Angliæ mutari.*"

"Upon the whole, the following are the characters which appertain in common to all the several arguments here distinguished by the name of fallacies:—

"1. Whatever be the measure in hand, they are, with relation to it, irrelevant.

"2. They are all of them such, that the application of these irrelevant arguments affords a presumption either of the weakness or total absence of relevant arguments on the side on which they are employed.

"3. To any good purpose they are all of them unnecessary.

"4. They are all of them not only capable of being applied, but actually in the habit of being applied, and with advantage, to bad purposes, viz., to the obstruction and defeat of all such measures as have for their object the removal of the abuses or other imperfections still discernible in the frame and practice of the government.

"5. By means of their irrelevancy, they all of them consume and misapply time, thereby obstructing the course and retarding the progress of all necessary and useful business.

"6. By that irritative quality which, in virtue of their irrelevancy, with the improbity or weakness of which it is indicative, they possess, all of them, in a degree more or less considerable, but in a more particular degree such of them as consist in personalities, they are productive of ill-humour, which in some instances has been productive of bloodshed, and is continually productive, as above, of waste of time and hinderance of business.

"7. On the part of those who, whether in spoken or written discourses, give utterance to them, they are indicative either of improbity or intellectual weakness, or of a contempt for the understanding of those on whose minds they are destined to operate.

"8. On the part of those on whom they operate, they are indicative of intellectual weakness; and on the part of those in and by whom they are pretended to operate, they are indicative of improbity, viz., in the shape of insincerity.

"The practical conclusion is, that in proportion as the acceptance, and thence the utterance, of them can be prevented, the understanding of the public will be strengthened, the morals of the public will be purified, and the practice of government improved."—(pp. 359, 360.)

WATERTON.*

[EDINBURGH REVIEW, 1826.]

MR. WATERTON is a Roman Catholic gentleman of Yorkshire, of good fortune, who, instead of passing his life at balls and assemblies, has preferred living with Indians and monkeys in the forests of Guiana. He appears in early life to have been seized with an unconquerable aversion to Piccadilly, and to that train of meteorological questions and answers, which forms the great staple of polite English conversation. From a dislike to the regular form of a journal, he throws his travels into detached pieces, which he, rather affectedly, calls Wanderings—and of which we shall proceed to give some account.

His first Wandering was in the year 1812, through the wilds of Demerara and Essequibo, a part of *ci-devant* Dutch Guiana, in South America. The sun exhausted him by day, the musquitoes bit him by night; but on went Mr. Charles Waterton!

The first thing which strikes us in this extraordinary chronicle, is the genuine zeal and inexhaustible delight with which all the barbarous countries he visits are described. He seems to love the forests, the tigers, and the apes;—to be rejoiced that he is the only man there; that he has left his species far away; and is at last in the midst of his blessed baboons! He writes with a considerable degree of force and vigour; and contrives to infuse into his reader that admiration of the great works, and undisturbed scenes of nature, which animates his style, and has influenced his life and practice. There is something, too, to be highly respected and praised in the conduct of a country gentleman, who, instead of exhausting life in the chase, has dedicated a considerable portion of it to the pursuit of knowledge. There are so many temptations to complete idleness in the life of a country gentleman, so many examples of it, and so much loss to the community from it,

* *Wanderings in South America, the North-West of the United States, and the Antilles, in the years* 1812, 1816, 1820, *and* 1824; *with Original Instructions for the perfect Preservation of Birds, &c., for Cabinets of Natural History.* By CHARLES WATERTON, Esq. London. Mawman. 4to. 1825.

that every exception from the practice is deserving of great praise. Some country gentlemen must remain to do the business of their counties; but, in general, there are many more than are wanted; and, generally speaking also, they are a class who should be stimulated to greater exertions. Sir Joseph Banks, a squire of large fortune in Lincolnshire, might have given up his existence to double-barrelled guns and persecutions of poachers—and all the benefits derived from his wealth, industry, and personal exertion in the cause of science would have been lost to the community.

Mr. Waterton complains, that the trees of Guiana are not more than six yards in circumference—a magnitude in trees which it is not easy for a Scotch imagination to reach. Among these, pre-eminent in height rises the mora—upon whose top branches, when naked by age, or dried by accident, is perched the toucan, too high for the gun of the fowler;—around this are the green heart, famous for hardness; the tough hackea; the ducalabali, surpassing mahogany; the ebony and letter-wood, exceeding the most beautiful woods of the Old World; the locust-tree, yielding copal; and the hayawa and olou-trees, furnishing sweet-smelling resin. Upon the top of the mora grows the fig-tree. The bush-rope joins tree and tree, so as to render the forest impervious, as, descending from on high, it takes root as soon as its extremity touches the ground, and appears like shrouds and stays supporting the mainmast of a line-of-battle ship.

Demerara yields to no country in the world in her birds. The mud is flaming with the scarlet curlew. At sunset, the pelicans return from the sea to the courada trees. Among the flowers are the humming-birds. The columbine, gallinaceous, and passerine tribes people the fruit-trees. At the close of day, the vampires, or winged bats, suck the blood of the traveller, and cool him by the flap of their wings. Nor has nature forgotten to amuse herself here in the composition of snakes:—the camoudi has been killed from thirty to forty feet long; he does not act by venom, but by size and convolution. The Spaniards affirm that he grows to the length of eighty feet, and that he will swallow a bull; but Spaniards love the superlative. There is a *whipsnake* of a beautiful green. The labarri snake of a dirty brown, who kills you in a few minutes. Every lovely colour under heaven is lavished upon the counachouchi, the most venomous of reptiles, and known by the name of the *bush-master*. Man and beast, says Mr. Waterton, fly before him, and allow him to pursue an undisputed path.

We consider the following description of the various sounds in these wild regions as very striking, and done with very considerable powers of style.

"He whose eye can distinguish the various beauties of uncultivated nature, and whose ear is not shut to the wild sounds in the woods, will be delighted in passing up the river Demerara. Every now and then, the maam or tinamou sends forth one long and plaintive whistle from the depth of the forest, and then stops; whilst the yelping of the toucan, and the shrill voice of the bird called pi-pi-yo, are heard during the interval. The campanero never fails to attract the attention of the passenger: at a distance of nearly three miles you may hear this snow-white bird tolling every four or five minutes, like the distant convent bell. From six to nine in the morning, the forests resound with the mingled cries and strains of the feathered race; after this they gradually die away. From eleven to three, all nature is hushed as in a midnight silence, and scarce a note is heard, saving that of the campanero and the pi-pi-yo; it is then that, oppressed by the solar heat, the birds retire to the thickest shade, and wait for the refreshing cool of evening.

"At sundown the vampires, bats, and goat-suckers, dart from their lonely retreat, and skim along the trees on the river's bank. The different kinds of frogs almost stun the ear with their hoarse and hollow-sounding croaking, while the owls and goatsuckers lament and mourn all night long.

"About two hours before daybreak you will hear the red monkey moaning as though in deep distress; the houtou, a solitary bird, and only found in the thickest recesses of the forest, distinctly articulates, 'houtou, houtou,' in a low and plaintive tone, an hour before sunrise; the maam whistles about the same hour; the hannaquoi, pataca, and maroudi announce his near approach to the eastern horizon, and the parrots and paroquets confirm his arrival there."—(pp. 13—15.)

Our good Quixote of Demerara is a little too fond of apostrophizing:—"Traveller! dost thou think? Reader! dost thou imagine?" Mr. Waterton should remember, that the whole merit of these violent deviations from common style depends upon their rarity, and that nothing does, for ten pages together, but the indicative mood. This fault gives an air of affectation to the writing of Mr. Waterton, which we believe to be foreign from his character and nature. We do not wish to deprive him of these indulgences altogether; but merely to put him upon an allowance, and upon such an allowance as will give to these figures of speech the advantage of surprise and relief.

This gentleman's delight and exultation always appear to increase as he loses sight of European inventions, and comes to something purely Indian. Speaking of an Indian tribe, he says,—

"They had only one gun, and it appeared rusty and neglected; but their poisoned weapons were in fine order. Their blow-pipes hung from the roof of the hut, carefully suspended by a silk grass cord; and on taking a nearer view of them, no dust seemed to have collected there, nor had the spider spun the smallest web on them; which showed that they were in constant use. The quivers were close by them, with the jaw-bone of the fish pirai tied by a string to their brim, and a small wicker-basket of wild cotton, which hung down to the centre; they were nearly full of poisoned arrows. It was with difficulty these Indians could be persuaded to part with any of the Wourali poison, though a good price was offered for it: they gave us to understand that it was powder and shot to them, and very difficult to be procured."—(pp. 34, 35.)

A wicker-basket of wild cotton, full of poisoned arrows, for shooting fish! This is Indian with a vengeance. We fairly admit that, in the contemplation of such utensils, every trait of civilized life is completely and effectually banished.

One of the strange and fanciful objects of Mr. Waterton's journey was, to obtain a better knowledge of the composition and nature of the *Wourali* poison, the ingredient with which the Indians poison their arrows. In the wilds of Essequibo, far away from any European settlements, there is a tribe of Indians known by the name of *Macoushi.* The *Wourali* poison is used by all the South American savages, betwixt the Amazon and the Oroonoque; but the Macoushi Indians manufacture it with the greatest skill, and of the greatest strength. A vine grows in the forest called Wourali; and from this vine, together with a good deal of nonsense and absurdity, the poison is prepared. When a native of Macoushia goes in quest of feathered game, he seldom carries his bow and arrows. It is the blow-pipe he then uses. The reed grows to an amazing length, as the part the Indians use is from 10 to 11 feet long, and no tapering can be perceived, one end being as thick as another; nor is there the slightest appearance of a knot or joint. The end which is applied to the mouth is tied round with a small silk grass cord. The arrow is from nine to ten inches long; it is made out of the leaf of a palm-tree, and pointed as sharp as a needle: about an inch of the pointed end is poisoned: the other end is burnt to make it still harder; and wild cotton is put round it for an inch and a half. The quiver holds from 500 to 600 arrows, is from 12 to 14 inches long, and in shape like a dice-box. With a quiver of these poisoned arrows over his shoulder, and his blow-pipe in his hand, the Indian stalks into the forest in quest of his feathered game.

"These generally sit high up in the tall and tufted trees, but still are not out of the Indian's reach; for his blow-pipe, at its greatest elevation, will send an arrow three hundred feet. Silent as midnight he steals under them, and so cautiously does he tread the ground, that the fallen leaves rustle not beneath his feet. His ears are open to the least sound, while his eye, keen as that of the lynx, is employed in finding out the game in the thickest shade. Often he imitates their cry, and decoys them from tree to tree, till they are within range of his tube. Then taking a poisoned arrow from his quiver, he puts it in the blow-pipe, and collects his breath for the fatal puff.

"About two feet from the end through which he blows, there are fastened two teeth of the acouri, and these serve him for a sight. Silent and swift the arrow flies, and seldom fails to pierce the object at which it is sent. Sometimes the wounded bird remains in the same tree where it was shot, but in three minutes falls down at the Indian's feet. Should he take wing, his flight is of short duration, and the Indian following in the direction he has gone, is sure to find him dead.

"It is natural to imagine that, when a slight wound only is inflicted, the game will make its escape. Far otherwise; the Wourali poison instantaneously mixes with blood or water, so that if you wet your finger, and dash it along the poisoned arrow in the quickest manner possible, you are sure to carry off some of the poison.

"Though three minutes generally elapse before the convulsions come on in the wounded bird, still a stupor evidently takes place sooner, and this stupor manifests itself by an apparent unwillingness in the bird to move. This was very visible in a dying fowl." (pp. 60—62.)

The flesh of the game is not in the slightest degree injured by the poison; nor does it appear to be corrupted sooner than that killed by the gun or knife. For the larger animals, an arrow with a poisoned spike is used.

"Thus armed with deadly poison, and hungry as the hyena, he ranges through the forest in quest of the wild beasts' track. No hound can act a surer part. Without clothes to fetter him, or shoes to bind his feet, he observes the footsteps of the game, where an European eye could not discern the smallest vestige. He pursues it through all its turns and windings, with astonishing perseverance, and success generally crowns his efforts. The animal, after receiving the poisoned arrow, seldom retreats two hundred paces before it drops.

"In passing over land from the Essequibo to the Demerara we fell in with a herd of wild hogs. Though encumbered with baggage, and fatigued with a hard day's walk, an Indian got his bow ready, and let fly a poisoned arrow at one of them. It entered the cheek-bone, and broke off. The wild hog was found quite dead about one hundred and seventy paces from the place where he had been shot. He afforded us an excellent and wholesome supper."—(p. 65.)

Being a *Wourali* poison fancier, Mr. Waterton has recorded several instances of the power of his favourite drug. A sloth poisoned by it went gently to sleep, and died! a large ox, weighing one thousand pounds, was shot with three arrows; the poison took effect in four minutes, and in twenty-five minutes he was dead. The death seems to be very gentle; and resembles more a quiet apoplexy, brought on by hearing a long story, than any other kind of death. If an Indian happens to be wounded with one of these arrows, he considers it as certain death. We have reason to congratulate ourselves, that our method of terminating disputes is by sword and pistol, and not by these medicated pins; which, we presume, will become the weapons of gentlemen in the new republics of South America.

The *second* journey of Mr. Waterton, in the year 1816, was to Pernambuco, in the southern hemisphere, on the coast of Brazil, and from thence he proceeds to Cayenne. His plan was to have ascended the Amazon from Para, and get into the Rio Negro, and from thence to have returned towards the source of the Essequibo, in order to examine the Crystal Mountains, and to look once more for Lake Parima, or the

White Sea; but on arriving at Cayenne, he found that to beat up the Amazon would be long and tedious; he left Cayenne, therefore, in an American ship for Paramaribo, went through the interior to Coryntin, stopped a few days at New Amsterdam, and proceeded to Demerara.

"Leave behind you" (he says to the traveller) "your high-seasoned dishes, your wines, and your delicacies; carry nothing but what is necessary for your own comfort, and the object in view, and depend upon the skill of an Indian, or your own, for fish and game. A sheet, about twelve feet long, ten wide, painted, and with loop-holes on each side, will be of great service: in a few minutes you can suspend it betwixt two trees in the shape of a roof. Under this, in your hammock, you may defy the pelting shower, and sleep heedless of the dews of night. A hat, a shirt, and a light pair of trowsers, will be all the raiment you require. Custom will soon teach you to tread lightly and barefoot on the little inequalities of the ground, and show you how to pass on, unwounded, amid the mantling briars."—(pp. 112, 113.)

Snakes are certainly an annoyance; but the snake, though high-spirited, is not quarrelsome; he considers his fangs to be given for defence, and not for annoyance, and never inflicts a wound but to defend existence. If you tread upon him, he puts you to death for your clumsiness, merely because he does not understand what your clumsiness means; and certainly a snake, who feels fourteen or fifteen stone stamping upon his tail, has little time for reflection, and may be allowed to be poisonous and peevish. American tigers generally run away—from which several respectable gentlemen in Parliament inferred, in the American war, that American soldiers would run away also!

The description of the birds is very animated and interesting; but how far does the gentle reader imagine the campanero may be heard, whose size is that of a jay? Perhaps 300 yards. Poor innocent, ignorant reader! unconscious of what nature has done in the forests of Cayenne, and measuring the force of tropical intonation by the sounds of a Scotch duck! The campanero may be heard three miles!—this single little bird being more powerful than the belfry of a cathedral, ringing for a new dean—just appointed on account of shabby politics, small understanding, and good family!

"The fifth species is the celebrated campanero of the Spaniards, called dara by the Indians, and bell-bird by the English. He is about the size of the jay. His plumage is white as snow. On his forehead rises a spiral tube nearly three inches long. It is jet black, dotted all over with small white feathers. It has a communication with the palate, and when filled with air, looks like a spire; when empty, it becomes pendulous. His note is loud and clear, like the sound of a bell, and may be heard at the distance of three miles. In the midst of these extensive wilds, generally on the dried top of an aged mora, almost out of gun reach, you will see the campanero. No sound or song from any of the winged inhabitants of the forest, not even the clearly pronounced 'Whip-poor Will,' from the goatsucker, causes such astonishment as the toll of the campanero.

"With many of the feathered race he pays the common tribute of a morning and an evening song; and even when the meridian sun has shut in silence the mouths of almost the whole of animated nature, the campanero still cheers the forest. You hear his toll, and then a pause for a minute, then another toll, and then a pause, again, and then a toll, and again a pause."—(pp. 117, 118.)

It is impossible to contradict a gentleman who has been in the forests of Cayenne; but we are determined, as soon as a campanero is brought to England, to make him toll in a public place, and have the distance measured. The toucan has an enormous bill, makes a noise like a puppy dog, and lays his eggs in hollow trees. How astonishing are the freaks and fancies of nature! To what purpose, we say, is a bird placed in the woods of Cayenne, with a bill a yard long, making a noise like a puppy dog, and laying eggs in hollow trees? The toucans, to be sure, might retort, to what purpose were gentlemen in Bond street created? To what purpose were certain foolish, prating members of Parliament created?—pestering the House of Commons with their ignorance and folly, and impeding the business of the country? There is no end of such questions. So we will not enter into the metaphysics of the toucan. The houtou ranks high in beauty; his whole body is green, his wings and tail blue; his crown is of black and blue; he makes no nest, but rears his young in the sand.

"The cassique, in size, is larger than the starling; he courts the society of man, but disdains to live by his labours. When nature calls for support, he repairs to the neighbouring forest, and there partakes of the store of fruits and seeds, which she has produced in abundance for her aërial tribes. When his repast is over, he returns to man, and pays the little tribute which he owes him for his protection; he takes his station on a tree close to his house; and there, for hours together, pours forth a succession of imitative notes. His own song is sweet, but very short. If a toucan be yelping in the neighbourhood, he drops it, and imitates him. Then he will amuse his protector with the cries of the different species of the woodpecker; and when the sheep bleat, he will distinctly answer them. Then comes his own song again, and if a puppy dog or a guinea fowl interrupt him, he takes them off admirably, and by his different gestures during the time, you would conclude that he enjoys the sport.

"The cassique is gregarious, and imitates any sound he hears with such exactness that he goes by no other name than that of mocking-bird amongst the colonists."—(pp. 127, 128.)

There is no end to the extraordinary noises of the forest of Cayenne. The woodpecker, in striking against the tree with his bill, makes a sound so loud, that Mr. Waterton says it reminds you more of a wood-cutter than a bird. While lying in your hammock, you hear the goatsucker lamenting like one in deep distress —a stranger would take it for a Weir murdered by Thurtell.

"Suppose yourself in hopeless sorrow, begin with a high loud note, and pronounce, 'ha, ha, ha, ha, ha, ha, ha,' each note lower and lower, till the last is scarcely heard, pausing a moment or two betwixt every note, and you will have some idea of the moaning of the largest goatsucker in Demerara."—(p. 141.)

One species of the goatsucker cries, "Who are you? who are you?" Another exclaims, "Work away, work away." A third, "Willy come go, Willy come go." A fourth, "Whip poor Will, whip poor Will." It is very flattering to us that they should all speak *English!*—though we cannot much commend the elegance of their selections. The Indians never destroy these birds, believing them to be the servants of Jumbo, the African devil.

Great travellers are very fond of triumphing over civilized life; and Mr. Waterton does not omit the opportunity of remarking, that nobody ever stopt him in the forests of Cayenne to ask him for his license, or to inquire if he had an hundred a year, or to take away his gun, or to dispute the limits of a manor, or to threaten him with a tropical justice of the peace. We hope, however, that in this point we are on the eve of improvement. Mr. Peel, who is a man of high character and principles, may depend upon it that the time is come for his interference, and that it will be a loss of reputation to him not to interfere. If any one else can and will carry an alteration through Parliament, there is no occasion that the hand of government should appear; but some hand *must* appear. The common people are becoming ferocious, and the perdricide criminals are more numerous than the violators of all the branches of the Decalogue.

"The king of the vultures is very handsome, and seems to be the only bird which claims regal honours from a surrounding tribe. It is a fact beyond all dispute, that when the scent of carrion has drawn together hundreds of the common vultures, they all retire from the carcass as soon as the king of the vultures makes his appearance. When his majesty has satisfied the cravings of his royal stomach with the choicest bits from the most stinking and corrupted parts, he generally retires to a neighbouring tree, and then the common vultures return in crowds to gobble down his leavings. The Indians, as well as the whites, have observed this; for when one of them, who has learned a little English, sees the king, and wishes you to have a proper notion of the bird, he says, 'There is the governor of the carrion crows.'

"Now, the Indians have never heard of a personage in Demerara higher than that of governor; and the colonists, through a common mistake, call the vultures carrion crows. Hence the Indian, in order to express the dominion of this bird over the common vultures, tells you he is governor of the carrion crows. The Spaniards have also observed it, for, through all the Spanish Main, he is called Rey de Zamuros, king of the vultures."—(p. 146.)

This, we think, explains satisfactorily the origin of kingly government. As men have "learnt from the dog the physic of the field," they may probably have learnt from the vulture those high lessons of policy upon which, in Europe, we suppose the whole happiness of society, and the very existence of the human race, to depend.

Just before his third journey, Mr. Waterton takes leave of Sir Joseph Banks, and speaks of him with affectionate regret. "I saw," (says Mr. W.) "with sorrow, that death was going to rob us of him. We talked of stuffing quadrupeds; I agreed that the lips and nose ought to be cut off, and stuffed with wax." This is the way great naturalists take an eternal farewell of each other! Upon stuffing animals, however, we have a word to say. Mr. Waterton has placed at the head of his book the picture of what he is pleased to consider a nondescript species of monkey. In this exhibition our author is surely abusing his stuffing talents, and laughing at the public. It is clearly the head of a master in chancery—whom we have often seen backing in the House of Commons after he has delivered his message. It is foolish thus to trifle with science aud natural history. Mr. Waterton gives an interesting account of the sloth, an animal of which he appears to be fond, and whose habits he has studied with peculiar attention.

"Some years ago I kept a sloth in my room for several months. I often took him out of the house and placed him upon the ground, in order to have an opportunity of observing his motions. If the ground were rough, he would pull himself forwards, by means of his fore legs, at a pretty good pace; and he invariably shaped his course towards the nearest tree. But if I put him upon a smooth and well-trodden part of the road, he appeared to be in trouble and distress: his favourite abode was the back of a chair; and after getting all his legs in a line upon the topmost part of it, he would hang there for hours together, and often, with a low and inward cry, would seem to invite me to take notice of him."—(p. 164.)

The sloth, in its wild state, spends its life in trees, and never leaves them but from force or accident. The eagle to the sky, the mole to the ground, the sloth to the tree; but what is most extraordinary, he lives not *upon* the branches, but *under* them. He moves suspended, rests suspended, sleeps suspended, and passes his life in suspense—like a young clergyman distantly related to a bishop. Strings of ants may be observed, says our good traveller, a mile long, each carrying in its mouth a green leaf the size of a sixpence! he does not say whether this is a loyal procession, like Oak-apple Day, or for what purpose these leaves are carried; but it appears, while they are carrying the leaves, that three sorts of ant-bears are busy in eating them. The habits of the largest of these three animals are curious, and to us new. We recommend the account to the attention of the reader.

He is chiefly found in the inmost recesses of the forest, and seems partial to the low and swampy parts near creeks, where the Troely tree grows. There he goes up and down in quest of ants, of which there is never the least scarcity; so that he soon obtains a sufficient supply of food, with very little trouble. He cannot travel fast; man is superior to him in speed. Without swiftness to enable him to escape from his enemies, without teeth, the possession of which would assist him in self-defence, and without the power of burrowing in the ground, by which he might conceal himself from his pursuers, he still is capable of ranging through these wilds in perfect safety; nor does he fear the fatal pressure of the serpent's fold, or the teeth of the famished jaguar. Nature has formed his fore legs wonderfully thick, and strong, and muscular, and armed his feet with three tremendous sharp and crooked claws. Whenever he seizes an animal with these formidable weapons, he hugs it close to his body and keeps it there till it dies through pressure, or through want of food. Nor does the ant-bear, in the mean time, suffer much from loss of aliment, as it is a well-known fact, that he can go longer without food than perhaps any other animal, except the land tortoise. His skin is of a texture that perfectly resists the bite of a dog; his hinder parts are protected by thick and shaggy hair, while his immense tail is large enough to cover his whole body.

"The Indians have a great dread of coming in contact with the ant-bear; and, after disabling him in the chase, never think of approaching him till he be quite dead."—(pp 171, 172.)

The vampire measures about 26 inches from wing to wing. There are two species, large and small. The large suck men, and the smaller, birds. Mr. W. saw some fowls which had been sucked the night before, and they were scarcely able to walk.

"Some years ago I went to the river Paumaron with a Scotch gentleman, by name Tarbet. We hung our hammocks in the thatched loft of a planter's house. Next morning I heard this gentleman muttering in his hammock, and now and then letting fall an imprecation or two, just about the time he ought to have been saying his morning prayers. 'What is the matter, sir?' said I, softly; 'is any thing amiss?'—'What's the matter?' answered he, surlily; 'why, the vampires have been sucking me to death.' As soon as there was light enough, I went to his hammock, and saw it much stained with blood. 'There,' said he, thrusting his foot out of the hammock, 'see how these infernal imps have been drawing my life's blood.' On examining his foot, I found the vampire had tapped his great toe: there was a wound somewhat less than that made by a leech; the blood was still oozing from it; I conjectured he might have lost from ten to twelve ounces of blood. Whilst examining it, I think I put him into a worse humour, by remarking, that an European surgeon would not have been so generous as to have blooded him without making a charge. He looked up in my face, but did not say a word: I saw he was of opinion that I had better have spared this piece of ill-timed levity."—(pp. 176, 177.)

The story which follows this account is vulgar, unworthy of Mr. Waterton, and should have been omitted.

Every animal has its enemies. The land tortoise has two enemies, man, and the boa-constrictor. The natural defence of the tortoise is to draw himself up in his shell, and to remain quiet. In this state, the tiger, however famished, can do nothing with him, for the shell is too strong for the stroke of his paw. Man, however, takes him home and roasts him—and the boa-constrictor swallows him whole, shell and all, and consumes him slowly in the interior, as the Court of Chancery does a great estate.

The danger seems to be much less with snakes and wild beasts, if you conduct yourself like a gentleman, and are not abruptly intrusive. If you will pass on gently, you may walk unhurt within a yard of the Labairi snake, who would put you to death if you rushed upon him. The taguan knocks you down with a blow of his paw, if suddenly interrupted, but will run away, if you will give him time to do so. In short, most animals look upon man as a very ugly customer; and, unless sorely pressed for food, or from fear of their own safety, are not fond of attacking him. Mr. Waterton, though much given to sentiment, made a Labairi snake bite itself, but no bad consequences ensued—nor would any bad consequences ensue, if a court-martial were to order a sinful soldier to give himself a thousand lashes. It is barely possible that the snake had some faint idea of whom and what he was biting.

Insects are the curse of tropical climates. The bête rouge lays the foundation of a tremendous ulcer. In a moment you are covered with ticks. Chigoes bury themselves in your flesh, and hatch a colony of young chigoes in a few hours. They will not live together, but every chigoe sets up a separate ulcer, and has his own private portion of pus. Flies get entry into your mouth, into your eyes, into your nose; you eat flies, drink flies, and breathe flies. Lizards, cockroaches, and snakes, get into the bed; ants eat up the books; scorpions sting you on the foot. Every thing bites, stings, or bruises; every second of your existence you are wounded by some piece of animal life that nobody has ever seen before, except Swammerdam and Meriam. An insect with eleven legs is swimming in your teacup, a nondescript with nine wings is struggling in the small beer, or a caterpillar with several dozen eyes in his belly is hastening over the bread and butter! All nature is alive, and seems to be gathering all her entomological hosts to eat you up, as you are standing, out of your coat, waistcoat, and breeches. Such are the tropics. All this reconciles us to our dews, fogs, vapour, and drizzle—to our apothecaries rushing about with gargles and tinctures—to our old, British, constitutional coughs, sore throats, and swelled faces.

We come now to the counterpart of St. George and the Dragon. Every one knows that the large snake of tropical climates throws himself upon his prey, twists the folds of his body round the victim, presses him to death, and then eats him. Mr. Waterton wanted a large snake for the sake of his skin; and it occurred to him that the success of this sort of combat depended upon who began first, and that if he could contrive to fling himself upon the snake, he was just as likely to send the snake to the British Museum, as the snake, if allowed the advantage of prior occupation, was to eat him up. The opportunities which Yorkshire squires have of combating with the boa constrictor are so few, that Mr. Waterton must be allowed to tell his own story in his own manner.

"We went slowly on in silence, without moving our arms or heads, in order to prevent all alarm as much as possible, lest the snake should glide off, or attack us in self-defence. I carried the lance perpendicularly before me, with the point about a foot from the ground. The snake had not moved; and on getting up to him, I struck him with the lance on the near side, just behind the neck, and pinned him to the ground. That moment the negro next to me seized the lance and held it firm in its place, while I dashed head foremost into the den to grapple with the snake, and to get hold of his tail before he could do any mischief.

"On pinning him to the ground with the lance, he gave a tremendous loud hiss, and the little dog ran away, howling as he went. We had a sharp fray in the den, the rotten sticks flying on all sides, and each party struggling for superiority. I called out to the second negro to throw himself upon me, as I found I was not heavy enough. He did so, and the additional weight was of great service. I had now got firm hold of his tail; and after a violent struggle or two, he gave in, finding himself overpowered. This was the moment to secure him. So, while the first negro continued to hold the lance firm to the ground, and the other was helping me, I contrived to unloose my braces, and with them tied up the snake's mouth.

"The snake, now finding himself in an unpleasant situation, tried to better himself, and set resolutely to work, but we overpowered him. We contrived to make him twist himself round the shaft of the lance, and then prepared to convey him out of the forest. I stood at his head, and held it firm under my arm; one negro supported the belly, and the other the tail. In this order we began to move slowly towards home, and reached it after resting ten times: for the snake was too heavy for us to support him without stopping to recruit our strength. As we proceeded onwards with him, he fought hard for freedom, but it was all in vain."—(pp. 202—204.)

One of these combats we should have thought sufficient for glory, and for the interest of the British Museum. But Hercules killed two snakes, and Mr. Waterton would not be content with less.

"There was a path where timber had formerly been dragged along. Here I observed a young coulacanara, ten feet long, slowly moving onwards; I saw he was not thick enough to break my arm, in case he got twisted round it. There was not a moment to be lost. I laid hold of his tail with the left hand, one knee being on the ground; with the right I took off my hat, and held it as you would hold a shield for defence.

"The snake instantly turned, and came on at me, with his head about a yard from the ground, as if to ask me what business I had to take liberties with his tail. I let him come, hissing and open-mouthed, within two feet of my face, and then, with all the force I was master of, I drove my fist, shielded by my hat, full in his jaws. He was stunned and confounded by the blow, and ere he could recover himself, I had seized his throat with both hands, in such a position that he could not bite me; I then allowed him to coil himself round my body, and marched off with him as my lawful prize. He pressed me hard, but not alarmingly so."—(pp. 206, 207.)

When the body of the large snake began to smell, the vultures immediately arrived. The king of the vultures first gorged himself, and then retired to a large tree, while his subjects consumed the remainder. It does not appear that there was any favouritism. When the king was full, all the mob vultures ate alike; neither could Mr. Waterton perceive that there was any division into Catholic and Protestant vultures, or that the majority of the flock thought it essentially vulturish to exclude one-third of their numbers from the blood and entrails. The vulture, it is remarkable, never eats live animals. He seems to abhor every thing which has not the relish of putrescence and flavour of death. The following is a characteristic specimen of the little inconveniences to which travellers are liable, who sleep on the feather beds of the forest. To see a rat in a room in Europe insures a night of horror. Every thing is by comparison.

"About midnight, as I was lying awake, and in great pain, I heard the Indian say, 'Massa, massa, you no hear tiger?' I listened attentively, and heard the softly sounding tread of his feet as he approached us. The moon had gone down; but every now and then we could get a glance of him by the light of our fire; he was the jaguar, for I could see the spots on his body. Had I wished to have fired at him, I was not able to take a sure aim, for I was in such pain that I could not turn myself in my hammock. The Indian would have fired, but I would not allow him to do so, as I wanted to see a little more of our new visitor; for it is not every day or night that the traveller is favoured with an undisturbed sight of the jaguar in his own forests.

"Whenever the fire got low, the jaguar came a little nearer, and when the Indian renewed it, he retired abruptly; sometimes he would come within twenty yards, and then we had a view of him, sitting on his hind legs like a dog; sometimes he moved slowly to and fro, and at other times we could hear him mend his pace, as if impatient. At last the Indian, not relishing the idea of having such company in the neighbourhood, could contain himself no longer, and set up a most tremendous yell. The jaguar bounded off like a race-horse, and returned no more; it appeared by the print of his feet next morning that he was a full-grown jaguar."—(pp. 212, 213.)

We have seen Mr. Waterton fling himself upon a snake; we shall now mount him upon a crocodile, undertaking that this shall be the last of his feats exhibited to the reader. He had baited for a cayman or crocodile, the hook was swallowed, and the object was to pull the animal up and to secure him. "If you pull him up," say the Indians, "as soon as he sees you on the brink of the river, he will run at you and destroy you." "Never mind," says our traveller, "pull away, and leave the rest to me." And accordingly he places himself upon the shore with the mast of the canoe in his hand, ready to force it down the throat of the crocodile as soon as he makes his appearance.

"By the time the cayman was within two yards of me, I saw he was in a state of fear and perturbation; I instantly dropped the mast, sprung up, and jumped on his back, turning half round as I vaulted, so that I gained my seat with my face in a right position. I immediately seized his fore legs, and, by main force, twisted them on his back; thus they served me for a bridle.

"He now seemed to have recovered from his surprise, and probably fancying himself in hostile company, he began to plunge furiously, and lashed the sand with his long and powerful tail. I was out of reach of the strokes of it, by being near his head. He continued to plunge and strike, and make my seat very uncomfortable. It must have been a fine sight for an unoccupied spectator.

"The people roared out in triumph, and were so vociferous, that it was some time before they heard me tell them to pull me and my beast of burden farther in land. I was apprehensive the rope might break, and then there would have been every chance of going down to the regions under water with the cayman. That would have been more perilous than Arion's marine morning ride:—

'Delphini insidens, vada cærula sulcat Arion.'

"The people now dragged us above forty yards on the sand; it was the first and last time I was ever on a cayman's back. Should it be asked how I managed to keep my seat, I would answer—I hunted some years with Lord Darlington's fox hounds."—(pp. 231, 232.)

The Yorkshire gentlemen have long been famous for their equestrian skill; but Mr. Waterton is the first among them of whom it could be said, that he has a fine hand upon a crocodile. This accursed animal, so ridden by Mr. Waterton, is the scourge and terror of all the large rivers in South America near the line. Their boldness is such, that a cayman has sometimes come out of the Oroonoque, at Angustura, near the public walks where the people were assembled, seized a full-grown man, as big as Sir William Curtis after dinner, and hurried him into the bed of the river for his food. The governor of Angustura witnessed this circumstance himself.

Our Eboracic traveller had now been nearly eleven months in the desert, and not in vain. Shall we express our doubts, or shall we confidently state at once the immense wealth he had acquired!—a prodigious variety of insects, two hundred and thirty birds, ten land-tortoises, five armadillos, two large serpents, a sloth, an ant-bear, and a cayman. At Liverpool, the custom-house officers, men ignorant of Linnæus, got hold of his collection, detained it six weeks, and, in spite of remonstrances to the treasury, he was forced to pay very high duties. This is really perfectly absurd; that a man of science cannot bring a pickled armadillo, for a collection of natural history, without paying a tax for it. This surely must have happened in the dark days of Nicolas. We cannot doubt but that such paltry exactions have been swept away, by the manly and liberal policy of Robinson and Huskisson. That a great people should compel an individual to make them a payment before he can be permitted to land a stuffed snake upon their shores, is, of all the paltry custom-house robberies we ever heard of, the most mean and contemptible—but *Major rerum ordo nascitur*.

The *fourth* journey of Mr. Waterton is to the United States. It is pleasantly written; but our author does not appear as much at home among men as among beasts. Shooting, stuffing, and pursuing are his occupations. He is lost in places where there are no bushes, snakes, nor Indians—but he is full of good and amiable feeling wherever he goes. We cannot avoid introducing the following passage:—

"The steamboat from Quebec to Montreal had above five hundred Irish emigrants on board. They were going 'they hardly knew whither,' far away from dear Ireland. It made one's heart ache to see them all huddled together, without any expectation of ever revisiting their native soil. We feared that the sorrow of leaving home for ever, the miserable accommodations on board the ship which had brought them away, and the tossing of the angry ocean, in a long and dreary voyage, would have rendered them callous to good behaviour. But it was quite otherwise. They conducted themselves with great propriety. Every American on board seemed to feel for them. And then 'they were so full of wretchedness. Need and oppression stared within their eyes. Upon their backs hung ragged misery. The world was not their friend.' 'Poor, dear Ireland,' exclaimed an aged female, as I was talking to her, 'I shall never see it any more!' "—(pp. 259, 260.)

And thus it is in every region of the earth! There is no country where an Englishman can set his foot, that he does not meet these miserable victims of English cruelty and oppression—banished from their country by the stupidity, bigotry, and meanness of the English people, who trample on their liberty and conscience, because each man is afraid, in another reign, of being out of favour, and losing his share in the spoil.

We are always glad to see America praised (slavery excepted). And yet there is still, we fear, a party in this country, who are glad to pay their court to the timid and the feeble, by sneering at this great spectacle of human happiness. We never think of it without considering it as a great lesson to the people of England, to look into their own affairs, to watch and to suspect their rulers, and not to be defrauded of happiness and money by pompous names, and false pretences.

"Our western brother is in possession of a country replete with every thing that can contribute to the happiness and comfort of mankind. His code of laws, purified by experience and common sense, has fully answered the expectations of the public. By acting up to the true spirit of this code, he has reaped immense advantages from it. His advancement, as a nation, has been rapid beyond all calculation; and, young as he is, it may be remarked, without any impropriety, that he is now actually reading a salutary lesson to the rest of the civilized world."—(p. 273.)

Now, what shall we say, after all, of Mr. Waterton? That he has spent a great part of his life in wandering in the wild scenes he describes, and that he describes them with entertaining zeal and real feeling. His stories draw largely sometimes on our faith; but a man who lives in the woods of Cayenne must do many odd things, and see many odd things—things utterly unknown to the dwellers in Hackney and Highgate. We do not want to rein up Mr. Waterton too tightly—because we are convinced he goes best with his head free. But a little less of apostrophe, and some faint suspicion of his own powers of humour, would improve this gentleman's style. As it is, he has a considerable talent at describing. He abounds with good feeling; and has written a very entertaining book, which hurries the reader out of his European parlour, into the heart of tropical forests, and gives, over the rules and the cultivation of the civilized parts of the earth, a momentary superiority to the freedom of the savage, and the wild beauties of nature. We honestly recommend the book to our readers: it is well worth the perusal.

MAN TRAPS AND SPRING GUNS.*

[Edinburgh Review, 1821.]

Most of our readers will remember, that we very lately published an article upon the use of steel traps and spring guns; and, in the course of discussion, had occasion to animadvert upon the report of Mr. Justice Best's judgment, in the case of Ilott and Wilkes, as reported in *Chetwynd's Edition of Burn's Justice*, published in the spring of the present year. In the Morning Chronicle, of the 4th of June, 1821, Mr. Justice Best is reported to have made the following observations in the King's Bench:—

"Mr. Justice Best said, Mr. Chetwynd's book having been mentioned by my learned brother Bayley, I must take this opportunity, not without some pain, of adverting to what I am reported, in his work, to have said in the case of Ilott *v.* Wilkes, and of correcting a most gross misrepresentation. I am reported to have concurred with the other judges, and to have delivered my judgment at considerable length, and then to have said, 'This case has been discussed at the bar, as if these engines were exclusively resorted to for the protection of game; but I consider them as lawfully applicable to the protection of every species of property against unlawful trespassers.' This is not what I stated; but the part which I wish more particularly to deny, as ever having said, or even conceived, is this—'But if even they might not lawfully be used for the protection of game, I, for one, should be extremely glad to adopt such means, if they were found sufficient for that purpose.' I confess I am surprised that this learned person should suppose, from the note of any one, that any person who ever sat in a court of justice as a judge could talk such wicked nonsense as I am made to talk; and I am surprised that he should venture to give the authority he does for what he has published; for I find, that the reference he gives in the appendix to his book is 3 Barn. and Ald. 304, where there is a correct report of that case, and where it will be found that every word uttered by me is directly contrary to what I am supposed, by Mr. Chetwynd's statement of the case, to have said. I don't trouble the court with reading the whole of what I did say on that occasion, but I will just say that I said 'My brother Bayley has illustrated this case by the question which he asked, namely, Can you indict a man for putting spring guns in his enclosed field? I think the question put by Lord Chief Justice Gibbs, in the case of Dean *v.* Clayton, in the Common Pleas, a still better illustration, viz. Can you justify entering into enclosed lands to take away guns so set? If both these questions must be answered in the negative, it cannot be unlawful to set spring guns in an enclosed field, at a distance from any road, giving such notice that they are set as to render it in the highest degree probable that all persons in the neighbourhood must know that they are so set. Humanity requires that the fullest notice possible should be given; and the law of England will not sanction what is inconsistent with humanity.' A popular work has quoted this report from Mr. Chetwynd's work, but has omitted this important line (which omission reminds one of the progress of a thing, the name of which one does not choose to mention), 'that I had concurred in what had fallen from the other judges; and omitting that line, they state, that one had said, 'It is my opinion, that with notice, or without notice, this might be done.' Now, concurring with the other judges, it is impossible I should say that. It is right that this should be corrected; not that I enter-

* *Reports of Cases argued and determined in the Court of King's Bench, in Hilary Term, 60th Geo. III.* 1820.—By Richard V. Barnewall, of Lincoln's Inn, Esq., Barrister-at-law, and Edward H. Alderson, of the Inner Temple, Esq., Barrister-at-Law. Vol. III. Part II. London, 1820.

tain any angry feeling, for too much time has elapsed since then for any anger to remain on my mind; but all I claim, with respect to the observations made in that work, severe as they are (and I, for one, feel that I should deserve no mercy if I should ever entertain such doctrines), is, that I may not be misrepresented. It is not necessary for me, in this place, to say, that no man entertains more horror of the doctrine than I am supposed to have laid down than I do, that the life of man is to be treated lightly and indifferently, in comparison with the preservation of game, and the amusement of sporting; that the laws of humanity are to be violated for the sake merely of preserving the amusement of game. I am sure no man can justly impute to me such wicked doctrines. It is unnecessary for me to say, that I entertain no such sentiments; and therefore I hope I shall be excused, not on account of my own feelings, but as far as the public are interested in the character of a judge, in saying, that no person should blame a judge for what has been unjustly put into his mouth."

His lordship's speech is reported in the New Times of the same date, as follows:—

"Mr. Justice Best said, 'My brother Bayley has quoted Mr. Chetwynd's edition of Burn: I am surprised that the learned author of that work should have made me talk such mischievous nonsense, as he has given to the public, in a report of my judgment, in the case of Ilott and Wilkes. I am still more surprised, that he should have suffered this judgment to remain uncorrected, after he had seen a true report of the case in Barnewall and Alderson, to which report he has referred in his appendix.' Mr. Chetwynd's report has the following passage:—'Mr. Justice Best concurred with the other judges.' His lordship concluded as follows:—'This case has been discussed at the bar, as if these inquiries were exclusively resorted to for the protection of game; but I considered them as lawfully applicable to the protection of every species of property against unlawful trespassers. *But if even they might not lawfully be used for the protection of game, I for one should be extremely glad to adopt such measures, if they were found sufficient for that purpose.*'

"A popular periodical work contains the passage just cited, with the omission of the words 'concurred with the other judges.' Of this omission I have reason to complain, because, if it had been inserted, the writer of the article could not have said, 'It follows, that a man may put his fellow-creatures to death for any infringement of his property, for picking the sloes and blackberries off his hedges; for breaking a few dead sticks out of them by night or by day, *with resistance or without resistance, with warning or without warning.*' The judges with whom Mr. Chetwynd makes me concur in opinion, all gave their judgment on the ground of due notice being given. I do not complain of the other observations contained in this work; they would have been deserved by me had I ever uttered such an opinion as the report of Mr. Chetwynd has stated me to have delivered. The whole of what I said will be found to be utterly inconsistent with the statement, by those who will read the case in 'Barnewall and Alderson.' I will only trouble the court with the passage which will be found in the report of my judgment, in '3 Barnewall and Alderson, 319:' 'It cannot be unlawful to set spring guns in an enclosed field, at a distance from any road, giving such notice that they are set, as to render it in the highest degree probable that all persons in the neighbourhood must know that they are so set. Humanity required that the fullest notice possible should be given; and the law of England will not sanction what is inconsistent with humanity.' I have taken the first opportunity of saying this, because I think it of importance to the public that such a misrepresentation of the opinion of one of the judges should not be circulated without some notice."

We subjoin the report of Messrs. Barnewall and Alderson, here alluded to, and allowed by Mr. Justice Best to be correct:—

"*Best*, J. The act of the plaintiff could only occasion mere nominal damage to the wood of the defendant. The injury that the plaintiff's trespass has brought upon himself is extremely severe. In such a case, one cannot, without pain, decide against the action. But we must not allow our feelings to induce us to lose sight of the principles which are essential to the rights of property. The prevention of intrusion upon property is one of these rights; and every proprietor is allowed to use the force that is *absolutely* necessary to vindicate it. If he uses more force than is *absolutely* necessary, he renders himself responsible for all the consequences of the excess. Thus, if a man comes on my land, I cannot lay hands on him to remove him, until I have desired him to go off. If he will not depart on request, I cannot proceed immediately to beat him, but must endeavour to push him off. If he is too powerful for me, I cannot use a dangerous weapon, but must first call in aid other assistance. I am speaking of out-door property, and of cases in which no felony is to be apprehended. It is evident, also, that this doctrine is only applicable to trespasses committed in the presence of the owner of the property trespassed on. When the owner and his servants are absent at the time of the trespass, it can only be repelled by the terror of spring guns, or other instruments of the same kind. There is, in such cases, no possibility of proportioning the resisting force to the obstinacy and violence of the trespasser, as the owner of the close may and is required to do where he is present. There is no distinction between the mode of defence of one species of out-door property and another (except in cases where the taking or breaking into the property amounts to felony). If the owner of woods cannot set spring guns in his woods, the owner of an orchard, or of a field with potatoes or turnips, or any other crop usually the object of plunder, cannot set them in such field. How, then, are these kinds of property to be protected, at a distance from the residence of the owner, in the night, and in the absence of his servants? It has been said, that the law has provided remedies for any injuries to such things by action. But the offender must be detected before he can be subjected to an action; and the expense of continual watching for this purpose would often exceed the value of the property to be protected. If we look at the subject in this point of view, we may find, amongst poor tenants, who are prevented from paying their rents by the plunder of their crops, men who are more objects of our compassion than the wanton trespasser, who brings on himself the injury which he suffers. If an owner of a close cannot set spring guns, he cannot put glass bottles or spikes on the top of a wall, or even have a savage dog, to prevent persons from entering his yard. It has been said, in argument, that you may see the glass bottles or spikes; and it is admitted, that if the exact spot where these guns are set was pointed out to the trespasser, he could not maintain any action for the injury he received from one of them. As to seeing the glass bottles or spikes, that must depend on the circumstance whether it be light or dark at the time of the trespass. But what difference does it make, whether the trespasser be told the gun is set in such a spot, or that there are guns in different parts of such a field, if he has no right to go on any part of that field? It is absurd to say you may set the guns, provided you tell the trespasser exactly where they are set, because then the setting them could answer no purpose. My brother *Bayley* has illustrated this case, by the question which he asked, namely, Can you indict a man for putting spring guns in his enclosed field? I think the question put by Lord C. J. *Gibbs*, in the case of the Common Pleas, a still better illustration, viz.: Can you justify entering into enclosed lands, to take away guns so set? If both these questions must be answered in the negative, it cannot be unlawful to set spring guns in an enclosed field, at a distance from any road, giving such notice that they are set as to render it in the highest degree probable that all persons in the neighbourhood must know that they are so set. Humanity requires that the fullest notice possible should be given: and the law of *England* will not sanction what is inconsistent with humanity. It has been said in argument, that it is a principle of law, that you cannot do indirectly what you are not permitted to do directly. This principle is not applicable to the case. You cannot shoot a man that comes on your land, because you may turn him off by means less hurtful to him; and, therefore, if you saw him walking in your field, and were to invite him to proceed on his walk, knowing that he must tread on a wire, and so shoot himself with a spring gun, you would be liable to all the consequences that would follow. The invitation to him to pursue his walk is doing indirectly what, by drawing the trigger of a gun with your own hand, is done directly. But the case is just the reverse, if, instead of inviting him to walk on your land, you tell him to keep off, and warn him of what will follow if he does not. It is also said, that it is a maxim of law, that you must so use your own property as not to injure another's. This maxim I admit; but I deny its application to the case of a man who comes to trespass on my property. It applies only to cases where a man has only a transient property, such as in the air or water that passes over his land, and which he must not corrupt by nuisance or where a man has a qualified property, as in land near another's ancient windows, or in land over which another has a right of way In the first case, he must do nothing on his land to stop the light of the windows, or, in the second, to obstruct the way. This case has been argued, as if it appeared in it that the guns were set to preserve game; but that is not so: they were set to prevent trespasses on the lands of the defendant. Without, however, saying in whom the property of game is vested, I say, that a man has a right to keep persons off his lands, in order to preserve the game. Much money is expended in the protection of game; and it would be hard, if, in one night, when the keepers are absent, a gang of poachers might destroy what has been kept at so much cost. If you do not allow men of landed estates to preserve their game, you will not prevail on them to reside in the country. Their poor neighbours will thus lose their protection and kind offices; and the government the support that it derives from an independent, enlightened, and unpaid magistracy."

As Mr. Justice Best denies that he did say what a very respectable and grave law publication reported him to have said, and as Mr. Chetwynd and his reporter have made no attempt to vindicate their report, of course our observations cease to be applicable. There is certainly nothing in the term report of Mr. Justice Best's speech which calls for any degree of moral criticism;—nothing but what a respectable and temperate judge might fairly have uttered. Had such been the report cited in Burn, it never would have drawn from us one syllable of reprehension.

We beg leave, however, to observe, that we have never said that it was Mr. Justice Best's opinion, as reported in Chetwynd, that a man might be put to death *without notice*, but without *warning;* by which we meant a very different thing. If notice was given on boards, that certain grounds were guarded by watchmen with fire-arms, the watchmen, feeling perhaps some little respect for human life, would probably call out to the man to stand and deliver himself up:—"Stop, or I'll shoot you!" "Stand, or you are a dead man!"—or some such compunctious phrases as the law compels living machines to use. But the trap can give no such warning—can present to the intruder no alternative of death or surrender. Now, these different modes of action in the dead or the living guard, is what we alluded to in the words *without warning*. We meant to characterize the ferocious, unrelenting nature of the means used—and the words are perfectly correct and applicable, after all the printed *notices* in the world. Notice is the communication of something about to happen, after some little interval of time. Warning is the communication of some imminent danger. Nobody gives another notice that he will immediately shoot him through the head—or warns him that he will be a dead man in less than thirty years. This, and not the disingenuous purpose ascribed to us by Mr. Justice Best, is the explanation of the offending words. We are thoroughly aware that Mr. Justice Best was an advocate for notice, and never had the most distant intention of representing his opinion otherwise: and we really must say, that (if the report had been correct) there never was a judicial speech where there was so little necessity for having recourse to the arts of misrepresentation. We are convinced, however, that the report is not correct—and we are heartily glad it is not. There is in the Morning Chronicle an improper and offensive phrase, which (now we know Mr. Justice Best's style better) we shall attribute to the reporters, and pass over without further notice. It would seem, from the complaint of the learned judge, that we had omitted something in the middle of the quotation from Chetwynd; whereas we have quoted every word of the speech as Chetwynd has given it, and only began our quotation after the preliminary observations, because we had not the most distant idea of denying that Mr. Justice Best considered ample notice as necessary to the legality of these proceedings.

There are passages in the Morning Chronicle already quoted, and in the term report, which we must take the liberty of putting in juxtaposition to each other.

Mr. Justice Best in the Morning Chronicle of the 4th of June, 1821.

It is not necessary for me in this place to say, that no man entertains more horror of the doctrine I am supposed to have laid down than I do, that the life of man is to be treated lightly and indifferently, in comparison with the preservation of game and the amusement of sporting—that the laws of humanity are to be violated for the sake merely of preserving the amusement of game. I am sure no man can justly impute to me such wicked doctrines; it is unnecessary for me to say I entertain no such sentiments.

In Barnewall and Alderson there is a correct report of that case.—*Morn. Chron.*

Mr. Justice Best in the Term Reports, Barnewall and Alderson.

When the owner and his servants are absent at the time of the trespass, it can only be repelled by the terror of spring guns, or other instruments of the same kind. There is, in such cases, no possibility of proportioning the resisting force to the obstinacy and violence of the trespasser, as the owner of the close may, and is required to do, when he is present.—317.

Without saying in whom the property of game is vested, I say that a man has a right to keep persons off his lands, in order to preserve the game. Much money is expended on the protection of game; and it would be hard if, in one night, when the *keepers are absent*, a gang of poachers might destroy what has been kept at so much cost.—320.

If an owner of a close cannot set spring guns, he cannot put glass bottles or spikes on the top of a wall.—318.

If both these questions must be answered in the negative, it cannot be unlawful to set spring guns in an enclosed field, at a distance from any road; giving such notice that they are set, as to render it in the highest degree probable that all persons in the neighbourhood must know they are so set. Humanity requires that the fullest notice possible should be given; and the law of England will not sanction what is inconsistent with humanity.—*Barnewall and Alderson*, 319.

There is, perhaps, some little inconsistency in these opposite extracts; but we have not the smallest wish to insist upon it. We are thoroughly and honestly convinced that Mr. Justice Best's horror at the destruction of human life for the mere preservation of game is quite sincere. It is impossible, indeed, that any human being, of common good nature, could entertain a different feeling upon the subject, when it is earnestly pressed upon him; and though, perhaps, there may be judges upon the bench more remarkable for imperturbable apathy, we never heard Mr. Justice Best accused of ill-nature. In condescending to notice our observations, in destroying the credit of Chetwynd's report, and in withdrawing the canopy of his name from the bad passions of country gentlemen; he has conferred a real favour upon the public.

Mr. Justice Best, however, must excuse us for saying, that we are not in the slightest degree convinced by his reasoning. We shall suppose a fifth judge to have delivered his opinion in the case of *Ilott against Wilkes*, and to have expressed himself in the following manner. But we must caution Mr. Chetwynd against introducing this fifth judge in his next edition of Burn's Justice; and we assure him that he is only an imaginary personage.

"My Brother Best justly observes, that prevention of intrusion upon private property is a right which every proprietor may act upon, and use force to vindicate—the force absolutely necessary for such vindication. If any man intrude upon another's lands, the proprietor must first desire him to go off, then lay hands upon the intruder, then push him off; and if that will not do, call in aid or other assistance, before he uses a dangerous weapon. If the proprietor uses more force than is absolutely necessary, he renders himself responsible for all the consequences of the excess. In this doctrine I cordially concur; and admire (I am sure, with him) the sacred regard which our law everywhere exhibits for the life and safety of man—its tardiness and reluctance to proceed to extreme violence; but my learned brother then observes as follows:—'It is evident, also, that this doctrine is only applicable to trespasses committed in the presence of the owner of the property trespassed upon. When the owner and his servants are absent at the time of the trespass, it can only be repelled by the terror of spring guns, or other instruments of the same kind.' If Mr. Justice Best means, by the *terror of the spring guns*, the mere alarm that the notice excites—or the powder without the bullets—noise without danger—it is not worth while to raise an argument upon the point; for, absent or present, notice or no notice, such means must always be lawful. But if my brother Best means that in the absence of the proprietor, the intruder may be killed by such instruments, after notice, this is a doctrine to which I never can assent; because it rests the life and security of the trespasser upon the accident of the proprietor's presence. In that presence there must be a most cautious and nicely graduated scale of admonition and harmless compulsion; the feelings and safety of the intruder are to be studiously consulted; but if business or pleasure call the proprietor away, the intruder may be instantly shot dead by machinery. Such a state of law, I must be permitted to say, is too incongruous for this or any other country.

"If the alternative is the presence of the owner and his servants or such dreadful consequences as these, why are the owner or his servants allowed to be absent? If the ultimate object in preventing such intrusions is pleasure in sporting, it is better that pleasure should be rendered more expensive, than that the life of man should be rendered so precarious. But why is it impossible to proportion the resisting force to the obstinacy of the trespasser in the absence of the proprietor? Why may not an intruder be let gently down into five feet of liquid mud?—why not caught in a box which shall detain him till the next morning?—why not held in a toothless trap till the proprietor arrives?—such traps as are sold in all the iron shops in this city? We are bound, according to my brother Best, to inquire if these means have been previously resorted to; for upon his own principle, greater violence must not be used, where less will suffice for the removal of the intruder.

"There are crops, I admit, of essential importance to agriculture, which will not bear the expense of eternal vigilance; and if there are districts where such crops are exposed to such serious and disheartening depredation, that may be a good reason for additional severity; but then it must be the severity of the legislator, and not of the proprietor. If the legislature enacts fine and imprisonment as the punishment for stealing turnips, it is not to be endured that the proprietor should award to this crime the punishment of death. If the fault is not sufficiently prevented by the punishments already in existence, he must wait till the frequency and flagrancy of the offence attract the notice, and stimulate the penalties of those who make laws. He must not make laws (and those very bloody laws) for himself.

"I do not say that the setter of the trap or gun allures the trespasser into it; but I say that the punishment he intends for the man who trespasses after notice, is death. He covers his spring gun with furze, and gives it the most natural appearance he can; and in that gun he places the slugs by which he means *to kill* the trespasser. This killing of an unchallenged, unresisting person, I really cannot help considering to be as much murder as if the proprietor had shot the trespasser with his gun. Giving it all the attention in my power, I am utterly at a loss to distinguish between the two cases. Does it signify whose hand or whose foot pulls the string which moves the trigger?—the real murderer is he who prepares the instrument of death, and places it in a position that such hand or foot may touch it, for the purposes of destruction. My brother Holroyd says, the trespasser who has had a notice of guns being set in the wood is the real voluntary agent who pulls the trigger. But I most certainly think that he is not. He is the animal agent, but not the rational agent—he does not intend to put himself to death; but he foolishly trusts in his chance of escaping, and is any thing but a voluntary agent in firing the gun. If a trespasser were to rush into a wood, meaning to seek his own destruction—to hunt for the wire, and when found, to pull it, he would indeed be the agent, in the most philosophical sense of the word. But, after entering the wood, he does all he can to avoid the gun keeps clear of every suspicious place, and is baffled only by the superior cunning of him who planted the gun. How the firing of the gun then can be called his act—his voluntary act—I am at a loss to conceive. The practice has unfortunately become so common, that the first person convicted of such a murder, and acting under the delusion of right, might be a fit object for royal mercy. Still, in my opinion, such an act must legally be considered as murder.

"It has been asked, if it be an indictable offence to set such guns in a man's own ground: but let me first put a much greater question—Is it murder to kill any man with such instruments? If it is, it must be indictable to set them. To place an instrument for the purpose of committing murder, and to surrender (as in such cases you must surrender) all control over its operation, is clearly an indictable offence.

"All my brother judges have delivered their opinions as if these guns were often set for the purposes of terror, and not of destruction. To this I can only say, that the moment any man puts a bullet into his spring gun, he has some other purpose than that of terror; and if he does not put a bullet there, he can never be the subject of argument in this court.

"My Lord Chief Justice can see no distinction between the case of tenter-hooks upon a wall, and the placing of spring guns, as far as the lawfulness of both is concerned. But the distinctions I take between the case of tenter-hooks upon a wall, and the setting of spring guns, are founded—1st, in the magnitude of the evil inflicted; 2dly, in the great difference of the notice which the trespasser receives; 3dly, in the very different evidence of criminal intention in the trespasser; 4thly, in the greater value of the property invaded; 5thly, in the greater antiquity of the abuse. To cut the fingers, or to tear the hand, is of course a more pardonable injury than to kill. The trespasser, in the daytime, sees the spikes; and by day or night, at all events, he sees or feels the wall. It is impossible he should not understand the nature of such a prohibition, or imagine that his path lies over this wall; whereas the victim of the spring gun may have gone astray, may not be able to read, or may first cross the armed soil in the night time, when he cannot read;—and so he is absolutely without any notice at all. In the next place, the slaughtered man may be perfectly innocent in his purpose, which the scaler of the walls cannot be. No man can get to the top of a garden wall without a criminal purpose. A garden, by the common consent and feeling of mankind, contains more precious materials than a wood, or a field, and may seem to justify a greater jealousy and care. Lastly, and for these reasons, perhaps, the practice of putting spikes and glass bottles has prevailed for this century past; and the right so to do has become, from time, and the absence of cases, (for the plaintiff, in such a case, must acknowledge himself a thief,) inveterate. But it is quite impossible, because in some trifling instances, and in much more pardonable circumstances, private vengeance has usurped upon the province of law, that I can, from such slight abuses, confer upon private vengeance the power of life and death. On the contrary, I think it my imperious duty to contend, that punishment for such offences as these is to be measured by the law, and not by the exaggerated notions which any individual may form of the importance of his own pleasures. It is my duty, instead of making one abuse a reason for another, to recall the law back to its perfect state, and to restrain as much as possible the invention and use of private punishments. Indeed, if this wild sort of justice is to be tolerated, I see no sort of use in the careful adaptation of punishments to crimes, in the humane labours of the lawgiver. Every lord of a manor is his own Lycurgus, or rather his own Draco, and the great purpose of civil life is defeated. *Inter nova tormentorum genera machinasque exitiales, silent leges.*

"Whatever be the law, the question of humanity is a separate question. I shall not state all I think of that person, who, for the preservation of game, would doom the innocent—or the guilty intruder, to a sudden death. I will not, however (because I am silent respecting individuals), join in any undeserved panegyric of the humanity of the English law. I cannot say, at the same moment, that the law of England allows such machines to be set after public notice; and that the law of England sanctions nothing but what is humane. If the law sanctions such practices, it sanctions, in my opinion, what is to the last degree odious, unchristian, and inhumane.

"The case of the dog or bull I admit to be an analogous case to this: and I say, if a man were to keep a dog of great ferocity and power, for the express purpose of guarding against trespass in woods or fields, and that dog was *to kill* a trespasser, it would be murder in the person placing him there for such a purpose. It is indifferent to me whether the trespasser is slain by animals or machines, intentionally brought there for that purpose: he ought not to be *slain* at all. It is murder to use such a punishment for such an offence. If a man puts a ferocious dog in his *yard*, to guard his *house* from burglary, and that dog strays into the neighbouring field and there worries the man, there wants, in this case, the murderous and malicious spirit. The dog was placed in the yard for the legal purpose of guarding the house against burglary; for which crime, if caught in the act of perpetrating it, a man may legally be put to death. There was no primary intention here of putting *a mere trespasser* to death. So, if a man keep a ferocious bull, not for agricultural purposes, but for the *express purpose* of repelling trespassers, and that bull occasion the death of a trespasser, it is murder: the *intentional infliction of death by any means for such sort of offences constitutes the murder:* a right to kill for such reasons cannot be acquired by the foolhardiness of the trespasser, nor by any sort of notice or publicity. If a man were to blow a trumpet all over the country, and say that he would shoot any man who asked him how he did, would he acquire a right to do so by such notice? Does mere publication of an unlawful intention make the action lawful which follows? If notice is the principle which consecrates this mode of destroying human beings, I wish my brothers had been a little more clear, or a little more unanimous, as to what is meant by this notice. Must the notice be always actual, or is it sufficient that it is probable? May these guns act only against those who *have* read the notice, or against all who *might* have read the notice? The truth is, that the practice is so enormous, and the opinions of the most learned men so various, that a declaratory law upon the subject is imperiously required.* Common humanity required it, after the extraordinary difference of opinion which occurred in the case of Dean and Clayton.

"For these reasons, I am compelled to differ from my learned brothers. We have all, I am sure, the common object of doing justice in such cases as these; we can have no possible motive for doing otherwise. Where such a superiority of talents and numbers is against me, I must of course be wrong; but I think it better to publish my own errors, than to subscribe to opinions of the justice of which I am not convinced. To destroy a trespasser with such machines, I think would be murder; to set such uncontrollable machines for the purpose of committing this murder, I think would be indictable; and I am, therefore, of opinion, that he who suffers from such machines has a fair ground of action, in spite of any notice; for it is not in the power of notice to make them lawful."

* This has been done.

HAMILTON'S METHOD OF TEACHING LANGUAGES.*

[Edinburgh Review, 1826.]

We have nothing whatever to do with Mr. Hamilton personally. He may be the wisest or the weakest of men; most dexterous or most unsuccessful in the exhibition of his system; modest and proper, or prurient and preposterous in its commendation;—by none of these considerations is his system itself affected.

The proprietor of Ching's Lozenges must necessarily have recourse to a newspaper, to rescue from oblivion the merit of his vermifuge medicines. In the same manner, the Amboyna tooth-powder must depend upon the Herald and the Morning Post. Unfortunately, the system of Mr. Hamilton has been introduced to the world by the same means, and has exposed itself to those suspicions which hover over splendid discoveries of genius, detailed in the daily papers, and sold in sealed boxes at an infinite diversity of prices—but with a perpetual inclusion of the stamp, and with an equitable discount for undelayed payment.

It may have been necessary for Mr. Hamilton to have had recourse to these means of making known his discoveries, since he may not have had friends whose names and authority might have attracted the notice of the public; but it is a misfortune to which his system has been subjected, and a difficulty which it has still to overcome. There is also a singular and somewhat ludicrous condition of giving *warranted lessons;* by which is meant, we presume, that the money is to be returned, if the progress is not made. We should be curious to know how poor Mr. Hamilton would protect himself from some swindling scholar, who, having really learnt all that the master professed to teach, should counterfeit the grossest ignorance of the Gospel of St. John, and refuse to construe a single verse, or to pay a farthing?

Whether Mr. Hamilton's translations are good or bad, is not the question. The point to determine is, whether very close interlineal translations are helps in learning a language? not whether Mr. Hamilton has executed these translations faithfully and judiciously. Whether Mr. Hamilton is or is not the inventor of the system which bears his name, and what his claims to originality may be, are also questions of very second-rate importance; but they merit a few observations. That man is not the discoverer of any art who first says the thing; but he who says it so long, and so loud, and so clearly, that he compels mankind to hear him—the man who is so deeply impressed with the importance of the discovery that he will take no denial, but, at the risk of fortune and fame, pushes through all opposition, and is determined that what he thinks he has discovered shall not perish for want of a fair trial. Other persons had noticed the effect of coal-gas in producing light; but Winsor worried the town with bad English for three winters before he could attract any serious attention to his views. Many persons broke stone before Macadam, but Macadam felt the discovery more strongly, stated it more clearly, persevered in it with greater tenacity, wielded his hammer, in short, with greater force than other men, and finally succeeded in bringing his plan into general use.

Literal translations are not only not used in our public schools, but are generally discountenanced in them. A literal translation, or any translation of a school-book, is a contraband article in English schools, which a school-master would instantly seize, as a custom-house officer would a barrel of gin. Mr. Hamilton, on the other hand, maintains, by books and lectures, that all boys ought to be allowed to work with literal translations, and that it is by far the best method of learning a language. If Mr. Hamilton's system is just, it is sad trifling to deny his claim to originality, by stating that Mr. Locke has said the same thing, or that others have said the same thing, a century earlier than Hamilton. They have all said it so feebly, that their observations have passed *sub silentio;* and if Mr. Hamilton succeeds in being heard and followed, to him be the glory—because from him have proceeded the utility and the advantage.

The works upon this subject on this plan, published before the time of Mr. Hamilton, are Montanus's edition of the Bible, with Pignini's interlineary Latin version; Lubin's New Testament having the Greek interlined with Latin and German; Abbé L'Olivet's Pensées de Ciceron; and a French work by the Abbé Radonvilliers, Paris, 1768—and Locke upon Education.

One of the first principles of Mr. Hamilton is, to introduce very strict literal, interlinear translations, as aids to lexicons and dictionaries, and to make so much use of them as that the dictionary or lexicon will be for a long time little required. We will suppose the language to be the Italian, and the book selected to be the Gospel of St. John. Of this Gospel Mr. Hamilton has published a key, of which the following is an extract:—

"1 Nel principio era il Verbo, e il
In the beginning was the Word, and the
Verbo era appresso Dio, e il Verbo era Dio
Word was near to God, and the Word was God

* 1. *The Gospel of St. John, in Latin, adapted to the Hamiltonian System, by an Analytical and Interlineary Translation.* Executed under the immediate Direction of James Hamilton. London, 1824.

2. *The Gospel of St. John, adapted to the Hamiltonian System, by an Analytical and Interlineary Translation from the Italian, with full Instructions for its Use, even by those who are wholly ignorant of the Language. For the Use of Schools.* By James Hamilton, Author of the Hamiltonian System. London, 1825.

"2 Questo era nel principio appresso Dio.
This was in the beginning near to God.
"3 Per mezzo di lui tutte le cose furon
By means of him all the things were
fatte: e senza di lui nulla fu fatto di
made: and without of him nothing was made of
ciò, che è stato fatto.
that, which is been made.
"4 In lui era la vita, e la vita era
In him was the life, and the life was
la luce degli uomini:
the light of the men:
"5 E la luce splende tra le tenebre,
And the light shines among the darknesses,
e la tenebre hanno non ammessa la.
and the darknesses have not admitted her.
"6 Vi fu un uomo mandato da Dio che
There was a man sent by God, who
nomava si Giovanni.
did name himself John.
"7 Questo venne qual testimone, affin di
This came like as witness, in order of
rendere testimonianza alla luce, onde per
to render testimony to the light, whence by
mezzo di lui tutti credessero.
means of him all might believe."

In this way Mr. Hamilton contends (and appears to us to contend justly), that the language may be acquired with much greater ease and despatch, than by the ancient method of beginning with grammar, and proceeding with the dictionary. We will presume at present, that the only object is to read, not to write, or speak Italian, and that the pupil instructs himself from the key without a master, and is not taught in a class. We wish to compare the plan of finding the English word in such a literal translation, to that of finding it in dictionaries—and the method of ending with grammar, or of taking the grammar at an advanced period of knowledge in the language, rather than at the beginning. Every one will admit, that of all the disgusting labours of life, the labour of lexicon and dictionary is the most intolerable. Nor is there a greater object of compassion than a fine boy, full of animal spirits, set down in a bright sunny day, with an heap of unknown words before him, to be turned into English, before supper, by the help of a ponderous dictionary alone. The object in looking into a dictionary can only be to exchange an unknown sound for one that is known. Now, it seems indisputable, that the sooner this exchange is made the better. The greater the number of such exchanges which can be made in a given time, the greater is the progress, the more abundant the *copia verborum* obtained by the scholar. Would it not be of advantage if the dictionary at once opened at the required page, and if a self-moving index at once pointed to the requisite word? Is any advantage gained to the world by the time employed first in finding the letter P, and then in finding the three guiding letters P R I? This appears to us to be pure loss of time, justifiable only if it is inevitable; and even after this is done, what an infinite multitude of difficulties are heaped at once upon the wretched beginner! Instead of being reserved for his greater skill and maturity in the language, he must employ himself in discovering in which of many senses which his dictionary presents the word is to be used; in considering the case of the substantive, and the syntaxical arrangement in which it is to be placed, and the relation it bears to other words. The loss of time in the merely mechanical part of the old plan is immense. We doubt very much, if an average boy, between ten and fourteen, will look out or find more than sixty words in an hour; we say nothing at present of the time employed in thinking of the meaning of each word when he has found it, but of the mere naked discovery of the word in the lexicon or dictionary. It must be remembered, we say an *average* boy—not what Master Evans, the show boy, can do, nor what Master Macarthy, the boy who is whipt every day, can do, but some boy between Macarthy and Evans; and not what this medium boy can do, while his mastigophorous superior is frowning over him; but what he actually does, when left in the midst of noisy boys, and with a recollection, that, by sending to the neighbouring shop, he can obtain any quantity of unripe gooseberries upon credit. Now, if this statement be true, and if there are 10,000 words in the Gospel of St. John, here are 160 hours employed in the mere digital process of turning over leaves! But, in much less time than this, any boy of average quickness might learn, by the Hamiltonian method, to construe the whole four Gospels, with the greatest accuracy, and the most scrupulous correctness. The interlineal translation of course spares the trouble and time of this mechanical labour. Immediately under the Italian word is placed the English word. The unknown sound therefore is *instantly* exchanged for one that is known. The labour here spared is of the most irksome nature; and it is spared at a time of life the most averse to such labour; and so painful is this labour to many boys, that it forms an insuperable obstacle to their progress. They prefer to be flogged, or to be sent to sea. It is useless to say of any medicine that it is valuable, if it is so nauseous that the patient flings it away. You must give me, not the best medicine you have in your shop, but the best you can get me to take.

We have hitherto been occupied with finding the word; we will now suppose, after running a dirty finger down many columns, and after many sighs and groans, that the word is found. We presume the little fellow working in the true orthodox manner without any translation; he is in pursuit of the Greek word Βαλλω, and, after a long chase, seizes it as greedily as a bailiff possesses himself of a fugacious captain. But alas! the vanity of human wishes!—the never sufficiently to be pitied stripling has scarcely congratulated himself upon his success, when he finds Βαλλω to contain the following meanings in Hederick's Lexicon:—1. Jacio; 2. Jaculor; 3. Ferio; 4. Figo; 5. Saucio; 6. Attingo; 7. Projicio; 8. Emitto; 9. Profundo; 10. Pono; 11. Immitto; 12. Trado; 13. Committo; 14. Condo; 15. Ædifico; 16. Verso; 17. Flecto. Suppose the little rogue, not quite at home in the Latin tongue, to be desirous of affixing English significations to these various words, he has then, at the moderate rate of six meanings to every Latin word, one hundred and two meanings to the word Βαλλω; or if he is content with the Latin, he has then only seventeen.*

Words, in their origin, have a natural or primary sense. The accidental associations of the people who use it, afterwards give to that word a great number of secondary meanings. In some words the primary meaning is very common, and the secondary meaning very rare. In other instances it is just the reverse; and in very many the particular secondary meaning is pointed out by some preposition which accompanies it, or some case by which it is accompanied. But an accurate translation points these things out gradually as it proceeds. The common and most probable meanings of the word Βαλλω, or of any other word, are, in the Hamiltonian method, insensibly but surely fixed on the mind, which, by the lexicon method, must be done by a tentative process, frequently ending in gross error, noticed with peevishness, punished with severity, consuming a great deal of time, and for the most part only corrected, after all, by the accurate *vivâ voce* translation of the master—or, in other words, by the Hamiltonian method.

The recurrence to a translation is treated in our schools as a species of imbecility and meanness; just as if there was any other dignity here than utility, any other object in learning languages, than to turn something you do not understand, into something you do understand, and as if that was not the best method which effected this object in the shortest and simplest manner. Hear upon this point the judicious Locke:—"But if such a man cannot be got, who speaks good Latin, and being able to instruct your son in all these parts of knowledge, will undertake it by this method, the next best is to have him taught as near this way as may be—which is by taking some easy and pleasant book, such as Æsop's Fables, and writing the English translation (made as literal as it can be) in one line, and the Latin words which answer each of them just over it in another. These let him read every day over and over again, till he perfectly understands the Latin; and then go on to another fable, till he be also perfect in that, not omitting what he is already perfect in, but sometimes reviewing that, to keep it in his memory; and when he comes to write, let these be set him for copies, which, with the exercise of his hand, will also advance him in Latin. This being a more imperfect way than by talking Latin unto him, the formation of the verbs first, and afterwards the declensions of the nouns and pronouns perfectly learned by heart, may facilitate his acquaintance with the genius and manner of the Latin tongue, which varies the signification of verbs and nouns, not as the modern languages do, by particles prefixed, but by changing the last syllables. More than this of grammar I think he need not have till he can read himself 'Sanctii Minerva'—with Scioppius and Perigonius's notes."—*Locke on Education*, p. 74, folio.

Another recommendation which we have not mentioned in the Hamiltonian system is, that it can be combined, and is constantly combined, with the system of Lancaster. The Key is probably sufficient for those who have no access to classes and schools: but in an Hamiltonian school during the lesson, it is not left to the option of the child to trust to the Key alone. The master stands in the middle, translates accurately and literally the whole verse, and then asks the boys the English of separate words, or challenges them to join the words together, as he has done. A perpetual attention and activity is thus kept up. The master, or a scholar (turned into a temporary Lancasterian master), acts as a living lexicon; and, if the thing is well done, as a lively and animating lexicon. How is it possible to compare this with the solitary wretchedness of a poor lad of the desk and lexicon, suffocated with the nonsense of grammarians, overwhelmed with every species of difficulty disproportioned to his age, and driven by despair to peg top or marbles?

"Taking these principles as a basis, the teacher forms his class of *eight*, *ten*, *twenty* or *one hundred*. The number is of little moment, it being as easy to teach a greater as a smaller one, and brings them at once to the language itself, by reciting, with a loud articulate voice, the first verse thus:—*In* in, *principio* in beginning, *Verbum* Word, *erat* was, *et* and, *Verbum* Word, *erat* was, *apud* at, *Deum* God, *et* and, *Verbum* Word, *erat* was, *Deus* God. Having recited the verse once or twice himself, it is then recited *precisely* in the same manner by any person of the class whom he may judge most capable; the person copying his manner and intonations as much as possible.—When the verse has been thus recited, by *six* or *eight* persons of the class, the teacher recites the 2d verse in the same manner, which is recited as the former by any members of the class; and thus continues until he has recited from *ten* to *twelve* verses, which usually constitute the first lesson of one hour.—In three lessons, the first Chapter may be thus readily translated, the teacher gradually diminishing the number of repetitions of the same verse till the *fourth* lesson, when each member of the class translates his verse in turn from the mouth of the teacher; from which period *fifty*, *sixty*, or even *seventy*, verses may be translated in the time of a lesson, or one hour. At the *seventh* lesson, it is invariably found that the class can translate without the assistance of the teacher, farther than for occasional correction, and for those words which they may not have met in the preceding chapters. But, to accomplish this, it is absolutely necessary that every member of the class know *every word* of all the preceding lessons; which is, however, an easy task, the words being always taught him in class, and the pupil besides being able to refer

* In addition to the other needless difficulties and miseries entailed upon children who are learning languages, their Greek Lexicons give a Latin instead of an English translation; and a boy of twelve or thirteen years of age, whose attainments in Latin are of course but moderate, is expected to make it the vehicle of knowledge for other languages. This is setting the short-sighted and blear-eyed to lead the blind; and is one of those afflicting pieces of absurdity which escape animadversion, because they are, and have long been, of daily occurrence. Mr. Jones has published an English and Greek Lexicon, which we recommend to the notice of all persons engaged in education, and not sacramented against all improvement.

to the key whenever he is at a loss—the key translated in the very words which the teacher has used in the class, from which, as was before remarked, he must never deviate.—In *ten* lessons, it will be found that the class can readily translate the whole of the Gospel of St. John, which is called the first section of the course.—Should any delay, from any cause, prevent them, it is in my classes always for account of teacher, who gives the extra lesson or lessons always *gratis*.—It cannot be too deeply impressed on the mind of the pupil, that *a perfect knowledge of every word* of his first section is most important to the ease and comfort of his future progress.—At the end of *ten* lessons, or first section, the custom of my establishments is to give the pupil the *Epitome Historiæ Sacræ*, which is provided with a key in the same manner.—It was first used in our classes for the first and second sections; we now teach it in one section of *ten* lessons, which we find easier than to teach it in two sections before the pupil has read the Testament.—When he has read the Epitome, it will be then time to give him the theory of the verbs and other words which change their terminations.—He has already acquired a good practical knowledge of these things; the theory becomes then very easy.—A grammar containing the declensions and conjugations, and printed specially for my classes, is then put into the pupil's hands, (not to be got by heart, nothing is ever got by rote on this system,) but that he may comprehend more readily his teacher who lectures on grammar generally, but especially on the verbs. From this time, that is, from the beginning of the *third* section, the pupil studies the theory and construction of the language as well as its practice. For this purpose he reads the ancient authors, beginning with Cæsar, which, together with the *Selecta e Profanis*, fills usefully the *third* and *fourth* sections. When these with the preceding books are well known, the pupil will find little difficulty in reading the authors usually read in schools. The *fifth* and *sixth* sections consist of Virgil and Horace, enough of which is read to enable the pupil to read them with facility, and to give him correct ideas of Prosody and Versification. Five or six months, with mutual attention on the part of the pupil and teacher, will be found sufficient to acquire a knowledge of this language, which hitherto has *rarely* been the result of as many years."

We have before said, that the Hamiltonian system must not depend upon Mr. Hamilton's method of carrying it into execution; for instance, he banishes from his schools the effects of emulation. The boys do not take each other's places. This, we think, is a sad absurdity. A cook might as well resolve to make bread without fermentation, as a pedagogue to carry on a school without emulation. It must be a sad doughy lump without this vivifying principle. Why are boys to be shut out from a class of feelings to which society owes so much, and upon which their conduct in future life must (if they are worth any thing) be so closely constructed? Poet A writes verses to outshine poet B. Philosopher C sets up roasting Titanium, and boiling Chromium, that he may be thought more of than philosopher D. Mr. Jackson strives to out-paint Sir Thomas; Sir Thomas Lethbridge to overspeak Mr. Canning; and so society gains good chemists, poets, painters, speakers, and orators; and why are not boys to be emulous as well as men?

If a boy were in Paris, would he learn the language better by shutting himself up to read French books with a dictionary, or by conversing freely with all whom he met? and what is conversation but an Hamiltonian school? Every man you meet is a living lexicon and grammar—who is perpetually changing your English into French, and perpetually instructing you, in spite of yourself, in the terminations of French substantives and verbs. The analogy is still closer, if you converse with persons of whom you can ask questions, and who will be at the trouble of correcting you. What madness would it be to run away from these pleasing facilities, as too dangerously easy—to stop your ears, to double-lock the door, and to look out *chickens*, *taking a walk*, and *fine weather*, in Boyer's Dictionary—and then, by the help of Chambaud's Grammar, to construct a sentence which should signify, "*Come to my house, and eat some chickens, if it is fine?*" But there is in England almost a love of difficulty and needless labour. We are so resolute and industrious in raising up impediments which ought to be overcome, that there is a sort of suspicion against the removal of these impediments, and a notion that the advantage is not fairly come by without the previous toil. If the English were in a paradise of spontaneous productions, they would continue to dig and plough, though they were never a peach nor a pine-apple the better for it.

A principal point to attend to in the Hamiltonian system, is the prodigious number of words and phrases which pass through the boy's mind, compared with those which are presented to him by the old plan. As a talkative boy learns French sooner in France than a silent boy, so a translator of books learns sooner to construe, the more he translates. An Hamiltonian makes, in six or seven lessons, three or four hundred times as many exchanges of English for French or Latin, as a grammar schoolboy can do; and if he loses 50 per cent. of all he hears, his progress is still, beyond all possibility of comparison, more rapid.

As for pronunciation of living languages, we see no reason why that consideration should be introduced in this place. We are decidedly of opinion, that all living languages are best learned in the country where they are spoken, or by living with those who come from that country; but if that cannot be, Mr. Hamilton's method is better than the grammar and dictionary method. *Cæteris paribus*, Mr. Hamilton's method, as far as French is concerned, would be better in the hands of a Frenchman, and his Italian method in the hands of an Italian; but all this has nothing to do with the system.

"Have I read through Lilly?—have I learned by heart that most atrocious momument of absurdity, the Westminster Grammar?—have I been whipt for the substantives?—whipt for the verbs?—and whipt for and with the interjections?—have I picked the sense slowly, and word by word, out of Hederick?—and shall my son Daniel be exempt from all this misery?—Shall a little unknown person in Cecil Street, Strand, No. 25, pretend to tell me that all this is unnecessary?—Was it possible that I might have been spared all this?—The whole system is nonsense, and the man an impostor. If there had been any truth in it, it must have occurred to some one else before this period."—This is a very common style of observation upon Mr. Hamilton's system, and by no means an uncommon wish of the mouldering and decaying part of mankind, that the next generation should not enjoy any advantages from which they themselves have been precluded.—*"Ay, ay, it's all mighty well—but I went through this myself, and I am determined my children shall do the same."* We are convinced that a great deal of opposition to improvement proceeds from this principle. Crabbe might make a good picture of an unbenevolent old man, slowly retiring from this sublunary scene, and lamenting that the coming race of men would be less bumped on the roads, better lighted in the streets, and less tormented with grammars and lexicons, than in the preceding age. A great deal of compliment to the wisdom of ancestors, and a great degree of alarm at the dreadful spirit of innovation, are soluble into mere jealousy and envy.

But what is to become of a boy who has no difficulties to grapple with? How enervated will that understanding be, to which every thing is made so clear, plain, and easy;—no hills to walk up, no chasms to step over; every thing graduated, soft, and smooth. All this, however, is an objection to the multiplication table, to Napier's bones, and to every invention for the abridgment of human labour. There is no dread of any lack of difficulties. Abridge intellectual labour by any process you please—multiply mechanical powers to any extent—there will be sufficient, and infinitely more than sufficient, of laborious occupation for the mind and body of man. Why is the boy to be idle?—By and by comes the book without a key; by and by comes the lexicon. They do come at last—though at a better period. But if they did not come—if they were useless, if language could be attained without them—would any human being wish to retain difficulties for their own sake, which led to nothing useful, and by the annihilation of which our faculties were left to be exercised, by difficulties which *do* lead to something useful—by mathematics, natural philosophy, and every branch of useful knowledge? Can any one be so anserous as to suppose, that the faculties of young men cannot be exercised, and their industry and activity called into proper action, because Mr. Hamilton teaches, in three or four years, what has (in a more vicious system) demanded seven or eight? Besides, even in the Hamiltonian method it is very easy for one boy to outstrip another. Why may not a clever and ambitious boy employ three hours upon his key by himself, while another boy has only employed one? There is plenty of corn to thrash, and of chaff to be winnowed away, in Mr. Hamilton's system; the difference is, that every blow tells, because it is properly directed. In the old way, half their force was lost in air. There is a mighty foolish apophthegm of Dr. Bell's,* that it is not what is done for a boy that is of importance, but what a boy does for himself. This is just as wise as to say, that it is not the breeches which are made for a boy that can cover his nakedness, but the breeches he makes for himself. All this entirely depends upon a comparison of the time saved, by showing the boy how to do a thing, rather than by leaving him to do it for himself. Let the object be, for example, to make a pair of shoes. The boy will effect this object much better if you show him how to make the shoes, than if you merely give him wax, thread, and leather, and leave him to find out all the ingenious abridgments of labour which have been discovered by experience. The object is to turn Latin into English. The scholar will do it much better and sooner if the word is found for him, than if he finds it—much better and sooner if you point out the effect of the terminations, and the nature of the syntax, than if you leave him to detect them for himself. The thing *is* at last done *by the pupil himself*—for he reads the language—which was the thing to be done. All the help he has received has only enabled him to make a more economical use of his time, and to gain his end sooner. Never be afraid of wanting difficulties for your pupil; if means are rendered more easy, more will be expected. The animal will be compelled, or induced to do all that he can do. Macadam has made the roads better. Dr. Bell would have predicted, that the horses would get too fat; but the actual result is, that they are compelled to go ten miles an hour instead of eight.

"For teaching children, this, too, I think is to be observed, that, in most cases, where they stick, they are not to be farther puzzled, by putting them upon finding it out themselves; as by asking such questions as these, viz.—which is the nominative case in the sentence they are to construe? or demanding what 'aufero' signifies, to lead them to the knowledge what 'abstulere' signifies, &c., when they cannot readily tell. This wastes time only in disturbing them; for whilst they are learning, and apply themselves with attention, they are to be kept in good humour, and every thing made easy to them, and as pleasant as possible. Therefore, wherever they are at a stand, and are willing to go forwards, help them presently over the difficulty, without any rebuke or chiding; remembering that, where harsher ways are taken, they are the effect only of pride and peevishness in the teacher, who expects children should instantly be masters of as much as he knows; whereas he should rather consider, that his business is to settle in them *habits*, not angrily to inculcate *rules*."—*Locke on Education*, p. 74.

* A very foolish old gentleman, seized on eagerly by the Church of England to defraud Lancaster of his discovery.

Suppose the first five books of Herodotus to be acquired by a key, or literal translation after the method of Hamilton, so that the pupil could construe them with the greatest accuracy;—we do not pretend, because the pupil could construe this book, that he could construe any other book equally easy; we merely say, that the pupil has acquired, by these means, a certain *copia verborum*, and a certain practical knowledge of grammar, which must materially diminish the difficulty of reading the next book; that his difficulties diminish in a compound ratio with every fresh book he reads with a key—till at last he reads any common book, without a key—and that he attains this last point of perfection in a time incomparably less, and with difficulties incomparably smaller, than in the old method.

There are a certain number of French books, which when a boy can construe accurately, he may be said, for all purposes of reading, to be master of the French language. No matter how he has attained this power of construing the books. If you try him thoroughly, and are persuaded he is perfectly master of the books—then he possesses the power in question—he understands the language. Let these books, for the sake of the question, be Telemachus, the History of Louis XIV., the Henriade, the Plays of Racine, and the Revolutions of Vertot. We would have Hamiltonian keys to all these books, and the Lancasterian method of instruction. We believe these books would be mastered in one-sixth part of the time, by these means, that they would be by the old method of looking out the words in the dictionary, and then coming to say the lesson to the master; and we believe that the boys, long before they came to the end of this series of books, would be able to do without their keys—to fling away their cork-jackets, and to swim alone. But boys who learn a language in four or five months, it is said, are apt to forget it again. Why, then, does not a young person, who has been five or six months in Paris, forget his French four or five years afterwards? It has been obtained without any of that labour, which the objectors to the Hamiltonian system deem to be so essential to memory. It has been obtained in the midst of tea and bread and butter, and yet is in a great measure retained for a whole life. In the same manner, the pupils of this new school use a colloquial living dictionary, and, from every principle of youthful emulation, contend with each other in catching the interpretation, and in applying to the lesson before them.

"If you wish boys to remember any language, make the acquisition of it very tedious and disgusting." This seems to be an odd rule: but if it is good for language, it must be good also for every species of knowledge—music, mathematics, navigation, architecture. In all these sciences aversion should be the parent of memory—impediment the cause of perfection. If difficulty is the cause of memory, the boy who learns with the greatest difficulty will remember with the greatest tenacity;—in other words, the acquisitions of a dunce will be greater and more important than those of a clever boy. Where is the love of difficulty to end? Why not leave a boy to compose his own dictionary and grammar? It is not what is done for a boy, but what he does for himself, that is of any importance. Are there difficulties enough in the old method of acquiring languages? Would it be better if the difficulties were doubled, and thirty years given to languages, instead of fifteen? All these arguments presume the difficulty to be got over, and then the memory to be improved. But what if the difficulty is shrunk from? What if it puts an end to power, instead of increasing it; and extinguishes, instead of exciting, application? And when these effects are produced, you not only preclude all hopes of learning, or language, but you put an end for ever to all literary habits, and to all improvements from study. The boy who is lexicon-struck in early youth looks upon all books afterwards with horror, and goes over to the blockheads. Every boy would be pleased with books, and pleased with school, and be glad to forward the views of his parents, and obtain the praise of his master, if he found it possible to make tolerably easy progress; but he is driven to absolute despair by gerunds, and wishes himself dead! Progress is pleasure—activity is pleasure. It is impossible for a boy not to make progress, and not to be active in the Hamiltonian method; and this pleasing state of mind we contend to be more favourable to memory, than the languid, jaded spirit which much commerce with lexicons never fails to produce.

Translations are objected to in schools justly enough, when they are paraphrases and not translations. It is impossible, from a paraphrase or very loose translation, to make any useful progress—they retard rather than accelerate a knowledge of the language to be acquired, and are the principal causes of the discredit into which translations have been brought, as instruments of education.

> Infandum Regina jubes renovare dolorem.
> Regina, jubes renovare dolorem infandum.

Oh! Queen, thou orderest to renew grief not to be spoken of.

Oh! Queen, in pursuance of your commands, I enter upon the narrative of misfortunes almost too great for utterance.

The first of these translations leads us directly to the explication of a foreign language, as the latter insures a perfect ignorance of it.

It is difficult enough to introduce any useful novelty in education without enhancing its perils by needless and untenable paradox. Mr. Hamilton has made an assertion in his Preface to the Key of the Italian Gospel, which has no kind of foundation in fact, and which has afforded a conspicuous mark for the aim of his antagonists.

"I have said that each word is translated by its *one sole* undeviating meaning, assuming, as an incontrovertible principle in all languages, that, with very few exceptions, each word has one meaning only, and can usually be rendered correctly into another by one word only, which one word should serve for its representative at at all times and on all occasions."

Now, it is probable that each word had one

meaning only in its origin; but metaphor and association are so busy with human speech, that the same word comes to serve in a vast variety of senses, and continues to do so long after the metaphors and associations which called it into this state of activity are buried in oblivion. Why may not *jubeo* be translated order as well as command, or *dolorem* rendered *grief* as well as *sorrow?* Mr. Hamilton has expressed himself loosely; but he perhaps means no more than to say, that in school translations, the metaphysical meaning should never be adopted, when the word can be rendered by its primary signification. We shall allow him, however, to detail his own method of making the translation in question.

"Translations on the Hamiltonian system, according to which this book is translated, must not be confounded with translations made according to Locke, Clarke, Sterling, or even according to Dumarsais, Fremont, and a number of other Frenchmen, who have made what have been and are yet sometimes called *literal*, and interlineal translations. The latter are, indeed, *interlineal*, but no *literal* translation had ever appeared in any language before those called Hamiltonian, that is, before my Gospel of St. John from the French, the Greek, and Latin Gospels, published in London, and L'Hommond's Epitome of the Historia Sacra. These and these only were and are truly literal; that is to say, that every word is rendered in English by a corresponding part of speech, that the grammatical analysis of the phrase is never departed from; that the case of every noun, pronoun, adjective, or particle, and the mood, tense, and person of every verb, are accurately pointed out by appropriate and unchanging signs, so that a grammarian not understanding one word of Italian, would, on reading any part of the translation here given, be instantly able to parse it. In the translations above alluded to, an attempt is made to preserve the correctness of the language into which the different works are translated, but the wish to conciliate this correctness with a literal translation, has only produced a barbarous and uncouth idiom, while it has in every case deceived the unlearned pupil by a translation altogether false and incorrect. Such translations may, indeed, give an idea of what is contained in the book translated, but they will not assist, or at least very little, in enabling the pupil to make out the exact meaning of each word, which is the principal object of Hamiltonian translations. The reader will understand this better by an illustration: A gentleman has lately given a translation of Juvenal according to the plan of the above-mentioned authors, beginning with the words *semper ego*, which he joins and translates, 'shall I always be'—if his intention were to teach Latin words, he might as well have said, 'shall I always eat beef-steaks?'—True, there is nothing about beef-steaks in *semper ego*, but neither is there about 'shall be:' the whole translation is on the same plan, that is to say, that there is not one line of it correct, I had almost said one word, on which the pupil can rely, as the exact equivalent in English of the Latin word above it. Not so the translation here given.

"As the object of the author has been that the pupil should know every word as well as he knows it himself, he has uniformly given it the one sole, precise meaning which it has in our language, sacrificing everywhere the beauty, the idiom, and the correctness of the English language to the original, in order to show the perfect idiom, phraseology, and picture of that original as in a glass. So far is this carried, that where the English language can express the precise meaning of the Italian phrase only by a barbarism, this barbarism is employed without scruple—as thus; 'e le tenebre non l'hanno ammessa.'—Here the word *tenebre* being plural, if you translate it darkness, you not only give a false translation of the word itself, which is used by the Italians in the plural number, but what is much more important, you lead the pupil into an error about its government, it being the nominative case to *hanno*, which is the third person plural; it is therefore translated not darkness, but darknesses."

To make these keys perfect, we rather think there should be a free translation added to the literal one. Not a paraphrase, but only so free as to avoid any awkward or barbarous expression. The comparison between the free and the literal translation would immediately show to young people the peculiarities of the language in which they were engaged.

Literal translation or key—*Oh! Queen, thou orderest me to renew grief not to be spoken of.*

Free—"Oh! Queen, thou orderest me to renew my grief, too great for utterance."

The want of this accompanying free translation is not felt in keys of the Scriptures, because, in fact, the English Bible is a free translation, great part of which the scholar remembers. But in a work entirely unknown, of which a key was given, as full of awkward and barbarous expressions as a key certainly ought to be, a scholar might be sometimes puzzled to arrive at the real sense. We say as full of awkward and barbarous expressions as it ought to be, because we thoroughly approve of Mr. Hamilton's plan, of always sacrificing English and elegance to sense, when they cannot be united in the key. We are rather sorry Mr. Hamilton's first essay has been in a translation of the Scriptures, because every child is so familiar with them, that it may be difficult to determine whether the apparent progress is ancient recollection or recent attainment; and because the Scriptures are so full of Hebraisms and Syriacisms, and the language so different from that of Greek authors, that it does not secure a knowledge of the language equivalent to the time employed upon it.

The keys hitherto published by Mr. Hamilton are the Greek, Latin, French, Italian, and German keys to the Gospel of St. John, Perrin's Fables, Latin Historia Sacra, Latin, French, and Italian Grammar, and Studia Metrica. One of the difficulties under which the system is labouring, is a want of more keys. Some of the best Greek and Roman classics should be immediately published, with keys, and by very good scholars. We shall now lay before our readers an extract from one of the public papers respecting the progress made in the Hamiltonian schools.

"*Extract from the Morning Chronicle of Wednesday, November,* 16*th*, 1825.—*Hamiltonian System.*—We yesterday were present at an examination of eight lads who have been under Mr. Hamilton since some time in the month of May last, with a view to ascertain the efficacy of his system in communicating a knowledge of languages. These eight lads, all of them between the ages of twelve and fourteen, are the children of poor people, who, when they were first placed under Mr. Hamilton, possessed no other instruction than common reading and writing. They were obtained from a common country school, through the interposition of a member of Parliament, who takes an active part in promoting charity schools throughout the country; and the choice was determined by the consent of the parents, and not by the cleverness of the boys.

"They have been employed in learning Latin, French, and latterly Italian; and yesterday they were examined by several distinguished individuals, among whom we recognized John Smith, Esq. M. P.; G. Smith, Esq. M. P.; Mr. J. Mill, the historian of British India; Major Camac; Major Thompson; Mr. Cowell, &c. &c. They first read different portions of the Gospel of St. John in Latin, and of Cæsar's Commentaries, selected by the visitors. The translation was executed with an ease which it would be in vain to expect in any of the boys who attend our common schools, even in their third or fourth year; and proved, that the principle of exciting the attention of boys to the utmost, during the process by which the meaning of the words is fixed in their memory, had given them a great familiarity with so much of the language as is contained in the books above alluded to. Their knowledge of the parts of speech was respectable, but not so remarkable; as the Hamiltonian system follows the natural mode of acquiring language, and only employs the boys in analyzing, when they have already attained a certain familiarity with any language.

"The same experiments were repeated in French and Italian with the same success, and, upon the whole, we cannot but think the success has been complete. It is impossible to conceive a more impartial mode of putting any system to the test, than to make such an experiment on the children of our peasantry."

Into the truth of this statement we have personally inquired, and it seems to us to have fallen short of the facts, from the laudable fear of overstating them. The lads selected for the experiment were parish boys of the most ordinary description, reading English worse than Cumberland curates, and totally ignorant of the rudiments of any other language. They were purposely selected for the experiment by a gentleman who defrayed its expense, and who had the strongest desire to put strictly to the test the efficacy of the Hamiltonian system. The experiment was begun the middle of May, 1825, and concluded on the day of November in the same year mentioned in the extract, exactly six months after. The Latin books set before them were the Gospel of St. John, and parts of Cæsar's Commentaries; some Italian book or books (what we know not), and a selection of French histories. The visitors put the boys on where they pleased, and the translation was (as the reporter says) executed with an ease which it would be vain to expect in any of the boys who attend our common schools, even in their third or fourth year.*

From experiments and observations which have fallen under our own notice, we do not scruple to make the following assertions. If there were keys to the four Gospels, as there is to that of St. John, any boy or girl of thirteen years of age, and of moderate capacity, studying four hours a day, and beginning with an utter ignorance even of the Greek character, would learn to construe the four Gospels with the most perfect and scrupulous accuracy, in six weeks. Some children, utterly ignorant of French or Italian, would learn to construe the four Gospels, in either of these languages, in three weeks; the Latin in four weeks; the German in five weeks. We believe they would do it in a class; but not to run any risks, we will presume a master to attend upon one student alone for these periods. We assign a master principally, because the application of a solitary boy at that age could not be depended upon; but if the sedulity of the child were certain, he would do it nearly as well alone. A greater time is allowed for German and Greek, on account of the novelty of the character. A person of mature habits, eager and energetic in his pursuits, and reading seven or eight hours per day, might, though utterly ignorant of a letter of Greek, learn to construe the four Gospels, with the most punctilious accuracy in three weeks, by the key alone. These assertions we make, not of the Gospels alone, but of any tolerably easy book of the same extent. We mean to be very accurate; but suppose we are wrong—add 10, 20, 30 per cent. to the time, an average boy of thirteen, in an average school, cannot construe the four Gospels in two years from the time of his beginning the language.

All persons would be glad to read a foreign language, but all persons do not want the same scrupulous and comprehensive knowledge of grammar which a great Latin scholar possesses. Many persons may, and do derive great pleasure and instruction from French, German, and Italian books, who can neither speak nor write these languages—who know that certain terminations, when they see them, signify present or past time, but who, if they wished to signify present or past time, could not recall these terminations. For many purposes and objects, therefore, very little grammar is wanting.

The Hamiltonian method begins with what all persons want, a facility of construing, and leaves every scholar to become afterwards

* We have left with the bookseller the names of two gentlemen who have verified this account to us, and who were present at the experiment. Their names will at once put an end to all scepticism as to the fact. Two more candid and enlightened judges could not be found.

as profound in grammar as he (or those who educate him) may choose; whereas the old method aims at making all more profound grammarians than three-fourths wish to be, or than nineteen-twentieths *can* be. One of the enormous follies of the enormously foolish education in England, is, that all young men —dukes, fox-hunters, and merchants—are educated as if they were to keep a school, and serve a curacy; while scarcely an hour in the Hamiltonian education is lost for any variety of life. A grocer may learn enough of Latin to taste the sweets of Virgil; a cavalry officer may read and understand Homer, without knowing that ἵημι comes from ἕω with a smooth breathing, and that it is formed by an improper reduplication. In the mean time, there is nothing in that education which prevents a scholar from knowing (if he wishes to know) what Greek compounds draw back their accents. He may trace verbs in ιμι from polysyllables in ιω, or derive endless glory from marking down derivatives in πτω, changing the ε of their primitives into iota.

Thus in the Hamiltonian method, a good deal of grammar necessarily impresses itself upon the mind (*chemin faisant*), as it does in the vernacular tongue, without any rule at all, and merely by habit. How is it possible to read many Latin keys, for instance, without remarking, willingly or unwillingly, that the first person of verbs end in *o*, the second in *s*, the third in *t*?—that the same adjective ends in *us* or *a*, accordingly as the connected substantive is masculine or feminine, and other such gross and common rules? An Englishman who means to say, *I will go to London*, does not say, *I could go to London*. He never read a word of grammar in his life; but he has learnt by habit, that the word *go*, signifies to proceed or set forth, and by the same habit he learns that future intentions are expressed by *I will*; and by the same habit the Hamiltonian pupil, reading over, and comprehending twenty times more words and phrases than the pupil of the ancient system, insensibly but infallibly fixes upon his mind many rules of grammar. We are far from meaning to say, that the grammar thus acquired will be sufficiently accurate for a first-rate Latin and Greek scholar; but there is no reason why a young person arriving at this distinction, and educated in the Hamiltonian system, may not carry the study of grammar to any degree of minuteness and accuracy. The only difference is, that he begins grammar as a study, after he has made a considerable progress in the language, and not before—a very important feature in the Hamiltonian system, and a very great improvement in the education of children.

The imperfections of the old system proceed in a great measure from a bad and improvident accumulation of difficulties, which must all, perhaps, though in a less degree, at one time or another be encountered, but which may be, and in the Hamiltonian system are, much more wisely distributed. A boy who sits down to Greek with lexicon and grammar, has to master an unknown character of an unknown language—to look out words in a lexicon, in the use of which he is inexpert—to guess, by many trials, in which of the numerous senses detailed in the lexicon he is to use the word—to attend to the inflexions of cases and tense—to become acquainted with the syntax of the language—and to become acquainted with these inflexions and this syntax from books written in foreign languages, and full of the most absurd and barbarous terms, and this at the tenderest age, when the mind is utterly unfit to grapple with any great difficulty; and the boy, who revolts at all this folly and absurdity, is set down for a dunce, and must go into a marching regiment, or on board a man of war! The Hamiltonian pupil has his word looked out for him, its proper sense ascertained, the case of the substantive, the inflexions of the verb pointed out, and the syntaxical arrangement placed before his eyes. Where, then, is he to encounter these difficulties? Does he hope to escape them entirely? Certainly not, if it is his purpose to become a great scholar; but he will enter upon them when the character is familiar to his eye—when a great number of Greek words are familiar to his eye and ear—when he has practically mastered a great deal of grammar—when the terminations of verbs convey to him different modifications of time, the terminations of substantives different varieties of circumstance—when the rules of grammar, in short, are a confirmation of previous observation, not an irksome multitude of directions, heaped up without any opportunity of immediate application.

The real way of learning a dead language, is to imitate, as much as possible, the method in which a living language is naturally learnt. When do we ever find a well-educated Englishman or Frenchman embarrassed by an ignorance of the grammar of their respective languages? They first learn it practically and unerringly; and then, if they choose to look back and smile at the idea of having proceeded by a number of rules without knowing one of them by heart, or being conscious that they had any rule at all, this is a philosophical amusement: but whoever thinks of learning the grammar of their own tongue before they are very good grammarians? Let us hear what Mr. Locke says upon this subject:—"If grammar ought to be taught at any time, it must be to one that can speak the language already; how else can he be taught the grammar of it? This at least is evident, from the practice of the wise and learned nations amongst the ancients. They made it a part of education to cultivate their own, not foreign languages. The Greeks counted all other nations barbarous, and had a contempt for their languages. And though the Greek learning grew in credit amongst the Romans towards the end of their commonwealth, yet it was the Roman tongue that was made the study of their youth: their own language they were to make use of, and therefore it was their own language they were instructed and exercised in.

"But, more particularly, to determine the proper season for grammar, I do not see how it can reasonably be made any one's study, but as an introduction to rhetoric. When it is thought time to put any one upon the care of polishing his tongue, and of speaking better than the illiterate, then is the time for him to be instructed in the rules of grammar, and not before. For grammar being to teach men not to speak, but to speak correctly, and according to the exact rules of the tongue, which is one part of elegancy, there is little use of the one to him that has no need of the other. Where rhetoric is not necessary, grammar may be spared. I know not why any one should waste his time, and beat his head about the Latin grammar, who does not intend to be a critic, or make speeches, and write despatches in it. When any one finds in himself a necessity or disposition to study any foreign language to the bottom, and to be nicely exact in the knowledge of it, it will be time enough to take a grammatical survey of it. If his use of it be only to understand some books writ in it, without a critical knowledge of the tongue itself, reading alone, as I have said, will attain that end, without charging the mind with the multiplied rules and intricacies of grammar."—*Locke on Education*, p. 78, folio.

In the Eton Grammar, the following very plain and elementary information is conveyed to young gentlemen utterly ignorant of every syllable of the language:—

"Nomina anomala quæ contrahuntur sunt, Ὁλοπαθῆ, quæ contrahuntur in omnibus, ut γοος γούς, &c. Ολιγοπαθῆ, quæ in paucioribus casibus contrahuntur, ut substantiva Barytonia in ὑϛ. Imparyllatria in ουϛ," &c. &c.

From the Westminster Grammar we make the following extract—and some thousand rules, conveyed in poetry of equal merit, must be fixed upon the mind of the youthful Grecian, before he advances into the interior of the language.

"ω finis thematis finis utriusque futuri est
Post liquidam in primo, vel in unoquoque secundo,
ω circumflexum est. Ante ω finale character
Explicitus σε primi est implicitusque futuri
ω itaque in quo σ quasi plexum est solitu in σω."
Westminster Greek Grammar, 1814.

Such are the easy initiations of our present methods of teaching. The Hamiltonian system, on the other hand, 1. teaches an unknown tongue by the closest interlinear translation, instead of leaving a boy to explore his way by the lexicon or dictionary. 2. It postpones the study of grammar till a considerable progress has been made in the language, and a great degree of practical grammar has been acquired. 3. It substitutes the cheerfulness and competition of the Lancasterian system for the dull solitude of the dictionary. By these means, a boy finds he is making a progress, and learning something from the very beginning. He is not overwhelmed with the first appearance of insuperable difficulties; he receives some little pay from the first moment of his apprenticeship, and is not compelled to wait for remuneration till he is out of his time. The student having acquired the great art of understanding the sense of what is written in another tongue, may go into the study of the language as deeply and as extensively as he pleases. The old system aims at beginning with a depth and accuracy which many men never will want, which disgusts many from arriving even at moderate attainments, and is a less easy, and not more certain road to a profound skill in languages, than if attention to grammar had been deferred to a later period.

In fine, we are strongly persuaded, that the time being given, this system will make better scholars; and the degree of scholarship being given, a much shorter time will be needed. If there is any truth in this, it will make Mr. Hamilton one of the most useful men of his age; for if there is any thing which fills reflecting men with melancholy and regret, it is the waste of mortal time, parental money, and puerile happiness, in the present method of pursuing Latin and Greek.

COUNSEL FOR PRISONERS.*

[EDINBURGH REVIEW, 1826.]

ON the sixth of April, 1824, Mr. George Lamb (a gentleman who is always the advocate of whatever is honest and liberal) presented the following petition from several jurymen in the habit of serving on juries at the Old Bailey:—

"That your petitioners, fully sensible of the invaluable privilege of jury trials, and desirous of seeing them as complete as human institutions will admit, feel it their duty to draw the attention of the House to the restrictions imposed on the prisoner's counsel, which, they humbly conceive, have strong claims to a legislative remedy. With every disposition to decide justly, the petitioners have found, by experience, in the course of their attendances as jurymen in the Old Bailey, that the opening statements for the prosecution too frequently leave an impression more unfavourable to the prisoner at the bar than the evidence of itself could have produced; and it has always sounded harsh to the petitioners to hear it announced from the bench, that the counsel, to whom the prisoner has committed his defence, cannot be permitted to address the jury in his behalf, nor reply to the charges which have, or have not, been substantiated by the witnesses. The petitioners have felt their situation peculiarly painful and embarrassing when the prisoner's faculties, perhaps surprised by such an intimation, are too much absorbed in the difficulties of his unhappy circumstances to admit of an effort towards his own justification, against the statements of the prosecutor's counsel, often unintentionally aggravated through zeal or misconception; and it is purely with a view to the attainment of impartial justice, that the petitioners humbly submit to the serious consideration of the House the expediency of allowing every accused person the full benefit of counsel, as in cases of misdemeanour, and according to the practice of the civil courts."

With the opinions so sensibly and properly expressed by these jurymen, we most cordially agree. We have before touched incidentally on this subject; but shall now give to it a more direct and a fuller examination. We look upon it as a very great blot in our over-praised criminal code; and no effort of ours shall be wanting, from time to time, for its removal.

We have now the benefit of discussing these subjects under the government of a home secretary of state, whom we may (we believe) fairly call a wise, honest, and high principled man—as he appears to us, without wishing for innovation, or having any itch for it, not to be afraid of innovation,† when it is gradual and well considered. He is, indeed, almost the only person we remember in his station, who has not considered sound sense to consist in the rejection of every improvement, and loyalty to be proved by the defence of every accidental, imperfect, or superannuated institution.

If this petition of jurymen be a real *bonâ fide* petition, not the result of solicitation—and we have no reason to doubt it—it is a warning which the legislature cannot neglect, if it mean to avoid the disgrace of seeing the lower and middle orders of mankind making laws for themselves, which the government is at length compelled to adopt as measures of their own. The judges and the Parliament would have gone on to this day, hanging, by wholesale, for the forgeries of bank notes, if juries had not become weary of the continual butchery, and resolved to acquit. The proper execution of laws must always depend, in great measure, upon public opinion; and it is undoubtedly most discreditable to any men intrusted with power, when the governed turn round upon their governors, and say, "Your laws are so cruel, or so foolish, we cannot, and *will not* act upon them."

The particular improvement, of allowing counsel to those who are accused of felony, is so far from being unnecessary, from any extraordinary indulgence shown to English prisoners, that we really cannot help suspecting, that not a year elapses in which many innocent persons are not found guilty. How is it possible, indeed, that it can be otherwise? There are seventy or eighty persons to be tried for various offences at the assizes, who have lain in prison for some months; and fifty of whom, perhaps, are of the lowest order of the people, without friends in any better condition than themselves, and without one single penny to employ in their defence. How are they to obtain witnesses? No attorney can be employed—no subpœna can be taken out; the witnesses are fifty miles off, perhaps—totally uninstructed—living from hand to mouth—utterly unable to give up their daily occupation to pay for their journey, or for their support when arrived at the town of trial—and, if they could get there, not knowing where to go, or what to do. It is impossible but that a human being, in such a helpless situation, must be found guilty; for, as he cannot give evidence for himself, and has not a penny to fetch those who can give it for him, any story told against him must be taken for true (however false);

* *Stockton on the Practice of not allowing Counsel for Prisoners accused of Felony.* 8vo. London, 1826.

† We must always except the Catholic question. Mr. Peel's opinions on this subject (giving him credit for sincerity) have always been a subject of real surprise to us. It must surely be some mistake between the right honourable gentleman and his chaplain! They have been travelling together; and some of the parson's notions have been put in Mr. Peel's head by mistake. We yet hope he will return them to their rightful owner.

since it is impossible for the poor wretch to contradict it. A brother or a sister may come —and support every suffering and privation themselves in coming; but the prisoner cannot often have such claims upon the persons who have witnessed the transaction, nor any other claims but those which an unjustly accused person has upon those whose testimony can exculpate him—and who probably must starve themselves and their families to do it. It is true, a case of life and death will rouse the poorest persons, every now and then, to extraordinary exertions, and they may tramp through mud and dirt to the assize town to save a life—though even this effort is precarious enough: but imprisonment, hard labour, or transportation, appeal less forcibly than death, —and would often appeal for evidence in vain, to the feeble and limited resources of extreme poverty. It is not that a great proportion of those accused are not guilty—but that some are not —and are utterly without means of establishing their innocence. We do not believe they are often accused from wilful and corrupt perjury: but the prosecutor is himself mistaken. The crime has been committed; and in his thirst for vengeance, he has got hold of the wrong man. The wheat was stolen out of the barn; and, amidst many other collateral circumstances, the witnesses (paid and brought up by a wealthy prosecutor, who is repaid by the county) swear that they saw a man, very like the prisoner, with a sack of corn upon his shoulder, at an early hour of the morning, going from the barn in the direction of the prisoner's cottage! Here is one link, and a very material link, of a long chain of circumstantial evidence. Judge and jury must give it weight, till it is contradicted. In fact, the prisoner did not steal the corn; he was, to be sure, out of his cottage at the same hour—and that also is proved—but travelling in a totally different direction,—and was seen to be so travelling by a stage coachman passing by, and by a market gardener. An attorney with money in his pocket, whom every moment of such employ made richer by six-and-eight pence, would have had the two witnesses ready, and at rack and manger, from the first day of the assize; and the innocence of the prisoner would have been established: but by what possible means is the destitute, ignorant wretch himself to find or to produce such witnesses? or how can the most humane jury, and the most acute judge, refuse to consider him as guilty, till his witnesses *are* produced? We have not the slightest disposition to exaggerate, and, on the contrary, should be extremely pleased to be convinced that our apprehensions were unfounded: but we have often felt extreme pain at the hopeless and unprotected state of prisoners; and we cannot find any answer to our suspicions, or discover any means by which this perversion of justice, under the present state of the law, can be prevented from taking place. Against the prisoner are arrayed all the resources of an angry prosecutor, who has certainly (let who will be the culprit) suffered a serious injury. He has his hand, too, in the public purse; for he prosecutes at the expense of the county. He cannot even relent; for the magistrate is bound over to indict. His witnesses cannot fail him; for they are all bound over by the same magistrate to give evidence. He is out of prison, too, and can exert himself.

The prisoner, on the other hand, comes into court, squalid and depressed from long confinement—utterly unable to tell his own story from want of words and want of confidence, and is unable to produce evidence for want of money. His fate accordingly is obvious;—and that there are many innocent men punished every year, for crimes they have not committed, appears to us to be extremely probable. It is, indeed, scarcely possible it should be otherwise: and, as if to prove the fact, every now and then, a case of this kind *is* detected. Some circumstances come to light between sentence and execution; immense exertions are made by humane men; time is gained, and the innocence of the condemned person completely established. In Elizabeth Caning's case, two women were capitally convicted, ordered for execution—and at last found innocent, and respited. Such, too, was the case of the men who were sentenced ten years ago, for the robbery of Lord Cowper's steward. "I have myself (says Mr. Scarlett) *often* seen persons I thought innocent convicted, and the guilty escape, for want of some acute and intelligent counsel to show the bearings of the different circumstances on the conduct and situation of the prisoner."—(*House of Commons Debates, April 25th,* 1826.) We were delighted to see, in this last debate, both Mr. Brougham and Mr. Scarlett profess themselves friendly to Mr. Lamb's motion.

But in how many cases has the injustice proceeded without any suspicion being excited? and even if we could reckon upon men being watchful in capital cases, where life is concerned, we are afraid it is in such cases alone that they ever besiege the secretary of state, and compel his attention. We never remember any such interference to save a man unjustly condemned to the hulks or the treadmill; and yet there are certainly more condemnations to these minor punishments than to the gallows: but then it is all one—who knows or cares about it? If Harrison or Johnson has been condemned, after regular trial by jury, to six months' treadmill, because Harrison and Johnson were without a penny to procure evidence—who knows or cares about Harrison or Johnson? how can they make themselves heard? or in what way can they obtain redress? It worries rich and comfortable people to hear the humanity of our penal laws called in question. There is talk of a society for employing discharged prisoners: might not something be effected by a society instituted for the purpose of providing to poor prisoners a proper defence, and a due attendance of witnesses? But we must hasten on from this disgraceful neglect of poor prisoners, to the particular subject of complaint we have proposed to ourselves.

The proposition is, *That the prisoner accused of felony ought to have the same power of select-*

ing counsel to speak for him as he has in cases of treason and misdemeanour, and as defendants have in all civil actions.

Nothing can be done in any discussion upon any point of law in England, without quoting Mr. Justice Blackstone. Mr. Justice Blackstone, we believe, generally wrote his Commentaries late in the evening, with a bottle of wine before him; and little did he think, as each sentence fell from the glass and pen, of the immense influence it might hereafter exercise upon the laws and usages of his country. "It is" (says this favourite writer) "not at all of a piece with the rest of the humane treatment of prisoners by the English law; for upon what face of reason can that assistance be denied to save the life of a man, which yet is allowed him in prosecutions for every petty trespass?" Nor, indeed, strictly speaking, is it a part of our ancient law; for the Mirror, having observed the necessity of counsel in civil suits, who know how to forward and defend the cause by the rules of law and customs of the realm, immediately subjoins "and more necessary are they for defence upon indictment and appeals of felony, than upon any other venial crimes." To the authority of Blackstone may be added that of Sir John Hall, in Hollis's case; of Sir Robert Atkyns, in Lord Russell's case; and of Sir Bartholomew Shower, in the arguments for a New Bill of Rights, in 1682. "In the name of God," says this judge, "what harm can accrue to the public in general, or to any man in particular, that, in cases of State-treason, counsel should not be allowed to the accused? What rule of justice is there to warrant its denial, when, in a civil case of a halfpenny cake, he may plead either by himself or by his advocate? That the court is counsel for the prisoner can be no effectual reason; for so they are for each party, that right may be done."—(*Somer's Tracts*, vol. ii. p. 568.) In the trial of Thomas Rosewell, a dissenting clergyman, for high treason in 1684, *Judge Jeffries*, in summing up, confessed to the jury, "that he thought it a hard case, that a man should have counsel to defend himself for a twopenny trespass, and his witnesses be examined upon oath; but if he stole, committed murder or felony, nay, high treason, where life, estate, honour, and all were concerned, that he should neither have counsel, nor have his witnesses examined upon oath."—*Howell's State Trials*, vol. x. p. 207.

There have been two capital errors in the criminal codes of feudal Europe, from which a great variety of mistake and injustice have proceeded; the one, a disposition to confound accusation with guilt; the other, to mistake a defence of prisoners accused by the crown, for disloyalty and disaffection to the crown; and from these errors our own code has been slowly and gradually recovering, by all those struggles and exertions which it always costs to remove *folly sanctioned by antiquity*. In the early periods of our history, the accused person could call no evidence:—then, for a long time, his evidence against the king could not be examined upon oath; consequently, he might as well have produced none, as all the evidence against him was upon oath. Till the reign of Anne, no one accused of felony could produce witnesses upon oath; and the old practice was vindicated, in opposition to the new one, introduced under the statute of that day, on the grounds of humanity and tenderness to the prisoner! because, as his witnesses were not restricted by an oath, they were at liberty to indulge in simple falsehood as much as they pleased;—so argued the blessed defenders of nonsense in those days. Then it was ruled to be indecent and improper that counsel should be employed against the crown; and, therefore, the prisoner accused of treason could have no counsel. In like manner, a party accused of felony could have no counsel to assist him in the trial. Counsel might indeed stay in the court, but apart from the prisoner, with whom they could have no communication. They were not allowed to put any question, or to suggest any doubtful point of law; but if the prisoner (likely to be a weak, unlettered man) could himself suggest any doubt in matter of law, the court determined first if the question of law should be entertained, and then assigned counsel to argue it. In those times, too, the jury were punishable if they gave a false verdict against the king, but were *not* punishable if they gave a false verdict against the prisoner. The preamble of the Act of 1696 runs thus,—"Whereas it is expedient that persons charged with high treason should make a full and sufficient defence." Might it not be altered to *persons charged with any species or degree of crime?* All these errors have given way to the force of truth, and to the power of common sense and common humanity—the Attorney and Solicitor General, for the time being, always protesting against each alteration, and regularly and officially prophesying the utter destruction of the whole jurisprudence of Great Britain. There is no man now alive, perhaps, so utterly foolish, as to propose that prisoners should be prevented from producing evidence upon oath, and being heard by their counsel in cases of high treason; and yet it cost a struggle for *seven* sessions to get this measure through the two houses of Parliament. But mankind are much like the children they beget—they always make wry faces at what is to do them good; and it is necessary sometimes to hold the nose, and force the medicine down the throat. They enjoy the health and vigour consequent upon the medicine; but cuff the doctor, and sputter at his stuff!

A most absurd argument was advanced in the honourable house, that the practice of employing counsel would be such an expense to the prisoner!—just as if any thing was so expensive as being hanged! What a fine topic for the ordinary! "You are going" (says that exquisite divine) "to be hanged to-morrow, it is true, but consider what a sum you have saved! Mr. Scarlett or Mr. Brougham might certainly have presented arguments to the jury which would have insured your acquittal; but do you forget that gentlemen of their eminence must be recompensed by large fees, and that, if your life had been saved, you would actually have been out of pocket above 20*l.*? You will now die with the consciousness of having obeyed the dictates of a wise economy; and with a grateful reverence for the laws of your country, which prevents you from running into such unbounded expense—so let us now go to prayers."

It is ludicrous enough to recollect, when the employment of counsel is objected to on account of the expense to the prisoner, that the same merciful law which, to save the prisoner's money, has *denied* him counsel, and produced his conviction, seizes upon all his savings the moment he is convicted.

Of all false and foolish *dicta*, the most trite and the most absurd is that which asserts that the judge is counsel for the prisoner. We do not hesitate to say that this is merely an unmeaning phrase, invented to defend a pernicious abuse. The judge *cannot* be counsel for the prisoner, *ought not* to be counsel for the prisoner, never *is* counsel for the prisoner. To force an ignorant man into a court of justice, and to tell him that the judge is his counsel, appears to us quite as foolish as to set a hungry man down to his meals, and to tell him that the table was his dinner. In the first place, a counsel should always have private and previous communication with the prisoner, which the judge, of course, cannot have. The prisoner reveals to his counsel how far he is guilty, or he is not; states to him all the circumstances of his case—and might often enable his advocate, if his advocate were allowed to speak, to explain a long string of circumstantial evidence, in a manner favourable to the innocence of his client. Of all these advantages, the judge, if he had every disposition to befriend the prisoner, is of course deprived. Something occurs to a prisoner in the course of the cause; he suggests it in a whisper to his counsel, doubtful if it is a wise point to urge or not. His counsel thinks it of importance, and would urge it, if his mouth were not shut. Can a prisoner have this secret communication with a judge, and take his advice, whether or not he, the judge, shall mention it to the jury? The counsel has (after all the evidence has been given) a bad opinion of his client's case; but he suppresses that opinion; and it is his duty to do so. He is not to decide; that is the province of the jury: and, in spite of his own opinion—his client may be innocent. He is brought there (or would be brought there if the privilege of speech were allowed) for the express purpose of saying all that could be said on one side of the question. He is a weight in *one* scale, and some one else holds the balance. This is the way in which truth is elicited in civil, and would be in criminal cases. But does *the Judge* ever assume the appearance of believing a prisoner to be innocent whom he thinks to be guilty? If the prisoner advances inconclusive or weak arguments, does not the judge say they are weak and inconclusive, and does he not often sum up against his own client? How then is he counsel for the prisoner? If the counsel for the prisoner were to see a strong point, which the counsel for the prosecution had missed, would he supply the deficiency of his antagonist, and urge what had been neglected to be urged? But is it not the imperious duty of the judge to do so? How then can these two functionaries stand in the same relation to the prisoner? In fact the only meaning of the phrase is this, that the judge will not suffer any undue advantage to be taken of the ignorance and helplessness of the prisoner—that he will point out any evidence or circumstance in his favour—and see that equal justice is done to both parties. But in this sense he is as much the counsel of the prosecutor as of the prisoner. This is all the judge can do, or even pretends to do; but he can have no previous communication with the prisoner—he can have no confidential communication in court with the prisoner before he sums up; he cannot fling the whole weight of his understanding into the opposite scale against the counsel for the prosecution, and produce that collision of faculties, which, in all other cases but those of felony, is supposed to be the happiest method of arriving at truth. Baron Garrow, in his charge to the grand jury at Exeter, on the 16th of August, 1824, thus expressed his opinion of a judge being counsel for the prisoner. "It has been said, and truly said, that in criminal courts, judges were counsel for the prisoners. So undoubtedly they were, as far as they could to prevent undue prejudice, to guard against improper influence being excited against prisoners; but it was impossible for them to go farther than this; for they could not suggest the course of defence prisoners ought to pursue; for judges only saw the depositions so short a time before the accused appeared at the bar of their country, that it was quite impossible for them to act fully in that capacity." The learned Baron might have added, that it would be more correct to call the judge counsel for the prosecution; for his only previous instructions were the depositions for the prosecution, from which, in the absence of counsel, he examined the evidence against the prisoner. On the prisoner's behalf he had no instructions at all.

Can any thing, then, be more flagrantly and scandalously unjust, than, in a long case of circumstantial evidence, to refuse to a prisoner the benefit of counsel? A foot-mark, a word, a sound, a tool dropped, all gave birth to the most ingenious inferences; and the counsel for the prosecution is so far from being blameable for entering into all these things, that they are all essential to the detection of guilt, and they are all links of a long and intricate chain: but if a close examination into, and a logical statement of, all these circumstances be necessary for the establishment of guilt, is not the same closeness of reasoning and the same logical statement necessary for the establishment of innocence? If justice cannot be done to society without the intervention of a practised and ingenious mind, who may connect all these links together, and make them clear to the apprehension of a jury, *can* justice be done to the prisoner, unless similar practice and similar ingenuity are employed to detect the flaws of the chain, and to point out the disconnection of the circumstances?

Is there any one gentleman in the House of Commons, who, in yielding his vote to this paltry and perilous fallacy of the judge being counsel for the prisoner, does not feel, that, were he himself a criminal, he would prefer almost any counsel at the bar, to the tender mercies of the judge? How strange that any man who could make his election would eagerly and diligently surrender this exquisite privilege, and addict himself to the perilous practice of giving fees to counsel? Nor let us forget, in considering judges as counsel for the prisoner, that there have been such men as Chief Justice Jeffries, Mr. Justice Page, and Mr. Justice Alybone, and that, in bad times, such men may reappear. "If you do not allow me counsel, my lords (says Lord Lovat), it is impossible for me to make any defence, by reason of my infirmity. I do not see, I do not hear. I come up to the bar at the hazard of my life. I have fainted several times, I have been up so early, ever since four o'clock this morning. I therefore ask for assistance; and if you do not allow me counsel, or such aid as is necessary, it will be impossible for me to make any defence at all." Though Lord Lovat's guilt was evident, yet the managers of the impeachment felt so strongly the injustice which was done, that, by the hands of Sir W. Young, the chief manager, a bill was brought into parliament, to allow counsel to persons impeached by that house, which was not previously the case; so that the evil is already done away with, in a great measure, to persons of rank: it so happens in legislation, when a gentleman suffers, public attention is awakened to the evil of laws. Every man who makes laws says, "This may be my case:" but it requires the repeated efforts of humane men, or, as Mr. North calls them, dilettanti philosophers, to awaken the attention of lawmakers to evils from which they are themselves exempt. We do not say this to make the leaders of mankind unpopular, but to rouse their earnest attention in cases where the poor only are concerned, and where neither good nor evil can happen to themselves.

A great stress is laid upon the moderation of the opening counsel; that is, he does not conjure the farmers in the jury-box, by the love which they bear to their children—he does not declaim upon blood-guiltiness—he does not describe the death of Abel by Cain, the first murderer—he does not describe scattered brains, ghastly wounds, pale features, and hair clotted with gore—he does not do a thousand things, which are not in English taste, and which it would be very foolish and very vulgar to do. We readily allow all this. But yet, if it be a cause of importance, it is essentially necessary to our counsellor's reputation that his man should be hung! And accordingly, with a very calm voice, and composed manner, and with many expressions of candour, he sets himself to comment astutely upon the circumstances. Distant events are immediately connected; meaning is given to insignificant facts; new motives are ascribed to innocent actions; farmer gives way after farmer in the jury-box: and a rope of eloquence is woven round the prisoner's neck! Every one is delighted with the talents of the advocate; and because there has been no noise, no violent action, and no consequent perspiration, he is praised for his candour and forbearance, and the lenity of our laws is the theme of universal approbation. In the mean time, the speech-maker and the prisoner know better.

We should be glad to know of any nation in the world, taxed by kings, or even imagined by poets (except the English), who have refused to prisoners the benefit of counsel. Why is the voice of humanity heard every where else, and disregarded here? In Scotland, the accused have not only counsel to speak for them, but a copy of the indictment, and a list of the witnesses. In France, in the Netherlands, in the whole of Europe, counsel are allotted as a matter of course. Every where else but here, accusation is considered as unfavourable to the exercise of human faculties. It is admitted to be that crisis in which, above all others, an unhappy man wants the aid of eloquence, wisdom, and coolness. In France, the Napoleon code has provided not only that counsel should be allowed to the prisoner, but that, as with us in Scotland, his counsel should have the last word.

It is a most affecting moment in a court of justice, when the evidence has all been heard, and the judge asks the prisoner what he has to say in his defence. The prisoner, who has (by great exertions, perhaps of his friends) saved up money enough to procure counsel, says to the judge, "that he leaves his defence to his counsel." We have often blushed for English humanity to hear the reply. "Your counsel cannot speak for you, you must speak for yourself;" and this is the reply given to a poor girl of eighteen—to a foreigner—to a deaf man—to a stammerer—to the sick—to the feeble—to the old—to the most abject and ignorant of human beings! It is a reply, we must say, at which common sense and common feeling revolt:—for it is full of brutal cruelty, and of base inattention, of those who make laws, to the happiness of those for whom laws were made. We wonder that any juryman can convict under such a shocking violation of all natural justice. The iron age of Clovis and Clottaire can produce no more atrocious violation of every good feeling, and every good principle. Can a sick man find strength and nerves to speak before a large assembly?—can an ignorant man find words?—can a low man find confidence? Is not he afraid of becoming an object of ridicule?—can he believe that his expressions will be understood? How often have we seen a poor wretch, struggling against the agonies of his spirit, and the rudeness of his conceptions, and his awe of better dressed men and better taught men, and the shame which the accusation has brought upon his head, and the sight of his parents and children gazing at him in the court, for the last time, perhaps, and after a long absence? The mariner sinking in the wave does not want a helping hand more than does this poor wretch. But help is denied to all! Age cannot have it, nor ignorance, nor the modesty of women! One hard, uncharitable rule silences the defenders of the wretched, in the worst of human evils; and at the bitterest of human moments, mercy is blotted out from the ways of men!

Suppose a crime to have been committed under the influence of insanity; is the insane man, now convalescent, to plead his own insanity?—to offer arguments to show that he must have been mad?—and, by the glimmerings of his returning reason, to prove that, at a former period, that same reason was utterly extinct? These are the cruel situations into which judges and courts of justice are thrown by the present state of the law.

There is a judge now upon the bench, who never took away the life of a fellow creature without shutting himself up alone and giving the most profound attention to every circumstance of the case! and this solemn act he always premises with his own beautiful prayer to God, that he will enlighten him with his Divine Spirit in the exercise of this terrible privilege! Now would it not be an immense satisfaction to this feeling and honourable magistrate, to be sure that every witness on the side of the prisoner had been heard, and that every argument which could be urged in his favour had been brought forward, by a man whose duty it was to see only on one side of the question, and whose interest and reputation were thoroughly embarked in this partial exertion? If a judge fails to get at the truth, after these instruments of investigation are used, his failure must be attributed to the limited powers of man—not to the want of good inclination, or wise institutions. We are surprised that such a measure does not come into Parliament, with the strong recommendation of the judges. It is surely better to be a day longer on the circuit, than to murder rapidly in ermine.

It is argued, that, among the various pleas for mercy that are offered, no prisoner has ever urged to the secretary of state the disadvantage of having no counsel to plead for him; but a prisoner who dislikes to undergo his sentence, naturally addresses to those who can reverse it such arguments only as will produce, in the opinion of the referee, a pleasing effect. He does not therefore find fault with the established system of jurisprudence, but brings forward facts and arguments to prove his own innocence. Besides, how few people there are who can elevate themselves from the acquiescence in what *is*, to the consideration of what *ought to be;* and if they could do so, the way to get rid of a punishment is not (as we have just observed) to say, "You have no right to punish me in this manner," but to say, "I am innocent of the offence." The fraudulent baker at Constantinople, who is about to be baked to death in his own oven, does not complain of the severity of baking bakers, but promises to use more flour and less fraud.

Whence comes it (we should like to ask Sir John Singleton Copley, who seems to dread so much the conflicts of talent in criminal cases) that a method of getting at truth which is found so serviceable in civil cases, should be so much objected to in criminal cases? Would you have all this wrangling and bickering, it is asked, and contentious eloquence, when the life of a man is concerned? Why not, as well as when his property is concerned? It is either a good means of doing justice, or it is not, that two understandings should be put in opposition to each other, and that a third should decide between them. Does this open every view which can bear upon the question? Does it in the most effectual manner watch the judge, detect perjury, and sift evidence? If not, why is it suffered to disgrace our civil institutions? If it effect all these objects, why is it not incorporated into our criminal law? Of what importance is a little disgust at professional tricks, if the solid advantage gained is a nearer approximation to truth? Can any thing be more preposterous than this preference of taste to justice, and of solemnity to truth? What an eulogium of a trial to say, "I am by no means satisfied that the jury were right in finding the prisoner guilty; but every thing was carried on with the utmost decorum. The verdict was wrong; but there was the most perfect propriety and order in the proceedings. The man will be unfairly hanged; but all was genteel!" If solemnity is what is principally wanted in a court of justice, we had better study the manners of the old Spanish Inquisition; but if battles with the judge, and battles among the counsel, are the best method, as they certainly are, of getting at the truth, better tolerate this philosophical Billingsgate, than persevere, *because* the life of a man is at stake, in solemn and polished injustice.

Why would it not be just as wise and equitable to leave the defendant without counsel in civil cases—and to tell him that the judge was his counsel? And if the reply is to produce such injurious effects as are anticipated upon the minds of the jury in criminal cases, why not in civil cases also? In twenty-eight cases out of thirty, the verdict in civil cases is correct; in the two remaining cases, the error may proceed from other causes than the right of reply; and yet the right of reply has existed in all. In a vast majority of cases, the verdict is for the plaintiff, not because there is a right of reply, but because he who has it in his power to decide whether he will go to law or not, and resolves to expose himself to the expense and trouble of a lawsuit, has probably a good foundation for his claim. Nobody, of course, can intend to say that the majority of verdicts in favour of plaintiffs are against justice, and merely attributable to the advantage of a last speech. If this were the case, the sooner advocates are turned out of court the better—and then the improvement of both civil and criminal law would be an abolition of all speeches; for those who dread the effect of the last word upon the fate of the prisoner, must remember that there is at present always a last speech against the prisoner; for, as the counsel for the prosecution cannot be replied to, *his* is the last speech.

There is certainly this difference between a civil and a criminal case—that in one a new trial can be granted, in the other not. But you must first make up your mind whether this system of contentious investigation by opposite advocates is or is not the best method of getting at truth: if it be, the more irremediable the decision, the more powerful and perfect should be the means of deciding; and then it would be a less oppression if the civil defendant were deprived of counsel than the criminal prisoner. When an error has been committed, the advantage is greater to the latter of these persons than to the former;—the criminal is not tried again, but pardoned; while the civil defendant must run the chance of another jury.

If the effect of reply, and the contention of counsel, have all these baneful consequences in felony, why not also in misdemeanour and high treason? Half the cases at sessions are cases of misdemeanour, where counsel are employed, and half-informed justices preside instead of learned judges. There are no complaints of the unfairness of verdicts, though there are every now and then of the severity of punishments. Now, if the reasoning of Mr. Lamb's opponents were true, the disturbing force of the prisoner's counsel must fling every thing into confusion. The court for misdemeanours must be a scene of riot and perplexity; and the detection and punishment of crime must be utterly impossible: and yet in the very teeth of these objections, such courts of justice are just as orderly in one set of offences as the other; and the conviction of a guilty person just as certain and as easy.

The prosecutor (if this system were altered) would have the choice of counsel; so he has now—with this difference, that, at present, his counsel cannot be answered nor opposed. It would be better, in all cases, if two men of exactly equal talent could be opposed to each other; but as this is impossible, the system must be taken with this inconvenience; but there can be no inequality between counsel so great as that between any counsel and the prisoner pleading for himself. "It has been lately my lot," says Mr. Denman, "to try two prisoners who were deaf and dumb, and who could only be made to understand what was passing by the signs of their friends. The cases were clear and simple; but if they had been circumstantial cases, in what a situation would the judge and jury be placed, when the prisoner could have no counsel to plead for him."—*Debates of the House of Commons, April* 25, 1826.

The folly of being counsel for yourself is so notorious in civil cases, that it has grown into a proverb. But the cruelty of the law compels a man, in criminal cases, to be guilty of a much greater act of folly, and to trust his life to an advocate, who, by the common sense of mankind, is pronounced to be inadequate to defend the possession of an acre of land.

In all cases it must be supposed, that reasonably convenient instruments are selected to effect the purpose in view. A judge may be commonly presumed to understand his profession, and a jury to have a fair allowance of common sense; but the objectors to the improvement we recommend appear to make no such suppositions. Counsel are always to make flashy addresses to the passions. Juries are to be so much struck with them, that they are always to acquit or to condemn, contrary to justice; and judges are always to be so biassed, that they are to fling themselves rashly into the opposite scale against the prisoner. Many cases of misdemeanour consign a man to infamy, and cast a blot upon his posterity. Judges and juries must feel these cases as strongly as any cases of felony; and yet, in spite of this, and in spite of the free permission of counsel to speak, they preserve their judgment, and command their feelings surprisingly. Generally speaking, we believe none of these evils would take place. Trumpery declamation would be considered as discreditable to the counsel, and would be disregarded by the jury. The judge and jury (as in civil cases) would gain the habit of looking to the facts, selecting the arguments, and coming to reasonable conclusions. It is so in all other countries—and it would be so in this. But the vigilance of the judge is to relax, if there is counsel for the prisoner. Is, then, the relaxed vigilance of the judges complained of, in high treason, in misdemeanour, or in civil cases? This appears to us really to shut up the debate, and to preclude reply. *Why* is the practice so good in all other cases, and so pernicious in felony alone? This question has never received even the shadow of an answer. There is no one objection against the allowance of counsel to prisoners in felony, which does not apply to them in all cases. If the vigilance of judges depend upon this injustice to the prisoner, then, the greater injustice to the prisoner, the more vigilance; and so the true method of perfecting the Bench would be, to deny the prisoner the power of calling witnesses, and to increase as much as possible the disparity between the accuser and the accused. We hope men are selected for *the Judges of Israel*, whose vigilance depends upon better and higher principles.

There are three methods of arranging a trial, as to the mode of employing counsel—that both parties should have counsel, or neither—or only one. The first method is the best; the second is preferable to the last; and the last, which is our present system, is the worst possible. If counsel were denied to either of the parties, if it be necessary that any system of jurisprudence should be disgraced by such an act of injustice, they should rather be denied to the prosecutor than to the prisoner.

But the most singular caprice of the law is, that counsel are permitted in very high crimes, and in very small crimes, and denied in crimes of a sort of medium description. In high treason, where you mean to murder Lord Liverpool, and to levy war against the people, and to blow up the two houses of Parliament, all the lawyers of Westminster Hall may talk themselves dry, and the jury deaf. Lord Eldon, when at the bar, has been heard for nine hours on such subjects. If, instead of producing the destruction of five thousand people, you are indicted for the murder of one person, here human faculties, from the diminution of guilt, are supposed to be so clear and so unclouded, that the prisoner is quite adequate to make his own defence, and no counsel are allowed. Take it then upon that principle; and let the rule, and the reason of it, pass as sufficient. But if, instead of murdering the man, you have only libelled him, then, for some reason or another, though utterly unknown to us, the original imbecility of faculties in accused persons i respected, and counsel *are* allowed. Was ever such nonsense defended by public men in grave assemblies? The prosecutor, too (as Mr. Horace Twiss justly observes), can either allow or disallow counsel, by selecting his form of prosecution;—as where a mob has assembled to repeal, by riot and force, some unpopular statute, and certain persons had continued in that assembly for more than an hour after proclamation to disperse. That might be treated as levying war against the king, and then the prisoner would be entitled to receive (as Lord George Gordon did receive) the benefit of counsel. It might also be treated as a seditious riot; then it would be a misdemeanour, and counsel would still be allowed. But if government had a mind to destroy the prisoner effectually, they have only to abstain from the charge of treason, and to introduce into the indictment the aggravation, that the prisoner had continued with the mob for an hour after proclamation to disperse; this is a felony, the prisoner's life is in jeopardy, and counsel are effectually excluded. It produces, in many other cases disconnected with treason, the most scandalous injustice. A receiver of stolen goods, who employs a young girl to rob her master, may be tried for the misdemeanour; the young girl taken afterwards would be tried for the felony. The receiver would be punishable only with fine, imprisonment, or whipping, and he could have counsel to defend him. The girl indicted for felony, and liable to death, would enjoy no such advantage.

In the comparison between felony and treason, there are certainly some arguments why counsel should be allowed in felony rather than in treason. Persons accused of treason are generally persons of education and rank, accustomed to assemblies, and to public speaking, while men accused of felony are commonly of the lowest of the people. If it be true, that judges, in cases of high treason, are more liable to be influenced by the crown, and to lean against the prisoner, this cannot apply to cases of misdemeanour, or to the defendants in civil cases; but if it be necessary, that judges should be watched in political cases, how often are cases of felony connected with political disaffection? Every judge, too, has his idiosyncrasies, which require to be watched. Some hate Dissenters—some mobs; some have one weakness, some another; and the ultimate truth is, that no court of justice is safe, unless there is some one present whose occupation and interest it is to watch the safety of the prisoner. Till then, no man of right feeling can be easy at the administration of justice, and the punishment of death.

Two men are accused of one offence; the one dexterous, bold, subtile, gifted with speech, and remarkable for presence of mind; the other timid, hesitating, and confused—is there any reason why the chances of these two men for acquittal should be, as they are, so very different? Inequalities there will be in the means of defence under the best system, but there is no occasion the law should make these greater than they are left by chance or nature.

But (it is asked) what practical injustice is done—what practical evil is there in the present system? The great object of all law is, that the guilty should be punished, and that the innocent should be acquitted. A very great majority of prisoners, we admit, are guilty—and so clearly guilty, that we believe they would be found guilty under any system; but among the number of those who are tried, *some* are innocent, and the chance of establishing their innocence is very much diminished by the privation of counsel. In the course of twenty or thirty years, among the whole mass of English prisoners, we believe *many* are found guilty who are innocent, and who would not have been found guilty, if an able and intelligent man had watched over their interest, and represented their case. If this happen only to two or three every year, it is quite a sufficient reason why the law should be altered. That such cases exist we firmly believe; and this is the practical evil—perceptible to men of sense and reflection; but not likely to become the subject of general petition. To ask why there are not petitions—why the evil is not more noticed, is mere parliamentary froth and ministerial juggling. Gentlemen are rarely hung. If they were so, there would be petitions without end for counsel. The creatures exposed to the cruelties and injustice of the law are dumb creatures, who feel the evil without being able to express their feeling. Besides, the question is not, whether the evil is found out, but whether the evil exist. Whoever thinks it is an evil, should vote against it, whether the sufferer from the injustice discover it to be an injustice, or whether he suffer in ignorant silence. When the bill was enacted, which allowed counsel for treason, there was not a petition from one end of England to the other. Can there be a more shocking answer from the ministerial bench, than to say, For real evil we care nothing—only for detected evil? We will set about curing any wrong which affects our popularity and power: but as to any other evil, we wait till the people find it out; and, in the mean time, commit such evils to the care of Mr. George Lamb, and of Sir James Mackintosh. We are sure so good a man as Mr. Peel can never feel in this manner.

Howard devoted himself to his country. It was a noble example. Let two gentlemen on the ministerial side of the house (we only ask for two) commit some crimes, which will render their execution a matter of painful necessity Let them feel, and report to the house, all the injustice and inconvenience of having neither a copy of the indictment, nor a list of witnesses, nor counsel to defend them. We will venture to say, that the evidence of two such persons would do more for the improvement of the criminal law, than all the orations of Mr. Lamb or the lucubrations of Beccaria. Such evidence would save time, and bring the question to an issue. It is a great duty, and ought to be fulfilled—and, in ancient Rome, would have been fulfilled.

The opponents always forget that Mr. Lamb's plan is not to *compel* prisoners to have counsel, but to *allow* them to have counsel, if they choose to do so. Depend upon it, as Dr. Johnson says, when a man is going to be hanged, his faculties are wonderfully concentrated. If it be really true, as the defenders of *Mumpsimus* observe, that the judge is the best counsel for the prisoner, the prisoner will soon learn to employ him, especially as his lordship works without fees. All that we want is an option given to the prisoner—that a man, left to adopt his own means of defence in every trifling civil right, may have the same power of selecting his own auxiliaries for higher interests.

But nothing can be more unjust than to speak of judges, as if they were of one standard, and one heart and head pattern. The great majority of judges, we have no doubt, are upright and pure; but some have been selected for flexible politics—some are passionate—some are in a hurry—some are violent churchmen—some resemble ancient females—some have the gout—some are eighty years old—some are blind, deaf, and have lost the power of smelling. All one to the unhappy prisoner—he has no choice.

It is impossible to put so gross an insult upon judges, jurymen, grand jurymen, or any person connected with the administration of justice, as to suppose that the longer time to be taken up by speeches of counsel constitutes the grand bar to the proposed alteration. If three hours would acquit a man, and he is hanged because he is only allowed two hours for his defence, the poor man is as much murdered as if his throat had been cut before he came into court. If twelve judges cannot do the most perfect justice, other twelve must be appointed. Strange administration of criminal law, to adhere obstinately to an inadequate number of judges, and to refuse any improvement which is incompatible with this arbitrary and capricious enactment. Neither is it quite certain that the proposed alteration would create a greater demand upon the time of the court. At present the counsel makes a defence by long cross-examinations and examinations in chief of the witnesses, and the judge allows a greater latitude than he would do, if the counsel of the prisoner were permitted to speak. The counsel by these oblique methods, and by stating false points of law for the express purpose of introducing facts, endeavours to obviate the injustice of the law, and takes up more time by this oblique, than he would do by a direct defence. But the best answer to this objection of time (which, if true, is no objection at all) is, that as many misdemeanours as felonies are tried in a given time, though counsel are allowed in the former, and not in the latter case.

One excuse for the absence of counsel is, that the evidence upon which the prisoner is convicted is always so clear, that the counsel cannot gainsay it. This is mere absurdity. There is not, and cannot be, any such rule. Many a man has been hung upon a string of circumstantial evidence, which not only very ingenious men, but very candid and judicious men, might criticise and call in question. If no one were found guilty but upon such evidence as would not admit of a doubt, half the crimes in the world would be unpunished. This dictum, by which the present practice has often been defended, was adopted by Lord Chancellor Nottingham. To the lot of this chancellor, however, it fell to pass sentence of death upon Lord Stafford, whom (as Mr. Denman justly observes) no court of justice, not even the house of lords (constituted as it was in those days), could have put to death, if he had had counsel to defend him.

To improve the criminal law of England, and to make it really deserving of the incessant eulogium which is lavished upon it, we would assimilate trials for felony to trials for high treason. The prisoner should not only have counsel, but a copy of the indictment and a list of the witnesses, many days antecedent to the trial. It is in the highest degree unjust that I should not see and study the description of the crime with which I am charged, if the most scrupulous exactness be required in that instrument which charges me with crime. If the place *where*, the time *when*, and the manner *how*, and the persons by whom, must all be specified with the most perfect accuracy, if any deviation from this accuracy is fatal, the prisoner, or his legal advisers, should have a full opportunity of judging whether the scruples of the law have been attended to in the formation of the indictment; and they ought not to be confined to the hasty and imperfect consideration which can be given to an indictment exhibited for the first time in court. Neither is it possible for the prisoner to repel accusation till he knows who is to be brought against him. He may see suddenly, stuck up in the witness's box, a man who has been writing him letters, to extort money from the threat of evidence he could produce. The character of such a witness would be destroyed in a moment, if the letters were produced; and the letters would have been produced, of course, if the prisoner had imagined such a person would have been brought forward by the prosecutor. It is utterly impossible for a prisoner to know in what way he may be assailed, and against what species of attacks he is to guard. Conversations may be brought against him which he has forgotten, and to which he could (upon notice) have given another colour and complexion. Actions are made to bear upon his case, which (if he had known they would have been referred to) might have been explained in the most satisfactory manner. All these modes of attack are pointed out by the list of witnesses transmitted to the prisoner, and he has time to prepare his answer, as it is perfectly just he should have. This is justice, when a prisoner has ample means of compelling the attendance of his witnesses; when his written accusation is put into his hand, and he has time to study it—when he knows in what manner his guilt is to be proved, and when he has a man of practised understanding to state his facts, and prefer his arguments. Then criminal justice may march on boldly. The judge has no stain of blood on his ermine; and the phrases which English people are so fond of lavishing upon the humanity of their laws will have a real foundation. At present this part of the law is a mere relic of the barbarous injustice by which accusation in the early part of our jurisprudence was always confounded with guilt. The greater part of these abuses have been brushed away, as this cannot fail soon to be. In the mean time, it is defended (as every other abuse has been defended) by men who think it their duty to defend every thing which *is*, and to dread every thing which *is not*. We are told that the judge does what he does not do, and ought not to do. The most pernicious effects are anticipated in trials of felony, from that which is found to produce the most perfect justice in civil causes, and in cases of treason and misdemeanour: we are called upon to continue a practice without example in any other country, and are required by lawyers to consider that custom as humane, which every one who is not a lawyer pronounces to be most cruel and unjust—and which has not been brought forward to general notice, only because its bad effects are confined to the last and lowest of mankind.*

* All this nonsense is now put an end to. Counsel is allowed to the prisoner, and they are permitted to speak in his defence.

CATHOLICS.*

[Edinburgh Review, 1827.]

If a poor man were to accept a guinea upon the condition that he spoke all the evil he could of another whom he believed to be innocent, and whose imprisonment he knew he should prolong, and whose privations he knew he should increase by his false testimony, would not the person so hired be one of the worst and basest of human beings? And would not his guilt be aggravated, if, up to the moment of receiving his *aceldama*, he had spoken in terms of high praise of the person whom he subsequently accused? Would not the latter feature of the case prove him to be as much without shame as the former evinced him to be without principle? Would the guilt be less, if the person so hired were a man of education? Would it be less if he were above want? Would it be less, if the profession and occupation of his life were to decide men's rights, or to teach them morals and religion? Would it be less by the splendour of the bribe? Does a bribe of 3000*l.* leave a man innocent, whom a bribe of 30*l.* would cover with infamy? You are of a mature period of life, when the opinions of an honest man ought to be, and are fixed. On Monday you were a barrister or a country clergyman, a serious and temperate friend to religious liberty and Catholic emancipation. In a few weeks from this time you are a bishop, or a dean, or a judge—publishing and speaking charges and sermons against the poor Catholics, and explaining away this sale of your soul by every species of falsehood, shabbiness, and equivocation. You may carry a bit of ermine on your shoulder, or hide the lower moiety of the body in a silken petticoat—and men may call you Mr. Dean, or My Lord; but you have sold your honour and your conscience for money; and, though better paid, you are as base as the witness who stands at the door of the judgment-hall, to swear whatever the suborner will put into his mouth, and to receive whatever he will put in his pocket.†

When soldiers exercise, there stands a goodly portly person out of the ranks, upon whom all eyes are directed, and whose signs and motions, in the performance of the manual exercise, all the soldiers follow. The Germans, we believe, call him a *Flugelman.* We propose Lord Nugent as a political flugelman;—he is always consistent, plain and honest, steadily and straightly pursuing his object without hope or fear, under the influence of good feelings and high principle. The House of Commons does not contain within its walls a more honest, upright man.

We seize upon the opportunity which this able pamphlet of his lordship affords us, to renew our attention to the Catholic question. There is little new to be said; but we must not be silent, or, in these days of baseness and tergiversation, we shall be supposed to have deserted our friend the Pope; and they will say of us, *Prostant venales apud Lambeth et Whitehall.* God forbid it should ever be said of us with justice—it is pleasant to loll and roll, and to accumulate—to be a purple and fine linen man, and to be called by some of those nicknames which frail and ephemeral beings are so fond of accumulating upon each other;—but the best thing of all is to live like honest men, and to add something to the cause of liberality, justice, and truth.

The Letter to Lord Milton is very well and very pleasantly written. We were delighted with the liberality and candour of the Archbishop of Cashel. The charge is in the highest degree creditable to him. He must lay his account for the furious hatred of bigots, and the incessant gnawing of rats.

There are many men who (thoroughly aware that the Catholic question must be ultimately carried) delay their acquiescence till the last moment, and wait till the moment of peril and civil war before they yield. That this moment is not quite so remote as was supposed a twelvemonth since, the events now passing in the world seem to afford the strongest proof. The truth is, that the disaffected state of Ireland is a standing premium for war with every cabinet in Europe which has the most distant intention of quarrelling with this country for any other cause. "*If we are to go to war, let us do so when the discontents of Ireland are at their greatest height, before any spirit of concession has been shown by the British cabinet.*" Does any man imagine that so plain and obvious a principle has not been repeatedly urged on the French cabinet?—that the eyes of the Americans are shut upon the state of Ireland—and that that great and ambitious republic will not, in case of war, aim a deadly blow at this most sensitive part of the British empire? We should really say that England has fully as much to fear from Irish fraternization with America as with France. The language is the same; the Americans have preceded them in the struggle; the number of emigrant and rebel Irish is very great in America; and all parties are sure of perfect toleration under the protection of America. We are astonished at the madness and folly of Englishmen, who do not perceive that both France and America are only waiting for a con-

* 1. *A Plain Statement in support of the Political Claims of the Roman Catholics; in a Letter to the Rev. Sir George Lee, Bart.* By Lord Nugent, Member of Parliament for Aylesbury. London, Hookham. 1826.
2. *A Letter to Viscount Milton, M. P.* By One of his Constituents. London, Ridgway. 1827.
3. *Charge by the Archbishop of Cashel.* Dublin, Milliken.

† It is very far from our intention to say that all who were for the Catholics, and are now against them, have made this change from base motives; it is equally far from our intention not to say that many men of both professions have subjected themselves to this shocking imputation.

venient opportunity to go to war with this country; and that one of the first blows aimed at our independence would be the invasion of Ireland.

We should like to argue this matter with a regular tory lord, whose members vote steadily against the Catholic question. "I wonder that mere fear does not make you give up the Catholic question! Do you mean to put this fine place in danger—the venison—the pictures—the pheasants—the cellars—the hot-house and the grapery? Should you like to see six or seven thousand French or Americans landed in Ireland, and aided by a universal insurrection of the Catholics? Is it worth your while to run the risk of their success? What evil from the possible encroachment of Catholics, by civil exertions, can equal the danger of such a position as this? How can a man of your carriages, and horses, and hounds, think of putting your high fortune in such a predicament, and crying out, like a schoolboy or a chaplain, "Oh, we shall beat them! we shall put the rascals down!" No Popery, I admit to your lordship, is a very convenient cry at an election, and has answered your end; but do not push the matter too far: to bring on a civil war for no popery is a very foolish proceeding in a man who has two courses, and a remove! As you value your side-board of plate, your broad riband, your pier glasses—if obsequious domestics and large rooms are dear to you—if you love ease and flattery, titles and coats of arms—if the labour of the French cook, the dedication of the expecting poet, can move you—if you hope for a long life of side-dishes—if you are not insensible to the periodical arrival of the turtle fleets—emancipate the Catholics! Do it for your ease, do it for your indolence, do it for your safety—emancipate and eat, emancipate and drink—emancipate, and preserve the rent-roll and the family estate!"

The most common excuse of the *Great Shabby* is, that the Catholics are their own enemies—that the violence of Mr. O'Connell and Mr. Shiel have ruined their cause—that, but for these boisterous courses, the question would have been carried before this time. The answer to this nonsense and baseness is, that the very reverse is the fact. The mild and the long-suffering may suffer for ever in this world. If the Catholics had stood with their hands before them simpering at the Earls of Liverpool and the Lords Bathurst of the moment, they would not have been emancipated till the year of our Lord four thousand. As long as the patient will suffer, the cruel will kick. No treason—no rebellion—but as much stubbornness and stoutness as the law permits—a thorough intimation that you know what is your due, and that you are determined to have it if you can *lawfully* get it. This is the conduct we recommend to the Irish. If they go on withholding, and forbearing, and hesitating whether this is the time for the discussion or that is the time, they will be laughed at for another century as fools—and kicked for another century as slaves. "I must have my bill paid (says the sturdy and irritated tradesman); your master has put me off twenty times under different pretences. I know he is at home, and I will not quit the premises till I get the money." Many a tradesman gets paid in this manner who would soon smirk and smile himself into the gazette, if he trusted to the promises of the great.

Can any thing be so utterly childish and foolish as to talk of the bad taste of the Catholic leaders?—as if, in a question of conferring on, or withholding important civil rights from seven millions of human beings, any thing could arrest the attention of a wise man but the good or evil consequences of so great a measure. Suppose Mr. S. does smell slightly of tobacco—admit Mr. L. to be occasionally stimulated by rum and water—allow that Mr. F. was unfeeling in speaking of the Duke of York—what has all this nonsense to do with the extinction of religious hatred and the pacification of Ireland? Give it if it is right, refuse it if it is wrong. How it is asked, or how it is given or refused, is less than the dust of the balance.

What is the real reason why a good honest tory, living at ease on his possessions, is an enemy to Catholic emancipation? He admits the Catholic of his own rank to be a gentleman, and not a bad subject—and about theological disputes an excellent tory never troubles his head. Of what importance is it to him whether an Irish Catholic or an Irish Protestant is a judge in the King's Bench at Dublin? None; but *I am afraid for the church of Ireland*, says our alarmist. Why do you care so much for the church of Ireland, a country you never live in?—*Answer—I do not care so much for the church of Ireland, if I was sure the church of England would not be destroyed.*—And is it for the Church of England alone that you fear?—*Answer—Not quite to that, but I am afraid we should all be lost, that every thing would be overturned, and that I should lose my rank and my estate.* Here, then, we say, is a long series of dangers, which (if there were any chance of their ever taking place) would require half a century for their development; and the danger of losing Ireland by insurrection and invasion, which may happen in six months, is utterly overlooked and forgotten. And if a foreign influence should ever be fairly established in Ireland, how many hours would the Irish church, how many months would the English church, live after such an event? How much is any English title worth after such an event—any English family—any English estate? We are astonished that the brains of rich Englishmen do not fall down into their bellies in talking of the Catholic question—that they do not reason through the cardia and the pylorus—that all the organs of digestion do not become intellectual. The descendants of the proudest noblemen in England may become beggars in a foreign land from this disgraceful nonsense of the Catholic question—fit only for the ancient females of a market town.

What alarms us in the state of England is the uncertain basis on which its prosperity is placed—and the prodigious mass of hatred which the English government continues, by its obstinate bigotry, to accumulate—eight hundred and forty millions sterling of debt. The revenue depending upon the demand for the shoes, stockings, and breeches of Europe—and seven millions of Catholics in a state of the greatest fury and exasperation. We persecute as if we did not *owe* a shilling—we spend as if we had no disaffection. This, by possibility, may go on; but it is dangerous walking—the chance is, there will be a fall. No wise man should take such a course. All probabilities are against it. We are astonished that Lord Hertford and Lord Lowther, shrewd and calculating tories, do not see that it is nine to one against such a game.

It is not only the event of war we fear in the military struggle with Ireland; but the expense of war, and the expenses of the English government, are paving the way for future revolutions. The world never yet saw so extravagant a government as the government of England. Not only is economy not practised—but it is despised; and the idea of it connected with disaffection, Jacobinism, and Joseph Hume. Every rock in the ocean where a cormorant can perch is occupied by our troops—has a governor, deputy-governor, store-keeper, and deputy-store-keeper—and will soon have an archdeacon and a bishop. Military colleges, with thirty-four professors, educating seventeen ensigns per annum, being half an ensign for each professor, with every species of nonsense, athletic, sartorial, and plumigerous. A just and necessary war costs this country about one hundred pounds a minute; whipcord fifteen thousand pounds; red tape seven thousand pounds; lace for drummers and fifers, nineteen thousand pounds; a pension to one man who has broken his head at the Pole; to another who has shattered his leg at the Equator; subsidies to Persia; secret service-money to Thibet; an annuity to Lady Henry Somebody and her seven daughters—the husband being shot at some place where we never ought to have had any soldiers at all; and the elder brother returning four members to Parliament. Such a scene of extravagance, corruption, and expense as must paralyze the industry, and mar the fortunes, of the most industrious, spirited people that ever existed.

Few men consider the historical view which will be taken of present events. The bubbles of last year; the fishing for half-crowns in Vigo Bay; the Milk Muffin and Crumpet Companies; the Apple, Pear, and Plum Associations; the National Gooseberry and Current Company; will all be remembered as instances of that partial madness to which society is occasionally exposed. What will be said of all the intolerable trash which is issued forth at public meetings of No Popery? The follies of one century are scarcely credible in that which succeeds it. A grandmamma of 1827 is as wise as a very wise man of 1727. If the world lasts till 1927, the grandmammas of that period will be far wiser than the tip-top No-Popery men of this day. That this childish nonsense will have got out of the drawing-room, there can be no doubt. It will most probably have passed through the steward's room —and butler's pantry, into the kitchen. This is the case with ghosts. They no longer loll on couches and sip tea; but are down on their knees scrubbing with the scullion—or stand sweating, and basting with the cook. Mrs. Abigail turns up her nose at them, and the housekeeper declares for flesh and blood, and will have none of their company.

It is delicious to the persecution-fanciers to reflect that no general bill has passed in favour of the Protestant Dissenters. They are still disqualified from holding any office—and are only protected from prosecution by an annual indemnity act. So that the sword of Damocles still hangs over them—not suspended, indeed, by a thread, but by a cart-rope—still it hangs there an insult, if not an injury, and prevents the painful idea from presenting itself to the mind of perfect toleration, and pure justice. There is the larva of tyranny, and the skeleton of malice. Now this is all we presume to ask for the Catholics—admission to Parliament, exclusion from every possible office by law, and annual indemnity for the breach of law This is surely much more agreeable to feebleness, to littleness, and to narrowness, than to say the Catholics are as free and as eligible as ourselves.

The most intolerable circumstance of the Catholic dispute is, the conduct of the Dissenters. Any man may dissent from the Church of England, and preach against it, by paying sixpence. Almost every tradesman in a market town is a preacher. It must absolutely be ride and tie with them; the butcher must hear the baker in the morning, and the baker listen to the butcher in the afternoon, or there would be no congregation. We have often speculated upon the peculiar trade of the preacher from his style of action. Some have a tying-up or parcel-packing action; some strike strongly against the anvil of the pulpit some screw, some bore, some act as if they were managing a needle. The occupation of the preceding week can seldom be mistaken In the country, three or four thousand Ranters are sometimes encamped, supplicating in religious platoons, or roaring psalms out of waggons. Now all this freedom is very proper; because, though it is abused, yet in truth there is no other principle in religious matters, than to let men alone as long as they keep the peace. Yet we should imagine this unbounded license of Dissenters should teach them a little charity towards the Catholics, and a little respect for their religious freedom. But the picture of sects is this—there are twenty fettered men in a jail, and every one is employed in loosening his own fetters with one hand, and riveting those of his neighbour with the other.

"'If, then,' says a minister of our own church, the Reverend John Fisher, rector of Wavenden, in this county, in a sermon published some years ago, and entitled 'The Utility of the Church Establishment, and its Safety consistent with Religious Freedom'—'If, then, the Protestant religion could have originally worked its way in this country against numbers, prejudices, bigotry, and interest; if, in times of its infancy, the power of the prince could not prevail against it; surely, when confirmed by age, and rooted in the affections of the people—when invested with authority, and in full enjoyment of wealth and power—when cherished by a sovereign who holds his very throne by this sacred tenure, and whose conscientious attachment to it well warrants the title of Defender of the Faith—surely any attack upon it must be contemptible, any alarm of danger must be imaginary.' "—*Lord Nugent's Letter*, p. 18.

To go into a committee upon the state of the Catholic laws is to reconsider, as Lord Nugent justly observes, passages in our domestic history, which bear date about 270 years ago. Now, what human plan, device, or invention, 270 years old, does not require reconsideration? If a man drest as he drest 270 years ago, the pug-dogs in the street would tear him to pieces. If he lived in the houses of 270 years ago, unrevised and uncorrected, he would die of rheumatism in a week. If he listened to the sermons of 270 years ago, he would perish with sadness and fatigue; and when a man cannot make a coat or a cheese, for 50 years together, without making them better, can it be said that laws made in those days of ignorance, and framed in the fury of religious hatred, need no revision, and are capable of no amendment.

We have not the smallest partiality for the Catholic religion; quite the contrary. That it should exist at all—that all Catholics are not converted to the Protestant religion—we consider to be a serious evil; but there they are, with their spirit as strong, and their opinions as decided, as your own; the Protestant part of the cabinet have quite given up all idea of putting them to death; what remains to be done? We all admit the evil; the object is to make it as little as possible. One method commonly resorted to, we are sure, does not lessen, but increase the evil; and that is, to falsify history, and deny plain and obvious facts, to the injury of the Catholics. No true friend to the Protestant religion, and to the Church of England, will ever have recourse to such disingenuous arts as these.

"Our histories have not, I believe, stated what is untrue of Queen Mary, nor, perhaps, have they very much exaggerated what is true of her; but our arguers, whose only talk is of Smithfield, are generally very uncandid in what they conceal. It would appear to be little known that the statutes which enabled Mary to burn those who had conformed to the church of her father and brother, were Protestant statutes, declaring the common law against heresy, and framed by her father Henry the Eighth, and confirmed and acted upon by order of council of her brother Edward the Sixth, enabling that mild and temperate young sovereign to burn divers misbelievers, by sentence of commissioners (little better, says Neale, than a Protestant Inquisition) appointed to 'examine and search after all Anabaptists, Heretics, or contemners of the Book of Common Prayer.' It would appear to be seldom considered, that her zeal might very possibly have been warmed by the circumstance of both her chaplains having been imprisoned for their religion, and herself arbitrarily detained, and her safety threatened, during the short but persecuting reign of her brother. The sad evidences of the violence of those days are by no means confined to her acts. The fagots of persecution were not kindled by Papists only, nor did they cease to blaze when the power of using them as instruments of conversion ceased to be in Popish hands. Cranmer himself, in his dreadful death, met with but equal measure for the flames to which he had doomed several who denied the *spiritual* supremacy of Henry the Eighth; to which he had doomed also a Dutch Arian, in Edward the Sixth's reign; and to which, with great pains and difficulty, he had persuaded that prince to doom another miserable enthusiast, Joan Bocher, for some metaphysical notions of her own on the divine incarnation. 'So that on both sides' (says Lord Herbert of Cherbury) 'it grew a bloody time.' Calvin burned Servetus at Geneva, for 'discoursing concerning the Trinity contrary to the sense of the whole church; and thereupon set forth a book wherein he giveth an account of his doctrine, and of whatever else had passed in this affair, and teacheth that the sword may be lawfully employed against heretics.' Yet Calvin was no Papist. John Knox extolled in his writings, as 'the godly fact of James Melvil,' the savage murderer by which Cardinal Beaton was made to expiate his many and cruel persecutions; a murder to which, by the great popular eloquence of Knox, his fellow labourers in the vineyard of reformation, Lesly and Melvil, had been excited; and yet John Knox, and Lesly and Melvil, were no Papists. Henry the Eighth, whose one virtue was impartiality in these matters, (if an impartial and evenly balanced persecution of all sects be a virtue,) beheaded a chancellor and a bishop, because having admitted his civil supremacy, they doubted his spiritual. Of the latter of them Lord Herbert says, 'The pope, who suspected not perchance, that the bishop's end was so near, had, for more testimony of his favour to him as disaffection to our king, sent him a cardinal's hat; but unseasonably, his head being off.' He beheaded the Countess of Salisbury, because at upwards of eighty years old she wrote a letter to Cardinal Pole, her own son: and he burned Barton, the 'Holy Maid of Kent,' for a prophecy of his death. He burned four Anabaptists in one day for opposing the doctrine of infant baptism; and he burned Lambert, and Anne Ascue, and Belerican, and Lassells, and Adams, on another day, for opposing that of transubstantiation; with many others of lesser note, who refused to subscribe to his Six Bloody Articles, as they were called, or whose opinions fell short of his, or exceeded them, or who abided by opinions after he had abandoned them; and all this after the Reformation. And yet Henry the Eighth was the sovereign who first delivered us from the yoke of Rome.

"In later times, thousands of Protestant Dissenters of the four great sects were made to languish in loathsome prisons, and hundreds to perish miserably, during the reign of Charles the Second, under a Protestant high church government, who then first applied, in the prayer for the Parliament, the epithets of 'most religious and gracious,' to a sovereign whom they knew to be profligate and unprincipled beyond example, and had reason to suspect to be a concealed Papist.

"Later still, Archbishop Sharpe was sacrificed by the murderous enthsiasm of certain Scotch Covenanters, who yet appear to have sincerely believed themselves inspired by Heaven to this act of cold-blooded barbarous assassination.

"On subjects like these, silence on all sides, and a mutual interchange of repentance, forgiveness, and oblivion, is wisdom. But to quote grievances on one side only, is not honesty."—*Lord Nugent's Letter*, pp. 24—27.

Sir Richard Birnie can only attend to the complaints of individuals; but no cases of swindling are brought before him so atrocious as the violation of the treaty of Limerick, and the disappointment of those hopes, and the frustration of that arrangement; which hopes, and which arrangements, were held out as one of the great arguments for the union. The chapter of English fraud comes next to the chapter of English cruelty, in the history of Ireland—and both are equally disgraceful.

Nothing can be more striking than the conduct of the parent legislature to the legislature of the West Indian Islands. "We cannot leave you to yourselves upon these points" (says the English government); "the wealth of the planter and the commercial prosperity of the island are not the only points to be looked to. We must look to the general rights of humanity, and see that they are not outraged in the case of the poor slave. It is impossible we can be satisfied, till we know that he is placed in a state of progress and amelioration." How beautiful is all this! and how wise, and how humane and affecting are our efforts throughout Europe to put an end to the slave trade? Wherever three or four negotiators are gathered together, a British diplomate appears among them, with some article of kindness and pity for the poor negro. All is mercy and compassion, except when wretched Ireland is concerned. The saint who swoons at the lashes of the Indian slave is the encourager of No-Popery meetings, and the hard, bigoted, domineering tyrant of Ireland.

See the folly of delaying to settle a question which, in the end, must be settled, and, ere long, to the advantage of the Catholics. How the price rises by delay! This argument is extremely well put by Lord Nugent.

"I should observe that two occasions have already been lost of granting these claims, coupled with what were called securities, such as never can return. In 1808, the late Duke of Norfolk and Lord Grenville, in the one house, and Mr. Ponsonby and Mr. Grattan, in the other, were authorized by the Irish Catholic body to propose a negative to be vested in the crown upon the appointment of their bishops. Mr. Perceval, the chancellor, and the spiritual bench, did not see the importance of this opportunity. It was rejected; the Irish were driven to despair; and in the same tomb with the question of 1808 lies forever buried the veto. The same was the fate with what were called the 'wings' attached to Sir Francis Burdett's bill of last year. I voted for them, not for the sake certainly of extending the patronage of the crown over a new body of clergy, nor yet for the sake of diminishing the popular character of elections in Ireland, but because Mr. O'Connell, and because some of the Protestant friends of the measure who knew Ireland the best, recommended them; and because I believed, from the language of some who supported it only on these conditions, that they offered the fairest chance for the measure being carried. I voted for them as the price of Catholic emancipation, for which I can scarcely contemplate any Irish price that I would not pay. With the same object, I would vote for them again; but I shall never again have the opportunity. For these also, if they were thought of any value as securities, the events of this year in Ireland have shown you that you have lost for ever. And the necessity of the great measure becomes every day more urgent and unavoidable."—*Lord Nugent's Letter*, pp. 71, 72.

Can any man living say that Ireland is not in a much more dangerous state than it was before the Catholic convention began to exist? that the inflammatory state of that country is not becoming worse and worse?—that those men whom we call demagogues and incendiaries have not produced a very considerable and alarming effect upon the Irish population? Where is this to end? But the fool lifteth up his voice in the coffee-house, and sayeth, "We shall give them an hearty thrashing: let them arise—the sooner the better—we will soon put them down again." The fool sayeth this in the coffee-house, and the greater fool praiseth him. But does Lord Stowell say this? does Mr. Peel say this? does the Marquis of Hertford say this? do sensible, calm, and reflecting men like these, not admit the extreme danger of combating against invasion and disaffection, and this with our forces spread in active hostility over the whole face of the globe? Can they feel this vulgar, hectoring certainty of success, and stupidly imagine that a thing cannot be because it has never yet been? because we have hitherto maintained our tyranny in Ireland against all Europe, that we are always to maintain it? And then, what if the struggle does at last end in our favour? Is the loss of English lives and of English money not to be taken into account? Is this the way in which a nation overwhelmed with debt, and trembling whether its looms and ploughs will not be overmatched by the looms and ploughs of the rest of Europe—is this the way in which such a country is to husband its resources? Is the best blood of the land to be flung away in a war of hassocks and surplices? Are cities to be summoned for the Thirty-nine Articles, and men to be led on to the charge by professors of divinity? The expense of *keeping* such a country must be added to all other enormous expenses. What is really possessed of a country so subdued? four or five yards round a sentry-box, and no more. And in twenty years' time it is all to do over again—another war—another rebellion, and another enormous and ruinously expensive contest, with the same dreadful uncertainty of the issue! It is forgotten, too, that a new feature has arisen in the history of this country. In all former insurrections in Ireland no democratic party existed in England. The efforts of government were left free and unimpeded. But suppose a stoppage in your manufactures coincident with a rising of the Irish Catholics, when every soldier is employed in the sacred duty of Papist-hunting. Can any man contemplate such a state of things without horror? Can any man say that he is taken by surprise for such a combination? Can any man say that any danger to church or state is comparable to this? But for the prompt interference of the military in the early part of 1826, three or four hundred thousand starving manufacturers would have carried ruin and destruction over the north of England, and over Scotland. These dangers are inseparable from an advanced state of manufactures—but they need not the addition of other and greater perils, which need not exist in any country too wise and too enlightened for persecution.

Where is the weak point in these plain arguments? Is it the remoteness of the chance of foreign war? Alas! we have been at war 35 minutes out of every hour since the peace of Utrecht. The state of war seems more natural to man than the state of peace; and if we turn from general probabilities to the state of Europe—Greece to be liberated—Turkey to be destroyed—Portugal and Spain to be made free—the wounded vanity of the French, the increasing arrogance of the Americans, and our own philopolemical folly, are endless scenes of war. We believe it at all times a better speculation to make ploughshares into swords than swords into ploughshares. If war is certain, we believe insurrection to be quite as certain. We cannot believe but that the French or Americans would, in case of war, make a serious attempt upon Ireland, and that all Ireland would rush, tail foremost, into insurrection.

A new source of disquietude and war has lately risen in Ireland. Our saints are evangelical people, or serious people, or by whatever name they are to be designated, have taken the field in Ireland against the pope, and are converting in the large way. Three or four Irish Catholic prelates take a post-chaise, and curse the converters and the converted. A battle royal ensues with shillelas: the policeman comes in, and, reckless of Lambeth or the Vatican, makes no distinction between what is perpendicular, and what is hostile, but knocks down every body and every thing which is upright; and so the feud ends for the day. We have no doubt but that these efforts will tend to bring things to a crisis much sooner between the parties, than the disgraceful conduct of the cabinet alone would do.

"It is a charge not imputed by the laws of England, nor by the oaths which exclude the Catholics: for those oaths impute only spiritual errors. But it is imputed, which is more to the purpose, by those persons who approve of the excluding oaths, and wish them retained. But, to the whole of this imputation, even if no other instance could be adduced, as far as a strong and remarkable example can prove the negative of an assumption which there is not a single example to support—the full, and sufficient, and incontestable answer is Canada. Canada, which, until you can destroy the memory of all that now remains to you of your sovereignty on the North American continent, is an answer practical, memorable, difficult to be accounted for, but blazing as the sun itself in sight of the whole world, to the whole charge of divided allegiance. At your conquest of Canada, you found it Roman Catholic; you had to choose for her a constitution in church and state. You were wise enough not to thwart public opinion. Your own conduct towards Presbyterianism in Scotland was an example for imitation; your own conduct towards Catholocism in Ireland was a beacon for avoidance; and in Canada you established and endowed the religion of the people. Canada was your only Roman Catholic colony. Your other colonies revolted; they called on a Catholic power to support them, and they achieved their independence. Catholic Canada, with what Lord Liverpool would call her half-allegiance, *alone* stood by you. She fought by your side against the interference of Catholic France. To reward and encourage her loyalty, you endowed in Canada bishops to say mass, and to ordain others to say mass, whom, at that very time, your laws would have hanged for saying mass in England; and Canada is still yours in spite of Catholic France, in spite of her spiritual obedience to the pope, in spite of Lord Liverpool's argument, and in spite of the independence of all the states that surround her. This is the only trial you have made. Where you allow to the Roman Catholics their religion undisturbed, it has proved itself to be compatible with the most faithful allegiance. It is only where you have placed allegiance and religion before them as a dilemma, that they have preferred (as who will say they ought not?) their religion to their allegiance. How then stands the imputation? Disproved by history, disproved in all states where both religions co-exist, and in both hemispheres, and asserted in an exposition by Lord Liverpool, solemnly and repeatedly abjured by all Catholics, of the discipline of *their* church."—*Lord Nugent's Letter*, pp. 35, 36.

Can any man who has gained permission to take off his strait-waistcoat, and been out of Bedlam three weeks, believe that the Catholic question will be set to rest by the conversion of the Irish Catholics to the Protestant religion? The best chance of conversion will be gained by taking care that the point of honour is not against conversion.

"We may, I think, collect from what we know of the ordinary feelings of men that, by admitting all to a community of political benefits, we should remove a material impediment that now presents itself to the advances of proselytism to our established mode of worship; particularly assuming, as we do, that it is the purest, and that the disfranchised mode is supported only by superstition and priestcraft. By external pressure and restraint, things are compacted as well in the moral as in the physical world. Where a sect is at spiritual variance with the established church, it only requires an abridgment of civil privileges to render it at once a political faction. Its members become instantly pledged, some from enthusiasm, some from resentment, and many from honourable shame, to cleave with desperate fondness to the suffering fortunes of an hereditary religion. Is this human nature, or is it not? Is it a natural or an unnatural feeling for the representative of an ancient Roman Catholic family, even if in his heart he rejected the controverted tenets of his early faith, to scorn an open conformity to ours, so long as such conformity brings with it the irremovable suspicion that faith and conscience may have bowed to the base hope of temporal advantage? Every man must feel and act for himself: but, in my opinion, a good man might be put to difficulty to determine whether more harm is not done by the example of one changing his religion to his worldly advantage, than good by his openly professing conformity from what we think error to what we think truth."—*Lord Nugent's Letter*, pp. 54, 55.

"We will not be bullied out of the Catholic question." This is a very common text, and requires some comment. If you mean that the sense of personal danger shall not prevent you from doing what you think right—this is a worthy and proper feeling, but no such motive is suspected, and no such question is at issue. Nobody doubts but that any English gentleman would be ready to join his No-Popery corps, and to do his duty to the community, if the government required it; but the question is, Is it worth while in the government to require it? Is it for the general advantage that such a war should be carried on for such an object? It is a question not of personal valour, but of political expediency. Decide seriously if it is worth the price of civil war to exclude the Catholics, and act accordingly; taking it for granted that you possess, and that every body supposes you to possess, the vulgar attribute of personal courage; but do not draw your sword like a fool, from the unfounded apprehension of being called a coward.

We have great hopes of the Duke of Clarence. Whatever else he may be, he is not a bigot—not a person who thinks it necessary to show respect to his royal father, by prolonging the miseries and incapacities of six millions of people. If he ascends the throne of these realms, he must stand the fire of a few weeks' clamour and unpopularity. If the measure is passed by the end of May, we can promise his royal highness it will utterly be forgotten before the end of June. Of all human nonsense, it is surely the greatest to talk of respect to the late king—respect to the memory of the Duke of York—by not voting for the Catholic question. Bad enough to burn widows when the husband dies—bad enough to burn horses, dogs, butlers, footmen, and coachmen, on the funeral pile of a Scythian warrior—but to offer up the happiness of seven millions of people to the memory of the dead, is certainly the most insane sepulchral oblation of which history makes mention. The best compliment to these deceased princes, is to remember their real good qualities, and to forget (as soon as we can forget it) that these good qualities were tarnished by limited and mistaken views of religious liberty.

Persecuting gentlemen forget the expense of persecution; whereas, of all luxuries, it is the most expensive. The Ranters do not cost us a farthing, because they are not disqualified by ranting. The Methodists and Unitarians are gratis. The Irish Catholics, supposing every alternate year to be war, as it has been for the last century, will cost us within these next twenty years, forty millions of money. There are 20,000 soldiers there in time of peace; in war, including the militia, their numbers will be doubled—and there must be a very formidable fleet in addition. Now, when the tax paper comes round, and we are to make a return of the greatest number of horses, buggies, ponies, dogs, cats, bulfinches, and canary birds, &c., and to be taxed accordingly, let us remember how well and wisely our money has been spent, and not repine that we have purchased, by severe taxation, the high and exalted pleasures of intolerance and persecution.

It is mere unsupported and unsupportable nonsense to talk of the exclusive disposition of the Catholics to persecute. The Protestants have murdered, and tortured, and laid waste as much as the Catholics. Each party, as it gained the upper hand, tried death as the remedy for heresy—both parties have tried it in vain.

A distinction is set up between civil rights, and political power, and applied against the Catholics: the real difference between these two words is, that civil comes from a Latin word, and political from a Greek one; but if there is any difference in their meaning, the Catholics do not ask for political power, but for eligibility to political power. The Catholics have never prayed, or dreamt of praying, that so many of the judges and king's counsel should necessarily be Catholics; but that no law should exist which prevented them from becoming so, if a Protestant king chose to make them so. Eligibility to political power is a civil privilege, of which we have no more right to deprive any man than of any other civil privilege. The good of the state may require that all civil rights may be taken from Catholics; but to say that eligibility to political power is not a civil right, and that to take it away without grave cause, would not be a great act of injustice, is mere declamation. Besides, what is called political power, and what are called civil rights, are given or withholden, without the least reference to any principle, but by mere caprice. A right of voting is given—this is political power; eligibility to the office of alderman or bank director is refused—this is a civil right: the distinction is perpetually violated, just as it has suited the state of parties for the moment. And here a word or two on the manner of handling the question. Because some offices must be filled with Catholics, all would be: this is one topic. A second is, because there might be inconvenience from a Catholic king or chancellor, that, therefore, there would be no inconvenience from Catholic judges or serjeants. In talking of establishments, they always take care to blend the Irish and English establishments, and never to say which is meant, though the circumstances of both are as different as possible. It is always presumed, that sects holding opinions contrary to the establishment, are *hostile* to the establishment; meaning by the word hostile, that they are combined, or ready to combine, for its destruction. It is contended that the Catholics would not be satis fied by these concessions; meaning, thereby, that many would not be so—but forgetting to add, that many *would* be quite satisfied—all *more* satisfied, and less likely to run into rebellion. It is urged that the mass of Catholics are indifferent to the question; whereas (never mind the cause) there is not a Catholic ploughboy, at this moment, who is not ready to risk his life for it, nor a Protestant stable-boy, who does not give himself airs of superiority over any papistical cleaner of horses, who is scrubbing with him under the same roof.

The Irish were quiet under the severe code of Queen Anne—so the half-murdered man left on the ground bleeding by thieves is quiet; and he only moans, and cries for help as he recovers. There was a method which would have made the Irish still more quiet, and effectually have put an end to all further solicitation respecting the Catholic question. It was adopted in the case of the wolves.

They are forming societies in Ireland for the encouragement of emigration, and striving, and successfully striving, to push their redundant population into Great Britain. Our business is to pacify Ireland—to give confidence to capitalists—and to keep their people where they are. On the day the Catholic question was passed, all property in Ireland would rise 20 per cent.

Protestants admit that there are sectaries sitting in Parliament, who differ from the Church of England as much as the Catholics; but it is forgotten that, according to the doctrine of the Church of England, the Unitarians are considered as condemned to eternal punishment in another world—and that many such have seats in Parliament. And can any thing be more preposterous (as far as doctrine has any influence in these matters) than that men, whom we believe to be singled out as objects of God's eternal vengeance, should have a seat in our national councils: and that Catholics, whom we believe may be saved, should not?

The only argument which has any *appearance of weight*, is the question of divided allegiance; and, generally speaking, we should say it is the argument which produces the greatest effect in the country at large. England, in this respect, is in the same state, at least, as the whole of Catholic Europe. Is not the allegiance of every French, every Spanish, and every Italian Catholic (who is not a Roman,) divided? His king is in Paris, or Madrid, or Naples, while his high-priest is at Rome. We speak of it as an anomaly in politics; whereas, it is the state, and condition of almost the whole of Europe. The danger of this divided allegiance, they admit, is nothing, as long as it is confined to purely spiritual concerns; but it may extend itself to temporal matters, and so endanger the safety of the state. This danger, however, is greater in a Catholic than in a Protestant country; not only on account of the greater majority upon whom it might act: but because there are objects in a Catholic country much more desirable, and attainable, than in a country like England, where Popery does not exist, or Ireland, where it is humbled, and impoverished. Take, for instance, the freedom of the Gallican Church. What eternal disputes did this object give birth to? What a temptation to the Pope to infringe in rich Catholic countries! How is it possible his holiness can keep his hands from picking and stealing? It must not be imagined that Catholicism has been any defence against the hostility and aggression of the Pope; he has cursed and excommunicated every Catholic state in Europe, in their turns. Let that eminent Protestant, Lord Bathurst, state any one instance where, for the last century, the Pope has interfered with the temporal concerns of Great Britain. We can mention, and his lordship will remember, innumerable instances where he might have done so, if such were the modern habit and policy of the court of Rome. But the fact is, there is no court of Rome, and no Pope. There is a wax-work Pope, and a wax-work court of Rome. But popes of flesh and blood have long since disappeared; and in the same way, those great giants of the city exist no more, but their truculent images are at Guildhall. We doubt if there is in the treasury of the Pope change for a guinea—we are sure there is not in his armory one gun which will go off. We believe, if he attempted to bless any body whom Dr. Doyle cursed, or to curse any body whom Dr. Doyle blessed, that his blessings and curses would be as powerless as his artillery. Dr. Doyle* is the Pope of Ireland; and the ablest ecclesiastic of that country will always be its Pope—and that Lord Bathurst ought to know—most likely does know. But what a waste of life and time, to combat such arguments! Can my Lord Bathurst be ignorant? Can any man, who has the slightest knowledge of Ireland, be ignorant, that the portmanteau which sets out every quarter for Rome, and returns from it, is an heap of ecclesiastical matters, which have no more to do with the safety of the country, than they have to do with the safety of the moon—and which but for the respect to individual feelings, might all be published at Charing Cross? Mrs. *Flanagan*, intimidated by stomach complaints, wants a dispensation for eating flesh. *Cornelius Oh Bowel* has intermarried by accident with his grandmother; and finding that she is really his grandmother, his conscience is uneasy. *Mr. Mac Tooley*, the priest, is discovered to be married: and to have two sons, *Castor* and *Pollux Mac Tooley*. Three or four schools-full of little boys have been cursed for going to hear a Methodist preacher. Bargains for shirts and toe-nails of deceased saints—surplices and trencher-caps blessed by the Pope. These are the fruits of double allegiance—the objects of our incredible fear, and the cause of our incredible folly. There is not a syllable which goes to or comes from the court of Rome, which, by a judicious expenditure of sixpence by the year, would not be open to the examination of every member of the

* "Of this I can with great truth assure you; and my testimony, if not entitled to respect, should not be utterly disregarded, that papal influence will never induce the Catholics of this country either to continue tranquil, or to be disturbed, either to aid or to oppose the government; and that your lordship can contribute much more than the Pope to secure their allegiance, or to render them disaffected."—*Dr. Doyle's Letter to Lord Liverpool*, 115.

cabinet. Those who use such arguments know the answer to them as well as we do. The real evil they dread is the destruction of the church of Ireland, and, through that, of the Church of England. To which we reply, that such danger must proceed from the regular proceedings of Parliament, or be effected by insurrection and rebellion. The Catholics, restored to civil functions, would, we believe, be more likely to cling to the church than to Dissenters. If not, both Catholics and Dissenters must be utterly powerless against the overwhelming English interests and feelings in the house. Men are less inclined to run into rebellion, in proportion as they have less to complain of; and, of all other dangers, the greatest to the Irish and English church establishments, and to the Protestant faith throughout Europe, is *to leave Ireland in its present state of discontent.*

If the intention is to wait to the last, before concession is made, till the French or Americans have landed, and the holy standard has been unfurled, we ought to be sure of the terms which can be obtained at such a crisis. This game was played in America. Commissioners were sent in one year to offer and to press what would have been most thankfully received the year before; but they were always too late. The rapid concessions of England were outstripped by the more rapid exactions of the colonies; and the commissioners returned with the melancholy history, that they had humbled themselves before the rebels in vain. If you ever mean to concede at all, do it when every concession will be received as a favour. To wait till you are forced to treat, is as mean in principle as it is dangerous in effect.

Then, how many thousand Protestant Dissenters are there who pay a double allegiance to the king, and to the head of their church, who is not the king? Is not Mr. William Smith, member for Norwich, the head of the Unitarian Church? Is not Mr. Wilberforce the head of the Clapham Church? Are there not twenty preachers at Leeds, who regulate all the proceedings of the Methodists? The gentlemen we have mentioned are eminent, and most excellent men; but if any thing at all is to be apprehended from this divided allegiance, we should be infinitely more afraid of some Jacobinical fanatic at the head of Protestant votaries—some man of such character as Lord George Gordon—than we should of all the efforts of the Pope.

As so much evil is supposed to proceed from not obeying the king as head of the church, it might be supposed to be a very active office—that the king was perpetually interfering with the affairs of the church—and that orders were in a course of emanation from the throne which regulated the fervour, and arranged the devotion, of all the members of the Church of England. But we really do not know what orders are ever given by the king to the church, except the appointment of a fast-day once in three or four years;—nor can we conceive (for appointment to bishoprics is out of the question) what duties there would be to perform, if this allegiance were paid, instead of being withholden. Supremacy appears to us to be a mere name, without exercise of power—and allegiance to be a duty without any performance annexed. If any one will say what ought to be done, which is not done, on account of this divided allegiance, we shall better understand the magnitude of the evil. Till then, we shall consider it as a lucky Protestant phrase, good to look at, like the mottos and ornaments on cake, but not fit to be eaten.

Nothing can be more unfair than to expect, in an ancient church like that of the Catholics, the same uniformity as in churches which have not existed for more than two or three centuries. The coats and waistcoats of the reign of Henry VIII. bear some resemblance to the same garments of the present day; but, as you recede, you get to the skins of wild beasts, or the fleeces of sheep, for the garments of savages. In the same way, it is extremely difficult for a church, which has to do with the counsels of barbarous ages, not to be detected in some discrepancy of opinion; while in younger churches, every thing is fair and fresh, and of modern date and figure; and it is not the custom among theologians to own their church in the wrong. "No religion can stand, if men, without regard to their God, and with regard only to controversy, shall rake out of the rubbish of antiquity the obsolete and quaint follies of the sectarians, and affront the majesty of the Almighty, with the impudent catalogue of their devices; and it is a strong argument against the proscriptive system, that it helps to continue this shocking contest. Theologian against theologian, polemic against polemic, until the two madmen defame their common parent, and expose their common religion."—*Grattan's Speech on the Catholic Question*, 1805.

A good-natured and well-conditioned person has pleasure in keeping and distributing any thing that is good. If he detects any thing with superior flavour, he presses and invites, and is not easy till others participate;—and so it is with political and religious freedom. It is a pleasure to possess it, and a pleasure to communicate it to others. There is something shocking in the greedy, growling, guzzling monopoly of such a blessing.

France is no longer a nation of atheists; and therefore, a great cause of offence to the Irish Roman Catholic clergy is removed. Navigation by steam renders all shores more accessible. The union among Catholics is consolidated; all the dangers of Ireland are redoubled; every thing seems tending to an event fatal to England—fatal (whatever Catholics may foolishly imagine) to Ireland—and which will subject them both to the dominion of France.

Formerly a poor man might be removed from a parish if there was the slightest danger of his becoming chargeable; a hole in his coat or breeches excited suspicion. The churchwardens said, "He *has* cost us nothing, but he *may* cost us something; and we must not live even in the apprehension of evil." All this is changed; and the law now says, "Wait till you are hurt; time enough to meet the evil when it comes; you have no right to do a certain evil to others, to prevent an uncertain evil to yourselves." The Catholics, however, are told that what they *do* ask is objected to, from the fear of what they *may* ask; that they must do without that which is *reasonable*, for fear they should ask what is *unreasonable*. "I would give you a penny (says the miser to the beggar), if I was quite sure you would not ask me for half a crown."

"Nothing, I am told, is now so common on the continent as to hear our Irish policy discussed. Till of late the extent of the disabilities was but little understood, and less regarded, partly because, having less liberty themselves, foreigners could not appreciate the deprivations, and partly because the pre-eminence of England was not so decided as to draw the eyes of the world on all parts of our system. It was scarcely credited that England, that knight-errant abroad, should play the exclusionist at nome; that every where else she should declaim against oppression, but contemplate it without emotion at her doors. That her armies should march, and her orators philippize, and her poets sing against continental tyranny, and yet that laws should remain extant, and principles be operative within our gates, which are a bitter satire on our philanthropy, and a melancholy negation of our professions. Our sentiments have been so lofty, our deportment to foreigners so haughty, we have set up such liberty and such morals, that no one could suppose that we were hypocrites. Still less could it be foreseen that a great moralist, called Joseph Surface, kept a 'little milliner' behind the scenes, we too should be found out at length in taking the diversion of private tyranny after the most approved models for that amusement."—*Letter to Lord Milton*, pp. 50, 51.

We sincerely hope—we firmly believe—it never will happen; but if it were to happen, why cannot England be just as happy with Ireland being Catholic, as it is with Scotland being Presbyterian? Has not the Church of England lived side by side with the Kirk, without crossing or jostling, for these last hundred years? Have the Presbyterian members entered into any conspiracy for mincing bishoprics and deaneries into synods and presbyteries? And is not the Church of England tenfold more rich and more strong than when the separation took place? But however this may be, the real danger, even to the church of Ireland, as we have before often remarked, is the refusal of Catholic emancipation.

It would seem, from the phrenzy of many worthy Protestants, whenever the name of Catholic is mentioned, that the greatest possible diversity of religious opinions existed between the Catholic and the Protestant—that they were as different as fish and flesh—as alkali and acid —as cow and cart-horse; whereas it is quite clear, that there are many Protestant sects whose difference from each other is much more marked, both in church discipline and in tenets of faith, than that of Protestants and Catholics. We maintain that Lambeth, in these two points, is quite as near to the Vatican as it is to the Kirk—if not much nearer.

Instead of lamenting the power of the priests over the lower orders of the Irish, we ought to congratulate ourselves that any influence can affect or control them. Is the tiger less formidable in the forest than when he has been caught and taught to obey a voice, and tremble at an hand? But we overrate the power of the priest, if we suppose that the upper orders are to encounter all the dangers of treason and rebellion, to confer the revenues of the Protestant church upon the Catholic clergy. If the influence of the Catholic clergy upon men of rank and education is so unbounded, why cannot the French and Italian clergy recover their possessions, or acquire an equivalent for them? They are starving in the full enjoyment of an influence which places (as we think) all the wealth and power of the country at their feet—an influence which, in our opinion, overpowers avarice, fear, ambition, and is the master of every passion which brings on change and movement in the Protestant world.

We conclude with a few words of advice to the different opponents of the Catholic question.

To the No-Popery Fool.

You are made use of by men who laugh at you, and despise you for your folly and ignorance; and who, the moment it suits their purpose, will consent to emancipation of the Catholics, and leave you to roar and bellow No Popery! to vacancy and the moon.

To the No-Popery Rogue.

A shameful and scandalous game, to sport with the serious interests of the country, in order to gain some increase of public power!

To the Honest No-Popery People.

We respect you very sincerely—out are astonished at your existence.

To the Base.

Sweet children of turpitude, beware! the old anti-popery people are fast perishing away. Take heed that you are not surprised by an emancipating king, or an emancipating administration. Leave a *locus pœnitentiæ!*—prepare a place for retreat—get ready your equivocations and denials. The dreadful day may yet come, when liberality may lead to place and power. We understand these matters here. It is the safest to be moderately base—to be flexible in shame, and to be always ready for what is generous, good, and just, when any thing is to be gained by virtue.

To the Catholics.

Wait. Do not add to your miseries by a mad and desperate rebellion. Persevere in civil exertions, and concede all you can concede. All great alterations in human affairs are produced by compromise.

NECKAR'S LAST VIEWS.*

[Edinburgh Review, 1803.]

If power could be measured by territory, or counted by population, the inveteracy, and the disproportion which exists between France and England, must occasion to every friend of the latter country the most serious and well-founded apprehensions. Fortunately however for us, the question of power is not only what is the amount of population? but, how is that population governed? How far is a confidence in the *stability* of political institutions established by an experience of their *wisdom?* Are the various interests of society adjusted and protected by a system of laws thoroughly tried, gradually ameliorated, and purely administered? What is the degree of general prosperity evinced by that most perfect of all *criteria*, general credit? These are the considerations to which an enlightened politician, who speculates on the future destiny of nations, will direct his attention, more than to the august and imposing exterior of territorial dominion, or to those brilliant moments, when a nation, under the influence of great passions, rises above its neighbours, and above itself, in military renown.

If it be visionary to suppose the grandeur and safety of the two nations as compatible and co-existent, we have the important (though the cruel) consolation of reflecting, that the French have yet to put together the very elements of a civil and political constitution; that they have to experience all the danger and all the inconvenience which result from the rashness and the imperfect views of legislators, who have every thing to conjecture, and every thing to create; that they must submit to the confusion of repeated change, or the greater evil of obstinate perseverance in error; that they must live for a century in that state of perilous uncertainty in which every revolutionized nation remains, before rational liberty becomes feeling and habit, as well as law, and is written in the hearts of men as plainly as in the letter of the statute; and that the opportunity of beginning this immense edifice of human happiness is so far from being presented to them at present, that it is extremely problematical whether or not they are to be bandied from one vulgar usurper to another, and remain for a century subjugated to the rigour of a military government, at once the scorn and the scourge of Europe.†

To the more pleasing supposition, that the First Consul will make use of his power to give his country a free constitution, we are indebted for the work of M. Neckar now before us, a work of which good temper is the characteristic excellence: it every where preserves that cool impartiality which it is so difficult to retain in the discussion of subjects connected with recent and important events; modestly proposes the results of reflection; and, neither deceived nor wearied by theories, examines the best of all that mankind have said or done for the attainment of rational liberty.

The principal object of M. Neckar's book is to examine this question, "An opportunity of election supposed, and her present circumstances considered—what is the best form of government which France is capable of receiving?" and he answers his own query by giving the preference to a Republic One and Indivisible.

The work is divided into four parts.

1. An Examination of the present constitution of France.

2. On the best form of a Republic One and Indivisible.

3. On the best form of a Monarchical Government.

4. Thoughts upon Finance.

From the misfortune which has hitherto attended all discussions of *present* constitutions in France, M. Neckar has not escaped. The subject has proved too rapid for the author; and its existence has ceased before its properties were examined. This part of the work, therefore, we shall entirely pass over: because, to discuss a mere name, is an idle waste of time; and no man pretends that the present constitution of France can, with propriety, be considered as any thing more. We shall proceed to a description of that form of a republican government which appears to M. Neckar best calculated to promote the happiness of that country.

Every department is to be divided into five parts, each of which is to send one member. Upon the eve of an election, all persons paying 200 livres of government taxes in direct contribution, are to assemble together, and choose 100 members from their own number, who form what M. Neckar calls a chamber of indication. This chamber of indication is to present five candidates, of whom the people are to elect one; and the right of voting in this latter election is given to every body engaged in a wholesale or retail business; to all superintendents of manufactures and trades; to all commissioned and non-commissioned officers and soldiers who have received their discharge; and to all citizens paying, in direct contribution, to the amount of twelve livres. Votes are not to be given in one spot, but before the chief magistrate of each *commune* where the voter resides, and there inserted in registers; from a comparison of which, the successful candidate is to be determined. The municipal officers are to enjoy the right of *recommending* one of these candidates to the people, who are free to adopt their recommendation or not, as

* *Dernières Vues de Politiques, et de Finance.* Par M. Neckar. An 10, 1802.

† All this is, unfortunately, as true now as it was when written thirty years ago.

they may think proper. The right of voting is confined to qualified single men of twenty-five years of age: married men of the same description may vote at any age.

To this plan of election we cannot help thinking there are many great and insuperable objections. The first and infallible consequence of it would be, a devolution of the whole elective franchise upon the chamber of indication, and a complete exclusion of the people from any share in the privilege: for the chamber bound to return five candidates, would take care to return four out of the five so thoroughly objectionable, that the people would be compelled to choose the fifth. Such has been the constant effect of all elections so constituted in Great Britain, where the power of conferring the office has always been found to be vested in those who named the candidates, not in those who selected an individual from the candidates named.

But if such were not the consequences of a double election; and if it were so well constituted, as to retain that character which the legislature meant to impress upon it, there are other reasons which would induce us to pronounce it a very pernicious institution. The only foundation of political liberty is the spirit of the people; and the only circumstance which makes a lively impression upon their senses, and powerfully reminds them of their importance, their power, and their rights, is the periodical choice of their representatives. How easily that spirit may be totally extinguished, and of the degree of abject fear and slavery to which the human race may be reduced for ages, every man of reflection is sufficiently aware: and he knows that the preservation of that feeling is, of all other objects of political science, the most delicate and the most difficult. It appears to us, that a people who did not choose their representatives, but only those who chose their representatives, would very soon become indifferent to their elections altogether. To deprive them of their power of nominating their own candidate, would be still worse. The eagerness of the people to vote, is kept alive by their occasional expulsion of a candidate who has rendered himself objectionable, or the adoption of one who knows how to render himself agreeable to them. They are proud of being solicited *personally* by a man of family or wealth. The uproar even, and the confusion and the clamour of a popular election in England, have their use: they give a stamp to the names, *Liberty, Constitution*, and *People:* they infuse sentiments which nothing but violent passions and gross objects of sense *could* infuse; and which would never exist, perhaps, if the sober constituents were to sneak, one by one, into a notary's office to deliver their votes for a representative, or were to form the first link in that long chain of causes and effects, which, in this compound kind of elections, ends with choosing a member of parliament.

"Above all things (says M. Neckar) languor is the most deadly to a republican government; for when such a political association is animated neither by a kind of instinctive affection for its beauty, nor by the continual homage of reflection to the happy union of order and liberty, the public spirit is half lost, and with it the republic. The rapid brilliancy of despotism is preferred to a mere complicated machine, from which every symptom of life and organization is fled."

Sickness, absence, and nonage, would (even under the supposition of universal suffrage) reduce the voters of any country to one fourth of its population. A qualification much lower than that of the payment of twelve livres in direct contribution, would reduce that fourth one half, and leave the number of voters in France three millions and a half, which, divided by 600, gives between five and six thousand constituents for each represensative; a number not amounting to a third part of the voters for many counties in England, and which certainly is not so unwieldy as to make it necessary to have recourse to the complex mechanism of double elections. Besides, too, if it could be believed that the peril were considerable, of gathering men together in such masses, we have no hesitation in saying, that it would be infinitely preferable to thin their numbers, by increasing the value of the qualification, than to obviate the apprehended bad effects, by complicating the system of election.

M. Neckar (much as he has seen and observed,) is clearly deficient in that kind of experience which is gained by living under free governments: he mistakes the riots of a free, for the insurrections of an enslaved people; and appears to be impressed with the most tremendous notions of an English election. The difference is, that the tranquillity of an arbitrary government is rarely disturbed, but from the most serious provocations, not to be expiated by any ordinary vengeance. The excesses of a free people are less important, because their resentments are less serious; and they can commit a great deal of apparent disorder with very little real mischief. An English mob, which, to a foreigner, might convey the belief of an impending massacre, is often contented by the demolition of a few windows.

The idea of diminishing the number of constituents, rather by extending the period of nonage to twenty-five years, than by increasing the value of the qualification, appears to us to be new and ingenious. No person considers himself as so completely deprived of a share in the government, who is to enjoy it when he becomes older, as he would do, were that privilege deferred till he became richer; time comes to all, wealth to few.

This assembly of representatives, as M. Neckar has constituted it, appears to us to be in extreme danger of turning out to be a mere collection of country gentlemen. Every thing is determined by territorial extent and population; and as the voters in towns must, in any single division, be almost always inferior to the country voters, the candidates will be returned in virtue of large landed property; and that infinite advantage which is derived to a popular assembly, from the *variety* of characters of which it is composed, would be entirely lost under the system of M. Neckar. The sea-ports, the universities, the great commercial towns, should all have their separate organs in the parliament of a great country. There should be some means of bringing in active, able, young men, who would submit to the labour of business, from the stimulus of honour and wealth. Others should be there, expressly to speak the sentiments, and defend the interests of the executive. Every popular assembly must be grossly imperfect, that is not composed of such heterogeneous materials as these. Our own parliament may perhaps contain within itself *too many* of that species of representatives, who could never have arrived at the dignity under a pure and perfect system of election; but, for all the practical purposes of government, amidst a great majority fairly elected by the people, we should always wish to see a certain number of the legislative body representing interests very distinct from those of the people.

The legislative part of his constitution M. Neckar manages in the following manner. There are two councils, the great and the little. The great council is composed of five members from each department, elected in the manner we have just described, and amounting to the number of six hundred. The assembly is re-elected every five years. No qualification* of property is necessary to its members, who receive each a salary of 12,000 livres. No one is eligible to the assembly before the age of twenty-five years. The little national council consists of one hundred members, or from that number to one hundred and twenty; one for each department. It is re-elected every ten years; its members must be thirty years of age; and they receive the same salary as the members of the great council. For the election of the little council, each of the five chambers of indication, in every department, gives in the name of one candidate; and, from the five so named, the same voters who choose the great council select one.

The municipal officers enjoy, in this election, the same right of *recommending* one of the candidates to the people; a privilege which they would certainly exercise indirectly, without a law, wherever they could exercise it with any effect, and the influence of which the sanction of the law would at all times rather diminish than increase.

The grand national council commences all deliberations which concern public order, and the interest of the state, with the exception of those only which belong to finance. Nevertheless, the executive and the little council have it in their power to *propose* any law for the consideration of the grand council. When a law has passed the two councils, and received the sanction of the executive senate, it becomes binding upon the people. If the executive senate disapprove of any law presented to them for their adoption, they are to send it back to the two councils for their reconsideration; but if it pass these two bodies again, with the approbation of two-thirds of the members of each assembly, the executive has no longer the power of withholding its assent. All measures of finance are to initiate with government.

* Nothing can be more absurd than our qualification for parliament: it is nothing but a foolish and expensive lie on parchment.

We believe M. Neckar to be right in his idea of not exacting any qualification of property in his legislative assemblies. When men are left to choose their own governors, they are guided in their choice by some one of those motives which has always commanded their homage and admiration:—if they do not choose wealth, they choose birth or talents, or military fame; and of all these species of pre-eminence, a large popular assembly should be constituted. In England, the laws, requiring that members of parliament should be possessed of certain property, are (except in the instance of members for counties) *practically* repealed.

In the salaries of the members of the two councils, with the exception of the expense, there is, perhaps, no great balance of good or harm. To some men it would be an inducement to become senators; to others, induced by more honourable motives, it would afford the means of supporting that situation without disgrace. Twenty-five years of age is certainly too late a period for the members of the great council. Of what astonishing displays of eloquence and talent should we have been deprived in this country under the adoption of a similar rule!

The institution of two assemblies constitutes a check upon the passion and precipitation by which the resolutions of any single popular assembly may occasionally be governed. The chances, that one will correct the other, do not depend solely upon their dividuality, but upon the different ingredients of which they are composed, and that difference of system and spirit, which results from a difference of conformation. Perhaps M. Neckar has not sufficiently attended to this consideration. The difference between his two assemblies is not very material; and the same popular fury which marked the proceedings of the one, would not be very sure of meeting with an adequate corrective in the dignified coolness and wholesome gravity of the other.

All power which is tacitly allowed to devolve upon the executive part of a government, from the experience that it is most conveniently placed there, is both safer, and less likely to be complained of, than that which is conferred upon it by law. If M. Neckar had placed some agents of the executive in the great council, all measures of finance would, *in fact*, have originated in them, without any exclusive right to such initiation; but the *right* of initiation, from M. Neckar's contrivance, is likely to excite that discontent in the people, which alone can render it dangerous and objectionable.

In this plan of a republic, every thing seems to depend upon the purity and the moderation of its governors. The executive has no connection with the great council; the members of the great council have no motive of hope, or interest, to consult the wishes of the executive. The assembly, which is to give example to the nation, and enjoy its confidence, is composed of six hundred men, whose passions have no other control than that pure love of the public, which it is *hoped* they may possess, and that cool investigation of interests, which it is *hoped* they may pursue.

Of the effects of such a constitution, every

thing must be conjectured; for experience enables us to make no assertion respecting it. There is only one government in the modern world, which, from the effects it has produced, and the time it has endured, can with justice be called good and free. Its constitution, in books, contains the description of a legislative assembly, similar to that of M. Neckar's. Happily, perhaps, for the people, the share they have *really* enjoyed in its election, is much less ample than that allotted to them in this republic of the closet. How long a really popular assembly would tolerate any rival and co-existing power in the state—for what period the feeble executive, and the untitled, unblazoned peers of a republic, could not stand against it—whether any institutions, compatible with the essence and meaning of a republic, could prevent it from absorbing all the dignity, the popularity and the power of the state,—are questions that we leave for the resolution of wiser heads; with the sincerest joy, that we have only a theoretical interest in stating them.*

The executive senate is to consist of seven; and the right of presenting the candidates, and selecting *from* the candidates alternately from one assembly to the other, *i. e.* on a vacancy, the great council present three candidates to the little council, who select one from that number; and, on the next vacancy, by the inversion of this process, the little council present, and the great council select; and so alternately. The members of the executive must be thirty-five years of age. Their measures are determined by a majority. The president, called the Consul, has a casting vote: his salary is fixed at 300,000 livres; that of all the other senators at 60,000 livres. The office of consul is annual. Every senator enjoys it in his turn. Every year one senator goes out, unless re-elected; which he may be once, and even twice, if he unites three-fourths of the votes of each council in his favour. The executive shall name to all civil and military offices, except to those of mayors and municipalities. Political negotiations, and connections with foreign countries, fall under the direction of the executive. Declarations of war or peace, when presented by the executive to the legislative body, are to be adopted, the first by a majority of three-fifths, the last by a simple majority. The parade, honours, and ceremonies of the executive, devolve upon the consul alone. The members of the senate, upon going out of office, become members of the little council, to the number of seven. Upon the vacation of an eighth senator, the oldest ex-senator in the little council resigns his seat to make room for him. All responsibility rests upon the consul alone, who has a right to stop the proceedings of a majority of the executive senate, by declaring them unconstitutional; and if the majority persevere, in spite of this declaration, the dispute is referred to and decided by a secret committee of the little council.

M. Neckar takes along with him the same mistake through the whole of his constitution, by conferring the choice of candidates on one body, and the election of the member on another: so that though the alternation would take place between the two councils, it would turn out to be in an order directly opposite to that which was intended.

We perfectly acquiesce in the reasons M. Neckar has alleged for the preference given to an executive constituted of many individuals, rather than of one. The prize of supreme power is too tempting to admit of fair play in the game of ambition; and it is wise to lessen its value by dividing it: at least it is wise to do so under a form of government that cannot admit the better expedient of rendering the executive hereditary; an expedient (gross and absurd as it seems to be) the best calculated, perhaps, to obviate the effects of ambition upon the stability of governments, by narrowing the field on which it acts, and the object for which it contends. The Americans have determined otherwise, and adopted an elective presidency: but there are innumerable circumstances, as M. Neckar very justly observes, which render the example of America inapplicable to other governments. America is a federative republic, and the extensive jurisdiction of the individual states exonerates the president from so great a portion of the cares of domestic government, that he may almost be considered as a mere minister of foreign affairs. America presents such an immediate, and such a seducing species of provision to all its inhabitants, that it has no idle discontented populace, its population amounts only to six millions, and it is not condensed in such masses as the population of Europe. After all, an experiment of twenty years is never to be cited in politics; nothing can be built upon such a slender inference. Even if America were to remain stationary, she might find that she had presented too fascinating and irresistible an object to human ambition: of course, that peril is increased by every augmentation of a people, who are hastening on, with rapid and irresistible pace, to the highest eminences of human grandeur. Some contest for power there must be in every free state: but the contest for vicarial and deputed power, as it implies the presence of a moderator and a master, is more prudent than the struggle for that which is original and supreme.

The difficulty of reconciling the responsibility of the executive with its dignity, M. Neckar foresees; and states, but does not remedy. An irresponsible executive, the jealousy of a republic would never tolerate; and its amenability to punishment, by degrading it in the eyes of the people, diminishes its power.

All the leading features of *civil liberty* are copied from the constitution of this country, with hardly any variation.

Having thus finished his project of a republic, M. Neckar proposes the government of this country as the best model of a temperate and hereditary monarchy; pointing out such alterations in it as the genius of the French people, the particular circumstances in which they are placed, or the abuses which have crept into our policy, may require. From one or the other of these motives he re-establishes the

* That interest is at present not quite so theoretical as it was.

salique law;* forms his elections after the same manner as that previously described in his scheme of a republic; and excludes the clergy from the house of peers. This latter *assembly* M. Neckar composes of 250 hereditary peers chosen from the best families in France, and of 50 assistant peers enjoying that dignity for life only, and nominated by the crown. The number of hereditary peers is limited as above; the peerage goes only in the male line; and upon each peer is perpetually entailed landed property to the amount of 30,000 livres. This partial creation of peers for life only, appears to remedy a very material defect in the English constitution. An hereditary legislative aristocracy not only adds to the dignity of the throne, and establishes that gradation of ranks which is, perhaps, absolutely necessary to its security, but it transacts a considerable share of the business of the nation, as well in the framing of laws as in the discharge of its juridical functions. But men of rank and wealth, though they are interested by a splendid debate, will not submit to the drudgery of business, much less can they be supposed conversant in all the niceties of law questions. It is therefore necessary to add to their number a certain portion of *novi homines*, men of established character for talents, and upon whom the previous tenor of their lives has necessarily impressed the habits of business. The evil of this is, that the title descends to their posterity, without the talents and the utility that procured it; and the dignity of the peerage is impaired by the increase of its numbers: not only so, but as the peerage is the reward of military, as well as the earnest of civil services, and as the annuity commonly granted with it is only for one or two lives, we are in some danger of seeing a race of nobles wholly dependent upon the crown for their support, and sacrificing their political freedom to their necessities. These evils are effectually, as it should seem, obviated by the creation of a *certain*† *number* of peers for life only; and the increase of power which it seems to give to the crown, is very fairly counteracted by the exclusion of the episcopacy, and the limitation of the hereditary peerage. As the weight of business in the upper house would principally devolve upon the created peers, and as they would hardly arrive at that dignity without having previously acquired great civil or military reputation, the consideration they would enjoy would be little inferior to that of the other part of the aristocracy. When the *noblesse* of nature are fairly opposed to the *noblesse* created by political institutions, there is little fear that the former should suffer by the comparison.

If the clergy are suffered to sit in the lower house, the exclusion of the episcopacy from the upper house is of less importance: but, in some part of the legislative bodies, the interests of the church ought unquestionably to be represented. This consideration M. Neckar wholly passes over.*

Though this gentleman considers an hereditary monarchy as preferable in the abstract, he deems it impossible that such a government could be established in France, under her present circumstances, from the impracticability of establishing with it an hereditary aristocracy; because the property, and the force of opinion, which constituted their real power, are no more, and cannot be restored. Though we entirely agree with M. Neckar, that an hereditary aristocracy is a *necessary* part of temperate monarchy, and that the latter must exist upon the base of the former, or not at all—we are by no means converts to the very decided opinion he has expressed of the impossibility of restoring them both to France.

We are surprised that M. Neckar should attempt to build any strong argument upon the durability of opinions in nations that are about to undergo, or that have recently undergone, great political changes. What opinion was there in favour of a republic in 1780? Or against it in 1794? Or, what opinion is there now in favour of it in 1802? Is not the tide of opinions, at this moment, in France, setting back with a strength equal to its flow? and is there not reason to presume, that, for some time to come, their ancient institutions may be adored with as much fury as they were destroyed? If opinion can revive in favour of kings (and M. Neckar allows it may), why not in favour of nobles? It is true their property is in the hands of other persons; and the whole of that species of proprietors will exert themselves to the utmost to prevent a restoration so pernicious to their interests. The obstacle is certainly of a very formidable nature. But why this weight of property, so weak a weapon of defence to its *ancient*, should be deemed so irresistible in the hands of its *present* possessors, we are at a loss to conceive; unless, indeed, it be supposed, that antiquity of possession diminishes the sense of right and the vigour of retention; and that men will struggle harder to keep what they have acquired only yesterday, than that which they have possessed, by themselves or their ancestors, for six centuries.

In France, the inferiority of the price of revolutionary lands to others, is immense. Of the former species, church land is considerably dearer than the forfeited estates of emigrants. Whence the difference of price, but from the estimated difference of security? Can any fact display more strongly the state of public opinion with regard to the probability of a future restoration of these estates, either partial or total? and can any circumstance facilitate the execution of such a project more than the general belief that it will be executed? M. Neckar allows, that the impediments to the formation of a republic are very serious; but thinks they would all yield to the talents and activity of Buonaparte, if he were to dedicate himself to

* A most sensible and valuable law, banishing gallantry and chivalry from cabinets, and preventing the amiable antics of grave statesmen.

† The most useless and offensive tumour in the body politic, is the titled son of a great man whose merit has placed him in the peerage. The name, face, and perhaps the pension, remain. The dæmon is gone; or there is a slight flavour from the cask, but it is empty.

* The parochial clergy are as much unrepresented in the English Parliament as they are in the Parliament of Brobdignag. The bishops make just what laws they please, and the bearing they may have on the happiness of the clergy at large never for one moment comes into the serious consideration of Parliament.

the superintendence of such a government during the period of its infancy: of course, therefore, he is to suppose the same power dedicated to the formation of an hereditary monarchy: or his parallel of difficulties is unjust, and his preference irrational. Buonaparte could represent the person of a monarch, during his life, as well as he could represent the executive of a republic; and if he could overcome the turbulence of electors, to whom freedom was new, he could appease the jealousy that his generals would entertain of the returning nobles. Indeed, without such powerful intervention, this latter objection does not appear to us to be by any means insuperable. If the history of our own restoration were to be acted over again in France, and royalty and aristocracy brought back by the military successor of Buonaparte, it certainly could not be done without a very liberal distribution of favours among the great leaders of the army.

Jealousy of the executive is one feature of a republic; in consequence, that government is clogged with a multiplicity of safeguards and restrictions, which render it unfit for investigating complicated details, and managing extensive relations with vigour, consistency, and despatch. A republic, therefore, is better fitted for a little state than a large one.

A love of equality is another very strong principle in a republic; therefore it does not tolerate hereditary honour or wealth; and all the effect produced upon the minds of the people by this factitious power is lost, and the government weakened; but, in proportion as the government is less able to command, the people should be more willing to obey; therefore a republic is better suited to a moral than an immoral people.

A people who have *recently* experienced great evils from the privileged orders and from monarchs, love republican forms so much, that the warmth of their inclination supplies, in some degree, the defect of their institutions. *Immediately*, therefore, upon the destruction of despotism, a republic *may be* preferable to a limited monarchy.

And yet, though narrowness of territory, purity of morals, and recent escape from despotism, appear to be the circumstances which most strongly recommend a republic, M. Neckar proposes it to the most numerous and the most profligate people in Europe, who are disgusted with the very name of liberty, from the incredible evils they have suffered in pursuit of it.

Whatever be the species of free government adopted by France, she can adopt none without the greatest peril. The miserable dilemma in which men living under bad governments are placed, is, that, without a radical revolution, they may never be able to gain liberty at all; and, with it, the attainment of liberty appears to be attended with almost insuperable difficulties. To call upon a nation, on a sudden, totally destitute of such knowledge and experience, to perform all the manifold functions of a free constitution, is to entrust valuable, delicate, and abstruse mechanism, to the rudest skill and the grossest ignorance. Public acts may confer liberty; but experience only can teach a people to use it; and, till they have gained that experience, they are liable to tumult, to jealousy, to collision of powers, and to every evil to which men are exposed, who are desirous of preserving a great good, without knowing how to set about it. In an old established system of liberty, like our own, the encroachments which one department of the state makes on any other, are slow, and hardly intentional; the political feelings and the constitutional knowledge which every Englishman possesses, create a public voice, which tends to secure the tranquillity of the whole. Amid the crude sentiments and new-born precedents of sudden liberty, the crown might destroy the commons, or the commons the crown, almost before the people had formed any opinion of the nature of their contention. A nation grown free in a single day, is a child born with the limbs and the vigour of a man, who would take a drawn sword for his rattle, and set the house in a blaze, that he might chuckle over the splendour.

Why can factious eloquence produce such limited effects in this country? Partly because we are accustomed to it, and know how to appreciate it. We are acquainted with popular assemblies; and the language of our Parliament produces the effect it ought upon public opinion, because long experience enables us to conjecture the real motives by which men are actuated; to separate the vehemence of party spirit from the language of principle and truth; and to discover whom we can trust, and whom we cannot. The want of all this, and of much more than this, must retard, for a very long period, the practical enjoyment of liberty in France, and present very serious obstacles to her prosperity; obstacles little dreamed of by men who seem to measure the happiness and future grandeur of France by degrees of longitude and latitude, and who believe she might acquire liberty with as much facility as she could acquire Switzerland or Naples.

M. Neckar's observations on the finances of France, and on finance in general, are useful, entertaining, and not above the capacity of every reader. France, he says, at the beginning of 1781, had 438 millions of revenue; and, at present, 540 millions. The state paid, in 1781, about 215 millions in pensions, the interest of perpetual debts, and debts for life. It pays, at present, 80 millions in interests and pensions; and owes about 12 millions for anticipations on the public revenue. A considerable share of the increase of the revenue is raised upon the conquered countries; and the people are liberated from tithes, corvées, and the tax on salt. This, certainly, is a magnificent picture of finance. The best informed people at Paris, who would be very glad to consider it as a copy from life, dare not contend that it is so. At least, we sincerely ask pardon of M. Neckar, if our information as to this point be not correct: but we believe he is generally considered to have been misled by the public financial reports.

In addition to the obvious causes which keep the interest of money so high in France, M. Neckar states one which we shall present to our readers:—

"There is one means for the establishment of credit," he says, "equally important with the others which I have stated—a sentiment of respect for morals, sufficiently diffused to overawe the government, and intimidate it from treating with bad faith any solemn engagements contracted in the name of the state. *It is this respect for morals which seems at present to have disappeared?* a respect which the Revolution has destroyed, and which is unquestionably one of the firmest supports of national faith."

The terrorists of this country are so extremely alarmed at the power of Buonaparte, that they ascribe to him resources which M. Neckar very justly observes to be incompatible—despotism and credit. Now, clearly, if he is so omnipotent in France as he is represented to be, there is an end of all credit; for nobody will trust *him* whom nobody can compel to pay; and if he establishes a credit, he loses all that temporary vigour which is derived from a revolutionary government. Either the despotism or the credit of France directed against this country would be highly formidable; but, both together, can never be directed at the same time.

In this part of his work, M. Neckar very justly points out one of the most capital defects of Mr. Pitt's administration; who always supposed that the power of France was to cease with her credit, and measured the period of her existence by the depreciation of her assignats. Whereas, France was never more powerful than when she was totally unable to borrow a single shilling in the whole circumference of Europe, and when her assignats were not worth the paper on which they were stamped.

Such are the principal contents of M. Neckar's very respectable work. Whether, in the course of that work, his political notions appear to be derived from a successful study of the passions of mankind, and whether his plan for the establishment of a republican government in France, for the ninth or tenth time, evinces a more sanguine, or a more sagacious mind, than the rest of the world, we would rather our readers should decide for themselves, than expose ourselves to any imputation of arrogance, by deciding for them. But when we consider the pacific and impartial disposition which characterizes the *Last Views on Politics and Finance*, the serene benevolence which it always displays, and the pure morals which it always inculcates, we cannot help entertaining a high respect for its venerable author, and feeling a fervent wish, that the last views of every public man may proceed from a heart as upright, and be directed to objects as good.

CATTEAU, TABLEAU DES ETATS DANOIS.*

[Edinburgh Review, 1803.]

The object of this book is to exhibit a picture of the kingdom of Denmark, under all its social relations, of politics, statistics, science, morals, manners, and every thing which can influence its character and importance, as a free and independent collection of human beings.

This book is, upon the whole, executed with great diligence and good sense. Some subjects of importance are passed over, indeed, with too much haste; but if the publication had exceeded its present magnitude, it would soon have degenerated into a mere book of reference, impossible to be read, and fit only, like a dictionary, for the purposes of occasional appeal: It would not have been a picture presenting us with an interesting epitome of the whole; but a typographical plan, detailing, with minute and fatiguing precision, every trifling circumstance, and every subordinate feature. We should be far from objecting to a much more extended and elaborate performance than the present; because those who read, and those who write, are now so numerous, that there is room enough for varieties and modifications of the same subject: but information of this nature, conveyed in a form and in a size adapted to continuous reading, gains in surface what it loses in depth,—and gives general notions to many, though it cannot afford all the knowledge which a few have it in their power to acquire, from the habits of more patient labour, and more profound research.

This work, though written at a period when enthusiasm or disgust had thrown most men's minds off their balance, is remarkable, upon the whole, for sobriety and moderation. The observations, though seldom either strikingly ingenious or profound, are just, temperate, and always benevolent. We are so far from perceiving any thing like extravagance in Mr. Catteau, that we are inclined to think he is occasionally too cautious for the interests of truth; that he manages the court of Denmark with too much delicacy; and exposes, by distant and scarcely perceptible touches, that which it was his duty to have brought out boldly and strongly. The most disagreeable circumstance in the style of the book is, the author's compliance with that irresistible avidity of his country to declaim upon common-place subjects. He goes on, mingling bucolic details and sentimental effusions, melting and measuring, crying and calculating, in a manner which is very bad, if it is poetry, and worse if it is prose. In speaking of the mode of cultivating potatoes, he cannot avoid calling the potato *a modest vegetable:* and when he comes to the exportation of horses from the duchy of Holstein, we learn that "these animals are dragged from the bosom of their peaceable and modest country, to hear, in foreign regions, the sound of the warlike trumpet; to carry the combatant amid the hostile ranks; to increase the éclat of some pompous procession; or drag, in gilded car, some favourite of fortune."

We are sorry to be compelled to notice these untimely effusions, especially as they may lead to a suspicion of the fidelity of the work; of which fidelity, from actual examination of many of the authorities referred to, we have not the most remote doubt. Mr. Catteau is to be depended upon as securely as any writer, going over such various and extensive ground, can ever be depended upon. He is occasionally guilty of some trifling inaccuracies; but what he advances is commonly derived from the most indisputable authorities; and he has condensed together a mass of information, which will render his book the most accessible and valuable road of knowledge, to those who are desirous of making any researches respecting the kingdom of Denmark.

Denmark, since the days of piracy, has hardly been heard of out of the Baltic. Margaret, by the union of Calmar, laid the foundation of a monarchy, which (could it have been preserved by hands as strong as those which created it) would have exercised a powerful influence upon the destinies of Europe, and have strangled, perhaps in the cradle, the infant force of Russia. Denmark, reduced to her ancient bounds by the patriotism and talents of Gustavus Vasa, has never since been able to emerge into notice by her own natural resources, or the genius of her ministers and her monarchs. During that period, Sweden has more than once threatened to give laws to Europe; and, headed by Charles and Gustavus, has broke out into chivalrous enterprises, with an heroic valour, which merited wiser objects, and greater ultimate success. The spirit of the Danish nation has, for the last two or three centuries, been as little carried to literature or to science, as to war. They have written as little as they have done. With the exception of Tycho Brahé and a volume of shells, there is hardly a Danish book, or a Danish writer, known five miles from the Great Belt. It is not sufficient to say, that there are many authors read and admired in Denmark: there are none that have passed the Sound, none that have had energy enough to force themselves into the circulation of Europe, to extort universal admiration, and live, without the aid of municipal praise, and local approbation. From the period, however, of the first of the Bernstorffs, Denmark has made a

* *Tableaux des Etats Danois.* Par Jean Pierre Catteau. 3 tomes. 1802. à Paris.

great spring, and has advanced more within the last twenty or thirty years, than for the three preceding centuries. The peasants are now emancipated; the laws of commerce, foreign and interior, are simplified and expanded; the transport of corn and cattle is made free; a considerable degree of liberty is granted to the press; and slavery is to cease this very year in their West Indian possessions. If Ernest Bernstorff was the author of some less considerable measures, they are to be attributed more to the times, than to the defects of his understanding, or of his heart. To this great minister succeeded the favourite Struensee, and to him Ove Guildberg: the first, with views of improvements, not destitute of liberality or genius, but little guided by judgment, or marked by moderation; the latter, devoid of that energy and firmness which were necessary to execute the good he intended. In 1788, when the king became incapable of business, and the crown-prince assumed the government, Count Andrew Bernstorff, nephew of Ernest, was called to the ministry: and, while some nations were shrinking from the very name of innovation, and others overturning every establishment and violating every principle, Bernstorff steadily pursued, and ultimately effected, the gradual and bloodless amelioration of his country. His name will ever form a splendid epoch in the history of Denmark. The spirit of economical research and improvement which emanated from him still remains; while the personal character of the prince of Denmark, and the zeal with which he seconded the projects of his favourite minister, seem to afford a guarantee for the continuation of the same system of administration.

In his analysis of the present state of Denmark, Mr. Catteau, after a slight historical sketch of that country, divides his subject into sixteen sections.

1. Geographical and physical qualities of the Danish territory: 2. Form of Government: 3. Administration: 4. Institutions relative to government and administration: 5. Civil and criminal laws, and judiciary institutions: 6. Military system, land, army, and marine: 7. Finance: 8. Population: 9. Productive industry, comprehending agriculture, the fisheries, and the extraction of mineral substances: 10. Manufacturing industry: 11. Commerce, interior and exterior, including the state of the great roads, the canals of navigation, the maritime insurances, the bank, &c. &c.: 12. Establishments of charity and public utility: 13. Religion: 14. Education: 15. Language, character, manners, and customs: 16. Sciences and arts.—This division we shall follow.

From the southern limits of Holstein to the southern extremity of Norway, the Danish dominions extend to 300 miles* in length, and are, upon an average, from about 50 to 60 in breadth; the whole forms an area of about 8000 square miles. The western coast of Jutland, from Riba to Lemvig, is principally alluvial, and presents much greater advantages to the cultivator than he has yet drawn from it. The eastern coast is also extremely favourable to vegetation. A sandy and barren ridge stretching from north to south, between the two coasts, is unfavourable to every species of culture, and hardly capable of supporting the wild and stunted shrubs which languish upon its surface. Towards the north, where the Jutland peninsula terminates in the Baltic, every thing assumes an aspect of barrenness and desolation. It is Arabia, without its sun or its verdant islands; but not without its tempests or sands, which sometimes overwhelm what little feeble agriculture they may encounter, and convert the habitual wretchedness of the Jutlanders into severe and cruel misfortune. The Danish government has attempted to remedy this evil, in some measure, by encouraging the cultivation of those kinds of shrubs which grow on the sea-shore, and by their roots give tenacity and aggregation to the sand. The *Elymus Arenaria*, though found to be the most useful for that purpose, is still inadequate to the prevention of the calamity.*

The Danish isles are of a green and pleasant aspect. The hills are turfed up to the top, or covered with trees; the valleys animated by the passage of clear streams; and the whole strikingly contrasted with the savage sterility, or imposing grandeur, of the scenes on the opposite coast of Jutland. All the seas of Denmark are well stored with fish; and a vast number of deep friths and inlets affords a cheap and valuable communication with the interior of the country.

The Danish rivers are neither numerous nor considerable. The climate, generally speaking, is moist and subject to thick fogs, which almost obscure the horizon. Upon a mean of twenty-six years, it has rained for a hundred and thirty days every year, and thundered for thirteen. Their summer begins with June, and ends with September. A calm serene sky, and an atmosphere free from vapours, are very rarely the lot of the inhabitants of Denmark; but the humidity with which the air is impregnated is highly favourable to vegetation; and all kinds of corn and grass are cultivated there with great success. To the south of Denmark are the countries of Sleswick and Holstein. Nature has divided these countries into two parts; the one of which is called *Geetsland*, the other *Marschland*. Geetsland is the elevated ground situated along the Baltic. The soil resembles that of Denmark. The division of Marschland forms a band or stripe, which extends from the Elbe to the frontiers of Jutland, an *alluvium* gained and preserved from the sea, by a labour which, though vigilant and severe, is repaid by the most ample

* The mile alluded to here, and through the whole of the book, is the Danish mile, 15 to a degree, or 4000 toises in round numbers: the ancient mile of Norway is much more considerable. It may be as well to mention here, that the Danes reckon their money by rixdollars, marks, and schellings. A rixdollar contains 6 marks, and a mark 16 schellings; 20 schellings are equal to one livre; consequently, the pound sterling is equal to 4 r. 4 m. 14 sch., or nearly 5 rixdollars.

* There is a Danish work, by Professor Viborg, upon those plants which grow in sand. It has been very actively distributed in Jutland, by the Danish administration, and might be of considerable service in Norfolk, and other parts of Great Britain

profits. The sea, however, in all these alluvial countries, seldom forgets his original rights. Marschland, in the midst of all its tranquillity, fat, and silence, was invaded by this element in the year 1634, with the loss of whole villages, many thousands of horned cattle, and 1500 human beings.

Nature is as wild and grand in Norway as she is productive in Marschland. Cataracts amid the dark pines; the eternal snow on the mountains; seas that bid adieu to the land, and stretch out to the end of the world; an endless succession of the great and the terrible,—leave the eye and the mind without repose. The climate of Norway is extremely favourable to the longevity of the human race, and sufficiently so to the life of many animals domesticated by man. The horses are of good breed; the horned cattle excellent, though small. Crops of grain are extremely precarious, and often perish before they come to maturity.*

In 1660, the very year in which this happier country was laying the foundations of rational liberty by the wise restrictions imposed upon its returning monarch, the people of Denmark, by a solemn act, surrendered their natural rights into the hands of their sovereign, endowed him with absolute power, and, in express words, declared him, for all his political acts, accountable only to him to whom all kings and governors are accountable. This revolution, similar to that effected by the king and people at Stockholm in 1772, was not a change from liberty to slavery; but from a worse sort of slavery to a better; from the control of an insolent and venal senate, to that of one man: it was a change which simplified their degradation, and, by lessening the number of their tyrants, put their servitude more out of sight. There ceased immediately to be an arbitrary monarch in every parish, and the distance of the oppressor either operated as a diminution of the oppression, or was thought to do so. The same spirit, to be sure, which urged them to victory over one evil, might have led them on a little farther to the subjugation of both; and they might have limited the king, by the same powers which enabled them to dissolve the senate. But Europe, at that period, knew no more of liberty than of galvanism; and the peasants of Denmark no more dreamt of becoming free than the inhabitants of Paris do at this moment.

At present, Denmark is in theory one of the most arbitrary governments on the face of the earth. It has remained so ever since the revolution to which we have just alluded; in all which period the Danes have not, by any important act of rebellion, evinced an impatience of their yoke, or any sense that the enormous power delegated to their monarchs has been improperly exercised. In fact, the Danish government enjoys great reputation for its forbearance and mildness; and sanctifies, in a certain degree, its execrable constitution, by the moderation with which it is administered.

* We shall take little notice of Iceland in this review, from the attention we mean to pay to that subject in the review of "Voyage en Iceland, fait par ordre de sa Majesté Danoise," 5 vols. 1802.

We regret extremely that Mr. Catteau has given us, upon this curious subject of the Danish government, such a timid and sterile dissertation. Many governments are despotic in law, which are not despotic in fact; not because they are restrained by their own moderation, but because, in spite of their theoretical omnipotence, they are compelled, in many important points, to respect either public opinion or the opinion of other balancing powers, which, without the express recognition of law, have gradually sprung up in the state. Russia, and Imperial Rome, had its prætorian guards. Turkey has its uhlema. Public opinion almost always makes some exceptions to its blind and slavish submission; and in bowing its neck to the foot of a sultan, stipulates how hard he shall tread. The very fact of enjoying a mild government for a century and a half, must, in their own estimation, have given the Danes a sort of right to a mild government. Ancient possession is a good title in all cases; and the King of Denmark may have completely lost the power of doing many just and many unjust actions, from never having exercised it in particular instances. What he has not done for so long a period, he may not dare to do now; and he may in vain produce constitutional parchment, abrogated by the general feelings of those whom they were intended to control. Instead of any information of this kind, the author of the Tableau has given us at full length the constitutional act of 1660, and has afforded us no other knowledge than we could procure from the most vulgar histories; as if state papers were the best place to look for constitutions, and as if the rights of king and people were really adjusted, by the form and solemnity of covenant and pacts; by oaths of allegiance, or oaths of coronation.

The king has his privy council, to which he names whom he pleases, with the exception of the heir-apparent, and the princes of the blood, who sit there of right. It is customary, also, that the heads of colleges should sit there. These colleges are the offices in which the various business of the state is carried on. The chancelry of Denmark interprets all laws which concern privileges in litigation, and the different degrees of authority belonging to various public bodies. It watches over the interests of church and poor: issues patents, edicts, grants, letters of naturalization, legitimacy, and nobility. The archives of the state are also under its custody. The German chancelry has the same powers and privileges in Sleswick and Holstein, which are fiefs of the empire. There is a college for foreign affairs; two colleges of finance; and a college of economy and commerce; which, divided into four parts, directs its attention to four objects: 1. Manufacturing industry: 2. Commerce: 3. Productions: 4. Possessions in the East Indies. All projects and speculations, relative to any of these objects, are referred to this college; and every encouragement given to the prosecution of such as it may approve. There are two other colleges, which respectively manage the army and navy. The total number is nine.

The court of Denmark is on a footing of great simplicity. The pomp introduced by Christian IV., who modelled his establishments after those of Louis XIV., has been laid aside, and a degree of economy adopted, much more congenial to the manners of the people, and the resources of the country. The hereditary nobility of Denmark may be divided into those of the ancient, those of the modern fiefs, and the personal nobility. The first class are only distinguished from the second, by the more extensive privileges annexed to their fiefs; as it has been the policy of the court of Denmark, in latter times, not to grant such immunities to the possessors of noble lands as had been accorded to them at earlier periods. Both of these classes, however, derive their nobility from their estates, which are inalienable, and descend according to the laws of primogeniture. In the third class, nobility derives from the person, and not from the estate. To prevent the female noblesse from marrying beneath their rank, and to preserve the dignity of their order, nine or ten Protestant nunneries have been from time to time endowed, in each of which about twelve noble women are accommodated, who, not bound by any vow, find in these societies an economical and elegant retirement. The nobility of Norway have no fiefs. The nobility of Holstein and Sleswick derive their nobility from their fiefs, and are possessed of very extensive privileges. Every thing which concerns their common interest is discussed in a convention held periodically in the town of Keil; during the vacations of the convention, there is a permanent deputation resident in the same town. Interests so well watched by the nobles themselves, are necessarily respected by the court of Denmark. The same institution of free nunneries for the female nobility prevails in these provinces. Societies of this sort might perhaps be extended to other classes, and to other countries with some utility. The only objection to a nunnery is, that those who change their mind cannot change their situation. That a number of unmarried females should collect together into one mass, and subject themselves to some few rules of convenience, is a system which might afford great resources and accommodation to a number of helpless individuals, without proving injurious to the community; unless, indeed, any very timid statesman shall be alarmed at the progress of celibacy, and imagine that the increase and multiplication of the human race may become a mere antiquated habit.

The lowest courts in Denmark are composed of a judge and a secretary, both chosen by the landed proprietors within the jurisdiction, but confirmed by the king, in whose name all their proceedings are carried on. These courts have their sessions once a week in Denmark, and are attended by four or five burgesses or farmers, in the capacity of assessors, who occasionally give their advice upon subjects of which their particular experience may entitle them to judge. From this jurisdiction there is appeal to a higher court, held every month in different places in Denmark, by judges paid by the crown. The last appeal for Norway and Denmark is to the *Hoieste Rett*, or supreme court, fixed at Copenhagen, which is occupied for nine months in the year, and composed half of noble, half of plebeian judges. This is the only tribunal in which the advocates plead *vivâ voce;* in all the others, litigation is carried on by writing. The king takes no cognisance of pecuniary suits determined by this court, but reserves to himself a revision of all its sentences which affect the life or honour of the subject. It has always been the policy of the court of Denmark to render justice as cheap as possible. We should have been glad to have learned from Mr. Catteau, whether or not the cheapness of justice operates as an encouragement to litigation; and whether (which we believe is most commonly the case) the quality of Danish justice is not in the ratio of the price. But this gentleman, as we have before remarked, is so taken up by the formal part of institutions, that he has neither leisure nor inclination to say much of their spirit. The *Tribunal of Conciliation*, established since 1795, is composed of the most intelligent and respectable men in the vicinage, and its sessions are private. It is competent to determine upon a great number of civil questions; and if both parties agree to the arrangement proposed by the court, its decree is registered, and has legal authority. If the parties cannot be brought to agreement by the amicable interference of the mediators, they are at full liberty to prosecute their suit in a court of justice. All the proceedings of the Tribunal of Conciliation are upon unstamped paper, and they cannot be protracted longer than fifteen days in the country, and eight days in the towns, unless both parties consent to a longer delay. The expenses, which do not exceed three shillings, are not payable, but in case of reconciliation. During the three years preceding this institution, there came before the courts of law, 25,521 causes; and, for the three years following, 9653, *making the astonishing difference of fifteen thousand eight hundred and sixty-three lawsuits.* The idea of this court was taken from the Dutch, among whom it likewise produced the most happy effects. And when we consider what an important point it is, that there should be time for disputants to cool; the strong probability there is, that four or five impartial men from the vicinage will take a right view of the case, and the reluctance that any man must feel to embark his reputation and property in opposition to their opinion, we cannot entertain a doubt of the beauty and importance of the invention. It is hardly possible that it should be bad justice which satisfies both parties, and this species of mediation has no validity but upon such condition. It is curious, too, to remark, how much the progress of rancour obstructs the natural sense of justice; it appears that plaintiff and defendant were *both* satisfied in 15,868 causes: if all these causes had come on to a regular hearing, and the parties been inflamed by the expense and the publicity of the quarrel, we doubt if there would have been one single man out of the whole number who would have acknowledged that his cause was justly given against him.

There are some provisions in the criminal law of Denmark, for the personal liberty of the subject, which cannot be of much importance, so long as the dispensing power is vested in the crown; however, though they are not much, they are better than nothing; and have probably some effect in offences merely criminal, where the passions and interests of the governors do not interfere. Mr. Catteau considers the law which admits the accused to bail, upon finding proper security, to be unjust, because the poor cannot avail themselves of it. But this is bad reasoning: for every country has a right to impose such restrictions and liens upon the accused, that they shall be forthcoming for trial; at the same time, those restrictions are not to be more severe than the necessity of the case requires. The primary and most obvious method of security is imprisonment. Whoever can point out any other method of effecting the same object, less oppressive to himself and as satisfactory to the justice of the country, has a right to require that it be adopted; whoever cannot, must remain in prison. It is a principle that should never be lost sight of, that an accused person is presumed to be innocent; and that no other vexation should be imposed upon him than what is absolutely necessary for the purposes of future investigation. The imprisonment of a poor man, because he cannot find bail, is not a gratuitous vexation, but a necessary severity; justified only, because no other nor milder mode of security can, in that particular instance, be produced.

Inquisitorial and penal torture is, in some instances, allowed by the laws of Denmark: the former, after having been abolished, was re-established in 1771. The corporations have been gradually and covertly attacked in Denmark, as they have been in Great Britain. The peasants, who had before been attached to the soil, were gradually enfranchised between 1788 and 1800; so that, on the first day of the latter year, there did not remain a single slave in the Danish dominions; or, to speak more correctly, slavery was equalized among all ranks of people. We need not descant on the immense impertance of this revolution; and if Mr. Catteau had been of the same opinion, we should have been spared two pages of very bad declamation; beginning, in the true French style, with "oh toi," and going on with what might be expected to follow such a beginning.

The great mass of territorial proprietors in Denmark are the signiors, possessing fiefs with very extensive privileges and valuable exemptions from taxes. Many persons hold lands under these proprietors, with interests in the land of very different descriptions. There are some cultivators who possess freeholds, but the number of these is very inconsiderable. The greater number of farmers are what the French call Metayers, put in by the landlord, furnished with stock and seed at his expense, and repaying him in product, labour, or any other manner agreed on in the contract. This is the first, or lowest stage of tenantry, and is the surest sign of a poor country. The feudal system never took root very deeply in Norway: the greater part of the lands are freehold, and cultivated by their owners. Those which are held under the few privileged fiefs which still exist in Norway, are subjected to less galling conditions than farms of a similar tenure in Denmark. Marriage is a mere civil contract among the privileged orders: the presence of a priest is necessary for its celebration among the lower orders. In every large town, there are two public tutors appointed, who, in conjunction with the magistrates, watch over the interests of wards, at the same time that they occupy themselves with the care of the education of children within the limits of their jurisdiction. Natural children are perhaps more favoured in Denmark than in any other kingdom of Europe, they have half the portion which the law allots to legitimate children, and the whole if there are no legitimate.

A very curious circumstance took place in the kingdom of Denmark, in the middle of the last century, relative to the infliction of capital punishments upon malefactors. They were attended from the prison to the place of execution by priests, accompanied by a very numerous procession, singing psalms, &c. &c.: which ended, a long discourse was addressed by the priest to the culprit, who was hung as soon as he had heard it. This spectacle, and all the pious cares bestowed upon the criminals, so far seduced the imaginations of the common people, that many of them committed murder purposely to enjoy such inestimable advantages, and the government was positively obliged to make hanging dull as well as deadly, before it ceased to be an object of popular ambition.

In 1796, the Danish land forces amounted to 74,654, of which 50,880 were militia.* Amongst the troops on the Norway establishment, is a regiment of skaters. The pay of a colonel in the Danish service is about 1740 rixdollars *per annum*, with some perquisites; that of a private 6 schellings a day. The entry into the Danish states from the German side is naturally strong. The passage between Lubeck and Hamburg is only eight miles, and the country intersected by marshes, rivers, and lakes. The straits of the Baltic afford considerable security to the Danish isles; and there are very few points in which an army could penetrate through the Norway mountains to overrun that country. The principal fortresses of Denmark are Copenhagen, Rendsbhurg, Gluchstadt, and Frederickshall. In 1801, the Danish navy consisted of 3 ships of 80 guns, 12 of 74, 2 of 70, 3 of 64, and 2 of 60; 4 frigates of 40, 3 of 36, 3 of 24, and a number of small vessels; in all, 22 of the line, and 10 frigates.†

* The militia is not embodied in regiments by itself, but divided among the various regiments of the line.

† In 1791, the Swedish army amounted to 47,000 men, regulars and militia; their navy to not more than 16 ships of the line: before the war it was about equal to the Danish navy. The author of *Voyage des deux Français* places the regular troops of Russia at 250,000 men exclusive of guards and garrisons; and her navy, as it existed in 1791, at 30 frigates, and 50 sail of the line, of which 8 were of 110 guns. This is a brief picture of the forces of the Baltic powers.

The revenues of Denmark are derived from the interest of a capital formed by the sale of crown lands; from a share in the tithes; from the rights of fishing and hunting let to farm; from licenses granted to the farmers to distil their own spirits; from the mint, post, turnpikes, lotteries, and the passage of the Sound. About the year 1750, the number of vessels which passed the Sound both ways, was annually from 4000 to 5000; in 1752, the number of 6000 was considered as very extraordinary. They have increased since in the following ratio:—

1770	7,736
1777	9,047
1783	11,166
1790	9,734
1796	12,113
1800	9,048

In 1770, the Sound duties amounted to 459,890 rixdollars; and they have probably been increased since that period to about half a million. To these sources of revenue are to be added, a capitation tax, a land tax, a tax on rank, a tax on places, pensions, and the clergy; the stamps, customs, and excise; constituting a revenue of 7,270,172 rixdollars.* The following is a table of the expenses of the Danish government.

	Rixdollars.
The court	250,000
The minor branches of the royal family	180,000
Civil servants	707,500
Secret service money and pensions	231,000
Army	2,080,000
Navy	1,200,000
East India colonies	180,000
Bounties to commerce and manufactures	300,000
Annuities	27,000
Buildings and repairs	120,000
Interest of the public debt	1,100,000
Sinking fund	150,000
Total	6,525,500

The state of the Danish debt does not appear to be well ascertained. *Voyage des deux Français* makes it amount to 13,645,046 rixdollars. Catteau seems to think it must have been above 20,000,000 rixdollars at that period. The Danish government has had great recourse to the usual expedient of issuing paper money. So easy a method of getting rich has of course been abused; and the paper was, in the year 1790, at a discount of 8, 9, and 10 *per cent.* There is, in general, a great want of specie in Denmark; for, though all the Sound duties are paid in gold and silver, the government is forced to export a considerable quantity of the precious metals, for the payment of its foreign debts and agents; and, in spite of the rigid prohibitions to the contrary, the Jews, who swarm at Copenhagen, export Danish ducats to a large value. The court of Denmark has no great credit out of its own dominions, and has always experienced a considerable difficulty in raising its loans in Switzerland, Genoa, and Holland, the usual markets it has resorted to for that purpose.

In the census taken in 1769, the return was as follows:—

In Denmark	785,690
Norway	722,141
Iceland	46,201
Ferro Isles	4,754
Sleswick	243,605
Holstein	134,665
Oldenbourg and Delmenhurst	79,071
	2,017,127

This census was taken during the summer a season in which great numbers of sailors are absent from their families; and as it does not include the army, the total ought, perhaps, to be raised to 2,225,000. The present population of the Danish states, calculating from the tables of life and death, should be about two millions and a half; the census lately taken has not yet been published. From registers kept for a number of years, it appears that the number of marriages were to the whole population, as 1 to 125; and the number of births to the whole population, were as 1 to 32 or 33; of deaths, as 1 to 38. In 1797, in the diocese of Vibourg, out of 8600 children, 80 were bastard: in the diocese of Fionia, 280 out of 1146. Out of 1356, dead in the first of these dioceses, 100 had attained the age of 80, and one of 100. In 1769, the population of the towns was 144,105; in 1787, it was 142,880. In the first of these years, the population of the country was 641,485; and in the latter, 667,165. The population of Copenhagen consisted, in the year 1799, of 42,142 males, and 41,476 females. The deaths exceeded the births, says Mr. Catteau; and to prove it, he exhibits a table of deaths and births for six years. Upon calculating this table, however, it appears, that the sum of the births, at Copenhagen, during that period, exceeds the sum of the deaths by 491, or nearly 82 *per annum;* about $\frac{1}{1000}$ of the whole population of the city. The whole kingdom increases $\frac{6}{1216}$, or nearly $\frac{1}{202}$ in a year.* There is no city in Denmark proper, except Copenhagen, which has a population of more than 5000 souls. The density of population in Denmark proper is about 1300 to the square mile.† The proportion of births and deaths in the duchies is the same as in Denmark; that of marriages, as 1 to 115. Altona, the second city in the Danish dominions, has a population of 20,000. The density of population in Marschland is 6000 per square mile. The paucity of inhabitants in Norway is not merely referable to the difficulties of subsistence, but to the administrative system established there, and to the bad state of its civil and economical laws. It has been more than once exposed to the horrors of famine, by the monopoly of the commerce of grain established there, from which, however, it has at length been delivered. The proportion of births to the living, is as 1 to 35; that of deaths to the living, as 1 to 49.‡ So that the whole

* Upon the subject of the Danish revenues, see Toze's Introduction to the Statistics, edited and improved by Heinz, 1799, tom. xi. From this work, Mr. Catteau has taken his information concerning the Danish revenues. See also the 10th cap. vol. ii. of *Voyage des deux Français,* which is admirable for extent and precision of information. In general, indeed, this work cannot be too much attended to by those who wish to become acquainted with the statistics of the north of Europe.

* The average time in which old countries double their population is stated by Adam Smith to be about 500 years.

† The same rule is used here as in p. 279.

‡ This proportion is very remarkable proof of the longevity of the Norwegians.

Danish dominions increase, every year, by about $\frac{1}{203}$; and Norway, which has the worst climate and soil, by about $\frac{1}{222}$; exceeding the common increase by nearly $\frac{1}{300}$ of the whole population. Out of 26,197 persons who died in Denmark in 1799, there were 165 between 80 and 100; and out of 18,354 who died in Norway the same year, there were 208 individuals of the same advanced age. The country population is to the town population in the ratio of 13 to 137. In some parts of Nordland and Finmarken, the population is as low as 15 to the square mile.

Within the last twenty or thirty years, the Danes have done a great deal for the improvement of their country. The peasants, as we have before mentioned, are freed from the soil. The greater part of the clerical, and much of the lay tithes are redeemed, and the corvées and other servile tenures begin to be commuted for money. A bank of credit is established at Copenhagen, for the loan of money to persons engaged in speculations of agriculture and mining. The interest is 4 *per cent.*, and the money is repaid by instalments in the course of from 21 to 28 years. In the course of 12 years, the bank has lent about three millions of rixdollars. The external and domestic commerce of grain is now placed upon the most liberal footing. The culture of potatoes (*ce fruit modeste*) has at length found its way into Denmark, after meeting with the same objections which it experienced at its first introduction from every nation in Europe. Hops are a good deal attended to in Fionia, though enough are not yet grown for the supply of the country. Tobacco is cultivated in the environs of Fredericia, in Jutland, by the industrious descendants of a French colony planted there by Frederick IV. Very little hemp and flax are grown in the Danish dominions. They had veterinary schools previous to the present establishment of them in Great Britain. Indeed, there was a greater necessity for them in Denmark; as no country in Europe has suffered so severely from diseases among its animals. The decay of the woods begins to be very perceptible; and great quantities, both for fuel and construction, are annually imported from the other countries bordering the Baltic. They have pit-coal; but, either from its inferior quality, or their little skill in working it, they are forced to purchase to a considerable amount from England. The Danes have been almost driven out of the herring market by the Swedes. Their principal export of this kind is dried fish; though, at Altona, their fisheries are carried on with more appearance of enterprise than elsewhere. The districts of Hedemarken, Hodeland, Toten, and Romerige, are the parts of Norway most celebrated for the cultivation of grain, which principally consists of oats. The distress in Norway is sometimes so great, that the inhabitants are compelled to make bread of various sorts of lichens, mingled with their grain. It has lately been discovered that the *Lichen rangiferus*, or rein-deer's moss, is extremely well calculated for that purpose. The Norway fisheries bring to the amount of a million and a half of rixdollars annually into the country. The most remarkable mines in Norway are the gold mines of Edsvold, the silver mines of Konigsberg, the copper mines of Rœraas, and the iron mines of Arendal and Krageræ, the cobalt mines of Fossum, and the black-lead mines of Englidal. The court of Denmark is not yet cured of the folly of entering into commercial speculations on its own account. From the year 1769 to 1792, 78,000 rixdollars *per annum* have been lost on the royal mines alone. Norway produces marble of different colours, very beautiful granites, mill, and whet-stones, and alum.

The principal manufactures of Denmark are those of cloth, cotton-printing, sugar refining, and porcelain; of which latter manufactures, carried on by the crown, the patient proprietors hope that the profits may at some future period equal the expenses. The manufactories for large and small arms are at Frederickwaerk and Elsineur; and, at the gates of Copenhagen, there has lately been erected a cotton spinning-mill upon the construction so well known in England. At Tendern, in Sleswick, there is a manufacture of lace; and very considerable glass manufactories in several parts of Norway. All the manufacturing arts have evidently travelled from Lubeck and Hamburg; the greater part of the manufacturers are of German parentage; and vast numbers of manufacturing Germans are to be met with, not only in Denmark, but throughout Sweden and Russia.

The Holstein canal, uniting the Baltic and the North Sea, is extremely favourable to the interior commerce of Denmark, by rendering unnecessary the long and dangerous voyage round the peninsula of Jutland. In the year 1785, there passed through this canal 409 Danish, and 44 foreign ships. In the year 1798, 1086 Danish, and 1164 foreign. This canal is so advantageous, and the passage round Jutland so very bad, that goods, before the creation of the canal, were very often sent by land from Lubeck to Hamburg. The amount of cargoes despatched from Copenhagen for Iceland, between the years 1764 and 1784, was 2,560,000 rixdollars; that of the returns, 4,665,000. The commerce with the isles of Foeroe is quite inconsiderable. The exports from Greenland, in the year 1787, amounted to 168,475 rixdollars; its imports to 74,427. None of these possessions are suffered to trade with foreign nations, but through the intervention of the mother country. The cargoes despatched to the Danish West Indies consist of all sorts of provisions, of iron, of copper, of various Danish manufactures, and of some East India goods. The returns are made in sugar, rum, cotton, indigo, tobacco, and coffee. There are about 75 vessels employed in this commerce, from the burden of 40 to 200 tons.

If the slave trade, in pursuance of the laws to that effect, ceases in the Danish colonies, the establishments on the coast of Africa will become rather a burden than a profit. What measures have been taken to insure the abolition, and whether or not the philanthropy of the mother country is likely to be defeated by the interested views of the colonists, are delicate points, which Mr. Catteau, who often seems to think more of himself than of his reader, passes over with his usual timidity and caution. The present year is the period at which all further importation of negroes ought to cease; and if this wise and noble law be really carried into execution, the Danes will enjoy the glory of having been the first to erase this foulest blot in the morality of Europe, and to abolish a wicked and absurd traffic, which purchases its luxuries at the price of impending massacre, and present oppression. Deferred revenge is always put out to compound interest, and exacts its dues with more than Judaical rigour. The Africans have begun with the French:

——Jam proximus ardet
Ucalegon.

Tea, rhubarb, and porcelain are the principal articles brought from China. The factories in the East Indies send home cotton cloths, silk, sugar, rice, pepper, ginger, indigo, opium, and arrack. Their most important East Indian settlement is Fredericksnager.* Denmark, after having been long overshadowed by the active industry of the Hanseatic towns, and embarrassed by its ignorance of the true principles of commerce, has at length established important commercial connections with all the nations of Europe, and has regulated those connections by very liberal and enlightened principles. The regulations for the customs, published in 1791, are a very remarkable proof of this assertion. Every thing is there arranged upon the most just and simple principles; and the whole code evidences the striking progress of mercantile knowledge in that country. In looking over the particulars of the Danish commerce, we were struck with the immense increase of their freightage during the wars of this country; a circumstance which should certainly have rendered them rather less disposed to complain of the vexations imposed upon the neutral powers during such periods.† In the first six months of the year 1796, 5032 lasts of Danish shipping were taken up by strangers for American voyages only. The commercial tonnage of Denmark is put at about 85,000 lasts.

There appears to exist in the kingdom of Denmark, according to the account of Mr. Catteau, a laudable spirit of religious toleration; such as, in some instances, we might copy, with great advantage, in this island. It is not, for instance, necessary in Denmark, that a man should be a Lutheran, before he can be the mayor of a town; and, incredible as it may seem to some people, there are many officers and magistrates, who are found capable of civil trusts, though they do not take the sacraments, exactly in the forms prescribed by the established church. There is no doubt, however, of the existence of this very extraordinary fact; and, if Mr. Catteau's authority is called in question, we are ready to corroborate it by the testimony of more than one dozen German statists. The Danish church consists of 13 bishops, 227 archpriests, and 2462 priests. The principal part of the benefices are, in Norway, in the gift of the crown. In some parts of Denmark, the proprietors of the privileged lands are the patrons; in other parts, the parishes. The revenues of the clergy are from the same sources as our own clergy. The sum of the church revenues is computed to be 1,391,895 rixdollars; which is little more than 500 for each clergyman.* The court of Denmark is so liberal upon the subject of sectaries, that the whole royal family and the Bishop of Seland assisted at the worship of the Calvinists in 1789, when they celebrated, in the most public manner, the centenary of the foundation of their church. In spite of this tolerant spirit, it is computed that there are not more than 1800 Calvinists in the whole Danish dominions. At Christianfield, on the frontiers of Sleswick and Jutland, there is a colony of Northern Quakers, or Hernhutes, of which Mr. Catteau has given a very agreeable account. They appear to be characterized by the same neatness, order, industry, and absurdity, as their brethren in this country; taking the utmost care of the sick and destitute, and thoroughly persuaded that by these good deeds, aided by long pockets and slouched hats, they are acting up to the true spirit of the Gospel. The Greenlanders were converted to Christianity by a Norwegian priest, named John Egede. He was so eminently successful in the object of his mission, and contrived to make himself so very much beloved, that his memory is still held among them in the highest veneration; and they actually date their chronology from the year of his arrival, as we do ours from the birth of our Saviour.

There are, in the University of Copenhagen, seven professors of theology, two of civil law, two of mathematics, one of Latin and rhetoric, one of Greek, one of oriental languages, one of history, five of medicine, one of agriculture, and one of statistics. They enjoy a salary of from 1000 to 1500 rixdollars, and are well lodged in the university. The University of Copenhagen is extremely rich, and enjoys an income of 3,000,000 rixdollars. Even Mr. Catteau admits that it has need of reform. In fact, the reputation of universities is almost always short-lived, or else it survives their merit. If they are endowed, professors become fat-witted, and never imagine that the arts and sciences are any thing else but incomes. If universities, slenderly endowed, are rendered famous by the accidental occurrence of a few great teachers, the number of scholars attracted there by the reputation of the place, makes the situation of a professor worth intriguing for. The learned pate is not fond of ducking to the golden fool. He who has the best talents for getting the office, has most commonly the least for filling it; and

* We should very willingly have gone through every branch of the Danish commerce, if we had not been apprehensive of extending this article too far. Mr. Catteau gives no general tables of the Danish exports and imports. A German work places them, for the year 1768, as follows:—Exports, 3,067,051 rixdollars; imports, 3,215,085.—*Ur. Kunden, par Gatspari.*

† To say nothing of the increased sale of Norway timber, out of 86,000 lasts exported from Norway, 1799, 76,000 came to Great Britain.

* The Jews, however, are still prohibited from entering the kingdom of Norway.

men are made moral and mathematical teachers by the same trick and filthiness with which they are made tide-waiters, and clerks of the kitchen.

The number of students in the University of Copenhagen is about 700: they come not only from Denmark, but from Norway and Iceland: the latter are distinguished as well for the regularity of their manners, as for the intensity of their application; the instruments of which application are furnished to them by a library containing 60,000 volumes. The Danes have primary schools established in the towns, but which have need of much reform, before they can answer all the beneficial ends of such an institution. We should have been happy to have learned from Mr. Catteau, the degree of information diffused among the lower orders in the Danish dominions; but upon this subject he is silent. In the University of Keil there is an institution for the instruction of schoolmasters; and in the list of students in the same university, we were a good deal amused to find only one student dedicating himself to belles lettres.

The people of Holstein and Sleswick are Dutch in their manners, character, and appearance. Their language is in general the low German; though the better sort of people in the towns begin to speak high German.* In Jutland and the isles, the Danish language is spoken: within half a century this language has been cultivated with some attention: before that period, the Danish writers preferred to make use of the Latin or the German language. It is in the island of Finland that it is spoken with the greatest purity. The Danish character is not agreeable. It is marked by silence, phlegm, and reserve. A Dane is the excess and extravagance of a Dutchman; more breeched, more ponderous, and more saturnine. He is not often a bad member of society in the great points of morals, and seldom a good one in the lighter requisites of manners. His understanding is alive only to the useful and the profitable; he never lives for what is merely gracious, courteous, and ornamental. His faculties seem to be drenched and slackened by the eternal fogs in which he resides; he is never alert, elastic, nor serene. His state of animal spirits is so low, that what in other countries would be deemed dejection, proceeding from casual misfortune, is the habitual tenour and complexion of his mind. In all the operations of his understanding, he must have time. He is capable of undertaking great journeys; but he travels only a foot pace, and never leaps nor runs. He loves arithmetic better than lyric poetry, and affects Cocker rather than Pindar. He is slow to speak of fountains and amorous maidens; but can take a spell at porisms as well as another; and will make profound and extensive combinations of thought, if you pay him for it, and do not insist that he shall either be brisk or brief. There is something, on the contrary, extremely pleasing in the Norwegian style of character. The Norwegian expresses firmness and elevation in all that he says and does. In comparison with the Danes, he has always been a free man; and you read his history in his looks. He is not apt, to be sure, to forgive his enemies; but he does not deserve any; for he is hospitable in the extreme, and prevents the needy in their wants. It is not possible for a writer of this country to speak ill of the Norwegians; for, of all strangers, the people of Norway love and admire the British the most. In reading Mr. Catteau's account of the congealed and blighted Laplanders, we were struck with the infinite delight they must have in dying; the only circumstance in which they can enjoy any superiority over the rest of mankind; or which tends, in their instance, to verify the theory of the equality of human condition.

If we pass over Tycho Brahé, and the well known history of the Scaldes, of the chronicles of Isleif, Sæmunder, Hiinfronde, Snorro, Sturleson, and other Islandic worthies, the list of Danish literati will best prove that they have no literati at all. Are there twenty persons in Great Britain who have ever heard of Longomontanus, Nicholas Stenaonis, Sperling Laurenburg, Huitfeild, Gramn, Holberg, Langebeck, Carstens, Suhm, Kofod, Anger? or of the living Wad, Fabricius, Hanch, Tode, and Zæga? We do not deny merit to these various personages; many of them may be much admired by those who are more conversant in Danish literature than we can pretend to be: but they are certainly not names on which the learned fame of any country can be built very high. They have no classical celebrity and diffusion: they are not an universal language; they have not enlarged their original dominion, and become the authors of Europe instead of the authors of Denmark. It would be loss of time to speak of the fine arts in Denmark: they hardly exist.

We have been compelled to pass over many parts of Mr. Catteau's book more precipitately than we could have wished; but we hope we have said and exhibited enough of it, to satisfy the public that it is, upon the whole, a very valuable publication. The two great requisites for his undertaking, moderation and industry, we are convinced this gentleman possesses in an eminent degree. He represents every thing without prejudice, and he represents every thing authentically. The same cool and judicious disposition which clears him from the spirit of party, makes him perhaps cautious in excess. We are convinced that every thing he says is true; but we have been sometimes induced to suspect that we do not see the whole truth. After all, perhaps, he has told as much truth as he could do, compatibly with the opportunity of telling any. A person more disposed to touch upon critical and offensive subjects might not have submitted as diligently to the investigation of truth, with which passion was not concerned. How few writers are, at the same time, laborious, impartial, and intrepid!

We cannot conclude this article without expressing the high sense we entertain of the

* Mr. Catteau s description of Heligoland is entertaining. In an island containing a population of 2000, there is neither horse, cart, nor plough. We could not have imagined the possibility of such a fact in any part of Europe.

importance of such researches as those in which Mr. Catteau has been engaged. They must form the basis of all interior regulations, and ought principally to influence the conduct of every country in its relations towards foreign powers. As they contain the best estimate of the wealth and happiness of a people, they bring theory to the strictest test; and measure, better than all reasoning, the wisdom with which laws are made, and the mildness with which they are administered. If such judicious and elaborate surveys of the state of this and other countries in Europe, had been made from time to time for the last two centuries, they would have quickened and matured the progress of knowledge, and the art of governing by throwing light on the spirit and tendency of laws; they would have checked the spirit of officious interference in legislation; have softened persecution, and expanded narrow conceptions of national policy. The happiness of a nation would have been proclaimed by the fulness of its garners, and the multitudes of its sheep and oxen; and rulers might sometimes have sacrificed their schemes of ambition, or their unfeeling splendour, at the detail of silent fields, empty harbours, and famished peasants.

THOUGHTS ON THE RESIDENCE OF THE CLERGY.*

[Edinburgh Review, 1803.]

This pamphlet is the production of a gentleman who has acquired a right to teach the duties of the clerical character by fulfilling them; and who has exercised that right in the present instance, with honour to himself, and benefit to the public. From the particular character of understanding evinced in this work, we should conceive Dr. Sturges to possess a very powerful claim to be heard on all questions referable to the decision of practicable good sense. He has availed himself of his experience to observe; and of his observation, to judge well: he neither loves his profession too little, nor too much; is alive to its interests, without being insensible to those of the community at large; and treats of those points where his previous habits might render a little intemperance venial, as well as probable, with the most perfect good humour and moderation.

As exceptions to the general and indisputable principle of residence, Dr. Sturges urges the smallness of some livings; the probability that their incumbents be engaged in the task of education, or in ecclesiastical duty, in situations where their talents may be more appropriately and importantly employed. Dr. Sturges is also of opinion, that the power of enforcing residence, under certain limits, should be invested in the bishops; and that the acts prohibiting the clergy to hold or cultivate land should be in a great measure repealed.

We sincerely hope that the two cases suggested by Dr. Sturges, of the clergyman who may keep a school, or be engaged in the duty of some parish not his own, will be attended to in the construction of the approaching bill, and admitted as pleas for non-residence. It certainly is better that a clergyman should do the duty of his own benefice, rather than of any other. But the injury done to the community, is not commensurate with the vexation imposed upon the individual. Such a measure is either too harsh, not to become obsolete; or, by harassing the clergy with a very severe restriction, to gain a very disproportionate good to the community, would bring the profession into disrepute, and have a tendency to introduce a class of men into the church, of less liberal manners, education, and connection; points of the utmost importance, in our present state of religion and wealth. Nothing has enabled men to do wrong with impunity so much as the extreme severity of the penalties with which the law has threatened them. The only method to insure success to the bill for enforcing ecclesiastical residence, is to consult the convenience of the clergy in its construction, as far as is possibly consistent with the object desired, and even to sacrifice something that *ought* to be done, in order that much *may* be done. Upon this principle, the clergyman should not be confined to his parsonage-house, but to the precincts of his parish. Some advantage would certainly attend the residence of the clergy in their official mansions; but, as we have before observed, the good one party would obtain, bears no sort of proportion to the evil the other would suffer.

Upon the propriety of investing the bench of bishops with a power of enforcing residence, we confess ourselves to entertain very serious doubts. A bishop has frequently a very temporary interest in his diocese: he has favours to ask; and he must grant them. Leave of absence will be granted to powerful intercession; and refused, upon stronger pleas, to men without friends. Bishops are frequently men advanced in years, or immersed in study. A single person who compels many others to their duty, has much odium to bear, and much activity to exert. A bishop is subject to caprice, and enmity, and passion, in common with other individuals; there is some danger, also, that his power over the clergy may be converted to a political purpose. From innumerable causes, which might be reasoned upon to great length, we are apprehensive the object of the legislature will be entirely frus-

* *Thoughts on the Residence of the Clergy.* By John Sturges, LL. D.

trated in a few years, if it be committed to espiscopal superintendence and care; though, upon the first view of the subject, no other scheme can appear so natural and so wise.

Dr. Sturges observes, that after all the conceivable justifications of non-residence are enumerated in the act, many others must from time to time occur, and indicate the propriety of vesting somewhere a discretionary power. If this be true of the penalties by which the clergy are governed, it is equally true of all other penal laws; and the law should extend to every offence the contingency of discretionary omission. The objection to this system is, that it trusts too much to the sagacity and the probity of the judge, and exposes a country to the partial, lax, and corrupt administration of its laws. It is certainly inconvenient, in many cases, to have no other guide to resort to but the unaccommodating mandates of an act of Parliament: yet, of the two inconveniences, it is the least. It is some palliation of the evils of discretionary power, that it should be exercised (as by the court of chancery) in the face of day, and that the moderator of law should himself be moderated by the force of precedent and opinion. A bishop will exercise his discretionary power in the dark; he is at full liberty to depart to-morrow from the precedent he has established to-day; and to apply the same decisions to different, or different decisions to the same circumstances, as his humour or interest may dictate. Such power may be exercised well under one judge of extraordinary integrity; but it is not very probable he will find a proper successor. To suppose a series of men so much superior to temptation, and to construct a system of church government upon such a supposition, is to build upon sand, with materials not more durable than the foundation.

Sir William Scott has made it very clear, by his excellent speech, that it is not possible, in the present state of the revenues of the English church, to apply a radical cure to the evil of non-residence. It is there stated, that out of 11,700 livings, there are 6000 under 80*l. per annum;* many of those, 20*l.*, 30*l.*, and some as low as 2*l.* or 3*l. per annum.* In such a state of endowment, all idea of rigid residence is out of the question. Emoluments which a footman would spurn, can hardly recompense a scholar and a gentleman. A mere palliation is all that can be applied; and these are the ingredients of which we wish such a palliation should be composed:—

1. Let the clergymen have the full liberty of farming, and be put in this respect exactly upon a footing with laymen.

2. Power to reside in any other house in the parish, as well as the parsonage-house, and to be absent five months in the year.

3. Schoolmasters, and ministers *bonâ fide* discharging ministerial functions in another parish, exempt from residence.

4. Penalties in proportion to the value of livings, and number of times the offence has been committed.

5. Common informers to sue as at present; though *probably* it might be right to make the name of one parishioner a necessary addition; and a proof of non-residence might be made to operate as a nonsuit in an action for tithes.

6. No action for non-residence to lie where the benefice was less than 80*l. per annum;* and the powers of bishops to remain precisely as they are.

These indulgences would leave the clergy without excuse, would reduce the informations to a salutary number, and diminish the odium consequent upon them, by directing their effects against men who regard church preferment merely as a source of revenue, not as an obligation to the discharge of important duties.

We venture to prognosticate, that a bill of greater severity either will not pass the House of Commons, or will fail of its object. Considering the times and circumstances, we are convinced we have stated the greatest quantum of *attainable* good; which of course will not be attained, by the customary error, of attending to what is desirable to be done, rather than to what it is practicable to do.

TRAVELS FROM PALESTINE.*

[Edinburgh Review, 1807.]

In the year 1432, many great lords in the dominions of Burgundy, holding offices under Duke Philip le Bon, made a pilgrimage to Jerusalem. Among them was his first esquire-carver La Brocquière, who, having performed many devout pilgrimages in Palestine, returned sick to Jerusalem, and during his convalescence, formed the bold scheme of returning to France over land. This led him to traverse the western parts of Asia, and Eastern Europe; and, during the whole journey, except towards the end of it, he passed through the dominions of the Musselmen. The execution of such a journey, even at this day, would not be without difficulty; and it was then thought to be impossible. It was in vain that his companions attempted to dissuade him; he was obstinate; and, setting out, overcame every obstacle; returned in the course of the year 1433, and presented himself to the Duke in his Saracen dress, and on the horse which had carried him during the whole of his journey. The duke, after the fashion of great people, conceiving that the glory of his esquire-carver was his own, caused the work to be printed and published.

The following is a brief extract of this valiant person's peregrinations. "After performing the customary pilgrimages, we went," says La Brocquière, "to the mountain where Jesus fasted forty days; to Jordan, where he was baptized; to the church of St. Martha, where Lazarus was raised from the dead; to Bethlehem, where he was born; to the birth-place of St. John the Baptist; to the house of Zachariah; and, lastly, to the holy cross, where the tree grew that formed the real cross." From Jerusalem the first gentleman-carver betook himself to Mount Sinai, paying pretty handsomely to the Saracens for that privilege. These infidels do not appear to have ever prevented the Christian pilgrims from indulging their curiosity and devotion in visiting the most interesting evangelical objects in the Holy Land; but, after charging a good round price for this gratification, contented themselves with occasionally kicking them, and spitting upon them. In his way to Mount Sinai, the esquire-carver passed through the Valley of Hebron, where he tells us, Adam was created; and from thence to Gaza, where they showed him the columns of the building which Samson pulled down; though, of the identity of the building, the esquire seems to entertain some doubts. At Gaza five of his companions fell sick and returned to Jerusalem. The second day's journey in the desert the carver fell ill also,—returned to Gaza, where he was cured by a Samaritan,—and finding his way back to Jerusalem, hired some pleasant lodgings on Mount Sion.

Before he proceeded on his grand expedition over land, he undertook a little expedition to Nazareth, hearing, first of all, divine service at the Cordeliers, and imploring, at the tomb of our lady, her protection for his journey. From Jerusalem their first stage was Acre, where they gave up their intended expedition, and repaired to Baruth, whence Sir Samson de Lalaing and the author sallied afresh, under better auspices, to Damascus. He speaks with great pleasure of the valley where Noah built the ark, through which valley he passed in his way to Damascus; upon entering which town he was knocked down by a Saracen for wearing an ugly hat,—as he probably would be in London for the same offence in the year 1807. At Damascus, he informs us the Christians are locked up every night,—as they are in English workhouses, night and day, when they happen to be poor. The greatest misfortune attendant upon this Damascene incarceration, is the extreme irregularity with which the doors are opened in the morning, their janitor having no certain hour of quitting his bed. At Damascus, he saw the place where St. Paul had a vision. "I saw also," says he, "the stone from which St. George mounted his horse, when he went to combat the dragon. It is two feet square; and they say that, when formerly the Saracens attempted to carry it away, in spite of all the strength they employed, they could not succeed." After having seen Damascus, he returns with Sir Samson to Baruth; and communicates his intentions of returning over land to France to his companions. They state to him the astonishing difficulties he will have to overcome in the execution of so extraordinary a project; but the admirable carver, determined to make no bones, and to cut his way through every obstacle, persists in his scheme, and bids them a final adieu. He is determined, however, not to be baffled in his subordinate expedition to Nazareth; and, having now got rid of his timid companions, accomplishes it with ease. We shall here present our readers with an extract from this part of his journal, requesting them to admire the naïf manner in which he speaks of the vestiges of ecclesiastical history.

"Acre, though in a plain of about four leagues in extent, is surrounded on three sides by mountains, and on the fourth by the sea. I made acquaintance there with a Venetian merchant called Aubert Franc, who received me well, and procured me much useful information respecting my two pilgrimages, by which I profited. With the aid of his advice, I took the road to Nazareth; and, having crossed an extensive plain, came to the foun-

* *The Travels of Bertrandon de la Brocquière, First Esquire-Carver to Philip le Bon, Duke of Burgundy, during the years* 1432, 1433.—Translated from the French, by Thomas Johnes, Esq.

tain, the water of which our Lord changed into wine at the marriage of Archétréclin; it is near a village where St. Peter is said to have been born.

"Nazareth is another large village, built between two mountains; but the place where the angel Gabriel came to announce to the Virgin Mary that she would be a mother, is in a pitiful state. The church that had been there built is entirely destroyed; and of the house wherein our lady was when the angel appeared to her, not the smallest remnant exists.

"From Nazareth I went to Mount Tabor, the place where the transfiguration of our Lord, and many other miracles took effect. These pasturages attract the Arabs who come thither with their beasts; and I was forced to engage four additional men as an escort, two of whom were Arabs. The ascent of the mountain is rugged, because there is no road; I performed it on the back of a mule, but it took me two hours. The summit is terminated by an almost circular plain of about two bow-shots in length, and one in width. It was formerly enclosed with walls, the ruins of which, and the ditches, are still visible: within the wall, and around it, were several churches, and one especially, where, although in ruins, full pardon for vice and sin is gained.

"We went to lodge at Samaria, because I wished to see the lake of Tiberias, where it is said St. Peter was accustomed to fish; and, by so doing, some pardons may be gained, for it was the ember week of September. The Moucre left me to myself the whole day. Samaria is situated on the extremity of a mountain. We entered at the close of day, and left it at midnight to visit the lake. The Moucre had proposed this hour to evade the tribute exacted from all who go thither; but the night hindered me from seeing the surrounding country.

"I went first to Joseph's Well, so called from his being cast into it by his brethren. There is a handsome mosque near it, which I entered with my Moucre, pretending to be a Saracen.

"Further on is a stone bridge over the Jardon, called Jacob's Bridge, on account of a house hard by, said to be the residence of that patriarch. The river flows from a gentle lake situated at the foot of a mountain to the north-west, on which Namcardin has a very handsome castle."—(pp. 122—128.)

From Damascus, to which he returns after his expedition to Nazareth, the first carver of Philip le Bon sets out with the caravan for Bursa. Before he begins upon his journey, he expatiates with much satisfaction upon the admirable method of shoeing horses at Damascus,—a panegyric which certainly gives us the lowest ideas of that art in the reign of Philip le Bon; for it appears that, out of fifty days, his horse was lame for twenty-one, owing to this ingenious method of shoeing. As a mark of gratitude to the leader of the caravan, the esquire presents him with a pot of green ginger; and the caravan proceeds. Before it has advanced one day's journey, the esquire, however, deviates from the road, to pay his devoirs to a miraculous image of our Lady of Serdenay, which always sweats—not ordinary sudorific matter—but an oil of great ecclesiastical efficacy. While travelling with the caravan, he learnt to sit cross-legged, got drunk privately, and was nearly murdered by some Saracens, who discovered that he had money. In some parts of Syria, M. de la Brocquière met with an opinion, which must have been extremely favourable to the spirit of proselytism, in so very hot a country—an opinion that the infidels have a very bad smell, and that this is only to be removed by baptism. But as the baptism was according to the Greek ritual, by total immersion, Bertrandon seems to have a distant suspicion that this miracle may be resolved into the simple phenomenon of washing. He speaks well of the Turks, and represents them, to our surprise, as a very gay, laughing people. We thought Turkish gravity had been almost proverbial. The natives of the countries through which we passed pray (says he) for the conversion of Christians; and especially request that there may be never sent among them again such another terrible man as Godfrey of Boulogne. At Couhongue the caravan broke up; and here he quitted a Mameluke soldier, who had kept him company during the whole of the journey, and to whose courage and fidelity Europe, Philip le Bon, and Mr. Johnes of Hafod, are principally indebted for the preservation of the first esquire-carver.

"I bade adieu," he says, "to my Mameluke. This good man, whose name was Mohammed, had done me innumerable services. He was very charitable, and never refused alms when asked in the name of God. It was through charity he had been so kind to me; and I must confess that, without his assistance, I could not have performed my journey without incurring the greatest danger; and that had it not been for his kindness, I should often have been exposed to cold and hunger, and much embarrassed with my horse.

"On taking leave of him, I was desirous of showing my gratitude; but he would not accept of any thing except a piece of our fine European cloth to cover his head, which seemed to please him much. He told me all the occasions that had come to his knowledge, on which, if it had not been for him, I should have run risks of being assassinated, and warned me to be very circumspect in my connections with the Saracens, for that there were among them some as wicked as the Franks. I write this to recall to my reader's memory, that the person who, from his love to God, did me so many and essential kindnesses, was a man not of our faith."—(pp. 196, 197.)

For the rest of the journey, he travelled with the family of the leader of the caravan, without any occurrence more remarkable than those we have already noticed;—arrived at Constantinople, and passed through Germany to the court of Philip le Bon. Here his narrative concludes. Nor does the carver vouchsafe to inform us of the changes which time had made in the appetite of that great prince,—whether veal was more pleasing to him than lamb,—if his favourite morsels were still in request,—if animal succulence were as grateful to him as before the departure of the carver,—or if this semisanguineous partiality had given way to a taste for cinereous and torrefied meats. All these things the first esquire-carver might have said,—none of them he does say,—nor does Mr. Johnes of Hafod supply, by any antiquarian conjectures of his own, the distressing silence of the original. Saving such omissions, there is something pleasant in the narrative of this arch-divider of fowls. He is an honest, brave, liberal man; and tells his singular story with great brevity and plainness. We are obliged to Mr. Johnes for the amusement he has afforded us; and we hope he will persevere in his gentlemanlike, honourable, and useful occupations.

LETTER* ON THE CURATE'S SALARY BILL.†

[EDINBURGH REVIEW, 1808.]

THE poverty of curates has long been a favourite theme with novelists, sentimental tourists, and elegiac poets. But notwithstanding the known accuracy of this class of philosophers, we cannot help suspecting that there is a good deal of misconception in the popular estimate of the amount of the evil.

A very great proportion of all the curacies in England are filled with men to whom the emolument is a matter of subordinate importance. They are filled by young gentlemen who have recently left college, who of course are able to subsist as they had subsisted for seven years before, and who are glad to have an opportunity, on any terms, of acquiring a practical familiarity with the duties of their profession. They move away from them to higher situations as vacancies occur; and make way for a new race of ecclesiastical apprentices. To those men, the smallness of the appointment is a grievance of no very great magnitude; nor is it fair with relation to them, to represent the ecclesiastical order as degraded by the indigence to which some of its members are condemned. With regard, again, to those who take curacies merely as a means of subsistence, and with the prospect of remaining permanently in that situation, it is certain that by far the greater part of them are persons born in a very humble rank in society, and accustomed to no greater opulence than that of an ordinary curate. There are scarcely any of those persons who have taken a degree in an university, and not very many who have resided there at all. Now the son of a small Welsh farmer, who works hard every day for less than 40*l.* a year, has no great reason to complain of degradation or disappointment, if he get from 50*l.* to 100*l.* for a moderate portion of labour one day in seven. The situation, accordingly, is looked upon by these people as extremely eligible; and there is a great competition for curacies, even as they are now provided. The amount of the evil, then, as to the curates themselves, cannot be considered as very enormous, when there are so few who either actually feel, or are entitled to feel, much discontent on the subject. The late regulations about residence, too, by diminishing the total number of curates, will obviously throw that office chiefly into the hands of the well educated and comparatively independent young men, who seek for the situation rather for practice than profit, and do not complain of the want of emolument.

Still we admit it to be an evil, that the resident clergyman of a parish should not be enabled to hold a respectable rank in society from the regular emoluments of his office. But it is an evil which does not exist exclusively among curates; and which, wherever it exists, we are afraid is irremediable, without the destruction of the Episcopal church, or the augmentation of its patrimony. More than one-half of the livings in England are under 80*l.* a year; and the whole income of the church, including that of the bishops, if thrown into a common fund, would not afford above 180*l.* for each living. Unless Mr. Perceval, therefore, will raise an additional million or two for the church, there *must* be poor curates,—and poor rectors also; and unless he is to reduce the Episcopal hierarchy to the republican equality of our Presbyterian model, he must submit to very considerable inequalities in the distribution of this inadequate provision.

Instead of applying any of these remedies, however,—instead of proposing to increase the income of the church, or to raise a fund for its lowest servants by a *general* assessment upon those who are more opulent,—instead of even trying indirectly to raise the pay of curates, by raising their qualifications in respect of regular education, Mr. Perceval has been able, after long and profound study, to find no better cure for the endemic poverty of curates, than to ordain all rectors of a certain income to pay them one-fifth part of their emoluments, and to vest certain alarming powers in the bishops for the purpose of controlling their appointment. Now this scheme, it appears to us, has all the faults which it is possible for such a scheme to have. It is unjust and partial in its principle,—it is evidently altogether and utterly inefficient for the

* *A Letter to the Right Honourable Spencer Perceval, on a Subject connected with his Bill, now under Discussion in Parliament, for improving the Situation of Stipendiary Curates.* 8vo. Hatchard, London. 1808.

† Now we are all dead, it may be amusing to state that I was excited to this article by Sir William Scott, who brought me the book in his pocket; and begged I would attend to it, carefully concealing his name; my own opinions happened entirely to agree with his.

correction of the evil in question,—and it introduces other evils infinitely greater than that which it vainly proposes to abolish.

To this project, however, for increasing the salary of curates, Mr. Perceval has been so long and so obstinately partial, that he returned to the charge in the last session of Parliament, for the third time; and experienced, in spite of his present high situation, the same defeat which had baffled him in his previous attempts.

Though the subject is gone by once more for the present, we cannot abstain from bestowing a little gentle violence to aid its merited descent into the gulf of oblivion, and to extinguish, if possible, that resurgent principle which has so often disturbed the serious business of the country, and averted the attention of the public from the great scenes that are acting in the world—to search for some golden medium between the selfishness of the sacred principal, and the rapacity of the sacred deputy.

If church property is to be preserved, that precedent is not without danger which disposes at once of a fifth of all the valuable livings in England. We do not advance this as an argument of any great importance against the bill, but only as an additional reason why its utility should be placed in the clearest point of view, before it can attain the assent of well-wishers to the English establishment.

Our first and greatest objection to such a measure, is the increase of power which it gives to the bench of bishops,—an evil which may produce the most serious effects, by placing the whole body of the clergy under the absolute control of men who are themselves so much under the influence of the crown. This, indeed, has been pretty effectually accomplished, by the late residence bill of Sir William Scott; and our objection to the present bill is, that it tends to augment that excessive power before conferred on the prelacy.

If a clergyman lives in a situation which is destroying his constitution, he cannot exchange with a brother clergyman without the consent of the bishop; in whose hands, under such circumstances, his life and death are actually placed. If he wishes to cultivate a little land for his amusement or better support,—he cannot do it without the license of the bishop. If he wishes to spend the last three or four months with a declining wife or child at some spot where better medical assistance can be procured—he cannot do so without permission of the bishop. If he is struck with palsy, or racked with stone—the bishop can confine him in the most remote village in England. In short, the power which the bishops at present possess over their clergy is so enormous, that none but a fool or a madman would think of compromising his future happiness, by giving the most remote cause of offence to his diocesan. We ought to recollect, however, that the clergy constitute a body of 12 or 15,000 educated persons; that the whole concern of education devolves upon them; that some share of the talents and information which exist in the country must naturally fall to their lot; and that the complete subjugation of such a body of men cannot, in any point of view, be a matter of indifference to a free country.

It is in vain to talk of the good character of bishops. Bishops are men; not always the wisest of men; not always preferred for eminent virtues and talents, or for any good reason whatever known to the public. They are almost always devoid of striking and indecorous vices; but a man may be very shallow, very arrogant, and very vindictive, though a bishop; and pursue with unrelenting hatred a subordinate clergyman, whose principles he dislikes,* and whose genius he fears. Bishops, besides, are subject to the infirmities of old age, like other men; and in the decay of strength and understanding, will be governed as other men are, by daughters and wives, and whoever ministers to their daily comforts. We have no doubt that such cases sometimes occur; and produce, whenever they do occur, a very capricious administration of ecclesiastical affairs.† As the power of enforcing residence must be lodged somewhere, why not give the bishop a council, consisting of two-thirds ecclesiastics, and one-third laymen: and meeting at the same time as the sessions and deputy sessions;—the bishop's license for non-residence to issue, of course, upon their recommendation. Considering the vexatious bustle of a new, and the laxity of an aged bishop, we cannot but think that a diocese would be much more steadily administered under this system than by the present means.

Examine the constitutional effects of the power now granted to the bench. What hinders a bishop from becoming in the hands of the court a very important agent in all county elections? what clergyman would dare to refuse him his vote? But it will be said that no bishop will ever condescend to such sort of intrigues:—a most miserable answer to a most serious objection. The temptation is admitted,—the absence of all restraint; the dangerous consequences are equally admitted; and the only preservative is the personal character of the individual. If this style of reasoning were general, what would become of law, constitution, and every wholesome restraint which we have been accumulating for so many centuries? We have no intention to speak disrespectfully of constituted authorities; but when men can abuse power with impunity, and recommend themselves to their superiors by abusing it, it is but common sense to suppose that power will be abused; if it is, the country will hereafter be convulsed to its very entrails, in tearing away that power from the prelacy which has been so improvidently conferred upon them. It is useless to talk of the power they anciently possessed. They have never possessed it since England has been what it now is. Since we have enjoyed practically a free constitution, the bishops have, in point of fact, possessed little or no power of oppression over their clergy.

* Bold language for the year 1808.

† I have seen in the course of my life, as the mind of the prelate decayed, wife bishops, daughter bishops, butler bishops, and even cook and housekeeper bishops

It must be remembered, however, that we are speaking only of probabilities: the fact may turn out to be quite the reverse; the power vested in the bench may be exercised for spiritual purposes only, and with the greatest moderation. We shall be extremely happy to find that this is the case; and it will reflect great honour upon those who have corrected the improvidence of the legislature by their own sense of propriety.

It is contended by the friends of this law, that the respectability of the clergy depends in some measure on their wealth; and that, as the rich bishop reflects a sort of worldly consequence upon the poor bishop, and the rich rector upon the poor rector;—so, a rich class of curates could not fail to confer a greater degree of importance upon that class of men in general. This is all very well, if you intend to raise up some new fund in order to enrich curates: but you say that the riches of some constitute the dignity of the whole; and then you immediately take away from the rector the superfluous wealth which, according to your own method of reasoning, is to decorate and dignify the order of men to whom he belongs! The bishops constitute the first class in the church; the beneficed clergy the second; the curates the last. Why are you to take from the second to give to the last? Why not as well from the first* to give to the second—if you really mean to contend that the first and second are already too rich?

It is not true, however, that the class of rectors is generally either too rich, or even rich enough. There are 6000 livings below 80*l.* per annum, which is not very much above the average allowance of a curate. If every rector, however, who has more than 500*l.* is obliged to give a fifth part to a curate, there seems to be no reason why every bishop who has more than 1000*l.* should not give a fifth part among the poor rectors in his diocese. It is in vain to say this assessment upon rectors is reasonable and right, because they may reside and do duty themselves, and then they will not need a curate;—that their non-residence, in short, is a kind of delinquency for which they compound by this fine to the parish. If more than half of the rectories in England are under 80*l.* a year, and some thousands of them under 40*l.*, pluralities are *absolutely necessary;* and clergymen, who have not the gift of ubiquity, *must* be non-resident at some of them. Curates, therefore, are not the deputies of negligent rectors;—they are an order of priests absolutely necessary in the present form of the Church of England: and a rector incurs no shadow of delinquency by employing one, more than the king does by appointing a lord-lieutenant of Ireland, or a commissioner to the General Assembly of the Church of Scotland, instead of doing the duty of these offices in person. If the legislature, therefore, is to interfere to raise the natural, *i. e.* the actual wages of this order of men, at the expense of the more opulent ministers of the Gospel, there seems to be no sort of reason for exempting the bishops from their share in this pious contribution, or for refusing to make a similar one for the benefit of all rectors who have less than 100*l.* per annum.

The true reason, however, for exempting my lords the bishops from this imposition is, that they have the privilege of voting upon all bills brought in by Mr. Perceval, and of materially affecting his comfort and security by their parliamentary control and influence. This, however, is to cure what you believe to be unjust, by means which you must know to be unjust; to fly out against abuses which may be remedied without peril, and to connive at them when the attempt at a remedy is attended with political danger; to be mute and obsequious towards men who enjoy church property to the amount of 8 or 19,000*l.* per annum; and to be so scandalized at those who possess as many hundreds, that you must melt their revenues down into curacies, and save to the eye of political economy the spectacle of such flagrant inequality!

In the same style of reasoning, it may be asked why the lay improprietors are not compelled to advance the salary of their perpetual curacies, up to a fifth of their estates? The answer, too, is equally obvious—Many lay improprietors have votes in both houses of Parliament; and the only class of men this cowardly reformation attacks, is that which has no means of saying any thing in its own defence.

Even if the enrichment of curates were the most imperious of all duties, it might very well be questioned, whether a more unequal and pernicious mode of fulfilling it could be devised than that enjoined by this bill. Curacies are not granted for the life of the curate; but for the life or incumbency or good-liking of the rector. It is only rectors worth 500*l.* a-year who are compelled by Mr. Perceval to come down with a fifth to their deputy; and these form but a very small proportion of the whole non-resident rectors; so that the great multitude of curates must remain as poor as formerly,—and probably a little more discontented. Suppose, however, that one has actually entered on the enjoyment of 250*l.* *per annum.* His wants, and his habits of expense, are enlarged by this increase of income. In a year or two his rector dies, or exchanges his living; and the poor man is reduced, by the effects of comparison, to a much worse state than before the operation of the bill. Can any person say that this is a wise and effectual mode of ameliorating the condition of the lower clergy? To us it almost appears to be invented for the express purpose of destroying those habits of economy and caution, which are so indispensably necessary to their situation. If it is urged that the curate, knowing his wealth only to be temporary, will make use of it as a means of laying up a fund for some future day,—we admire the good sense of the man: but what becomes of all the provisions of the bill? what becomes of that opulence which is to confer respectability upon all around it, and to radiate even upon the curates of Wales? The money was expressly given to blacken his coat,—to render him convex and rosy,—to give him a sort of pseudo-rectorial appearance, and to dazzle th

* The first unfortunately make the laws.

parishioners at the rate of 250*l.* *per annum.* The poor man, actuated by those principles of common sense which are so contrary to all the provisions of the bill, chooses to make a good thing of it, because he knows it will not last; wears his old coat, rides his lean horse, and defrauds the class of curates of all the advantages which they were to derive from the sleekness and splendour of his appearance.

It is of some importance to the welfare of a parish, and the credit of the church, that the curate and his rector should live upon good terms together. Such a bill, however, throws between them elements of mistrust and hatred, which must render their agreement highly improbable. The curate would be perpetually prying into every little advance which the rector made upon his tithes, and claiming his proportionate increase. No respectable man could brook such inquisition; some, we fear, would endeavour to prevent its effects by clandestine means. The church would be a perpetual scene of disgraceful animosities; and the ears of the bishop never free from the clamours of rapacity and irritation.

It is some slight defect in such a bill, that it does not proportion reward to the labour done, but to the wealth of him for whom it is done. The curate of a parish containing 400 persons, may be paid as much as another person who has the care of 10,000; for, in England, there is very little proportion between the value of a living, and the quantity of duty to be performed by its clergyman.

The bill does not attain its object in the best way. Let the bishop refuse to allow of any curate upon a living above 500*l.* *per annum,* who is not a Master of Arts of one of the universities. Such curates will then be obtained at a price which will render it worth the while of such men to take curacies; and such a degree and situation in society will secure good curates much more effectually than the complicated provisions of this bill: for, *primâ facie,* it appears to us much more probable, that a curate should be respectable, who is a Master of Arts in some English university, than if all that we knew about him was, that he had a fifth of the profits of the living. The object is, to fix a good clergyman in a parish. The law will not trust the non-resident rector to fix both the price and the person; but fixes the price, and then leaves him the choice of the person. Our plan is, to fix upon the description of person, and then to leave the price to find its level; for the good price by no means implies a good person, but the good person will be sure to get a good price.

Where the living will admit of it, we have commonly observed that the English clergy are desirous of putting in a proper substitute. If this is so, the bill is unnecessary; for it proceeds on the very contrary supposition, that the great mass of opulent clergy consult nothing but economy in the choice of their curates.

It is very galling and irksome to any class of men to be compelled to disclose their private circumstances; a provision contained in, and absolutely necessary to this bill, under which the diocesan can always compel the minister to disclose the full value of his living.

After all, however, the main and conclusive objection to the bill is, that its provisions are drawn from such erroneous principles, and betray such gross ignorance of human nature, that though it would infallibly produce a thousand mischiefs foreseen and not foreseen, it would evidently have no effect whatsoever in raising the salaries of curates. We do not put this as a case of common buyer and seller; we allow that the parish is a third party, having an interest;* we fully admit *the right* of the legislature to interfere for their relief. We only contend, that such interference would be necessarily altogether ineffectual, so long as men can be found capable of doing the duty of curates, and willing to do it for less than the statutory *minimum.*

If there is a competition of rectors for curates, it is quite unnecessary and absurd to make laws in favour of curates. The demand for them will do their business more effectually than the law. If, on the contrary (as the fact plainly is), there is a competition of curates for employment, is it possible to prevent this order of men from labouring under the regulation price? Is it possible to prevent a curate from pledging himself to his rector, that he will accept only half the legal salary, if he is so fortunate as to be preferred among an host of rivals, who are willing to engage on the same terms? You may make these contracts illegal: What then? Men laugh at such prohibitions; and they always become a dead letter. In nine instances out of ten, the contract would be honourably adhered to; and then what is the use of Mr. Perceval's law? Where the contract was not adhered to, whom would the law benefit?—A man utterly devoid of every particle of honour and good faith. And this is the new species of curate, who is to reflect dignity and importance upon his poorer brethren! The law encourages breach of faith between gambler and gambler; it arms broker against broker:—but it cannot arm clergyman against clergyman. Did any human being before, ever think of disseminating such a principle among the teachers of Christianity? Did any ecclesiastic law, before this, ever depend for its success upon the mutual treachery of men who ought to be examples to their fellow-creatures of every thing that is just and upright.

We have said enough already upon the absurdity of punishing all rich rectors for non-residence, as for a presumptive delinquency. A law is already passed, fixing what shall be legal and sufficient causes for non-residence. Nothing can be more unjust, then, than to punish that absence which you admit to be legal. If the causes of absence are too numerous, lessen them; but do not punish him who has availed himself of their existence. We deny, however, that they are too numerous. There are 6000 livings out of 11,000 in the English church under 80*l.* *per annum;* many

* We remember Horace's description of the misery of a parish where there is no resident clergyman.

———— "Illacrymabiles
Urgentur, ignotique longâ
Nocte, *carent quia vate sacro.*"

of these 20*l.*, many 30*l. per annum*. The whole task of education at the university, public schools, private families, and in foreign travel, devolves upon the clergy. A great part of the literature of their country is in their hands. Residence is a very proper and necessary measure; but, considering all these circumstances, it requires a great deal of moderation and temper to carry it into effect, without doing more mischief than good. At present, however, the torrent sets the other way. Every lay plunderer, and every fanatical coxcomb, is forging fresh chains for the English clergy; and we should not be surprised, in a very little time, to see them absenting themselves from their benefices by a kind of day-rule, like prisoners in the king's bench. The first bill, which was brought in by Sir William Scott, always saving and excepting the power granted to the bishops, is full of useful provisions, and characterized throughout by great practical wisdom. We have no doubt but that it has, *upon the whole*, improved the condition of the English church. Without caution, mildness, or information, however, it was peculiarly unfortunate to follow such a leader. We are extremely happy the bill was rejected. We have seldom witnessed more of ignorance and error stuffed and crammed into so very narrow a compass. Its origin, we are confident, is from the Tabernacle; and its consequences would have been, to have sown the seeds of discord and treachery in an ecclesiastical constitution, which, under the care of prudent and honest men, may always be rendered a source of public happiness.

One glaring omission in this bill we had almost forgotten to mention. The chancellor of the exchequer has entirely neglected to make any provision for that very meritorious class of men, the *lay curates*, who do all the business of those offices, of which lazy and non-resident placemen receive the emoluments. So much delicacy and conscience, however, are here displayed on the subject of pocketing unearned emoluments, that we have no doubt the moral irritability of this servant of the crown will speedily urge him to a species of reform, of which he may be the object as well as the mover.

PROCEEDINGS OF THE SOCIETY FOR THE SUPPRESSION OF VICE.*

[EDINBURGH REVIEW, 1809.]

A SOCIETY that holds out as its object the suppression of vice, must at first sight conciliate the favour of every respectable person; and he who objects to an institution calculated apparently to do so much good, is bound to give very clear and satisfactory reasons for his dissent from so popular an opinion. We certainly have, for a long time, had doubts of its utility; and now think ourselves called upon to state the grounds of our distrust.

Though it were clear that individual informers are useful auxiliaries to the administration of the laws, it would by no means follow that hese informers should be allowed to combine,—to form themselves into a body,—to make a public purse,—and to prosecute under a common name. An informer, whether he is paid by the week, like the agents of this society—or by the crime, as in common cases—is, in general, a man of a very indifferent character. So much fraud and deception are necessary for carrying on his trade—it is so odious to his fellow subjects,—that no man of respectability will ever undertake it. It is evidently impossible to make such a character otherwise than odious. A man who receives weekly pay for prying into the transgressions of mankind, and bringing them to consequent punishment, will always be hated by mankind; and the office must fall to the lot of some men of desperate fortunes and ambiguous character. The multiplication, therefore, of such officers, and the extensive patronage of such characters, may, by the management of large and opulent societies, become an evil nearly as great as the evils they would suppress. The alarm which a private and disguised accuser occasions in a neighbourhood, is known to be prodigious, not only to the guilty, but to those who may be at once innocent, and ignorant, and timid. The destruction of social confidence is another evil, the consequence of information. An informer gets access to my house or family,—worms my secret out of me,—and then betrays me to the magistrate. Now, all these evils may be tolerated in a small degree, while, in a greater degree, they would be perfectly intolerable. Thirty or forty informers roaming about the metropolis, may frighten the mass of offenders a little, and do some good: ten thousand informers would either create an insurrection, or totally destroy the confidence and cheerfulness of private life. Whatever may be said, therefore, of the single and insulated informer, it is quite a new question when we come to a corporation of informers supported by large contributions. The one may be a good, the other a very serious evil; the one legal, the other wholly out of the contemplation of law,-

* *Statement of the Proceedings of the Society for the Suppression of Vice, from July* 9 *to November* 12, *read at their General Meeting, held November* 12, 1804. *With an Appendix, containing the Plan of the Society, &c. &c.* London. 1804.

An Address to the Public from the Society for the Suppression of Vice, instituted in London, 1802. *Part the Second. Containing an Account of the Proceedings of the Society from its original Institution.* London. 1804.

which often, and very wisely, allows individuals to do what it forbids to many individuals assembled.

If once combination is allowed for the suppression of vice, where are its limits to be? Its capital may as well consist of 100,000*l. per annum*, as of a thousand: its numbers may increase from a thousand subscribers, which this society, it seems, had reached in its second year, to twenty thousand: and, in that case, what accused persons of an inferior condition of life would have the temerity to stand against such a society? Their mandates would very soon be law; and there is no compliance into which they might not frighten the common people, and the lower orders of tradesmen. The idea of a society of gentlemen, calling themselves an association for the suppression of vice, would alarm any small offender to a degree that would make him prefer any submission to any resistance. He would consider the very fact of being accused by them, as almost sufficient to ruin him.

An individual accuser accuses at his own expense; and the risk he runs is a good security that the subject will not be harassed by needless accusations,—a security which, of course, he cannot have against such a society as this, to whom pecuniary loss is an object of such little consequence. It must never be forgotten, that this is not a society for *punishing* people who have been found to transgress the law, but for *accusing* persons of transgressing the law; and that before trial, the accused person is to be considered as innocent, and is to have every fair chance of establishing his innocence. He must be no common defendant, however, who does not contend against such a society with very fearful odds;—the best counsel engaged for his opponents,—great practice in the particular court, and particular species of cause,—witnesses thoroughly hackneyed in a court of justice,—and an unlimited command of money. It by no means follows, that the legislature, in allowing individuals to be informers, meant to subject the accused person to the superior weight and power of such societies. The very influence of names must have a considerable weight with the jury. Lord Dartmouth, Lord Radstock, and the Bishop of Durham, *versus* a Whitechapel butcher or a publican! Is this a fair contest before a jury? It is not so even in London; and what must it be in the country, where a society for the suppression of vice may consist of all the principal persons in the neighbourhood? These societies are now established in York, in Reading, and in many other large towns. Wherever this is the case, it is far from improbable that the same persons, at the Quarter or Town Sessions, may be both judges and accusers; and still more fatally so, if the offence is tried by a special jury. This is already most notoriously the case in societies for the preservation of game. They prosecute a poacher;—the jury is special; and the poor wretch is found guilty by the very same persons who have accused him.

If it is lawful for respectable men to combine for the purpose of turning informers, it is lawful for the lowest and most despicable race of informers to do the same thing; and then it is quite clear that every species of wickedness and extortion would be the consequence. We are rather surprised that no society of perjured attorneys and fraudulent bankrupts has risen up in this metropolis, for the suppression of vice. A chairman, deputy-chairman, subscriptions, and an annual sermon would give great dignity to their proceedings; and they would soon begin to take some rank in the world.

It is true that it is the duty of grand juries to inform against vice; but the law knows the probable number of grand jurymen, the times of their meeting, and the description of persons of whom they consist. Of voluntary societies it can know nothing,—their numbers, their wealth, or the character of their members. It may therefore trust to a grand jury what it would by no means trust to an unknown combination. A vast distinction is to be made, too, between official duties and voluntary duties. The first are commonly carried on with calmness and moderation; the latter often characterized, in their execution, by rash and intemperate zeal.

The present society receives no members but those who are of the Church of England. As we are now arguing the question generally, we have a right to make any supposition. It is equally free, therefore, upon general principles, for a society of sectarians to combine and exclude members of the Church of England; and the suppression of vice may thus come in aid of Methodism, Jacobinism, or of any set of principles, however perilous, either to church or state. The present society may, perhaps, consist of persons whose sentiments on these points are rational and respectable. Combinations, however, of this sort may give birth to something far different; and such a supposition is the fair way of trying the question.

We doubt if there be not some mischief in averting the fears and hopes of the people from the known and constituted authorities of the country to those self-created powers;—a society that punishes in the Strand,—another which rewards at Lloyd's Coffee-house! If these things get to any great height, they throw an air of insignificance over those branches of the government to whom these cares properly devolve, and whose authority is by these means assisted, till it is superseded. It is supposed that a project must necessarily be good, because it is intended for the aid of law and government. At this rate, there should be a society in aid of the government, for procuring intelligence from foreign parts, with accredited agents all over Europe. There should be a voluntary transport board, and a gratuitous victualling office. There should be a duplicate, in short, of every department of the state,—the one appointed by the king, the other by itself. There should be a real Lord Glenbervie in the woods and forests,—and with him a monster, a voluntary Lord Glenbervie, serving without pay, and guiding *gratis*, with secret counsel, the axe of his prototype. If it be asked, who are the constituted authorities who are legally appointed to watch over morals, and whose functions the society usurp? our answer is, that there are in England about 12,000 clergy, not unhandsomely paid for persuading the people, and about 4000 justices, 30 grand juries, and 40,000 constables, whose duty and whose inclination it is to compel them to do right. Under such circumstances, a voluntary moral society does indeed seem to be the purest result of volition; for there certainly is not the smallest particle of necessity mingled with its existence.

It is hardly possible that a society for the suppression of vice can ever be kept within the bounds of good sense and moderation. If there are many members who have really become so from a feeling of duty, there will necessarily be some who enter the society to hide a bad character, and others whose object it is to recommend themselves to their betters by a sedulous and bustling inquisition into the immoralities of the public. The loudest and noisiest suppressors will always carry it against the more prudent part of the community; the most violent will be considered as the most moral; and those who see the absurdity will, from the fear of being thought to encourage vice, be reluctant to oppose it.

It is of great importance to keep public opinion on the side of virtue. To their authorized and legal correctors, mankind are, on common occasions, ready enough to submit; but there is something in the self-erection of a voluntary magistracy which creates so much disgust, that it almost renders vice popular, and puts the offence at a premium. We have no doubt but that the immediate effect of a voluntary combination for the suppression of vice, is an involuntary combination in favour of the vices to be suppressed; and this is a very serious drawback from any good of which such societies may be the occasion; for the state of morals, at any one period, depends much more upon opinion than law; and to bring odious and disgusting auxiliaries to the aid of virtue, is to do the utmost possible good to the cause of vice. We regret that mankind are as they are; and we sincerely wish, that the species at large were as completely devoid of every vice and infirmity as the president, vice-president, and committee of the suppressing society; but, till they are thus regenerated, it is of the greatest consequence to teach them virtue and religion in a manner which will not make them hate both the one and the other. The greatest delicacy is required in the application of violence to moral and religious sentiment. We forget that the object is, not to produce the outward compliance, but to raise up the inward feeling, which secures the outward compliance. You may drag men into church by main force, and prosecute them for buying a pot of beer,—and cut them off from the enjoyment of a leg of mutton;—and you may do all this, till you make the common people hate Sunday, and the clergy, and religion, and every thing which relates to such subjects. There are many crimes, indeed, where persuasion cannot be waited for, and where the untaught feelings of all men go along with the violence of the law. A robber and a murderer must be knocked on the head like mad dogs; but we have no great opinion of the possibility of indicting men into piety, or of calling in the quarter sessions to the aid of religion. You may produce outward conformity by these means; but you are so far from producing (the only thing worth producing) the inward feeling, that you incur a great risk of giving birth to a totally opposite sentiment.

The violent modes of making men good, just alluded to, have been resorted to at periods when the science of legislation was not so well understood as it now is; or when the manners of the age have been peculiarly gloomy or fanatical. The improved knowledge, and the improved temper of later times, push such laws into the back ground, and silently repeal them. A suppressing society, hunting every where for penalty and information, has a direct tendency to revive ancient ignorance and fanaticism,—and to re-enact laws, which, if ever they ought to have existed at all, were certainly calculated for a very different style of manners, and a very different degree of information. To compel men to go to church, under a penalty, appears to us to be absolutely absurd. The bitterest enemy of religion will necessarily be that person who is driven to a compliance with its outward ceremonies, by informers and justices of the peace. In the same manner, any constable who hears another swear an oath, has a right to seize him, and carry him before a magistrate, where he is to be fined so much for each execration. It is impossible to carry such laws into execution; and it is lucky that it is impossible,—for their execution would create an infinitely greater evil than it attempted to remedy. The common sense and common feeling of mankind, if left to themselves, would silently repeal such laws; and it is one of the evils of these societies, that they render absurdity eternal, and ignorance indestructible. Do not let us be misunderstood: upon the object to be accomplished, there can be but one opinion;—it is only upon the means employed, that there can be the slightest difference of sentiment. To go to church is a duty of the greatest possible importance; and on the blasphemy and vulgarity of swearing, there can be but one opinion. But such duties are not the objects of legislation; they must be left to the general state of public sentiment; which sentiment must be influenced by example, by the exertions of the pulpit and the press, and, above all, by education. The fear of God can never be taught by constables, nor the pleasures of religion be learnt from a common informer.

Beginning with the best intentions in the world, such societies must, in all probability, degenerate into a receptacle for every species of tittle-tattle, impertinence, and malice. Men, whose trade is rat-catching, love to catch rats; the bug-destroyer seizes on his bug with delight; and the suppressor is gratified by finding his vice. The last soon becomes a mere tradesman like the others; none of them moralize, or lament that their respective evils should exist in the world. The public feeling is swallowed up in the pursuit of a daily occupation, and in the display of a technical skill. Here, then, is a society of men, who invite accusation,—who receive it (almost unknown to themselves) with pleasure,—and who, if they hate dulness and inoccupation, can have very little pleasure in the innocence of their fellow-creatures. The natural consequence of all this is, that (besides that portion of rumour which every member contributes at the weekly meeting), their table must be covered with anonymous lies against the character of individuals. Every servant discharged from his master's service,—every villain who hates the man he has injured,—every cowardly assassin of character,—now knows where his accusations will be received, and where they cannot fail to produce some portion of the mischievous effects which he wishes. The very first step of such a society should be, to declare, in the plainest manner, that they would never receive any anonymous accusation. This would be the only security to the public, that they were not degrading themselves into a receptacle for malice and falsehood. Such a declaration would inspire some species of confidence; and make us believe that their object was neither the love of power, nor the gratification of uncharitable feelings. The society for the suppression, however, have done no such thing. They request, indeed, the signature of the informers whom they invite; but they do not (as they ought) make that signature an indispensable condition.

Nothing has disgusted us so much in the proceedings of this society, as the control which they exercise over the amusements of the poor. One of the specious titles under which this legal meanness is gratified is, *Prevention of Cruelty to Animals.*

Of cruelty to animals, let the reader take the following specimens:—

Running an iron hook in the intestines of an animal; presenting this first animal to another as his food; and then pulling this second creature up, and suspending him by the barb in his stomach.

Riding a horse till he drops, in order to see an innocent animal torn to pieces by dogs.

Keeping a poor animal upright for many weeks, to communicate a peculiar hardness to his flesh.

Making deep incisions into the flesh of another animal, while living, in order to make the muscles more firm.

Immersing another animal, while living, in hot water.

Now we do fairly admit, that such abominable cruelties as these are worthy of the interference of the law: and that the society should have punished them, cannot be matter of surprise to any feeling mind.—But stop, gentle reader! these cruelties are the cruelties of the suppressing committee, not of the poor. You must not think of punishing these.—The first of these cruelties passes under the pretty name of *angling*;—and therefore there can be no harm in it—the more particularly as the president himself has one of the best preserved trout streams in England.—The next is *hunting*;—and as many of the vice-presidents and of the committee hunt, it is not possible there can be any cruelty in hunting.* The next is, a process for making *brawn*—a dish never tasted by the poor, and therefore not to be disturbed by indictment. The fourth is the mode of *crimping* cod; and the fifth of boiling lobsters; all high-life cruelties, with which a justice of the peace has no business to meddle. The real thing which calls forth the sympathies, and harrows up the soul, is to see a number of boisterous artisans baiting a bull, or a bear; not a savage hare, or a carnivorous stag,—but a poor, innocent, timid bear;—not pursued by magistrates, and deputy lieutenants, and men of education,—but by those who must necessarily seek their relaxation in noise and tumultuous merriment,—by men whose feelings are blunted, and whose understanding is wholly devoid of refinement. The society detail, with symptoms of great complacency, their detection of a bear-beating in Black-boy Alley, Chick Lane, and the prosecution of the offenders before a magistrate. It appears to us, that nothing can be more partial and unjust than this kind of proceedings. A man of ten thousand a year may worry a fox as much as he pleases,—may encourage the breed of a mischievous animal on purpose to worry it; and a poor labourer is carried before a magistrate for paying sixpence to see an exhibition of courage between a dog and a bear! Any cruelty may be practised to gorge the stomachs of the rich,—none to enliven the holidays of the poor. We venerate those feelings which really protect creatures susceptible of pain, and incapable of complaint. But heaven-born pity, now-a-days, calls for the income tax, and the Court Guide; and ascertains the rank and fortune of the tormentor before she weeps for the pain of the sufferer. It is astonishing how the natural feelings of mankind are distorted by false theories. Nothing can be more mischievous than to say, that the pain inflicted by the dog of a man of quality is not (when the strength of the two animals is the same) equal to that produced by the cur of a butcher. Haller, in his Pathology, expressly says, *that the animal bitten knows no difference in the quality of the biting animal's master;* and it is now the universal opinion among all enlightened men, that the misery of the brawner would be very little diminished, if he could be made sensible that he was to be eaten up only by persons of the first fashion. The contrary supposition seems to us to be absolute nonsense; it is the desertion of the true *Baconian* philosophy, and the substitution of mere unsupported conjecture in its place. The trespass, however, which calls forth all the energies of a suppressor, is the sound of a fiddle. That the

* "How reasonable creatures" (says the society) "can enjoy a pastime which is the cause of such sufferings to brute animals, or how they can consider themselves entitled, for their own amusement, to stimulate those animals, by means of the antipathies which Providence has thought proper to place between them, to worry and tear, and often to destroy each other, it is difficult to conceive. So inhuman a practice, by a retribution peculiarly just, tends obviously to render the human character brutal and ferocious," &c. &c. (*Address*, p. 71, 72.) We take it for granted, that the reader sees clearly that no part of this description can possibly apply to the case of *hunting*.

common people are really enjoying themselves, is now beyond all doubt: and away rush secretary, president, and committee, to clap the cotillon into the compter, and to bring back the life of the poor to its regular standard of decorous gloom. The gambling houses of St. James's remain untouched. The peer ruins himself and his family with impunity; while the Irish labourer is privately whipped for not making a better use of the excellent moral and religious education which he has received in the days of his youth!

It is not true, as urged by the society, that the vices of the poor are carried on in houses of public resort, and those of the rich in their own houses. The society cannot be ignorant of the innumerable gambling houses resorted to by men of fashion. Is there one they have suppressed, or attempted to suppress? Can any thing be more despicable than such distinctions as these? Those who make them seem to have for other persons' vices all the rigour of the ancient Puritans—without a particle of their honesty, or their courage. To suppose that any society will ever attack the vices of people of fashion, is wholly out of the question. If the society consisted of tradesmen, they would infallibly be turned off by the vicious customers whose pleasures they interrupted: and what gentlemen so fond of suppressing, as to interfere with the vices of good company, and inform against persons who were really genteel? He knows very well that the consequence of such interference would be a complete exclusion from elegant society; that the upper classes could not and would not endure it; and that he must immediately lose his rank in the world, if his zeal subjected fashionable offenders to the slightest inconvenience from the law. Nothing, therefore, remains, but to rage against the Sunday dinners of the poor, and to prevent a bricklayer's labourer from losing, on the seventh day, that beard which has been augmenting the other six. We see at the head of this society the names of several noblemen, and of other persons moving in the fashionable world. Is it possible they can be ignorant of the innumerable offences against the law and morality which are committed by their own acquaintances and connections? Is there one single instance where they have directed the attention of the society to this higher species of suppression, and sacrificed men of consideration to that zeal for virtue which watches so acutely over the vices of the poor? It would give us very little pleasure to see a duchess sent to the Poultry compter; but if we saw the society flying at such high game, we should at least say they were honest and courageous, whatever judgment we might form of their good sense. At present they should denominate themselves a society for suppressing the vices of persons whose income does not exceed 500*l.* *per annum;* and then, to put all classes upon an equal footing, there must be another society of barbers, butchers, and bakers, to return to the higher classes that moral character, by which they are so highly benefited.

To show how impossible it is to keep such societies within any kind of bounds, we shall quote a passage respecting circulating libraries, from their proceedings.

"Your committee have good reasons for believing, that the circulation of their notices among the printsellers, warning them against the sale or exhibition of indecent representations, has produced, and continues to produce, the best effects.

"But they have to lament that the extended establishments of circulating libraries, however useful they may be, in a variety of respects, to the easy and general diffusion of knowledge, are extremely injurious to morals and religion, by the indiscriminate admission which they give to works of a prurient and immoral nature. It is a toilsome task to any virtuous and enlightened mind, to wade through the catalogues of these collections, and much more to select such books from them as have only an apparent bad tendency. But your committee being convinced that their attention ought to be directed to those institutions which possess such powerful and numerous means of poisoning the minds of young persons, and especially of the female youth, have therefore begun to make some endeavours towards their better regulation."—*Statement of the Proceedings for* 1804, pp. 11, 12.

In the same spirit, we see them writing to a country magistrate in Devonshire, respecting a wake advertised in the public papers. Nothing can be more presumptuous than such conduct, or produce, in the minds of impartial men, a more decisive impression against the society.

The natural answer from the members of the society (the only answer they have ever made to the enemies of their institution) will be, that we are lovers of vice,—desirous of promoting indecency, of destroying the Sabbath, and of leaving mankind to the unrestrained gratification of their passions. We have only very calmly to reply, that we are neither so stupid nor so wicked as not to concur in every scheme which has for its object the preservation of rational religion and sound morality;—but the scheme must be well concerted,—and those who are to carry it into execution must deserve our confidence, from their talents and their character. Upon religion and morals depends the happiness of mankind;—but the fortune of knaves and the power of fools are sometimes made to rest on the same apparent basis; and we will never (if we can help it) allow a rogue to get rich, or a blockhead to get powerful, under the sanction of these awful words. We do not by any means intend to apply these contemptuous epithets to the Society for the Suppression. That there are among their number some very odious hypocrites, is not impossible; that many men who believe they come there from the love of virtue, do really join the society from the love of power, we do not doubt: but we see no reason to doubt that the great mass of subscribers consists of persons who have very sincere intentions of doing good. That they have, in some instances, done a great deal of good, we admit with the greatest pleasure. We believe, that in the hands of truly honest, intrepid, and above all, discreet men, such a society might become a valuable institution, improve in some degree the public morals, and increase the public happiness. So many qualities, however, are required to carry it on well,—the temptations to absurdity and impertinence are so very great,—that we ever despair of seeing our wishes upon this subject realized. In the present instance, our object has been to suppress the arrogance of suppressors,—to keep them within due bounds,—to show them that to do good requires a little more talent and reflection than they are aware of,—and, above all, to impress upon them that true zeal for virtue knows no distinction between the rich and the poor; and that the cowardly and the mean can never be the true friends of morality, and the promoters of human happiness. If they attend to these rough doctrines, they will ever find in the writers of this journal their warmest admirers, and their most sincere advocates and friends.

CHARACTERS OF FOX.*

[Edinburgh Review, 1809.]

This singular work consists of a collection of all the panegyrics passed upon Mr. Fox, after his decease, in periodical publications, speeches, sermons, or elsewhere,—in a panegyric upon Mr. Fox by Philopatris himself,—and in a volume of notes by the said Philopatris upon the said panegyric.

Of the panegyrics, that by Sir James Mackintosh appears to us to be by far the best. It is remarkable for good sense, acting upon a perfect knowledge of his subject, for simplicity, and for feeling. Amid the languid or turgid efforts of mediocrity, it is delightful to notice the skill, attention, and resources, of a superior man,—of a man, too, who seems to feel what he writes,—who does not aim at conveying his meaning in rhetorical and ornamental phrases, but who uses plain words to express strong sensations. We cannot help wishing, indeed, that Sir James Mackintosh had been more diffuse upon the political character of Mr. Fox, the great feature of whose life was the long and unwearied opposition which he made to the low cunning, the profligate extravagance, the sycophant mediocrity, and the stupid obstinacy of the English court.

To estimate the merit and the difficulty of this opposition, we must remember the enormous influence which the crown, through the medium of its patronage, exercises in the remotest corners of the kingdom,—the number of subjects whom it pays,—the much greater number whom it keeps in a state of expectation,—and the ferocious turpitude of those mercenaries whose present profits and future hopes are threatened by honest, and exposed by eloquent men. It is the easiest of all things, too, in this country, to make Englishmen believe that those who oppose the government wish to ruin the country. The English are a very busy people; and, with all the faults of their governors, they are still a very happy people. They have, as they ought to have, a perfect confidence in the administration of justice. The rights which the different classes of mankind exercise the one over the other are arranged upon equitable principles. Life, liberty, and property are protected from the violence and caprice of power. The visible and immediate stake, therefore, for which English politicians play, is not large enough to attract the notice of the people, and to call them off from their daily occupations, to investigate thoroughly the characters and motives of men engaged in the business of legislation. The people can only understand, and attend to the last results of a long series of measures. They are impatient of the details which lead to these results; and it is the easiest of all things to make them believe that those who insist upon such details are actuated only by factious motives. We are all now groaning under the weight of taxes: but how often was Mr. Fox followed by the curses of his country for protesting against the two wars which have loaded us with these taxes?—the one of which wars has made America independent, and the other rendered France omnipotent. The case is the same with all the branches of public liberty. If the broad and palpable question were, whether every book which issues from the press should be subjected to the license of a general censor, it would be impossible to blacken the character of any man who, so called upon, defended the liberty of publishing opinions. But, when the attorney-general for the time being ingratiates himself with the court, by nibbling at this valuable privilege of the people, it is very easy to treat hostility to his measures as a minute and frivolous opposition to the government, and to persuade the mass of mankind that it is so. In fact, when a nation has become free, it is extremely difficult to persuade them that their freedom is only to be preserved by perpetual and minute jealousy. They do not observe that there is a constant, perhaps an unconscious, effort, on the part of their governors, to diminish, and so ultimately to destroy, that freedom. They stupidly imagine that what is, will always be; and, contented with the good they have already gained, are easily persuaded to suspect and vilify those

---

* *Characters of the late Charles James Fox.* By Philopatris Varvicensis. 2 vols. 8vo.

friends—the object of whose life it is to preserve that good, and to increase it.

It was the lot of Mr. Fox to fight this battle for the greater part of his life; in the course of which time he never was seduced by the love of power, wealth, or popularity, to sacrifice the happiness of the many to the interest of the few. He rightly thought, that kings, and all public officers, were instituted only for the good of those over whom they preside; and he acted as if this conviction was always present to his mind; disdaining and withstanding that idolatrous tendency of mankind, by which they so often not only suffer, but invite ruin from that power which they themselves have wisely created for their own happiness. He loved, too, the happiness of his countrymen more than their favour; and while others were exhausting the resources, by flattering the ignorant prejudices and foolish passions of the country, Mr. Fox was content to be odious to the people, so long as he could be useful also. It will be long before we witness again such pertinacious opposition to the alarming power of the crown, and to the follies of our public measures, the necessary consequence of that power. That such opposition should ever be united again with such extraordinary talents, it is, perhaps, in vain to hope.

One little exception to the eulogium of Sir James Mackintosh upon Mr. Fox, we cannot help making. We are no admirers of Mr. Fox's poetry. His *Vers de Société* appears to us flat and insipid. To write verses was the only thing which Mr. Fox ever attempted to do, without doing it well. In that single instance he seems to have mistaken his talent.

Immediately after the collection of panegyrics which these volumes contain, follows the eulogium of Mr. Fox by Philopatris himself; and then a volume of notes upon a variety of topics which this eulogium has suggested. Of the laudatory talents of this Warwickshire patriot, we shall present our readers with a specimen.

"Mr. Fox, though not an adept in the use of political wiles, was very unlikely to be the dupe of them. He was conversant in the ways of man, as well as in the contents of books. He was acquainted with the peculiar language of states, their peculiar forms, and the grounds and effects of their peculiar usages. From his earliest youth, he had investigated the science of politics in the greater and the smaller scale; he had studied it in the records of history, both popular and rare—in the conferences of ambassadors—in the archives of royal cabinets—in the minuter detail of memoirs—and in collected or straggling anecdotes of the wrangles, intrigues, and cabals, which, springing up in the secret recesses of courts, shed their baneful influence on the determinations of sovereigns, the fortune of favourites, and the tranquillity of kingdoms. But that statesmen of all ages, like priests of all religions, are in all respects alike, is a doctrine the propagation of which he left, as an inglorious privilege, to the misanthrope, to the recluse, to the factious incendiary, and to the unlettered multitude. For himself he thought it no very extraordinary stretch of penetration or charity, to admi that human nature is everywhere nearly as capable of emulation in good, as in evil. He boasted of no very exalted heroism, in opposing the calmness and firmness of conscious integrity to the shuffling and slippery movements, the feints in retreat, and feints in advance, the dread of being over-reached, or detected in attempts to over-reach, and all the other humiliating and mortifying anxieties of the most accomplished proficients in the art of diplomacy. He reproached himself for no guilt, when he endeavoured to obtain that respect and confidence which the human heart unavoidably feels in its intercourse with persons who neither wound our pride, nor take aim at our happiness, in a war of hollow and ambiguous words. He was sensible of no weakness in believing that politicians, who, after all, 'knew only as they are known,' may, like other human beings, be at first the involuntary creatures of circumstances, and seem incorrigible from the want of opportunities or incitements to correct themselves; that, bereft of the pleas usually urged in vindication of deceit, by men who are fearful of being deceived, they, in their official dealings with him, would not wantonly lavish the stores they had laid up for huckstering in a traffic, which, ceasing to be profitable, would begin to be infamous; and that, possibly, here and there, if encouraged by example, they might learn to prefer the shorter process, and surer results of plain dealing, to the delays, the vexations, and the uncertain or transient success, both of old-fashioned and new-fangled chicanery."—(I. 209—211.)

It is impossible to read this singular book without being everywhere struck with the lofty and honourable feelings, the enlightened benevolence, and sterling honesty with which it abounds. Its author is everywhere the circumspect friend of those moral and religious principles upon which the happiness of society rests. Though he is never timid, nor prejudiced, nor bigoted, his piety, not prudish and full of antiquated and affected tricks, presents itself with an earnest aspect, and in a manly form; obedient to reason, prone to investigation, and dedicated to honest purposes The writer, a clergyman, speaks of himself as a very independent man, who has always expressed his opinion without any fear of consequences, or any hope of bettering his condition. We sincerely believe he speaks the truth; and revere him for the life he has led. Political independence—discouraged enough in these times among all classes of men—is sure, in the timid profession of the church, to doom a man to eternal poverty and obscurity.

There are occasionally, in Philopatris, a great vigour of style and felicity of expression. His display of classical learning is quite unrivalled—his reading various and good; and we may observe, at intervals, a talent for wit, of which he might have availed himself to excellent purpose, had it been compatible with the dignified style in which he generally conveys his sentiments. With all these excellent qualities of head and heart, we have seldom met with a writer more full of faults than Philopatris. There is an event recorded in the Bible, which men who write books should keep constantly in their remembrance. It is there set forth, that many centuries ago, the earth was covered with a great flood, by which the whole of the human race, with the exception of one family, were destroyed. It appears also, that from thence, a great alteration was made in the longevity of mankind, who, from a range of seven or eight hundred years, which they enjoyed before the flood, were confined to their present period of seventy or eighty years. This epoch in the history of man gave birth to the twofold division of the antediluvian and postdiluvian style of writing, the latter of which naturally contracted itself into those inferior limits which were better accommodated to the abridged duration of human life and literary labour. Now, to forget this event,—to write without the fear of the deluge before his eyes, and to handle a subject as if mankind could lounge over a pamphlet for ten years, as before their submersion,—is to be guilty of the most grievous error into which a writer can possibly fall. The author of this book should call in the aid of some brilliant pencil, and cause the distressing scenes of the deluge to be portrayed in the most lively colours for his use. He should gaze at Noah and be brief. The ark should constantly remind him of the little time there is left for reading; and he should learn, as they did in the ark, to crowd a great deal of matter into a very little compass.

Philopatris must not only condense what he says into a narrower compass, but he must say it in a more natural manner. Some persons can neither stir hand nor foot without making it clear that they are thinking of themselves, and laying little traps for approbation. In the course of two long volumes, the Patriot of Warwick is perpetually studying modes and postures:—the subject is the second consideration, and the mode of expression the first. Indeed, whole pages together seem to be mere exercises upon the English language, to evince the copiousness of our synonymes, and to show the various methods in which the parts of speech can be marshalled and arrayed. This, which would be tiresome in the ephemeral productions of a newspaper, is intolerable in two closely printed volumes.

Again, strange as it may appear to this author to say so, he must not fall into the frequent mistake of rural politicians, by supposing that the understandings of all Europe are occupied with him and his opinions. His ludicrous self-importance is perpetually destroying the effect of virtuous feeling and just observation, leaving his readers with a disposition to laugh, where they might otherwise learn and admire.

"I have been asked, why, after pointing out by name the persons who seemed to me most qualified for reforming our penal code, I declined mentioning such ecclesiastics as might with propriety be employed in preparing for the use of the churches a grave and impressive discourse on the authority of human laws; and as other men may ask the same question which my friend did, I have determined, after some deliberation, to insert the substance of my answer in this place.

"If the public service of our church should ever be directly employed in giving effect to the sanctions of our penal code, the office of drawing up such a discourse as I have ventured to recommend would, I suppose, be assigned to more than one person. My ecclesiastical superiors will, I am sure, make a wise choice. But they will hardly condemn me for saying, that the best sense expressed in the best language may be expected from the Bishops of Landaff, Lincoln, St. David's, Cloyne, and Norwich, the Dean of Christ Church, and the President of Magdalen College, Oxford. I mean not to throw the slightest reproach upon other dignitaries whom I have not mentioned. But I should imagine that few of my enlightened contemporaries hold an opinion different from my own, upon the masculine understanding of a Watson, the sound judgment of a Tomlin, the extensive erudition of a Burgess, the exquisite taste and good nature of a Bennet, the calm and enlightened benevolence of a Bathurst, the various and valuable attainments of a Cyril Jackson, or the learning, wisdom, integrity, and piety of a Martin Routh."—(pp. 524, 525.)

In the name of common modesty, what could it have signified whether this author had given a list of ecclesiastics whom he thought qualified to preach about human laws? what is his opinion worth? who called for it? who wanted it? how many millions will be influenced by it?—and who, oh gracious Heaven! who are *a* Burgess,—*a* Tomlin,—*a* Bennet,—*a* Cyril Jackson,—*a* Martin Routh?—A *Tom*,—a *Jack*,—a Harry,—a Peter? All good men enough in their generation doubtless they are. But what have they done for the broad *a?* what has any one of them perpetrated, which will make him be remembered, out of the sphere of his private virtues, six months after his decease? Surely, scholars and gentlemen can drink tea with each other, and eat bread and butter, without all this laudatory crackling.

Philopatris has employed a great deal of time upon the subject of capital punishments, and has evinced a great deal of very laudable tenderness and humanity in discussing it. We are scarcely, however, converts to that system which would totally abolish the punishment of death. That it is much too frequently inflicted in this country, we readily admit; but we suspect it will be always necessary to reserve it for the most pernicious crimes. Death is the most terrible punishment to the common people, and therefore the most preventive. It does not perpetually outrage the feelings of those who are innocent, and likely to remain innocent, as would be the case from the spectacle of convicts working in the highroads and public places. Death is the most irrevocable punishment, which is in some sense a good; for, however necessary it might be to inflict labour and imprisonment for life, it would never be done. Kings and legislatures would take pity after a great lapse of years;

the punishment would be remitted, and its preventive efficacy, therefore, destroyed. We agree with Philopatris, that the executions should be more solemn; but still the English are not of a very dramatic turn, and the thing must not be got up too finely. Philopatrist and Mr. Jeremy Bentham before him, lay a vast stress upon the promulgation of laws, and treat the inattention of the English government to this point as a serious evil. It may be so—but we do not happen to remember any man punished for an offence which he did not know to be an offence; though he might not know exactly the degree in which it was punishable. Who are to read the laws to the people? who would listen to them if they were read? who would comprehend them if they listened? In a science like law there must be technical phrases known only to professional men: business could not be carried on without them: and of what avail would it be to repeat such phrases to the people? Again, what laws are to be repeated, and in what places? Is a law respecting the number of threads on the shuttle of a Spitalfields weaver to be read to the corn-growers of the Isle of Thanet? If not, who is to make the selection? If the law cannot be comprehended by listening to the *vivâ voce* repetition, is the reader to explain it, and are there to be law lectures all over the kingdom? The fact is, that the evil does not exist. Those who are most likely to commit the offence soon scent out the newly devised punishments, and have been long thoroughly acquainted with the old ones. Of the nice applications of the law they are indeed ignorant; but they purchase the requisite skill of some man whose business it is to acquire it; and so they get into less mischief by trusting to others than they would do if they pretended to inform themselves. The people, it is true, are ignorant of the laws; but they are ignorant only of the laws that do not concern them. A poacher knows nothing of the penalties to which he exposes himself by stealing ten thousand pounds from the public. Commissioners of public boards are unacquainted with all the decretals of our ancestors respecting the wiring of hares; but the one pockets his extra per centage, and the other his leveret, with a perfect knowledge of the laws—the particular laws which it is his business to elude. Philopatris will excuse us for differing from him upon a subject where he seems to entertain such strong opinions. We have a real respect for all his opinions:—no man could form them who had not a good heart and a sound understanding. If we have been severe upon his style of writing, it is because we know his weight in the commonwealth: and we wish that the many young persons who justly admire and imitate him should be turned to the difficult task of imitating his many excellences, rather than the useless and easy one of copying his few defects.

OBSERVATIONS ON THE HISTORICAL WORK OF THE RIGHT HONOURABLE CHARLES JAMES FOX.*

[Edinburgh Review, 1809.]

This is an extraordinary performance in itself;—but the reasons assigned for its publication are still more extraordinary. A person of Mr. Rose's consequence—incessantly occupied, as he assures us, "with official duties, which take equally," according to his elegant expression, "from the disembarrassment of the mind and the leisure of time,"—thinks it absolutely necessary to explain to his country the motives which have led him to do so idle a thing as to write a book. He would not have it supposed, however, that he could be tempted to so questionable an act by any light or ordinary consideration. Mr. Fox and other literary loungers may write from a love of fame, or a relish for literature; but the official labours of Mr. Rose can only be suspended by higher calls. All his former publications, he informs us, originated in a "sense of public duty;" and the present, in "an impulse of private friendship." An ordinary reader may, perhaps, find some difficulty in comprehending how Mr. Rose could be "*impelled* by private friendship," to publish a heavy quarto of political observations on Mr. Fox's history:—and for our own part, we must confess, that after the most diligent perusal of his long explanation, we do not in the least comprehend it yet. The explanation, however, which is very curious, it is our duty to lay before our readers.

Mr. Rose was much patronised by the late Earl of Marchmont, who left him his family papers, with an injunction to make use of them, "if it should ever become necessary." Among these papers was a narrative by Sir Patrick Hume, the earl's grandfather, of the occurrences which befell him and his associates in the unfortunate expedition undertaken by the Earl of Argyle in 1685. Mr. Fox, in detailing the history of that expedition, has passed a censure, as Mr. Rose thinks, on the character of Sir Patrick; and, to obviate the effects of that censure, he now finds it "necessary" to publish this volume.

All this sounds very chivalrous and affec-

* *Observations on the Historical Work of the Right Honourable Charles James Fox.* By the Right Honourable George Rose. pp. 215. *With a Narrative of the Events which occurred in the Enterprise of the Earl of Argyle in 1685.* By Sir Patrick Hume. London. 1809.

tionate; but we have three little remarks to make. In the first place, Mr. Fox passes no censure on Sir Patrick Hume. In the second place, this publication does by no means obviate the censure of which Mr. Rose complains. And, thirdly, it is utterly absurd to ascribe Mr. Rose's part of the volume, in which Sir Patrick Hume is scarcely ever mentioned, to any anxiety about *his* reputation.

In the first place, it is quite certain that Mr. Fox passes no censure on Sir Patrick Hume. On the contrary, he says of him, that "he had early distinguished himself in the cause of liberty;" and afterwards rates him so very highly as to think it a sufficient reason for construing some doubtful points in Sir John Cochrane's conduct favourably, that "he had always acted in conjunction with Sir Patrick Hume, who is proved by the subsequent events, and, indeed, *by the whole tenour of his life and conduct, to have been uniformly sincere and zealous in the cause of his country*." Such is the deliberate and unequivocal testimony which Mr. Fox has borne to the character of this gentleman; and such the historian, whose unjust censures have compelled the Right Honourable George Rose to indite 250 quarto pages, out of pure regard to the injured memory of this ancestor of his deceased patron.

Such is Mr. Fox's opinion, then, of Sir Patrick Hume; and the only opinion he *anywhere* gives of his *character*. With regard to his *conduct*, he observes, indeed, in one place, that he and the other gentlemen engaged in the enterprise appear to have paid too little deference to the opinion of their noble leader; and narrates, in another, that, at the breaking up of their little army, they did not even stay to reason with him, but crossed the Clyde with such as would follow them. Now, Sir Patrick's own narrative, so far from contradicting either of these statements, confirms them both in the most remarkable manner. There is scarcely a page of it that does not show the jealous and controlling spirit which was exercised towards their leader; and, with regard to the concluding scene, Sir Patrick's own account makes infinitely more strongly against himself and Sir John Cochrane, than the general statement of Mr. Fox. So far from staying to argue with their general before parting with him, it appears that Sir Patrick did not so much as see him; and that Cochrane, at whose suggestion he deserted him, had in a manner ordered that unfortunate nobleman to leave their company. The material words of the narrative are these:—

"On coming down to Kilpatrick, I met Sir John (Cochrane), with others accompanieing him; who *takeing mee by the hand, turned mee*, saying, My heart, goe you with mee? Whither goe you, said I? Over Clide by boate, said he.—I: Wher is Argyle? I must see him.—He: He is gone away to his owne countrey, you cannot see him.—I: How comes this change of resolution, and that wee went not together to Glasgow?—He: It is no time to answer questions, but I shall satisfy you afterward. To the boates wee came, filled 2, and rowed over," &c.—"An honest gentleman who was present, told mee afterward the manner of his parting with the Erle. Argyle being in the roome with Sir John, the gentleman coming in, found confusion in the Erle's countenance and speach. In end he said, Sir John, I pray advise mee what shall I doe; shall I goe over Clide with you, or shall I goe to my owne countrey? Sir John answered, My Lord, I have told you my opinion; *you have some Highlanders here about you; it is best you goe to your owne countrey with them, for it is to no purpose for you to go over Clide. My lord, faire you well.* Then call'd the gentleman, *Come away, Sir; who followed him when I met with him*."—Sir P. Hume's *Narrative*, pp. 63, 64.

Such are all the censures which Mr. Fox passes upon this departed worthy; and such the *contradiction* which Mr. Rose now thinks it necessary to exhibit. It is very true that Mr. Fox, in the course of his narrative, is under the necessity of mentioning, on the credit of all the historians who have treated of the subject, that Argyle, after his capture, did express himself in terms of strong disapprobation both of Sir Patrick Hume and of Sir John Cochrane; and said, that their ignorance and misconduct were, *though not designedly*, the chief cause of his failure. Mr. Fox neither adopts nor rejects this sentiment. He gives his own opinion, as we have already seen, in terms of the highest encomium, on the character of Sir Patrick Hume, and merely repeats the expressions of Argyle as he found them in Wodrow and the other historians, and as he was under the necessity of repeating them, if he was to give any account of the last words of that unfortunate nobleman. It is this censure of Argyle, then, perhaps, and not any censure of Mr. Fox's, that Mr. Rose intended to obviate by the publication before us. But, upon this supposition, how did the appearance of Mr. Fox's book constitute that *necessity* which compelled the tender conscience of Lord Marchmont's executor to give to the world this long-lost justification of his ancestor? The censure did not appear for the first time in Mr. Fox's book. It was repeated, during Sir Patrick's own life, in all the papers of the time, and in all the historians since. Sir Patrick lived nearly forty good years after this accusation of Argyle was made public; and thirty-six of those years in great credit, honour, and publicity. If he had thought that the existence of such an accusation constituted a kind of moral *necessity* for the publication of his narrative, it is evident that he would himself have published it; and if it was not necessary then, while he was alive, to suffer by the censure of his leader, or to profit by its refutation, it is not easy to understand how it should be necessary now, when 130 years have elapsed from the date of it, and the bones of its author have reposed for nearly a century in their peaceful and honoured monument.

That the narrative never was published before, though the censure, to which it is supposed to be an antidote, had been published for more than a century, is a pretty satisfactory proof that those who were most interested and best qualified to judge, either did not consider the censure as very deadly, or the antidote as very effectual. We are very well contented to leave it doubtful which of these was the case; and we are convinced that all the readers of Mr. Rose's book will agree that it is still very doubtful. Sir Patrick, in his narrative, no doubt, says that Argyle was extremely arrogant, self-willed, and obstinate; but it is equally certain, that the earl said to him that he was jealous, disobedient, and untractable. Both were men of honour and veracity; and, we doubt not, believed what they said. It is even possible that both may have said truly; but, at this distance of time, and with no new evidence but the averment of one of the parties, it would be altogether ridiculous to pretend to decide which may have come nearest to an impartial statement. Before the publication of the present narrative, it is plain from Wodrow, Burnet, and other writers, that considerable blame was generally laid on Argyle for his peremptoriness and obstinacy; and, now that the narrative is published, it is still more apparent than ever that he had some ground for the charges he made against his officers. The whole tenour of it shows that they were constantly in the habit of checking and thwarting him; and we have already seen that it gives a very lame and unsatisfactory account of their strange desertion of him, when their fortunes appeared to be desperate.

It is perfectly plain, therefore, we conceive, that the publication of Mr. Fox's book constituted neither a necessity nor an intelligible inducement for the publication of this narrative; and that the narrative, now that it is published, has no tendency to remove any slight shade of censure that history may have thrown over the temper or prudence of Sir Patrick Hume. But, even if all this had been otherwise—if Mr. Fox had, for the first time, insinuated a censure on this defunct whig, and if the narrative had contained the most complete refutation of such a censure,—this might, indeed, have accounted for the publication of Sir Patrick's narrative; but it could not have accounted at all for the publication of Mr. Rose's book—the only thing to be accounted for. The narrative is given as an appendix of 65 pages to a volume of upwards of 300. In publishing the narrative, Mr. Rose did not assume the character of "an author," and was not called upon, by the responsibility of that character, to explain to the world his reasons for "submitting himself to their judgment." It is only for his book, then, exclusive of the narrative, that Mr. Rose can be understood to be offering any apology; and the apology he offers is, that it sprung from the impulse of private friendship. When the matter is looked into, however, it turns out, that though private friendship may, by a great stretch, be supposed to have dictated the publication of the appendix, it can by no possibility account, or help to account, for the composition of the book. Nay, the tendency and tenour of the book are such as this ardent and romantic friendship must necessarily condemn. It contains nothing whatever in praise or in defence of Sir Patrick Hume; but it contains a very keen, and not a very candid, attack upon his party and his principles. Professing to be published from anxiety to vindicate and exalt the memory of an insurgent revolution whig, it consists almost entirely of an attempt to depreciate whig principles, and openly to decry and vilify such of Mr. Fox's opinions as Sir Patrick Hume constantly exemplified in his actions. There never was an effect, we believe, imputed to so improbable a cause.

Finally, we may ask, if Mr. Rose's view, in this publication, was merely to vindicate the memory of Sir Patrick Hume, why he did not put into Mr. Fox's hands the information which would have rendered all vindication unnecessary? It was known to all the world, for several years, that Mr. Fox was engaged in the history of that period; and if Mr. Rose really thought that the papers in his custody gave a different view of Sir Patrick's conduct from that exhibited in the printed authorities, was it not his duty to put Mr. Fox upon his guard against being misled by them, and to communicate to him those invaluable documents to which he could have access in no other way? Did he doubt that Mr. Fox would have candour to state the truth, or that he would have stated with pleasure any thing that could exalt the character of a revolution whig? Did he imagine that any statement of his could ever obtain equal notoriety and effect with a statement in Mr. Fox's history? Or did he poorly withhold this information, that he might detract from the value of that history, and have to boast to the public that there was one point upon which he was better informed than that illustrious statesman? As to the preposterous apology which seems to be hinted at in the book itself, viz., that it was Mr. Fox's business to have asked for these papers, and not Mr. Rose's to have offered them, we shall only observe, that it stands on a point of etiquette, which would scarcely be permitted to govern the civilities of tradesmen's wives; and that it seems not a little unreasonable to lay Mr. Fox under the necessity of asking for papers, the very existence of which he could have no reason to expect. This narrative of Sir Patrick Hume has now lain in the archives of his family for 130 years, unknown and unsuspected to all but its immediate proprietor; and, distinguished as Sir Patrick was in his day in Scotland, it certainly does not imply any extraordinary stupidity in Mr. Fox, not to know, by intuition, that there were papers of his in existence which might afford him some light on the subject of his history.

We may appear to have dwelt too long on these preliminary considerations, since the intrinsic value of Mr. Rose's observations certainly will not be affected by the truth or the fallacy of the motives he has assigned for publishing them. It is impossible, however, not to see that, when a writer assigns a false motive for his coming forward, he is commonly conscious that the real one is discreditable: and that to expose the hollowness of such a pretence, is to lay the foundation of a wholesome distrust of his general fairness and temper. Any body certainly had a right to publish remarks on Mr. Fox's work—and nobody a better right than Mr. Rose; and if he had stated openly, that all the habits and connections of his life had led him to wish to see that work discredited, no one would have been entitled to complain of his exertions in the cause. When he chooses to disguise this motive, however, and to assign another which does not at all account for the phenomenon, we are so far from forgetting the existence of the other, that we are internally convinced of its being much stronger than we should otherwise have suspected; and that it is only dissembled, because it exists in a degree that could not have been decently avowed. For the same reason, therefore, of enabling our readers more distinctly to appreciate the intellect and temper of this right honourable author, we must say a word or two more of his Introduction, before proceeding to the substance of his remarks.

Besides the edifying history of his motive for writing, we are favoured, in that singular piece, with a number of his opinions upon points no way connected with Mr. Fox or his history; and with a copious account of his labours and studies in all kinds of juridical and constitutional learning. In order to confirm an opinion that a minute knowledge of our ancient history is not necessary to understand our actual constitution, he takes an unintelligible survey of the progress of our government, from the days of King Alfred,—and quotes Lord Coke, Plowden, Doomsday Book, Lord Ellesmere, Rymer's Fœdera, Dugdale's Origines, the Rolls of Parliament, Whitelock, and Abbot's Records; but, above all, "a report which *I* made several years ago on the state of the records in *my* custody." He then goes on, in the most obliging manner, to inform his readers that "Vertot's Account of the Revolutions of Rome has been found very useful by persons who have read the Roman History; but the best model that I have met with for such a work as appears to me to be much wanted, is a short History of Poland, which I translated nearly forty years ago, but did not publish; the manuscript of which his majesty at the time did me the honour to accept; and it probably is still in his majesty's library."—Introduction, pp. xxiv. xxv.

Truly all this is very interesting, and very much to the purpose:—but scarcely more so than eight or nine pages that follow, containing a long account of the conversations which Lord Marchmont had with Lord Bolingbroke, about the politics of Queen Anne's ministers, and which Mr. Rose now gives to the world from his recollection of various conversations between himself and Lord Marchmont. He tells us, moreover, that, "accustomed as he has been to *official accuracy* in statement," he had naturally a quick eye for mistakes in fact or in deduction;—that "having long enjoyed the confidence and affectionate friendship of Mr. Pitt," he has been more scrupulous than he would otherwise have been in ascertaining the grounds of his animadversions on the work of his great rival;—and that, notwithstanding all this anxiety, and the want of "disembarrassment of mind" and "leisure of time," he has compiled this volume in about as many *weeks* as Mr. Fox took *years* to the work on which it comments!

For the Observations themselves, we must say that we have perused them with considerable pleasure—not certainly from any extraordinary gratification which we derived from the justness of the sentiments, or the elegance of the style, but from a certain agreeable surprise which we experienced on finding how few parts of Mr. Fox's doctrine were considered as vulnerable, even by Mr. Rose; and in how large a proportion of his freest and strongest observations that jealous observer has expressed his most cordial concurrence. The Right Honourable George Rose, we rather believe, is commonly considered as one of the least whiggish or democratical of all the public characters who have lived in our times; and he has himself acknowledged, that a long habit of political opposition to Mr. Fox had perhaps given him a stronger bias against his favourite doctrines than he might otherwise have entertained. It was, therefore, no slight consolation to us to find that the true principles of English liberty had made so great a progress in the opinions of all men in upper life, as to extort such an ample admission of them, even from a person of Mr. Rose's habits and connections. As we fear, however, that the same justness and liberality of thinking are by no means general among the more obscure retainers of party throughout the country, we think it may not be without its use to quote a few of the passages to which we have alluded, just to let the vulgar tories in the provinces see how much of their favourite doctrines has been abjured by their more enlightened chief and leaders in the seat of government.

In the first place, there are all the passages (which it would be useless and tedious to recite) in which the patriotism and public virtue of Sir P. Hume are held up to the admiration of posterity. Now, Sir P. Hume, that true and sincere lover of his country, whose "talents and virtues his sovereign acknowledged and rewarded," and "whose honours have been attended by the suffrage of his country and the approbation of good men," was, even in the reign of Charles, concerned in designs analogous to those of Russell and Sydney;—and, very soon after the accession of James, and (as Mr. Rose thinks) before that monarch had done any thing in the least degree blameable, rose up openly in arms, and endeavoured to stir up the people to overthrow the existing government. Even Mr. Fox hesitated as to the wisdom and the virtue of those engaged in such enterprises;—and yet Mr. Rose, professing to see danger in that writer's excessive zeal for liberty, writes a book to extol the patriotism of a premature insurgent.

After this we need not quote our author's warm panegyrics on the Revolution—"that *glorious* event to which the measures of James *necessarily* led,"—or on the character of Lord Sommers, "whose wisdom, talents, political *courage* and *virtue*, would alone have been sufficient to insure the success of that measure." It may surprise some of his political admirers a little more, however, to find him professing that he "*concurs* with Mr. Fox as to the expediency of the bill of exclusion," (that boldest and most decided of all whig measures); and thinks "that the events which took place in the next reign afford a strong justification of the conduct of the promoters of that measure." When his tory friends have digested that sentiment, they may look at his patriotic invectives against the degrading connection of the two last of the Stuart princes with the court of France, and the "scandalous profligacy by which Charles and his successor betrayed the best interests of their country for miserable stipends." There is something very edifying, indeed, though we should fear a little alarming to courtly tempers, in the warmth with which our author winds up his diatribe on this interesting subject. "Every one," he observes, "who carries on a clandestine correspondence with a foreign power, in matters touching the interests of Great Britain, is *primâ facie* guilty of a great moral, as well as political, crime. If a subject, he is a traitor to his king and his country; and if a monarch, *he is a traitor to the crown which he wears*, and to the empire which he governs. There may, by possibility, be circumstances to extenuate the former; there can be none to lessen our detestation of the latter."—(pp. 149, 150.)

Conformably to these sentiments, Mr. Rose expresses his concurrence with all that Mr. Fox says of the arbitrary and oppressive measures which distinguished the latter part of Charles's reign;—declares that "he has manifested great temperance and forbearance in the character which he gives of Jefferies;—and *understated* the enormity of the cruel and detestable proceedings of the Scottish government, in its unheard of acts of power, and the miseries and persecutions which it inflicted;" admits that Mr. Fox's work treated of a period "in which the *tyranny of the sovereign* at home was not redeemed by any glory or success abroad;"—and speaks of the Revolution as the era "when the full measure of *the monarch's tyrannical usurpations made resistance a duty paramount to every consideration* of personal or public danger."

It is scarcely possible, we conceive, to read these, and many other passages which might be quoted from the work before us, without taking the author for a whig; and it certainly is not easy to comprehend how the writer of them could quarrel with any thing in Mr. Fox's history, for want of deference and veneration for the monarchical part of our constitution. To say the truth, we have not always been able to satisfy ourselves of the worthy author's consistency; and holding, as we are inclined to do, that his natural and genuine sentiments are liberal and manly, we can only account for the narrowness and unfairness of some of his remarks, by supposing them to originate from the habits of his practical politics, and of that long course of opposition, in which he learned to consider it a duty to his party to discredit every thing that came from the advocate of the people. We shall now say a word or two on the remarks themselves, which, as we have already noticed, will be found to be infinitely fewer, and more insignificant, than any one, looking merely at the bulk of the volume, could possibly have conjectured.

The first, of any sort of importance, is made on those passages in which Mr. Fox calls the execution of the king "a far less violent measure than that of Lord Strafford;" and says, "that there was something in the splendour and magnanimity of the act, which has served to raise the character of the nation in the opinion of Europe in general." Mr. Rose takes great offence at both these remarks; and says, that the constitution itself was violated by the execution of the king, while the case of Lord Strafford was but a private injury. We are afraid Mr. Rose does not perfectly understand Mr. Fox,—otherwise it would be difficult not to agree with him. The grossness of Lord Strafford's case consisted in this, that a bill of attainder was brought in, *after* a regular proceeding by impeachment had been tried against him. He was substantially *acquitted*, by the most unexceptionable process known in our law, *before* the bill of attainder came to declare him guilty, and to punish him. There was here, therefore, a most flagrant violation of all law and justice, and a precedent for endless abuses and oppressions. In the case of the king, on the other hand, there could be no violation of settled rules or practice; because the case itself was necessarily out of the purview of every rule, and could be drawn into no precedent. The constitution, no doubt, was necessarily destroyed or suspended by the trial; but Mr. Rose appears to forget that it had been destroyed or suspended before, by the *war*, or by the acts of the king which brought on the war. If it was lawful to fight against the king, it must have been lawful to take him prisoner: after he was a prisoner, it was both lawful and necessary to consider what should be done with him; and every deliberation of this sort had all the assumption, and none of the fairness of a trial. Yet Mr. Rose has himself told us, that "there are cases in which resistance becomes a paramount duty;" and probably is not prepared to say, that it was more violent and criminal to drive King James from the throne in 1688, than to wrest all law and justice to take the life of Lord Strafford in 1641. Yet the constitution was as much violated by the forfeiture of the one sovereign, as by the trial and execution of the other. It was impossible that the trial of King Charles might have terminated in a sentence of mere deprivation; and if James had fought against his people, and been conquered, he might have been tried and executed. The constitution was gone for the time, in both cases, as soon as force was mutually appealed to; and the violence that followed thereafter, to the person of the monarch, can receive no aggravation from any view of that nature.

With regard, again, to the loyal horror which Mr. Rose expresses, when Mr. Fox speaks of the splendour and magnanimity of the proceedings against the king, it is probable that this zealous observer was not aware, that his favourite "prerogative writer," Mr. Hume, had used the same, or still loftier expressions, in relation to the same event. Some of the words of that loyal and unsuspected historian are as follows:—"the pomp, the dignity, the ceremony of this transaction, correspond to the greatest conceptions that are suggested in the annals of human kind;—the delegates of a great people sitting in judgment upon their supreme magistrate, and trying him for his mismanagement and breach of trust."* Cordially as we agree with Mr. Fox in the unprofitable severity of this example, it is impossible, we conceive, for any one to consider the great, grave, and solemn movement of the nation that led to it, or the stern and dispassionate temper in which it was conducted, without feeling that proud contrast between this execution and that of all other deposed sovereigns in history,—which led Mr. Fox, in common with Mr. Hume, and every other writer on the subject, to make use of the expressions which have been alluded to.

When Mr. Rose, in the close of his remarks upon this subject, permits himself to insinuate, that if Mr. Fox thought such high praise due to the publicity, &c., of King Charles's trial, he must have felt unbounded admiration at that of Lewis XVI., he has laid himself open to a charge of such vulgar and uncandid unfairness, as was not to have been at all expected from a person of his rank and description. If Lewis XVI. had been openly in arms against his people,—if the Convention had required no other victim—and had settled into a regular government as soon as he was removed,—there might have been more room for a parallel,—to which, as the fact actually stands, every Briton must listen with indignation. Lewis XVI. was wantonly sacrificed to the rage of an insane and bloodthirsty faction, and tossed to the executioner among the common supplies for the guillotine. The publicity and parade of his trial were assumed from no love of justice, or sense of dignity; but from a low principle of profligate and clamorous defiance to every thing that had become displeasing: and ridiculous and incredible as it would appear of any other nation, we have not the least doubt that a certain childish emulation of the avenging liberty of the English had its share in producing this paltry copy of our grand and original daring. The insane coxcombs who blew out their brains, after a piece of tawdry declamation, in some of the provincial assemblies, were about as like Cato or Hannibal, as the trial and execution of Lewis was like the condemnation of King Charles. Our regicides were serious and original at least, in the bold, bad deeds which they committed. The regicides of France were poor theatrical imitators,—intoxicated with blood and with power, and incapable even of forming a sober estimate of the guilt or the consequences of their actions. Before leaving this subject, we must remind our readers that Mr. Fox unequivocally condemns the execution of the king; and spends some time in howing that it was excusable neither on the ground of present expediency nor future warning. After he had finished that statement, he proceeds to say, that notwithstanding what the more reasonable part of mankind may think, it is to be doubted, whether that proceeding has not served to raise the national character in the eyes of foreigners, &c.; and then goes on to refer to the conversations he had himself witnessed on that subject abroad. A man must be a very zealous royalist, indeed, to disbelieve or be offended with this.

Mr. Rose's next observation is in favour of General Monk; upon whom he is of opinion that Mr. Fox has been by far too severe,—at the same time that he fails utterly in obviating any of the grounds upon which that severity is justified. Monk was not responsible *alone*, indeed, for restoring the king, without taking any security for the people; but as wielding the whole power of the army, by which that restoration was effected, he is certainly *chiefly* responsible for that most criminal omission. As to his indifference to the fate of his companions in arms, Mr. Rose does, indeed, quote the testimony of *his chaplain*, who wrote a complimentary life of his patron, to prove that, on the trial of the regicides, he behaved with great moderation. We certainly do not rate this testimony very highly; and do think it far more than compensated by that of Mrs. Hutchinson, who, in the life of her husband, says, that on the first proceedings against the regicides in the House of Commons, "Monk sate still, and had not one word to interpose for any man, *but was as forward to set vengeance on foot as any one*."* And a little afterwards she adds, apparently from her own personal knowledge and observation, that "before the prisoners were brought to the Tower, Monk and his wife came one evening to the garden, and caused them to be brought down, only to stare at them,—which was such a behaviour for that man, who had betrayed so many of those that had honoured and trusted him, &c., as no story can parallel the inhumanity of."†

With regard again to Mr. Fox's charge of Monk's tamely acquiescing in the insults so meanly put on the illustrious corps of his old commander Blake, it is perfectly evident, even from the authorities referred to by Mr. Rose, that Blake's body was dug up by the king's order, among others, and removed out of the hallowed precincts of Westminster, to be reinterred, with twenty more, in one pit at St. Margaret's.

But the chief charge is, that on the trial of Argyle, Monk spontaneously sent down some confidential letters, which turned the scale of evidence against that unfortunate nobleman. This statement, to which Mr. Fox is most absurdly blamed for giving credit, is made on the authority of the three historians who lived nearest to the date of the transaction, and who all report it as quite certain and notorious. These historians are Burnet, Baillie, and Cunningham; nor are they contradicted by any one writer on the subject, except Dr. Campbell, who, at a period comparatively recent, and without pretending to have discovered any new document on the subject, is pleased to disbelieve them upon certain hypothetical and argumentative reasons of his own. These reasons Mr. Laing has examined and most satisfactorily obviated in his history; and Mr. Rose

* Hume's History, vol. vii. p. 141.

* Life of Colonel Hutchinson, p. 372. † Ibid. p. 373.

has exerted incredible industry to defend. The Scottish records for that period have perished; and for this reason, and because a collection of pamphlets and newspapers of that age, in Mr. Rose's possession, make no mention of the circumstance, he thinks fit to discredit it altogether. If this kind of scepticism were to be indulged, there would be an end of all reliance on history. In this particular case, both Burnet and Baillie speak quite positively, from the information of contemporaries; and state a circumstance that would very well account for the silence of the formal accounts of the trial, if any such had been preserved, viz., that Monk's letters were not produced till after the evidence was finished on both sides, and the debate begun on the result;—an irregularity, by the way, by much too gross to have been charged against a public proceeding without any foundation.

Mr. Rose's next observation is directed rather against Judge Blackstone than against Mr. Fox; and is meant to show, that this learned person was guilty of great inaccuracy in representing the year 1679 as the era of good laws and bad government. It is quite impossible to follow him through the dull details and feeble disputations by which he labours, to make it appear that our laws were not very good in 1679, and that they, as well as the administration of them, were much mended after the Revolution. Mr. Fox's, or rather Blackstone's remark is too obviously and strikingly true in substance, to admit of any argument or illustration.*

The next charge against Mr. Fox is for saying, that if Charles II.'s ministers betrayed him, he betrayed them in return; keeping, from some of them at least, the secret of what he was pleased to call his religion, and the state of his connections with France. After the furious attack which Mr. Rose has made in another place upon this prince and his French connections, it is rather surprising to see with what zeal he undertakes his defence against this very venial sort of treachery, of concealing his shame from some of his more respectable ministers. The attempt, however, is at least as unsuccessful as it is unaccountable. Mr. Fox says only, that *some* of the ministers were not trusted with the secret; and both Dalrymple and Macpherson say, that none but the *Catholic* counsellors were admitted to this confidence. Mr. Rose mutters, that there is no evidence of this; and himself produces an abstract of the secret treaty between Lewis and Charles, of May, 1670, to which the subscriptions of four *Catholic* ministers of the latter are affixed!

Mr. Fox is next taxed with great negligence for saying, that he does not know what proof there is of Clarendon's being privy to Charles receiving money from France; and very long quotations are inserted from the correspondence printed by Dalrymple and Macpherson—which do *not* prove Clarendon's knowledge of any money being *received*, though they do seem to establish that he must have known of its being stipulated for.

After this comes Mr. Rose's grand attack; in which he charges the historian with his whole heavy artillery of argument and quotation, and makes a vigorous effort to drive him from the position, that the early and primary object of James's reign was not to establish popery in this country, but in the first place to render himself absolute: and that, for a considerable time, he does not appear to have aimed at any thing more than a complete toleration for his own religion. The grounds upon which this opinion is maintained by Mr. Fox are certainly very probable. There is, in the first place, his zeal for the Church of England during his brother's life, and the violent oppressions by which he enforced a Protestant test in Scotland; secondly, the fact of his carrying on the government and the persecution of nonconformist's by Protestant ministers; and, thirdly, his addresses to his Parliament, and the tenour of much of his correspondence with Lewis. In opposition to this, Mr. Rose quotes an infinite variety of passages from Barillon's correspondence, to show in general the unfeigned zeal of this unfortunate prince for his religion, and his constant desire to glorify and advance it. Now, it is perfectly obvious, in the first place, that Mr. Fox never intended to dispute James's zeal for popery; and, in the second place, it is very remarkable, that in the first *seven* passages quoted by Mr. Rose, nothing more is said to be in the king's contemplation than the complete *toleration* of that religion. "The free exercise of the Catholic religion in their own houses,"—the abolition of the penal laws against Catholics,—"the free exercise of that religion," &c. &c., are the only objects to which the zeal of the king is said to be directed; and it is not till after the suppression of Monmouth's rebellion, that these phrases are exchanged for "a resolution to *establish the*

---

* Mr. Rose talks a great deal, and justly, about the advantages of the judges not being removable at pleasure; and, with a great air of erudition, informs us, that after 6 Charles, all the commissions were made *quamdiu nobis placuerit*. Mr. Rose's researches, we fear, do not often go beyond the records in his custody. If he had looked into Rushworth's Collection, he would have found, that, in 1641, King Charles agreed to make the commission, *quamdiu se bene gesserint*; and that some of those illegally removed in the following reign, though not officiating in court, still retained certain functions in consequence of that appointment. The following is the passage, at p. 1265, vol. iii. of Rushworth: "After the passing of these votes (16th December, 1640) against the judges, and transmitting them to the House of Peers, and their concurring with the House of Commons therein, an address was made unto the king shortly after, that his majesty, for the future, would not make any judge by patent *during pleasure*; but that they may hold their places hereafter, *quamdiu se bene gesserint*; and his majesty *did really grant the same*. And in his speech to both houses of Parliament, at the time of giving his royal assent to two bills, one to take away the High Commission Court, and the other the Court of Star-Chamber, and regulating the power of the council table, he hath this passage; 'If you consider what I have done this Parliament, discontents will not sit in your hearts; for I hope you remember, that I have granted, that the judges hereafter shall hold their places *quamdiu se bene gesserint*.' And likewise, his gracious majesty King Charles the Second observed the same rule and method in granting patents to judges, *quamdiu se bene gesserint*; as appears upon record in the Rolls; viz., to Sergeant Slide to be Lord Chief Justice of the King's Bench, Sir Orlando Bridgeman to be Lord Chief Baron, and afterwards to be Lord Chief Justice of Common Pleas; to Sir Robert Forster, and others. Mr. Sergeant Archer, now living, *notwithstanding his removal, still enjoys his patent*, being *quamdiu se bene gesserint*; and receives *a share in the profits of the court*, as to fees and other proceedings, by virtue of his said patent: and his name is used in those fines, &c., as a judge of that court."

Catholic religion," or "to get that religion established;" though it would be fair, perhaps, to interpret some even of these phrases with reference to those which precede them in the correspondence; especially as, in a letter from Lewis to Barillon, so late as 20th August, 1685, he merely urges the great expediency of James establishing "*the free exercise*" of that religion.

After all, in reality, there is not much substantial difference as to this point between the historian and his observer. Mr. Fox admits most explicitly, that James was zealous in the cause of popery; and that after Monmouth's execution, he made attempts equally violent and undisguised to restore it. Mr. Rose, on the other hand, admits that he was exceedingly desirous to render himself absolute; and that one ground of his attachment to popery probably was, its natural affinity with an arbitrary government. Upon which of these two objects he set the chief value, and which of them he wished to make subservient to the other, it is not perhaps now very easy to determine. In addition to the authorities referred to by Mr. Fox, however, there are many more which tend directly to show that one great ground of his antipathy to the reformed religion was, his conviction that it led to rebellion and republicanism. There are very many passages in Barillon to this effect; and, indeed, the burden of all Lewis's letters is to convince James that "the existence of monarchy" in England depended on the protection of the Catholics. Barillon says (Fox, App. p. 125), that "the king often declares publicly, that all Calvinists are naturally enemies to royalty, and above all, to royalty in England." And Burnet observes (vol. i. p. 73), that the king told him, "that among other prejudices he had against the Protestant religion, this was one, that his brother and himself being in many companies in Paris *incognito* (during the Commonwealth), where there were Protestants, he found they were all alienated from them, and great admirers of Cromwell; *so he believed they were all rebels in their hearts.*" It will not be forgotten either, that in his first address to the council, on his accession, he made use of those memorable words:—"I know the principles of the Church of England are for monarchy, and *therefore* I shall always take care to defend and support it." While he retained this opinion of its loyalty, accordingly, he did defend and support it; and did persecute all dissidents from its doctrine, at least as violently as he afterwards did those who opposed popery. It was only when he found that the orthodox doctrines of non-resistance and *jus divinum* would not go all lengths, and that even the bishops would not send his proclamation to their clergy, that he came to class them with the rest of the heretics, and to rely entirely upon the slavish votaries of the Roman superstition.

The next set of remarks is introduced for the purpose of showing that Mr. Fox has gone rather too far, in stating that the object both of Charles and James in taking money from Lewis was to render themselves independent of Parliament, and to enable them to govern without those assemblies. Mr. Rose admits that this was the point which both monarchs were *desirous* of attaining; and merely says, that it does not appear that either of them expected that the calling of Parliaments could be entirely dispensed with. There certainly is not here any worthy subject of contention.

The next point is, as to the sums of money which Barillon says he distributed to the whig leaders, as well as to the king's ministers. Mr. Rose is very liberal and rational on this subject; and thinks it not unfair to doubt the accuracy of the account which this minister renders of his disbursements. He even quotes two passages from Mad. de Sevigné, to show that it was the general opinion that he had enriched himself greatly by his mission to England. In a letter written during the continuance of that mission, she says, "Barillon s'en va, &c.; *son emploi est admirable cette année; il mangera cinquante mille francs; mais il sait bien où les prendre.*" And after his final return, she says he is old and rich, and looks without envy on the brilliant situation of M. D'Avaus. The only inference he draws from the discussion is, that it should have a little shaken Mr. Fox's confidence in his accuracy. The answer to which obviously is, that his mere dishonesty, where his private interest was concerned, can afford no reason for doubting his accuracy where it was not affected.

In the concluding section of his remarks, Mr. Rose resumes his eulogium on Sir Patrick Hume,—introduces a splendid encomium on the Marquis of Montrose,—brings authority to show that torture was used to extort confession in Scotland even after the Revolution,—and then breaks out into a high tory rant against Mr. Fox, for supposing that the councillors who condemned Argyle might not be very easy in their consciences, and for calling those who were hunting down that nobleman's dispersed followers "authorized assassins." James, he says, was their *lawful sovereign;* and the parties in question having been in open rebellion, it was the evident duty of all who had not joined with them to suppress them. We are not very fond of arguing general points of this nature; and the question here is fortunately special and simple. If the tyranny and oppression of James in Scotland—the unheard-of enormity of which Mr. Rose owns that Mr. Fox has understated—had already given that country a far juster title to renounce him than England had in 1688; then James was *not* "their lawful sovereign" in any sense in which that phrase can be understood by a free people; and those whose cowardice or despair made them submit to be the instruments of the tyrant's vengeance on one who had armed for their deliverance, may very innocently be presumed to have suffered some remorse for their compliance. With regard, again, to the phrase of "authorized assassins," it is plain, from the context of Mr. Fox, that it is not applied to the regular forces acting against the remains of Argyle's *armed* followers, but to those individuals, whether military or not, who pursued the disarmed and solitary fugitives, for the purpose of butchering them in cold blood, in their caverns and mountains.

Such is the substance of Mr. Rose's observations; which certainly do not appear to us of any considerable value—though they indicate, throughout, a laudable industry, and a still more laudable consciousness of inferiority,—together with (what we are determined to believe) a natural disposition to liberality and moderation, counteracted by the littleness of party jealousy and resentment. We had noted a great number of petty misrepresentations and small inaccuracies; but in a work which is not likely either to be much read, or long remembered, these things are not worth the trouble of correction.

Though the book itself is very dull, however, we must say that the Appendix is very entertaining. Sir Patrick's narrative is clear and spirited; but what delights us far more, is another and more domestic and miscellaneous narrative of the adventures of his family, from the period of Argyle's discomfiture till their return in the train of King William. This is from the hand of Lady Murray, Sir Patrick's grand-daughter; and is mostly furnished from the information of her mother, his favourite and exemplary daughter. There is an air of cheerful magnanimity and artless goodness about this little history, which is extremely engaging: and a variety of traits of *Scottish* simplicity and homeliness of character, which recommend it, in a peculiar manner, to our *national* feelings. Although we have already enlarged this article beyond its proper limits, we must give our readers a few specimens of this singular chronicle.

After Sir Patrick's escape, he made his way to his own castle, and was concealed for some time in a vault under the church, where his daughter, then a girl under twenty, went alone, every night, with an heroic fortitude, to comfort and feed him. The gaiety, however, which lightened this perilous intercourse, is to us still more admirable than its heroism.

"She went every night by herself, at midnight, to carry him victuals and drink; and stayed with him as long as she could to get home before day. In all this time, my grandfather showed the same constant composure, and cheerfulness of mind, that he continued to possess to his death, which was at the age of eighty-four; all which good qualities she inherited from him in a high degree. *Often did they laugh heartily in that doleful habitation*, at different accidents that happened. She at that time had a terror for a churchyard, especially in the dark, as is not uncommon at her age, by idle nursery stories; but when engaged by concern for her father, she stumbled over the graves every night alone, without fear of any kind entering her thoughts, but for soldiers and parties in search of him, which the least noise or motion of a leaf put her in terror for. The minister's house was near the church. The first night she went, his dogs kept such a barking as put her in the utmost fear of a discovery. My grandmother sent for the minister next day, and, upon pretence of a mad dog, got him to hang all his dogs. There was also difficulty of getting victuals to carry him, without the servants suspecting: the only way it was done, was by stealing it off her plate at dinner, into her lap. Many a diverting story she has told about this, and other things of the like nature. Her father liked sheep's head; and, while the children were eating their broth, she had conveyed most of one into her lap. When her brother Sandy (the late Lord Marchmont) had done, he looked up with astonishment and said, 'Mother, will you look at Grizzel; while we have been eating our broth, she has eat up the whole sheep's head.' *This occasioned so much mirth among them, that her father, at night, was greatly entertained by it; and desired Sandy might have a share in the next.*"—App. p. [v.]

They then tried to secrete him in a low room in his own house; and, for this purpose, to contrive a bed concealed under the floor, which this affectionate and light-hearted girl secretly excavated herself, by scratching up the earth with her nails, "till she left not a nail on her fingers," and carrying it into the garden at night in bags. At last, however, they all got over to Holland, where they seem to have lived in great poverty,—but in the same style of magnanimous gaiety and cordial affection, of which some instances have been recited. This admirable young woman, who lived afterwards with the same simplicity of character in the first society in England, seems to have exerted herself in a way that nothing but affection could have rendered tolerable, even to one bred up to drudgery.

"All the time they were there" (says his daughter), "there was not a week my mother did not sit up two nights, to do the business that was necessary. She went to market; went to the mill to have their corn ground, which, it seems, is the way with good managers there; dressed the linen; cleaned the house; made ready dinner; mended the children's stockings, and other clothes; made what she could for them; and, in short, did every thing. Her sister Christian, who was a year or two younger, diverted her father and mother, and the rest, who were fond of music. Out of their small income they bought a harpsichord for little money (but is a Rucar*), now in my custody, and most valuable. My aunt played and sung well, and had a great deal of life and humour, but no turn to business. Though my mother had the same qualifications, and liked it as well as she did, she was forced to drudge; and *many jokes used to pass betwixt the sisters about their different occupations*."—p. [ix.]

"Her brother soon afterwards entered into the Prince of Orange's guards: and her constant attention was to have him appear right in his linen and dress. They wore little point cravats and cuffs, which many a night she sat up to have in as good order for him as any in the place; and one of their greatest expenses was in dressing him as he ought to be. As their house was always full of the unfortunate banished people like themselves, they seldom went to dinner, without three, or four, or five of them, to share with them; and many a hundred times I have heard her say, she could

* An eminent maker of that time.

never look back upon their manner of living there, without thinking it a miracle. They had no want, but plenty of every thing they desired, and much contentment; and always declared it the most pleasing part of her life, though they were not without their little distresses; *but to them they were rather jokes than grievances.* The professors, and men of learning in the place, came often to see my grandfather. The best entertainment he could give them was a glass of alabast beer, which was a better kind of ale than common. He sent his son Andrew, the late Lord Kimmerghame, a boy, to draw some for them in the cellar: he brought it up with great diligence; but in the other hand the spigot of the barrel. My grandfather said, 'Andrew, what is that in your hand?' When he saw it he run down with speed; but the beer was all run out before he got there. *This occasioned much mirth;* though, perhaps, they did not well know where to get more."—pp. [x. xi.]

Sir Patrick, we are glad to hear, retained this kindly cheerfulness of character to the last; and, after he was an earl and chancellor of Scotland, and unable to stir with gout, had himself carried to the room where his children and grandchildren were dancing, and insisted on beating time with his foot. Nay, when *dying* at the advanced age of eighty-four, he could not resist his old propensity to joking, but uttered various pleasantries on the disappointment the worms would meet with, when, after boring through his thick coffin, they would find little but bones.

There is, in the Appendix, besides these narrations, a fierce attack upon Burnet, which is full of inaccuracies and ill temper; and some interesting particulars of Monmouth's imprisonment and execution. We dare say Mr. Rose could publish a volume or two of very interesting tracts; and can venture to predict that his collections will be much more popular than his observations.

DISTURBANCES AT MADRAS.*

[EDINBURGH REVIEW, 1810.]

THE disturbances which have lately taken place in our East Indian possessions, would, at any period, have excited a considerable degree of alarm; and those feelings are, of course, not a little increased by the ruinous aspect of our European affairs. The revolt of an army of eighty thousand men is an event which seems to threaten so nearly the ruin of the country in which it happens, that no common curiosity is excited as to the causes which could have led to it, and the means by which its danger was averted. On these points, we shall endeavour to exhibit to our readers the information afforded to us by the pamphlets whose titles we have cited. The first of these is understood to be written by an agent of Sir George Barlow, sent over for the express purpose of defending his measures; the second is most probably the production of some one of the dismissed officers, or, at least, founded upon their representations; the third statement is by Mr. Petrie,—and we most cordially recommend it to the perusal of our readers. It is characterized, throughout, by moderation, good sense, and a feeling of duty. We have seldom read a narrative, which, on the first face of it, looked so much like truth. It has, of course, produced the ruin and dismissal of this gentleman, though we have not the shadow of doubt, that if his advice had been followed, every unpleasant occurrence which has happened in India might have been effectually prevented.

In the year 1802, a certain monthly allowance, proportioned to their respective ranks, was given to each officer of the coast army, to enable him to provide himself with camp equipage; and a monthly allowance was also made to the commanding officers of the native corps, for the provision of the camp equipage of these corps. This arrangement was commonly called the *tent contract.* Its intention (as the pamphlet of Sir George Barlow's agent very properly states) was to combine facility of movement in military operations with views of economy. In the general revision of its establishments, set on foot for the purposes of economy by the Madras government, this contract was considered as entailing upon them a very unnecessary expense; and the then commander-in-chief, General Craddock, directed Colonel Munro, the quartermaster-general, to make a report to him upon the subject. The report, which was published almost as soon as it was made up, recommends the abolition of this contract; and, among other passages for the support of this opinion, has the following one:—

"Six years' experience of the practical effects of the existing system of the camp equipage equipment of the native army, has afforded means of forming a judgment relative to its advantages and efficiency which were not possessed by the persons who proposed its introduction; and an attentive examination of its operations during that period of time has suggested the following observations regarding it:—"

After stating that the contract is needlessly

---

* *Narrative of the Origin and Progress of the Dissensions at the Presidency of Madras, founded on Original Papers and Correspondence.* Lloyd, London, 1810.

Account of the Origin and Progress of the late Discontents of the Army on the Madras Establishment. Cadell and Davies, London, 1810.

Statement of Facts delivered to the Right Honourable Lord Minto. By WILLIAM PETRIE Esq. Stockdale, London, 1810.

expensive—that it subjects the Company to the same charges for troops in garrison as for those in the field—the report proceeds to state the following observation, made on the authority of *six years' experience and attentive examination.*

"Thirdly. By granting the same allowances in peace and war for the equipment of native corps, while the expenses incidental to that charge are unavoidably much greater in war than peace, it places the interest and duty of officers commanding native corps in direct opposition to one another. It makes it their interest that their corps should not be in a state of efficiency fit for field service, and therefore furnishes strong inducements to neglect their most important duties."—*Accurate and Authentic Narrative*, pp. 117, 118.

Here, then, is not only a proposal for reducing the emoluments of the principal officers of the Madras army, but a charge of the most flagrant nature. The first they might possibly have had some right to consider as a hardship; but, when severe and unjust invective was superadded to strict retrenchment—when their pay and their reputation were diminished at the same time—it cannot be considered as surprising, that such treatment, on the part of the government, should lay the foundation for a spirit of discontent in those troops who had recently made such splendid additions to the Indian empire, and established, in the progress of these acquisitions, so high a character for discipline and courage. It must be remembered, that an officer on European and one on Indian service are in very different situations, and propose to themselves very different objects. The one never thinks of making a fortune by his profession, while the hope of ultimately gaining an independence is the principal motive for which the Indian officer banishes himself from his country. To diminish the emoluments of his profession is to retard the period of his return, and to frustrate the purpose for which he exposes his life and health in a burning climate, on the other side of the world. We make these observations, certainly without any idea of denying the right of the East India Company to make any retrenchments they may think proper, but to show that it is a right which ought to be exercised with great delicacy and with sound discretion—that it should only be exercised when the retrenchment is of real importance—and above all, that it should always be accompanied with every mark of suavity and conciliation. Sir George Barlow, on the contrary, committed the singular imprudence of stigmatizing the honour, and wounding the feelings of the Indian officers. At the same moment that he diminishes their emoluments he tells them, that the India Company take away their allowances for tents, because those allowances have been abused in the meanest, most profligate, and most unsoldier-like manner; for this and more than this is conveyed in the report of Colonel Munro, published by order of Sir George Barlow. If it was right, in the first instance, to diminish the emoluments of so vast an army, it was certainly indiscreet to give such reasons for it. If any individual had abused the advantages of the tent-contract, he might have been brought to a court-martial; and, if his guilt had been established, his punishment, we will venture to assert, would not have occasioned a moment of complaint or disaffection in the army; but that a civilian, a gentleman accustomed only to the details of commerce, should begin his government, over a settlement with which he was utterly unacquainted, by telling one of the bravest set of officers in the world, that, for six years past, they had been, in the basest manner, sacrificing their duty to their interest, does appear to us an instance of indiscretion which, if frequently repeated, would soon supersede the necessity of any further discussion upon Indian affairs.

The whole transaction, indeed, appears to have been gone into with a disregard to the common professional feelings of an army, which is to us utterly inexplicable. The opinion of the commander-in-chief, General Macdowall, was never asked upon the subject; not a single witness was examined; the whole seems to have depended upon the report of Colonel Munro, the youngest staff-officer of the army, published in spite of the earnest remonstrance of Colonel Capper, the adjutant-general, and before three days had been given him to substitute his own plan, which Sir George Barlow had promised to read before the publication of Colonel Munro's report. Nay, this great plan of reduction was never even submitted to the military board, by whom all subjects of that description were, according to the orders of the court of directors, and the usage of the service, to be discussed and digested, previous to their coming before government.

Shortly after the promulgation of this very indiscreet paper, the commander-in-chief, General Macdowall, received letters from almost all the officers commanding native corps, representing, in terms adapted to the feelings of each, the stigma which was considered to attach to them individually, and appealing to the authority of the commander-in-chief for redress against such charges, and to his personal experience for their falsehood. To these letters the general replied, that the orders in question had been prepared *without any reference to his opinion*, and that, as the matter was so far advanced, he deemed it inexpedient to interfere. The officers commanding corps, finding that no steps were taken to remove the obnoxious insinuations, and considering that, while they remained, an indelible disgrace was cast upon their characters, prepared charges against Colonel Munro. These charges were forwarded to General Macdowall, referred by him to the judge advocate general, and returned, with his objections to them, to the officers who had preferred the charges. For two months after this period, General Macdowall appears to have remained in a state of uncertainty, as to whether he would or would not bring Colonel Munro to a court-martial upon the charges preferred against him by the commanders of corps. At last, urged by the discontents of the army, he determined in the affirmative; and Colonel Munro was put in arrest, preparatory to his trial. Colonel Munro then appealed directly to the governor, Sir George Barlow; and was released by a positive order from him. It is necessary to state, that all appeals of officers to the government in India always pass through the hands of the commander-in-chief; and this appeal, therefore, of Colonel Munro, directed to the government, was considered by General Macdowall as a great infringement of military discipline. We have very great doubts whether Sir George Barlow was not guilty of another great mistake in preventing this court-martial from taking place. It is undoubtedly true, that no servant of the public is amenable to justice for doing what the government orders him to do; but he is not entitled to protection under the pretence of that order, if he has done something which it evidently did not require of him. If Colonel Munro had been ordered to report upon the conduct of an individual officer,—and it could be proved that, in gratification of private malice, he had taken that opportunity of stating the most infamous and malicious falsehoods,—could it be urged that his conduct might not be fairly scrutinized in a court of justice, or a court-martial? If this were otherwise, any duty delegated by government to an individual would become the most intolerable source of oppression: he might gratify every enmity and antipathy—indulge in every act of malice—vilify and traduce every one whom he hated—and then shelter himself under the plea of public service. Every body has a right to do what the supreme power orders him to do; but he does not thereby acquire a right to do what he has not been ordered to do. Colonel Munro was directed to make a report upon the state of the army: the officers whom he has traduced accuse him of reporting something utterly different from the state of the army—something which he and every body else knew to be different—and this for the malicious purpose of calumniating their reputation. If this was true, Colonel Munro could not plead the authority of government; for the authority of government was afforded to him for a very different purpose. In this view of the case, we cannot see how the dignity of government was attacked by the proposal of the court-martial, or to what other remedy those who had suffered from his abuse of his power could have had recourse. Colonel Munro had been promised, by General Macdowall, that the court-martial should consist of king's officers: there could not, therefore, have been any rational suspicion that his trial would have been unfair, or his judges unduly influenced.

Soon after Sir George Barlow had shown this reluctance to give the complaining officers an opportunity of re-establishing their injured character, General Macdowall sailed for England, and left behind him, for publication, an order, in which Colonel Munro was reprimanded for a violent breach in military discipline, in appealing to the governor otherwise than through the customary and prescribed channel of the commander-in-chief. As this paper is very short, and at the same time very necessary to the right comprehension of this case, we shall lay it before our readers.

"G. O. by the Commander-in-chief.

"The immediate departure of Lieutenant General Macdowall from Madras will prevent his pursuing the design of bringing Lieutenant-Colonel Munro, quartermaster-general, to trial, for disrespect to the commander-in-chief, for disobedience of orders, and for contempt of military authority, in having resorted to the power of the civil government, in defiance of the judgment of the officer at the head of the army, who had placed him under arrest, on charges preferred against him by a number of officers commanding native corps, in consequence of which appeal *direct* to the honourable the president in council, Lieutenant-General Macdowall has received positive orders from the chief secretary to liberate Lieutenant-Colonel Munro from arrest.

"Such conduct on the part of Lieutenant-Colonel Munro, being destructive of subordination, subversive of military discipline, a violation of the sacred rights of the commander-in-chief, and holding out a most dangerous example to the service, Lieutenant-General Macdowall, in support of the dignity of the profession, and his own station and character, feels it incumbent on him to express his strong disapprobation of Lieutenant-Colonel Munro's unexampled proceedings, and considers it a solemn duty imposed upon him to reprimand Lieutenant-Colonel Munro in general orders; and he is hereby reprimanded accordingly. (Signed) T. Boles, D. A. G."—*Accur. & Auth. Nar.* pp. 68, 69.

Sir George Barlow, in consequence of this paper, immediately deprived General Macdowall of his situation of commander-in-chief, which he had not yet resigned, though he had quitted the settlement; and as the official signature of the deputy adjutant-general appeared to the paper, that officer also was suspended from his situation. Colonel Capper, the adjutant-general, in the most honourable manner informed Sir George Barlow, that he was the culpable and responsible person; and that the name of his deputy only appeared to the paper in consequence of his positive order, and because he himself happened to be absent on shipboard with General Macdowall. This generous conduct on the part of Colonel Capper involved himself in punishment, without extricating the innocent person whom he intended to protect. The Madras government, always swift to condemn, doomed him to the same punishment as Major Boles; and he was suspended from his office.

This paper we have read over with great attention; and we really cannot see wherein its criminality consists, or on what account it could have drawn down upon General Macdowall so severe a punishment as the privation of the high and dignified office which he held. The censure upon Colonel Munro was for a violation of the regular etiquette of the army, in appealing to the governor otherwise than through the channel of the commander-in-chief. This was an entirely new offence on the part of Colonel Munro.

Sir George Barlow had given no opinion upon it; it had not been discussed between him and the commander-in-chief; and the commander-in-chief was clearly at liberty to act in this point as he pleased. He does not reprimand Colonel Munro for obeying Sir George Barlow's orders; for Sir George had given no orders upon the subject; but he blames him for transgressing a well-known and important rule of the service. We have great doubts if he was not quite right in giving this reprimand. But at all events, if he was wrong,—if Colonel Munro was not guilty of the offence imputed, still the errôneous punishment which the general had inflicted merited no such severe retribution as that resorted to by Sir George Barlow. There are no reflections in the paper on the conduct of the governor or the government. The reprimand is grounded entirely upon the breach of that military discipline which it was undoubtedly the business of General Macdowall to maintain in the most perfect purity and vigour. Nor has the paper any one expression in it foreign to this purpose. We were, indeed, not a little astonished at reading it. We had imagined that a paper, which drew after it such a long train of dismissals and suspensions, must have contained a declaration of war against the Madras government,—an exhortation to the troops to throw off their allegiance,—or an advice to the natives to drive their intrusive masters away, and become as free as their forefathers had left them. Instead of this, we find nothing more than a common reprimand from a commander-in-chief to a subordinate officer, for transgressing the bounds of his duty. If Sir George Barlow had governed kingdoms six months longer, we cannot help thinking he would have been a little more moderate.

But whatever difference of opinion there may be respecting the punishment of General Macdowall, we can scarcely think there can be any with regard to the conduct observed towards the adjutant-general and his deputy. They were the subordinates of the commander-in-chief, and were peremptorily bound to publish any general orders which he might command them to publish. They would have been liable to very severe punishment if they had not; and it appears to us the most flagrant outrage against all justice to convert their obedience into a fault. It is true, no subordinate officer is bound to obey any order which is plainly, and to any common apprehension, illegal; but then the illegality must be quite manifest; the order must imply such a contradiction to common sense, and such a violation of duties superior to the duty of military obedience, that there can be scarcely two opinions on the subject. Wherever any fair doubt can be raised, the obedience of the inferior officer is to be considered as proper and meritorious. Upon any other principle, his situation is the most cruel imaginable: he is liable to the severest punishment, even to instant death, if he refuses to obey; and if he does obey, he is exposed to the animadversion of the civil power, which teaches him that he ought to have canvassed the order,—to have remonstrated against it,—and, in case this opposition proved ineffectual, to have disobeyed it. We have no hesitation in pronouncing the imprisonment of Colonel Capper and Major Boles to have been an act of great severity and great indiscretion, and such as might very fairly give great offence to an army, who saw themselves exposed to the same punishments, for the same adherence to their duties.

"The measure of removing Lieutenant-Colonel Capper and Major Boles," says Mr. Petrie, "was universally condemned by the most respectable officers in the army, and not more so by the officers in the Company's service, than by those of his majesty's regiments. It was felt by all as the introduction of a most dangerous principle, and setting a pernicious example of disobedience and insubordination to all the gradations of military rank and authority; teaching inferior officers to question the legality of the orders of their superiors, and bringing into discussion questions which may endanger the very existence of government. Our proceedings at the time operated like an electric shock, and gave rise to combinations, associations, and discussions, pregnant with danger to every constituted authority in India. It was observed that the removal of General Macdowall (admitting the expediency of the measure) sufficiently vindicated the authority of government, and exhibited to the army a memorable proof that the supreme power is vested in the civil authority.

"The offence came from the general, and he was punished for it; but to suspend from the service the mere instruments of office, for the ordinary transmission of an order to the army, was universally condemned as an act of inapplicable severity, which might do infinite mischief, but could not accomplish any good or beneficial purpose. It was to court unpopularity, and adding fuel to the flame, which was ready to burst forth in every division of the army; that to vindicate the measure on the assumed illegality of the order, is to resort to a principle of a most dangerous tendency, capable of being extended in its application to purposes subversive of the foundations of all authority, civil as well as military. If subordinate officers are encouraged to judge of the legality of the orders of their superiors, we introduce a precedent of incalculable mischief, neither justified by the spirit nor practice of the laws. Is it not better to have the responsibility on the head of the authority which issues the order, except in cases so plain that the most common capacity can judge of their being direct violations of the established and acknowledged laws? Is the intemperance of the expressions, the indiscretions of the opinions, the inflammatory tendency of the order, so eminently dangerous, so evidently calculated to excite to mutiny and disobedience, so strongly marked with features of criminality, as not to be mistaken? Was the order, I beg leave to ask, of this description, of such a nature as to justify the adjutant-general and his deputy in their refusal to publish it, to disobey the order of the commander-in-chief, to revolt from his authority, and to complain of him to the government? Such were the views I took of that unhappy transaction; and, as I foresaw serious mischief from the measure, not only to the discipline of the army, but even to the security of the civil government, it was my duty to state my opinion to Sir G. Barlow, and to use every argument which my reason suggested, to prevent the publication of the order. In this I completely failed; the suspension took effect; and the match was laid that has communicated the flame to almost every military mind in India. I recorded no dissent; for, as a formal opposition could only tend to exonerate myself from a certain degree of responsibility, without effecting any good public purpose, and might probably be misconstrued or misconceived by those to whom our proceedings were made known, it was a more honourable discharge of my duty to relinquish this advantage, than to comply with the mere letter of the order respecting dissents. I explained this motive of my conduct to Sir G. Barlow."—*Statement of Facts*, pp. 20—23.

After these proceedings on the part of the Madras government, the disaffection of the troops rapidly increased; absurd and violent manifestoes were published by the general officers; government was insulted; and the army soon broke out into open mutiny.

When the mutiny was fairly begun, the conduct of the Madras government in quelling it, seems nearly as objectionable as that by which it had been excited. The governor, in attempting to be dignified, perpetually fell into the most puerile irritability; and wishing to be firm, was guilty of injustice and violence. Invitations to dinner were made an affair of state. Long negotiations appear respecting whole corps of officers who refused to dine with Sir George Barlow; and the first persons in the settlement were employed to persuade them to eat the repast which his excellency had prepared for them. A whole school of military lads were sent away, for some trifling display of partiality to the cause of the army; and every unfortunate measure recurred to, which a weak understanding and a captious temper could employ to bring a government into contempt. Officers were dismissed; but dismissed without trial, and even without accusation. The object seemed to be to punish somebody: whether it was the right or the wrong person was less material. Sometimes the subordinate was selected, where the principal was guilty; sometimes the superior was sacrificed for the ungovernable conduct of those who were under his charge. The blows were strong enough; but they came from a man who shut his eyes, and struck at random:—conscious that he must do something to repel the danger;—but so agitated by its proximity that he could not look at it, or take a proper aim.

Among other absurd measures resorted to by this new eastern emperor, was the notable expedient of imposing a test upon the officers of the army, expressive of their loyalty and attachment to the government; and as this was done at a time when some officers were in open rebellion, others fluctuating, and many almost resolved to adhere to their duty, it had the very natural and probable effect of uniting them all in opposition to government. To impose a test, or trial of opinions, is at all times an unpopular species of inquisition; and at a period when men were hesitating whether they should obey or not, was certainly a very dangerous and rash measure. It could be no security; for men who would otherwise rebel against their government, certainly would not be restrained by any verbal barriers of this kind; and, at the same time that it promised no effectual security, it appeared to increase the danger of irritated combination. This very rash measure immediately produced the strongest representations and remonstrances *from king's officers of the most unquestionable loyalty.*

"Lieutenant-Colonel Vesey, commanding at Palamcotah, apprehends the most fatal consequences to the tranquillity of the southern provinces, if Colonel Wilkinson makes any hostile movements from Trichinopoly. In different letters he states, that such a step must inevitably throw the company's troops into open revolt. He has ventured to write in the strongest terms to Colonel Wilkinson, entreating him not to march against the southern troops, and pointing out the ruinous consequences which may be expected from such a measure.

"Lieutenant-Colonel Stuart in Travancore, and Colonel Forbes in Malabar, have written, that they are under no apprehension for the tranquillity of those provinces, or for the fidelity of the company's troops, if government does not insist on enforcing the orders for the signature of the test; but that, if this is attempted, the security of the country will be imminently endangered. These orders are to be enforced; and I tremble for the consequences."—*Statement of Facts*, pp. 53, 54.

The following letter from the Honourable Colonel Stuart, commanding a king's regiment, was soon after received by Sir George Barlow:—

"The late measures of government, as carried into effect at the Presidency and Trichinopoly, have created a most violent ferment among the corps here. At those places where the European force was so far superior in number to the native, the measure probably was executed without difficulty; but here, where there are seven battalions of sepoys, and a company and a half of artillery, to our one regiment, I found it totally impossible to carry the business to the same length, particularly as any tumult among our own corps would certainly bring the people of Travancore upon us.

"It is in vain, therefore, for me, with the small force I can depend upon, to attempt to stem the torrent here by any acts of violence.

"Most sincerely and anxiously do I wish that the present tumult may subside, without fatal consequences; which, if the present violent measures are continued, I much fear will not be the case. If blood is once spilt in the cause, there is no knowing where it may end; and the probable consequences will be, that India will be lost for ever. So many officers of the army have gone to such lengths, that, unless a general amnesty is granted, tranquillity can never be restored.

"The honourable the governor in council will not, I trust, impute to me any other motives for having thus given my opinion. I am actuated solely by anxiety for the public good and the benefit of my country; and I think it my duty, holding the responsible situation I now do, to express my sentiments at so awful a period.

"Where there are any prospects of success, it might be right to persevere; but, where every day's experience proves, that the more coercive the measures adopted, the more violent are the consequences, a different and more conciliatory line of conduct ought to be adopted. I have the honour, &c."—*Statement of Facts*, pp. 55, 56.

"A letter from Colonel Forbes, commanding in Malabar, states, that to prevent a revolt in the province, and the probable march of the company's troops towards Seringapatam, he had accepted of a modification in the test, to be signed by the officers on their parole, to make no hostile movements until the pleasure of the government was known.—Disapproved by government, and ordered to enforce the former orders."—*Statement of Facts*, p. 61.

It can scarcely be credited, that in spite of these repeated remonstrances from officers, whose loyalty and whose knowledge of the subject could not be suspected, this test was ordered to be enforced, and the severest rebukes inflicted upon those who had presumed to doubt of its propriety, or suspend its operation. Nor let any man say that the opinionative person who persevered in this measure saw more clearly and deeply into the consequence of his own measures than those who were about him; for unless Mr. Petrie has been guilty, and repeatedly guilty, of a most downright and wilful falsehood, Sir George Barlow had not the most distant conception, during all these measures, that the army would ever venture upon revolt.

"Government, or rather the head of the government, was never correctly informed of the actual state of the army, or I think he would have acted otherwise; he was told, and he was willing to believe, that the discontents were confined to a small part of the troops; that a great majority disapproved of their proceedings, and were firmly and unalterably attached to government."—*Statement of Facts*, pp. 23, 24.

In a conversation which Mr. Petrie had with Sir George Barlow upon the subject of the army—and in the course of which he recommends to that gentleman more lenient measures, and warns him of the increasing disaffection of the troops—he gives us the following account of Sir George Barlow's notions of the then state of the army:—

"Sir G. Barlow assured me I was greatly misinformed; that he could rely upon his intelligence; and would produce to council the must satisfactory and unequivocal proofs of the fidelity of nine-tenths of the army; that discontents were confined almost exclusively to the southern division of the army; that the troops composing the subsidiary force, those in the ceded districts, in the centre, and a part of the northern division, were all untainted by those principles which had misled the rest of the army."—*Statement of Facts*, pp. 27, 28.

All those violent measures, then, the spirit and wisdom of which have been so much extolled, were not measures of the consequences of which their author had the most distant suspicion. They were not the acts of a man who knew that he must unavoidably, in the discharge of his duty, irritate, but that he could ultimately overcome that irritation. They appear, on the contrary, to have proceeded from a most gross and scandalous ignorance of the opinions of the army. He expected passive submission, and met with universal revolt. So far, then, his want of intelligence and sagacity are unquestionably proved. He did not proceed with useful measures, and run the risk of a revolt, for which he was fully prepared; but he carried these measures into execution, firmly convinced that they would occasion no revolt at all.*

The fatal nature of this mistake is best exemplified by the means recurred to for its correction. The grand expedient relied upon was to instigate the natives, men and officers, to disobey their European commanders; an expedient by which present safety was secured at the expense of every principle upon which the permanence of our Indian empire rests. There never was in the world a more singular spectacle than to see a few thousand Europeans governing so despotically fifty or sixty millions of people, of different climate, religion, and habits—forming them into large and well-disciplined armies—and leading them out to the further subjugation of the native powers of India. But can any words be strong enough to paint the rashness of provoking a mutiny, which could only be got under by teaching these armies to act against their European commanders, and to use their actual strength in overpowering their officers?—or, is any man entitled to the praise of firmness and sagacity, who gets rid of a present danger by encouraging a principle which renders that danger more frequent and more violent? We will venture to assert, that a more unwise or a more unstatesmanlike action was never committed by any man in any country; and we are grievously mistaken, if any length of time elapse before the evil consequences of it are felt and deplored by every man who deems the welfare of our Indian colonies of any importance to the prosperity of the mother country. We cannot help contrasting the management of the discontent of the Madras army, with the manner in which the same difficulty was got over with the army at Bengal. A little increase of attention and emolument to the head of that army, under the management of a man of rank and talents, dissipated ap

* We should have been alarmed to have seen Sir George Barlow, junior, churchwarden of St. George's, Hanover Square,—an office so nobly filled by Giblet and Leslie: it was an huge affliction to see so incapable a man at the head of the Indian empire.

pearances which the sceptred pomp of a merchant's clerk would have blown up into a rebellion in three weeks; and yet the Bengal army is at this moment in as good a state of discipline, as the English fleet to which Lord Howe made such abject concessions—and in a state to be much more permanently depended upon than the army which has been so effectually ruined by the inconveniently great soul of the present governor of Madras.

Sir George Barlow's agent, though faithful to his employment of calumniating those who were in any degree opposed to his principal, seldom loses sight of sound discretion, and confines his invectives to whole bodies of men, except where the dead are concerned. Against Colonel Capper, General Macdowall, and Mr. Roebuck, who are now no longer alive to answer for themselves, he is intrepidly severe; in all these instances he gives a full loose to his sense of duty, and inflicts upon them the severest chastisement. In his attack upon the civilians, he is particularly careful to keep to generals; and so rigidly does he adhere to this principle, that he does not support his assertion, that the civil service was disaffected as well as the military, by one single name, one single fact, or by any other means whatever, than his own affirmation of the fact. The truth (as might be supposed to be the case from such sort of evidence) is diametrically opposite. Nothing could be more exemplary, during the whole of the rebellion, than the conduct of the civil servants; and though the courts of justice were interfered with,—though the most respectable servants of the company were punished for the verdicts they had given as jurymen,—though many were dismissed for the slightest opposition to the pleasure of government, even in the discharge of official duties, where remonstrance was absolutely necessary,—though the greatest provocation was given, and the greatest opportunity afforded to the civil servants for revolt,—there is not a single instance in which the shadow of disaffection has been proved against any civil servant. This we say, from an accurate examination of all the papers which have been published on the subject; and we do not hesitate to affirm, that there never was a more unjust, unfounded, and profligate charge made against any body of men; nor have we often witnessed a more complete scene of folly and violence, than the conduct of the Madras government to its civil servants, exhibited during the whole period of the mutiny.

Upon the whole, it appears to us, that the Indian army was ultimately driven into revolt by the indiscretion and violence of the Madras government; and that every evil which has happened might, with the greatest possible facility, have been avoided.

We have no sort of doubt that the governor always meant well; but, we are equally certain that he almost always acted ill; and where incapacity rises to a certain height, for all practical purposes the motive is of very little consequence. That the late Gen. Macdowall was a weak man, is unquestionable. He was also irritated (and not without reason), because he was deprived of a seat in council, which the commanders before him had commonly enjoyed. A little attention, however, on the part of the government—the compliment of consulting him upon subjects connected with his profession—any of those little arts which are taught, not by a consummate political skill, but dictated by common good nature, and by the habit of mingling with the world, would have produced the effects of conciliation, and employed the force of General Macdowall's authority in bringing the army into a better temper of mind. Instead of this, it appears to have been almost the object, and if not the object, certainly the practice of the Madras government, to neglect and insult this officer. Changes of the greatest importance were made without his advice, and even without any communication with him; and it was too visible to those whom he was to command, that he himself possessed no sort of credit with his superiors. As to the tour which General Macdowall is supposed to have made for the purpose of spreading disaffection among the troops, and the part which he is represented by the agents to have taken in the quarrels of the civilians with the government, we utterly discredit these imputations. They are unsupported by any kind of evidence; and we believe them to be mere inventions, circulated by the friends of the Madras government. General Macdowall appears to us to have been a weak, pompous man; extremely out of humour; offended with the slights he had experienced; and whom any man of common address might have managed with the greatest ease: but we do not see, in any part of his conduct, the shadow of disloyalty and disaffection; and we are persuaded that the assertion would never have been made, if he himself had been alive to prove its injustice.

Besides the contemptuous treatment of Gen. Macdowall, we have great doubts whether the Madras government ought not to have suffered Colonel Munro to be put upon his trial; and to punish the officers who solicited that trial for the purgation of their own characters, appears to us (whatever the intention was) to have been an act of mere tyranny. We think, too, that General Macdowall was very hastily and unadvisedly removed from his situation, and upon the unjust treatment of Colonel Capper and Major Boles there can scarcely be two opinions. In the progress of the mutiny, instead of discovering in the Madras government any appearances of temper and wisdom, they appear to us to have been quite as much irritated and heated as the army, and to have been betrayed into excesses nearly as criminal, and infinitely more contemptible and puerile. The head of a great kingdom bickering with his officers about invitations to dinner—the commander-in-chief of the forces negotiating that the dinner should be loyally eaten—the obstinate absurdity of the test—the total want of selection in the objects of punishment—and the wickedness, or the insanity, of teaching the Sepoy to rise against his European officer—the contempt of the decision of juries in civil cases—and the punishment of the juries themselves; such a system of conduct as this would infallibly doom any individual to punishment, if it did not, fortunately for him, display precisely that contempt of men's feelings, and that passion for insulting multitudes, which is so congenial to our present government at home, and which passes now so currently for wisdom and courage. By these means, the liberties of great nations are frequently destroyed—and destroyed with impunity to the perpetrators of the crime. In distant colonies, however, governors who attempt the same system of tyranny are in no little danger from the indignation of their subjects; for though men will often yield up their happiness to kings who have been always kings, they are not inclined to show the same deference to men who have been merchants' clerks yesterday, and are kings to-day. From a danger of this kind, the governor of Madras appears to us to have very narrowly escaped. We sincerely hope that he is grateful for his good luck; and that he will now awake from his gorgeous dreams of mercantile monarchy, to good nature, moderation, and common sense.

BISHOP OF LINCOLN'S* CHARGE.†

[Edinburgh Review, 1813.]

It is a melancholy thing to see a man, clothed in soft raiment, lodged in a public palace, endowed with a rich portion of the product of other men's industry, using all the influence of his splendid situation, however conscientiously, to deepen the ignorance, and inflame the fury, of his fellow-creatures. These are the miserable results of that policy which has been so frequently pursued for these fifty years past, of placing men of mean, or middling abilities, in high ecclesiastical stations. In ordinary times, it is of less importance who fills them; but when the bitter period arrives, in which the people must give up some of their darling absurdities;—when the senseless clamour, which has been carefully handed down from father fool to son fool, can be no longer indulged;—when it is of incalculable importance to turn the people to a better way of thinking; the greatest impediments to all amelioration are too often found among those to whose councils, at such periods, the country ought to look for wisdom and peace. We will suppress, however, the feelings of indignation which such productions, from such men, naturally occasion. We will give the Bishop of Lincoln credit for being perfectly sincere;—we will suppose, that every argument he uses has not been used and refuted ten thousand times before; and we will sit down as patiently to defend the religious liberties of mankind, as the reverend prelate has done to abridge them.

We must begin with denying the main position upon which the Bishop of Lincoln has built his reasoning—*The Catholic religion is not tolerated in England.* No man can be fairly said to be permitted to enjoy his own worship who is punished for exercising that worship. His lordship seems to have no other idea of punishment, than lodging a man in the *Poultry compter*, or flogging him at the cart's tail, or fining him a sum of money;—just as if incapacitating a man from enjoying the dignities and emoluments to which men of similar condition, and other faith, may fairly aspire, was not frequently the most severe and galling of all punishments. This limited idea of the nature of punishments is the more extraordinary, as *incapacitation* is actually one of the most common punishments in some branches of our law. The sentence of a court-martial frequently purports, that a man is rendered for ever *incapable* of serving his majesty, &c. &c.; and a person not in holy orders, who performs the functions of a clergyman, is rendered for ever *incapable* of holding any preferment in the church. There are, indeed, many species of offence for which no punishment more apposite and judicious could be devised. It would be rather extraordinary, however, if the court, in passing such a sentence, were to assure the culprit, "that such incapacitation was not by them considered as a punishment; that it was only exercising a right inherent in all governments, of determining who should be eligible for office and who ineligible." His lordship thinks the toleration complete, because he sees a permission in the statutes for the exercise of the Roman Catholic worship. He sees the permission—but he does not choose to see the consequences to which they are exposed who avail themselves of this permission. It is the liberality of a father who says to a son, "Do as you please, my dear boy; follow your own inclination. Judge for yourself; you are free as air. But remember, if you marry that lady, I will cut you off with a shilling." We have scarcely ever read a more solemn and frivolous statement than the Bishop of Lincoln's antithetical distinction between persecution and the denial of political power.

"It is sometimes said, that Papists, being excluded from power, are consequently persecuted; as if exclusion from power and religious persecution were convertible terms. But surely this is to confound things totally distinct in their nature. Persecution inflicts positive punishment upon persons who hold certain religious tenets, and endeavours to accomplish the renunciation and extinction of those tenets by forcible means: exclusion from power is entirely negative in its operation—it only de-

---

* *A Charge delivered to the Clergy of the Diocese of Lincoln, at the Triennial Visitation of that Diocese in May, June, and July,* 1812. By George Tomline, D.D., F.R.S., Lord Bishop of Lincoln. London. Cadell and Co. 4to.

† It is impossible to conceive the mischief which this mean and cunning prelate did at this period.

clares that those who hold certain opinions shall not fill certain situations; but it acknowledges men to be perfectly free to hold those opinions. Persecution compels men to adopt a prescribed faith, or to suffer the loss of liberty, property, or even life: exclusion from power prescribes no faith; it allows men to think and believe as they please, without molestation or interference. Persecution requires men to worship God in one and in no other way: exclusion from power neither commands nor forbids any mode of divine worship—it leaves the business of religion, where it ought to be left, to every man's judgment and conscience. Persecution proceeds from a bigoted and sanguinary spirit of intolerance; exclusion from power is founded in the natural and rational principle of self-protection and self-preservation, equally applicable to nations and to individuals. History informs us of the mischievous and fatal effects of the one, and proves the expediency and necessity of the other."—(pp. 16, 17.)

We will venture to say, there is no one sentence in this extract which does not contain either a contradiction, or a misstatement. For how can that law acknowledge men to be perfectly free to hold an opinion, which excludes from desirable situations all who do hold that opinion? How can that law be said neither to molest, nor interfere, which meets a man in every branch of industry and occupation, to institute an inquisition into his religious opinions? And how is the business of religion left to every man's judgment and conscience, where so powerful a *bonus* is given to one set of religious opinions, and such a mark of infamy and degradation fixed upon all other modes of belief? But this is comparatively a very idle part of the question. Whether the present condition of the Catholics is or is not to be denominated a perfect state of toleration, is more a controversy of words than things. That they are subject to some restraints, the bishop will admit: the important question is, whether or not these restraints are necessary? For his lordship will, of course, allow, that every restraint upon human liberty is an evil in itself; and can only be justified by the superior good which it can be shown to produce. My lord's fears upon the subject of Catholic emancipation are conveyed in the following paragraph:—

"It is a principle of our constitution, that the king should have advisers in the discharge of every part of his royal functions—and is it to be imagined that Papists would advise measures in support of the cause of Protestantism? A similar observation may be applied to the two Houses of Parliament: would popish peers or popish members of the House of Commons, enact laws for the security of the Protestant government? Would they not rather repeal the whole Protestant code, and make Popery again the established religion of the country?"—(p. 14.)

And these are the apprehensions which the clergy of the diocese have prayed my lord to make public.

Kind Providence never sends an evil without a remedy:—and arithmetic is the natural cure for the passion of fear. If a coward can be made to count his enemies, his terrors may be reasoned with, and he may think of ways and means of counteraction. Now, might it not have been expedient that the reverend prelate, before he had alarmed his country clergy with the idea of so large a measure as the repeal of Protestantism, should have counted up the probable number of Catholics who would be seated in both houses of Parliament? Does he believe that there would be ten Catholic peers, and thirty Catholic commoners? But, admit double that number (and more, Dr. Duigenan himself would not ask),—will the Bishop of Lincoln seriously assert, that he thinks the whole Protestant code in danger of repeal from such an admixture of Catholic legislators as this? Does he forget, amid the innumerable answers which may be made to such sort of apprehensions, what a picture he is drawing of the weakness and versatility of Protestant principles?—that an handful of Catholics, in the bosom of a Protestant legislature, is to overpower the ancient jealousies, the fixed opinions, the inveterate habits of twelve millions of people?—that the king is to apostatize, the clergy to be silent, and the Parliament be taken by surprise?—that the nation is to go to bed over night, and to see the Pope walking arm in arm with Lord Castlereagh the next morning?—One would really suppose, from the bishop's fears, that the civil defences of mankind were, like their military bulwarks transferred, by superior skill and courage, in a few hours, from the vanquished to the victor—that the destruction of a church was like the blowing up of a mine,—deans, prebendaries, churchwardens and overseers, all up in the air in an instant. Does his lordship really imagine, when the mere dread of the Catholics becoming legislators has induced him to charge his clergy, and his agonized clergy, to extort from their prelate the publication of the charge, that the full and mature danger will produce less alarm than the distant suspicion of it has done in the present instance?—that the Protestant writers, whose pens are now up to the feather in ink, will, at any future period, yield up their church, without passion, pamphlet, or pugnacity? We do not blame the Bishop of Lincoln for being afraid; but we blame him for not rendering his fears intelligible and tangible—for not circumscribing and particularizing them by some individual case—for not showing us how it is possible that the Catholics (granting their intentions to be as bad as possible) should ever be able to ruin the Church of England. His lordship appears to be in a fog; and, as daylight breaks in upon him, he will be rather disposed to disown his panic. The noise he hears is not roaring,—but braying; the teeth and the mane are all imaginary; there is nothing but ears. It is not a lion that stops the way, but an ass.

One method his lordship takes, in handling this question, is by pointing out dangers that are *barely possible*, and then treating of them as if they deserved the active and present attention of serious men. But if no measure is to be carried into execution, and if no provision is safe in which the minute inspection of an ingenious man cannot find the *possibility* of danger, then all human action is impeded, and no human institution is safe or commendable. The king has the power of pardoning,—and so every species of gulit may remain unpunished: he has a negative upon legislative acts, and so no law may pass. None but Presbyterians may be returned to the House of Commons,—and so the Church of England may be voted down. The Scottish and Irish members may join together in both houses, and dissolve both unions. If probability is put out of sight,—and if, in the enumeration of dangers, it is sufficient to state any which, by remote contingency, *may* happen, then is it time that we should begin to provide against all the host of perils which we have just enumerated, and which are many of them as likely to happen, as those which the reverend prelate has stated in his charge. His lordship forgets that the Catholics are not asking for election but for *eligibility*—not to be admitted into the cabinet, but not to be excluded from it. A century may elapse before any Catholic actually becomes a member of the cabinet; and no event can be more utterly destitute of probability, than that they should gain an ascendency there, and direct that ascendency against the Protestant interest. If the bishop really wishes to know upon what our security is founded; it is *upon the prodigious and decided superiority of the Protestant interest in the British nation, and in the United Parliament.* No Protestant king would select such a cabinet, or countenance such measures; no man would be mad enough to attempt them; the English Parliament and the English people would not endure it for a moment. No man, indeed, but under the sanctity of the mitre, would have ventured such an extravagant opinion.—Wo to him, if he had been *only* a dean. But, in spite of his venerable office, we must express our decided belief, that his lordship (by no means averse to a good bargain) would not pay down five pounds, to receive fifty millions for his posterity, whenever the majority of the cabinet should be (Catholic emancipation carried) members of the Catholic religion. And yet, upon such terrors as these, which, when put singly to him, his better senses would laugh at, he has thought fit to excite his clergy to petition, and done all in his power to increase the mass of hatred against the Catholics.

It is true enough, as his lordship remarks, that events do not depend upon laws alone, but upon the wishes and intentions of those who administer these laws. But then his lordship totally puts out of sight two considerations—the improbability of Catholics ever reaching the highest offices of the state—and those fixed Protestant opinions of the country, which would render any attack upon the established church so hopeless, and therefore, so improbable. Admit a supposition (to us perfectly ludicrous, but still necessary to the bishop's argument), that the cabinet council consisted entirely of Catholics, we should even then have no more fear of their making the English people Catholics, than we should have of a cabinet of butchers making the Hindoos eat beef. The bishop has not stated the true and great security for any course of human actions. It is not the word of the law, nor the spirit of the government, but the general way of thinking among the people, especially when that way of thinking is ancient, exercised upon high interests, and connected with striking passages in history. The Protestant church does not rest upon the little narrow foundations where the Bishop of Lincoln supposes it to be placed: if it did, it would not be worth saving. It rests upon the general opinion entertained by a free and reflecting people, that the doctrines of the church are true, her pretensions moderate, and her exhortations useful. It is accepted by a people who have, from good taste, an abhorrence of sacerdotal mummery; and from good sense, a dread of sacerdotal ambition. Those feelings, so generally diffused, and so clearly pronounced on all occasions, are our real bulwarks against the Catholic religion, and the real cause which makes it so safe for the best friends of the church to diminish (by abolishing the test laws) so very fertile a source of hatred to the state.

In the 15th page of his lordship's charge, there is an argument of a very curious nature.

"Let us suppose," (says the Bishop of Lincoln), "that there had been no test laws, no disabling statutes, in the year 1745, when an attempt was made to overthrow the Protestant government, and to place a popish sovereign upon the throne of these kingdoms; and let us suppose, that the leading men in the houses of Parliament, that the ministers of state, and the commanders of our armies, had then been Papists. Will any one contend, that that formidable rebellion, supported as it was by a foreign enemy, would have been resisted with the same zeal, and suppressed with the same facility, as when all the measures were planned and executed by sincere Protestants?" (p. 15.)

And so his lordship means to infer, that it would be foolish to abolish the laws against the Catholics *now*, because it would have been foolish to have abolished them at some other period;—that a measure must be bad, because there was formerly a combination of circumstances, when it *would* have been bad. His lordship might, with almost equal propriety, debate what ought to be done if Julius Cæsar were about to make a descent upon our coasts; or lament the impropriety of emancipating the Catholics, because the Spanish Armada was putting to sea. The fact is that Julius Cæsar is dead—the Spanish Armada was defeated in the reign of Queen Elizabeth—for half a century there has been no disputed succession—the situation of the world is changed—and, because it is changed, we can do now what we could not do then. And nothing can be more lamentable than to see this respectable prelate wasting his resources in putting imaginary and inapplicable cases, and reasoning upon their solution, as if they had any thing to do with present affairs.

These remarks entirely put an end to the common mode of arguing *à Gulielmo.* What did King William do?—what would King William say? &c. King William was in a very different situation from that in which we are placed. The whole world was in a very different situation. The great and glorious authors of the Revolution (as they are commonly denominated) acquired their greatness and their glory, not by a superstitious reverence for inapplicable precedents, but by taking hold of present circumstances to lay a deep foundation for liberty; and then using old names for new things, they left the Bishop of Lincoln, and other good men, to suppose that they had been thinking all the time about ancestors.

Another species of false reasoning, which pervades the Bishop of Lincoln's charge, is this: He states what the interests of men are, and then takes it for granted that they will eagerly and actively pursue them; laying totally out of the question the probability or improbability of their effecting their object, and the influence which this balance of chances must produce upon their actions. For instance, it is the interest of the Catholics that our church should be subservient to theirs. Therefore, says his lordship, the Catholics will enter into a conspiracy against the English church. But, is it not also the decided interest of his lordship's butler that he should be bishop, and the bishop his butler? That the crozier and the corkscrew should change hands,—and the washer of the bottles which they had emptied become the diocesan of learned divines? What has prevented this change, so beneficial to the upper domestic, but the extreme improbability of success, if the attempt were made; an improbability so great that we will venture to say, the very notion of it has scarcely once entered into the understanding of the good man. Why, then, is the reverend prelate, who lives on so safely and contentedly with *John*, so dreadfully alarmed at the Catholics? And why does he so completely forget, in their instance alone, that men do not merely strive to obtain a thing because it is good, but always mingle with the excellence of the object a consideration of the chance of gaining it?

The Bishop of Lincoln (p. 19) states it as an argument against concession to the Catholics, that we have enjoyed "internal peace and entire freedom from all religious animosities and feuds since the Revolution." The fact, however, is not more certain than conclusive against his view of the question. For, since that period, the worship of the church of England has been abolished in Scotland—the corporation and test acts repealed in Ireland—and the whole of this king's reign has been one series of concessions to the Catholics. Relaxation, then (and we wish this had been remembered at the charge), of penal laws, on subjects of religious opinion, is perfectly compatible with *internal peace* and exemption from religious animosity. But the bishop is always fond of lurking in generals, and cautiously avoids coming to any specific instance of the dangers which he fears.

"It is declared in one of the 39 Articles, that the king is head of our church, without being subject to any foreign power; and it is expressly said that the Bishop of Rome has no jurisdiction within these realms. On the contrary, Papists assert, that the pope is supreme head of the whole Christian church, and that allegiance is due to him from every individual member, in all spiritual matters. This direct opposition to one of the fundamental principles of the ecclesiastical part of our constitution, is alone sufficient to justify the exclusion of Papists from all situations of authority. They acknowledge, indeed, that obedience in civil matters is due to the king. But cases must arise, in which civil and religious duties will clash; and he knows but little of the influence of the Popish religion over the mind of its votaries, who doubts which of these duties would be sacrificed to the other. Moreover, the most subtle casuistry cannot always discriminate between temporal and spiritual things; and in truth, the concerns of this life not unfrequently partake of both characters."—(pp. 21, 22.)

We deny entirely that any case can occur, where the exposition of a doctrine purely speculative, or the arrangement of a mere point of church discipline, can interfere with civil duties. The Roman Catholics are Irish and English citizens at this moment; but no such case has occurred. There is no instance in which obedience to the civil magistrate has been prevented, by an acknowledgment of the spiritual supremacy of the pope. The Catholics have given (in an oath which we suspect the bishop never to have read) the most solemn pledge, that their submission to their spiritual ruler should never interfere with their civil obedience. The hypothesis of the Bishop of Lincoln is, that it must very often do so. The fact is, that it has never done so.

His lordship is extremely angry with the Catholics for refusing to the crown a *veto* upon the appointment of their bishops. He forgets, that in those countries of Europe where the crown interferes with the appointment of bishops, the reigning monarch is a Catholic,—which makes all the difference. We sincerely wish that the Catholics would concede this point; but we cannot be astonished at their reluctance to admit the interference of a Protestant prince with their bishops. What would his lordship say to the interference of any Catholic power with the appointment of the English sees?

Next comes the stale and thousand times refuted charge against the Catholics, that they think the pope has the power of dethroning heretical kings; and that it is the duty of every Catholic to use every possible means to root out and destroy heretics, &c. To all of which may be returned this one conclusive answer, that the Catholics are ready to deny these doctrines upon oath. And as the whole controversy is, whether the Catholic shall, by means of oaths, be excluded from certain offices in the state;—those who contend that the continuation of these excluding oaths is essential to the public safety, must admit, that oaths are binding upon Catholics, and a security to the state that what they swear to is true.

It is right to keep these things in view—and

to omit no opportunity of exposing and counteracting that spirit of intolerant zeal or intolerable time-serving, which has so long disgraced and endangered this country. But the truth is, that we look upon this cause as already gained;—and while we warmly congratulate the nation on the mighty step it has recently made towards increased power and entire security, it is impossible to avoid saying a word upon the humiliating and disgusting, but at the same time most edifying spectacle, which has lately been exhibited by the anti-Catholic addressers. That so great a number of persons should have been found with such a proclivity to servitude (for honest bigotry had but little to do with the matter), as to rush forward with clamours in favour of intolerance, upon a mere surmise that this would be accounted as acceptable service by the present possessors of patronage and power, affords a more humiliating and discouraging picture of the present spirit of the country, than any thing else that has occurred in our remembrance. The edifying part of the spectacle is the contempt with which their officious devotions have been received by those whose favour they were intended to purchase,—and the universal scorn and derision with which they were regarded by independent men of all parties and persuasions. The catastrophe, we think, teaches two lessons;—one to the time-servers themselves, not to obtrude their servility on the government, till they have reasonable ground to think it is wanted;—and the other to the nation at large, not to imagine that a base and interested clamour in favour of what is supposed to be agreeable to government, however loudly and extensively sounded, affords any indication at all, either of the general sense of the country, or even of what is actually contemplated by those in the administration of its affairs. The real sense of the country has been proved, on this occasion, to be directly against those who presumptuously held themselves out as its organs;—and even the ministers have made a respectable figure, compared with those who assumed the character of their champions.

MADAME D'EPINAY.*

[Edinburgh Review, 1818.]

There used to be in Paris, under the ancient regime, a few women of brilliant talents, who violated all the common duties of life, and gave very pleasant little suppers. Among these supped and sinned Madame d'Epinay—the friend and companion of Rousseau, Diderot, Grimm, Holbach, and many other literary persons of distinction of that period. Her principal lover was Grimm; with whom was deposited, written in feigned names, the history of her life. Grimm died—his secretary sold the history—the feigned names have been exchanged for the real ones—and her works now appear abridged in three volumes octavo.

Madame d'Epinay, though far from an immaculate character, has something to say in palliation of her irregularities. Her husband behaved abominably; and alienated, by a series of the most brutal injuries, an attachment which seems to have been very ardent and sincere, and which, with better treatment, would probably have been lasting. For, in all her aberrations, Mad. d'Epinay seems to have had a tendency to be constant. Though extremely young when separated from her husband, she indulged herself with but two lovers for the rest of her life;—to the first of whom she seems to have been perfectly faithful, till he left her at the end of ten or twelve years;—and to Grimm, by whom he was succeeded, she appears to have given no rival till the day of her death. The account of the life she led, both with her husband and her lovers, brings upon the scene a great variety of French characters, and lays open very completely the interior of French life and manners. But there are some letters and passages which ought not to have been published; which a sense of common decency and morality ought to have suppressed; and which, we feel assured, would never have seen the light in this country.

A French woman seems almost always to have wanted the flavour of prohibition, as a necessary condiment to human life. The provided husband was rejected, and the forbidden husband introduced in ambiguous light, through posterns and secret partitions. It was not the union to one man that was objected to—for they dedicated themselves with a constancy which the most household and parturient woman in England could not exceed;—but the thing wanted was the wrong man, the gentleman without the ring—the master unsworn to at the altar—the person unconsecrated by priests—

"Oh! let me taste thee unexcised by kings."

The following strikes us as a very lively picture of the ruin and extravagance of a fashionable house in a great metropolis.

"M. d'Epinay a complété son domestique. Il a trois laquais, et moi deux; je n'en ai pas voulu davantage. Il a un valet de chambre; et il vouloit aussi que je prisse une seconde femme, mais comme je n'en ai que faire, j'ai tenu bon. Enfin les officiers, les femmes, les valets se montent au nombre de seize. Quoique la vie que je mène soit assez uniforme, j'espère

* *Mémoires et Correspondence de Madame d'Epinay.* 3 vols. 8vo. Paris, 1818.

n'être pas obligée d'en changer. Celle de M. d'Epinay est différente. Lorsqu'il est levé, son valet de chambre se met en devoir de l'accommoder. Deux laquais sont debout à attendre ordres. Le premier secrétaire vient avec l'intention de lui rendre compte des lettres qu'il a reçues de son département, et qu'il est chargé d'ouvrir; il doit lire les réponses et les faire signer; mais il est interrompu deux cents fois dans cette occupation par toutes sortes d'espèces imaginables. C'est un maquignon qui a des chevaux uniques à vendre, mais qui sont retenus par un seigneur; ainsi il est venu pour ne pas manquer à sa parole; car on lui en donneroit le double, qu'on ne pourroit faire affaire. Il en fait une description séduisante, on demande le prix. Le seigneur un tel en offre soixante louis.—Je vous en donne cent.—Cela est inutile, à moins qu'il ne se dédise. Cependant l'on conclut à cent louis sans les avoir vus, car le lendemain le seigneur ne manque pas de se dédire: voilà ce que j'ai vu et entendu la semaine dernière.

"Ensuite c'est un polisson qui vient brailler un air, et à qui on accorde sa protection pour le faire entrer à l'Opéra, après lui avoir donné quelques leçons de bon goût, et lui avoir appris ce que c'est que la propreté du chant françois; c'est une demoiselle qu'on fait attendre pour savoir si je suis encore là. Je me lève et je m'en vais; les deux laquais ouvrent les deux battans pour me laisser sortir, moi qui passerois alors par le trou d'une aiguille; et les deux estafiers crient dans l'anti-chambre: Madame, messieurs, voilà madame. Tout le monde se range en haie, et ces messieurs sont des marchands d'étoffes, des marchands d'instrumens, des bijoutiers, des colporteurs, des laquais, des décroteurs, des créanciers; enfin tout ce que vous pouvez imaginer de plus ridicule et de plus affligeant. Midi ou une heure sonne avant que cette toilette soit achevée, et le secrétaire, qui, sans doute, sait par expérience l'impossibilité de rendre un compte détaillé des affaires, a un petit bordereau qu'il remet entre les mains de son maître pour l'instruire de ce qu'il doit dire à l'assemblée. Une autre fois il sort à pied ou en fiacre, rentre à deux heures, fait comme un brûleur de maison, dîne tête à tête avec moi, ou admet en tiers son premier secrétaire qui lui parle de la nécessité de fixer chaque article de dépense, de donner des délégations pour tel ou tel objet. La seule réponse est: Nous verrons cela. Ensuite il court le monde et les spectacles; et il soupe en ville quand il n'a personne à souper chez lui. Je vois que mon temps de repos est fini."—I. pp. 308—310.

A very prominent person among the early friends of Madame d'Epinay is Mademoiselle d'Ette, a woman of great French respectability, and circulating in the best society; and, as we are painting French manners, we shall make no apology to the serious part of our English readers, for inserting this sketch of her history and character by her own hand.

'Je connois, me dit-elle ensuite, votre franchise et votre discrétion: dites-moi naturellement quelle opinion on a de moi dans le monde. La meilleure, lui dis-je, et telle que vous ne pourriez la conserver si vous pratiquiez la morale que vous venez de me prêcher. Voilà où je vous attendois, me dit-elle. Depuis dix ans que j'ai perdu ma mère, je fus séduite par le chevalier de Valory qui m'avoit vu, pour ainsi dire, elever; mon extrême jeunesse et la confiance que j'avois en lui ne me permirent pas d'abord de me défier de ses veus. Je fus longtemps à m'en apercevoir, et lorsque je m'en aperçus, j'avois pris tant de goût pour lui, que je n'eus pas la force de lui résister. Il me vint des scrupules; il les leva, en me promettant de m'épouser. Il y travailla en effet; mais voyant l'opposition que sa famille y apportoit, à cause de la disproportion d'âge et de mon peu de fortune; et me trouvant, d'ailleurs, heureuse comme j'étois, je fus la première à étouffer mes scrupules, d'autant plus qu'il est assez pauvre. Il commençoit à faire des réflexions, je lui proposai de continuer à vivre comme nous étions; il l'accepta. Je quittai ma province, et je le suivis à Paris; vous voyez comme j'y vis. Quatre fois la semaine il passe sa journée chez moi; le reste du temps nous nous contentons réciproquement d'apprendre de nos nouvelles, à moins que le hasard ne nous fasse rencontrer. Nous vivons heureux, contens; peut-être ne le serions nous pas tant si nous étions mariés."—I. pp. 111, 112.

This seems a very spirited, unincumbered way of passing through life; and it is some comfort, therefore, to a matrimonial English reader, to find Mademoiselle d'Ette kicking the chevalier out of doors towards the end of the second volume. As it is a scene very edifying to rakes, and those who decry the happiness of the married state, we shall give it in the words of Madame d'Epinay.

"Une nuit, dont elle avoit passé la plus grande partie dans l'inquiétude, elle entre chez le chevalier: il dormoit; elle le réveille, s'assied sur son lit, et entame une explication avec toute la violence et la fureur qui l'animoient. Le chevalier, après avoir employé vainement, pour le calmer, tous les moyens que sa bonté naturelle lui suggéra, lui signifia enfin très-précisément qu'il alloit se séparer d'elle pour toujours, et fuir un enfer auquel il ne pouvoit plus tenir. Cette confidence, qui n'étoit pas faite pour l'appaiser, redoubla sa rage. Puis-qu'il est ainsi, dit-elle, sortez tout à l'heure de chez moi; vous deviez partir dans quatre jours, c'est vous rendre service de vous faire partir dans l'instant. Tout ce qui est ici m'appartient; le bail est en mon nom: il ne me convient plus de vous souffrir chez moi: levez-vous, monsieur, et songez à ne rien emporter sans ma permission."—II. pp. 193, 194.

Our English method of asking leave to separate from Sir William Scott and Sir John Nicol is surely better than this.

Any one who provides good dinners for clever people, and remembers what they say, cannot fail to write entertaining Mémoires. Among the early friends of Madame d'Epinay was Jean Jacques Rousseau,—she lived with him in considerable intimacy; and no small part of her book is taken up with accounts of his eccentricity, insanity, and vice.

"Nous avons débuté par *l'Engagement téméraire*, comédie nouvelle, de M. Rousseau, ami de Francueil qui nous l'a présenté. L'auteur a joué un rôle dans sa pièce. Quoique ce ne soit qu'une comédie de société, elle a eu un grand succès. Je doute cependant qu'elle pût réussir au théâtre; mais c'est l'ouvrage d'un homme de beaucoup d'esprit, et peut-être d'un homme singulier. Je ne sais pas trop cependant si c'est ce que j'ai vu de l'auteur ou de la pièce qui me fait juger ainsi. Il est complimenteur sans être poli, ou au moins sans en avoir l'air. Il paroît ignorer les usages du monde; mais il est aisé de voir qu'il a infiniment d'esprit. Il a le teint brun: et des yeux pleins de feu animent sa physionomie. Lorsqu'il a parlé et qu'on le regarde, il paroît joli; mais lorsqu'on se le rappelle, c'est toujours en laid. On dit qu'il est d'une mauvaise santé, et qu'il a des souffrances qu'il cache avec soin, par je ne sais quel principe de vanité; c'est apparemment ce qui lui donne, de temps en temps, l'air farouche. M. de Bellegarde, avec qui il a causé long-temps, ce matin, en est enchanté, et l'a engagé à nous venir voir souvent. J'en suis bien aise; je me promets de profiter beaucoup de sa conversation."—I. pp. 175, 176.

Their friendship so formed, proceeded to a great degree of intimacy. Madame d'Epinay admired his genius, and provided him with hats and coats; and, at last, was so far deluded by his declamations about the country, as to fit him up a little hermit cottage, where there were a great many birds, and a great many plants and flowers—and where Rousseau was, as might have been expected, supremely miserable. His friends from Paris did not come to see him. The postman, the butcher, and the baker, hate romantic scenery; duchesses and marchionesses were no longer found to scramble for him. Among the real inhabitants of the country, the reputation of reading and thinking is fatal to character; and Jean Jacques cursed his own successful eloquence which had sent him from the suppers and flattery of Paris to smell to daffodils, watch sparrows, or project idle saliva into the passing stream. Very few men who have gratified, and are gratifying their vanity in a great metropolis, are qualified to quit it. Few have the plain sense to perceive that they must soon inevitably be forgotten,—or the fortitude to bear it when they are. They represent to themselves imaginary scenes of deploring friends and dispirited companies,—but the ocean might as well regret the drops exhaled by the sunbeams. Life goes on; and whether the absent have retired into a cottage or a grave, is much the same thing.—In London, as in law, *de non apparentibus, et non existentibus eadem est ratio.*

This is the account Madame d'Epinay gives of Rousseau soon after he had retired into the hermitage.

"J'ai été il y a deux jours à la Chevrette, pour terminer quelques affaires avant de m'y établir avec mes enfans. J'avois fait prévenir Rousseau de mon voyage: il est venu me voir. Je crois qu'il a besoin de ma présence, et que la solitude a déjà agité sa bile. Il se plaint de tout le monde. Diderot doit toujours aller, et ne va jamais le voir; M. Grimm le néglige; le Baron d'Holbach l'oublie; Gauffecourt et moi seulement avons encore des égards pour lui, dit-il; j'ai voulu les justifier; cela n'a pas réussi. J'espère qu'il sera beaucoup plus à la Chevrette qu'à l'Hermitage. Je suis persuadée qu'il n'y a que façon de prendre cet homme pour le rendre heureux; c'est de feindre de ne pas prendre garde à lui, et s'en occuper sans cesse; c'est pour cela que je n'insistai point pour le retenir, lorsqu'il m'eut dit qu'il vouloit s'en retourner à l'Hermitage, quoiqu'il fût tard et malgré le mauvais temps."—II. pp. 253, 254.

Jean Jacques Rousseau seems, as the reward of genius and fine writing, to have claimed an exemption from all moral duties. He borrowed and begged, and never paid;—put his children in a poor-house—betrayed his friends—insulted his benefactors—and was guilty of every species of meanness and mischief. His vanity was so great, that it was almost impossible to keep pace with it by any activity of attention; and his suspicion of all mankind amounted nearly, if not altogether, to insanity. The following anecdote, however, is totally clear of any symptom of derangement, and carries only the most rooted and disgusting selfishness.

"Rousseau vous a donc dit qu'il n'avoit pas porté son ouvrage à Paris? Il en a menti, car il n'a fait son voyage que pour cela. J'ai reçu hier une lettre de Diderot, qui peint votre hermite comme si je le voyois. Il a fait ces deux lieues à pied, est venu s'établir chez Diderot sans l'avoir prévenu, le tout pour faire avec lui la revision de son ouvrage. Au point où ils en étoient ensemble, vous conviendrez que cela est assez étrange. Je vois, par certains mots échappés à mon ami dans sa lettre, qu'il y a quelque sujet de discussion entre eux; mais comme il ne s'explique point, je n'y comprends rien. Rousseau l'a tenu impitoyablement à l'ouvrage depuis le Samedi dix heures du matin jusqu'au Lundi onze heures du soir, sans lui donner à peine le temps de boire ni manger. La revision finie, Diderot cause avec lui d'un plan qu'il a dans la tête, et prie Rousseau de l'aider à arranger un incident qui n'est pas encore trouvé à sa fantaisie. Cela est trop difficile, répond froidement l'hermite, il est tard, je ne suis point accoutumé à veiller. Bon soir, je pars demain à six heures du matin, il est temps de dormir. Il se lève, va se coucher, et laisse Diderot pétrifié de son procédé. Voilà cet homme que vous croyez si pénétré de vos leçons. Ajoutez à cette reflexion un propos singulier de la femme de Diderot, dont je vous prie de faire votre profit. Cette femme n'est qu'une bonne femme, mais elle a la tact juste. Voyant son mari désolé le jour du départ de Rousseau, elle lui en demande la raison; il la lui dit: C'est le manque de délicatesse de cet homme, ajoute-t-il, qui m'afflige; il me fait travailler comme un manœuvre, je ne m'en serois, je crois, pas aperçu, s'il ne m'avoit refusé aussi sèchement de s'occuper pour moi un quart-d'heure . . . Vous êtes étonné de cela, lui répond sa femme, vous ne le connoissez donc pas? Il est dévors d'envie; il enrage quand il paroit quelque chose de beau qui n'est pas de lui. On lui verra faire un jour quelques grands forfaits plutôt que de se laisser ignorer. Tenez, je ne jurerois pas qu'il ne se rangeât du parti des Jésuites, et qu'il n'enterprît leur apologie."—II. pp. 60, 61.

The horror which Diderot ultimately conceived for him, is strongly expressed in the following letter to Grimm,—written after an interview which compelled him, with many pangs, to renounce all intercourse with a man who had, for years, been the object of his tenderest and most partial feelings.

"Cet homme est un forcené. Je l'ai vu, je lui ai reproché, avec toute la force que donne l'honnêteté et une sorte d'intérêt qui reste au fond du cœur d'un ami qui lui est dévoué depuis long-temps, l'énormité de sa conduite; les pleurs versés aux pieds de Madame d'Epinay, dans le moment même oû il la chargeoit près de moi des accusations les plus graves; cette odieuse apologie qu'il vous a envoyee, et où il n'y pas une seule des raisons qu'il avoit à dire; cette lettre projectée pour Saint-Lambert, qui devoit le tranquilliser sur des sentimens qu'il se reprochoit, et où, loin d'avouer une passion née dans son cœur son malgré lui, il s'excuse d'avoir alarmé Madame d'Houdetot sur la sienne. Que sais-je encore? Je ne suis point content de ses résponses; je n'ai pas eu le courage de le lui témoigner j'ai mieux aimé lui laisser la misérable consolation de croire qu'il m'a trompé. Qu'il vive! Il a mis dans sa défense un emportement froid qui m'a affligé. J'ai peur qu'il ne soit endurci.

"Adieu, mon ami; soyons et continuons d'être honnêtes gens: l'état de ceux qui ont cessé à l'être me fait peur. Adieu, mon ami; je vous embrasse bien tendrement. . . . . Je ne jette dans vos bras comme un homme effrayé; je tâche en vain de faire de la poésie, mais cet homme me revient tout à travers mon travail; il me trouble, et je suis comme si j'avois à côté de moi un damné; il est damné, cela est sûr. Adieu, mon ami. . . . . Grimm, violà l'effet que je ferois sur vous, si je devenois jamais un méchant: en vérité, j'aimerois mieux être mort. Il n'y a peut-être pas le sens commun dans tout ce que je vous écris, mais je vous avoue que je n'ai jamais éprouvé un trouble d'ame si terrible que cela que j'ai.

"Oh! mon ami, quel spectacle que celui d'un homme méchant et bourrelé! Brûlez, déchirez ce papier, qu'il ne retombe plus sous vos yeux; que je ne revoie plus cet homme là, il me feroit croire aux diables et à l'enfer. Si je suis jamais forcé de retourner chez lui, je suis sûr que je frémirai tout le long du chemin: j'avois la fiévre en revenant. Je suis fâché de ne lui avoir pas laissé voir l'horreur qu'il m'inspiroit, et je ne me réconcilie avec moi qu'en pensant, que vous, avec toute votre fermeté, vous ne l'auriez pas pu à ma place; je ne sais pas s'il ne m'auroit pas tué. On entendoit ses cris jusqu'au bout du jardin; et je le voyois! Adieu, mon ami, j'irai demain vous voir; j'irai chercher un homme de bien, aupres duquel je m'asséye, qui me rassure, et qui chasse de mon ame je ne sais quoi d'infernal qui la tourmente et qui s'y est attaché. Les poëtes ont bien fait de mettre un intervalle immense entre le ciel et les enfers. En vérité, la main me tremble."—III. pp. 148, 149

Madame d'Epinay lived, as we before observed, with many persons of great celebrity. We could not help smiling, among many others, at this anecdote of our countryman, David Hume. At the beginning of his splendid career of fame and fashion at Paris, the historian was persuaded to appear in the character of a sultan; and was placed on a sofa between two of the most beautiful women of Paris, who acted for that evening the part of inexorables, whose favour he was supposed to be soliciting. The absurdity of this scene can easily be conceived.

"Le célèbre David Hume, grand et gros historiographe d'Angleterre, connu et estimé par ses écrits, n'a pas autant de talens pour ce genre d'amusemens auquel toutes nos jolies femmes l'avoient décidé propre. Il fit son début chez Madame de T* * *; on lui avoit destiné le rôle d'un sultan assis entre deux esclaves, employant toute son éloquence pour s'en faire aimer; les trouvant inexorables, il devoit chercher le sujet de leurs peines et de leur résistance: on le place sur un sopha entre les deux plus jolies femmes de Paris, il les regarde attentivement, il se frappe le ventre et les genoux à plusieurs reprises, et ne trouve jamais autre chose à leur dire que: *Eh bien! mes demoiselles . . . . Eh bien! vous voilà donc . . . . Eh bien! vous voilà . . . . vous voilà ici?* . . . . Cette phrase dura un quart-d'heure, sans qu'il pût en sortir. Une d'elles se leva d'impatience: Ah! dit-elle, je m'en étois bien doutée, cet homme n'est bon qu'à manger du veau! Dupuis ce temps il est relégué au rôle de spectateur, et n'en est pas moins fêté et cajolé. C'est en vérité une chose plaisante que le rôle qu'il joue ici; malheureusement pour lui, ou plutôt pour la dignité philosophique, car, pour lui, il paroît s'accommoder fort de ce train de vie; il n'y avoit aucune manie dominante dans ce pays lorsqu'il y est arrivé; on l'a regardé comme une trouvaille dans cette circonstance, et l'effervescence de nos jeunes têtes s'est tournée de son côté. Toutes les jolies femmes s'en sont emparées; il est de tous les soupers fins, et il n'est point de bonne fête sans lui: en un mot, il est pour nos agréables ce que les Genevois sont pour moi."—III. pp. 284, 285.

There is always some man, of whom the human viscera stand in greater dread than of any other person, who is supposed, for the time being, to be the only person who can dart his pill into their inmost recesses; and bind them over, in medical recognisance, to assimilate and digest. In the Trojan war, Podalirius and Machaon were what Dr. Baillie and Sir Henry Halford now are—they had the fashionable practice of the Greek camp; and, in all probability, received many a guinea from Agamemnon dear to Jove, and Nestor the tamer of horses. In the time of Madame d'Epinay, Dr. Tronchin, of Geneva, was in vogue, and no lady of fashion could recover without writing to him, or seeing him in person. To the Esculapius of this very small and irritable republic, Madame d'Epinay repaired; and, after a struggle between life and death, and Dr. Tronchin, recovered her health. During her residence at Geneva, she became acquainted with Voltaire, of whom she has left the following admirable and original account—the truth, talent, and simplicity of which, are not a little enhanced by the tone of adulation or abuse which has been so generally employed in speaking of this celebrated person.

"Eh bien! mon ami, je n'aimerois pas à vivre de suite avec lui; il n'a nul principe arrêté, il compte trop sur sa mémoire, et il en abuse souvent; je trouve qu'elle fait tort quelquefois à sa conversation; il redit plus qu'il ne dit, et ne laisse jamais rien à faire aux autres. Il ne sait point causer, et il humilie l'amour-propre; il dit le pour et le contre, tant qu'on veut, toujours avec de nouvelles graces à la vérité, et néanmoins il a toujours l'air de se moquer de tout, jusqu'à lui-même. Il n'a nulle philosophie dans la tête; il est tout hérissé de petits préjugés d'enfans; on les lui passeroit peut-être en faveur de ses graces, du brilliant de son esprit et de son originalité, s'il ne s'affichoit pas pour les secouer tous. Il a des inconséquences plaisantes, et il est au milieu de tout cela très-amusant à voir. Mais je n'aime point les gens qui ne font que m'amuser. Pour madame sa nièce, elle est tout-à-fait comique.

"Il paroît ici depuis quelques jours un livre qui a vivement échauffe les têtes, et qui cause des discussions fort intéressantes entre différentes personnes de ce pays, parce que l'on prétend que la constitution de leur gouvernement y est intéressée: Voltaire s'y trouve mêlé pour des propos assez vifs qu'il a tenu à ce sujet contre les prêtres. La grosse nièce trouve fort mauvais que tous les magistrats n'ayent pas pris fait et cause pour son oncle. Elle jette tour à tour ses grosses mains et ses petits bras par dessus sa tête, maudissant avec des cris inhumains les lois, les républiques, et surtout ces polissons de républicains qui vont à pied, qui sont obligés de souffrir les criailleries de leurs prêtres, et qui se croient libres. Cela est tout-à-fait bon à entendre et à voir." III. pp. 196, 197.

Madame D'Epinay was certainly a woman of very considerable talent. Rousseau accuses her of writing bad plays and romances. This may be; but her epistolary style is excellent—her remarks on passing events lively, acute, and solid—and her delineation of character admirable. As a proof of this, we shall give her portrait of the Marquis de Croismare, one of the friends of Diderot and the Baron d'Holbach.

"Je lui crois bien soixante ans; il ne les paroît pourtant pas. Il est d'une taille médiocre, sa figure a dû être très-agréable: elle se distingue encore par un air de noblesse et d'aisance, qui répand de la grace sur tout sa personne. Sa physionomie a de la finesse. Ses gestes, ses attitudes ne sont jamais recherchés; mais ils sont si bien d'accord avec la tournure de son esprit, qu'ils semblent ajouter à son originalité. Il parle des choses les plus sérieuses et les plus importantes d'un ton si gai, qu'on est souvent tenté de ne rien croire de ce qu'il dit. On n'a presque jamais rien a citer de ce qu'on lui entend dire; mais lorsqu'il parle, on ne veut rien perdre de ce qu'il dit; s'il se tait, on désire qu'il parle encore. Sa prodigieuse vivacité, et une singulière aptitude à toutes sortes de talens et de connoissances, l'ont porté à tout voir et à tout connoître; au moyen de quoi vous comprenez qu'il est fort instruit. Il a bien lu, bien vu, et n'a retenu que ce qui valoit la peine de l'être. Son esprit annonce d'abord plus d'agrément que de solidité, mais je crois que quiconque le jugeroit frivole lui feroit tort. Je le soupçonne de renfermer dans son cabinet les épines des roses qu'il distribue dans la société: assez constamment gai dans le monde, seul je le crois mélancolique. On dit qu'il a l'ame aussi tendre qu'honnête; qu'il sent vivement et qu'il se livre avec impetuosité à ce qui trouve le chemin de son cœur. Tout le monde ne lui plaît pas; il faut pour cela de l'originalité, ou des vertus distinguées, ou de certains vices qu'il appelle passions; néanmoins dans le courant de la vie, il s'accommode de tout. Beaucoup de curiosité et de la facilité dans le caractère (ce qui va jusqu'à la foiblesse) l'entraînent souvent à négliger ses meilleurs amis et à les perdre de vue, pour se livrer à des goûts factices et passagers: il en rit avec eux; mais on voit si clairement qu'il en rougit avec lui-même, qu'on ne peut lui savoir mauvais gré de ses disparates."—III. pp. 324—326.

The portrait of Grimm, the French Boswell, vol. iii. p. 97, is equally good, if not superior; but we have already extracted enough to show the nature of the work, and the talents of the author. It is a lively, entertaining book,—relating in an agreeable manner the opinions and habits of many remarkable men—mingled with some very scandalous and improper passages, which degrade the whole work. But if all the decencies and delicacies of life were in one scale, and five francs in the other, what French bookseller would feel a single moment of doubt in making his selection?

POOR-LAWS.*

[EDINBURGH REVIEW, 1820.]

OUR readers, we fear, will require some apology for being asked to look at anything upon the poor-laws. No subject, we admit, can be more disagreeable, or more trite. But, unfortunately, it is the most important of all the important subjects which the distressed state of the country is now crowding upon our notice.

A pamphlet on the poor-laws generally contains some little piece of favourite nonsense, by which we are gravely told this enormous evil may be perfectly cured. The first gentleman recommends little gardens; the second cows; the third a village shop; the fourth a spade; the fifth Dr. Bell, and so forth. Every man rushes to the press with his small morsel of imbecility; and is not easy till he sees his impertinence stitched in blue covers. In this list of absurdities, we must not forget the project of supporting the poor from national funds, or, in other words, of immediately doubling the expenditure, and introducing every possible abuse into the administration of it.

Then there are worthy men, who call upon gentlemen of fortune and education to become overseers—meaning, we suppose, that the present overseers are to perform the higher duties of men of fortune. Then merit is set up as the test of relief; and their worships are to enter into a long examination of the life and character of each applicant, assisted, as they doubtless would be, by candid overseers, and neighbours divested of every feeling of malice and partiality. The children are next to be taken from their parents, and lodged in immense pedagogueries of several acres each, where they are to be carefully secluded from those fathers and mothers they are commanded to obey and honour, and are to be brought up in virtue by the churchwardens.—And this is gravely intended as a corrective of the poor-laws; as if (to pass over the many other objections which might be made to it,) it would not set mankind populating faster than carpenters and bricklayers could cover in their children, or separate twigs to be bound into rods for their flagellation. An extension of the poor-laws to personal property is also talked of. We should be very glad to see any species of property exempted from these laws, but have no wish that any which is now exempted should be subjected to their influence. The case would infallibly be like that of the income-tax, —the more easily the tax was raised, the more profligate would be the expenditure. It is proposed also that alehouses should be diminished, and that the children of the poor should be catechized publicly in the church,—both very respectable and proper suggestions but of themselves hardly strong enough for the evil. We have every wish that the poor should accustom themselves to habits of sobriety; but we cannot help reflecting, sometimes, that an alehouse is the only place where a poor tired creature, haunted with every species of wretchedness, can purchase three or four times a year three pennyworth of ale—a liquor upon which wine-drinking moralists are always extremely severe. We must not forget, among other nostrums, the eulogy of small farms—in other words, of small capital, and profound ignorance in the arts of agriculture;—and the evil is also thought to be curable by periodical contributions from men who have nothing, and can earn nothing without charity. To one of these plans, and perhaps the most plausible, Mr. Nicol has stated, in the following passage, objections that are applicable to almost all the rest.

"The district school would no doubt be well superintended and well regulated; magistrates and country gentlemen would be its visitors. The more excellent the establishment, the greater the mischief; because the greater the expense. We may talk what we will of economy, but where the care of the poor is taken exclusively into the hands of the rich, comparative extravagance is the necessary consequence: to say that the gentleman, or even the overseer, would never permit the poor to live at the district school, as they live at home, is saying far too little. English humanity will never see the poor in any thing like want, when that want is palpably and visibly brought before it: first, it will give necessaries, next comforts; until its fostering care rather pampers, than merely relieves. The humanity itself is highly laudable; but if practised on an extensive scale, its consequences must entail an almost unlimited expenditure.

"Mr. Locke computes that the labour of a child from 3 to 14, being set against its nourishment and teaching, the result would be exoneration of the parish from expense. Nothing could prove more decisively the incompetency of the board of trade to advise on this question. Of the productive labour of the workhouse, I shall have to speak hereafter; I will only observe in this place, that after the greatest care and attention bestowed on the subject, after expensive looms purchased, &c., the 50 boys of the blue coat school earned in the year 1816, 59*l.* 10*s.* 3*d.*; the 40 girls earned, in the same time, 40*l.* 7*s.* 9*d.* The ages of these children are from 8 to 16. They earn about one pound in the year, and cost about twenty.

---

* 1. *Safe Method for rendering Income arising from Personal Property available to the Poor-Laws.* Longman & Co. 1819.
2. *Summary Review of the Report and Evidence relative to the Poor-Laws.* By S. W. Nicol. York.
3. *Essay on the Practicability of modifying the Poor-Laws.* Sherwood. 1819.
4. *Considerations on the Poor-Laws.* By John Davison, A. M. Oxford.

"The greater the call for labour in public institutions, be they prisons, workhouses, or schools, the more difficult to be procured that labour must be. There will thence be both much less of it for the comparative numbers, and it will afford a much less price; to get any labour at all, one school must underbid another.

"It has just been observed, that 'the child of a poor cottager, half clothed, half fed, with the enjoyment of home and liberty, is not only happier but better than the little automaton of a parish workhouse:' and this I believe is accurately true. I scarcely know a more cheering sight, though certainly many more elegant ones, than the youthful gambols of a village green. They call to mind the description given by Paley of the shoals of the fry of fish: 'They are so happy that they know not what to do with themselves; their attitude, their vivacity, their leaps out of the water, their frolics in it, all conduce to show their excess of spirits, and are simply the effects of that excess.'

"Though politeness may be banished from the cottage, and though the anxious mother may sometimes chide a little too sharply, yet here both maternal endearments and social affection exist in perhaps their greatest vigour: the attachments of lower life, where independent of attachment there is so little to enjoy, far outstrip the divided if not exhausted sensibility of the rich and great; and in depriving the poor of these attachments, we may be said to rob them of their little all.

"But it is not to happiness only I here refer; it is to morals. I listen with great reserve to that system of moral instruction, which has not social affection for its basis, or the feelings of the heart for its ally. It is not to be concealed, that every thing may be taught, yet nothing learned, that systems planned with care, and executed with attention, may evaporate into unmeaning forms, where the imagination is not roused, or the sensibility impressed.

"Let us suppose the children of the 'district school,' nurtured with that superabundant care which such institutions, when supposed to be well conducted, are wont to exhibit; they rise with the dawn; after attending to the calls of cleanliness, prayers follow; then a lesson; then breakfast; then work, till noon liberates them, for perhaps an hour, from the walls of their prison to the walls of their prison court. Dinner follows; and then, in course, work, lessons, supper, prayers; at length, after a day dreary and dull, the counterpart of every day which has preceded, and of all that are to follow, the children are dismissed to bed.—This system may construct a machine, but it will not form a man. Of what does it consist? of prayers parroted without one sentiment in accord with the words uttered: of moral lectures which the understanding does not comprehend, or the heart feel; of endless bodily constraint, intolerable to youthful vivacity, and injurious to the perfection of the human frame.—The cottage day may not present so imposing a scene; no decent uniform; no well trimmed locks; no glossy skin; no united response of hundreds of conjoined voices; no lengthened procession, misnamed exercise; but if it has less to strike the eye, it has far more to engage the heart. A trifle in the way of cleanliness must suffice; the prayer is not forgot; it is perhaps imperfectly repeated, and confusedly understood; but it is not muttered as a vain sound; it is an earthly parent that tells of a heavenly one; duty, love, obedience, are not words without meaning, when repeated by a mother to her child: to God, the great unknown Being that made all things, all thanks, all praise, all adoration is due. The young religionist may be in some measure bewildered by all this; his notions may be obscure, but his feelings will be roused, and the foundation at least of true piety will be laid.

"Of moral instruction, the child may be taught less at home than at school, but he will be taught better; that is, whatever he is taught he will feel: he will not have abstract propositions of duty coldly presented to his mind; but precept and practice will be conjoined; what he is told it is right to do will be instantly done. Sometimes the operative principle on the child's mind will be love, sometimes fear, sometimes habitual sense of obedience; it is always something that will impress, always something that will be remembered."

There are two points which we consider as now admitted by all men of sense,—*1st*, That the poor-laws must be abolished; *2dly*, That they must be *very gradually* abolished.* We hardly think it worth while to throw away pen and ink upon any one who is still inclined to dispute either of these propositions.

With respect to the gradual abolition, it must be observed, that the present redundant population of the country has been entirely produced by the poor-laws: and nothing could be so grossly unjust as to encourage people to such a vicious multiplication, and then, when you happen to discover your folly, immediately to starve them into annihilation. You have been calling upon your population for two hundred years to beget more children—furnished them with clothes, food, and houses—taught them to lay up nothing for matrimony, nothing for children, nothing for age—but to depend upon justices of the peace for every human want. The folly is now detected; but the people, who are the fruit of it, remain. It was madness to call them in this manner into existence; but it would be the height of cold-blooded cruelty to get rid of them by any other than the most gentle and gradual means; and not only would it be cruel, but extremely dangerous, to make the attempt. Insurrections of the most sanguinary and ferocious nature would be the immediate consequence of any very sudden change in the system of the poor-laws; not partial, like those which proceeded from an impeded or decaying state of manufactures, but as universal as the poor-laws themselves,

* I am not quite so wrong in this as I seem to be, nor after all our experience am I satisfied that there has not been a good deal of rashness and precipitation in the conduct of this admirable measure. You have not been able to carry the law into manufacturing countries. Parliament will compel you to soften some of the more severe clauses. It has been the nucleus of general insurrection and chartism. The Duke of Wellington wisely recommended that the experiment should be first tried in a few counties round the metropolis.

and as ferocious as insurrections always are which are led on by hunger and despair.

These observations may serve as an answer to those angry and impatient gentlemen, who are always crying out, What has the committee of the House of Commons done?—What have they to show for their labours?—Are the rates lessened?—Are the evils removed? The committee of the House of Commons would have shown themselves to be a set of the most contemptible charlatans, if they had proceeded with any such indecent and perilous haste, or paid the slightest regard to the ignorant folly which required it at their hands. They have very properly begun, by collecting all possible information upon the subject; by consulting speculative and practical men; by leaving time for the press to contribute whatever it could of thought or knowledge to the subject; and by introducing measures, the effects of which will be, and are intended to be, gradual. The lords seemed at first to have been surprised that the poor-laws were not abolished before the end of the first session of Parliament; and accordingly set up a little rival committee of their own, which did little or nothing, and will not, we believe, be renewed. We are so much less sanguine than those noble legislators, that we shall think the improvement immense, and a subject of very general congratulation, if the poor-rates are perceptibly diminished, and if the system of pauperism is clearly going down in twenty or thirty years hence.

We think, upon the whole, that government has been fortunate in the selection of the gentleman who is placed at the head of the committee for the revision of the poor-laws; or rather, we should say, (for he is a gentleman of very independent fortune), who has consented that he should be placed there. Mr. Sturges Bourne is undoubtedly a man of business, and of very good sense: he has made some mistakes; but, upon the whole, sees the subject as a philosopher and a statesman ought to do. Above all, we are pleased with his good nature and good sense in adhering to his undertaking, after the Parliament has flung out two or three of his favourite bills. Many men would have surrendered so unthankful and laborious an undertaking in disgust; but Mr. Bourne knows better what appertains to his honour and character, and, above all, what he owes to his country. It is a great subject; and such as will secure to him the gratitude and favour of posterity, if he brings it to a successful issue.

We have stated our opinion that all remedies, without gradual abolition, are of little importance. With a foundation laid for such gradual abolition, every auxiliary improvement of the poor-laws (while they do remain) is worthy the attention of Parliament: and, in suggesting a few alterations as fit to be immediately adopted, we wish it to be understood, that we have in view the gradual destruction of the system, as well as its amendment while it continues to operate.

It seems to us, then, that one of the first and greatest improvements of this unhappy system would be a complete revision of the law of settlement. Since Mr. East's act for preventing the removal of the poor till they are actually chargeable, any man may live where he pleases, until he becomes a beggar, and asks alms of the place where he resides. To gain a settlement, then, is nothing more than to gain a right of begging: it is not, as it used to be before Mr. East's act, a power of residing where, in the judgment of the resident, his industry and exertion will be best rewarded; but a power of taxing the industry and exertions of other persons in the place where his settlement falls. This privilege produces all the evil complained of in the poor-laws; and instead, therefore, of being conferred with the liberality and profusion which it is at present, it should be made of very difficult attainment, and liable to the fewest possible changes. The constant policy of our courts of justice has been, to make settlements easily obtained. Since the period we have be fore alluded to, this has certainly been a very mistaken policy. It would be a far wiser course to abolish all other means of settlement than those of birth, parentage, and marriage—not for the limited reason stated in the committee, that it would diminish the law expenses, (though that, too, is of importance,) but because it would invest fewer residents with the fatal privilege of turning beggars, exempt a greater number of labourers from the moral corruption of the poor-laws, and stimulate them to exertion and economy, by the fear of removal if they are extravagant and idle. Of ten men who leave the place of their birth, four, probably, get a settlement by yearly hiring, and four others by renting a small tenement; while two or three may return to the place of their nativity, and settle there. Now, under the present system, here are eight men settled where they have a right to beg without being removed. The probability is, that they will all beg; and that their virtue will give way to the incessant temptation of the poor-laws: but if these men had felt from the very beginning, that removal from the place where they wished most to live would be the sure consequence of their idleness and extravagance, the probability is, that they would have escaped the contagion of pauperism, and been much more useful members of society than they now are. The best labourers in a village are commonly those who are living where they are legally settled, and have therefore no right to ask charity—for the plain reason, that they have nothing to depend upon but their own exertions: in short, for them the poor-laws hardly exist; and they are such as the great mass of English peasantry would be, if we had escaped the curse of these laws altogether.

It is incorrect to say, that no labourer would settle out of the place of his birth, if the means of acquiring a settlement were so limited. Many men begin the world with strong hope and much confidence in their own fortune, and without any intention of subsisting by charity; but they see others subsisting in greater ease, without their toil—and their spirit gradually sinks to the meanness of mendicity.

An affecting picture is sometimes drawn of a man falling into want in the decline of life, and compelled to remove from the place where he has spent the greatest part of his days. These things are certainly painful enough to him who has the misfortune to witness them. But they must be taken upon a large scale; and the whole good and evil which they produce diligently weighed and considered. The question then will be, whether any thing can be more really humane, than to restrain a system which relaxes the sinews of industry, and places the dependence of laborious men upon any thing but themselves. We must not think only of the wretched sufferer who is removed, and, at the sight of his misfortunes, call out for fresh facilities to beg. We must remember the industry, the vigour, and the care which the dread of removal has excited, and the number of persons who owe their happiness and their wealth to that salutary feeling. The very person, who, in the decline of life, is removed from the spot where he has spent so great a part of his time, would, perhaps, have been a pauper half a century before, if he had been afflicted with the right of asking alms in the place where he lived.

It has been objected, that this plan of abolishing all settlements but those of birth, would send a man, the labour of whose youth had benefited some other parish, to pass the useless part of his life in a place for which he existed only as a burden. Supposing that this were the case, it would be quite sufficient to answer, that any given parish would probably send away as many useless old men as it received; and, after all, little inequalities must be borne for the general good. But, in truth, it is rather ridiculous to talk of a parish not having benefited by the labour of the man who is returned upon their hands in his old age. If such parish resembles most of those in England, the absence of a man for thirty or forty years has been a great good instead of an evil; they have had many more labourers than they could employ; and the very man whom they are complaining of supporting for his few last years, would, in all probability, have been a beggar forty years before, if he had remained among them; or, by pushing him out of work, would have made some other man a beggar. Are the benefits derived from prosperous manufactures limited to the parishes which contain them? The industry of Halifax, Huddersfield, or Leeds, is felt across the kingdom as far as the Eastern Sea. The prices of meat and corn at the markets of York and Malton are instantly affected by any increase of demand and rise of wages in the manufacturing districts to the west. They have benefited these distant places, and found labour for their superfluous hands by the prosperity of their manufactures. Where, then, would be the injustice, if the manufacturers, in the time of stagnation and poverty, were returned to their birth settlements? But as the law now stands, *population tumors*, of the most dangerous nature, may spring up in a parish:—a manufacturer, concealing his intention, may settle there, take 200 or 300 apprentices, fail, and half ruin the parish which has been the scene of his operations. For these reasons, we strongly recommend to Mr. Bourne to narrow as much as possible, in all his future bills, the means of acquiring settlements,* and to reduce them ultimately to parentage, birth and marriage—convinced that, in so doing, he will in furtherance of the great object of abolishing the poor-laws, be only *limiting the right of begging*, and preventing the resident and almsman from being (as they now commonly are) one and the same person. But, before we dismiss this part of the subject, we must say a few words upon the methods by which settlements are now gained.

In the settlement by hiring it is held, that a man has a claim upon the parish for support where he has laboured for a year; and yet another, who has laboured there for twenty years by short hirings, gains no settlement at all. When a man was not allowed to live where he was not settled, it was wise to lay hold of any plan for extending settlements. But the whole question is now completely changed; and the only point which remains is, to find out what mode of conferring settlements produces the least possible mischief. We are convinced it is by throwing every possible difficulty in the way of acquiring them. If a settlement hereafter should not be obtained in that parish in which labourers have worked for many years, it will be because it contributes materially to their happiness that they should not gain a settlement there; and this is a full answer to the apparent injustice.

Then, upon what plea of common sense should a man gain a power of taxing a parish to keep him, because he has rented a tenement of ten pounds a year there? or, because he has served the office of clerk, or sexton, or hog-ringer, or bought an estate of thirty pounds value? However good these various pleas might be for conferring settlements, if it was desirable to increase the facility of obtaining them, they are totally inefficacious if it can be shown that the means of gaining new settlements should be confined to the limits of the strictest necessity.

These observations (if they have the honour of attracting his attention) will show Mr. Bourne our opinion of his bill for giving the privilege of settlement only to a certain length of residence. In the *first* place, such a bill would be the cause of endless vexation to the poor, from the certainty of their being turned out of their cottages, before they pushed their legal taproot into the parish; and, *secondly*, it would rapidly extend all the evils of the poor laws, by identifying, much more than they are at present identified, the resident and the settled man—the very opposite of the policy which ought to be pursued.

Let us suppose, then, that we have got rid of all the means of gaining a settlement, or right to become a beggar, except by birth, parentage, and marriage; for the wife, of course, must fall into the settlement of the husband; and the children, till emancipated, must be removed, if their parents are removed. This point gained, the task of regulating the law expenses of the poor-laws would be nearly accomplished: for the most fertile causes of dispute would be removed. Every first settlement is an inexhaustible source of litigation and expense to the miserable rustics. Upon the simple fact, for example, of a farmer hiring a ploughman for a year, arise the following afflicting ques-

* This has been done.

tions:—Was it an expressed contract? Was it an implied contract? Was it an implied hiring of the ploughman, rebutted by circumstances? Was the ploughman's contract for a year's prospective service? Was it a customary hiring of the ploughman? Was it a retrospective hiring of the ploughman? Was it a conditional hiring? Was it a general hiring? Was it a special, or a special yearly hiring, or a special hiring with wages reserved weekly?—Did the farmer make it a special conditional hiring with warning, or an exceptive hiring? Was the service of the ploughman actual or contructive? Was there any dispensation expressed or implied?—or was there a dissolution implied?—by new agreement?—or mutual consent?—or by justices?—or by any other of the ten thousand means which the ingenuity of lawyers has created? Can any one be surprised, after this, to learn, that the amount of appeals for removals, in the four quarter sessions ending Mid-summer, 1817, were *four thousand seven hundred?** Can any man doubt that it is necessary to reduce the hydra to as few heads as possible? or can any other objection be stated to such reduction, than the number of attorneys and provincial counsel, whom it will bring into the poor-house? Mr. Nicol says, that the greater number of modes of settlement do not increase litigation. He may just as well say, that the number of the streets in the Seven Dials does not increase the difficulty of finding the way. The modes of settlement we leave, are by far the simplest, and the evidence is assisted by registers.

Under the head of law expenses, we are convinced a great deal may be done, by making some slight alteration in the law of removals. At present, removals are made without any warning to the parties to whom the pauper is removed; and the first intimation which the defendant parish receives of the projected increase of their population is, by the arrival of the father, mother, and eight or nine children at the overseer's door—where they are tumbled out, with the justice's order about their necks, and left as a spectacle to the assembled and indignant parishioners. No sooner have the poor wretches become a little familiarized to their new parish, than the order is appealed against, and they are recarted with the same precipitate indecency—*Quo fata trahunt, retrahuntque.*

No removal should ever take place without due notice to the parish to which the pauper is to be removed, nor till the time in which it may be appealed against is passed by. Notice to be according to the distance—either by letter, or personally; and the decision should be made by the justices at their petty sessions, with as much care and attention as if there were no appeal from their decision. An absurd notion prevails among magistrates, that they need not take much trouble in the investigation of removals, because their errors may be corrected by a superior court; whereas, it is an object of great importance, by a fair and diligent investigation in the nearest and cheapest court, to convince the country people which party is right and which is wrong: and in this manner to prevent them from becoming the prey of law vermin. We are convinced that this subject of the removal of poor is well worthy a short and separate bill. Mr. Bourne thinks it would be very difficult to draw up such a bill. We are quite satisfied we could draw up one in ten minutes that would completely answer the end proposed, and cure the evil complained of.

We proceed to a number of small details, which are well worth the attention of the legislature. Overseers' accounts should be given in quarterly, and passed by the justices, as they now are, annually. The office of overseer should be triennial. The accounts which have nothing to do with the poor, such as the constable's account, should be kept and passed separately from them; and the vestry should have the power of ordering a certain portion of the superfluous poor upon the roads. But we beseech all speculators in poor-laws to remember, that the machinery they must work with is of a very coarse description. An overseer must always be a limited, uneducated person, but little interested in what he is about, and with much business of his own on his hands. The extensive interference of gentlemen with those matters is quite visionary and impossible. If gentlemen were tide-waiters, the custom-house would be better served; if gentlemen would become petty constables, the police would be improved; if bridges were made of gold, instead of iron, they would not rust. But there are not enough of these articles for such purposes.

A great part of the evils of the poor-laws, has been occasioned by the large powers intrusted to individual justices. Every body is full of humanity and good-nature when he can relieve misfortune by putting his hand—in his neighbour's pocket. Who can bear to see a fellow-creature suffering pain and poverty, when he can order other fellow-creatures to relieve him? Is it in human nature, that A should see B in tears and misery, and not order C to assist him? Such a power must, of course, be liable to every degree of abuse; and the sooner the power of ordering relief can be taken out of the hands of magistrates, the sooner shall we begin to experience some mitigation of the evils of the poor-laws. The special-vestry bill is good for this purpose, as far as it goes; but it goes a very little way; and we much doubt if it will operate as any sort of abridgment to the power of magistrates granting relief. A single magistrate must not act under this bill but in cases of special emergency. But every case of distress is a case of special emergency: and the double magistrates, holding their petty sessions at some little alehouse, and overwhelmed with all the monthly business of the hundred, cannot possibly give to the pleadings of the overseer and pauper half the attention they would be able to afford them at their own houses.

The common people have been so much accustomed to resort to magistrates for relief, that it is certainly a delicate business to wean them from this bad habit; but it is essential to the great objects which the poor-committee have in view, that the power of magistrates of

* Commons' Report, 1817.

ordering relief should be gradually taken away. When this is once done, half the difficulties of the abolition are accomplished. We will suggest a few hints as to the means by which this desirable end may be promoted.

A poor man now comes to a magistrate any day in the week, and any hour in any day, to complain of the overseers, or of the select committee. Suppose he were to be made to wait a little, and to feel for a short time the bitterness of that poverty which, by idleness, extravagance, and hasty marriage, he has probably brought upon himself. To effect this object, we would prohibit all orders for relief, by justices, between the 1st and 10th of the month; and leave the poor entirely in the hands of the overseers, or of the select vestry, for that period. Here is a beginning—a gradual abolition of one of the first features of the poor-laws. And it is without risk of tumult; for no one will run the risk of breaking the laws for an evil to which he anticipates so speedy a termination. This Decameron of overseers' despotism, and paupers' suffering, is the very thing wanted. It will teach the parishes to administer their own charity responsibly, and to depend upon their own judgment. It will teach the poor the miseries of pauperism and dependence; and will be a warning to unmarried young men not hastily and rashly to place themselves, their wives and children, in the same miserable situation; and it will effect all these objects gradually, and without danger. It would of course be the same thing on principle, if relief were confined to three days between the 1st and the 10th of each month; three between the 10th and the 20th; three between the 20th and the end of the month;—or in any other manner that would gradually* crumble away the power, and check the gratuitous munificence of justices,—give authority over their own affairs to the heads of the parish, and teach the poor, by little and little, that they must suffer if they are imprudent. It is understood in all these observations, that the overseers are bound to support their poor without any order of justices; and that death arising from absolute want should expose those officers to very severe punishments, if it could be traced to their inhumanity and neglect. The time must come when we must do without this; but we are not got so far yet—and are at present only getting rid of justices, not of overseers.

Mr. Davison seems to think that the plea of old age stands upon a different footing, with respect to the poor-laws, from all other pleas. But why should this plea be more favoured than that of sickness? why more than losses in trade, incurred by no imprudence? In reality, this plea is less entitled to indulgence. Every man knows he is exposed to the helplessness of age; but sickness and sudden ruin are very often escaped—comparatively seldom happen. Why is a man exclusively to be protected against that evil which he must have foreseen longer than any other, and has had the longest time to guard against? Mr. Davison's objections to a limited expenditure are much more satisfactory. These we shall lay before our readers; and we recommend them to the attention of the committee.

"I shall advert next to the plan of a limitation upon the amount of rates to be assessed in future. This limitation, as it is a pledge of some protection to the property now subjected to the maintenance of the poor against the indefinite encroachment which otherwise threatens it, is, in that light, certainly a benefit; and supposing it were rigorously adhered to, the very knowledge, among the parish expectants, that there was some limit to their range of expectation, some barrier which they could not pass, might incline them to turn their thoughts homeward again to the care of themselves. But it is an expedient, at the best, far from being satisfactory. In the first place, there is much reason to fear that such a limitation would not eventually be maintained, after the example of a similar one having failed before, and considering that the urgency of the applicants as long as they retain the principle of dependence upon the parish unqualified in any one of its main articles, would probably overbear a mere barrier of figures in the parish account. Then there would be much real difficulty in the proceedings, to be governed by such a limiting rule. For the use of the limitation would be chiefly, or solely, in cases where there is some struggle between the ordinary supplies of the parish rates, and the exigencies of the poor, or a kind of run and pressure upon the parish by a mass of indigence: and in circumstances of this kind, it would be hard to know how to distribute the supplies under a fair proportion to the applicants, known or expected; hard to know how much might be granted for the present, and how much should be kept in reserve for the remainder of the year's service. The real intricacy in such a distribution of account would show itself in disproportions and inequalities of allowance, impossible to be avoided; and the applicants would have one pretext more for discontent.

"The limitation itself in many places would be only in words and figures. It would be set, I presume, by an average of certain preceding years. But the average taken upon the preceding years might be a sum exceeding in its real value the highest amount of the assessments of any of the averaged years, under the great change which has taken place in the value of money itself. A given rate, or assessment nominally the same, or lower, might in this way be a greater real money value than it was some time before. In many of the most distressed districts, where the parochial rates have nearly equalled the rents, a nominal average would, therefore, be no effectual benefit; and yet it is in those districts that the alleviation of the burthen is the most wanted.

"It is manifest also that a peremptory restriction of the whole amount of money applicable to the parochial service, though abundantly justified in many districts by their particular condition being so impoverished as to make the measure, for them, almost a measure of necessity, if nothing can be substituted for it; and where the same extreme necessity does not exist, still justified by the prudence of pre

* All gradation and caution have been banished since the reform bill—rapid high-pressure wisdom is the only agent in public affairs.

venting in some way the interminable increase of the parochial burthens; still, that such a restriction is an ill-adjusted measure in itself, and would, in many instances, operate very inequitably. It would fall unfairly in some parishes, where the relative state of the poor and the parish might render an increase of the relief as just and reasonable as it is possible for any thing to be under the poor-laws at all. It would deny to many possible fair claimants the whole, or a part, of that degree of relief commonly granted elsewhere to persons in their condition, on this or that account of claim. Leaving the reason of the present demands wholly unimpeached, and unexplained; directing no distinct warning or remonstrance to the parties, in the line of their affairs, by putting a check to their expectations upon positive matters implicated in their conduct; which would be speaking to them in a definite sense, and a sense applicable to all: this plan of limitation would nurture the whole mass of the claim in its origin, and deny the allowance of it to thousands, on account of reasons properly affecting a distant quarter, of which they know nothing. The want of a clear method, and of a good principle at the bottom of it, in this direct compulsory restriction, renders it, I think, wholly unacceptable, unless it be the only possible plan that can be devised for accomplishing the same end. If a parish had to keep its account with a single dependant, the plan would be much more useful in that case. For the ascertained fact of the total amount of his expectations might set his mind to rest, and put him on a decided course of providing for himself. But, in the limitation proposed to be made, the ascertained fact is of a general amount only, not of each man's share in it. Consequently, each man has his indefinite expectations left to him, and every separate specific ground of expectation remaining as before."

Mr. Davison talks of the propriety of refusing to find labour for able labourers after the lapse of ten years, as if it was some ordinary bill he was proposing, unaccompanied by the slightest risk. It is very easy to make such laws, and to propose them; but it would be of immense difficulty to carry them into execution. Done it must be, every body knows that; but the real merit will consist in discovering the gradual and gentle means by which the difficulties of getting parish labour may be increased, and the life of a parish pauper be rendered a life of salutary and deterring hardship. A law that rendered such request for labour perfectly lawful for ten years longer, and then suddenly abolished it, would merely bespeak a certain, general, and violent insurrection for the year 1830. The legislator, thank God, is in his nature a more cunning and gradual animal.

Before we drop Mr. Davison, who writes like a very sensible man, we wish to say a few words about his style. If he would think less about it, he would write much better. It is always as plethoric and full-dressed as if he were writing a treatise *de finibus bonorum et malorum*. He is sometimes obscure; and is occasionally apt to dress up common-sized thoughts in big clothes, and to dwell a little too long in proving what every man of sense knows and admits. We hope we shall not offend Mr. Davison by these remarks; and we have really no intention of doing so. His views upon the poor-laws are, generally speaking, very correct and philosophical; he writes like a gentleman, a scholar, and a man capable of eloquence; and we hope he will be a bishop. If his mitred productions are as enlightened and liberal as this, we are sure he will confer as much honour on the bench as he receives from it. There is a good deal, however, in Mr. Davison's book about the "virtuous marriages of the poor." To have really the charge of a family as a husband and father, we are told—to have the privilege of laying out his life in their service, is the poor man's boast,—"his home is the school of his sentiments," &c. &c. This is viewing human life through a Claude Lorraine glass, and decorating it with colours which do not belong to it. A ploughman marries a ploughwoman because she is plump; generally uses her ill; thinks his children an incumbrance; very often flogs them; and, for sentiment, has nothing more nearly approaching to it, than the ideas of broiled bacon and mashed potatoes. This is the state of the lower orders of mankind—deplorable, but true—and yet rendered much worse by the poor-laws.

The system of roundsmen is much complained of; as well as that by which the labour of paupers is paid, partly by the rate, partly by the master—and a long string of Sussex justices send up a petition on the subject. But the evil we are suffering under is an excess of population. There are ten men applying for work, when five only are wanted; of course, such a redundance of labouring persons must depress the rate of their labour far beyond what is sufficient for the support of their families. And how is that deficiency to be made up but from the parish rates, unless it is meant suddenly and immediately to abolish the whole system of the poor-laws? To state that the rate of labour is lower than a man can live by, is merely to state that we *have had*, and *have*, poor-laws—of which this practice is at length the inevitable consequence; and nothing could be more absurd than to attempt to prevent, by acts of Parliament, the natural depreciation of an article which exists in much greater abundance than it is wanted. Nor can any thing be more unjust than the complaint, that roundsmen are paid by their employers at an inferior rate, and that the difference is made up by the parish funds. A roundsman is commonly an inferior description of labourer who cannot get regularly hired;—he comes upon his parish for labour commonly at those periods when there is the least to do;—he is not a servant of the farmer's choice, and probably does not suit him;—he goes off to any other labour at a moment's warning, when he finds it more profitable;—and the farmer is forced to keep nearly the same number of labourers as if there were no roundsmen at all. Is it just, then, that a labourer, combining every species of imperfection, should receive the same wages as a chosen, regular, stationary person, who is always ready at hand, and whom the farmer has selected for his dexterity and character?

Those persons who do not, and cannot em

ploy labourers, have no kind of right to complain of the third or fourth part of the wages being paid by the rates; for if the farmers did not agree among themselves to take such occasional labourers, the whole of their support must be paid by the rates, instead of one-third. The order is, that the pauper shall be paid such a sum as will support himself and family; and if this agreement to take roundsmen was not entered into by the farmers, they must be paid, by the rates, the whole of the amount of the order, for doing nothing. If a circulating labourer, therefore, with three children, to whom the justices would order 12*s.* per week, receives 8*s.* from his employer, and 4*s.* from the rates, the parish is not burdened by this system to the amount of 4*s.*, but relieved to the amount of 8*s.* A parish manufacture, conducted by overseers, is infinitely more burdensome to the rates than any system of roundsmen. There are undoubtedly a few instances to the contrary. Zeal and talents will cure the original defects of any system; but to suppose that average men can do what extraordinary men have done, is the cause of many silly projects and extravagant blunders. Mr. Owen may give his whole heart and soul to the improvement of one of his parochial parallelograms; but who is to succeed to Mr. Owen's enthusiasm? Before we have quite done with the subject of roundsmen, we cannot help noticing a strange assertion of Mr. Nicol, that the low rate of wages paid by the master is an injustice to the pauper—that he is cheated, forsooth, out of 8*s.* or 10*s.* per week by this arrangement. Nothing, however, can possibly be more absurd than such an allegation. The whole country is open to him. Can he gain more anywhere else? If not, this is the market price of his labour; and what right has he to complain? or how can he say he is defrauded? A combination among farmers to lower the price of labour would be impossible, if labour did not exist in much greater quantities than was wanted. All such things, whether labour, or worsted stocking, or broadcloth, are, of course, always regulated by the proportion between the supply and demand. Mr. Nicol cites an instance of a parish in Suffolk, where the labourer receives sixpence from the farmers, and the rest is made up by the rates; and for this he reprobates the conduct of the farmers. But why are they not to take labour as cheap as they can get it? Why are they not to avail themselves of the market price of this, as of any other commodity? The rates are a separate consideration; let them supply what is wanting; but the farmer is right to get his iron, his wood, and his labour, as cheap as he can. It would, we admit, come nearly to the same thing, if 100*l.* were paid in wages rather than 25*l.* in wages, and 75*l.* by rate; but then, if the farmers were to agree to give wages above the market price, and sufficient for the support of the labourers without any rate, such an agreement could never be adhered to. The base and the crafty would make their labourers take less, and fling heavier rates upon those who adhered to the contract; whereas, the agreement, founded upon giving as little as can be given, is pretty sure of being adhered to; and he who breaks it, lessens the rate to his neighbour, and does not increase it. The problem to be solved is this: If you have ten or twenty labourers who say they can get no work, and you cannot dispute this, and the poor-laws remain, what better scheme can be devised, than that the farmers of the parish should employ them in their turns?—and what more absurd than to suppose that farmers so employing them should give one farthing more than the market price for their labour?

It is contended, that the statute of Elizabeth, rightly interpreted, only compels the overseer to assist the sick and old, and not to find labour for strong and healthy men. This is true enough; and it would have been eminently useful to have attended to it a century past: but to find employment for all who apply, is now, by long use, become a practical part of the poor-laws, and will require the same care and dexterity for its abolition as any other part of that pernicious system. It would not be altogether prudent suddenly to tell a million of stout men, with spades and hoes in their hands, that the 43d of Elizabeth had been misconstrued, and that no more employment would be found for them. It requires twenty or thirty years to state such truths to such numbers.

We think, then, that the diminution of the claims of settlement, and of the authority of justices, coupled with the other subordinate improvements we have stated, will be the best steps for beginning the abolition of the poor-laws. When these have been taken, the description of persons entitled to relief may be narrowed by degrees. But let no man hope to get rid of these laws, even in the gentlest and wisest method, without a great deal of misery, and some risk of tumult. If Mr. Bourne thinks only of avoiding risk, he will do nothing. Some risk must be incurred: but the secret is gradation; and the true reason for abolishing these laws is, not that they make the rich poor, but that they make the poor poorer.*

---

* The boldness of modern legislation has thrown all my caution into the background. Was it wise to encounter such a risk? Is the danger over? Can the vital parts of the bill be maintained?

PUBLIC CHARACTERS OF 1801, 1802.*

[Edinburgh Review, 1802.]

The design of this book appeared to us so extremely reprehensible, and so capable, even in the hands of a blockhead, of giving pain to families and individuals, that we considered it as a fair object of literary police, and had prepared for it a very severe chastisement. Upon the perusal of the book, however, we were entirely disarmed. It appears to be written by some very innocent scribbler, who feels himself under the necessity of dining, and who preserves, throughout the whole of the work, that degree of good humour, which the terror of indictment by our lord the king is so well calculated to inspire. It is of some importance, too, that grown-up country gentlemen should be habituated to read printed books; and such may read a story book about their living friends, who would read nothing else.

We suppose the booksellers have authors at two different prices. Those who do write grammatically, and those who do not; and that they have not thought fit to put any of their best hands upon this work. Whether or not there may be any improvement on this point in the next volume, we request the biographer will at least give us some means of ascertaining when he is comical, and when serious. In the life of Dr. Rennell, we find this passage:—

"Dr. Rennell might well look forward to the highest dignities in the establishment; but, if our information be right, and we have no reason to question it, this is what he by no means either expects or courts. There is a primitive simplicity in this excellent man, which much resembles that of the first prelates of the Christian church, who were with great difficulty prevailed upon to undertake the episcopal office."

* *Public Characters of* 1801—1802. Richard Phillips, St. Paul's. 1 vol. 8vo.

ANASTASIUS.*

[EDINBURGH REVIEW, 1821.]

ANASTASIUS is a sort of oriental Gil Blas, who is tossed about from one state of life to another,—sometimes a beggar in the streets of Constantinople, and, at others, an officer of the highest distinction under an Egyptian Bey,—with that mixture of good and evil, of loose principles and popular qualities, which, against our moral feelings and better judgment, render a novel pleasing, and an hero popular. Anastasius is a greater villain than Gil Blas, merely because he acts in a worse country, and under a worse government. Turkey is a country in the last stage of *Castlereagh-ery* and *Vansittartism;* it is in that condition to which we are steadily approaching—a political *finish;*—the sure result of just and necessary wars, interminable burthens upon affectionate people, green bags, strangled sultanas, and murdered mobs. There are, in the world, all shades and gradations of tyranny. The Turkish, or last, puts the pistol and stiletto in action. Anastasius, therefore, among his other pranks, makes nothing of two or three murders; but they are committed in character, and are suitable enough to the temper and disposition of a lawless Turkish soldier; and this is the justification of the book, which is called wicked but for no other reason than because it accurately paints the manners of a people become wicked from the long and uncorrected abuses of their government.

One cardinal fault which pervades this work is, that it is too long; in spite of the numerous fine passages with which it abounds, there is too much of it;—and it is a relief, not a disappointment, to get to the end. Mr. Hope, too, should avoid humour, in which he certainly does not excel. His attempts of that nature are among the most serious parts of the book. With all these objections, (and we only mention them in case Mr. Hope writes again,) there are few books in the English language which contain passages of greater power, feeling, and eloquence than this novel,—which delineate frailty and vice with more energy and acuteness, or describe historical scenes with such bold imagery, and such glowing language. Mr. Hope will excuse us,—but we could not help exclaiming, in reading it, Is this Mr. Thomas Hope?—Is this the man of chairs and tables—the gentleman of sphinxes—the Œdipus of coal-boxes—he who meditated on muffineers and planned pokers?—Where has he hidden all this eloquence and poetry up to this hour?—How is it that he has, all of a sudden, burst out into descriptions which would not disgrace the pen of Tacitus—and displayed a depth of feeling and a vigour of imagination which Lord Byron could not excel? We do not shrink from one syllable of this eulogium. The work now before us places him at once in the highest list of eloquent writers, and of superior men.

Anastasius, the hero of the tale, is a native of Chios, the son of the drogueman to the French consul. The drogueman, instead of bringing him up to make Latin verses, suffered him to run wild about the streets of Chios, where he lives for some time a lubberly boy, and then a profligate youth. His first exploit is to debauch the daughter of his acquaintance, from whom (leaving her in a state of pregnancy) he runs away, and enters as a cabin boy in a Venetian brig. The brig is taken by Maynote pirates: the pirates by a Turkish frigate, by which he is landed at Nauplia, and marched away to Argos, where the captain, Hassan Pacha, was encamped with his army.

"I had never seen an encampment: and the novel and striking sight absorbed all my faculties in astonishment and awe. There seemed to me to be forces sufficient to subdue the whole world: and I knew not which most to admire, the endless clusters of tents, the enormous piles of armour, and the rows of threatening cannon, which I met at every step, or the troops of well mounted spahees, who, like dazzling meteors, darted by us on every side, amid clouds of stifling dust. The very dirt with which the nearer horsemen bespattered our humble troop, was, as I thought, imposing; and every thing upon which I cast my eyes gave me a feeling of nothingness, which made me shrink within myself like a snail in its cell. I envied not only those who were destined to share in all the glory and success of the expedition, but even the meanest follower of the camp, as a being of a superior order to myself; and, when suddenly there arose a loud flourish of trumpets, which, ending a concert of cymbals and other warlike instruments, re-echoed in long peals from all the surrounding mountains, the clank shook every nerve in my body, thrilled me to the very soul, and infused in all my veins a species of martial ardour so resistless, that it made me struggle with my fetters, and try to tear them asunder. Proud as I was by nature, I would have knelt to whoever had offered to liberate my limbs, and to arm my hands with a sword or a battleaxe."—(I. 36, 37.)

From his captive state he passes into the service of Mavroyeni, Hassan's drogueman, with whom he ingratiates himself, and becomes a person of consequence. In the service of this person, he receives from old Demo, a brother domestic, the following admirable lecture on masters:—

"'Listen, young man,' said he, 'whether you like it or not. For my own part, I have always

* *Anastasius; or, Memoirs of a Greek, written in the 18th Century.* London Murr[illegible]. 3 vols. 8vo.

had too much indolence, not to make it my study throughout life rather to secure ease than to labour for distinction. It has, therefore, been my rule to avoid cherishing in my patron any outrageous admiration of my capacity, which would have increased my dependence while it lasted, and expose me to persecution on wearing out:—but you, I see, are of a different mettle: I therefore may point out to you the surest way to that more perilous height, short of which your ambition, I doubt, will not rest satisfied. When you have compassed it, you may remember old Demo, if you please.

"'Know first that all masters, even the least lovable, like to be loved. All wish to be served from affection rather than duty. It flatters their pride, and it gratifies their selfishness. They expect from this personal motive a greater devotion to their interest, and a more unlimited obedience to their commands. A master looks upon mere fidelity in his servant as his due—as a thing scarce worth his thanks: but attachment he considers as a compliment to his merit, and if at all generous, he will reward it with liberality. Mavroyeni is more open than any body to this species of flattery. Spare it not, therefore. If he speak to you kindly, let your face brighten up. If he talk to you of his own affairs, though it should only be to dispel the tedium of conveying all day long other men's thoughts, listen with the greatest eagerness. A single yawn, and you are undone! Yet let not curiosity appear your motive, but the delight only of being honoured with his confidence. The more you appear grateful for the least kindness, the oftener you will receive important favours. Our ostentatious drogueman will feel a pleasure in raising your astonishment. His vanity knows no bounds. Give it scope, therefore. When he comes home choking with its suppressed ebullitions, be their ready and patient receptacle:—do more; discreetly help him on in venting his conceit; provide him with a cue; hint what you heard certain people, not knowing you to be so near, say of his capacity, his merit, and his influence. He wishes to persuade the world that he completely rules the pasha. Tell him not flatly he does, but assume it as a thing of general notoriety. Be neither too candid in your remarks, nor too fulsome in your flattery. Too palpable deviations from fact might appear a satire on your master's understanding. Should some disappointment evidently ruffle his temper, appear not to conceive the possibility of his vanity having received a mortification. Preserve the exact medium between too cold a respect, and too presumptuous a forwardness. However much Mavroyeni may caress you in private, never seem quite at ease with him in public. A master still likes to remain master, or, at least, to appear so to others. Should you get into some scrape, wait not to confess your imprudence, until concealment becomes impossible; nor try to excuse the offence. Rather than that you should, by so doing, appear to make light of your guilt, exaggerate your self-upbraidings, and throw yourself entirely upon the drogueman's mercy. On all occasions take care how you appear cleverer than your lord, even in the splitting of a pen; or, if you cannot avoid excelling him in some trifle, give his own tuition all the credit of your proficiency. Many things he will dislike, only because they come not from himself. Vindicate not your innocence when unjustly rebuked: rather submit for the moment; and trust that, though Mavroyeni never will expressly acknowledge his error, he will in due time pay you for your forbearance.'"—(I. 43—45.)

In the course of his service with Mavroyeni, he bears arms against the Arnoots, under the Captain Hassan Pacha; and a very animated description is given of his first combat.

"I undressed the dead man completely.—When, however, the business which engaged all my attention was entirely achieved, and that human body, of which, in the eagerness for its spoil, I had only thus far noticed the separate limbs one by one, as I stripped them, all at once struck my sight in its full dimensions, as it lay naked before me;—when I contemplated that fine athletic frame, but a moment before full of life and vigour unto its fingers' ends, now rendered an insensible corpse by the random shot of a raw youth whom in close combat its little finger might have crushed, I could not help feeling, mixed with my exultation, a sort of shame, as if for a cowardly advantage obtained over a superior being; and, in order to make a kind of atonement to the shade of an Epirote—of a kinsman—I exclaimed with outstretched hands, 'Cursed be the paltry dust which turns the warrior's arm into a mere engine, and, striking from afar an invisible blow, carries death no one knows whence to no one knows whom; levels the strong with the weak, the brave with the dastardly; and, enabling the feeblest hand to wield its fatal lightning, makes the conqueror slay without anger, and the conqueror die without glory.'"—(I. 54, 55.)

The campaign ended, he proceeds to Constantinople with the drogueman, where his many intrigues and debaucheries end with the drogueman's turning him out of doors. He lives for some time at Constantinople in great misery; and is driven, among other expedients, to the trade of quack-doctor.

"One evening, as we were returning from the Blacquernes, an old woman threw herself in our way, and, taking hold of my master's garments, dragged him almost by main force after her into a mean-looking habitation just by, where lay on a couch, apparently at the last gasp, a man of foreign features. 'I have brought a physician,' said the female to the patient, 'who, perhaps, may relieve you.' 'Why will you'—answered he faintly—'still persist to feed idle hopes! I have lived an outcast: suffer me at least to die in peace; nor disturb my last moments by vain illusions. My soul pants to rejoin the Supreme Spirit; arrest not its flight; it would only be delaying my eternal bliss!'

"As the stranger spoke these words—which struck even Yacoob sufficiently to make him suspend his professional grimace—the last beams of the setting sun darted across the casement of the window upon his pale yet swarthy features. Thus visited, he seemed for a moment to revive. 'I have always,' said he, 'considered my fate as connected with the great luminary that rules the creation. I have always paid it due worship, and firmly believed I could not breathe my last while its rays shone upon me. Carry me, therefore, out, that I may take my last farewell of the heavenly ruler of my earthly destinies!'

"We all rushed forward to obey the mandate; but the stairs being too narrow, the woman only opened the window, and placed the dying man before it, so as to enjoy the full view of the glorious orb, just in the act of dropping beneath the horizon. He remained a few moments in silent adoration; and mechanically we all joined him in fixing our eyes on the object of his worship. It set in all its splendour; and when its golden disk had entirely disappeared, we looked round at the Parsee. He, too, had sunk into everlasting rest."—(I. 103, 104.)

From the dispensation of chalk and water, he is then ushered into a Turkish jail, the description of which, and of the plague with which it is visited, are very finely written; and we strongly recommend them to the attention of our readers.

"Every day a capital, fertile in crimes, pours new offenders into this dread receptacle; and its high walls and deep recesses resound every instant with imprecations and curses, uttered in all the various idioms of the Ottoman empire. Deep moans and dismal yells leave not its frightful echoes a moment's repose. From morning till night, and from night till morning, the ear is stunned with the clang of chains, which the galley-slaves wear while confined in their cells, and which they still drag about when toiling at their tasks. Linked together two and two for life, should they sink under their sufferings, they still continue unsevered after death; and the man doomed to live on, drags after him the corpse of his dead companion. In no direction can the eye escape the spectacle of atrocious punishments and of indescribable agonies. Here, perhaps, you see a wretch whose stiffened limbs refuse their office, stop suddenly short in the midst of his labour, and as if already impassible, defy the stripes that lay open his flesh, and wait in total immobility the last merciful blow that is to end his misery; while there, you view his companion foaming with rage and madness, turn against his own person his desperate hands, tear his clotted hair, rend his bleeding bosom, and strike his skull, until it burst, against the wall of his dungeon."—(I. 110, 111.)

A few survived.

"I was among these scanty relics. I who, indifferent to life, had never stooped to avoid the shafts of death, even when they flew thickest around me, had more than once laid my finger on the livid wound they inflicted, had probed it as it festered; I yet remained unhurt: for sometimes the plague is a magnanimous enemy, and, while it seldom spares the pusillanimous victim whose blood, running cold ere it is tainted, lacks the energy necessary to repel the infection when at hand, it will pass him by who dares its utmost fury, and advances undaunted to meet its raised dart."—(I. 121.)

In this miserable receptacle of guilty and unhappy beings, Anastasius forms and cements the strongest friendship with a young Greek, of the name of Anagnosti. On leaving the prison, he vows to make every exertion for the liberation of his friend—vows that are forgotten as soon as he is clear from the prison walls. After being nearly perished with hunger, and after being saved by the charity of an hospital, he gets into an intrigue with a rich Jewess—is detected—pursued—and, to save his life, turns Mussulman. This exploit performed, he suddenly meets his friend Anagnosti—treats him with disdain—and, in a quarrel which ensues between them, stabs him to the heart.

"'Life,' says the dying Anagnosti, 'has long been bitterness: death is a welcome guest: I rejoin those that love me, and in a better place. Already, methinks, watching my flight, they stretch out their arms from heaven to their dying Anagnosti. Thou,—if there be in thy breast one spark of pity left for him thou once namedst thy brother; for him to whom a holy tie, a sacred vow .... Ah! suffer not the starving hounds in the street .... See a little hallowed earth thrown over my wretched corpse.' These words were his last."—(I. 209.)

The description of the murderer's remorse is among the finest passages in the work.

"From an obscure aisle in the church I beheld the solemn service; saw on the field of death the pale stiff corpse lowered into its narrow cell, and hoping to exhaust sorrow's bitter cup, at night, when all mankind hushed its griefs, went back to my friend's final resting-place, lay down upon his silent grave, and watered with my tears the fresh-raised hollow mound.

"In vain! Nor my tears nor my sorrows could avail. No offerings nor penance could purchase me repose. Wherever I went, the beginning of our friendship and its issue still alike rose in view; the fatal spot of blood still danced before my steps, and the reeking dagger hovered before my aching eyes. In the silent darkness of the night I saw the pale phantom of my friend stalk round my watchful couch, covered with gore and dust: and even during the unavailing riots of the day, I still beheld the spectre rise over the festive board, glare on me with piteous look, and hand me whatever I attempted to reach. But whatever it presented seemed blasted by its touch. To my wine it gave the taste of blood, and to my bread the rank flavour of death!"—(I. 212, 213.)

We question whether there is in the English language a finer description than this. We request our readers to look at the very beautiful and affecting picture of remorse, pp. 214, 215, vol. i.

Equally good, but in another way, is the description of the opium coffee-house.

"In this tchartchee might be seen any day a numerous collection of those whom private sorrows have driven to a public exhibition of insanity. There each reeling idiot might take his neighbour by the hand, and say, 'Brother, and what ailed thee, to seek so dire a cure?' There did I, with the rest of its familiars, now take my habitual station in my solitary niche, like an insensible, motionless idol, sitting with sightless eyeballs staring on vacuity.

"One day, as I lay in less entire absence than usual under the purple vines of the porch, admiring the gold-tipped domes of the majestic Sulimanye, the appearance of an old man with a snow-white beard, reclining on the couch beside me, caught my attention. Half plunged in stupor, he every now and then burst out into a wild laugh, occasioned by the grotesque phantasms which the ample dose of madjoon he had just swallowed was sending up to his brain. I sat contemplating him with mixed curiosity and dismay, when, as if for a moment roused from his torpor, he took me by the hand, and fixing on my countenance his dim, vacant eyes, said, in an impressive tone, 'Young man, thy days are yet few; take the advice of one who, alas! has counted many. Lose no time; hie thee hence, nor cast behind one lingering look: but if thou hast not the strength, why tarry even here? Thy journey is but half achieved. At once go on to that large mansion before thee. It is thy ultimate destination: and by thus beginning where thou must end at last, thou mayest at least save both thy time and thy money.'"—(I. 215, 216.)

Lingering in the streets of Constantinople, Anastasius hears that his mother is dead, and proceeds to claim that heritage which, by the Turkish law in favour of proselytes, had devolved upon him.

"How often," he exclaims (after seeing his father in the extremity of old age)—"how often does it happen in life, that the most blissful moments of our return to a long-left home are those only that just precede the instant of our arrival; those during which the imagination still is allowed to paint in its own unblended colours the promised sweets of our reception! How often, after this glowing picture of the phantasy, does the reality which follows appear cold and dreary! How often do even those who grieved to see us depart, grieve more to see us return! and how often do we ourselves encounter nothing but sorrow, on again beholding the once happy, joyous promoters of our own hilarity, now mournful, disappointed, and themselves needing what consolation we may bring!"—(I. 239, 240.)

During his visit to Chios, he traces and describes the dying misery of Helena, whom he had deserted, and then debauches her friend Agnes. From thence he sails to Rhodes, the remnants of which produce a great deal of eloquence and admirable description.—(pp. 275, 276, vol. i.) From Rhodes he sails to Egypt; and chap. 16 contains a short and very well written history of the origin and progress of the Mameluke government. The flight of Mourad, and the pursuit of this chief in the streets of Cairo (p. 325, vol. i.), would be considered as very fine passages in the best histories of antiquity. Our limits prevent us from quoting them. Anastasius then becomes a Mameluke; marries his master's daughter, and is made a kiashef. In the numerous skirmishes into which he falls in his new military life, it falls to his lot to shoot, from an ambush, Assad, his inveterate enemy.

"Assad, though weltering in his blood, was still alive: but already the angel of death flapped his dark wings over the traitor's brow. Hearing footsteps advance, he made an effort to raise his head, probably in hopes of approaching succour: but beholding, but recognising only me, he felt that no hopes remained, and gave a groan of despair. Life was flowing out so fast, that I had only to stand still—my arms folded in each other,—and with a steadfast eye to watch its departure. One instant I saw my vanquished foe, agitated by a convulsive tremor, open his eyes and dart at me a glance of impotent rage; but soon he averted them again, then gnashed his teeth, clenched his fist, and expired."—(II. 92.)

We quote this, and such passages as these, to show the great power of description which Mr. Hope possesses. The vindictive man standing with his arms folded, and watching the blood flowing from the wound of his enemy, is very new and very striking.

After the death of his wife, he collects his property, quits Egypt, and visits Mekkah, and acquires the title and prerogatives of an Hadjee. After this he returns to the Turkish capital, renews his acquaintance with Spiridion, the friend of his youth, who in vain labours to reclaim him, and whom he at last drives away, disgusted with the vices and passions of Anastasius. We then find our oriental profligate fighting as a Turkish captain in Egypt, against his old friends the Mamelukes; and afterwards employed in Wallachia, under his old friend Mavroyeni, against the Russians and Austrians. In this part of the work, we strongly recommend to our readers to look at the Mussulmans in a pastry-cook's shop during the Rhamadam, vol. ii. p. 164; the village of beggars, vol. ii. p. 266; the death of the Hungarian officer, vol. ii. p. 327; and, in the last days of Mavroyeni, vol. ii. p. 356;—not forgetting the walk over a field of battle, vol. ii. p. 252. The character of Mavroyeni is extremely well kept up through the whole of the book; and his decline and death are drawn in a very spirited and masterly manner. The Spiridion part of the novel we are not so much struck with; we entirely approve of Spiridion, and ought to take more interest in him; but we cannot disguise the melancholy truth that he is occasionally a little long and tiresome. The next characters assumed by Anastasius are, a Smyrna debauchee, a robber of the desert, and a Wahabee. After serving some time with these sectaries, he returns to Smyrna,—finds his child missing whom he had left there,—traces the little boy to Egypt,—recovers him,—then loses him by sickness,—and wearied of life, retires to end his days in a cottage in Carinthia. For striking passages in this part of the novel, we refer our readers to the description of the burial places near Constantinople, vol. iii. 11—13;

the account of Djezzar Pacha's retirement to his harem during the revolt,—equal to any thing in Tacitus; and, above all, to the landing of Anastasius with his sick child, and the death of the infant. It is impossible not to see that this last picture is faithfully drawn from a sad and cruel reality. The account of the Wahabees is very interesting, vol. iii. 128; and nothing is more so than the story of Euphrosyne. Anastasius had gained the affections of Euphrosyne, and ruined her reputation; he then wishes to cast her off, and to remove her from his house.

"'Ah no!' now cried Euphrosyne, convulsively clasping my knees, 'be not so barbarous! Shut not your own door against her against whom you have barred every once friendly door. Do not deny her whom you have dishonoured the only asylum she has left. If I cannot be your wife, let me be your slave, your drudge. No service, however mean, shall I recoil from when you command. At least before you I shall not have to blush. In your eyes I shall not be what I must seem in those of others; I shall not from you incur the contempt which I must expect from my former companions; and my diligence to execute the lowest offices you may require, will earn for me, not only as a bare alms at your hands, that support which, however scanty, I can elsewhere only receive as an unmerited indulgence. Since I did a few days please your eye, I may still please it a few days longer:—perhaps a few days longer, therefore, I may still wish to live; and when that last blessing, your love, is gone by,—when my cheek, faded with grief, has lost the last attraction that could arrest your favour, then speak, then tell me so, that, burthening you no longer, I may retire—and die!'"—(III. 64, 65.)

Her silent despair, and patient misery, when she finds that she has not only ruined herself with the world, but lost his affections also, have the beauty of the deepest tragedy.

"Nothing but the most unremitting tenderness on my part could in some degree have revived her drooping spirits.—But when, after my excursion, and the act of justice on Sophia, in which it ended, I reappeared before the still trembling Euphrosyne, she saw too soon that that cordial of the heart must not be expected. One look she cast upon my countenance, as I sat down in silence, sufficed to inform her of my total change of sentiments;—and the responsive look by which it was met, tore for ever from her breast the last seeds of hope and confidence. Like the wounded snail, she shrunk within herself, and thenceforth, cloaked in unceasing sadness, never more expanded to the sunshine of joy. With her buoyancy of spirits she seemed even to lose all her quickness of intellect, nay, all her readiness of speech: so that, not only fearing to embark with her in serious conversation, but even finding no response in her mind to lighter topics, I at last began to nauseate her seeming torpor and dulness, and to roam abroad even more frequently than before a partner of my fate remained at home, to count the tedious hours of my absence; while she, poor, miserable creature, dreading the sneers of an unfeeling world, passed her time under my roof in dismal and heart-breaking solitude.—Had the most patient endurance of the most intemperate sallies been able to soothe my disappointment and to soften my hardiness, Euphrosyne's angelic sweetness must at last have conquered: but, in my jaundiced eye, her resignation only tended to strengthen the conviction of her shame; and I saw in her forbearance nothing but the consequence of her debasement, and the consciousness of her guilt. 'Did her heart,' thought I, 'bear witness to a purity on which my audacity dared first to cast a blemish, she could not remain thus tame, thus spiritless, under such an aggravation of my wrongs; and either she would be the first to quit my merciless roof, or, at least, she would not so fearfully avoid giving me even the most unfounded pretence for denying her its shelter.—She must merit her sufferings, to bear them so meekly!'—Hence, even when moved to real pity by gentleness so enduring, I seldom relented in my apparent sternness."—(III. 72—74.)

With this, we end our extracts from Anastasius. We consider it as a work in which great and extraordinary talent is evinced. It abounds in eloquent and sublime passages,—in sense,—in knowledge of history,—and in knowledge of human character;—but not in wit. It is too long; and if this novel perishes, and is forgotten, it will be solely on that account. If it is the picture of vice, so is Clarissa Harlowe, and so is Tom Jones. There are no sensual and glowing descriptions in Anastasius,—nothing which corrupts the morals by inflaming the imagination of youth; and we are quite certain that every reader ends this novel with a greater disgust at vice, and a more thorough conviction of the necessity of subjugating passion, than he feels from reading either of the celebrated works we have just mentioned. The sum of our eulogium is, that Mr. Hope, without being very successful in his story, or remarkably skilful in the delineation of character, has written a novel, which all clever people of a certain age should read, because it is full of marvellously fine things.

SCARLETT'S POOR BILL.*

[EDINBURGH REVIEW, 1821.]

WE are friendly to the main principle of Mr. Scarlett's bill; but are rather surprised at the unworkmanlike manner in which he has set about it.

To fix a maximum for the poor-rates, we should conceive to be an operation of sufficient difficulty and novelty for any one bill. There was no need to provoke more prejudice, to rouse more hostility, and create more alarm, than such a bill would naturally do. But Mr. Scarlett is a very strong man; and before he works his battering-ram, he chooses to have the wall made of a thickness worthy of his blow—capable of evincing, by the enormity of its ruins, the superfluity of his vigour, and the certainty of his aim. Accordingly, he has introduced into his bill a number of provisions, which have no necessary, and, indeed, no near connection with his great and main object; but which are sure to draw upon his back all the Sir Johns and Sir Thomases in the House of Commons. It may be right, or it may be wrong, that the chargeable poor should be removed; but why introduce such a controverted point into a bill framed for a much more important object, and of itself calculated to produce so much difference of opinion! Mr. Scarlett appears to us to have been not only indiscreet in the introduction of such heterogeneous matter, but very much mistaken in the enactments which that matter contains.

"And be it further enacted, that from and after the passing of this act, it shall not be lawful for any justice of peace or other person to remove, or cause to be removed, any poor person or persons from any parish, township or place, to any other, by reason of such person or persons being chargeable to such parish, township or place, or being unable to maintain him or themselves, or under colour of such person or persons being settled in any other parish, township or place, any law or statute to the contrary notwithstanding: Provided always, that nothing in this act shall in any wise be deemed to alter any law now in force for the punishment of vagrants, or for removing poor persons to Scotland, Ireland, or the Isles of Guernsey, Jersey, and Man.—And be it further enacted, that in all cases where any poor person, at the time of the passing of this act, shall be resident in any parish, township or place, where he is not legally settled, and shall be receiving relief from the overseers, guardians, or directors of the poor of the place of his legal settlement, the said overseers, guardians, or directors, are hereby required to continue such relief, in the same manner, and by the same means, as the same is now administered, until one of his majesty's justices of the peace, in or near the place of residence of such poor person, shall, upon application to him, either by such poor person, or any other person on his behalf, for the continuance thereof, or by the said overseers, guardians, or directors of the poor, paying such relief, for the discharge thereof, certify that the same is no longer necessary."—*Bill*, pp. 3, 4.)

Now, here is a gentleman, so thoroughly and so justly sensible of the evils of the poor-laws, that he introduces into the House of Commons a very plain, and very bold measure to restrain them; and yet, in the very same bill, he abrogates the few impediments that remain to universal mendicity. The present law says, "Before you can turn beggar in the place of your residence, you must have been born there, or you must have rented a farm there, or served an office;" but Mr. Scarlett says, "You may beg anywhere where you happen to be. I will have no obstacles to your turning beggar; I will give every facility and every allurement to the destruction of your independence." We are quite confident that the direct tendency of Mr. Scarlett's enactments is to produce these effects. Labourers living in one place, and settled in another, are uniformly the best and most independent characters in the place. Alarmed at the idea of being removed from the situation of their choice, and knowing they have nothing to depend upon but themselves, they are alone exempted from the degrading influence of the poor-laws, and frequently arrive at independence by their exclusion from that baneful privilege which is offered to them by the inconsistent benevolence of this bill. If some are removed, after long residence in parishes where they are not settled, these examples only insure the beneficial effects of which we have been speaking. Others see them, dread the same fate, quit the mug, and grasp the flail. Our policy, as we have explained in a previous article, is directly the reverse of that of Mr. Scarlett. Considering that a poor man, since Mr. East's bill, if he asks no charity, has a right to live where he pleases, and that a settlement is now nothing more than a beggar's ticket, we would gradually abolish all means of gaining a settlement, but those of birth, parentage, or marriage; and this method would destroy litigation as effectually as the method proposed by Mr. Scarlett.*

* 1. *Letter to James Scarlett, Esq., M. P., on his Bill relating to the Poor-Laws.* By a Surrey Magistrate. London, 1821.

2. *An Address to the Imperial Parliament, upon the Practical Means of gradually Abolishing the Poor-Laws, and Educating the Poor Systematically. Illustrated by an Account of the Colonies of Fredericks-Oord in Holland, and of the Common Mountain in the South of Ireland. With General Observations.* Third Edition. By WILLIAM HERBERT SAUNDERS, Esq. London, 1821.

3. *On Pauperism and the Poor-Laws. With a Supplement.* London, 1821.

* This has since been done.

Mr. Scarlett's plan, too, we are firmly persuaded, would completely defeat his own intentions; and would inflict a greater injury upon the poor than this very bill, intended to prevent their capricious removal. If his bill had passed, he could not have passed. His post-chaise on the northern circuit would have been impeded by the crowds of houseless villagers, driven from their cottages by landlords rendered merciless by the bill. In the mud—all in the mud (for such cases made and provided) would they have rolled this most excellent counsellor. Instigated by the devil and their own malicious purposes, his wig they would have polluted, and tossed to a thousand winds the parchment bickerings of Doe and Roe. Mr. Scarlett's bill is so powerful a motive to proprietors for the depopulation of a village—for preventing the poor from living where they wish to live,—that nothing but the conviction that such a bill would never be suffered to pass, has prevented those effects from already taking place. Landlords would, in the contemplation of such a bill, pull down all the cottages of persons not belonging to the parish, and eject the tenants; the most vigorous measures would be taken to prevent any one from remaining or coming who was not absolutely necessary to the lord of the soil. At present, cottages are let to anybody: because, if they are burthensome to the parish, the tenants can be removed. But the impossibility of doing this would cause the immediate demolition of cottages; prevent the erection of fresh ones where they are really wanted; and chain a poor man for ever to the place of his birth, without the possibility of moving. If everybody who passed over Mr. Scarlett's threshold were to gain a settlement for life in his house, he would take good care never to be at home. We all boldly let our friends in, because we know we can easily get them out. So it is with the residence of the poor. Their present power of living where they please, and going where they please, entirely depends upon the possibility of their removal when they become chargeable. If any mistaken friend were to take from them this protection, the whole power and jealousy of property would be turned against their locomotive liberty; they would become *adscripti glebæ*, no more capable of going out of the parish than a tree is of proceeding, with its roots and branches, to a neighbouring wood.

The remedy here proposed for these evils is really one of the most extraordinary we ever remember to have been introduced into any act of Parliament.

"And whereas it may happen, that in several parishes or townships now burdened with the maintenance of the poor settled and residing therein, the owners of lands or inhabitants may, *in order to remove the residence of the labouring poor* from such parishes or places, destroy the cottages and habitations therein, now occupied by the labourers and their families: And whereas, also, it may happen, that certain towns and villages, maintaining their own poor, may, by the residence therein of labourers employed and working in other parishes or townships lying near the said towns and villages, be charged with the burden of maintaining those who do not work, and before the passing of this act were not settled therein: For remedy thereof, be it enacted, by the authority aforesaid, that, in either of the above cases, it shall be lawful for the justices, at any quarter-sessions of the peace held for the county in which such places shall be, upon the complaint of the overseers of the poor of any parish, town or place, that by reason of either of the causes aforesaid, the rates for the relief of the poor of such parish, town, or place, have been materially increased, whilst those of any other parish or place have been diminished, to hear and fully to inquire into the matter of such complaint; and in case they shall be satisfied of the truth thereof, then to make an order upon the overseers of the poor of the parish or township, whose rates have been diminished by the causes aforesaid, to pay to the complainants such sum or sums, from time to time, as the said justices shall adjudge reasonable, not exceeding, in any case, together with the existing rates, the amount limited by this act, as a contribution towards the relief of the poor of the parish, town, or place, whose rates have been increased by the causes aforesaid; which order shall continue in force until the same shall be discharged by some future order of sessions, upon the application of the overseers paying the same, and proof that the occasion for it no longer exists: Provided, always, that no such order shall be made, without proof of notice in writing of such intended application, and of the grounds thereof, having been served upon the overseers of the poor of the parish or place, upon whom such order is prayed, fourteen days at the least before the first day of the quarter-sessions, nor unless the justices making such order shall be satisfied that no money has been improperly or unnecessarily expended by the overseers of the poor praying for such order; and that a separate and distinct account has been kept by them of the additional burden which has been thrown upon their rates by the causes alleged."—(*Bill*, pp. 4, 5.)

Now this clause, we cannot help saying, appears to us to be a receipt for universal and interminable litigation all over England—a perfect law-hurricane—a conversion of all flesh into plaintiffs and defendants. The parish A. has pulled down houses, and burthened the parish B.; B. has demolished to the misery of C.; which has again misbehaved itself in the same manner to the oppression of other letters of the alphabet. All run into parchment, and pant for revenge and exoneration. Though the fact may be certain enough, the causes which gave rise to it may be very uncertain; and assuredly will not be admitted to have been those against which the statute has denounced these penalties. It will be alleged, therefore, that the houses were not pulled down to get rid of the poor, but because they were not worth repair—because they obstructed the squire's view—because rent was not paid. All these motives must go before the sessions, the last resource of legislators—the unhappy quarter-sessions pushed to the ex tremity of their wit by the plump contradictions of parish perjury.

Another of the many sources of litigation, in this clause, is as follows:—A certain number of workmen live in a parish M., not being settled in it, and not working in it before the passing of this act. After the passing of this act, they become chargeable to M., whose poor-rates are increased. M. is to find out the parishes relieved from the burthen of these men, and to prosecute at the quarter-sessions for relief. But suppose the burthened parish to be in Yorkshire, and the relieved parish in Cornwall, are the quarter-sessions in Yorkshire to make an order of annual payment upon a parish in Cornwall? and Cornwall, in turn, upon Yorkshire? How is the money to be transmitted? What is the easy and cheap remedy, if neglected to be paid? And if all this could be effected, what is it, after all, but the present system of removal rendered ten times more intricate, confused and expensive! Perhaps Mr. Scarlett means, that the parishes where these men worked, and which may happen to be within the jurisdiction of the justices, are to be taxed in aid of the parish M., in proportion to the benefit they have received from the labour of men whose distresses they do not relieve. We must have, then, a detailed account of how much a certain carpenter worked in one parish, how much in another; and enter into a species of evidence absolutely interminable. We hope Mr. Scarlett will not be angry with us: we entertain for his abilities and character the highest possible respect; but great lawyers have not leisure for these trifling details. It is very fortunate that a clause so erroneous in its view should be so inaccurate in its construction. If it were easy to comprehend it, and possible to execute it, it would be necessary to repeal it.

The shortest way, however, of mending all this, will be entirely to omit this part of the bill. We earnestly, but with very little hopes of success, exhort Mr. Scarlett not to endanger the really important part of his project, by the introduction of a measure which has little to do with it, and which any quarter-session country squire can do as well or better than himself. The real question introduced by his bill is, whether or not a limit shall be put to the poor-laws; and not only this, but whether their amount shall be gradually diminished. To this better and higher part of the law, we shall now address ourselves.

In this, however, as well as in the former part of his bill, Mr. Scarlett becomes frightened at his own enactments, and repeals himself. Parishes are first to relieve every person actually resident within them. This is no sooner enacted than a provision is introduced to relieve them from this expense, tenfold more burthensome and expensive than the present system of removal. In the same manner, a maximum is very wisely and bravely enacted; and in the following clause is immediately repealed.

"Provided, also, and be it further enacted, that if, by reason of any unusual scarcity of provisions, epidemic disease, or any other cause of a temporary or local nature, it shall be deemed expedient by the overseers of the poor, or other persons having, by virtue of any local act of Parliament, the authority of overseers of the poor of any parish, township, or place, to make any addition to the sum assessed for the relief of the poor, beyond the amount limited by this act, it shall be lawful for the said overseers, or such other persons, to give public notice in the several churches, and other places of worship, within the same parish, township, or place, and if there be no church or chapel within such place, then in the parish church or chapel next adjoining the same, of the place and time of a general meeting to be held by the inhabitants paying to the relief of the poor within such parish, township, or place, for the purpose of considering the occasion and the amount of the proposed addition; and, if it shall appear to the majority of the persons assembled at such meeting, that such addition shall be necessary, then it shall be lawful to the overseers, or other persons having power to make assessments, to increase the assessment by the additional sum proposed and allowed, at such meeting, and for the justices, by whom such rate is to be allowed, upon due proof upon oath to be made before them, of the resolution of such meeting, and that the same was held after sufficient public notice to allow such rate with the proposed addition, specifying the exact amount thereof, with the reasons for allowing the same, upon the face of the rate."—(*Bill*, p. 3.)

It would really seem, from these and other qualifying provisions, as if Mr. Scarlett had never reflected upon the consequences of his leading enactments till he had penned them; and that he then set about finding how he could prevent himself from doing what he meant to do. To what purpose enact a maximum, if that maximum may at any time be repealed by the majority of the parishioners? How will the compassion and charity which the poor-laws have set to sleep be awakened, when such a remedy is at hand as the repeal of the maximum by a vote of the parish? Will ardent and amiable men form themselves into voluntary associations to meet any sudden exigency of famine and epidemic disease, when this sleepy and sluggish method of overcoming the evil can be had recourse to? As soon as it becomes *really impossible* to increase the poor fund by law—when there is but little, and there *can* be no more, that little will be administered with the utmost caution; claims will be minutely inspected; idle manhood will not receive the scraps and crumbs which belong to failing old age; distress will make the poor provident and cautious; and all the good expected from the abolition of the poor-laws will begin to appear. But these expectations will be entirely frustrated, and every advantage of Mr. Scarlett's bill destroyed, by this fatal facility of eluding and repealing it.

The danger of insurrection is a circumstance worthy of the most serious consideration, in discussing the propriety of a maximum. Mr. Scarlett's bill is an infallible receipt for tumult and agitation, whenever corn is a little dearer than common. "Repeal the maximum," will be the clamour in every village; and woe be to those members of the village vestry who should oppose the measure. Whether it was really a year of scarcity, and whether it was a proper season for expanding the bounty of the law, would be a question constantly and fiercely agitated between the farmers and the poor. If the maximum is to be quietly submitted to, its repeal must be rendered impossible but to the legislature. "Burn your ships, Mr. Scarlett. You are doing a wise and necessary thing; don't be afraid of yourself. Respect your own nest. Don't let clause A repeal clause B. Be stout. Take care that the rat lawyers on the treasury bench do not take the oysters out of your bill, and leave you the shell. Do not yield one particle of the wisdom and philosophy of your measure to the country gentlemen of the earth."

We object to a *maximum* which is not rendered a decreasing maximum. If definite sums were fixed for each village, which they could not exceed, that sum would, in a very few years, become a minimum, and an established claim. If 80*s.* were the sum allotted for a particular hamlet, the poor would very soon come to imagine that they were entitled to that precise sum, and the farmers that they were compelled to give it. Any maximum established should be a decreasing, but a very slowly decreasing maximum,—perhaps it should not decrease at a greater rate than 10*s.* per cent. per annum.

It may be doubtful also, whether the first bill should aim at repealing more than 20 per cent. of the present amount of the poor-rates. This would be effected in forty years. Long before that time, the good or bad effects of the measure would be fairly estimated; if it is wise that it should proceed, let posterity do the rest. It is by no means necessary to destroy, in one moment, upon paper, a payment which cannot, without violating every principle of justice, and every consideration of safety and humanity, be extinguished in less than two centuries.

It is important for Mr. Scarlett to consider whether he will make the operation of his bill immediate, or interpose two or three years between its enactment and first operation.

We entirely object to the following clause; the whole of which ought to be expunged:—

"And be it further enacted, that it shall not be lawful for any churchwarden, overseer, or guardian of the poor, or any other person having authority to administer relief to the poor, to allow or give, or for any justice of the peace to order, any relief to any person whatsoever, who shall be married after the passing of this act, for himself, herself, or any part of his or her family, unless such poor person shall be actually, at the time of asking such relief, by reason of age, sickness, or bodily infirmity, unable to obtain a livelihood, and to support his or her family by work: Provided, always, that nothing in this clause contained shall be construed so as to authorize the granting relief, or making any order for relief, in cases where the same was not lawful before the passing of this act."

Nothing in the whole bill will occasion so much abuse and misrepresentation as this clause. It is upon this that the radicals will first fasten. It will, of course, be explained into a prohibition of marriage to the poor; and will, in fact, create a marked distinction between two classes of paupers, and become a rallying point for insurrection. In fact, it is wholly unnecessary. As the funds for the relief of pauperism decrease, under the operation of a diminishing maximum, the first to whom relief is refused will be the young and the strong; in other words, the most absurd and extravagant consequences of the present poor-laws will be the first cured.

Such, then, is our conception of the bill which ought to be brought into Parliament—a maximum regulated by the greatest amount of poor-rates ever paid, and annually diminishing at the rate of 10*s.* per cent. till they are reduced 20 per cent. of their present value; with such a preamble to the bill as will make it fair and consistent for any future Parliament to continue the reduction. If Mr. Scarlett will bring in a short and simple bill to this effect, and not mingle with it any other parochial improvements, and will persevere in such a bill for two or three years, we believe he will carry it; and we are certain he will confer, by such a measure, a lasting benefit upon his country—and upon none more than upon its labouring poor.

We presume there are very few persons who will imagine such a measure to be deficient in vigour. That the poor-laws should be stopped in their fatal encroachment upon property, and unhappy multiplication of the human species, —and not only this, but that the evil should be put in a state of diminution, would be an improvement of our condition almost beyond hope. The tendency of fears and objections will all lie the other way; and a bill of this nature will not be accused of inertness, but of rashness, cruelty, and innovation. We cannot now enter into the question of the poor-laws, of all others that which has undergone the most frequent and earnest discussion. Our whole reasoning is founded upon the assumption, that no system of laws was ever so completely calculated to destroy industry, foresight, and economy in the poor; to extinguish compassion in the rich; and, by destroying the balance between the demand for, and supply of, labour, to spread a degraded population over a ruined land. Not to attempt the cure of this evil, would be criminal indolence; not to cure it gradually and compassionately, would be very wicked. To Mr. Scarlett belongs the real merit of introducing the bill. He will forgive us the freedom, perhaps the severity, of some of our remarks. We are sometimes not quite so smooth as we ought to be; but we hold Mr. Scarlett in very high honour and estimation. He is the greatest advocate, perhaps, of his time; and without the slightest symptom of *tail* or *whiskers*—decorations, it is reported, now as characteristic of the English bar as wigs and gowns in days of old—he has never carried his soul to the treasury, and said, What will you give me for this?—he has never sold the warm feelings and honourable motives of his youth and manhood for an annual sum of money and an office—he has never taken a price for public liberty and public happiness—he has never touched the political Aceldama, and signed the devil's bond for cursing to-morrow what he has blessed to-day. Living in the midst of men who have disgraced it, he has cast honour upon his honourable profession; and has sought dignity, not from the ermine and the mace, but from a straight path and a spotless life.

MEMOIRS OF CAPTAIN ROCK.*

[Edinburgh Review, 1824.]

This agreeable and witty book is generally supposed to have been written by Mr. Thomas Moore, a gentleman of small stature, but full of genius, and a steady friend of all that is honourable and just. He has here borrowed the name of a celebrated Irish leader, to typify that spirit of violence and insurrection which is necessarily generated by systematic oppression, and rudely avenges its crimes; and the picture he has drawn of its prevalence in that unhappy country is at once piteous and frightful. Its effect in exciting our horror and indignation is in the long run increased, we think,—though at first it may seem counteracted, by the tone of levity, and even jocularity, under which he has chosen to veil the deep sarcasm and substantial terrors of his story. We smile at first, and are amused—and wonder, as we proceed, that the humorous narrative should produce conviction and pity—shame, abhorrence, and despair!

England seems to have treated Ireland much in the same way as Mrs. Brownrigg treated her apprentice—for which Mrs. Brownrigg is hanged in the first volume of the Newgate Calendar. Upon the whole, we think the apprentice is better off than the Irishman: as Mrs. Brownrigg merely starves and beats her, without any attempt to prohibit her from going to any shop, or praying at any church, apprentice might select; and once or twice, if we remember rightly, Brownrigg appears to have felt some compassion. Not so Old England, who indulges rather in a steady baseness, uniform brutality, and unrelenting oppression.

Let us select from this entertaining little book a short history of dear Ireland, such as even some profligate idle member of the House of Commons, voting as his master bids him, may perchance throw his eye upon, and reflect for a moment upon the iniquity to which he lends his support.

For some centuries after the reign of Henry II. the Irish were killed like game, by persons qualified or unqualified. Whether dogs were used does not appear quite certain, though it is probable they were, spaniels as well as pointers; and that, after a regular point by Basto, well backed by Ponto and Cæsar, Mr. O'Donnel or Mr. O'Leary bolted from the thicket, and were bagged by the English sportsman. With Henry II. came in tithes, to which, in all probability, about one million of lives may have been sacrificed in Ireland. In the reign of Edward I., the Irish who were settled near the English requested that the benefit of the English laws might be extended to them but the remonstrance of the barons with the hesitating king was in substance this:—"You have made us a present of these wild gentlemen, and we particularly request that no measures may be adopted to check us in that full range of tyranny and oppression in which we consider the value of such a gift to consist. You might as well give us sheep, and prevent us from shearing the wool, or roasting the meat." This reasoning prevailed, and the Irish were kept to their barbarism, and the barons preserved their live-stock.

"Read 'Orange faction' (says Captain Rock) here, and you have the wisdom of our rulers, at the end of near six centuries, *in statu quo.*—The grand periodic year of the stoics, at the close of which every thing was to begin again, and the same events to be all reacted in the same order, is, on a miniature scale, represented in the history of the English government in Ireland—every succeeding century being but a renewed revolution of the same follies, the same crimes, and the same turbulence that disgraced the former. But 'Vive l'ennemi!' say I: whoever may suffer by such measures, Captain Rock, at least, will prosper.

"And such was the result at the period of which I am speaking. The rejection of a petition, so humble and so reasonable, was followed, as a matter of course, by one of those daring rebellions into which the revenge of an insulted people naturally breaks forth. The M'Cartys, the O'Briens, and all the other Macs and O's, who have been kept on the alert by similar causes ever since, flew to arms under the command of a chieftain of my family; and. as the proffered *handle* of the sword had been rejected, made their inexorable masters at least feel its *edge*."—(pp. 23—25.)

Fifty years afterwards the same request was renewed and refused. Up again rose Mac and O,—a *just and necessary war* ensued; and after the usual murders, the usual chains were replaced upon the Irishry. All Irishmen were excluded from every species of office. It was high treason to marry with the Irish blood, and highly penal to receive the Irish into religious houses. War was waged also against their

* *Memoirs of Captain Rock, the celebrated Irish Chieftain; with some Account of his Ancestors.* Written by himself. Fourth Edition. 12mo. London, 1824.

Thomas Moores, Samuel Rogerses, and Walter Scotts, who went about the country harping and singing against English oppression. No such turbulent guests were to be received. The plan of making them poets-laureate, or converting them to loyalty by pensions of 100*l.* per annum, had not then been thought of. They debarred the Irish even from the pleasure of running away, and fixed them to the soil like negroes.

"I have thus selected," says the historian of Rock, "cursorily and at random a few features of the reigns preceding the Reformation, in order to show what good use was made of those three or four hundred years in attaching the Irish people to their English governors; and by what a gentle course of alternatives they were prepared for the inoculation of a new religion, which was now about to be attempted upon them by the same skilful and friendly hands.

"Henry the Seventh appears to have been the first monarch to whom it occurred, that matters were not managed exactly as they ought in this part of his dominions; and we find him—with a simplicity which is still fresh and youthful among our rulers—expressing his *surprise* that 'his subjects of this land should be so prone to faction and rebellion, and that so little advantage had been hitherto derived from the acquisitions of his predecessors, notwithstanding the fruitfulness and natural advantages of Ireland.'—Surprising, indeed, that a policy, such as we have been describing, should not have converted the whole country into a perfect Atalantis of happiness—should not have made it like the imaginary island of Sir Thomas More, where '*tota insula velut una familia est!*'—most stubborn, truly, and ungrateful must that people be, upon whom, up to the very hour in which I write, such a long and unvarying course of penal laws, confiscations, and insurrection acts has been tried, without making them in the least degree in love with their rulers.

"Heloïse tells her tutor Abelard, that the correction which he inflicted upon her only served to increase the ardour of her affection for him; but bayonets and hemp are no such '*amoris stimuli.*'—One more characteristic anecdote of those times, and I have done. At the battle of Knocktow, in the reign of Henry VII., when that remarkable man, the Earl of Kildare, assisted by the great O'Neal and other Irish chiefs, gained a victory over Clanricard of Connaught, most important to the English government, Lord Gormanstown, after the battle, in the first insolence of success, said, turning to the Earl of Kildare, 'We have now slaughtered our enemies, but to complete the good deed, we must proceed yet further, and—cut the throats of those Irish of our own party!'* Who can wonder that the Rock family were active in those times?"—(pp. 33—35.)

Henry VIII. persisted in all these outrages, and aggravated them by insulting the prejudices of the people. England is almost the only country in the world (even at present), where there is not some favourite religious spot, where absurd lies, little bits of cloth, feathers, rusty nails, splinters, and other invaluable relics, are treasured up, and in defence of which the whole population are willing to turn out and perish as one man. Such was the shrine of St. Kieran, the whole treasures of which the satellites of that corpulent tyrant turned out into the street, pillaged the sacred church of Clonmacnoise, scattered the holy nonsense of the priests to the winds, and burnt the real and venerable crosier of St. Patrick, fresh from the silversmith's shop, and formed of the most costly materials. Modern princes change the uniform of regiments; Henry changed the religion of kingdoms, and was determined that the belief of the Irish should undergo a radical and Protestant conversion. With what success this attempt was made, the present state of Ireland is sufficient evidence.

"Be not dismayed," said Elizabeth, on hearing that O'Neal meditated some designs against her government; "tell my friends, if he arise, it will turn to their advantage—*there will be estates for those who want.*" Soon after this prophetic speech, Munster was destroyed by famine and the sword, and near 600,000 acres forfeited to the crown, and distributed among Englishmen. Sir Walter Raleigh (the virtuous and good) butchered the garrison of Limerick in cold blood, after Lord Deputy Gray had selected 700 to be hanged. There were, during the reign of Elizabeth, three invasions of Ireland by the Spaniards, produced principally by the absurd measures of this princess for the reformation of its religion. The Catholic clergy, in consequence of these measures, abandoned their cures, the churches fell to ruin, and the people were left without any means of instruction. Add to these circumstances the murder of M'Mahon, the imprisonment of M'Toole* and O'Dogherty, and the kidnapping of O'Donnel—all truly Anglo-Hibernian proceedings. The execution of the laws was rendered detestable and intolerable by the queen's officers of justice. The spirit raised by these transactions, besides innumerable smaller insurrections, gave rise to the great wars of Desmond and Hugh O'Neal; which, after they had worn out the ablest generals, discomfited the choicest troops, exhausted the treasure, and embarrassed the operations of Elizabeth, were terminated by the destruction of these two ancient families, and by the confiscation of more than half the territorial surface of the island. The two last years of O'Neal's wars cost Elizabeth 140,000*l.* per annum, though the whole revenue of England at that period fell considerably short of 500,000*l.* Essex, after the destruction of Norris, led into Ireland an army of above 20,000 men, which was totally baffled and de-

* Leland gives this anecdote on the authority of an Englishman.

* There are not a few of the best and most humane Englishmen of the present day, who, when under the influence of fear or anger, would think it no great crime to put to death people whose names begin with O or Mac The violent death of Smith, Green, or Thomson, would throw the neighbourhood into convulsions, and the regular forms would be adhered to—but little would be really thought of the death of any body called O'Dogherty or O'Toole.

stroyed by Tyrone, within two years of their landing. Such was the importance of Irish rebellions two centuries before the time in which we live. Sir G. Carew attempted to assassinate the Lugan earl—Mountjoy compelled the Irish rebels to massacre each other. In the course of a few months, 3000 men were starved to death in Tyrone. Sir Arthur Chichester, Sir Richard Manson, and other commanders, saw three children feeding on the flesh of their dead mother. Such were the golden days of good queen Bess!

By the rebellions of Dogherty in the reign of James I., six northern counties were confiscated, amounting to 500,000 acres. In the same manner, 64,000 acres were confiscated in Athlone. The whole of his confiscations amount to nearly a million of acres; and if Leland means plantation acres, they constitute a twelfth of the whole kingdom according to Newenham, and a tenth according to Sir W. Petty. The most shocking and scandalous action in the reign of James, was his attack upon the whole property of the province of Connaught, which he would have effected, if he had not been bought off by a sum greater than he hoped to gain by his iniquity, besides the luxury of confiscation. The Irish, during the reign of James I., suffered under the *double* evils of a licentious soldiery, and a religious persecution.

Charles the First took a bribe of 120,000*l.* from his Irish subjects, to grant them what in those days were called *graces*, but in these days would be denominated the elements of justice. The money was paid, but the graces were never granted. One of these graces is curious enough: "That the clergy were not to be permitted to keep henceforward any private prisons of their own, but delinquents were to be committed to the public jails." The idea of a rector, with his own private jail full of dissenters, is the most ludicrous piece of tyranny we ever heard of. The troops in the beginning of Charles's reign were supported by the weekly fines levied upon the Catholics for non-attendance upon established worship. The Archbishop of Dublin went himself, at the head of a file of musketeers, to disperse a Catholic congregation in Dublin,—which object he effected, after a considerable skirmish with the priests. "The favourite object" (says Dr. Leland, a Protestant clergyman, and dignitary of the Irish church) "of the Irish government and the English Parliament, was *the utter extermination* of all the Catholic inhabitants of Ireland." The great rebellion took place in this reign, and Ireland was one scene of blood and cruelty and confiscation.

Cromwell began his career in Ireland by massacreing for five days the garrison of Drogheda, to whom quarter had been promised. Two millions and a half of acres were confiscated. Whole towns were put up in lots, and sold. The Catholics were banished from three-fourths of the kingdom, and confined to Connaught. After a certain day, every Catholic found out of Connaught was to be punished with death. Fleetwood complains peevishly "that the people *do not transport readily*,"—but adds. "*it is doubtless a work in which the Lord will appear.*" Ten thousand Irish were sent as recruits to the Spanish army.

"Such was *Cromwell's* way of settling the affairs of Ireland—and if a nation *is* to be ruined, this method is, perhaps, as good as any. It is, at least, more humane than the slow lingering process of exclusion, disappointment, and degradation, by which their hearts are worn out under more specious forms of tyranny; and that talent of despatch which Molière attributes to one of his physicians, is no ordinary merit in a practitioner like Cromwell:—'C'est un homme expéditif, qui aime à depêcher ses malades; et quand on a à mourir, cela se fait avec lui le plus vite du monde.' A certain military duke, who complains that Ireland is but half conquered, would, no doubt, upon an emergency, try his hand in the same line of practice, and, like that 'stern hero,' Mirmillo, in the Dispensary,

> 'While others meanly take whole months to slay,
> Despatch the grateful patient in a day!'

"Among other amiable enactments against the Catholics at this period, the price of five pounds was set on the head of a Romish priest—being exactly the same sum offered by the same legislators for the head of a wolf. The Athenians, we are told, encouraged the destruction of wolves by a similar reward (five drachmas); but it does not appear that these heathens bought up the heads of priests at the same rate—such zeal in the cause of religion being reserved for times of Christianity and Protestantism."—(pp. 97—99.)

Nothing can show more strongly the light in which the Irish were held by Cromwell, than the correspondence with Henry Cromwell, respecting the peopling of Jamaica from Ireland. Secretary Thurloe sends to Henry, the lord-deputy in Ireland, to inform him, that "a stock of Irish girls, and Irish young men, are wanting for the peopling of Jamaica." The answer of Henry Cromwell is as follows:—"Concerning the supply of young men, although we must use force in taking them up, *yet it being so much for their own good*, and likely to be of so great advantage to the public, it is not the least doubted but that you may have such a number of them as you may think fit to make use of on this account.

"I shall not need repeat any thing respecting the girls, not doubting to answer your expectations to the full *in that;* and I think it might be of like advantage to your affairs there, and ours here, if you should think fit to send 1500 or 2000 boys to the place above mentioned. *We can well spare them;* and who knows that it may be the means of making them Englishmen, I mean rather Christians. As for the girls, I suppose you will make provisions of clothes, and other accommodations for them." Upon this, Thurloe informs Henry Cromwell, that the council have voted 4000 *girls, and as many boys*, to go to Jamaica.

Every Catholic priest found in Ireland was hanged, and five pounds paid to the informer.

"About the year 1652 and 1653," says Colonel Lawrence in his *Interests of Ireland*, "the plague and famine had so swept away whole counties, that a man might travel twenty or thirty miles and not see a living creature, either man, or beast, or bird,—they being all dead, or had quitted those desolate places. Our soldiers would tell stories of the places where they saw smoke—it was so rare to see either smoke by day, or fire or candle by night." In this manner did the Irish live and die under Cromwell, suffering by the sword, famine, pestilence, and persecution, beholding the confiscation of a kingdom and the banishment of a race. "So that there perished (says S. W. Petry) in the year 1641, 650,000 human beings, whose blood somebody must atone for to God and the king!!"

In the reign of Charles II., by the Act of Settlement, four millions and a half of acres were for ever taken from the Irish. "This country," says the Earl of Essex, lord-lieutenant in 1675, "has been perpetually rent and torn, since his majesty's restoration. I can compare it to nothing better than the flinging the reward on the death of a deer among the packs of hounds —where every one pulls and tears where he can for himself." All wool grown in Ireland was, by act of Parliament, compelled to be sold to England; and Irish cattle were excluded from England. The English, however, were pleased to accept 30,000 head of cattle, sent as a gift from Ireland to the sufferers in the great fire!—and the first day of the sessions, after this act of munificence, the Parliament passed fresh acts of exclusion against the productions of that country.

"Among the many anomalous situations in which the Irish have been placed, by those 'marriage vows, false as dicers' oaths,' which bind their country to England, the dilemma in which they found themselves at the Revolution was not the least perplexing or cruel.* If they were loyal to the king *de jure*, they were hanged by the king, *de facto*; and if they escaped with life from the king *de facto*, it was but to be plundered and proscribed by the king *de jure* afterwards.

"Hac *gener* atque *socer* coeant mercede suorum."—
VIRGIL.

"In a manner so summary, prompt, and high-mettled,
'Twixt father and son-in-law matters were settled."

"In fact, most of the outlawries in Ireland were for treason committed the very day on which the Prince and Princess of Orange accepted the crown in the banqueting-house; though the news of this event could not possibly have reached the other side of the Channel on the same day, and the lord-lieutenant of King James, with an army to enforce obedience, was at that time in actual possession of the government,—so little was common sense consulted, or the mere decency of forms observed by that rapacious spirit, which nothing less than the confiscation of the whole island could satisfy; and which having, in the reign of James I. and at the restoration, despoiled the natives of no less than ten millions six hundred and thirty-six thousand eight hundred and thirty-seven acres, now added to its plunder one million sixty thousand seven hundred and ninety-two acres more, being the amount, altogether, (according to Lord Clare's calculation), of the whole superficial contents of the island.

"Thus not only had *all* Ireland suffered confiscation in the course of this century, but no inconsiderable portion of it had been twice and even thrice confiscated. Well might Lord Clare say, 'that the situation of the Irish nation, at the revolution, stands unparalleled in the history of the inhabited world.'"—(pp. 111—113.)

By the articles of Limerick, the Irish were promised the free exercise of their religion, but from that period till the year 1788, every year produced some fresh penalty against that religion—some liberty was abridged, some right impaired, or some suffering increased. By acts in King William's reign, they were prevented from being solicitors. No Catholic was allowed to marry a Protestant; and any Catholic who sent a son to Catholic countries for education was to forfeit all his lands. In the reign of Queen Anne, any son of a Catholic who chose to turn Protestant got possession of his father's estate. No Papist was allowed to purchase freehold property, or to take a lease for more than thirty years. If a Protestant dies intestate, the estate is to go to the next *Protestant* heir, though all to the tenth generation should be Catholic. In the same manner, if a Catholic dies intestate, his estate is to go to the next Protestant. No Papist is to dwell in Limerick or Galway. No Papist is to take an annuity for life. The widow of a Papist turning Protestant to have a portion of the chattels of deceased, in spite of any will. Every Papist teaching schools to be presented as a regular Popish convict. Prices of catching Catholic priests from 50*s.* to 10*l.*, according to rank. Papists are to answer all questions respecting other Papists, or to be committed to jail for twelve months. No trust to be undertaken for Papists. No Papist to be on grand juries. Some notion may be formed of the spirit of those times, from an order of the House of Commons, "that the sergeant-at-arms should take into custody all Papists that should presume to come into *the gallery!*" (*Commons' Journal*, vol. iii. fol. 976.) During this reign, the English Parliament legislated as absolutely for Ireland as they do now for Rutlandshire—an evil not to be complained of, if they had done it as justly. In the reign of George I. the horses of Papists were seized for the militia, and rode by Protestants, towards which the Catholics paid double, and were compelled to find Protestant substitutes. They were prohibited from voting at vestries, or being high or petty constables. An act of the English Parliament in this reign opens as follows:—"Whereas attempts have been lately made to shake off the subjection of Ireland to the imperial crown of these realms, be it enacted," &c. &c. In the reign of George II four-sixths of the population were cut off from the rights of voting at elections, by the neces

* "Among the persons most puzzled and perplexed by the two opposite royal claims on their allegiance, were the clergymen of the established church; who, having first prayed for King James as their lawful sovereign, as soon as William was proclaimed, took to praying for *him;* but again, on the success of the Jacobite forces in the north, very prudently prayed for King James once more, till the arrival of Schomberg, when, as far as his quarters reached, they returned to praying for King William again."

sity under which they were placed of taking the oath of supremacy. Barristers and solicitors marrying Catholics are exposed to all the penalties of Catholics. Persons robbed by privateers during a war with a Catholic state, are to be indemnified by a levy on the Catholic inhabitants of the neighbourhood. All marriages between Catholics and Protestants are annulled. All Popish priests celebrating them are to be hanged. "This system" (says Arthur Young) "has no other tendency than that of driving out of the kingdom all the personal wealth of the Catholics, and extinguishing their industry within it! and the face of the country, every object which presents itself to travellers, tell him how effectually this has been done."—*Young's Tour in Ireland*, vol. ii. p. 48.

Such is the history of Ireland—for we are now at our own times; and the only remaining question is, whether the system of improvement and conciliation begun in the reign of George III. shall be pursued, and the remaining incapacities of the Catholics removed, or all these concessions be made insignificant by an adherence to that spirit of proscription which they professed to abolish? Looking to the sense and reason of the thing, and to the ordinary working of humanity and justice, when assisted, as they are here, by self-interest and worldly policy, it might seem absurd to doubt of the result. But looking to the facts and the persons by which we are now surrounded, we are constrained to say that we greatly fear that these incapacities never will be removed, till they are removed by fear. What else, indeed, can we expect when we see them opposed by such enlightened men as Mr. Peel—faintly assisted by men of such admirable genius as Mr. Canning—when royal dukes consider it as a compliment to the memory of their fathers to continue this miserable system of bigotry and exclusion,—when men act ignominiously and contemptibly on this question, who do so on no other question,—when almost the only persons zealously opposed to this general baseness and fatuity are a few whigs and reviewers, or here and there a virtuous poet, like Mr. Moore? We repeat again, that the measure never will be effected but by fear. In the midst of one of our just and necessary wars, the Irish Catholics will compel this country to grant them a great deal more than they at present require, or even contemplate. We regret most severely the protraction of the disease, and the danger of the remedy;—but in this way it is that human affairs are carried on!

We are sorry we have nothing for which to praise the administration on the subject of the Catholic question—but, it is but justice to say, that they have been very zealous and active in detecting fiscal abuses in Ireland, in improving mercantile regulations, and in detecting Irish jobs. The commission on which Mr. Wallace presided has been of the greatest possible utility, and does infinite credit to the government. The name of Mr. Wallace, in any commission, has now become a pledge to the public that there is a real intention to investigate and correct abuse. He stands in the singular predicament of being equally trusted by the rulers and the ruled. It is a new era in government, when such men are called into action; and, if there were not proclaimed and fatal limits to that ministerial liberality—which, so far as it goes, we welcome without a grudge, and praise without a sneer—we might yet hope that, for the sake of mere consistency, they might be led to falsify our forebodings. But alas! there are motives more immediate, and therefore irresistible; and the time is not yet come, when it will be believed easier to govern Ireland by the love of the many than by the power of the few—when the paltry and dangerous machinery of bigoted faction and prostituted patronage may be dispensed with, and the vessel of the state be propelled by the natural current of popular interests and the breath of popular applause. In the mean time, we cannot resist the temptation of gracing our conclusion with the following beautiful passage, in which the author alludes to the hopes that were raised at another great era of partial concession and liberality—that of the revolution of 1782,—when, also, benefits were conferred which proved abortive because they were incomplete—and balm poured into the wound, where the envenomed shaft was yet left to rankle.

"And here," says the gallant Captain Rock,—"as the free confession of weaknesses constitutes the chief charm and use of biography—I will candidly own that the dawn of prosperity and concord, which I now saw breaking over the fortunes of my country, so dazzled and deceived my youthful eyes, and so unsettled every hereditary notion of what I owed to my name and family, that—shall I confess it?—I even hailed with pleasure the prospects of peace and freedom that seemed opening around me; nay, was ready, in the boyish enthusiasm of the moment, to sacrifice all my own personal interest in all future riots and rebellions, to the one bright, seducing object of my country's liberty and repose.

"When I contemplated such a man as the venerable Charlemont, whose nobility was to the people like a fort over a valley—elevated above them solely for their defence; who introduced the polish of the courtier into the camp of the freeman, and served his country with all that pure, Platonic devotion, which a true knight in the times of chivalry proffered to his mistress;—when I listened to the eloquence of Grattan, the very music of freedom—her first, fresh matin song, after a long night of slavery, degradation, and sorrow;—when I saw the bright offerings which he brought to the shrine of his country,—wisdom, genius, courage, and patience, invigorated and embellished by all those social and domestic virtues, without which the loftiest talents stand isolated in the moral waste around them, like the pillars of Palmyra towering in a wilderness!—when I reflected on all this, it not only disheartened me for the mission of discord which I had undertaken, but made me secretly hope that it might be rendered unnecessary; and that a country, which could produce such men and achieve such a revolution, might yet—in spite of the joint efforts of the government and my family—take her rank in the scale of nations, and be happy!

"My father, however, who saw the momentary dazzle by which I was affected, soon drew me out of this false light of hope in which I lay basking, and set the truth before me in a way but too convincing and ominous. 'Be not deceived, boy,' he would say, 'by the fallacious appearances before you. Eminently great and good as is the man to whom Ireland owes this short era of glory, *our* work, believe me, will last longer than his. We have a power on our side that 'will not willingly let us die;' and, long after Grattan shall have disappeared from earth,—like that arrow shot into the clouds by Alcestes, effecting nothing, but leaving a long train of light behind him,—the family of the Rocks will continue to flourish in all their native glory, upheld by the ever-watchful care of the legislature, and fostered by that 'nursing-mother of Liberty,' the Church.' "

GRANBY.*

[Edinburgh Review, 1826.]

There is nothing more amusing in the spectacles of the present day, than to see the Sir Johns and Sir Thomases of the House of Commons struck aghast by the useful science and wise novelties of Mr. Huskisson and the chancellor of the exchequer. Treason, Disaffection, Atheism, Republicanism, and Socinianism—the great guns in the Noodle's park of artillery—they cannot bring to bear upon these gentlemen. Even to charge with a regiment of ancestors is not quite so efficacious as it used to be; and all that remains, therefore, is to rail against Peter M'Culloch and political economy! In the mean time, day after day, down goes one piece of nonsense or another. The most approved trash, and the most trusty clamours, are found to be utterly powerless. Twopenny taunts and trumpery truisms have lost their destructive omnipotence; and the exhausted commonplace-man, and the afflicted fool, moan over the ashes of imbecility, and strew flowers on the urn of ignorance! General Elliot found the London tailors in a state of mutiny, and he raised from them a regiment of light cavalry, which distinguished itself in a very striking manner at the battle of Minden. In humble imitation of this example, we shall avail ourselves of the present political disaffection and unsatisfactory idleness of many men of rank and consequence, to request their attention to the Novel of Granby—written, as we have heard, by a young gentleman of the name of Lister,† and from which we have derived a considerable deal of pleasure and entertainment.

The main question as to a novel is—did it amuse? were you surprised at dinner coming so soon? did you mistake eleven for ten, and twelve for eleven? were you too late to dress? and did you sit up beyond the usual hour? If a novel produces these effects, it is good; if it does not—story, language, love, scandal itself, cannot save it. It is only meant to please; and it must do that, or it does nothing. Now Granby seems to us to answer this test extremely well; it produces unpunctuality, makes the reader too late for dinner, impatient of contradiction, and inattentive,—even if a bishop is making an observation, or a gentleman lately from the Pyramids, or the Upper Cataracts, is let loose upon the drawing-room. The objection, indeed, to these compositions, when they are well done, is, that it is impossible to do any thing, or perform any human duty, while we are engaged in them. Who can read Mr. Hallam's Middle Ages, or extract the root of an impossible quantity, or draw up a bond, when he is in the middle of Mr. Trebeck and Lady Charlotte Duncan? How can the boy's lesson be heard, about the Jove-nourished Achilles, or his six miserable verses upon Dido be corrected, when Henry Granby and Mr. Courtenay are both making love to Miss Jermyn? Common life palls in the middle of these artificial scenes. All is emotion when the book is open—all dull, flat, and feeble when it is shut.

Granby, a young man of no profession, living with an old uncle in the country, falls in love with Miss Jermyn, and Miss Jermyn with him; but Sir Thomas and Lady Jermyn, as the young gentleman is not rich, having discovered, by long living in the world and patient observation of its ways, that young people are commonly Malthus-proof and have children, and that young and old must eat, very naturally do what they can to discourage the union. The young people, however, both go to town—meet at balls—flutter, blush, look and cannot speak—speak and cannot look,—suspect, misinterpret, are sad and mad, peevish and jealous, fond and foolish; but the passion, after all, seems less near to its accomplishment at the end of the season than the beginning. The uncle of Granby, however, dies, and leaves to his nephew a statement accompanied with the requisite proofs—that Mr. Tyrrel, the supposed son of Lord Malton, is illegitimate, and that he, Granby, is the heir to Lord Malton's fortune. The second volume is now far advanced, and it is time for Lord Malton to die. Accordingly Mr. Lister very judiciously despatches

* *Granby. A Novel in Three Volumes.* London, Colburn, 1826.

† This is the gentleman who now keeps the keys of Life and Death, the Janitor of the world.

him; Granby inherits the estate—his virtues (for what shows off virtue like land?) are discovered by the Jermyns—and they marry in the last act.

Upon this slender story, the author has succeeded in making a very agreeable and interesting novel; and he has succeeded, we think, chiefly, by the very easy and natural picture of manners, as they really exist among the upper classes; by the description of new characters judiciously drawn and faithfully preserved; and by the introduction of many striking and well-managed incidents; and we are particularly struck throughout the whole with the discretion and good sense of the author. He is never *nimious;* there is nothing in excess; there is a good deal of fancy and a great deal of spirit at work, but a directing and superintending judgment rarely quits him.

We would instance, as a proof of his tact and talent, the visit at Lord Daventry's, and the description of characters of which the party is composed. There are absolutely no events; nobody runs away, goes mad, or dies. There is little of love, or of hatred; no great passion comes into play; but nothing can be farther removed from dulness and insipidity. Who has ever lived in the world without often meeting the Miss Cliftons?

"The Miss Cliftons were good-humoured girls; not handsome, but of pleasing manners, and sufficiently clever to keep up the ball of conversation very agreeably for an occasional half hour. They were always *au courant du jour*, and knew and saw the first of every thing—were in the earliest confidence of many a bride elect, and could frequently tell that a marriage was 'off' long after it had been announced as 'on the tapis' in the morning papers—always knew something of the new opera, or the new Scotch novel, before any body else did—were the first who made fizgigs, or acted charades—contrived to have private views of most exhibitions, and were supposed to have led the fashionable throng to the Caledonian Chapel, Cross Street, Hatton Garden. Their employments were like those of most other girls; they sang, played, drew, rode, read occasionally, spoiled much muslin, manufactured purses, handscreens, and reticules for a repository, and transcribed a considerable quantity of music out of large fair print into diminutive manuscript.

"Miss Clifton was clever and accomplished; rather cold, but very conversable; collected seals, franks, and anecdotes of the day; and was a greater retailer of the latter. Anne was odd and entertaining; was a formidable quizzer, and no mean caricaturist; liked fun in most shapes; and next to making people laugh, had rather they stared at what she said. Maria was the echo of the other two: vouched for all Miss Clifton's anecdotes, and led the laugh at Anne's repartees. They were plain, and they knew it; and cared less about it than young ladies usually do. Their plainness, however, would have been less striking, but for that hard, pale, par-boiled town look,—that stamp of fashion, with which late hours and hot rooms generally endow the female face."—(pp. 103—105.)

Having introduced our reader to the Miss Cliftons, we must make him acquainted with Mr. Trebeck, one of those universally appearing gentlemen and tremendous table tyrants, by whom London society is so frequently governed:—

"Mr. Trebeck had great powers of entertainment, and a keen and lively turn for satire; and could talk down his superiors, whether in rank or talent, with very imposing confidence. He saw the advantages of being formidable, and observed with derision how those whose malignity he pampered with ridicule of others, vainly thought to purchase by subserviency exemption for themselves. He had sounded the gullibility of the world; knew the precise current value of pretension; and soon found himself the acknowledged umpire, the last appeal, of many contented followers.

"He seldom committed himself by praise or recommendation, but rather left his example and adoption to work its way. As for censure he had both ample and witty store; but here too he often husbanded his remarks, and where it was needless or dangerous to define a fault, could check admiration by an incredulous smile, and depress pretensions of a season's standing by the raising of an eyebrow. He had a quick perception of the foibles of others, and a keen relish for bantering and exposing them. No keeper of a menagerie could better show off a monkey than he could an 'original.' He could ingeniously cause the unconscious subject to place his own absurdities in the best point of view, and would cloak his derision under the blandest cajolery. Imitators he loved much; but to baffle them—more. He loved to turn upon the luckless adopters of his last folly, and see them precipitately back out of the scrape into which himself had led them.

"In the art of cutting he shone unrivalled: he knew the 'when,' the 'where,' and the 'how.' Without affecting useless short-sightedness, he could assume that calm but wandering gaze which veers, as if unconsciously, round the proscribed individual; neither fixing, nor to be fixed; not looking on vacancy, nor on any one object; neither occupied nor abstracted; a look which perhaps excuses you to the person *cut*, and, at any rate, prevents him from accosting you. Originality was his idol. He wished to astonish, even if he did not amuse; and had rather say a silly thing than a commonplace one. He was led by this sometimes even to approach the verge of rudeness and vulgarity; but he had considerable tact, and a happy hardihood, which generally carried him through the difficulties into which his fearless love of originality brought him. Indeed, he well knew that what would, in the present condition of his reputation, be scouted in any body else, would pass current with the world in him. Such was the far-famed and redoubtable Mr. Trebeck."—(pp. 109—112.)

This sketch we think exceedingly clever. But we are not sure that its merit is fully sustained by the actual presentment of its subject.

He makes his debut at dinner very characteristically, by gliding in quietly after it is half over; but in the dialogue which follows with Miss Jermyn, he seems to us a little too resolutely witty, and somewhat affectedly odd—though the whole scene is executed with spirit and talent.

"The duke had been discoursing on cookery, when Mr. Trebeck turned to her, and asked in a low tone if she had ever met the duke before—'I assure you,' said he, 'that upon *that* subject he is well worth attending to. He is supposed to possess more true science than any amateur of his day. By the bye, what is the dish before you? It looks well, and I see you are eating some of it. Let me recommend it to him upon your authority; I dare not upon my own.'—'Then pray do not use mine.'—'Yes, I will, with your permission; I'll tell him you thought, by what dropped from him in conversation, that it would exactly suit the genius of his taste. Shall I? Yes.—Duke,' (raising his voice a little, and speaking across the table,)—'Oh, no! how can you?'—'Why not?—Duke,' (with a glance at Caroline,) 'will you allow me to take wine with you?'—'I thought,' said she, relieved from her trepidation, and laughing slightly, 'you would never say any thing so very strange.'—'You have too good an opinion of me; I blush for my unworthiness. But confess, that in fact you were rather alarmed at the idea of being held up to such a critic as the recommender of a bad dish.'—'Oh, no, I was not thinking of that; but I hardly know the duke: and it would have seemed so odd; and perhaps he might have thought that I had really told you to say something of that kind.'—'Of course he would; but you must not suppose that he would have been at all surprised at it. I'm afraid you are not aware of the full extent of your privileges, and are not conscious how many things young ladies can, and may, and will do.'—'Indeed I am not—perhaps you will instruct me.'—'Ah, I never do that for any body. I like to see young ladies instruct themselves. It is better for them, and much more amusing to me. But, however, for once I will venture to tell you, that a very competent knowledge of the duties of women may, with proper attention, be picked up in a ball room.'—'Then I hope,' said she, laughing, 'you will attribute my deficiency to my little experience of ball. I have only been at two.'—'Only two! and one of them I suppose a race ball. Then you have not yet experienced any of the pleasures of a London season? Never had the dear delight of seeing and being seen, in a well of tall people at a rout, or passed a pleasant hour at a ball upon a staircase? I envy you. You have much to enjoy.'—'You do not mean that I really have?'—'Yes—really. But let me give you a caution or two. Never dance with any man without first knowing his character and condition, on the word of two credible chaperons. At balls, too, consider what you come for—to dance of course, and not to converse; therefore, never talk yourself, nor encourage it in others.'—'I'm afraid I can only answer for myself.'—'Why, if foolish, well-meaning people will choose to be entertaining, I question if you have the power of frowning them down in a very forbidden manner: but I would give them no countenance nevertheless.'—'Your advice seems a little ironical.'—'Oh, you may either follow it or reverse it—that is its chief beauty. It is equally good taken either way.'—After a slight pause, he continued—'I hope you do not sing, or play, or draw, or do any thing that every body else does.'—'I am obliged to confess that I do a little—very little—in each.'—'I understand your "very little:" I'm afraid you are accomplished.'—'You need have no fear of that. But why are you an enemy to all accomplishments?'—'All accomplishments? Nay, surely, you do not think me an enemy to all? What can you possibly take me for?'—'I do not know,' said she, laughing slightly.—'Yes, I see you do not know exactly what to make of me—and you are not without your apprehensions. I can perceive that, though you try to conceal them.—But never mind. I am a safe person to sit near—sometimes. I am to-day. This is one of my lucid intervals. I'm much better, thanks to my keeper. There he is, on the other side of the table—the tall man in black,' (pointing out Mr. Bennet,) 'a highly respectable kind of person. I came with him here for change of air. How do you think I look at present?'—Caroline could not answer him for laughing.—'Nay,' said he, 'it is cruel to laugh on such a subject. It is very hard that you should do that, and misrepresent my meaning too.'—'Well then,' said Caroline, resuming a respectable portion of gravity, 'that I may not be guilty of that again, what accomplishments do you allow to be tolerable?'—'Let me see,' said he, with a look of consideration; 'you may play a waltz with one hand, and dance as little as you think convenient. You may draw caricatures of your intimate friends. You may *not* sing a note of Rossini; nor sketch gateposts and donkeys after nature. You may sit to a harp, but you need not play it. You must not paint miniatures nor copy Swiss costumes. But you may manufacture any thing—from a cap down to a pair of shoes—always remembering that the less useful your work the better. Can you remember all this?'—'I do not know,' said she, 'it comprehends so much; and I am rather puzzled between the "mays" and "must nots." However, it seems, according to your code, that very little is to be required of me; for you have not mentioned any thing that I positively *must* do'—'Ah, well, I can reduce all to a very small compass. You must be an archeress in the summer, and a skater in the winter, and play well at billiards all the year; and if you do these extremely well, my admiration will have no bounds.'—'I believe I must forfeit all claim to your admiration then, for unfortunately I am not so gifted.'—'Then you must place it to the account of your other gifts.'—'Certainly—when it comes.'—'Oh it is sure to come, as you well know: but, nevertheless, I like that incredulous look extremely.'—He then turned away, thinking probably that he had paid her the compliment of sufficient attention, and began a conversation with the duchess, which was carried on in such a well-regulated under tone, as to be perfectly inaudible to any but themselves."—(pp. 92—99.)

The bustling importance of Sir Thomas Jermyn, the fat duke and his right hand man, the blunt toad-eater, Mr. Charlecote, a loud noisy sportsman, and Lady Jermyn's worldly prudence, are all displayed and managed with considerable skill and great power of amusing. One little sin against good taste, our author sometimes commits—an error from which Sir Walter Scott is not exempt. We mean the humour of giving characteristic names to persons and places; for instance, Sir Thomas Jermyn is Member of Parliament for the town of Rottenborough. This very easy and appellative jocularity seems to us, we confess, to savour a little of vulgarity; and is therefore quite as unworthy of Mr. Lister, as Dr. Dryasdust is of Sir Walter Scott. The plainest names which can be found (Smith, Thomson, Johnson, and Simson, always excepted) are the best for novels. Lord Chesterton we have often met with; and suffered a good deal from his lordship: a heavy, pompous, meddling peer, occupying a great share of the conversation—saying things in ten words which required only two, and evidently convinced that he is making a great impression; a large man, with a large head, and very landed manner; knowing enough to torment his fellow-creatures, not to instruct them—the ridicule of young ladies, and the natural butt and target of wit. It is easy to talk of carnivorous animals and beasts of prey; but does such a man, who lays waste a whole party of civilized beings by prosing, reflect upon the joy he spoils, and the misery he creates, in the course of his life? and that any one who listens to him through politeness, would prefer toothache or earache to his conversation? Does he consider the extreme uneasiness which ensues, when the company have discovered a man to be an extremely absurd person, at the same time that it is absolutely impossible to convey, by words or manner, the most distant suspicion of the discovery? And then, who punishes this bore? What sessions and what assizes for him? What bill is found against him? Who indicts him? When the judges have gone their vernal and autumnal rounds—the sheep-stealer disappears—the swindler gets ready for the Bay—the solid parts of the murderer are preserved in anatomical collections. But, after twenty years of crime, the bore is discovered in the same house, in the same attitude, eating the same soup,—unpunished, untried, undissected—no scaffold, no skeleton—no mob of gentlemen and ladies to gape over his last dying speech and confession.

The scene of quizzing the country neighbours is well imagined, and not ill executed; though there are many more fortunate passages in the book. The elderly widows of the metropolis beg, through us, to return their thanks to Mr. Lister for the following agreeable portrait of Mrs. Dormer.

"It would be difficult to find a more pleasing example than Mrs. Dormer, of that much libelled class of elderly ladies of the world, who are presumed to be happy only at the card table; to grow in bitterness as they advanced in years, and to haunt, like restless ghosts, those busy circles which they no longer either enliven or adorn. Such there may be; but of these she was not one. She was the frequenter of society, but not its slave. She had great natural benevolence of disposition; a friendly vivacity of manners, which endeared her to the young, and a steady good sense, which commanded the respect of her contemporaries; and many, who did not agree with her on particular points, were willing to allow that there was a good deal of reason in Mrs. Dormer's *prejudices.* She was, perhaps, a little blind to the faults of her friends; a defect of which the world could not cure her; but she was very kind to their virtues. She was fond of young people, and had an unimpaired gaiety about her, which seemed to expand in the contact with them; and she was anxious to promote, for their sake, even those amusements for which she had lost all taste herself. She was—but after all, she will be best described by negatives. She was not a match-maker, or mischief-maker; nor did she plume herself upon her charity, in implicitly believing only just half of what the world says. She was no retailer of scandalous '*on dits.*' She did not combat wrinkles with rouge; nor did she labour to render years less respected by a miserable affectation of girlish fashions. She did not stickle for the inviolable exclusiveness of certain sects; nor was she afraid of being known to visit a friend in an unfashionable quarter of the town. She was no worshipper of mere rank. She did not patronize oddities; nor sanction those who delight in braving the rules of common decency. She did not evince her sense of propriety, by shaking hands with the recent defendant in a crim. con. cause; nor exhale her devotion in Sunday routs."—(pp. 243, 244.)

Mrs. Clotworthy, we are afraid, will not be quite so well pleased with the description of her rout. Mrs. Clotworthy is one of those ladies who have ices, fiddlers, and fine rooms, but no fine friends. But fine friends may always be had, where there are ices, fiddlers, and fine rooms: and so, with ten or a dozen stars and an Oonalaska chief; and, followed by all vicious and salient London, Mrs. Clotworthy takes the field.

"The poor woman seemed half dead with fatigue already; and we cannot venture to say whether the prospect of five hours more of this high-wrought enjoyment tended much to brace her to the task. It was a brilliant sight, and an interesting one, if it could have been viewed from some fair vantage ground, with ample space, in coolness and in quiet. Rank, beauty, and splendour, were richly blended. The gay attire; the glittering jewels; the more resplendent features they adorned, and too frequently the rouged cheek of the sexagenarian; the vigilant chaperon; the fair but languid form which she conducted; well curled heads, well propped with starch; well whiskered guardsmen; and here and there fat, good-humoured, elderly gentlemen, with stars upon their coats;—all these united in one close medley—a curious piece of living mosaic. Most of them came to see and be seen; some of the most youthful professedly to dance; yet how could they? at any rate they tried.—They stood, if they could, with their vis-à-vis facing them,—and sidled across—and back again, and made one step—or two if there was room, to the right or left, and joined hands, and set—perhaps, and turned their partners, or dispensed with it if necessary—and so on to the end of 'La Finale;' and then comes a waltz for the few who choose it—and then another squeezy quadrille—and so on—and on, till the weary many 'leave ample room and verge enough' for the persevering few to figure in with greater freedom.

"But then they talk; oh! ay! true, we must not forget the charms of conversation. And what passes between nine-tenths of them! Remarks on the heat of the room; the state of the crowd; the impossibility of dancing, and the propriety nevertheless of attempting it; that on last Wednesday was a bad Almack's, and on Thursday a worse Opera; that the new ballet is supposed to be good; mutual inquiries how they like Pasta, or Catalani, or whoever the syren of the day may be; whether they have been at Lady A.'s, and whether they are going to Mrs. B.'s; whether they think Miss Such-a-one handsome! and what is the name of the gentleman talking to her; whether Rossini's music makes the best quadrilles, and whether Collinet's band are the best to play them. There are many who pay in better coin; but the small change is much of this description."—(I. 249—251.)

We consider the following description of London, as it appears to a person walking home after a rout, at four or five o'clock in the morning, to be as poetical as any thing written on the forests of Guiana, or the falls of Niagara:—

"Granby followed them with his eyes; and now, too full of happiness to be accessible to any feelings of jealousy or repining, after a short reverie of the purest satisfaction, he left the ball, and sallied out into the fresh cool air of a summer morning—suddenly passing from the red glare of lamp-light, to the clear sober brightness of returning day. He walked cheerfully onward, refreshed and exhilarated by the air of morning, and interested with the scene around him. It was broad day-light, and he viewed the town under an aspect in which it is alike presented to the late retiring votary of pleasure, and to the early rising sons of business. He stopped on the pavement of Oxford street, to contemplate the effect. The whole extent of that long vista, unclouded by the mid-day smoke, was distinctly visible to his eye at once. The houses shrunk to half their span, while the few visible spires of the adjacent churches seemed to rise less distant than before, gaily tipped with early sunshine, and much diminished in apparent size, but heightened in distinctness and in beauty. Had it not been for the cool gray tint which slightly mingled with every object, the brightness was almost that of noon. But the life, the bustle the busy din, the flowing tide of human existence, were all wanting to complete the similitude. All was hushed and silent; and this mighty receptacle of human beings, which a few short hours would wake into active energy and motion, seemed like a city of the dead.

"There was little to break this solemn illusion. Around were the monuments of human exertion, but the hands which formed them were no longer there. Few, if any, were the symptoms of life. No sounds were heard but the heavy creaking of a solitary wagon; the twittering of an occasional sparrow; the monotonous tone of the drowsy watchman; and the distant rattle of the retiring carriage, fading on the ear till it melted into silence: and the eye that searched for living objects fell on nothing but the grim great-coated guardian of the night, muffled up into an appearance of doubtful character between bear and man, and scarcely distinguishable, by the colour of his dress, from the brown flags along which he sauntered."—(pp. 297—299.)

One of the most prominent characters of the book, and the best drawn, is that of Tyrrel, son of Lord Malton, a noble blackleg, a titled gamester, and a profound plotting villain—a man, in comparison of whom, nine-tenths of the persons hung in Newgate are pure and perfect. The profound dissimulation and wicked artifices of this diabolical person are painted with great energy and power of description. The party at whist made to take in Granby is very good, and that part of the story where Granby compels Tyrrel to refund what he has won of Courtenay is of first-rate dramatic excellence; and if any one wishes for a short and convincing proof of the powers of the writer of this novel—to that scene we refer him. It shall be the taster of the cheese, and we are convinced it will sell the whole article. We are so much struck with it, that we advise the author to consider seriously whether he could not write a good play. It is many years since a good play has been written. It is about time, judging from the common economy of nature, that a good dramatic writer should appear. We promise Mr. Lister sincerely, that the Edinburgh Review shall rapidly undeceive him if he mistakes his talents; and that his delusion shall not last beyond the first tragedy or comedy.

The picture at the exhibition is extremely well managed, and all the various love-tricks of attempting to appear indifferent, are, as well as we can remember, from the life. But it is thirty or forty years since we have been in love.

The horror of an affectionate and dexterous mamma is a handsome young man without money: and the following lecture deserves to be committed to memory by all managing mothers, and repeated at proper intervals to the female progeny.

"'True, my love, but understand me. I don't wish you positively to *avoid* him. I would not go away, for instance, if I saw him coming, or even turn my head that I might not see him as he passed. That would be too *broad* and marked. People might notice it. It would look *particular.* We should never do any thing that looks *particular.* No, I would answer him civilly and composedly whenever he spoke to me, and then pass on, just as you might in the case of any body else. But I leave all this to your own tact and discretion, of which nobody has more for her age. I am sure you can enter into all these niceties, and that my observations will not be lost upon you. And now, my love, let me mention another thing. You must get over that little embarrassment which I see you show whenever you meet him. It was very natural and excusable the first time, considering our long acquaintance with him and the General: but we must make our conduct conform to circumstances; so try to get the better of this little flutter: it does not look well, and might be observed. There is no quality more valuable in a young person than self-possession. So you must keep down these blushes,' said she, patting her on the cheek, 'or I believe I must rouge you:—though it would be a thousand pities, with the pretty natural colour you have. But you must remember what I have been saying. Be more composed in your behaviour. Try to adopt the manner which I do. It may be difficult; but you see I contrive it, and I have known Mr. Granby a great deal longer than you have, Caroline.' "—(pp. 21, 22.)

These principles are of the highest practical importance in an age when the art of marrying daughters is carried to the highest pitch of excellence, when love must be made to the young men of fortune, not only by the young lady, who must appear to be dying for him, but by the father, mother, aunts, cousins, tutor, gamekeeper, and stable-boy—assisted by the parson of the parish, and the churchwardens. If any of these fail, Dives pouts, and the match is off.

The merit of this writer is, that he catches delicate portraits, which a less skilful artist would pass over, from not thinking the features sufficiently marked. We are struck, however, with the resemblance, and are pleased with the conquest of difficulties—we remember to have seen such faces, and are sensible that they form an agreeable variety to the expression of more marked and decided character. Nobody, for instance, can deny that he is acquainted with Miss Darrell.

"Miss Darrell was not strictly a beauty. She had not, as was frequently observed by her female friends, and unwillingly admitted by her male admirers, a single truly good feature in her face. But who could quarrel with the *tout ensemble?* who but must be dazzled with the graceful animation with which those features were lighted up? Let critics hesitate to pronounce her beautiful; at any rate they must allow her to be fascinating. Place a perfect stranger in a crowded assembly, and she would first attract his eye; correcter beauties would pass unnoticed, and his first attention would be riveted by her. She was all brilliancy and effect; but it were hard to say she studied it; so little did her spontaneous, airy graces convey the impression of premeditated practice. She was a sparkling tissue of little affectations, which, however, appeared so interwoven with herself, that their seeming artlessness disarmed one's censure. Strip them away, and you destroyed at once the brilliant being that so much attracted you; and it thus became difficult to condemn what you felt unable, and, indeed, unwilling, to remove. With positive affectation, malevolence itself could rarely charge her; and prudish censure seldom exceeded the guarded limits of a dry remark, that Miss Darrell had 'a good deal of *manner.*'

"Eclat she sought and gained. Indeed, she was both formed to gain it, and disposed to desire it. But she required an extensive sphere. A ball-room was her true arena; for she waltzed '*à ravir,*' and could talk enchantingly about nothing. She was devoted to fashion, and all its fickleness, and went to the extreme whenever she could do so consistently with grace. But she aspired to be a leader as well as a follower; seldom, if ever, adopted a mode that was unbecoming to herself, and dressed to suit the genius of her face."—(pp. 28, 29.)

Tremendous is the power of a novelist! If four or five men are in a room, and show a disposition to break the peace, no human magistrate (not even Mr. Justice Bayley) could do more than bind them over to keep the peace, and commit them if they refused. But the writer of the novel stands with a pen in his hand, and can run any of them through the body,—can knock down any one individual, and keep the others upon their legs; or, like the last scene in the first tragedy written by a young man of genius, can put them all to death. Now, an author possessing such extraordinary privileges, should not have allowed Mr. Tyrrel to strike Granby. This is ill-managed; particularly as Granby does not return the blow, or turn him out of the house. Nobody should suffer his hero to have a black eye, or to be pulled by the nose. The Iliad would never have come down to these times if Agamemnon had given Achilles a box on the ear. We should have trembled for the Æneid, if any Tyrian nobleman had kicked the pious Æneas in the 4th book. Æneas may have deserved it; but he could not have founded the Roman empire after so distressing an accident

ISLAND OF CEYLON.*

[EDINBURGH REVIEW, 1803.]

It is now little more than half a century since the English first began to establish themselves in any force upon the peninsula of India; and we at present possess in that country a more extensive territory, and a more numerous population, than any European power can boast of at home. In no instance has the genius of the English, and their courage, shone forth more conspicuously than in their contest with the French for the empire of India. The numbers on both sides were always inconsiderable; but the two nations were fairly matched against each other, in the cabinet and in the field; the struggle was long and obstinate; and, at the conclusion, the French remained masters of a dismantled town, and the English of the grandest and most extensive colony that the world has ever seen. To attribute this success to the superior genius of Clive, is not to diminish the reputation it confers on his country, which reputation must of course be elevated by the number of great men to which it gives birth. But the French were by no means deficient in casualties of genius at that period, unless Bussy is to be considered as a man of common stature of mind, or Dupleix to be classed with the vulgar herd of politicians. Neither was Clive (though he clearly stands forward as the most prominent figure in the group) without the aid of some military men of very considerable talents. Clive extended our Indian empire; but General Lawrence preserved it to be extended; and the former caught, perhaps, from the latter, that military spirit by which he soon became a greater soldier than him, without whom he never would have been a soldier at all.

Gratifying as these reflections upon our prowess in India are to national pride, they bring with them the painful reflection, that so considerable a portion of our strength and wealth is vested upon such precarious foundations, and at such an immense distance from the parent country. The glittering fragments of the Portuguese empire, scattered up and down the East, should teach us the instability of such dominion. We are (it is true) better capable of preserving what we have obtained, than any other nation which has ever colonized in Southern Asia: but the object of ambition is so tempting, and the perils to which it is exposed so numerous, that no calculating mind can found any durable conclusions upon this branch of our commerce, and this source of our strength.

In the acquisition of Ceylon, we have obtained the greatest of all our wants—a good harbour. For it is a very singular fact, that, in the whole peninsula of India, Bombay is alone capable of affording a safe retreat to ships during the period of the monsoons.

The geographical figure of our possessions in Ceylon is whimsical enough: we possess the whole of the sea-coast, and enclose in a periphery the unfortunate King of Candia, whose rugged and mountainous dominions may be compared to a coarse mass of iron, set in a circle of silver. The Popilian ring, in which this votary of Buddha has been so long held by the Portuguese and Dutch, has infused the most vigilant jealousy into the government, and rendered it as difficult to enter the kingdom of Candia, as if it were Paradise or China; and yet, once there, always there; for the difficulty of departing is just as great as the difficulty of arriving; and his Candian excellency, who has used every device in his power to keep them out, is seized with such an affection for those who baffle his defensive artifices, that he can on no account suffer them to depart. He has been known to detain a string of four or five Dutch embassies, till various members of the legation died of old age at his court, while they were expecting an answer to their questions, and a return to their presents:* and his majesty once exasperated a little French ambassador to such a degree, by the various pretences under which he kept him at his court, that this lively member of the corps diplomatique, one day, in a furious passion, attacked six or seven of his majesty's largest elephants sword in hand, and would, in all probability, have reduced them to mince-meat, if the poor beasts had not been saved from the unequal combat

The best and most ample account of Ceylon is contained in the narrative of Robert Knox, who, in the middle of the 17th century, was taken prisoner there (while refitting his ship) at the age of nineteen, and remained nineteen years on the island, in slavery to the King of Candia. During this period, he learnt the language, and acquired a thorough knowledge of the people. The account he has given of them is extremely entertaining, and written in a very simple and unaffected style; so much so, indeed, that he presents his reader with a very grave account of the noise the devil makes in the woods of Candia, and of the frequent opportunities he has had of hearing him.

Mr. Percival does not pretend to deal with the devil; but appears to have used the fair and natural resources of observation and good sense, to put together an interesting description of Ceylon. There is nothing in the book very animated, or very profound, but it is without

* *An Account of the Island of Ceylon.* By ROBERT PERCIVAL, Esq., of his Majesty's Nineteenth Regiment of Foot London, C. and R. Baldwin.

* Knox's Ceylon.

pretensions; and if it does not excite attention by any unusual powers of description, it never disgusts by credulity, wearies by prolixity, or offends by affectation. It is such an account as a plain military man of diligence and common sense might be expected to compose; and narratives like these we must not despise. To military men we have been, and must be, indebted for our first acquaintance with the interior of many countries. Conquest has explored more than ever curiosity has done; and the path for science has been commonly opened by the sword.

We shall proceed to give a very summary abstract of the principal contents of Mr. Percival's book.

The immense accessions of territory which the English have acquired in the East Indies since the American war, rendered it absolutely necessary, that some effort should be made to obtain possession of a station where ships might remain in safety during the violent storms incidental to that climate. As the whole of that large tract which we possess along the Coromandel coast presents nothing but open roads, all vessels are obliged, on the approach of the monsoons, to stand out in the open seas; and there are many parts of the coast that can be approached only during a few months of the year. As the harbour of Trincomalee, which is equally secure at all seasons, afforded the means of obviating these disadvantages, it is evident that, on the first rupture with the Dutch, our countrymen would attempt to gain possession of it. A body of troops was, in consequence, detached in the year 1795, for the conquest of Ceylon, which (in consequence of the indiscipline which political dissension had introduced among the Dutch troops) was effected almost without opposition.

Ceylon is now inhabited by the English; the remains of the Dutch, and Portuguese, the Cinglese or natives, subject to the dominion of the Europeans; the Candians, subject to the king of their own name; and the Vaddahs, or wild men, subject to no power. A Ceylonese Dutchman is a course, grotesque species of animal, whose native apathy and phlegm is animated only by the insolence of a colonial tyrant: his principal amusement appears to consist in smoking; but his pipe, according to Mr. Percival's account, is so seldom out of his mouth, that his smoking appears to be almost as much a necessary function of animal life as his breathing. His day is eked out with gin, ceremonious visits, and prodigious quantities of gross food, dripping with oil and butter; his mind, just able to reach from one meal to another, is incapable of farther exertion; and, after the panting and deglutition of a long protracted dinner, reposes on the sweet expectation that, in a few hours, the carnivorous toil will be renewed. He lives only to digest, and, while the organs of gluttony perform their office, he has not a wish beyond; and is the happy man which Horace describes:—

——— *in seipso totus, teres, atque rotundus.*

The descendants of the Portuguese differ materially from the Moors, Malabars, and other Mahometans. Their great object is to show the world they are Europeans and Christians. Unfortunately, their ideas of Christianity are so imperfect, that the only mode they can hit upon of displaying their faith, is by wearing hats and breeches, and by these habiliments they consider themselves as showing a proper degree of contempt, on various parts of the body, towards Mahomet and Buddha. They are lazy treacherous, effeminate, and passionate to excess; and are, in fact, a locomotive and animated farrago of the bad qualities of all tongues, people, and nations, on the face of the earth.

The Malays, whom we forgot before to enumerate, form a very considerable portion of the inhabitants of Ceylon. Their original empire lies in the peninsula of Malacca, from whence they have extended themselves over Java, Sumatra, the Moluccas, and a vast number of other islands in the peninsula of India. It has been many years customary for the Dutch to bring them to Ceylon, for the purpose of carrying on various branches of trade and manufacture, and in order also to employ them as soldiers and servants. The Malays are the most vindictive and ferocious of living beings. They set little or no value on their own existence, in the prosecution of their odious passions; and having thus broken the great tie which renders man a being capable of being governed, and fit for society, they are a constant source of terror to all those who have any kind of connection or relation with them. A Malay servant, from the apprehension excited by his vindictive disposition, often becomes the master of his master. It is as dangerous to dismiss him as to punish him; and the rightful despot, in order to avoid assassination, is almost compelled to exchange characters with his slave. It is singular, however, that the Malay, incapable of submission on any other occasion, and ever ready to avenge insult with death, submits to the severest military discipline with the utmost resignation and meekness. The truth is, obedience to his officers forms part of his religious creed; and the same man who would repay the most insignificant insult with death, will submit to be lacerated at the halbert with the patience of a martyr. This is truly a tremendous people! When assassins and blood-hounds will fall in rank and file, and the most furious savages submit (with no diminution of their ferocity) to the science and discipline of war, they only want a Malay Bonaparte to lead them to the conquest of the world. Our curiosity has always been very highly excited by the accounts of this singular people; and we cannot help thinking, that, one day or another, when they are more full of opium than usual, they *will run a muck* from Cape Comorin to the Caspian.

Mr. Percival does not consider the Ceylonese as descended from the continentals of the peninsula, but rather from the inhabitants of the Maldive Islands, whom they very much resemble in complexion, features, language, and manners.

"The Ceylonese (says Mr. Percival) are courteous and polite in their demeanour, even to a degree far exceeding their civilization. In several qualities they are greatly superior to all other Indians who have fallen within the sphere of my observation. I have already exempted them from the censure of stealing and lying, which seem to be almost inherent in the nature of an Indian. They are mild, and by no means captious or passionate in their intercourse with each other; though, when once their anger is roused, it is proportionably furious and lasting. Their hatred is indeed mortal, and they will frequently destroy themselves to obtain the destruction of the detested object. One instance will serve to show the extent to which this passion is carried. If a Ceylonese cannot obtain money due to him by another, he goes to his debtor, and threatens to kill himself if he is not instantly paid. This threat, which is sometimes put in execution, reduces the debtor, if it be in his power, to immediate compliance with the demand: as, by their law, if any man causes the loss of another man's life, his own is the forfeit. 'An eye for an eye, and a tooth for a tooth,' is a proverbial expression continually in their mouths. This is, on other occasions, a very common mode of revenge among them; and a Ceylonese has often been known to contrive to kill himself in the company of his enemy, that the latter might suffer for it.

"This dreadful spirit of revenge, so inconsistent with the usually mild and humane sentiments of the Ceylonese, and much more congenial to the bloody temper of a Malay, still continues to be fostered by the sacred customs of the Candians. Among the Cinglese, however, it has been greatly mitigated by their intercourse with Europeans. The desperate mode of obtaining revenge which I have just described, has been given up, from having been disappointed of its object; as, in all those parts under our dominion, the European modes of investigating and punishing crimes are enforced. A case of this nature occurred at Caltura in 1799. A Cinglese peasant happening to have a suit or controversy with another, watched an opportunity of going to bathe in company with him, and drowned himself, with the view of having his adversary put to death. The latter was upon this taken up, and sent to Columbo to take his trial for making away with the deceased, upon the principle of having been the last seen in his company. There was, however, nothing more than presumptive proof against the culprit, and he was of course acquitted. This decision, however, did not by any means tally with the sentiments of the Cinglese, who are as much inclined to continue their ancient barbarous practice, as their brethren the Candians, although they are deprived of the power."—(pp. 70—72.)

The warlike habits of the Candians make them look with contempt on the Cinglese, who are almost entirely unacquainted with the management of arms. They have the habit and character of mountaineers—warlike, hardy, enterprising, and obstinate. They have, at various times, proved themselves very formidable enemies to the Dutch; and in that kind of desultory warfare, which is the only one their rugged country will admit of, have cut off large parties of the troops of both these nations. The King of Candia, as we have before mentioned, possesses only the middle of the island, which nature, and his Candian majesty, have rendered as inaccessible as possible. It is traversable only by narrow wood-paths, known to nobody but the natives, strictly watched in peace and war, and where the best troops in the world might be shot in any quantities by the Candian marksmen, without the smallest possibility of resisting their enemies; because there would not be the smallest possibility of finding them. The King of Candia is of course despotic; and the history of his life and reign presents the same monotonous ostentation, and baby-like caprice, which characterize oriental governments. In public audiences he appears like a great fool, squatting on his hams; far surpassing gingerbread in splendour; and, after asking some such idiotical question, as whether Europe is in Asia or Africa, retires with a flourish of trumpets very much out of tune. For his private amusements, he rides on the nose of an elephant, plays with his jewels, sprinkles his courtiers with rose-water, and feeds his gold and silver fish. If his tea is not sweet enough, he impales his footman; and smites off the heads of half a dozen of his noblemen, if he has a pain in his own.

—ὥσπερ γαρ (says Aristotle) *τελεωθεν βελτιστον των ζωων ανθρωπος εστι, οὑτω και χωρισθεν νομου, και δικης χειριστον παντων.* Polit.

The only exportable articles of any importance which Ceylon produces, are pearls, cinnamon, and elephants. Mr. Percival has presented us with an extremely interesting account of the pearl fishery, held in Condatchy Bite, near the island of Manaar, in the straits which separate Ceylon from the main land.

"There is perhaps no spectacle which the island of Ceylon affords more striking to an European, than the bay of Condatchy, during the season of the pearl fishery. This desert and barren spot is at that time converted into a scene, which exceeds, in novelty and variety, almost any thing I ever witnessed. Several thousands of people of different colours, countries, castes, and occupations, continually passing and repassing in a busy crowd; the vast number of small tents and huts erected on the shore, with the bazaar or market-place before each; the multitude of boats returning in the afternoon from the pearl banks, some of them laden with riches; the anxious expecting countenances of the boat-owners, while the boats are approaching the shore, and the eagerness and avidity with which they run to them when arrived, in hopes of a rich cargo; the vast numbers of jewellers, brokers, merchants of all colours and all descriptions, both natives and foreigners, who are occupied in some way or other with the pearls, some separating and assorting them, others weighing and ascertaining their number and value, while others are hawking them about, or drilling and boring them for future use;—all these circumstances tend to impress the mind with the value and importance of that object, which can of itself create this scene.

"The bay of Condatchy is the most central rendezvous for the boats employed in the fishery. The banks where it is carried on extend several miles along the coast from Manaar southward off Arippo, Condatchy, and Pompa-ripo. The principal bank is opposite to Condatchy, and lies out at sea about twenty miles. The first step, previous to the commencement of the fishery, is to have the different oyster banks surveyed, the state of the oysters ascertained, and a report made on the subject to government. If it has been found that the quantity is sufficient, and that they are arrived at a proper degree of maturity, the particular banks to be fished that year are put up for sale to the highest bidder, and are usually purchased by a black merchant. This, however, is not always the course pursued: government sometimes judges it more advantageous to fish the banks on its own account, and to dispose of the pearls afterwards to the merchants. When this plan is adopted, boats are hired for the season on account of government, from different quarters; the price varies considerably according to circumstances, but is usually from five to eight hundred pagodas for each boat. There are, however, no stated prices, and the best bargain possible is made for each boat separately. The Dutch generally followed this last system; the banks were fished on government account, and the pearls disposed of in different parts of India or sent to Europe. When this plan was pursued, the governor and council of Ceylon claimed a certain per centage on the value of the pearls; or, if the fishing of the banks was disposed of by public sale, they bargained for a stipulated sum to themselves over and above what was paid on account of government. The pretence on which they founded their claims for this perquisite, was their trouble in surveying and valuing the banks."—(pp. 59—61.)

The banks are divided into six or seven portions, in order to give the oysters time to grow, which are supposed to attain their maturity in about seven years. The period allowed to the merchant to complete his fishery is about six weeks, during which period all the boats go out and return together, and are subject to very rigorous laws. The dexterity of the divers is very striking; they are as adroit in the use of their feet as their hands; and can pick up the smallest object under water with their toes. Their descent is aided by a great stone, which they slip from their feet when they arrive at the bottom, where they can remain about two minutes. There are instances, however, of divers, who have so much of the aquatic in their nature, as to remain under water for five or six minutes. Their great enemy is the ground-shark; for the rule of eat and be eaten, which Dr. Darwin called the great law of nature, obtains in as much force fathoms deep beneath the waves as above them: this animal is as fond of the legs of Hindoos, as Hindoos are of the pearls of oysters; and as one appetite appears to him much more natural, and less capricious than the other, he never fails to indulge it. Where fortune has so much to do with peril and profit, of course there is no deficiency of conjurers, who, by divers enigmatical grimaces, endeavour to *ostracise* this submarine invader. If they are successful they are well paid in pearls and when a shark indulges himself with the leg of a Hindoo, there is a witch, who lives at Colang, on the Malabar coast, who always bears the blame.

A common mode of theft practised by the common people engaged in the pearl fishery, is by swallowing the pearls. Whenever any one is suspected of having swallowed these precious pills of Cleopatra, the police apothecaries are instantly sent for; a *brisk* cathartic is immediately despatched after the truant pearl, with the strictest orders to apprehend it, in whatever corner of the *viscera* it may be found lurking. Oyster lotteries are carried on here to a great extent. They consist in purchasing a quantity of the oysters unopened, and running the chance of either finding or not finding pearls in them. The European gentlemen and officers who attend the pearl fishery, through duty or curiosity, are particularly fond of these lotteries, and frequently make purchases of this sort. The whole of this account is very well written, and has afforded us a great degree of amusement. By what curious links, and fantastical relations, are mankind connected together! At the distance of half the globe, a Hindoo gains his support by groping at the bottom of the sea, for the morbid concretion of shell-fish, to decorate the throat of a London alderman's wife. It is said that the great Linnæus had discovered the secret of infecting oysters with this perligenous disease: what is become of the secret we do not know, as the only interest we take in oysters is of a much more vulgar, though, perhaps, a more humane nature.

The principal woods of cinnamon lie in the neighbourhood of Columbo. They reach to within half a mile of the fort, and fill the whole surrounding prospect. The grand garden near the town is so extensive, as to occupy a tract of country from 10 to 15 miles in length.

"Nature has here concentrated both the beauty and the riches of the island. Nothing can be more delightful to the eye than the prospect which stretches around Columbo. The low cinnamon trees which cover the plain, allow the view to reach the groves of evergreens, interspersed with tall clumps, and bounded everywhere with extensive ranges of cocoa-nut and other large trees. The whole is diversified with small lakes and green marshes, skirted all round with rice and pasture fields. In one part, the intertwining cinnamon trees appear completely to clothe the face of the plain; in another, the openings made by the intersecting footpaths just serve to show that the thick underwood has been penetrated. One large road, which goes out at the west gate of the fort, and returns by the gate on the south, makes a winding circuit of seven miles among the woods. It is here that the officers and gentlemen belonging to the garrison of Columbo take their morning ride, and enjoy one of the finest scenes in nature."—(pp. 336, 337.)

As this spice constitutes the wealth of Ceylon, great pains are taken to ascertain its qualities, and propagate its choicest kinds. The prime sort is obtained from the Laurus Cinnamonum. The leaf resembles the laurel in shape, but is not of so deep a green. When chewed it has the smell and taste of cloves. There are several different species of cinnamon trees on the island; but four sorts only are cultivated and barked. The picture which we have just quoted from Mr. Percival, of a morning ride in a cinnamon wood, is so enchanting, that we are extremely sorry the addition of aromatic odours cannot with veracity be made to it. The cinnamon has, unfortunately, no smell at all but to the nostrils of the poet. Mr. Percival gives us a very interesting account of the process of making up cinnamon for the market, in which we are sorry our limits will not permit us to follow him. The different qualities of the cinnamon bundles can only be estimated by the taste; an office which devolves upon the medical men of the settlement, who are employed for *several days together in chewing cinnamon*, the acrid juice of which excoriates the mouth, and puts them to the most dreadful tortures.

The island of Ceylon is completely divided into two parts by a very high range of mountains, on the two sides of which the climate and the seasons are entirely different. These mountains also terminate completely the effect of the monsoons, which set in periodically from opposite sides of them. On the west side, the rains prevail in the months of May, June, and July, the season when they are felt on the Malabar coast. This monsoon is usually extremely violent during its continuance. The northern parts of the island are very little affected. In the months of October and November, when the opposite monsoon sets in on the Coromandel coast, the north of the island is attacked; and scarcely any impression reaches the southern parts. The heat during the day is nearly the same throughout the year: the rainy season renders the nights much cooler. The climate, upon the whole, is much more temperate than on the continent of India. The temperate and healthy climate of Ceylon is, however, confined to the seacoast. In the interior of the country, the obstructions which the thick woods oppose to the free circulation of air, render the heat almost insupportable, and generate a low and malignant fever, known to Europeans by the name of the Jungle fever. The chief harbours of Ceylon are Trincomalee, Point de Galle, and, at certain seasons of the year, Columbo. The former of these, from its nature and situation, is that which stamps Ceylon one of our most valuable acquisitions in the East Indies. As soon as the monsoons commence, every vessel caught by them in any other part of the Bay of Bengal is obliged to put to sea immediately, in order to avoid destruction. At these seasons, Trincomalee alone, of all the parts on this side of the peninsula, is capable of affording to vessels a safe retreat; which a vessel from Madras may reach in two days. These circumstances render the value of Trincomalee much greater than that of the whole island; the revenue of which will certainly be hardly sufficient to defray the expense of the establishments kept up there. The agriculture of Ceylon is, in fact, in such an imperfect state, and the natives have so little availed themselves of its natural fertility, that great part of the provisions necessary for its support are imported from Bengal.

Ceylon produces the elephant, the buffalo, tiger, elk, wild-hog, rabbit, hare, flying-fox, and musk-rat. Many articles are rendered entirely useless by the smell of musk, which this latter animal communicates in merely running over them. Mr. Percival asserts (and the fact has been confirmed to us by the most respectable authority), that if it even pass over a bottle of wine, however well corked and sealed up, the wine becomes so strongly tainted with musk, that it cannot be used; and a whole cask may be rendered useless in the same manner. Among the great variety of birds, we were struck with Mr. Percival's account of the honey-bird, into whose body the soul of a common informer appears to have migrated. It makes a loud and shrill noise, to attract the notice of anybody whom it may perceive; and thus inducing him to follow the course it points out, leads him to the tree where the bees have concealed their treasure; after the apiary has been robbed, this feathered scoundrel gleans his reward from the hive. The list of Ceylonese snakes is hideous; and we become reconciled to the crude and cloudy land in which we live, from reflecting, that the indiscriminate activity of the sun generates what is loathsome, as well as what is lovely; that the asp reposes under the rose; and the scorpion crawls under the fragrant flower and the luscious fruit.

The usual stories are repeated here, of the immense size and voracious appetite of a certain species of serpent. The best history of this kind we ever remember to have read, was of a serpent killed near one of our settlements, in the East Indies; in whose body they found the chaplain of the garrison, all in black, the Rev. Mr.——(somebody or other, whose name we have forgotten), and who, after having been missing for above a week, was discovered in this very inconvenient situation. The dominions of the King of Candia are partly defended by leeches, which abound in the woods, and from which our soldiers suffered in the most dreadful manner. The Ceylonese, in compensation for their animated plagues, are endowed with two vegetable blessings, the cocoa-nut tree and the talipot tree. The latter affords a prodigious leaf, impenetrable to sun or rain, and large enough to shelter ten men. It is a natural umbrella, and is of as eminent service in that country as a great-coat tree would be in this. A leaf of the talipot tree is a tent to the soldier, a parasol to the traveller, and a book to the scholar.* The cocoa tree affords bread, milk, oil, wine, spirits, vinegar, yeast, sugar, cloth, paper, huts, and ships.

We could with great pleasure proceed to give a farther abstract of this very agreeable and interesting publication, which we very strongly recommend to the public. It is written with great modesty, entirely without pre

* All books are written upon it in Ceylon

tensions, and abounds with curious and important information. Mr. Percival will accept our best thanks for the amusement he has afforded us. When we can praise with such justice, we are always happy to do it; and regret that the rigid and independent honesty which we have made the very basis of our literary undertaking, should so freqnently compel us to speak of the authors who come before us, in a style so different from that in which we have vindicated the merits of Mr. Percival.

DELPHINE.*

[Edinburgh Review, 1803.]

This dismal trash, which has nearly dislocated the jaws of every critic among us with gaping, has so alarmed Bonaparte, that he has seized the whole impression, sent Madame de Staël out of Paris, and, for aught we know, sleeps in a night-cap of steel, and dagger-proof blankets. To us it appears rather an attack upon the Ten Commandments than the government of Bonaparte, and calculated not so much to enforce the rights of the Bourbons, as the benefits of adultery, murder, and a great number of other vices, which have been somehow or other strangely neglected in this country, and too much so (according to the apparent opinion of Madame de Staël) even in France.

It happens, however, fortunately enough, that her book is as dull as it could have been if her intentions had been good; for wit, dexterity, and the pleasant energies of the mind, seldom rank themselves on the side of virtue and social order; while vice is spiritual, eloquent, and alert, ever choice in expression, happy in allusion, and judicious in arrangement.

The story is simply this.—Delphine, a rich young widow, presents her cousin Matilda de Vernon with a considerable estate, in order to enable her to marry Leonce Mondeville. To this action she is excited by the arts and the intrigues of Madame de Vernon, an hackneyed Parisian lady, who hopes, by this marriage, to be able to discharge her numerous and pressing debts. Leonce, who, like all other heroes of novels, has fine limbs, and fine qualities, comes to Paris—dislikes Matilda—falls in love with Delphine, Delphine with him; and they are upon the eve of jilting poor Matilda, when, from some false reports spread abroad respecting the character of Delphine (which are aggravated by her own imprudences, and by the artifices of Madame Vernon), Leonce, not in a fit of honesty, but of revenge, marries the lady whom he came to marry. Soon after, Madame de Vernon dies—discovers the artifices by which she had prevented the union of Leonce and Delphine—and then, after this catastrophe, which ought to have terminated the novel, come two long volumes of complaint and despair. Delphine becomes a nun—runs away from the nunnery with Leonce, who is taken by some French soldiers, upon the supposition that he has been serving in the French emigrant army against his country—is shot, and upon his dead body falls Delphine as dead as he.

Making every allowance for reading this book in a translation, and in a very bad translation, we cannot but deem it a heavy performance. The incidents are vulgar; the characters vulgar, too, except those of Delphine and Madame de Vernon. Madame de Staël has not the artifice to hide what is coming. In travelling through a flat country, or a flat book, we see our road before us for half the distance we are going. There are no agreeable sinuosities, and no speculations whether we are to ascend next, or descend; what new sight we are to enjoy, or to which side we are to bend. Leonce is robbed and half murdered; the apothecary of the place is certain he will not live; we were absolutely certain that he would live, and could predict to an hour the time of his recovery. In the same manner we could have prophesied every event of the book a whole volume before its occurrence.

This novel is a perfect *Alexandrian*. The two last volumes are redundant, and drag their wounded length: it should certainly have terminated where the interest ceases, at the death of Madame de Vernon; but, instead of this, the scene-shifters come and pick up the dead bodies, wash the stage, sweep it, and do every thing which the timely fall of the curtain should have excluded from the sight, and left to the imagination of the audience. We humbly apprehend, that young gentlemen do not in general make their tutors the confidants of their passion; at least we can find no rule of that kind laid down either by Miss Hamilton or Miss Edgeworth, in their treatises on education. The tutor of Leonce is Mr. Barton, a grave old gentleman, in a peruke and snuff-coloured clothes. Instead of writing to this solemn personage about second causes, the ten categories, and the eternal fitness of things the young lover raves to him, for whole pages, about the white neck and auburn hair of his Delphine; and, shame to tell! the liquorish old pedagogue seems to think these amorous ebullitions the pleasantest sort of writing *in usum Delphini* that he has yet met with.

By altering one word, and making *only* one

* *Delphine.* By Madame de Staël Holstein. London, Mawman. 6 vols. 12mo.

false quantity,* we shall change the rule of Horace to

> "Nec *febris* intersit nisi dignus vindice nodus
> Inciderit."——

Delphine and Leonce have eight very bad *typhus* fevers between them, besides *hæmoptoe, hemorrhage, deliquium animi, singultus, hysteria,* and *fœminei ululatus,* or screams innumerable. Now, that there should be a reasonable allowance of sickness in every novel, we are willing to admit, and will cheerfully permit the heroine to be once given over, and at the point of death; but we cannot consent, that the interest which ought to be excited by the feelings of the mind should be transferred to the sufferings of the body, and a crisis of perspiration be substituted for a crisis of passion. Let us see difficulties overcome, if our approbation is required; we cannot grant it to such cheap and sterile artifices as these.

The characters in this novel are all said to be drawn from real life; and the persons for whom they are intended are loudly whispered at Paris. Most of them we have forgotten; but Delphine is said to be intended for the authoress, and *Madame de Vernon* (by a slight sexual metamorphosis) for Talleyrand, minister of the French republic for foreign affairs. As this lady (once the friend of the authoress) may probably exercise a considerable influence over the destinies of this country, we shall endeavour to make our readers a little better acquainted with her; but we must first remind them that she was once a bishop, a nigher dignity in the church than was ever attained by any of her sex since the days of Pope Joan; and that though she swindles Delphine out of her estate with a considerable degree of address, her dexterity sometimes fails her, as in the memorable instance of the American commissioners. Madame de Staël gives the following description of this pastoral metropolitan female:

"Though she is at least forty, she still appears charming even among the young and beautiful of her own sex. The paleness of her complexion, the slight relaxation of her features, indicate the languor of indisposition, and not the decay of years; the easy negligence of her dress accords with this impression. Every one concludes, that when her health is recovered, and she dresses with more care, she must be completely beautiful: this change, however, never happens, but it is always expected; and that is sufficient to make the imagination still add something more to the natural effect of her charms."—(Vol. I. p. 21.)

Nothing can be more execrable than the manner in which this book is translated. The bookseller has employed one of our countrymen for that purpose, who appears to have been very *lately caught.* The contrast between the passionate exclamations of Madame de Staël, and the barbarous vulgarities of poor Sawney, produces a mighty ludicrous effect. One of the heroes, a man of high fastidious temper, exclaims in a letter to Delphine, "I cannot endure this Paris; I have met *with ever so many people* whom my soul abhors." And the accomplished and enraptured Leonce terminates one of his letters thus: "*Adieu! Adieu, my dearest Delphine! I will give you a call* to-morrow." We doubt if Grub street ever imported from Caledonia a more abominable translator.

We admit the character of Madame de Vernon to be drawn with considerable skill. There are occasional traits of eloquence and pathos in this novel, and very many of those observations upon manners and character, which are totally out of the reach of all who have lived not long in the world, and observed it well.

The immorality of any book (in our estimation) is to be determined by the general impression it leaves on those minds, whose principles, not yet *ossified,* are capable of affording a less powerful defence to its influence. The most dangerous effect that any fictitious character can produce, is when two or three of its popular vices are varnished over with every thing that is captivating and gracious in the exterior, and ennobled by association with splendid virtues: this apology will be more sure of its effect, if the faults are not against nature, but against society. The aversion to murder and cruelty could not perhaps be so overcome; but a regard to the sanctity of marriage vows, to the sacred and sensitive delicacy of the female character, and to numberless restrictions important to the well-being of our species, may easily be relaxed by this subtle and voluptuous confusion of good and evil. It is in vain to say the fable evinces, in the last act, that vice is productive of misery. We may decorate a villain with graces and felicities for nine volumes, and hang him in the last page. This is not teaching virtue, but gilding the gallows, and raising up splendid associations in favour of being hanged. In such an union of the *amiable* and the vicious, (especially if the vices are such, to the commission of which there is no want of natural disposition,) the vice will not degrade the man, but the man will ennoble the vice. We shall wish to be him we admire, *in spite* of his vices, and, if the novel be well written, even *in consequence* of his vice. There exists, through the whole of this novel, a show of exquisite sensibility to the evils which individuals suffer by the inflexible rules of virtue prescribed by society, and an eager disposition to apologize for particular transgressions. Such doctrine is not confined to Madame de Staël; an Arcadian cant is gaining fast upon Spartan gravity; and the happiness diffused, and the beautiful order established in society, by this unbending discipline, are wholly swallowed up in compassion for the unfortunate and interesting individual. Either the exceptions or the rule must be given up: every highwayman who thrusts his pistol into a chaise window has met with *unforeseen misfortunes;* and every loose matron who flies into the arms of her *Greville* was compelled to marry an old man whom she detested, by an avaricious and unfeeling father. The passions want not accelerating, but retarding machinery. This fatal and foolish

* Perhaps a fault of all others which the English are least disposed to pardon. A young man, who, on a public occasion, makes a false quantity at the outset of life, can seldom or never get over it.

sophistry has power enough over every heart, not to need the aid of fine composition, and well-contrived incident—auxiliaries which Madame de Staël intended to bring forward in the cause, though she has fortunately not succeeded.

M. de Serbellone is received as a guest into the house of M. d'Ervins, whose wife he debauches as a recompense for his hospitality. Is it possible to be disgusted with ingratitude and injustice, when united to such an assemblage of talents and virtues as this man of paper possesses? Was there ever a more delightful, fascinating adulteress than Madame d'Ervins is intended to be? or a *povero cornuto* less capable of exciting compassion than her husband? The morality of all this is the old morality of Farquhar, Vanburgh, and Congreve—that every witty man may transgress the seventh commandment, which was never meant for the protection of husbands who labour under the incapacity of making repartees. In Matilda, religion is always as unamiable as dissimulation is graceful in Madame de Vernon, and imprudence generous in Delphine. This said Delphine, with her fine auburn hair, and her beautiful blue or green eyes (we forget which), cheats her cousin Matilda out of her lover, alienates the affections of her husband, and keeps a sort of assignation house for Serbellone and his *chère amie*, justifying herself by the most touching complaints against the rigour of the world, and using the customary phrases, *union of souls, married in the eye of heaven*, &c. &c. &c., and such like diction, the types of which Mr. Lane, of the Minerva Press, very prudently keeps ready composed, in order to facilitate the printing of the Adventures of Captain C—— and Miss F——, and other interesting stories, of which he, the said inimitable Mr. Lane, of the Minerva Press, well knows these sentiments must make a part. Another perilous absurdity which this *useful* production tends to cherish, is the common notion, that contempt of rule and order is a proof of greatness of mind. Delphine is everywhere a great spirit struggling with the shackles imposed upon her in common with the little world around her; and it is managed so that her contempt of restrictions shall always appear to flow from the extent, variety, and splendour of her talents. The vulgarity of this heroism ought in some degree to diminish its value. Mr. Colquhoun, in his Police of the Metropolis, reckons up above 40,000 heroines of this species, most of whom, we dare to say, have at one time or another reasoned like the sentimental Delphine about the judgments of the world.

To conclude—Our general opinion of this book is, that it is calculated to shed a mild lustre over adultery; by gentle and convenient gradation, to destroy the modesty and the caution of women; to facilitate the acquisition of easy vices, and encumber the difficulty of virtue. What a wretched qualification of this censure to add, that the badness of the principle is alone corrected by the badness of the style, and that this celebrated lady would have been very guilty, if she had not been very dull!

MISSION TO ASHANTEE.*

[EDINBURGH REVIEW, 1819.]

CAPE COAST CASTLE, or Cape Corso, is a factory of Africa, on the Gold Coast. The Portuguese settled here in 1610, and built the citadel; from which, in a few years afterwards, they were dislodged by the Dutch. In 1661, it was demolished by the English under Admiral Holmes; and by the treaty of Breda, it was made over to our government. The latitude of Cape Coast Castle is 5° 6′ north; the longitude 1° 51′ west. The capital of the kingdom of Ashantee is Coomassie, the latitude of which is about 6° 30′ 20″ north, and the longitude 2° 6′ 30″ west. The mission quitted Cape Coast Castle on the 22d of April, and arrived at Coomassie about the 16th of May—halting two or three days on the route, and walking the whole distance, or carried by hammock-bearers at a foot-pace. The distance between the fort and the capital is not more than 150 miles, or about as far as from Durham to Edinburgh; and yet the kingdom of Ashantee was, before the mission of Mr. Bowdich, almost as much unknown to us as if it had been situated in some other planet. The country which surrounds Cape Coast Castle belongs to the Fantees; and, about the year 1807, an Ashantee army reached the coast for the first time. They invaded Fantee again in 1811, and, for the third time, in 1816. To put a stop to the horrible cruelties committed by the stronger on the weaker nation; to secure their own safety, endangered by the Ashantees; and to enlarge our knowledge of Africa—the government of Cape Coast Castle persuaded the African committee to send a deputation to the kingdom of Ashantee; and of this embassy the publication now before us is the narrative. The embassy walked through a beautiful country, laid waste by the recent wars, and arrived in the time we have mentioned, and without meeting with any remarkable accident at Coomassie, the capital. The account of their first reception there we shall lay before our readers.

"We entered Coomassie at two o'clock, pass-

* *Mission from Cape Coast Castle to Ashantee, with a Statistical Account of that Kingdom, and Geographical Notices of other Parts of the Interior of Africa.* By T. EDWARD BOWDICH, Esq., Conductor. London, Murray, 1819.

ing under a fetish, or sacrifice of a dead sheep, wrapped up in red silk, and suspended between two lofty poles. Upwards of 5000 people, the greater part warriors, met us with awful bursts of martial music, discordant only in its mixture; for horns, drums, rattles, and gong-gongs, were all exerted with a zeal bordering on frenzy, to subdue us by the first impression. The smoke which encircled us from the incessant discharges of musketry, confined our glimpses to the foreground; and we were halted whilst the captains performed their Pyrrhic dance, in the centre of a circle formed by their warriors; where a confusion of flags, English, Dutch, and Danish, were waved and flourished in all directions; the bearers plunging and springing from side to side, with a passion of enthusiasm only equalled by the captains, who followed them, discharging their shining blunderbusses so close, that the flags now and then were in a blaze; and emerging from the smoke with all the gesture and distortion of maniacs. Their followers kept up the firing around us in the rear. The dress of the captains was a war cap, with gilded rams' horns projecting in front, the sides extended beyond all proportion by immense plumes of eagles' feathers, and fastened under the chin with bands of cowries. Their vest was of red cloth, covered with fetishes and saphies in gold and silver; and embroidered cases of almost every colour, which flapped against their bodies as they moved, intermixed with small brass bells, the horns and tails of animals, shells, and knives; long leopards' tails hung down their backs, over a small bow covered with fetishes. They wore loose cotton trowsers, with immense boots of a dull red leather, coming half way up the thigh, and fastened by small chains to their cartouch or waist belt; these were also ornamented with bells, horses' tails, strings of amulets, and innumerable shreds of leather; a small quiver of poisoned arrows hung from their right wrist, and they held a long iron chain between their teeth with a scrap of Moorish writing affixed to the end of it. A small spear was in their left hands, covered with red cloth and silk tassels; their black countenances heightened the effect of this attire and completed a figure scarcely human.

"This exhibition continued about half an hour, when we were allowed to proceed, encircled by the warriors, whose numbers, with the crowds of people, made our movement as gradual as if it had taken place in Cheapside; the several streets branching off to the right presented long vistas crammed with people; and those on the left hand being on an acclivity, innumerable rows of heads rose one above another: the large open porches of the houses, like the fronts of stages in small theatres, were filled with the better sort of females and children, all impatient to behold white men for the first time; their exclamations were drowned in the firing and music, but their gestures were in character with the scene. When we reached the palace, about half a mile from the place where we entered, we were again halted, and an open file was made, through which the bearers were passed, to deposit the presents and baggage in the house assigned to us. Here we were gratified by observing several of the caboceers (chiefs) pass by with their trains, the novel splendour of which astonished us. The bands, principally composed of horns and flutes, trained to play in concert, seemed to soothe our hearing into its natural tone again by their wild melodies; whilst the immense umbrellas, made to sink and rise from the jerkings of the bearers, and the large fans waving around, refreshed us with small currents of air, under a burning sun, clouds of dust, and a density of atmosphere almost suffocating. We were then squeezed, at the same funeral pace, up a long street, to an open-fronted house, where we were desired by a royal messenger to wait a further invitation from the king."—(pp. 31—33.)

The embassy remained about four months, leaving one of their members behind as a permanent resident. Their treatment, though subjected to the fluctuating passions of barbarians, was, upon the whole, not bad; and a foundation appears to have been laid for future intercourse with the Ashantees, and a mean opened, through them, of becoming better acquainted with the interior of Africa.

The Moors, who seem (barbarians as they are) to be the civilizers of internal Africa, have penetrated to the capital of the Ashantees: they are bigoted and intolerant to Christians, but not sacrificers of human victims in their religious ceremonies;—nor averse to commerce; and civilized in comparison to most of the idolatrous natives of Africa. From their merchants who resorted from various parts of the interior, Mr. Bowdich employed himself in procuring all the geographical details which their travels enabled them to afford. Timbuctoo they described as inferior to Houssa, and not at all comparable to Boornoo. The Moorish influence was stated to be powerful in it, but not predominant. A small river goes nearly round the town, overflowing in the rains, and obliging the people of the suburbs to move to an eminence in the centre of the town where the king lives. The king, a Moorish negro called Billabahada, had a few double-barrelled guns, which were fired on great occasions; and gunpowder was as dear as gold. Mr. Bowdich calculates Houssa to be N. E. from the Niger 20 days' journey of 18 miles each day; and the latitude and longitude to be 18° 59′ N. and 3° 59′ E. Boornoo was spoken of as the first empire in Africa. The Mahometans of Sennaar reckon it among the four powerful empires of the world; the other three being Turkey, Persia, and Abyssinia.

The Niger is only known to the Moors by the name of the *Quolla*, pronounced as *Quorra* by the negroes, who, from whatever countries they come, all spoke of this as the largest river with which they were acquainted; and it was the grand feature in all the routes to Ashantee, whether from *Houssa*, *Boornoo*, or the intermediate countries. The Niger, after leaving the lake Dibbri, was invariably described as dividing into two large streams; the Quolla, or the greater division, pursuing its course southeastward, till it joined the *Bahr Abiad* and the other branch running northward of east, near to Timbuctoo, and dividing again soon afterwards—the smaller division running northwards by *Yahoodee*, a place of great trade, and the larger running directly eastward, and entering the lake *Caudi* under the name of Gambaroo. "The variety of this concurrent evidence respecting the *Gambaroo*, made an impression on my mind," says Mr. Bowdich, "almost amounting to conviction." The same author adds, that he found the Moors very cautious in their accounts; declining to speak unless they were positive—and frequently referring doubtful points to others whom they knew to be better acquainted with them.

The character of the present king is, upon the whole, respectable; but he is ambitious, has conquered a great deal, and is conquering still. He has a love of knowledge; and was always displeased when the European objects which attracted his attention were presented to him as gifts. His motives, he said, ought to be better understood, and more respect paid to his dignity and friendship. He is acute, capricious, and severe, but not devoid of humanity; and has incurred unpopularity on some occasions, by limiting the number of human sacrifices more than was compatible with strict orthodoxy. His general subjects of discourse with the mission were war, legislation, and mechanics. He seemed very desirous of standing well in the estimation of his European friends; and put off a conversation once because he was a little tipsy, and at another time because he felt himself cross and out of temper.

The king, four aristocratical assessors, and the assembly of captains, are the three estates of the Ashantee government. The noble quartumvirate, in all matters of foreign policy, have a veto on the king's decisions. They watch, rather than share, the domestic administration; generally influencing it by their opinion, rather than controlling it by their authority. In exercising his judicial functions, the king always retires in private with the aristocracy, to hear their opinions. The course of succession in Ashantee is the brother, the sister's son, the son, and the chief slave.

The king's sisters may marry, or intrigue with any person they please, provided he is very strong and handsome; and these elevated and excellent women are always ready to set an example of submission to the laws of their country. The interest of money is about 300 per cent. A man may kill his own slave; or an inferior, for the price of seven slaves. Trifling thefts are punished by exposure. The property of the wife is distinct from that of the husband—though the king is heir to it. Those accused of witchcraft are tortured to death. Slaves, if ill treated, are allowed the liberty of transferring themselves to other masters.

The Ashantees believe that an higher sort of god takes care of the whites, and that they are left to the care of an inferior species of deities. Still the black kings and black nobility are to go to the upper gods after death, where they are to enjoy eternally the state and luxury which was their portion on earth. For this reason a certain number of cooks, butlers, and domestics of every description, are sacrificed on their tombs. They have two sets of priests: the one dwell in the temples, and communicate with the idols; the other species do business as conjurors and cunning men, tell fortunes, and detect small thefts. Half the offerings to the idols are (as the priests say) thrown into the river, the other half they claim as their own. The doors of the temples are, from motives of the highest humanity, open to runaway slaves; but shut, upon a fee paid by the master to the priest. Every person has a small set of household gods, bought of the Fetishmen. They please their gods by avoiding particular sorts of meat; but the prohibited viand is not always the same. Some curry favour by eating no veal; some seek protection by avoiding pork; others say, that the real monopoly which the celestials wish to establish, is that of beef—and so they piously and prudently rush into a course of mutton. They have the customary nonsense of lucky days, trial by ordeal, and libations and relics. The most horrid and detestable of their customs is their sacrifice of human victims, and the tortures preparatory to it. This takes place at all their great festivals, or customs, as they are called.—Some of these occur every twenty-one days; and there are not fewer than a hundred victims immolated at each. Besides these, there are sacrifices at the death of every person of rank, more or less bloody according to their dignity. On the death of his mother, the king butchered no less than *three thousand* victims; and on his own death this number would probably be doubled. The funeral rites of a great captain were repeated weekly for three months; and 200 persons, it is said, were slaughtered each time, or 2400 in all. The author gives an account of the manner of these abominations, in one instance of which he was an unwilling spectator. On the funeral of the mother of Quatchie Quofie, which was by no means a great one,—

"A dash of sheep and rum was exchanged between the king and Quatchie Quofie, and the drums announced the sacrifice of the victims. All the chiefs first visited them in turn; I was not near enough to distinguish wherefore. The executioners wrangled and struggled for the office: and the indifference with which the first poor creature looked on, in the torture he was from the knife passed through his cheeks, was remarkable. The nearest executioner snatched the sword from the others, the right hand of the victim was then lopped off, he was thrown down, and his head was sawed rather than cut off: it was cruelly prolonged, I will not say wilfully. Twelve more were dragged forward, but we forced our way through the crowd, and retired to our quarters. Other sacrifices, principally female, were made in the bush where the body was buried. It is usual to 'wet the grave' with the blood of a freeman of respectability. All the retainers of the family being present, and the heads of all the victims deposited in the bottom of the grave, several are unsuspectingly called on in a hurry to assist in placing the coffin or basket; and just as it rests on the head or skulls a slave from behind stuns one of these freemen by a violent blow, followed by a deep gash in the back part of the neck, and he is rolled in on the top of the body, and the grave instantly filled up."—(pp. 287, 288.)

"About a hundred persons, mostly culprits reserved, are generally sacrificed, in different quarters of the town, at this custom (that is, at the feast for the new year). Several slaves were also sacrificed at Bantama, over the large brass pan, their blood mingling with the various vegetable and animal matter within (fresh and putrefied), to complete the charm, and produce invincible fetish. All the chiefs kill several slaves, that their blood may flow into the hole from whence the new yam is taken. Those who cannot afford to kill slaves, take the head of one already sacrificed, and place it on the hole."—(p. 279.)

The Ashantees are very superior in discipline and courage to the water-side Africans: they never pursue when it is near sunset; the general is always in the rear, and the fugitives are instantly put to death. The army is prohibited, during the active part of the campaign, from all food but meal, which each man carries in a small bag by his side, and mixes in his hands with the first water he comes to; no fires are allowed, lest their position should be betrayed; they eat little select bits of the first enemy's heart whom they kill; and all wear ornaments of his teeth and bones.

In their buildings, a mould is made for receiving the clay, by two rows of stakes placed at a distance equal to the intended thickness of the wall: the interval is then filled with gravelly clay mixed with water, which, with the outward surface of the frame-work, is plastered so as to exhibit the appearance of a thick mud wall. The captains have pillars which assist to support the roof, and form a proscenium, or open front. The steps and raised floors of the rooms are clay and stone, with a thick layer of red earth, washed and painted daily.

"While the walls are still soft, they formed moulds or frame-works of the patterns in delicate slips of cane, connected by grass. The two first slips (one end of each being inserted in the soft wall) projected the relief, commonly mezzo: the interstices were then filled up with the plaster, and assumed the appearance depicted. The poles or pillars were sometimes encircled by twists of cane, intersecting each other, which, being filled up with thin plaster, resembled the lozenge and cable ornaments of the Anglo-Norman order; the quatre-foil was very common, and by no means rude, from the symmetrical bend of the cane which formed it. I saw a few pillars (after they had been squared with the plaster), with numerous slips of cane pressed perpendicularly on to the wet surface, which, being covered again with a very thin coat of plaster, closely resembled fluting. When they formed a large arch, they inserted one end of a thick piece of cane in the wet clay of the floor or base, and, bending the other over, inserted it in the same manner; the entablature was filled up with wattle-work plastered over. Arcades and piazzas were common. A white wash, very frequently renewed, was made from a clay in the neighbourhood. Of course the plastering is very frail, and in the relief frequently discloses the edges of the cane, giving, however, a piquant effect, auxiliary to the ornament. The doors were an entire piece of cotton wood, cut with great labour out of the stems or buttresses of that tree; battens variously cut and painted were afterwards nailed across. So disproportionate was the price of labour to that of provision, that I gave but two tokoos for a slab of cotton wood, five feet by three. The locks they use are from Houssa, and quite original: one will be sent to the British Museum. Where they raised a first floor, the under room was divided into two by an intersecting wall, to support the rafters for the upper room, which were generally covered with a frame-work thickly plastered over with red ochre. I saw but one attempt at flooring with plank; it was cotton wood shaped entirely with an adze, and looked like a ship's deck. The windows were open wood-work, carved in fanciful figures and intricate patterns, and painted red; the frames were frequently cased in gold, about as thick as cartridge paper. What surprised me most, and is not the least of the many circumstances deciding their great superiority over the generality of negroes, was the discovery that every house had its cloacæ, besides the common ones for the lower orders without the town."—(pp. 305, 306.)

The rubbish and offal of each house are burnt every morning at the back of the street; and they are as nice in their dwellings as in their persons. The Ashantee loom is precisely on the same principles as the English: the firmness, variety, brilliancy, and size of their cloths are astonishing. They paint white cloths, not inelegantly, as fast as an European can write. They excel in pottery, and are good goldsmiths. Their weights are very neat brass casts of almost every animal, fruit, and vegetable, known in the country. The king's scales, blow-pan, boxes, weights, and pipe-tongs were neatly made of the purest gold. They work finely in iron, tan leather, and are excellent carpenters.

Mr. Bowdich computes the number of men capable of bearing arms to be 204,000. The disposable force is 150,000; the population a million; the number of square miles 14,000. Polygamy is tolerated to the greatest extent; the king's allowance is 3333 wives; and the full complement is always kept up. Four of the principal streets in Coomassie are half a mile long, and from 50 to 100 yards wide. The streets were all named, and a superior captain in charge of each. The street where the mission was lodged was called Apperemsoo, or *Cannon Street;* another street was called Daebrim, or *Great Market Street;* another, *Prison Street*, and so on. A plan of the town is given. The Ashantees persisted in saying that the population of Coomassie was above 100,000; but this is thought, by the gentlemen of the mission, to allude rather to the population collected on great occasions, than the permanent residents, not computed by them at more than 15,000. The markets were daily; and the articles for sale, beef, mutton, wild-hog, deer, monkeys' flesh, fowls, yams, plantains, corn, sugarcane, rice, peppers, vegetable butter, oranges, papaus, pine-apples, bananas, salt and dried fish, large snails smoke-dried; palm wine, rum, pipes, beads, looking-glasses; sandals, silk, cotton cloth, powder, small pillars, white and blue thread, and calabashes. The cattle in Ashantee are as large as English cattle; their sheep are hairy. They have no implement but the hoe; have two crops of corn in the year; plant their yams at Christmas, and dig them up in September. Their plantations, extensive and orderly, have the appearance of hop gardens well fenced in, and regularly planted in lines, with a broad walk around, and a hut at each wicker-gate, where a slave and his family reside to protect the plantation. All the fruits mentioned as sold in the market grew in spontaneous abundance, as did the sugarcane. The oranges were of a large size and exquisite flavour. There were no cocoa trees. The berry which gives to acids the flavour of sweets, making limes taste like honey, is common here. The castor-oil plant rises to a large tree. The cotton tree sometimes rises to the height of 150 feet.

The great obstacle to the improvement of commerce with the Ashantee people (besides the jealousy natural to barbarians) is our rejection of the slave trade, and the continuance of that detestable traffic by the Spaniards. While the mission was in that country, one thousand slaves left Ashantee for two Spanish schooners on the coast.—How is an African monarch to be taught that he has not a right to turn human creatures into rum and tobacco? or that the nation which prohibits such an intercourse are not his enemies? To have free access to Ashantee, would command Dagwumba. The people of Inta and Dagwumba being commercial, rather than warlike, an intercourse with them would be an intercourse with the interior, as far as Timbuctoo and Houssa northwards, and Cassina, if not Boornoo, eastwards.

After the observations of Mr. Bowdich, senior officer of the mission, follows the narrative of Mr. Hutchinson, left as chargé d'affaires, upon the departure of the other gentlemen. Mr. Hutchinson mentions some white men residing at Yenné, whom he supposes to have been companions of Park; and Ali Baba, a man of good character and consideration, upon the eve of departure from these regions, assured him, that there were two Europeans then resident at Timbuctoo.—In his observations on the river Gaboon, Mr. Bowdich has the following information on the present state of the slave trade:—

"Three Portuguese, one French, and two large Spanish ships, visited the river for slaves during our stay; and the master of a Liverpool vessel assured me that he had fallen in with twenty-two between Gaboon and the Congo. Their grand rendezvous is Mayumba. The Portuguese of St. Thomas's and Prince's Islands send small schooner boats to Gaboon for slaves, which are kept, after they are transported this short distance, until the coast is clear for shipping them to America. A third large Spanish ship, well armed, entered the river the night before we quitted it, and hurried our exit, for one of that character was committing piracy in the neighbouring rivers. Having suffered from falling into their hands before, I felicitated myself on the escape. We were afterwards chased and boarded by a Spanish armed schooner, with three hundred slaves on board; they only desired provisions."

These are the most important extracts from this publication, which is certainly of considerable importance, from the account it gives us of a people hitherto almost entirely unknown; and from the light which the very diligent and laborious inquiries of Mr. Bowdich have thrown upon the geography of Africa, and the probability held out to us of approaching the great kingdoms on the Niger, by means of an intercourse by no means difficult to be established with the kingdoms of Inta and Dagwumba. The river Volta flows into the Gulf of Guinea, in latitude 7° north. It is navigable, and by the natives navigated for ten days, to Odentee. Now, from Odentee to Sallagha, the capital of the kingdom of Inta, is but four days' journey; and seven days' journey from Sallagha, through the Inta Jam of Zengoo, is Yahndi, the capital of Dagwumba. Yahndi is described to be beyond comparison larger than Coomassie, the houses much better built and ornamented. The Ashantees who had visited it, told Mr. Bowdich they had frequently lost themselves in the streets. The king has been converted by the Moors, who have settled themselves there in great numbers. Mr. Lucas calls it the Mahometan kingdom of Degomba; and it was represented to him as peculiarly wealthy and civilized. The markets of Yahndi are described as animated scenes of commerce, constantly crowded with merchants from almost all the countries of the interior. It seems to us, that the best way of becoming acquainted with Africa, is not to plan such sweeping expeditions as have been lately sent out by government, but to submit to become acquainted with it by degrees, and to acquire by little and little a knowledge of the best methods of arranging expeditions. The kingdom of Dagwumba, for instance, is not 200 miles from a well-known and regular water carriage, on the Volta. Perhaps it is nearer, but the distance is not greater than this. It is one of the most commercial nations in Africa, and one of the most civilized; and yet it is utterly unknown, except by report, to Europeans. Then why not plan an expedition to Dagwumba? The expense of which would be very trifling, and the issue known in three or four months. The information procured from such a wise and moderate undertaking, would enable any future mission to proceed with much greater ease and safety into the interior; or prevent them from proceeding, as they hitherto have done to their own destruction. We strongly believe, with Mr. Bowdich, that this is the right road to the Niger.

Nothing in this world is created in vain: lions, tigers, conquerors, have their use. Ambitious monarchs, who are the curse of civilized nations, are the civilizers of savage people.

With a number of little independent hordes, civilization is impossible. They must have a common interest before there can be peace; and be directed by one will before there can be order. When mankind are prevented from daily quarrelling and fighting, they first begin to improve; and all this, we are afraid, is only to be accomplished, in the first instance, by some great conqueror. We sympathize, therefore, with the victories of the King of Ashantee—and feel ourselves, for the first time, in love with military glory. The ex-emperor of the French would, at Coomassie, Dagwumba, or Inta, be an eminent benefactor to the human race.

WITTMAN'S TRAVELS.*

[EDINBURGH REVIEW, 1803.]

DR. WITTMAN was sent abroad with the military mission to Turkey, towards the spring of 1799, and remained attached to it during its residence in the neighbourhood of Constantinople, its march through the desert, and its short operations in Egypt. The military mission, consisting of General Koehler, and some officers and privates of the artillery and engineers, amounting on the whole to seventy, were assembled at Constantinople, June, 1799, which they left in the same month of the following year, joined the grand vizier at Jaffa in July, and entered Egypt with the Turks in April, 1801. After the military operations were concluded there, Dr. Wittman returned home by Constantinople, Vienna, &c.

The travels are written in the shape of a journal, which begins and concludes with the events which we have just mentioned. It is obvious that the route described by Dr. Wittman is not new: he could make no cursory and superficial observations upon the people whom he saw, or the countries through which he passed, with which the public are not already familiar. If his travels were to possess any merit at all, they were to derive that merit from accurate physical researches, from copious information on the state of medicine, surgery, and disease in Turkey; and above all, perhaps, from gratifying the rational curiosity which all inquiring minds must feel upon the nature of the plague, and the indications of cure. Dr. Wittman, too, was passing over the same ground trodden by Bonaparte in his Syrian expedition, and had an ample opportunity of inquiring its probable object, and the probable success which (but for the heroic defence of Acre) might have attended it; he was on the theatre of Bonaparte's imputed crimes, as well as his notorious defeat; and might have brought us back, not anile conjecture, but sound evidence of events which must determine his character, who may determine our fate. We should have been happy also to have found in the travels of Dr. Wittman a full account of the tactics and manœuvres of the Turkish army; and this it would not have been difficult to have obtained through the medium of his military companions. Such appear to us to be the subjects, from an able discussion of which, Dr. Wittman might have derived considerable reputation, by gratifying the ardour of temporary curiosity, and adding to the stock of permanent knowledge.

Upon opening Dr. Wittman's book, we turned, with a considerable degree of interest, to the subject of Jaffa; and to do justice to the doctor, we shall quote all that he has said upon the subject of Bonaparte's conduct at this place.

"After a breach had been effected, the French troops stormed and carried the place. It was probably owing to the obstinate defence made by the Turks, that the French commander-in-chief was induced to give orders for the horrid massacre which succeeded. Four thousand of the wretched inhabitants who had surrendered, and who had in vain implored the mercy of their conquerors, were, together with a part of the late Turkish garrison of El-Arish (amounting, it has been said, to five or six hundred), dragged out in cold blood, *four days after the French had obtained possession of Jaffa*, to the sand hills, about a league distant, in the way to Gaza, and there most inhumanly put to death. I have seen the skeletons of these unfortunate victims, which lie scattered over the hills; a modern Golgotha, which remains a lasting disgrace to a nation calling itself civilized. It would give pleasure to the author of this work, as well as to every liberal mind, to hear these facts contradicted on substantial evidence. Indeed, I am sorry to add, that the charge of cruelty against the French general does not rest here. It having been reported, that, previously to the retreat of the French army from Syria, their commander-in-chief had ordered all the French sick at Jaffa to be poisoned, I was led to make the inquiry to which every one who should have visited the spot would naturally have been directed, respecting an act of such singular, and, it should seem, wanton inhumanity. It concerns me to have to state, not only that such a circumstance was positively asserted to have happened, but that, while in Egypt, an individual was pointed out to us, as having been the executioner of these diabolical commands."—(p. 128.)

Now, in this passage, Dr. Wittman offers no

* *Travels in Turkey, Asia Minor, and Syria, &c., and into Egypt.* By WILLIAM WITTMAN, M. D. 1803. London. Phillips.

other evidence whatever of the massacre, than that he had seen the skeletons scattered over the hills, and that the fact was universally believed. But how does Dr. Wittman know what skeletons those were which he saw? An oriental camp, affected by the plague, leaves as many skeletons behind it as a massacre. And though the Turks bury their dead, the doctor complains of the very little depth at which they are interred; so that jackals, high winds, and a sandy soil, might, with great facility, undo the work of Turkish sextons. Let any one read Dr. Wittman's account of the camp near Jaffa, where the Turks remained so long in company with the military mission, and he will immediately perceive that, a year after their departure, it might have been mistaken, with great ease, for the scene of a massacre. The spot which Dr. Wittman saw might have been the spot where a battle had been fought. In the turbulent state of Syria, and amidst the variety of its barbarous inhabitants, can it be imagined that every bloody battle, with its precise limits and circumscription, is accurately committed to tradition, and faithfully reported to inquirers? Besides, why scattered among hills? If 5000 men were marched out to a convenient spot and massacred, their remains would be heaped up in a small space, a mountain of the murdered, a vast bridge of bones and rottenness. As the doctor has described the bone scenery, it has much more the appearance of a battle and pursuit than of a massacre. After all, this gentleman lay eight months under the walls of Jaffa; whence comes it he has given us no better evidence? Were 5000 men murdered in cold blood by a division of the French army, a year before, and did no man remain in Jaffa, who said, I saw it done—I was present when they were marched out—I went the next day, and saw the scarcely dead bodies of the victims? If Dr. Wittman received any such evidence, why did he not bring it forward? If he never inquired for such evidence, how is he qualified to write upon the subject? If he inquired for it and could not find it, how is the fact credible?

This author cannot make the same excuse as Sir Robert Wilson, for the suppression of his evidence, as there could be no probability that Bonaparte would wreak his vengeance upon Soliman Aga, Mustapha Cawn, Sidi Mahomet, or any given Turks, upon whose positive evidence Dr. Wittman might have rested his accusation. Two such wicked acts as the poisoning and the massacre, have not been committed within the memory of man;—within the same memory, no such extraordinary person has appeared, as he who is said to have committed them; and yet, though their commission must have been public, no one has yet said, *Vidi ego.* The accusation still rests upon hearsay.

At the same time, widely disseminated as this accusation has been over Europe, it is extraordinary that it has not been contradicted in print: and, though Sir Robert Wilson's book must have been read in France, that no officer of the division of Bon has come forward in vindication of a criminal who could repay incredulity so well. General Andreossi, who was with the First Consul in Syria, treats the accusations as contemptible falsehoods. But though we are convinced he is a man of character, his evidence has certainly less weight, as he may have been speaking in the mask of diplomacy. As to the general circulation of the report, he must think much higher of the sagacity of multitudes than we do, who would convert this into a reason of belief. Whoever thinks it so easy to get at truth in the midst of passion, should read the various histories of the recent rebellion in Ireland; or he may, if he chooses, believe, with thousands of worthy Frenchmen, that the *infernale* was planned by Mr. Pitt and Lord Melville. As for us, we will state what appears to us to be the truth, should it even chance to justify a man in whose lifetime Europe can know neither happiness nor peace.

The story of the poisoning is given by Dr. Wittman precisely in the same desultory manner as that of the massacre. "An individual was pointed out to us as the executioner of these diabolical commands." By how many persons was he pointed out as the executioner? by persons of what authority? and of what credibility? Was it asserted from personal knowledge, or merely from rumour? Whence comes it that such an agent, after the flight of his employer, was not driven away by the general indignation of the army? If Dr. Wittman had combined this species of information with his stories, his conduct would have been more just, and his accusations would have carried greater weight. At present, when he, who had the opportunity of telling us so much, has told us so little, we are rather less inclined to believe than we were before. We do not say these accusations are not true, but that Dr. Wittman has not proved them to be true.

Dr. Wittman did not see more than two cases of plague: he has given both of them at full length. The symptoms were, thirst, headache, vertigo, pains in the limbs, bilious vomitings, and painful tumours in the groins. The means of cure adopted were, to evacuate the primæ viæ; to give diluting and refreshing drinks; to expel the redundant bile by emetics; and to assuage the pain in the groin by fomentations and anodynes; both cases proved fatal. In one of the cases, the friction with warm oil was tried in vain; but it was thought useful in the prevention of plague: the immediate effect produced was, to throw the person rubbed into a very copious perspiration. A patient in typhus, who was given over, recovered after this discipline was administered.

The boldness and enterprise of medical men are quite as striking as the courage displayed in battle, and evinces how much the power of encountering danger depends upon habit.—Many a military veteran would tremble to feed upon *pus;* to sleep in sheets running with water; or to draw up the breath of feverish patients. Dr. White might not, perhaps, have marched up to a battery with great alacrity; but Dr. White, in the year 1801, inoculated himself in the arms, with recent matter taken from the bubo of a pestiferous patient, and rubbed the same matter upon different parts of his body. With somewhat less of courage, and more of injustice, he wrapt his Arab servant in the bed of a person just dead of the plague. The doctor died; and the doctor's man (perhaps to prove his master's theory, that the plague was not contagious) ran away. The bravery of our naval officers never produced any thing superior to this therapeutic heroism of the doctor's.

Dr. Wittman has a chapter which he calls *An Historical Journal of the Plague;* but the information which it contains amounts to nothing at all. He confesses that he has had no experience in the complaint; that he has no remedy to offer for its cure, and no theory for its cause.* The treatment of the minor plague of Egypt, ophthalmia, was precisely the method common in this country; and was generally attended with success, where the remedies were applied in time.

Nothing can be conceived more dreadful than was the situation of the military mission in the Turkish camp; exposed to a mutinous Turkish soldiery, to infection, famine, and a scene of the most abominable filth and putrefaction; and this they endured for a year and a half, with the patience of apostles of peace, rather than war. Their occupation was to teach diseased barbarians, who despised them, and thought it no small favour that they should be permitted to exist in their neighbourhood. They had to witness the cruelties of despotism, and the passions of armed and ignorant multitudes; and all this embellished with the fair probability of being swept off, in some grand engagement, by the superior tactics and activity of the enemy to whom the Turks were opposed. To the filth, irregularity, and tumult of a Turkish camp, as it appeared to the British officers in 1800, it is curious to oppose the picture of one drawn by Busbequius in the middle of the sixteenth century: "Turcæ in proximis campis tendebant; cum vero in eo loco tribus mensibus vixerim, fuit mihi facultas videndorum ipsorum castrorum, et cognoscendæ aliqua ex parte disciplinæ; qua de re nisi pauca attingam, habeas fortasse quod me accuses. Sumpto habitu Christianis hominibus in illis locis usitato, cum uno aut altero comite quacunque vagabar ignotus: primum videbam summo ordine cujusque corporis milites suis locis distributos, et, quod vix credat, qui nostratis militiæ consuetudinem novit, summum erat ubique silentium, summa quies, rixa nulla, nullum cujusquam insolens factum: sed ne nox quidem aut vitulatio per lasciviam aut ebrietatem emissa. *Ad hæc summa mundities, nulla sterquilinia, nulla purgamenta,* nihil quod oculos aut nares offenderet. Quicquid est hujusmodi, aut defodiunt Turcæ, aut procul à conspectu submovent. Sed nec ullas compotationes aut convivia, nullum aleæ genus, magnum nostratis militiæ flagitium, videre erat: nulla lusoriarum chartarum, neque tesserarum damna norunt Turcæ."—*Augeri Busbequii, Epist.* 3, p. 187. *Hanoviæ.* 1622. There is at present, in the Turkish army, a curious mixture of the severest despotism in the commander, and the most rebellious insolence in the soldier. When the soldier misbehaves, the vizier cuts his head off, and places it under his arm. When the soldier is dissatisfied with his vizier, he fires his ball through his tent, and admonishes him, by these messengers, to a more pleasant exercise of his authority. That such severe punishments should not confer a more powerful authority, and give birth to a better discipline, is less extraordinary, if we reflect, that we hear only that the punishments are severe, not that they are steady, and that they are just; for, if the Turkish soldiers were always punished with the same severity when they were in fault, and never but then, it is not in human nature to suppose, that the Turkish army would long remain in as contemptible a state as it now is. But the governed soon learn to distinguish between systematic energy, and the excesses of casual and capricious cruelty; the one awes them into submission, the other rouses them to revenge.

Dr. Wittman, in his chapter on the Turkish army, attributes much of its degradation to the altered state of the corps of Janissaries; the original constitution of which corps was certainly both curious and wise. The children of Christians made prisoners in the predatory incursions of the Turks, or procured in any other manner, were exposed in the public markets of Constantinople. Any farmer or artificer was at liberty to take one into his service, contracting with government to produce him again when he should be wanted: and in the mean time to feed and clothe him, and to educate him to such works of labour as are calculated to strengthen the body. As the Janissaries were killed off, the government drew upon this stock of hardy orphans for its levies; who, instead of hanging upon weeping parents at their departure, came eagerly to the camp, as the situation which they had always been taught to look upon as the theatre of their future glory, and towards which all their passions and affections had been bent, from their earliest years. Arrived at the camp, they received at first low pay, and performed menial offices for the little division of Janissaries to which they were attached: "Ad Gianizaros rescriptus primo meret menstruo stipendio, paulo plus minus, unius ducati cum dimidio. Id enim militi novitio, et rudi satis esse censent. Sed tamen ne quid victus necessitati desit, cum ea decuria, in cujus contuernium adscitus est, gratis cibum capit, eâ conditione, ut in culinâ reliquoque ministerio ei decuriæ serviat; usum armorum adeptus tyro, cnedum tamen suis contubernalibus honore neque stipendio par unam in solâ virtute, se illis æquandi, spem habet: utpote si militiæ quæ prima se obtulerit, tale specimen sui dederit, ut dignus judicetur, qui tyrocinio exemptus, honoris gradu et stipendii magnitudine, reliquis Gianizaris par habeatur. Quâ quidem spe plerique tyrones impulsi, multa præclare audent, et fortitudine cum veteranis certant."—*Busbequius, De Re Mil. cont. Turc. Instit. Consilium.** The

* One fact mentioned by Dr. Wittman appears to be curious;—that Constantinople was nearly free from plague during the interruption of its communication with Egypt.

* This is a very spirited appeal to his countrymen on the tremendous power of the Turks; and, with the sub-

same author observes, that there was no rank or dignity in the Turkish army, to which a common Janissary might not arrive, by his courage or his capacity. This last is a most powerful motive to exertion, and is, perhaps, one leading cause of the superiority of the French arms. Ancient governments promote, from numberless causes which ought to have no concern with promotion: revolutionary governments, and military despotisms, can make generals of persons who are fit for generals: to enable them to be unjust in all other instances, they are forced to be just in this. What, in fact, are the sultans and pashas of Paris, but Janissaries raised from the ranks? At present, the Janissaries are procured from the lowest of the people, and the spirit of the corps is evaporated. The low state of their armies is in some degree imputable to this; but the principal reason why the Turks are no longer as powerful as they were, is, that they are no longer enthusiasts, and that war is now become more a business of science than of personal courage.

The person of the greatest abilities in the Turkish empire is the capitan pasha; he has disciplined some ships and regiments in the European fashion, and would, if he were well seconded, bring about some important reforms in the Turkish empire. But what is become of all the reforms of the famous Gazi Hassan? The blaze of partial talents is soon extinguished. Never was there so great a prospect of improvement as that afforded by the exertions of this celebrated man, who, in spite of the ridicule thrown upon him by Baron de Tott, was such a man as the Turks cannot expect to see again once in a century. He had the whole power of the Turkish empire at his disposal for fifteen years; and, after repeated efforts to improve the army, abandoned the scheme as totally impracticable. The celebrated Bonneval, in his time, and De Tott since, made the same attempt with the same success. They are not to be taught; and six months after his death, every thing the present capitan pasha has done will be immediately pulled to pieces. The present grand vizier is a man of no ability. There are some very entertaining instances of his gross ignorance cited in the 133d page of the Travels. Upon the news being communicated to him that the earth was round, he observed that this could not be the case: for the people and the objects on the other side would in that case fall off; and that the earth could not move round the sun; for if so, a ship bound from Jaffa to Constantinople, instead of proceeding to the capital, would be carried to London, or elsewhere. We cannot end this article without confessing with great pleasure the entertainment we have received from the work which occasions it. It is an excellent lounging-book, full of pleasant details, never wearying by prolixity, or offending by presumption, and is apparently the production of a respectable, worthy man. So far we can conscientiously recommend it to the public; for any thing else,

Non cuivis homini contingit adire, &c. &c. &c.

stitution of France for Turkey, is so applicable to the present times that it might be spoken in Parliament with great effect.

SPEECHES.

CATHOLIC CLAIMS.

A Speech at a Meeting of the Clergy of the Archdeaconry of the East Riding of Yorkshire, held at Beverley, in that Riding, on Monday, April 11, 1825, *for the Purpose of Petitioning Parliament, &c.**

Mr. Archdeacon,—It is very disagreeable to me to differ from so many worthy and respectable clergymen here assembled, and not only to differ from them, but, I am afraid, to stand alone among them. I would much rather vote in majorities, and join in this, or any other political chorus, than to stand unassisted and alone, as I am now doing. I dislike such meetings for such purposes—I wish I could reconcile it to my conscience to stay away from them, and to my temperament to be silent at them; but if they are called by others, I deem it right to attend—if I attend I must say what I think. If it is unwise in us to meet in taverns to discuss political subjects, the fault is not mine, for I should never think of calling such a meeting. If the subject is trite, no blame is imputable to me: it is as dull to me to handle such subjects, as it is to you to hear them. The customary promise on the threshold of an inn is good entertainment for man and horse. — If there is any truth in any part of this sentence at the Tiger, at Beverley, our horses at this moment must certainly be in a state of much greater enjoyment than the masters who rode them.

It will be some amusement, however, to this meeting, to observe the schism which this question has occasioned in my own parish of Londesborough. My excellent and respectable curate, Mr. Milestones, alarmed at the effect of the pope upon the East Riding, has come here to oppose me, and there he stands, breathing war and vengeance on the Vatican. We had some previous conversation on this subject, and, in imitation of our superiors, we agreed not to make it a cabinet question.—Mr. Milestones, indeed, with that delicacy and propriety which belong to his character, expressed some scruples upon the propriety of voting against his rector, but I insisted he should come and vote against me. I assured him nothing would give me more pain than to think I had prevented, in any man, the free assertion of honest opinions. That such conduct, on his part, instead of causing jealousy and animosity between us, could not, and would not fail to increase my regard and respect for him.

I beg leave, sir, before I proceed on this subject, to state what I mean by Catholic emancipation. I mean eligibility of Catholics to all civil offices, with the usual exceptions introduced into all bills—jealous safeguards for the preservation of the Protestant church, and for the regulation of the intercourse with Rome—and, lastly, provision for the Catholic clergy.

I object, sir, to the law as it stands at present, because it is impolitic, and because it is unjust. It is impolitic, because it exposes this country to the greatest danger in time of war. Can you believe, sir, can any man of the most ordinary turn for observation, believe, that the monarchs of Europe mean to leave this country in the quiet possession of the high station which it at present holds? Is it not obvious that a war is coming on between the governments of law and the governments of despotism?—that the weak and tottering race of the Bourbons will (whatever our wishes may be) be compelled to gratify the wounded vanity of the French, by plunging them into a war with England. Already they are pitying the Irish people, as you pity the West Indian slaves—already they are opening colleges for the reception of Irish priests. Will they wait for your tardy wisdom and reluctant liberality? Is not the present state of Ireland a premium upon early invasion? Does it not hold out the most alluring invitation to your enemies to begin? And if the flag of any hostile power in Europe is unfurled in that unhappy country, is there one Irish peasant who will not hasten to join it?—and not only the peasantry, sir; the peasantry begin these things, but the peasantry do not end them—they are soon joined by an order a little above them—and then, after a trifling success, a still superior class think it worth while to try the risk: men are hurried into a rebellion, as the oxen are pulled into the cave of Cacus—tail foremost. The mob first, who have nothing to lose but their lives, of which every Irishman has nine—then comes the shopkeeper—then the parish priest—then the vicar-general—then Dr. Doyle, and, lastly, Daniel O'Connell. But if the French were to make the same blunders respecting Ireland as Napoleon committed, if wind and weather preserved Ireland for you a second time, still all your resources would be crippled by watching Ireland. The force employed for this might liberate Spain and Portugal, protect India, or accomplish any great purpose of offence or defence.

War, sir, seems to be almost as natural a state to mankind as peace; but if you could hope to escape war, is there a more powerful receipt for destroying the prosperity of any country than these eternal jealousies and dis-

* I was left at this meeting in a minority of one. A poor clergyman whispered to me, that he was quite of my way of thinking, but had nine children. I begged he would remain a Protestant.

tinctions between the two religions? What man will carry his industry and his capital into a country where his yard measure is a sword, his pounce-box a powder-flask, and his ledger a return of killed and wounded? Where a cat will get, there I know a cotton-spinner will penetrate; but let these gentlemen wait till a few of their factories have been burnt down, till one or two respectable merchants of Manchester have been carded, and till they have seen the cravatists hanging the shanavists in cotton twist. In the present fervour for spinning, ourang-outangs, sir, would be employed to spin, if they could be found in sufficient quantities; but miserably will those reasoners be disappointed who repose upon cotton—not upon justice—and who imagine this great question can be put aside, because a few hundred Irish spinners are gaining a morsel of bread by the overflowing industry of the English market.

But what right have you to continue these rules, sir, these laws of exclusion? What necessity can you show for it? Is the reigning monarch a concealed Catholic?—Is his successor an open one?—Is there a disputed succession?—Is there a Catholic pretender? If some of these circumstances are said to have justified the introduction, and others the continuation of these measures, why does not the disappearance of all these circumstances justify the repeal of the restrictions? If you must be unjust—if it is a luxury you cannot live without—reserve your injustice for the weak, and not for the strong—persecute the Unitarians, muzzle the Ranters, be unjust to a few thousand sectaries, not to six millions—galvanize a frog, don't galvanize a tiger.

If you go into a parsonage house in the country, Mr. Archdeacon, you see sometimes a style and fashion of furniture which does very well for us, but which has had its day in London. It is seen in London no more; it is banished to the provinces; from the gentlemen's houses of the provinces these pieces of furniture, as soon as they are discovered to be unfashionable, descend to the farm-houses, then to cottages, then to the faggot-heap, then to the dunghill. As it is with furniture, so is it with arguments. I hear at country meetings many arguments against the Catholics which are never heard in London; their London existence is over—they are only to be met with in the provinces, and there they are fast hastening down, with clumsy chairs and ill-fashioned sofas, to another order of men. But, sir, as they are not yet gone where I am sure they are going, I shall endeavour to point out their defects, and to accelerate their descent.

Many gentlemen now assembled at the Tiger Inn, at Beverley, believe that the Catholics do not keep faith with heretics; these gentlemen ought to know that Mr. Pitt put this very question to six of the leading Catholic universities in Europe. He inquired of them whether this tenet did or did not constitute any part of the Catholic faith. The question received from these universities the most decided negative; they denied that such doctrine formed any part of the creed of Catholics. Such doctrine, sir, is denied upon oath, in the bill now pending in Parliament, a copy of which I hold in my hand. The denial of such a doctrine upon oath is the only means by which a Catholic can relieve himself from his present incapacities. If a Catholic, therefore, sir, will not take the oath, he is not relieved, and remains where you wish him to remain; if he does take the oath, you are safe from his peril: if he has no scruple about oaths, of what consequence is it whether this bill passes, the very object of which is to relieve him from oaths? Look at the fact, sir. Do the Protestant cantons of Switzerland, living under the same state with the Catholic cantons, complain that no faith is kept with heretics? Do not the Catholics and Protestants in the kingdom of the Netherlands meet in one common Parliament? Could they pursue a common purpose, have common friends, and common enemies, if there was a shadow of truth in this doctrine imputed to the Catholics? The religious affairs of this last kingdom are managed with the strictest impartiality to both sects? ten Catholics and ten Protestants (gentlemen need not look so much surprised to hear it), positively meet together, sir, in the same room. They constitute what is called the religious committee for the kingdom of the Netherlands, and so extremely desirous are they of preserving the strictest impartiality, that they have chosen a Jew for their secretary. Their conduct has been unimpeachable and unimpeached; the two sects are at peace with each other; and the doctrine, that no faith is kept with heretics, would, I assure you, be very little credited at Amsterdam or the Hague, cities as essentially Protestant as the town of Beverley.

Wretched is our condition, and still more wretched the condition of Ireland, if the Catholic does not respect his oath. He serves on grand and petty juries in both countries; we trust our lives, our liberties, and our properties, to his conscientious reverence of an oath, and yet, when it suits the purposes of party to bring forth this argument, we say he has no respect for oaths. The right to a landed estate of 3000*l.* per annum was decided last week, in York, by a jury, the foreman of which was a Catholic; does any human being, harbour a thought, that this gentleman, whom we all know and respect, would, under any circumstances, have thought more lightly of the obligation of an oath, than his Protestant brethren of the box? We all disbelieve these arguments of Mr. A. the Catholic, and of Mr. B. the Catholic: but we believe them of Catholics in general, of the abstract Catholics, of the Catholic of the Tiger Inn, at Beverley, the formidable unknown Catholic, that is so apt to haunt our clerical meetings.

I observe that some gentlemen who argue this question, are very bold about other offices, but very jealous lest Catholic gentlemen should become justices of the peace. If this jealousy is justifiable anywhere, it is justifiable in Ireland, where some of the best and most respectable magistrates are Catholics

It is not true that the Roman Catholic religion is what it was. I meet that assertion with a plump denial. The pope does not dethrone kings, nor give away kingdoms, does not extort money, has given up, in some instances, the nomination of bishops to Catholic princes, in some, I believe, to Protestant princes; Protestant worship is now carried on at Rome. In the Low Countries, the seat of the Duke of Alva's cruelties, the Catholic tolerates the Protestant, and sits with him in the same Parliament—the same in Hungary—the same in France. The first use which even the Spanish people made of their ephemeral liberty, was to destroy the Inquisition. It was destroyed also by the mob of Portugal. I am so far from thinking the Catholic not to be more tolerant than he was, that I am much afraid the English, who gave the first lesson of toleration to mankind, will very soon have a great deal to learn from their pupils.

Some men quarrel with the Catholics, because their language was violent in the Association; but a groan or two, sir, after two hundred years of incessant tyranny, may surely be forgiven. A few warm phrases to compensate the legal massacre of a million of Irishmen are not unworthy of our pardon. All this hardly deserves the eternal incapacity of holding civil offices. Then they quarrel with the Bible Society; in other words they vindicate that ancient tenet of their church, that the Scriptures are not to be left to the unguided judgment of the laity. The objection to Catholics is, that they did what Catholics ought to do—and do not many prelates of our church object to the Bible Society, and contend that the Scriptures ought not to be circulated without the comment of the Prayer Book and the Articles? If they are right, the Catholics are not wrong; and if the Catholics are wrong, they are in such good company, that we ought to respect their errors.

Why not pay their clergy? the Presbyterian clergy in the north of Ireland are paid by the state: the Catholic clergy of Canada are provided for: the priests of the Hindoos are, I believe, in some of their temples, paid by the Company. You must surely admit that the Catholic religion (the religion of two-thirds of Europe), is better than no religion. I do not regret that the Irish are under the dominion of the priests. I am glad that so savage a people as the lower orders of Irish are under the dominion of their priests; for it is a step gained to place such beings under any influence, and the clergy are always the first civilizers of mankind. The Irish are deserted by their natural aristocracy, and I should wish to make their priesthood respectable in their appearance, and easy in their circumstances. A government provision has produced the most important changes in the opinions of the Presbyterian clergy of the north of Ireland, and has changed them from levellers and Jacobins into reasonable men; it would not fail to improve most materially the political opinions of the Catholic priests. This cannot, however, be done, without the emancipation of the laity. No priest would dare to accept a salary from government, unless this preliminary was settled. I am aware it would give to government a tremendous power in that country; but I must choose the least of two evils. The great point, as physicians say, in some diseases, is to resist the tendency to death. The great object of our day is to prevent the loss of Ireland, and the consequent ruin of England; to obviate the tendency to death; we will first keep the patient alive, and then dispute about his diet and his medicine.

Suppose a law were passed, that no clergyman who had ever held a living in the East Riding, could be made a bishop. Many gentlemen here (who have no hopes of ever being removed from their parishes) would feel the restriction of the law as a considerable degradation. We should soon be pointed at as a lower order of clergymen. It would not be long before the common people would find some fortunate epithet for us, and it would not be long either before we should observe in our brethren of the north and west an air of superiority, which would aggravate not a little the justice of the privation. Every man feels the insult thrown upon his *caste;* the insulted party falls lower, every body else becomes higher. There are heart-burnings and recollections. Peace flies from that land. The volume of parliamentary evidence I have brought here is loaded with the testimony of witnesses of all ranks and occupations, stating to the House of Commons the undoubted effects produced upon the lower order of Catholics by these disqualifying laws, and the lively interest they take in their removal. I have seventeen quotations, sir, from this evidence, and am ready to give any gentleman my references; but I forbear to read them, from compassion to my reverend brethren, who have trotted many miles to vote against the pope, and who will trot back in the dark, if I attempt to throw additional light upon the subject.

I have also, sir, a high-spirited class of gentlemen to deal with, who will do nothing from fear, who admit the danger, but think it disgraceful to act as if they feared it. There is a degree of fear, which destroys a man's faculties, renders him incapable of acting, and makes him ridiculous. There is another sort of fear, which enables a man to foresee a coming evil, to measure it, to examine his powers of resistance, to balance the evil of submission against the evils of opposition or defeat, and if he thinks he must be ultimately overpowered, leads him to find a good escape in a good time. I can see no possible disgrace in feeling this sort of fear, and in listening to its suggestions. But it is mere cant to say, that men will not be actuated by fear in such questions as these. Those who pretend not to fear now, would be the first to fear upon the approach of danger; it is always the case with this distant valour. Most of the concessions which have been given to the Irish have been given to fear. Ireland would have been lost to this country, if the British legislature had not, with all the rapidity and precipitation of the truest panic, passed those acts which Ireland did not ask, but demanded in the time of her armed associations. I should not think a man brave, but mad, who did not fear the treasons and rebellions of Ireland in time of war. I should think him not dastardly, but consummately wise, who provided against them in time of peace. The Catholic question has made a greater progress since the opening of this Parliament than I ever remember it to have made, and it has made that progress from fear alone. The House of Commons were astonished by the union of the Irish Catholics. They saw that Catholic Ireland had discovered her strength, and stretched out her limbs, and felt manly powers, and called for manly treatment; and the House of Commons wisely and practically yielded to the innovations of time, and the shifting attitude of human affairs.

I admit the church, sir, to be in great danger. I am sure the state is so also. My remedy for these evils is, to enter into an alliance with the Irish people—to conciliate the clergy, by giving them pensions—to loyalize the laity, by putting them on a footing with the Protestant. My remedy is the old one, approved of from the beginning of the world, to lessen dangers, by increasing friends, and appeasing enemies. I think it most probable, that under this system of crown patronage, the clergy will be quiet. A Catholic layman, who finds all the honours of the state open to him, will not, I think, run into treason and rebellion—will not live with a rope about his neck, in order to turn our bishops out, and put his own in; he may not, too, be of opinion that the utility of his bishop will be four times as great, because his income is four times as large; but whether he is or not, he will never endanger his sweet acres (large measure) for such questions as these. Anti-Trinitarian Dissenters sit in the House of Commons, whom we believe to be condemned to the punishments of another world. There is no limit to the introduction of Dissenters into both houses—Dissenting Lords or Dissenting Commons. What mischief have Dissenters for this last century and a half plotted against the Church of England? The Catholic lord and the Catholic gentleman (restored to their fair rights) will never join with levellers and Iconoclasts. You will find them defending you hereafter against your Protestant enemies.—The crosier in any hand, the mitre on any head, are more tolerable in the eyes of a Catholic than doxological Barebones and tonsured Cromwell.

We preach to our congregations, sir, that a tree is known by its fruits. By the fruits it produces I will judge your system. What has it done for Ireland? New Zealand is emerging—Otaheite is emerging—Ireland is not emerging—she is still veiled in darkness—her children, safe under no law, live in the very shadow of death. Has your system of exclusion made Ireland rich? Has it made Ireland loyal? Has it made Ireland free? Has it made Ireland happy? How is the wealth of Ireland proved? Is it by the naked, idle, suffering savages, who are slumbering on the mud floor of their cabins? In what does the loyalty of Ireland consist? Is it in the eagerness with which they would range themselves under the hostile banner of any invader, for your destruction and for your distress? Is it liberty when men breathe and move among the bayonets of English soldiers? Is their happiness and their history any thing but such a tissue of murders, burnings, hanging, famine, and disease, as never existed before in the annals of the world?—This is the system which, I am sure, with very different intentions, and different views of its effects, you are met this day to uphold. These are the dreadful consequences, which those laws your petition prays may be continued, have produced upon Ireland. From the principles of that system, from the cruelty of those laws, I turn, and turn with the homage of my whole heart, to that memorable proclamation which the head of our church—the present monarch of these realms—has lately made to his hereditary dominions of Hanover—*That no man should be subjected to civil incapacities on account of religious opinions.* Sir, there have been many memorable things done in this reign. Hostile armies have been destroyed; fleets have been captured; formidable combinations have been broken to pieces—*but this sentiment, in the mouth of a king,* deserves more than all glories and victories the notice of that historian who is destined to tell to future ages the deeds of the English people. I hope he will lavish upon it every gem which glitters in the cabinet of genius, and so uphold it to the world that it will be remembered when Waterloo is forgotten, and when the fall of Paris is blotted out from the memory of man. Great as it is, sir, this is not the only pleasure I have received in these latter days. I have seen, within these few weeks, a degree of wisdom in our mercantile laws, such superiority to vulgar prejudice, views so just and so profound, that it seemed to me as if I was reading the works of a speculative economist, rather than the improvement of a practical politician, agreed to by a legislative assembly, and upon the eve of being carried into execution, for the benefit of a great people. Let who will be their master, I honour and praise the ministers who have learnt such a lesson. I rejoice that I have lived to see such an improvement in English affairs—that the stubborn resistance to all improvement—the contempt of all scientific reasoning, and the rigid adhesion to every stupid error which so long characterized the proceedings of this country, are fast giving away to better things, under better men, placed in better circumstances.

I confess it is not without severe pain that, in the midst of all this expansion and improvement, I perceive that in our profession we are still calling for the same exclusion—still asking that the same fetters may be riveted on our fellow-creatures—still mistaking what constitutes the weakness and misfortune of the church, for that which contributes to its glory, its dignity, and its strength. Sir, there are two petitions at this moment in this house, against two of the wisest and best measures which ever came into the British Parliament, against the impending corn law and against the Catholic emancipation—the one bill intended to increase the comforts, and the other to allay the bad passions of man.—Sir, I am not in a situation of life to do much good, but I will take care that I will not willingly do any evil.—The wealth of the Riding should not tempt me to petition against either of those bills. With the corn bill, I have nothing to do at this time. Of the Catholic emancipation bill, I shall say, that it will be the foundation stone of a lasting religious peace; that it will give to Ireland not all that it wants, but what it most wants, and without which no other boon will be of any avail.

When this bill passes, it will be a signal to

all the religious sects of that unhappy country to lay aside their mutual hatred, and to live in peace, as equal men should live under equal law—when this bill passes, the Orange flag will fall—when this bill passes, the Green flag of the rebel will fall—when this bill passes, no other flag will fly in the land of Erin than that flag which blends the lion with the harp—that flag which, wherever it does fly, is the sign of freedom and of joy—the only banner in Europe which floats over a limited king and a free people.

SPEECH AT THE TAUNTON REFORM MEETING.*

Mr. Bailiff,—This is the greatest measure which has ever been before Parliament in my time, and the most pregnant with good or evil to the country; and though I seldom meddle with political meetings, I could not reconcile it to my conscience to be absent from this.

Every year, for this half century, the question of reform has been pressing upon us, till it has swelled up at last into this great and awful combination; so that almost every city and every borough in England are at this moment assembled for the same purpose, and are doing the same thing we are doing. It damps the ostentation of argument and mitigates the pain of doubt, to believe (as I believe) that the measure is inevitable; the consequences may be good or bad, but done it must be; I defy the most determined enemy of popular influence, either now or a little time from now, to prevent a reform in Parliament. Some years ago, by timely concession, it might have been prevented. If members had been granted to Birmingham, Leeds, and Manchester, and other great towns, as opportunities occurred, a spirit of conciliation would have been evinced, and the people might have been satisfied with a reform, which though remote would have been gradual; but with the customary blindness and insolence of human beings, the day of adversity was forgotten, the rapid improvement of the people was not noticed; the object of a certain class of politicians was to please the court and to gratify their own arrogance by treating every attempt to expand the representation, and to increase the popular influence, with every species of contempt and obloquy: the golden opportunity was lost; and now proud lips must swallow bitter potions.

The arguments and the practices (as I remember to have heard Mr. Huskisson say), which did very well twenty years ago, will not do now. The people read too much, think too much, see too many newspapers, hear too many speeches, have their eyes too intensely fixed upon political events. But if it was possible to put off parliamentary reform a week ago, is it possible now? When a monarch (whose amiable and popular manners have, I verily believe, saved us from a revolution) approves the measure—when a minister of exalted character plans and fashions it—when a cabinet of such varied talent and disposition protects it—when such a body of the aristocracy vote for it—when the hundred-horse power of the press is labouring for it;—who does not know, after this, (whatever be the decision of the present Parliament,) that the measure is virtually carried—and that all the struggle between such annunciation of such a plan, and its completion, is tumult, disorder, disaffection, and (it may be) political ruin?

An honourable member of the honourable house, much connected with this town, and once its representative, seems to be amazingly surprised, and equally dissatisfied, at this combination of king, ministers, nobles, and people, against his opinion:—like the gentleman who came home from serving on a jury very much disconcerted, and complaining he had met with eleven of the most obstinate people he had ever seen in his life, whom he found it absolutely impossible by the strongest arguments to bring over to his way of thinking.

They tell you, gentlemen, that you have grown rich and powerful with these rotten boroughs, and that it would be madness to part with them, or to alter a constitution which had produced such happy effects. There happens, gentlemen, to live near my parsonage a labouring man, of very superior character and understanding to his fellow-labourers; and who has made such good use of that superiority, that he has saved what is (for his station in life) a very considerable sum of money, and if his existence is extended to the common period, he will die rich. It happens, however, that he is (and long has been) troubled with violent stomachic pains, for which he has hitherto ob-

* I was a sincere friend to reform; I am so still. It was a great deal too violent—but the only justification is, that you cannot reform as you wish, by degrees; you must avail yourself of the few opportunities that present themselves. The reform carried, it became the business of every honest man to turn it to good, and to see that the people (drunk with their new power) did not ruin our ancient institutions. We have been in considerable danger, and that danger is not over. What alarms me most is the large price paid by both parties for popular favour. The yeomanry were put down: nothing could be more grossly absurd—the people were rising up against the poor-laws, and such an excellent and permanent force was abolished because they were not deemed a proper force to deal with popular insurrections. You may just as well object to put out a fire with pond water because pump water is better for the purpose: I say, put out the fire with the first water you can get; but the truth is, radicals don't like armed yeomen: they have an ugly homicide appearance. Again, —a million of revenue is given up in the nonsensical penny-post scheme, to please my old, excellent, and universally dissentient friend, Noah Warburton. I admire the whig ministry, and think tney have done more good things than all the ministries since the Revolution; but these concessions are sad and unworthy marks of weakness, and fill reasonable men with just alarm. All this folly has taken place since they have become ministers upon principles of chivalry and gallantry; and the tories, too, for fear of the people, have been much too quiet. There is only one principle of public conduct—*Do what you think right, and take place and power as an accident.* Upon any other plan, office is habbiness, labour, and sorrow

tained no relief, and which really are the bane and torment of his life. Now, if my excellent labourer were to send for a physician, and to consult him respecting this malady, would it not be very singular language if our doctor were to say to him, "My good friend, you surely will not be so rash as to attempt to get rid of these pains in your stomach. Have you not grown rich with these pains in your stomach? have you not risen under them from poverty to prosperity? has not your situation, since you were first attacked, been improving every year? You surely will not be so foolish and so indiscreet as to part with the pains in your stomach?"—Why, what would be the answer of the rustic to this nonsensical monition? "Monster of rhubarb! (he would say) I am not rich in consequence of the pains in my stomach, but in spite of the pains in my stomach; and I should have been ten times richer, and fifty times happier, if I had never had any pains in my stomach at all." Gentlemen, these rotten boroughs are your pains in the stomach—and you would have been a much richer and greater people if you had never had them at all. Your wealth and your power have been owing, not to the debased and corrupted parts of the House of Commons, but to the many independent and honourable members whom it has always contained within its walls. If there had been a few more of these very valuable members for close boroughs, we should, I verily believe, have been by this time about as free as Denmark, Sweden, or the Germanized states of Italy.

They tell you of the few men of name and character who have sat for boroughs; but nothing is said of those mean and menial men who are sent down every day by their aristocratic masters to continue unjust and unnecessary wars, to prevent inquiring into profligate expenditure, to take money out of your pockets, or to do any other bad or base thing which the minister of the day may require at their unclean hands. What mischief, it is asked, have these boroughs done? I believe there is not a day of your lives in which you are not suffering in all the taxed commodities of life from the accumulation of bad votes of bad men. But, Mr. Bailiff, if this *were otherwise*, if it really were a great political invention, that cities of 100,000 men should have no representatives, because those representatives were wanted for political ditches, political walls, and political parks; that the people should be bought and sold like any other commodity; that a retired merchant should be able to go into the market and buy ten shares in the government of twenty millions of his fellow-subjects; yet can such asseverations be made openly before the people? Wise men, men conversant with human affairs, may whisper such theories to each other in retirement; but can the people ever be taught that it is right they should be bought and sold? Can the vehemence of eloquent democrats be met with such arguments and theories? Can the doubts of honest and limited men be met by such arguments and theories? The moment such a government is looked at by all the people it is lost. It is impossible to explain, defend, and recommend it to the mass of mankind. And true enough it is, that as often as misfortune threatens us at home, or imitation excites us from abroad, political reform is clamored for by the people—there it stands, and ever will stand, in the apprehension of the multitude—reform, the cure of every evil—corruption, the source of every misfortune—famine, defeat, decayed trade, depressed agriculture, will all lapse into the question of reform. Till that question is set at rest (and it may be set at rest), all will be disaffection, tumult, and perhaps (which God avert!) destruction.

But democrats and agitators (and democrats and agitators there are in the world), will not be contented with this reform. Perhaps not, sir; I never hope to content men whose game is never to be contented—but if they are not contented, I am sure their discontent will then comparatively be of little importance. I am afraid of them now; I have no arguments to answer them: but I shall not be afraid of them after this bill, and would tell them boldly, in the middle of their mobs, that there was no longer cause for agitation and excitement, and that they were intending wickedly to the people. You may depend upon it such a measure would destroy their trade, as the repeal of duties would destroy the trade of the smuggler; their functions would be carried on faintly, and with little profit; you would soon feel that your position was stable, solid, and safe.

All would be well, it is urged, if they would but let the people alone. But what chance is there, I demand, of these wise politicians, that the people will ever be let alone; that the orator will lay down his craft, and the demagogue forget his cunning? If many things were let alone, which never will be let alone, the aspect of human affairs would be a little varied. If the winds would let the waves alone, there would be no storms. If gentlemen would let ladies alone, there would be no unhappy marriages, and deserted damsels. If persons who can reason no better than this, would leave speaking alone, the school of eloquence might be improved. I have little hopes, however, of witnessing any of these acts of forbearance, particularly the last, and so we must (however foolish it may appear), proceed to make laws for a people who, we are sure, will not be let alone.

We might really imagine, from the objections made to the plan of reform, that the great mass of Englishmen were madmen, robbers, and murderers. The kingly power is to be destroyed, the House of Lords is to be annihilated, the church is to be ruined, estates are to be confiscated. I am quite at a loss to find in these perpetrators of crimes—in this mass of pillagers and lunatics—the steady and respectable tradesmen and farmers, who will have votes to confer, and the steady and respectable country gentlemen, who will probably have votes to receive;—it may be true of the tradesmen of *Mauritania*, it may be just of the country gentlemen of *Fez*—it is any thing but true of the English people. The English are a tranquil, phlegmatic, money-loving, money-getting people, who want to be quiet—and would be quiet if they were not surrounded by evils of such magnitude, that it would be baseness and pusillanimity not to oppose to them the strongest constitutional resistance.

Then it is said that there is to be a lack of talent in the new Parliament: it is to be composed of ordinary and inferior persons, who will bring the government of the country into contempt. But the best of all talents, gentlemen, is to conduct our affairs honestly, diligently, and economically—and this talent will, I am sure, abound as much in the new Parliament as in many previous parliaments. Parliament is not a school for rhetoric and declamation, where a stranger would go to hear a speech, as he would go to the opera to hear a song; but if it were otherwise—if eloquence be a necessary ornament of, and an indispensable adjunct to, popular assemblies—can it ever be absent from popular assemblies? I have always found that all things moral or physical grow in the soil best suited for them. Show me a deep and tenacious earth—and I am sure the oak will spring up in it. In a low and damp soil I am equally certain of the alder and the willow. Gentlemen, the free Parliament of a free people is the native soil of eloquence—and in that soil will it ever flourish and abound—there it will produce those intellectual effects which drive before them whole tribes and nations of the human race, and settle the destinies of man. And, gentlemen, if a few persons of a less elegant and aristocratic description were to become members of the House of Commons, where would be the evil? They would probably understand the common people a great deal better, and in this way the feelings and interests of all classes of people would be better represented. The House of Commons, thus organized, will express more faithfully the opinions of the people.

The people are sometimes, it is urged, grossly mistaken; but are kings never mistaken? Are the higher orders never mistaken?—never wilfully corrupted by their own interests? The people have at least this superiority, that they always intend to do what is right.

The argument of fear is very easily disposed of: he who is afraid of a knock on the head or a cut on the cheek is a coward; he who is afraid of entailing greater evils on the country by refusing the remedy than by applying it, and who acts in pursuance of that conviction, is a wise and prudent man—nothing can be more different than personal and political fear; it is the artifice of our opponents to confound them together.

The right of disfranchisement, gentlemen, must exist somewhere, and where but in Parliament? If not, how was the Scotch union, how was the Irish union, effected? The Duke of Wellington's administration disfranchised at one blow 200,000 Irish voters—for no fault of theirs, and for no other reason than the best of all reasons, that public expediency required it. These very same politicians are now looking in an agony of terror at the disfranchisement of corporations containing twenty or thirty persons, sold to their representatives, who are themselves perhaps sold to the government: and to put an end to these enormous abuses is called *corporation robbery*, and there are some persons wild enough to talk of compensation. This principle of compensation you will consider perhaps in the following instance to have been carried as far as sound discretion permits. When I was a young man, the place in England I remember as most notorious for highwaymen and their exploits was Finchley Common, near the metropolis; but Finchley Common, gentlemen, in the progress of improvement, came to be enclosed, and the highwaymen lost by these means the opportunity of exercising their gallant vocation. I remember a friend of mine proposed to draw up for them a petition to the House of Commons for compensation, which ran in this manner—"We, your loyal highwaymen of Finchley Common, and its neighbourhood, having, at great expense, laid in a stock of blunderbusses, pistols, and other instruments for plundering the public, and finding ourselves impeded in the exercise of our calling by the said enclosure of the said Common of Finchley, humbly petition your honourable house will be pleased to assign to us such compensation as your honourable house in its wisdom and justice may think fit." Gentlemen, I must leave the application to you.

An honourable baronet says, if Parliament is dissolved, I will go to my borough with the bill in my hand, and will say, "I know of no crime you have committed, I found nothing proved against you: I voted against the bill, and am come to fling myself upon your kindness, with the hope that my conduct will be approved, and that you will return me again to Parliament." That honourable baronet may, perhaps, receive from his borough an answer he little expects—"We are above being bribed by such a childish and unworthy artifice; we do not choose to consult our own interest at the expense of the general peace and happiness of the country; we are thoroughly convinced a reform ought to take place; we are very willing to sacrifice a privilege we ought never to have possessed to the good of the community, and we will return no one to Parliament who is not deeply impressed with the same feeling." This I hope is the answer that gentleman will receive, and this, I hope, will be the noble and generous feeling of every borough in England.

The greater part of human improvements, gentlemen, I am sorry to say, are made after war, tumult, bloodshed, and civil commotion: mankind seem to object to every species of gratuitous happiness, and to consider every advantage as too cheap, which is not purchased by some calamity. I shall esteem it as a singular act of God's providence, if this great nation, guided by these warnings of history, not waiting till tumult for reform, nor trusting reform to the rude hands of the lowest of the people, shall amend their decayed institutions at a period when they are ruled by a popular monarch, guided by an upright minister, and blest with profound peace.

SPEECH AT TAUNTON.

Mr. Chairman,—I am particularly happy to assist on this occasion, because I think that the accession of the present king is a marked and important era in English history. Another coronation has taken place since I have been in the world, but I never assisted at its celebration. I saw in it a change of masters, not a change of system. I did not understand the joy which it occasioned. I did not feel it, and I did not counterfeit what I did not feel.

I think very differently of the accession of his present majesty. I believe I see in that accession a great probability of serious improvement, and a great increase of public happiness. The evils which have been long complained of by bold and intelligent men are now universally admitted. The public feeling, which has been so often appealed to, is now intensely excited. The remedies which have so often been called for are now at last vigorously, wisely and faithfully applied. I admire, gentlemen, in the present king, his love of peace—I admire in him his disposition to economy, and I admire in him, above all, his faithful and honorable conduct to those who happen to be his ministers. He was, I believe, quite as faithful to the Duke of Wellington as to Lord Grey, and would, I have no doubt, be quite as faithful to the political enemies of Lord Grey (if he thought fit to employ them), as he is to Lord Grey himself. There is in this reign, no secret influence, no double ministry—on whomsoever he confers the office, to him he gives that confidence without which the office cannot be holden with honour, nor executed with effect. He is not only a peaceful king, and an economical king, but he is an honest king. So far, I believe, every individual of this company will go with me. There is another topic of eulogium, on which, before I sit down, I should like to say a few words—I mean the willingness of our present king to investigate abuses and to reform them. If this subject is not unpleasant, I will offer upon it a very few observations—a few, because the subject is exhausted, and because, if it were not, I have no right, from my standing or my situation in this county, to detain you long upon that or any other subject.

In criticising this great question of reform, I think there is some injustice done to its authors. Men seem to suppose that a minister can sit down and make a plan of reform with as much ease and as much exactness, and with as complete a gratification of his own will, as an architect can do in building or altering a house. But a minister of state (it should be in justice observed), works in the midst of hatred, injustice, violence, and the worst of human passions—his works are not the works of calm and unembarrassed wisdom—they are not the best that a dreamer of dreams can imagine. It is enough if they are the best plans which the passions, parties, and prejudices of the times in which he acts will permit. In passing a reform bill, the minister overthrows the long and deep interest which powerful men have in existing abuses—he subjects himself to the deepest hatred, and encounters the bitterest opposition. Auxiliaries he must have, and auxiliaries he can only find among the people—not the mob—but the great mass of those who have opinions worth hearing, and property worth defending—a greater mass, I am happy to say, in this country than exists in any other country on the face of the earth. Now, before the middling orders will come forward with one great impulse, they must see that something is offered them worth the price of contention; they must see that the object is great and the gain serious. If you call them in at all, it must not be to displace one faction at the expense of another, but to put down all factions—to substitute purity and principle for corruption—to give to the many that political power which the few have unjustly taken to themselves—to get rid of evils so ancient and so vast that any other arm than the public arm would be lifted up against them in vain. This, then, I say, is one of the reasons why ministers have been compelled to make their measures a little more vigorous and decisive than a speculative philosoper, sitting in his closet, might approve of. They had a mass of opposition to contend with which could be encountered only by a general exertion of public spirit—they had a long-suffering and an often deceived public to appeal to, who were determined to suffer no longer, and to be deceived no more. The alternative was to continue the ancient abuses, or to do what they have done—and most firmly do I believe that you and I, and the latest posterity of us all, will rejoice in the decision they have made. Gradation has been called for in reform: we might, it is said, have taken thirty or forty years to have accomplished what we have done in one year. 'It is not so much the magnitude of what you are doing we object to, as the suddenness.' But was not gradation tendered? Was it not said by the friends of reform—'Give us Birmingham and Manchester, and we will be satisfied?' and what was the answer? 'No Manchester, no Birmingham, no reform in any degree—all abuses as they are—all perversions as we found them—the corruptions which our fathers bequeathed us we will hand down unimpaired and unpurified to our children.' But I would say to the graduate philosopher,—'How often does a reforming minister occur?' and if such are so common that you can command them when you please, how often does a reforming monarch occur? and how often does the conjunction occur? Are you sure that a people, bursting into new knowledge, and speculating on every public event, will wait for your protracted reform? Strike while the iron is hot—up with the arm, and down with the hammer, and up again with the arm, and down again with the hammer. The iron is hot—the opportunity exists now—if you neglect it, it may not return for an hundred years to come.

There is an argument I have often heard, and

that is this—Are we to be afraid?—is this measure to be carried by intimidation?—is the House of Lords to be overawed? But this style of argument proceeds from confounding together two sets of feelings which are entirely distinct—personal fear and political fear. If I am afraid of voting against this bill, because a mob may gather about the house of Lords—because stones may be flung at my head—because my house may be attacked by a mob, I am a poltroon, and unfit to meddle with public affairs; but I may rationally be afraid of producing great public agitation—I may be honourably afraid of flinging people into secret clubs and conspiracies—I may be wisely afraid of making the aristocracy hateful to the great body of the people. This surely has no more to do with fear than a loose identity of name; it is in fact prudence of the highest order; the deliberate reflection of a wise man who does not like what he is going to do, but likes still less the consequence of not doing it, and who, of two evils, chooses the least.

There are some men much afraid of what is to happen: my lively hope of good is, I confess, mingled with very little apprehension, but of one thing I must be candid enough to say that I am much afraid, and that is of the opinion now increasing, that the people are become indifferent to reform; and of that opinion I am afraid, because I believe in an evil hour it may lead some misguided members of the upper house of Parliament to vote against the bill. As for the opinion itself, I hold it in the utmost contempt. The people are waiting in virtuous patience for the completion of the bill, because they know it is in the hands of men who do no mean to deceive them. I do not believe they have given up one atom of reform—I do not believe that a great people were ever before so firmly bent upon any one measure. I put it to any man of common sense, whether he believes it possible, after the king and Parliament have acted as they have done, that the people will ever be content with much less than the present bill contains. If a contrary principle is acted upon, and the bill attempted to be got rid of altogether, I confess I tremble for the consequences, which I believe will be of the worst and most painful description; and this I say deliberately, after the most diligent and extensive inquiry.—Upon that diligent inquiry I repeat again my firm conviction, that the desire of reform has increased, not diminished; that the present repose is not indifference, but the calmness of victory, and the tranquillity of success. When I see all the wishes and appetites of created beings changed, when I see an eagle, that after long confinement, has escaped into the air, come back to his cage and his chains,—when I see the emancipated negro asking again for the hoe which has broken down his strength, and the lash which has tortured his body, I will then, and not till then, believe that the English people will return to their ancient degradation—that they will hold out their repentant hands for those manacles which at this moment lay broken into links at their feet.

SPEECH AT TAUNTON.

[From the "Taunton Courier" of October 12th, 1831.]

The Reverend Sydney Smith rose and said: Mr. Bailiff, I have spoken so often on this subject, that I am sure both you and the gentlemen here present will be obliged to me for saying but little, and that favour I am as willing to confer, as you can be to receive it. I feel most deeply the event which has taken place, because, by putting the two houses of Parliament in collision with each other, it will impede the public business, and diminish the public prosperity. I feel it as a churchman, because I cannot but blush to see so many dignitaries of the church arrayed against the wishes and happiness of the people. I feel it more than all, because I believe it will sow the seeds of deadly hatred between the aristocracy and the great mass of the people. The loss of the bill I do not feel, and for the best of all possible reasons—because I have not the slightest idea that it is lost. I have no more doubt, before the expiration of the winter, that this bill will pass, than I have that the annual tax bills will pass, and greater certainty than this no man can have, for Franklin tells us, there are but two things certain in this world—death and taxes. As for the possibility of the House of Lords preventing ere long a reform of Parliament, I hold it to be the most absurd notion that ever entered into human imagination. I do not mean to be disrespectful, but the attempt of the lords to stop the progress of reform, reminds me very forcibly of the great storm of Sidmouth, and of the conduct of the excellent Mrs. Partington on that occasion. In the winter of 1824, there set in a great flood upon that town—the tide rose to an incredible height—the waves rushed in upon the houses, and every thing was threatened with destruction. In the midst of this sublime and terrible storm, Dame Partington, who lived upon the beach, was seen at the door of her house with mop and pattens, trundling her mop, squeezing out the sea-water, and vigorously pushing away the Atlantic Ocean. The Atlantic was roused. Mrs. Partington's spirit was up; but I need not tell you that the contest was unequal. The Atlantic Ocean beat Mrs. Partington. She was excellent at a slop, or a puddle, but she should not have meddled with a tempest. Gentlemen, be at your ease—be quiet and steady. You will beat Mrs. Partington.

They tell you, gentlemen, in the debates by which we have been lately occupied, that the bill is not justified by experience. I do not think this true, but if it were true, nations are sometimes compelled to act without experience for their guide, and to trust to their own sagacity for the anticipation of consequences. The instances where this country has been compelled thus to act have been so eminently successful, that I see no cause for fear, even if we were acting in the manner imputed to us by our enemies. What precedents and what experience were there at the Reformation, when the country, with one unanimous effort, pushed out the pope, and his grasping and ambitious clergy?—What experience, when, at the Revolution, we drove away our ancient race of kings, and chose another family more congenial to our free principles?—And yet to those two events, contrary to experience, and unguided by precedents, we owe all our domestic happiness, and civil and religious freedom—and having got rid of corrupt priests and despotic kings, by our sense and our courage, are we now to be intimidated by the awful danger of extinguishing boroughmongers, and shaking from our necks the ignominious yoke which their baseness has imposed upon us? Go on, they say, as you have done for these hundred years last past. I answer, it is impossible—five hundred people now write and read where one hundred wrote and read fifty years ago. The iniquities and enormities of the borough system are now known to the meanest of the people. You have a different sort of men to deal with—you must change because the beings whom you govern are changed. After all, and to be short, I must say that it has always appeared to me to be the most absolute nonsense that we cannot be a great, or a rich and happy nation, without suffering ourselves to be bought and sold every five years like a pack of negro slaves. I hope I am not a very rash man, but I would launch boldly into this experiment without any fear of consequences, and I believe there is not a man here present who would not cheerfully embark with me. As to the enemies of the bill, who pretend to be reformers, I know them, I believe, better than you do, and I earnestly caution you against them. You will have no more of reform than they are compelled to grant—you will have no reform at all, if they can avoid it—you will be hurried into a war to turn your attention from reform. They do not understand you—they will not believe in the improvement you have made—they think the English of the present day are as the English of the times of Queen Anne or George the First. They know no more of the present state of their own country, than of the state of the Esquimaux Indians. Gentlemen, I view the ignorance of the present state of the country with the most serious concern, and I believe they will one day or another waken into conviction with horror and dismay. I will omit no means of rousing them to a sense of their danger; for this object I cheerfully sign the petition proposed by Dr. Kinglake, which I consider to be the wisest and most moderate of the two.

SPEECH BY THE REV. SYDNEY SMITH.

Stick to the bill—it is your Magna Charta, and your Runnymede. King John made a present to the barons. King William has made a similar present to you. Never mind, common qualities good in common times. If a man does not vote for the bill he is unclean—the plague-spot is upon him; push him into the lazaretto of the last century, with Wetherell and Saddler; purify the air before you approach him; bathe your hands in chloride of lime, if you have been contaminated by his touch.

So far from its being a merely theoretical improvement, I put it to any man, who is himself embarked in a profession, or has sons in the same situation, if the unfair influence of boroughmongers has not perpetually thwarted him in his lawful career of ambition, and professional emolument? "I have been in three general engagements at sea," said an old sailor —"have been twice wounded;—I commanded the boats when the French frigate, the Astrolabe, was cut out so gallantly." "Then you are made a post captain?" "No. I was very near it; but—Lieutenant Thomson cut me out, as I cut out the French frigate; his father is town clerk of the borough of which Lord F———— is member, and there my chance was finished." In the same manner, all over England, you will find great scholars rotting on curacies—brave captains starving in garrets—profound lawyers decayed and mouldering in the inns of court, because the parsons, warriors, and advocates of boroughmongers must be crammed to saturation, before there is a morsel of bread for the man who does not sell his votes, and put his country up to auction; and though this is of every day occurrence, the borough system, we are told, is no practical evil.

Who can bear to walk through a slaughter-house? blood, garbage, stomachs, entrails, legs, tails, kidneys, horrors—I often walk a mile about to avoid it. What a scene of disgust and horror is an election—the base and infamous traffic of principles—a candidate of high character reduced to such means—the perjury and evasion of agents—the detestable rapacity of voters—the ten days' dominion of mammon and Belial. The bill lessens it—begins the destruction of such practices—affords some chance, and some means of turning public opinion against bribery, and of rendering it infamous.

But the thing I cannot, and will not bear, is this;—what right has *this* lord, or *that* marquis to buy ten seats in Parliament, in the shape of boroughs, and then to make laws to govern me? And how are these masses of power re-distributed? The eldest son of my lord is just come from Eton—he knows a good deal about Æneas, and Dido, Apollo, and Daphne—and that is all;

and to this boy, his father gives a six hundredth part of the power of making laws, as he would give him a horse, or a double-barreled gun. Then Vellum, the steward, is put in—an admirable man;—he has raised the estates—watched the progress of the family road, and canal bills—and Vellum shall help to rule over the people of Israel. A neighbouring country gentleman, Mr. Plumpkin, hunts with my lord—opens him a gate or two, while the hounds are running—dines with my lord—agrees with my lord—wishes he could rival the Southdown sheep of my lord—and upon Plumpkin is conferred a portion of the government. Then there is a distant relation of the same name, in the county militia, with white teeth, who calls up the carriage at the opera, and is always wishing O'Connell was hanged, drawn, and quartered—then a barrister, who has written an article in the Quarterly, and is very likely to speak, and refute M'Culloch; and these five people, in whose nomination I have no more agency than I have in the nomination of the toll-keepers of the Bosphorus, are to make laws for me and my family—to put their hands in my purse, and to sway the future destinies of this country; and when the neighbours step in, and beg permission to say a few words before these persons are chosen, there is an universal cry of ruin, confusion, and destruction;—we have become a great people under Vellum and Plumpkin—under Vellum and Plumpkin our ships have covered the ocean—under Vellum and Plumpkin our armies have secured the strength of the hills—to turn out Vellum and Plumpkin is not reform, but revolution.

Was there ever such a ministry? Was there ever before a real ministry of the people? Look at the condition of the country when it was placed in their hands: the state of the house when the incoming tenant took possession: windows broken, chimneys on fire, mobs round the house threatening to pull it down, roof tumbling, rain pouring in. It was courage to occupy it; it was a miracle to save it; it will be the glory of glories to enlarge and expand it, and to make it the eternal palace of wise and temperate freedom.

Proper examples have been made among the unhappy and misguided disciples of Swing: a rope had been carried round O'Connell's legs, and a ring inserted in Cobbett's nose. Then the game laws!!! Was ever conduct so shabby as that of the two or three governments which preceded that of Lord Grey? The cruelties and enormities of this code had been thoroughly exposed; and a general conviction existed of the necessity of a change. Bills were brought in by various gentlemen, containing some trifling alteration in this abominable code, and even these were sacrificed to the tricks and manœuvres of some noble Nimrod, who availed himself of the emptiness of the town in July, and flung out the bill. Government never stirred a step. The fulness of the prisons, the wretchedness and demoralization of the poor, never came across them. The humane and considerate Peel never once offered to extend his ægis over them. It had nothing to do with the state of party; and some of their double-barreled voters might be offended. In the mean time, for every ten pheasants which fluttered in the wood, one English peasant was rotting in jail. No sooner is Lord Althorp chancellor of the exchequer, than he turns out of the house a trumpery and (perhaps) an insidious bill for the improvement of the game laws; and in an instant offers the assistance of government for the abolition of the whole code.

Then look at the gigantic Brougham, sworn in at 12 o'clock, and before 6, has a bill on the table abolishing the abuses of a court which has been the curse of the people of England for centuries. For twenty-five long years did Lord Eldon sit in that court, surrounded with misery and sorrow, which he never held up a finger to alleviate. The widow and the orphan cried to him as vainly as the town crier cries when he offers a small reward for a full purse; the bankrupt of the court became the lunatic of the court; estates mouldered away, and mansions fell down; but the fees came in, and all was well. But in an instant the iron mace of Brougham shivered to atoms this house of fraud and of delay; and this is the man who will help to govern you; who bottoms his reputation on doing good to you; who knows, that to reform abuses is the safest basis of fame and the surest instrument of power; who uses the highest gifts of reason, and the most splendid efforts of genius, to rectify those abuses, which all the genius and talent of the profession* have hitherto been employed to justify, and to protect. Look to Brougham, and turn you to that side where he waves his long and lean finger; and mark well that face which nature has marked so forcibly—which dissolves pensions—turns jobbers into honest men—scares away the plunderer of the public—and is a terror to him who doeth evil to the people. But, above all, look to the northern earl, victim, before this honest and manly reign, of the spitefulness of the court. You may now, for the first time, learn to trust in the professions of a minister; you are directed by a man who prefers character to place, and who has given such unequivocal proofs of honesty and patriotism, that his image ought to be amongst your household gods, and his name to be lisped by your children; two thousand years hence it will be a legend like the fable of Perseus and Andromeda; Britannia changed to a mountain—two hundred rotten animals menacing her destruction, till a tall earl, armed with schedule A., and followed by his page Russell, drives them into the deep, and delivers over Britannia in safety to crowds of ten-pound renters, who deafen the air with their acclamations. Forthwith, Latin verses upon this—school exercises—boys whipt, and all the usual absurdities of education. Don't part with an administration composed of Lord Grey and Lord Brougham; and not only these, but look at them all—the mild wisdom of Lansdowne—the genius and extensive knowledge of Holland, in whose bold and honest life there is no varying or shadow of change—the unexpected and exemplary activity of Lord Melbourne—and the rising parliamentary talents of Stanley. You are ignorant of your best interests,

* Lord Lyndhurst is an exception; I firmly believe he had no wish to perpetuate the abuses of the Court of Chancery.

if every vote you can bestow is not given to such a ministry as this.

You will soon find an alteration of behaviour in the upper orders when elections become real. You will find that you are raised to the importance to which you ought to be raised. The merciless ejector, the rural tyrant, will be restrained within the limits of decency and humanity, and will improve their own characters, at the same time that they better your condition.

It is not the power of aristocracy that will be destroyed by these measures, but the unfair power. If the Duke of Newcastle is kind and obliging to his neighbours, he will probably lead his neighbours; if he is a man of sense, he will lead them more certainly, and to a better purpose. All this is as it should be; but the Duke of Newcastle, at present, by buying certain old houses, could govern his neighbours, and legislate for them, even if he had not five grains of understanding, and if he were the most churlish and brutal man under heaven. The present state of things renders unnecessary all those important virtues, which rich and well-born men, under a better system, would exercise for the public good. The Duke of Newcastle (I mention him only as an instance,) Lord Exeter will do as well, but either of those noblemen, depending not upon walls, arches, and abutments, for their power—but upon mercy, charity, forbearance, indulgence, and example—would pay this price, and lead the people by their affections; one would be the god of Stamford, and the other of Newark. This union of the great with the many is the real healthy state of a country; such a country is strong to invincibility—and this strength the borough system entirely destroys.

Cant words creep in, and affect quarrels; the changes are rung between revolution and reform; but, first settle whether a wise government ought to attempt the measure—whether any thing is wanted—whether less would do—and, having settled this, mere nomenclature becomes of very little consequence. But, after all, if it is revolution, and not reform, it will only induce me to receive an old political toast, in a twofold meaning, and with twofold pleasure. When King William and the great and glorious Revolution are given, I shall think not only of escape from bigotry, but exemption from corruption; and I shall thank Providence, which has given us a second King William for the destruction of vice, as the other, of that name, was given us for the conservation of freedom.

All formal political changes, proposed by these very men, it is said, were mild and gentle, compared to this; true, but are you on Saturday night to seize your apothecary by the throat, and to say to him, "Subtle compounder, fraudulent posologist, did not you order me a drachm of this medicine on Monday morning, and now you declare that nothing short of an ounce can do me any good?" "True enough," would he of the phials reply, "*but you did not take the drachm on Monday morning*—that makes all the difference, my dear sir; if you had done as I advised you at first, the small quantity of medicine would have sufficed; and instead of being in a night-gown and slippers up stairs, you would have been walking vigorously in Piccadilly. Do as you please—and die if you please; but don't blame me because you despised my advice, and by your own ignorance and obstinacy have entailed upon yourself tenfold rhubarb, and unlimited infusion of senna."

Now see the consequences of having a manly leader, and a manly cabinet. Suppose they had come out with a little ill-fashoned seven months' reform; what would have been the consequence? The same opposition from the tories—that would have been quite certain—and not a single reformer in England satisfied with the measure. You have now a real reform, and a fair share of power delegated to the people.

The anti-reformers cite the increased power of the press—this is the very reason why I want an increased power in the House of Commons. The Times, Herald, Advertiser, Globe, Sun, Courier, and Chronicle, are an heptarchy, which govern this country, and govern it because the people are so badly represented. I am perfectly satisfied, that with a fair and honest House of Commons the power of the press would diminish—and that the greatest authority would centre in the highest place.

Is it possible for a gentleman to get into Parliament, at present, without doing things he is utterly ashamed of—without mixing himself up with the lowest and basest of mankind? Hands, accustomed to the scented lubricity of soap, are defiled with pitch, and contaminated with filth. Is there not some inherent vice in a government, which cannot be carried on but with such abominable wickedness, in which no gentleman can mingle without moral degradation; and the practice of crimes, the very imputation of which, on other occasions, he would repel at the hazard of his life?

What signifies a small majority in the house? The miracle is, that there should have been any majority at all; that there was not an immense majority on the other side. It was a very long period before the courts of justice in Jersey could put down smuggling; and why? The judges, counsel, attorneys, crier of the court, grand and petty jurymen, were all smugglers, and the high sheriff and the constable were running goods every moonlight night.

How are you to do without a government? And what other government, if this bill is ultimately lost, could possibly be found? How could any country defray the ruinous expense of protecting with troops and constables, the Duke of Wellington and Sir Robert Peel, who literally would not be able to walk from the Horse Guards to Grosvenor Square, without two or three regiments of foot to screen them from the mob; and in these hollow squares the hero of Waterloo would have to spend his political life. By the whole exercise of his splendid military talents, by strong batteries at Bootle's, and White's, he might, on nights of great debate, reach the House of Lords; but Sir Robert would probably be cut off, and nothing could save his Twist and Lewis.

The great majority of persons returned by the new boroughs would either be men of high reputation for talents, or persons of fortune known in the neighborhood; they have property and character to lose. Why are they to plunge into mad and revolutionary projects of pillaging the public creditor? It is not the interest of any such man to do it; he would lose more by the destruction of public credit than what he would gain by a remission of what he paid for the interest of the public debt. And if it is not the interest of any one to act in this manner, it is not the interest of the mass. How many, also, of these new legislators would there be, who were not themselves creditors of the state? Is it the interest of such men to create a revolution, by destroying the constitutional power of the House of Lords, or of the king? Does there exist in persons of that class, any disposition for such changes? Are not all feelings, and opinions, and prejudices, on the opposite side? The majority of the new members will be landed gentlemen: their genus is utterly distinct from the revolutionary tribe; they have molar teeth; they are destitute of the carnivorous and incisive jaws of political adventurers.

There will be mistakes at first, as there are in all changes. All young ladies will imagine (as soon as this bill is carried) that they will be instantly married. Schoolboys believe that gerunds and supines will be abolished, and that currant tarts must ultimately come down in price; the corporal and sergeant are sure of double pay; bad poets will expect a demand for their epics; fools will be disappointed, as they always are; reasonable men, who know what to expect, will find that a very serious good has been obtained.

What good to the hewer of wood and the drawer of water? How is he benefited, if Old Sarum is abolished, and Birmingham members created? But if you ask this question of reform, you must ask it of a great number of other measures. How is he benefited by Catholic emancipation, by the repeal of the Corporation and Test Act, by the Revolution of 1688, by any great political change? by a good government? In the first place, if many are benefited, and the lower orders are not injured, this alone is reason enough for the change. But the hewer of wood and the drawer of water *are* benefited by reform. Reform will produce economy and investigation; there will be fewer jobs, and a less lavish expenditure; wars will not be persevered in for years after the people are tired of them; taxes will be taken off the poor and laid upon the rich: democratic habits will be more common in a country where the rich are forced to court the poor for political power; cruel and oppressive punishments (such as those for night poaching), will be abolished. If you steal a pheasant, you will be punished as you ought to be, but not sent away from your wife and children for seven years. Tobacco will be 2*d*. per lb. cheaper. Candles will fall in price. These last results of an improved government will be felt. We do not pretend to abolish poverty or to prevent wretchedness; but if peace, economy, and justice are the results of reform, a number of small benefits, or rather of benefits which appear small to us but not to them, will accrue to millions of people; and the connection between the existence of John Russell, and the reduced price of bread and cheese, will be as clear as it has been the object of his honest, wise, and useful life to make it.

Don't be led away by such nonsense; all things are dearer under a bad government, and cheaper under a good one. The real question they ask you is, What difference can any change of government make to you? They want to keep the bees from buzzing and stinging, in order that they may rob the hive in peace.

Work well! How does it work well, when every human being in doors and out (except the Duke of Wellington), says it must be made to work better, or it will soon cease to work at all? It is little short of absolute nonsense to call a government good, which the great mass of Englishmen would before twenty years were elapsed, if reform were denied, rise up and destroy. Of what use have all the cruel laws been of Perceval, Eldon, and Castlereagh, to extinguish reform? Lord John Russell and his abettors, would have been committed to jail twenty years ago for half only of his present reform; and now relays of the people would drag them from London to Edinburgh; at which latter city we are told by Mr. Dundas, that there is no eagerness for reform. Five minutes before Moses struck the rock, this gentleman would have said that there was no eagerness for water.

There are two methods of making alterations: the one is to despise the applicants, to begin with refusing every concession, then to relax by making concessions which are always too late; by offering in 1831 what is then too late, but would have been cheerfully accepted in 1830—gradually to O'Connellize the country, till at last, after this process has gone on for some time, the alarm becomes too great, and every thing is conceded in hurry and confusion. In the mean time fresh conspiracies have been hatched by the long delay, and no gratitude is expressed for what has been extorted by fear. In this way, peace was concluded with America, and emancipation granted to the Catholics; and in this way the war of complexion will be finished in the West Indies. The other method is, to see at a distance that the thing must be done, and to do it effectually, *and at once;* to take it out of the hands of the common people, and to carry the measure in a manly liberal manner, so as to satisfy the great majority.—The merit of this belongs to the administration of Lord Grey. He is the only minister I know of who has begun a great measure in good time, conceded at the beginning of twenty years what would have been extorted at the end of it, and prevented that folly, violence, and ignorance, which emanate from a long denial and extorted concession of justice to great masses of human beings. I believe the question of reform, or any dangerous agitation of it, is set at rest for thirty or forty years; and this is an eternity in politics.

Boroughs are not the power proceeding from wealth. Many men, who have no boroughs, are infinitely richer than those who have—but it is the artifice of wealth in seizing hold of certain localities. The boroughmonger is like rheumatism, which owes its power not so much to the intensity of the pain as to its peculiar position; a little higher up, or a little lower down, the same pain would be trifling; but it fixes in the joints, and gets into the head-quarters of motion and activity. The boroughmonger knows the importance of arthritic positions; he disdains muscle, gets into the joints, and lords it over the whole machine by felicity of place. Other men are as rich—but those riches are not fixed in the critical spot.

I live a good deal with all ranks and descriptions of people; I am thoroughly convinced that the party of democrats and republicans is very small and contemptible; that the English love their institutions—that they love not only this king, (who would not love him?) but the kingly office—that they have no hatred to the aristocracy. I am not afraid of trusting English happiness to English gentlemen. I believe that the half million of new voters will choose much better for the public than the twenty or thirty peers, to whose usurped power they succeed.

If any man doubts the power of reform, let him take these two memorable proofs of its omnipotence. First, but for the declaration against it, I believe the Duke of Wellington might this day have been in office; and, secondly, in the whole course of the debates at county meetings, and in Parliament, there are not twenty men who have declared against reform. Some advance an inch, some a foot, some a yard—but nobody stands still—nobody says, We ought to remain just where we were—every body discovers that he is a reformer, and has long been so—and appears infinitely delighted with this new view of himself. Nobody appears without the cockade—bigger or less—but always the cockade.

An exact and elaborate census is called for—vast information should have been laid upon the table of the House—great time should have been given for deliberation. All these objections, being turned into English, simply mean, that the chances of another year should have been given for defeating the bill. In that time the Poles may be crushed, the Belgians organized, Louis Philip dethroned; war may rage all over Europe—the popular spirit may be diverted to other objects. It is certainly provoking that the ministry foresaw all these possibilities, and determined to model the iron while it was red and glowing.

It is not enough that a political institution works well practically: it must be defensible; it must be such as will bear discussion, and not excite ridicule and contempt. It might work well for aught I know, if, like the savages of Onelashka, we sent out to catch a king: but who could defend a coronation by chase? who can defend the payment of 40,000*l.* for the three-hundredth part of the power of Parliament, and the re-sale of this power to government for places to the Lord Williams, and Lord Charles's, and others of the Anglophagi? Teach a million of the common people to read—and such a government (work it ever so well) must perish in twenty years. It is impossible to persuade the mass of mankind, that there are not other and better methods of governing a country. It is so complicated, so wicked, such envy and hatred accumulate against the gentlemen who have fixed themselves on the joints, that it cannot fail to perish, and to be driven as it *is* driven from the country, by a general burst of hatred and detestation. I meant, gentlemen, to have spoken for another half-hour, but I am old and tired. Thank me for ending—but, gentlemen, bear with me for another moment; one word before I end. I am old, but I thank God I have lived to see more than my observations on human nature taught me I had any right to expect. I have lived to see an honest king, in whose word his ministers can trust; who disdains to deceive those men whom he has called to the public service, but makes common cause with them for the common good; and exercises the highest powers of a ruler for the dearest interests of the state. I have lived to see a king with a good heart, who, surrounded by nobles, thinks of common men; who loves the great mass of English people, and wishes to be loved by them; who knows that his real power, as he feels that his happiness, is founded on their affection. I have lived to see a king, who, without pretending to the pomp of superior intellect, has the wisdom to see, that the decayed institutions of human policy require amendment; and who, in spite of clamor, interest, prejudice, and fear, has the manliness to carry these wise changes into immediate execution. Gentlemen, farewell: shout for the king.

BALLOT.

It is possible, and perhaps not very difficult, to invent a machine, by the aid of which electors may vote for a candidate, or for two or three candidates, out of a greater number, without its being discovered for whom they vote; it is less easy than the rabid and foaming radical supposes; but I have no doubt it may be accomplished. In Mr. Grote's dagger ballot box, which has been carried round the country by eminent patriots, you stab the card of your favourite candidate with a dagger. I have seen another, called the mouse-trap ballot box, in which you poke your finger into the trap of the member you prefer, and are caught and detained till the trap-clerk below (who knows by means of a wire when you are caught) marks your vote, pulls the liberator, and releases you. Which may be the most eligible of these two methods I do not pretend to determine, nor do I think my excellent friend Mr. Babbage has as yet made up his mind on the subject; but, by some means or other, I have no doubt the thing may be done.

Landed proprietors imagine they have a right to the votes of their tenants; and instances, in every election, are numerous where tenants have been dismissed for voting contrary to the wishes of their landlords. In the same manner strong combinations are made against tradesmen who have chosen to think and act for themselves in political matters, rather than yield their opinions to the solicitations of their customers. There is a great deal of tyranny and injustice in all this. I should no more think of asking what the political opinions of a shopkeeper were, than of asking whether he was tall or short, or large or small: for a difference of 2½ per cent., I would desert the most aristocratic butcher that ever existed, and deal with one who

"Shook the arsenal and fulmined over Greece."

On the contrary, I would not adhere to the man who put me in uneasy habiliments, however great his veneration for trial by jury, or however ardent his attachment to the liberty of the subject. A tenant I never had; but I firmly believe that if he had gone through certain pecuniary formalities twice a year, I should have thought it a gross act of tyranny to have interfered either with his political or his religious opinions.

I distinctly admit that every man has a right to do what he pleases with his own. I cannot, by law, prevent any one from discharging his tenants and changing his tradesmen for political reasons; but I may judge whether that man exercises his right to the public detriment, or for the public advantage. A man has a right to refuse dealing with any tradesman who is not five feet eleven inches high; but if he acts upon this rule, he is either a madman or a fool. He has a right to lay waste his own estate, and to make it utterly barren; but I have also a right to point him out as one who exercises his right in a manner very injurious to society. He may set up a religious or a political test for his tradesmen but admitting his right, and deprecating all interference of law, I must tell him he is making the aristocracy odious to the great mass, and that he is sowing the seeds of revolution. His purse may be full, and his fields may be wide; but the moralist will still hold the rod of public opinion over his head, and tell the money-bloated blockhead that he is shaking those laws of property which it has taken ages to extort from the wretchedness and rapacity of mankind; and that what he calls his own will not long be his own, if he tramples too heavily upon human patience.

All these practices are bad; but the facts and the consequences are exaggerated.

In the first place, the plough is not a political machine: the loom and the steam-engine are furiously political, but the plough is not. Nineteen tenants out of twenty care nothing about their votes, and pull off their opinions as easily to their landlords as they do their hats. As far as the great majority of tenants are concerned, these histories of persecution are mere declamatory nonsense; they have no more predilection for whom they vote than the organ pipes have for what tunes they are to play. A tenant dismissed for a fair and just cause often attributes his dismissal to political motives, and endeavours to make himself a martyr with the public: a man who ploughs badly, or who pays badly, says he is dismissed for his vote. No candidate is willing to allow that he has lost his election by his demerits; and he seizes hold of these stories, and circulates them with the greatest avidity: they are stated in the House of Commons; John Russel and Spring Rice fall a-crying: there is lamentation of liberals in the land; and many groans for the territorial tyrants.

A standing reason against the frequency of dismissal of tenants is, that it is always injurious to the pecuniary interests of a landlord to dismiss a tenant; the property always suffers in some degree by a going off tenant; and it is therefore always the interest of a landlord not to change when the tenant does his duty as an agriculturalist.

To part with tenants for political reasons always makes a landlord unpopular. The Constitutional, price 4*d.*; the Cato, at 3½*d.*; and the Lucius Junius Brutus, at 2*d.*, all set upon the unhappy scutiger; and the squire, unused to be pointed at, and thinking that all Europe and part of Asia are thinking of him and his farmers, is driven to the brink of suicide and despair. That such things are done is not denied; that they are scandalous when they are done is equally true; but these are reasons why such acts are less frequent than they are commonly represented to be. In the same manner, there are instances of shopkeepers being materially injured in their business from the votes they have given; but the facts themselves, as well as the consequences, are grossly exaggerated. If shopkeepers lose tory, they gain whig customers; and it is not always the vote which does the mischief, but the low, vulgar impertinence and the unbridled scurrility of a man who thinks that, by dividing to mankind their rations of butter and of cheese, he has qualified himself for legislation, and that he can hold the rod of empire because he has wielded the yard of mensuration. I detest all inquisition into political opinions, but I have very rarely seen a combination against any tradesman who modestly, quietly, and conscientiously took his own line in politics. But Brutus and butterman, cheesemonger and Cato, do not harmonize well together; good taste is offended, the coxcomb loses his friends, and general disgust is mistaken for combined oppression. Shopkeepers, too, are very apt to cry out before they are hurt: a man who sees, after an election, one of his customers buying a pair of gloves on the opposite side of the way, roars out that his honesty will make him a bankrupt, and the county papers are filled with letters from Brutus, Publicola, Hampden, and Pym.

This interference with the freedom of voting, bad as it is, produces no political deliberation; it does not make the tories stronger than the whigs, nor the whigs than the tories, for both are equally guilty of this species of tyranny; and any particular system of measure fails or prevails, much as if no such practice existed. The practice had better not be at all, but if a certain quantity of the evil does exist, it is better that it should be equally divided among both parties, than that it should be exercised by one for the depression of the other. There are politicians always at a white heat, who suppose that there are landed tyrants only on one side of the question; but human life has been distressingly abridged by the flood: there is no time to spare; it is impossible to waste it upon such senseless bigotry.

If a man is sheltered from intimidation, is it at all clear that he would vote from any better motive than intimidation? If you make so tremendous an experiment, are you sure of attaining your object? The landlord has perhaps said a cross word to the tenant; the candidate for whom the tenant votes in opposition to his landlord has taken his second son for a footman, or his father knew the candidate's grandfather: how many thousand votes, sheltered (as the ballotists suppose) from intimidation, would be given from such silly motives as these? how many would be given from the mere discontent of inferiority? or from that strange simious schoolboy passion of giving pain to others, even when the author cannot be found out?—motives as pernicious as any which could proceed from intimidation. So that all voters screened by ballot would not be screened for any public good.

The radicals, (I do not use this word in any offensive sense, for I know many honest and excellent men of this way of thinking),—but the radicals praise and admit the lawful influence of wealth and power. They are quite satisfied if a rich man of popular manners gains the votes and affections of his dependants but why is this not as bad as intimidation? The real object is to vote for the good politician, not for the kind-hearted or agreeable man the mischief is just the same to the country whether I am smiled into a corrupt choice or frowned into a corrupt choice,—what is it to me whether my landlord is the best of landlords, or the most agreeable of men? I must vote for Joseph Hume, if I think Joseph more honest than the marquis. The more mitigated radical may pass over this, but the real carnivorous variety of the animal should declaim as loudly against the fascinations as against the threats of the great. The man who possesses the land should never speak to the man who tills it. The intercourse between landlord and tenant should be as strictly guarded as that of the sexes in Turkey. A funded duenna should be placed over every landed grandee.—And then intimidation! Is intimidation confined to the aristocracy? Can any thing be more scandalous and atrocious than the intimidation of mobs? Did not the mob of Bristol occasion more ruin, wretchedness, death, and alarm, than all the ejection of tenants, and combinations against shopkeepers, from the beginning of the century? and did not the Scotch philosophers tear off the clothes of the tories in Mintoshire? or at least such clothes as the customs of the country admit of being worn?—and did not they, without any reflection at all upon the customs of the country, wash the tory voters in the river?

Some sanguine advocates of the ballot contend that it would put an end to all canvassing: why should it do so? Under the ballot, I canvass (it is true) a person who may secretly deceive me. I cannot be sure he will not do so—but I am sure it is much less likely he will vote against me, when I have paid him all the deference and attention which a representative bestows on his constituents, than if I had totally neglected him: to any other objections he may have against me, at least I will not add that of personal incivility.

Scarcely is any great virtue practised without some sacrifice; and the admiration which virtue excites seems to proceed from the contemplation of such sufferings, and of the exertions by which they are endured: a tradesman suffers some loss of trade by voting for his country; is he not to vote? he might suffer some loss of blood in fighting for his country; is he not to fight? Every one would be a good Samaritan, if he was quite sure his compassion would cost him nothing. We should all be heroes, if it was not for blood and fractures; all saints, if it were not for the restrictions and privations of sanctity; all patriots, if it were not for the losses and misrepresentations to which patriotism exposes us. The ballotists are a set of Englishmen glowing with the love of England and the love of virtue, but determined to hazard the most dangerous experiments in politics, rather than run the risk of losing a penny in defence of their exalted feelings.

An abominable tyranny exercised by the ballot is, that it compels those persons to conceal their votes, who hate all concealment, and who glory in the cause they support. If you are afraid to go in at the front door, and to say in a clear voice what you have to say, go in at the back door, and say it in a whisper—but this is not enough for you; you make me, who am bold and honest, sneak in at the back door as well as yourself: because you are afraid of selling a dozen or two of gloves less than usual, you compel me, who have no gloves to sell, or who would dare and despise the loss, if I had, to hide the best feelings of my heart, and to lower myself down to your mean morals. It is as if a few cowards, who could only fight behind walls and houses, were to prevent the whole regiment from showing a bold front in the field: what right has the coward to degrade me who am no coward, and put me in the same shameful predicament with himself? If ballot is established, a zealous voter cannot do justice to his cause; there will be so many false Hampdens, and spurious Catos, that all men's actions and motives will be mistrusted. It is in the power of any man to tell me that my colours are false, that I declaim with stimulated warmth, and canvass with fallacious zeal; that I am a tory, though I call *Russell* for ever, or a whig, in spite of my obstreperous panegyrics of *Peel.* It is really a curious condition that all men must imitate the defects of a few, in order that it may not be known who have the natural imperfection, and who put it on from conformity. In this way, in former days, to hide the gray hairs of the old, every body was forced to wear powder and pomatum.

It must not be forgotten that, in the ballot, concealment must be absolutely *compulsory.* It would never do to let one man vote openly, and another secretly. You may go to the edge of the box, and say, "I vote for A.," but who knows that your ball is not put in for B.? There must be a clear, plain opportunity for telling an undiscoverable lie, or the whole invention is at an end. How beautiful is the progress of man! printing has abolished ignorance—gas put an end to darkness—steam has conquered time and distance—it remained for Grote and his box to remove the incumbrance of truth from human transactions. May we not look now for more little machines to abolish the other cardinal virtues.

But if all men are suspected; if things are so contrived that it is impossible to know what men really think, a serious impediment is created to the formation of good public opinion in the multitude. There is a town (No. 1.) in which live two very clever and respectable men, Johnson and Pelham, small tradesmen, men always willing to run some risk for the public good, and to be less rich, and more honest than their neighbours. It is of considerable consequence to the formation of opinion in this town, as an example, to know how Johnson and Pelham vote. It guides the affections, and directs the understandings, of the whole population, and materially affects public opinion in this town; and in another borough, No. 2, it would be of the highest importance to public opinion if it were certain how Mr. Smith, the ironmonger, and Mr. Rodgers, the London carrier, voted; because they are both thoroughly honest men, and of excellent understanding for their condition of life. Now, the tendency of ballot would be to destroy all the Pelhams, Johnsons, Rodgers's, and Smiths, to sow a universal mistrust, and to exterminate the natural guides and leaders of the people: political influence, founded upon honour and ancient honesty in politics, could not grow up under such a system. No man's declarations could get believed. It would be easy to whisper away the character of the best men; and to assert, that in spite of all his declarations, which are nothing but a blind, the romantic Rodgers has voted on the other side, and is in secret league with our enemies.

"Who brought that mischievous profligate villain into Parliament? Let us see the names of his real supporters. Who stood out against the strong and uplifted arm of power? Who discovered this excellent and hitherto unknown person? Who opposed the man whom we all know to be one of the first men in the country?" Are these fair and useful questions to be veiled hereafter in impenetrable mystery? Is this sort of publicity of no good as a restraint? is it of no good as an incitement to and a reward for exertions? Is not public opinion formed by such feelings? and is it not a dark and demoralizing system to draw this veil over human actions; to say to the mass, be base, and you will not be despised; be virtuous, and you will not be honoured? Is this the way in which Mr. Grote would foster the spirit of a bold and indomitable people? Was the liberty of that people established by fraud? Did America lie herself into independence? Was it treachery which enabled Holland to shake off the yoke of Spain? Is there any instance since the beginning of the world where human liberty has been established by little systems of trumpery and trick? These are the weapons of monarchs against the people, not of the people against monarchs. With their own right hand, and with their mighty arm, have the people gotten to themselves the victory, and upon them may they ever depend; and then comes Mr. Grote, a scholar and gentleman, and knowing all the histories of public courage, preaches cowardice and treachery to England; tells us that the bold cannot be free, and bids us seek for liberty by clothing ourselves in the mask of falsehood, and trampling on the cross of truth.*

If this shrinking from the performance of duties is to be tolerated, voters are not the only persons who would recur to the accommodating convenience of ballot. A member of Parliament, who votes against government, can get nothing in the army, navy, or church, or at the bar, for his children or himself; they are placed on the north wall, and starved for their honesty. Judges, too, suffer for their unpopularity—Lord Kilwarden was murdered, Lord Mansfield burnt down; but voters, forgetting that they are only trustees for those who have no vote, require that they themselves should be virtuous with impunity, and that all the penalties of austerity and Catonism should fall upon others. I am aware that it is of the greatest consequence to the constituent that

* Mr. Grote is a very worthy, honest, and able man; and, if the world were a chess-board, would be an important politician.

he should be made acquainted with the conduct of his representative; but I maintain, that to know, without the fear of mistake, what the conduct of individuals has been in their fulfilment of the great trust of electing members of Parliament, is also of the greatest importance in the formation of public opinion; and that, when men acted in the dark, the power of distinguishing between the bad and the good would be at an end.

To institute ballot, is to apply a very dangerous innovation to a temporary evil; for it is seldom, but in very excited times, that these acts of power are complained of which the ballot is intended to remedy. There never was an instance in this country where parties were so nearly balanced; but all this will pass away, and, in a very few years, either Peel will swallow Lord John, or Lord John will pasture upon Peel; parties will coalesce, the Duke of Wellington and Viscount Melbourne meet at the same board, and the lion lie down with the lamb. In the mean time a serious and dangerous political change is resorted to for the cure of a temporary evil, and we may be cursed with ballot when we do not want it, and cannot get rid of it.

If there is ballot there can be no scrutiny, the controlling power of Parliament is lost, and the members are entirely in the hands of returning officers.

An election is hard run—the returning officer lets in twenty votes which he ought to have excluded, and the opposite candidate is unjustly returned. I petition, and as the law now stands, the return would be amended, and I, who had the legitimate majority, should be seated in Parliament. But how could justice be done if the ballot obtained, and if the returning officer were careless or corrupt? Would you put all the electors upon their oath? Would it be advisable to accept any oath where detection was impossible? and could any approximation to truth be expected under such circumstances, from such an inquisition? It is true, the present committees of the House of Commons are a very unfair tribunal, but that tribunal may and will be amended; and bad as that tribunal is, nobody can be insane enough to propose that we are to take refuge in the blunders or the corruptions of 600 returning officers, 100 of whom are Irish.

It is certainly in the power of a committee, when incapacity or villany of the returning officer has produced an unfair return, to annul the whole election, and to proceed again *de novo;* but how is this just? or what satisfaction is this to me, who have unquestionably a lawful majority, and who ask of the House of Commons to examine the votes, and to place in their house the man who has combined the greatest number of suffrages? The answer of the House of Commons is, "One of you is undoubtedly the rightful member, but we have so framed our laws of election, that it is impossible to find out which that man is; the loss and penalties ought only to fall upon one, but they must fall upon both; we put the well-doer and the evil-doer precisely in the same situation; there shall be no election;" and this may happen ten times running.

Purity of election, the fair choice of representatives, must be guarded either by the coercing power of the House of Commons exercised upon petitions, or it must be guarded by the watchful jealousy of opposite parties a the registrations; but if (as the radicals suppose) ballot gives a power of perfect concealment, whose interest is it to watch the registrations? If I despair of distinguishing my friends from my foes, why should I take any trouble about registrations? Why not leave every thing to that great *primum mobile* of all human affairs, the barrister of six years' standing?

The answer of the excellent Benthamites to all this is, "What you say may be true enough in the present state of registrations, but we have another scheme of registration to which these objections will not apply." There is really no answering this paulo-post legislation. I reason now upon registration and reform which are in existence, which I have seen at work for several years. What new improvements are in the womb of time, or (if time has no womb) in the more capacious pockets of the followers of Bentham, I know not: when I see them tried, I will reason upon them. There is no end to these eternal changes; we have made an enormous revolution within the last ten years,—let us stop a little and secure it, and prevent it from being turned into ruin; I do not say the reform bill is final, but I want a little time for breathing; and if there are to be any more changes, let them be carried into execution hereafter by those little legislators who are now receiving every day after dinner a cake or a plumb, in happy ignorance of Mr. Grote and his ballot. I long for the quiet times of *Log*, when all the English common people are making calico, and all the English gentlemen are making long and short verses, with no other interruption of their happiness than when false quantities are discovered in one or the other.

What is to become of petitions if ballot is established? Are they to be open as they now are, or are they to be conducted by ballot? Are the radical shopkeepers and the radical tenant to be exposed (as they say) to all the fury of incensed wealth and power, and is that protection to be denied to them in petitions, which is so loudly demanded in the choice of representatives? Are there to be two distinct methods of ascertaining the opinions of the people, and these completely opposed to each other? A member is chosen this week by a large majority of voters who vote in the dark, and the next week, when men vote in the light of day, some petition is carried totally opposite to all those principles for which the member with invisible votes was returned to Parliament. How, under such a system, can Parliament ever ascertain what the wishes of the people really are? The representatives are radicals, the petitioners eminently conservative; the voice is the voice of Jacob, but the hands are the hands of Esau.

And if the same protection is adopted for petitions as is given in elections, and if both are conducted by ballot, how is the House of Commons to deal with petitions? When it is intended particularly that a petition should attract the attention of the House of Commons, some member bears witness to the respectability or the futility of the signatures; and how is it possible, without some guides of this kind, that the House could form any idea of the value and importance of the petition?

These observations apply with equal force to the communications between the representative and the constituent. It is the radical doctrine that a representative is to obey the instructions of his constituents. He has been elected under the ballot by a large majority; an open meeting is called, and he receives instructions in direct opposition to all those principles upon which he has been elected. Is this the real opinion of his constituents? and if he receives his instructions for a ballot meeting, who are his instructors? The lowest men in the town, or the wisest and the best?—But if ballot is established for elections only, and all communications between the constituents on one side, and Parliament and the representatives on the other, are carried on in open meetings, then are there two publics according to the radical doctrines, essentially different from each other; the one acting under the influence of the rich and powerful, the other free; and if all political petitions are to be carried on by ballot, how is Parliament to know who petitions, or the member to know who instructs?

I have hitherto spoken of ballot, as if it were, as the radicals suppose it to be, a mean of secrecy; their very cardinal position is, that landlords, after the ballot is established, will give up in despair all hopes of commanding the votes of their tenants. I scarcely ever heard a more foolish and gratuitous assumption. Given up? Why should they be given up? I can give many reasons why landlords should never exercise this unreasonable power, but I can give no possible reason why a man determined to do so should be baffled by the ballot. When two great parties in the empire are combating for the supreme power, does Mr. Grote imagine, that the man of woods, forests, and rivers,—that they who have the strength of the hills,—are to be baffled by bumpkins thrusting a little pin into a little card in a little box? that England is to be governed by political acupuncturation?

A landlord who would otherwise be guilty of the oppression will not change his purpose, because you attempt to outwit him by the invention of the ballot; he will become, on the contrary, doubly vigilant, inquisitive, and severe. "I am a professed radical," said the tenant of a great duke to a friend of mine, "and the duke knows it; but if I vote for his candidates, he lets me talk as I please, live with whom I please, and does not care if I dine at a radical dinner every day in the week. If there was a ballot, nothing could persuade the duke, or the duke's master, the steward, that I was not deceiving them, and I should lose my farm in a week." This is the real history of what would take place. The single lie on the hustings would not suffice; the concealed democrat who voted against his landlord must talk with the wrong people, subscribe to the wrong club, huzza at the wrong dinner, break the wrong head, lead (if he wished to escape from the watchful jealousy of his landlord) a long life of lies between every election; and he must do this, not only *eundo*, in his calm and prudential state, but *redeundo* from the market, warmed with beer and expanded by alcohol; and he must not only carry on his seven years of dissimulation before the world, but in the very bosom of his family, or he must expose himself to the dangerous garrulity of wife, children, and servants, from whose indiscretion every kind of evil report would be carried to the ears of the watchful steward. And when once the ballot is established, mere gentle, quiet lying will not do to hide the tenant who secretly votes against his landlord; the quiet passive liar will be suspected, and he will find, if he does not wave his bonnet and strain his throat in furtherance of his bad faith, and lie loudly, that he has put in a false ball in the dark to very little purpose. I consider a long concealment of political opinion from the landlord to be nearly impossible for the tenant; and if you conceal from the landlord the only proof he can have of his tenant's sincerity, you are taking from the tenant the only means he has of living quietly upon his farm. You are increasing the jealousy and irascibility of the tyrant, and multiplying instead of lessening the number of his victims.

Not only you do not protect the tenant who wishes to deceive his landlord, by promising one way and voting another, but you expose all the other tenants who have no intention of deceiving, to all the evils of mistake and misrepresentation. The steward hates a tenant, and a rival wants his farm: they begin to whisper him out of favour, and to propagate rumours of his disaffection to the blue or the yellow cause; as matters now stand he can refer to the poll-book, and show how he has voted. Under the ballot his security is gone, and he is exposed, in common with his deceitful neighbour, to that suspicion from which none can be exempt when all vote in secret. If ballot then answered the purpose for which it was intended, the number of honest tenants whom it exposed to danger would be as great as the number of deceitful tenants whom it screened.

But if landlords could be prevented from influencing their tenants in voting, by threatening them with the loss of farms;—if public opinion were too strong to allow of such threats, what would prevent a landlord from refusing to take, as a tenant, a man whose political opinion did not agree with his own? what would prevent him from questioning, long before the election, and cross-examining his tenant, and demanding certificates of his behaviour and opinions, till he had, according to all human probability, found a man who felt as strongly as himself upon political subjects, and who would adhere to those opinions with as much firmness and tenacity? What would prevent, for instance, an Orange landlord from filling his farms with Orange tenants, and from cautiously rejecting every Catholic tenant who presented himself plough in hand? But if this practice were to obtain generally, of cautiously selecting tenants from their political opinion, what would become of the sevenfold shield of the ballot? Not only this tenant is not continued in the farm he already holds, but he finds, from the severe inquisition into which men of property are driven by the invention of ballot, that it is extremely difficult for a man whose principles are opposed to those of his landlord, to get any farm at all.

The noise and jollity of a ballot mob must be such as the very devils would look on with delight. A set of deceitful wretches, wearing the wrong colours, abusing their friends, pelting the man for whom they voted, drinking their enemies' punch, knocking down persons with whom they entirely agreed, and roaring out eternal duration to principles they abhorred. A scene of wholesale bacchanalian fraud, a *posse comitatus* of liars, which would disgust any man with a free government, and make him sigh for the monocracy of Constantinople.

All the arguments which apply to suspected tenants apply to suspected shopkeepers. Their condition under the ballot would be infinitely worse than under the present system; the veracious shopkeeper would be suspected, perhaps without having his vote to appeal to for his protection, and the shopkeeper who meant to deceive must prop up his fraud, by accommodating his whole life to the first deceit, or he would have told a disgraceful falsehood in vain. The political persecutors would not be baffled by the ballot; customers, who think they have a right to persecute tradesmen now, would do it then; the only difference would be that more would be persecuted then on suspicion, than are persecuted now from a full knowledge of every man's vote. Inquisitors would be exasperated by this attempt of their victims to become invisible, and the search for delinquents would be more sharp and incessant.

A state of things may (to be sure) occur where the aristocratic part of the voters may be desirous, by concealing their votes, of protecting themselves from the fury of the multitude; but precisely the same objection obtains against ballot, whoever may be the oppressor or the oppressed. It is no defence; the single falsehood at the hustings will not suffice. Hypocrisy for seven years is impossible; the multitude will be just as jealous of preserving the power of intimidation, as aristocrats are of preserving the power of property, and will in the same way redouble their vicious activity from the attempt at destroying their empire by ballot.

Ballot could not prevent the disfranchisement of a great number of voters. The shopkeeper, harassed by men of both parties, equally consuming the articles in which he dealt, would seek security in not voting at all, and of course, the ballot could not screen the disobedient tenant whom the landlord requested to stay away from the poll. Mr. Grote has no box for this; but a remedy for securing the freedom of election, which has no power to prevent the voter from losing the exercise of his franchise altogether, can scarcely be considered as a remedy at all. There is a method, indeed, by which this might be remedied, if the great soul of Mr. Grote will stoop to adopt it. Why are the acts of concealment to be confined to putting in a ball? Why not vote in a domino, taking off the vizor to the returning officer only? or as tenant Jenkins or tenant Hodge might be detected by their stature, why not poll in sedan chairs with the curtains closely drawn, choosing the chairman by ballot?

What a flood of deceit and villany comes in with ballot! I admit there are great moral faults under the present system. It is a serious violation of duty to vote for A. when you think B. the more worthy representative; but the open voter, acting under the influence of his landlord, commits only this one fault, great as it is:—if he vote for his candidate, the landlord is satisfied, and asks no other sacrifice of truth and opinion; but if the tenant votes against his landlord under the ballot, he is practising every day some fraud to conceal his first deviation from truth. The present method may produce a vicious act, but the ballot establishes a vicious habit; and then it is of some consequence, that the law should not range itself on the side of vice. In the open voting, the law leaves you fairly to choose between the dangers of giving an honest, or the convenience of giving a dishonest vote; but the ballot law opens a booth and asylum for fraud, calling upon all men to lie by beat of drum, forbidding open honesty, promising impunity for the most scandalous deceit, and encouraging men to take no other view of virtue than whether it pays or does not pay; for it must always be remembered and often repeated, and said and sung to Mr. Grote, that it is to the degraded liar only that the box will be useful. The man who performs what he promises needs no box. The man who refuses to do what he is asked to do despises the box. The liar, who says he will do what he never means to do, is the only man to whom the box is useful, and for whom this leaf out of the Punic pandects is to be inserted in our statute book; the other vices will begin to look up, and to think themselves neglected, if falsehood obtains such flattering distinction, and is thus defended by the solemn enactments of law.

Old John Randolph, the American orator, was asked one day at a dinner party in London, whether the ballot prevailed in his state of Virginia—"I scarcely believe," he said, "we have such a fool in all Virginia, as to mention even the vote by ballot; and I do not hesitate to say that the adoption of the ballot would make any nation a nation of scoundrels, if it did not find them so." John Randolph was right; he felt that it was not necessary that a people should be false in order to be free; universal hypocrisy would be the consequence of ballot: we should soon say on deliberation what David only asserted in his haste, *that all men were liars.*

This exclamation of old Randolph applied to the method of popular elections, which I believe has always been by open voice in Virginia; but the assemblies voted, and the judges were chosen by ballot; and in the year 1830, upon a solemn review of their institutions, ballot was entirely abolished in every instance throughout the state, and open voting substituted in its place.

Not only would the tenant under ballot be constantly exposed to the suspicions of the landlord, but the landlord would be exposed to the constant suspicions and the unjust misrepresentation of the tenant. Every tenant who was dismissed for a fair and a just cause, would presume he was suspected, would attribute his dismissal to political motives, and endeavour to make himself a martyr with the public; and in this way violent hatred would be by the ballot disseminated among classes of men on whose agreement the order and happiness of England depend.

All objections to ballot which are important in England apply with much greater force to Ireland, a country of intense agitation, fierce passions, and quick movements. Then how would the ballot box of Mr. Grote harmonize with the confessional box of Father O'Leary?

I observe Lord John Russell, and some important men as well as him, saying, "We hate ballot, but if these practices continue, we shall be compelled to vote for it." What! vote for it, if ballot is no remedy of these evils? Vote for it, if ballot produces still greater evils than it cures? That is (says the physician), if fevers increase in this alarming manner, I shall be compelled to make use of some medicine which will be of no use to fevers, and will at the same time bring on diseases of a much more serious nature. I shall be under the absolute necessity of putting out your eyes, because I cannot prevent you from being lame. In fact, this sort of language is utterly unworthy of the sense and courage of Lord John; he gives hopes where he ought to create absolute despair. This is that hovering between two principles which ruins political strength by lowering political character, and creates a notion that his enemies need not fear such a man, and that his friends cannot trust him. No opinion could be more unjust as applied to Lord John; but such an opinion will grow if he begins to value himself more upon his dexterity and finesse, than upon those fine, manly, historico-Russell qualities he most undoubtedly possesses. There are two beautiful words in the English language,—yes and no; he must pronounce them boldly and emphatically; stick to yes and no to the death; for yes and no lay his head down upon the scaffold, where his ancestors have laid their heads before, and cling to his yes and no in spite of Robert Peel and John Wilson, and Joseph, and Daniel, and Fergus, and Stevens himself. He must do as the Russells always have done, advance his firm foot on the field of honour, plant it on the line marked out by justice, and determine in that cause to perish or to prevail.

In clubs, ballot preserves secrecy; but in clubs, after the barrister has blackballed the colonel, he most likely never hears of the colonel again: he does not live among people who are calling out for seven years *the colonel for ever;* nor is there any one who, thinking he has a right to the barrister's suffrage, exercises the most incessant vigilance to detect whether or not he has been defrauded of it. I do not say that ballot can never in any instance be made a mean of secrecy and safety, but that it cannot be so in popular elections. Even in elections, a consummate hypocrite who was unmarried, and drank water, might perhaps exercise his timid patriotism with impunity; but the instances would be so rare, as to render ballot utterly inefficient as a general protection against the abuses of power.

In America, ballot is nearly a dead letter; no protection is wanted: if the ballot protects any one, it is the master, not the man. Some of the states have no ballot,—some have exchanged the ballot for open voting.

Bribery carried on in any town now would probably be carried on with equal success under the ballot. The attorney (if such a system prevailed) would say to the candidate, "There is my list of promises; if you come in I will have 5000*l*., and if you do not, you shall pay me nothing." To this list, to which I suppose all the venal rabble of the town to have put their names, there either is an opposition bribery list, or there is not: if there is not, the promisers, looking only to make money by their vote, have every inducement to keep their word. If there is an opposite list, the only trick which a promiser can play is to put down his name upon both lists: but this trick would be so easily detected, so much watched and suspected, and would even in the vote market render a man so infamous, that it never would be attempted to any great extent. At present, if a man promises his vote to A., and votes for B., because he can get more money by it, he does not become infamous among the bribed, because they lose no money by him; but where a list is found, and a certain sum of money is to be divided among that list, every interloper lessens the receipts of all the rest; it becomes their interest to guard against fraudulent intrusion; and a man who puts his name upon more lists than the votes he was entitled to give, would soon be hunted down by those he had robbed. Of course there would be no pay till after the election, and the man who having one vote had put himself down on two lists, or having two votes had put himself down on three lists, could hardly fail to be detected, and would, of course, lose his political *aceldama.* There must be honour among thieves; the mob regularly inured to bribery under the canopy of the ballot, would for their own sake soon introduce rules for the distribution of the plunder, and infuse, with their customary energy, the morality of not being sold more than once at every election.

If ballot were established, it would be received by the upper classes with the greatest possible suspicion, and every effort would be made to counteract it and to get rid of it. Against those attacks the inferior orders would naturally wish to strengthen themselves, and the obvious means would be by extending the number of voters; and so comes on universal suffrage. The ballot would fail: it would be found neither to prevent intimidation nor bribery. Universal suffrage would cure both, as a teaspoonful of prussic acid is a certain cure for the most formidable diseases; but universal suffrage would in all probability be the next step. "The 200 richest voters of Bridport shall not beat the 400 poorest voters. Every body who has a house shall vote, or every body who is twenty-one shall vote, and then the people will be sure to have their way —we will blackball every member standing for Bridgewater who does not promise to vote for universal suffrage."

The ballot and universal suffrage are never mentioned by the radicals without being coupled together. Nobody ever thinks of separating them. Any person who attempted to separate them at torchlight or sunlight meetings would be hooted down. It is professedly avowed that ballot is only wanted for ulterior purposes, and no one makes a secret of what those ulterior purposes are: not only would the gift of ballot, if universal suffrage were refused, not be received with gratitude, but it would be received with furious indignation and contempt, and universal suffrage be speedily extorted from you.

There would be this argument also for universal suffrage, to which I do not think it very easy to find an answer. The son of a man who rents a house of ten pounds a year is often a much cleverer man than his father; the wife more intelligent than the husband. Under the system of open voting, these persons are not excluded from want of intellect, but for want of independence, for they would necessarily vote with their principal; but the moment the ballot is established, according to the reasoning of the Grote school, one man is as independent as another, because all are concealed, and so all are equally entitled to offer their suffrages. This cannot sow dissensions in families; for how, ballotically reasoning, can the father find it out? or, if he did find it out, how has any father, ballotically speaking, a right to control the votes of his family?

I have often drawn a picture in my own mind of a Balloto-Grotical family voting and promising under the new system. There is one vacancy, and three candidates, tory, whig, and radical. Walter Wiggins, a small artificer of shoes, for the moderate gratuity of five pounds promises his own vote, and that of the chaste Arabella his wife, to the tory candidate; he, Walter Wiggins, having also sold, for one sovereign, the vote of the before-named Arabella to the whigs. Mr. John Wiggins, a tailor, the male progeny of Walter and Arabella, at the solicitation of his master, promises his vote to the whigs, and persuades his sister Honoria to make a similar promise in the same cause. Arabella, the wife, yields implicitly to the wishes of her husband. In this way, before the election, stand committed the highly moral family of Mr. Wiggins. The period for lying arrives, and the mendacity machine is exhibited to the view of the Wigginses. What happens? Arabella, who has in the interim been chastised by her drunken husband, votes secretly for the radicals, having been sold both to whig and tory. Mr. John Wiggins, pledged beyond redemption to whigs, votes for the tory; and Honoria, extrinsically furious in the cause of whigs, is persuaded by her lover to vote for the radical member. The following table exhibits the state of this moral family before and after the election:—

Walter Wiggins sells himself once and his wife twice.
Arabella Wiggins, sold to tory and whig, votes for radical.
John Wiggins, promised to whig, votes for tory.
Honoria Wiggins, promised to whig, votes for radical.

In this way the families of the poor, under the legislation of Mr. Grote, will become schools for good faith, openness, and truth. What are Chrysippus and Crantor, and all the moralists of the whole world, compared to Mr. Grote?

It is urged that the lower order of voters, proud of such a distinction, will not be anxious to extend it to others; but the lower order of voters will often find that they possess this distinction in vain—that wealth and education are too strong for them; and they will call in the multitude as auxiliaries, firmly believing that they can curb their inferiors and conquer their superiors. Ballot is a mere illusion, but universal suffrage is not an illusion. The common people will get nothing by the one, but they will gain every thing, and ruin every thing, by the last.

Some members of Parliament who mean to vote for ballot, in the fear of losing their seats, and who are desirous of reconciling to their conscience such an act of disloyalty to mankind, are fond of saying that ballot is harmless; that it will neither do the good nor the evil that is expected from it; and that the people may fairly be indulged in such an innocent piece of legislation. Never was such folly and madness as this; ballot will be the cause of interminable hatred and jealousy among the different orders of mankind; it will familiarize the English people to a long tenour of deceit; it will not answer its purpose of protecting the independent voter; and the people, exasperated and disappointed by the failure, will indemnify themselves by insisting upon unlimited suffrage. And then it is talked of as an experiment, as if men were talking of acids and alkalies, and the galvanic pile; as if Lord John could get on the hustings and say, "Gentlemen, you see this ballot does not answer; do me the favour to give it up, and to allow yourselves to be replaced in the same situation as the ballot found you." Such, no doubt, is the history of nations and the march of human affairs; and, in this way, the error of a sudden and foolish largess of power to the people might, no doubt, be easily retrieved. The most unpleasant of all bodily feelings is a cold sweat; nothing brings it on so surely as perilous nonsense in politics. I lose all warmth from the bodily frame when I hear the ballot talked of as an *experiment.*

I cannot at all understand what is meant by this indolent opinion. Votes are coerced now; if votes are free, will the elected be the same? if not, will the difference of the elected be unimportant? Will not the ballot stimulate the upper orders to fresh exertions? and are their increased jealousy and interference of no importance? If ballot, after all, is found to hold out a real protection to the voter, is universal lying of no importance? I can understand what is meant by calling ballot a great good, or a great evil; but, in the mighty contention for power which is raging in this country, to call it indifferent appears to me extremely foolish in all those in whom it is not extremely dishonest.

If the ballot did succeed in enabling the lower order of voters to conquer their betters, so much the worse. In a town consisting of 700 voters, the 300 most opulent and powerful (and therefore probably the best instructed) would make a much better choice than the remaining 400; and the ballot would, in that case, do more harm than good. In nineteen cases out of twenty, the most numerous party would be in the wrong. If this is the case, why give the franchise to all? why not confine it to the first division? *because even with all the abuses which occur, and in spite of them, the great mass of the people are much more satisfied with having a vote occasionally controlled than with having none.* Many agree with their superiors, and therefore feel no control. Many are persuaded by their superiors, and not controlled. Some are indifferent which way they exercise the power, though they would not like to be utterly deprived of it. Some guzzle away their vote, some sell it, some brave their superiors, a few are threatened and controlled. The election, in different ways, is affected by the superior influence of the upper orders; and the great mass (occasionally and justly complaining) are, beyond all doubt, better pleased than if they had no votes at all. The lower orders always have it in their power to rebel against their superiors; and occasionally they will do so, and have done so, and occasionally and justly carried elections* against gold, and birth, and education. But it is madness to make laws of society which attempt to shake off the great laws of nature. As long as men love bread, and mutton, and broadcloth, wealth, in a long series of years, must have enormous effects upon human affairs, and the strong box will beat the ballot box. Mr. Grote has both, but he miscalculates their respective powers. Mr. Grote knows the relative values of gold and silver; but by what moral rate of exchange is he able to tell us the relative values of liberty and truth?

It is hardly necessary to say any thing about universal suffrage, as there is no act of folly or madness which it may not in the beginning produce. There would be the greatest risk that the monarchy, as at present constituted, the funded debt, the established church, titles, and hereditary peerage, would give way before it. Many really honest men may wish for these changes; I know, or at least believe, that wheat and barley would grow if there was no Archbishop of Canterbury, and domestic fowls would breed if our Viscount Melbourne was again called Mr. Lamb; but they have stronger nerves than I have who would venture to bring these changes about. So few nations have been free, it is so difficult to guard freedom from kings, and mobs, and patriotic gentlemen; and we are in such a very tolerable state of happiness in England, that I think such changes would be very rash; and I have an utter mistrust in the sagacity and penetration of political reasoners who pretend to foresee all the consequences to which they would give birth. When I speak of the tolerable state of happiness in which we live in England, I do not speak merely of nobles, squires, and canons of St. Paul's, but of drivers of coaches, clerks in offices, carpenters, blacksmiths, butchers, and bakers, and most men who do not marry upon nothing, and become burdened with large families before they have arrived at years of maturity. The earth is not sufficiently fertile for this:

Difficilem victum fundit durissima tellus.

After all, the great art in politics and war is to choose a good position for making a stand. The Duke of Wellington examined and fortified the lines of Torres Vedras a year before he had any occasion to make use of them, and he had previously marked out Waterloo as the probable scene of some future exploit. The people seem to be hurrying on through all the well-known steps to anarchy; they must be stopped at some pass or another: the first is the best and most easily defended. The people have a right to ballot or to any thing else which will make them happy; and they have a right to nothing which will make them unhappy. They are the best judges of their immediate gratifications, and the worst judges of what would best conduce to their interests for a series of years. Most earnestly and conscientiously wishing their good, I say, No Ballot.

* The 400 or 500 voting against the 200 are right about as often as juries are right in differing from judges; and that is very seldom.

FIRST LETTER TO ARCHDEACON SINGLETON,

ON THE

ECCLESIASTICAL COMMISSION.

My dear Sir,

As you do me the honour to ask my opinion respecting the constitution and proceedings of the ecclesiastical commission, and of their conduct to the dignitaries of the church, I shall write to you without any reserve upon this subject.

The first thing which excited my surprise, was the constitution of the commission. As the reform was to comprehend every branch of churchmen, bishops, dignitaries, and parochial clergymen, I cannot but think it would have been much more advisable to have added to the commission some members of the two lower orders of the church—they would have supplied that partial knowledge which appears in so many of the proceedings of the commissioners to have been wanting—they would have attended to those interests (not episcopal) which appear to have been so completely overlooked—and they would have screened the commission from those charges of injustice and partiality which are now so generally brought against it. There can be no charm in the name of bishop—the man who was a curate yesterday is a bishop to-day. There are many prebendaries, many rectors, and many vicars, who would have come to the reform of the church with as much integrity, wisdom, and vigour as any bishop on the bench; and I believe, with a much stronger recollection that all the orders of the church were not to be sacrificed to the highest; and that to make their work respectable, and lasting, it should in all (even in its minutest provisions), be founded upon justice.

All the interests of the church in the commutation of tithes are entrusted to one parochial clergyman;* and I have no doubt, from what I hear of him, that they will be well protected. Why could not one or two such men have been added to the commission, and a general impression been created, that government in this momentous change had a parental feeling for all orders of men whose interests might be affected by it? A ministry may laugh at this, and think if they cultivate bishops, that they may treat the other orders of the church with contempt and neglect; but I say, that to create a general impression of justice, if it be not what common honesty requires from any ministry, is what common sense points out to them. t is strength and duration—it is the only power which is worth having—in the struggle of parties it gives victory, and is remembered, and goes down to other times.

A mixture of different orders of clergy in the commission would at least have secured a decent attention to the representations of all; for of seven communications made to the commission by cathedrals, and involving very serious representations respecting high interests, six were totally disregarded, and the receipt of the papers not even acknowledged.

I cannot help thinking that the commissioners have done a great deal too much. Reform of the church was absolutely necessary—it cannot be avoided, and ought not to be postponed; but I would have found out what really gave offence, have applied a remedy, removed the nuisance, and done no more. I would not have operated so largely on an old, and (I fear) a decaying building. I would not, in days of such strong political excitement, and amidst such a disposition to universal change, have done one thing more than was absolutely necessary to remove the odium against the establishment, the only sensible reason for issuing any commission at all; and the means which I took to effect this, should have agreed, as much as possible, with institutions already established. For instance, the public were disgusted with the spectacle of rich prebendaries enjoying large incomes, and doing little or nothing for them. The real remedy for this would have been to have combined wealth and labour; and as each of the present prebendaries fell off, to have annexed the stall to some large and populous parish. A prebendary of Canterbury or of St. Paul's, in his present state, may make the church unpopular; but place him as rector of a parish, with 8000 or 9000 people, and in a benefice of little or no value, he works for his wealth, and the odium is removed. In like manner the prebends, which are not the property of the residentiaries, might have been annexed to the smallest livings of the neighbourhood where the prebendal estate was situated. The interval which has elapsed since the first furious demand for reform, would have enabled the commissioners to adopt a scheme of much greater moderation than might perhaps have been possible at the first outbreak of popular indignation against the church; and this sort of distribution would have given much more general satisfaction than the plan adopted by commissioners; for though money, in the estimation of philosophers, has no ear-mark, it

* The Rev. Mr. Jones is the commissioner appointed by the Archbishop of Canterbury to watch over the interests of the church.

has a very deep one in the opinion of the multitude. The riches of the church of Durham were most hated in the neighbourhood of Durham; and there such changes as I have pointed out would have been most gladly received, *and would have conciliated the greatest favour* to the church. The people of Kent cannot see why their Kentish estates, given to the cathedral of Canterbury, are to augment livings in Cornwall. The citizens of London see some of their ministers starving in the city, and the profits of the extinguished prebends sent into Northumberland. These feelings may be very unphilosophical, but they are the feelings of the mass; and to the feelings of the mass the reforms of the church ought to be directed. In this way the evil would have been corrected where it was most seen and noticed. All patronage would have been left as it was. One order of the church would not have plundered the other. Nor would all the cathedrals in England have been subjected to the unconciliating empire, and unwearied energy of one man.

Instead of this quiet and cautious mode of proceeding, all is change, fusion and confusion. New bishops, new dioceses, confiscated prebends—clergymen changing bishops, and bishops clergymen—mitres in Manchester, Gloucester turned into Bristol. Such a scene of revolution and commutation as has not been seen since the days of Ireton and Cromwell! and the singularity is, that all this has been effected by men selected from their age, their dignity, and their known principles, and from whom the considerate part of the community expected all the caution and calmness which these high requisites seemed to promise, and ought to have secured.

The plea of making a fund is utterly untenable—the great object was not to make a fund; and there is the mistake into which the commission have fallen: the object was not to add 10*l.* or 20*l.* per annum to a thousand small livings, and to diminish inequalities in a ratio so trifling that the public will hardly notice it; a very proper thing to do if higher interests were not sacrificed to it; but the great object was to remove the causes of hatred from the church, by lessening such incomes as those of Canterbury, Durham, and London, exorbitantly and absurdly great—by making idleness work—and by these means to lessen the envy of laymen. It is impossible to make a fund which will raise the smaller livings of the church into any thing like a decent support for those who possess them. The whole income of the church, episcopal, prebendal, and parochial, divided among the clergy, would not give to each clergyman an income equal to that which is enjoyed by the upper domestic of a great nobleman. The method in which the church has been paid, and must continue to be paid, is by unequal divisions. All the enormous changes which the commission is making will produce a very trifling difference in the inequality, while it will accustom more and more those enemies of the church, who are studying under their right rev. masters, to the boldest revolutions in ecclesiastical affairs. Out of 10,478 benefices, there are 297 of about 40*l.* per annum value, 1,629 at about 75*l.* and 1,602 at about 125*l.*; to raise all these benefices to 200*l.* per annum, would require an annual sum of 371,293*l.*; and upon 2,878 of those benefices there are no houses; and upon 1,728 no houses fit for residence. What difference in the apparent inequality of the church would this sum of 371,293*l.* produce, *if it could* be raised? or in what degree would it lessen the odium which that inequality creates? The case is utterly hopeless; and yet with all their confiscations the commissioners are so far from being able to raise the annual sum of 371,000*l.*, that the utmost they expect to gain is 130,000*l.* per annum.

It seems a paradoxical statement, but the fact is, that the respectability of the church, as well as of the bar, is almost entirely preserved by the unequal division of their revenues. A bar of one hundred lawyers travel the northern circuit, enlightening provincial ignorance, curing local partialities, diffusing knowledge, and dispensing justice in their route: it is quite certain that all they gain is not equal to all that they spend; if the profits were equally divided there would not be six and eight-pence for each person, and there would be no bar at all. At present, the success of the leader animates them all—each man hopes to be a Scarlett or a Brougham—and takes out his ticket in a lottery by which the mass must infallibly lose, trusting (as mankind are so apt to do) to his good fortune, and believing that the prize is reserved for him, disappointment and defeat for others. So it is with the clergy; the whole income of the church, if equally divided, would be about 250*l.* for each minister. Who would go into the church and spend 1,200*l.* or 1,500*l.* upon his education, if such were the highest remuneration he could ever look to? At present, men are tempted into the church by the prizes of the church, and bring into that church a great deal of capital, which enables them to live in decency, supporting themselves, not with the money of the public, but with their own money, which, but for this temptation, would have been carried into some retail trade. The officers of the church would then fall down to men little less coarse and ignorant than agricultural labourers—the clergyman of the parish would soon be seen in the squire's kitchen; and all this would take place in a country where poverty is infamous.

In fact, nothing can be more unjust and idle than the reasoning of many laymen upon church matters. You choose to have an establishment—God forbid you should choose otherwise! and you wish to have men of decent manners, and good education, as the ministers of that establishment; all this is very right: but are you willing to pay them as such men ought to be paid? Are you willing to pay to each clergyman, confining himself to one spot, and giving up all his time to the care of one parish, a salary of 500*l.* per annum? To do this would require three millions to be added to the present revenues of the church; and such an expenditure is impossible! What then remains, if you will have a clergy and will not pay them equitably and separately than to pay them unequally and by lottery? and yet this very inequality, which secures to you a respectable clergy upon the most economical terms, is considered by laymen as a gross abuse. It is an abuse, however, which they have not the spirit to extinguish by increased munificence to their clergy, nor justice to consider as the only other method by which all the advantages of a respectable establishment can be procured; but they use it at the same time as a topic for sarcasm, and a source of economy.

This, it will be said, is a mammonish view of the subject; it is so, but those who make this objection, forget the immense effect which mammon produces upon religion itself. Shall the Gospel be preached by men paid by the state? shall these men be taken from the lower orders and be meanly paid? shall they be men of learning and education? and shall there be some magnificent endowments to allure such men into the church? Which of these methods is the best for diffusing the rational doctrines of Christianity? not in the age of the apostles, not in the abstract, timeless, nameless, placeless land of the philosophers, but in the year 1837, in the porter-brewing, cotton-spinning, tallow-melting kingdom of Great Britain, bursting with opulence, and flying from poverty as the greatest of human evils. Many different answers may be given to these questions, but they are questions which, not ending in mammon, have a powerful bearing on religion, and deserve the deepest consideration from its disciples and friends. Let the comforts of the clergy go for nothing. Consider their state only as religion is affected by it. If upon this principle I am forced to allot to some an opulence which my clever friend the Examiner would pronounce to be apostolical, I cannot help it; I must take this people with all their follies, and prejudices, and circumstances, and carve out an establishment best suited for them, however unfit for early Christianity in barren and conquered Judea.

Not only will this measure of the commission bring into the church a lower and worse educated set of men, but it will have a tendency to make the clergy fanatical. You will have a set of ranting, raving pastors, who will wage war against all the innocent pleasures of life, vie with each other in extravagance of zeal, and plague your heart out with their nonsense and absurdity: cribbage must be played in caverns, and sixpenny whist take refuge in the howling wilderness. In this way low men doomed to hopeless poverty, and galled by contempt, will endeavour to force themselves into station and significance.

There is an awkward passage in the memorial of the church of Canterbury, which deserves some consideration from him to whom it is directed. The Archbishop of Canterbury, at his consecration, takes a solemn oath that he will maintain the rights and liberties of the church of Canterbury; as chairman, however, of the new commission, he seizes the patronage of that church, takes two-thirds of its revenues, and abolishes two-thirds of its members. That there is an answer to this I am very willing to believe, but I cannot at present find out what it is; and this attack upon the revenues and members of Canterbury, is not obedience to an act of Parliament, but the very act of Parliament, which takes away, is recommended, drawn up, and signed by the person who has sworn he will never take away; and this little apparent inconsistency is not confined to the Archbishop of Canterbury, but is shared equally by all the bishop commissioners, who have all (unless I am grievously mistaken) taken similar oaths for the preservation of their respective chapters. It would be more easy to see our way out of this little embarrassment, if some of the embarrassed had not, unfortunately, in the parliamentary debates on the Catholic question, laid the greatest stress upon the king's oath, applauded the sanctity of the monarch to the skies, rejected all comments, called for the oath in its plain meaning, and attributed the safety of the English church to the solemn vow made by the king at the altar to the Archbishops of Canterbury and York, and the other bishops. I should be very sorry if this were not placed on a clear footing, as fools will be imputing to our church the *pia et religiosa Calliditas*, which is so commonly brought against the Catholics.

> Urbem quam dicunt Romam, Melibœe, putavi
> Stultus ego huic nostræ similem.

The words of Henry VIII., in endowing the cathedral of Canterbury, are thus given in the translation. "We, therefore, dedicating the aforesaid close, site, circle, and precinct to the honour and glory of the Holy and undivided Trinity, Father, Son, and Holy Spirit, have decreed that a certain Cathedral and Metropolitan Church, with one Dean, Presbyter, and twelve Prebendaries Presbyters; these verily and for ever to serve Almighty God shall be created, set up, settled, and established; and the same aforesaid Cathedral and Metropolitan Church, with one Dean, Presbyter, and twelve Prebendaries Presbyters, with other Ministers necessary for divine worship, by the tenor of these presents in reality, and plenitude of force, we do create, set up, settle, and establish, and do command to be established and to be in perpetuity, and inviolably maintained and upheld by these presents." And this is the church, the rights and liberties of which the archbishop at his consecration swears to maintain. Nothing can be more ill-natured among politicians, than to look back into Hansard's Debates, to see what has been said by particular men upon particular occasions, and to contrast such speeches with present opinions—and therefore I forbear to introduce some inviting passages upon taking oaths in their plain and obvious sense, both in debates on the Catholic question and upon that fatal and *Mezentian* oath which binds the Irish to the English church.

It is quite absurd to see how all the cathedrals are to be trimmed to an exact *Procrustes* pattern;—*quieta movere* is the motto of the commission:—there is to be everywhere a dean, and four residentiaries; but St. Paul's and Lincoln have at present only three residentiaries, and a dean, who officiates in his turn as a canon:—a fourth must be added to each. Why? nobody wants more prebendaries; St. Paul's and Lincoln go on very well as they are. It is not for the lack of prebendaries, it is for idleness, that the Church of England is unpopular; but in the lust of reforming, the commission cut and patch property as they would cut figures in pasteboard. This little piece of wanton change, however, gives to two of the bishops, who are commissioners as well as bishops, patronage of a thousand a year each; and though I am willing not to consider this as the cause of the recommendation, yet I must observe it is not very common that the same persons should bring in the verdict and receive the profits of the suit. No other archdeacons are paid in such a manner, and no other bishops out of the commission have received such a bonus.*

I must express my surprise that nothing in this commission of bishops, either in the bill which has passed, or in the report which preceded it, is said of the duties of bishops. A bishop is not now forced by law to be in his diocese or to attend his duty in Parliament—he may be entirely absent from both; nor are there wanting instances within these six years where such has been the case. It would have been very easy to have placed the repairs of episcopal palaces (as the concurrent leases of bishops are placed) under the superintendence of deans and chapters; but though the bishops' bill was accompanied by another bill, containing the strictest enactments for the residence of the clergy, and some very arbitrary and unjust rules for the repair of their houses, it did not appear upon the face of the law that the bishops had any such duties to perform; and yet I remember the case of a bishop, dead not six years ago, who was scarcely ever seen in the House of Lords, or in his diocese; and I remember well also the indignation with which the inhabitants of a great cathedral town spoke of the conduct of another bishop (now also deceased), who not only never entered his palace, but turned his horses into the garden. When I mention these instances, I am not setting myself up as the satirist of bishops. I think, upon the whole, they do their duty in a very exemplary manner, but they are not, as the late bills would have us to suppose, *impeccable*. The church commissioners should not have suffered their reports and recommendations to paint the other branches of the church as such slippery transgredient mortals, and to leave the world to imagine that bishops may be safely trusted to their own goodness without enactment or control.

This squabble about patronage is said to be disgraceful. Those who mean to be idle, and insolent, because they are at peace, may look out of the window and say, "This is a disgraceful squabble between bishops and chapters;" but those who mean to be just, should ask, *Who begins?* the *real* disgrace of the squabble is in the attack, and not in the defence. If any man puts his hand into my pocket to take my property, am I disgraced if I prevent him? Churchmen are ready enough to be submissive to their superiors; but were they to submit to a spoliation so gross, accompanied with ignominy and degradation, and to bear all this in submissive silence;—to be accused of nepotism by nepotists, who were praising themselves indirectly by the accusation, and benefiting themselves directly by the confiscation founded on it;—the real disgrace would have been to have submitted to this: and men are to be honoured, not disgraced, who come forth, contrary to their usual habits, to oppose those masters whom, in common seasons, they would willingly obey; but who, in this matter, have tarnished their dignity, and forgotten what they owe to themselves and to us.

It is a very singular thing that the law always suspects judges, and never suspects bishops. If there is any way in which the partialities of the judge may injure laymen, the subject is fenced round with all sorts of jealousies, and enactments, and prohibitions—all partialities are guarded against, and all propensities watched. Where bishops are concerned, acts of Parliament are drawn up for beings who can never possibly be polluted by pride, prejudice, passion, or interest. Not otherwise would be the case with judges, if they, like the heads of the church, legislated for themselves.

Then comes the question of patronage; can any thing be more flagrantly unjust, than that the patronage of cathedrals should be taken away and conferred upon the bishops? I do not want to go into a long and tiresome history of episcopal nepotism, but it is notorious to all, that bishops confer their patronage upon their sons, and sons-in-law, and all their relations; and it is really quite monstrous in the face of the world, who see this every day, and every hour, to turn round upon deans and chapters, and to say to them, "We are credibly informed that there are instances in your chapters where preferment has not been given to the most learned men you can find, but to the sons and brothers of some of the prebendaries. These things must not be—we must take these benefices into our own keeping;" and this is the language of men swarming themselves with sons and daughters, and who, in enumerating the advantages of their stations, have always spoken of the opportunities of providing for their families as the greatest and most important. It is, I admit, the duty of every man, and of every body, to present the best man that can be found to any living of which he is the patron; but if this duty has been neglected, it has been neglected by bishops quite as much as by chapters; and no man can open the "Clerical Guide" and read two pages of it, without seeing that the bench of bishops are the last persons from whom any remedy of this evil is to be expected.

The legislature has not always taken the same view of the comparative trust-worthiness of bishops and chapters as is taken by the commission. Bishops' leases for years are for twenty-one years, renewable every seven When seven years are expired, if the present tenant will not renew, the bishop may grant a concurrent lease. How does his lordship act on such occasions? He generally asks two

* This extravagant pay of archdeacons is taken, remember, from that fund for the augmentation of small livings, for the establishment of which all the divisions and confiscations have been made

years' income for the renewal, when chapters, not having the privilege of granting such concurring leases, ask only a year and a half; and if the bishop's price is not given, he puts a son, or a daughter, or a trustee, into the estate, and the price of the lease deferred is money saved for his family. But unfair and exorbitant terms may be asked by his lordship, and the tenant may be unfairly dispossessed—therefore, the legislature enacts that all those concurrent leases must be countersigned by the dean and chapter of the diocese—making them the safeguards against episcopal rapacity; and, as I hear from others, not making them so in vain. These sorts of laws do not exactly correspond with the relative views taken of both parties by the ecclesiastical commission. This view of chapters is of course overlooked by a commission of bishops, just as all mention of bridles would be omitted in a meeting of horses; but in this view, chapters might be made eminently useful. In what profession, too, are there no gradations? Why is the Church of England to be nothing but a collection of beggars and bishops—the Right Reverend Dives in the palace, and Lazarus in orders at the gate, doctored by dogs, and comforted with crumbs?

But to take away the patronage of existing prebendaries is objectionable for another class of reasons. If it is right to take away the patronage of my cathedral and to give it to the bishop, it is at least unjust to do so with my share of it during my life. Society have a right to improve, or to do what they think an improvement, but then they have no right to do so suddenly and hastily, to my prejudice! After securing to me certain possessions by one hundred statutes passed in six hundred years—after having clothed me in fine garments, and conferred upon me pompous names, they have no right to turn round upon me all of a sudden to say, You are not a dean nor a canon-residentiary, but a vagabond and an outcast, and a morbid excrescence upon society. This would not be a reform, but the grossest tyranny and oppression. If a man cannot live under the canopy of ancient law, where is he safe? how can he see his way, or lay out his plan of life?

"Dubitant homines serere atque impendere curas."

You tolerated, for a century, the wicked traffic in slaves, legislated for that species of property, encouraged it by premiums, defended it in your courts of justice—West Indians bought and sold, trusting (as Englishmen always ought to trust) in parliaments. Women went to the altar, promised that they should be supported by that property; and children were born to it, and young men were educated with it: but God touched the hearts of the English people, and they would have no slaves. The scales fell from their eyes, and they saw the monstrous wickedness of the traffic; but then they said, and said magnificently, to the West Indians, "We mean to become wiser and better, but not at your expense; the loss shall be ours, and we will not involve you in ruin, because we are ashamed of our former cruelties, and have learnt a better lesson of humanity and wisdom." And this is the way in which improving nations ought to act, and this is the distinction between reform and revolution.

Justice is not changed by the magnitude or minuteness of the subject. The old cathedrals have enjoyed their patronage for seven hundred years, and the new ones since the time of Henry VIII.; which latter period even gives a much longer possession than ninety-nine out of a hundred of the legislators, who are called upon to plunder us, can boast for their own estates. And these rights, thus sanctioned, and hallowed by time, are torn from their present possessors without the least warning, or preparation, in the midst of all that fever of change which has seized upon the people, and which frightens men to the core of their hearts; and this spoliation is made, not by low men rushing into the plunder of the church and state, but by men of admirable and unimpeached character in all the relations of life—not by rash men of new politics, but by the ancient conservators of ancient law—by the archbishops and bishops of the land, high official men, invented and created, and put in palaces to curb the lawless changes, and the mutations, and the madness of mankind; and to crown the whole, the ludicrous is added to the unjust, and what they take from the other branches of the church they confer upon *themselves*.

Never dreaming of such sudden revolutions as these, a prebendary brings up his son to the church, and spends a large sum of money in his education, which, perhaps, he can ill afford. His hope is (wicked wretch!) that, according to the established custom of the body to which he (immoral man!) belongs, the chapter will (when his turn arrives), if his son be of fair attainments and good character, attend to his nefarious recommendation, and confer the living upon the young man; and in an instant all his hopes are destroyed, and he finds his preferment seized upon, under the plea of public good, by a stronger churchman than himself. I can call this by no other name than that of tyranny and oppression. I know very well that this is not the theory of patronage; but who does better?—do individual patrons?—do colleges who give in succession?—and as for bishops, lives there the man so weak and foolish, so little observant of the past, as to believe (when this tempest of purity and perfection has blown over) that the name of Bloomfield will not figure in those benefices from which the names of Copleston, Blomberg, Taite, and Smith, have been so virtuously excluded? I have no desire to make odious comparisons between the purity of one set of patrons and another, but they are forced upon me by the injustice of the commissioners. I must either make such comparisons or yield up, without remonstrance, those rights to which I am fairly entitled.

It may be said that the bishops will do better in future; that now the *public eye* is upon them, they will be ashamed into a more lofty and anti-nepotic spirit; but, if the argument of past superiority is given up, and the hope of future amendment resorted to, why may we not improve as well as our masters? but the commission says, "These excellent men (meaning themselves) have promised to do better, and we have an implicit confidence in their word: we must have the patronage of the cathedrals." In the mean time we are ready to promise as well as the bishops.

With regard to that common newspaper phrase, *the public eye*—there's nothing (as the bench well know) more wandering and slippery than the *public eye*. In five years hence, the public eye will no more see what description of men are promoted by bishops, than it will see what doctors of law are promoted by the Turkish Ulhema; and at the end of this period (such is the example set by the commission), the *public eye*, turned in every direction, may not be able to see any bishops at all.

In many instances, chapters are better patrons than bishops, because their preferment is not given exclusively to one species of incumbents. I have a diocese now in my private eye which has undergone the following changes. The first of three bishops whom I remember was a man of careless, easy temper, and how patronage went in those early days may be conjectured by the following letters; which are not his, but serve to illustrate a system:

THE BISHOP TO LORD A——.

My dear Lord,

I have noticed with great pleasure the behaviour of your lordship's second son, and am most happy to have it in my power to offer to him the living of * * *. He will find it of considerable value; and there is, I understand, a very good house upon it, &c. &c.

This is to confer a living upon a man of real merit out of the family; into which family, apparently sacrificed to the public good, the living is brought back by the second letter:—

THE SAME TO THE SAME, A YEAR AFTER.

My dear Lord,

Will you excuse the liberty I take in soliciting promotion for my grandson? He is an officer of great skill and gallantry, and can bring the most ample testimonials from some of the best men in the profession: the Arethusa frigate is, I understand, about to be commissioned; and if, &c. &c.

Now I am not saying that hundreds of prebendaries have not committed such enormities and stupendous crimes as this (a declaration which will fill the whig cabinet with horror); all that I mean to contend for is, that such is the practice of bishops quite as much as it is of inferior patrons.

The second bishop was a decided enemy of Calvinistical doctrines, and no clergyman so tainted had the slightest chance of preferment in his diocese.

The third bishop could endure no man whose principles were not strictly Calvinistic, and who did not give to the articles that kind of interpretation. Now here were a great mass of clergy naturally alive to the emoluments of their profession and not knowing which way to look or stir, because they depended so entirely upon the will of one person. Not otherwise is it with a very whig bishop, or a very tory bishop; but the worst case is that of a superannuated bishop; here the preferment is given away, and must be given away by wives and daughters, or by sons, or by butlers, perhaps, and valets, and the poor dying patron's paralytic hand is guided to the signature of papers, the contents of which he is utterly unable to comprehend. In all such cases as these, the superiority of bishops as patrons will not assist that violence which the commissioners have committed upon the patronage of cathedrals.

I never heard that cathedrals had sold the patronage of their preferment; such a practice, however, is not quite unknown among the higher orders of the church. When the Archbishop of Canterbury consecrates an inferior bishop, he marks some piece of preferment in the gift of the bishop as his own. This is denominated an *option;* and when the preferment falls, it is not only in the gift of the archbishop, if he is alive, but in the gift of his representatives if he is not. It is an absolute chattel, which, like any other chattel, is part of the archbishop's assets; and if he died in debt, might be taken and sold for the benefit of his creditors—and within the memory of man such options have been publicly sold by auction—and if the present Archbishop of Canterbury were to die in debt to-morrow, such might be the fate of his options. What Archbishop Moore did with his options I do not know, but the late Archbishop Sutton very handsomely and properly left them to the present—a bequest, however, which would not have prevented such options from coming to the hammer, if Archbishop Sutton had not cleared off, before his death, those incumbrances which, at one period of his life, sat so heavily upon him.

What the present archbishop means to do with them, I am not informed. They are not alluded to in the church returns, though they must be worth some thousand pounds. The commissioners do not seem to know of their existence—at least they are profoundly silent on the subject; and the bill which passed through Parliament in the summer for the regulation of the emoluments of bishops, does not make the most distant allusion to them. When a parallel was drawn between two species of patrons—which ended in the confiscation of the patronage of cathedrals—when two archbishops helped to draw the parallel, and profited by the parallel, I have a perfect right to state this corrupt and unabolished practice of their own sees—a practice which I never heard charged against deans and chapters.*

I do not mean to imply, in the most remote degree, that either of the present archbishops have sold their options, or ever thought of it. Purer and more high-minded gentlemen do not exist, nor men more utterly incapable of doing any thing unworthy of their high station; and

* Can any thing be more shabby in a government legislating upon church abuses, than to pass over such scandals as these existing in high places? Two years have passed, and they are unnoticed

I am convinced the Archbishop of Canterbury* will imitate or exceed the munificence of his predecessor: but when twenty-four public bodies are to be despoiled of their patronage, we must look not only to present men, but historically, to see how it has been administered in times of old, and in times also recently past; and to remember, that at this moment, when bishops are set up as the most admirable lispensers of patronage—as the only persons fit to be intrusted with it—as marvels, for whom law and justice and ancient possessions ought to be set aside, that this patronage (very valuabl because selected from the whole diocese) of the two heads of the church is liable to all the accidents of succession—that it may fall into the hands of a superannuated wife, of a profligate son, of a weak daughter, or a rapacious creditor—that it may be brought to the hammer, and publicly bid for at an auction, like all the other chattels of the palace; and that such have been the indignities to which this optional patronage has been exposed, from the earliest days of the church to this moment. Truly, men who live in houses of glass (especially where the panes are so large) ought not to fling stones; or if they do, they should be specially careful at whose head they are flung.

And then the patronage which is not seized —the patronage which the chapter is allowed to present to its own body—may be divided without their consent. Can any thing be more thoroughly lawless, or unjust than this—that my patronage during my life shall be divided without my consent? How do my rights during my life differ from those of a lay patron, who is tenant for life? and upon what principle of justice or common sense is his patronage protected from the commissioners' dividing power to which mine is subjected? That one can sell, and the other cannot sell, the next presentation, would be bad reasoning if it were good law; but it is not law, for an ecclesiastical corporation, aggregate or sole, can sell a next presentation as legally as a lay life-tenant can do. They have the same power of selling as laymen, but they never do so; that is, they dispense their patronage with greater propriety and delicacy, which, in the estimate of the commissioners, seems to make their right weaker, and the reasons for taking it away more powerful.

Not only are laymen guarded by the same act which gives the power of dividing livings to the commissioners, but bishops are also guarded. The commissioners may divide the livings of chapters without their consent; but before they can touch the living of a bishop, his consent must be obtained. It seems, after a few of those examples, to become a little clearer, and more intelligible, why the appointment of any other ecclesiastics than bishops was so disagreeable to the bench.

* The options of the Archbishop of York are comparatively trifling. I never heard, at any period, that they have been sold; but they remain, like those of Canterbury, in the absolute possession of the archbishop's representatives after his death. I will answer for it that the present archbishop will do every thing with them which becomes his high station and high character. They ought to be abolished by act of Parliament.

The reasoning, then, is this: If a good living is vacant in the patronage of a chapter, they will only think of conferring it on one of their body or their friends. If such a living falls to the gift of a bishop, he will totally overlook the interests of his sons and daughters, and divide the living into small portions for the good of the public; and with these sort of anilities, whig leaders, whose interest it is to lull the bishops into a reform, pretend to be satisfied; and upon this intolerable nonsense they are not ashamed to justify spoliation.*

A division is set up between public and private patronage, and it is pretended that one is holden in trust for the public, the other is private property. This is mere theory—a slight film thrown over convenient injustice. Henry VIII. gave to the Duke of Bedford much of his patronage. Roger de Hoveden gave to the church of St. Paul's much of his patronage before the Russells were in existence. The duke has the legal power to give his preferment to whom he pleases—so have we. We are both under the same moral and religious restraint to administer that patronage properly —the trust is precisely the same to both; and if the public good requires it, the power of dividing livings without the consent of patrons should be given in all instances, and not confined as a mark of infamy to cathedrals alone. This is not the real reason of the difference: bishops are the active members of the commission—they do not choose that their own patronage should be meddled with, and they know that the laity would not allow for a moment that their livings should be pulled to pieces by bishops; and that if such a proposal were made, there would be more danger of the bishop being pulled to pieces than the living. The real distinction is, between the weak and the strong—between those who have power to resist encroachment, and those who have not. This is the reason why we are selected for experiment, and so it is with all the bill from beginning to end. There is purple and fine linen in every line of it.

Another strong objection to the dividing power of the commission is this: according to the printed bill brought forward last session, if the living is not taken by some members of the body, it lapses to the bishop. Suppose, then, the same person to be bishop and commissioner, he breaks the living into little pieces as a commissioner, and after it is rejected in its impoverished state by the chapter, he gives it away as bishop of the diocese. The only answer that is given to such objections is, the *impeccability of bishops;* and upon this principle the whole bill has been constructed, and here is the great mistake about bishops. They are, upon the whole, very good and worthy men; but they are not (as many ancient ladies suppose) wholly exempt from human infirmities; they have their malice, hatred, uncharitableness, persecution and interest like other men; and an administration who did not think it more magnificent to laugh at the lower clergy, than to protect them,

* These reasonings have had their effect, and many early acts of injustice of the commission have been subsequently corrected.

should suffer no ecclesiastical bill to pass through Parliament without seriously considering how its provisions may affect the happiness of poor clergymen pushed into living tombs, and pining in solitude—

> Vates procul atque in sola relegant
> Pascua, post montem oppositum, et trans flumina lata.

There is a practice among some bishops, which may as well be mentioned here as anywhere else, but which, I think, cannot be too severely reprobated. They send for a clergyman, and insist upon his giving evidence respecting the character and conduct of his neighbour. Does he hunt? Does he shoot? Is he in debt? Is he temperate? Does he attend to his parish? &c. &c. Now what is this, but to destroy for all clergymen the very elements of social life—to put an end to all confidence between man and man—and to disseminate among gentlemen, who are bound to live in concord, every feeling of resentment, hatred and suspicion? But the very essence of tyranny is to act as if the finer feelings, like the finer dishes, were delicacies only for the rich and great, and that little people have no taste for them and no right to them. A good and honest bishop (I thank God there are many who deserve that character!) ought to suspect himself, and carefully to watch his own heart. He is all of a sudden elevated from being a tutor, dining at an early hour with his pupil (and occasionally, it is believed, on cold meat), to be a spiritual lord; he is dressed in a magnificent dress, decorated with a title, flattered by chaplains, and surrounded by little people looking up for the things which he has to give away; and this often happens to a man who has had no opportunities of seeing the world, whose parents were in very humble life, and who has given up all his thoughts to the Frogs of Aristophanes and the Targum of Onkelos. How is it possible that such a man should not lose his head? that he should not swell? that he should not be guilty of a thousand follies, and worry and tease to death (before he recovers his common sense) an hundred men as good and as wise and as able as himself?*

The history of the division of Edmonton has, I understand, been repeatedly stated in the commission—and told, as it has been, by a decided advocate, and with no sort of evidence called for on the other side of the question, has produced an unfair impression against chapters. The history is shortly this:—Besides the mother church of Edmonton, there are two chapels—Southgate and Winchmore Hill chapel. Winchmore Hill chapel was built by the society for building churches upon the same plan as the portions of Marylebone are arranged; the clergyman was to be remunerated by the lease of the pews, and if curates with talents for preaching had been placed there, they might have gained 200*l.* per annum. Though men of perfectly respectable and honourable character, they were not endowed with this sort of talent, and they gained no more than 90*l.* to 100*l.* per annum. The Bishop of London applied to the cathedral of St. Paul's, to consent to 250*l.* per annum in addition to the proceeds from the letting of the pews, or that proportion of the whole of the value of the living, should be allotted to the chapel of Winchmore; and at the same time we received an application from the chapel at Southgate, that another considerable portion, I forget what, but believe it to have been rather less (perhaps 200*l.*), should be allotted to them, and the whole living severed into three parishes. Now the living of Edmonton is about 1,350*l.* per annum, besides surplice fees; but this 1,350*l.* depends upon a corn rent of 10*s.* 3*d.* per bushel, present valuation, which, at the next valuation would, in the opinion of eminent land surveyors whom we consulted, be reduced to about 6*s.* per bushel, so that the living, considering the reduction also of all voluntary offerings to the church, would be reduced one half, and this half was to be divided into three, and one or two curates (two curates by the present bill) to be kept by the vicar of the old church; and thus three clerical beggars were, by the activity of the Bishop of London, to be established in a district where the extreme dearness of all provisions is the plea for making the see of London double in value to that of any bishopric in the country. To this we declined to agree; and this, heard only on one side, with the total omission of the changing value of the benefice from the price of corn, has most probably been the parent of the clause in question. The right cure for this and all similar cases would be to give the bishop a power of allotting to such chapels as high a salary as to any other curate in the diocese, taking, as part of that salary, whatever was received from the lease of the pews, and to this no reasonable man could or would object: but this is not enough—all must bow to one man—"Chapters must be taught submission. No pamphlets, no meeting of independent prebendaries, to remonstrate against the proceedings of their superiors—no opulence and ease but mine."

Some effect was produced also upon the commission, by the evidence of a prelate, who is both dean and bishop,* and who gave it as his opinion that the patronage of bishops was given upon better principles than that of chapters, which, translated into fair English, is no more than this—that the said witness, not meaning to mislead, but himself deceived, has his own way entirely in his diocese, and can only have it partially in his chapter.

There is a rumour that these reasonings, with which they were assailed from so many quarters in the last session of Parliament, have not been without their effect, and that it is the intention of the commissioners only to take away the patronage from the cathedrals exactly in proportion as the numbers of their members are reduced. Such may be the intention of the commissioners; but as that inten-

* Since writing this, and after declining the living for myself, I have had the pleasure of seeing it presented in an undivided state to my amiable and excellent friend, Mr. Taite, who, after a long life of moods and tenses, has acquired (as he has deserved) ease and opulence in his old age.

* This prelate stated it as his opinion to the commission, that in future all prelates ought to declare that they held their patronage in trust for the public.

tion has not been publicly notified, it depends only upon report; and the commissioners have changed their minds so often, that they may alter their intentions twenty times again before the meeting of Parliament. The whole of my observations in this letter are grounded upon their *bills of last year*—which Lord John Russell stated his intention of re-introducing at the beginning of this session. If they have any new plans, they ought to have published them three months ago—and to have given to the clergy an ample opportunity of considering them: but this they take the greatest care never to do. The policy of the government and of the commissioners is to hurry their bills through with such rapidity, that very little time is given to those who suffer by them for consideration and remonstrance, and we must be prepared for the worst beforehand. You are cashiered and confiscated before you can look about you—if you leave home for six weeks, in these times, you find a commissioner in possession of your house and office.

A report has reached my ears, that though all other cathedrals are to retain patronage exactly equal to their reduced numbers, a separate measure of justice is to be used for St. Paul's; that our numbers are to be augmented by a fifth; and our patronage reduced by a third; and this immediately on the passing of the bill. That the Bishop of Exeter, for instance, is to receive his augmentation of patronage only in proportion as the prebendaries die off, and the prebendaries themselves will, as long as they live, remain in the same proportional state as to patronage; and that when they are reduced to four (their stationary number), they will retain one-third of all the patronage the twelve now possess. Whether this is wise or not, is a separate question, but at least it is just; the four who remain cannot with any colour of justice complain that they do not retain all the patronage which was divided among twelve; but at St. Paul's not only are our numbers to be augmented by a fifth, but the patronage of fifteen of our best livings is to be instantly conferred upon the Bishop of London. This little *episode of plunder* involves three separate acts of gross injustice: in the first place, if only our numbers had been augmented by a fifth (in itself a mere bonus to commissioners), our patronage would have been reduced one-fifth in value. Secondly, one-third of the preferment is to be taken away immediately, and these two added together make eight-fifteenths, or more than one-half of our whole patronage. So that, when all the cathedrals are reduced to their reformed numbers, each cathedral will enjoy precisely the same proportion of patronage as it now does, and each member of every other cathedral will have precisely the same means of promoting men of merit or men of his own family, as is now possessed; while less than half of these advantages will remain to St. Paul's. Thirdly, if the Bishop of London were to wait (as all the other bishops by this arrangement must wait) till the present patrons die off, the injustice would be to the future body; but by this scheme, every present incumbent of St. Paul's is instantly deprived of eight-fifteenths of his patronage; while every other member of every other cathedral (as far as patronage is concerned) remains precisely in the same state in which he was before. Why this blow is levelled against St. Paul's I cannot conceive; still less can I imagine why the Bishop of London is not to wait, as all other bishops are forced to wait, for the death of the present patrons. There is a reason, indeed, for not waiting, by which (had I to do with a person of less elevated character than the Bishop of London) I would endeavour to explain this precipitate seizure of patronage—and that is, that the livings assigned to him in this remarkable scheme are all very valuable, and the incumbents all very old. But I shall pass over this scheme as a mere supposition, invented to bring the commission into disrepute, a scheme to which it is utterly impossible the commissioners should ever affix their names.

I should have thought, if the love of what is just had not excited the commissioner bishops, that the ridicule of men voting such comfortable things to themselves as the prebendal patronage would have alarmed them; but they want to sacrifice with other men's hecatombs, and to enjoy, at the same time, the character of great disinterestedness, and the luxury of unjust spoliation. It was thought necessary to make a fund; and the prebends in the gift of the bishops* were appropriated to that purpose. The bishops who consented to this have then made a great sacrifice—true, but they have taken more out of our pockets than they have disbursed from their own; where then is the sacrifice? They must either give back the patronage or the martyrdom, if they choose to be martyrs—which I hope they will do—let them give us back our patronage: if they prefer the patronage, they must not talk of being martyrs—they cannot effect this double sensuality, and combine the sweet flavour of rapine with the aromatic odour of sanctity.

We are told, if you agitate these questions among yourselves, you will have the democratic Philistines come down upon you, and sweep you all away together. Be it so; I am quite ready to be swept away when the time comes. Every body has his favourite death; some delight in apoplexy, and others prefer marasmus. I would infinitely rather be crushed by democrats, than, under the plea of the public good, be mildly and blandly absorbed by bishops.

I met the other day, in an old Dutch chronicle, with a passage so apposite to this subject, that though it is somewhat too light for the occasion, I cannot abstain from quoting it. There was a great meeting of all the clergy at Dordrecht, and the chronicler thus describes it, which I give in the language of the translation:—"And there was great store of bishops in the town, in their robes goodly to behold,

* The bishops have, however, secured for themselves all the livings which were in the separate gifts of prebendaries and deans, and they have received from the crown a very large contribution of valuable patronage; why or wherefore, is known only to the unfathomable wisdom of ministers. The glory of martyrdom can be confined only at best to the bishops of the old cathedrals, for there are scarcely any separate prebends in the new cathedrals.

and all the great men of the state were there, and folks poured in in boats on the Meuse, the Merve, the Rhine, and the Linge, coming from the Isle of Beverlandt, and Isselmond, and from all quarters in the Bailiwick of Dort; Arminians and Gomarists, with the friends of John Barneveldt and of Hugh Grote. And before my lords the bishops, Simon of Gloucester, who was a bishop in those parts, disputed with Vorstius, and Leoline the Monk, and many texts of Scripture were bandied to and fro; and when this was done, and many propositions made, and it waxed towards twelve of the clock, my lords the bishops prepared to set them down to a fair repast, in which was great store of good things—and among the rest a roasted peacock, having, in lieu of a tail, the arms and banners of the archbishop, which was a goodly sight to all who favoured the church—and then the archbishop would say a grace, as was seemly to do, he being a very holy man; but ere he had finished, a great mob of townspeople and folks from the country, who were gathered under the window, cried out, *Bread! bread!* for there was a great famine, and wheat had risen to three times the ordinary price of the *sleich;** and when they had done crying *Bread! bread!* they called out *No bishops!*—and began to cast up stones at the windows. Whereat my lords the bishops were in a great fright, and cast their dinner out of the window to appease the mob, and so the men of that town were well pleased, and did devour the meats with great appetite; and then you might have seen my lords standing with empty plates, and looking wistfully at each other, till Simon of Gloucester, he who disputed with Leoline the Monk, stood up among them and said, '*Good my lords, it is your pleasure to stand here fasting, and that those who count lower in the church than you do should feast and fluster? Let us order to us the dinner of the deans and canons, which is making ready for them in the chamber below.*' And this speech of Simon of Gloucester pleased the bishops much; and so they sent for the host, one William of Ypres, and told him it was for the public good, and he, much fearing the bishops, brought them the dinner of the deans and canons; and so the deans and canons went away without dinner, and were pelted by the men of the town, because they had not put any meat out of the window like the bishops; and when the count came to hear of it, he said it was a pleasant conceit, *and that the bishops were right cunning men, and had ding'd the canons well.*"

When I talk of sacrifices, I mean the sacrifices of the bishop commissioners, for we are given to understand that the great mass of bishops were never consulted at all about these proceedings; that they are contrary to every thing which consultations at Lambeth, previous to the commission, had led them to expect; and that they are totally disapproved of by them. The voluntary sacrifice, then (for it is no sacrifice, if it is not voluntary), is in the bishop commissioners only; and besides the indemnification which they have voted to themselves out of the patronage of the cathedrals, they will have all that never-ending patronage, which is to proceed from the working of the commission, and the endowments bestowed upon different livings. So much for episcopal sacrifices!

And who does not see the end and meaning of all this? The lay commissioners, who are members of the government, cannot and will not attend—the Archbishops of York and Canterbury are quiet and amiable men, going fast down in the vale of life—some of the members of the commission are expletives—some must be absent in their dioceses—the Bishop of London is passionately fond of labour, has certainly no aversion to power, is of quick temper, great ability, thoroughly versant in ecclesiastical law, and always in London. He will become the commission, and when the church of England is mentioned, it will only mean *Charles James, of London*, who will enjoy a greater power than has ever been possessed by any churchman since the days of Laud, and will become the *Church of England here upon earth.* As for the commission itself, there is scarcely any power which is not given to it. They may call for every paper in the world, and every human creature who possesses it; and do what they like to one or the other. It is hopeless to contend with such a body; and most painful to think that it has been established under a whig government.* A commission of tory churchmen, established for such purposes, should have been framed with the utmost jealousy, and with the most cautious circumscription of its powers, and with the most earnest wish for its extinction when the purposes of its creation were answered. The government have done every thing in their power to make it vexatious, omnipotent, and everlasting. This immense power, flung into the hands of an individual, is one of the many foolish consequences which proceed from the centralization of the bill, and the unwillingness to employ the local knowledge of the bishops in the process of annexing dignified to parochial preferment.

There is a third bill concocted by the commission-bishops, in which the great principle of increasing the power of the bench has certainly not been lost sight of. ——— ———, a brother clergyman, falls ill suddenly in the country, and he begs his clerical neighbour to do duty for him in the afternoon, thinking it better that there should be single service in two churches, than two services in one, and none in the other. The clergyman who accedes to this request, is liable to a penalty of 5*l.* There is an harshness and ill nature in this—a gross ignorance of the state of the poorer clergy—an hard-heartedness produced by the long enjoyment of wealth and power, which makes it quite intolerable. I speak of it as it stands in the bill of last year.†

If a clergyman has a living of 400*l.* per annum, and a population of two thousand per-

* A measure in the Bailiwick of Dort, containing two gallons one pint English dry measure

* I am speaking here of the permanent commission established by act of Parliament in 1835. The commission for reporting had come to an end six months before this letter was written.

† This is also given up.

sons, the bishop can compel him to keep a curate, to whom he can allot any salary which he may allot to any other curate; in other words, he may take away half the income of the clergyman, and instantly ruin him—and this without any complaint from the vestry; with every testimonial of the most perfect satisfaction of the parish in the labours of a minister, who may, perhaps, be dedicating his whole life to their improvement. I think I remember that the Bishop of London once attempted this before he was a commissioner, and was defeated. I had no manner of doubt that it would speedily become the law, after the commission had begun to operate. The Bishop of London is said to have declared, after this trial, that *if it was not law it should soon be law;** and *law*, you will see, it will become. In fact he can slip into any ecclesiastical act of Parliament any thing he pleases. There is nobody to heed or contradict him; provided the power of bishops is extended by it; no bishop is so ungenteel as to oppose the act of his right reverend brother; and there are not many men who have knowledge, eloquence, or force of character to stand up against the Bishop of London, and, above all, of industry to watch him. The ministry, and the lay lords, and the House of Commons, care nothing about the matter; and the clergy themselves, in a state of the greatest ignorance as to what is passing in the world, find their chains heavier and heavier, without knowing who or what has produced the additional incumbrance. A good honest whig minister should have two or three stout-hearted parish priests in his train to watch the bishop's bills, and to see that they were constructed on other principles than that *bishops can do no wrong, and cannot have too much power.* The whigs do nothing of this, and yet they complain that they are hated by the clergy, and that in all elections the clergy are their bitterest enemies. Suppose they were to try a little justice, a little notice, and a little protection. It would take more time than quizzing, and contempt, but it might do some good.

The bishop puts a great number of questions to his clergy, which they are to be compelled, by this new law of the commission, to answer, under a penalty; and if they do answer them, they incur, perhaps, a still heavier penalty. "Have you had two services in your church all the year?"—"I decline to answer."—"Then I fine you 20*l.*"—"I have only had one service."—"Then I fine you 250*l.*" In what other profession are men placed between this double fire of penalties, and compelled to criminate themselves? It has been disused in England, I believe, ever since the time of Laud and the Star Chamber.†

By the same bill, as it first emanated from the commission, a bishop could compel a clergyman to expend three years' income upon a house in which he had resided, perhaps, fifty years, and in which he had brought up a large family. With great difficulty, some slight modification of this enormous power was obtained, and it was a little improved in the amended bill.* In the same way an attempt was made to try delinquent clergymen, by a jury of clergymen, nominated by the bishop, but this was too bad, and was not endured for an instant; still it showed the same love of power and the same principle of *impeccability*, for the bill is expressly confined to all suits and complaints against persons *below the dignity and degree of bishops.* The truth is, that there are very few men in either House of Parliament (ministers, or any one else), who ever think of the happiness and comfort of the working clergy, or bestow one thought upon guarding them from the increased and increasing power of their encroaching masters. What is called taking care of the church is taking care of the bishops; and all bills for the management of the clergy are left to the concoction of men who very naturally believe they are improving the church when they are increasing their own power. There are many bishops too generous, too humane, and too Christian, to oppress a poor clergyman; but I have seen (I am sorry to say) many grievous instances of partiality, rudeness, and oppression.† I have seen clergymen treated by them with a violence and contempt which the lowest servant in the bishop's establishment would not have endured for a single moment; and if there is a helpless, friendless, wretched being in the community, it is a poor clergyman in the country with a large family. If there is an object of compassion, he is one. If there is any occasion in life where a great man should lay aside his office, and put on those kind looks, and use those kind words which raise the humble from the dust, these are the occasions when those best parts of the Christian character ought to be displayed.

I would instance the unlimited power which a bishop possesses over a curate, as a very unfair degree of power for any man to possess. Take the following dialogue which represents a real event.

Bishop.—Sir, I understand you frequent the meetings of the Bible Society.

Curate.—Yes, my lord, I do.

Bishop.—Sir, I tell you plainly, if you continue to do so, I shall silence you from preaching in my diocese.

Curate.—My lord, I am very sorry to incur your indignation, but I frequent that society

* The Bishop of London denies that he ever said this; but the Bishop of London affects short sharp sayings, seasoned, I am afraid, sometimes with a little indiscretion; and these sayings are not necessarily forgotten because he forgets them.

† This attempt upon the happiness and independence of the clergy has been abandoned.

* I perceive that the Archbishop of Canterbury borrows money for the improvement of his palace, and pays the principal off in forty years. This is quite as soon as a debt incurred for such public purposes ought to be paid off, and the archbishop has done rightly to take that period. In process of time I think it very likely that this indulgence will be extended to country clergymen, who are compelled to pay off the debts for buildings (which they are compelled to undertake) in twenty years; and by the new bill, not yet passed, this indulgence is extended to thirty years. Why poor clergymen have been compelled for the last five years to pay off the incumbrances at the rate of one-twentieth per annum, and are now compelled to pay them off, or will, when the bill passes, be so compelled, at the rate of one-thirtieth per annum, when the archbishop takes forty years to do the same thing, and has made that bargain in the year 1831, I really cannot tell. A clergyman who does not reside, is forced to pay off his building debt in ten years.

† What bishops like best in their clergy is a dropping-down deadness of manner.

upon principle, because I think it eminently serviceable to the cause of the Gospel.

Bishop.—Sir, I do not enter into your reasons, but tell you plainly, if you continue to go there you shall be silenced.

The young man did go, and was silenced—and as bishops have always a great deal of clever machinery at work of testimonials and *bene-decessits*, and always a lawyer at their elbow, under the name of a secretary, a curate excluded from one diocese is excluded from all. His remedy is an appeal to the archbishop from the bishop; his worldly goods, however, amount to ten pounds; he never was in London; he dreads such a tribunal as an archbishop—he thinks, perhaps, in time, the bishop may be softened—if he is compelled to restore him, the enmity will be immortal. It would be just as rational to give to a frog or a rabbit, upon which the physician is about to experiment, an appeal to the Zoological Society, as to give to a country curate an appeal to the archbishop against his purple oppressor.

The errors of the bill are a public concern—the injustice of the bill is a private concern. Give us our patronage for life.* Treat the cathedrals all alike, with the same measure of justice. Don't divide livings in the patronage of present incumbents without their consent—or do the same with all livings. If these points are attended to in the forthcoming bill, *all complaint of unfairness and injustice will be at an end.* I shall still think, that the commissioners have been very rash and indiscreet, that they have evinced a contempt for existing institutions, and a spirit of destruction which will be copied to the life hereafter, by commissioners of a very different description. Bishops live in high places with high people, or with little people who depend upon them. They walk delicately, like Agag. They hear only one sort of conversation, and avoid bold, reckless men, as a lady veils herself from rough breezes. I am half inclined to think, sometimes, that the bishop-commissioners really think that they are finally settling the church; that the House of Lords will be open to the bench for ages; and that many archbishops in succession will enjoy their fifteen thousand pounds a year in Lambeth. I wish I could do for the bishop-commissioners what his mother did for Æneas, in the last days of Troy:—

> "Omnem quæ nunc obducta tuenti
> Mortales hebetat visus tibi, et humida circum
> Caligat, nubem eripiam.
> Apparent diræ facies," &c. &c.

It is ominous for liberty, when Sydney and Russell cannot agree; but when Lord John Russell, in the House of Commons, said, that we showed no disposition to make any sacrifices for the good of the church, I took the liberty to remind that excellent person that he must first of all prove it to be for the good of the church that our patronage should be taken away by the bishops, and then he might find fault with us for not consenting to the sacrifice.

I have little or no personal nor pecuniary interest in these things, and have made all possible exertion (as two or three persons in the power well know) that they should no come before the public. I have no son nor son-in-law in the church, for whom I want any patronage. If I were young enough to survive any incumbent of St. Paul's, my own preferment is too agreeably circumstanced to make it at all probable I should avail myself of the opportunity. I am a sincere advocate for church reform; but I think it very possible, and even very easy, to have removed all odium from the establishment in a much less violent and revolutionary manner, without committing or attempting such flagrant acts of injustice, and without leaving behind an odious court of inquisition, which will inevitably fall into the hands of a single individual, and will be an eternal source of vexation, jealousy, and change. I give sincere credit to the commissioners for good intentions—how can such men have intended any thing but good? And I firmly believe that they are hardly conscious of the extraordinary predilection they have shown for bishops in all their proceedings; it is like those errors in tradesmen's bills of which the retail arithmetician is really unconscious, but which, somehow or another, always happen to be in his own favour. Such men as the commissioners do not say this patronage belongs justly to the cathedrals, and we will take it away unjustly for ourselves; but, after the manner of human nature, a thousand weak reasons prevail, which would have no effect, if self-interest were not concerned; they are practising a deception on themselves, and sincerely believe they are doing right. When I talk of spoil and plunder, I do not speak of the intention, but of the effect, and the precedent.

Still the commissioners are on the eve of entailing an immense evil upon the country, and unfortunately, they have gone so far, that it is necessary they should ruin the cathedrals, to preserve their character for consistency. They themselves have been frightened a great deal too much by the mob; have overlooked the chances in their favour produced by delay; have been afraid of being suspected (as tories) of not doing enough; and have allowed themselves to be hurried on by the constitutional impetuosity of one man, who cannot be brought to believe that wisdom often consists in leaving alone, standing still and doing nothing. From the joint operation of all these causes, all the cathedrals of England will, in a few weeks, be knocked about our ears. You, Mr. Archdeacon Singleton, will sit like Caius Marius on the ruins, and we shall lose for ever the wisest scheme for securing a well-educated clergy upon the most economical terms, and for preventing that low fanaticism which is the greatest curse upon human happiness, and the greatest enemy of true religion. We shall have all the evils of an establishment, and none of its good.

You tell me I shall be laughed at as a rich and overgrown churchman; be it so. I have been laughed at a hundred times in my life, and care little or nothing about it. If I am well provided for now—I have had my full share of the blanks in the lottery as the prizes. Till thirty years of age I never received a farthing from the church; then 50*l.* per annum

* This has now been given to us.

for two years—then nothing for ten years—then 500*l.* per annum, increased for two or three years to 800*l.*, till, in my grand climacteric, I was made canon of St. Paul's; and before that period, I had built a parsonage-house with farm offices for a large farm, which cost me 4,000*l.*, and had reclaimed another from ruins at the expense of 2,000*l.* A lawyer, or a physician in good practice, would smile at this picture of great ecclesiastical wealth, and yet I am considered as a perfect monster of ecclesiastical prosperity.

I should be very sorry to give offence to the dignified ecclesiastics who are in the commission; I hope they will allow for the provocation, if I have been a little too warm in the defence of St. Paul's, which I have taken a solemn oath to defend. I was at school and college with the Archbishop of Canterbury; fifty-three years ago he knocked me down with the chess-board for check-mating him—and now he is attempting to take away my patronage. I believe these are the only two acts of violence he ever committed in his life: the interval has been one of gentleness, kindness, and the most amiable and high-principled courtesy to his clergy. For the Archbishop of York, I feel an affectionate respect—the result of that invariable kindness I have received from him: and who can see the Bishop of London without admiring his superior talents—being pleased with his society, without admitting that, *upon the whole,** the public is benefited by his ungovernable passion for business; and without receiving the constant workings of a really good heart, as an atonement for the occasional excesses of an impetuous disposition? I am quite sure if the tables had been turned, and if it had been his lot, as a canon, to fight against the encroachments of bishops, that he would have made as stout a defence as I have done—the only difference is that he would have done it with much greater talent.

As for my friends the whigs, I neither wish to offend them nor any body else. I consider myself to be as good a whig as any amongst them. I was a whig before many of them were born—and while some of them were tories and waverers. I have always turned out to fight their battles, and when I saw no other clergyman turn out but myself—and this in times before liberality was well recompensed, and therefore in fashion, when the smallest appearance of it seemed to condemn a churchman to the grossest of obloquy, and the most hopeless poverty. It may suit the purpose of the ministers to flatter the bench; it does not suit mine. I do not choose in my old age to be tossed as a prey to the bishops; I have not deserved this of my whig friends. I know very well there can be no justice for deans and chapters, and that the momentary lords of the earth will receive our statement with derision and *persiflage*—the great principle which is now called in for the government of mankind. Nobody admires the general conduct of the whig administration more than I do. They have conferred, in their domestic policy, the most striking benefits on the country. To say that there is no risk in what they have done is mere nonsense—there is great risk; and all honest men must balance to counteract it—holding back as firmly down hill as they pulled vigorously up hill. Still, great as the risk is, it was worth while to incur it in the poor-law bill, in the tithe bill, in the corporation bill, and in the circumscription of the Irish Protestant Church. In all these matters, the whig ministry, after the heat of party is over, and when Joseph Hume and Wilson Croker* are powdered into the dust of death, will gain great and deserved fame. In the question of the church commission they have behaved with the grossest injustice; delighted to see this temporary delirium of archbishops and bishops, scarcely believing their eyes, and carefully suppressing their laughter, when they saw these eminent conservatives laying about them with the fury of Mr. Tyler or Mr. Straw; they have taken the greatest care not to disturb them, and to give them no offence: "Do as you like, my lords, with the chapters and the parochial clergy; you will find some pleasing morsels in the ruins of the cathedrals. Keep for yourselves any thing you like—whatever is agreeable to you cannot be unpleasant to us." In the mean time, the old friends of, and the old sufferers for, liberty, do not understand this new meanness, and are not a little astonished to find their leaders prostrate on their knees before the lords of the church, and to receive no other answer from them than that, if they are disturbed in their adulation, they will immediately resign!

I remain, my dear Sir, with sincere good will and respect, yours,

SYDNEY SMITH.

* I have heard that the Bishop of London employs eight hours per day in the government of his diocese—in which no part of Asia, Africa, or America is included. The world is, I believe, taking one day with another, governed in about a third of that time.

* I meant no harm by the comparison, but I have made two bitter enemies by it.

SECOND LETTER TO ARCHDEACON SINGLETON.

My dear Sir,

It is a long time since you heard from me, and in the mean time the poor Church of England has been trembling, from the bishop who sitteth upon the throne, to the curate who rideth upon the hackney horse. I began writing on the subject to avoid bursting from indignation; and, as it is not my habit to recede, I will go on till the Church of England is either up or down—semianimous on its back, or vigorous on its legs.

Two or three persons have said to me—"Why, after writing an entertaining and successful letter to Archdeacon Singleton, do you venture upon another, in which you may probably fail, and be weak or stupid?" All this I utterly despise; I write upon these matters not to be entertaining, but because the subjects are very important, and because I have strong opinions upon them. If what I write is liked, so much the better; but liked or not liked, sold or not sold, Wilson Crockered or not Wilson Crockered, I will write. If you ask me who excites me, I answer you, it is that judge who stirs good thoughts in honest hearts—under whose warrant I impeach the wrong, and by whose help I hope to chastise it.

There are, in most cathedrals, two sorts of prebendaries—the one resident, the other non-resident. It is proposed by the church commission to abolish all the prebendaries of the latter and many of the former class; and it is the prebendaries of the former class, the resident prebendaries, whom I wish to save.

The non-resident prebendaries never come near the cathedral; they are just like so many country gentlemen; the difference is, that their appointments are elective, not hereditary. They have houses, manors, lands, and every appendage of territorial wealth and importance. Their value is very different. I have one, Neasdon, near Willesdon, which consists of a quarter of an acre of land, worth a few shillings per annum, but animated by the burden of repairing a bridge, which sometimes costs the unfortunate prebendary fifty or sixty pounds. There are other non-resident prebendaries, however, of great value; and one, I believe, which would be worth, if the years or lives were run out, from 40,000*l.* to 60,000*l.* per annum.

Not only do these prebendaries do nothing, and are never seen, but the existence of the preferment is hardly known; and the abolition of the preferment, therefore, would not in any degree lessen the temptation to enter into the church, while the mass of these preferments would make an important fund for the improvement of small livings. The residentiary prebendaries, on the contrary, perform all the services of the cathedral church; their existence is known, their preferment coveted, and to get a stall, and to be preceded by men with silver rods, is the bait which the ambitious squire is perpetually holding out to his second son. What prebendary is next to come into residence, is as important a topic to the cathedral town, and ten miles around it, as what the evening or morning star may be to the astronomer. I will venture to say, there is not a man of good humour, sense, and worth, within ten miles of Worcester, who does not hail the rising of Archdeacon Singleton in the horizon as one of the most agreeable events of the year. If such sort of preferments are extinguished, a very serious evil (as I have often said before) is done to the church—the service becomes unpopular, further spoliation is dreaded, the whole system is considered to be altered and degraded, capital is withdrawn from the church, and no one enters into the profession but the sons of farmers and little tradesmen, who would be footmen if they were not vicars—or figure on the coach-box if they were not lecturing from the pulpit.

But what a practical rebuke to the commissioners, after all their plans and consultations and carvings of cathedral preferment, to leave it integral, and untouched! It is some comfort, however, to me, to think that the persons of all others to whom this preservation of cathedral property would give the greatest pleasure, are the ecclesiastical commissioners themselves. Can any one believe that the Archbishop of Canterbury, or the Bishop of London, really wishes for the confiscation of any cathedral property, or that they were driven to it by any thing but fear, mingled, perhaps, with a little vanity of playing the part of great reformers? They cannot, of course, say for themselves what I say for them; but of what is really passing in the ecclesiastical minds of these great personages, I have no more doubt than I have of what passes in the mind of the prisoner when the prosecutor recommends and relents, and the judge says he shall attend to the recommendation.

What harm does a prebend do, in a politico-economical point of view? The alienation of the property for three lives, or twenty-one years, and the almost certainty that the tenant has of renewing, give him sufficient interest in the soil for all purposes of cultivation,* and a long series of elected clergymen is rather

* The church, it has been urged, do not plant—they do not extend their woods; but almost all cathedrals possess woods, and regularly plant a succession, so as to keep them up. A single evening of dice and hazard does not doom their woods to sudden destruction; a life tenant does not cut down all the timber to make the most of his estate; the woods of ecclesiastical bodies are managed upon a fixed and settled plan, and considering the sudden prodigalities of laymen, I should not be afraid of a comparison.

more likely to produce valuable members of the community than a long series of begotten squires. Take, for instance, the cathedral of Bristol, the whole estates of which are about equal to keeping a pack of fox-hounds. If this had been in the hands of a country gentleman; instead of precentor, succentor, dean, and canons, and sexton, you would have had huntsman, whipper-in, dog-feeders, and stoppers of earths; the old squire full of foolish opinions, and fermented liquids, and a young gentleman of gloves, waistcoats and pantaloons: and how many generations might it be before the fortuitous concourse of noodles would produce such a man as Professor Lee, one of the prebendaries of Bristol, and by far the most eminent oriental scholar in Europe? The same argument might be applied to every cathedral in England. How many hundred coveys of squires would it take to supply as much knowledge as is condensed in the heads of Dr. Copplestone or Mr. Taite, of St. Paul's? and what a strange thing it is that such a man as Lord John Russell, the whig leader, should be so squirrel-minded as to wish for a movement without object or end! Saving there can be none, for it is merely taking from one ecclesiastic to give it to another; public clamour, to which the best men must sometimes yield, does not require it: and so far from doing any good, it would be a source of infinite mischief to the establishment.

If you were to gather a parliament of curates on the hottest Sunday in the year, after all the services, sermons, burials, and baptisms of the day were over, and to offer them such increase of salary as would be produced by the confiscation of the cathedral property, I am convinced they would reject the measure, and prefer splendid hope, and the expectation of good fortune in advanced life, to the trifling improvement of poverty which such a fund could afford. Charles James, of London, was a curate; the Bishop of Winchester was a curate; almost every rose-and-shovel man has been a curate in his time. All curates hope to draw great prizes.

I am surprised it does not strike the mountaineers how very much the great emoluments of the church are flung open to the lowest ranks of the community. Butchers, bakers, publicans, schoolmasters, are perpetually seeing their children elevated to the mitre. Let a respectable baker drive through the city from the west end of the town, and let him cast an eye on the battlements of Northumberland House, has his little muffin-faced son the smallest chance of getting in among the Percies, enjoying a share of their luxury and splendour, and of chasing the deer with hound and horn upon the Cheviot Hills? But let him drive his alum-steeped loaves a little farther, till he reaches St. Paul's churchyard, and all his thoughts are changed when he sees that beautiful fabric; it is not impossible that his little penny roll may be introduced into that splendid oven. Young Crumpet is sent to school—takes to his books—spends the best years of his life, as all eminent Englishmen do, in making Latin verses—knows that the *crum* in crum-pet is long, and the *pet* short—goes to the University—gets a prize for an Essay on the Dispersion of the Jews—takes orders—becomes a bishop's chaplain—has a young nobleman for his pupil—publishes an useless classic, and a serious call to the unconverted—and then goes through the Elysian translations of prebendary, dean, prelate, and the long train of purple, profit, and power.

It will not do to leave only four persons in each cathedral, upon the supposition that such a number will be sufficient for all the men of real merit who ought to enjoy such preferment; we ought to have a steady confidence that the men of real merit will always bear a small proportion to the whole number; and that in proportion as the whole number is lessened, the number of men of merit provided for will be lessened also. If it were quite certain that ninety persons would be selected, the most remarkable for conduct, piety, and learning, ninety offices might be sufficient; but out of these ninety are to be taken tutors to dukes and marquises, paid in this way by the public; bishop's chaplains, running tame about the palace; elegant clergymen, of small understanding, who have made themselves acceptable in the drawing-rooms of the mitre? Billingsgate controversialists, who have tossed and gored an Unitarian. So that there remain but a few rewards for men of real merit—yet these rewards do infinite good; and in this mixed, checkered way, human affairs are conducted.

No man at the beginning of the reform could tell to what excesses the new power conferred upon the multitude would carry them; it was not safe for a clergyman to appear in the streets. I bought a blue coat, and did not despair in time of looking like a layman. All this is passed over. Men are returned to their senses upon the subject of the church, and I utterly deny that there is any public feeling whatever which calls for the destruction of the resident prebends. Lord John Russell has pruned the two luxuriant bishoprics, and has abolished pluralities: he has made a very material alteration in the state of the church: not enough to please Joseph Hume, and the tribunes of the people, but enough to satisfy every reasonable and moderate man, and, therefore, enough to satisfy himself. What another generation may choose to do, is another question: I am thoroughly convinced that enough has been done for the present.

Viscount Melbourne declared himself quite satisfied with the church as it is; but if the public had any desire to alter it, they might do as they pleased. He might have said the same thing of the monarchy, or of any other of our institutions; and there is in the declaration a permissiveness and good humour which, in public men, have seldom been exceeded. Carelessness, however, is but a poor imitation of genius, and the formation of a wise and well-reflected plan of reform conduces more to the lasting fame of a minister than that affected contempt of duty which every man sees to be mere vanity, and a vanity of no very high description.

But, if the truth must be told, our viscount is somewhat of an impostor. Every thing about him seems to betoken careless desolation: any one would suppose from his manner that he was playing at chuck-farthing with human happiness; that he was always on the heel of pastime; that he would giggle away the great charter, and decide by the method of tee-totum whether my lords the bishops should or should not retain their seats in the House of Lords. All this is the mere vanity of surprising, and making us believe that he can play with kingdoms as other men can with nine-pins. Instead of this lofty nebulo, this miracle of moral and intellectual felicities, he is nothing more than a sensible, honest man, who means to do his duty to the sovereign and to the country: instead of being the ignorant man he pretends to be, before he meets the deputation of tallow-chandlers in the morning, he sits up half the night talking with Thomas Young about melting and skimming, and then, though he has acquired knowledge enough to work off a whole vat of prime Leicester tallow, he pretends next morning not to know the difference between a dip and a mould. In the same way, when he has been employed in reading acts of Parliament, he would persuade you that he has been reading *Cleghorn on the Beatitudes*, or *Pickler on the Nine Difficult Points.* Neither can I allow to this minister (however he may be irritated by the denial) the extreme merit of indifference to the consequences of his measures. I believe him to be conscientiously alive to the good or evil that he is doing, and that his caution has more than once arrested the gigantic projects of the Lycurgus of the Lower House. I am sorry to hurt any man's feelings, and to brush away the magnificent fabric of levity and gaiety he has reared; but I accuse our minister of honesty and diligence; I deny that he is careless or rash: he is nothing more than a man of good understanding, and good principle, disguised in the eternal and somewhat wearisome affectation of a political roué.

One of the most foolish circumstances attending this destruction of cathedral property, is the great sacrifice of the patronage of the crown; the crown gives up eight prebends of Westminster, two at Worcester, 1,500*l.* per annum at St. Paul's, two prebends at Bristol, and a great deal of other preferment all over the kingdom; and this at a moment when such extraordinary power has been suddenly conferred upon the people, and when every atom of power and patronage ought to be husbanded for the crown. A prebend of Westminster for my second son would soften the Catos of Cornhill, and lull the Gracchi of the metropolitan boroughs. Lives there a man so absurd as to suppose that government can be carried on without those gentle allurements? You may as well attempt to poultice off the humps of a camel's back, as to cure mankind of these little corruptions.

I am terribly alarmed by a committee of cathedrals now sitting in London, and planning a petition to the legislature to be heard by counsel. They will take such high ground, and talk a language so utterly at variance with the feelings of the age about church property, that I am much afraid they will do more harm than good. In the time of Lord George Gordon's riots, the Guards said they did not care for the mob, if the gentlemen volunteers behind would be so good as not to hold their muskets in such a dangerous manner. I don't care for popular clamour, and think it might now be defied; but I confess the gentlemen volunteers alarm me. They have, unfortunately too, collected their addresses, and published them in a single volume!!!

I should like to know how many of our institutions at this moment, besides the cathedrals, are under notice of destruction. I will, before I finish my letter, endeavour to procure a list; in the mean time I will give you the bill of fare with which the last session opened, and I think that of 1838 will not be less copious. But at the opening of the session of 1837, when I addressed my first letter to you, this was the state of our intended changes:—The law of copyright was to be recreated by Serjeant Talfourd; church rates abolished by Lord John Russell, and imprisonment for debt by the attorney-general; the Archbishop of Canterbury kindly undertook to destroy all the cathedrals, and Mr. Grote was to arrange our voting by ballot; the septennial act was to be repealed by Mr. Williams, corn laws abolished by Mr Clay, and the House of Lords reformed by Mr. Ward; Mr. Hume remodelled county rates, Mr. Ewart put an end to primogeniture, and Mr. Tooke took away the exclusive privileges of Dublin, Oxford, and Cambridge; Thomas Duncombe was to put an end to the proxies of the lords, and Serjeant Prime to turn the universities topsy-turvy. Well may it be said that

"Man never continueth in one stay."

See how men accustom themselves to large and perilous changes. Ten years ago, if a cassock or a hassock had been taken from the establishment, the current of human affairs would have been stopped till restitution had been made. In a fortnight's time, Lord John Russell is to take possession of, and to re-partition all the cathedrals in England; and what a prelude for the young queen's coronation! what a medal for the august ceremony!—the fallen Gothic buildings on one side of the gold, the young Protestant queen on the other:—

"Victoria Ecclesiæ Victrix."

And then, when she is full of noble devices, and of all sorts enchantingly beloved, and amid the solemn swell of music, when her heart beats happily, and her eyes look majesty, she turns them on the degraded ministers of the Gospel, and shudders to see she is stalking to the throne of her Protestant ancestors over the broken altars of God.

Now, remember, I hate to overstate my case. I do not say that the destruction of cathedrals will put an end to railroads: I believe that good mustard and cress, sown after Lord John's bill is passed, will, if duly watered, continue to grow. I do not say that the country has no *right*, after the death of individual incumbents, to do what they propose to do;—I merely say that it is inexpedient, uncalled for, and mischievous—that the lower clergy, for whose sake it is proposed to be done, do not desire it—that the bishop commissioners, who proposed it, would be heartily glad if it was put an end to—that it will lower the character of those who enter into the church, and accustom the English people to large and dangerous confiscations: and I would not have gentlemen of the money-bags, and of wheat and bean land, forget that the church means many other things than Thirty-nine Articles, and a discourse of five-and-twenty minutes' duration on the Sabbath. It means a check to the conceited rashness of experimental reasoners—an adhesion to old moral landmarks—an attachment to the happiness we have gained from tried institutions, greater than the expectation of that which is promised by novelty and change. The loud cry of ten thousand teachers of justice and worship, that cry which masters the *Borgias* and *Catilines* of the world, and guards from devastation the best works of God—

Magnâ testantur voce per orbem
Discite justitiam moniti et non temnere divos.

In spite of his uplifted chess-board, I cannot let my old school-fellow, the Archbishop of Canterbury, off, without harping a little upon his oath, which he has taken to preserve the rights and property of the church of Canterbury: I am quite sure so truly good a man, as from the bottom of my heart I believe him to be, has some line of argument by which he defends himself; but till I know it, I cannot of course say I am convinced by it. The common defence for breaking oaths is, that they are contracts made with another party, which the Creator is called to witness, and from which the swearer is absolved, if those for whom the oath is taken choose to release him from his obligation. With whom, then, is the contract made by the archbishop? Is it with the community at large? If so, nothing but an act of Parliament (as the community at large have no other organ) could absolve him from his oath; but three years before any act is passed, he puts his name to a plan for taking away two-thirds of the property of the church of Canterbury. If the contract is not made with the community at large, but with the church of Canterbury, every member of it is in decided hostility to his scheme. O'Connell takes an oath that he will not injure nor destroy the Protestant church; but in promoting the destruction of some of the Irish bishoprics, he may plead that he is sacrificing a part to preserve the whole, and benefiting, not injuring, the Protestant establishment. But the archbishop does not swear to a general truth, where the principle may be preserved, though there is an apparent deviation from the words; but he swears to a very narrow and limited oath, that he will not alienate the possessions of the church of Canterbury. A friend of mine has suggested to me that his grace has, perhaps, forgotten the oath; but this cannot be, for the first Protestant in Europe of course makes a memorandum in his pocket-book of all the oaths he takes to do, or to abstain. The oath, however, may be less present to the archbishop's memory, from the fact of his not having taken the oath in person, but by the medium of a gentleman sent down by the coach to take it for him—a practice which, though I believe it to have been long established in the church, surprised me, I confess, not a little. A proxy to vote, if you please—a proxy to consent to arrangements of estates, if wanted; but a proxy sent down in the Canterbury fly, to take the Creator to witness that the archbishop, detained in town by business or pleasure, will never violate that foundation of piety over which he presides—all this seems to me an act of the most extraordinary indolence ever recorded in history. If an ecclesiastic, not a bishop, may express any opinion on the reforms of the church, I recommend that archbishops and bishops should take no more oaths by proxy; but as they do not wait upon the sovereign or the prime minister, or even any of the cabinet, by proxy, that they should also perform all religious acts in their own person. This practice would have been abolished in Lord John's first bill, if other grades of churchmen as well as bishops had been made commissioners. But the motto was—

"Peace to the palaces—war to the manses."

I have been informed, though I will not answer for the accuracy of the information, that this vicarious oath is likely to produce a scene which would have puzzled the *Ductor Dubitantium.* The attorney who took the oath for the archbishop, is, they say, seized with religious horrors at the approaching confiscation of Canterbury property, and has in vain tendered back his 6*s.* 8*d.* for taking the oath. The archbishop refuses to accept it; and feeling himself light and disencumbered, wisely keeps the saddle upon the back of the writhing and agonized scrivener. I have talked it over with several clergymen, and the general opinion is, that the scrivener will suffer.

I cannot help thinking that a great opportunity opens itself for improving the discipline of the church, by means of those chapters which Lord John Russell* is so anxious to destroy; divide the diocese among the members of the chapter, and make them responsible for the superintendence and inspection of the clergy in their various divisions under the supreme control of the bishop; by a few additions they might be made the bishops' council for the trial of delinquent clergymen. They might be made a kind of college for the general care of education in the diocese, and ap-

* I only mention Lord John Russell's name so often, because the management of the church measures devolves upon him. He is, beyond all comparison, the ablest man in the whole administration, and to such a degree is he superior, that the government could not exist a moment without him. If the foreign secretary were to retire, we should no longer be nibbling ourselves into disgrace on the coast of Spain. If the amiable Lord Glenelg were to leave us, we should feel secure in our colonial possessions. If Mr. Spring Rice were to go into holy orders, great would be the joy of the three per cents. A decent, good-looking head of the government might easily enough be found in lieu of Viscount Melbourne; but in five minutes after the departure of Lord John, the whole whig government would be dissolved into sparks of liberality and splinters of reform. There are six remarkable men, who, in different methods and in different degrees, are now affecting the interests of this country—the Duke of Wellington, Lord John Russell, Lord Brougham, Lord Lyndhurst, Sir Robert Peel, and O'Connell. Greater powers than all these are the phlegm of the English people—the great mass of good sense and intelligence diffused among them—and the number of those who have something to lose, and have not the slightest intention of losing it.

plied to a thousand useful purposes, which would have occurred to the commissioners, if they had not been so dreadfully frightened, and to the government, if their object had been, not to please the dissenters, but to improve the church.

The Bishop of Lincoln has lately published a pamphlet on the church question. His lordship is certainly not a man full of felicities and facilities, imitating none, and inimitable of any; nor does he work with infinite agitation of wit. His creation has blood without head, bones without marrow, eyes without speculation. He has the art of saying nothing in many words beyond any man that ever existed; and when he seems to have made a proposition, he is so dreadfully frightened at it, that he proceeds as quickly as possible, in the ensuing sentence, to disconnect the subject and the predicate, and to avert the dangers he has incurred:—but as he is a bishop, and will be therefore more read than I am, I cannot pass him over. His lordship tells us, that it was at one time under consideration of the commissioners whether they should not tax all benefices above a certain value, in order to raise a fund for the improvement of smaller livings; and his lordship adds, with the greatest innocence, that the considerations which principally weighed with the commissioners in inducing them not to adopt the plan of taxation, was that they understood the clergy in general to be decidedly averse to it; so that the plan of the commission was, that the greater benefices should pay to the little, while the bishops themselves—the Archbishop of Canterbury with his 15,000*l.* a year, and the Bishop of London with his 10,000*l.* a year—were not to subscribe a single farthing for that purpose. Why does John, Bishop of Lincoln, mention these distressing schemes of the commission, which we are certain would have been met with a general yell of indignation from one end of the kingdom to another? Surely it must have occurred to this excellent prelate that the bishops would have been compelled, by mere shame, to have contributed to the fund which they were about to put upon the backs of the more opulent parochial clergy; surely a moment's reflection must have taught them that the safer method by far was to confiscate cathedral property.

The idea of abandoning this taxation, because it was displeasing to the clergy at large, is not unentertaining as applied to a commission who treated the clergy with the greatest contempt, and did not even notice the communications from cathedral bodies upon the subject of the most serious and extensive confiscations.*

"The plan of taxation, therefore," says the bishop, "being abandoned, it was evident that the funds for the augmentation of poor livings, and for the supply of the spiritual wants of populous districts, must be drawn from the episcopal and cathedral revenues; that is, from the revenues from which the legislature seems to have a peculiar right to draw the funds for the general supply of the religious wants of the people; because they arise from benefices, of which the patronage is either actually in the crown, or is derivative from the crown. In the case of the episcopal revenues, the commissioners had already carried the principle of redistribution as far as they thought that it could, with due allowance for the various demands upon the incomes of the bishops, be carried. The only remaining source, therefore, was to be found in the cathedral revenues; and the commissioners proceeded, in the execution of the duties prescribed to them, to consider in what manner

* Upon this subject I think it right to introduce the following letters, the first of which was published Jan. 23, 1838:—

TO THE EDITOR OF THE TIMES.

"Sir,—I feel it to be consistent with my duty, as secretary to the church commissioners, to notice a statement emanating from a quarter which would seem to give it authenticity—that, of seven chapter memorials addressed to the board, the receipt of one was only acknowledged.

"It is strictly within my province to acknowledge communications made to the commissioners as a body, either directly or through me; and it is part of their general instructions to me that I should do so in all cases.

"To whatever extent, therefore, the statement may be true, or whatever may be its value, it is clear that it cannot attach to the commissioners, but that I alone am responsible.

"In the execution of my office, I have endeavoured, in the midst of my other duties, to conduct an extensive correspondence in accordance to what I knew to be the feelings and wishes of the commissioners, and to treat every party in communication with them with attention and respect.

"If, at some period of more than usual pressure, any accidental omission may have occurred, or may hereafter occur, involving an appearance of discourtesy, it is for me to offer, as I now do, explanation and apology.

"I am, sir, your obedient humble servant,

"C. K. MURRAY.

"*Whitehall Place, Jan.* 21."

TO THE EDITOR OF THE TIMES.

"Sir,—A more indiscreet and extraordinary communication than that which appears in your own paper of the 23d instant, signed by Mr. C. K. Murray, I never read. '*Apparet domus intus.*' It is now clear how the commission has been worked. Where communications from the oldest ecclesiastical bodies, upon the most important of all subjects to them and to the kingdom, were received by the greatest prelates and noblemen of the land, acting under the king's commission, I should have thought that answers suitable to the occasion would, in each case, have been dictated by the commission; that such answers would have been entered on the minutes, and read on the board-day next ensuing.

"Is Mr. C. K. Murray quite sure that this, which is done at all boards on the most trifling subjects, was not done at his board, in the most awful confiscation ever known in England? Is he certain that spoliation was in no instance sweetened by civility, and injustice never vanished by forms? Were all the decencies and proprieties, which ought to regulate the intercourse of such great bodies, left without a single inquiry from the commissioner, to a gentleman who seems to have been seized with six distinct fits of oblivion on six separate occasions, any one of which required all that attention to decorum and that accuracy of memory for which secretaries are selected and paid?

"According to Mr. C. K. Murray's account, the only order he received from the board was, 'If any prebendary calls, or any cathedral writes, desiring not to be destroyed, just say the communication has been received;' and even this, Mr. Murray tells us, he has not done, and that no one of the king's commissioners—archbishops, bishops, marquises, earls—ever asked him whether he had done it or not—though any one of these great people would have swooned away at the idea of not answering the most trifling communication from any other of these great people.

"Whatever else these commissioners do, they had better not bring their secretary forward again. They may feel wind-bound by public opinion, but they must choose, as a sacrifice, a better Iphigenia than Mr. C. K. Murray.

"SYDNEY SMITH."

those revenues might be rendered conducive to the efficiency of the established church."

This is very good episcopal reasoning; but is it true? The bishops and commissioners wanted a fund to endow small livings; they did not touch a farthing of their own incomes, only distributed them a little more equally; and proceeded lustily at once to confiscate cathedral property. But why was it necessary, if the fund for small livings was such a paramount consideration, that the future archbishops of Canterbury should be left with two palaces, and 15,000*l.* per annum? Why is every future bishop of London to have a palace in Fulham, a house in St. James's Square, and 10,000*l.* a-year? Could not all the episcopal functions be carried on well and effectually with the half of these incomes? Is it necessary that the Archbishop of Canterbury should give feasts to aristocratic London; and that the domestics of the prelacy should stand with swords and bag-wigs round pig, and turkey, and venison, to defend, as it were, the orthodox gastronome from the fierce Unitarian, the fell Baptist, and all the famished children of dissent? I don't object to all this; because I am sure that the method of prizes and blanks is the best method of supporting a church, which must be considered as very slenderly endowed, if the whole were equally divided among the parishes; but if my opinion were different—if I thought the important improvement was to equalize preferment in the English church—that such a measure was not the one thing foolish, but the one thing needful—I should take care, as a mitred commissioner, to reduce my own species of preferment to the narrowest limits, before I proceeded to confiscate the property of any other grade of the church. I could not, as a conscientious man, leave the Archbishop of Canterbury with 15,000*l.* a-year, and make a fund by annihilating residentiaries at Bristol of 500*l.* This comes of calling a meeting of one species of cattle only. The horned cattle say,—"If you want any meat, kill the sheep; don't meddle with us, there is no beef to spare." They said this, however, to the lion; and the cunning animal, after he had gained all the information necessary for the destruction of the muttons, and learned how well and widely they pastured, and how they could be most conveniently eaten up, turns round and informs the cattle, who took him for their best and tenderest friend, that he means to eat them up also. Frequently did Lord John meet the destroying bishops; much did he commend their daily heaps of ruins; sweetly did they smile on each other, and much charming talk was there of meteorology and catarrh, and the particular cathedral they were pulling down at each period;* till one fine day, the home secretary, with a voice more bland, and a look more ardently affectionate, than that which the masculine mouse bestows on his nibbling female, informed them that the government meant to take all the church property into their own hands, to pay the rates out of it, and deliver the residue to the rightful possessors. Such an effect, they say, was never before produced by a *coup de théâtre.* The commission was separated in an instant: London clinched his fist; Canterbury was hurried out by his chaplains, and put into a warm bed; a solemn vacancy spread itself over the face of Gloucester; Lincoln was taken out in strong hysterics.—What a noble scene Serjeant Talfourd would have made of this! Why are such talents wasted on *Ion* and the *Athenian Captive?*

But, after all, what a proposition! "You don't make the most of your money: I will take your property into my hands, and see if I cannot squeeze a penny out of it: you shall be regularly paid all you now receive, only if any thing more can be made of it, that we will put into our own pockets."—"Just pull off your neck-cloth, and lay your head under the guillotine, and I will promise not to do you any harm: just get ready for confiscation; give up the management of all your property; make us the ostensible managers of every thing; let us be informed of the most minute value of all, and depend upon it, we will never injure you to the extent of a single farthing."—"Let me get my arms about you," says the bear; "I have not the smallest intention of squeezing you."—"Trust your finger in my mouth," says the mastiff; "I will not fetch blood."

Where is this to end? If government are to take into their own hands all property which is not managed with the greatest sharpness and accuracy, they may squeeze 1-8th per cent. out of the Turkey Company; Spring Rice would become director of the Hydro-impervious Association, and clear a few hundreds for the treasury. The British Roasted Apple Society is notoriously mismanaged, and Lord John and Brother Lister, by a careful selection of fruit, and a judicious management of fuel, would soon get it up to par.

I think, however, I have heard at the Political Economy Club, where I have sometimes had the honour of being a guest, that no trades should be carried on by governments. That they have enough to do of their own, without undertaking other persons' business. If any savings in the mode of managing ecclesiastical leases could be made, great deduction from these savings must be allowed for the jobbing and *Gaspillage* of general boards, and all the old servants of the church, displaced by this measure, must receive compensation.

The whig government, they will be vexed to hear, would find a great deal of patronage forced upon them by this measure. Their favourite human animal, the barrister of six years' standing, would be called into action.—The whole earth is, in fact, in commission, and the human race, saved from the flood, are delivered over to barristers of six years' standing. *The onus probandi* now lies upon any man who says he is not a commissioner; the only doubt on seeing a new man among the whigs is, not whether he is a commissioner or not, but whether it is tithes, poor-laws, boundaries of boroughs, church leases, charities, or any of the thousand human concerns which are now worked by commissioners, to the infinite comfort and satisfaction of mankind, who seem

* "What cathedral are we pulling down to-day?" was the standing question at the commission.

in these days to have found out the real secret of *life*—*the* one *thing* wanting to sublunary happiness—the great principle of commission, and six years' barristration.

Then, if there is a better method of working ecclesiastical estates—if any thing can be gained for the church—why is not the church to have it? why is it not applied to church purposes? what right has the state to seize it? If I give you an estate, I give it you not only in its present state, but I give to you all the improvements which can be made upon it—all that mechanical, botanical, and chemical knowledge may do hereafter for its improvement—all the ameliorations which care and experience can suggest, in setting, improving, and collecting your rents. Can there be such miserable equivocation as to say—I leave you your property, but I do not leave to you all the improvements which your own wisdom, or the wisdom of your fellow-creatures, will enable you to make of your property? How utterly unworthy of a whig government is such a distinction as this!

Suppose the same sort of plan had been adopted in the reign of Henry VIII., and the legislature had said,—You shall enjoy all you now have, but every farthing of improved revenue, after this period, shall go into the pocket of the state—it would have been impossible by this time that the church could have existed at all: and why may not such a measure be as fatal hereafter to the existence of a church, as it would have been to the present generation, if it had been brought forward at the time of the Reformation?

There is some safety in dignity. A church is in danger when it is degraded. It costs mankind much less to destroy it when an institution is associated with mean, and not with elevated ideas. I should like to see the subject in the hands of H. B. I would entitle the print—

"The Bishops' Saturday Night; or, Lord John Russell at the Pay-Table."

The bishops should be standing before the pay-table, and receiving their weekly allowance; Lord John and Spring Rice counting, ringing, and biting the sovereigns, and the Bishop of Exeter insisting that the chancellor of the exchequer has given him one which was not weight. Viscount Melbourne, in high chuckle, should be standing, with his hat on, and his back to the fire, delighted with the contest; and the deans and canons should be in the back-ground, waiting till their turn came, and the bishops were paid; and among them a canon, of large composition, urging them on not to give way too much to the bench. Perhaps I should add the president of the board of trade, recommending the truck principle to the bishops, and offering to pay them in hassocks, cassocks, aprons, shovel-hats, sermon-cases, and such like ecclesiastical gear.

But the madness and folly of such a measure are in the revolutionary feeling which it excites. A government taking into its hands such an immense value of property! What a lesson of violence and change to the mass of mankind! Do you want to accustom Englishmen to lose all confidence in the permanence of their institutions—to inure them to great acts of plunder—and to draw forth all the latent villanies of human nature? The whig leaders are honest men, and cannot mean this, but these foolish and inconsistent measures are the horn-book and infantile lessons of revolution; and remember, it requires no great time to teach mankind to rob and murder on a great scale.

I am astonished that these ministers neglect the common precaution of a foolometer,* with which no public man should be unprovided; I mean, the acquaintance and society of three or four regular British fools as a test of public opinion. Every cabinet minister should judge of all his measures by his foolometer, as a navigator crowds or shortens sail by the barometer in his cabin. I have a very valuable instrument of that kind myself, which I have used for many years; and I would be bound to predict, with the utmost nicety, by the help of this machine, the precise effect which any measure would produce upon public opinion. Certainly, I never saw any thing so decided as the effects produced upon my machine by the rate bill. No man who had been accustomed in the smallest degree to handle philosophical instruments could have doubted of the storm which was coming on, or of the thoroughly un-English scheme in which the ministry had so rashly engaged themselves.

I think, also, that it is a very sound argument against this measure of church rates, that estates have been bought liable to these payments, and that they have been deducted from the purchase-money. And what, also, if a dissenter were a republican as well as a dissenter—a case which has sometimes happened; and what if our anti-monarchical dissenter were to object to the expenses of kingly government? Are his scruples to be respected, and his taxes diminished, and the queen's privy purse to be subjected and exposed to the intervening and economical squeeze of government commissioners?

But these lucubrations upon church rates are an episode; I must go back to John, Bishop of Lincoln. All other cathedrals are fixed at four prebendaries; St. Paul's and Lincoln, having only three, are increased to the regulation pattern of four. I call this useless and childish. The Bishop of Lincoln says, there were more residentiaries before the Reformation; but if for three hundred years three residentiaries have been found to be sufficient, what a strangely feeble excuse it is for adding another, and diverting 3000*l.* per annum from the small living fund, to say, that there were more residentiaries three hundred years ago.

Must every thing be good and right that is

* Mr. Fox very often used to say, "I wonder what Lord B. will think of this." Lord B. happened to be a very stupid person, and the curiosity of Mr. Fox's friends was naturally excited to know why he attached such importance to the opinion of such an ordinary common-place person. "His opinion," said Mr. Fox, "is of much more importance than you are aware of. He is an exact representative of all common-place English prejudices, and what Lord B. thinks of any measure, the great majority of English people will think of it." It would be a good thing if every cabinet of philosophers had a Lord B among them.

done by bishops? Is there one rule of right for them, and another for the rest of the world? Now here are two commissioners, whose express object is to constitute, out of the large emoluments of the dignitaries, a fund for the poorer parochial clergy; and in the very heat and fervour of confiscation, they build up two new places, utterly useless and uncalled for, take 3000*l.* from the charity fund to pay them, and they give patronage of these places to themselves. Is there a single epithet in the language of invective which would not have been levelled at lay commissioners who had attempted the same thing? If it is necessary to do so much for archdeacons, why might not one of the three residentaries be archdeacon in virtue of his prebend? If government make bishops, they may surely be trusted to make archdeacons. I am very willing to ascribe good motives to these commissioners, who are really worthy and very sensible men, but I am perfectly astonished that they were not deterred from such a measure by appearances, and by the motives which, whether rightly or wrongly, would be imputed to them. In not acting so as to be suspected, the Bishop of London should resemble Cæsar's wife. In other respects, this excellent prelate would not have exactly suited for the partner of that great and self-willed man; and an idea strikes me, that it is not impossible he might have been in the senate-house instead of Cæsar.

Lord John Russell gives himself great credit for not having confiscated church property, but merely remodelled and redivided it. I accuse him not of plunder, but I accuse him of taking the Church of England, rolling it about as a cook does a piece of dough, with a rolling pin, cutting a hundred different shapes with all the plastic fertility of a confectioner, and without the most distant suspicion that he can ever be wrong, or ever be mistaken: with a certainty that he can anticipate the consequences of every possible change in human affairs. There is not a better man in England than Lord John Russell; but his failure is, that he is utterly ignorant of all moral fear; there is nothing he would not undertake. I believe he would perform the operation for the stone—build St. Peter's—or assume (with or without ten minutes' notice) the command of the Channel fleet; and no one would discover by his manner that the patient had died—the church tumbled down—and the Channel fleet been knocked to atoms. I believe his motives are always pure, and his measures often able; but they are endless, and never done with that pedetentous pace and pedetentous mind in which it behoves the wise and virtuous improver to walk. He alarms the wise liberals; and it is impossible to sleep soundly while he has the command of the watch.*

Do not say, my dear Lord John, that I am too severe upon you. A thousand years have scarce sufficed to make our blessed England what it is; an hour may lay it in the dust; and can you, with all your talents, renovate its shattered splendour—can you recall back its virtues—can you vanquish time and fate? But, alas! you want to shake the world, and to be the thunderer of the scene!

Now what is the end of what I have written? Why every body was in a great fright; and a number of bishops, huddled together, and talking of their great sacrifices, began to destroy other people's property, and to take other people's patronage: and all the fright is over now; and all the bishops are very sorry for what they have done, and regret extremely the destruction of the cathedral dignitaries, but don't know how to get out of the foolish scrape. The whig ministry persevere to please Joseph and his brethren, and the destroyers; and the good sense of the matter is to fling out the dean and chapter bill, as it now stands, and to bring in another next year—making a fund out of all the non-resident prebends, annexing some of the others, and adopting many of the enactments contained in the present bill.

THIRD LETTER TO ARCHDEACON SINGLETON.

My dear Sir,

I hope this is the last letter you will receive from me on church matters. I am tired of the subject; so are you; so is every body. In spite of many bishops' charges, I am unbroken; and remain entirely of the same opinion as I was two or three years since—that the mutilation of deans and chapters is a rash, foolish, and imprudent measure.

I do not think the charge of the Bishop of London successful, in combating those arguments which have been used against the impending dean and chapter bill; but it is quiet, gentleman-like, temperate, and written in a manner which entirely becomes the high office and character which he bears.

I agree with him in saying that the plurality and residence bill is, upon the whole, a very good bill;—nobody, however, knows better than the Bishop of London the various changes it has undergone, and the improvements it has received. I could point out fourteen or fifteen very material alterations for the better, since it came out of the hands of the commission, and all *bearing materially upon the happiness and*

* Another peculiarity of the Russells is, that they never alter their opinions: they are an excellent race, but they must be trepanned before they can be convinced.

comfort of the parochial clergy. I will mention only a few:—the bill, as originally introduced, gave the bishop a power, when he considered the duties of the parish to be improperly performed, to suspend the clergyman and appoint a curate with a salary. Some impious persons thought it not impossible that occasionally such a power might be maliciously and vindictively exercised, and that some check to it should be admitted into the bill; accordingly, under the existing act, an ecclesiastical jury is to be summoned, and into that jury the defendant clergyman may introduce a friend of his own.

If a clergyman, from illness or any other overwhelming necessity, was prevented from having two services, he was exposed to an information and penalty. In answering the bishop, he was subjected to two opposite sets of penalties—the one for saying *yes;* the other for saying *no:* he was amenable to the needless and impertinent scrutiny of a rural dean before he was exposed to the scrutiny of the bishop. Curates might be forced upon him by subscribing parishioners, and the certainty of a schism established in the parish; a curate might have been forced upon *present* incumbents by the bishop without any complaint made; upon men who took, or, perhaps, bought their livings under very different laws; all these acts of injustice are done away with, but it is not to the credit of the framers of the bill that they were ever admitted, and they completely justify the opposition with which the bill was received by me and by others. I add, however, with great pleasure, that when these and other objections were made, they were heard with candour, and promised to be remedied by the Archbishop of Canterbury and the Bishop of London and Lord John Russell.

I have spoken of the power to issue a commission to inquire into the well-being of any parish: a vindictive and malicious bishop might, it is true, convert this, which was intended for the protection, to the oppression of the clergy—afraid to dispossess a clergyman of his own authority, he might attempt to do the same thing under the cover of a jury of his ecclesiastical creatures. But I can hardly conceive such baseness in the prelate, or such infamous subserviency in the agents. An honest and respectable bishop will remember that the very issue of such a commission is a serious slur upon the character of a clergyman; he will do all he can to prevent it by private monition and remonstrance; and if driven to such an act of power, he will, of course, state to the accused clergyman the subjects of accusation, the names of his accusers, and give him ample time for his defence. If, upon anonymous accusation, he subjects a clergyman to such an investigation, or refuses to him any advantage which the law gives to every accused person, he is an infamous, degraded, and scandalous tyrant: but I cannot believe there is such a man to be found upon the bench.

There is in this new bill a very humane clause, (though not introduced by the commission), enabling the widow of the deceased clergyman to retain possession of the parsonage-house for two months after the death of the incumbent. It ought, in fairness, to be extended to the heirs, executors, and administrators of the incumbent. It is a great hardship that a family settled in a parish for fifty years, perhaps, should be torn up by the roots in eight or ten days; and the interval of two months, allowing time for repairs, might put to rest many questions of dilapidation.

To the bishop's power of intruding a curate, without any complaint on the part of the parish that the duty has been inadequately performed, I retain the same objections as before. It is a power which, without this condition, will be unfairly and partially exercised. The first object I admit is not the provision of the clergyman, but the care of the parish; but one way of taking care of parishes is to take care that clergymen are not treated with tyranny, partiality, and injustice; and the best way of effecting this is to remember that their superiors have the same human passions as other people, and not to trust them with a power which may be so grossly abused, and which (incredible as the Bishop of London may deem it) *has been*, in some instances, grossly abused.

I cannot imagine what the bishop means by saying, that the members of cathedrals do not, in virtue of their office, bear any part in the parochial instruction of the people. This is a fine deceitful word, the word *parochial*, and eminently calculated to coax the public. If he means simply that cathedrals do not belong to parishes, that St. Paul's is not the parish church of Upper Puddicomb, and that the vicar of St. Fiddlefrid does not officiate in Westminster Abbey: all this is true enough, but do they not in the most material points instruct the people precisely in the same manner as the parochial clergy? Are not prayers and sermons the most important means of spiritual instruction? And are there not eighteen or twenty services in every cathedral for one which is heard in parish churches? I have very often counted in the afternoon of week days in St. Paul's 150 people, and on Sundays it is full to suffocation. Is all this to go for nothing? and what right has the Bishop of London to suppose that there is not as much real piety in cathedrals, as in the most roadless, postless, melancholy, sequestered hamlet preached to by the most provincial, sequestered, bucolic clergyman in the queen's dominions?

A number of little children, it is true, do not repeat a catechism of which they do not comprehend a word; but it is rather rapid and wholesale to say, that the parochial clergy are spiritual instructors of the people, and that the cathedral clergy are only so in a very restricted sense. I say that in the most material points and acts of instruction, they are much more laborious and incessant than any parochial clergy. It might really be supposed, from the Bishop of London's reasoning, that some other methods of instruction took place in cathedrals than prayers and sermons can afford; that lectures were read on chemistry, or lessons given on dancing; or that it was a Mechanics' Institute, or a vast receptacle for hexameter and pentameter boys. His own most respectable chaplain, who is often there as a member of the body, will tell him that the prayers are strictly adhered to, according to the rubric, with the difference only that the service is beautifully chanted instead of being badly read; that instead of the atrocious bawling of parish churches, the anthems are sung with great taste and feeling: and if the preaching is not good, it is the fault of the Bishop of London, who has the whole range of London preachers from whom to make his selection. The real fact is, that, instead of being something materially different from the parochial clergy, as the commissioners wish to make them, the cathedral clergy are fellow-labourers with the parochial clergy, outworking them ten to one; but the commission having provided snugly for the bishops, have, by *the merest accident in the world*, entangled themselves in this quarrel with cathedrals.

"Had the question," says the bishop, "been proposed to the religious part of the community, whether, if no other means were to be found, the effective cure of souls should be provided for by the total suppression of those ecclesiastical corporations which have no cure of souls, nor bear any part in the parochial labours of the clergy; that question, I verily believe, would have been carried in the affirmative by an immense majority of suffrages." But suppose no other means could be found for the effective cure of souls than the suppression of bishops, does the Bishop of London imagine that the majority of suffrages would have been less immense? How idle to put such cases.

A pious man leaves a large sum of money in Catholic times for some purposes which are superstitious, and for others, such as preaching and reading prayers, which are applicable to all times; the superstitious usages are abolished, the pious usages remain: now the bishop must admit, if you take half or any part of this money from clergymen to whom it was given, and divide it for similar purposes among clergy to whom it was not given, you deviate materially from the intentions of the founder. These foundations are made *in loco;* in many of them the *locus* was, perhaps, the original cause of the gift. A man who founds an almshouse at Edmonton does not mean that the poor of Tottenham should avail themselves of it; and if he could have anticipated such a consequence, he would not have endowed any almshouse at all. Such is the respect for property, that the Court of Chancery, when it becomes impracticable to carry the will of the donor into execution, always attend to the *cy pres*, and apply the charitable fund to a purpose as germane as possible to the intention of the founder; but here, when men of Lincoln have left to Lincoln cathedral, and men of Hereford to Hereford, the commissioners seize it all, melt it into a common mass, and disperse it over the kingdom. Surely the Bishop of London cannot contend that this is not a greater deviation from the will of the founder than if the same people, remaining in the same place, receiving all the founder gave them, and doing all things not forbidden by the law, which the founder ordered, were to do something more than the founder ordered, were to become the guardians of education, the counsel to the bishop, and the curators of the diocese in his old age and decay.

The public are greater robbers and plunderers than any one in the public; look at the whole transaction; it is a mixture of meanness and violence. The country choose to have an established religion, and a resident parochial clergy, but they do not choose to build houses for their parochial clergy, or to pay them in many instances more than a butler or a coachman receives. How is this deficiency to be supplied? The heads of the church propose to this public to seize upon estates which never belonged to the public, and which were left for another purpose; and by the seizure of these estates to save that which ought to come out of the public purse.

Suppose Parliament were to seize upon all the almshouses in England, and apply them to the diminution of the poor-rate, what a number of ingenious arguments might be pressed into the service of this robbery: "Can any thing be more revolting than that the poor of Northumberland should be starving while the poor of the suburban hamlets are dividing the benefactions of the pious dead? '*We want for these purposes all that we can obtain from whatever sources derived.*'" I do not deny the right of parliament to do this, or any thing else; but I deny that it would be expedient, because I think it better to make any sacrifices, and to endure any evil, than to gratify this rapacious spirit of plunder and confiscation. Suppose these commissioner prelates firm and unmoved, when we were all alarmed, had told the public that the parochial clergy were badly provided for, and that it was the duty of that public to provide a proper support for their ministers;—suppose the commissioners, instead of leading them on to confiscations, had warned their fellow subjects against the base economy, and the perilous injustice of seizing on that which was not their own;—suppose they had called for water and washed their hands, and said, "We call you all to witness that we are innocent of this great ruin;"—does the Bishop of London imagine that the prelates who made such a stand would have gone down to posterity less respected and less revered than those men upon whose tombs it must (after all the enumerations of their virtues) be written, *that under their auspices and by their counsels the destruction of the English church began?* Pity that the Archbishop of Canterbury had not retained those feelings, when, at the first meeting of bishops, the Bishop of London proposed this *holy innovation* upon cathedrals, and the head of our church declared, with vehemence and indignation, that nothing in the earth would induce him to consent to it.

Si mens non læva fuisset,
Trojaque nunc stares, Priamique arx alta maneres.

"But," says the Lord Bishop of London, "you admit the principle of confiscation by proposing the confiscation and partition of prebends in the possession of non-residents."

I am thinking of something else, and I see all of a sudden a great blaze of light; I behold a great number of gentlemen in short aprons, neat purple coats, and gold buckles, rushing about with torches in their hands, calling each other "my lord," and setting fire to all the rooms in the house, and the people below delighted with the combustion; finding it impossible to turn them from their purpose, and finding that they are all what they are, by divine permission; I endeavour to direct their *holy innovations* into another channel; and I say to them, "my lords, had not you better set fire to the out of door offices, to the barns and stables, and spare this fine library and this noble drawing-room? Yonder are several cow-houses of which no use is made; pray direct your fury against them, and leave this beautiful and venerable mansion as you found it." If I address the divinely permitted in this manner, has the Bishop of London any right to call me a brother incendiary?

Our *holy innovator*, the Bishop of London, has drawn a very affecting picture *of sheep having no shepherd*, and of millions who have no *spiritual food;* our wants, he says, are most imperious; even if we were to tax large livings, we must still have the money of the cathedrals: no plea will exempt you, nothing can stop us, for the formation of benefices, and the endowment of new ones. We want (and he prints it in italics) for these purposes "*all that we can obtain from whatever sources derived.*" I never remember to have been more alarmed in my life than by this passage. I said to myself, the necessities of the church have got such complete hold of the imagination of this energetic prelate, who is so captivated by the holiness of his innovations, that all grades and orders of the church and all present and future interests will be sacrificed to it. I immediately rushed to the acts of Parliament, which I always have under my pillow, to see at once the worst of what had happened. I found present revenues of the bishops all safe; that is some comfort, I said to myself; Canterbury, 24,000*l.* or 25,000*l.* per annum; London, 18,000*l.* or 20,000*l.* I began to feel some comfort: "things are not so bad; the bishops do not mean to sacrifice to *sheep and shepherds' money* their present revenues; the Bishop of London is less violent and headstrong than I thought he would be." I looked a little further, and found that 15,000*l.* per annum is allotted to the future Archbishop of Canterbury, 10,000*l.* to the Bishop of London, 8000*l.* to Durham, and 8000*l.* each to Winchester and Ely. "Nothing of *sheep and shepherd* in all this," I exclaimed, and felt still more comforted. It was not till after the bishops were taken care of, and the revenues of the cathedrals came into full view, that I saw the perfect development of the *sheep and shepherd principle*, the deep and heartfelt compassion for spiritual labourers, and that inward groaning for the destitute state of the church, and that firm purpose, printed in italics, of taking *for these purposes all that could be obtained from whatever source derived;* and even in this delicious rummage of cathedral property, where all the fine church feelings of the bishop's heart could be indulged without costing the poor sufferer a penny, stalls for archdeacons in Lincoln and St. Paul's are, to the amount of 2000*l.* per annum, taken from the *sheep and shepherd fund*, and the patronage of them divided between two commissioners, the Bishop of London, and the Bishop of Lincoln, instead of being paid to additional *labourers in the vineyard.*

Has there been any difficulty, I would ask, in procuring archdeacons upon the very moderate pay they now receive? Can any clergyman be more thoroughly respectable than the present archdeacons in the see of London? but men bearing such an office in the church, it may be said, should be highly paid, and archbishops, who could very well keep up their dignity upon 7000*l.* per annum, are to be allowed 15,000*l.* I make no objection to all this; but then what becomes of all these heart-rending phrases of *sheep and shepherd*, and *drooping vineyards, and flocks without spiritual consolation?* The bishop's argument is, that the superfluous must give way to the necessary; but in fighting, the bishop should take great care that his cannons are not seized, and turned against himself. He has awarded to the bishops of England a superfluity as great as that which he intends to take from the cathedrals; and then, when he legislates for an order to which he does not belong, begins to remember the distresses of the lower clergy, paints them with all the colours of impassioned eloquence, and informs the cathedral institutions that he must have *every farthing he can lay his hand upon.* Is not this as if one, affected powerfully by a charity sermon, were to put his hands into another man's pocket, and cast, from what he had extracted, a liberal contribution into the plate?

I beg not to be mistaken; I am very far from considering the Bishop of London as a sordid and interested person; but this is a complete instance of how the best of men deceive themselves, where their interests are concerned. I have no doubt the bishop firmly imagined he was doing his duty; but there should have been men of all grades in the commission, some one to say a word for cathedrals and against bishops.

The bishop says "his antagonists have allowed three canons to be sufficient for St. Paul's, and, therefore, four must be sufficient for other cathedrals." Sufficient to read the prayers and preach the sermons, certainly, and so would *one* be; but not sufficient to excite, by the hope of increased rank and wealth, eleven thousand parochial clergy.

The most important and cogent arguments against the dean and chapter confiscations are passed over in silence in the bishop's charge This, in reasoning, is always the wisest and most convenient plan, and which all young bishops should imitate after the manner of this wary polemic. I object to the confiscation *because it will throw a great deal more of capital out of the parochial church than it will bring into it.* I am very sorry to come forward with so homely an argument, which shocks so many clergymen, and particularly those with the largest incomes, and the best bishoprics; but the truth is, the greater number of clergymen go into the church in order that they may derive a comfortable income *from* the church. Such men intend to do their duty, and they do it; but the duty is, however, not the motive, but the adjunct. If I was writing in gala and parade, I would not hold this language; but we are in earnest, and on business; and as very rash and hasty changes are founded upon contrary suppositions of the pure disinterestedness and perfect inattention to temporals in the clergy, we must get down at once to the solid rock without heeding how we disturb the turf and the flowers above. The parochial clergy maintain their present decent appearance quite as much by their own capital as by the income they derive from the church. I will now state the income and capital of seven clergymen, taken promiscuously in this neighbourhood:—No. 1. Living 200*l*., capital 12,000*l*.; No. 2. Living 800*l*., capital 15,000*l*.; No. 3. Living 500*l*., capital 12,000*l*.; No. 4. Living 150*l*., capital 10,000*l*.; No. 5. Living 800*l*., capital 12,000*l*.; No. 6. Living 150*l*., capital 1000*l*.; No. 7. Living 600*l*., capital 16,000*l*. I have diligently inquired into the circumstances of seven Unitarian and Wesleyan ministers, and I question much if the whole seven could make up 6000*l*. between them; and the zeal of enthusiasm of this last division is certainly not inferior to that of the former. Now here is a capital of 72,000*l*. carried into the church, which the confiscations of the commissioners would force out of it, by taking away the good things which were the temptation to its introduction. So that, by the old plan of paying by lottery, instead of giving a proper competence to each, not only do you obtain a parochial clergy upon much cheaper terms; but, from the gambling propensities of human nature, and the irresistible tendency to hope that they shall gain the great prizes, you tempt men into your service who keep up their credit and yours, not by your allowance, but by their own capital; and to destroy this wise and well-working arrangement, a great number of bishops, marquises, and John Russells, are huddled into a chamber, and, after proposing a scheme which will turn the English church into a collection of consecrated beggars, we are informed by the Bishop of London that it is an *holy innovation.*

I have no manner of doubt, that the immediate effect of passing the dean and chapter bill will be, that a great number of fathers and uncles, judging, and properly judging, that the church is a very altered and deterioriated profession, will turn the industry and capital of their *élèves* into another channel. My friend, Robert Eden, says "this is of the earth earthy:" be it so; I cannot help it, I paint mankind as I find them, and am not answerable for their defects. When an argument, taken from real life, and the actual condition of the world, is brought among the shadowy discussions of ecclesiastics, it always occasions terror and dismay; it is like Æneas stepping into Charon's boat, which carried only ghosts and spirits.

> Gemuit sub pondere cymba
> Sutilis.

The whole plan of the Bishop of London is a ptochogony—a generation of beggars. He purposes, out of the spoils of the cathedral, to create a thousand livings, and to give to the thousand clergymen 130*l*. per annum each; a Christian bishop proposing, in cold blood, to create a thousand livings of 130*l*. per annum each;—to call into existence a thousand of the most unhappy men on the face of the earth,—the sons of the poor, without hope, without the assistance of private fortune, chained to the soil, ashamed to live with their inferiors, unfit for the society of the better classes, and dragging about the English curse of poverty, without the smallest hope that they can ever shake it off. At present, such livings are filled by young men who have better hopes—who have reason to expect good property—who look forward to a college or a family living—who are the sons of men of some substance, and hope so to pass on to something better—who exist under the delusion of being hereafter deans and prebendaries—who are paid once by money, and three times by hope. Will the Bishop of London promise to the progeny of any of these thousand victims of the *holy innovation* that, if they behave well, one of them shall have his butler's place; another take care of the cedars and hyssops of his garden? Will he take their daughters for his nursery-maids? and may some of the sons of these "labourers of the vineyard" hope one day to ride the leaders from St. James's to Fulham? Here is hope—here is room for ambition—a field for genius, and a ray of amelioration! If these beautiful feelings of compassion are throbbing under the cassock of the bishop, he ought, in common justice to himself, to make them known.

If it were a scheme for giving ease and independence to any large bodies of clergymen, it might be listened to; but the revenues of the English church are such as to render this wholly and entirely out of the question. If you place a man in a village in the country, require that he should be of good manners and well educated; that his habits and appearance should be above those of the farmers to whom he preaches, if he has nothing else to expect (as would be the case in a church of equal division); and if, upon his village income, he is to support a wife and educate a family, without any power of making himself known in a remote and solitary situation, such a person ought to receive 500*l*. per annum, and be furnished with a house. There are about 10,700 parishes in England and Wales, whose average income is 285*l*. per annum. Now, to provide these incumbents with decent houses, to keep them in repair, and to raise the income of the incumbent to 500*l*. per annum, would require (if all the incomes of the bishops, deans and chapters of separate dignitaries, of sinecure rectories, were confiscated, and if the excess of all the livings in England above 500*l*. per annum were added to them,) a sum of two millions and a half in addition to the present income of the whole church; and no power on earth could persuade the present Parliament of Great Britain to grant a single shilling for that purpose. Now, is it possible to pay such a church upon any other principle than that of unequal division? The proposed pillage of the cathedral and college churches (omitting all consideration of the separate estate of dignitaries) would amount, divided among all the benefices in England, to about 5*l.* 12*s.* 6½*d.* per man: and this, which would not stop an hiatus in a cassock, and would drive out of the parochial church ten times as much as it brought into it, is the panacea for pauperism recommended by her majesty's commissioners.

But if this plan were to drive men of capital out of the church, and to pauperize the English clergy, where would the harm be? Could not all the duties of religion be performed as well by poor clergymen as by men of good substance? My great and serious apprehension is, that such would not be the case. There would be the greatest risk that your clergy would be fanatical, and ignorant; that their habits would be low and mean, and that they would be despised.

Then a picture is drawn of a clergyman with 130*l.* per annum, who combines all moral, physical, and intellectual advantages, a learned man, dedicating himself intensely to the care of his parish—of charming manners and dignified deportment—six feet two inches high, beautifully proportioned, with a magnificent countenance, expressive of all the cardinal virtues and the Ten Commandments,—and it is asked, with an air of triumph, if such a man as this will fall into contempt on account of his poverty? But substitute for him an average, ordinary, uninteresting minister; obese, dumpy, neither ill-natured nor good-natured; neither learned nor ignorant, striding over the stiles to church, with a second-rate wife—dusty and deliquescent—and four parochial children, full of catechism and bread and butter; or let him be seen in one of those Shem-Ham-and-Japhet buggies—made on Mount Ararat soon after the subsidence of the waters, driving in the High Street of Edmonton;*—among all his pecuniary, saponaceous, oleaginous parishioners. Can any man of common sense say that all these outward circumstances of the ministers of religion have no bearing on religion itself?

I ask the Bishop of London, a man of honour and conscience as he is, if he thinks five years will elapse before a second attack is made upon deans and chapters? Does he think, after reformers have tasted the flesh of the church, that they will put up with any other diet? Does he forget that deans and chapters are but mock turtle—that more delicious delicacies remain behind? Five years hence he will attempt to make a stand, and he will be laughed at and eaten up. In this very charge the bishop accuses the lay commissioners of another intended attack upon the property of the church, contrary to the clearest and most explicit stipulations (as he says) with the heads of the establishment.

Much is said of the conduct of the commissioners, but that is of the least possible consequence. They may have acted for the best, according to the then existing circumstances: they may seriously have intended to do their duty to the contrary; and I am far from saying or thinking they did not; but without the least reference to the commissioners, the question is, Is it wise to pass this bill, and to justify such an open and tremendous sacrifice of church property? Does public opinion now call for any such measure? is it a wise distribution of the funds of an ill-paid church? and will it not force more capital out of the parochial part of the church than it brings into it? If the bill is bad, it is surely not to pass out of compliment to the feelings of the Archbishop of Canterbury. If the project is hasty, it is not to be adopted to gratify the Bishop of London. The mischief to the church is surely a greater evil than the stultification of the commissioners, &c. If the physician has prescribed hastily, is the medicine to be taken to the death or disease of the patient? If the judge has condemned improperly, is the criminal to be hung, that the wisdom of the magistrate may not be impugned?*

But why are the commissioners to be stultified by the rejection of the measure? The measure may have been very good when it was recommended, and very objectionable now. I thought, and many men thought, that the church was going to pieces—that the affections of the common people were lost to the establishment; and that large sacrifices must be instantly made, to avert the effects of this temporary madness; but those days are gone by—and with them ought to be put aside measures, which might have been wise in those days, but are wise no longer.

After all, the Archbishop of Canterbury and the Bishop of London are good and placable men; and will ere long forget and forgive the successful efforts of their enemies in defeating this mis-ecclesiastic law.

Suppose the commission were now beginning to sit for the first time, will any man living say that they would make such reports as they have made? and that they would seriously propose such a tremendous revolution in church property? And if they would not, the inference is irresistible, that, to consult the feelings of two or three churchmen, we are complimenting away the safety of the church. Milton asked where the nymphs were when Lycidas perished? I ask where the bishops are when the remorseless deep is closing over the head of their beloved establishment?†

You must have read an attack upon me by the Bishop of Gloucester, in the course of which he says that I have not been appointed to my situation as canon of St. Paul's for my piety and learning, but because I am a scoffer and a jester. Is not this rather strong for a bishop, and does it not appear to you, Mr. Archdeacon, as rather too close an imitation of that language which is used in the apostolic

* A parish which the Bishop of London has the greatest desire to divide into little bits; but which appears quite as fit to preserve its integrity as St. James's, St. George's, or Kensington, all in the patronage of the bishop.

* "After the trouble the commissioners have taken (says Sir Robert), after the obloquy they have incurred," &c. &c. &c.

† What is the use of publishing separate charges, as the Bishops of Winchester, Oxford, and Rochester have done? Why do not the dissentient bishops form into a firm phalanx to save the church and fling out the bill?

occupation of trafficking in fish? Whether I have been appointed for my piety or not, must depend upon what this poor man means by piety. He means by that word, of course, a defence of all the tyrannical and oppressive abuses of the church which have been swept away within the last fifteen or twenty years of my life; the corporation and test acts; the penal laws against the Catholics; the compulsory marriages of dissenters, and all those disabling and disqualifying laws which were the disgrace of our church, and which he has always looked up to as the consummation of human wisdom. If piety consisted in the defence of these—if it was impious to struggle for their abrogation, I have, indeed, led an ungodly life.

There is nothing pompous gentlemen are so much afraid of as a little humour. It is like the objection of certain cephalic animalculæ to the use of small-tooth combs,—"Finger and thumb, precipitate powder, or any thing else you please; but for Heaven's sake no small-tooth combs!" After all, I believe, Bishop Monk has been the cause of much more laughter than ever I have been; I cannot account for it, but I never see him enter a room without exciting a smile on every countenance within it.

Dr. Monk is furious at my attacking the heads of the church; but how can I help it? If the heads of the church are at the head of the mob; if I find the best of men doing that which has in all times drawn upon the worst enemies of the human race the bitterest curses of history, am I to stop because the motives of these men are pure, and their lives blameless? I wish I could find a blot in their lives, or a vice in their motives. The whole power of the motion is in the character of the movers: feeble friends, false friends, and foolish friends, all cease to look upon the measure, and say, Would such a measure have been recommended by such men as the prelates of Canterbury and London, if it were not for the public advantage? And in this way, the great good of a religious establishment, now rendered moderate and compatible with all men's liberties and rights, is sacrificed to names; and the church destroyed from good breeding and etiquette! the real truth is, that Canterbury and London have been frightened—they have overlooked the effect of time and delay—they have been betrayed into a fearful and ruinous mistake. Painful as it is to teach men who ought to teach us, the legislature ought, while there is yet time, to awake and read them this lesson.

It is dangerous for a prelate to write; and whoever does it ought to be a very wise one. He has speculated why I was made a canon of St. Paul's. Suppose I were to follow his example, and, going through the bench of bishops, were to ask for what reason each man had been made a bishop; suppose I were to go into the county of Gloucester, &c. &c. &c.!!!!

I was afraid the bishop would attribute my promotion to the Edinburgh Review; but upon the subject of promotion by reviews, he preserves an impenetrable silence. If my excellent patron Earl Grey had any reasons of this kind, he may at least be sure that the reviews commonly attributed to me were really written by me. I should have considered myself as the lowest of created beings to have disguised myself in another man's wit, and to have received a reward to which I was not entitled.*

I presume that what has drawn upon me the indignation of this prelate, is the observations I have from time to time made on the conduct of the commissioners; of which he positively asserts himself to have been a member; but whether he was, or was not a member, I utterly acquit him of all possible blame, and of every species of imputation which may attach to the conduct of the commissioner. In using that word, I have always meant the Archbishop of Canterbury, the Bishop of London, and Lord John Russell; and have, honestly speaking, given no more heed to the Bishop of Gloucester than if he had been sitting in a commission of Bonzes in the court of Pekin.

To read, however, his lordship a lesson of good manners, I had prepared for him a chastisement which would have been echoed from the *Seagrave*, who banqueteth in the castle, to the idiot who spitteth over the bridge at Gloucester; but the following appeal struck my eye, and stopped my pen:—"Since that time, my inadequate qualifications have sustained an appalling diminution, by the affection of my eyes, which have impaired my vision, and the progress of which threatens to consign me to darkness; I beg the benefit of your prayers to the Father of all mercies, that he will restore me to better use of the visual organs, to be employed on his service; or that he will inwardly illumine the intellectual vision, with a particle of that divine ray, which his Holy Spirit can alone impart."

It might have been better taste, perhaps, if a mitred invalid, in describing his bodily infirmities before a church full of clergymen, whose prayers he asked, had been a little more sparing in the abuse of his enemies; but a good deal must be forgiven to the sick. I wish that every Christian was as well aware as this poor bishop of what he needed from divine assistance; and in the supplication for the restoration of his sight and the improvement of his understanding, I must fervently and cordially join.

I was much amused with what old Hermann† says of the Bishop of London's Æschylus. "We find," he says, "*a great arbitrariness of proceeding, and much boldness of innovation, guided by no sure principle;*" here it is: *qualis ab incepto.* He begins with Æschylus, and ends with the Church of England; begins with profane, and ends with holy innovations—scratch-

---

* I understand that the bishop bursts into tears every now and then, and says that I have set him the name of Simon, and that all the bishops now call him Simon. Simon of Gloucester, however, after all, is a real writer, and how could I know that Dr. Monk's name was Simon? When tutor in Lord Corrington's family, he was called by the endearing, though somewhat unmajestic name of *Dick;* and if I had thought about his name at all, I should have called him Richard of Gloucester.

† Ueber die behandlung der Griechischen Dichter be den Engländern, Von Gottfried Hermann. Wiemar Jahrbucher, vol. liv. 1831.

ing out old readings which every commentator had sanctioned, abolishing ecclesiastical dignities which every reformer had spared; thrusting an anapest into a verse which will not bear it; and intruding a canon into a cathedral which does not want it; and this is the prelate by whom the proposed reform of the church has been principally planned, and to whose practical wisdom the legislature is called upon to defer. The Bishop of London is a man of very great ability, humane, placable, generous, munificent, very agreeable, but not to be trusted with great interests where calmness and judgment are required; unfortunately, my old and amiable school-fellow, the Archbishop of Canterbury, has melted away before him, and sacrificed that wisdom on which we all founded our security.

Much writing and much talking are very tiresome; and, above all, they are so to men who, living in the world, arrive at those rapid and just conclusions which are only to be made by living in the world. This bill passed, every man of sense acquainted with human affairs must see, that, as far as the church is concerned, the thing is at an end. From Lord John Russell, the present improver of the church, we shall descend to Hume, from Hume to Roebuck, and after Roebuck we shall receive our last improvements from Dr. Wade: plunder will follow after plunder, degradation after degradation. The church is gone, and what remains is not life, but sickness, spasm, and struggle.

Whatever happens, I am not to blame; I have fought my fight.—Farewell.

SYDNEY SMITH.

LETTER

ON THE

CHARACTER OF SIR JAMES MACKINTOSH.

My dear Sir,

You ask for some of your late father's letters: I am sorry to say I have none to send you. Upon principle, I keep no letters except those on business. I have not a single letter from him, nor from any human being in my possession.

The impression which the great talents and amiable qualities of your father made upon me, will remain as long as I remain. When I turn from living spectacles of stupidity, ignorance, and malice, and wish to think better of the world—I remember my great and benevolent friend Mackintosh.

The first points of character which every body noticed in him were the total absence of envy, hatred, malice, and uncharitableness. He could not hate—he did not know how to set about it. The gall-bladder was omitted in his composition, and if he could have been persuaded into any scheme of revenging himself upon an enemy, I am sure (unless he had been narrowly watched) it would have ended in proclaiming the good qualities, and promoting the interests of his adversary. Truth had so much more power over him than anger, that (whatever might be the provocation) he could not misrepresent, nor exaggerate. In questions of passion and party, he stated facts as they were, and reasoned fairly upon them, placing his happiness and pride in equitable discrimination. Very fond of talking, he heard patiently, and, not averse to intellectual display, did not forget that others might have the same inclination as himself.

Till subdued by age and illness, his conversation was more brilliant and instructive than that of any human being I ever had the good fortune to be acquainted with. His memory (vast and prodigious as it was) he so managed as to make it a source of pleasure and instruction, rather than that dreadful engine of colloquial oppression into which it is sometimes erected. He remembered things, words, thoughts, dates, and every thing that was wanted. His language was beautiful, and might have gone from the fireside to the press; but though his ideas were always clothed in beautiful language, the clothes were sometimes too big for the body, and common thoughts were dressed in better and larger apparel than they deserved. He certainly had this fault, but it was not one of frequent commission.

He had a method of putting things so mildly and interrogatively, that he always procured the readiest reception for his opinions. Addicted to reasoning in the company of able men, he had two valuable habits, which are rarely met with in great reasoners—he never broke in upon his opponent, and always avoided strong and vehement assertions. His reasoning commonly carried conviction, for he was cautious in his positions, accurate in his deductions, aimed only at truth. The ingenious side was commonly taken by some one else; the interests of truth were protected by Mackintosh.

His good-nature and candour betrayed him into a morbid habit of eulogizing every body—a habit which destroyed the value of commendations, that might have been to the young (if more sparingly distributed) a reward of virtue and a motive to exertion. Occasionally he took fits of an opposite nature; and I have seen him abating and dissolving pompous gentlemen with the most successful ridicule. He certainly had a good deal of humour; and I remember, amongst many other examples of it, that he kept us for two or three hours in a roar of laughter, at a dinner-party at his own house, playing upon the simplicity of a Scotch cousin, who had mistaken me for my gallant synonym, the hero of Acre. I never saw a more perfect comedy, nor heard ridicule so long and so well sustained. Sir James had not only humour, but he had wit also; at least, new and sudden relations of ideas flashed across his mind in reasoning, and produced the same effect as wit, and would have been called wit, if a sense of their utility and importance had not often overpowered the admiration of novelty, and entitled them to the higher name of wisdom. Then the great thoughts and fine sayings of the great men of all ages were intimately present to his recollection, and came out dazzling and delighting in his conversation. Justness of thinking was a strong feature in his understanding; he had a head in which nonsense and error could hardly vegetate: it was a soil utterly unfit for them. If his display in conversation had been only in maintaining splendid paradoxes, he would soon have wearied those he lived with; but no man could live long and intimately with your father without finding that he was gaining upon doubt, correcting error, enlarging the boundaries, and strengthening the foundations of truth. It was worth while to listen to a master, whom not himself, but nature had appointed to the office, and who taught what it was not easy to forget, by methods which it was not easy to resist.

Curran, the master of the rolls, said to Mr. Grattan, "You would be the greatest man of your age, Grattan, if you would buy a few yards of red tape, and tie up your bills and papers." This was the fault or misfortune of your excellent father; he never knew the use of red tape, and was utterly unfit for the common business of life. That a guinea represented a quantity of shillings, and that it would barter for a quantity of cloth, he was well aware; but the accurate number of the baser coin, or the just measurement of the manufactured article, to which he was entitled for his gold, he could never learn, and it was impossible to teach him. Hence his life was often an example of the ancient and melancholy struggle of genius, with the difficulties of existence.

I have often heard Sir James Mackintosh say of himself, that he was born to be the professor of an university. Happy, and for ages celebrated, would have been the university, which had so possessed him, but in this view he was unjust to himself. Still, however, his style of speaking in Parliament was certainly more academic than forensic; it was not sufficiently short and quick for a busy and impatient assembly. He often spoke over the heads of his hearers—was too much in advance of feeling for their sympathies, and of reasoning for their comprehension. He began too much at the beginning, and went too much to the right and left of the question, making rather a lecture or a dissertation than a speech. His voice was bad and nasal; and though nobody was in reality more sincere, he seemed not only not to feel, but hardly to think what he was saying.

Your father had very little science, and no great knowledge of physics. His notions of his early pursuit—the study of medicine—were imperfect and antiquated, and he was but an indifferent classical scholar, for the Greek language has never crossed the Tweed in any great force. In history the whole stream of time was open before him; he had looked into every moral and metaphysical question from Plato to Paley, and had waded through morasses of international law, where the step of no living man could follow him. Political economy is of modern invention; I am old enough to recollect when every judge on the bench (Lord Eldon and Serjeant Runnington excepted,) in their charges to the grand juries, attributed the then high prices of corn to the scandalous combination of farmers. Sir James knew what is commonly agreed upon by political economists, without taking much pleasure in the science, and with a disposition to blame the very speculative and metaphysical disquisitions into which it has wandered, but with a full conviction also (which many able men of his standing are without) of the immense importance of the science to the welfare of society.

I think (though, perhaps, some of his friends may not agree with me in this opinion) that he was an acute judge of character, and of the good as well as evil in character. He was, in truth, with the appearance of distraction and of one occupied with other things, a very minute observer of human nature; and I have seen him analyze, to the very springs of the heart, men who had not the most distant suspicion of the sharpness of his vision, nor a belief that he could read any thing but books.

Sufficient justice has not been done to his political integrity. He was not rich, was from the northern part of the island, possessed great facility of temper, and had therefore every excuse for political lubricity, which that vice (more common in those days than I hope it will ever be again) could possibly require. Invited by every party, upon his arrival from India, he remained steadfast to his old friends the whigs, whose admission to office, or enjoyment of political power, would at that period have been considered as the most visionary of all human speculations; yet, during his lifetime, every body seemed more ready to have forgiven the tergiversation of which he was not guilty, than to admire the actual firmness he had displayed. With all this he never made the slightest efforts to advance his interests with his political friends, never mentioned his sacrifices nor his services, expressed no resentment at neglect, and was therefore pushed into such situations as fall to the lot of the feeble and delicate in a crowd.

A high merit in Sir James Mackintosh was his real and unaffected philanthropy. He did not make the improvement of the great mass of mankind an engine of popularity, and a stepping stone to power, but he had a genuine love of human happiness. Whatever might assuage the angry passions, and arrange the conflicting interests of nations; whatever could promote peace, increase knowledge, extend commerce, diminish crime, and encourage industry; whatever could exalt human character, and could enlarge human understanding; struck at once at the heart of your father, and roused all his faculties. I have seen him in a moment when this spirit came upon him—like a great ship of war—cut his cable, and spread his enormous canvass, and launch into a wide sea of reasoning eloquence.

But though easily warmed by great schemes of benevolence and human improvement, his manner was cold to individuals. There was an apparent want of heartiness and cordiality. It seemed as if he had more affection for the species than for the ingredients of which it was composed. He was in reality very hospitable, and so fond of company, that he was hardly happy out of it; but he did not receive his friends with that honest joy which warms more than dinner or wine.

This is the good and evil of your father which comes uppermost. If he had been arrogant and grasping; if he had been faithless and false; if he had always been eager to strangle infant genius in its cradle; always ready to betray and to blacken those with whom he sat at meat; he would have passed many men, who, in the course of his long life, have passed him; but, without selling his soul for pottage, if he only had had a little more prudence for the promotion of his interests, and more of angry passions for the punishment of those detractors who envied his fame and presumed upon his sweetness; if he had been more aware of his powers, and of that space which nature intended him to occupy: he would have acted a great part in life, and remained a character in history. As it is, he has left, in many of the best men in England, and of the continent, the deepest admiration of his talents, his wisdom, his knowledge and his benevolence.

I remain, my dear Sir,

Very truly yours,

SYDNEY SMITH.

A LETTER

TO

LORD JOHN RUSSELL.

My Lord,

Though, upon the whole, your residence and plurality bill is a good bill, and although I think it (thanks to your kind attention to the suggestions of various clergymen) a much better bill than that of last year, there are still some important defects in it, which deserve amendment and correction.

Page 13, *Sec.* 31.—It would seem, from this section, that the repairs are to depend upon the will of the bishop, and not upon the present law of the land. A bishop enters into the house of a non-resident clergyman, and finds it neither papered, nor painted—he orders these decorative repairs. In the mean time the court of Queen's Bench have decided that substantial repairs, only, and not decorative repairs, can be recovered by an incumbent from his predecessor; the following words should be added;—'Provided, always, that no other repairs shall be required by the bishop, than such as any incumbent could recover as dilapidations from the person preceding him in the said benefice.

Page 19, *Sec.* 42.—Incumbents are to answer questions transmitted by the bishop, and these are to be countersigned by the rural dean.—This is another vexation to the numerous catalogue of vexations entailed upon the rural clergy. Is every man to go before the rural dean, twenty or thirty miles off, perhaps? Is he to go through a cross examination by the rural dean, as to the minute circumstance of twenty or thirty questions, to enter into reasonings upon them, and to produce witnesses? This is a most degrading and vexatious enactment, if all this is intended; but if the rural dean is to believe the assertion of every clergyman upon his word only, why may not the bishop do so: and what is gained by the enactment? But the commissioners seem to have been a set of noblemen and gentlemen, who met once a-week, to see how they could harass the working clergy, and how they could make every thing smooth and pleasing to the bishops.

The clause for holding two livings, at the interval of ten miles, is perfectly ridiculous. If you are to abolish pluralities, do it at once, or leave a man only in possession of such benefices as he can serve himself; and then the distance should be two miles, and not a yard more.

But common justice requires that there should be exceptions to your rules. For two hundred years pluralities within certain distances have been allowed; acting under the faith of these laws, livings have been bought and bequeathed to clergymen, tenable with other preferments in their possession—upon faith in these laws, men and women have married—educated their children—laid down a certain plan of life, and adopted a certain rate of expense, and ruin comes upon them in a moment from this thoughtless inattention to existing interests. I know a man whose father dedicated all he had saved in a long life of retail trade, to purchase the next presentation to a living of 800*l*. per annum, tenable under the old law, with another of 500*l*. given to the son by his college. The whole of this clergyman's life and prospects (and he has an immense family of children) are cut to pieces by your bill. It is a wrong thing, you will say, to hold two livings; I think it is, but why did not you, the legislature, find this out fifty years ago? Why did you entice this man into the purchase of pluralities, by a venerable laxity of two hundred years, and then clap him into gaol from the new virtue of yesterday? Such reforms as these make wisdom and carefulness useless, and turn human life into a mere scramble.

Page 32, *Sec.* 69.—There are the strongest possible objections to this clause. The living is 410*l*. per annum, the population above 2000—perhaps, as is often the case, one third of them dissenters. A clergyman does his duty in the most exemplary manner—dedicates his life to his parish, from whence he derives his whole support—there is not the shadow of a complaint against him. The bishop has, by this clause, acquired a right of thrusting a curate upon the rector at the expense of a fifth part of his whole fortune. This, I think, an abominable piece of tyranny; and it will turn out to be an inexhaustible source of favouritism and malice. In the bishop's bill I have in vain looked for a similar clause,—"That if the population is above 800,000, and the income amounts to 10,000*l*., an assistant to the bishop may be appointed by the commissioners, and a salary of 2000*l*. per annum allotted to him." This would have been honest and manly, to have begun with the great people.

But mere tyranny and episcopal malice are not the only evils of this clause, nor the greatest evils. Every body knows the extreme activity of that part of the English church which is denominated evangelical, and their industry in bringing over every body to their habits of thinking and acting; now see what will happen from the following clause: "And whenever the population of any benefice shall amount to 2000, and it shall be made appear to the satisfaction of the bishop, that a stipend can be provided for the payment of a curate, by voluntary contribution or otherwise, without charge to the incumbent, it shall be lawful for the bishop to require the spiritual person, holding the same, to nominate a fit person to be licensed as such curate, whatever may be the annual value of such benefice; and if, in either of the said cases, a fit person shall not be nominated to the bishop within two months after his requisition for that purpose shall have been delivered to the incumbent, it shall be lawful for the bishop to appoint and license a curate." A clause worthy of the Vicar of Wrexhill himself. Now what will happen? The bishop is a Calvinistic bishop; wife, children, chaplains, Calvinized up to the teeth. The *serious* people of the parish meet together, and agree to give an hundred pounds per annum, if Mr. Wilkinson is appointed. It requires very little knowledge of human nature to predict, that at the expiration of two months Mr. Wilkinson will be the man; and then the whole parish is torn to pieces with jealousies, quarrels, and comparisons between the rector and the delightful Wilkinson. The same scene is acted (mutatis mutandis), where the bishop sets his face against Calvinistic principles. The absurdity consists in suffering the appointment of a curate by private subscription; in other words, one clergyman in a parish by *nomination*, the other by *election;* and, in this way, religion is brought into contempt by their jealousies and quarrels. Little do you know, my dear lord, of the state of that country you govern, if you suppose this will not happen. I have now a diocese in my eye, where, I am positively certain, that in less than six months after the passing of this bill, there will not be a single parish of 2000 persons, in which you will not find a subscription curate, of evangelical habits, canting and crowing over the regular and established clergyman of the parish.

In the draft of the fifth report, upon which, I presume your dean and chapter bill is to be founded, I see the rights of patronage are to be conceded to present incumbents. This is very high and honourable conduct in the commissioners, and such as deserves the warmest thanks of the clergy; it is always difficult to retract, much more difficult to retract to inferiors; but it is very virtuous to do so when there can be no motive for it but a love of justice.

Your whole bill is to be one of retrenchment, and amputation; why add fresh canons to St. Paul's and Lincoln? Nobody wants them; the cathedrals go on perfectly well without them; they take away each of them 1500*l.* or 1600*l.* per annum, from the fund for the improvement of small livings; they give, to be sure, a considerable piece of patronage to the Bishops of London and Lincoln, who are commissioners, and they preserve a childish and pattern-like uniformity in cathedrals. But the first of these motives is corrupt, and the last silly: and, therefore, they cannot be your motives.

You cannot plead the recommendation of the commission for the creation of these new canons, for you have flung the commission overboard; and the reformers of the church are no longer archbishops and bishops, but Lord John Russell—not those persons to whom the crown has entrusted the task, but Lord Martin Luther, bred and born in our own island, and nourished by the Woburn spoils and confiscations of the church. The church is not without friends, but those friends have said there can be no danger of measures which are sanctioned by the highest prelates of the church; but you have chased away the bearers, and taken the ark into your own possession. Do not forget, however, if you have deviated from the plan of your brother commissioners, that you have given to them a perfect right to oppose you.

This unfair and wasteful creation of new canons, produces a great and scandalous injustice to St. Paul's and Lincoln, in the distribution of their patronage. The old members of all other cathedrals will enjoy the benefit of survivorship, till they subside into the magic number of four; up to that point, then, every fresh death will add to the patronage of the remaining old members; but in the churches of Lincoln and St. Paul's, the old members will immediately have one-fifth of their patronage taken away by the creation of a fifth canon to share it. This injustice and partiality are so monstrous, that the two prelates in question will see that it is necessary to their own character to apply a remedy. Nothing is more easy than to do so. Let the bishop's canon have no share in the distribution of the patronage, till after the death of all those who were residentiaries at the passing of the bill.

Your dean and chapter bill will, I am afraid, cut down the great preferments of the church too much.

Take for your fund only the non-resident prebends, and leave the number of resident prebends as they are, annexing some of them to poor livings with large populations. I am sure this is all (besides the abolition of pluralities), which ought to be done, and all that would be done, if the commissioners were to begin *de novo* from this period, when bishops have recovered from their fright, dissenters shrunk into their just dimensions, and the foolish and exaggerated expectations from reform have vanished away. The great prizes of the church induce men to carry, and fathers and uncles to send into the church considerable capitals, and in this way, enable the clergy to associate with gentlemen, and to command that respect which, in all countries, and above all in this, depends so much on appearances. Your bill, abolishing pluralities, and taking away, at the same time, so many dignities, leaves the Church of England so destitute of great prizes, that, as far as mere emolument has any influence, it will be better to dispense cheese and butter in small quantities to the public, than to enter into the church.

There are admirable men, whose honest and beautiful zeal carries them into the church without a moment's thought of its emoluments. Such a man, combining the manners of a gentleman with the acquirements of a scholar, and the zeal of an apostle, would overawe mercantile grossness, and extort respect from insolent opulence; but I am talking of average vicars, mixed natures, and eleven thousand parish priests. If you divide the great emoluments of the church into little portions, such as butlers and head game-keepers receive, you very soon degrade materially the style and character of the English clergy. If I were dictator of the church, as Lord Durham is to be of Canada, I would preserve the resident, and abolish, for the purposes of a fund, the non-resident prebends. This is the principal and most important alteration in your dean and chapter bill, which it is not too late to make, and for which every temperate and rational man ought to strive.

You will, of course, consider me as a defender of abuses. I have all my life been just the contrary, and I remember, with pleasure, thirty years ago, old Lord Stowell saying to me, "Mr. Smith, you would have been a much richer man if you had joined us." I like, my dear lord, the road you are travelling, but I don't like the pace you are driving; too similar to that of the son of Nimshi. I always feel inclined to cry out, Gently, John, gently down hill. Put on the drag. We shall be over if you go so quick—you'll do us a mischief.

Remember, as a philosopher, that the Church of England now is a very different institution from what it was twenty years ago. It then oppressed every sect; they are now all free—all exempt from the tyranny of an establishment; and the only real cause of complaint for dissenters is, that they can no longer find a grievance and enjoy the distinction of being persecuted. I have always tried to reduce them to this state, and I do not pity them.

You have expressed your intention of going beyond the fifth report, and limiting deans to 2000*l.* per annum, and canons to 1000*l.* This is, I presume, in conformity with the treatment of the bishops, who are limited to from 4500*l.*, to 5000*l.* per annum; and it wears a fine appearance of impartial justice; but for the dean and canon the sum is a maximum—in bishops it is a maximum and minimum too; a bishop cannot have less than 4500*l.*, a canon may have as little as the poverty of his church dooms him to, but he cannot have more than 1000*l.*; but there may be canonries of 500*l.*, or 600*l.*, or 700*l.* per annum, and a few only of 1000*l.*; many deaneries of from 1000*l.* to 1500*l.* per annum; and only a very few above 2000*l.* If you mean to make the world believe that you are legislating for men without votes, as benevolently as you did for those who have votes in Parliament, you should make up the allowance of every canon to 1000*l.*, and every dean to 2000*l.* per annum, or leave them to the present lottery of blanks and prizes. Besides, too, do I not recollect some remarkable instances, in your bishop's act, of deviation from this rigid standard of episcopal wealth? Are not the archbishops to have the enormous sums of 15,000*l.* and 12,000*l.* per annum? is not the Bishop of London to have 10,000*l* per annum? Are not all these three prelates commissioners? And is not the reason alleged for the enormous income of the Bishop of London, that everything is so expensive in the metropolis? Do not the deans of St. Paul's and Westminster, then, live in London also? And can the Bishop of London sit in his place in the House of Lords, and not urge for those dignitaries the same reasons which were so successful in securing such ample emoluments for his own see? My old friend, the Bishop of Durham, has 8000*l.* per annum secured to him. I am heartily glad of it; what possible reason can there be for giving him more than other bishops, and not giving the Dean of Durham more than other deans? that is, of leaving to him one half of his present income. It is impossible this can be a clap-trap for Joseph Hume, or a set-off against the disasters of Canada; you are too honest and elevated for this. I cannot comprehend what is meant by such gross partiality and injustice.

Why are the economists so eagerly in the field? The public do not contribute one halfpenny to the support of deans and chapters; it is not proposed by any one to confiscate the revenues of the church; the whole is a question of distribution, in what way the revenues of the church can be best administered for the public good. But whatever may bethe respective shares of Peter or Paul, the public will never be richer or poorer by one shilling.

When your dean and chapter bill is printed, I shall take the liberty of addressing you again. The clergy naturally look with the greatest anxiety to these two bills; they think that you will avail yourself of this opportunity to punish them for their opposition to your government in the last elections. They are afraid that your object is not so much to do good as to gratify your vanity, by obtaining the character of a great reformer, and that (now the bishops are provided for) you will varnish over your political mistakes by increased severity against the church, or, apparently struggling for their good, see with inexpressible delight the clergy delivered over to the tender mercies of the radicals. These are the terrors of the clergy. I judge you with a very different judgment. You are a religious man, not unfriendly to the church; and but for that most foolish and fatal error of the church rates (into which you were led by a man who knows no more of England than of Mesopotamia), I believe you would have gone on well with the church to the last. There is a genius in action, as well as diction; and because you see political evils clearly, and attack them bravely, and cure them wisely, you are a man of real genius, and are most deservedly looked up to as the leader of the whig party in this kingdom. I wish, I must confess, you were rather less afraid of Joseph and Daniel; but God has given you a fine understanding, and a fine character; and I have so much confidence in your spirit and honour, that I am sure you would rather abandon your bills altogether, than suffer the enemies of the church to convert them into an engine of spoil and oppression.

I am, &c.

SYDNEY SMITH.

SERMON

ON THE

DUTIES OF THE QUEEN

DANIEL, IV. 31.

"OH KING, THY KINGDOM IS DEPARTED FROM THEE."

I DO not think I am getting out of the fair line of duty of a minister of the gospel, if, at the beginning of a new reign, I take a short review of the moral and religious state of the country; and to point out what those topics are which deserve the most serious consideration of a wise and a Christian people.

The death of a king is always an awful lesson to mankind; and it produces a more solemn pause, and creates more profound reflection than the best lessons of the best teachers.

From the throne to the tomb—wealth, splendour, flattery, all gone! The look of favour—the voice of power, no more;—the deserted palace—the wretched monarch on his funeral bier—the mourners ready—the dismal march of death prepared. Who are we, and what are we? and for what has God made us? and why are we doomed to this frail and unquiet existence? Who does not feel all this? in whose heart does it not provoke appeal to and dependence on God? before whose eyes does it not bring the folly and nothingness of all things human?

But a good king must not go to his grave without that reverence from the people which his virtues deserved. And I will state to you what those virtues were, state it to you honestly and fairly; for I should heartily despise myself, if from this chair of truth I would utter one word of panegyric of the great men of the earth, which I could not aver before the throne of God.

The late monarch, whose loss we have to deplore, was sincere and honest in his political relations; he put his trust really where he put his trust ostensibly—and did not attempt to undermine, by secret means, those to whom he trusted publicly the conduct of affairs; and I must beg to remind you that no vice and no virtue are indifferent in a monarch; human beings are very imitative; there is a fashion in the higher qualities of our minds, as there is in the lesser considerations of life. It is by no means indifferent to the morals of the people at large, whether a tricking perfidious king is placed on the throne of these realms, or whether the sceptre is swayed by one of plain and manly character, walking ever in a straight line, on the firm ground of truth, under the searching eye of God.

The late king was of a sweet and Christian disposition; he did not treasure up little animosities, and indulge in vindictive feelings; he had no enemies but the enemies of the country; he did not make the memory of a king a fountain of wrath; the feelings of the individual (where they required any control) were in perfect subjection to the just conception he had formed of his high duties; and every one near him found it was a government of principle, and not of temper; not of caprice, not of malice couching in high places, and watching an opportunity of springing on its victim.

Our late monarch had the good nature of Christianity; he loved the happiness of all the individuals about him, and never lost an opportunity of promoting it; and where the heart is good, and the mind active, and the means ample, this makes a luminous and beautiful life, which gladdens the nations, and leads them, and turns men to the exercise of virtue, and the great work of salvation.

We may honestly say of our late sovereign that he loved his country, and was sensibly alive to its glory and its happiness. When he entered into his palaces he did not say, "All this is my birthright; I am entitled to it—it is my due—how can I gain more splendour? how can I increase all the pleasures of the senses?" but he looked upon it all as a memorial that he was to repay by example, by attention, and by watchfulness over the public interests, the affectionate and lavish expenditure of his subjects; and this was not a decision of reason, but a feeling, which hurried him away. Whenever it was pointed out to him that England could be made more rich, or more happy, or rise higher in the scale of nations, or be better guided in the straight path of the Christian faith, on all such occasions he rose above himself; there was a warmth, and a truth, and an honesty, which it was impossible to mistake; the gates of his heart were flung open, and that heart throbbed and beat for the land which his ancestors had rescued from slavery, and governed with justice:—but he is gone—and let fools praise conquerors, and say the great Napoleon pulled down this kingdom and destroyed that army, we will thank God for a king who has derived his quiet glory from the peace of his realm, and who has founded his own happiness upon the happiness of his people.

But the world passes on, and a new order of things arises. Let us take a short view of those duties which devolve upon the young queen, whom Providence has placed over us—what ideas she ought to form of her duties—and on what points she should endeavour to place the glories of her reign.

First and foremost, I think, the new queen should bend her mind to the very serious consideration of educating the people. Of the importance of this, I think no reasonable doubt can exist; it does not, in its effects, keep pace with the exaggerated expectations of its injudicious advocates, but it presents the best chance of national improvement.

Reading and writing are mere increase of power. They may be turned, I admit, to a good, or a bad purpose; but for several years of his life the child is in your hands, and you may give to that power what bias you please: thou shalt not kill—thou shalt not steal—thou shalt not bear false witness;—by how many fables, by how much poetry, by how many beautiful aids of imagination, may not the fine morality of the Sacred Scriptures be engraven on the minds of the young? I believe the arm of the assassin may be often stayed by the lessons of his early life. When I see the village school, and the tattered scholars, and the aged master or mistress teaching the mechanical art of reading or writing, and thinking that they are teaching that alone, I feel that the aged instructor is protecting life, insuring property, fencing the altar, guarding the throne, giving space and liberty to all the fine powers of man, and lifting him up to his own place in the order of creation.

There are, I am sorry to say, many countries in Europe, which have taken the lead of England in the great business of education, and it is a thoroughly commendable, and legitimate object of ambition in a sovereign to overtake them. The names too, of malefactors, and the nature of their crimes are subjected to the sovereign;—how is it possible that a sovereign, with the fine feelings of youth, and with all the gentleness of her sex, should not ask herself, whether the human being whom she dooms to death, or at least does not rescue from death, has been properly warned in early youth of the horrors of that crime for which his life is forfeited? "Did he ever receive any education at all?——did a father and mother watch over him?—was he brought to places of worship?—was the Word of God explained to him?—was the book of knowledge opened to him?—Or am I, the fountain of mercy, the nursing-mother of my people, to send a forsaken wretch from the streets to the scaffold, and to prevent, by unprincipled cruelty, the evils of unprincipled neglect?"

Many of the objections found against the general education of the people are utterly untenable; where all are educated, education cannot be a source of distinction and a subject for pride. The great source of labour is want; and as long as the necessities of life call for labour—labour is sure to be supplied. All these fears are foolish and imaginary; the great use and the great importance of education properly conducted are, that it creates a great bias in favour of virtue and religion, at a period of life when the mind is open to all the impressions which superior wisdom may choose to affix upon it; the sum and mass of these tendencies and inclinations make a good and virtuous people, and draw down upon us the blessing and protection of Almighty God.

A second great object which I hope will be impressed upon the mind of this royal lady is, a rooted horror of war—an earnest and passionate desire to keep her people in a state of profound peace. The greatest curse which can be entailed upon mankind is a state of war. All the atrocious crimes committed in years of peace—all that is spent in peace by the secret corruptions, or by the thoughtless extravagance of nations, are mere trifles compared with the gigantic evils which stalk over the world in a state of war. God is forgotten in war—every principle of Christian charity trampled upon—human labour destroyed—human industry extinguished;—you see the son and the husband and the brother dying miserably in distant lands—you see the waste of human affections—you see the breaking of human hearts—you hear the shrieks of widows and children after the battle—and you walk over the mangled bodies of the wounded calling for death. I would say to that royal child, worship God, by loving peace—it is not *your* humanity to pity a beggar by giving him food or raiment—*I* can do that; that is the charity of the humble, and the unknown—widen you your heart for the more expanded miseries of mankind—pity the mothers of the peasantry who see their sons torn away from their families—pity your poor subjects crowded into hospitals, and calling in their last breath upon their distant country and their young queen—pity the stupid, frantic folly of human beings who are always ready to tear each other to pieces, and to deluge the earth with each other's blood; this is your extended humanity—and this the great field of your compassion. Extinguish in your heart the fiendish love of military glory, from which your sex does not necessarily exempt you, and to which the wickedness of flatterers may urge you. Say upon your death-bed, "I have made few orphans in my reign—I have made few widows—my object has been peace. I have used all the weight of my character, and all the power of my situation, to check the irascible passions of mankind, and to turn them to the arts of honest industry: this has been the Christianity of my throne, and this the Gospel of my sceptre; in this way I have strove to worship my Redeemer and my Judge."

I would add (if any addition were wanted as a part of the lesson to youthful royalty), the utter folly of all wars of ambition, where the object sought for—if attained at all—is commonly attained at manifold its real value, and often wrested, after short enjoyment, from its possessor, by the combined indignation and just vengeance of the other nations of the world. It is all misery, and folly, and impiety, and cruelty. The atrocities, and horrors, and disgusts of war, have never been half enough insisted upon by the teachers of the people; but the worst of evils and the greatest of follies, have been varnished over with specious names, and the gigantic robbers and murderers of the world have been holden up, for their imitation, to the weak eyes of youth. May honest counsellors keep this poison from the mind of the young queen. May she love what God bids, and do what makes men happy!

I hope the queen will love the national church, and protect it; but it must be impressed upon her mind, that every sect of Christians have as perfect a right to the free exercise of their worship as the church itself—that there must be no invasion of the privileges of other sects, and no contemptuous disrespect of their feelings—that the altar is the very ark and citadel of freedom.

Some persons represent old age as miserable, because it brings with it the pains and infirmities of the body; but what gratification to the mind may not old age bring with it in this country of wise and rational improvement? I have lived to see the immense improvements of the Church of England; all its powers of persecution destroyed—its monopoly of civil offices expunged from the book of the law, and all its unjust and exclusive immunities leveled to the ground. The Church of England is now a rational object of love and admiration—it is perfectly compatible with civil freedom—it is an institution for worshipping God, and not a cover for gratifying secular insolence, and ministering to secular ambition. It will be the duty of those to whom the sacred trust of instructing our youthful queen is entrusted, to lead her attention to these great improvements in our religious establishments; and to show to her how possible, and how wise it is, to render the solid advantages of a national church compatible with the civil rights of those who cannot assent to its doctrines.

Then again, our youthful ruler must be very slow to believe all the exaggerated and violent abuse which religious sects indulge in against each other. She will find, for instance, that the Catholics, the great object of our horror and aversion, have (mistaken as they are) a great deal more to say in defence of their tenets than those imagine who indulge more in the luxury of invective than in the labour of inquiry—she will find in that sect, men as enlightened, talents as splendid, and probity as firm, as in our own church; and she will soon learn to appreciate, at its just value, that exaggerated hatred of sects which paints the Catholic faith (the religion of two-thirds of Europe) as utterly incompatible with the safety, peace and order of the world.

It will be a sad vexation to all loyal hearts and to all rationally pious minds, if our sovereign should fall into the common error of mistaken fanaticism for religion: and in this way fling an air of discredit upon real devotion. It is, I am afraid, unquestionably the fault of the age; her youth and her sex do not make it more improbable, and the warmest efforts of that description of persons will not be wanting to gain over a convert so illustrious, and so important. Should this take place, the consequences will be serious and distressing—the land will be inundated with hypocrisy—absurdity will be heaped upon absurdity—there will be a race of folly and extravagance for royal favour, and he who is farthest removed from reason will make the nearest approach to distinction; and then follow the usual consequences; a weariness and disgust of religion itself, and the foundation laid for an age of impiety and infidelity. Those, then, to whom these matters are delegated, will watch carefully over every sign of this excess, and guard from the mischievous intemperance of enthusiasm those feelings and that understanding, the healthy state of which bears so strongly and intimately upon the happiness of a whole people.

Though I deprecate the bad effects of fanaticism, I earnestly pray that our young sovereign may evince herself to be a person of deep religious feeling: what other cure has she for all the arrogance and vanity which her exalted position must engender? for all the flattery and falsehood with which she must be surrounded? for all the soul-corrupting homage with which she is met at every moment of her existence? what other cure than to cast herself down in darkness and solitude before God—to say that she is dust and ashes—and to call down the pity of the Almighty upon her difficult and dangerous life? This is the antidote of kings against the slavery and the baseness which surround them—they should think often of death—and the folly and nothingness of the world, and they should humble their souls before the Master of masters, and the King of kings; praying to Heaven for wisdom and calm reflection, and for that spirit of Christian gentleness which exalts command into an empire of justice, and turns obedience into a service of love.

A wise man struggling with adversity is said by some heathen writer to be a spectacle on which the gods might look down with pleasure—but where is there a finer moral and religious picture, or one more deserving of divine favour, than that of which, perhaps, we are now beginning to enjoy the blessed reality?

A young queen, at that period of life which is commonly given up to frivolous amusement, sees at once the great principles by which she should be guided, and steps at once into the great duties of her station. The importance of educating the lower orders of the people is never absent from her mind; she takes up this principle at the beginning of her life, and in all the change of servants, and in all the struggle of parties, looks to it as a source of permanent improvement. A great object of her affections is the preservation of peace; she regards a state of war as the greatest of all human evils, thinks that the lust of conquest is not a glory but a bad crime; despises the folly and miscalculations of war, and is willing to sacrifice every thing to peace, but the clear honour of her land.

The patriot queen, whom I am painting, reverences the national church—frequents its worship, and regulates her faith by its precepts; but she withstands the encroachments, and keeps down the ambition natural to establishments, and, by rendering the privileges of the church compatible with the civil freedom of all sects, confers strength upon, and adds duration to, that wise and magnificent institution. And then this youthful monarch, profoundly but wisely religious, disdaining hypocrisy, and far above the childish follies of false piety, casts herself upon God, and seeks from the Gospel of his blessed Son a path for her steps and a comfort for her soul. Here is a picture which warms every English heart, and would bring all this congregation upon their bended knees before Almighty God to pray it may be realized. What limits to the glory and happiness of our native land, if the Creator should in his mercy have placed in the heart of this royal woman the rudiments of wisdom and mercy; and if, giving them time to expand, and to bless our children's children with her goodness, He should grant to her a long sojourning upon earth, and leave her to reign over us till she is well stricken in years? What glory! what happiness! what joy! what bounty of God! I of course can only expect to see the beginning of such a splendid period; but when I do see it, I shall exclaim with the Psalmist,—"Lord, now lettest thou thy servant depart in peace, for mine eyes have seen thy salvation."

THE LAWYER THAT TEMPTED CHRIST.

A SERMON PREACHED IN THE CATHEDRAL CHURCH AT ST. PETER, YORK, BEFORE THE HON. SIR JOHN BAYLEY, KNT., ONE OF HIS MAJESTY'S JUSTICES OF THE COURT OF KING'S BENCH, AND THE HON. SIR JOHN HULLOCK, KNT., ONE OF HIS MAJESTY'S BARONS OF THE COURT OF EXCHEQUER.—AUG. 1, 1824.

LUKE X. 25.

"*And, behold, a certain lawyer stood up, and tempted him, saying, Master, what shall I do to inherit eternal life?*"

THIS lawyer, who is thus represented to have tempted our blessed Saviour, does not seem to have been very much in earnest in the question which he asked: his object does not appear to have been the acquisition of religious knowledge, but the display of human talent. He did not say to himself, I will now draw near to this august being; I will inform myself from the fountain of truth, and from the very lips of Christ; I will learn a lesson of salvation; but it occurred to him that in such a gathering together of the Jews, in such a moment of public agitation, the opportunity of display was not to be neglected: full of that internal confidence which men of talents so ready, and so exercised, are sometimes apt to feel, he approaches our Saviour with all the apparent modesty of interrogation, and, saluting him with the appellation of Master, prepares, with all professional acuteness, for his humiliation and defeat.

Talking humanly, and we must talk humanly, for our Saviour was then acting an human part, the experiment ended as all must wish an experiment to end, where levity and bad faith are on one side, and piety, simplicity, and goodness on the other: the objector was silenced, and one of the brightest lessons of the Gospel elicited, for the eternal improvement of mankind.

Still, though we wish the motive for the question had been better, we must not forget the question, and we must not forget who asked the question, and we must not forget who answered it, and what that answer was. The question was the wisest and best that ever came from the mouth of man; the man who asked it was the very person who ought to have asked it; a man overwhelmed, probably, with the intrigues, the bustle, and business of life, and, therefore, most likely to forget the interests of another world: the answerer was our blessed Saviour, through whose mediation, you, and I, and all of us, hope to live again; and the answer, remember, was plain and practical: not flowery, not metaphysical, not doctrinal; but it said to the man of the law, if you wish to live eternally, do your duty to God and man; live in this world as you ought to live; make yourself fit for eternity; and then, and then only, God will grant to you eternal life.

There are, probably, in this church, many persons of the profession of the law, who have often asked before, with better faith than their brother, and who do now ask this great question, "What shall I do to inherit eternal life?" I shall, therefore, direct to them some observations on the particular duties they owe to society, because I think it suitable to this particular season, because it is of much more importance to tell men how they are to be Christians in detail, than to exhort them to be Christians generally; because it is of the highest utility to avail ourselves of these occasions, to show to classes of mankind what those virtues are which they have more frequent and valuable opportunities of practising, and what those faults and vices are to which they are more particularly exposed.

It falls to the lot of those who are engaged in the active and arduous profession of the law, to pass their lives in great cities, amidst severe and incessant occupation, requiring all the faculties, and calling forth, from time to time, many of the strongest passions of our nature. In the midst of all this, rivals are to be watched, superiors are to be cultivated, connections cherished; some portion of life must be given to society, and some little to relaxation and amusement. When, then, is the question to be asked, "What shall I do to inherit eternal life?" what leisure for the altar, what time for God? I appeal to the experience of men engaged in this profession, whether religious feelings and religious practices are not, without any speculative disbelief, perpetually sacrificed to the business of the world. Are not the habits of devotion gradually displaced by other habits of solicitude, hurry, and care, totally incompatible with habits of devotion? Is not the taste for devotion lessened? Is not the time for devotion abridged? Are you not more and more conquered against your warnings and against your will, not, perhaps, without pain and compunction, by the mammon of life? and what is the cure for this great evil to which your profession exposes you? The cure is, to keep a sacred place in your heart, where Almighty God is enshrined, and where nothing human can enter; to say to the world, "Thus far shalt thou go, and no farther;" to remember you are a lawyer, without forgetting you are a Christian; to wish for no more wealth than ought to be possessed by an inheritor of the kingdom of heaven; to covet no more honour than is suitable to a child of God; boldly and bravely to set yourself limits, and to show to others you have limits, and that no professional eagerness and no professional activity shall ever induce ou to infringe upon the rules and practices of religion: remember the text; put the great ques-'on really, which the tempter of Christ only pretended to put. In the midst of your highest success, in the most perfect gratification of your vanity, in the most ample increase of your wealth, fall down at the feet of Jesus, and say, "Master, what shall I do to inherit eternal life?"

The genuine and unaffected piety of a lawyer is, in one respect, of great advantage to the general interests of religion; inasmuch as to the highest member of that profession a great share of church patronage is entrusted, and to him we are accustomed to look up in the senate, for the defence of our venerable establishment; and great and momentous would be the loss to this nation, if any one, called to so high and honourable an office, were found deficient in this ancient, pious, and useful zeal for the established church. In talking to men of your active lives and habits, it is not possible to anticipate the splendid and exalted stations for which any one of you may be destined. Fifty years ago, the person at the head of his profession, the greatest lawyer now in England, perhaps in the world, stood in this church, on such occasions as the present, as obscure, as unknown, and as much doubting of his future prospects, as the humblest individual of the profession here present. If Providence reserve such honours for any one who may now chance to hear me, let him remember that there is required at his hands a zeal for the established church, but a zeal tempered by discretion, compatible with Christian charity, and tolerant of Christian freedom. All human establishments are liable to err, and are capable of improvement: to act as if you denied this, to perpetuate any infringement upon the freedom of other sects, however vexatious that infringement, and however safe its removal, is not to defend an establishment, but to expose it to unmerited obloquy and reproach. Never think it necessary to be weak and childish in the highest concerns of life; the career of the law opens to you many great and glorious opportunities of promoting the Gospel of Christ, and of doing good to your fellow-creatures; there is no situation of that profession in which you can be more great and more glorious than when, in the fulness of years, and the fulness of honours, you are found defending that church which first taught you to distinguish between good and evil, and breathed into you the elements of religious life; but when you defend that church, defend it with enlarged wisdom, and with the spirit of magnanimity; praise its great excellencies; do not perpetuate its little defects; be its liberal defender, be its wise patron, be its real friend. If you can be great and bold in human affairs, do not think it necessary to be narrow and timid in spiritual concerns; bind yourself up with the real and important interests of the church, and hold yourself accountable to God for its safety; but yield up trifles to the altered state of the world. Fear no change which lessens the enemies of that establishment, fear no change which increases the activity of that establishment, fear no change which draws down upon it the more abundant prayers and blessings of the human race.

Justice is found, experimentally, to be most effectually promoted by the opposite efforts of practised and ingenious men, presenting to the selection of an impartial judge the best arguments for the establishment and explanation of truth. It becomes, then, under such an arrangement, the decided duty of an advocate to use all the arguments in his power to defend the cause he has adopted, and to leave the effects of those arguments to the judgment of others. However useful this practice may be for the promotion of public justice, it is not without danger to the individual whose practice it becomes. It is apt to produce a profligate indifference to truth in higher occasions of life, where truth cannot, for a moment, be trifled with, much less callously trampled on, much less suddenly and totally yielded up to the basest of human motives. It is astonishing what unworthy and inadequate notions men are apt to form of the Christian faith. Christianity does not insist upon duties to an individual, and forget the duties which are owing to the great mass of individuals, which we call our country; it does not teach you how to benefit your neighbour, and leave you to inflict the most serious injuries upon all whose interest is bound up with you in the same land: I need not say to this congregation that there is a wrong and a right in public affairs, as there is a wrong and a right in private affairs. I need not prove that in any vote, in any line of conduct which affects the public interest, every Christian is bound, most solemnly and most religiously, to follow the dictates of his conscience. Let it be for, let it be against, let it please, let it displease, no matter with whom it sides, or what it thwarts, it is a solemn duty, on such occasions, to act from the pure dictates of conscience, and to be as faithful to the interests of the great mass of your fellow-creatures, as you would be to the interests of any individual of that mass. Why, then, if there is any truth in these observations, can that man be pure and innocent before God, can he be quite harmless and respectable before men, who, in mature age, at a moment's notice, sacrifices to wealth and power all the fixed and firm opinions of his life; who puts his moral principles to sale, and barters his dignity and his soul for the baubles of the world? If these temptations come across you, then remember the memorable words of the text, "What shall I do to inherit eternal life?" not this—don't do this; it is no title to eternity to suffer deserved shame among men; endure any thing rather than the loss of character, cling to character as your best possession, do not envy men who pass you in life, only because they are under less moral and religious restraint than yourself. Your object is not fame, but honourable fame; your object is not wealth, but wealth worthily obtained; your object is not power, but power gained fairly and exercised virtuously. Long-suffering is a great and important lesson in human life; in no part of human life is it more necessary than in your arduous profession. The greatest men it has produced have been at some period of their professional lives ready to faint at the long and apparently fruitless journey; and if you look at those lives, you will find they have been supported by a confidence (under God) in the general effects of character and industry. They have withstood the allurement of pleasure, which is the first and most common cause of failure; they have disdained the little arts and meannesses which carry base men a certain way, and no further; they have sternly rejected, also, the sudden means of growing basely rich and dishonourably great, with which every man is at one time or another sure to be assailed; and then they have broken out into light and glory at the last, exhibiting to mankind the splendid spectacle of great talents long exercised by difficulties, and high principles never tainted with guilt.

After all, remember that your profession is a lottery, in which you may lose as well as win; and you must take it as a lottery, in which, after every effort of your own, it is impossible to command success; for this you are not accountable, but you are accountable for your purity: you are accountable for the preservation of your character. It is not in every man's power to say, I will be a great and successful lawyer, but it is in every man's power to say, that he will (with God's assistance) be a good Christian, and an honest man. Whatever is moral and religious is in your own power. If fortune deserts you, do not desert yourself; do not undervalue inward consolation; connect God with your labour; remember you are Christ's servant; be seeking always for the inheritance of immortal life.

I must urge you by another motive, and bind you by another obligation, against the sacrifice of public principle. A proud man, when he has obtained the reward, and accepted the wages of baseness, enters into a severe account with himself, and feels clearly that he has suffered degradation; he may hide it by increased zeal and violence, or varnish it over by simulated gaiety; he may silence the world, but he cannot always silence himself. If this is only a beginning, and you mean, henceforward, to trample all principle under foot, that is another thing; but a man of fine parts and nice feelings is trying a very dangerous experiment with his happiness, who means to preserve his general character, and indulge in one act of baseness. Such a man is not made to endure scorn and self-reproach; it is far from being certain that he will be satisfied with that unscriptural bargain in which he has gained the honours of the world, and lost the purity of his soul.

It is impossible in the profession of the law but that many opportunities must occur for the exertion of charity and benevolence. I do not mean the charity of money, but the charity of time, labour and attention; the protection of those whose resources are feeble, and the information of those whose knowledge is small. In the hands of bad men, the law is sometimes an artifice to mislead, and sometimes an engine to oppress. In your hands it may be, from time to time, a buckler to shield, and a sanctuary to save; you may lift up oppressed humility, listen patiently to the injuries of the wretched, vindicate their just claims, maintain their fair rights, and show, that in the hurry of business and the struggles of ambition, you have not forgotten the duties of a Christian, and the feelings of a man. It is in your power, above all other Christians, to combine the wisdom of the serpent with the innocence of the dove, and to fulfil, with greater acuteness and more perfect effect than other men can pretend to, the love, the lessons and the law of Christ.

I should caution the younger part of this profession (who are commonly selected for it on account of their superior tatents) to cultivate a little more diffidence of their own powers, and a little less contempt for received opinions, than is commonly exhibited at the beginning of their career; mistrust of this nature teaches moderation in the formation of opinions, and prevents the painful necessity of inconsistency and recantation in future life. It is not possible that the ablest young men, at the beginning of their intellectual existence, can anticipate all those reasons, and dive into all those motives, which induce mankind to act as they do act, and make the world such as we find it to be; and though there is, doubtless, much to alter, and much to improve in human affairs, yet you will find mankind not quite so wrong as, in the first ardour of youth, you supposed them to be; and you will find, as you advance in life, many new lights to open upon you, which nothing but advancing in life could ever enable you to observe. I say this, not to check originality and vigour of mind, which are the best chattels and possessions of the world, but to check that eagerness which arrives at conclusions without sufficient premises; to prevent that violence which is not uncommonly atoned for in after-life by the sacrifice of all principle and all opinions; to lessen that contempt which prevents a young man from improving his own understanding, by making a proper and prudent use of the understandings of his fellow-creatures.

There is another unchristian fault which must be guarded against in the profession of the law, and that is, misanthropy, an exaggerated opinion of the faults and follies of mankind. It is naturally the worst part of mankind who are seen in courts of justice, and with whom the professors of the law are most conversant. The perpetual recurrence of crime and guilt insensibly connects itself with the recollections of the human race: mankind are always painted in the attitude of suffering and inflicting. It seems as if men were bound together by the relations of fraud and crime; but laws are not made for the quiet, the good, and the just; you see and know little of them in your profession, and, therefore you forget them; you see the oppressor, and you let loose your eloquence against him; but you do not see the man of silent charity, who is always seeking out objects of compassion: the faithful guardian does not come into a court of justice, nor the good wife, nor the just servant, nor the dutiful son; you punish the robbers who ill-treated the wayfaring man, but you know nothing of the good Samaritan who bound up his wounds. The lawyer who tempted his Master, had heard, perhaps, of the sins of the woman at the feast, without knowing that she had poured her store of precious ointment on the feet of Jesus.

Upon those who are engaged in studying the laws of their country, devolves the honourable and Christian task of defending the accused; a sacred duty never to be yielded up, never to be influenced by any vehemence, nor intensity of public opinion. In these times of profound peace, and unexampled prosperity, there is little danger in executing this duty, and little temptation to violate it; but human affairs change like the clouds of heaven; another year may find us, or may leave us, in all the perils and bitterness of internal dissension, and upon one of you may devolve the defence of some accused person, the object of men's hopes and fears, the single point on which the eyes of a whole people are bent. These are the occasions which try a man's inward heart, and separate the dross of human nature from the gold of human nature. On these occasions, never mind being mixed up for a moment with the criminal and the crime; fling yourself back upon great principles, fling yourself back upon God; yield not one atom to violence, suffer not the slightest encroachments of injustice, retire not one step before the frowns of power, tremble not, for a single instant, at the dread of misrepresentation. The great interests of mankind are placed in your hands; it is not so much the individual you are defending; it is not so much a matter of consequence whether this or that is proved to be a crime, but on such occasions, you are often called upon to defend the occupation of a defender, to take care that the sacred rights belonging to that character are not destroyed, that that best privilege of your profession, which so much secures our regard, and so much redounds to your credit, is never soothed by flattery, never corrupted by favour, never chilled by fear. You may practise this wickedness secretly, as you may any other wickedness; you may suppress a topic of defence, or soften an attack upon opponents, or weaken your own argument, and sacrifice the man who has put his trust in you, rather than provoke the powerful by the triumphant establishment of unwelcome innocence; but if you do this, you are a guilty man before God. It is better to keep within the pale of honour, it is better to be pure in Christ, and to feel that you are pure in Christ; and if the praises of mankind are sweet, if it is ever allowable to a Christian to breathe the incense of popular favour, and to say it is grateful, and good, it is when the honest, temperate, unyielding advocate, who has protected innocence from the grasp of power, is followed from the hall of judgment by the prayers and blessings of a grateful people.

These are the Christian excellencies which the members of the profession of the law have, above all, an opportunity of cultivating; this is your tribute to the happiness of your fellow-creatures, and these your preparations for eternal life. Do not lose God in the fervour and business of the world; remember that the churches of Christ are more solemn and more sacred than your tribunals; bend not before the judges of the king, and forget the Judge of judges; search not other men's hearts without heeding that your own hearts will be searched; be innocent in the midst of subtilty; do not carry the lawful arts of your profession beyond your profession; but when the robe of the advocate is laid aside, so live that no man shall dare to suppose your opinions venal, or that your talents and energy may be bought for a price; do not heap scorn and contempt upon your declining years, by precipitate ardour for success in your profession; but set out with a firm determination to be unknown, rather than ill-known; and to rise honestly if you rise at all. Let the world see that you have risen, because the natural probity of your heart leads you to truth; because the precision and extent of your legal knowledge enable you to find the right way of doing the right thing; because a thorough knowledge of legal art and legal form is, in your hands, not an instrument of chicanery, but the plainest, easiest and shortest way to the end of strife. Impress upon yourselves the importance of your profession; consider that some of the greatest and most important interests of the world are committed to your care; that you are our protectors against the encroachments of power: that you are the preservers of freedom, the defenders of weakness, the unravellers of cunning, the investigators of artifice, the humblers of pride and the scourges of oppression; when you are silent, the sword leaps from its scabbard, and nations are given up to the madness of eternal strife. In all the civil difficulties of life, men depend upon your exercised faculties, and your spotless integrity; and they require of you an elevation above all that is mean, and a spirit which will never yield when it ought not to yield. As long as your profession retains its character for learning, the rights of mankind will be well arranged; as long as it retains its character for virtuous boldness, those rights will be well defended; as long as it preserves itself pure and incorruptible on other occasions not connected with your professions, those talents will never be used to the public injury which were intended and nurtured for the public good. I hope you will weigh these observations, and apply them to the business of the ensuing week, and beyond that, in the common occupations of your professions; always bearing in your minds the emphatic words of the text, and often in the hurry of your busy, active lives, honestly, humbly, heartily exclaiming to the Son of God, "Master, what shall I do to inherit eternal life?"

THE JUDGE THAT SMITES CONTRARY TO THE LAW.

A SERMON PREACHED IN THE CATHEDRAL CHURCH OF SAINT PETER, YORK, BEFORE THE HON. SIR JOHN BAYLEY, KNT., AND THE HON. SIR GEORGE SOWLEY HOLROYD, KNT., JUSTICES OF THE COURT OF KING'S BENCH, MARCH 28, 1824.

ACTS XXIII. 3.

"Sittest thou here to judge me after the law, and commandest thou me to be smitten, contrary to the law?"

WITH these bold words St. Paul repressed the unjust violence of that ruler who would have silenced his arguments and extinguished his zeal for the Christian faith. Knowing well the misfortunes which awaited him, prepared for deep and various calamity, not ignorant of the violence of the Jewish multitude, not unused to suffer, not unwilling to die, he had not prepared himself for the monstrous spectacle of perverted justice; but loosing that spirit to whose fire and firmness we owe the very existence of the Christian faith, he burst into that bold rebuke which brought back the extravagance of power under the control of law, and branded it with the feelings of shame: "Sittest thou here to judge me after the law, and commandest thou me to be smitten, contrary to the law?"

I would observe that, in the Gospels, and the various parts of the New Testament, the words of our Saviour and of St. Paul, when they contain any opinion, are always to be looked upon as lessons of wisdom to us, however incidentally they may have been delivered, and however shortly they may have been expressed. As their words were to be recorded by inspired writers, and to go down to future ages, nothing can have been said without reflection and design. Nothing is to be lost, every thing is to be studied: a great moral lesson is often conveyed in a few words. Read slowly, think deeply, let every word enter into your soul, for it was intended for your soul.

I take these words of St. Paul as a condemnation of that man who smites contrary to the law; as a praise of that man who judges according to the law; as a religious theme upon the importance of human justice to the happiness of mankind; and, if it be that theme, it is appropriate to this place, and to the solemn public duties of the past and the ensuing week, over which some here present will preside, at which many here present will assist, and which almost all here present will witness.

I will discuss, then, the importance of judging, according to the law, or, in other words, of the due administration of justice upon the character and happiness of nations. And in so doing, I will begin with stating a few of those circumstances which may mislead even good and conscientious men, and subject them to the unchristian sin of smiting contrary to the law. I will state how that justice is purified and perfected by which the happiness and character of nations are affected to a good purpose.

I do this with less fear of being misunderstood, because I am speaking before two great magistrates, who have lived much among us; and whom—because they have lived much among us—we have all learned to respect and regard, and to whom no man fears to consider himself as accountable, because all men see that they, in the administration of their high office, consider themselves as deeply and daily accountable to God.

And let no man say, "Why teach such things? do you think they must not have occurred to those to whom they are a concern?" I answer to this, that no man preaches novelties and discoveries; the object of preaching is, constantly to remind mankind of what mankind are constantly forgetting; not to supply the defects of human intelligence, but to fortify the feebleness of human resolutions, to recall mankind from the by-paths where they turn, into that broad path of salvation which all know, but few tread. These plain lessons the humblest ministers of the Gospel may teach, if they are honest, and the most powerful Christians will ponder, if they are wise. No man, whether he bear the sword of the law, or whether he bear that sceptre which the sword of the law cannot reach, can answer for his own heart to-morrow, and can say to the teacher,—"Thou warnest me, thou teachest me, in vain."

A Christian judge, in a free land, should, with the most scrupulous exactness, guard himself from the influence of those party feelings, upon which, perhaps, the preservation of political liberty depends, but by which the better reason of individuals is often blinded and the tranquillity of the public disturbed. I am not talking of the ostentatious display of such feelings; I am hardly talking of any gratification of which the individual himself is conscious, but I am raising up a wise and useful jealousy of the encroachment of those feelings, which, when they do encroach, lessen the value of the most valuable, and lower the importance of the most important men in the country. I admit it to be extremely difficult to live amidst the agitations, contests, and discussions of a free people, and to remain in that state of cool, passionless, Christian candour which society expect from their great magistrates; but it is the pledge that magistrate has given, it is the life he has taken up, it is the class of qualities which he has promised us, and for which he has rendered himself responsible; it is the same fault in him which want of courage would be in some men, and want of moral regularity in others. It runs counter to those very purposes, and sins against those utilities for which the very office was created; without these qualities, he who ought to be cool, is heated; he who ought to be neutral, is partial; the ermine of justice is spotted; the balance of justice is unpoised; the fillet of justice is torn off; and he who sits to judge after the law, smites contrary to the law.

And if the preservation of calmness amidst the strong feelings by which a judge is surrounded be difficult, is it not also honourable? and would it be honourable if it were not difficult? Why do men quit their homes, and give up their common occupations, and repair to the tribunal of justice? Why this bustle and business, why this decoration and display, and why are we all eager to pay our homage to the dispensers of justice? Because we all feel that there must be, somewhere or other, a check to human passions; because we all know the immense value and importance of men in whose placid equity and mediating wisdom we can trust in the worst of times; because we cannot cherish too strongly and express too plainly that reverence we feel for men who can rise up in the ship of the state, and rebuke the storms of the mind, and bid its angry passions be still.

A Christian judge, in a free land, should not only keep his mind clear from the violence of party feelings, but he should be very careful to preserve his independence, by seeking no promotion, and asking no favours from those who govern; or at least, to be (which is an experiment not without danger to his salvation) so thoroughly confident of his motives and his conduct, that he is certain the hope of favour to come, or gratitude for favour past, will never cause him to swerve from the strict line of duty. It is often the lot of a judge to be placed, not only between the accuser and the accused, not only between the complainant and him against whom it is complained, but between the governors and the governed, between the people and those whose lawful commands the people are bound to obey. In these sort of contests it unfortunately happens that the rulers are sometimes as angry as the ruled; the whole eyes of a nation are fixed upon one man, and upon his character and conduct the stability and happiness of the times seem to depend. The best and firmest magistrates cannot tell how they may act under such circumstances, but every man may prepare himself for acting well under such circumstances, by cherishing that quiet feeling of independence, which removes one temptation to act ill. Every man may avoid putting himself in a situation where his hopes of advantage are on one side, and his sense of duty on the other; such a temptation may be withstood, but it is better it should not be encountered. Far better that feeling which says, "I have vowed a vow before God; I have put on the robe of justice; farewell avarice, farewell ambition; pass me who will, slight me who will, I live henceforward only for the great duties of life; my business is on earth, my hope and my reward are in God."

He who takes the office of a judge, as it now exists in this country, takes in his hands a splendid gem, good and glorious, perfect and pure. Shall he give it up mutilated, shall he mar it, shall he darken it, shall it emit no light, shall it be valued at no price, shall it excite no wonder? Shall he find it a diamond, shall he leave it a stone? What shall we say to the man who would wilfully destroy with fire the magnificent temple of God, in which I am now preaching? Far worse is he who ruins the moral edifices of the world, which time and toil, and many prayers to God, and many sufferings of men, have reared; who puts out the light of the times in which he lives, and leaves us to wander amid the darkness of corruption and the desolation of sin. There may be, there probably is, in this church, some young man who may hereafter fill the office of an English judge, when the greater part of those who hear me are dead, and mingled with the dust of the grave. Let him remember my words, and let them form and fashion his spirit; he cannot tell in what dangerous and awful times he may be placed; but as a mariner looks to his compass in the calm, and looks to his compass in the storm, and never keeps his eyes off his compass, so, in every vicissitude of a judicial life, deciding for the people, deciding against the people, protecting the just rights of kings, or restraining their unlawful ambition, let him ever cling to that pure, exalted and Christian independence which towers over the little motives of life; which no hope of favour can influence, which no effort of power can control.

A Christian judge in a free country should respect, on every occasion, those popular institutions of justice which were intended for his control, and for our security; to see humble men collected accidentally from the neighbourhood, treated with tenderness and courtesy by supreme magistrates of deep learning and practised understanding, from whose views they are, perhaps, at that moment differing and whose directions they do not choose to follow; to see at such times every disposition to warmth restrained, and every tendency to contemptuous feeling kept back; to witness this submission of the great and wise, not when it is extorted by necessity, but when it is practised with willingness and grace, is a spectacle which is very grateful to Englishmen, which no other country sees, which, above all things, shows that a judge has a pure, gentle, and Christian heart, and that he never wishes to smite contrary to the law.

May I add the great importance in a judge of courtesy to all men, and that he should, on all occasions, abstain from unnecessary bitterness and asperity of speech. A judge always speaks with impunity, and always speaks with effect. His words should be weighed, because they entail no evil upon himself, and much evil upon others. The language of passion, the language of sarcasm, the language of satire, is not, on such occasions, Christian language; it is not the language of a judge. There is a propriety of rebuke and condemnation, the justice of which is felt even by him who suffers under it; but when magistrates, under the mask of law, aim at the offender more than the offence, and are more studious of inflicting pain than repressing error or crime, the office suffers as much as the judge; the respect for justice is lessened; and the school of pure reason becomes the hated theatre of mischievous passion.

A Christian judge who means to be just, must not fear to smite according to the law; he must remember that he beareth not the sword in vain. Under his protection we live, under his protection we acquire, under his protection we enjoy. Without him, no man would defend his character, no man would preserve his substance; proper pride, just gains, valuable exertions, all depend upon his firm wisdom. If he shrink from the severe duties of his office, he saps the foundation of social life, betrays the highest interests of the world, and sits not to judge according to the law.

The topics of mercy are the smallness of the offence—the infrequency of the offence; the temptations to the culprit, the moral weakness of the culprit, the severity of the law, the error of the law, the different state of society, the altered state of feeling, and, above all, the distressing doubt whether a human being in the lowest abyss of poverty and ignorance has not done injustice to himself, and is not perishing away from the want of knowledge, the want of fortune, and the want of friends. All magistrates feel these things in the early exercise of their judicial power, but the Christian judge always feels them, is always tender when he is going to shed human blood; retires from the business of men, communes with his own heart, ponders on the work of death, and prays to that Saviour who redeemed him, that he may not shed the blood of man in vain.

These, then, are those faults which expose a man to the danger of smiting contrary to the law; a judge must be clear from the spirit of party, independent of all favour, well inclined to the popular institutions of his country; firm in applying the rule, merciful in making the exception; patient, guarded in his speech, gentle and courteous to all. Add his learning, his labour, his experience, his probity, his practised and acute faculties, and this man is the light of the world, who adorns human life, and gives security to that life which he adorns.

Now we see the consequence of that state of justice which this character implies, and the explanation of all that deserved honour we confer on the preservation of such a character, and all the wise jealousy we feel at the slightest injury or deterioration it may experience.

The most obvious and important use of this perfect justice is, that it makes nations safe: under common circumstances, the institutions of justice seem to have little or no bearing upon the safety and security of a country, but in periods of real danger, when a nation, surrounded by foreign enemies, contends not for the boundaries of empire, but for the very being and existence of empire, then it is that the advantages of just institutions are discovered. Every man feels that he has a country, that he has something worth preserving, and worth contending for. Instances are remembered where the weak prevailed over the strong; one man recalls to mind when a just and upright judge protected him from unlawful violence, gave him back his vineyard, rebuked his oppressor, restored him to his rights, published, condemned, and rectified the wrong. This is what is called country. Equal rights to unequal possessions, equal justice to the rich and poor; this is what men come out to fight for, and to defend. Such a country has no legal injuries to remember, no legal murders to revenge, no legal robbery to redress; it is strong in its justice; it is then that the use and object of all this assemblage of gentlemen and arrangement of juries, and the deserved veneration in which we hold the character of English judges, are understood in all their bearings, and in their fullest effects: men die for such things—they cannot be subdued by foreign force where such just practices prevail. The sword of ambition is shivered to pieces against such a bulwark. Nations fall where judges are unjust, because there is nothing which the multitude think worth defending; but nations do not fall which are treated as we are treated, but they rise as we have risen, and they shine as we have shone, and die as we have died, too much used to justice, and too much used to freedom, to care for that life which is not just and free. I call you all to witness if there is any exaggerated picture in this; the sword is just sheathed, the flag is just furled, the last sound of the trumpet has just died away. You all remember what a spectacle this country exhibited: one heart, one voice—one weapon, one purpose. And why? Because this country is a country of the law; because the judge is a judge for the peasant as well as for the palace; because every man's happiness is guarded by fixed rules from tyranny and caprice. This town, this week, the business of the few next days, would explain to any enlightened European why other nations *did* fall in the storms of the world, and why we did *not* fall. The Christian patience you may witness, the impartiality of the judgment-seat, the disrespect of persons, the disregard of consequences. These attributes of justice do not end with arranging your conflicting rights, and mine; they give strength to the English people, duration to the English name; they turn the animal courage of this people into moral and religious courage, and present to the lowest of mankind plain reasons and strong motives why they should resist aggression from without, and bend themselves a living rampart round the land of their birth.

There is another reason why every wise man is so scrupulously jealous of the character of English justice. It puts an end to civil dissension. What other countries obtain by bloody wars, is here obtained by the decisions of our own tribunals; unchristian passions are laid to rest by these tribunals; brothers are brothers again; the Gospel resumes its empire, and because all confide in the presiding magistrate, and because a few plain men are allowed to decide upon their own conscientious impression of facts, civil discord, years of convulsion, endless crimes are spared; the storm is laid, and those who came in clamouring for revenge, go back together in peace from the hall of judgment to the loom and the plough, to the senate and the church.

The whole tone and tenour of public morals are affected by the state of supreme justice; it extinguishes revenge, it communicates a spirit of purity and uprightness to inferior magistrates; it makes the great good, by taking away impunity; it banishes fraud, obliquity, and solicitation, and teaches men that the law is their right. Truth is its handmaid, freedom is its child, peace is its companion; safety walks in its steps, victory follows in its train: it is the brightest emanation of the Gospel; it is the greatest attribute of God; it is that centre round which human motives and passions turn: and justice, sitting on high, sees genius and power, and wealth and birth, revolving round her throne; and teaches their paths, and marks out their orbits, and warns with a loud voice, and rules with a strong arm, and carries order and discipline into a world, which, but for her, would only be a wild waste of passions. Look what we are, and what just laws have done for us:—a land of piety and charity;—a land of churches and hospitals and altars;—a nation of good Samaritans;—a people of universal compassion. All lands, all seas, have heard we are brave. We have just sheathed that sword which defended the world; we have just laid down that buckler which covered the nations of the earth. God blesses the soil with fertility; English looms labour for every climate. All the waters of the globe are covered with English ships. We are softened by fine arts, civilized by humane literature, instructed by deep science; and every people, as they break their feudal chains, look to the founders and fathers of freedom for examples which may animate, and rules which may guide. If ever a nation was happy—if ever a nation was visibly blessed by God—if ever a nation was honoured abroad, and left at home under a government (which we can now conscientiously call a liberal government) to the full career of talent, industry, and vigour, we are at this moment that people—and this is our happy lot.—First, the Gospel has done it, and then justice has done it; and he who thinks it his duty to labour that this happy condition of existence may remain, must guard the piety of these times, and he must watch over the spirit of justice which exists in these times. First he must take care that the altars of God are not polluted, that the Christian faith is retained in purity and in perfection; and then turning to human affairs, let him strive for spotless, incorruptible justice;—praising, honouring, and loving the just judge, and abhorring, as the worst enemy of mankind, him who is placed there to "judge after the law, and who smites contrary to the law."

A LETTER TO THE ELECTORS,

UPON

THE CATHOLIC QUESTION.

Why is not a Catholic to be believed on his oath?

What says the law of the land to this extravagant piece of injustice? It is no challenge against a juryman to say he is a Catholic; he sits in judgment upon your life and your property. Did any man ever hear it said that such or such a person was put to death, or that he lost his property, because a Catholic was among the jurymen? Is the question ever put? Does it ever enter into the mind of the attorney or the counsellor to inquire of the faith of the jury? If a man sell a horse, or a house, or a field, does he ask if the purchaser is a Catholic? Appeal to your own experience, and try by that fairest of all tests, the justice of this enormous charge.

We are in treaty with many of the powers of Europe, because we believe in the good faith of Catholics. Two-thirds of Europe are, in fact, Catholics; are they all perjured? For the first fourteen centuries all the Christian world were Catholics; did they live in a constant state of perjury? I am sure these objections against the Catholics are often made by very serious and honest men, but I much doubt if Voltaire has advanced any thing against the Christian religion so horrible, as to say that two-thirds of those who profess it are unfit for all the purposes of civil life; for who is fit to live in society who does not respect oaths? But if this imputation be true, what folly to agitate such questions as the civil emancipation of the Catholics. If they are always ready to support falsehood by an appeal to God, why are they suffered to breathe the air of England, or to drink of the waters of England? Why are they not driven into the howling wilderness? But now they possess, and bequeath, and witness, and decide civil rights; and save life as physicians, and defend property as lawyers, and judge property as jurymen; and you pass laws, enabling them to command all your fleets and armies,* and then you turn round upon the very man whom you have made the master of the European seas, and the arbiter of nations, and tell him he is not to be believed on his oath.

I have lived a little in the world, but I never happened to hear a single Catholic even suspected of getting into office by violating his oath; the oath which they are accused of violating is an insuperable barrier to them all. Is there a more disgraceful spectacle in the world than that of the Duke of Norfolk hovering round the House of Lords in the execution of his office, which he cannot enter as a peer of the realm? disgraceful to the bigotry and injustice of his country, to his own sense of duty, honourable in the extreme; he is the leader of a band of ancient and high-principled gentlemen, who submit patiently to obscurity and privation, rather than do violence to their conscience. In all the fury of party, I never heard the name of a single Catholic mentioned, who was suspected of having gained, or aimed at, any political advantage, by violating his oath. I have never heard so bitter a slander supported by the slightest proof. Every man in the circle of his acquaintance has met with Catholics, and lived with them probably as companions. If this immoral lubricity were their characteristic, it would surely be perceived in common life. Every man's experience would corroborate the imputation; but I can honestly say that some of the best and most excellent men I have ever met with have been Catholics; perfectly alive to the evil and inconvenience of their situation, but thinking themselves bound by the law of God and the law of honour, not to avoid persecution by falsehood and apostasy. But why (as has been asked ten thousand times before) do you lay such a stress upon these oaths of exclusion, if the Catholics do not respect oaths? You compel me, a Catholic, to make a declaration against transubstantiation, for what purpose but to keep me out of Parliament? Why, then, I respect oaths and declarations, or else I should perjure myself, and get into Parliament; and if I do not respect oaths, of what use is it to enact them in order to keep me out? A farmer has some sheep, which he chooses to keep from a certain field, and to effect this object, he builds a wall: there are two objections to his proceeding; the first is, that it is for the good of the farm that the sheep should come into the field; and so the wall is not only useless, but pernicious. The second is, that he himself thoroughly believes at the time of building the wall, that all the sheep are in the constant habit of leaping over such walls. His first intention with respect to the sheep is absurd, his means more absurd, and his error is perfect in all its parts. He tries to do that which, if he succeeds, will be very foolish, and tries to do it by means which he himself, at the time of using them, admits to be inadequate to the purpose; but I hope this objection

* There is no law to prevent a Catholic from having the command of a British fleet or a British army.

to the oaths of Catholics is disappearing; I believe neither Lord Liverpool nor Mr. Peel (a very candid and honourable man), nor the archbishops (who are both gentlemen), nor Lord Eldon, nor Lord Stowell (whose Protestantism nobody calls in question), would make such a charge. It is confined to provincial violence, and to the politicians of the second table. I remember hearing the Catholics from the hustings of an election accused of disregarding oaths, and within an hour from that time, I saw five Catholic voters rejected, because they would not take the oath of supremacy; and these were not men of rank who tendered themselves, but ordinary tradesmen. The accusation was received with loud huzzas; the poor Catholics retired unobserved and in silence. No one praised the conscientious feelings of the constituents; no one rebuked the calumny of the candidate. This is precisely the way in which the Catholics are treated; the very same man who encourages among his partisans the doctrine that Catholics are not to be believed upon their oaths, directs his agents upon the hustings to be very watchful that all Catholics should be prevented from voting, by tendering to them the oath of supremacy, which he is certain not one of them will take. If this is not calumny and injustice, I know not what human conduct can deserve the name.

If you believe the oath of a Catholic, see what he will swear, and what he will not swear; read the oaths he already takes, and say whether, in common candour or in common sense, you can require more security than he offers you. Before the year 1793, the Catholic was subject to many more vexatious laws than he now is; in that year an act passed in his favour, but before the Catholic could exempt himself from his ancient pains and penalties, it was necessary to take an oath. This oath was, I believe, drawn up by Dr. Duigenan, the bitter and implacable enemy of the sect; and it is so important an oath, so little known and read in England, that I cannot, in spite of my wish to be brief, abstain from quoting it. I deny your right to call no Popery, till you are master of its contents.

"I do swear, that I do abjure, condemn, and detest, as unchristian and impious, the principle, that it is lawful to murder, destroy, or any ways injure, any person whatsoever, for or under the pretext of being a heretic; and I do declare solemnly, before God, that I believe no act, in itself unjust, immoral, or wicked, can ever be justified or excused by or under pretence or colour, that it was done either for the good of the church, or in obedience to any ecclesiastical power whatsoever. I also declare that it is not an article of the Catholic faith, neither am I thereby required to believe or profess, that the pope is infallible; or that I am bound to obey any order, in its own nature immoral, though the pope, or any ecclesiastical power, should issue or direct such order; but, on the contrary, I hold that it would be sinful in me to pay any respect or obedience thereto. I further declare, that I do not believe that any sin whatsoever committed by me, can be forgiven at the mere will of any pope or any priest, or of any persons whatsoever; but that sincere sorrow for past sins, a firm and sincere resolution to avoid future guilt, and to atone to God, are previous and indispensable requisites to establish a well-founded expectation of forgiveness; and that any person who receives absolution, without these previous requisites, so far from obtaining thereby any remission of his sins, incurs the additional guilt of violating a sacrament; and I do swear, that I will defend, to the utmost of my power, the settlement and arrangement of property in this country, as established by the laws now in being.—I do hereby disclaim, disavow, and solemnly abjure any intention to subvert the present church establishment, for the purpose of substituting a Catholic establishment in its stead; and I do solemnly swear, that I will not exercise any privilege to which I am or may become entitled, to disturb and weaken the Protestant religion, and Protestant government in this kingdom.' So help me God."

This oath is taken by every Catholic in Ireland, and a similar oath, allowing for the difference of circumstances of the two countries, is taken in England.

It appears from the evidence taken before the two houses and lately printed, that if Catholic emancipation were carried, there would be little or no difficulty in obtaining from the pope an agreement, that the nomination of the Irish Catholic bishops should be made at home constitutionally by the Catholics, as it is now in fact,* and in practice, and that the Irish prelates would go a great way, in arranging a system of general education, if the spirit of proselytism, which now renders such a union impossible, were laid aside. This great measure carried, the Irish Catholics would give up all their endowments abroad, if they receive for them an equivalent at home; for now Irish priests are fast resorting to the continent for education, allured by the endowments which the French government are cunningly restoring and augmenting. The intercourse with the see of Rome might and would, after Catholic emancipation, be so managed, that it should be open, upon grave occasions, or, if thought proper, on every occasion, to the inspection of commissioners. There is no security *compatible with the safety of their faith*, which the Catholics are not willing to give. But what is Catholic emancipation as far as England is concerned? not an equal right to office with the member of the Church of England, but a participation in the same pains and penalties as those, to which the Protestant dissenter is subjected by the corporation and test acts. If the utility of these last-mentioned laws is to be measured by the horror and perturbation their repeal would excite, they are laws of the utmost importance to the defence of the English Church; but if it be of importance to the church that pains and penalties should be thus kept suspended over men's heads, then these bills are

* The Catholic bishops, since the death of the Pretender, are recommended either by the chapters or the parochial clergy, to the pope; and there is no instance of his deviating from their choice.

an effectual security against Catholics as well as Protestants; and the manacles so much confided in are not taken off, but loosened, and the prayer of a Catholic is this:—"I cannot now become an alderman without perjury. I pray of you to improve my condition so far, that if I become an alderman I may be only exposed to a penalty of 500*l*." There are two common errors upon the subject of Catholic emancipation; the one, that the emancipated Catholic is to be put on a better footing than the Protestant dissenter, whereas he will be put precisely on the same footing; the other, that he is to be admitted to civil offices, without any guard, exception, or reserve; whereas, in the various bills which have been from time to time brought forward, the legal wit of man has been exhausted to provide against every surmise, suspicion, and whisper of the most remote danger to the Protestant church.

The Catholic question is not an English question, but an Irish one; or rather it is no otherwise an English question than as it is an Irish one. As for the handful of Catholics that are in England, no one, I presume, can be so extravagant as to contend, if they were the only Catholics we had to do with, that it would be of the slightest possible consequence to what offices of the state they were admitted. It would be quite as necessary to exclude the Sandemanians, who are sixteen in number, or to make a test act against the followers of Joanna Southcote, who amount to one hundred and twenty persons. A little chalk on the wall, and a profound ignorance of the subject, soon raise a cry of no Popery; but I question if the danger of admitting five popish peers and two commoners to the benefits of the constitution could raise a mob in any market-town in England. Whatever good may accrue to England from the emancipation, or evil may befall this country for withholding emancipation, will reach us only through the medium of Ireland.

I beg to remind you, that in talking of the Catholic religion, you must talk of the Catholic religion as it is carried on in Ireland; you have nothing to do with Spain, or France, or Italy: the religion you are to examine is the Irish Catholic religion. You are not to consider what it was, but what it is; not what individuals profess, but what is generally professed; not what individuals do, but what is generally practised. I constantly see, in advertisements from county meetings, all these species of monstrous injustice played off against the Catholics. The Inquisition exists in Spain and Portugal, therefore I confound place, and vote against the Catholics of Ireland, where it never did exist, nor was purposed to be instituted.* There have been many cruel persecutions of Protestants by Catholic governments; and, therefore, I will confound time and place, and vote against the Irish, who live centuries after these persecutions, and in a totally different country. Doctor this, or Doctor that, of the Catholic Church, has written a very violent and absurd pamphlet; therefore I will confound persons, and vote against the whole Irish Catholic church, which has neither sanctioned nor expressed any such opinions. I will continue the incapacities of men of this age, because some men, in distant ages, deserved ill of other men in distant ages. They shall expiate the crimes committed, before they were born, in a land they never saw, by individuals they never heard of. I will charge them with every act of folly which they have never sanctioned and cannot control. I will sacrifice space, time, and identity, to my zeal for the Protestant Church. Now, in the midst of all this violence, consider, for a moment, how you are imposed upon by words, and what a serious violation of the rights of your fellow-creatures you are committing. Mr. Murphy lives in Limerick, and Mr. Murphy and his son are subjected to a thousand inconveniences and disadvantages because they are Catholics. Murphy is a wealthy, honourable, excellent man; he ought to be in the corporation; he cannot get in because he is a Catholic. His son ought to be king's counsel for his talents, and his standing at the bar; he is prevented from reaching this dignity because he is a Catholic. Why, what reasons do you hear for all this? Because Queen Mary, three hundred years before the natal day of Mr. Murphy, murdered Protestants in Smithfield; because Louis XIV. dragooned his Protestant subjects, when the predecessor of Murphy's predecessor was not in being; because men are confined in prison in Madrid, twelve degrees more south than Murphy has ever been in his life; all ages, all climates, are ransacked to perpetuate the slavery of Murphy, the ill-fated victim of political anachronisms.

Suppose a barrister, in defending a prisoner, were to say to the judge, "My lord, I humbly submit to your lordship that this indictment against the prisoner cannot stand good in law; and as the safety of a fellow-creature is concerned, I request your lordship's patient attention to my objections. In the first place, the indictment does not pretend that the prisoner at the bar is himself guilty of the offence, but that some persons of the same religious sect as himself are so; in whose crime he cannot (I submit), by any possibility, be implicated, as these criminal persons lived three hundred years before the prisoner was born. In the next place, my lord, the *venue* of several crimes imputed to the prisoner is laid in countries to which the jurisdiction of this court does not extend; in France, Spain, and Italy, where also the prisoner has never been; and as to the argument used by my learned brother, that it is only want of power, and not want of will, and that the prisoner *would* commit the crime *if* he *could;* I humbly submit, that the custom of England has been to wait for the overt act before pain and penalty are inflicted, and that your lordship would pass a most doleful assize, if punishment depended upon evil volition; if men were subjected to legal incapacities from the mere suspicion that they *would* do harm *if* they *could;* and if it were admitted to be sufficient proof of this suspicion, that men of this faith in distant ages, different countries,

* While Mary was burning Protestants in England, not a single Protestant was executed in Ireland: and yet the terrors of that reign are, at this moment, one of the most operative causes of the exclusion of Irish Catholics.

and under different circumstances, had planned evil, and when occasion offered, done it."

When are mercy and justice, in fact, ever to return upon the earth, if the sins of the elders are to be for ever visited on these who are not even their children? Should the first act of liberated Greece be to recommence the Trojan war? Are the French never to forget the Sicilian vespers; or the Americans the long war waged against their liberties? Is any rule wise, which may set the Irish to recollect what they have suffered?

The real danger is this—that you have four Irish Catholics for one Irish Protestant. That is the matter of fact, which none of us can help. Is it better policy to make friends, rather than enemies, of this immense population? I allow there is danger to the Protestant Church, but much more danger, I am sure there is, in resisting than admitting the claims of the Catholics. If I might indulge in visions of glory, and imagine myself an Irish dean or bishop, with an immense ecclesiastical income; if the justice or injustice of the case were entirely indifferent to me, and my only object were to live at ease in my possessions, *there is no measure for which I should be so anxious as that of Catholic emancipation.* The Catholics are now extremely angry and discontented at being shut out from so many offices and honours; the incapacities to which they are subjected thwart them in all their pursuits; they feel they are a degraded caste. The Protestant feels he is a privileged caste, and not only the Protestant gentleman feels this, but every Protestant servant feels it, and takes care that his Catholic fellow-servant shall perceive it. The difference between the two religions is an eternal source of enmity, ill-will, and hatred, and the Catholic remains in a state of permanent disaffection to the government under which he lives. I repeat that if I were a member of the Irish church, I should be afraid of this position of affairs. I should fear it in peace, on account of riot and insurrection, and in war on account of rebellion. I should think that my greatest security consisted in removing all just cause of complaint from the Catholic society, in endearing them to the English constitution, by making them feel, as soon as possible, that they shared in its blessings. I should really think my tithes and my glebe, upon such a plan, worth twenty years' purchase more than under the present system. Suppose the Catholic layman were to think it an evil, that his own church should be less splendidly endowed than that of the Protestant Church, whose population is so inferior; yet if he were free himself, and had nothing to complain of, he would not rush into rebellion and insurrection, merely to augment the income of his priest. At present you bind the laity and clergy in one common feeling of injustice; each feels for himself, and talks of the injuries of the other. The obvious consequence of Catholic emancipation would be to separate their interests. But another important consequence of Catholic emancipation would be to improve the condition of the clergy. Their chapels would be put in order, their incomes increased, and we should hear nothing more of the Catholic Church. If this measure were carried in March, I believe by the January following, the whole question would be as completely forgotten as the sweating sickness, and that nine Doctor Doyles, at the rate of thirty years to a Doyle, would pass away one after the other, before any human being heard another syllable on the subject. All men gradually yield to the comforts of a good income. Give the Irish archbishop 1200*l.* per annum; the bishop 800*l.*, the priest 200*l.*, the coadjutor 100*l.*, per annum, and the cathedral of Dublin is almost as safe as the Cathedral of York.* This is the real secret of putting an end to the Catholic question; there is no other; but, remember, I am speaking of provision for the Catholic clergy after emancipation, not before. There is not an Irish clergyman of the Church of Rome who would touch one penny of the public money before the laity were restored to civil rights, and why not pay the Catholic clergy as well as the Presbyterian clergy? Ever since the year 1803, the Presbyterian clergy in the North of Ireland have been paid by the government, and the grant is annually brought forward in Parliament; and not only are the Presbyterians paid, but one or two other species of Protestant dissenters. The consequence has been loyalty and peace. This way of appeasing dissenters you may call expensive, but is there no expense in injustice? You have at this moment an army of 20,000 men in Ireland, horse, foot, and artillery, at an annual expense of a million and a half of money; about one-third of this sum would be the expense of the allowance to the Catholic clergy; and this army is so necessary, that the government dare not at this moment remove a single regiment from Ireland. Abolish these absurd and disgraceful distinctions, and a few troops of horse to help the constables on fair days will be more than sufficient for the catholic limb of the empire.

Now for a very few of the shameful misrepresentations circulated respecting the Irish Catholics, for I repeat again that we have nothing to do with Spanish or Italian, but with Irish Catholics; it is not true that the Irish Catholics refuse to circulate the Bible in English; on the contrary, they have in Ireland circulated several editions of the Scriptures in English. In the last year, the Catholic prelates prepared and put forth a stereotype edition of the Bible, of a small print and low price, to insure its general circulation. They circulate the Bible with their own notes, and how, as Catholics, can they act otherwise? Are not our prelates and Bartlett's buildings acting in the same manner? And must not all churches, if they are consistent, act in

* I say *almost*, because I hate to overstate an argument, and it is impossible to deny that there is danger to a church, to which seven millions contribute largely, and in which six millions disbelieve; my argument merely is, that such a church would be more safe in proportion as it interfered less with the comforts and ease of its natural enemies, and rendered their position more desirable and agreeable. I firmly believe the Toleration Act to be quite as conducive to the security of the Church of England as it is to the dissenters. Perfect toleration and the abolition of every incapacity as a consequence of religious opinions, are not, what is commonly called, a receipt for innovation, but a receipt for the quiet and permanence of every establishment which has the real good sense to adopt it.

the same manner? The Bibles Catholics quarrel with, are Protestant Bibles without notes, or Protestant Bibles with Protestant notes, and how can they do otherwise without giving up their religion? They deny, upon oath, that the infallibility of the pope is any necessary part of the Catholic faith. They, upon oath, declare that Catholic people are forbidden to worship images, and saints, and relics. They, upon oath, abjure the temporal power of the pope, or his right to absolve any Catholic from his oath. They renounce, upon oath, all right to forfeit lands, and covenant, upon oath, not to destroy or plot against the Irish Protestant Church. What more can any man want whom any thing will content?

Some people talk as if they were quite teased and worried by the eternal clamours of the Catholics; but if you are eternally unjust, can you expect any thing more than to be eternally vexed by the victims of your injustice? You want all the luxury of oppression without any of its inconvenience. I should think the Catholics very much to blame, if they ever ceased to importune the legislature for justice, so long as they could find one single member of Parliament who would advocate their cause.

The putting the matter to rest by an effort of the county of York, or by any decision of Parliament against them, is utterly hopeless. Every year increases the Catholic population, and the Catholic wealth, and the Catholic claims, till you are caught in one of those political attitudes to which all countries are occasionally exposed, in which you are utterly helpless, and must give way to their claims; and if you do it then, you will do it badly; you may call it an arrangement, but arrangements made at such times are much like the bargains between an highwayman and a traveller, a pistol on one side, and a purse on the other; the rapid scramble of armed violence, and the unqualified surrender of helpless timidity. *If you think the thing must be done at some time or another, do it when you are calm and powerful, and when you need not do it.*

There are a set of high-spirited men who are very much afraid of being afraid; who cannot brook the idea of doing any thing from fear, and whose conversation is full of fire and sword, when any apprehension of resistance is alluded to. I have a perfect confidence in the high and unyielding spirit, and in the military courage of the English; and I have no doubt but that many of the country gentlemen, who now call out no Popery, would fearlessly put themselves at the head of their embattled yeomanry, to control the Irish Catholics. My objection to such courage is, that it would certainly be exercised unjustly, and probably exercised in vain. I should deprecate any rising of the Catholics as the most grievous misfortune which could happen to the empire and to themselves. They had far better endure all they do endure, and a great deal worse, than try the experiment. *But if they do try it, you may depend upon it, they will do it at their own time, and not at yours.* They will not select a fortnight in the summer, during a profound peace, when corn and money abound, and when the Catholics of Europe are unconcerned spectators. If you make a resolution to be unjust, you must make another resolution to be always strong, always vigilant, and always rich; you must commit no blunders, exhibit no deficiencies, and meet with no misfortunes; you must present a square phalanx of impenetrable strength, for keen-eyed revenge is riding round your ranks; and if one heart falters, or one hand trembles, you are lost.

You may call all this threatening; I am sure I have no such absurd intention; but wish only, in sober sadness, to point out what appears to me to be the inevitable consequences of the conduct we pursue. If danger be not pointed out and insisted upon, how is it to be avoided? My firm belief is, that England will be compelled to grant ignominiously what she now refuses haughtily. Remember what happened respecting Ireland in the American war. In 1779, the Irish, whose trade was completely restricted by English laws, asked for some little relaxation, some liberty to export her own products, and to import the products of other countries; their petition was flung out of the house with the utmost disdain, and by an immense majority. In April, 1782, 70,000 Irish volunteers were under arms, the representatives of 170 armed corps met at Ulster, and the English Parliament (the Lords and Commons, both on the same day and with only one dissentient voice, the ministers moving the question) were compelled, in the most disgraceful and precipitate manner, to acknowledge the complete independence of the Irish nation, *and nothing but the good sense and moderation of Grattan prevented the separation of the two crowns.*

It is no part of my province to defend every error of the Catholic Church: I believe it has many errors, though I am sure these errors are grievously exaggerated and misrepresented. I should think it a vast accession to the happiness of mankind, if every Catholic in Europe were converted to the Protestant faith. The question is not, whether there shall be Catholics, but the question (as they do exist and you cannot get rid of them) is, what are you to do with them? Are you to make men rebels because you cannot make them Protestants? and are you to endanger your state, because you cannot enlarge your church? England is the ark o liberty: the English Church I believe to be one of the best establishments in the world; but what is to become of England, of its church, of its free institutions, and the beautiful political model it holds out to mankind, if Ireland should succeed in connecting itself with any other European power hostile to England? I join in the cry of no Popery as lustily as any man in the streets who does not know whether the pope lives in Cumberland or Westmoreland; but I know that it is impossible to keep down European Popery, and European tyranny, without the assistance, or with the opposition of Ireland. If you give the Irish their privileges, the spirit of the nation will overcome the spirit of the church; they will cheerfully serve you against all enemies, and chant a *Te Deum* for your victories over all the Catholic armies of Europe. If it be true, as her enemies say, that the Roman Catholic Church is waging war all over Europe, against common sense, against public liberty; selling the people to the kings and nobles, and labouring for the few against the many; all this is an additional reason why I would fortify England and Protestantism by every concession to Ireland: why I should take care that our attention was not distracted, nor our strength wasted by internal dissension; why I would not paralyze those arms which wield the sword of justice among the nations of the world, and lift up the buckler of safety. If the Catholic religion in Ireland is an abuse, you must tolerate that abuse, to prevent its extension and tyranny over the rest of Europe. If you will take a long view instead of a confined view, and look generally to the increase of human happiness, *the best check upon the increase of Popery, the best security for the establishment of the Protestant Church is, that the British empire shall be preserved in a state of the greatest strength, union and opulence.* My cry, then, is, *no Popery;* therefore emancipate the Catholics, that they may not join with foreign Papists in time of war. *Church for ever;* therefore emancipate the Catholics, that they may not help to pull it down. *King for ever;* therefore emancipate the Catholics, that they may become his loyal subjects. *Great Britain for ever;* therefore emancipate the Catholics, that they may not put an end to its perpetuity. *Our government is essentially Protestant;* therefore, by emancipating the Catholics, give up a few circumstances which have nothing to do with the essence. *The Catholics are disguised enemies;* therefore, by emancipation, turn them into open friends. *They have a double allegiance;* therefore, by emancipation, make their allegiance to their king so grateful, that they will never confound it with the spiritual allegiance to their pope. It is very difficult for electors, who are much occupied by other matters, to choose the right path amid the rage and fury of faction; but I give you one mark, *vote for a free altar;* give what the law compels you to give to the establishment; (that done,) no chains, no prisons, no bonfires for a man's faith; and, above all, no modern chains and prisons under the names of disqualifications and incapacities, which *are only the cruelty and tyranny of a more civilized age;* civil offices open to all, a Catholic or a Protestant alderman, a Moravian, or a Church of England, or a Wesleyan justice; *no oppression, no tyranny in belief: a free altar, an open road to heaven; no human insolence, no human narrowness, hallowed by the name of God.*

Every man in trade must have experienced the difficulty of getting in a bill from an unwilling paymaster. If you call in the morning, the gentleman is not up; if in the middle of the day, he is out; if in the evening, there is company. If you ask mildly, you are indifferent to the time of payment; if you press, you are impertinent. No time and no manner can render such a message agreeable. So it is with the poor Catholics; their message is so disagreeable, that their time and manner can never be right. "Not this session. Not *now;* on no account at the present time; any other time than this. The great mass of the Catholics are so torpid on the subject, that the question is clearly confined to the ambition of the few, or the whole Catholic population are so leagued together, that the object is clearly to intimidate the mother-country." In short, the Catholics want justice, and we do not mean to be just, and the most specious method of refusal is, to have it believed that they are refused from their own folly, and not from our fault.

What if O'Connell (a man certainly of extraordinary talents and eloquence) is sometimes violent and injudicious? What if O'Gorman and O'Sullivan have spoken ill of the Reformation? Is a great stroke of national policy to depend on such childish considerations as these? If these chains ought to remain, could I be induced to remove them by the chaste language and humble deportment of him who wears them? If they ought to be struck away, would I continue them, because my taste was offended by the coarse insolence of a goaded and injured captive? Would I make that great measure to depend on the irritability of my own feelings, which ought to depend upon policy and justice? The more violent and the more absurd the conduct of the Catholics, the greater the wisdom of emancipation. If they were always governed by men of consummate prudence and moderation, your justice in refusing would be the same, but your danger would be less. The levity and irritability of the Irish character are pressing reasons why all just causes of provocation should be taken away, and those high passions enlisted in the service of the empire.

In talking of the spirit of the papal empire, it is often argued that the *will* remains the same; that the pontiff *would,* if he *could,* exercise the same influence in Europe; that the Catholic Church *would, if it could,* tyrannize over the rights and opinions of mankind; but if the power is taken away, what signifies the will? If the pope thunders in vain against the kingdoms of the earth, of what consequence is his disposition to thunder? If mankind are too enlightened and too humane to submit to the cruelties and hatreds of a Catholic priesthood; if the Protestants of the empire are sufficiently strong to resist it, why are we to alarm ourselves with the barren volition, unseconded by the requisite power? I hardly know in what order or description of men I should choose to confide, if they *could* do as they *would;* the best security is, that the rest of the world will not let them do as they wish to do; and having satisfied myself of this, I am not very careful about the rest.

Our government is called essentially Protestant; but if it be essentially Protestant in the imposition of taxes, it should be essentially Protestant in the distribution of offices. The treasury is open to all religions, Parliament only to one. The tax-gatherer is the most indulgent and liberal of human beings: he excludes no creed, imposes no articles; but counts Catholic cash, pockets Protestant paper; and is candidly and impartially oppressive to every description of the Christian world. Can any thing be more base than when you want the blood or the money of the

Catholics, to forget that they are Catholics, and to remember only that they are British subjects; and when they ask for the benefits of the British constitution, to remember only that they are Catholics, and to forget that they are British subjects?

No Popery was the cry of the great English Revolution, because the increase and prevalence of Popery in England would, at that period, have rendered this island tributary to France. The Irish Catholics were, at that period, broken to pieces by the severity and military execution of Cromwell, and by the penal laws. They are since become a great and formidable people. The same dread of foreign influence makes it now necessary that they should be restored to political rights. Must the friends of rational liberty join in a clamour against the Catholics now, because, in a very different state of the world, they excited that clamour a hundred years ago? I remember a house near Battersea Bridge which caught fire, and there was a general cry of "Water, water!" Ten years after, the Thames rose, and the people of the house were nearly drowned. Would it not have been rather singular to have said to the inhabitants, "I heard you calling for water ten years ago, why don't you call for it now?"

There are some men who think the present times so incapable of forming any opinions, that they are always looking back to the wisdom of our ancestors. Now, as the Catholics sat in the English Parliament to the reign of Charles II. and in the Irish Parliament, I believe, till the reign of King William, the precedents are more in their favour than otherwise; and to replace them in the Parliament seems rather to return to, than to deviate from the practice of our ancestors.

If the Catholics are priest-ridden, pamper the rider, and he will not stick so close; don't torment the animal ridden, and his violence will be less dangerous.

The strongest evidence against the Catholics is that of Colonel John Irvine; he puts every thing against them in the strongest light, and Colonel John (with great actual, though, I am sure, with no intentional exaggeration) does not pretend to say there would be more than forty-six members returned for Ireland who were Catholics; but how many members are there in the House now returned by Catholics, and compelled, from the fear of losing their seats, to vote in favour of every measure which concerns the Catholic Church? The Catholic party, as the colonel justly observes, was formed when you admitted them to the elective franchise. The Catholic party are increasing so much in boldness, that they will soon require of the members they return, to oppose generally any government hostile to Catholic emancipation, and they will turn out those who do not comply with this rule. If this is done, the phalanx so much dreaded from emancipation is found at once without emancipation. This consequence of resistance to the Catholic claims is well worth the attention of those who make use of the cry of no Popery, as a mere political engine.

We are taunted with our prophetical spirit, because it is said by the advocates of the Catholic question that the thing must come to pass; that it is inevitable: our prophecy, however, is founded upon experience and common sense, and is nothing more than the application of the past to the future. In a few years' time, when the madness and wretchedness of war are forgotten, when the greater part of those who have lost in war, legs and arms, health and sons, have gone to their graves, the same scenes will be acted over again in the world. France, Spain, Russia, and America, will be upon us. The Catholics will watch their opportunity, and soon settle the question of Catholic emancipation. To suppose that any nation can go on in the midst of foreign wars, denying common justice to seven millions of men, in the heart of the empire, awakened to their situation, and watching for the critical moment of redress, does, I confess, appear to me to be the height of extravagance. To foretell the consequence of such causes, in my humble apprehension, demands no more of shrewdness than to point out the probable results of leaving a lighted candle stuck up in an open barrel of gunpowder.

It is very difficult to make the mass of mankind believe that the state of things is ever to be otherwise than they have been accustomed to see it. I have very often heard old persons describe the impossibility of making any one believe that the American colonies could ever be separated from this country. It was always considered as an idle dream of discontented politicians, good enough to fill up the periods of a speech, but which no practical man, devoid of the spirit of party, considered to be within the limits of possibility. There was a period when the slightest concession would have satisfied the Americans; but all the world was in heroics; one set of gentlemen met at the Lamb, and another at the Lion: blood and treasure men, breathing war, vengeance, and contempt; and in eight years afterwards, an awkward-looking gentleman in plain clothes walked up to the drawing-room of St. James's, in the midst of the gentlemen of the Lion and Lamb, and was introduced as the *ambassador from the United States of America.*

You must forgive me if I draw illustrations from common things—but in seeing swine driven, I have often thought of the Catholic question and of the different methods of governing mankind. The object, one day, was to drive some of these animals along a path, to a field where they had not been before. The man could by no means succeed; instead of turning their faces to the north, and proceeding quietly along, they made for the east and west, rushed back to the south, and positively refused to advance; a reinforcement of rustics was called for; maids, children, neighbours, all helped; a general rushing, screaming, and roaring ensued; but the main object was not in the slightest degree advanced; after a long delay, we resolved (though an hour before we should have disdained such a compromise) to have recourse to Catholic emancipation; a little boy was sent before them with a handful of barley: a few grains were scattered in the path, and the bristly herd were speedily and safely conducted to the place of their destination. If, instead of putting Lord Stowell out of breath with driving, compelling the Duke of York to swear, and the chancellor to strike at them with the mace, Lord Liverpool would condescend, in his graceful manner, to walk before the Catholic doctors with a basket of barley, what a deal of ink and blood would be saved to mankind.

Because the Catholics are intolerant we will be intolerant; but did any body ever hear before that a government is to imitate the vices of its subjects? If the Irish were a rash, violent, and intemperate race, are they to be treated with rashness, violence, and intemperance? If they were addicted to fraud and falsehood, are they to be treated by those who rule them with fraud and falsehood? Are there to be perpetual races in error and vice between the people and the lords of the people? Is the supreme power always to find virtues among the people; never to teach them by example, or improve them by laws and institutions? Make all sects free, and let them learn the value of the blessing to others, by their own enjoyment of it; but if not, let them learn it by your vigilance and firm resistance to every thing intolerant. Toleration will then become a habit and a practice, ingrafted upon the manners of a people, when they find the law too strong for them, and that there is no use in being intolerant.

It is very true that the Catholics have a double allegiance,* but it is equally true that their second or spiritual allegiance has nothing to do with civil policy, and does not, in the most distant manner, interfere with their allegiance to the crown. What is meant by allegiance to the crown, is, I presume, obedience to acts of Parliament, and a resistance to those who are constitutionally proclaimed to be the enemies of the country. I have seen and heard of no instance, for this century and a half last past, where the spiritual sovereign has presumed to meddle with the affairs of the temporal sovereign. The Catholics deny him such power by the most solemn oaths which the wit of man can devise. In every war, the army and navy are full of Catholic officers and soldiers; and if their allegiance in temporal matters is unimpeachable and unimpeached, what matters to whom they choose to pay spiritual obedience, and to adopt as their guide in genuflexion and psalmody? Suppose these same Catholics were foolish enough to be governed by a set of Chinese moralists in their diet, this would be a third allegiance; and if they were regulated by Brahmins in their dress, this would be a fourth allegiance; and if they received the directions of the Patriarch of the Greek Church, in educating their children, here is another allegiance: and as long as they fought, and paid taxes, and kept clear of the quarter sessions and assizes, what matters how many fanciful supremacies and frivolous allegiances they choose to manufacture or accumulate for themselves?

A great deal of time would be spared, if gentlemen, before they ordered their post-chaises for a no-Popery meeting, would read the most elementary defence of these people, and inform themselves even of the rudiments of the question. If the Catholics meditate the resumption of the Catholic property, why do they purchase that which they know (if the fondest object of their political life succeed) must be taken away from them? Why is not an attempt made to purchase a quietus from the rebel who is watching the blessed revolutionary moment for regaining his possessions, and revelling in the unbounded sensuality of mealy and waxy enjoyments? But after all, who are the descendants of the rightful possessors? The estate belonged to the O'Rourkes, who were hanged, drawn and quartered in the time of Cromwell: true, but before that, it belonged to the O'Connors, who were hanged, drawn and quartered in the time of Henry VII. The O'Sullivans have a still earlier plea of suspension, evisceration and division. Who is the rightful possessor of the estate? We forget that Catholic Ireland has been murdered three times over by its Protestant masters.

Mild and genteel people do not like the idea of persecution, and are advocates for toleration; but then they think it no act of intolerance to deprive Catholics of political power. The history of all this is, that all men secretly like to punish others for not being of the same opinion with themselves, and that this sort of privation is the only species of persecution, of which the improved feeling and advanced cultivation of the age will admit. Fire and fagot, chains and stone walls, have been clamoured away; nothing remains but to mortify a man's pride, and to limit his resources, and to set a mark upon him, by cutting him off from his fair share of political power. By this receipt, insolence is gratified, and humanity is not shocked. The gentlest Protestant can see, with dry eyes, Lord Stourton excluded from Parliament, though he would abominate the most distant idea of personal cruelty to Mr. Petre. This is only to say that he lives in the nineteenth, instead of the sixteenth century, and that he is as intolerant in religious matters as the state of manners existing in his age will permit. Is it not the same spirit which wounds the pride of a fellow-creature on account of his faith, or which casts his body into the flames? Are they any thing else but degrees and modifications of the same principle? The minds of these two men no more differ because they differ in their degrees of punishment, than their bodies differ, because one wore a doublet in the time of Mary, and the other wears a coat in the reign of George. I do not accuse them of intentional cruelty and injustice; I am sure there are very many excellent men who would be shocked if they could conceive themselves to be guilty of any thing like cruelty; but they innocently give a wrong name to the bad spirit which is within them, and think they are tolerant, because they are not as intolerant as they could have been in other times, but cannot be now. The true spirit is to search after God and for another life with lowliness of heart; to fling down no man's altar, to punish no man's prayer; to heap no penalties and no pains on those solemn supplications which, in divers

* The same double allegiance exists in every Catholic country in Europe. The spiritual head of the country among French, Spanish, and Austrian Catholics, is the pope; the political head, the king or emperor.

tongues, and in varied forms, and in temples of a thousand shapes, but with one deep sense of human dependence, men pour forth to God.

It is completely untrue that the Catholic religion is what it was three centuries ago, or that it is unchangeable and unchanged. These are mere words, without the shadow of truth to support them. If the pope were to address a bull to the kingdom of Ireland, excommunicating the Duke of York, and cutting him off from the succession, for his Protestant effusion in the House of Lords, he would be laughed at as a lunatic in all the Catholic chapels in Dublin. The Catholics would not now burn Protestants as heretics. In many parts of Europe, Catholics and Protestants worship in one church—Catholics at eleven, Protestants at one; they sit in the same Parliament, are elected to the same office, live together without hatred or friction, under equal laws. Who can see and know these things, and say that the Catholic religion is unchangeable and unchanged?

I have often endeavoured to reflect upon the causes which, from time to time, raised such a clamour against the Catholics, and I think the following are among the most conspicuous:

1. Historical recollections of the cruelties inflicted upon the Protestants.

2. Theological differences.

3. A belief that the Catholics are unfriendly to liberty.

4. That their morality is not good.

5. That they meditate the destruction of the Protestant Church.

6. An unprincipled clamour by men who have no sort of belief in the danger of emancipation, but who make use of no Popery as a political engine.

7. A mean and selfish spirit of denying to others the advantages we ourselves enjoy.

8. A vindictive spirit or love of punishing others, who offend our self-love by presuming, on important points, to entertain opinions opposite to our own.

9. Stupid compliance with the opinions of the majority.

10. To these I must, in justice and candour, add, as a tenth cause, a real apprehension on the part of honest and reasonable men, that it is dangerous to grant farther concessions to the Catholics.

To these various causes I shall make a short reply, in the order in which I have placed them.

1. Mere historical recollections are very miserable reasons for the continuation of penal and incapacitating laws, and one side has as much to recollect as the other.

2. The state has nothing to do with questions purely theological.

3. It is ill to say this in a country whose free institutions were founded by Catholics, and it is often said by men who care nothing about free institutions.

4. It is not true.

5. Make their situation so comfortable, that it will not be worth their while to attempt an enterprise so desperate.

6. This is an unfair political trick, because it is too dangerous; it is spoiling the table in order to win the game.

The 7th and 8th causes exercise a great share of influence in every act of intolerance. The 9th must, of course, comprehend the greatest number.

10. Of the existence of such a class of no Poperists as this, it would be the height of injustice to doubt, but I confess it excites in me a very great degree of astonishment.

Suppose, after a severe struggle, you put the Irish down, if they are mad and foolish enough to recur to open violence; yet are the retarded industry, and the misapplied energies of so many millions of men to go for nothing? Is it possible to forget all the wealth, peace and happiness which are to be sacrificed for twenty years to come, to these pestilential and disgraceful squabbles? Is there no horror in looking forward to a long period in which men, instead of ploughing and spinning, will curse and hate, and burn and murder?

There seems to me a sort of injustice and impropriety in our deciding at all upon the Catholic question. It should be left to those Irish Protestants whose shutters are bullet-proof; whose dinner-table is regularly spread with knife, fork, and cocked pistol; salt cellar and powder-flask. Let the opinion of those persons be resorted to, who sleep in sheet-iron night-caps; who have fought so often and so nobly before their scullery door, and defended the parlour passage as bravely as Leonidas defended the pass of Thermopylæ. The Irish Protestant members see and know the state of their own country. Let their votes decide* the case. We are quiet and at peace; our homes may be defended with a feather, and our doors fastened with a pin; and as ignorant of what armed and insulted Popery is, as we are of the state of New Zealand, we pretend to regulate by our clamours the religious factions of Ireland.

It is a very pleasant thing to trample upon Catholics, and it is also a very pleasant thing to have an immense number of pheasants running about your woods; but there come thirty or forty poachers in the night, and fight with thirty or forty game preservers; some are killed, some fractured, some scalped, some maimed for life. Poachers are caught up and hanged; a vast body of hatred and revenge accumulates in the neighbourhood of the great man; and he says "the sport is not worth the candle. The preservation of game is a very agreeable thing, but I will not sacrifice the happiness of my life to it. This amusement, like any other, may be purchased too dearly." So it is with the Irish Protestants; they are finding out that Catholic exclusion may be purchased too dearly. Maimed cattle, fired ricks, threatening letters, barricadoed houses, to endure all this, is to purchase superiority at too dear a rate, and this is the inevitable state of two parties, the one of whom are unwilling to relinquish their ancient monopoly of power, while the other party have, at length, discovered their strength, and are determined to be free.

Gentlemen (with the best intentions, I am

---

* A great majority of Irish members voted for Catholic emancipation.

sure) meet together in a county town, and enter into resolutions that no farther concessions are to be made to the Catholics; but if you will not let them into Parliament, why not allow them to be king's counsel, or serjeants at law? Why are they excluded by law from some corporations in Ireland, and admissible, though not admitted, to others? I think, before such general resolutions of exclusion are adopted, and the rights and happiness of so many millions of people disposed of, it would be decent and proper to obtain some tolerable information of what the present state of the Irish Catholics is, and of the vast number of insignificant offices from which they are excluded. Keep them from Parliament, if you think it right, but do not, therefore, exclude them from any thing else, to which you think Catholics may be fairly admitted without danger; and as to their content or discontent, there can be no sort of reason why discontent should not be lessened, though it cannot be removed.

You are shocked by the present violence and abuse used by the Irish Association; by whom are they driven to it? and whom are you to thank for it? Is there a hope left to them? Is any term of endurance alluded to? any scope or boundary to their patience? Is the minister waiting for opportunities? Have they reason to believe that they are wished well to by the greatest of the great? Have they brighter hopes in another reign? Is there one clear spot in the horizon? any thing that you have left to them, but that disgust, hatred and despair, which, breaking out into wild eloquence, and acting upon a wild people, are preparing every day a mass of treason and disaffection, which may shake this empire to its very centre? and you may laugh at Daniel O'Connell, and treat him with contempt, and turn his metaphors into ridicule; but Daniel has, after all, a great deal of real and powerful eloquence; and a strange sort of misgiving sometimes comes across me, that Daniel and the doctor are not quite so great fools as many most respectable country clergymen believe them to be.

You talk of their abuse of the Reformation, but is there any end to the obloquy and abuse with which the Catholics are upon every point, and from every quarter, assailed? Is there any one folly, vice, or crime, which the blind fury of Protestants does not lavish upon them? and do you suppose all this is to be heard in silence, and without retaliation? Abuse as much as you please, if you are going to emancipate, but if you intend to do nothing for the Catholics but to call them names, you must not be put out of temper if you receive a few ugly appellations in return.

The great object of men who love party better than truth, is to have it believed that the Catholics alone have been persecutors; but what can be more flagrantly unjust than to take our notions of history only from the conquering and triumphant party? If you think the Catholics have not their Book of Martyrs as well as the Protestants, take the following enumeration of some of their most learned and careful writers.

The whole number of Catholics who have suffered death in England for the exercise of the Roman Catholic religion since the Reformation:

Henry VIII.,	59
Elizabeth,	204
James I.,	25
Charles I., and Commonwealth,	23
Charles II.,	8
Total,	319

Henry VIII., with consummate impartiality, burnt three Protestants and hanged four Catholics for different errors in religion on the same day, and the same place. Elizabeth burnt two Dutch Anabaptists for some theological tenets, July 22, 1575, Fox the martyrologist vainly pleading with the queen in their favour. In 1579, the same Protestant queen cut off the hand of Stubbs, the author of a tract against popish connection, of Singleton, the printer, and Page, the disperser of the book. Camden saw it done. Warburton properly says it exceeds in cruelty any thing done by Charles I. On the 4th of June, Mr. Elias Thacker and Mr. John Capper, two ministers of the Brownist persuasion, were hanged at St. Edmundsbury, for dispersing books against the Common Prayer. With respect to the great part of the Catholic victims, the law was fully and literally executed; after being hanged up, they were cut down alive, dismembered, ripped up, and their bowels burnt before their faces; after which, they were beheaded and quartered. The time employed in this butchery was very considerable, and, in one instance, lasted more than half an hour.

The uncandid excuse for all this is, that the greater part of these men were put to death for political, not for religious crimes. That is, a law is first passed making it high treason for a priest to exercise his function in England, and so, when he is caught and burnt, this is not religious persecution, but an offence against the state. We are, I hope, all too busy to need any answer to such childish, uncandid reasoning as this.

The total number of those who suffered capitally in the reign of Elizabeth, is stated by Dodd, in his Church History,* to be one hundred and ninety-nine; further inquiries made their number to be two hundred and four: fifteen of these were condemned for denying the queen's supremacy; one hundred and twenty-six for the exercise of priestly functions; and the others for being reconciled to the Catholic faith, or for aiding and assisting priests. In this list, no person is included who was executed for any plot, real or imaginary, except eleven, who suffered for the pretended plot of Rheims; a plot, which Dr. Milner justly observes, was so daring a forgery, that even Camden allows the sufferers to have been po-

* The total number of sufferers in the reign of Queen Mary, varies, I believe, from 200 in the Catholic to 280 in the Protestant accounts. I recommend all young men who wish to form some notion of what answer the Catholics have to make, to read Milner's "Letters to a Prebendary," and to follow the line of reading to which his references lead. They will then learn the importance of that sacred maxim, *Audi alteram partem.*

litical victims. Besides these, mention is made in the same work of ninety Catholic priests, or laymen, who died in prison in the same reign. "About the same time," he says, "I find fifty gentlemen lying prisoners in York Castle; *most of them perished there*, of vermin, famine, hunger, thirst, dirt, damp, fever, whipping, and broken hearts, the inseparable circumstances of prisons in those days. These were every week, for a twelve-month together, dragged by main force to hear the established service performed in the castle chapel." The Catholics were frequently, during the reign of Elizabeth, tortured in the most dreadful manner. In order to extort answers from Father Campian, he was laid on the rack, and his limbs stretched a little, to show him, as the executioner termed it, what the rack was. He persisted in his refusal; then for several days successively, the torture was increased, and on the last two occasions he was so cruelly rent and torn, that he expected to expire under the torment. While under the rack, he called continually upon God. In the reign of the Protestant Edward VI., Joan Knell was burnt to death, and the year after, George Parry was burnt also. In 1575, two Protestants, Peterson and Turwort, (as before stated,) were burnt to death by Elizabeth. In 1589, under the same queen, Lewes, a Protestant, was burnt to death at Norwich, where Francis Kett was also burnt for religious opinions in 1589, under the same great queen, who, in 1591, hanged the Protestant Hacket for heresy, in Cheapside, and put to death Greenwood, Barrow, and Penry, for being *Brownists*. Southwell, a Catholic, was racked ten times during the reign of this sister of bloody Queen Mary. In 1592, Mrs. Ward was hanged, drawn and quartered, for assisting a Catholic priest to escape in a box. Mrs. Lyne suffered the same punishment for harbouring a priest; and in 1586, Mrs. Clitheroe, who was accused of relieving a priest, and refused to plead, was pressed to death in York Castle; a sharp stone being placed underneath her back.

Have not Protestants persecuted both Catholics and their fellow Protestants in Germany, Switzerland, Geneva, France, Holland, Sweden, and England? Look to the atrocious punishment of Leighton under Laud, for writing against prelacy; first, his ear was cut off, then his nose slit; then the other ear cut off, then whipped again. Look to the horrible cruelties exercised by the Protestant Episcopalians on the Scottish Presbyterians, in the reign of Charles II., of whom 8000 are said to have perished in that persecution. Persecutions of Protestants by Protestants, are amply detailed by Chandler, in his History of Persecution; by Neale, in his History of the Puritans; by Laing, in his History of Scotland; by Penn, in his Life of Fox; and in Brandt's History of the Reformation in the Low Countries; which furnishes many very terrible cases of the sufferings of the Anabaptists and Remonstrants. In 1560, the Parliament of Scotland decreed, at one and the same time, the establishment of Calvinism, and the punishment of death against the ancient religion: "With such indecent haste (says Robertson) did the very persons who had just escaped ecclesiastical tyranny, proceed to imitate their example." Nothing can be so absurd as to suppose, that in barbarous ages, the excesses were all committed by one religious party, and none by the other. The Huguenots of France burnt churches, and hung priests, wherever they found them. Froumenteau, one of their own writers, confesses, that in the single province of Dauphiny, they killed two hundred and twenty priests, and one hundred and twelve friars. In the Low Countries, wherever Vandemerk and Sonoi, lieutenants of the Prince of Orange, carried their arms, they uniformly put to death, and in cold blood, all the priests and religious they could lay their hands on. The Protestant Servetus was put to death by the Protestants of Geneva, for denying the doctrine of the Trinity, as the Protestant Gentilis was, on the same score, by those of Berne; add to these, Felix Mans, Rotman, and Barnevald. Of Servetus, Melancthon, the mildest of men, declared that he deserved to have his bowels pulled out, and his body torn to pieces. The last fires of persecution which were lighted in England, were by Protestants. Bartholomew Legate, an Arian, was burnt by order of King James in Smithfield, on the 18th of March, 1612; on the 11th of April, in the same year, Edward Weightman was burnt at Litchfield, by order of the Protestant Bishop of Litchfield and Coventry; and this man was, *I believe*, the last person who was burnt in England for heresy. There was another condemned to the fire for the same heresy, but as pity was excited by the constancy of these sufferers, it was thought better to allow him to linger on a miserable life in Newgate. Fuller, who wrote in the reign of Charles II., and was a zealous Church of England man, speaking of the burnings in question, says, "It may appear that God was well pleased with them."

There are, however, grievous faults on both sides: and as there are a set of men, who, not content with retaliating upon Protestants, deny the persecuting spirit of the Catholics, I would ask them what they think of the following code, drawn up by the French Catholics against the French Protestants, and carried into execution for one hundred years, and as late as the year 1765, and not repealed till 1782?

"Any Protestant clergyman remaining in France three days, without coming to the Catholic worship, to be punished with death. If a Protestant sends his son to a Protestant schoolmaster for education, he is to forfeit 250 livres a month, and the schoolmaster who receives him, 50 livres. If they sent their children to any seminary abroad, they were to forfeit 2000 livres, and the child so sent, became incapable of possessing property in France. To celebrate Protestant worship, exposed the clergyman to a fine of 2800 livres. The fine to a Protestant for hearing it, was 1300 livres. If any Protestant denied the authority of the pope in France, his goods were seized for the first offence, and he was hanged for the second. If any Common Prayer-book, or book of Protestant worship be found in the possession of any Protestant, he shall forfeit 20 livres for the first offence, 40 livres for the second, and shall be imprisoned at pleasure for the third. Any person bringing from beyond sea, or selling any Protestant books of worship, to forfeit 100 livres. Any magistrates may search Protestant houses for such articles. Any person, required by a magistrate to take an oath against the Protestant religion, and refusing, to be committed to prison, and if he afterwards refuse again, to suffer forfeiture of goods. Any person, sending any money over sea to the support of a Protestant seminary, to forfeit his goods, and be imprisoned at the king's pleasure. Any person going over sea, for Protestant education, to forfeit goods and lands for life. The vessel to be forfeited which conveyed any Protestant woman or child over sea, without the king's license. Any person converting another to the Protestant religion, to be put to death. Death to any Protestant priest to come into France; death to the person who receives him; forfeiture of goods and imprisonment to send money for the relief of any Protestant clergyman: large rewards for discovering a Protestant parson. Every Protestant shall cause his child, within one month after birth, to be baptized by a Catholic priest, under a penalty of 2000 livres. Protestants were fined 4000 livres a-month for being absent from Catholic worship, were disabled from holding offices and employments, from keeping arms in their houses, from maintaining suits at law, from being guardians, from practising in law or physic, and from holding offices, civil or military. They were forbidden (bravo, Louis XIV.!) to travel more than five miles from home without license, under pain of forfeiting all their goods, and they might not come to court under pain of 2000 livres. A married Protestant woman when convicted of being of that persuasion was liable to forfeit two-thirds of her jointure; she could not be executrix to her husband, nor have any part of his goods; and during her marriage, she might be kept in prison, unless her husband redeemed her at the rate of 200 livres a-month, or the third part of his lands. Protestants convicted of being such, were, within three months after their conviction, either to submit, and renounce their religion, or, if required by four magistrates, to abjure the realm, and if they did not depart, or departing returned, were to suffer death. All Protestants were required, under the most tremendous penalties, to swear that they considered the pope as the head of the church. If they refused to take this oath, which might be tendered at pleasure by any two magistrates, they could not act as advocates, procureurs, or notaries public. Any Protestant taking any office, civil or military, was compelled to abjure the Protestant religion; to declare his belief in the doctrine of transubstantiation, and to take the Roman Catholic sacrament within six months, under the penalty of 10,000 livres. Any person professing the Protestant religion, and educated in the same, was required, in six months after the age of sixteen, to declare the pope to be the head of the church; to declare his belief in transubstantiation, and that the invocation of saints was according to the doctrine of the Christian religion; failing this, he could not hold, possess, or inherit landed property; his lands were given to the nearest Catholic relation. Many taxes were doubled upon Protestants. Protestants keeping schools were imprisoned for life, and all Protestants were forbidden to come within ten miles of Paris or Versailles. If any Protestant had a horse worth more than 100 livres, any Catholic magistrate might take it away, and search the house of the said Protestant for arms." Is not this a monstrous code of persecution? Is it any wonder, after reading such a spirit of tyranny as is here exhibited, that the tendencies of the Catholic religion should be suspected, and that the cry of no Popery should be a rallying sign to every Protestant nation in Europe? .... Forgive, gentle reader, and gentle elector, the trifling deception I have practised upon you. This code is not a code made by French Catholics against French Protestants, but by English and Irish Protestants against English and Irish Catholics; I have given it to you, for the most part, as it is set forth in Burns' "Justice" of 1780: it was acted upon in the beginning of the last king's reign, and was notorious through the whole of Europe, as the most cruel and atrocious system of persecution ever instituted by one religious persuasion against another. Of this code, Mr. Burke says, that "it is a truly barbarous system; where all the parts are an outrage on the laws of humanity, and the rights of nature; it is a system of elaborate contrivance, as well fitted for the oppression, imprisonment, and degradation of a people, and the debasement of human nature itself, as ever proceeded from the perverted ingenuity of man." It is in vain to say that these cruelties were laws of political safety; such has always been the plea for all religious cruelties; by such arguments the Catholics defended the massacre of St. Bartholomew, and the burnings of Mary.

With such facts as these, the cry of persecution will not do; it is unwise to make it, because it can be so very easily, and so very justly retorted. The business is, to forget and forgive, to kiss and be friends, and to say nothing of what has past, which is to the credit of neither party. There have been atrocious cruelties, and abominable acts of injustice on both sides. It is not worth while to contend who shed the most blood, or whether (as Dr. Sturgess objects to Dr. Milner) death by fire is worse than hanging or starving in prison As far as England itself is concerned, the balance may be better preserved. Cruelties exercised upon the Irish go for nothing in English reasoning; but if it were not uncandid and vexatious to consider Irish persecutions* as part of the case, I firmly believe there have been two Catholics put to death for religious causes in Great Britain for one Protestant who has suffered; not that this proves much, because the Catholics have enjoyed the sovereign power for so few years between this period

* Thurloe writes to Henry Cromwell to *catch* up some thousand Irish boys, to send to the colonies. Henry writes back he has done so; and desires to know whether his highness would choose as many girls to be caught up. and he adds, "doubtless it is a business, in which God will appear." Suppose *bloody Queen Mary* had caught up and transported three or four thousand Protestant boys and girls from the three ridings of Yorkshire!!!!!!

and the Reformation, and certainly it must be allowed that they were not inactive, during that period, in the great work of pious combustion.

It is, however, some extenuation of the Catholic excesses, that their religion was the religion of the whole of Europe, when the innovation began. They were the ancient lords and masters of faith, before men introduced the practice of thinking for themselves in these matters. The Protestants have less excuse, who claimed the right of innovation, and then turned round upon other Protestants who acted upon the same principle, or upon Catholics who remained as they were, and visited them with all the cruelties from which they had themselves so recently escaped.

Both sides, as they acquired power, abused it; and both learnt, from their sufferings, the great secret of toleration and forbearance. If you wish to do good in the times in which you live, contribute your efforts to perfect this grand work. I have not the most distant intention to interfere in local politics, but I advise you never to give a vote to any man, whose only title for asking it is, that he means to continue the punishments, privations, and incapacities of any human beings, merely because they worship God in the way they think best: the man who asks for your vote upon such a plea, is, *probably*, a very weak man, who believes in his own bad reasoning, or a very artful man, who is laughing at you for your credulity: at all events, he is a man who, knowingly or unknowingly, exposes his country to the greatest dangers, and hands down to posterity all the foolish opinions and all the bad passions which prevail in those times in which he happens to live. Such a man is so far from being that friend to the church which he pretends to be, that he declares its safety cannot be reconciled with the franchises of the people; for what worse can be said of the Church of England than this, that wherever it is judged necessary to give it a legal establishment, it becomes necessary to deprive the body of the people, if they adhere to their old opinions, of their liberties, and of all their free customs, and to reduce them to a state of civil servitude?

SYDNEY SMITH.

A SERMON

ON THOSE

RULES OF CHRISTIAN CHARITY BY WHICH OUR OPINIONS OF OTHER SECTS SHOULD BE FORMED:

PREACHED

BEFORE THE MAYOR AND CORPORATION, IN THE CATHEDRAL CHURCH OF BRISTOL, ON WEDNESDAY, NOVEMBER 5, 1828.

I publish this sermon (or rather allow others to publish it), because many persons, who know the city of Bristol better than I do, have earnestly solicited me to do so, and are convinced it will do good. It is not without reluctance (as far as I myself am concerned) that I send to the press such plain rudiments of common charity and common sense.

Sydney Smith.

Nov. 8, 1828.

Col. iii. 12, 13.

"*Put on, as the elect of God, kindness, humbleness of mind, meekness, long-suffering, forbearing one another, and forgiving one another.*"

The Church of England, in its wisdom and piety, has very properly ordained that a day of thanksgiving should be set apart, in which we may return thanks to Almighty God for the mercies vouchsafed to this nation in their escape from the dreadful plot planned for the destruction of the sovereign and his Parliament,—the forerunner, no doubt, of such sanguinary scenes as were suited to the manners of that age, and must have proved the inevitable consequence of such enormous wickedness and cruelty. Such an escape is a fair and lawful foundation for national piety. And it is a comely and Christian sight to see the magistrates and high authorities of the land obedient to the ordinances of the church, and holding forth to their fellow-subjects a wise example of national gratitude and serious devotion. This use of this day is deserving of every commendation. The idea that Almighty God does sometimes exercise a special providence for the preservation of a whole people is justified by Scripture, is not repugnant to reason, and can produce nothing but feelings and opinions favourable to virtue and religion.

Another wise and lawful use of this day is an honest self-congratulation that we have burst through those bands which the Roman Catholic priesthood would impose upon human judgment; that the Protestant Church not only permits, but exhorts, every man to appeal from human authority to the Scriptures; that it makes of the clergy guides and advisers, not masters and oracles; that it discourages vain and idle ceremonies, unmeaning observances, and hypocritical pomp; and encourages freedom in thinking upon religion, and simplicity in religious forms. It is impossible that any candid man should not observe the marked superiority of the Protestants over the Catholic faith in these particulars; and difficult that any pious man should not feel grateful to Almighty Providence for escape from danger which would have plunged this country afresh into so many errors and so many absurdities.

I hope, in this condemnation of the Catholic religion (in which I most sincerely join its bitterest enemies), I shall not be so far mistaken as to have it supposed that I would convey the slightest approbation of any laws which disqualify or incapacitate any class of men from civil offices on account of religious opinions. I regard all such laws as fatal and lamentable mistakes in legislation; they are mistakes of troubled times, and half-barbarous ages. All Europe is gradually emerging from their influence. This country has lately, with the entire consent of its prelates, made a noble and successful effort, by the abolition of some of the most obnoxious laws of this class. In proportion as such example is followed, the enemies of church and state will be diminished, and the foundation of peace, order, and happiness be strengthened. These are my opinions, which I mention, not to convert you, but to guard myself from misrepresentation. It is my duty,—it is my wish,—it is the subject of this day to point out those evils of the Catholic religion from which we have escaped; but I should be to the last degree concerned, if a condemnation of theological errors were to be construed into an approbation of laws which I cannot but consider as deeply marked by a spirit of intolerance. Therefore, I beg you to remember that I record these opinions not for the purpose of converting any one to them, which would be an abuse of the privilege of addressing you from the pulpit; not that I attach the slightest degree of importance to them because they are mine; but merely to guard myself from misrepresentation upon a point on which all men's passions are, at this moment, so powerfully excited.

I have said that, at this moment, all men's passions are powerfully excited on this subject. If this is true, it points out to me my line of duty. I must use my endeavours to guard against the abuse of this day; to take care that the principles of sound reason are not lost sight of; and that such excitement, instead of rising into dangerous vehemence, is calmed into active and useful investigation of the subject.

I shall, therefore, on the present occasion, not investigate generally the duties of charity and forbearance, but of charity and forbearance in religious matters; of that Christian meekness and humility which prevent the intrusion of bad passions into religious concerns, and keep calm and pure the mind intent upon eternity. And remember, I beg of you, that the rules I shall offer you for the observation of Christian charity are general, and of universal application. What you choose to do, and which way you incline upon any particular question, are, and can be, no concern of mine. It would be the height of arrogance and presumption in me, or in any other minister of God's word, to interfere on such points; I only endeavour to teach that spirit of forbearance and charity, which (though it cannot always prevent differences upon religious points) will ensure that these differences are carried on with Christian gentleness. I have endeavoured to lay down these rules for difference with care and moderation; and, if you will attend to them patiently, I think you will agree with me, that, however the practice of them may be forgotten, the propriety of them cannot be denied.

It would always be easier to fall in with human passions than to resist them; but the ministers of God must do their duty through evil report, and through good report; neither prevented nor excited by the interests of the present day. They must teach those general truths which the Christian religion has committed to their care, and upon which the happiness and peace of the world depend.

In pressing upon you the great duty of religious charity, the inutility of the opposite defect of religious violence first offers itself to, and, indeed, obtrudes itself upon my notice. The evil of difference of opinion must exist; it admits of no cure. The wildest visionary does not now hope he can bring his fellow-creatures to one standard of faith. If history has taught us any one thing, it is that mankind, on such sort of subjects, will form their own opinions. Therefore, to want charity in religious matters is at least useless; it hardens error and provokes recrimination; but it does not enlighten those whom we wish to reclaim, nor does it extend doctrines which to us appear so clear and indisputable. But to do wrong, and to gain nothing by it, are surely to add folly to fault, and to proclaim an understanding not led by the rule of reason, as well as a disposition unregulated by the Christian faith.

Religious charity requires that we should not judge any sect of Christians by the representations of their enemies alone, without hearing and reading what they have to say in their own defence; it requires only, of course, to state such a rule to procure for it general admission. No man can pretend to say that such a rule is not founded upon the plainest principles of justice—upon those plain principles of justice which no one thinks of violating in the ordinary concerns of life; and yet I fear that rule is not always very strictly adhered to in religious animosities. Religious hatred is often founded on tradition, often on hearsay, often on the misrepresentations of notorious enemies; without inquiry, without the slightest examination of opposite reasons and authorities, or consideration of that which the accused party has to offer for defence or explanation. It is impossible, I admit, to examine every thing; many have not talents, many have not leisure, for such pursuits; many must be contented with the faith in which they have been brought up, and must think it the best modification of the Christian faith, because they are told it is so. But this imperfect acquaintance with religious controversy, though not blameable when it proceeds from want of power, and want of opportunity, can be no possible justification of violent and acrimonious opinions. I would say to the ignorant man, "It is not your ignorance I blame; you have had no means, perhaps, of acquiring knowledge: the circumstances of your life have not led to it—may have prevented it; but then I must tell you, if you have not had leisure to inquire, you have no right to accuse. If you are unacquainted with the opposite arguments,—or, knowing, cannot balance them, it is not upon you the task devolves of exposing the errors, and impugning the opinions of other sects." If charity is ever necessary, it is in those who know accurately neither the accusation nor the defence. If invective,—if rooted antipathy, in religious opinions, is ever a breach of Christian rules, it is so in those who, not being able to become wise, are not willing to become charitable and modest.

Any candid man, acquainted with religious controversy, will, I think, admit that he has frequently, in the course of his studies, been astonished by the force of arguments with which that cause has been defended, which he at first thought to be incapable of any defence at all. Some accusations he has found to be utterly groundless; in others the facts and arguments have been mis-stated; in other instances the accusation has been retorted; in many cases the tenets have been defended by strong arguments and honest appeal to Scripture; in many with consummate acuteness and deep learning. So that religious studies often teach to opponents a greater respect for each other's talents, motives, and acquirements; exhibit the real difficulties of the subject; lessen the surprise and anger which are apt to be excited by opposition; and, by these means, promote that forgiving one another, and forbearing one another, which are so powerfully recommended by the words of my text.

A great deal of mischief is done by not attending to the limits of interference with each other's religious opinions,—by not leaving to the power and wisdom of God that which belongs to God alone. Our holy religion consists of some doctrines which influence practice, and of others which are purely speculative. If religious errors are of the former description, they may, perhaps, be fair objects of human interference; but, if the opinion is merely theological and speculative, there the right of human interference seems to end, because the necessity for such interference does not exist. Any error of this nature is between the Creator and the creature,—between the Redeemer and the redeemed. If such opinions are not the best opinions which can be found, God Almighty will punish the error, if mere error seemeth to the Almighty a fit object of punishment. Why may not man wait if God waits? Where are we called upon in Scripture to pursue men for errors purely speculative?—to assist Heaven in punishing those offences which belong only to Heaven?—in fighting unasked for what we deem to be the battles of God,—of that patient and merciful God, who pities the frailties we do not pity—who forgives the errors we do not forgive,—who sends rain upon the just and the unjust, and maketh his sun to shine upon the evil and the good?

Another canon of religious charity is to revise, at long intervals, the bad opinions we have been compelled, or rather our forefathers have been compelled, to form of other Christian sects; to see whether the different bias of the age, the more general diffusion of intelligence, do not render those tenets less pernicious: that which might prove a very great evil under other circumstances, and in other times, may, perhaps, however weak and erroneous, be harmless in these times, and under these circumstances. We must be aware, too, that we do not mistake recollections for apprehensions, and confound together what has passed with what is to come,—history with futurity. For instance, it would be the most enormous abuse of this religious institution to imagine that such dreadful scenes of wickedness are to be apprehended from the Catholics of the present day, because the annals of this country were disgraced by such an event two hundred years ago. It would be an enormous abuse of this day to extend the crimes of a few desperate wretches to a whole sect; to fix the passions of dark ages upon times of refinement and civilization. All these are mistakes and abuses of this day, which violate every principle of Christian charity, endanger the peace of society, and give life and perpetuity to hatreds, which must perish at one time or another, and had better, for the peace of society, perish now.

It would be religiously charitable, also, to consider whether the objectionable tenets, which different sects profess, are in their hearts as well as in their books. There is, unfortunately, so much pride where there ought to be so much humility, that it is difficult, if not almost impossible, to make religious sects abjure or recant the doctrines they have once professed. It is not in this manner, I fear, that the best and purest churches are ever reformed. But the doctrine gradually becomes obsolete; and, though not disowned, ceases in fact to be a distinguishing characteristic of the sect which professes it. These modes of reformation,—this silent antiquation of doctrines,—this real improvement, which the parties themselves are too wise not to feel, though not wise enough to own, must, I am afraid, be generally conceded to human infirmity. They are indulgences not unnecessary to many sects of Christians. The more generous method would be to admit error where error exists, to say these were the tenets and interpretations of dark and ignorant ages; wider inquiry, fresh discussion, superior intelligence have convinced us we are wrong; we will act in future upon better and wiser principles. This is what men do in laws, arts, and sciences; and happy for them would it be if they used the same modest docility in the highest of all concerns. But it is, I fear, more than experience will allow us to expect; and therefore the kindest and most charitable method is to allow religious sects silently to improve without reminding them of, and taunting them with, the improvement; without bringing them to the humiliation of former disavowal, or the still more pernicious practice of defending what they know to be indefensible. The triumphs which proceed from the neglect of these principles are not (what they pretend to be) the triumphs of religion, but the triumphs of personal vanity. The object is not to extinguish the dangerous errors with as little pain and degradation as possible to him who has fallen into the error, but the object is to exalt ourselves, and to depreciate our theological opponents, as much as possible, at any expense to God's service, and to the real interests of truth and religion.

There is another practice not less common than this, and equally uncharitable; and that is to represent the opinions of the most violent and eager persons who can be met with, as the common and received opinions of the whole sect. There are, in every denomination of Christians, individuals, by whose opinion or by whose conduct the great body would very reluctantly be judged. Some men aim at attracting notice by singularity; some are deficient in temper; some in learning; some push every principle to the extreme; distort, overstate, pervert; fill every one to whom their cause is dear with concern that it should have been committed to such rash and intemperate advocates. If you wish to gain a victory over your antagonists, these are the men whose writings you should study, whose opinions you should dwell on, and should carefully bring forward to notice; but if you wish, as the elect of God, to put on kindness and humbleness, meekness and long-suffering,—if you wish to forbear and to forgive, it will then occur to you that you should seek the true opinions of any sect from those only who are approved of, and reverenced by that sect; to whose authority that sect defer, and by whose arguments they consider their tenets to be properly defended. This may not suit your purpose, if you are combating for victory; but it is your duty if you are combating for truth; it is the safe, honest, and splendid conduct of him who never writes nor speaks on religious subjects, but that he may diffuse the real blessings of religion among his fellow-creatures, and restrain the bitterness of controversy by the feelings of Christian charity and forbearance.

Let us also ask ourselves, when we are sitting in severe judgment upon the faults, follies, and errors of other Christian sects, whether it is not barely possible that we have fallen into some mistakes and misrepresentations? Let us ask ourselves, honestly and fairly, whether we are wholly exempt from prejudice, from pride, from obstinate adhesion to what candour calls upon us to alter, and to yield? Are there no violent and mistaken members of our own community, by whose conduct we should be loath to be guided,—by whose tenets we should not choose our faith should be judged? Has time, that improves all, found nothing in us to change for the better? Amid all the manifold divisions of the Christian world, are we the only Christians who, without having any thing to learn from the knowledge and civilization of the last three centuries, have started up, without infancy, and without error, into consummate wisdom and spotless perfection?

To listen to enemies as well as friends is a rule which not only increases sense in common life, but is highly favourable to the increase of religious candour. You find that you are not so free from faults as your friends suppose, nor so full of faults as your enemies suppose. You begin to think it not impossible that you may be as unjust to others as they are to you; and that the wisest and most Christian scheme is that of mutual indulgence; that it is better to put on, as the elect of God, kindness, humbleness of mind, meekness, long-suffering, forbearing one another, and forgiving one another.

Some men cannot understand how they are to be zealous if they are candid in religious matters; how the energy necessary for the one virtue is compatible with the calmness which the other requires. But remember that the Scriptures carefully distinguish between laudable zeal and indiscreet zeal; that the apostles and epistolary writers knew they had as much to fear from the over-excitement of some men as from the supineness of others; and in nothing have they laboured more than in preventing religion from arming human passions instead of allaying them, and rendering those principles a source of mutual jealousy and hatred which were intended for universal peace. I admit that indifference sometimes puts on the appearance of candour; but, though there is a counterfeit, yet there is a reality; and the imitation proves the value of the original, because men only attempt to multiply the appearances of useful and important things. The object is to be at the same time pious to God and charitable to man; to render your own faith as pure and perfect as possible, not only without hatred of those who differ from you, but with a constant recollection that it is possible, in spite of thought and study, that you may have been mistaken,—that other sects may be right, and that a zeal in his service, which God does not want, is a very bad excuse for those bad passions which his sacred word condemns.

Lastly, I would suggest that many differences between sects are of less importance than the furious zeal of many men would make them. Are the tenets of any sect of such a description, that we believe they will be saved under the Christian faith? Do they fulfil the common duties of life? Do they respect property? Are they obedient to the laws? Do they speak the truth? If all these things are right, the violence of hostility may surely submit to some little softness and relaxation; honest difference of opinion cannot call for such entire separation and complete antipathy; such zeal as this, if it be zeal, and not something worse, is not surely zeal according to discretion.

The arguments, then, which I have adduced in support of the great principles of religious charity are, that violence upon such subjects is rarely or ever found to be useful; but generally to produce effects opposite to those which are intended. I have observed that religious sects are not to be judged from the representations of their enemies; but that they are to be heard for themselves, in the pleadings of their best writers, not in the representations of those whose intemperate zeal is a misfortune to the sect to which they belong. If you will study the principles of your religious opponents, you will often find your contempt and hatred lessened in proportion as you are better acquainted with what you despise. Many religious opinions, which are purely speculative, are without the limits of human interference. In the numerous sects of Christianity, interpreting our religion in very opposite manners, all cannot be right. Imitate the forbearance and long-suffering of God, who throws the mantle of his mercy over all, and who will probably save, on the last day, the piously right and the piously wrong, seeking Jesus in humbleness of mind. Do not drive religious sects to the disgrace (or to what they foolishly think the disgrace) of formally disavowing tenets they once professed, but concede something to human weakness; and, when the tenet is virtually given up, treat it as if it were actually given up; and always consider it to be very possible that you yourself may have made mistakes, and fallen into erroneous opinions, as well as any other sect to which you are opposed. If you put on these dispositions, and this tenor of mind, you cannot be guilty of any religious fault, take what part you will in the religious disputes which appear to be coming on the world. If you choose to perpetuate the restrictions upon your fellow creatures, no one has a right to call you bigoted; if you choose to do them away, no one has any right to call you lax and indifferent; you have done your utmost to do right, and, whether you err, or do not err, in your mode of interpreting the Christian religion, you show at least that you have caught its heavenly spirit,—that you have put on, as the elect of God, kindness, humbleness of mind, meekness, long-suffering, forbearing one another, and forgiving one another.

I have thus endeavoured to lay before you the uses and abuses of this day; and, having stated the great mercy of God's interference, and the blessings this country has secured to itself in resisting the errors, and follies, and superstitions of the Catholic Church, I have endeavoured that this just sense of our own superiority should not militate against the sacred principles of Christian charity. That charity which I ask for others, I ask also for myself. I am sure I am preaching before those who will think (whether they agree with me or not) that I have spoken conscientiously, and from good motives, and from honest feelings, on a very difficult subject,—not sought for by me, but devolving upon me in the course of duty;—in which I should have been heartily ashamed of myself (as you would have been ashamed of me), if I had thought only how to flatter and please, or thought of any thing but what I hope I always do think of in the pulpit,—that I am placed here by God to tell the truth, and to do good.

I shall conclude my sermon, (pushed, I am afraid, already to an unreasonable length,) by reciting to you a very short and beautiful apologue, taken from the rabbinical writers. It is, I believe, quoted by Bishop Taylor in his "Holy Living and Dying." I have not now access to that book, but I quote it to you from memory; and should be made truly happy if you would quote it to others from memory also.

"As Abraham was sitting in the door of his tent, there came unto him a wayfaring man; and Abraham gave him water for his feet, and set bread before him. And Abraham said unto him, 'Let us now worship the Lord our God before we eat of this bread.' And the wayfaring man said unto Abraham, 'I will not worship the Lord thy God, for thy God is not my God, but I will worship my God, even the God of my fathers.' But Abraham was exceeding wroth; and he rose up to put the wayfaring man forth from the door of his tent. And the voice of the Lord was heard in the tent,—Abraham, Abraham! have I borne with this man for threescore and ten years, and canst not thou bear with him for one hour?"

LETTERS ON THE SUBJECT OF THE CATHOLICS,

TO

MY BROTHER ABRAHAM, WHO LIVES IN THE COUNTRY.

BY PETER PLYMLEY.

LETTER I.

Dear Abraham,

A worthier and better man than yourself does not exist; but I have always told you, from the time of our boyhood, that you were a bit of a goose. Your parochial affairs are governed with exemplary order and regularity; you are as powerful in the vestry as Mr. Perceval is in the House of Commons,—and, I must say, with much more reason; nor do I know any church where the faces and smock-frocks of the congregation are so clean, or their eyes so uniformly directed to the preacher. There is another point upon which I will do you ample justice; and that is, that the eyes so directed towards you are wide open; for the rustic has, in general, good principles, though he cannot control his animal habits; and, however loud he may snore, his face is perpetually turned towards the fountain of orthodoxy.

Having done you this act of justice, I shall proceed, according to our ancient intimacy and familiarity, to explain to you my opinions about the Catholics, and to reply to yours.

In the first place, my sweet Abraham, the pope is not landed nor are there any curates sent out after him—nor has he been hid at St. Alban's by the Dowager Lady Spencer—nor dined privately at Holland House—nor been seen near Dropmore. If these fears exist (which I do not believe), they exist only in the mind of the chancellor of the exchequer; they emanate from his zeal for the Protestant interest; and, though they reflect the highest honour upon the delicate irritability of his faith, must certainly be considered as more ambiguous proofs of the sanity and vigour of his understanding. By this time, however, the best informed clergy in the neighbourhood of the metropolis are convinced that the rumour is without foundation; and, though the pope is probably hovering about our coast in a fishing smack, it is most likely he will fall a prey to the vigilance of our cruisers; and it is certain he has not yet polluted the Protestantism of our soil.

Exactly in the same manner, the story of the wooden gods seized at Charing Cross, by an order from the Foreign Office, turns out to be without the shadow of a foundation; instead of the angels and archangels, mentioned by the informer, nothing was discovered but a wooden image of Lord Mulgrave, going down to Chatham, as a head-piece for the Spanker gun-vessel; it was an exact resemblance of his lordship in his military uniform; and *therefore* as little like a god as can well be imagined.

Having set your fears at rest as to the extent of the conspiracy formed against the Protestant religion, I will now come to the argument itself.

You say these men interpret the Scriptures in an orthodox manner; and that they eat their God.—Very likely. All this may seem very important to you, who live fourteen miles from a market-town, and, from long residence upon your living, are become a kind of holy vegetable; and, in a theological sense, it is highly important. But I want soldiers and sailors for the state; I want to make a greater use than I now can do of a poor country full of men; I want to render the military service popular among the Irish; to check the power of France; to make every possible exertion for the safety of Europe, which in twenty years' time will be nothing but a mass of French slaves; and then you, and ten thousand other such boobies as you, call out—"For God's sake, do not think of raising cavalry and infantry in Ireland! . . . . They interpret the Epistle to Timothy in a different manner from what we do! . . . . They eat a bit of wafer every Sunday, which they call their God!" . . . . I wish to my soul they would eat you, and such reasoners as you are. What! when Turk, Jew, Heretic, Infidel, Catholic, Protestant, are all combined against this country; when men of every religious persuasion, and no religious persuasion; when the population of half the globe is up in arms against us; are we to stand examining our generals and armies as a bishop examines a candidate for holy orders? and to suffer no one to bleed for England who does not agree with you about the 2d of Timothy? You talk about the Catholics! If you and your brotherhood have been able to persuade the country into a continuation of this grossest of all absurdities, you have ten times the power which the Catholic clergy ever had in their best days. Louis XIV., when he revoked the Edict of Nantes, never thought of preventing the Protestants from fighting his battles; and gained accordingly some of his most splendid victories by the talents of his Protestant generals. No power in Europe, but yourselves, has ever thought, for these hundred years past, of asking whether a bayonet is Catholic, or Presbyterian, or Lutheran; but whether it is sharp and well-tempered. A bigot delights in public ridicule; for he begins to think he is a martyr. I can promise you the full enjoyment of this pleasure, from one extremity of Europe to the other.

I am as disgusted with the nonsense of the Roman Catholic religion as you can be; and no man who talks such nonsense shall ever tithe the product of the earth, nor meddle with the ecclesiastical establishment in any shape;—but what have I to do with the speculative nonsense of his theology, when the object is to elect the mayor of a country town, or to appoint a colonel of a marching regiment? Will a man discharge the solemn impertinences of the one office with the less zeal, or shrink from the bloody boldness of the other with greater timidity, because the blockhead believes in all the Catholic nonsense of the real presence. I am sorry there should be such impious folly in the world, but I should be ten times a greater fool than he is, if I refused, in consequence of his folly, to lead him out against the enemies of the state. Your whole argument is wrong; the state has nothing whatever to do with theological errors which do not violate the common rules of morality, and militate against the fair power of the ruler: it leaves all these errors to you, and to such as you. You have every tenth porker in your parish for refuting them; and take care that you are vigilant and logical in the task.

I love the church as well as you do; but you totally mistake the nature of an establishment, when you contend that it ought to be connected with the military and civil career of every individual in the state. It is quite right that there should be one clergyman to every parish interpreting the Scriptures after a particular manner, ruled by a regular hierarchy, and paid with a rich proportion of haycocks and wheatsheafs. When I have laid this foundation for a rational religion in the state—when I have placed ten thousand well-educated men in different parts of the kingdom to preach it up, and compelled every body to pay them, whether they hear them or not—I have taken such measures as I know must always procure an immense majority in favour of the established church; but I can go no farther. I cannot set up a civil inquisition, and say to one, you shall not be a butcher, because you are not orthodox; and prohibit another from brewing, and a third from administering the law, and a fourth from defending the country. If common justice did not prohibit me from such a conduct, common sense would. The advantage to be gained by quitting the heresy would make it shameful to abandon it; and men who had once left the church would continue in such a state of alienation from a point of honour, and transmit that spirit to the latest posterity. This is just the effect your disqualifying laws have produced. They have fed Dr. Rees and Dr. Kippis; crowded the congregation of the Old Jewry to suffocation; and enabled every sublapsarian, and supralapsarian, and semipelagian clergyman, to build himself a neat brick chapel, and live with some distant resemblance to the state of a gentleman.

You say the king's coronation oath will not allow him to consent to any relaxation of the Catholic laws—Why not relax the Catholic laws as well as the laws against Protestant dissenters? If one is contrary to his oath, the other must be so too; for the spirit of the oath is, to defend the church establishment; which the Quaker and the Presbyterian differ from as much or more than the Catholic; and yet his majesty has repealed the Corporation and Test Act in Ireland, and done more for the Catholics of both kingdoms than had been done for them since the Reformation. In 1778 the ministers said nothing about the roya con science; in 1793* no conscience; in 1804 no conscience; the common feeling of humanity and justice then seem to have had their fullest influence upon the advisers of the crown; but in 1807—a year, I suppose, eminently fruitful in moral and religious scruples, (as some years are fruitful in apples, some in hops,—it is contended by the well-paid John Bowles, and by Mr. Perceval (who tried to be well paid), that that is now perjury which we had hitherto called policy and benevolence! Religious liberty has never made such a stride as under the reign of his present majesty; nor is there any instance in the annals of our history, where so many infamous and damnable laws have been repealed as those against the Catholics, which have been put an end to by him; and then, at the close of this useful policy, his advisers discover that the very measures of concession and indulgence, or (to use my own language), the measures of justice, which he has been pursuing through the whole of his reign, are contrary to the oath he takes at its commencement! That oath binds his majesty not to consent to any measure contrary to the interests of the established church; but who is to judge of the tendency of each particular measure? Not the king alone; it can never be the intention of this law that the king, who listens to the advice of his Parliament upon a road bill, should reject it upon the most important of all measures. Whatever be his own private judgment of the tendency of any ecclesiastical bill, he complies most strictly with his oath, if he is guided in that particular point by the advice of his Parliament, who may be presumed to understand its tendency better than the king, or any other individual. You say, if Parliament had been unanimous in their opinion of the absolute necessity for Lord Howick's bill, and the king had thought it pernicious, he would have been perjured if he had not rejected it. I say, on the contrary, his majesty would have acted in the most conscientious manner, and have complied most scrupulously with his oath, if he had sacrificed his own opinion to the opinion of the great council of the nation; because the probability was that such opinion was better than his own; and upon the same principle, in common life, you give up your opinion to your physician, your lawyer, and your builder.

You admit this bill did not compel the king to elect Catholic officers, but only gave him the option of doing so if he pleased; but you add, that the king was right in not trusting such dangerous power to himself or his successors. Now, you are either to suppose that the king, for the time being, has a zeal for the Catholic establishment, or that he has not. If he has not, where is the danger of giving such an option? If you suppose that he may be influenced by such an admiration of the Catholic religion, why did his present majesty, in the year 1804, consent to that bill which empowered the crown to station ten thousand Catholic soldiers in any part of the kingdom, and placed them absolutely at the disposal of the crown? If the King of England for the time being is a good Protestant, there can be no danger in making the Catholic *eligible* to any thing; if he is not, no power can possibly be so dangerous as that conveyed by the bill last quoted; to which, in point of peril, Lord Howick's bill is a mere joke. But the real fact is, one bill opened a door to his majesty's advisers for trick, jobbing, and intrigue; the other did not.

Besides, what folly to talk to me of an oath, which, under all possible circumstances, is to prevent the relaxation of the Catholic laws! for such a solemn appeal to God sets all conditions and contingencies at defiance. Suppose Bonaparte was to retrieve the only very great blunder he has made, and were to succeed, after repeated trials, in making an impression upon Ireland, do you think we should hear any thing of the impediment of a coronation oath? or would the spirit of this country tolerate for an hour such ministers, and such unheard-of nonsense, if the most distant prospect existed of conciliating the Catholics by every species even of the most abject concession? And yet, if your argument is good for any thing, the coronation oath ought to reject, at such a moment, every tendency to conciliation, and to bind Ireland forever to the crown of France.

I found in your letter the usual remarks about fire, fagot, and bloody Mary. Are you aware, my dear priest, that there were as many persons put to death for religious opinions under the mild Elizabeth as under the bloody Mary? The reign of the former was, to be sure, ten times as long; but I only mention the fact, merely to show you that something depends upon the age in which men live, as well as on their religious opinions. Three hundred years ago, men burnt and hanged each other for these opinions. Time has softened Catholic as well as Protestant; they both required it; though each perceives only his own improvement, and is blind to that of the other. We are all the creatures of circumstances. I know not a kinder and better man than yourself; but you (if you had lived in those times) would certainly have roasted your Catholic; and I promise you, if the first exciter of this religious mob had been as powerful then as he is now, you would soon have been elevated to the mitre. I do not go the length of saying that the world has suffered as much from Protestant as from Catholic persecution; far from it: but you should remember the Catholics had all the power, when the idea first started up in the world that there could be two modes of faith; and that it was much more natural they should attempt to crush this diversity of opinion by great and cruel efforts, than that the Protestants should rage against those who differed from them, when the very basis of their system was complete freedom in all spiritual matters.

I cannot extend my letter any further at present, but you shall soon hear from me again. You tell me I am a party man. I hope I shall always be so, when I see my country in the hands of a pert London joker and a second-rate lawyer. Of the first, no other good

* These feelings of humanity and justice were at some periods a little quickened by the representations of 40,000 armed volunteers.

is known than that he makes pretty Latin verses; the second seems to me to have the head of a country parson, and the tongue of an Old Bailey lawyer.

If I could see good measures pursued, I care not a farthing who is in power; but I have a passionate love for common justice, and for common sense, and I abhor and despise every man who builds up his political fortune upon their ruin.

God bless you, reverend Abraham, and defend you from the pope, and all of us from that administration who seek power by opposing a measure which Burke, Pitt, and Fox all considered as absolutely necessary to the existence of the country.

LETTER II.

Dear Abraham,

The Catholic not respect an oath! why not? What upon earth has kept him out of Parliament, or excluded him from all the offices whence he is excluded, but his respect for oaths? There is no law which prohibits a Catholic to sit in Parliament. There could be no such law; because it is impossible to find out what passes in the interior of any man's mind. Suppose it were in contemplation to exclude all men from certain offices who contended for the legality of taking tithes: the only mode of discovering that fervid love of decimation which I know you to possess would be to tender you an oath "against that damnable doctrine, that it is lawful for a spiritual man to take, abstract, appropriate, subduct, or lead away the tenth calf, sheep, lamb, ox, pigeon, duck," &c., &c., &c., and every other animal that ever existed, which of course the lawyers would take care to enumerate. Now this oath I am sure you would rather die than take; and so the Catholic is excluded from Parliament because he will not swear that he disbelieves the leading doctrines of his religion! The Catholic asks you to abolish some oaths which oppress him; your answer is, that he does not respect oaths. Then why subject him to the test of oaths? The oaths keep him out of Parliament; why then he respects them. Turn which way you will, either your laws are nugatory, or the Catholic is bound by religious obligations as you are; but no eel in the well-sanded fist of a cook-maid, upon the eve of being skinned, ever twisted and writhed as an orthodox parson does when he is compelled by the gripe of reason to admit any thing in favour of a dissenter.

I will not dispute with you whether the pope be or be not the Scarlet Lady of Babylon. I hope it is not so; because I am afraid it will induce his majesty's chancellor of the exchequer to introduce several severe bills against Popery, if that is the case; and though he will have the decency to appoint a previous committee of inquiry as to the fact, the committee will be garbled, and the report inflammatory. Leaving this to be settled as he pleases to settle it, I wish to inform you, that previously to the bill last passed in favour of the Catholics, at the suggestion of Mr. Pitt, and for his satisfaction, the opinions of six of the most celebrated of the foreign Catholic universities were taken as to the right of the pope to interfere in the temporal concerns of any country. The answer cannot possibly leave the shadow of a doubt, even in the mind of Baron Maseres; and Dr. Rennel would be compelled to admit it, if three bishops lay dead at the very moment the question were put to him. To this answer might be added also the solemn declaration and signature of all the Catholics in Great Britain.

I should perfectly agree with you, if the Catholics admitted such a dangerous dispensing power in the hands of the pope; but they all deny it, and laugh at it, and are ready to abjure it in the most decided manner you can devise. They obey the pope as the spiritual head of their church; but are you really so foolish as to be imposed upon by mere names?—What matters it the seven-thousandth part of a farthing who is the spiritual head of any church? Is not Mr. Wilberforce at the head of the church of Clapham? Is not Dr. Letsom at the head of the Quaker church? Is not the general assembly at the head of the church of Scotland? How is the government disturbed by these many-headed churches? or in what way is the power of the crown augmented by this almost nominal dignity?

The king appoints a fast-day once a year, and he makes the bishops; and if the government would take half the pains to keep the Catholics out of the arms of France that it does to widen Temple Bar, or improve Snow Hill, the king would get into his hands the appointments of the titular bishops of Ireland.—Both Mr. C——'s sisters enjoy pensions more than sufficient to place the two greatest dignitaries of the Irish Catholic Church entirely at the disposal of the crown.—Every body who knows Ireland knows perfectly well, that nothing would be easier, with the expenditure of a little money, than to preserve enough of the ostensible appointment in the hands of the pope to satisfy the scruples of the Catholics, while the real nomination remained with the crown. But, as I have before said, the moment the very name of Ireland is mentioned, the English seem to bid adieu to common feeling, common prudence, and to common sense, and to act with the barbarity of tyrants, and the fatuity of idiots.

Whatever your opinion may be of the follies of the Roman Catholic religion, remember they are the follies of four millions of human beings, increasing rapidly in numbers, wealth and intelligence, who, if firmly united with this country, would set at defiance the power of France, and if once wrested from their alliance with England, would in three years render its existence as an independent nation absolutely impossible. You speak of danger to the establishment: I request to know when the establishment was ever so much in danger as when Hoche was in Bantry Bay, and whether all the books of Bossuet, or the arts of the Jesuits, were half so terrible? Mr. Perceval and his parsons forgot all this, in their horror lest twelve or fourteen old women may be converted to holy water, and Catholic nonsense. They never see that, while they are saving these venerable ladies from perdition, Ireland may be lost, England broken down, and the Protestant Church, with all its deans, prebendaries, Percevals and Rennels, be swept into the vortex of oblivion.

Do not, I beseech you, ever mention to me again the name of Dr. Duigenan. I have been in every corner of Ireland, and have studied its present strength and condition with no common labour. Be assured Ireland does not contain at this moment less than five millions of people. There were returned in the year 1791 to the hearth tax 701,000 houses, and there is no kind of question that there were about 50,000 houses omitted in that return. Taking, however, only the number returned for the tax, and allowing the average of six to a house (a very small average for a potato-fed people), this brings the population to 4,200,000 people in the year 1791; and it can be shown from the clearest evidence, (and Mr. Newenham in his book shows it,) that Ireland for the last fifty years has increased in its population at the rate of 50 or 60,000 per annum; which leaves the present population of Ireland at about five millions, after every possible deduction for *existing circumstances, just and necessary wars, monstrous and unnatural rebellions*, and all other sources of human destruction. Of this population, two out of ten are Protestants; and the half of the Protestant population are dissenters, and as inimical to the church as the Catholics themselves. In this state of things, thumb-screws and whipping—admirable engines of policy, as they must be considered to be—will not ultimately avail. The Catholics will hang over you; they will watch for the moment; and compel you hereafter to give them ten times as much, against your will, as they would now be contented with, if it was voluntarily surrendered. Remember what happened in the American war: when Ireland compelled you to give her every thing she asked, and to renounce, in the most explicit manner, your claim of sovereignty over her. God Almighty grant the folly of these present men may not bring on such another crisis of public affairs!

What are your dangers which threaten the establishment?—Reduce this declamation to a point, and let us understand what you mean. The most ample allowance does not calculate that there would be more than twenty members who were Roman Catholics in one house, and ten in the other, if the Catholic emancipation were carried into effect. Do you mean that these thirty members would bring in a bill to take away the tithes from the Protestant, and to pay them to the Catholic clergy? Do you mean that a Catholic general would march his army into the House of Commons and purge it of Mr. Perceval and Mr. Duigenan? or, that the theological writers would become all of a sudden more acute and more learned, if the present civil incapacities were removed? Do you fear for your tithes, or your doctrines, or your person, or the English constitution? Every fear, taken separately, is so glaringly absurd, that no man has the folly or the boldness to state it. Every one conceals his ignorance, or his baseness, in a stupid general panic, which, when called on, he is utterly incapable of explaining. Whatever you think of the Catholics, there they are—you cannot get rid of them; your alternative is, to give them a lawful place for stating their grievances, or an unlawful one: if you do not admit them to the House of Commons, they will hold their Parliament in Potato-place, Dublin, and be ten times as violent and inflammatory as they would be in Westminster. Nothing would give me such an idea of security, as to see twenty or thirty Catholic gentlemen in Parliament, looked upon by all the Catholics as the fair and proper organ of their party. I should have thought it the height of good fortune that such a wish existed on their part, and the very essence of madness and ignorance to reject it. Can you murder the Catholics?—Can you neglect them? They are too numerous for both these expedients. What remains to be done is obvious to every human being—but to that man who, instead of being a Methodist preacher, is, for the curse of us, and our children, and for the ruin of Troy, and the misery of good old Priam and his sons, become a legislator and a politician.

A distinction, I perceive, is taken, by one of the most feeble noblemen in Great Britain, between persecution and the deprivation of political power; whereas, there is no more distinction between these two things than there is between him who makes the distinction and a booby. If I strip off the relic-covered jacket of a Catholic, and give him twenty stripes .... I persecute; if I say, every body in the town where you live shall be a candidate for lucrative and honourable offices, but you who are a Catholic .... I do not persecute!—What barbarous nonsense is this! as if degradation was not as great an evil as bodily pain, or as severe poverty; as if I could not be as great a tyrant by saying, You shall not enjoy—as by saying, You shall suffer. The English, I believe, are as truly religious as any nation in Europe; I know no greater blessing; but it carries with it this evil in its train, that any villain who will bawl out "*The church is in danger!*" may get a place, and a good pension; and that any administration who will do the same thing may bring a set of men into power who, at a moment of stationary and passive piety, would be hooted by the very boys in the streets. But it is not all religion; it is, in great part, that narrow and exclusive spirit which delights to keep the common blessings of sun, and air, and freedom from other human beings. "Your religion has always been degraded; you are in the dust, and I will take care you never rise again. I should enjoy less the possession of an earthly good, by every additional person to whom it was extended." You may not be aware of it yourself, most reverend Abraham, but you deny their freedom to the Catholics upon the same principle that Sarah your wife refuses to give the receipt for a ham or a gooseberry dumpling; she values her receipts, not because they secure to her a certain flavour, but because they remind her that her neighbours want it:—a feeling laughable in a priestess, shameful in a priest; venial when it withholds the blessings of a ham, tyrannical and execrable when it narrows the boon of religious freedom.

You spend a great deal of ink about the character of the present prime-minister. Grant you all that you write; I say, I fear he will ruin Ireland, and pursue a line of policy destructive to the true interest of his country; and then you tell me, he is faithful to Mrs. Perceval, and kind to the Master Percevals! These are, undoubtedly, the first qualifications to be looked to in a time of the most serious public danger; but somehow or another (if public and private virtues must always be incompatible), I should prefer that he destroyed the domestic happiness of Wood or Cockell, owed for the veal of the preceding year, whipped his boys, and saved his country.

The late administration did not do right; they did not build their measures upon the solid basis of facts. They should have caused several Catholics to have been dissected after death by surgeons of either religion; and the report to have been published with accompanying plates. If the viscera, and other organs of life, had been found to be the same as in Protestant bodies; if the provision of nerves, arteries, cerebrum, and cerebellum, had been the same as we are provided with, or as the dissenters are now known to possess; then, indeed, they might have met Mr. Perceval upon a proud eminence, and convinced the country at large of the strong probability that the Catholics are really human creatures, endowed with the feelings of men, and entitled to all their rights. But instead of this wise and prudent measure, Lord Howick, with his usual precipitation, brings forward a bill in their favour, without offering the slightest proof to the country that they were any thing more than horses and oxen. The person who shows the lama at the corner of Piccadilly has the precaution to write up—*Allowed by Sir Joseph Banks to be a real quadruped:* so his lordship might have said—*Allowed by the Bench of Bishops to be real human creatures* . . . . I could write you twenty letters upon this subject: but I am tired, and so I suppose are you. Our friendship is now of forty years' standing; you know me to be a truly religious man; but I shudder to see religion treated like a cockade, or a pint of beer, and made the instrument of a party. I love the king, but I love the people as well as the king; and if I am sorry to see his old age molested, I am much more sorry to see four millions of Catholics baffled in their just expectations. If I love Lord Grenville, and Lord Howick, it is because they love their country; if I abhor ******, it is because I know there is but one man among them who is not laughing at the enormous folly and credulity of the country, and that he is an ignorant and mischievous bigot. As for the light and frivolous jester, of whom it is your misfortune to think so highly, learn, my dear Abraham, that this political Killigrew, just before the breaking-up of the last administration, was in actual treaty with them for a place; and if they had survived twenty-four hours longer, he would have been now declaiming against the cry of No Popery! instead of inflaming it.—With this practical comment on the baseness of human nature, I bid you adieu!

LETTER III.

All that I have so often told you, Mr. Abraham Plymley, is now come to pass. The Scythians, in whom you and the neighbouring country gentlemen placed such confidence, are smitten hip and thigh; their Benningsen put to open shame; their magazines of train oil intercepted, and we are waking from our disgraceful drunkenness to all the horrors of Mr. Perceval and Mr. Canning . . . . We shall now see if a nation is to be saved by schoolboy jokes and doggerel rhymes, by affronting petulance, and by the tones and gesticulations of Mr. Pitt. But these are not all the auxiliaries on which we have to depend; to these his colleague will add the strictest attention to the smaller parts of ecclesiastical government, to hassocks, to psalters, and to surplices; in the last agonies of England, he will bring in a bill to regulate Easter-offerings; and he will adjust the stipends of curates,* when the flag of France is unfurled on the hills of Kent. Whatever can be done by very mistaken notions of the piety of a Christian, and by very wretched imitation of the eloquence of Mr. Pitt, will be done by these two gentlemen. After all, if they both really were what they both either wish to be or wish to be thought; if the one were an enlightened Christian, who drew from the Gospel the toleration, the charity, and the sweetness which it contains; and if the other really possessed any portion of the great understanding of his Nisus who guarded him from the weapons of the whigs, I should still doubt if they could save us. But I am sure we are not to be saved by religious hatred, and by religious trifling; by any psalmody, however sweet; or by any persecution, however sharp: I am certain the sounds of Mr. Pitt's voice, and the measure of his tones, and the movement of his arms, will do nothing for us; when these tones, and movements, and voice bring us always declamation without sense or knowledge, and ridicule without good humour or conciliation. Oh, Mr. Plymley, Mr. Plymley, this never will do. Mrs. Abraham Plymley, my sister, will be led away captive by an amorous Gaul; and Joel Plymley, your first-born, will be a French drummer.

Out of sight, out of mind, seems to be a proverb which applies to enemies as well as friends. Because the French army was no longer seen from the cliffs of Dover; because the sound of cannon was no longer heard by the debauched London bathers on the Sussex coast; because the *Morning Post* no longer fixed the invasion sometimes for Monday, sometimes for Tuesday, sometimes (positively for the last time of invading) on Saturday; because all these causes of terror were suspended, you

---

* The reverend the chancellor of the exchequer has, since this was written, found time, in the heat of the session, to write a book on the stipends of curates.

conceived the power of Bonaparte to be at an end, and were setting off for Paris, with Lord Hawkesbury the conqueror.—This is precisely the method in which the English have acted during the whole of the revolutionary war. If Austria or Prussia armed, doctors of divinity immediately printed those passages out of Habakkuk, in which the destruction of the usurper by General Mack, and the Duke of Brunswick, are so clearly predicted. If Bonaparte halted, there was a mutiny, or a dysentery. If any one of his generals were eaten up by the light troops of Russia, and picked (as their manner is) to the bone, the sanguine spirit of this country displayed itself in all its glory. What scenes of infamy did the Society for the Suppression of Vice lay open to our astonished eyes: tradesmen's daughters dancing; pots of beer carried out between the first and second lesson; and dark and distant rumours of indecent prints. Clouds of Mr. Canning's cousins arrived by the waggon; all the contractors left their cards with Mr. Rose; and every plunderer of the public crawled out of his hole, like slugs and grubs, and worms, after a shower of rain.

If my voice could have been heard at the late changes, I should have said, "Gently; patience; stop a little; the time is not yet come; the mud of Poland will harden, and the bowels of the French grenadiers will recover their tone. When honesty, good sense, and liberality have extricated you out of your present embarrassment, then dismiss them as a matter of course; but you cannot spare them just now; don't be in too great a hurry, or there will be no monarch to flatter, and no country to pillage; only submit for a little time to be respected abroad; overlook the painful absence of the tax-gatherer for a few years; bear up nobly under the increase of freedom and of liberal policy for a little time, and I promise you, at the expiration of that period, you shall be plundered, insulted, disgraced, and restrained to your heart's content. Do not imagine I have any intention of putting servility and canting hypocrisy permanently out of place, or of filling up with courage and sense those offices which naturally devolve upon decorous imbecility and inflexible cunning: give us only a little time to keep off the hussars of France, and then the jobbers and jesters shall return to their birth-right, and public virtue be called by its old name of fanaticism."* Such is the advice I would have offered to my infatuated countrymen; but it rained very hard in November, Brother Abraham, and the bowels of our enemies were loosened, and we put our trust in white fluxes, and wet mud; and there is nothing now to oppose to the conqueror of the world, but a small table wit, and the sallow surveyor of the meltings.

You ask me, if I think it possible for this country to survive the recent misfortunes of Europe?—I answer you without the slightest degree of hesitation, that, if Bonaparte lives, and a great deal is not immediately done for the conciliation of the Catholics, it does seem to me absolutely impossible but that we must perish; and take this with you, that we shall perish without exciting the slightest feeling of present or future compassion, but fall amidst the hootings and revilings of Europe, as a nation of blockheads, Methodists, and old women. If there were any great scenery, any heroic feelings, any blaze of ancient virtue, any exalted death, any termination of England that would be ever remembered, ever honoured in that western world, where liberty is now retiring, conquest would be more tolerable, and ruin more sweet; but it is doubly miserable to become slaves abroad, because we would be tyrants at home; to persecute, when we are contending against persecution; and to perish, because we have raised up worse enemies within, from our own bigotry, than we are exposed to without from the unprincipled ambition of France. It is, indeed, a most silly and afflicting spectacle to rage at such a moment against our own kindred and our own blood; to tell them they cannot be honourable in war, because they are conscientious in religion; to stipulate (at the very moment when we should buy their hearts and swords at any price) that they must hold up the right hand in prayer, and not the left; and adore one common God, by turning to the east rather than to the west.

What is it the Catholics ask of you? Do not exclude us from the honours and emoluments of the state, because we worship God in one way, and you worship him in another,—in a period of the deepest peace, and the fattest prosperity, this would be a fair request; it should be granted, if Lord Hawkesbury had reached Paris, if Mr. Canning's interpreter had threatened the Senate in an opening speech, or Mr. Perceval explained to them the improvements he meant to introduce into the Catholic religion; but to deny the Irish this justice now, in the present state of Europe, and in the summer months, just as the season for destroying kingdoms is coming on, is (beloved Abraham), whatever you may think of it, little short of positive insanity.

Here is a frigate attacked by a corsair of immense strength and size, rigging cut, masts in danger of coming by the board, four foot water in the hold, men dropping off very fast; in this dreadful situation how do you think the captain acts (whose name shall be Perceval)? He calls all hands upon deck; talks to them of king, country, glory, sweethearts, gin, French prison, wooden shoes, old England, and hearts of oak; they give three cheers, rush to their guns, and, after a tremendous conflict, succeed in beating off the enemy. Not a syllable of all this; this is not the manner in which the honourable commander goes to work; the first thing he does is to secure 20 or 30 of his prime sailors who happen to be Catholics, to clap

* This is Mr. Canning's term for the detection of public abuses; a term invented by him, and adopted by that simious parasite who is always grinning at his heels.—Nature descends down to infinite smallness. Mr. Canning has his parasites; and if you take a large buzzing blue-bottle fly, and look at it in a microscope, you may see 20 or 30 little ugly insects crawling about it, which doubtless think their fly to be the bluest, grandest, merriest, most important animal in the universe, and are convinced the world would be at an end if it ceased to buzz.

them in irons, and set over them a guard of as many Protestants; having taken this admirable method of defending himself against his infidel opponents, he goes upon deck, reminds the sailors, in a very bitter harangue, that they are of different religions; exhorts the Episcopal gunner not to trust to the Presbyterian quarter-master; issues positive orders that the Catholics should be fired at upon the first appearance of discontent; rushes through blood and brains, examining his men in the catechism and 39 Articles, and positively forbids every one to spunge or ram who has not taken the sacrament according to the Church of England. Was it right to take out a captain made of excellent British stuff, and to put in such a man as this? Is not he more like a parson, or a talking lawyer, than a thorough-bred seaman? And built as she is of heart of oak, and admirably manned, is it possible, with such a captain, to save this ship from going to the bottom?

You have an argument, I perceive, in common with many others, against the Catholics, that their demands complied with would only lead to farther exactions, and that it is better to resist them now, before any thing is conceded, than hereafter, when it is found that all concessions are in vain. I wish the chancellor of the exchequer, who uses this reasoning to exclude others from their just rights, had tried its efficacy, not by his understanding, but by (what are full of much better things) his pockets. Suppose the person to whom he applied for the meltings had withstood every plea of wife and fourteen children, no business, and good character, and refused him this paltry little office, because he might hereafter attempt to get hold of the revenues of the Duchy of Lancaster for life; would not Mr. Perceval have contended eagerly against the injustice of refusing moderate requests, because immoderate ones may hereafter be made? Would he not have said, (and said truly,) leave such exorbitant attempts as these to the general indignation of the Commons, who will take care to defeat them when they do occur; but do not refuse me the irons, and the meltings now, because I may totally lose sight of all moderation hereafter. Leave hereafter to the spirit and the wisdom of hereafter; and do not be niggardly now, from the apprehension that men as wise as you should be profuse in times to come.

You forget, Brother Abraham, that it is a vast art (where quarrels cannot be avoided) to turn the public opinion in your favour and to the prejudice of your enemy; a vast privilege to feel that you are in the right, and to make him feel that he is in the wrong: a privilege which makes you more than a man, and your antagonist less; and often secures victory, by convincing him who contends, that he must submit to injustice if he submits to defeat. Open every rank in the army and navy to the Catholic; let him purchase at the same price as the Protestant (if either Catholic or Protestant can purchase such refined pleasures) the privilege of hearing Lord Castlereagh speak for three hours; keep his clergy from starving, soften some of the most odious powers of the tithing-man, and you will for ever lay this formidable question to rest. But if I am wrong, and you must quarrel at last, quarrel upon just rather than unjust grounds; divide the Catholic, and unite the Protestant; be just, and your own exertions will be more formidable and their exertions less formidable; be just, and you will take away from their party all the best and wisest understandings of both persuasions, and knit them firmly to your own cause. "Thrice is he armed who has his quarrel just;" and ten times as much may he be taxed. In the beginning of any war, however destitute of common sense, every mob will roar, and every lord of the bedchamber address; but if you are engaged in a war that is to last for years, and to require important sacrifices, take care to make the justice of your case so clear and so obvious, that it cannot be mistaken by the most illiterate country gentleman who rides the earth. Nothing, in fact, can be so grossly absurd as the argument which says, I will deny justice to you now, because I suspect future injustice from you. At this rate, you may lock a man up in your stable, and refuse to let him out because you suspect that he has an intention, at some future period, of robbing your hen-roost. You may horsewhip him at Lady-day, because you believe he will affront you at Midsummer. You may commit a greater evil, to guard against a less, which is merely contingent, and may never happen. You may do what you have done a century ago in Ireland, made the Catholics worse than Helots, because you suspected that they might hereafter aspire to be more than fellow-citizens; rendering their sufferings certain from your jealousy, while yours were only doubtful from their ambition; an ambition sure to be excited by the very measures which were taken to prevent it.

The physical strength of the Catholics will not be greater because you give them a share of political power. You may, by these means, turn rebels into friends; but I do not see how you make rebels more formidable. If they taste of the honey of lawful power, they will love the hive from whence they procure it; if they will struggle with us like men in the same state for civil influence, we are safe. All that I dread is, the physical strength of four millions of men combined with an invading French army. If you are to quarrel at last with this enormous population, still put it off as long as you can; you must gain, and cannot lose, by the delay. The state of Europe cannot be worse; the conviction which the Catholics entertain of your tyranny and injustice cannot be more alarming, nor the opinions of your own people more divided. Time, which produces such effect upon brass and marble, may inspire one minister with modesty, and another with compassion; every circumstance may be better; some certainly will be so, none can be worse; and, after all, the evil may never happen.

You have got hold, I perceive, of all the vulgar English stories respecting the hereditary transmission of forfeited property, and seriously believe that every Catholic beggar wears the terriers of his father's land next his skin, and is only waiting for better times to cut the throat of the Protestant professor, and get drunk in the hall of his ancestors. There is one irresistible answer to this mistake, and that is, that the forfeited lands are purchased indiscriminately by Catholic and Protestant, and that the Catholic purchaser never objects to such a title. Now the land (so purchased by a Catholic) is either his own family estate, or it is not. If it is, you suppose him so desirous of coming into possession, that he resorts to the double method of rebellion and purchase; if it is not his own family estate of which he becomes the purchaser, you suppose him first to purchase, then to rebel, in order to defeat the purchase. These things may happen in Ireland; but it is totally impossible they can happen anywhere else. In fact, what land can any man of any sect purchase in Ireland, but forfeited property? In all other oppressed countries which I have ever heard of, the rapacity of the conqueror was bounded by the territorial limits in which the objects of his avarice were contained; but Ireland has been actually confiscated twice over, as a cat is twice killed by a wicked parish-boy.

I admit there is a vast luxury in selecting a particular set of Christians, and in worrying them as a boy worries a puppy dog; it is an amusement in which all the young English are brought up from their earliest days. I like the idea of saying to men who use a different hassock from me, that till they change their hassock, they shall never be colonels, aldermen, or Parliament-men. While I am gratifying my personal insolence respecting religious forms, I fondle myself into an idea that I am religious, and that I am doing my duty in the most exemplary (as I certainly am in the most easy) way. But then, my good Abraham, this sport, admirable as it is, is become, with respect to the Catholics, a little dangerous; and if we are not extremely careful in taking the amusement, we shall tumble into the holy water, and be drowned. As it seems necessary to your idea of an established church to have somebody to worry and torment, suppose we were to select for this purpose William Wilberforce, Esq., and the patent Christians of Clapham. We shall by this expedient enjoy the same opportunity for cruelty and injustice, without being exposed to the same risks; we will compel them to abjure vital clergymen by a public test, to deny that the said William Wilberforce has any power of working miracles, touching for barrenness or any other infirmity, or that he is endowed with any preternatural gift whatever. We will swear them to the doctrine of good works, compel them to preach common sense, and to hear it; to frequent bishops, deans, and other high churchmen; and to appear (once in the quarter at the least) at some melodrame, opera, pantomime, or other light scenical representation; in short, we will gratify the love of insolence and power; we will enjoy the old orthodox sport of witnessing the impotent anger of men compelled to submit to civil degradation, or to sacrifice their notions of truth to ours. And all this we may do without the slightest risk, because their numbers are (as yet) not very considerable. Cruelty and injustice must, of course, exist; but why connect them with danger? Why torture a bull-dog when you can get a frog or a rabbit? I am sure my proposal will meet with the most universal approbation. Do not be apprehensive of any opposition from ministers. If it is a case of hatred, we are sure that one man will defend it by the Gospel; if it abridges human freedom, we know that another will find precedents for it in the Revolution.

In the name of Heaven, what are we to gain by suffering Ireland to be rode by that faction which now predominates over it? Why are we to endanger our own church and state, not for 500,000 Episcopalians, but for ten or twelve great Orange families, who have been sucking the blood of that country for these hundred years last past? and the folly of the Orangemen* in playing this game themselves, is almost as absurd as ours in playing it for them. They ought to have the sense to see that their business now is to keep quietly the lands and beeves of which the fathers of the Catholics were robbed in days of yore; they must give to their descendants the sop of political power; by contending with them for names, they will lose realities, and be compelled to beg their potatoes in a foreign land, abhorred equally by the English, who have witnessed their oppression, and by the Catholic Irish, who have smarted under them

LETTER IV.

Then comes Mr. Isaac Hawkins Brown (the gentleman who danced† so badly at the court of Naples), and asks, if it is not an anomaly to educate men in another religion than your own? It certainly is our duty to get rid of error, and above all, of religious error; but this is not to be done *per saltum*, or the measure will miscarry, like the queen. It may be very easy to dance away the royal embryo of a great kingdom; but Mr. Hawkins Brown must look before he leaps, when his object is to crush an opposite sect in religion; false steps aid the one effect as much as they are fatal to the other; it will require not only the lapse of Mr. Hawkins Brown, but the lapse of centuries, before the absurdities of the Catholic religion are laughed at as much as they deserve to be; but surely, in the mean time, the Catholic religion is better than none; four millions of Catholics are better than four millions of wild beasts; two hundred priests, educated by our own government, are better than the same number educated by the man who means to destroy us.

The whole sum now appropriated by government to the religious education of four millions of Christians is 13,000*l.*; a sum about one

* This remark begins to be sensibly felt in Ireland. The Protestants in Ireland are fast coming over to the Catholic cause.

† In the third year of his present majesty, and in the 30th of his own age, Mr. Isaac Hawkins Brown, then upon his travels, danced one evening at the court of Naples. His dress was a volcanic silk with lava buttons. Whether (as the Neapolitan wits said) he had studied dancing under St. Vitus, or whether David, dancing in a linen vest, was his model, is not known; but Mr. Brown danced with such inconceivable alacrity and vigour, that he threw the Queen of Naples into convulsions of laughter, which terminated in a miscarriage, and changed the dynasty of the Neapolitan throne.

hundred times as large being appropriated in the same country to about one-eighth part of this number of Protestants. When it was proposed to raise this grant from 8,000*l.* to 13,000*l.*, its present amount, this sum was objected to by that most indulgent of Christians, Mr. Spencer Perceval, as enormous; he himself having secured for his own eating and drinking, and the eating and drinking of the Master and Miss Percevals, the reversionary sum of 21,000*l.* a year of the public money, and having just failed in a desperate and rapacious attempt to secure to himself for life the revenues of the Duchy of Lancaster; and the best of it is, that this minister, after abusing his predecessors for their impious bounty to the Catholics, has found himself compelled, from the apprehension of immediate danger, to grant the sum in question; thus dissolving his pearl* in vinegar, and destroyiug all the value of the gift by the virulence and reluctance with which it was granted.

I hear from some persons in Parliament, and from others in the sixpenny societies for debate, a great deal about unalterable laws passed at the Revolution. When I hear any man talk of an unalterable law, the only effect it produces upon me is to convince me that he is an unalterable fool. A law passed when there were Germany, Spain, Russia, Sweden, Holland, Portugal, and Turkey; when there was a disputed succession; when four or five hundred acres were won and lost after ten years' hard fighting; when armies were commanded by the sons of kings, and campaigns passed in an interchange of civil letters and ripe fruit; and for these laws, when the whole state of the world is completely changed, we are now, according to my Lord Hawkesbury, to hold ourselves ready to perish. It is no mean misfortune, in times like these, to be forced to say any thing about such men as Lord Hawkesbury, and to be reminded that we are governed by them; but as I am driven to it, I must take the liberty of observing, that the wisdom and liberality of my Lord Hawkesbury are of that complexion which always shrinks from the present exercise of these virtues, by praising the splendid examples of them in ages past. If he had lived at such periods, he would have opposed the Revolution by praising the Reformation, and the Reformation by speaking handsomely of the crusades. He gratifies his natural antipathy to great and courageous measures, by playing off the wisdom and courage which have ceased to influence human affairs against that wisdom and courage which living men would employ for present happiness. Besides, it happens unfortunately for the warden of the Cinque Ports, that to the principal incapacities under which the Irish suffer, they were subjected after that great and glorious revolution, to which we are indebted for so many blessings, and his lordship for the termination of so many periods. The Catholics were not excluded from the Irish House of Commons, or military commands, before the 3d and 4th of William and Mary, and he 1st and 2d of Queen Anne.

If the great mass of the people, environed as they are on every side with Jenkinsons, Percevals, Melvilles, and other perils, were to pray for divine illumination and aid, what more could Providence in its mercy do than send them the example of Scotland? For what a length of years was it attempted to compel the Scotch to change their religion: horse, foot, artillery, and armed prebendaries, were sent out after the Presbyterian parsons and their congregations. The Percevals of those days called for blood; this call is never made in vain, and blood was shed; but, to the astonishment and horror of the Percevals of those days, they could not introduce the Book of Common Prayer, nor prevent that metaphysical people from going to heaven their true way, instead of our true way. With a little oatmeal for food, and a little sulphur for friction, allaying cutaneous irritation with the one hand, and holding his Calvinistical creed in the other, Sawney ran away to his flinty hills, sung his psalm out of tune his own way, and listened to his sermon of two hours long, amid the rough and imposing melancholy of the tallest thistles. But Sawney brought up his unbreeched offspring in a cordial hatred of his oppressors; and Scotland was as much a part of the weakness of England then as Ireland is at this moment. The true and the only remedy was applied; the Scotch were suffered to worship God after their own tiresome manner, without pain, penalty, and privation. No lightnings descended from heaven; the country was not ruined; the world is not yet come to an end; the dignitaries, who foretold all these consequences, are utterly forgotten; and Scotland has ever since been an increasing source of strength to Great Britain. In the six hundredth year of our empire over Ireland, we are making laws to transport a man, if he is found out of his house after eight o'clock at night. That this is necessary, I know too well; but tell me why it is necessary? It is not necessary in Greece, where the Turks are masters.

Are you aware, that there is at this moment an universal clamour throughout the whole of Ireland against the union? It is now one month since I returned from that country; I have never seen so extraordinary, so alarming, and so rapid a change in the sentiments of any people. Those who disliked the union before are quite furious against it now; those who doubted doubt no more; those who were friendly to it have exchanged that friendship for the most rooted aversion; in the midst of all this (which is by far the most alarming symptom), there is the strongest disposition on the part of the northern dissenters to unite with the Catholics, irritated by the faithless injustice with which they have been treated. If this combination does take place (mark what I say to you), you will have meetings all over Ireland for the cry of *No Union;* that cry will spread like wild-fire, and blaze over every opposition; and if this is the case, there is no use in mincing the matter, Ireland is gone, and the death-blow of England is struck; and this

* Perfectly ready at the same time to follow the other half of Cleopatra's example, and to swallow the solution himself.

event may happen *instantly*—before Mr. Canning and Mr. Hookham Frere have turned Lord Howick's last speech into doggerel rhyme; before "*the near and dear relations*" have received another quarter of their pension, or Mr. Perceval conducted the curates' salary bill safely to a third reading.—If the mind of the English people, cursed as they now are with that madness of religious dissension which has been breathed into them for the purpose of private ambition, can be alarmed by any remembrances, and warned by any events, they should never forget how nearly Ireland was lost to this country during the American war; that it was saved merely by the jealousy of the Protestant Irish towards the Catholics, then a much more insignificant and powerless body than they now are. The Catholic and the dissenter have since combined together against you. Last war, the winds, those ancient and unsubsidized allies of England; the winds, upon which English ministers depend as much for saving kingdoms as washerwomen do for drying clothes; the winds stood your friends; the French could only get into Ireland in small numbers, and the rebels were defeated. Since then, all the remaining kingdoms of Europe have been destroyed; and the Irish see that their national independence is gone, without having received any single one of those advantages which they were taught to expect from the sacrifice. All good things were to flow from the union; they have none of them gained any thing. Every man's pride is wounded by it; no man's interest is promoted. In the seventh year of that union, four million Catholics, lured by all kinds of promises to yield up the separate dignity and sovereignty of their country, are forced to squabble with such a man as Mr. Spencer Perceval for five thousand pounds with which to educate their children in their own mode of worship; he, the same Mr. Spencer, having secured to his own Protestant self a reversionary portion of the public money amounting to four times that sum. A senior proctor of the University of Oxford, the head of a house, or the examining chaplain to a bishop, may believe these things can last; but every man of the world, whose understanding has been exercised in the business of life, must see (and see with a breaking heart) that they will soon come to a fearful termination.

Our conduct to Ireland, during the whole of this war, has been that of a man who subscribes to hospitals, weeps at charity sermons, carries out broth and blankets to beggars, and then comes home and beats his wife and children. We had compassion for the victims of all other oppression and injustice, except our own. If Switzerland was threatened, away went a treasury clerk with a hundred thousand pounds for Switzerland; large bags of money were kept constantly under sailing orders; upon the slightest demonstration towards Naples, down went Sir William Hamilton upon his knees, and begged for the love of St. Januarius they would help us off with a little money; all the arts of Machiavel were resorted to, to persuade Europe to borrow; troops were sent off in all directions to save the Catholic and Protestant world; the pope himself was guarded by a regiment of English dragoons; if the Grand Lama had been at hand, he would have had another; every Catholic clergyman, who had the good fortune to be neither English nor Irish, was immediately provided with lodgings, soup, crucifix, missal, chapel-beads, relics, and holy water; if Turks had landed, Turks would have received an order from the treasury for coffee, opium, korans, and seraglios. In the midst of all this fury of saving and defending, this crusade for conscience and Christianity, there was an universal agreement among all descriptions of people to continue every species of internal persecution; to deny at home every just right that had been denied before; to pummel poor Dr. Abraham Rees and his dissenters; and to treat the unhappy Catholics of Ireland as if their tongues were mute, their heels cloven, their nature brutal, and designedly subjected by Providence to their Orange masters.

How would my admirable brother, the Rev. Abraham Plymley, like to be marched to a Catholic chapel, to be sprinkled with the sanctified contents of a pump, to hear a number of false quantities in the Latin tongue, and to see a number of persons occupied in making right angles upon the breast and forehead? And if all this would give you so much pain, what right have you to march Catholic soldiers to a place of worship where there is no aspersion, no rectangular gestures, and where they understand every word they hear, having first, in order to get him to enlist, made a solemn promise to the contrary? Can you wonder, after this, that the Catholic priest stops the recruiting in Ireland, as he is now doing to a most alarming degree?

The late question concerning military rank did not individually affect the lowest persons of the Catholic persuasion; but do you imagine that they do not sympathize with the honour and disgrace of their superiors? Do you think that satisfaction and dissatisfaction do not travel down from Lord Fingal to the most potatoless Catholic in Ireland, and that the glory or shame of the sect is not felt by many more than these conditions personally and corporally affect? Do you suppose that the detection of Sir H. M., and the disappointment of Mr. Perceval *in the matter* of the Duchy of Lancaster, did not affect every dabbler in public property? Depend upon it these things were felt through all the gradations of small plunderers, down to him who filches a pound of tobacco from the king's warehouses; while, on the contrary, the acquittal of any noble and official thief would not fail to diffuse the most heartfelt satisfaction over the larcenous and burglarious world. Observe, I do not say because the lower Catholics are affected by what concerns their superiors, that they are not affected by what concerns themselves. There is no disguising the horrid truth; *there must be some relaxation with respect to tithe:* this is the cruel and heart-rending price which must be paid for national preservation. I feel how little existence will be worth having, if any alteration, however slight, is made in the property of Irish rectors; I am conscious how much such changes must affect the daily and hourly comforts of every Englishman; I shall feel too happy if they leave Europe untouched, and are not ultimately fatal to the destinies of America; but I am madly bent upon keeping foreign enemies out of the British empire, and my limited understanding presents me with no other means of effecting my object.

You talk of waiting till another reign, before any alteration is made; a proposal full of good sense and good nature, if the measure in question were to pull down St. James's Palace, or to alter Kew Gardens. Will Bonaparte agree to put off his intrigues, and his invasion of Ireland? If so, I will overlook the question of justice, and finding the danger suspended, agree to the delay. I sincerely hope this reign may last many years, yet the delay of a single session of Parliament may be fatal; but if another year elapses without some serious concession made to the Catholics, I believe, before God, that all future pledges and concessions will be made in vain. I do not think that peace will do you any good under such circumstances; if Bonaparte gives you a respite, it will only be to get ready the gallows on which he means to hang you. The Catholic and the dissenter can unite in peace as well as war. If they do, the gallows is ready; and your executioner, in spite of the most solemn promises, will turn you off the next hour.

With every disposition to please (where to please within fair and rational limits is an high duty), it is impossible for public men to be long silent about the Catholics: pressing evils are not got rid of because they are not talked of. A man may command his family to say nothing more about the stone, and surgical operations; but the ponderous malice still lies upon the nerve, and gets so big, that the patient breaks his own law of silence, clamours for the knife, and expires under its late operation. Believe me, you talk folly, when you talk of suppressing the Catholic question. I wish to God the case admitted of such a remedy: bad as it is, it does not admit of it. If the wants of the Catholics are not heard in the manly tones of Lord Grenville, or the servile drawl of Lord Castlereagh, they will be heard ere long in the madness of mobs, and the conflicts of armed men.

I observe, it is now universally the fashion to speak of the first personage in the state as the great obstacle to the measure. In the first place, I am not bound to believe such rumours because I hear them; and in the next place, I object to such language as unconstitutional. Whoever retains his situation in the ministry, while the incapacities of the Catholics remain, is the advocate for those incapacities; and to him, and to him only, am I to look for responsibility. But waive this question of the Catholics, and put a general case: How is a minister of this country to act when the conscientious scruples of his sovereign prevent the execution of a measure deemed by him absolutely necessary to the safety of the country? His conduct is quite clear—he should resign. But what is his successor to do?—Resign. But is the king to be left without ministers, and is he in this manner to be compelled to act against his own conscience? Before I answer this, pray tell me, in my turn, what better defence is there against the machinations of a wicked, or the errors of a weak monarch, than the impossibility of finding a minister who will lend himself to vice and folly? Every English monarch, in such a predicament, would sacrifice his opinions and views to such a clear expression of the public will; and it is one method in which the constitution aims at bringing about such a sacrifice. You may say, if you please, the ruler of a state is forced to give up his object, when the natural love of place and power will tempt no one to assist him in its attainment. This may be force; but it is force without injury, and therefore without blame. I am not to be beat out of these obvious reasonings, and ancient constitutional provisions, by the term conscience. There is no fantasy, however wild, that a man may not persuade himself that he cherishes from motives of conscience; eternal war against impious France, or rebellious America, or Catholic Spain, may in times to come be scruples of conscience. One English monarch may, from scruples of conscience, wish to abolish every trait of religious persecution; another monarch may deem it his absolute and indispensable duty to make a slight provision for dissenters out of the revenues of the Church of England. So that you see, Brother Abraham, there are cases where it would be the duty of the best and most loyal subjects to oppose the conscientious scruples of their sovereign, still taking care that their actions were constitutional, and their modes respectful. Then you come upon me with personal questions, and say, that no such dangers are to be apprehended now under our present gracious sovereign, of whose good qualities we must be all so well convinced. All these sorts of discussions I beg leave to decline; what I have said upon constitutional topics, I mean of course for general, not for particular application. I agree with you in all the good you have said of the powers that be, and I avail myself of the opportunity of pointing out general dangers to the constitution, at a moment when we are so completely exempted from their present influence. I cannot finish this letter without expressing my surprise and pleasure at your abuse of the servile addresses poured in upon the throne; nor can I conceive a greater disgust to a monarch, with a true English heart, than to see such a question as that of Catholic emancipation argued, not with a reference to its justice or its importance, but universally considered to be of no farther consequence than as it affects his own private feelings. That these sentiments should be mine, is not wonderful; but how they come to be yours, does, I confess, fill me with surprise. Are you moved by the arrival of the Irish brigade at Antwerp, and the amorous violence which awaits Mrs. Plymley?

LETTER V.

Dear Abraham,

I never met a parson in my life who did not consider the Corporation and Test Acts as the great bulwarks of the church; and yet it is now just sixty-four years since bills of indemnity to destroy their penal effects, or, in other words, to repeal them, have been passed annually as a matter of course.

Heu vatum ignaræ mentes.

These bulwarks, without which no clergyman thinks he could sleep with his accustomed soundness, have actually not been in existence since any man now living has taken holy orders. Every year the indemnity act pardons past breaches of these two laws, and prevents any fresh actions of informers from coming to a conclusion before the period for the next indemnity bill arrives; so that these penalties, by which alone the church remains in existence, have not had one moment's operation for sixty-four years. You will say the legislature, during the whole of this period, has reserved to itself the discretion of suspending, or not suspending. But had not the legislature the right of re-enacting, if it was necessary? And now, when you have kept the rod over these people (with the most scandalous abuse of all principle) for sixty-four years, and not found it necessary to strike once, is not that the best of all reasons why the rod should be laid aside? You talk to me of a very valuable hedge running across your fields which you would not part with on any account. I go down, expecting to find a limit impervious to cattle, and highly useful for the preservation of property; but, to my utter astonishment, I find that the hedge was cut down half a century ago, and that every year the shoots are clipped the moment they appear above ground: it appears, upon farther inquiry, that the hedge never ought to have existed at all; that it originated in the malice of antiquated quarrels, and was cut down because it subjected you to vast inconvenience, and broke up your intercourse with a country absolutely necessary to your existence. If the remains of this hedge serve only to keep up an irritation in your neighbours, and to remind them of the feuds of former times, good nature and good sense teach you that you ought to grub it up, and cast it into the oven. This is the exact state of these two laws; and yet it is made a great argument against concession to the Catholics, that it involves their repeal; which is to say, Do not make me relinquish a folly that will lead to my ruin; because, if you do, I must give up other follies ten times greater than this.

I confess, with all our bulwarks and hedges, it mortifies me to the very quick, to contrast with our matchless stupidity and inimitable folly, the conduct of Bonaparte upon the subject of religious persecution. At the moment when we are tearing the crucifixes from the necks of the Catholics, and washing pious mud from the foreheads of the Hindoos; at that moment this man is assembling the very Jews at Paris, and endeavouring to give them stability and importance. I shall never be reconciled to mending shoes in America; but I see it must be my lot, and I will then take a dreadful revenge upon Mr. Perceval, if I catch him preaching within ten miles of me. I cannot for the soul of me conceive whence this man has gained his notions of Christianity; he has the most evangelical charity for errors in arithmetic, and the most inveterate malice against errors in conscience. While he rages against those whom, in the true spirit of the Gospel, he ought to indulge, he forgets the only instance of severity which that Gospel contains, and leaves the jobbers, and contractors, and money-changers at their seats, without a single stripe.

You cannot imagine, you say, that England will ever be ruined and conquered; and for no other reason that I can find, but because it seems so very odd it should be ruined and conquered. Alas! so reasoned, in their time, the Austrian, Russian and Prussian Plymleys. But the English are brave; so were all these nations. You might get together an hundred thousand men individually brave; but without generals capable of commanding such a machine, it would be as useless as a first-rate man-of-war manned by Oxford clergymen, or Parisian shopkeepers. I do not say this to the disparagement of English officers; they have had no means of acquiring experience; but I do say it to create alarm; for we do not appear to me to be half alarmed enough, or to entertain that sense of our danger which leads to the most obvious means of self-defence. As for the spirit of the peasantry, in making a gallant defence behind hedge-rows, and through plate-racks and hen-coops, highly as I think of their bravery, I do not know any nation in Europe so likely to be struck with panic as the English; and this from their total unacquaintance with the science of war. Old wheat and beans blazing for twenty miles round; cart mares shot; sows of Lord Somerville's breed running wild over the country; the minister of the parish wounded solely in his hinder parts; Mrs. Plymley in fits; all these scenes of war an Austrian or a Russian has seen three or four times over; but it is now three centuries since an English pig has fallen in a fair battle upon English ground, or a farm-house been rifled, or a clergyman's wife been subjected to any other proposals of love than the connubial endearments of her sleek and orthodox mate. The old edition of Plutarch's Lives, which lies in the corner of your parlour window, has contributed to work you up to the most romantic expectations of our Roman behaviour. You are persuaded that Lord Amherst will defend Kew Bridge like Cocles; that some maid of honour will break away from her captivity, and swim over the Thames; that the Duke of York will burn his capitulating hand; and little Mr. Sturges Bourne* give forty years' purchase for Moulsham Hall, while the French are encamped upon it. I hope we shall witness all this, if the French do come; but in the mean time I am so enchanted with the ordinary English behaviour of these invaluable persons, that I earnestly pray no opportunity may be given them for Roman valour, and for those very un-Roman pensions which they would all, of course, take especial care to claim in

* There is nothing more objectionable in Plymley's Letters than the abuse of Mr. Sturges Bourne, who is an honourable, able, and excellent person; but such are the malevolent effects of party spirit.

consequence. But whatever was our conduct, if every ploughman was as great a hero as he who was called from his oxen to save Rome from her enemies, I should still say, that at such a crisis you want the affections of all your subjects in both islands; there is no spirit which you must alienate, no heart you must avert; every man must feel he has a country, and that there is an urgent and pressing cause why he should expose himself to death.

The effects of penal laws, in matters of religion, are never confined to those limits in which the legislature intended they should be placed; it is not only that I am excluded from certain offices and dignities because I am a Catholic, but the exclusion carries with it a certain stigma, which degrades me in the eyes of the monopolizing sect, and the very name of my religion becomes odious. These effects are so very striking in England, that I solemnly believe blue and red baboons to be more popular here than Catholics and Presbyterians; they are more understood, and there is a greater disposition to do something for them. When a country squire hears of an ape, his first feeling is to give it nuts and apples; when he hears of a dissenter, his immediate impulse is to commit it to the county jail, to shave its head, to alter its customary food, and to have it privately whipped. This is no caricature, but an accurate picture of national feelings, as they degrade and endanger us at this very moment. The Irish Catholic gentleman would bear his legal disabilities with greater temper, if these were all he had to bear—if they did not enable every Protestant cheesemonger and tidewaiter to treat him with contempt. He is branded on the forehead with a red-hot iron, and treated like a spiritual felon, because, in the highest of all considerations, he is led by the noblest of all guides, his own disinterested conscience.

Why are nonsense and cruelty a bit the better because they are enacted? If Providence, which gives wine and oil, had blessed us with that tolerant spirit which makes the countenance more pleasant and the heart more glad than these can do; if our statute book had never been defiled with such infamous laws, the sepulchral Spencer Perceval would have been hauled through the dirtiest horse-pond in Hampstead, had he ventured to propose them. But now persecution is good, because it exists; every law which originated in ignorance and malice, and gratifies the passions from whence it sprang, we call the wisdom of our ancestors; when such laws are repealed, they will be cruelty and madness; till they are repealed, they are policy and caution.

I was somewhat amused with the imputation brought against the Catholics by the University of Oxford, that they are enemies to liberty. I immediately turned to my history of England, and marked as an historical error that passage in which it is recorded that, in the reign of Queen Anne, the famous decree of the University of Oxford, respecting passive obedience, was ordered, by the House of Lords, to be burnt by the hands of the common hangman, as contrary to the liberty of the subject, and the law of the land. Nevertheless, I wish, whatever be the modesty of those who impute, that the imputation was a little more true; the Catholic cause would not be quite so desperate with the present administration. I fear, however, that the hatred to liberty in these poor devoted wretches may ere long appear more doubtful than it is at present to the vice-chancellor and his clergy, inflamed, as they doubtless are, with classical examples of republican virtue, and panting, as they always have been, to reduce the power of the crown within narrower and safer limits. What mistaken zeal to attempt to connect one religion with freedom, and another with slavery! Who laid the foundations of English liberty? What was the mixed religion of Switzerland? What has the Protestant religion done for liberty in Denmark, in Sweden, throughout the north of Germany, and in Prussia? The purest religion in the world, in my humble opinion, is the religion of the Church of England; for its preservation (so far as it is exercised without intruding upon the liberties of others), I am ready at this moment to venture my present life, and but through that religion I have no hopes of any other; yet I am not forced to be silly because I am pious; nor will I ever join in eulogiums on my faith, which every man of common reading and common sense can so easily refute.

You have either done too much for the Catholics (worthy Abraham), or too little; if you had intended to refuse them political power, you should have refused them civil rights. After you had enabled them to acquire property, after you had conceded to them all that you did concede in 78 and 93, the rest is wholly out of your power; you may choose whether you will give the rest in an honourable or a disgraceful mode, but it is utterly out of your power to withhold it.

In the last year, land to the amount of *eight hundred thousand pounds* was purchased by the Catholics in Ireland. Do you think it possible to be-Perceval, and be-Canning, and be-Castlereagh such a body of men as this out of their common rights and their sense? Mr. George Canning may laugh and joke at the idea of Protestant bailiffs ravishing Catholic ladies, under the 9th clause of the sunset bill; but if some better remedy is not applied to the distractions of Ireland than the jocularity of Mr. Canning, they will soon put an end to his pension, and to the pension of those "near and dear relatives," for whose eating, drinking, washing, and clothing, every man in the United Kingdoms now pays his two-pence or three-pence a year. You may call these observations coarse, if you please; but I have no idea that the Sophias and Carolines of any man breathing are to eat national veal, to drink public tea, to wear treasury ribands, and then that we are to be told that it is coarse to animadvert upon this pitiful and eleemosynary splendour. If this is right, why not mention it? If it is wrong, why should not he who enjoys the ease of supporting his sisters in this manner bear the shame of it? Every body seems hitherto to have spared a man who never spares any body.

As for the enormous wax candles, and superstitious mummeries, and painted jackets of the Catholic priests, I fear them not. Tell me that the world will return again under the influence of the small-pox; that Lord Castlereagh will hereafter oppose the power of the court; that Lord Howick and Mr. Grattan will do each of them a mean and dishonourable action; that any body who has heard Lord Redesdale speak once will knowingly and willingly hear him again; that Lord Eldon has assented to the fact of two and two making four, without shedding tears, or expressing the smallest doubt or scruple; tell me any other thing absurd or incredible, but, for the love of common sense, let me hear no more of the danger to be apprehended from the general diffusion of Popery. It is too absurd to be reasoned upon; every man feels it is nonsense when he hears it stated, and so does every man while he is stating it.

I cannot imagine why the friends to the church establishment should entertain such an horror of seeing the doors of Parliament flung open to the Catholics, and view so passively the enjoyment of that right by the Presbyterians, and by every other species of dissenter. In their tenets, in their church government, in the nature of their endowments, the dissenters are infinitely more distant from the Church of England than the Catholics are; yet the dissenters have never been excluded from Parliament. There are 45 members in one house and 16 in the other, who always are dissenters. There is no law which would prevent every member of the Lords and Commons from being dissenters. The Catholics could not bring into Parliament half the number of the Scotch members; and yet one exclusion is of such immense importance, because it has taken place; and the other no human being thinks of, because no one is accustomed to it. I have often thought, if the *wisdom of our ancestors* had excluded all persons with red hair from the House of Commons, of the throes and convulsions it would occasion to restore them to their natural rights. What mobs and riots would it produce? To what infinite abuse and obloquy would the capillary patriot be exposed? what wormwood would distil from Mr. Perceval, what froth would drop from Mr. Canning; how (I will not say *my*, but *our* Lord Hawkesbury, for he belongs to us all), how our Lord Hawkesbury would work away about the hair of King William and Lord Somers, and the authors of the great and glorious Revolution; how Lord Elton would appeal to the Deity and his own virtues, and to the hair of his children: some would say that red-haired men were superstitious; some would prove they were atheists; they would be petitioned against as the friends of slavery, and the advocates for revolt; in short, such a corrupter of the heart and the understanding is the spirit of persecution, and these unfortunate people (conspired against by their fellow-subjects of every complexion), if they did not emigrate to countries where hair of another colour was persecuted, would be driven to the falsehood of perukes, or the hypocrisy of the Tricosian fluid.

As for the dangers of the church (in spite of the staggering events which have lately taken place), I have not yet entirely lost my confidence in the power of common sense, and I believe the church to be in no danger at all; but if it is, that danger is not from the Catholics, but from the Methodists, and from that patent Christianity which has been for some time manufacturing at Clapham, to the prejudice of the old and admirable article prepared by the church. I would counsel my lords the bishops to keep their eyes upon that holy village, and its hallowed vicinity; they will find there a zeal in making converts far superior to any thing which exists among the Catholics; a contempt for the great mass of English clergy much more rooted and profound; and a regular fund to purchase livings for those groaning and garrulous gentlemen, whom they denominate (by a standing sarcasm against the regular church) gospel preachers, and vital clergymen. I am too firm a believer in the general propriety and respectability of the English clergy, to believe they have much to fear either from old nonsense, or from new; but if the church must be supposed to be in danger, I prefer that nonsense which is grown half venerable from time, the force of which I have already tried and baffled, which at least has some excuse in the dark and ignorant ages in which it originated. The religious enthusiasm manufactured by living men before my own eyes disgusts my understanding as much, influences my imagination not at all, and excites my apprehensions much more.

I may have seemed to you to treat the situation of public affairs with some degree of levity; but I feel it deeply, and with nightly and daily anguish; because I know Ireland; I have known it all my life; I love it, and I foresee the crisis to which it will soon be exposed. Who can doubt but that Ireland will experience ultimately from France a treatment to which the conduct they have experienced from England is the love of a parent, or a brother? Who can doubt but that five years after he has got hold of the country, Ireland will be tossed away by Bonaparte as a present to some one of his ruffian generals, who will knock the head of Mr. Keogh against the head of Cardinal Troy, shoot twenty of the most noisy block heads of the Roman persuasion, wash his pug-dogs in holy water, and confiscate the salt butter of the Milesian republic to the last tub? But what matters this? or who is wise enough in Ireland to heed it? or when had common sense much influence with my poor dear Irish? Mr. Perceval does not know the Irish; but I know them, and I know that at every rash and mad hazard, they will break the union, revenge their wounded pride and their insulted religion, and fling themselves into the open arms of France, sure of dying in the embrace. And now, what means have you of guarding against this coming evil, upon which the future happiness or misery of every Englishman depends? Have you a single ally in the whole world? Is there a vulnerable point in the French empire where the astonishing resources of that people can be attracted and employed? Have you a ministry wise enough to comprehend the danger, manly enough to believe unpleasant intelligence, honest enough to state their apprehensions at the peril of their places? Is there anywhere the slightest disposition to join any measure of love, or conciliation, or hope, with that dreadful bill which the distractions of Ireland have rendered necessary? At the very moment that the last monarchy in Europe has fallen, are we not governed by a man of pleasantry, and a man of theology? In the six hundredth year of our empire over Ireland, have we any memorial of ancient kindness to refer to? any people, any zeal, any country on which we can depend? Have we any hope, but in the winds of heaven, and the tides of the sea? any prayer to prefer to the Irish, but that they should forget and forgive their oppressors, who, in the very moment that they are calling upon them for their exertions, solemnly assure them that the oppression shall still remain?

Abraham, farewell! If I have tired you, remember how often you have tired me and others. I do not think we really differ in politics so much as you suppose; or at least, if we do, that difference is in the means, and not in the end. We both love the constitution, respect the king, and abhor the French. But though you love the constitution, you would perpetuate the abuses which have been engrafted upon it; though you respect the king, you would confirm his scruples against the Catholics; though you abhor the French, you would open to them the conquest of Ireland. My method of respecting my sovereign is by protecting his honour, his empire, and his lasting happiness; I evince my love of the constitution, by making it the guardian of all men's rights and the source of their freedom; and I prove my abhorrence of the French, by uniting against them the disciples of every church in the only remaining nation in Europe. As for the men of whom I have been compelled, in this age of mediocrity, to say so much, they cannot of themselves be worth a moment's consideration to you, to me, or to any body. In a year after their death, they will be forgotten as completely as if they had never been; and are now of no farther importance than as they are the mere vehicles of carrying into effect the common-place and mischievous prejudices of the times in which they live.

LETTER VI.

Dear Abraham,

What amuses me the most is, to hear of the *indulgences* which the Catholics have received, and their exorbitance in not being satisfied with those indulgences: now if you complain to me that a man is obtrusive and shameless in his requests, and that it is impossible to bring him to reason, I must first of all hear the whole of your conduct towards him; for you may have taken from him so much in the first instance, that, in spite of a long series of restitution, a vast latitude for petition may still remain behind.

There is a village (no matter where) in which the inhabitants, on one day in the year, sit down to a dinner prepared at the common expense; by an extraordinary piece of tyranny (which Lord Hawkesbury would call the wisdom of the village ancestors), the inhabitants of three of the streets, about an hundred years ago, seized upon the inhabitants of the fourth street, bound them hand and foot, laid them upon their backs, and compelled them to look on while the rest were stuffing themselves with beef and beer; the next year, the inhabitants of the persecuted street (though they contributed an equal quota of the expense) were treated precisely in the same manner. The tyranny grew into a custom; and (as the manner of our nature is) it was considered as the most sacred of all duties to keep these poor fellows without their annual dinner; the village was so tenacious of this practice, that nothing could induce them to resign it; every enemy to it was looked upon as a disbeliever in Divine Providence, and any nefarious churchwarden who wished to succeed in his election had nothing to do but to represent his antagonist as an abolitionist, in order to frustrate his ambition, endanger his life, and throw the village into a state of the most dreadful commotion. By degrees, however, the obnoxious street grew to be so well peopled, and its inhabitants so firmly united, that their oppressors, more afraid of injustice, were more disposed to be just. At the next dinner they are unbound, the year after allowed to sit upright, then a bit of bread and a glass of water; till at last, after a long series of concessions, they are emboldened to ask, in pretty plain terms, that they may be allowed to sit down at the bottom of the table, and to fill their bellies as well as the rest. Forthwith a general cry of shame and scandal: "Ten years ago, were you not laid upon your backs? Don't you remember what a great thing you thought it to get a piece of bread? How thankful you were for cheese parings? Have you forgotten that memorable era, when the lord of the manor interfered to obtain for you a slice of the public pudding? And now with an audacity only equalled by your ingratitude, you have the impudence to ask for knives and forks, and to request, in terms too plain to be mistaken, that you may sit down to table with the rest, and be indulged even with beef and beer: there are not more than half a dozen dishes which we have reserved for ourselves; the rest has been thrown open to you in the utmost profusion; you have potatoes, and carrots, suet dumplings, sops in the pan, and delicious toast and water, in incredible quantities. Beef, mutton, lamb, pork, and veal are ours; and if you were not the most restless and dissatisfied of human beings, you would never think of aspiring to enjoy them."

Is not this, my dainty Abraham, the very nonsense and the very insult which is talked to and practised upon the Catholics? You are surprised that men who have tasted of partial justice should ask for perfect justice; that he who has been robbed of coat and cloak will not be contented with the restitution of one of his garments. He would be a very lazy blockhead if he were content, and I (who, though an inhabitant of the village, have preserved, thank God, some sense of justice) most earnestly counsel these half-fed claimants to persevere in their just demands, till they are admitted to a more complete share of a dinner for which they pay as much as the others; and if they see a little attenuated lawyer squabbling at the head of their opponents, let them desire him to empty his pockets, and to pull out all the pieces of duck, fowl, and pudding, which he has filched from the public feast, to carry home to his wife and children.

You parade a great deal upon the vast concessions made by this country to the Irish before the union. I deny that any voluntary concession was ever made by England to Ireland.—What did Ireland ever ask that was granted? What did she ever demand that was refused? How did she get her mutiny bill—a limited Parliament—a repeal of Poyning's law—a constitution? Not by the concessions of England, but by her fears. When Ireland asked for all these things upon her knees, her petitions were rejected with Percevalism and contempt: when she demanded them with the voice of 60,000 armed men, they were granted with every mark of consternation and dismay. Ask of Lord Auckland the fatal consequences of trifling with such a people as the Irish. He himself was the organ of these refusals.—As secretary to the lord-lieutenant, the insolence and tyranny of this country passed through his hands. Ask him if he remembers the consequences. Ask him if he has forgotten that memorable evening, when he came down booted and mantled to the House of Commons, when he told the House he was about to set off for Ireland that night, and declared, before God, if he did not carry with him a compliance with all their demands, Ireland was for ever lost to this country. The present generation have forgotten this; but I have not forgotten it; and I know, hasty and undignified as the submission of England then was, that Lord Auckland was right, that the delay of a single day might very probably have separated the two people for ever. The terms submission and fear are galling terms, when applied from the lesser nation to the greater; but it is the plain historical truth, it is the natural consequence of injustice, it is the predicament in which every country places itself which leaves such a mass of hatred and discontent by its side. No empire is powerful enough to endure it; it would exhaust the strength of China, and sink it with all its mandarins and tea-kettles to the bottom of the deep. By refusing them justice now, when you are strong enough to refuse them any thing more than justice, you will act over again, with the Catholics, the same scene of mean and precipitate submission which disgraced you before America, and before the volunteers of Ireland. We shall live to hear the Hampstead Protestant pronouncing such extravagant panegyrics upon holy water, and paying such fulsome compliments to the thumbs and offals of departed saints, that parties will change sentiments, and Lord Henry Petty and Sam Whitbread take a spell at No-Popery. The wisdom of Mr. Fox was alike employed in teaching his country justice when Ireland was weak, and dignity when Ireland was strong. We are fast pacing round the same miserable circle of ruin and imbecility. Alas! where is our guide?

You say that Ireland is a millstone about our necks; that it would be better for us if Ireland were sunk at the bottom of the sea; that the Irish are a nation of irreclaimable savages and barbarians. How often have I heard these sentiments fall from the plump and thoughtless squire, and from the thriving English shopkeeper, who has never felt the rod of an Orange master upon his back. Ireland a millstone about your neck! Why is it not a stone of Ajax in your hand? I agree with you most cordially, that, governed as Ireland now is, it would be a vast accession of strength if the waves of the sea were to rise and ingulf her to-morrow. At this moment, opposed as we are to all the world, the annihilation of one of the most fertile islands on the face of the globe, containing five millions of human creatures, would be one of the most solid advantages which could happen to this country. I doubt very much, in spite of all the just abuse which has been lavished upon Bonaparte, whether there is any one of his conquered countries the blotting out of which would be as beneficial to him as the destruction of Ireland would be to us: of countries, I speak, differing in language from the French, little habituated to their intercourse, and inflamed with all the resentments of a recently conquered people. Why will you attribute the turbulence of our people to any cause but the right—to any cause but your own scandalous oppression? If you tie your horse up to a gate, and beat him cruelly, is he vicious because he kicks you? If you have plagued and worried a mastiff dog for years, is he mad because he flies at you whenever he sees you? Hatred is an active, troublesome passion. Depend upon it, whole nations have always some reason for their hatred. Before you refer the turbulence of the Irish to indurable defects in their character, tell me if you have treated them as friends and equals? Have you protected their commerce? Have you respected their religion? Have you been as anxious for their freedom as your own? Nothing of all this. What then?—Why, you have confiscated the territorial surface of the country twice over; you have massacred and exported her inhabitants; you have deprived four-fifths of them of every civil privilege; you have at every period made her commerce and manufactures slavishly subordinate to your own; and yet the hatred which the Irish bear to you is the result of an original turbulence of character, and of a primitive, obdurate wildness, utterly incapable of civilization. The embroidered inanities and the sixth-form effusions of Mr. Canning, are really not powerful enough to make me believe this; nor is there any authority on earth (always excepting the Dean of Christ-Church) which could make it credible to me. I am sick of Mr. Canning. There is not a ha'p'orth of bread to all this sugar and sack. I love not the cretaceous and incredible countenance of his colleague. The only opinion in which I agree with these two gentlemen, is that which they entertain of each other; I am sure that the insolence of Mr. Pitt, and the unbalanced accounts of Melville, were far better than the perils of this new ignorance:—

> Nonne fuit satius tristes Amaryllidis iras
> Atque superba pati fastidia—nonne Menalcam,
> Quamvis ille *niger*?

In the midst of the most profound peace, the secret articles of the treaty of Tilsit, in which the destruction of Ireland is resolved upon, induce you to rob the Danes of their fleet.—After the expedition sailed comes the treaty of Tilsit, containing no article,* public or private, alluding to Ireland. The state of the world, you tell me, justified us in doing this.—Just God! do we think only of the state of the world when there is an opportunity for robbery, for murder, and for plunder; and do we forget the state of the world when we are called upon to be wise, and good, and just? Does the state of the world never remind us, that we have four millions of subjects whose injuries we ought to atone for, and whose affections we ought to conciliate? Does the state of the world never warn us to lay aside our infernal bigotry, and to arm every man who acknowledges a God and can grasp a sword? Did it never occur to this administration, that they might virtuously get hold of a force ten times greater than the force of the Danish fleet? Was there no other way of protecting Ireland, but by bringing eternal shame upon Great Britain, and by making the earth a den of robbers? See what the men whom you have supplanted would have done. They would have rendered the invasion of Ireland impossible, by restoring to the Catholics their long-lost rights; they would have acted in such a manner that the French would neither have wished for invasion, nor dared to attempt it; they would have increased the permanent strength of the country while they preserved its reputation unsullied. Nothing of this kind your friends have done, because they are solemnly pledged to do nothing of this kind; because to tolerate all religions, and to equalize civil rights to all sects, is to oppose some of the worst passions of our nature—to plunder and to oppress is to gratify them all. They wanted the huzzas of mobs, and they have for ever blasted the fame of England to obtain them. Were the fleets of Holland, France, and Spain, destroyed by larceny? You resisted the power of 150 sail of the line by sheer courage, and violated every principle of morals from the dread of 15 hulks, while the expedition itself cost you three times more than the value of the larcenous matter brought away. The French trample upon the laws of God and man, not for old cordage, but for kingdoms, and always take care to be well paid for their crimes. We contrive, under the present administration, to unite moral with intellectual deficiency, and to grow weaker and worse by the same action. If they had any evidence of the intended hostility of the Danes, why was it not produced? Why have the nations of Europe been allowed to feel an indignation against this country beyond the reach of all subsequent information? Are these times, do you imagine, when we can trifle with a year of universal hatred, dally with the curses of Europe, and then regain a lost character at pleasure, by the parliamentary perspirations of the foreign secretary, or the solemn asseverations of the pecuniary Rose? Believe me, Abraham, it is not under such ministers as these that the dexterity of honest Englishmen will ever equal the dexterity of French knaves; it is not in their presence that the serpent of Moses will ever swallow up the serpents of the magicians.

* This is now completely confessed to be the case by ministers.

Lord Hawkesbury says, that nothing is to be granted to the Catholics from fear. What! not even justice? Why not? There are four millions of disaffected people within twenty miles of your own coast. I fairly confess, that the dread which I have of their physical power, is with me a very strong motive for listening to their claims. To talk of not acting from fear is mere parliamentary cant. From what motive but fear, I should be glad to know, have all the improvements in our constitution proceeded? I question if any justice has ever been done to large masses of mankind from any other motive. By what other motives can the plunderers of the Baltic suppose nations to be governed in their intercourse *with each other?* If I say, Give this people what they ask because it is just, do you think I should get ten people to listen to me? Would not the lesser of the two Jenkinsons be the first to treat me with contempt? The only true way to make the mass of mankind see the beauty of justice, is by showing to them in pretty plain terms the consequences of injustice. If any body of French troops land in Ireland, the whole population of that country will rise against you to a man, and you could not possibly survive such an event three years. Such, from the bottom of my soul, do I believe to be the present state of that country; and so far does it appear to me to be impolitic and unstatesmanlike to concede any thing to such a danger, that if the Catholics, in addition to their present just demands, were to petition for the perpetual removal of the said Lord Hawkesbury from his majesty's councils, I think, whatever might be the effect upon the destinies of Europe, and however it might retard our own individual destruction, that the prayer of the petition should be instantly complied with. Canning's crocodile tears should not move me; the hoops of the maids of honour should not hide him. I would tear him from the banisters of the back stairs, and plunge him in the fishy fumes of the dirtiest of all his Cinque Ports.

LETTER VII.

Dear Abraham,

In the correspondence which is passing between us, you are perpetually alluding to the foreign secretary; and in answer to the dangers of Ireland, which I am pressing upon your notice, you have nothing to urge but the confidence which you repose in the discretion and sound sense of this gentleman.* I can

* The attack upon virtue and morals in the debate upon Copenhagen is brought forward with great ostentation by this gentleman's friends. But is Harlequin less Harlequin because he acts well? I was present: he leaped about, touched facts with his wand, turned yes into no, and no into yes; it was a pantomime well played, but a pantomime; Harlequin deserves higher wages than he did two years ago; is he therefore fit for serious parts?

only say, that I have listened to him long and often, with the greatest attention; I have used every exertion in my power to take a fair measure of him, and it appears to me impossible to hear him upon any arduous topic without perceiving that he is eminently deficient in those solid and serious qualities upon which, and upon which alone, the confidence of a great country can properly repose. He sweats, and labours, and works for sense, and Mr. Ellis seems always to think it is coming, but it does not come; the machine can't draw up what is not to be found in the spring; Providence has made him a light, jesting, paragraph-writing man, and that he will remain to his dying day. When he is jocular he is strong, when he is serious he is like Samson in a wig; any ordinary person is a match for him; a song, an ironical letter, a burlesque ode, an attack in the newspaper upon Nicoll's eye, a smart speech of twenty minutes, full of gross misrepresentations and clever turns, excellent language, a spirited manner, lucky quotation, success in provoking dull men, some half information picked up in Pall Mall in the morning; these are your friend's natural weapons; all these things he can do; here I allow him to be truly great; nay, I will be just, and go still farther, if he would confine himself to these things, and consider the *facete* and the playful to be the basis of his character, he would, for that species of man, be universally regarded as a person of a very good understanding; call him a legislator, a reasoner, and the conductor of the affairs of a great nation, and it seems to me as absurd as if a butterfly were to teach bees to make honey. That he is an extraordinary writer of small poetry, and a diner out of the highest lustre, I do most readily admit. After George Selwyn, and perhaps Tickell, there has been no such man for this half century. The foreign secretary is a gentleman, a respectable as well as an highly agreeable man in private life; but you may as well feed me with decayed potatoes as console me for the miseries of Ireland by the resources of his *sense* and his *discretion*. It is only the public situation which this gentleman holds which entitles me or induces me to say so much about him. He is a fly in amber; nobody cares about the fly: the only question is, How the devil did it get there? Nor do I attack him from the love of glory, but from the love of utility, as a burgomaster hunts a rat in a Dutch dyke, for fear it should flood a province.

The friends of the Catholic question are, I observe, extremely embarrassed in arguing when they come to the loyalty of the Irish Catholics. As for me, I shall go straight forward to my object, and state what I have no manner of doubt, from an intimate knowledge of Ireland, to be the plain truth. Of the great Roman Catholic proprietors, and of the Catholic prelates, there may be a few, and but a few, who would follow the fortunes of England at all events; there is another set of men who, thoroughly detesting this country, have too much property and too much character to lose, not to wait for some very favourable event before they show themselves; but the great mass of Catholic population, upon the slightest appearance of a French force in tha country, would rise upon you to a man. It is the most mistaken policy to conceal the plain truth. There is no loyalty among the Catholics; they detest you as their worst oppressors, and they will continue to detest you till you remove the cause of their hatred. It is in your power in six months' time to produce a total revolution of opinions among this people; and in some future letter I will show you that this is clearly the case. At present, see what a dreadful state Ireland is in. The common toast among the low Irish is, the feast of the *passover*. Some allusion to *Bonaparte*, in a play lately acted at Dublin, produced thunders of applause from the pit and the galleries; and a politician should not be inattentive to the public feelings expressed in theatres. Mr. Perceval thinks he has disarmed the Irish; he has no more disarmed the Irish than he has resigned a shilling of his own public emoluments. An Irish* peasant fills the barrel of his gun full of tow dipped in oil, butters up the lock, buries it in a bog, and allows the Orange bloodhound to ransack his cottage at pleasure. Be just and kind to the Irish, and you will indeed disarm them: rescue them from the degraded servitude in which they are held by an handful of their own countrymen, and you will add four millions of brave and affectionate men to your strength. Nightly visits, Protestant inspectors, licenses to possess a pistol or a knife and fork, the odious vigour of the *evangelical* Perceval—acts of Parliament, drawn up by some English attorney, to save you from the hatred of four million people—the guarding yourselves from universal disaffection by a police; a confidence in the little cunning of Bow Street, when you might rest your security upon the eternal basis of the best feelings; this is the meanness and madness to which nations are reduced when they lose sight of the first elements of justice, without which a country can be no more secure than it can be healthy without air. I sicken at such policy and such men. The fact is, the ministers know nothing about the present state of Ireland; Mr. Perceval sees a few clergymen, Lord Castlereagh a few general officers, who take care, of course, to report what is pleasant rather than what is true. As for the joyous and lepid consul, he jokes upon neutral flags and feuds, jokes upon Irish rebels, jokes upon northern, and western, and southern foes, and gives himself no trouble upon any subject; nor is the mediocrity of the idolatrous deputy of the slightest use. Dis solved in grins, he reads no memorials upon the state of Ireland, listens to no reports, asks no questions, and is the

"*Bourn* from whom no traveller returns."

The danger of an immediate insurrection is now, *I believe*,† blown over. You have so strong

* No man who is not intimately acquainted with the Irish, can tell to what a curious extent this concealment of arms is carried. I have stated the exact mode in which it is done.

† I know too much, however, of the state of Ireland not to speak tremblingly about this. I hope to God I am right.

an army in Ireland, and the Irish are become so much more cunning from the last insurrection, that you may perhaps be tolerably secure just at present from that evil: but are you secure from the efforts which the French may make to throw a body of troops into Ireland? and do you consider that event to be difficult and improbable? From Brest Harbour to Cape St. Vincent, you have above three thousand miles of hostile sea-coast, and twelve or fourteen harbours quite capable of containing a sufficient force for the powerful invasion of Ireland. The nearest of these harbours is not two days' sail from the southern coast of Ireland, with a fair leading wind; and the farthest not ten. Five ships of the line, for so very short a passage, might carry five or six thousand troops with cannon and ammunition; and Ireland presents to their attack a southern coast of more than 500 miles, abounding in deep bays, admirable harbours, and disaffected inhabitants. Your blockading ships may be forced to come home for provisions and repairs, or they may be blown off in a gale of wind and compelled to bear away for their own coast;—and you will observe, that the very same wind which locks you up in the British Channel, when you are got there, is evidently favourable for the invasion of Ireland. And yet this is called government, and the people huzza Mr. Perceval for continuing to expose his country day after day to such tremendous perils as these; cursing the men who would have given up a question in theology to have saved us from such a risk. The British empire at this moment is in the state of a peach-blossom—if the wind blows gently from one quarter, it survives; if furiously from the other, it perishes. A stiff breeze may set in from the north, the Rochefort squadron will be taken, and the minister will be the most holy of men; if it comes from some other point, Ireland is gone, we curse ourselves as a set of monastic madmen, and call out for the unavailing satisfaction of Mr. Perceval's head. Such a state of political existence is scarcely credible; it is the action of a mad young fool standing upon one foot, and peeping down the crater of Mount Ætna, not the conduct of a wise and sober people deciding upon their best and dearest interests; and in the name, the much injured name, of Heaven, what is it all for that we expose ourselves to these dangers? Is it that we may sell more muslin? Is it that we may acquire more territory? Is it that we may strengthen what we have already acquired? No: nothing of all this; but that one set of Irishmen may torture another set of Irishmen—that Sir Phelim O'Callagan may continue to whip Sir Toby M'Tackle, his next-door neighbour, and continue to ravish his Catholic daughters; and these are the measures which the honest and consistent secretary supports; and this is the secretary whose genius, in the estimation of Brother Abraham, is to extinguish the genius of Bonaparte. Pompey was killed by a slave, Goliath smitten by a stripling, Pyrrhus died by the hand of a woman; tremble, thou great Gaul, from whose head an armed Minerva leaps forth in the hour of danger; tremble, thou scourge of God, a pleasant man is come out against thee, and thou shalt be laid low by a joker of jokes, and he shall talk his pleasant talk against thee, and thou shalt be no more!

You tell me, in spite of all this parade of sea-coast, Bonaparte has neither ships nor sailors: but this is a mistake. He has not ships and sailors to contest the empire of the seas with Great Britain, but there remains quite sufficient of the navies of France, Spain, Holland, and Denmark, for these short excursions and invasions. Do you think, too, that Bonaparte does not add to his navy every year? Do you suppose, with all Europe at his feet, that he can find any difficulty in obtaining timber, and that money will not procure for him any quantity of naval stores he may want? The mere machine, the empty ship, he can build as well, and as quickly, as you can; and though he may not find enough of practised sailors to man large fighting fleets—it is not possible to conceive that he can want sailors for such sort of purposes as I have stated? He is at present the despotic monarch of above twenty thousand miles of sea-coast, and yet you suppose he cannot procure sailors for the invasion of Ireland. Believe, if you please, that such a fleet met at sea by any number of our ships at all comparable to them in point of force, would be immediately taken; let it be so; I count nothing upon their power of resistance, only upon their power of escaping unobserved. If experience has taught us any thing, it is the impossibility of perpetual blockades. The instances are innumerable, during the course of this war, where whole fleets have sailed in and out of harbour in spite of every vigilance used to prevent it. I shall only mention those cases where Ireland is concerned. In December, 1796, seven ships of the line, and ten transports, reached Bantry Bay from Brest, without having seen an English ship in their passage. It blew a storm when they were off shore, and therefore England still continues to be an independent kingdom. You will observe that at the very time the French fleet sailed out of Brest harbour, Admiral Colpoys was cruising off there with a powerful squadron, and still, from the particular circumstances of the weather, found it impossible to prevent the French from coming out. During the time that Admiral Colpoys was cruising off Brest, Admiral Richery, with six ships of the line, passed him, and got safe into the harbour. At the very moment when the French squadron was lying in Bantry Bay, Lord Bridport with his fleet was locked up by a foul wind in the Channel, and for several days could not stir to the assistance of Ireland. Admiral Colpoys, totally unable to find the French fleet, came home. Lord Bridport, at the change of the wind, cruised for them in vain, and they got safe back to Brest, without having seen a single one of these floating bulwarks, the possession of which we believe will enable us with impunity to set justice and common sense at defiance. Such is the miserable and precarious state of an anemocracy, of a people who put their trust in hurricanes, and are governed by wind. In August, 1798, three forty-gun frigates landed 1100 men under Humbert, making the passage from Rochelle to Killala without seeing any English ship. In October of the same year, four French frigates anchored in Killala Bay with 2000 troops; and though they did not land their troops, they returned to France in safety. In the same month, a line of battle ship, eight stout frigates, and a brig, all full of troops and stores, reached the coast of Ireland, and were fortunately, in sight of land, destroyed, after an obstinate engagement, by Sir John Warren.

If you despise the little troop which, in these numerous experiments, did make good its landing, take with you, if you please, this *précis* of its exploits: eleven hundred men, commanded by a soldier raised from the ranks, put to rout a select army of 6000 men, commanded by General Lake, seized their ordinance, ammunition, and stores, advanced 150 miles into a country containing an armed force of 150,000 men, and at last surrendered to the viceroy, an experienced general, gravely and cautiously advancing at the head of all his chivalry and of an immense army to oppose him. You must excuse these details about Ireland, but it appears to me to be of all other subjects the most important. If we conciliate Ireland, we can do nothing amiss; if we do not, we can do nothing well. If Ireland was friendly, we might equally set at defiance the talents of Bonaparte and the blunders of his rival, Mr. Canning; we could then support the ruinous and silly bustle of our useless expeditions, and the almost incredible ignorance of our commercial orders in council. Let the present administration give up but this one point, and there is nothing which I would not consent to grant them. Mr. Perceval shall have full liberty to insult the tomb of Mr. Fox, and to torment every eminent dissenter in Great Britain; Lord Camden shall have large boxes of plums; Mr. Rose receive permission to prefix to his name the appellative of virtuous; and to the Viscount Castlereagh* a round sum of ready money shall be well and truly paid into his hand. Lastly, what remains to Mr. George Canning, but that he rides up and down Pall Mall glorious upon a white horse, and that they cry out before him, Thus shall it be done to the statesman who hath written "The Needy Knife-Grinder," and the German play? Adieu only for the present; you shall soon hear from me again; it is a subject upon which I cannot long be silent.

LETTER VIII.

Nothing can be more erroneous than to suppose that Ireland is not bigger than the Isle of Wight, or of more consequence than Guernsey or Jersey; and yet I am almost inclined to believe, from the general supineness which prevails here respecting the dangerous state of that country, that such is the rank which it holds in our statistical tables. I have been writing to you a great deal about Ireland, and perhaps it may be of some use to state to you concisely the nature and resources of the country which has been the subject of our long and strange correspondence. There were returned, as I have before observed, to the hearth tax, in 1791, 701,132* houses, which Mr. Newenham shows from unquestionable documents to be nearly 80,000 below the real number of houses in that country. There are 27,457 square English miles in Ireland,† and more than five millions of people.

By the last survey, it appears that the inhabited houses in England and Wales amount to 1,574,902, and the population to 9,343,578, which gives an average of $5\frac{7}{8}$ to each house, in a country where the density of population is certainly less considerable than in Ireland. It is commonly supposed that two-fifths of the army and navy are Irishmen, at periods when political disaffection does not avert the Catholics from the service. The current value of Irish exports in 1807 was 9,314,854*l.* 17*s.* 7*d.*; a state of commerce about equal to the commerce of England in the middle of the reign of George II. The tonnage of ships entered inward and cleared outward in the trade of Ireland, in 1807, amounted to 1,567,430 tons. The quantity of home spirits exported amounted to 10,284 gallons in 1796, and to 930,800 gallons in 1804. Of the exports, which I have stated, provisions amounted to four millions, and linen to about four millions and a half. There was exported from Ireland, upon an average of two years ending in January, 1804, 591,274 barrels of barley, oats, and wheat; and by weight 910,848 cwts. of flour, oatmeal, barley, oats and wheat. The amount of butter exported in 1804, from Ireland, was worth, in money, 1,704,680*l.* sterling. The importation of ale and beer from the immense manufactures now carrying on of these articles, was diminished to 3209 barrels, in the year 1804, from 111,920 barrels, which was the average importation per annum, taking from three years ending in 1792; and at present there is an export trade of porter. On an average of the three years, ending March, 1783, there were imported into Ireland, of cotton wool, 3326 cwts., of cotton yarn, 5405 lbs.; but on an average of three years, ending January, 1803, there were imported, of the first article, 13,159 cwts., and of the latter, 628,406 lbs. It is impossible to conceive any manufacture more flourishing. The export of linen has increased in Ireland from 17,776,862 yards, the average in 1770, to 43,534,971 yards, the amount in 1805. The tillage of Ireland has more then trebled within the last twenty-one years. The importation of coals has increased from 230,000 tons in 1783, to 417,030 in 1804; of tobacco, from 3,459,861 lbs. in 1783, to 6,611,543 in 1804; of tea, from 1,703,855 lbs. in 1783, to 3,358,256, in 1804; of sugar, from 143,117 cwts. in 1782, to 309,076, in 1804. Ireland now supports a funded debt of above 64 millions, and it is computed that more than three millions of money are annually remitted to Irish absentees resident in this country. In Mr. Foster's re-

* This is a very unjust imputation on Lord Castlereagh.

* The checks to population were very trifling from the rebellion. It lasted two months: of his majesty's Irish forces, there perished about 1600; of the rebels, 11,000 were killed in the field, and 2000 hanged or exported 400 loyal persons were assassinated.

† In England 49,450.

port, of 100 folio pages, presented to the House of Commons in the year 1806, the total expenditure of Ireland is stated at 9,760,013*l*. Ireland has increased about two-thirds in its population within twenty-five years, and yet, and in about the same space of time, its exports of beef, bullocks, cows, pork, swine, butter, wheat, barley, and oats, collectively taken, have doubled; and this in spite of two years' famine, and the presence of an immense army, that is always at hand to guard the most valuable appanage of our empire from joining our most inveterate enemies. Ireland has the greatest possible facilities for carrying on commerce with the whole of Europe. It contains, within a circuit of 750 miles, 66 secure harbours, and presents a western frontier against Great Britain, reaching from the Frith of Clyde north to the Bristol Channel south, and varying in distance from 20 to 100 miles; so that the subjugation of Ireland would compel us to guard with ships and soldiers a new line of coast, certainly amounting, with all its sinuosities, to more than 700 miles—an addition of polemics, in our present state of hostility with all the world, which must highly gratify the vigorists, and give them an ample opportunity of displaying that foolish energy upon which their claims to distinction are founded. Such is the country which the right reverend the chancellor of the exchequer would drive into the arms of France, and for the conciliation of which we are requested to wait, as if it were one of those sinecure places which were given to Mr. Perceval snarling at the breast, and which cannot be abolished till his decease.

How sincerely and fervently have I often wished that the Emperor of the French had thought as Mr. Spencer Perceval does upon the subject of government; that he had entertained doubts and scruples upon the propriety of admitting the Protestants to an equality of rights with the Catholics, and that he had left in the middle of his empire these vigorous seeds of hatred and disaffection: but the world was never yet conquered by a blockhead. One of the very first measures we saw him recurring to was the complete establishment of religious liberty; if his subjects fought and paid as he pleased, he allowed them to believe as they pleased; the moment I saw this, my best hopes were lost. I perceived in a moment the kind of man we had to do with. I was well aware of the miserable ignorance and folly of this country upon the subject of toleration; and every year has been adding to the success of that game which it was clear he had the will and the ability to play against us.

You say Bonaparte is not in earnest upon the subject of religion, and that this is the cause of his tolerant spirit; but is it possible you can intend to give us such dreadful and unamiable notions of religion? Are we to understand that the moment a man is sincere he is narrow-minded; that persecution is the child of belief; and that a desire to leave all men in the quiet and unpunished exercise of their own creed can only exist in the mind of an infidel? Thank God! I know many men whose principles are as firm as they are expanded, who cling tenaciously to their own modification of the Christian faith, without the slightest disposition to force that modification upon other people. If Bonaparte is liberal in subjects of religion because he has no religion, is this a reason why we should be illiberal because we are Christians? If he owes this excellent quality to a vice, is that any reason why we may not owe it to a virtue? Toleration is a great good and a good to be imitated, let it come from whom it will. If a sceptic is tolerant, it only shows that he is not foolish in practice as well as erroneous in theory. If a religious man is tolerant, it evinces that he is religious from thought and inquiry, because he exhibits in his conduct one of the most beautiful and important consequences of a religious mind,—an inviolable charity to all the honest varieties of human opinion.

Lord Sidmouth, and all the anti-Catholic people, little foresee that they will hereafter be the sport of the antiquary; that their prophecies of ruin and destruction from Catholic emancipation will be clapped into the notes of some quaint history, and be matter of pleasantry even to the sedulous housewife and the rural dean. There is always a copious supply of Lord Sidmouths in the world: nor is there one single source of human happiness against which they have not uttered the most lugubrious predictions. Turnpike roads, navigable canals, inoculation, hops, tobacco, the Reformation, the Revolution—there are always a set of worthy and moderately-gifted men, who bawl out death and ruin upon every valuable change which the varying aspect of human affairs absolutely and imperiously requires. I have often thought that it would be extremely useful to make a collection of the hatred and abuse that all those changes have experienced, which are now admitted to be marked improvements in our condition. Such an history might make folly a little more modest, and suspicious of its own decisions.

Ireland, you say, since the union, is to be considered as a part of the whole kingdom; and therefore, however Catholics may predominate in that particular spot, yet, taking the whole empire together, they are to be considered as a much more insignificant quota of the population. Consider them in what light you please, as part of the whole, or by themselves, or in what manner may be most consentaneous to the devices of your holy mind—I say in a very few words, if you do not relieve these people from the civil incapacities to which they are exposed, you will lose them; or you must employ great strength and much treasure in watching over them. In the present state of the world, you can afford to do neither the one nor the other. Having stated this, I shall leave you to be ruined, Puffendorf in hand, (as Mr. Secretary Canning says,) and to lose Ireland, just as you have found out what proportion the aggrieved people should bear to the whole population, before their calamities meet with redress. As for your parallel cases, I am no more afraid of deciding upon them than I am upon their prototype. If ever any one heresy should so far spread itself over the principality of Wales that the established church were left in a minority of one to four; if you had subjected these heretics to very severe civil privations; if the consequence of such privations were an universal state of disaffection among that caseous and wrathful people; and if, at the same time, you were at war with all the world, how can you doubt for a moment that I would instantly restore them to a state of the most complete civil liberty? What matters it under what name you put the same case? Common sense is not changed by appellations. I have said how I would act to Ireland, and I would act so to all the world.

I admit that, to a certain degree, the government will lose the affections of the Orangemen by emancipating the Catholics; much less, however, at present, than three years past. The few men, who have ill-treated the whole crew, live in constant terror that the oppressed people will rise upon them and carry the ship into Brest:—they begin to find that it is a very tiresome thing to sleep every night with cocked pistols under their pillows, and to breakfast, dine, and sup with drawn hangers. They suspect that the privilege of beating and kicking the rest of the sailors is hardly worth all this anxiety, and that if the ship does ever fall into the hands of the disaffected, all the cruelties which they have experienced will be thoroughly remembered and amply repaid. To a short period of disaffection among the Orangemen, I confess I should not much object: my love of poetical justice does carry me as far as that; one summer's whipping, only one: the thumb-screw for a short season; a little light, easy torturing between Lady-day and Michaelmas; a short specimen of Mr. Perceval's rigour. I have malice enough to ask this slight atonement for the groans and shrieks of the poor Catholics, unheard by any human tribunal, but registered by the angel of God against their Protestant and enlightened oppressors.

Besides, if you who count ten so often can count five, you must perceive that it is better to have four friends and one enemy than four enemies and one friend; and the more violent the hatred of the Orangemen, the more certain the reconciliation of the Catholics. The disaffection of the Orangemen will be the Irish rainbow; when I see it, I shall be sure that the storm is over.

If those incapacities, from which the Catholics ask to be relieved, were to the mass of them only a mere feeling of pride, and if the question were respecting the attainment of privileges which could be of importance only to the highest of the sect, I should still say, that the pride of the mass was very naturally wounded by the degradation of their superiors. Indignity to George Rose would be felt by the smallest nummary gentleman in the king's employ; and Mr. John Bannister could not be indifferent to any thing which happened to Mr. Canning. But the truth is, it is a most egregious mistake to suppose that the Catholics are contending merely for the fringes and feathers of their chiefs. I will give you a list, in my next letter, of those privations which are represented to be of no consequence to any body but Lord Fingal, and some twenty or thirty of the principal persons of their sect. In the mean time, adieu, and be wise.

LETTER IX.

Dear Abraham,

No catholic can be chief governor or governor of this kingdom, chancellor or keeper of the great seal, lord high-treasurer, chief of any of the courts of justice, chancellor of the exchequer, puisne judge, judge in the admiralty, master of the rolls, secretary of state, keeper of the privy seal, vice-treasurer or his deputy, teller or cashier of exchequer, auditor or general, governor or custos rotulorum of counties, chief governor's secretary, privy councillor, king's counsel, serjeant, attorney, solicitor-general, master in chancery, provost or fellow of Trinity College, Dublin, post-master-general, master and lieutenant-general of ordnance, commander-in-chief, general on the staff, sheriff, sub-sheriff, mayor, bailiff, recorder, burgess, or any other officer in a city, or a corporation. No Catholic can be guardian to a Protestant, and no priest guardian at all; no Catholic can be a gamekeeper, or have for sale, or otherwise, any arms or warlike stores; no Catholic can present to a living, unless he chooses to turn Jew in order to obtain that privilege; the pecuniary qualification of Catholic jurors is made higher than that of Protestants, and no relaxation of the ancient rigorous code is permitted, unless to those who shall take an oath prescribed by 13 & 14 Geo. III. Now if this is not picking the plums out of the pudding, and leaving the mere batter to the Catholics, I know not what is. If it were merely the privy council, it would be (I allow) nothing but a point of honour for which the mass of Catholics were contending, the honour of being chief mourners or pall-bearers to the country; but surely no man will contend that every barrister may not speculate upon the possibility of being a puisne judge; and that every shopkeeper must not feel himself injured by his exclusion from borough offices.

One of the greatest practical evils which the Catholics suffer in Ireland, is their exclusion from the offices of sheriff and deputy sheriff. Nobody who is unacquainted with Ireland can conceive the obstacles which this opposes to the fair administration of justice. The formation of juries is now entirely in the hands of the Protestants: the lives, liberties, and properties of the Catholics in the hands of the juries; and this is the arrangement for the administration of justice in a country where religious prejudices are inflamed to the greatest degree of animosity! In this country, if a man is a foreigner, if he sells slippers, and sealing wax and artificial flowers, we are so tender of human life, that we take care half the number of persons who are to decide upon his fate should be men of similar prejudices and feelings with himself: but a poor Catholic in Ireland may be tried by twelve Percevals, and destroyed according to the manner of that gentleman in the name of the Lord, and with all the insulting forms of justice. I do not go the length of saying that deliberate and wilful injustice is done. I have no doubt that the Orange deputy-sheriff thinks it would be a most unpardonable breach of his duty if he did not summon a Protestant panel. I can easily believe that the Protestant panel may conduct themselves very conscientiously in hanging the gentleman of the crucifix; but I blame the law which does not guard the Catholic against the probable tenour of those feelings which must unconsciously influence the judgments of mankind. I detest that state of society which extends unequal degrees of protection to different creeds and persuasions; and I cannot describe to you the contempt I feel for a man who, calling himself a statesman, defends a system which fills the heart of every Irishman with treason, and makes his allegiance prudence, not choice.

I request to know if the vestry taxes, in Ireland, are a mere matter of romantic feeling, which can affect only the Earl of Fingal? In a parish where there are four thousand Catholics and fifty Protestants, the Protestants may meet together in a vestry meeting, at which no Catholic has the right to vote, and tax all the lands in the parish 1s. 6*d.* per acre, or in the pound, I forget which, for the repairs of the church—and how has the necessity of these repairs been ascertained? A Protestant plumber has discovered that it wants new leading; a Protestant carpenter is convinced the timbers are not sound, and a glazier, who hates holy water, (as an accoucher hates celibacy because he gets nothing by it,) is employed to put in new sashes.

The grand juries in Ireland are the great scene of jobbing. They have a power of making a county rate to a considerable extent for roads, bridges, and other objects of general accommodation. "You suffer the road to be brought through my park, and I will have the bridge constructed in a situation where it will make a beautiful object to your house. You do my job, and I will do yours." These are the sweet and interesting subjects which occasionally occupy Milesian gentlemen while they are attendant upon this grand inquest of justice. But there is a religion, it seems, even in jobs; and it will be highly gratifying to Mr. Perceval to learn that no man in Ireland who believes in seven sacraments can carry a public road, or bridge, one yard out of the direction most beneficial to the public, and that nobody can cheat that public who does not expound the Scriptures in the purest and most orthodox manner. This will give pleasure to Mr. Perceval: but, from his unfairness upon these topics, I appeal to the justice and proper feelings of Mr. Huskisson. I ask him if the human mind can experience a more dreadful sensation than to see its own jobs refused, and the jobs of another religion perpetually succeeding? I ask him his opinion of a jobless faith, of a creed which dooms a man through life to a lean and plunderless integrity. He knows that human nature cannot and will not bear it; and if we were to paint a political Tartarus, it would be an endless series of snug expectations and cruel disappointments. These are a few of many dreadful inconveniences which the Catholics of all ranks suffer from the laws by which they are at present oppressed. Besides, look at human nature:—what is the history of all professions? Joel is to be brought up to the bar: has Mrs. Plymley the slightest doubt of his being chancellor? Do not his two shrivelled aunts live in the certainty of seeing him in that situation, and of cutting out with their own hands his equity habiliments? And I could name a certain minister of the Gospel who does not, in the bottom of his heart, much differ from these opinions. Do you think that the fathers and mothers of the holy Catholic Church are not as absurd as Protestant papas and mamas? The probability I admit to be, in each particular case, that the sweet little blockhead will in fact never get a brief;—but I will venture to say, there is not a parent from the Giant's causeway to Bantry Bay who does not conceive that his child is the unfortunate victim of the exclusion, and that nothing short of positive law could prevent his own dear pre-eminent Paddy from rising to the highest honours of the state. So with the army, and Parliament; in fact, few are excluded; but, in imagination, all: you keep twenty or thirty Catholics out, and you lose the affections of four millions; and, let me tell you, that recent circumstances have by no means tended to diminish in the minds of men that hope of elevation beyond their own rank which is so congenial to our nature; from pleading for John Roe to taxing John Bull, from jesting for Mr. Pitt and writing in the Anti-Jacobin, to managing the affairs of Europe—these are leaps which seem to justify the fondest dreams of mothers and aunts.

I do not say that the disabilities to which the Catholics are exposed amount to such intolerable grievances, that the strength and industry of a nation are overwhelmed by them; the increasing prosperity of Ireland fully demonstrates the contrary. But I repeat again, what I have often stated in the course of our correspondence, that your laws against the Catholic are exactly in that state in which you have neither the benefits of rigour nor of liberality; every law which prevented the Catholics from gaining strength and wealth is repealed; every law which can irritate remains; if you were determined to insult the Catholics, you should have kept them weak; if you resolved to give them strength, you should have ceased to insult them:—at present your conduct is pure, unadulterated folly.

Lord Hawkesbury says, we heard nothing about the Catholics till we began to mitigate the laws against them; when we relieved them in part from this oppression they began to be disaffected. This is very true; but it proves just what I have said, that you have either done too much, or too little; and as there lives not, I hope, upon earth, so depraved a courtier that he would load the Catholics with their ancient chains, what absurdity it is then not to render their dispositions friendly, when you leave their arms and legs free!

You know, and many Englishmen know, what passes in China; but nobody knows or cares what passes in Ireland. At the beginning of the present reign, no Catholic could realize property, or carry on any business; they were absolutely annihilated, and had no more agency in the country than so many trees. They were like Lord Mulgrave's eloquence, and Lord Camden's wit; the legislative bodies did not know of their existence. For these twenty-five years last past, the Catholics have been engaged in commerce; within that period the commerce of Ireland has doubled:—there are four Catholics at work for one Protestant, and eight Catholics at work for one Episcopalian; of course the proportion which Catholic wealth bears to Protestant wealth is every year altering rapidly in favour of the Catholics. I have already told you what their purchases of land were the last year; since that period, I have been at some pains to find out the actual state of the Catholic wealth; it is impossible, upon such a subject, to arrive at complete accuracy; but I have good reason to believe that there are at present 2000 Catholics in Ireland, possessing an income from 500*l.* upwards, many of these with incomes of one, two, three, and four thousand, and some amounting to fifteen and twenty thousand per annum:—and this is the kingdom, and these the people, for whose conciliation we are to wait Heaven knows when, and Lord Hawkesbury why! As for me, I never think of the situation of Ireland, without feeling the same necessity for immediate interference as I should do if I saw blood flowing from a great artery. I rush towards it with the instinctive rapidity of a man desirous of preventing death, and have no other feeling but that in a few seconds the patient may be no more.

I could not help smiling, in the times of No-Popery, to witness the loyal indignation of many persons at the attempt made by the last ministry to do something for the relief of Ireland. The general cry in the country was, that they would not see their beloved monarch used ill in his old age, and that they would stand by him to the last drop of their blood. I respect good feelings, however erroneous be the occasions on which they display themselves; and, therefore, I saw in all this as much to admire as to blame. It was a species of affection, however, which reminded me very forcibly of the attachment displayed by the servants of the Russian ambassador, at the beginning of the last century. His excellency happened to fall down in a kind of apoplectic fit, when he was paying a morning visit in the house of an acquaintance. The confusion was of course very great, and messengers were despatched, in every direction, to find a surgeon, who, upon his arrival, declared that his excellency must be immediately blooded, and prepared himself forthwith to perform the operation; the barbarous servants of the embassy, who were there in great numbers, no sooner saw the surgeon prepared to wound the arm of their master with a sharp shining instrument, than they drew their swords, put themselves in an attitude of defence, and swore in pure Sclavonic, "that they would murder any man who attempted to do him the slightest injury; he had been a very good master to them, and they would not desert him in his misfortunes, or suffer his blood to be shed while he was off his guard, and incapable of defending himself." By good fortune, the secretary arrived about this period of the dispute, and his excellency, relieved from superfluous blood and perilous affection, was, after much difficulty, restored to life.

There is an argument brought forward with some appearance of plausibility in the House of Commons, which certainly merits an answer. You know that the Catholics now vote for members of Parliament in Ireland, and that they outnumber the Protestants in a very great proportion; if you allow Catholics to sit in Parliament, religion will be found to influence votes more than property, and the greater part of the 100 Irish members who are returned to Parliament will be Catholics. Add to these the Catholic members who are returned in England, and you will have a phalanx of heretical strength which every minister will be compelled to respect, and occasionally to conciliate by concessions incompatible with the interests of the Protestant Church. The fact is, however, that you are at this moment subjected to every danger of this kind which you can possibly apprehend hereafter. If the spiritual interests of the voters are more powerful than their temporal interests, they can bind down their representatives to support any measures favourable to the Catholic religion, and they can change the objects of their choice till they have found Protestant members (as they easily may do) perfectly obedient to their wishes. If the superior possessions of the Protestants prevent the Catholics from uniting for a common political object, then the danger you fear cannot exist; if zeal, on the contrary, gets the better of acres, then the danger at present exists, from the right of voting already given to the Catholics, and it will not be increased by allowing them to sit in Parliament. There are, as nearly as I can recollect, thirty seats in Ireland for cities and counties, where the Protestants are the most numerous, and where the members returned must of course be Protestants. In the other seventy representations, the wealth of the Protestants is opposed to the number of the Catholics; and if all the seventy members returned were of the Catholic persuasion, they must still plot the destruction of our religion in the midst of 588 Protestants. Such terrors would disgrace a cook-maid, or a toothless aunt—when they fall from the lips of bearded and senatorial men, they are nauseous, antiperistaltic, and emetical.

How can you for a moment doubt of the rapid effects which would be produced by the emancipation?—In the first place, to my certain knowledge, the Catholics have long since expressed to his majesty's ministers their perfect readiness *to vest in his majesty, either with the consent of the pope, or without it, if it cannot be obtained, the nomination of the Catholic prelacy.* The Catholic prelacy in Ireland consists of twenty-six bishops and the warden of Galway, a dignitary enjoying Catholic jurisdiction. The number of Roman Catholic priests in Ireland exceeds one thousand. The expenses of his peculiar worship are, to a substantial farmer or mechanic, five shillings per annum, to a labourer (where he is not entirely excused), one shilling per annum; this includes the contribution of the whole family, and for this the priest is bound to attend them when sick, and to confess them when they apply to him: he is also to keep his chapel in order, to celebrate divine service, and to preach on Sundays and holydays. In the northern district a priest gains from 30*l.* to 50*l.*; in the other parts of Ireland from 60*l.* to 90*l.* per annum. The best paid Catholic bishops receive about 400*l.* per ann.; the others from 300*l.* to 350*l.* . My plan is very simple; I would have 300 Catholic parishes at 100*l.* per ann., 300 at 200*l.* per ann., and 400 at 300*l.* per ann.; this, for the whole thousand parishes, would amount to 190,000*l.* To the prelacy I would allot 20,000*l.* in unequal proportions, from 1000*l.* to 500*l.*; and I would appropriate 40,000*l.* more for the support of Catholic schools, and the repairs of Catholic churches: the whole amount of which sums is 250,000*l.*, about the expense of three days of one of our genuine, good, English, *just and necessary wars.* The clergy should all receive their salaries at the Bank of Ireland, and I would place the whole patronage in the hands of the crown. Now, I appeal to any human being, except Spencer Perceval, Esq., of the parish of Hampstead, what the disaffection of a clergy would amount to, gaping after this graduated bounty of the crown, and whether Ignatius Loyola himself, if he were a living blockhead instead of a dead saint, could withstand the temptation of bouncing from 100*l.* a year in Sligo, to 300*l.* in Tipperary? This is the miserable sum of money for which the merchants, and land-owners, and nobility of England are exposing themselves to the tremendous peril of losing Ireland. The sinecure places of the Roses and the Percevals, and the "dear and near relations," put up to auction at thirty years' purchase, would almost amount to the money.

I admit that nothing can be more reasonable than to expect that a Catholic priest should starve to death, genteelly and pleasantly, for the good of the Protestant religion; but is it equally reasonable to expect that he should do so for the Protestant pews, and Protestant brick and mortar? On an Irish Sabbath, the bell of a neat parish church often summons to church only the parson and an occasionally conforming clerk; while, two hundred yards off, a thousand Catholics are huddled together in a miserable hovel, and pelted by all the storms of heaven. Can any thing be more distressing than to see a venerable man pouring forth sublime truths in tattered breeches, and depending for his food upon the little offal he gets from his parishioners? I venerate a human being who starves for his principles, let them be what they may; but starving for any thing is not at all to the taste of the honourable flagellants; strict principles, and good pay, is the motto of Mr. Perceval; the one he keeps in great measure for the faults of his enemies, the other for himself.

There are parishes in Connaught in which a Protestant was never settled, nor even seen; in that province, in Munster, and in parts of Leinster, the entire peasantry for sixty miles are Catholics; in these tracts, the churches are frequently shut for want of a congregation, or opened to an assemblage of from six to twenty persons. Of what Protestants there are in Ireland, the greatest part are gathered together in Ulster, or they live in towns. In the country of the other three provinces the Catholics see no other religion but their own, and are at the least as fifteen to one Protestant. In the diocese of Tuam, they are sixty to one; in the parish of St. Mullins, diocese of Leghlin, there are four thousand Catholics and *one Protestant;* in the town of Grasgenamana, in the county of Kilkenny, there are between four and five hundred Catholic houses, and three Protestant houses. In the parish of Allen, county Kildare, there is no Protestant, though it is very populous. In the parish of Arlesin, Queen's county, the proportion is one hundred to one. In the whole county of Kilkenny, by actual enumeration, it is seventeen to one; in the diocese of Kilmacduagh, province of Connaught, fifty-two to one, by ditto. These I give you as a few specimens of the present state of Ireland;—and yet there are men impudent and ignorant enough to contend that such evils require no remedy, and that mild family man who dwelleth in Hampstead can find none but the cautery and the knife,

> ———— omne per ignem
> Excoquitur vitium.

I cannot describe the horror and disgust which I felt at hearing Mr. Perceval call upon the then ministry for measures of vigour in Ireland. If I lived at Hampstead upon stewed meats and claret; if I walked to church every Sunday before eleven young gentlemen of my own begetting, with their faces washed, and their hair pleasingly combed; if the Almighty had blessed me with every earthly comfort,—how awfully would I pause before I sent forth the flame and the sword over the cabins of the poor, brave, generous, open-hearted peasants of Ireland! How easy it is to shed human blood—how easy it is to persuade ourselves that it is our duty to do so—and that the decision has cost us a severe struggle—how much, in all ages, have wounds and shrieks and tears been the cheap and vulgar resources of the rulers of mankind—how difficult and how noble it is to govern in kindness, and to found an empire upon the everlasting basis of justice and affection!—But what do men call vigour? To let loose hussars and to bring up artillery, to govern with lighted matches, and to cut, and push, and prime—I call this, not vigour, but the *sloth of cruelty and ignorance.* The vigour I love consists in finding out wherein subjects are aggrieved, in relieving them, in studying the temper and genius of a people, in consulting their prejudices, in selecting proper persons to lead and manage them, in the laborious, watchful, and difficult task of increasing public happiness by allaying each particular discontent. In this way Hoche pacified La Vendée—and in this way only will Ireland ever be subdued. But this, in the eyes of Mr. Perceval, is imbecility and meanness; houses are not broken open—women are not insulted—the people seem all to be happy; they are not rode over by horses, and cut by whips. Do you call this vigour?—Is this government?

LETTER X. AND LAST.

You must observe that all I have said of the effects which will be produced by giving salaries to the Catholic clergy, only proceeds upon the supposition that the emancipation of the laity is effected:—without that, I am sure there is not a clergyman in Ireland who would receive a shilling from government; he could not do so, without an entire loss of credit among the members of his own persuasion.

What you say of the moderation of the Irish Protestant clergy in collecting tithes, is, I believe, strictly true. Instead of collecting what the law enables them to collect, I believe they seldom or ever collect more than two-thirds; and I entirely agree with you, that the abolition of agistment tithe in Ireland by a vote of the Irish House of Commons, and without any remuneration to the church, was a most scandalous and jacobinical measure. I do not blame the Irish clergy; but I submit to your common sense, if it is possible to explain to an Irish peasant upon what principle of justice, or common sense, he is to pay every tenth potato in his little garden to a clergyman in whose religion nobody believes for twenty miles around him, and who has nothing to preach to but bare walls. It is true, if the tithes are bought up, the cottager must pay more rent to his landlord; but the same thing, done in the shape of rent, is less odious than when it is done in the shape of tithe; I do not want to take a shilling out of the pockets of the clergy, but to leave the substance of things, and to change their names. I cannot see the slightest reason why the Irish labourer is to be relieved from the real onus, or from any thing else but the name of tithe. At present, he rents only nine-tenths of the produce of the land, which is all that belongs to the owner; this he has at the market price; if the landowner purchase the other tenth of the church, of course he has a right to make a correspondent advance upon his tenant.

I very much doubt, if you were to lay open all civil offices to the Catholics, and to grant salaries to their clergy, in the manner I have stated, if the Catholic laity would give themselves much trouble about the advance of their church; for they would pay the same tithes under one system that they do under another. If you were to bring the Catholics into the daylight of the world, to the high situations of the army, the navy, and the bar, numbers of them would come over to the established church, and do as other people do; instead of that you set a mark of infamy upon them, rouse every passion of our nature in favour of their creed, and then wonder that men are blind to the follies of the Catholic religion. There are hardly any instances of old and rich families among the Protestant dissenters; when a man keeps a coach, and lives in good company, he comes to church, and gets ashamed of the meeting-house; if this is not the case with the father, it is almost always the case with the son. These things would never be so, if the dissenters were in *practice* as much excluded from all the concerns of civil life, as the Catholics are. If a rich young Catholic were in Parliament, he would belong to White's and to Brooke's, would keep race-horses, would walk up and down Pall Mall, be exonerated of his ready money and his constitution, become as totally devoid of morality, honesty, knowledge, and civility, as Protestant loungers in Pall Mall, and return home with a supreme contempt for Father O'Leary and Father O'Callaghan. I am astonished at the madness of the Catholic clergy, in not perceiving that Catholic emancipation is Catholic infidelity; that to entangle their people in the intrigues of a Protestant Parliament, and a Protestant court, is to insure the loss of every man of fashion and consequence in their community. The true receipt for preserving their religion is Mr. Perceval's receipt for destroying it; it is to deprive every rich Catholic of all the objects of secular ambition, to separate him from the Protestant, and to shut him up in his castle, with priests and relics.

We are told, in answer to all our arguments, that this is not a fit period,—that a period of universal war is not the proper time for dangerous innovations in the constitution; this is as much as to say, that the worst time for making friends is the period when you have made many enemies; that it is the greatest of all errors to stop when you are breathless, and to lie down when you are fatigued. Of one thing I am quite certain: if the safety of Europe is once completely restored, the Catholics may for ever bid adieu to the slightest probability of effecting their object. Such men as hang about a court not only are deaf to the suggestions of mere justice, but they despise justice; they detest the word *right;* the only word which rouses them is *peril;* where they can oppress with impunity, they oppress for ever, and call it loyalty and wisdom.

I am so far from conceiving the legitimate strength of the crown would be diminished by these abolitions of civil incapacities in consequence of religious opinions, that my only objection to the increase of religious freedom is, that it would operate as a diminution of political freedom; the power of the crown is so overbearing at this period, that almost the only steady opposers of its fatal influence are men disgusted by religious intolerance. Our establishments are so enormous, and so utterly disproportioned to our population, that every second or third man you meet in society gains something from the public; my brother the commissioner,—my nephew the police justice,—purveyor of small beer to the army in Ireland,—clerk of the mouth,—yeoman to the left hand,—these are the obstacles which common sense and justice have now to overcome. Add to this, that the king, old and infirm, excites a principle of very amiable generosity in his favour; that he has led a good, moral, and religious life, equally removed from profligacy and methodistical hypocrisy; that he has been a good husband, a good father, and a good master; that he dresses plain, loves hunting and farming, hates the French, and is, in all his opinions and habits, quite English;—these feelings are heightened by the present situation of the world, and the yet unexploded clamour of Jacobinism. In short, from the various sources of interest, personal regard, and national taste, such a tempest of loyalty has set in upon the people, that the 47th proposition in Euclid might now be voted down with as much ease as any proposition in politics; and, therefore, if Lord Hawkesbury hates the abstract truths of science as much as he hates concrete truth in human affairs, now is his time for getting rid of the multiplication table, and passing a vote of censure upon the pretensions of the *hypothenuse.* Such is the history of English parties at this moment; you cannot seriously suppose that the people care for such men as Lord Hawkesbury, Mr. Canning, and Mr. Perceval, on their own account; you cannot really believe them to be so degraded as to look to their safety from a man who proposes to subdue Europe by keeping it without Jesuit's bark. The people, at present, have one passion, and but one—

A Jove principium, Jovis omnia plena.

They care no more for the ministers I have mentioned, than they do for those sturdy royalists who, for 60*l.* per annum, stand behind his majesty's carriage, arrayed in scarlet and in gold. If the present ministers opposed the court instead of flattering it, they would not command twenty votes.

Do not imagine by these observations, that I am not loyal; without joining in the common cant of the best of kings, I respect the king most sincerely as a good man. His religion is better than the religion of Mr. Perceval, his old morality very superior to the old morality of Mr. Canning, and I am quite certain he has a safer understanding than both of them put together. Loyalty, within the bounds of reason and moderation, is one of the great instruments of English happiness; but the love of the king may easily become more strong than the love of the kingdom, and we may lose sight of the public welfare in our exaggerated admiration of him who is appointed to reign only for its promotion and support. I detest Jacobinism; and if I am doomed to be a slave at all, I would rather be the slave of a king than a cobler. God save the king, you say, warms your heart like the sound of a trumpet. I cannot make use of so violent a metaphor; but I am delighted to hear it, when it is the cry of genuine affection; I am delighted to hear it, when they hail not only the individual man, but the outward and living sign of all English blessings. These are noble feelings, and the heart of every good man must go with them; but God save the king, in these times, too often means God save my pension and my place, God give my sisters an allowance out of the privy purse,—make me clerk of the irons, let me survey the meltings, let me live upon the fruits of other men's industry, and fatten upon the plunder of the public.

What is it possible to say to such a man as the gentleman of Hampstead, who really believes it feasible to convert the four million Irish Catholics to the Protestant religion, and considers this as the best remedy for the disturbed state of Ireland? It is not possible to answer such a man with arguments; we must come out against him with beads, and a cowl, and push him into an hermitage. It is really such trash, that it is an abuse of the privilege of reasoning to reply to it. Such a project is well worthy the statesman who would bring the French to reason by keeping them without rhubarb, and exhibit to mankind the awful spectacle of a nation deprived of neutral salts. This is not the dream of a wild apothecary indulging in his own opium; this is not the distempered fancy of a pounder of drugs, delirious from smallness of profits; but it is the sober, deliberate, and systematic scheme of a man to whom the public safety is entrusted, and whose appointment is considered by many as a masterpiece of political sagacity. What a sublime thought, that no purge can now be taken between the Weser and the Garonne; that the bustling pestle is still, the canorous mortar mute, and the bowels of mankind locked up for fourteen degrees of latitude! When, I should be curious to know, were all the powers of crudity and flatulence fully explained to his majesty's ministers? At what period was this great plan of conquest and constipation fully developed? In whose mind was the idea of destroying the pride and the plasters of France first engendered? Without castor oil they might, for some months, to be sure, have carried on a lingering war; but can they do without bark? Will the people live under a government where antimonial powders cannot be procured? Will they bear the loss of mercury? "There's the rub." Depend upon it, the absence of materia medica will soon bring them to their senses, and the cry of *Bourbon and bolus* burst forth from the Baltic to the Mediterranean.

You ask me for any precedent in our history where the oath of supremacy has been dispensed with. It was dispensed with to the Catholics of Canada, in 1774. They are only required to take a simple oath of allegiance. The same, I believe, was the case in Corsica. The reason of such exemption was obvious; you could not possibly have retained either of these countries without it. And what did it signify, whether you retained them or not? In cases where you might have been foolish without peril, you were wise; when nonsense and bigotry threaten you with destruction, it is impossible to bring you back to the alphabet of justice and common sense; if men are to be fools, I would rather they were fools in little matters than in great; dulness turned up with temerity, is a livery all the worse for the facings; and the most tremendous of all things is the magnanimity of a dunce.

It is not by any means necessary, as you contend, to repeal the Test Act if you give relief to the Catholic; what the Catholics ask for is to be put on a footing with the Protestant dissenters, which would be done by repealing that part of the law which compels them to take the oath of supremacy and to make the declaration against transubstantiation; they would then come into Parliament as all other dissenters are allowed to do, and the penal laws to which they were exposed for taking office would be suspended every year, as they have been for this half century past towards Protestant dissenters. Perhaps, after all, this is the best method,—to continue the persecuting law, and to suspend it every year,—a method which, while it effectually destroys the persecution itself, leaves to the great mass of mankind the exquisite gratification of supposing that they are enjoying some advantage from which a particular class of their fellow-creatures are excluded. We manage the Corporation and Test Acts at present much in the same manner as if we were to persuade parish boys, who had been in the habit of beating an ass, to spare the animal, and beat the skin of an ass stuffed with straw; this would preserve the semblance of tormenting without the reality, and keep boy and beast in good humour.

How can you imagine that a provision for the Catholic clergy affects the 5th article of the Union? Surely I am preserving the Protestant church in Ireland, if I put it in a better condition than that in which it now is. A tithe proctor in Ireland collects his tithes with a blunderbuss, and carries his tenth hay-cock by storm, sword in hand; to give him equal value in a more specific shape, cannot, I should imagine, be considered as injurious to the church of Ireland; and what right has that church to complain, if Parliament chooses to fix upon the empire the burthen of supporting a double ecclesiastical establishment? Are the revenues of the Irish Protestant clergy in the slightest degree injured by such provision? On the contrary, is it possible to confer a more serious benefit upon that church, than by quieting and contenting those who are at work for its destruction?

It is impossible to think of the affairs of Ireland without being forcibly struck with the parallel of Hungary. Of her seven millions of inhabitants, one-half were Protestants, Calvinists, and Lutherans, many of the Greek Church, and many Jews; such was the state of their religious dissensions, that Mahomet had often been called in to the aid of Calvin, and the crescent often glittered on the walls of Buda and of Presburg. At last, in 1791, during the most violent crisis of disturbance, a diet was called, and by a great majority of voices a decree was passed, which secured to all the contending sects the fullest and freest exercise of religious worship and education; ordained (let it be heard in Hampstead) that churches and chapels should be erected for all on the most perfectly equal terms, that the Protestants of both confessions should depend upon their spiritual superiors alone, liberated them from swearing by the usual oath, "the holy Virgin Mary, the saints, and chosen of God;" and then, the decree adds, "that *public offices and honours, high or low, great or small, shall be given to natural born Hungarians who deserve well of their country, and possess the other qualifications, let their religion be what it may.*" Such was the line of policy pursued in a diet consisting of four hundred members, in a state whose form of government approaches nearer to our own than any other, having a Roman Catholic establishment of great wealth and power, and under the influence of one of the most bigoted Catholic courts in Europe. This measure has now the experience of eighteen years in its favour; it has undergone a trial of fourteen years of revolution, such as the world never witnessed, and more than equal to a century less convulsed. What have been its effects? When the French advanced like a torrent within a few days' march of Vienna, the Hungarians rose in a mass; they formed what they called the sacred insurrection, to defend their sovereign, their rights and liberties, now common to all; and the apprehension of their approach dictated to the reluctant Bonaparte the immediate signature of the treaty of *Leoben:* the Romish hierarchy of Hungary exists in all its former splendour and opulence; never has the slightest attempt been made to diminish it; and those revolutionary principles, to which so large a portion of civilized Europe has been sacrificed, have here failed in making the smallest successful inroad.

The whole history of this proceeding of the Hungarian diet is so extraordinary, and such an admirable comment upon the Protestantism of Mr. Spencer Perceval, that I must compel you to read a few short extracts from the law itself:—"The Protestants of both confessions shall, in religious matters, depend upon their own spiritual superiors alone. The Protestants may likewise retain their trivial and grammar schools. The church dues which the Protestants have hitherto paid to the Catholic parish priests, schoolmasters, or other such officers, either in money, productions, or labour, shall in future entirely cease, and after three months from the publishing of this law, be no more anywhere demanded. In the building or repairing of churches, parsonage-houses, and schools, the Protestants are not obliged to assist the Catholics with labour, nor the Catholics the Protestants. The pious foundations and donations of the Protestants which already exist, or which in future may be made for their churches, ministers, schools and students, hospitals, orphan-houses and poor, cannot be taken from them under any pretext, nor yet the care of them; but rather the unimpeded administration shall be entrusted to those from among them to whom it legally belongs, and those foundations which may have been taken from them under the last government, shall be returned to them without delay; all affairs of marriage of the Protestants are left to their own consistories; all landlords and masters of families, under the penalty of public prosecution, are ordered not to prevent their subjects and servants, whether they be Catholic or Protestant, from the observance of the festivals and ceremonies of their religion," &c. &c. &c.—By what strange chances are mankind influenced! A little Catholic barrister of Vienna might have raised the cry of *no Protestantism,* and Hungary would have panted for the arrival of a French army as much as Ireland does at this moment; arms would have been searched for; Lutheran and Calvinist houses entered in the dead of the night; and the strength of Austria exhausted in guarding a country from which, under the present liberal system, she may expect, in a moment of danger the most powerful aid; and let it be remembered, that this memorable example of political wisdom took place at a period when many great monarchies were yet unconquered in

Europe; in a country where the two religious parties were equal in number; and where it is impossible to suppose indifference in the party which relinquished its exclusive privileges. Under all these circumstances, the measure was carried in the Hungarian diet by a majority of 280 to 120. In a few weeks, we shall see every concession denied to the Catholics by a much larger majority of Protestants, at a moment when every other power is subjugated but ourselves, and in a country where the oppressed are four times as numerous as their oppressors. So much for the wisdom of our ancestors—so much for the nineteenth century—so much for the superiority of the English over all the nations of the continent!

Are you not sensible, let me ask you, of the absurdity of trusting the lowest Catholics with offices correspondent to their situation in life, and of denying such privilege to the higher? A Catholic may serve in the militia, but a Catholic cannot come into Parliament; in the latter case you suspect combination, and in the former case you suspect no combination; you deliberately arm ten or twenty thousand of the lowest of the Catholic people;—and the moment you come to a class of men whose education, honour, and talents, seem to render all mischief less probable, then you see the danger of employing a Catholic, and cling to your investigating tests and disabling laws. If you tell me you have enough of members of Parliament, and not enough of militia, without the Catholics, I beg leave to remind you, that, by employing the physical force of any sect, at the same time when you leave them in a state of utter disaffection, you are not adding strength to your armies, but weakness and ruin:—if you want the vigour of their common people, you must not disgrace their nobility, and insult their priesthood.

I thought that the terror of the pope had been confined to the limits of the nursery, and merely employed as a means to induce young master to enter into his small clothes with greater speed, and to eat his breakfast with greater attention to decorum. For these purposes, the name of the pope is admirable; but why push it beyond? Why not leave to Lord Hawkesbury all farther enumeration of the pope's powers? For a whole century, you have been exposed to the enmity of France, and your succession was disputed in two rebellions; what could the pope do at the period when there was a serious struggle, whether England should be Protestant or Catholic, and when the issue was completely doubtful? Could the pope induce the Irish to rise in 1715? Could he induce them to rise in 1745? You had no Catholic enemy when half this island was in arms; and what did the pope attempt in the last rebellion in Ireland? But if he had as much power over the minds of the Irish as Mr. Wilberforce has over the mind of a young Methodist, converted the preceding quarter, is this a reason why we are to disgust men, who may be acted upon in such a manner by a foreign power? or is it not an additional reason why we should raise up every barrier of affection and kindness against the mischief of foreign influence? But the true answer is, the mischief does not exist. Gog and Magog have produced as much influence upon human affairs as the pope has done for this half century past; and by spoiling him of his possessions, and degrading him in the eyes of all Europe, Bonaparte has not taken quite the proper method of increasing his influence.

But why not a Catholic king, as well as a Catholic member of Parliament, or of the cabinet?—Because it is probable that the one would be mischievous, and the other not. A Catholic king might struggle against the Protestantism of the country, and if the struggle was not successful, it would at least be dangerous; but the efforts of any other Catholic would be quite insignificant, and his hope of success so small, that it is quite improbable the effort would ever be made; my argument is, that in so Protestant a country as Great Britain, the character of her Parliaments and her cabinet could not be changed by the few Catholics who would ever find their way to the one or the other. But the power of the crown is immeasurably greater than the power which the Catholics could obtain from any other species of authority in the state; and it does not follow, because the lesser degree of power is innocent, that the greater should be so too. As for the stress you lay upon the danger of a Catholic chancellor, I have not the least hesitation in saying, that his appointment would not do a ten-thousandth part of the mischief to the English church that might be done by a methodistical chancellor of the true Clapham breed; and I request to know, if it is really so very necessary that a chancellor should be of the religion of the Church of England, how many chancellors you have had within the last century who have been bred up in the Presbyterian religion?—And again, how many you have had who notoriously have been without any religion at all?

Why are you to suppose that eligibility and election are the same thing, and that all the cabinet *will* be Catholics, whenever all the cabinet *may* be Catholics? You have a right, you say, to suppose an extreme case, and to argue upon it—so have I: and I will suppose that the hundred Irish members will one day come down in a body, and pass a law compelling the king to reside in Dublin. I will suppose that the Scotch members, by a similar stratagem, will lay England under a large contribution of meal and sulphur; no measure is without objection, if you sweep the whole horizon for danger; it is not sufficient to tell me of what may happen, but you must show me a rational probability that it will happen: after all, I might, contrary to my real opinion, admit all your dangers to exist; it is enough for me to contend that all other dangers taken together are not equal to the danger of losing Ireland from disaffection and invasion.

I am astonished to see you, and many good and well-meaning clergymen beside you, painting the Catholics in such detestable colours; two-thirds, at least, of Europe are Catholics,—they are Christians, though mistaken Christians; how can I possibly admit that any sect of Christians, and above all, that the oldest and the most numerous sect of Christians, are incapable of fulfilling the common duties and relations of life: though I do differ from them in many particulars, God forbid I should give such a handle to infidelity, and subscribe to such blasphemy against our common religion!

Do you think mankind never change their opinions without formally expressing and confessing that change? When you quote the decisions of ancient Catholic councils, are you prepared to defend all the decrees of English convocations and universities since the reign of Queen Elizabeth? I could soon make you sick of your uncandid industry against the Catholics, and bring you to allow that it is better to forget times past, and to judge and be judged by present opinions and present practice.

I must beg to be excused from explaining and refuting all the mistakes about the Catholics made by my Lord Redesdale; and I must do that nobleman the justice to say, that he has been treated with great disrespect. Could any thing be more indecent than to make it a morning lounge in Dublin to call upon his lordship, and to cram him with Arabian-night stories about the Catholics? Is this proper behaviour to the representative of majesty, the child of Themis, and the keeper of the conscience in West Britain? Whoever reads the letters of the Catholic bishops, in the appendix to Sir John Hippesly's very sensible book, will see to what an excess this practice must have been carried with the pleasing and Protestant nobleman whose name I have mentioned, and from thence I wish you to receive your answer about excommunication, and all the trash which is talked against the Catholics.

A sort of notion has, by some means or another, crept into the world, that difference of religion would render men unfit to perform together the offices of common and civil life; that Brother Wood and Brother Grose could not travel together the same circuit if they differed in creed, nor Cockell and Mingay be engaged in the same cause if Cockell was a Catholic and Mingay a Muggletonian. It is supposed that Huskisson and Sir Harry Englefield would squabble behind the speaker's chair about the Council of Lateran, and many a turnpike bill miscarry by the sarcastical controversies of Mr. Hawkins Brown and Sir John Throckmorton upon the real presence. I wish I could see some of these symptoms of earnestness upon the subject of religion; but it really seems to me, that, in the present state of society, men no more think about inquiring concerning each other's faith than they do concerning the colour of each other's skins. There may have been times in England when the quarter sessions would have been disturbed by the theological polemics; but now, after a Catholic justice had once been seen on the bench, and it had been clearly ascertained that he spoke English, had no tail, only a single row of teeth, and that he loved port-wine,—after all the scandalous and infamous reports of his physical conformation had been clearly proved to be false,—he would be reckoned a jolly fellow, and very superior in flavour to a sly Presbyterian. Nothing, in fact, can be more uncandid and unphilosophical* than to say that a man has a tail, because you cannot agree with him upon religious subjects; it appears to be ludicrous, but I am convinced it has done infinite mischief to the Catholics, and made a very serious impression upon the minds of many gentlemen of large landed property.

In talking of the impossibility of Catholics and Protestants living together with equal privilege under the same government, do you forget the cantons of Switzerland? You might have seen there a Protestant congregation going into a church which had just been quitted by a Catholic congregation; and I will venture to say that the Swiss Catholics were more bigoted to their religion than any people in the whole world. Did the kings of Prussia ever refuse to employ a Catholic? Would Frederick the Great have rejected an able man on this account? We have seen Prince Czartorinski, a Catholic secretary of state in Russia; in former times, a Greek patriarch and an apostolic vicar acted together in the most perfect harmony in Venice; and we have seen the Emperor of Germany in modern times entrusting the care of his person and the command of his guard to a Protestant prince, Ferdinand of Wirtemberg. But what are all these things to Mr. Perceval? He has looked at human nature from the top of Hampstead Hill, and has not a thought beyond the little sphere of his own vision. "The snail," say the Hindoos, "sees nothing but its own shell, and thinks it the grandest palace in the universe."

I now take a final leave of this subject of Ireland; the only difficulty in discussing it is a want of resistance, a want of something difficult to unravel, and something dark to illumine; to agitate such a question is to beat the air with a club, and cut down gnats with a scimitar; it is a prostitution of industry, and a waste of strength. If a man says I have a good place, and I do not choose to lose it, this mode of arguing upon the Catholic question I can well understand; but that any human being with an understanding two degrees elevated above that of an Anabaptist preacher, should conscientiously contend for the expediency and propriety of leaving the Irish Catholics in their present state, and of subjecting us to such tremendous peril in the present condition of the world, it is utterly out of my power to conceive. Such a measure as the Catholic question is entirely beyond the common game of politics; it is a measure in which all parties ought to acquiesce, in order to preserve the place where, and the stake for which they play. If Ireland is gone, where are jobs? where are reversions? where is my brother, Lord Arden? where are my dear and near relations? The game is up, and the speaker of the House of Commons will be sent as a present to the menagerie at Paris. We talk of waiting from particular considerations, as if centuries of joy and prosperity were before us; in the next ten years our fate must be decided; we shall know, long before that period, whether we can

* *Vide* Lord Bacon, Locke, and Descartes.

bear up against the miseries by which we are threatened, or not; and yet, in the very midst of our crisis, we are enjoined to abstain from the most certain means of increasing our strength, and advised to wait for the remedy till the disease is removed by death or health. And now, instead of the plain and manly policy of increasing unanimity at home, by equalizing rights and privileges, what is the ignorant, arrogant, and wicked system which has been pursued? Such a career of madness and of folly was, I believe, never run in so short a period. The vigour of the ministry is like the vigour of a grave-digger,—the tomb becomes more ready and more wide for every effort which they make. There is nothing which it is worth while either to take or to retain, and a constant train of ruinous expeditions has been kept up. Every Englishman felt proud of the integrity of his country; the character of the country is lost for ever. It is of the utmost consequence to a commercial people at war with the greatest part of Europe, that there should be a free entry of neutrals into the enemy's ports; the neutrals who carried our manufactures we have not only excluded, but we have compelled them to declare war against us. It was our interest to make a good peace, or convince our own people that it could not be obtained; we have not made a peace, and we have convinced the people of nothing but of the arrogance of the foreign secretary; and all this has taken place in the short space of a year, because a King's Bench barrister and a writer of epigrams, turned into ministers of state, were determined to show country gentlemen that the late administration had no vigour. In the mean time commerce stands still, manufactures perish, Ireland is more and more irritated, India is threatened, fresh taxes are accumulated upon the wretched people, the war is carried on without it being possible to conceive any one single object which a rational being can propose to himself by its continuation; and in the midst of this unparalleled insanity we are told that the continent is to be reconquered by the want of rhubarb and plums.* A better spirit than exists in the English people never existed in any people in the world; it has been misdirected, and squandered upon party purposes in the most degrading and scandalous manner; they have been led to believe that they were benefiting the commerce of England by destroying the commerce of America, that they were defending their sovereign by perpetuating the bigoted oppression of their fellow-subject; their rulers and their guides have told them that they would equal the vigour of France by equalling her atrocity; and they have gone on wasting that opulence, patience, and courage, which, if husbanded by prudent and moderate counsels, might have proved the salvation of mankind. The same policy of turning the good qualities of Englishmen to their own destruction, which made Mr. Pitt omnipotent, continues his power to those who resemble him only in his vices; advantage is taken of the loyalty of Englishmen, to make them meanly submissive; their piety is turned into persecution, their courage into useless and obstinate contention; they are plundered because they are ready to pay, and soothed into asinine stupidity because they are full of virtuous patience. If England must perish at last, so let it be; that event is in the hands of God; we must dry up our tears and submit. But that England should perish swindling and stealing; that it should perish waging war against lazar-houses, and hospitals; that it should perish persecuting with monastic bigotry; that it should calmly give itself up to be ruined by the flashy arrogance of one man, and the narrow fanaticism of another; these events are within the power of human beings, and I did not think that the magnanimity of Englishmen would ever stoop to such degradations.

Longum vale!

PETER PLYMLEY.

* Even Allen Park (accustomed as he has always been to be delighted by all administrations) says it is too bad and Hall and Morris are said to have actually blushed in one of the divisions.

THE END.

www.ingramcontent.com/pod-product-compliance
Lightning Source LLC
LaVergne TN
LVHW020925110826
845150LV00004B/770

* 9 7 8 1 4 2 5 5 5 3 8 5 2 *